ISBN 978-1-333-24644-0
PIBN 10532310

1 MONTH OF
FREE
READING

at

www.ForgottenBooks.com

By purchasing this book you are eligible for one month membership to ForgottenBooks.com, giving you unlimited access to our entire collection of over 700,000 titles via our web site and mobile apps.

To claim your free month visit:
www.forgottenbooks.com/free532310

Hon. ELLERY BICKNELL CRANE.

Member Worcester City Council 1876-7-8-9. Board of Aldermen 1886-7. Representative
Massachusetts Legislature 1895-6. State Senator 1897 and 1898.

GENEALOGY

OF THE

CRANE FAMILY.

VOLUME II.

DESCENDANTS OF BENJAMIN CRANE,

OF

WETHERSFIELD, CONN.,

AND

JOHN CRANE, OF COVENTRY, CONN.

ALSO OF

JASPER CRANE, OF NEW HAVEN, CONN., AND NEWARK, N. J.

AND

STEPHEN CRANE, OF ELIZABETHTOWN, N. J.

WITH

FAMILIES OF THE NAME IN NEW HAMPSHIRE, MARYLAND AND VIRGINIA.

BY

ELLERY BICKNELL CRANE.

Worcester, Mass.

PRESS OF CHARLES HAMILTON,

311 MAIN STREET.

1900.

1142921

CONTENTS.

ILLUSTRATIONS.

EXPLANATION.

Two Indexes have been prepared for descendants of each of the four progenitors. One giving the *Christian names of Cranes*, the other, *names of persons* who have *intermarried with them;* alphabetically arranged.

Also an index of *Christian names of Cranes* found in the *Addenda*. In looking for a certain name, unless you know to which line the person belongs it will be necessary to examine each of the five indexes.

The number after the name is the consecutive number. Turn to this number in the body of the book and you will find the person's *family record*. If the person had no family the number will refer to the birth under the parent's name. If the Index does not give the name sought, find name of the parent, and look through the list of the children. Some names came too late for numbering. Where there are several names alike, the year of birth placed before the name may help to indicate the one sought.

The bracketed [—] number after the name of a parent refers to the number where the person appears as a child. After the name of a parent the pedigree is indicated in parentheses (——) with small figures above, showing to what generation the name belongs, and giving the names back as far as the progenitor of the line.

The following abbreviations have been used: b. for born, m. for married, unm. for unmarried, (s. settled), d. for died.

ERRATA.

Page 37, 5th line, read Glastonbury for Glassenbury.

Page 120, 3d line, read Parmele for Parnele.

Page 150, 5th to 11th line, read without parentheses.

Page 189, 1st line, read Mary for Maria.

Page 190, 34th line, read Edward Martin for Edward Norton.

Page 302, last two lines, read Huntington after Samuel and Hannah.

Page 323, 29th line, read Croes for Cross.

Page 333, last line, read William for Hugh.

Page 345, after 698, Hannah Crane, read [265].

Page 370, after 1132-2, read Frances for Francis.

Page 374, after 1184, Timothy Dwight Crane, read [588].

Page 385, 3d line from bottom, read 3 sons and 2 daughters.

Page 386, in 3d line, read 8 children for 6 children.

Page 386, after 1452-8, read Davis for Davie.

Page 430, after 2223, Stephen, omit V.

Page 465, after 2741, Isabel W. Crane, read [2570] for [2624]

Page 465, after 2742, Bessie K. Crane, read [2571], for [2625].

Page 486, 6th line from bottom, read Erastus D. Crosfield for Erastus P. Crosfield.   309-4, after Orpha M. read Erastus D.

Page 387, 315-10, after Samuel, read T. for F.

Page 488, 365-6, omit *in* before the word Boston.

Page 489, 392-4, read Bragaw for Brown.

Page 490, 408-2, omit the words *no children*.

Page 490, 414-2, read Heyt for Keyt.

Page 496, 530, after William Crane, read [213] for [212].

Page 510, 757-6, omit all after M. Moore.

Page 510, 759-8, omit all after Sarah Briggs.

Page 542, 1402, after Ann Maria Crane, read [919] for [917]

PREFACE.

VOLUME I. of the Crane Family Genealogy, published in 1895, contains an article on Origin of the name *Crane;* copies of five different armorials belonging to the family;.a sketch of the Crane family in England, with pedigrees covering thirteen generations, and a brief reference to the first of the name who came to New England, together with Henry Crane of Wethersfield and Guilford, Conn., and his descendants of nine generations; a list of Cranes who served in Connecticut as lawmakers and public officials; also a list of members of the family who served in the French and Indian, as well as the Revolutionary war, from that State. There has been considerable delay in issuing the second volume, and no doubt some interested persons have become impatient to see the work in print. But the task of tracing the lines from five different progenitors has been no easy one. Special care has been exercised in keeping each line of descendants independent of the other, although they have in some instances intermarried, and in many cases resided for years in close proximity to each other. Volume II. has exceeded in size our most sanguine expectations, for the reason that the descendants of Jasper and Stephen Crane of New Jersey have so willingly assisted in supplying records from private sources that could in no other way be furnished. The early public records of New Jersey, so far as the writer's experience extends, furnish a very unsatisfactory field for the genealogist. During the early settlements there seems to have been no fixed system for recording births, marriages and deaths for preservation. Probate Records have supplied the greater portion of the early records for the descendants of Jasper and Stephen Crane. Some of the early church records, from which much was expected, were found to have been destroyed by fire. The lack of dates has caused a vast amount of trouble in establishing the identity of certain members of the family. Where

there seemed any doubt of the identification it has been expressed in the context or by a foot-note.

Although the writer has given a vast amount of time, and a considerable sum from his means in prosecuting this work, still he is fully aware how difficult is the task of collecting material and compiling a work of this nature, and presenting it free from inaccuracies. Every effort has been made to avoid errors, and wherever different dates or conflicting statements have been received regarding the same event, which has frequently been the case, careful investigation has followed in order to determine if possible the correct statement to be used in the book. To the many friends who have in any way contributed to the encouragement of this work the writer would here express his profound gratitude. Among the names of those who have given special aid in its prosecution may be mentioned: Rev. Elias Nettleton Crane, Rev. Oliver Crane and James Eells Crane, all deceased; the latter died Nov. 19, 1893, in Philadelphia, Pa.; William M. Crane, Greenville, Mich.; Stephen S. Crane, Maple Hill Farm, High Ridge, Conn.; Harrison Horton Crane, Middletown, N. Y.; Augustus S. Crane, Elizabeth, N. J.; Miss A. J. Reed, Carmel, N. Y.; Dorothy N. Law, Dixon, Ill.; Anna Russell Vance, Milwaukee, Wis.; Henry Harmon Noble, Albany, N. Y.; Horatio Crain, Key West, Fla.: and J. M. Crane, Kingwood, West Va.

Records of several families needing further proof to define their position in the body of the book have been placed in the *Addenda* with the hope that some of the descendants may be able to find the connecting link. In some instances the peculiar spelling of names has been retained, believing members of the families would prefer to have them presented in that way.

ELLERY BICKNELL CRANE,
Worcester, Mass.

January, 1900.

BENJAMIN CRANE.

WINDSOR was probably the first town settled in Connecticut by the English, and Wethersfield next. The former made its beginning in the year 1633 and the latter in 1634. The people who planted these towns were almost without exception from Massachusetts. In the year 1621 and for many years thereafter practically all settlers bound for New England landed in the colony of New Plymouth or Massachusetts, and emigrated from there to the various settlements of their choice. For several years Windsor, Wethersfield and Hartford proved the chief attractions for settlers locating west of the Connecticut River, although a few planted themselves at Saybrook. Many of those who early settled at Wethersfield came from Watertown, Mass., while the towns of Cambridge and Dorchester furnished a considerable number of the families for Windsor, and Newtown furnished some for Hartford. The emigrants from Dorchester, Mass., named their town Dorchester, now Windsor. Wethersfield was called Watertown, and Hartford was called Newtown. But at the meeting of the General Court of the Connecticut colony in 1637 the present name was decided upon and adopted. This, however, was not the first session of the General Court of this colony. Their first session was held April 26, 1636.

Rev. Henry Smith was the first settled minister in Wethersfield; came there about the year 1636, but was not installed until the year 1640 or 1644, and died 1648.

The early records of Wethersfield are exceedingly interesting and voluminous, yet lack system and completeness. The records of births, with some deaths, are furnished from 1635 to about 1666; and after an interval of some years the record of deaths is again taken up with the year 1670, and the births and marriages about the year 1692. Subsequent to the year 1700 there seems to have been a more complete system of entries throughout all the departments. On the whole, however, the records at Wethersfield are perhaps in as good condition in all respects and

2

are as well preserved as the average of the early New England towns. The entries of dates of births of children of Benjamin Crane senior were apparently made eight years subsequent to the last birth, and records of lands assigned to or owned by Benjamin Crane, senior, in one or two instances, were also apparently entered some years after possession had been given; a fact which, to say the least, shows a slack method of making important records during the early life of the town. But the descendants of· this progenitor may congratulate themselves that so' much has been recorded and preserved to be used by them in rearing their genealogical tree.

FIRST GENERATION.

1. BENJAMIN CRANE, was in Wethersfield, Conn., as early as 1655, and may have been there a few years earlier. According to the Records of the Particular Court, held at Hartford, March, 1655, he is defendant in a civil suit with John Sadler, pltf.; also in June, 1656, he is defendant in another suit with Richard Montague. He was born about 1630; was made freeman May 12, 1658, at Wethersfield. It is not positively known from whence he came to Wethersfield, but Hinman in his "History of Connecticut Settlers" seems to think that he came from Massachusetts, which statement all investigations thus far seem to warrant. February 24, 1656, the town gave him a home lot of 2½ acres, more or less, bounded by the Common N. W., a brook and the home lot of John Graves N. E., the Common S. E., the highway S. W. He also bought John Dixon's or Dickenson's land in the West Field, Sept. 14, 1664. The latter is said to have removed to Hadley 1659 or 1660. It appears that this last mentioned tract of land was that on which the late home of Sam'l Coleman, deceased, stands, on Mud Lane. It was there when Mr. Crane built his dwelling-house and tanneries. The house was one of the six houses fortified by vote of the town in 1704. The town also gave him three acres of land on Beaver, now Tando's, Brook, in 1660; served as juror 1664; drew land in the allotment of 1670, and purchased land of Daniel Rose, Dec. 8, 1671. January 15, 1673, he is rated among inhabitants of Wethersfield to pay the town 0—4—5½; acquires more land next south of Job Whitcomb's, February 22, 1680, March 25, 1680, July 13, 1680; under latter date the land is located on the Connecticut River on road to Middletown and road to Rocky Hill.

May, 1682, Benjamin Crane with others petitioned the General Court for liberty to "erect a plantation in the Wabaynassit country" (Windham County). It was proposed to have a "Town Grant" ten miles square.

He married Mary Backus, daughter of William and Sarah (Charles) Backus, April 23, 1655, and carried on the tanning business about a mile below the village on the Middletown road. The spot for many years has been known as "Old Crane's Tannery Place." At his death, May 31, 1691, his son John succeeded to the business. She died July 8, 1717. Children:

2 —1. BENJAMIN, born March 1, 1656; drowned June 20, 1693.
3 —2. JONATHAN, born December 1, 1658.
4 —3. JOSEPH, born April 1, 1661.

5—4. JOHN, born April 30, 1663.
6—5. ELIJAH, born 1665.
7—6. ABRAHAM, born 1668.
8—7. JACOB, born 1670.
9—8. ISRAEL, born November 1, 1671.
10—9. MARY, born 1673.

AUGUST 22, 1689.

To all Christian persons to whom this present writing shall come, Greeting, Know ye that Benjamin Crane senior of Wethersfield co Hartford in his magesties Territory and Dominion of New England in America, husbandman, for and in consideration of the love and affection that he hath and beareth to his beloved son John Crane of Wethersfield aforesaid, Tanner, and for and in consideration that the said John Crane shall pay unto the said Benjamin Crane the full and just sum of three pounds in good and merchantable corn or pork at the current price yearly every year during the natural life of said Benjamin Crane and for and in consideration that if the said Benjamin Crane shall see cause to build a well on his own land for the conviency of his new dwelling house at any time before his or his wife's decease that the said John Crane is to bear and pay half the charges and cost of the same and for divers other good causes and considerations herein the said Benjamin Crane hereunto   hath given, granted, bargained,   assigned set over and confirmed and doth by these presents fully clearly and absolutely give, grant, bargain   assign, set over and confirm unto the said John Crane and unto his heirs and assigns forever all the estate right title, interest, use, property, possession, claim and demand whatever the said Benjamin Crane hath or   to come might, ought or should have in or to one piece of land situated in the bounds of Wethersfield.

Signed Feby. 28, 1688.   BENJAMIN B C CRANE, Senior.
his mark.

Under date of August 22, 1689, we find the following:

To all Christian people to whom this writing shall come, Greeting, Know ye that Benjamin Crane senior of Wethersfield husbandman, for and in consideration of the love &c for his son John Crane of Wethersfield Tanner, for and in consideration of the said John Crane shall pay to said Benjamin Crane three pounds in good and merchantable corn or pork at the current price yearly every year during the natural life of said Benjamin Crane and Mary the now wife of said Benjamin Crane I hereby give a part of the land where I live thirteen and one half rods in length from highway west to land of said Benjamin Crane, one and one half rod at east end and seven and one half rods wide at west end and joinds on land of Sgt John Kilnborne, with all workhouses, tan vats, water courses &c orchard trees &c

BENJAMIN B C CRANE.
his mark.

About two years later Benjamin Crane, senior, died, and two years and twenty days from the date of his death his son Benjamin Crane, Jr., was drowned.

February 13, 1692, an inventory of the estate of Benjamin senior, deceased, was returned by his brother Henry Crane of Guilford and Killingworth, Conn., Jonathan Deming and Nathaniel Foot. Amount of the real, 408 pounds; personal, 150 pounds.

September 7, 1693, an account of the estate was exhibited in court, and the widow, with James Treat, appointed to administer on the estate. March 13, 1693-4 the division was ordered; widow to have one-third, Benjamin, the eldest son, two parts, each of the other children one part; Mr. James Treat, Lieut. Henry Crane and Mr. Nathaniel Foot, or any two of them, to divide it.

An inuentory of the Estate of Beniamin Crane sener who Decesed May ye 31 in the year 1691. now 93

	£	s	d
In cash 8s and apparell £8 all att.	08	08	
the best bed and bedstad with furniture	10	00	
One down bed and bedstead and furniture to it	05	10	
the bed and bedstead in the chamber and furniture	02	10	
to one fether bed and bedstad with the furniture	05	10	
" One couerlid and rugg and blankit	01	05	
" 6 pilows bears 12s and 6 napkins 14s and table cloaths 12s	01	18	
" aleauen sheets at £5 and 2 bras cetels at £4 10s	09	10	
" One warming pan 8s one frying pan 4s. Stilyards 12s	01	04	
" One great Iron pot 18s one pot 10s a little pot 5s Iron Kettle 5s	01	18	
" tramiell and tongs 10s 2 tin pans 4s 2 tables 15s	01	09	
" puter £3 15s one hechel 5s earthen ware 3s 6d	04	03	06
" Wooden dishes and bouls and trenshers	00	08	
" 3 paels 6s and chars and cushens £1 04s	01	10	
" chest 9s and Wheals 8s bareals in seler £1	01	17	
" one balel pork, one barel beefe	05	15	
" to barels in the chamber and meal troughs meal sines	01	02	
" Arms and amunishion £4 one timber chain £1 5s	05	05	
" old Iron 8s branding Iron 1s one short chain 3s spaid 3s		15	
" Axes 9s one pillion 12s one sadle 10s one sadle 3s	01	14	
" one pannel 10s smoothing Iron and lamp 5s and sickles	100	15	
" books £1 20 bushel wheat £4 20 bushel corn £2 10s	07	10	00

to cart and wheals with the Iron work yoak and
     cart rope   03—00—00

" 2 collers and 2 hors chans £1 10s plow Irons   03—15

" 2 Oxen £11 10s 2 three year old steers £6 one
     steer £2   19—10

" 2 cows £8 and one cow £3 10s and one heifer £2   13—10

" One mare and colt £3 10s one hors £4 one gray
     hors £5   12—10

" one brake 4s one bell 4s two hoghs and one fork
     06s .   00—14

" to swine £2 15s and crop on the grounde £6   8—15

" a hay knife and ½ of crosecott saw and pease
     hook^s 10

" 3 sheep £1 10s   01—10

this inuentory was taken by us febrewery 13-1692.

                       HENRY CRANE

The Widow   JOHNATHAN DEMING

Benjamin   NATHANIEL FOOTE

Johnathan

Joseph

Jo   the hons and homestad that is with all the

Abram   bouldings the tan hous excepted that belongs to

Jacob   John which he clame in his own wright which

Isreal   is recorded to hime with the land he stands

Elijah   posit of in his own wright

Mary   the housing and barn with three acors

            of land at the frunt of whome lott with

            aportinances   100

                              L   s   d

17 acors of plowing land in the whome lott   120—00—00

from the highway that cros the Wests lott upon or
     near the West swamp hill containing sixteen
     acors or theirabouts at three pounds acor   48—00—00

the remainder of the lott containing about ten acors   10—00—00

the paustar ioyning to John Wadons his whome lott
     at ten pounds acor by estimation 4 acors   40—00—00

one parsel called the nek. near becile meadow 4
     acors   30—00—00

one parsel of swamp containing 3 acors   27

one parsel of land lying at rocke hill containing
     twelve acors at 20 shillings per acor   12

one parsel of land one the west sid conitocut riuer
     on lay dout   01

the West lot containing fifty acors and the adission   20

apised by us

Nathaniel Foot   }
James Treat Sener }

We add other entries which may be of interest in connection
with the settlement of this estate.

July 10, 1710. Whereas Benjamin Crane senior had a piece of land granted by the town near Rocky Hill, the court gave half to John and half to Jacob. Now John was dead, and Jacob agreed with John Chester for the estate of John Crane, and James Steel guardian for Josiah, son of John, to divide it, Josiah to have the north half and Jacob (his uncle) to have the south part.

June 11, 1711. Mary Crane of Wethersfield, for the love she bore for her grandson, Benonie Crane, son of Abraham, gave him 11½ acres, being on or near a place in Wethersfield known as or called Cow Plain, being one-half of that lot laid out to said widow Crane free and clear.

June 13, 1713. An agreement between the heirs of Benjamin Crane senior and Benjamin, Jr. Jonathan Crane owned three and one-half acres, for which he was to receive £20 current. The heirs of Abraham Crane paid the £20, and Jonathan Crane signed a release to all claims to the estate.

In the year 1693 we find the number of acres land held by the family in Wethersfield, as follows: Jacob Crane, 51 acres 10½ rods; John Crane, 102 acres 15½ rods; Widow Mary Crane, 106 acres 23 rods; Israel Crane, 109 acres 13 rods; Abraham Crane, 116 acres 9½ rods; Joseph Crane, 163 acres 24 rods.

SECOND GENERATION.

11. BENJAMIN CRANE[2] [2], Benjamin[1] was chosen Rate Maker in 1685. Married 1st Mary Chapman, May 12, 1686, Capt. Benjamin Newbury performing the ceremony. She died April 5, 1687, aged 22 years. He then married Martha Boardman, born August 12, 1666. He was drowned June 20, 1693, in his 38th year. His widow married Samuel Terry of Enfield, June 5, 1697-8, Capt. John Chester performing the ceremony. She died May 29, 1743, in her 77th year, having had five sons and a daughter by her last marriage.

Martha, his widow, exhibited Inventory of estate of Benj. Crane, Jr., January 13, 1693; was appointed administratrix 1693. November 5, 1693, his estate inventoried 55—13—10.

The widow drew land at the allotment in Wethersfield 1694. She was again after her marriage appointed administratrix April 19, 1698. Children :

12—1. BENJAMIN, born Nov. 7, 1690; d. May, 1693.
13—2. ISAAC, born Aug. 19, 1692, d. Sept. 16, 1712, and left his will, dated Sept. 15, 1712; mentions his four brothers by his mother, Widow Martha, who married Samuel Terry, quite likely children by Mr. Terry. After his debts are paid he wills that his four brothers by his mother have all his estate and to be equally divided, but if any of them are sickly or weakly they should have more than the rest, and further said that he counted that they were the nearest relatives that he had. He appeared before the court and made choice of Lt. Jonathan Borman or Boardman as his guardian. This Jonathan was brother of his mother Martha, and born February 4, 1660, at Wethersfield. Lt. Jonathan accepted the charge, and gave bond May 1, 1710. May 2, 1711, he asked the court to require Samuel Terry of Enfield and Martha, his wife, administratrix on estate late Benjamin Crane, Jr., to render an account of said estate. October 6, 1712, court issued the order to report before first Monday of June next. March 2, 1712-13, they exhibited the account. Nearly the whole estate had been expended on Isaac, the only child of said Benjamin. May 4, 1713, Samuel and Martha were discharged.

The life of Benjamin Crane [2], although brief, was rather an eventful one.

April 3, 1685, he purchased land of John Ryley, and his brother John Crane was witness to the transaction.

April 14, 1686, he took a deed from Nathaniel Foot of land situated in Wethersfield on the Connecticut River.

April 14, 1690, Daniel Sayre and his wife Sarah of Southampton, N. Y., deeded to Benjamin Crane, Jr., " Tanner," land in Wethersfield.

January 3, 1692, he took a deed of land situated in "South field," Wethersfield, of Thomas Hosmer of Northampton, Mass.

July 2, 1692, Benjamin Crane, Jr., son and heir of Benjamin, late of Wethersfield, deceased, quitclaimed land to his brother Joseph Crane dated "April 19, in ye 4th year of ye reign of our sovereign Lord and Lady, William and Mary" (1692). This document was witnessed by his brother John Crane, and to which both signed their full names. The reader will notice that Benjamin, Jr., was also a tanner; in fact the family seemed to adopt that occupation in connection with the tilling of the soil, Benjamin, Sr., with his brother Henry, Benjamin, Jr., and brother John, all being tanners, and there may have been others of the family who followed that line of business. According to accessible records Benjamin, Jr., seems to have deferred his marriage rather beyond the average for his time. Early marriages were the custom as well as rule in those days, and to defer such an important event until the age of thirty must have required no small degree of independence, fortified with a record of good moral character, for Mr. Royal R. Hinman, the historian, tells us that the general court of the Connecticut colony ordered that no young unmarried man, unless a public officer, or he keep a servant, should keep house alone, except by license of the town, under a penalty of twenty shillings per week; and that no head of a family should entertain such young man under a like penalty without liberty from the town.

Benjamin Crane, Jr., was enjoying the confidence of his fellow townsmen when Sir Edmund Andros appeared as the willing tool of King James II. in the capacity of Governor of New England, and whose subsequent actions, including the demand for the surrender of the charter of Connecticut, were so distasteful to the people that more or less criticism was expressed, sometimes it being not altogether complimentary to the Governor and his associates, and it came to the ears of the officials about Hartford that Benjamin Crane had used language. reflecting upon their good name and character.

Those familiar with our colonial history will remember that Sir Edmund Andros, who had been governor of New York, arrived in Boston, December 20, 1686 * with a commission from King James II. for the government of New England, apparently the object being to bring all the various colonies under one government, he to be governor-in-chief, with the seat of government at Boston.

December 22 Andros wrote Governor Robert Treat that he was ready to receive the surrender of the charter of Connecticut and

---

* History of the Colony of Massachusetts Bay.—*Hutchinson.*

assume control of all New England. Governor Treat replied
that his people were loyal people of his majesty, and wished to
continue as such, and should submit to his majesty's royal com-
mands, even if it be to conjoin his colony with the other colonies
and provinces. A very courteous letter, but rather non-com-
mittal. June 13, 1687, Andros again wrote, pressing his demand
a little harder.

October 22, 1687, he wrote, demanding annexation. October
31 he appeared in Hartford at the head of a troop of soldiers,
and formally took possession of the colony, appointed Governor.
Robert Treat and Capt. John Allen members of his council, and
renewed his demand for the charter; but during the debate in
the General Court, then assembled in Hartford in the evening,
suddenly the lights were extinguished and the charter was carried
and concealed in a hollow tree standing on the Willys estate;
and this tree was subsequently known as the "Charter Oak."

The people were not willing to give up their charter, upon
which all their property rights and privileges as citizens were
based. They were not pleased with the proposed changes in the
new form of government. They were willing to let well enough
alone. Dissensions continued, not alone in Connecticut, but in
Massachusetts as well; and after Andros had made his tour on
through to New York and return, he reached Boston in October,
1688, to find that public sentiment had become aroused against
him; the revolution came, and he was deposed and imprisoned.
Escaping from jail he fled to Rhode Island, was there re-arrested,
taken back to Massachusetts, and sent to England, and from
there he went to Virginia, where he was made governor, but
died in London, February 24, 1714. With the downfall of
Andros, Where did the power of government rest? was the question that occupied the minds of the people. Should the old
officers who were in power when Andros took possession be rein-
stated, or new ones elected, and who had authority to call an
election? These were perplexing questions; good people differed
as to the proper course to follow. In Hartford there was a sort
of public gathering, at which excitement ran high; votes were
taken and doubts expressed as to the result, but at last the vote
to reinstate old officers was declared carried, although many persons doubted the correctness of that decision. Governor Treat,
however, in October, 1690, when challenged as to his jurisdiction
in a trial before the court of assistants, claimed the election to
have been legal.

Now it seems that Benjamin Crane, Jr., was among those who
opposed Andros, and his assistants, and therefore belonged to
the party for retaining the old charter. Andros was no stranger
to the people of Connecticut. For many years while governor
of New York he had been harassing this colony with his unrea-
sonable demands, even going to the extent of appearing off
Saybrook, July 8, 1675, with two vessels filled with armed men

to press a landing for the purpose of taking possession of what was then one of the chief ports of that colony, thus attempting to rob the Connecticut people of valuable territory, of which they had held peaceable possession for nearly forty years. This bold action on the part of Andros aroused the blood of the Connecticut settlers, who were determined to hold every foot of land covered by their charter, and so impressed the would-be usurper with their firmness that he abandoned the scheme and went on his way for that time, but to appear in another rôle at a later date. Therefore, in view of the whole situation, it does not at this writing seem strange that when Andros came again to take from them, as they believed, the rights they enjoyed under the old charter the people should express their indignation and distrust. Many of these gentlemen were earnest and outspoken, even using words of contempt for those who were in authority under Andros. Governor Treat, who felt the rebuke most keenly, was determined that the dignity of the office should be maintained; therefore, as a warning to those who would speak ill of their superiors, an order was issued for the arrest of Benjamin Crane, Jr., he perhaps having been the most forcible or severe in his criticism.

Thus the persecution of Benjamin Crane was instituted, he avoiding arrest on the ground of want of jurisdiction. Those claiming authority had received commissions from Andros, he had been deposed, and they had thrown up their commissions; and the question, whether or not there had been a legal election to reinstate the present officials, had not, in the opinion of many people, been fairly settled.

A brief account is given in the following language: "The Court being informed that Benjamin Crane of Wethersfield had spoken some hard words of those gentlemen who had thrown up their commissions, &c., as if they were perjured, &c., they thought there was cause for slander or defamation, so issued a warrant to bring him into court. He resolved not to fall into their hands, absconded, so issued a special rit warrant as they called it to a man that was no officer to take a file of musketeers (musqueteers) and break open his house and serch for him there and aprehend Benjamin Crane and bring him into court. The honest man with the warrant did not know what to do. The people were enraged, and he was liable to be imprisoned if he did not act. So he sends Benjamin notice of it, and then goes with soldiers to the house. Benjamin's wife being big with child near her time, and naturally afraid of guns, kept the door shut against them, and told them her husband was not in the house. But while their leader was at the other end of the house some of the company fetched a log to break the door. She, not thinking they would break in the door, sat where she was near to it. Her brother, seeing them bring the log, told his sister; she no sooner removed than the log came violently against the door and break

it, and in they rushed with their arms, frightening her almost to death. Some of the men were ashamed, others very impudent. They found not Benjamin. This woman, though young and naturally robust, on account of the fright had a long and severe delivery, and a long infirmity after it."

This attempt to apprehend Mr. Crane must have been made in the autumn of 1690.

In the court records we find the following:

COURT HARTFORD, Nov. 28, 1690.

COL. ROBT. TREAT, ESQ., GOVERNOR.

Whereas the court October last had complaint made to them of Benjamin Crane of his notorious obsine speaking against the authority's, The said court ordered that as soon as they may, call him to account, and punish him for the same, which by the court was attended to, and the court called said Crane to appear before them, and showed him his charge which was for saying the authority was a company of fore sworn wretches, that it was not of the King nor of God but of the Divile, which he acknowledth in his passion he did say, and also his wishing himself anethema maranatha and that his soule may perish to all eternity if he submitted to this government which was testified against him which he acknowledged he submitted to the testimonie, and the court having considered the case and the circumstances thereof Do judge him worthy of severe punishment as could be well laid upon him, yet willing to be favorable as may be, Do sentence the said Benjamin Crane to pay a fine of £15 to the treasurer of this country and that the said Crane be committed to prison there to continue till the said 15 lbs is paid and at his release he is to give a £50 bond with sufficient security or sureties for his good behavior till the court in March next and that then he appear and take up his bond. The marshall was ordered upon his denyal of submitting to the servace of the court to convey said Crane to the common goale (and have his mittemus with him)."

The court, held Nov. 28, 1690, was made up as follows:

Col. Robert Treat, Esq., Governor,
Samuel Willys,
William Joanes,
Lt. Col. Jno. Allyn,
Capt. Samuel Talcott,
William Pitkin,
Nathaniel Stanley.

Judging from the following court record Benjamin Crane paid his fine of fifteen pounds, but did not appear before the court in March, 1691, and may not have been strictly on his good behavior, for his brother John Crane, who signed Benjamin's bond, was called upon to pay the fifty pounds.

APRIL 8, 1691.

The court ordered " that the clerk of the court do inform John

Crane that they require that he return Benjamin Crane to prison, that he do it within two days, and in failure thereof the court resolve to take the forfeiture of his bond."

APRIL 25, 1691.

"John Crane being called three times to appear in court and to bring his brother Benjamin according to his bond. He appeared not, so his bond of £50 is forfeited to the country treasury."

It is a fact worthy of notice that these brothers both died young, and soon after this rather unfortunate political entanglement; Benjamin was drowned June 20, 1693, and John died Oct. 21, 1694.

14. LIEUT. JONATHAN CRANE[2] [3], (Benjamin[1]), married Deborah Griswold, daughter of Francis Griswold, Dec. 19, 1678. She was born May, 1661, and died about 1704. Mr. Griswold was in Windsor in 1649. Went from there to Saybrook, and from thence, about 1660, to Norwich, where he was among the most enterprising of the early settlers. Was called of Windham, Norwich and Lebanon. He died June 6, 1735. He was one of the first settlers of Windham, Conn., erecting the first sawmill in the town. Mr. Weaver says he was known as a blacksmith in 1715.

Dec. 11, 1690, he purchased of John Calkins of Norwich 1000 acres right in S. E. Quarter No. 2. He was at that time called of Norwich.

October, 1696, he was appointed one of the Overseers of the estate of Robert Wade. Appointed by the Assistants a Lieutenant October, 1703. Was chosen Deputy to the General Court from Windham 1701, 1703, 1705, 1707 to 1714, 1717, 1718, 1721 and 1722. Children:

15—1. SARAH, b. Nov. 16, 1680.*
16—2. JONATHAN, b. Feb. 2, 1684.'
17—3. JOHN, b. Oct. 1. 1687.
18—4. MARY, b. Oct. 20, 1689, m. Jacob Simons April 4, 1710.
19—5. HANNAH, b. March 7, 1692.†
20—6. ISAAC, b. April 6, 1694.
21—7. JOSEPH, b. May 17, 1696.
22—8. ELIZABETH, } b. Feb., 1698; both died in 1698.
23—9. DEBORAH, }
24—10. ABIGAIL, b. Feb. 15, 1700; m. David Knight Dec. 24, 1718, and lived in Norwich, Conn.

At the first public meeting of the settlers of Windham, Conn., held May 18, 1691, Jonathan Crane was one of the four persons directed to run the town lines, which work had been accomplished by May 28, at which time another meeting was held, and he with Joshua Ripley and Jonathan Ginnings were chosen to make division of the meadows at four shillings per day for their services. During the summer he built and set in operation his grist-mill, which was on the site of what is now known as Brigham's Mills.

---

*Norwich Records by Mr. Weaver.　†Windham Records by Mr. Weaver.

Jonathan Crane with ten others petitioned the General Court sitting at Hartford, Oct. 6, 1691, to grant them a Town charter, the town to be called Windham. The petition was granted May 12, 1692. At the first public town meeting, held June 12, 1692, Mr. Crane was elected one of the "Townsmen," and at the same meeting he with Thomas Huntington were directed to take measures for securing a minister. Their efforts were not crowned with success until September of that year, when they agreed with Mr. Samuel Whiting to come and carry on the ministry in that town. He preached his first sermon there January 1, 1693, and the people were so well pleased with him that they ratified the agreement and chose Samuel Roberts and Jonathan Crane " to discourse with him." He was directed to go with two others "to set to rights the lots at the Ponds," also one of three persons appointed "Collectors" to levy and gather rate. He resided on the "Hither Place," now Windham Centre. Was on committee to provide a convenient place for a burying ground; also to run the town lines with Mr. Joshua Ripley and three others. In May, 1695, he was chosen Ensign of a military company, and commissioned Ensign by the General Court in October of that year. January 4, 1695, Mr. Crane exchanged property with Sergt. Wm. Backus, giving his grist-mill and receiving a new dwelling-house in Windham, situated on the house and home lot of Mr. Backus, four acres of meadow lying on the Nochog path by the brook to the little pine swamp, and one acre of meadow in the five-acre meadow. This house and lot was on what was called the Hither Place, and April 11, 1695, Mr. Crane sold it to Exercise Conant, who sold it about one year later to John Abbe of Wenham for £70 silver. In 1696 the town built a house for their minister, Mr. Whitney. The work, except building the chimneys, was accomplished by the townspeople, led in four separate companies or squads, Ensign Crane taking the lead of one of them. That Mr. Crane was one of Windham's most active and influential men there can be little doubt.

January 30, 1700, he with Rev. Samuel Whiting purchased the front portion of William Backus's home lot, it being eight by twenty rods square, and gave it to the town for a " meeting-house plat or common." This lot was afterwards called " Windham Green," and here the first meeting-house was erected. In 1698 he with Mr. Huntington purchased in behalf of the proprietors of Windham a tract of land containing about ten thousand acres, lying between Windham and Norwich, and west of the " Nipmuck Path," called the " Mamosyneage lands." In the year 1700 this tract was made over to Rev. Samuel Whiting and Jonathan Crane. They took the whole care of laying it out into lots and selling them to settlers. Lieut. Daniel Mason publicly made claim to this land on Training-day in Windham, May 13, 1701, he having received a deed of it from one of the pretended Indian owners. But the following September the General Court

ratified and confirmed the purchase of Crane and Whiting, and granted them a patent, thus preventing further controversy as to the rightful ownership of this tract of land. In the year 1700 Lieut. Crane received permission from the Court at Hartford "to keep a public victualing house for the entertainment of travelers and strangers, and the retailing of strong drink." Also appointed by the General Court to view Plainfield and see best place to erect a meeting-house; chosen on committee to see the miller and regulate the grinding of corn, it not being satisfactory. October, 1701, on committee to run the town line; October 20, 1702, on committee to see to completing the meeting-house, and April 19, 1703, on committee to arrange the seating of the same. This same year the town agreed to have but "one ordinary, Lieut. Crane to keep it," and the General Court commissioned him Lieutenant. In 1704 he was on committee to run out the line "from Appaynage to the southeast corner of the town and c."

The Indian war broke out afresh in 1704, and Windham reorganized her military company for the protection of the inhabitants. John Fitch was chosen Captain, Jonathan Crane Lieutenant, and Joseph Cary Ensign. Although the people at this time became somewhat alarmed, no serious inconvenience was experienced. In 1705 Mr. Crane was one of a committee to have charge of all town lands; to call meetings to vote on any matters necessary, and to sign the acts to lay out highways, &c. In 1713 the town voted to enlarge the meeting-house, and appropriated £40 to pay for doing the work. The matter was, however, reconsidered, and the subject finally disposed of by deciding to build a new house of worship to meet the demands of the rapidly increasing population. Deacons Cary, Brigham and Lieut. Crane were chosen a committee to agree with the workmen, Mr. Crane to serve as treasurer. The work was speedily and successfully accomplished, the new building having been erected on the site of the old one. In the year 1715 he served on a committee to settle the question whether or not to allow the north parish (Canada) to form a separate religious society. After careful consideration of the matter, the prayer of the petition was granted. In 1726 Jonathan Crane, Joshua Ripley and John Fitch were chosen as representatives of the brethren to act with the newly appointed deacons to constitute the "seven pillars" or councillors of the church. These men were recommended to the pastor, to be called together by him for consultation whenever occasion demanded. Mr. Crane was one of the first set of jurymen empaneled in the County of Windham at the first Court of Common Pleas, holden June 26, 1726. It is reasonable to suppose that more than one occasion demanded the attention of this constituted arm of the Church, the "seven pillars." But we will quote but one, Nov. 13, 1728: "Whereas, the work and business of the pastor of a Church is very great,

and particularly the enquiring into scandal and procuring evidence, and whereas, the Scripture informs us that God has set some in the Church to be helps in the government, voted, That it shall be the work of the Representatives of the Bretheren, and they are hereby desired, with all diligence, to attend upon it. That when there is a public and common report that any person belonging to the congregation hath committed any public scandalous evil, to enquire into such report and bring information and evidence to the pastor, provided that this be not understood to hinder the pastor from taking cognizance of any scandal that may otherwise clearly come to his knowledge, nor to hinder any private brother from bringing a complaint whenever there be occasion for it."

The following was taken from the records of Wethersfield: "July 3, 1734: Jonathan Crane of Lebanon Windham Co for the love &c. I have for my two grandsons as follows John Crane of Wethersfield and Abiah Crane of Windham, I give in equal part or share all my right or interest in any lot or lotment of land in Wethersfield. Acknowledged before Jonathan Huntington, Justice."

This John and Abiah were brothers and the two eldest children of Jonathan's son John.

The inscription upon the headstone over his grave in the cemetery at Lebanon, Conn., reads as follows: "Here lies Mr Jonathan Crane husband of Mrs Deborah Crane who lived a pious and Godly life and left y[e] earth for heaven March y[e] 12th Ano[c] 1735, and in y[e] 77th year of his age."

25. JOSEPH CRANE[2] [4], (Benjamin[1]), married Sarah, daughter of John Kilborne, Dec. 10, 1684. He died Nov. 28, 1707. aged 46 years. At the distribution his estate was given to his wife and children, as mentioned, "Benjamin, Isaac, Susan Pool, Hannah Purple, and Ester Crane." His widow married Mr. Leonard, and, Sept. 2, 1718, Joseph Talcott, Esq., Judge, appointed this Mrs. Leonard of Wethersfield guardian of her children, Esther, about 16, she desiring the same, and Isaac, about 11, she giving the necessary bond for £100.

Had land given him by his father Jan. 12, 1683, and acknowledged March 5 that year. It was located near south end of "Rocky Hill," in Wethersfield, on the highway towards Middletown.

He purchased of his brother Jacob 4½ acres of land located on "Bever Brook," receiving the deed Oct. 9, 1696. Lot No. 163 on Connecticut River fell to him in the distribution of town lots. Aug. 6, 1697, he purchased a lot containing 24 acres of Michael Griswold. He also owned 21 acres at or near "Tappin's hill." Sarah, widow of Joseph Crane, late of Wethersfield, exhibited an Inventory of the estate Jan. 5, 1707, and was appointed administratrix. Abraham Kilborne had been appointed guardian for

Joseph's son Benjamin. Kilborne having died, Benjamin, aged about 16, asked the Court, March 17, 1712-13, to appoint John Wright as guardian, which was done. April 16, 1714, Benjamin asked to have Abraham Morrison of Wethersfield appointed guardian, and that was done.

May 12, 1709, widow was allowed to sell land to pay debts against the estate, and October, same year, again allowed to sell land to pay debts, and save movable property so she and the children could subsist.

Feb. 5, 1710-11, the Court granted further time to Sarah, widow and administratrix, to administer the estate. June 7, 1714, Sarah Leonard reported on estate of Joseph Crane, whole amount £233—0—6. She was to have one-third, and each child their part. June 8, 1714, this appears: "Whereas, the administratrix of the estate of Joseph Crane, late of Wethersfield, is married and moved out of this government, the Court granted letters of administration to Joseph Kilbourn of Wethersfield, which he accepted and gave bonds."

Jan. 18, 1714-15, Abraham Morris was added to administer this estate. May 28, 1715, reported not enough movable property to pay the debts. July 5, 1715, Court ordered 9—6—10 of land to be sold to pay debts.

Joseph Crane, freeman, of Fairfield, Conn., March 18, 1689-90, was without doubt this Joseph, and his nephew and namesake, going there later, as early as 1715.

Widow married 3d Mr. Andrews. Children:

26—1. SARAH, b. Dec. 10, 1685; d. June.24, 1686.*
27—2. SARAH, b. March 15, 1687; m. Moses Goff, Jr., July 5, 1711; he d. Dec. 5, 1711, aged 24; his child Jan. 17, 1712-3; she m. 2d Mr. Toole.
28—3. HANNAH, b. Aug. 4, 1689; m. Mr. Purple.
29—4. MARY, b. Aug. 31, 1692; d. Sept. 28, 1701.
30—5. BENJAMIN, b. May 21, 1694.
31—6. JOSEPH, b. Nov., 1696; d. Sept. 28. 1712.
32—7. HESTER, b. Sept. 7, 1698; d. Sept. 6, 1701.
33—8. DAVID, b. April 27, 1701; d. Sept. 15, 1701.
34—9. ESTHER, b. Aug. 28, 1702.
35-10. SUSAN, b. 1704 or 5; m. Mr. Pool.
36-11. ISAAC, b. Oct. 20, 1707.

June 8, 1714, Joseph Kilbourn was appointed guardian for Isaac and Esther.

37. JOHN CRANE[2] [5], (Benjamin[1]), married Abigail, daughter of Nathaniel Butler, Oct. 27, 1692. He went with his brother Jonathan to Windham, and built a house there 1691-2. Was a blacksmith by trade. He returned, however, to Wethersfield, and succeeded to his father's business as tanner. He drew land in Wethersfield, 1694. He died Oct. 21, 1694, aged 31 years. She then married Samuel Walker Feb. 23, 1697, having one child by her first husband. May, 1697, the Court granted full power to Mr. Walker and Abigail his wife to sell such part of estate of

---

*Nov.—Wethersfield Records.

the late John Crane as necessary to pay debts. By second marriage she had Abigail, Elizabeth and Sarah. Child:

38—1. JOSIAH. b. March 22, 1694.

Nov. 2, 1694, widow Abigail was appointed administratrix, with John Chester, Nathan Butler and John Wyatt to assist her. April 8, 1695, Inventory was exhibited and the estate divided. Widow had one-half and rest to the son.

Nov. 4, 1697, Abigail Walker, relict of John Crane, according to list of estates, 1693, was granted lot 102, containing 15½ acres, on Cow Plain, Wethersfield. Inventory of his (John Crane's) estate was £417—06—04. The rent on the tanyard was due to Widow Crane, senior, from estate of John Crane, March, 1695.

April 3, 1710, William Pitkin, Judge, ordered a writ to require Samuel Walker, late of Wethersfield and now residing in Stratford, with his wife, administrators on the estate of John Crane, late of Wethersfield, deceased, to appear before the Court and render an account of said estate on the first Monday of July next, or sooner if they can.

June 5, 1710, Samuel Walker and Abigail his wife, administrators on estate of John Crane, late of Wethersfield, tanner, deceased, report all debts paid, and said Abigail ⅓ out of movable part, and there is still remaining in hands of administrators, of the movable part £23—9—9 and the real part £262—0—0 for the use of the son and said heir of said John Crane, deceased.

May, 1713, upon petition of John Wright of Wethersfield, guardian to heirs of Joseph Crane, late of Wethersfield, deceased; Jonathan Belding, guardian to heirs; Israel Crane of Wethersfield, deceased, requested that they, together with guardian that shall be appointed by the Probate Court instead of James Steel of Wethersfield, deceased, who was guardian to the heirs of John Crane, late of Wethersfield, deceased, may be empowered to sell such lands of the minors above said as are due from the estate of Isaac Crane, son of Benjamin, late of Wethersfield, deceased. It was granted.

Under date April 4, 1715, Samuel Walker, administrator of estate of John Crane, tanner, late of Wethersfield, deceased, now under bond. Josiah, now of full age, child of the said John Crane. "Whereas, Josiah received his full share of the estate, as the Court assigned, June 5, 1710, said Walker is discharged; also Isaac Ryley is discharged as guardian of said Josiah Crane." The General Court granted Samuel Walker and Abigail his wife to sell land from estate of John Crane to pay debts.

39. ELIJAH CRANE[2] [6], (Benjamin[1]). Married 1st Mary Sherman, who was born May 8, 1666, daughter of Samuel Sherman, Jr. Samuel, senior, lived in Wethersfield, Conn. She was sister of Theophilus Sherman of Wethersfield. Samuel, Jr., removed to Stratford, Conn, where Mary was born. Elijah Crane owned

eighteen acres of land in Great Westfield in Wethersfield, his
brother Benjamin signing a release of the same, under date of
July 27, 1692. This was witnessed by their brother John Crane.
Not many years afterward he removed to Fairfield; for he renewed his covenant with the Church there (Stratfield Parish),
town of Fairfield, Feb. 8, 1697; and his wife Mary was admitted
to full communion there Oct. 22, 1699. June 1, 1699, Mr. Crane,
then of Fairfield, took a deed of 18 acres of land at "Toylsome,"
in Stratford, of Samuel Sherman, also of Fairfield. Nov. 27,
1701, Mr. Crane deeded land in Wethersfield to his brother Jacob
Crane. In the year 1712 he made an inventory of the estate of
Moses Jackson, senior, of Stratfield, and witnessed his will. In
1716 he was appointed guardian of William and Benjamin Castle,
sons of Joseph, deceased. His wife Mary died previous to March
8, 1719-20, for on that date he with wife Abigail Adams joined
in a deed with Daniel, David and John Adams, Isaac Castle
(for his wife Sarah), to sell the homestead of Abraham Adams,
Jr., deceased, they being his heirs. All were of Fairfield except
Isaac Castle, who was of Woodbury, Conn. Mr. Crane's wife
Abigail was daughter of Samuel Adams and sister of Abraham.
Mr. Crane died just prior to Feb. 7, 1726-7, for on that date
Daniel Adams was appointed administrator of his estate and
guardian of his children by second wife. Dec. 25, 1734,
Theophilus Sherman of Wethersfield, for the love he bore for his
sister Mary Crane, deceased, deeded land in Stratfield to Elijah,
Jabez, Mary and Comfort, her children. By second wife Abigail
he had four children.

An inventory of his estate, dated Feb. 20, 1726-7, was presented
to the Court by Samuel Odell, Jonathan Morehouse and Daniel
Adams, administrators. In 1730 the estate of Elijah Crane was
declared insolvent, and Mr. Jonathan Sturgess and Thomas Han-
ford were appointed commissioners. 1727, his son Benjamin
was made the ward of Capt. Samuel Couch of Fairfield. But
Dec. 31, 1739, Benjamin made choice of John Olmstead as his
guardian. 1727, his son Israel was made the ward of Ralph
Keeler of Norwalk. Children:

    40—1. ABIGAIL, bapt. May 29, 1698; probably d. prior to 1716.
    41—2. DEBORAH, bapt. April 2, 1699; probably d. prior to 1734.
    42—3. MARY, bapt. Sept. 15, 1700.
    43—4. ISRAEL, bapt. March 28, 1703; probably d. prior to 1724.
    44—5. COMFORT, bapt. June 16, 1706; m. Joseph Goodwin.
    45—6. ELIJAH, bapt. Nov. 7, 1708.
    46—7. JABEZ, bapt. May 9, 1714.
    47—8. ABIGAIL, bapt. June 29, 1716; probably died prior to 1734.
    48—9. SARAH.
    49—10. ELIZABETH.
    50—11. ISRAEL.
    51—12. BENJAMIN.

52. ABRAHAM CRANE[2] [7], (Benjamin[1]). Married Hannah,
and died July 5, 1713, aged 45. Inventory of his estate taken
Nov. 19, 1713, gave a valuation of £345—03—07.

Drew land in the allotment of 1694. He owned 17½ acres in Westfield, 8 acres in Cedar Swamp and 9 acres in Field. Served as fence viewer in 1699.

Hannah, the widow, with Joseph Belding, were appointed, Aug. 3, 1713, to administer the estate. They reported to the Court Nov. 20, 1713.

The Wethersfield records show that he purchased of his brother Israel land located on the Connecticut River which formerly belonged to Benjamin, senior, Israel signing the deed.

Records of the Probate Court show that Jan. 25, 1731-2, Hannah Crane, administratrix, reported amount of estate of Abraham Crane, late of Wethersfield, £55—9—2, with debts due said estate of £10—8—6.

Oct. 4, 1737, Hannah, wife of Abraham Crane, asked the Court for dower. John, eldest son, had £5—7—10, Benoni, Abraham, Mary, Hannah and Lucy each £2—13—11, of the movable estate. Children :

53—1. MARY, b. Feb. 7, 1697.
54—2. JOHN, b. March 14, 1700.
55—3. BENONI, b. Aug. 20, 1704. Jan. 14, 1725-6, sold land in Newington to Ezra Belding. Jan. 11, 1754, gave land to his brother Abraham, lot in West Swamp, 29th tier late division. He lived in Wethersfield.
56—4. HANNAH, b. May 26. 1706.
57—5. LUCY, b. July 25, 1710; m. Joseph Forbs of Wethersfield, Dec. 23, 1732; they for £70 quitclaimed all their interest in their father's (Abraham Crane) estate to her brother John.
58—6. ABRAHAM, b. Oct. 5, 1713.

59. JACOB CRANE[2] [8J, (Benjamin[1]). He lived and died in Wethersfield, Conn. He owned land near Rocky Hill, and his brother Benjamin signed a release to it Sept. 16, 1692, which was witnessed by Abraham Crane and John Talcott. This Jacob Crane drew land in allotment in Wethersfield, 1694, and bought land of his brother Elijah. Deed dated Nov. 27, 1701.

An inventory of his estate was taken Jan. 2, 1718-19, in which his land at Rocky Hill was mentioned; total amount £77—02—04. In "May, 1719, upon prayer of Jonathan Crane of Windham and William Warner of Wethersfield, administrators of the estate of Jacob Crane of said Wethersfield, who died insolvent, the Assistants granted permit to sell the lands to highest bidder and report to Probate Court so that the debts or a portion of them can be paid."

Inventory of his estate taken Jan. 2, 1718-19 is as follows : Shock rye, half acre land at Rocky Hill, 4 acres in meadow; total, £77—02—04. He was probably the Jacob Crane who, Sept. 27, 1699, sold land in Springfield he got of Simon Beamon of Deerfield, March 8, 1694-5, to Tiely Merrick.

Sept. 16, 1718, Joseph Talcott, Esq., Judge. "The Court, granted letters of administration on the estate of Jacob Crane late of Wethersfield, deceased, unto Jonathan Crane of Wind-

ham and William Warner of Wethersfield, provided they give
necessary bond and exhibit true inventory of said estate on or
before first Tuesday in November next, and that they render account of their administration on the estate on or before the first
Tuesday of September, 1719." Bond was accordingly given and
letters of administration taken out.

60. ISRAEL CRANE[2] [9], (Benjamin[1]), drew land in the allotment of 1694. Married Lydia Wright, daughter of James Wright,
Sept. 13, 1695, ceremony was performed by Rev. Stephen Mix.
He was chosen collector 1700. He died in Wethersfield April
28, 1707, aged 35, leaving a large estate, amounting to £444—
18—10. At the division of lots in 1693 he drew lot No. 160,
containing 11 acres.

His homestead was valued £130, and he had 4 acres pasture at
Town end, 13 acres at Cow Plain, 26 acres at Goosberry Swamp,
about 72 acres, besides homestead.

His dwelling-house lot joined the land of Benjamin Crane, Jr.
His brother Israel Crane at one time owned north end of the
great island pertaining to Wethersfield, called "Wright's Island,"
in Connecticut River.

May, 1708, leave was granted wife Lydia to sell portion of
husband's estate, late Israel Crane of Wethersfield.

May 4, 1713, Lt. Jonathan B. Twing of Wethersfield was
asked to be appointed guardian for children. May, 1713,
Jonathan Belding was guardian for the children. One of them
may have declined to serve.

Mr. Crane bought land April 5, 1693, in Great Westfield.
June 2, 1697, bought land on the Connecticut River of Abraham
Crane, witnessed by Jonathan Crane; also bought land and small
tanyard joining and on south of land belonging to heirs of John
Crane, deceased, and north on land of Abraham Crane, westerly
on highway; also bought land of Jonathan Crane of Windham,
June 4, 1697, deed signed by Jonathan Crane and witnessed by
Abraham Crane. Again, he purchased land of Ebenezer Coleman Jan. 13, 1702. Lydia, his widow, made her mark to a deed
to Abraham Crane, July 31, 1710, which mentioned tan-vats,
buildings, &c. Children :

  61—1. LYDIA, b. Aug. 4, 1701. ·
  62—2. HANNAH, b. Nov. 24, 1702.
  63—3. ELIZABETH, b. Sept. 23, 1704.
  64—4. MARTHA, b. March 19, 1706. She probably never married, for
          Aug. 17, 1731, she asked the Court to set off ½ the house,
          presumably to herself and sister Lydia, the other half
          going to her mother, who had by distribution 1719-20 ⅓, the
          four daughters having ⅔.

Jan. 5, 1719-20, "Whereas administration was formerly granted
on estate of Israel Crane, some time of Wethersfield, deceased,
the estate remains unsettled, no account rendered, the administratrix being unable to manage it. The Court grants letters of

administration to Lt. Jonathan Belding, he giving bond," &c. He gave the bond, &c.

Feb. 9, 1719-20, "Lydia Crane and Jonathan Belding exhibited an account of the estate of Israel Crane. £7—0—0 amount paid out in debts. Whole estate £444—19—6, the movable part whereof is £42—9—6, leaving £437—19—6 to distribution. Lydia, the widow, to have £11—16—6, being one-third of the movable part and one-third of the landed estate, during natural life. To Lydia, Hannah, Elizabeth and Martha, daughters of said deceased, to each £106—10—9, which is their equal share of said estate. David Goodrich, Joshua Robbins and Thomas Wright, or any two of them, appointed to distribute and divide the same before first Tuesday of April next." April 5, 1720, report was made and accepted.

65. MARY CRANE[2] [10], (Benjamin[1]), married to William Warner, May 21, 1696, by Rev. Stephen Mix. Settled in Wethersfield, Conn.; where they were married.

She died March 18, 1714, about 40 years of age. He then married 2d Elizabeth ———, by whom he had William, born Dec. 4, 1717. Children:

66—1. JOHN (Warner), b. Oct. 24, 1697; d. Nov. 11, 1697.
67—2. MARY (Warner), b. Dec. 2, 1698.
68—3. ABIGAILE (Warner), b. June 14, 1701.
69—4. JOHN (Warner), b. Jan. 5, 1703.
70—5. HANNAH (Warner), b. Nov. 17, 1706.
71—6. WILLIAM (Warner), b. Jan. 27, 1709; d. March 11, 1714.
72—7. JONATHAN (Warner), b. Dec. 11, 1712.

73. SARAH CRANE[3] [15], (Jonathan,[2] Benjamin[1]), married Nathaniel Hibard, April 16, 1702. This was the first marriage recorded in Windham, and their eldest child was the first birth recorded in the records of the town. They had eight sons and three daughters. He was son of Robert Hibard, Jr., of Salem, Mass., who removed to Windham about 1700. Children:

1. NATHANIEL (Hibard), b. Jan. 3, 1703; d. May 16, 1704.
2. SAMUEL (Hibard), b. July 21, 1704, d. July 21, 1704.
3. ANNA (Hibard), b. May 30, 1705; m. John Gray.
4. DEBORAH (Hibard), b. May 28, 1707; m. Isaac Robinson.
5. NATHANIEL (Hibard), ⎫ b. Oct. 23, 1709; m. Abigail Couch.
   ⎬ twins.
6. JONATHAN (Hibard), ⎭ b. Oct. 23, 1709.
7. PAUL (Hibard), b. March 4, 1712,
8. ZEBULON (Hibard), b. Feb. 20, 1714; d. July, 1788.
9. SARAH (Hibard), b. June 27, 1717.
10. ELISHA (Hibard), b. Dec. 11, 1719.
11. GIDEON (Hibard), b. May 2, 1721.

74. JONATHAN CRANE[3] [16], (Jonathan,[2] Benjamin[1]), married Mary, daughter of Robert Hibard, senior, of Windham, July 31, 1705. She was born in Windham, Aug. 18, 1674. Jonathan Crane, Jr.'s will was dated Aug. 29, 1748, and certified Sept. 10, 1757. Amount £701—2—3, and names, "wife Mary, children Silas, Zerviah and Ann, children of Jonathan, grandson Timothy Buel, son of my daughter Mary, Sarah, Anna, Theoda and Jerusha, Anna and Azaria Bill, children of my daughter Mary."

He was buried in the cemetery in Lebanon, Conn. Inscription on his headstone is as follows:

Here lies ye body of Jonathan Crane, who was born Feby. 2, A. D. 1684, and departed this life Aug. 27, 1757, in the 74 year of his age.
> His body lies in shade of night
> His soul we trust is in ye light
> Before the throne in humble days
> Singing his blessed Redeemer's praise.

Children:

75—1. SARAH, b. May 11, 1707.*
76—2. MARY, b. April 13, 1709.
77—3. ANNA, b. May 24, 1711.
78—4. ZEBULON, b. April 26, 1713; d. Oct. 6, 1714.

*Windham Records, Mr. Weaver.

79—5. JONATHAN, b. July 6, 1715.
80—6. ELIJAH, b. Feb. 4, 1717-18.*
81—7. THEODA, b. May 10, 1720; m. Eiijah Brigham, March 8, 1739, at Lebanon, Conn.
82—8. SILAS, b. April 19, 1723; m. Lucy Waterman, Sept. 20, 1742, at Norwich.
83—9. JERUSHA; m. Lemuel Crane, May 13, 1757; family at Lebanon.

84. JOHN CRANE[3] [17], (Jonathan,[2] Benjamin[1]), married 1st, Sarah Spencer, Sept. 16, 1708, at Windham. She died Sept. 15, 1715; 2d, Prudence Belding, April 18, 1716. He lived near a place called Fort Hill, where his father gave him house and lands Jan. 18, 1710-11. April 10, 1728, he sold all his tract of land, dwelling-house, &c., to Joseph Walden for £300. He also quitclaimed to his brother Jonathan, May 16, 1735; at which time he was called of Coventry.

April 9, 1730, John Crane of Wethersfield, for himself and as attorney for Jonathan Crane of Windham, gave caution to Wethersfield town clerk not to record any "distribution or agreement in y[e] division of land formerly of Benjamin Crane, senior, and Benjamin, Jr., and also of y[e] land of Isaac Crane, son of Benjamin, Jr., lying in Wethersfield." Children:

85—1. JOHN, b. July 31, 1709; d. in Becket, Mass.†
86—2. ABIAH, b. Oct. 12, 1710.
87—3. EUNICE, b. May 13, 1712.
88—4. ELISHAM or ELISHA, b. March 13, 1718.‡
89—5. SYBIL, b. April 1, 1719.
90—6. HEZEKIAH, b. March 31, 1721.
91—7. PRUDENCE, b. July 24, 1723.
92—8. LEMUEL, b. July 12, 1725.
93—9. HANNAH, b. March 15, 1727.
94-10. RHODA, b. March 28, 1729.
95-11. ADONIJAH, b. May 12, 1731.

96. HANNAH CRANE[3] [19], (Jonathan,[2] Benjamin[1]), married Caleb Conant, Aug. 23, 1714. Resided in Windham and Mansfield, Conn. Mr. Conant was a member of the first church at Windham, and for a time lived on Mountain Meadow Hill. April 20, 1717, he sold his house and land there to Jabez Huntington. She died Oct. 11, 1726. He died in April, 1727. Children:

1. MALACHI (Conant), b. June 12, 1715.
2. BENAJAH (Conant), b. Feb. 13, 1716-17.
3. SARAH (Conant), b. Dec. 20, 1718; d. Sept. 8, 1742.
4. RUTH (Conant), b. Oct. 28, 1720; married Shubail Conant.
5. MARY (Conant), b. Jan. 6, 1722-3; d. Nov. 23, 1726.
6. JOSIAH (Conant), b. Dec. 9, 1724.
7. HANNAH (Conant), b. Sept. 25, 1726.

97. ISAAC CRANE[3] [20], (Jonathan,[2] Benjamin[1]), married Ruth, daughter of John Waldo, July 12, 1716, at Windham; m. 2d, Hannah ———. He was called Isaac senior of Windham;

---

* Lebanon Records, Mr. Weaver.　　† Windham Records.
‡ Coventry Records.

spelled on records Crain and Crane. His will, dated June 26, 1751,. certified Aug. 5, 1751, proved Sept. 10, 1751; inventory Sept. 3, 1751, £3337—7—10, names wife Hannah, children Isaac, Ruth Webb, Adrie Broughton, Ann Babcock, Deborah. It is related that he gained the favor of Ruth Waldo by gallantly conveying her on his own steed through the swollen waters of Merrick's Brook, when a sudden Sunday freshet had made it impassable for travelers on foot. Children:

98.—1. RUTH, b. April 12, 1718; m. Ebenezer Webb.
99.—2. ADRIE, b July 25, 1720; m. Thomas Broughton.
100.—3. ANNA, b. Feb. 1, 1723-4; m. Joseph Babcock, Nov. 8, 1744
101'—4. ISAAC, b. July 27, 1726; he was of Hebron.
102.—2. DEBORAH, b. Jan. 28, 1729; m. John Ormsby, Nov. 14, 1754. — *Tolland Town Records.*

103. JOSEPH CRANE[3] [21], (Jonathan,[2] Benjamin[1]). Born in Windham, Conn. When the new meeting-house was built there, he, with a few other young men, in the year 1713, built a pew for their own use. Just the date he left Windham does not appear, but he evidently while a young man followed his uncles Joseph and Elijah Crane to Fairfield, where he married about the year 1719 Mary, daughter of Samuel Couch of that place. She was born Dec. 15, 1695. Mr. Couch gave his son-in-law property in Fairfield, deed dated Sept. 8, 1725. It will be seen by referring to the notice of Joseph Crane's uncle Elijah that after the death of this uncle, Benjamin, his youngest son, was in 1727 made the ward of Capt. Samuel Couch of Fairfield. This Joseph Crane in 1725 took an inventory of the estate of John Allen of Fairfield. But later he appears to have removed to Norwalk, and from there to the place now known as South East, Putnam County, N. Y., locating in the town last mentioned about the year 1730 on the north side of "Joe's Hill," about one mile and a half east of Sodom Corners, where on the east branch of the Croton River he built "Crane's Mill." The site of this mill is now covered by the Sodom Reservoir. Miss Kate Crane, a descendant in this line, writes that recently an old English clock has been found in South East with the following mark inside the case: "Joseph Crane, 1620." This clock may have been a wedding present, and ought ever to be retained in the possession of the Crane family. Counterfeit money was reported in circulation quite early in the history of this new country; but Joseph Crane was among those who were completely exonerated from any connection or knowledge of the matter, as will be seen from the following:

New York Colonial MSS. LXXIV. 201 "Oblong in Dutchess County April y 5 1745 We The subscribers hereinunder written was brought before me Jacobus Swartwout Esq one of his majestys judges of the court of common pleas for the said county and I could find no reason that these persons should be brought upon their oaths because they could give me no account

about Daniel Hunt Esq making or passing any counterfeit money directly or indirectly or having any concern about the money or Platt of making the New England that is called counterfeit

& nine teen
    names here
·[Literal transcription.]

JACOBUS SWARTWOUT
JAS DUNCAN
JOSEPH CRANE "

This seems to have been first Joseph of Putnam Co.
In the year 1747 Mr. Crane was chosen highway master.
Mrs. Crane died January 9, 1766, aged 70 years. He died August 20, 1781. The following dates of births and deaths were copied from the family Bible by Mr. Carso Crane, and by him presented to the compiler. Children :

104—1. ZEBULAN, b. Jan. 25, 1721; d. Jan. 24, 1789.
105—2. JOSEPH, b. Oct. 2, 1722; d. Oct. 14, 1800.
106—3. MARY, b. May 30, 1726; d. March 17, 1805.
107—4. THADDEUS, b. March 27, 1728; d. Sept. 1, 1803.
108—5. ABIGAIL, b. April 3, 1730; d. Sept. 30, 1806.
109—6. ANNA, b. April 12, 1732; d. March 28, 1805.
110—7. STEPHEN, b. May 19, 1734; d. May 10, 1814.
111—8. ADAH, b. Oct. 25, 1736; d. April 18, 1810.

112. BENJAMIN CRANE[3] [30], (Joseph,[2] Benjamin[1]). In the distribution of his father Joseph Crane's estate Dec. 29, 1717, he was given double portion thereof, being the eldest son, his mother (the widow, now Mrs. Leonard,) of course receiving one-third of the whole estate during her natural life; Sarah Tooley, Hannah Purple, Esther Crane and Isaac Crane, younger children of Joseph, deceased, single portions. The distributers were Edward Bulkley, Capt. Ephraim Goodrich and Jonathan Smith.

There was a debt due from this estate of Joseph Crane to his brother Jacob Crane. Possibly the following sale was for the purpose of cancelling that debt, or a portion of it, for Benjamin agreed to pay his uncle a debt which was due.

January 28, 1717–8, this Benjamin Crane sold to his uncle Jacob Crane for £31—7—0, 4½ acres of land in what was called Dry Swamp, bounded on west and south by highway and Beaver Creek east and north.

113. ESTHER CRANE[3] [34], (Joseph,[2] Benjamin[1]), married ——Pullers.

April 4, 1721, Esther Crane of Wethersfield declared to the court she was satisfied with the management of her guardian, Joseph Kilborn of said town, and that she had received her estate, and Joseph Kilborn's bond was discharged.

Oct. 6, 1730, Probate Records of Wethersfield, Conn., estate of Joseph Crane, deceased. Joseph Rigley and Stephen Rigley, interested in said estate, asked to have the distribution set aside, because the daughter Esther Pullers' part of the lot on Toppin's hill was set out to the widow Sarah Andrews in her dower. The

court set the distribution aside, and appointed Deacon Jonathan Curtis, Lieut. Samuel Woolcot and Ensign Jacob Williams of Wethersfield, or any two of them, to set out the widow Sarah Andrews, formerly widow to Joseph Crane, &c.

114. ELIJAH CRANE[3] [45], (Elijah,[2] Benjamin[1]), married, Aug. 3, 1732, Elizabeth, daughter of Henry and Sarah (Frost) Wakely of Fairfield, Conn. Mr. Crane and wife renewed the covenant with the church, Stratford Parish, Fairfield, July 29, 1733. She was baptized May 11, 1712. He died Oct. 3, 1740, and his widow married Benajah Mallery, Jan. 20, 1742-3.

Mr. Crane lived in Stratford by the side of his brother-in-law Joseph Goodwin, Mr. Goodwin having sold him a lot March 6, 1734-5, in consideration of his coming there to live. Oct. 13, 1740, Henry Walkely or Walkele was appointed administrator of his estate. But in 1744 Benajah Mallery was appointed administrator. Children:

115—1. JABEZ, b. Feb. 13, 1733-4; bapt. Feb. 17, 1733-4.
116—2. SETH, b. Nov. 18, 1737.

117. JABEZ CRANE[3] [46], (Elijah,[2] Benjamin[1]). He was of Norwalk, Conn., and June 20, 1746, bought for £100 all right, title and interest of James Rowland and Mary Rowland in lands located in Rocky Hill Parish, Wethersfield, that formerly belonged to Theophilus Sherman, late of Wethersfield, deceased. The deed was acknowledged in Fairfield County by T. Burr, Justice, July 20, 1746. He sold all right, title and interest in lands owned by his uncle Theophilus Sherman, late of Wethersfield, now deceased, lying at Rocky Hill Parish, to Theophilus Nichols of Stratford, Conn., for £250. Deed was acknowledged by John Thompson, Justice.

118. MARY CRANE[3] [53], (Abraham,[2], Benjamin[1]), married James Treat, Jr., Aug. 11, 1731. He died May 1, 1762, and she married, 2d, Nathaniel Copley, also of Wethersfield, Conn. Nov. 7, 1752, James Treat and Mary his wife asked the Court why the estate of her father Abraham Crane should not be distributed, and it was ordered distributed, April 26, 1763, as follows: To John Crane, eldest son, double share. To Benoni and Abraham Crane, Mary Treat, Hannah Crane and Lucy Forbs, each a single share. Joseph Bingham, Judge. Hezekiah May and Joseph Boardman reported distribution of the estate. John Crane of Wethersfield appealed from judgment of this Court to the Superior Court.

July 2, 1771, Nathaniel Copley, whose wife was Mary, daughter of Abraham Crane, deceased, called attention of the Court to some unclaimed common land belonging to estate, and Court ordered it distributed. Sergt. John Crane, two shares; heirs of Abraham and Benoni, by law, Mary Copley, Lucy, wife of Joseph

Forbs, and Hannah Crane, one share each.   John appealed it to
the Superior Court.   Children :

   1. MARY (Treat), b. Feb. 8, 1732 ; d. Dec. 24, 1751.
   2. JAMES (Treat), b. June 18, 1733 ; d. Nov. 13, 1758.
   3. SARAH (Treat), ⎱ b. Oct. 4. 1734.
   4. JOHN (Treat),   ⎰ b. Oct. 4, 1734 ; d. April 17, 1736.
   5. JOHN (Treat), b. April 1, 1740 ; d. Sept. 24, 1758.

119. SERGT. JOHN CRANE[3] [54], (Abraham,[2] Benjamin[1]),
married Lydia Curtis, March 30, 1737.   They were married by
David Goodrich, Justice of the Peace.   She died Aug. 11, 1790,
78 years of age.   June 2, 1761, the Court granted administration on the estate of John Crane to Lydia, widow of said
Crane, and she, with Samuel Bement of Wethersfield gave necessary bonds.   Settled in Wethersfield, Conn.   His estate was settled Oct. 22, 1765.   Mrs. Crane joined the church at Wethersfield in 1741.   He was a large land owner for that period ; for,
according to the Wethersfield records, he purchased for £200 all
right, title and interest of his brother Abraham in their father's
estate, Feb. 5, 1745-6, and gave Epaphras Lord £551—5—0 for
another tract of land, May 14, 1751.   Besides there were several
other purchases made by him from the year 1733 to 1754.

Inventory Oct. 11, 1790.   Dec. 2, 1790, the estate was apportioned and distributed.   Exhibited March, 1792, the distribution
was approved.   John (probably the grandson) had two shares ;
the other children one share each.   This was the widow's share.
Widow Lydia made will, exhibited Sept. 7, 1790.   Children :

  120.—1. RUTH, b. Feb. 2, 1738.
  121.—2. JOHN, b. Sept. 10, 1739.
  122.—3. LYDIA, b. May 23, 1741.
  123.—4. HANNAH, b. Oct. 6, 1744.
  124.—5. CURTIS, b. March 27, 1747.
  125.—6. WILLIAM, b. April 7, 1749.
  126.—7. ELIZABETH, b. June 30, 1750.

127. ABRAHAM CRANE[3] [58], (Abraham,[2] Benjamin[1]), married Rebecca, daughter of Thomas and Rebeccah (Meekin)
Hurlburt, March 15, 1739, and died March 25, 1756, aged
43 years.   She died Nov. 13, 1794, aged 82.   United with
the church at Wethersfield in 1739.   He purchased land in
Wethersfield of Ephraim Williams, March 31, 1737, for £110 in
bills.   June 21, 1756, Court granted administration on estate of
Abraham Crane, late of Wethersfield, deceased, to Rebecca
Crane and Thomas Hurlburt of said Wethersfield, and they gave
bonds £300.

April 18, 1764, they reported collected £44—18—7¾ and paid
out £43—8—2, and the distribution was made, Rebecca to have
⅓ of whole movable estate, after charges and debts are paid, and
real estate during her natural life.   Abraham. eldest son, to have
double share ; David, Elijah, Benjamin, Hezekiah, Joseph and
Mary each one part.

April 28, 1749, Abraham Crane bought for £370 land in Wethersfield of Mehitabel Tracy of Deerfield, Hampshire Co., Mass. March 18, 1750, a lot of land of Timothy Bordman for £300. Aug. 16, 1751, a lot of Thomas Hurlburt for £90. Aug. 8, 1753, a lot on Connecticut River of Charles Riley of Glassenbury for £85. April 5, 1754, a lot of land in Tier No. 29, in late division, of Abraham Nutt of Wethersfield, butting east on Capt. John Warner and south on land of Benonie Crane, for £250. Children :

.28—1.] ABRAHAM, b. Dec. 16, 1739.
129—2. DAVID, b. Nov. 29, 1741. Served as a soldier during the Revolutionary War. Was corporal Capt. Dickinson's Co., Col. Elmore's Regt., June 24, 1776. Served in New York State about Albany. Again enlisted January, 1777, from Sandisfield for three years, and joined Capt. Allen's Co., Col. Wigglesworth's Regt. Was also private Capt. Noah Allen's Co., Col. Calvin Smith's Regt. (late Col. Wigglesworth's Regt.). Served from May 28, 1777, to Jan. 29, 1781 ; then 39 years old. Stature 6 feet, complexion light, hair and eyes light. Also served in Ebenezer Smith's Co., 6th Regt. Was at Valley Forge in March and May, 1778; at Providence, 1779; West Point, Jan. 29, 1781. Died without issue about 1820, in Sandisfield, Mass., a pensioner.*
130—3. ELIJAH, b. Jan. 9, 1744.
131—4. BENJAMIN, b. July 18, 1746; d. before Dec. 11, 1776, it is said.†
132—5. HEZEKIAH, b. Sept. 28, 1748; m. Mary Dix.
133—6. REBECCA, b. Nov. 22, 1750; d. Oct. 4, 1751.
134—7. MARY, b. Nov. 5, 1752; m. John Adams, Dec. 6, 1771.
135—8. JOSEPH, b. Aug. 13, 1755.

136. HANNAH CRANE[3] [62], (Israel,[2] Benjamin[1]), married Timothy Bordman of Wethersfield, Dec. 21, 1721. He was son of Daniel Bordman and born July 20, 1700. This Daniel was brother to Martha Bordman, who married Benjamin Crane, Jr. Hannah Crane Bordman died in Dalton, Mass., at the home of her son Daniel. "She was a very Godly woman, and her descendants fondly cherish her memory." Children :

1. DAMARIS (Bordman), b. Nov. 11, 1722.
2. CHARLES (Bordman), b. Sept. 4, 1725.
3. TIMOTHY (Bordman), b. Dec. 2, 1727.
4. HANNAH (Bordman)i b. Dec. 12, 1729.
5. ELIZABETH (Bordman), b. Oct. 14, 1731; d. Nov. 6, 1731.
6. DANIEL (Bordman), b. Sept. 29, 1732.
7. JOHN (Bordman), b. Aug. 6, 1735.
8. ELIZABETH (Bordman), b. Oct. 5, 1737.
9. SETH (Bordman), b. April 21, 1742.
10. OLIVE (Bordman), b. Nov. 3, 1745.

---

*Massachusetts Soldiers and Sailors in Revolutionary War.
†Although this Benjamin is reported as having died before 1776, there was a Benjamin Crane bought land in Hartford of John Smith, Jan. 1, 1795, of John Morgan, March 25, 1795; also a lot of Samuel Nevins, Dec. 11 that year. Mortgaged his place on Prison street, where he lived, to J. Ramsey. He sold the place to George Wells, March 25, 1797, for £2000.

137. ELIZABETH CRANE[3] [63], (Israel,[2] Benjamin[1]), married John Russell, Jr., Dec. 1, 1725. She died Nov. 10, 1745. Elizabeth Crane, daughter of Israel Crane, deeded to Martha, her sister, part of the home-lot of Israel Crane, March 19, 1727-8. Children:

1. DAVID (Russell), b. Aug. 29, 1726.
2. ELIZABETH (Russell), b. May 27, 1729.
3. JOHN (Russell), b. Sept. 8, 1731.
4. HEZEKIAH (Russell), b. Feb. 13, 1739.
5. WILLIAM (Russell), b. June 29, 1741.
6. TIMOTHY (Russell), b. Dec. 31, 1744.

FOURTH GENERATION.

138. SARAH CRANE[4] [75], (Jonathan,[3] Jonathan,[2] Benjamin[1].), married Daniel Abel of Lebanon, Conn., Dec. 25, 1727, where he was born Feb. 3, 1706; settled in Lebanon, Conn.
Children :

  1. DANIEL (Abel)), b. Nov. 13, 1728.
  2. ELIPHALET (Abel), b. Sept. 10, 1730.
  3. JONATHAN (Abel), b. April 26, 1733.
  4. MARY (Abel), b. Feb. 24, 1736.
  5. ELIZABETH (Abel), b. Jan. 19, 1739.
  6. SARAH (Abel), b. Jan. 19, 1741.
  7. ELIJAH (Abel), b. Feb. 1, 1744.
  8. SIMON (Abel) b. Sept. 5, 1746; d. Sept. 20, 1746.
  9. EZEKIEL (Abel), b. Oct. 12, 1747.

139. MARY CRANE[4] [76], (Jonathan,[3] Jonathan,[2] Benjamin[1]), married first —— Buel, second James Bill. Children :

  1. TIMOTHY (Buel).
  2. AZARIAH (Buel).
  3. ANNA (Buel).

140. JONATHAN CRANE[4] [79], (Jonathan,[3] Jonathan,[2] Benjamin1), married Sarah Armstrong at Lebanon, 1741–42. It appears from Lebanon records he died previous to March 15, 1765, and that his brother Silas Crane was executor of his will.
Children :

141—1. ZERVIAH, b. Feb. 11, 1742-3.
142—2. ANN, m. Ebenezer Williams.

This Jonathan Crane may have left other children who went to New Hampshire, where relatives of the family did go, settling in and about Surry, Alstead and Gilsum.

There was a Jonathan Crain of Wilton, N. H., who served in the Revolutionary war, engaged March 20 and September 17, 1781, and discharged Nov. 25, 1781; Capt. John Mills' company, Col. Reynolds' regiment. Was he son of the above? Also a Daniel Crain in Andover, N. H., 1771, had lot No. 15 in third division, on which he made improvements; Seth Crane, one of the grantees of Maidston, Oct. 12, 1761; Josiah Crane of Waterbury, N. H., June 7, 1763; also Jonathan Crane, same place; Benjamin Crane, one of the grantees of Middlesex, N. H., June 8, 1763.

These were without much doubt from Connecticut.

143. SILAS CRANE[4] [82], (Jonathan,[3] Jonathan,[2] Benjamin[1]), married Lucy Waterman, Sept. 20, 1742 (Norwich).

Whether Silas Crane was a soldier under Sir Wm. Pepperell of Kittery Point, Me., in the expedition that captured Louisbourg in June, 1745, we do not know of a certainty. But certain we are that he was attracted, as were many others, to that spot known and remembered as Acadia, that region made famous by the muse of Longfellow, and where the broad acres and fertile fields which those French exiles had been forced to abandon were ready to welcome the new hand that should come to toil within their borders. Connecticut furnished her quota of men for that expedition, and ever after that 17th day of June, when M. Chambon, governor of Louisbourg, surrendered to Commodore P. Warren and Sir Wm. Pepperell, some of those undisciplined soldiers, as they were called by the regulars, turned their eyes occasionally in the direction of that fair country which had so generously been offered them by the English government.

Although the right to control these lands had passed back and forth at various times, 1621 to 1755, between France and England, quite a French population were still residents there, and, siding as they naturally did with the Indians against the English, became a constant source of alarm and a serious obstruction to progress among the New England settlements. At last a determination was formed to get rid of them if possible. To that end an expedition was planned, with Sir Wm. Pepperell at its head. Lt.-Col. Wm. Vaughn of Portsmouth, N. H., has the distinction of having proposed the scheme of taking Cape Breton to Gov. Wm. Shirley, who immediately approved it. Mr. Vaughn traveled through the several provinces securing subscriptions of money and engaging men to enlist in the enterprise. Although a resolution was passed by a majority vote in the assembly of Massachusetts Bay Jan. 25, 1744–51, favoring a movement, all preliminaries were worked quite secretly. Virginia, Maryland, Pennsylvania, Rhode Island, Connecticut, New Hampshire and Massachusetts were called upon to furnish men and means, Connecticut sending about 500 men toward the nearly 4000 furnished by the colonies to act in conjunction with Commodore Sir Peter Warren, then commanding his majesty's fleet, stationed along the Atlantic coast, then at West Indies. Enlistments began February 2, and by the latter part of the following month 3000 men were on the way to Canso. They were followed by others, and April 30 the army was drawn up before Louisbourg demanding its surrender. Steady constant work was put in step by step, the lines were tightened, until June 16 the stronghold succumbed, and the following day the French governor surrendered to Commodore Peter Warren and Sir Wm. Pepperell, after a siege of 49 days. It was a great victory. It gave to New England a certain degree of security which hitherto she had not known, and opened the way for developing her outlying settlements. The newly conquered territory also became a prize for those who were desirous of receiving a share in the

spoils of war. Lord Halifax formed a project by which the English colony of Nova Scotia might be augmented, and in 1749, after being adopted by the government, was set in motion, and the Lords Commissioners of Trade and Plantations issued in March of that year a proclamation by which 50 acres of land was offered to every soldier and sailor who would settle in that part of America, free of rent for 10 years, and not more than one shilling per annum for the 50 acres afterwards. To every soldier and sailor who had a wife and children 10 acres more were offered for every individual in his family, and for every increase that should afterwards happen to the family; to each subaltern officer 80 acres, and 15 more for each of his family, 200 acres to each ensign, 300 to each lieutenant, 400 to captain, 600 to each officer in rank above captain, and 30 acres more for each person in his household. The government also engaged to transport and maintain the new settlers one year at its own expense, to furnish them with such arms, provisions, utensils, implements and tools as necessary to put them in condition to clear and cultivate their lands, build habitations, and commence a fishery. Carpenters and other handicraftsmen were offered same opportunities as soldiers and sailors; surgeons were to receive same as ensigns. Within two months 3750 persons embarked and located the place called Halifax, and for several years government expended large sums of money annually to assist settlers in locating in Nova Scotia. The increase in population was so rapid that in July, 1755, the French that had held on, not being willing to give up all, saw that it was of no use to further contend, and abandoned their possessions, and left the country quite free to the English settlers, and the people of Connecticut as well as other provinces were encouraged to try their fortunes in this new country. About the year 1751 the people of Norwich, Conn., entered into the coastwise trade, building of ships, &c., which opened up communication with Nova Scotia, and many of the people about the eastern portion of Connecticut were anxious to possess some of the abandoned farms left by the exiled Acadians, and Silas Crane with his family were among the number. In 1760 he with his son Silas drew certain lots in the township of Horton—one of 50 acres marked A No. 2, located in Wolfville, about three miles from Grand Pré; he also drew a town lot, one-half acre and three farm lots, Nos. 289, 290 and 291. Silas, Jr., drew farm lot No. 292. These four lots contained 245 acres each, and adjoined the river.

They also had other lands set off to them in the first division, record of which was made in a book which has since been burned. Mr. James Leard, government surveyor for Kings county, 1891, writes: "We know that a majority of the first settlers came from Connecticut; 240 came very soon after the expulsion of the Acadians, and it is said many of them were with Sir Wm. Pepperell at the taking of Louisbourg in 1745." Another

4

company of settlers, including Col. Noble of Boston, being attracted thither in 1755, were surprised by the French, and the colonel, with his two lieutenants and some 70 men, were killed. Mr. James Leard remembers when a boy (many years ago) James Noble Crane, son of Jonathan, who pointed out to him the spot on his (Leard's) farm where Col. Noble and his two lieutenants were buried between two old French apple trees; but the trees have now disappeared, and nothing remains to mark the spot where they were laid to rest.

In August, 1760, it was claimed that 6000 people from American settlements, principally from Long Island and Connecticut, had recently settled in Nova Scotia. Among the names of those who settled with the Cranes there we find those of John Allen, John Allen, Jr., Jas. Anderson, John Atwell, Benj. Beckwith, Derius, Elisha and Jacob Brown, William, Peter and John Bishop, Sr., and John Bishop, Jr., Obed Benjamin, Timothy Bishop, Richard and Christopher Best, Andrew Belcher, John Burbidge, Jeremiah Calkin, Sr. and Jr., Benj. Cleveland, Wm. Coldwell, John and Jonathan Davidson, Nathan, Jehial and Simeon DeWolfe, Daniel Dodge, Andrew and David Sherman, Robert, William, Samuel Dennison, and their father, Col. Robert Dennison, who went from Norwich, Conn., and were at the siege of Louisbourg, John Eagles, James, Jonathan and Joseph Elderkin, Benjamin Fitch, Wm. Foster, Col. Foster, Noah, Amos and Nathan, Sr, and Jr., Gilbert, and Timothy Forsythe, Samuel Griffin, David and Jonathan Godfrey, Ephraim, Joseph, Gerrish and Jonathan Graves, John, Daniel and Jonathan Hamilton, Sr. and Jr., Lebbeus, Thedens, Asa, Daniel, Alpheus, Peleg, Gilbert and Ephraim Harris, Sr. and Jr., Jedediah Jordan, David Johnson, Andrew Marsters, Brotherton Martin, Sylvanus Thomas, Christopher, Darius and Martha Miner, Elisha Nichols, Silas and Benj. Peck, Sr. and Jr., Elnathan Palmeter, Roland Rogers, William, Mary, Samuel and James Reid, Charles and Ann Randall, Amos Rathburn, Arthur and Nathan Schofield, John Turner, Jedediar Wickwire, Benjamin and Joseph Woodworth, Samuel Witter, six Dicksons, four Fullars, four Hardings, six Lathrops, three Hoveys, three Blackmans, one Peabody, Amos and Samuel Conover. The latter married Chloe, daughter of Silas Crane, Sr.

Of course it will be noticed that they were not "refugees." They did not leave their country to escape the results of the Revolutionary war, as many others did during that eventful period in American history, but removed to Nova Scotia many years prior to the Revolution, and when that event came it found them in quite different circumstances. Their environments were of quite another sort. Many if not all of them were living under patronage of the mother country. They had been given special privileges under the crown in the possession of their lands, and therefore, as honorable men, were under obligation to stand

by and uphold the power that had so recently and so signally befriended them.   Children :

144—1.   SILAS, b. Sept. 4, 1743.
145—2.   CHLOE, b. Sept. 24, 1745. She married James Noble Shannon. He was born in September, 1751, and died Nov. 7, 1822. Was son of Cutt Shannon, and adopted son of Major James Noble of Boston, Mass. He settled in Nova Scotia. Chloe had previously married Samuel Conover*, but had left no issue, although they adopted James Noble, a son of Thomas, a brother of her last husband.
146—3.   JONATHAN, b. 1750, in Lebanon, Conn.
147—4.   THEODOREY, b. 1752 or 1753; m. Alpheus Morse, Esq.
148—5.   ELIJAH.

149. JOHN CRANE[4] [85], (John,[3] Jonathan,[2] Benjamin[1]), married Rebeckah Huntington, born in Windham, Conn., Sept. 18, 1712, daughter of Joseph and Rebeckah (Adgate) Huntington, Jan. 24, 1733–4; lived in Tolland. She died Jan. 23, 1742. He married 2d, Sarah Hutchinson, Nov. 11, 1742; 3d, Hannah Bissel of Middlefield, Mass., in 1783. The publication of this marriage appears in the history of Middlefield under date of Sept. 10, 1783. She was alive there Oct. 16, 1798. He died at Becket, Mass., March 9, 1793, aged 84 years. Was given land in Wethersfield, July 3, 1734, by his grandfather Jonathan Crane of Windham. He purchased land there of Jonathan and Stephen Riley, Sept. 28, 1736. Was assessor in Becket in 1767.
Children :

150—1.   SARAH, b. Nov. 30, 1735, in Wethersfield.
150½—2. BENJAMIN, b. March 29, 1738, in Wethersfield; d. in infancy.
--151—3. BENJAMIN, b. March 8, 1740, in Wethersfield.
152—4.   JOHN, b. Jan. 12, 1742, in Tolland.
153—5.   AMOS, b. April 8, 1744, in Tolland; killed in French and Indian war in New York. An ingeniously carved powder-horn bearing date 1760, the property of this Amos Crane, and carried by him, is in the possession of Amos S. Crane of Chicago, Ill. Jan. 30, 1772, court at Hartford granted administration on estate of Amos Crane late of Tolland, deceased, to Elijah Crane of Hartwood, in Province of Massachusetts Bay, who gave bond with John Plumb o said Hartwood £200.
154—6.   ELIJAH, b. Feb. 22, 1746, at Lebanon, Conn.
155—7.   ABEL, b. March 27, 1748.
156—8.   REBECCA, b. May 18, 1750.
157—9.   SAMUEL, b. May 29, 1752.
158-10. RACHEL, b. Jan. 14, 1755; m. Deacon Enos Kinsley o f Becket, Mass.
159-11. LYDIA, b. Aug. 18, 1757.

160. ABIAH CRANE[4] [86], (John,[3] Jonathan[2], Benjamin[1]), of Tolland, married Mary Tyler, Feb. 23, 1741-2, and died at Alstead, N. H., April 1, 1790. She died March 26, 1789.

*Samuel Conover had a brother Amos, who was among the first settlers of Horton.

Children :

161—1. JONATHAN, b. Nov. 21, 1742. Probably was private in Capt.
        John Mills' Co., Col. Reynolds' Regt., from Wilton, N.
        H.; enlisted Sept. 17 and marched Sept. 20, 1781; dis-
        charged Nov. 25, 1781.
162—2. JOSHUA; b. ———; m. 1st, Miss Mary Brown; 2d, Mrs. Ladd.
163—3. ISAAC, b. March 17, 1745, in Tolland.
164—4. MARY, b. Oct. 28, 1747; m. Joshua Wood of Alstead, N. H.
165—5. ABIAH, b. Feb. 8, 1751; m. Experience Smith of Surry, N. H.
166—6. ELEAZER, b. ———; d. Dec. 27, 1757. ·
167—7. JOSEPH, b. May 19, 1759; m. 1st, Eleanor Buck of Williams-
        town, Vt.; 2d, Ruth Wilson.
168—8. EUNICE, b. July 3, 1762; m. Jos. Kingsbury of Alstead, N. H.
        She died Sept. 10, 1791.
169—9. JOHN, b. Oct. 10, 1766; m. Nabby ———; lived in Western.

170. ELISHAM or ELISHA CRANE[4] [88], (John,[3] Jonathan,[2]
Benjamin[1]), married Sarah Bissell, Dec. 31, 1741. She was
daughter of Jeremiah and Mehitable (White) Bissell. Mrs. Bissell was sister to Capt. Daniel White of Hartford, Conn. Mr.
Crane lived in East Windsor. Children :

171—1. ELISHA, b. ———.
172—2. ANNA, b. March 12, 1747.
173—3. MEHITABLE, b. ———; m. Ephraim Ely, East Windsor, Conn.
And probably other children.

174. HEZEKIAH CRANE[4] [90], (John,[3] Jonathan[2], Benjamin[1]),
married Rachel Rockwell, April 2, 1746. She died Oct. 7, 1809,
aged 83 years. He died Jan. 3, 1805, aged 84. He was called
of Windsor, Conn., but purchased land in Bolton, Conn., May 3,
1750; also in July, 1753, and April, 1754. The births of three
of his children are recorded there. But it would appear from
the records that he moved to Bolton about 1750, and was
living there April 8, 1754. He may have been the Hezekiah
Crane, private in Capt. Roswell Grant's Co., Col. Johnson's
Regt., in service in Providence, R. I.; enlisted Jan. 7, 1778,
serving a few months. It was he or his son. Feb. 1, 1805, his
will was admitted to probate in East Windsor, Conn. It names
wife Rachel, his son David, daughters Rachel, Rhoda and Anna,
sons Aaron and Rufus; also heirs of his son Hezekiah, viz.,
Abner, his grandson, Eunice, Rhoda and Lucretia. This will
was dated Oct. 20, 1796, David Crane, Executor. Distribution
ordered Jan. 15, 1810, widow being then deceased. Children :

175—1. HEZEKIAH, b. Aug. 7, 1747.
176—2. DAVID, b. Oct. 1, 1748; d. ———, 1815.
177—3. RACHEL, b. June 8, 1751.
178—4. RHODA, b. April 22, 1753.
179—5. RUFUS, b. ———, 1755; d. ———, 1820.
180—6. AARON, b. May 8, 1756.
181—7. ANNA, b. ———.

182. LEMUEL CRANE[4] [92], (John,[3] Jonathan,[2] Benjamin[1]),
married Jerusha Crane, daughther of Jonathan, as Lebanon town

records say, May 13, 1757, which no doubt should have been 1752. Settled in Lebanon, Conn. Children:

183—1. ZEBULON, b. Feb. 21, 1753.
184—2. PRUDENCE, b. Feb. 12, 1755.
185—3. LOUISA, b. Feb. 16, 1757.

At this point in the record we find an Obediah Crane, who served as corporal in Col. Samuel Ashley's regiment and 7th company (Capt. Elisha Mack's company), men from Gilsum and Surry, N. H.; they marched to reinforce the Continental army at Ticonderoga in June, 1777. They marched 50 miles to Black River, and returned home again; met the retreat, June 28; discharged July 3.

Samuel Crain, or Crane, of Gilsum, N. H., was drafted under the order passed June 16, 1780, and served from June 29, 1780, to Dec. 6, 1780, 5 mos. 18 days. Travelled to Worcester, 83 miles. Aged 23. Was at West Point July, 1780, there received half pint rum and one pound sugar from Joseph Bass, Commissary for New Hampshire. Six months' men; was mustered in by Major Wm. Scott; age then 23 years.

Francis Crane, of Chesterfield, N. H., served from June 28, 1780, to Jan. 1, 1781, travelled 73 miles to Worcester. An order was passed June 16, 1780, for a draft to raise six hundred men to serve until Dec. 31, 1780, each one drafted was to serve or pay five hundred dollars. Those who went were to receive 40 shillings per month in money equal to corn at 4 shillings per bushel, five pounds for clothing and 12 shillings per mile for travel. Was this the same Francis Crane that lived in Vermont, and had a son Francis, who had a son, N. P. Crane, residing Oct. 1, 1881, in Eagle Village, Wyoming County, N. Y., then 74 years of age?

186. RHODA CRANE[4] [94], (John,[3] Jonathan,[2], Benjamin[1]), married Job Thompson, July 12, 1750, and lived in East Windsor, Conn. Children:

1. RHODA (Thompson), b. April 9, 1752.
2. EUNICE (Thompson), b. Sept. 21, 1753.
3. ELIZABETH (Thompson), b. July 10, 1757; d. May 23, 1758.

187. ADONIJAH CRANE[4] [95], (John,[3] Jonathan,[2] Benjamin[1]), m. —— ——; had the following and perhaps other children:

188—1. LEMUEL; settled in Hamilton, N. Y., about the year 1800.
189—2. LUKE; a farmer in Hamilton, N. Y.; d. there 1855, leaving no male heirs.
190—3. GEORGE; settled in Hamilton, N. Y.

191. RUTH CRANE[4] [98], (Isaac,[3] Jonathan,[2] Benjamin[1]), married Ebenezer Webb. He died Feb. 11, 1803, aged 84. She died Feb. 28, 1796, aged 78. They lived and died in Windham, Conn. Children:

1. DARIUS (Webb), b. July 28, 1742.

2. JERUSHA (Webb), b. April 17, 1744.
3. ANN (Webb), b. March 13, 1746.
4 JONATHAN (Webb), b. Oct. 2, 1747.
5. ALICE (Webb), b. Aug. 3, 1749.
6. RUTH (Webb), b. Feb. 22, 1751.
7. ELIZABETH (Webb), b. Feb. 19, 1753.
8. CHRISTOPHER (Webb), b. June 14, 1755.
9. EBENEZER (Webb), b. May 29, 1757.
10. HANNAH (Webb), b. Aug. 31, 1759.

192. ADRIE CRANE[4] [99], (Isaac,[3] Jonathan,[2] Benjamin[1]),
married Thomas Broughton at Windham, Nov. 15, 1738.
Children :

1. EUNICE (Broughton), b. 1739.
2. JOANNA (Broughton), b. 1741.
3. LYDIA (Broughton), b. 1742.
4. KEZIAH (Broughton), b. 1744.
5. DELIGHT (Broughton), d. 1747.
6. PRUDENCE (Broughton), b. 1749.
7. JEMIMA (Broughton), b. 1751.
8. ALICE (Broughton), b. 1753.
9. EBENEZER (Broughton), b. ——, who went to Irisburg, Vt.

193. ANNA CRANE[4] [100], (Isaac,[3] Jonathan,[2] Benjamin[1]),
married Joseph Babcock, Nov. 8, 1744, and lived on Babcock
Hill. She died Jan. 10, 1805. He died Dec. 22, 1797.
Children :

1. ANNE (Babcock), b. Nov. 27, 1745; m. Amos Allen, Jr.
2. ABIJAH (Babcock), b. Jan. 18, 1749.
3. ELIJAH (Babcock), b. April 28, 1750.
4. JOSEPH (Babcock), b. May 26, 1752.
5. WILLIAM (Babcock), b. June 30, 1754; d. Sept. 21, 1775.
6. ABIGAIL (Babcock), b. July 18, 1756; d. Sept. 7, 1775.
7. NATHAN (Babcock), b. June 31, 1760.
8. DANIEL (Babcock), b. April 7, 1762.
9. JERUSHA (Babcock), b. May 10, 1764; m. Jonathan Wales.
10. SARAH (Babcock), b. May 6, 1768: m. Coggswell Kinne of
Plainfield, Conn.

194. ISAAC CRANE[4] [101], (Isaac,[3] Jonathan,[2] Benjamin[1]),
married Eunice Walcutt, May 8, 1763. He died Oct. 2, 1777,
aged 51; his estate inventory, £814—13—10—1, April 15, 1778.
His residence was in Windham, Conn. Administration granted
on his estate, March 19, 1778, to Eunice Crane, and she was appointed guardian over her six children. Children :

195—1. SARAH, b. Jan. 24, 1764.
196—2. EUNICE, b. Oct. 19, 1765.
197—3. ADRIE, b. July 7, 1770.
198—4. ISAAC W., b. July 1, 1772.
199—5. JOHN, b. April 21, 1774.
200—6. ANNA, b. April 3, 1776.

201. ZEBULON CRANE[4] [104], (Joseph,[3] Jonathan,[2] Benja-
min1), married Sarah, daughter of William Belden of Wilton,
Conn., who was resident of Deerfield, Mass., in fall of 1696,

when the French and Indians made a raid on the town ; and also at the last attack, Feb. 1703-4. In the latter part of the year 1769 Mr. Crane moved from Bedford, Westchester Co., N. Y., to Judeah, now Washington, in Litchfield Co., Conn., where soon after the mother and five children died within two months of each other. Mr. Crane was captain of a militia company of Westchester Co., N. Y., in 1758, from which men were taken for service in the French war for the purpose of "ranging and scouring the frontiers."* Children :

202—1.   JOHN, b. Nov. 24, 1742.
203—2.   WILLIAM, b. Oct., 1744.
204—3.   ZEBULON, b. Aug. 7, 1746; d. Dec. 31, 1814.
205—4.   ELIJAH, b. April 1, 1748.
206—5.   SARAH, b. July 12, 1750.
207—6.   MARY, b. Oct. 8, 1752; d. young.
208—7.   BELDEN, b. Nov. 30, 1754; d. young.
209—8.   SAMUEL, b. April 11, 1757.
210—9.   ABIGAIL, b. May 26, 1759.
211-10. STEPHEN, b. April 11, 1761; d. young.
212-11. ANNA, b. Aug. 3, 1763; d. young.
213-12. SETH, b. March 1, 1766; d. young.

214.   CAPT. JOSEPH CRANE[4] [105], (Joseph,[3] Jonathan,[2] Benjamin[1]), married Esther Belden. She was born Oct. 31, 1727, and daughter of Samuel Belden. He was a resident of South East, N. Y., and lived and died on the old homestead, and a physician and judge in Duchess Co. 16 years. She died Feb. 27, 1786, aged 58. He died Oct. 14, 1800, aged 78. He owned a large tract of land situated in South East; also some adjoining it, but over the line in Connecticut. It was called ".Joe's Hill." At the foot of this hill, located on the Croton River, stood "Crane's Mill," built by his father. Dates of births and deaths of this family were furnished by Carso Crane from the family Bible.

Feb. 24, 1776, Joseph Crane memorialized the New York delegates in Continental Congress, and the same was received Feb. 26, in which attention was called to his services in the last campaign, and praying the care of an artillery company. After the memorial had been read, action on the same was postponed until the appointment of artillery officers was resumed. March 16 he was appointed Captain Lieutenant to serve in the Artillery Company whereof John Grinnell is Captain, on his (Joseph Crane) producing a certificate that he has been examined and is duly qualified.†

" Head Quarters New York April 9 1776 a certificate from S. Badlam Capt of Artillery dated 8th instant was read and filed. He hereby certifies that he has examined Joseph Crane as to his knowledge in gunnery and considering his merits and experience,

---

*N. Y. Colonial MSS., Vol. 85.
†Vol. I. Archives State of New York in the Revolution.

thinks him qualified for a Captain Lieutenancy. Therefore ordered, that the said Joseph Crane pursuant to the order of the provincial Congress of the 16th of March last be Capt Lieutenant of the Continental Company of Artillery whereof Sebastian Beauman Esq is Captain."

Dr. Crane was one of the most prominent men in the county during the Revolutionary war. Was Chairman of the South East Precinct Committee in 1775 and 1777; also one of the Supervisors in 1773, 1787 and 1789. Was it this Dr. Crane or his son that was ordered by the Provincial Congress, Sept. 17, 1776, with Mr. Duane, Mr. Duer and Mr. Schenck, to inquire into the situation of the Light Horsemen and Lieut. Onderdonck, and report thereon?

From the wording of the above memorial to the Continental Congress by Joseph Crane we understand he had rendered his country service at some prior date, and in New York Colonial MSS., Vol. LXXXV., page 132, may be found the following:

"Muster Roll of a company of Provincials in ye pay of ye Province of New York for Dutchess County commanded by Joseph Crane Esq." Also, same volume, page 141, an order, the substance of which is here given: "Copy of warrant from the Honorable James De Lancey Esq, His Majesties Lieutenant Governor and Commander in Chief May first 1758 an order to pay to Captain Joseph Crane one thousand and seventeen pounds, being the amount of bounty money and inlisting money for Ninety four volunteers inlisted in the pay of the Provinces as part of the quota for Dutchess County etc etc.

"To Abraham De Peyster Esq Treasurer Colony of New York.
"By order of His Honour in Council."

Children :

215—1. JONATHAN, b. April 27, 1747; died Aug. 28, 1834.
216—2. JOSEPH, b. Feb. 13, 1749; d. Nov. 21, 1825.
217—3. SOLOMON, b. Dec. 26, 1750; d. July 4, 1829.
218—4. ISAAC, b. Jan. 26, 1753; d. March 6, 1810.
219—5. EUNICE, b. Nov. 20, 1754; m. Comfort Sears.
220—6. ESTHER, b. Dec. 26, 1756; d. Aug. 3, 1833.
221—7. JOSIAH, b. July 11, 1759; d. May 13, 1768.
222—8. IRA, b. Aug. 10, 1761; d. Aug., 1828.
223—9. DANIEL, b. Sept. 17, 1763.
224-10. NATHAN, b. Aug. 1, 1765; d. May 21, 1768.
225-11. MOLLY, b. May 21, 1767; m. —— Raymond; d. Feb. 25, 1805.
226-12. JOSIAH NATHAN, b. June 10, 1770; d. July, 1797.
227-13. ARZAH, b. Sept. 29, 1772.

228.   COL. THADDEUS CRANE[4] [107], (Joseph,[3] Jonathan,[2] Benjamin[1]), married 1st, Sarah, daughter of Peter Paddock of South East, Putnam County, N. Y., Feb. 24, 1751. He was a farmer. Died Sept. 1, 1803, aged 75, and was buried in North Salem, Westchester County, N. Y. His first wife having died Feb. 19, 1777, he married Lydia, the widow of John Baxter, Jan. 13, 1779; her maiden name was Read, she having had three children by Mr. Baxter—Mary Bell Baxter, born Oct. 6, 1772, died June,

1838; Daniel R. Baxter, born June 22, 1774, died Dec. 16, 1842; Huldah Baxter born June 22, 1776, died 1851. The widow Lydia died April 26, 1832. Col. Crane's home was in North Salem, and the house is still standing.

Col. Thaddeus Crane served in the war of the Revolution. Was 2d major of the 2d Reg., Westchester County, May 28, 1778 (also captain of North Salem company); major Sept. 29, 1780. April 26 he was shot through the hip during the engagement at Ridgefield, Conn. (expedition to Danbury), and he asked the Honorable Council to reimburse him for loss of time, costs, &c.

" Kingston Aug 9. 1777. To Egbert Benson Esq

Gentlemen. It being my misfortune, in repulsing the enemy at Ridgefield on the 26 of April last to meet with a wound from them, which confined me to my bed for a long time : and I was at great expense by loss of time and cost of doctor, I desire to know from your Honorable Council whether I am to receive any wages or relief from the State, and where to apply to get the same if any is allowed. These from your Honor's humble servant.

To Honorable Council of Safety
State of New York. THADDEUS CRANE."*

Nearly nine years later the legislature of New York passed, April 22, 1786, an act making provisions for officers, soldiers and seamen, who had been disabled in the service of the United States.

The payment of pensions to the soldiers of New York and other States began, according to the "Ledger Rev. Accounts," March, 1782. "Crane, Thaddeus, major (Col. Thomas' militia), shot through the body; expedition to Danbury, April 27, 1777."

It will be noticed that his petition to the Honorable Council of New York states that he was shot April 26, while subsequent entries give it as April 27.

According to published accounts† we learn that Danbury, Conn., was, in the latter part of the year 1776, selected by the commissioners of the American army as a place of deposit for military stores, and at this time, April, 1777, large quantities of pork, flour, beef, grain, rum, wine, rice, tents, army carriages, besides other valuable articles, had been collected here, and Gov. Tryon, at the head of 2000 men from New York, proceeded by sailing vessel to Fairfield, and landing there Friday, April 25, during the afternoon and night, marched the next day, the 26th, to Danbury, where they arrived at two o'clock in the afternoon. Tryon and his soldiers were met here by a small detachment of Continental troops, who were, owing to the vastly superior number of the British, obliged to evacuate the town; not, however, until they had secured or removed a considerable quantity of stores

*Correspondence of the Provincial Congress, Vol. II., page 499.
†Connecticut Journal, British to Danbury, April, 1777.

and provisions; and it would appear from the reading of Col. Thaddeus Crane's petition that it was in the act of holding the enemy at bay and in attempting to save some of these stores from destruction that he received his wound. The next day, April 27th, early in the morning Tryon and his men set fire to the buildings, and immediately marched from the town on their way back to their vessel, the object of their expedition having been accomplished. Of course a general alarm had been given soon as the enemy appeared at Fairfield, and Brigadier-General Silliman, with about five hundred militia, immediately started in pursuit of the enemy. They were joined at Reading with Major-General Wooster and Brigadier-General Arnold, but the wet condition of the roads prevented the Continentals from reaching the enemy until Tryon was on his way back to his vessel, about eleven o'clock in the forenoon, April 27, when General Wooster and his men held a smart skirmish with the enemy, and Wooster was shot through the groin. General Arnold also came up about the same time with his command and engaged the enemy, and a lively action lasting about an hour occurred. Arnold's horse was shot from under him, but the general, recovering himself, drew his pistol. and shot the soldier who was advancing on him with fixed bayonet. The Continentals could do no more than fall back and harass Tryon and his men until they succeeded the next day, April 28th, in reaching their vessel and setting sail for Long Island. Notwithstanding the fact that the Continental troops succeeded in saving some of the stores deposited at Danbury, there was a large quantity destroyed, a careful estimate placing the loss* at 3000 barrels of pork, something over 1000 barrels flour, several hundred barrels beef, 1600 tents, 2000 bushels of grain, besides quantities of rum, wine, rice, army carriages, &c. Nineteen dwellings, a meeting-house, twenty-two stores and barns were burned. The loss of men on the American side was judged to have been about sixty killed and wounded. The British loss was more than double that number; also about twenty prisoners. Thaddeus Crane was captain in the Westchester County militia under Col. Thomas Thomas, receiving his commission in 1775; afterwards second major, 2d Regt., 1775, and lieutenant-colonel Feb. 17, 1780, 4th Regt., Westchester County. He was delegate to the New York State Constitutional Convention in 1788, and voted for adoption of the Constitution. He was delegate to the New York Legislature 1777, 1778, 1779; member of the New York Assembly (Provincial Congress) in 1777–9, 1788, 1789. His sword is retained in the hands of his grandson, Thaddeus Crane of Somers, N. Y. The old Crane homestead is at North Salem, Westchester County, N. Y., where Col. Thaddeus Crane lived, and where his nineteen children were born.

---

*Barber's Conn. Hist. Collections.

THE HOME OF COL. THADDEUS CRANE,
North Salem, Westchester Co., N. Y.

From the original manuscript Revolutionary Records in the State Comptroller's Office, Albany, N. Y., in volume XV., at page 80, appears the following:

" State of New York } SS.
City of New York }

Thaddeus Crane of Upper Salem in the County of Westchester being duly sworn maketh oath that during the late war he was Major of the Regiment of Westchester County commanded by Col. Thomas Thomas; that in the Invasion of the State of Connecticut by the Enemy under the Command of Govr. Tryon in the month of April in the year 1777 he was requested by Col. Cooke of Connecticut Militia residing at Danbury to march & oppose the Enemy; that being in actual service in opposing the Enemy aforesaid & acting under the immediate command of Brigadier General David Wooster on or about the twenty seventh day of April 1777 he received a wound from the Enemy by a Musket Ball thro·his left hip by means whereof he is rendered in great measure incapable of obtaining his livelihood by Labour; that on the eighth Day of April last he was fifty eight years of age & that he actually resides in Upper Salem as aforesaid.

Sworn this fifteenth }
   day of November 1786 } (Signed) THADDEUS CRANE.
   Before me }
      RICHD VARICK Recorder "

As there seem to be conflicting statements we print the following:

14.82   Thaddeus
                          Pay and Subsistence

15.70 " 8 mos pay as a wounded major in Col Thomas Thomas Reg" April 27. 1777 to December 27. 1777 according to resolution of Senate and Assembly April 23. 1785

                      Thaddeus
13.173   Feby 15, 1779 Major " Now commanding 4 Reg. Westchester " on Court Martial duty

---

13.220   Promoted Lt Col October 21. 1780

15.7   June 1. 1786 Major, wounded in left hip Annual pay £96
        Pension £806.18.8

                     Thaddeus
15.80   Wounded in Tryons Raid (See copy of his deposition)
15.27.   C. 3,
        Pension £80

Children :
229—1. DAUGHTER, b. Jan. 28, 1752; d. Feb. 7, 1752.

230—2. THADDEUS, b. March 2, 1753; d. Oct. 19, 1776, from exposure in Revolutionary war; captain North Salem company. His father was 2d major 2d or middle regiment.

231—3. MARY, b. Sept. 24, 1754; d. June 30, 1830.

232—4. SARAH, b. Sept. 5, 1757; d. Oct. 20, 1829.

233—5. JARED, b. Oct. 23, 1759; d. Dec. 8, 1776.

234—6. PETER, b. Oct. 28, 1761; d. Nov. 12, 1818.

235—7. JAMES, b. Oct. 11, 1763; d. Aug. 17, 1829.

236—8. ELIZABETH, b. Nov. 7, 1765; m. Nathaniel Smith; d. March 18, 1844.

237—9. RUTH, b. Oct. 27, 1767; m. Jonathan Smith; d. March 18, 1844.

238—10. ABIGAIL, b. April 17, 1770; d. April 27, 1848.

239—11. THOMAS, b. Oct. 26, 1772; d. Jan. 15, 1777.

240—12. THADDEUS, b. Dec. 31, 1780; d. Oct. 16, 1849.

241—13. FANNY, b. Aug. 11, 1782; d. Oct. 26, 1865.

242—14. LYDIA, b. May 19, 1784; d. Jan. 4, 1852.

243—15. THEDA, b. May 3, 1786; d. May 17, 1842.

244—16. WELTHAM, b. Dec. 27, 1788; d. Feb. 11, 1872, in Somers, N. Y.

245—17. GERARD, b. Jan. 3, 1791.

246—18. SALLY, b. Sept. 14, 1793.

247-19. THOMAS, b. Feb. 13, 1797; d. Aug. 27, 1822, in North Carolina, while travelling there with his brother, and was buried in the family lot of Mr. Hill of Waynesville.

248. ABIGAIL CRANE[4] [108], (Joseph,[3] Jonathan,[2] Benjamin[1]), married May 16, 1751, Timothy Todd, a resident of East Guilford, Conn., son of Jonathan Todd. He was a graduate of Yale College, class of 1747, and merchant as well as magistrate. She died Sept. 30, 1806. He was born 1723, and died 1779. Children:

1. SARAH (Todd), b. March 30, 1752; m. James Evarts of Sunderland, Vt., and was the mother of Jeremiah Evarts, b. in Sunderland, Feb. 3, 1781. He was Corresponding Secretary of Board of Foreign Missions from 1821 until his death, and Treasurer of that body from 1812 to 1820; graduated at Yale College 1802; studied law, and admitted to practice 1806 at New Haven, Conn.; but about 1810 became editor of the *Panoplist*, a religious paper published in Boston, and in 1820 the *Missionary Herald*; d. in Charleston, S. C., May 10, 1831. Sarah Todd Evarts d. March 30, 1810. William Maxwell Evarts, LL.D., son of Jeremiah, was born in Boston, Feb. 6, 1818; he also graduated at Yale, 1837, and from Harvard Law School; became an eminent lawyer, beginning practice in New York city 1841; was principal counsel for President Johnson at his trial, April and May, 1868, before the senate of the United States; Attorney-General United States July, 1868, to March 4, 1869; appointed by President Grant to assist in defending interests of citizens of United States at Geneva in settlement of the "Alabama claims," 1872. He was styled one of the most eloquent advocates in the United States; was Secretary of State under President Hayes.

2. ELIZABETH (Todd), b. Feb. 10, 1754; m. Jonathan Wilcox of Madison, Conn.; d. Sept. 29, 1833.

3. JONATHAN (Todd), b. May 17, 1756; settled in Madison, Conn; physician; d. Feb. 10, 1819; m. 1st, May, 1784, Ruth Bishop; 2d. Aug. 15, 1790, Chloe Lee; 3d, Jan. 11, 1793, Sally Fowler; latter d. Sept. 19, 1858.

4. TIMOTHY (Todd), b. May 16, 1758; physician; lived in Arlington, and Rutland, Vt., and Clinton, Conn.; d. Dec. 1, 1806; m. Phebe Buel, Nov. 27, 1783.

5. ABIGAIL (Todd), b. July 26, 1760; m. Lyman Graves, Georgia, Vt.; d. Feb. 19, 1810.

6. MARY (Todd), b. Oct. 9, 1763; m. Benj. Wilcox; d. Oct. 26, 1847.

7. JOHN (Todd), b. Aug. 20, 1766; d. Sept., 1766.

8. JOHN (Todd), b. Feb. 18, 1768; m. Esther Bishop; removed to St. Albans, Vt., and Manlius, N. Y.; he d. Dec. 28, 1841; she d. Feb. 20, 1859.

9. MATILDA (Todd), b. May 21, 1773; m. John Hamilton of North Killingworth, Conn.; she d. June 25, 1849.

249. STEPHEN CRANE[4] [110], (Joseph,[3] Jonathan,[2] Benjamin1), married Mary Chapman, Jan. 22, 1762. She was born in South East, N. Y., Jan. 4, 1745. It is said her father was a clergyman and from Cape Cod, and settled in New Milford, Conn., but died May 10, 1814, at the home of his son Joseph in Kent, Conn., and was buried there. April 10, 1770, he purchased a house and lot, also a blacksmith shop, in New Milford, 1½ miles north of the meeting-house.

He was a private in Thompson's Co., Wessenfel's Regt.;* also Miller's Co., Philips' Regt., State troops, and Col. Spencer's Regt. Line L. B. T. 14.6.17.; also captain and commissary of artillery in the war of the Revolution.† His widow married Peter Smith of Harpersfield, N. Y. She died June 24, 1824. Mr. Crane was chosen overseer of highways at Carmel, at first town meeting, held at the house of John Crane, son of Zebulon, April 7, 1795, and this John Crane was chosen town clerk.

Rev. Ezra F., grandson of Stephen Crane, writes; "My grandmother Crane was one of the grandest women of her age, *a perfect heroine* in the Revolutionary war. My grandfather was living at Danbury, Conn., when the British burned the town. He and all his men from the shop left for the fort near by, but my grandmother stood her ground, and stood in the door of the house when the British officer rode up, who had his men search the house; finding she was alone, no men near, caused a guard to be placed around the house till the army passed, and thus saved her house." She was daughter of Isaac and Mary (Paddock) Chapman. Her father was born in Dennis, Mass., April 7, 1721, and settled in South East, N. Y., about the year 1740. Her mother, Mary Paddock, was daughter of Peter Paddock, who was born June 3, 1724, and died at South East, Nov. 8, 1776. Isaac Chapman, father of Mrs. Crane, was son of Isaac, who was born in Barnstable county, Mass., Dec. 29, 1692, and grandson of Isaac, born Aug. 4, 1647, and great-grandson of Ralph Chapman Southwark of Surrey county, England. Children:

250—1. EZRA, b. Dec. 22, 1763; went west.
251—2. ABIGAIL, b. Nov. 24, 1765; d. 1803.

*Enlisted April 14, 1777, for three years in N. Y. line.
†Colonial History of New York.

252—3. ISAAC CHAPMAN, b. Nov. 17, 1767.
253—4. STEPHEN, b. Jan. 16, 1769.
254—5. NOAH, b. May 6, 1771.
255—6. MARY, b. June 8, 1773; m. Fitch Welch; lived in Brookfield.
256—7. JOSEPH, b. Aug. 24, 1775.
257—8. THALIA, b. 1777.
258—9. JARED; never married.
259-10. DAVID BALDWIN, b. June, 1783.
260-11. SALLY, m. Mr. Carpenter.
261-12. IRAD; lived with his brother David B.
262-13. ANNA, b. 1790; m. Philip Chase of South East.

263.   ADAH CRANE[4] [111], (Joseph,[3] Jonathan,[2] Benjamin[1]), married Capt. Joshua Barnum of Danbury, Conn., and settled in South East, Putnam County, N. Y., in 1755.   She died April 17, 1810.   Capt. Barnum was born in 1737, and died Oct. 23, 1822. He was an officer in the war of the Revolution, rendering valuable service; was wounded during the engagement at " Ward's House," near White Plains.   In battle of White Plains he took the lock from the door of the prison, thereby liberating a number of federal soldiers confined there; was wounded, taken prisoner, marched to New York, and confined on board one of the prison ships at Wallabout near Brooklyn, which ships were called " Ships of Death."   After a time he was released, but crippled with a shattered limb and the loss of sight in one eye.   During the war the captain was necessarily absent from home much of the time, but the wife superintended the work on the farm while her boys did the work.   In the meantime the son of a neighbor (Doty by name) who had enlisted in the army deserted, which fact so grieved his mother that she went to Mrs. Barnum in her distress of mind, and Mrs. Barnum sent her eldest son, 16 years of age, who served through one campaign as a substitute for the Doty boy.   Children :

1.   STEPHEN CRANE (Barnum), d. Aug. 11, 1849.
2.   JOSHUA (Barnum).
3.   JONATHAN (Barnum).
*.   MARTHA (Barnum), m. Reuben Doane.
5.   ADAH (Barnum), m. Jeremiah Gage.

264.   SETH CRANE[4] [116], (Elijah,[3] Elijah,[2] Benjamin[1]), married Dec. 20, 1762, Dorcas Sherwood.   Jan. 17, 1746–7, Seth Crane and his brother Jabez Crane were given land at Stratford, Conn., by their kinsman, Theophilus Nichols of said Stratford. Children :

265—1, ELIJAH JABEZ, b. Oct. 18, 1763.
266—2. MARY SHERMAN, b. Aug. 24, 1765.
267—3. DORCAS, b. Feb. 4, 1767.

268.   RUTH CRANE[4] [120], (John,[3] Abraham,[2] Benjamin[1]). One Ruth Crane married Solomon Lattimer.   If this was the Ruth she married after Oct. 7, 1765.   Her mother made her will at that time; she was then Ruth Crane; settled in Wethersfield: perhaps had

. 1. SAMUEL (Lattimer).

2. LEONARD (Lattimer).
3. RHODA (Lattimer).
4. ELIZABETH (Lattimer).

269.. JOHN CRANE[4] [121], (John,[3] Abraham,[2] Benjamin[1]), married Ruth ——; settled in Wethersfield, Conn.; was private in Capt. Oliver Hanchett's company of Suffield (10th Co.), 2d Regt. Vol., Col. Joseph Spencer; served in and about Boston. A portion of this regiment was engaged in battle of Bunker Hill; enlisted May 11; discharged Dec. 17, 1775. Mr. Crane and his wife joined the church in 1765. March 4, 1770, he sold his home place to his brother-in-law Thomas Kilbey. At the time of the baptism of the two youngest children Mrs. Crane was a widow. His mother Lydia Crane says he died in camp.

The following shows how claims were collected in the 18th century: "Whereas Geo. Olcott recovered judgment against Ruth Crane first Tuesday of Nov., 1789, for £40—18—11 and costs, 0—17—11, and for want of money the officer is ordered to take the body of said Ruth to the Goal and put her in care of the keeper until she pay the full sum above mentioned. The officer levied on land lying in Wethersfield at lower end of Broad Street, with one-half the dwelling-house.

LT. JOHN FRANCIS, Constable."

She paid Geo. Olcott, Dec. 3, 1791.

Children :

270—1. RHODA, baptized Aug. 6, 1764.
271—2. REBECKAH, baptized June 23, 1765; perhaps m. Solomon Lattimer, June 6, 1782.
272—3. ASHBIL, b. June 30, 1766; baptized Nov. 14, 1770.
273—4. CHARLES.
274—5. JOHN, baptized Sept. 21, 1777.
275—6. RUTH, baptized Sept. 21, 1777.

276. LYDIA CRANE[4] [122], (John,[3] Abraham,[2] Benjamin[1]), married Simon Griffin at Wethersfield, Conn., Dec. 12, 1771, by Rev. Burrage Meriam at Rocky Hill Parish or Stepney.

Children :

1. GEORGE (Griffin), b. May 19, 1772.
2. ANNE (Griffin), b. Nov. 11, 1774.
3. JOHN (Griffin), Feb. 6, 1777.

277. HANNAH CRANE[4] [123], (John,[3] Abraham,[2] Benjamin[1]), married Thomas Kilbey, Aug. 23, 1764, at Wethersfield, and settled there. She with Curtis Crane signed a deed to James Blin, April 15, 1776. Mr. Kilbey purchased the home place of his wife's brother, John Crane, March 4, 1770. Mr. Crane died before receiving full settlement, and Mr. Kilbey settled with the heirs of his brother-in-law, and in the transaction deeded to them certain land he had of their father. Children :

1. SALOMI (Kilbey), b. March 7, 1765.
2. THOMAS (Kilbey), b. Jan. 15, 1768.

3. RHODA (Kilbey), b. April 13, 1770.
4. HOPE (Kilbey), b. March 24, 1773.
5. SAMUEL (Kilbey), b. May 6, 1778.

278. CURTIS CRANE[4] [124], (John[3], Abraham,[2] Benjamin[1]),
enlisted Feb. 28, 1778, during the war of the Revolution, as
private in Capt. Thos. Wooster's company, Col. Samuel B.
Webb's regiment, which was the 3d regiment, and known as
Additional Infantry of Connecticut Line, 1777-1781. June 1,
1781, he was promoted to corporal in Capt. Roger Alden's company, same regiment (3d), Additional Infantry of Connecticut
Line of 1781-1783. Lt.-Col. Wm. S. Livingston acted as
colonel of this regiment while Col. Webb was held as a prisoner,
having been captured by the enemy while in command of an
expedition against Long Island on Dec. 10, 1777, and confined
till Jan. 1, 1781. Col. Webb's regiment after the enlistment of
Mr. Crane was, during the summer of 1778, attached to
Varnam's brigade, and took part in the battle of Rhode Island,
August 29, and was complimented for its conduct at that time.
The Regiment remained in Rhode Island until the fall of
1779, when it proceeded to Morristown, N. J., where it passed
the winter of 1779-1780, having been assigned to Stark's
brigade, Lt.-Col. Ebenezer Huntington being then in command. June 23, 1780, was present at the battle of Springfield, N. J., and during the following summer served with the
main army on the Hudson. Col. Webb's regiment was afterwards styled the 9th Regiment Additional Infantry of the
Connecticut Line, and passed the winter of 1780 and 1781
with the division at camp "Connecticut Village," above the
Robinson House on the Hudson, where it was reorganized Jan.
1, 1781, into the 3d regiment of the Connecticut Line with the
2d and 9th late "Additional Infantry" regiments, formation of
1781-1783. Col. Webb's regiment continued in service until the
close of the war, Mr. Crane serving with it nearly five and one-
half years, from 1778 to 1783. He received an honorable discharge, but died prior to the passage of the act of congress granting pensions; his widow, however, became a pensioner,
beginning with the year 1837, and continued to receive it up to
the time of her death.

Mr. Crane married Oct. 6, 1774, Elizabeth Palmer. He died
at Eaton, N. Y., Oct. 10, 1828. She died at Milford, N. Y.,
June 15, 1848. He deeded land in Wethersfield, Conn., to Lieut.
Elisha Treat, Oct. 22, 1768, and land in Wethersfield, Conn., to
John Robbins of Wethersfield, April 18, 1786: also to Abraham
Chamberlin, Nov. 3, 1801, in New Hartford, Litchfield county,
Conn. Children:

279—1. WILLIAM, b. June 27, 1775; d. of yellow fever at Charleston,
        S. C., Nov. 25, 1795.
280—2. CURTIS, b. June 24, 1777.
281—3. ELIZABETH, b. March 28, 1784.
282—4. HENRY, b. Nov. 23, 1785.

283—5. NANCY, b. Nov. 4, 1788.
284—6. CHARLES, b. March 4, 1791; d. at Eaton, N. Y., Feb. 15, 1826.
285—7. LYDIA PLATT, b. July 14, 1794; m. David Crowfut, and d. at
Preble, N. Y., Dec., 1821.
286—8. JOHN WILLIAM, b. July 3, 1797, at New Hartford, Conn.; d.
at Southwick, Aug. 29, 1803.

287. WILLIAM CRANE[4] [125], (John,[3] Abraham,[2] Benjamin[1]).
Under date of May 27, 1773, we find the following, showing that
he then resided in Wethersfield, Conn. : " We, Thomas Kilbey and
wife Hannah, Curtis and William Crane, all of Wethersfield, sold
to Capt. Chas. Churchill of Wethersfield a piece of land in Wethersfield, in the Parish of Newington, in tier No. 19, thirteen
acres, bounded west on land of John Crane, north on land of said
Churchill, south on land of Simon Griffin and Lydia, his wife.
All signed this document on the above date." He was private
in Capt. John Chester's company, 116 men, who volunteered, in
response to the Lexington alarm, from Wethersfield ; discharged
after six days' service ; enlisted May 9th in Capt. John Chester's
company (9th), 2d Regt. Vol., Gen. Joseph Spencer ; served in
and about Boston at time of siege ; reported deserted Dec. 1,
1775 ; private in Capt. Jonathan Wells' company, Hartford, Col.
Erastus Wolcott's regiment, state militia ; served about Boston,
January to March, 1776.
It will be noticed that this William Crane is reported as
having deserted ; but it appears from records in existence that
a number of men entered as deserters about December 1,
explained in petitions to the General Assembly of the Colony of
Connecticut that they had no intention of deserting, but believing
their time had expired on that date instead of December 10.
The Assembly ordered them to be paid for full time. This
William Crane was among the number. His mother, Lydia Crane,
states in a petition at the May session of the Assembly, 1776, that
she had three sons in the service in 1775. (They were John, Curtis
and this William). "The oldest died in camp, the second returned,
and the third, William, who had enlisted in Capt. Chester's company, and fought at Bunker's Hill, left his regiment about
November 30th, supposing his time to be out, but, being taken
down with fever on the way, wandered in his delirium to Leicester,
Mass., and died there."*
A careful examination of the records at Leicester, Mass.,
failed to disclose the record of the death of this William Crane ;
and it is quite probable that the good mother was misinformed at
that time, and that her son William recovered and re-enlisted,
being in service at the time she prepared her petition. The
means of getting information from any considerable distance in
those days were such that it would not be strange if conflicting
reports had reached Wethersfield about these supposed deserters,
and that this widowed mother, who had furnished three soldiers

* Historical Collections of Connecticut in war of the Revolution.
5

for the cause of national freedom, all the sons she had, and one of those then deceased while in the service, was easily led to believe that this the youngest of her sons was dead; but, from the best information at hand, it appears that after the close of the Revolutionary war he settled in Great Barrington, Mass. May 25, 1818, William Crane of that place made his will, in which he mentions his wife Rebecca, and grandchildren Harriet Crain and William Whiting Crain, "children of my late son, William Crain; Albert Lewis Crain, Aurelia Loiza Crain, children of my late son, Whiting Crain, deceased;" and daughter, Sally Crain; his wife Rebecca to be executrix. She presented the will for probate June. 4, 1818   Dec. 31, 1829, Sally Crain, the daughter, and then the only child living, petitioned the court to appoint Timothy Turner administrator for her mother (Rebecca Crain's) estate, she then being deceased. The appointment was made, and inventory filed Feb. 9, 1830, the total amount being eighty-eight dollars and a few cents. Rebecca died Dec. 19, 1829.   Mr. Crain was a farmer and tailor by trade.   Children:

288—1. WILLIAM.
289—2. WHITING.
290—3. SALLY.

291.   CAPT. ABRAHAM CRANE[4] [128], (Abraham,[3] Abraham,[2] Benjamin[1]), married Mary, probably daughter of Joshua Robbins of Wethersfield, where they resided.   She died May 20, 1813, aged 67 years.   He died June 29, 1808, aged 69 years. He united with the church Feb. 5, 1774.   He was one of the executors of Joshua Robbins' estate, and Mary Crane was one of the heirs.   May 15, 1808, his will was exhibited in court, and Abraham and Benjamin Crane, both of Wethersfield, were named executors.   April 26, 1809, an inventory of the estate was filed, amounting to $4,809.57, including 33 sides sole-leather. Abraham and David Crane of Wethersfield and Elijah Crane of Sandisfield, Berkshire County, Mass., brothers, deeded land in Wethersfield, Conn., to Silas Deane of Wethersfield, which belonged to the heirs of Joseph Webb, deceased, March 1, 1769. March 25, 1771, Abraham deeds land to Wm. Loveland.   Jan. 26, 1773, David, then of Sandisfield, Mass., deeded to his brother Abraham land in Wethersfield, being one-half of the home lot that belonged to his honored father Abraham Crane, late deceased; it joined land of Jedediah Sanburn, with barn standing partly on said acre, "only reserving the right for my mother during her natural life."   June 9, 1777, David Crane of Sandisfield, Mass., deeded land to Abraham that formerly belonged to his brother Benjamin, deceased, adjoining his mother, Rebecca's, land.   He willed his tannery to his sons Abraham and Benjamin. Children:

292—1. MARY, b. 1767; d. Dec., 1773.
293—2. ABRAHAM, b. 1770.

294—3. HULDAH, b. 1774; d. May 25, 1813.
295—4. BENJAMIN, baptized Feb. 5, 1775.
296—5. MARY, baptized April 16, 1775; m. Simeon Hanmer, May 17, 1798, at Wethersfield.
297—6. LUCY, baptized Sept. 7, 1777; m. Samuel Hanmer, Jr., March 15, 1798, at Wethersfield.
298—7. EUNICE, baptized April 23, 1780; m. Samuel Lockwood, Sept. 27, 1809, at Wethersfield.

299. ELIJAH CRANE[4] [130], (Abraham,[3] Abraham,[2] Benjamin[1]), married Martha Bush of Colebrook, Conn.; was a tanner by trade. Feb. 25, 1767, he was residing in Wethersfield, for on that day he deeded land to his brother Abraham; same time his mother Rebecca released her dower by her mark [X], Benjamin and David being witnesses. He removed from Wethersfield to Sandisfield, Berkshire County, Mass., prior to March 1, 1769, where he carried on farming, and where he died Aug. 30, 1806. Abiah Bush was appointed guardian of his five youngest children. Dec. 11, 1776, he deeded to his brother Abraham all his right, title and interest in 24 acres lying in parish of Stepney in Wethersfield, lately the property of his brother Benjamin, deceased. He was corporal in Capt. Beardsly's company, 5th regiment, Col. David Waterbury; enlisted May 5th, discharged Oct. 8, 1775; marched to New York, and later served in Northern Department. He again enlisted Aug. 12, 1776, as private in Capt. Fuller's company, 13th regiment, Connecticut militia; discharged Sept. 4, 1776; April 22, 1775, marched from Pittsfield to Boston in Capt. David Noble's company; enlisted Aug. 14, 1777; served four days in Bennington. Children:

300—1. REBECKAH, b. Feb. 17, 1771; m. Rosseter Robbins; moved to Cincinnati, Ohio; he d. in South Carolina 1830.
301—2. MARTHA, b. May 24, 1772; joined the Shakers at Lebanon, N.Y.
302—3. DUMARAS, b. Jan. 1, 1774.
303—4. ELIJAH, b. May 25, 1775.
304—5. ELIAS, b. May 17, 1780.
305—6. BARNABAS, b. March 17, 1781; m. Elizabeth ———; d. Aug. 11, 1857; no family.
306—7. SILAS, b. April 18, 1784.
307—8. PRUDENCE, b. Oct. 31, 1786.
308—9. ABRAHAM, b. June 21, 1789.
309—10. LUCY, b. June 6, 1791.
310—11. MARY, b. Sept. 28, 1793.
311—12. HOPEFUL, b. March 16, 1796.

312. HEZEKIAH CRANE[4] [132], (Abraham,[3] Abraham,[2] Benjamin[1]), married Mary Dix, Dec. 29, 1771. She was born in 1750, and died Jan. 13, 1825. He died March 10, 1800. He was a blacksmith by trade. April 9, 1800, his will was presented to the court. March 16, 1801, some of the real estate was ordered to be sold to pay debts to the amount of $38.12. He deeded land in Wethersfield, situated on the road to Middletown, to Ezekiel Williams, adjoining land of Daniel and Wm. Worner and his mother Rebecca Crane; also to Richard Robbins of

Wethersfield land in parish of Stepney, Oct. 15, 1773. It is quite likely that he was the Hezekiah Crane, private in Connecticut militia, who marched under Gen. Gates to the northward in 1777.
  Children :

313—1. SARAH, b. May 7, 1772.
314—2. MARY, b. Jan. 17, 1774; m. Levi Hatch; one child, Samuel, b. July 15, 1795; d. July 18, 1798.
315—3. LEONARD, b. Aug. 15, 1776; d. 1797 or 1799; lost at sea.
316—4. SAMUEL, b. July 25, 1779.
317—5. HEZEKIAH, b. Jan. 5, 1781; d. May 19, 1827.
318—6. THOMAS, b. March 1, 1783; d. May 27, 1787.
319—7. LANCELOT, b. Feb. 12, 1785; unmarried; owned land on highway to Middletown, and sold to Sarah Williams, 1819.
320—8. REBECCA, b. March 14, 1788.
321—9. EMILY, b. Dec. 19, 1790.

322. MARY CRANE[4] [134], (Abraham,[3] Abraham,[2] Benjamin[1]), married John Adams, Dec. 6, 1771; resided in Wethersfield, Conn. She died May 21, 1794. He died Aug. 7, 1795.
  Children :

1. MARY (Adams), m. Roger Wolcott, April 11, 1799.
2. LUCY (Adams), m. Curtis Crane, Jr.
3. —— (Adams), d. Aug. 25, 1786, aged 9 months.
4. HANNAH (Adams), b. 1786. Oct. 15, 1802, then about 16 years of age, according to the Probate Records at Hartford she made choice of a guardian; and from a deed dated May 17, 1810, it appears that she may have removed with her sister (Mary), Mrs. Roger Wolcott, to Trenton, N. Y.

323. JOSEPH CRANE[4] [135], (Abraham,[3] Abraham,[2] Benjamin[1]), married Abigail, daughter of Jacob Dix, Dec. 3, 1778, and settled in Wethersfield, Conn. He died June 21, 1811. She died March 27, 1813. Oct. 5, 1811, an inventory of his estate was exhibited by George Crane (probably his son), one of the executors. May 7, 1819, the estate was distributed. June 6, 1812, Abigail and George Crane were appointed to administer the estate. His wife was to have one-third, and each child a share, and the children of Joseph, Jr., to have a single share. After the death of the mother the son George settled the estate. Jan. 17, 1818, Elisha Robbins was appointed guardian for David, then about 20 years old. May 3, 1777, he deeded land to Hezekiah Crane, in which reference is made to his honored mother Rebecca. This deed was witnessed by David Crane, his brother. He was private in Capt. John Chester's company, Wethersfield, 9th company, Gen. Spencer's regiment; enlisted May 3d; discharged Dec. 17, 1765; served in and about Boston. Children :

324—1.   JOSEPH, b. 1779; d. March 10, 1784.
325—2.   ABIGAIL, b. March, 1781; d. Oct. 2, 1783.
326—3.   JOSEPH, b. Aug. 17, 1784.
327—4.   ABIGAIL, b. Aug. 29, 1786; d. Oct. 5, 1819.
328—5.   GEORGE, b. Aug. 12, 1788; d. Nov. 27, 1824.
329—6.   JUSTUS, b. Nov. 22, 1790.
330—7.   SALLY, b. Dec. 29, 1792; m. John Harris before Feb. 16, 1820.
331—8.   JOHN, b. Nov. 13, 1794; d. Jan. 7, 1795.
332—9.   DAVID, b. May 28, 1797.
333-10. WILLIAM, b. July 4, 1800; d. Aug. 9, 1820.

334. SILAS CRANE[5] [144], (Silas,[4] Jonathan,[3] Jonathan,[2] Benjamin[1]), went to Horton, Nova Scotia, with his father about 1760 and drew farm lot 292, containing 245 acres; afterwards resided at Economy. Said to have had a daughter.

335—1. GRACE, m. James Pineo. He was b. Aug. 2, 1777.

336. COL. JONATHAN CRANE[5] [146], (Silas,[4] Jonathan,[3] Jonathan,[2] Benjamin[1]), went with his father from Lebanon, Conn., where he was born in the year 1750, to Horton, Nova Scotia. Married at Horton, Rebecca Allison, a native of Londonderry, Ireland. He was a magistrate, and also held a colonel's commission in the militia of the Province, and was a member of the Nova Scotia Parliament for the township of Horton for many years. It is related of him that one day coming out of the Government House, John Howe asked him, "What is going on?" "Oh," replied Crane, "'t is all a game of whist, the honors are divided and nothing is to be got except by tricks." He was on duty with his regiment one year, while stationed at Halifax. Col. Crane was the first person elected to represent his township, and continued to be re-elected until his death. He represented Kings County in the Provincial Parliament, and was in his day the most prominent man in that part of Nova Scotia. The house where he lived is the oldest in that part of the county, and was, in 1882, occupied by his grandson William Crane.

Col. Crane was a man of more than ordinary ability, became very popular and was held in high esteem by all who knew him. Many stories are related illustrating his characteristics. Among them the following: "On one occasion, while the Colonel was in charge of protecting the people against attacks from the enemy to King George III., an American privateer ran in shore for the purpose of foraging, when the Colonel hastily collected a number of his townsmen, armed them from the magazine, manned the Parrsboro packet, and put off in hot pursuit after the privateer. With their six-pounder of brass they felt confident they could capture their game. But their valor proved much greater than their discretion, for the well-armed privateer soon induced them to surrender, and putting a prize crew on board the packet she was headed down the basin for Boston, much to the dismay of the crowd of people who had collected on shore to witness the affray. But the Grand Pré men were not slow to improve their opportunities; although the greater portion of them were fastened

below as prisoners, several of them were depended upon to assist the prize crew in navigating the packet to Boston. When night came, William Bishop conceived a plan, which, though desperate, promised a chance for freedom. Having arranged matters with his comrades on deck, at a given signal, when there was but one watch on deck, Bishop dealt the steersman a blow with a marline-spike and threw his body into the Lazeretto, while other Grand Pré men were taking care of the victims assigned them, fastening below the remaining privateersmen, and liberating their Grand Pré associates below hatches, thus enabling them soon to regain possession of the packet, which they turned towards the basin, soon arriving home, to the surprise of their friends on shore, and acquiring no small degree of notoriety for themselves."

At another time the Colonel was successful in outwitting John Thomas Hill, sheriff and customs officer. The Colonel imported a cask of good old Jamaica, the flavor of which he believed would be very much injured were the government's blighting stamp placed upon it. But Mr. Hill, with the usual persistency of a customs officer, was determined that nothing should escape his notice, and that the King should have his own. The Colonel knowing full well the alertness with which Mr. Hill executed his official duties, drove with great parade of stealth to Horton Landing, where the schooner lay, with his oxen and cart, loaded a cask and proceeded on his return home, when he was met by Officer Hill, who demanded a surrender. The Colonel submitted with a very bad grace, and the oxen, cart, cask and contents were confiscated in the king's name. The officer's disgust can be better imagined than described, when, upon inspection next morning, he found the cask contained pure water with the smallest snifter of rum.

Colonel Crane had the honor of "dining and wining" his Royal Highness the Duke of Kent, father of the present Queen Victoria, while on a visit to Halifax as commander-in-chief of His Majesty's forces; and the report is handed down that the Colonel's wife, a very estimable lady, who some now living can recall to mind, when informed that the Duke had brought with him a French lady as companion of his joys, that she made it her business to make sundry calls on her neighbors, thereby escaping an introduction to His Royal Highness and Mademoiselle Kazenksky.

He died at Grand Pré, August, 1820. She died there in 1841, aged 89 years.

HIS WILL.

"I Jonathan Crane of Horton in Kings County being weak in Body but of a sound and perfect mind and memory blessed be Almighty God for the same do make and publish this my last Will and Testament in the following manner,

First, I give and bequeath to my beloved wife Rebecca Crane

the use and improvement of one third of my Real property during her natural life, also one third part of my Personal property after all my just debts are paid, to be at her sole use and disposal.

Second, I give and bequeath to my eldest son James N. Crane the one half of the whole of my property both real and personal after all my lawful debts are paid which I owe and the debts owed by James N. Crane or that he calls his own is to come into the valuation the same as my own property.

Thirdly, I give and bequeath the remaining half of my property to be divided into six equal parts or shares (to say) to my daughters Nancy Denison one and a half share to include about a quarter of a share I intended for her Daughter Rebecca Boyer, To James N. Crane one share, To William Crane one share, To Silas H. Crane one share, To my Daughter Rebecca Black one share, To my grandson Jonathan Black one quarter share, To Jonathan Crane son of James N. Crane one quarter share deducting from each one of their shares what they may have formerly received from my Estate, And it is to be understood that it is my will and pleasure that the half of my property which I have willed to my several children, James, Nancy, William, Silas, Rebecca, Jonathan Black and Jonathan Crane Should remain in the hands of James N. Crane and not be diverted till ten years after my decease except it should be convenient for said James N. Crane to pay some part thereof before that period, and at the end of ten years to be paid or delivered to the above mentioned persons.

Fourthly, I give and bequeath to my son William Crane, to my daughter Nancy Denison and to Rebecca Black Three quarters of an acre of land to each to be set off to them from the lower part of the lot on which I now live near the crooked apple tree ten years after my decease the valuation of the same to be deducted from their several shares.

Fifth, I give and bequeath to my beloved wife one horse and chaise to be at her disposal.

Sixth, Any property descending or falling to me not before mentioned to be at the sole disposal of James N. Crane.

And Lastly, I do hereby appoint my beloved wife Rebecca Crane, James N. Crane, William Crane, Silas H. Crane, Sherman Denison and Samuel Black as Executrix and Executors to this my last will and testament hereby revoking and entirely disannulling all former wills by me made.

Signed sealed Published and declared   JONATHAN CRANE (L.S)
by the said Jonathan Crane to be his last
will and testament in the presence of us who
have hereunto subscribed our names as witnesses
in the presence of the Testator, Horton Aug 9th 1820
Samuel Avery, Elihu Woodworth, Edward Boyer."

" Whereas by the foregoing Will and Testament I Jonathan Crane have named constituted and appointed certain persons

therein mentioned as Executors for the due execution thereof according to the true meaning and intent of the same, and whereas my said Executors may find it necessary to sell part of my Real Estate for the payment of my just debts, and I having considered it most expedient and convenient for two of my said Executors to have power and authority for that purpose do by this Codicil annexed to my said Will and Testament hereby nominate authorize and appoint James N. Crane and William Crane Two of my Executors named as aforesaid for the purpose of making sale of such part of my Real Estate as they may think most convenient for the payment of my debts as aforesaid and execute conveyances of the same hereby confirming all that the said James N. Crane and William Crane may lawfully do or cause to be done touching and concerning the sale of lands and premises as aforesaid. And I do further authorize and appoint the said James N. Crane and William Crane to collect all debts due to me of whatsoever nature or kind and take every proper measure for collection of the same and execute discharges for all monies so collected which said monies are to be applied to the payment of my just debts as aforesaid.

JONATHAN CRANE (L.S)

Signed sealed published and declared
by the said Jonathan Crane to be a codicil
to his last Will and Testament in the presence
of us who have hereunto subscribed our names
as witnesses in the presence of the Testator
and of each other, Samuel Avery Edward Boyer
Elijah Crane,

King County Court of Probate."

" Cornwallis Sept 2, 1820.

This day a probate of the aforesaid last Will and Testament of the late Jonathan Crane of Horton in the County aforesaid Yeoman was granted to James Noble Crane William Crane Silas H. Crane sons of the deceased and to Sherman Denison and Samuel Black sonsinlaw of the deceased they being duly sworn to execute the trust reposed in them. Inventory to be exhibited Dec 2, 1820. Acct March 2, 1822.

On the same day a warrant of apprizement was issued to Elihu Woodworth, James Harris Jur and Perry Borden all of Horton in the County aforesaid yeoman.

WM. C. CAMPBELL Regd."

Children of Jonathan Crane :

337—1. ANN, b. Nov. 25, 1772; d. previous to Aug. 9, 1820.
338—2. JOSEPH, b. Jan. 8, 1776; d. previous to Aug. 9, 1820.
339—3. JONATHAN, b. April 22, 1779; d. previous to Aug. 9, 1820.
340—4. JAMES NOBLE, b. July 6, 1782.
341—5. NANCY; m. Sherman Dennison.
342—6. WILLIAM, b. Feb. 15, 1785.
343—7. SILAS HIBERT, b. Oct. 17, 1787.
344—8. REBECCA, b. May 12, 1791; m. Samuel Black.

345. ELIJAH CRANE[5] [148], (Silas,[4] Jonathan,[3] Jonathan,[2] Benjamin[1]), married Mirriam Lockhart, at Horton, Nova Scotia, Dec. 30, 1777. Children:

346—1. LUCY, b. Nov. 3, 1778.
347—2. MIRRIAM, b. July 30, 1780.
348—3. SARAH, b. March 15, 1782.
349—4. REBECCA; m. ——— Fisher.

350. BENJAMIN CRANE[5] [151], (John,[4] John,[3] Jonathan,[2] Benjamin[1]). Under date of Feb. 6, 1762, there is a "purpose of marriage between Benjamin Crane of Western, Mass., and Sarah Witherbee who has lately dwelt at Western." The entry was made evidently by Simeon Dwight, then Town Clerk of that place, and that is all we have been able to get from the town records. From the office of Register of Deeds at Springfield, Mass., we learn that Benjamin Crain, cooper by trade, of Western, and Sarah his wife, sold land (110 acres) in Shutesbury, April 4, 1764. He also sold land on May 4, 1774, located in Merryfield (now Chester), at which time he was called of Brookfield. Again he sold land Jan. 16, 1777. At this time he is called "cooper of Western." As the family record gives evidence of twenty years residence in this locality it seems strange that not one at least of his children are mentioned in the records of either Western (now Warren) or Brookfield. From the archives at the State House, Boston, we learn that Benjamin Crane of Western was a private in Capt. Ezekiel Knowlton's company, Col. Dyke's Regiment, and served from Dec. 1, 1776, to March 1, 1777; and from Rev. Horace Alonzo Crane, M.A., his great-grandson, we find he married Sarah Witherbee, March 16, 1762. Children:

351—1. SARAH, b. Aug. 12, 1762, at Western.
352—2. JOHN, b. Oct. 30, 1763, at Western.
353—3. AMOS, b. Nov. 22, 1765, at Brookfield.
354—4. REBECCA, b. Sept. 7, 1767, at Brookfield.
355—5. ANNA, b. Aug. 20, 1769, at Brookfield.
356—6. ABEL, b. July 23, 1771, at Brookfield.
357—7. DARIUS, b. March 11, 1775, at Brookfield; d. April 9, 1776.
358—8. RUTH, b. Jan. 16, 1776, at Brookfield.
359—9. OLIVE, b. April 20, 1780, at Western.

On the town records of Tolland, Conn., we find Amos Crane [353], married Sarah Alling, June 30, 1785, at Abington. We are unable to positively connect this family. Children:

1. REPTY, b. Aug. 20, 1786.
2. SARAH, b. Aug. 6, 1789.
3. LAURA, b. April 9, 1792.
4. Amos, } b. May 15, 1794.
5. ASAHEL, }
6. ALLEN, b. July 5, 1796.
7. SOPHRONIA, b. Oct. 21, 1798.

360. JOHN CRANE[5] [152], (John,[4] John,[3] Jonathan,[2] Benjamin[1]). Dr. John Crane was born in Tolland, Conn. His

mother was Rebeckah Huntington. His grandmother on the
maternal side was Rebeckah Adgate. This relationship doubtless
brought him into association with Eleazer Wheelock, A.M.,
D.D., son of Deacon Ralph and Ruth (Huntington) Wheelock.
This Ruth Huntington's mother having been Sarah Adgate, sister
to Dr. Crane's grandmother. Mr. Wheelock was a graduate of
Yale College in 1733, was ordained pastor of the Second Congregational Church, Lebanon, Conn., in March, 1735. He was
very successful as a preacher and pastor. In addition to his
ministerial charge he was greatly interested in the education of
young men, especially the youth of the Indian nations. After
having taken into his family several of the latter for the purpose
of educating and training them to serve as missionaries among
their own people, he conceived the idea of establishing and conducting a missionary school, where Indian boys might be fitted
to perform missionary work; and a house and two acres of land
adjoining his own home place was given him in the year 1754 by
Joshua Moore of Mansfield for the purpose, and the school
established. After conducting "Moore's School," as it was
then called, for several years, Mr. Wheelock thought the advantages might be greatly increased by changing its location and
merging it into a college. Accordingly he obtained a charter
from John Wentworth, then Governor of New Hampshire, and
set out on a tour of inspection for the purpose of selecting a site
on which to locate his college. Dr. John Crane is said to have
accompanied Mr. Wheelock on this trip, and assisted in selecting
Hanover, N. H., as the location. Dr. Crane removed from
Connecticut with Rev. Eleazer Wheelock to Hanover in August,
1770, and in 1773 built one of the first houses erected there. It
stood on Main Street, first house south of Dartmouth Hotel.
The house with several others was consumed by fire in December, 1886. The lot, about an acre of land, on which Dr. Crane
built his house was presented to him by the College to encourage
him to locate here. He was the first resident physician and
apothecary in the place, and acquired considerable reputation as
such. In 1776 he joined the army as surgeon and served until
Dec. 31, 1783, serving in Col. Vose's 1st and Col. Smith's 13th
Regiments,—Continental Army pay accounts for service from
Oct. 24, 1777, to Dec. 31, 1779; also service from Jan. 1, 1780,
to Dec. 31, 1780; also Lieut. Calvin Smith's 6th Regiment, wages
allowed from January, 1781, to December, 1782, 24 months. He
was at the battle of Saratoga, and in winter quarters at Valley
Forge. He was a member of the Massachusetts Society of the
Cincinnati, and was succeeded in 1809 by his son, John Huntington Crane. Dr. Crane attended President Wheelock in his
last sickness, when he died April 24, 1779. Oct. 15, 1784, he
signed a petition for a road from Boscawen on Merrimack River
to the Connecticut River. Dr. Crane married Hannah Brown,
and died in February, 1786. His widow married Col. Aaron
Kinsman also a Revolutionary soldier. She died in 1817.

Child:

1. JOHN HUNTINGTON, b. 1779; graduated at Dartmouth College, 1799; read law and began practice at Stafford, Vt. But removed his office to Boston, Mass., thence to Sandusky, Ohio, and finally to Louisville, Ky., where he d. Sept. 26, 1822, aged 43 years. Never married.

361. ELIJAH CRANE[5] [154], (John,[4] John,[3] Jonathan,[2] Benjamin[1]), married Sarah Hill. She was a native of Woburn, Mass. Mr. Crane was one of the first ten settlers of the town of Washington, Mass., going there in 1760,—from 1762 until 1777 the place was called Hartwood,—and with the exception of two years spent his life there. Jan. 30, 1772, he was appointed to settle his brother Amos Crane's estate of Tolland, Conn., and gave £200 bond to the court for faithful performance of the trust. Elijah was then called of Hartwood, Mass. Amos is said to have been killed by the Indians. Shortly before his death he removed to Madrid, N. Y., at which place he died Jan. 15, 1818. His widow died in Canton, St. Lawrence County, N. Y., Sept. 11, 1819, aged 70 years. Children:

362—1. ELIJAH, b. Dec. 15, 1771; d. April 9, 1781.
363—2. SARAH, b. May 26, 1773.
364—3. AMOS, b. Dec. 17, 1774.
365—4. LOIS, b. March 2, 1777.
366—5. JOEL, b. Feb. 17, 1779.
367—6. EUNICE, b. Nov. 23, 1780.
368—7. LUCY, b. Aug. 23, 1782; d. July 3, 1783.
369—8. SUSANNA, b. April 8, 1784.
370—9. ELIJAH, b. Sept. 28, 1785.
371—10. LUCY, b. Sept. 18, 1787.

372. ABEL CRAIN[5] [155], (John,[4] John,[3] Jonathan,[2] Benjamin[1]), married Elizabeth ———, and settled in Becket, Mass. Abel Crain of Becket served as private in Capt. Ebenezer Webber's company, Lt.-Col. Saml. Williams' Regiment, Dec. 17, 1776, discharged March 20, 1777. Marched to the northward, probably in Major Clap's Regiment. He again served in Capt. Porter's company, Col. Rositer's Regiment. From July 1 to Dec. 31, 1779, he served as private in Major's company, Col. Ebenezer Sprout's Regiment, Continental army, for the town of Becket. He was a powerfully built man, "six feet two or three inches tall, dark complexion, black hair, about thirty years of age." This we learn from the description list of men who served in Continental army. A visit to the office of Registrar of Probate at Pittsfield, Mass., disclosed the fact that May 31, 1817, on petition of the widow Elizabeth Crane, George Conant, Esq., was appointed by the court to settle the estate of Abel Crane of Becket. Some of the children were minors, and Timothy Snow was appointed guardian for Edward and Saloma. The estate was settled Sept. 7, 1819, and after the payment of all debts, the widow was given her portion, and the balance remaining, thirty-three dollars and fifty-

four cents, was equally divided between the children, each receiving the sum of four dollars and seventy-nine cents.   Children :

    373 – 1. ABEL H.
    374—2. DORASTUS.
    375—3. EDWARD.
    376—4. RACHEL.
    377—5. REBECCA.
    378—6. SOBRINA.
    379—7. SALOMA.

Whether this Abel was father to Abel, John and Orange Crain, the records at Pittsfield do not show.   But Mr. Orange Crane of Fillmore, Minn.. stated in 1881 that he was a son of Abel Crain of Massachusetts, and that he was a descendant of this Benjamin Crane.   That he had brothers Abel and John, and one son Ozias then living in Colorado.

380.   SAMUEL CRANE[5] [157], (John,[4] John,[3] Jonathan,[2] Benjamin[1]), married Charity Higley Nov. 7, 1776.   She was born Sept. 13, 1756.   He settled in Simsbury, Conn., a farmer, but subsequently, in 1802, removed to Onondaga Hill, N. Y., where he died July 28, 1818.   She died at Bennington, N. Y., Oct. 10, 1842.   He enlisted April 26, 1777, private in Capt. Peter Porter's company, Col. Benjamin Simons' Berkshire County Regiment. Company marched to Saratoga by order of Gen. Gates.   He was discharged May 20, 1777.   Children :

    381—1. SAMUEL HIGLEY, b. Oct. 9, 1777.
    382—2. CHARITY THEODOSIA, b. June 19, 1779.
    383—3. ANNA MARIA, b. March 28, 1781.
    384—4. ABEL, b. April 4, 1783.
    385—5. ARCHER, b. March 26, 1785.
    386—6. AMHERST, } twins, b. June 2, 1787; { d. June 10, 1861.
    387—7. AMBROSE, }   { d. Oct. 15, 1857.
    388—8. DANIEL COLTON, b. May 2, 1789 ; d. May 9, 1872.
    389—9. ADONIJAH, b. Sept. 25, 1791 ; d. June 26, 1792.
    390—10. LUKE, b. July 15, 1793 ; d. Sept. 4, 1855.
    391—11. SYLVESTER RETURN, b. Jan. 6, 1796.
    392—12. LAMENT SAMUEL, b. Jan. 1, 1799 ; d. Nov. 14, 1799.

393.   JOSHUA CRANE[5] [162], (Abiah,[4] John,[3] Jonathan,[2] Benjamin[1]), married first, May 4, 1769, Mary Brown.   She was born in 1745 and died March 23, 1791.   Married second, Widow Ladd.   He settled at Alstead, N. H.; a farmer.   His will was dated May 25, 1814, probated June 12, 1816, and mentioned his eight children then living and three grandchildren belonging to his son Joshua.   Children :

    394—1. HEZEKIAH, b. April 3, 1770 ; d. Feb. 3, 1792.
    395—2. SAMUEL, b. Oct. 25, 1771 ; d. Oct. 24, 1773.
    396—3. ISAAC, b. March 25, 1774.
    397—4. JOSHUA, b. May 16, 1776.
    398—5. MARTHA, b. Sept. 25, 1778 ; m. a Mr. Smith and went west.
    399—6. SARAH, b. Aug. 6, 1781 ; unm.; d. at Alstead, N. H.
    400—7. RUTH, b. Feb. 16, 1784 ; d. Jan. 25, 1812 ; not married.
    401—8. ELEAZER, b. Feb. 22, 1786.

402—9. SAMUEL, b. Feb. 1, 1788.
403—10. POLLY, b. Sept. 5, 1790.
404—11. EUNICE, b. Sept. 1, 1793, by second wife.

405. ISAAC CRANE[5] [163], (Abiah,[4] John,[3] Jonathan,[2] Benjamin[1]). Born at Coventry, Tolland County, Conn.; married in 1768 Thankful Putnam. She was born in Western (now Warren), Worcester County, Mass., May 17, 1747; and the purpose of their marriage was recorded there Aug. 20, 1768. She was a daughter of Josiah and Lydia Wheeler Putnam, born May 6, 1747, old style. . He was a private in Capt. Josiah Putnam's company, Col. Jedediah Foster's Regiment; marched April 21, 1775, to Roxbury in response to the alarm of April 19, served 8 days. Also served in Capt. Joseph Cutter's company of volunteers, marched from Western and Oakham to join Gen. Gates Sept. 24, 1777; served 32 days in Northern department. For several years the family resided in Western, Worcester County, but subsequently removed to northern Vermont, where Mrs. Crane was drowned in Onion River. Mr. Crane died in New York State. Children:

406—1. JOSIAH, b. March 11, 1769.
407—2. EUNICE, b. Jan. 27, 1771.
408—3. RUFUS, b. March 19, 1774.
409—4. SABRA, b. June 28, 1776; m. Mr. Newton, said to have settled in Massachusetts.
410—5. ISAAC, b. April 10, 1778; d. in Alstead, N. H., July 15, 1824, adm. granted Patty his widow, no other heirs named.
411—6. TIRZAH, b. May 7, 1780.
412—7. ASA, b. Nov. 9, 1782.
413—8. LUCINDA, b. Feb. 23, 1785; d. young.
414—9. PUTNAM, b. May 2, 1787; d. young.
415—10. AMOS, b. Sept. 12, 1788.

416. MARY CRANE[5] [164], (Abiah,[4] John,[3] Jonathan,[2] Benjamin[1]), married Joshua Wood of Alstead, N. H. They both were of Western, Mass., as the records there contain memorandum of a purpose of marriage "betwixed" them dated Jan. 21, 1775.

417. ABIAH or ABIA CRANE[5] [165], (Abiah,[4] John,[3] Jonathan,[2] Benjamin[1]), married Experience Smith, and settled in Surry, N. H.; a farmer. He died Feb. 6, 1805, aged 53 years, 11 months, 13 days. He was, no doubt, the Abiah Crane, corporal in Capt. Davis Howlet's company, which was raised out of Col. Ashley's regiment of militia, and marched from Keene, N. H., to reinforce the Continental army at Ticonderoga, May, 1777. He was probably the same Abiah who was in John Houghton's company, Col. Baldwin's regiment of New York; paid Sept. 22, 1776, £7—13—4. Children:

418—1. JOSHUA.
419—2. ICHABOD, m. 1st, Feb. 15, 1816, Fannie Watts of Alstead, N. H.; 2d, Clarissa Anderson of Walpole; he d. 1866; will dated Aug. 25. His widow m. Mr. Bragg; lives in Walpole, N. H.; no children. His will was contested, with the

result that the court distributed the property among the heirs-at-law, namely: John W. Crane of Saratoga, a son of Justus and Juliette C. Whitney, Fanny W. Godfrey, Nelly Ingalls, and Wm. C. Thompson, nephews and nieces of Ichabod.

420—3. THEODOSHA, m. Mr. Witherby; settled in Surry, N. H.

421—4. ZINA or EUNICE, b. Aug. 28, 1790; m. 1810 William Thompson, and removed to Ohio.

422—5. JUSTUS, m. and removed to New York State, settling in Saratoga; d. 1860, leaving an only child, John W. Crane, now (1898) residing at Saratoga Springs. He is a judge and counsellor-at-law.

423. JOSEPH CRANE,[5] [167], (Abiah,[4] John,[3] Jonathan,[2] Benjamin[1]), married 1st, Aug. 21, 1783, Ruth Wilson. She was in the 23d year of her age. She died about 1791, and in December, 1792, he married 2d, Eleanor Buck, who was born 1765, and died in Williamstown, May 13, 1832. He died March 31, 1819. He was enrolled among the list of Revolutionary soldiers in Williamstown, Vt. He was one of the first settlers of Williamstown, Vt. His wife was drawn in on a hand-sled. She was given a lot of land for being the first woman to settle in the town. Here Mr. Crane purchased 300 acres of land, and with his axe felled the first tree cut in the town. All his children were born here. He was a member of the Legislature of Vermont, and went from Tolland, Conn. Eleanor Buck taught first school in Williamstown, 1793. Children:

424—1. JOSEPH, b. Aug 8,1784; died in Wheelock, Vt.; unmarried; over 70 years of age. He served in war of 1812, enlisting in navy.

425—2. RUTH, b. Oct. 31, 1786.

426—3. ANNA, b. Dec. 17, 1788.

427—4. ABIA, b. Feb. 6, 1790; d. Nov. 9, 1814, of fever contracted while serving in war of 1812.

428—5. ARIEL, b. Oct. 24, 1793.

429—6. HORATIO, b. Feb. 23, 1795.

430—7. OREN, b. Jan. 18, 1797.

431—8. ARBA, b. Nov. 5, 1798.

432—9. LUCINA, b. May 8, 1800.

433—10. ADALINE, b. April 10, 1802; m. Jacob S. Martin, Williamstown, Vt., and d. March 30, 1878; no children.

434—11. PORTER, b. Feb. 27, 1804.

435—12. LUCY, b. May 9, 1806; d. March 7, 1816.

436—13. CHAUNCY, b. March 7, 1810.

437—14. CHARLES, b. Sept. 29, 1812.

438—15. ABIA WILSON, b. June 25, 1815; m. Emily Lease of Waterbury, Vt., and died July 14, 1869; no children.

439. JOHN CRANE[5] [169], (Abiah,[4] John,[3] Jonathan,[2] Benjamin[1]), married Sarah, daughter of Solomon and Anna Prentice, born Jan. 23, 1775, and settled in Glover, Vt. He must, however, have lived for a time in Williamstown, for it is recorded that Rev. Jesse Olds, Congregational minister, was ordained in John Crane's barn, Williamstown, 1797.

---

* Hemingway's Vermont, II., 1141, 1144, 1145.

Children :

440—1. EUNICE, b. May 1, 1798.
441—2. SALLY, b. April 27, 1800.
442—3. ASA PRENTICE. b. April 24, 1803; d. March 16, 1806.
443—4. JOHN, b. Nov. 14, 1805.
444—5. NANCY, b. June 14, 1808.
445—6. AVIS, b. Oct. 14, 1810; d. Jan. 1, 1815.
446—7. LAURA, b. Sept. 1, 1812.
447—8. PERSIS, b. March 3, 1815.

448. ELISHA CRANE[5] [171], (Elisham,[4] John,[3] Jonathan,[2] Benjamin[1]), married Lydia Owen, and settled in Bolton, Conn., where the eldest son was born. He then removed to Norwich, Vt., where Daniel was born. The family then went to Haverhill, N. H. Mr. Crane subsequently returned to Connecticut, and went from there to Albany, N. Y., and married again, having a son and a daughter at that place, where he died in 1822. He served as clerk in the commissary department at the time of the French and Indian war. He was living in Albany, N. Y., April 26, 1785, where he was a merchant, and then bought land in Goshen, Hampshire County, Mass., recorded at Springfield; was private in Capt. Amos Rathborne's company, Col. Benj. Simons' detachment, Berkshire County militia, Jan. 6 to March 15, 1777; at Ticonderoga, Feb. 25, 1777. Children :

449—1. WILLIAM, b. 1767.
450—2. DANIEL O., b. Sept. 6, 1769.
451—3. ELISHA, resided in Albany, N. Y.
452—4. ELIZABETH, m. John Mead of Albany, N. Y.

453. ANNA CRANE[5] [172], (Elisham,[4] John,[3] Jonathan,[2] Benjamin[1]), married Samuel Bartlett, Sept. 14, 1767, at Windsor, Conn. He was born Jan. 15, 1744-5, and died in East Windsor, Nov. 29, 1825. He was a farmer. She died March 17, 1831. Children :

1. COL. JONATHAN (Bartlett), b. July 25, 1769.
2. ANNA (Bartlett), m. James Harper of Enfield.
3. ABIGAIL (Bartlett), b. June 25, 1772; m. Joshua Allen.
4. SARAH (Bartlett), m. Capt Clark Foster of Ellington, Conn.
5. SAMUEL (Bartlett), b. —— 6, 1779.

454. HEZEKIAH CRANE[5] [175], (Hezekiah,[4] John,[3] Jonathan,[2] Benjamin[1]), married Sybil Lamphire. He enlisted Sept. 7, and was discharged Nov. 2, 1776, serving as private in Capt. Isaac Sergeant's company, Major Backus' regiment, Light Horse; served in and about New York city; also may have been private in Capt. Roswell Grant's company, Col. Johnson's regiment; served in Rhode Island; enlisted Jan. 7, 1778. Distribution of his estate was made in Probate Court in East Windsor, March 14, 1796; one-eighth part each to Wareham, Joel, Abner, Hezekiah, Russell, Eunice, Rhoda and Lucretia; widow Sibbel Crane her dower. Joel was administrator; administration granted Jan. 13, 1794. Children :

455—1. WAREHAM, b. 1770.

456—2. JOEL, b. Jan. 19, 1772.
457—3. HEZEKIAH, b. 1773.
458—4. EUNICE, m. John Hill.
459—5. ABNER, b. Jan. 3, 1776.
460—6. RHODA, b. Jan. 8, 1783.
461—7. RUSSELL WILLIS.
462—8. LUCRETIA.

463. DAVID CRANE[5] [176,] (Hezekiah,[4] John,[3] Jonathan,[2] Benjamin[1]), married 1st. Theodocia Pitkin; 2d, Jan. 7, 1779, Jerusha Smith of Ellington, Conn., daughter of David Smith. She was born Dec. 18, 1759, and settled in East Windsor, one mile south of Ketch mills. He was a carpenter and builder, as well as farmer; served in the Revolutionary war, and died in Scantic parish in 1841, about 92 years of age. March 12, 1850, administration was granted on estate of Mrs. Jerusha Crane of East Windsor. Children:

464—1. DAVID, b. Oct. 5, 1774–5.
465—2. SAMUEL PITKIN, b. Jan. 15, 1780.
466—3. CHAUNCEY, b. 1782.
467—4. CURTIS, b. Nov. 9, 1781.
468—5. JERUSHA, b. 1784.
469—6. CHARLOTTE, b. 1786; d. Jan. 14, 1813.
470—7. THEODOCIA, b. 1789; probably m. Josiah Blodgett, b. at Ellington, Conn., Jan. 12, 1789; d. in Monroeville, Ohio, Oct. 11, 1847. She d. there Nov. 11, 1849; had 12 children.
471—8. LEMUEL, b. 1791.
472—9. BETSY, b. 1793.
473–10. JOHN W., b. 1796; d. Feb. 24, 1799.
474–11. JOHN WASHINGTON, b. March 24, 1800.
475–12. WARREN S., b. Feb. 24, 1802.

476. RUFUS CRANE[5] [179], (Hezekiah,[4] John,[3] Jonathan,[2] Benjamin[1]), married Rachel Grant; born in Ellington 1761; settled in East Windsor. Conn. He died Nov. 30, 1820. She died April 1, 1849. He served in the Revolutionary war, and his widow drew a pension for many years; was private in Capt. Roswell Grant's company, Col. Roger Enos' regiment; served along the Hudson River in 1778; also in 2d regiment Connecticut Line, Col. Charles Webb; served in New York, New Jersey and Pennsylvania; at battle of Monmouth; enlisted July 19, discharged Dec. 9, 1780; served probably as private in Capt. Joseph Richards' company Aug. 17, 1779, and in Capt. Samuel Fisher's company in Rhode Island one month and three days. He was a carpenter and joiner by trade. Children:

477—1. RUFUS, b. Sept. 21, 1786. May 2, 1826, administration was granted to Rufus Crane on the estate of his father Rufus, late of East Windsor. June 26 dower was set to widow Rachel Crane. The estate was insolvent. Among the creditors of the estate were Hosea Crane, Rufus Crane, Lemuel Crane and James Crane. April 11, 1849, administration was granted on estate of Mrs. Rachel Crane to Rufus Crane. Distribution was ordered June 26, 1850, to eight heirs, names not given.

478—2. JAMES. m. Electa ——, and d. Jan. 2, 1843, aged 48. Electa
          d. July 16, 1845, aged 49.
479—3. PRUDENCE.
480—4. ACHSAH.
481—5. HOSEA, b. Feb. 3, 1802.
482—6. HARVEY.
483—7. JAMES GRANT.

484. AARON CRAIN[5] [180], (Hezekiah,[4] John,[3] Jonathan,[2]
Benjamin[1]), married June 16, 1778, Mary, daughter of Thomas
and Jane Barber, born Aug. 14, 1754. April 17, 1817, he
married widow Dorcas Munn of Springfield, Mass., and resided at
Longmeadow. Will dated May 13, 1826, and mentions his wife
Dorcas. He died July 3, 1826, aged 70 years. Was private
in Capt. Jonathan Johnson's company, Middletown, Col.
Philip B. Bradley's battalion, Wadsworth's brigade; enlisted
June 22, 1776; discharged Dec. 28 that year; served at Paulus
Hook, Bergen Heights and Fort Washington, where a portion of
the regiment was captured. He is, we presume, the Aaron Crane
who marched to the northward under Gen. Walcott's detachment
to join Gen. Gates, then surrounding Burgoyne's army. He sold
land July 7, 1803, to Joseph Brown. Children:

485—1. POLLY, b. May 10, 1779.
486—2. AARON, b. March 24, 1781. There was a Lodice Crane of
          Longmeadow, widow of Aaron, June 16, 1816.
487—3. TIMOTHY, b. Jan. 28, 1783.
488—4. ZIBA, b. April 16, 1785.
489—5. ELI, b. Aug. 3, 1787.
490—6. JANE, b. Dec. 24, 1789.
491—7. LUCINA. b. Aug. 19, 1792.
492—8. ELIHU, b. Nov. 17, 1794.
493—9. HEZEKIAH, b. Feb. 1, 1797.
494-10. ALMIRA, b. July 18, 1799; d. Sept. 6, 1808.

495. ZEBULON CRANE[5] [183], (Lemuel,[4] John,[3] Jonathan,[2]
Benjamin[1]), married Rhoda ——; served in Capt. Jason Wait's
company, Col. Bedel's regiment; paid for this service February,
1776; June 9, 1777, he is reported as serving one month and
three days at Ticonderoga in Col. Benj. Bellows' regiment, New
Hampshire militia; again from Sept. 21 to Oct. 22, 1777, at
Saratoga, same regiment, to reinforce the Continental army under
Gen. Gates; was wounded, and lived for a time in Williamstown,
Vt. Children:

496—1. THEDOSIA, b. Sept. 21, 1779; m. Edmund Wetherbee.
497—2. EBENEZER, b. April 1, 1781.
498—3. TRYPHENA, b. April 2, 1783; d. May 13, 1785.
499—4. EUNICE, b. July 6, 1785; m. Elisha Williams.
500—5. ELIJAH, b. Dec. 4, 1786; d. in Brookfield, Vt., or Williams-
          town, Vt.

501. ISAAC W. CRANE[5] [198], (Isaac,[4] Isaac,[3] Jonathan,[2]
Benjamin[1]), went from Windham, Conn., to Hebron, and was
6 •

there married Nov. 26, 1797, to Constantia Young of that place; children all born there.   Children :

502—1. LUCY MARIA, b. July 27, 1798; d. March 11, 1822.
503—2. GEORGE, b. April 14, 1801; m. Lovina Blackman, Sept. 12, 1822.
504—3. ERASTUS, b. April 16, 1803.
505—4. RALPH, b. June 8, 1805.
506—5. CHARLES, b. June 23, 1807; never married.
507—6. LUCY MARIA, b. Feb. 18, 1811; m. Alfred Theodore Lilly, a silk manufacturer at Florence, Mass. She d. Nov. 2, 1886. He d. 1890.
508—7. HARVEY, b. Sept. 1, 1817.

509.   JOHN CRAIN⁵ [199], (Isaac,⁴ Isaac,³ Jonathan,² Benjamin¹), married Abigail Faulkner, a native of Brooklyn, Conn. Mr. Crane was born in Windham and spelled his name Crain. He died in Windham, Conn. Children :

510—1. JOHN, b. July 25, 1800; never married; was a merchant in Pawtucket, R. I.; d. 1872.
511—2. LUCIUS, b. Nov. 22, 1801.
512—3. LUCY HARRIET, b. ———; m. Charles Trescott, lived in Providence, R. I.; d. 1877.
513—4. MARY, b. Nov. 28, 1805.
514—5. HARVEY H., b. May 10, 1811.
515—6. CHARLES, ⎫ twins, ⎧ m. Susan Philips, lived in
                b.   Sterling, Ct.
516—7. CAROLINE, ⎬ . Feb. 10, ⎨ m. Herbert Parkhurst, lived
                ⎭ 1813; ⎩ in Wauregan or Plainfield, Ct.

517.   JOHN CRANE⁵ [202], (Zebulon,⁴ Joseph,³ Jonathan,² Benjamin¹), married March 1, 1764, Tamar, daughter of John and Hannah Carpenter of New Castle, Westchester County. She was born Dec. 1, 1747.   Rev. Eliphalet Ball, the first settled minister of Ballston, N. Y., performed the marriage ceremony. Served in Revolutionary war in 3d company, New York Line, private from March 2 to July 15, 1777; was Captain of 4th company, 7th Regiment (Luddington's Regiment), elected March 12, 1776.   He was Judge for Dutchess County, N. Y.   Chosen Town Clerk of Carmel at first town meeting, April 7, 1795 (held at his house) ; also Commissioner of Highways.   She died at Carmel, N. Y., Jan. 1, 1823.   He died at same place June 9, 1827.

" My grandfather was living at the commencement of the Revolutionary war that separated the then thirteen colonies from the government of Great Britain.   At the commencement of that war, the people were divided into two classes,—Whigs and Tories.   The Whig party were those who were opposed to the black arts of the British Parliament;   and the Tories took sides with the king.   My grandfather was then about eighty years old, very strong and active for a man of that age, and a warm Whig; and, what is very remarkable, his eight children were all living, and heads of families.   He had many grandchildren and great-grandchildren, and not an individual, who had arrived at

the years of understanding, failed to take an active part in the American cause. I was the eldest grandchild, and had an ensign's commission under King George III., in the year 1775. I took a captain's commission under the Provincial Congress of the Province of New York, and on the fourth of July following, our Independence was declared, Clinton became our Governor, then I received a commission from him, and held it through the war. Such was the general conduct of the family, which was the cause of many of them receiving both Civil and Military commissions.; not on account of our extraordinary abilities, but as recognition of our *engagedness* in that blessed cause. I hope whoever reads the foregoing will erase the incorrectness as I want but six days of being eighty-three years of age and am almost blind."

(Signed)   "JOHN CRANE."

Judge John Crane, or Capt. John as he is frequently spoken of, was the eldest of twelve children of Zebulon and Sarah Belden Crane. On March 1, 1764, be married Tamar, daughter of John and Hannah Carpenter of New Castle, Westchester Co., N. Y. Five years later, with his wife and two small children, he came from New Castle to a farm of 250 acres, situated near Lake Mahopac, where, in 1772, he built the first frame house which was erected in this part of the country. His house was a public inn, where the business of the town was transacted, and town meetings were held. He held the office of justice of the peace, and was associate judge of the court of common pleas in Dutchess County, before the county was divided, and also of Putnam County after it was established. The military commissions are mentioned in his " Fragment of Family History." The commission he received from Clinton is now in the possession of Benj. T. Crane, his youngest grandson, who owns and occupies the old homestead near Mahopac.

During the Revolution, Gen. Charles Scott, with his staff, made his headquarters for a time at John Crane's inn. The troops in going to and from the headquarters at Salem, Westchester Co., and West Point, on the Hudson, passed that way, and often tarried over night there. Conspicuous among them was " Capt. Poll," a young Irish woman.

Beside being an unflinching patriot and noted for his integrity and superior business capacity in the management of public affairs, in his private life Judge Crane was a person of great benevolence and kindly feeling; a firm friend and an indulgent parent. He was medium-sized, well-proportioned, with mild blue eyes and a dignity of manner which commanded the respect of all with whom he came in contact.

In a letter written by a grand-nephew of his, Dr. Geo. B. Crane of St. Helena, Cal., who died recently at the advanced age of more than ninety years, he said: "Judge Crane came to our house, dressed as usual; silk stockings, and breeches, buckled

above his knees, and ending there; silver shoe-buckles, and a large brimmed fine fur hat. He was a gentleman of the old school, and such fashions went out with the old men of his time."

Judge Crane and his family were all active church workers, going on horseback, from their home near Mahopac to the old log church, near "Tilly Foster Mines," to attend service, and later, aiding in the erection and support of the Gilead Presbyterian Church at Carmel. Nor did the good work die with him; he left children and grandchildren of unusual attainments, of sterling worth, and high personal character. His sons Joseph and John were very influential men in the Gilead Church, and his grandson Azor B. Crane was during his whole life one of the most prominent citizens of Putnam County. In 1843, he was appointed judge of the court of common pleas, and was the first county judge and surrogate elected under the new constitution of 1847. Children :

518—1. JOSEPH, b. June 3, 1766.
519—2. ADAH, b. June 6, 1768.
520—3. STEPHEN, b. Nov. 1, 1770.
521—4. JOHN, b. June 6, 1773.
522—5. ZILLAH, b. Oct. 3, 1775.
523—6. NATHANIEL, b. Feb. 28, 1778.
524—7. SARAH, b. June 27, 1780.
525—8. ARABELLA, b. Dec. 25, 1784.
526—9. CLORINDA, b. Oct. 2, 1787.

527. WILLIAM CRANE[5] [203], (Zebulon,[4] Joseph,[3] Jonathan,[2] Benjamin[1]), served in Revolutionary war as private in Capt. Daniel Williams' company, Col. Albert Pawling's Regiment, for year 1779; also private in Barnum's company or Capt. Joseph Dyckman's company, Col. John Field's Regiment, two days, May 11, 1777. [L. B. P., Vol. 8, 65; Vol. 3, 156]. According to records at Albany, Land Bounty Papers, Vol. 1, 79 and 80, was private in 4th Battalion of New York Line, Col. James Holmes, Capt. David Palmer's company. On duty at Montreal Aug. 3, 1775; also on rolls of Jan. 1, and Feb. 13, 1776, before Quebec. He is also called 1st Lieutenant in the records at Albany, and served in Capt. Andrew White's company. [L. and B. P., 21, 98].

528. ZEBULON CRANE[5] [204], (Zebulon,[4] Joseph,[3] Jonathan,[2] Benjamin[1]), married first ——— Holmes, sister of David Holmes of Bedford, N. Y., by whom he had six children; married second Mrs. Elizabeth (Wood) Townsend. He was a soldier in the Revolutionary war. The following story is told of him : "After a skirmish with the Indians, the next day he with a few picked men were scouting and came upon a lone Indian two miles from camp. They took him prisoner, disarmed him, and Crane was left to guard him; but he let the Indian get behind him, when the Indian clinched Crane by the hair and tried to cut his throat with a knife he had concealed about his person. Crane

took the knife away from the Indian, and when the latter started to run away, Crane shot the Indian with his own gun. He returned to camp nearly dead from loss of blood, having received a severe gash across his forehead and temples and his hand half cut off in getting away the knife." His son Elijah gave this account in 1871, being then an old man. He died Dec. 31, 1814. Children :

529—1. BELDEN, b. Aug. 23, 1770.
530—2. SETH, b. April 16, 1773.
531—3. ELISHA, b. Jan. 20, 1775; d. young.
532—4. ELISHA, b. Dec. 18, 1776.
533—5. SAMUEL, b. Sept. 9, 1778.
534—6. DAVID, b. Dec. 23, 1782.
535—7. ZEBULON, b. Dec. 28, 1787.
536—8. LEWIS, b. Dec. 23, 1789.
537—9. AMZI, b. Oct. 7, 1791.
538-10. SALLY, b. June 8, 1793.
539-11. JESSE, b. Oct. 19, 1795.
540-12. POLLY, b. Oct. 18, 1797.
541-13. ELIJAH, b. Aug. 23, 1800.

542. ELIJAH CRANE[5] [205], (Zebulon,[4] Joseph,[3] Jonathan,[2] Benjamin[1]). He lived for a time on a farm about a mile north of Lake Mahopac. It is also related that he resided in Connecticut not far from New Haven; that he married Miss —— Bradley and had two daughters, and perhaps other children.*
Children :

543—1. NERISSA.
544—2. SARAH.

545. NERISSA CRANE[6] [543], (Elijah,[5] Zebulon,[4] Joseph,[3] Jonathan,[2] Benjamin[1]), married Zerah Tousey. Children :

1. SINCLAIR (Tousey), b. Jan. 18, 1815, in New Haven, Conn.
2. ARABELLA (Tousey).
3. GEORGE (Tousey).
4. MARY ANN (Tousey.)
5. HENRY (Tousey).

546. SINCLAIR TOUSEY [1] began his business career very early in life, going to New York city in 1833; he engaged in carrying newspapers. Three years later went west as agent for sale of patent medicines, making Louisville, Ky., his headquarters. In 1840 returned to New York State, and for some years carried on farming. In 1853 he entered into partnership with Messrs. Ross & Jones, wholesale news agents and booksellers, on Nassau street, New York city. Some years later he bought out his partners, and Feb. 1, 1864, the American News Company was established, and Mr. Tousey became the first president, and continued to hold that office until his death, June 16, 1887; an active anti-slavery man, and one of the first to join the republican party; a frequent writer for the press; member of the Union League Club, the Society for Prevention of Cruelty to Animals, and the Society for Prevention of Cruelty to Children; vice-president of the Hahne-

* It is exceedingly difficult to fix this with absolute certainty.

mann Hospital Association, and many years chairman of the
executive committee of the New York Prison Association,
and devoted a large share of his time to the work of the
latter institution. He married. Children :

    1. BENJAMIN (Tousey).
    2. CHARLES (Tousey).
    3. JOHN E. (Tousey).
    4. WILLIAM (Tousey).

547. GEORGE TOUSEY [3], married —— ——. Children :

    1. GEORGE (Tousey).
    2. EDWARD (Tousey).
    3. FRANK (Tousey), a publisher, New York city.
    4. SINCLAIR (Tousey).
    5. AMANDA (Tousey).

548. SARAH CRANE[6] [544], (Elijah,[5] Zebulon,[4] Joseph,[3]
Jonathan,[2] Benjamin[1]), married Joseph Henderson. Children :

    1. MARY ANN (Henderson), m. Dr. Richard Dennison.
    2. CAROLINE (Henderson).
    3. SARAH JANE (Henderson).

    CAROLINE HENDERSON [2]; m. Henry Miller. Children :

        1. ARABELLA (Miller).
        2. JOSEPH (Miller).
        3. HENRY (Miller).

    SARAH JANE HENDERSON [3], married John S. Park. Children :

        1. R. H. (Park), the sculptor.
        2. SARAH CRANE (Park), m. Samuel I. Avery; residence
           New York city.

549. SARAH CRANE[5] [206], (Zebulon,[4] Joseph,[3] Jonathan,[2]
Benjamin[1]). She was familiarly known as Sally Crane. She
married Elisha, son of Asahel and Catherine (Peet) Noble, a
lineal descendant of Thomas Noble, who was admitted an inhabitant of Boston, January 5, 1653, settled in Springfield,
Mass., the same year and died in Westfield, Mass., January 20,
1704, where his son John, the first settler in New Milford, Conn.,
1707, was born. Subsequently they made New Milford their
home. Here Mr. Noble was born, Oct. 25, 1750, and where
he identified himself with the church and town affairs. About
1796 he removed to Skeenesborough, now Whitehall, N. Y.,
where, about two years later, his wife died. Mrs. Noble was a
woman of rare personal virtues, greatly beloved not only by those
near and dear to her, but by all who became associated with her
in church and social life. He subsequently removed to Essex,
Essex County, N. Y., where he died at the home of his eldest
daughter Annis. Children :

    1. ANNIS (Noble) b. Nov. 23, 1773; m. Daniel Warner.
    2. BELDEN (Noble), baptized March 9, 1777; m. Mary Skinner.
    3. RANSOM (Noble), b. Aug. 16, 1778; m. Anna McNeil.
    4. ASAHEL.
    5. DANIEL, b. Dec. 21, 1792.

550. ANNIS NOBLE [1]; m., about 1793, Daniel Warner, a native of New Milford, Conn., b. January 7, 1768, son of Orange and Abigail (Prindle) Warner. He was a farmer and maker of weaver's reeds; settled first in New Milford, but subsequently resided in Brookfield and New Fairfield, Conn., Essex, N. Y.; again in New Milford, Conn., and from there they removed to Pike, Bradford County, Pa., where he d. Jan. 25, 1841; she d. May 7, 1848. Children:

    1. HARRIET (Warner), b. Dec. 26, 1795; m. Asa Fairchild.
    2. SALLY (Warner), b. Sept. 17, 1797; m. Jonathan Nichols.
    3. BELDEN NOBLE (Warner), b. Dec. 28, 1805; m. Polly Anna Pulford.

551. BELDEN NOBLE [2]; m. Mary Skinner, daughter of Adonijah and Judith (Raleigh) Skinner. He d. in Essex, N. Y., Sept. 8, 1808. His widow m. 2d, Samuel Andrews, and d. in Easton, N. Y., April 20, 1838. Children:

    1. SARAH (Noble), b. Feb. 7, 1800; m. Jacob V. Becker.
    2. HIRAM RALEIGH (Noble), b. June 1, 1801; m. Lydia Lovett.
    3. MARIA (Noble), b. May 8, 1804; m. Geo. M. Skellie.
    4. PHILOMELA.
    5. ADONIJAH SKINNER BELDEN (Noble), b. March 20, 1808; m. 1st, A. S. Loomis; 2d, A. E. Hay.

552. ADONIJAH SKINNER BELDEN NOBLE [5]; m. 1st, Abigail Sarah Loomis, b. September, 1809; dau. of Jeduthan and Abigail (Adams) Loomis of Cambridge, N. Y.; she d. June 17, 1834. Married 2d, Eveline Eliza Hay, b. April 22, 1811; dau. of Henry and Sarah (Hay) Hay of Cambridge; she d. there Aug. 21, 1877. Children:

    1. ABIGAIL SARAH (Noble), b. March 9, 1833; m. Squier W. Allen.
    2. HENRY (Noble), b. Dec. 21, 1836; m. Sarah I. Barton.
    3. CHARLES (Noble), b. Jan. 11, 1840; d. Oct. 26, 1857.
    4. ANN MARIA (Noble), b. Sept. 20, 1841; d. 1886.
    5. MARY E. (Noble), b. March 25, 1843; m. Chas. J. G. Hall.

553. HENRY NOBLE [2]; b. in Cambridge, N. Y., Dec. 21, 1836; was a printer, and editor of the *Washington County Post*; d. May 21, 1883. He m. Sept. 20, 1859, Irene Barton, b. Aug. 4, 1841; d. April 28, 1873. Children:

    1. CHARLES HALMER (Noble), b. Aug. 4, 1860; d. April 28, 1863.
    2. ANTOINETTE (Noble), b. Jan. 16, 1864; m. June 16, 1883, Albert Harvey Green. They reside in Shushan, N. Y. Children:

        1. HENRY NOBLE GREEN, b. June 8, 1884; d. June 8, 1884.
        2. LILLIAN ACHSAH GREEN, b. May 13, 1885.
        3. HOWARD ALMON GREEN, b. Jan. 26, 1889.
        4. HELEN, b. Dec. 15, 1893.
        5. ALBERT HARVEY GREEN, JR., b. March 26, 1896.

554. MARY E. NOBLE [5]; b. in Cambridge, N. Y.; d. Oct. 29, 1885, buried in Cambridge Nov. 1. 1885; m. Sept. 4, 1872, Charles Joseph Goulding Hall. He practices law at 261 Broadway,

New York City; resides 124 West 73d Street. Is a member of the Manhattan and Colonial Clubs. Children:

1. HARRY NOBLE (Hall), b. May 25, 1873.
2. CHARLES WAITE (Hall), b. April 14, 1880.
3. GEORGE BATCHELDER (Hall), b. Aug. 22, 1881.

555. Gen. RANSOM NOBLE [3]; m. 1st, Oct. 10, 1800, Anna McNeil, of Litchfield, Conn., b. July 25, 1780, dau. of Capt. Charles and Thankful Wooster McNeil, and granddaughter of Capt. Archibald McNeil, of Litchfield, who served six years in the old French war; Charles McNeil settled in Charlotte, Vt., in 1786, and d. in Three Rivers, Canada, Aug. 13, 1810. Thankful McNeil d. at the house of her son Hiram, Cambria, N. Y., May 5, 1841, aged 85 yrs. 9 mos. and 23 days. Anna McNeil d. in Essex, N. Y., March 29, 1831. He m. 2d, Aug. 21, 1831, widow Eliza Tobey, dau. of Hon. Daniel and Elizabeth (Gilliland) Ross, of Essex. She perished at the burning of the steamer *Empire*, on her passage from New York to Albany, May 17, 1849. She was the widow of Capt. Charles Edward Tobey, 21st Infantry, U. S. A. He was in the war of 1812. Mr. Noble removed from New Milford, Conn., Dec. 22, 1799, and drove to Essex (then Willsborough), Essex County, N. Y., arriving Jan. 3, 1800, and opened a store on a limited scale. But soon became actively engaged in the tanning of leather, and subsequently in the manufacture of lumber and later of iron, and through his skill and energy accumulated a handsome property. As a member of the State militia and a commissioned officer he was several times mustered into the United States service, and took part in the war of 1812 and was present at the battle of Plattsburgh, serving as 2d Major of the 8th Regiment Detached Militia, 1812; Major Commandant, 37th Regiment, 1813; Lt.-Col. Commandant, same Regiment, 40th Brigade of Infantry (Gen. Daniel Wright), Clinton and Essex Counties, N. Y. Militia, 3d Division, Maj.-Gen. Benjamin Mooers. While serving with the 8th Regiment he was stationed, a portion of the time during the year 1812, both at Chateaugay and St. Regis, on the Canadian frontier. He commanded the Militia in an encounter with the British, when they were repulsed, May 13, 1814, at the mouth of the Boquet River. March 22, 1816, he was commissioned Brigadier-General and served until 1821, when he resigned. The business capacity displayed by Gen, Noble was quite remarkable. Coming out from New Milford, Conn., into a new and unreclaimed country, with but the trade of a shoemaker upon which to rely for the support of his family, and with no powerful connections, such as favored many of the early settlers of Essex County, the outlook at first seemed anything but comforting. But with the keen perception of a skilful tradesman he saw about him priceless forests of timber, valuable mines of iron, nature's storehouse of wealth, if he could but unlock it with the keys of skill and personal unremitting industry. This he proceeded to do, and through the means of the little store, he moved on step by step, enlarging, as he went, until at one time he could count a half-score of sawmills located on various streams, cutting large quantities of lumber, which he brought to Essex to be shipped to the different markets. This industry, together with his tannery and iron business, thrived and prospered under his management, showing a business capacity of rare quality; and what brought as much satisfaction to his family as all else, and made the home more fascinating and

enjoyable, was the fact that he who had been so bountifully rewarded for his wise judgment and faithful application to business, was allowed to live to an advanced age, and thereby enjoy the fruits of his labors, and see his sons all honorable and thorough-going business men, well established on the way to success, in following the footsteps of their father. Gen. Noble died at the home of his son Harmon, in Essex. June 5, 1863. His name will ever remain conspicuous among the annals of the Champlain Valley. He was always interested in public matters, although he had little time to give to political life; yet no worthy cause escaped his notice, and he was always ready to assist in furthering any good work. He was supervisor of the town of Essex 1825-1826. He was a liberal subscriber toward the erection of both the Congregational and Presbyterian church edifices in Essex, and subsequently united with the latter church. Gen. Noble was a master Mason and a member of Essex Lodge, No. 152, F. & A. M., and his first sign-board, now in the possession of his grandson. Henry Harmon Noble, bears the square and compass, emblems of the Masonic fraternity. He was a Royal Arch Mason, having been exalted March 28, 1811, in Jerusalem Chapter, No. 2, R. A. M., Vergennes, Vt. In politics he was a Federalist, later a Whig, and eventually a Republican, and a staunch supporter of the Union during the war, as were his sons. With a reputation for business honor and integrity, which extended throughout the State, he was fittingly described as the " foremost business man of Northern New York." Children by first wife:

1. CHARLES (Noble), b. Dec. 25, 1801; m. 1st, Sarah Jane Ross; 2d, Elizabeth Burritt.
2. HARMON (Noble), b. Nov. 1, 1803; m. Laura A. Weleh.
3. HENRY RANSOM (Noble), b. Dec. 17, 1807; m. Cornelia Gould.
4. BELDEN (Noble), b. Jan. 11, 1810; m. Adeline M. Ferris.
5. DAVID (Noble), b. Oct. 10, 1813; d. Dec. 23, 1813,

556. CHARLES NOBLE [1]; m. 1st, Oct. 15, 1832, Sarah Jane, dau. of Hon. Daniel and Elizabeth (Gilliland) Ross, a native of Essex, N. Y., b. Feb. 9, 1804. He settled in Elizabethtown, Essex County, N. Y. He was commissioned, March 17, 1821, Paymaster 37th Regiment Infantry, New York State Militia; Feb. 1, 1828, Major and Quartermaster, 40th Brigade of Infantry, resigned Sept. 30, 1828; Feb. 14, 1831, Lt.-Col. and Quartermaster 11th Division of Infantry, New York State Militia, serving on the staff of Colonel, Brigadier-General and Major-General Henry H. Ross. He was a Master Mason, being a member of Valley Lodge, No. 314, F. & A. M., Elizabethtown, N. Y., and a Royal Arch Mason, having been exalted in Jerusalem Chapter, No. 2, R. A. M., Vergennes, Vt., May 15, 1825. He was associated with his brother Henry Ransom Noble in the lumber, iron and general mercantile business. He was supervisor of Elizabethtown 1832-34. In 1834 he removed to New York City and engaged in the iron trade under the firm name of Smith & Noble, commission merchants, at No. 76 Broad Street. At the close of his business life he removed to New Milford, Conn., where he d. Oct. 20, 1867. His first wife d. Nov. 18, 1834, and he m. 2d, June 10, 1845, Elizabeth Burritt, of New Haven, Conn., daughter of Abel and Nancy (Hotchkiss) Burritt. Children:

1. CORNELIA (Noble), b. Jan. 27, 1847.

2. JULIA STRONG (Noble), b. Nov. 6, 1849; d. at Santa Barbara, Cal., Jan. 13, 1892.
3. HENRIETTA BURRITT (Noble), b. March 24, 1851; m. at Grand Rapids, Feb. 9, 1882, Charles A. Boynton; resides (1899) at Fargo, N. D.
4. ELLA (Noble), b. May 30, 1853.

557. Major HARMON NOBLE [2]; m. Oct. 16, 1855, Laura A., dau. of Peter and Martha (Frazier) Welch, b. in Vergennes, Vt., Aug. 31, 1823, where her grandfather Paul Welch, with Abigail Crane, his wife, settled in 1808. It was the purpose of Gen. Ransom Noble to give each of his children a thorough English and business education; and from the easy manner in which he managed enterprises of considerable magnitude, we may reasonably infer that he did not fail in this undertaking. After Harmon had returned from seeking his education at Lansingburgh (N. Y.) Academy, preparatory to assuming a business life, he was placed in charge of the store and office at Essex, with the books of the firm his father had established, and which, at this time, was conducting a very large business. The young man at once developed an unusual capacity for his responsible position, and the prosperity of the firm assumed yet larger proportions than it had previously known. The lumbering interest, as well as the tannery and iron industries, were conspicuously enlarged under his careful and wise guidance, while the financial success of the business was of a most flattering nature. Mr. Noble was one of those useful persons who could turn his hands to almost any kind of an enterprise, and through skill, integrity and close application make a success of it. Whatever he undertook was carried out with unflinching persistence, while all his dealings were conducted on principles of thorough honesty and justice. Like his father, he never sought office of any kind, outside the State Militia. But in that department he was prominent, Governor DeWitt Clinton granting him a commission as Major, March 9, 1825, with rank from Dec. 11, 1824, and serving from time to time on the staff of Gen. H. H. Ross. The death of Mr. Noble caused a severe shock among those who enjoyed the pleasure of his acquaintance, for he was stricken down, amid the scenes of active business life. Returning home from his office on the evening of May 23, 1864, after reading his paper he retired for the night. A few moments later he uttered his last words to his heartbroken wife. The breaking of an abscess in the lungs caused his death, which occurred early in the morning of May 24. We quote the following from a sketch of Mr. Noble written at the time of his death by a person who knew him well:

"During his long intercourse with his fellow citizens as merchant no man ever had cause to doubt his honor and probity. But his worth did not arise merely from his capacity as a man of business. His kindly disposition, his support of the church, his tenderness and kindness as a son, parent, husband, relative and friend endeared him to all his relatives, and won the esteem of his acquaintances. His loss will be deeply felt in the extensive concerns in which he was engaged, and by the community generally, and the bereavement falls heavily upon his relatives, and doubly so on the beloved wife and young children." Children:

1. SARAH ELIZABETH (Noble), b. Aug. 29, 1856; m. Chas. Burritt Waite; d. Nov. 4, 1888.

2. ANNA LAURA (Noble), b. Jan. 26, 1858; m. Henry
   Howard Ross; d. July 12, 1886.
3. JENNIE (Noble), b. Aug. 29, 1859; m. Holland Stratford
   Whiting.
4. HENRY HARMON (Noble), b. May 9, 1861; m. Cora
   Sherman.
5. MARTHA FRASER (Noble), } b. May 5, 1863; d. August,
6. MARY MCNEIL (Noble), } 1863.

558. SARAH ELIZABETH NOBLE [1]; m. Oct. 18, 1876, Charles Burritt
   Waite, a native of New Haven, Conn.; b. March 31, 1851, and
   son of Charles C. Waite of New York, at one time proprietor
   of the old Brevoort House. She d. in San Francisco, Cal.,
   Nov. 4, 1888; buried in Essex. Child:

   1. JULIA NOBLE (Waite), b. Aug. 14, 1877; resides in
      Albany, N. Y. (1899).

559. ANNA LAURA NOBLE [2]; m. July 7, 1881, Henry Howard Ross,
   who was b. May 9, 1857, son of James B. Ross, and grandson
   of Gen. Henry H. Ross, a family of considerable distinction,
   and among the early settlers of Essex, N. Y. Mr. Ross was
   forced to relinquish his studies just before graduation at
   Hobart College, Geneva, N. Y., on account of failing health;
   but, continuing the study of law, was admitted to the bar of
   Colorado in the summer of 1881 at Denver, where he completed his studies in the office of Symes & Foote. In April,
   1882, he was admitted to practice in the Supreme Court of
   that State. After passing the summer of 1882 in Essex, N.
   Y., Mr. and Mrs. Ross returned to Denver, Col., where he
   engaged in practice with his father, James B. Ross, under
   the firm name of Ross & Ross, still hoping for health to come
   with the change of climate. But the brilliant and talented
   young lawyer was unable to throw off the disease that had
   now secured a firm hold, and on the 14th of December, 1882,
   he passed to his eternal rest, deeply lamented by a wide circle
   of relatives and friends. His widow d. in Essex, July 12,
   1886. Child:

   1. JAMES HENRY HOWARD (Ross), b. Dec. 13, 1882; resides
      (1899) at Denver, Col., with his grandfather, James
      B. Ross.

560. JENNIE NOBLE [3]; m. June 20, 1883, Holland Stratford
   Whiting; settled first in New York city. Their residence,
   1899, was Larchmont Manor, Westchester Co., N. Y.
   Children:

   1. JEAN NOBLE (Whiting), b. March 18, 1884.
   2. MARJORIE NOBLE (Whiting), b. Oct. 21, 1885.
   3. FRANCIS HOLLAND NICOLL (Whiting), b. Oct. 29, 1886.

561. HENRY HARMON NOBLE [4]; m. Nov. 15, 1887, Cora Sherman,
   dau. of Henry Dow and Sally Maria (Whitney) Sherman, a
   direct descendant of John and Elinor Whitney, who came from
   Isleworth, England, 1635, to Watertown, Mass. She is
   also a great-granddaughter of Joel French; he was a
   direct descendant of Lieut. William French and Corp. John
   French, who served in King Philip's war. He was b. in
   Billerica, Mass., 1780, settled in Lewis, N. Y.; was a soldier in the war of 1812 in Lt.-Col. Ransom Noble's regiment, and was present at the battle of Plattsburgh. She
   was b. Aug. 15, 1869, at Essex, N. Y. Her grandfather,
   Capt. Titus G. Sherman of Westport, N. Y., was son of

Humphrey, from Danby, Vt., who served in war of 1812 as private in Capt. Trowbridge's company, Lt.-Col. Henry Bloom's regiment, Brig.-Gen. William Wadsworth's brigade, New York detached militia, from September 7 to Dec. 6, 1813, at Fort Niagara. Titus G. Sherman was commissioned ensign July 25, 1840, by Gov. William H. Seward, lieutenant March 26, 1842; and captain by Gov. William C. Bouck, Aug. 17, 1843. He d. March 22, 1859, aged 46 years.

Mr. Noble is a gentleman of fine culture, having been educated at Selleck School, Norwalk, Conn., and in England. He is much interested in historical subjects; is thorough and exhaustive in all his researches. He has travelled quite extensively in Europe, and is at present (1899) employed in the State Historian's office at Albany, N.Y. His residence is still in Essex, Essex County, where he is now the only representative of the family name. He is a member of the "Society of Colonial Wars in the State of New York"; "Sons of the Revolution"; "Companion of the New York Commandery of the Military Order of Foreign Wars"; "The General Society of the war of 1812"; an incorporator and Registrar of the "Society of the War of 1812 in the State of New York"; a Master Mason; Royal Arch Mason; Knight Templar; member Iroquois Lodge 715, Essex; Cedar Point Chapter 269, Port Henry, N.Y.; De Soto Commandery 49, Plattsburgh, N.Y.; one of the original organizers of the Lake Champlain Yacht Club, and for several years member of its Executive Committee. He is also a member of the Benedict Club, Port Henry, and Fort Orange Club of Albany, N.Y. He was baptized in the Presbyterian Church at Essex, Nov. 10, 1861, by Rev. Joseph T. Millett, but a communicant of the Episcopal Church; has always been a republican in politics. Children:

1. JOHN HARMON (Noble), b. Sept: 6, 1888.
2. LAURA ANNE (Noble), b. Oct. 25, 1889.
3. KATHERINE RUTH (Noble), b. Oct. 2, 1892.
   All baptized at the Presbyterian Church.

562. HENRY RANSOM NOBLE [3]; m. Cornelia Gould, Feb. 6. 1837, dau. of Judge John and Theodocia (Nichols) Gould. She was b. April 9, 1815, at Essex, N.Y. Judge Gould served in the war of 1812 as major and aid-de-camp to Brig.-Gen. Daniel Wright, and was at the battle of Plattsburgh. She d. March 5, 1895.

Mr. Noble settled in Elizabethtown, Essex, N.Y., about the year 1827. He was an iron-master and lumberman. He was supervisor of Elizabethtown 1840–1841; d. Sept. 13, 1863. Children:

1. CHARLES HENRY (Noble), b. Jan. 15, 1838; m. Lavinia Felicia de Hass.
2. MARY ELIZABETH (Noble), b. Sept. 25, 1841; m. Richard L. Hand.
3. JOHN GOULD (Noble), b. May 25, 1847.

563. CHARLES HENRY NOBLE [1]; m. August 18, 1868, Lavinia Felicia de Hass, dau. of Dr. Wills and Lavinia (Hoblitzell) de Hass, residence Elizabethtown, N.Y. Children:

1. LAVINIA DE HASS (Noble), b. Nov. 27, 1871; d. Dec. 30. 1886.
2. MARIA MARGUERITE DE HASS (Noble), b. 1876.

564. MARY ELIZABETH NOBLE [2]; m. July 29, 1868, Richard Lockhart Hand, son of Judge Augustus Cincinnatus and Marcia Selye (Northrup) Hand. He graduated at Union College 1858, and now (1899) practices law in Elizabethtown, N. Y. Children:

1. AUGUSTUS NOBLE (Hand), b. July 26, 1869; graduated at Harvard University 1890, Harvard Law School 1894, and now (1899) member of firm of Curtis, Mallet-Prevost & Colt, 30 Broad street, New York city.
2. CORNELIA ELLEN (Hand), b. March 21, 1872; m. June 22, 1897, Henry Martin Baird, Jr.; residence (1899) Yonkers, N. Y.; practices law in New York city. Child:

   1. ARMENIA PALMER, b. August 4, 1898; d. Aug. 28, 1898.
3. MARCIA ELIZABETH (Hand), b. Sept. 29, 1875.
4. MARY EMILY THEODOCIA (Hand), b. March 11, 1881.

565. JOHN GOULD NOBLE [3], graduated at Union College 1868; studied at Carolina College, Braunschweig, Germany; graduated at College of Physicians and Surgeons, New York city, 1875; now (1899) practices medicine at 222 West 34th street, New York city; m. Jan. 25, 1888, Gertrude Begalow Pollard. Children:

1. RANSOM NOBLE, b. Feb. 4, 1889.
2. KATHERINE NOBLE, b. Sept. 4, 1890.

566. BELDEN NOBLE [4]; m. Aug. 28, 1856, Adeline M., dau. of Charles Ferris. He resided in Essex, N. Y., where he was associated in business with his father and brother Harmon, but removed to Washington, D. C. He was supervisor of the town of Essex 1843-1844, 1861-1862. He was an iron-master and lumberman. Like his father and brothers, he took an active interest in the State militia, serving in various grades as a commissioned officer, and was colonel of the late 37th regiment in 1840-41, the same regiment of which his father had been colonel in the war of 1812. In politics he was a whig, then a republican, An ardent supporter of the Union during the Civil war, he served on the Union Defence Committee of Essex County, and was active in raising the different quotas of volunteers which were apportioned to that County, notably the 118th New York. The firm of H. & B. Noble contributed liberally to the large sums of money which were raised in Essex County by voluntary contribution. He was to the last an uncompromising supporter of the republican party. He d. at Alburgh Springs, Vt., July 15, 1881; buried at Essex. Mrs. Noble resides at Essex, N. Y. Children:

1. RANSOM FERRIS (Noble), b. May 23, 1858; d. 1859.
2. WILLIAM BELDEN (Noble), b. Oct. 17, 1860.
3. CLARA LOUISE (Noble), b. Feb. 23, 1863: d. 1863.
4. MARY MAUDE (Noble), b. June 1, 1867.
5. ISABEL ELIZABETH (Noble), b. July 10, 1868; d. 1868.

567. WILLIAM BELDEN NOBLE [2]; graduated at Harvard University 1885; m. Nov. 30, 1889, dau. of Hon. David and ——— (Wickliff) Yulee. He d. July 28, 1896, at Glenwood Springs Colorado. His widow resides (1899) at Washington, D. C Child:

1. YULEE (Noble), b. Nov. 23, 1888.

568. MARY MAUDE (Noble) [4]; m. Nov. 3, 1897, at St. John's
Church, Washington, D. C., James Shanklin, son of Hon.
John M. Harlan, justice of the Supreme Court of the United
States. He graduated at Princeton College and is a lawyer.
They reside (1889) in Chicago, Ill.

569. ASAHEL NOBLE [4.]; m. Philomelia Skinner, sister of his
brother Belden's wife. He removed to western New York,
where he d. about 1814. His widow m. Mr. Hawes of
Shaftsbury, Vt.; and d. near Rochester, N. Y. Child:

    1. GARRY SKINNER (Noble), b. Feb. 27, 1807; m. 1st, S.
       Fowler; 2d, E. Freeman.

570. DANIEL NOBLE [5]; m. Nov. 4, 1817, Mary McNeil; b. in Charlotte, Vt., Dec. 13, 1792, dau. of Charles and Thankful
(Wooster) McNeil, and sister to Anna, wife of Gen. Ransom
Noble. He resided in Whitehall, Plattsburgh and Fort Covington, N. Y.; was a tanner and currier of leather; also
carried on the boot, shoe and dry goods trade. She d. in
Fort Covington, March 8, 1863, aged 70 years. He served
in the war of 1812 as sergeant in Capt. Ezra Parkill's company, Lt.-Col. Ransom Noble's regiment, in 1813, and as a
volunteer; at the battle of Plattsburgh he was taken
prisoner by the British, but escaped. He d. in Fort Covington, April 9, 1871. Children:

    1. CHARLOTTE (Noble), b. May 29, 1819.
    2. SARAH (Noble), b. May 16, 1823; d. 1824.
    3. SARAH (Noble), b. Dec. 14, 1824; m. Wm. C. Peck.
    4. RANSOM (Noble), b. July 10, 1829; d. 1848.

571. SARAH NOBLE [3]: m. Sept. 1, 1845, William Cary Peck, a native
of Lawrence. N. Y.; b. May 30, 1823; son of Myron Graves
and Electa (Royce) Peck. He was a practitioner of law
and dentistry; resided in Ravenna, Canal Dover, Ohio,
and Nicholville, N. Y.; in 1849 removed to Fort Covington;
and 1864 removed to Washington, D. C. He d. in Philadelphia, Pa., April 20, 1864. His widow subsequently resided
in Washington, D. C. Children:

    1. WILLIAM NOBLE (Peck), b. Nov. 9, 1846, in Canal Dover,
       Ohio; m. Sept. 10, 1867, Mary Elizabeth Greer; resi-
       dence Washington, D. C.; has for many years been
       connected with the Adjt.-General's office; enlisted in
       United States Army Feb. 25, 1864, for three years;
       is now (1899) Chief of Bureau of Military Informa-
       tion of Adjt.-General's office, War Department.
    2. SARAH FRANCES (Peck), b. July 30, 1854, in Fort Cov-
       ington, N. Y.; m. at Malone, N. Y., Oct. 4, 1894,
       Tom A. Klohs. Child:

        1. ETHEL JEANNE, b. May 11, 1895; resides (1899)
          at Malone, N. Y.

572. SAMUEL CRANE[5] [209], (Zebulon,[4] Joseph,[3] Jonathan,[2]
Benjamin[1]), was a private in Revolutionary war, serving in
Capt Joel Mead's company, Col. Luddington's Regiment. [Land
Bounty Papers, Vol. 22, page 150]. He is said to have married
his cousin Esther Crane, daughter of Joseph,[4] see page 48.

573. ABIGAIL CRANE[5] [210], (Zebulon,[4] Joseph,[3] Jonathan,[2]
Benjamin[1]), married Paul Welch, Jr., of New Milford, Conn.,
where they settled. In 1808 the family removed to Vergennes,

Vt. He was born Jan. 10, 1754, and died Sept. 19, 1815. She died April 6, 1842.

Paul Welch was a lineal descendant from Thomas Welch, Senior, an early settler at New Haven, Conn., who was also one of the founders of Milford, Nov. 20, 1639; Deputy to the General Court of New Haven Colony for twelve sessions, from May, 1654, to May, 1664, inclusive; also Deputy to the General Court of the Connecticut Colony 1665, after the union. The wife of Thomas Welch was Hannah, daughter of Thomas Buckingham, who was also one of the founders of Milford. She was born in England in 1632. Thomas Welch, Jr., had a son Paul, born 1696, who removed when a young man to New Milford, Litchfield County, Conn., and became one of the original proprietors of that place. Paul Welch, Esquire, as he was styled, was one of the leading men in New Milford, Deputy, Justice of the Peace, Lieutenant in the Militia, and it is stated of him in Orcutt's "History of New Milford" that "probably there was not another man of so much influence in the town when Rev. Nathaniel Taylor was settled here as pastor." His epitaph says:

"In memory of Paul Welch, Esqre., one of the first principal settlers of the town, and an original proprietor of the same. Departed this life, August 26, 1778, in the 82d year of his age.

"In his day he served the town in most offices of trust and honor, gave good satisfaction, and died possessed of a large estate."

Paul Welch, Jr., was born in New Milford, Jan. 9, 1759; married Abigail Crane, and established a home in his native town. Here they remained until the fall of 1808, when they removed to Vergennes, Vt., whither two of their children had already taken up their residence. Mrs. Welch was one of the twelve persons who in April, 1810, united with the Congregational Church of Vergennes; and at the time of her decease, was the oldest person in the church, being then 86 years of age. Sept. 15, 1815, Mr. Welch died. She died April 6, 1842. It is recorded of her (as also of her sister Sarah [Crane] Noble): "She was a mother in the broadest, truest sense, with a nature so kind and true as to command the admiration and respect of everyone who came in contact with her." Children:

1. MARVIN (Welch), b. Jan. 7, 1780; d. March, 1852.
2. JOHN (Welch), b. Nov. 7, 1781. Child:
    1. WILLIAM (Welch), b. Sept. 14, 1803; d. April 15, 1885.
3. BETSEY (Welch), b. Oct. 25, 1783; d. Aug. 31, 1827; m. Samuel B. Graves.
4. SALLY (Welch), b. Oct. 25, 1785: d. Feb. 3, 1786.
5. RACHEL (Welch), b. Dec. 13, 1786: d. May 10, 1810.
6. SAMUEL (Welch), b. May 12, 1789; d. Nov. 9, 1808.
7. PETER (Welch), b. Aug. 11, 1792; d. Feb. 28, 1865; m. Martha Frazer.
8. SALLY (Welch), 2d, b. Oct. 25, 1794; d. Sept. 20, 1808.
9. ABIGAIL (Welch), b. June 10, 1797; d. Nov. 15, 1808.

10. LAURA (Welch), b. Jan. 6, 1800; d. May 9, 1879, at the residence of her niece Mrs. Laura A. Noble, Essex, N. Y.

574. MARVIN WELCH [1] b. New Milford, Conn.; d. March, 1850, Masonville, N. Y.; m. 1st, —— Castle. "They had two sons and one daughter." Married 2d, at Masonville, Delaware Co., N. Y., Susannah, widow of Israel Kneeland. Child:

   1. AUSTIN LEE (Welch), b. ——; m. July 2, 1864. Has resided at Bainbridge, Chenango Co., N. Y., and Texas. He is at present engaged in the dry goods business in Wilson, Niagara Co., N. Y. Children:

      1. ALFRED M. (Welch), b. 1865.
      2. FLORENCE I. (Welch), b. ——; m. June, 1896, W. G. Gates; resides Niagara Falls, N. Y.·

575. BETSEY WELCH [3]; b. New Milford, Conn. Oct. 20, 1783; d. Aug. 31, 1827. Married Samuel B. Graves, b. Brandon, Vt., Nov. 22, 1776; d. at Adrian, Mich., April 11, 1861. Children:

   1. SARAH ANN (Graves), b. Oct. 13, 1823, Wheatland, N. Y.; resides (1899) San Diego, Cal. Married Sterling A. Hebbard, b. New Milford, Conn., March 25, 1814; d. Wheatland, N. Y., Feb. 14, 1876. Child:

      1. WILLIAM STERLING (Hebbard), b. Milford, Mich., April 13, 1863; graduated Cornell University 1887; is an architect; resides (1899) San Diego, Cal. Married Sept. 9, 1893, Jessie Miller. Children:

         1. DOROTHY (Hebbard) b. July 9, 1894.
         2. WILLIAM STERLING (Hebbard), Jr., b. Nov. 27, 1896.

   2. NANCY D. (Graves), b. ——; d. 1878. She m. 1826, Alvah Hall, b. Sept. 16, 1802, Windsor, Mass.; d. Dec. 2, 1888, Honeoye Falls, N. Y. Children:

      1. CHARLES FRANKLIN (Hall), b. June 15, 1829; m. June 17, 1868, Mary Jane Kidder, who d. Feb. 1, 1892.
      2. MARY JANE (Hall), b. June 29, 1831; m. Sept. 7, 1831, Asher Leroy Conger, who d. May 25, 1884.
      3. JULIA JUSTINA (Hall), b. July 16, 1833; d. March 4, 1895.
      4. MARTHA CAROLINE (Hall), b. June 18, 1835; m. Addison Shaw, Sept. 20, 1865, who d. Feb. 12, 1895.
      5. FRANCES ABIGAIL (Hall), b. Aug. 2, 1844; m. Luther Rogers, Feb. 13, 1867; reside Honeoye Falls, N. Y.

576. PETER WELCH [7]; b. New Milford, Conn., Aug. 11, 1792; d. at Essex, N. Y., Feb. 28, 1865; buried at Vergennes, Vt.; He m. at Vergennes, Vt., March 23, 1820, Martha Frazer. She d. April 30, 1836. Peter Welch was initiated Entered Apprentice, Dec. 29, 1817, passed to the degree of Fellow Craft, Jan. 15, 1818, and raised to the Sublime Degree of Master Mason, Feb. 19, 1818, in Dorchester Lodge, Vergennes, Vt. He took his Mark Master Degree Nov. 15, 1819, his Past and Most Excellent Master and Royal Arch Degrees, Jan. 21, 1822, in Jerusalem Chapter, Vergennes, Vt., and he took the de-

grees of Royal and Select Master, March 11, 1824, in Vergennes Council, Vergennes, Vt. He was an old time Mason
and was faithful and true all through the troublous times of
the Morgan excitement, and kept up his membership in the
Masonic bodies at Vergennes to the last. After he had gone
to make his home with his daughter Mrs. Noble in Essex, he
often visited Vergennes to attend Masonic meetings. His
grandson Henry Harmon Noble has in his possession many
letters to Mr. Welch from brethren of that place. Children:

1. MARVIN JOHN (Welch), b. Dec. 25, 1821; d. in Boston,
   Mass., May 5, 1858; buried in St. John's Lot, Mt.
   Auburn Cemetery, Boston, Mass.
2. LAURA ANN (Welch), b. Aug. 31, 1823; d. Essex, N. Y.,
   July 28, 1895. She m. Oct. 18, 1855, Harmon Noble
   (which see).
3. WILLIAM HOMER (Welch), b. Aug. 20, 1825; d. at Galveston, Texas, of yellow fever, Sept. 5, 1854.
4. FRAZER (Welch), b. Oct. 1, 1826; d. Oct. 15, 1856.
5. BELDEN FRAZER (Welch), b. March 16, 1828; d. at Boston, Mass., Jan. 27, 1891; buried in Mt. Hope Cemetery, Boston, Mass.
6. SAMUEL LOVEMAN (Welch), b. Sept. 24, 1835; resides
   (1899) Concord Junction, Mass.

577. Lt.-Col. JONATHAN CRANE[5] [215], (Joseph,[4] Joseph,[3]
Jonathan,[2] Benjamin[1]), married Feb. 28, 1771, Bethiah Baldwin
of Mansfield, Conn., born Jan. 1, 1752, and who came to Putnam County, N. Y., when a young child with her parents. The
beginning of the Revolutionary war found Mr. Crane ensign in
a company of minute-men, and he continued in service throughout the period of seven years. March 1, 1776, he was ensign in
5th South East company, Capt. Joshua Barnum, Jr., Col. Jacobus
Swartwout, 2d regiment. He was at the battle of Ridgefield,
April, 1777; also the engagement at Ward's House, near White
Plains. Mr. Crane was frequently employed in carrying mes-
sages to General Washington while located at the Highlands. His
widow received a pension. He was a farmer, and spent his life
on the farm he purchased from the State, it having been confiscated as the property of a tory. It was located in the southerly
portion of the town of South East, and known as "Crane's
Ridge," about three miles southeast from Brewster. He died
Aug. 27, 1834. She died May 14, 1839. Children:

578—1. MATILDA.
579—2. JOSIAH, b. May 21, 1773.
580—3. DEBORAH, b. June 9, 1775.
581—4. ISAAC.
582—5. ANSON, b. Jan. 25, 1783.
583—6. JONATHAN, b. 1785.
584—7. ESTHER.
585—8. SALLY BETSY.
586—9. ORRIN B., lived and d. in South East; unmarried.

587. JOSEPH CRANE[5] [216], (Joseph,[4] Joseph,[3] Jonathan,[2]
Benjamin[1]), was a physician, judge and captain. He was sur-

7

geon 3d regiment, Dutchess County, N. Y., active service* May
31 to June 11, 1779, June 26 to June 30, 1780, latter time on staff
of Col. John Field's regiment, Dutchess County Militia. In the
proceedings of Provincial Congress we find that Sept. 17, 1776,
ordered that Messrs. Duane, Duer, Schenck and Doctor Crane be a
committee to inquire into the situation of the Light Horsemen and
Lieut. Onderdonk and report thereon. A portion of the time he
was stationed on Long Island, where he married Rosanna Cock,
Aug. 6, 1775. She was born 1756. He married 2d, Feb. 14,
1798, Aner Leggitt, daughter of Capt. Hackaliah Brown of
Somers, Winchester County, N. Y., and settled at South East.
He was Judge of the Court of Common Pleas for Dutchess and
Putnam Counties. He inherited his father's library, the family
records and coat of arms. He died Nov. 21, 1825.

Dr. Joseph Crane, Jr., was Assistant Surgeon militia and additional officer in New York troops. He was Surgeon in 3d
regt. of Dutchess County, which was in active service May 31
to June 17, 1779, and June 26 to June 30, 1780, his brother
Solomon being Adjutant of this regiment at the same time, it
having been called out on a general alarm to repel the enemy.
He was a member of the Provincial Congress of the Province of
New York in 1776, and member of the Assembly 1778, 1779 and
1796. His home was about two miles east of Brewster, it being
the place now (1898) owned by Mr. George Sears. There has
been more or less confusion in reports from various members of
the family as to honors enjoyed by Joseph Crane, and it has
been no light task to know just where to place them. It must
be remembered that there were three Joseph Cranes, father, son
and grandson. No doubt all three performed well their part
during the trials connected with the stand for national independence. Joseph, senior, died Aug. 20, 1781; so it is fair to
presume that his son and grandson were most active during the
war. They were both doctors, which perhaps adds to the confusion. It would seem that possibly the eldest Dr. Joseph Crane
would have been the one chosen to attend the Provincial Congress, he being then fifty-four years of age, while his son Dr.
Crane, Jr., was but twenty-seven. But as descendants of the
family place this honor to the young Doctor, there may be no
good reason for changing it.

Child :

588—1. CARSO, b. June 15, 1800.

589. SOLOMON CRANE[5] [217], (Joseph,[4] Joseph,[3] Jonathan,[2]
Benjamin[1]) was adjutant† in 3d regiment, Dutchess County, May
31 to June 11, 1779, and June 26 to June 31, 1780. This was
Col. John Field's regiment, in which his brother Joseph was surgeon. He was chosen highway commissioner at the first town

* Archives of New York in Revolution. Land Bounty Papers, Vol. 8,
pages 56-67. †Ibid.

meeting of the inhabitants of Franklin, held April 7, 1795. Mr. Crane lived and died in Putnam County, N. Y. Children:

590—1. CHARLOTTE.
591—2. POLLY.
592—3. JAMES.
593—4. OLIVER.

594. ISAAC CRANE[5] [218], (Joseph,[4] Joseph,[3] Jonathan,[2] Benjamin[1]). Served in Revolutionary war, and was a prisoner on the ship *Jersey*; held a prisoner four months, then paroled in New York, and boarded with Thomas Arden there. Charles A. Crane says he was Adjt.-General of a brigade raised in Putnam and Dutchess Counties. That he was taken prisoner at the battle of White Plains, Nov. 16, 1776, and held *four months*. He was adjutant in Col. John Field's regiment, May 18, 1776, of Dutchess County, and in Lieut. Barnum's company, Col. Humphrey's regiment; entered March 3, 1777, taken prisoner in Westchester County, March 16, 1777, and remained in prison four years.* He married Anna Sears in 1783. She was born June 30, 1760, and died in 1858, aged 98. He lived at Crane's Corners for a time, but removed to Oswego County, N. Y. He died March 6, 1810. Children:

595—1. HENRY, b. June 21, 1784.
596—2. SARAH, b. 1786.
597—3. CHARLES, b. 1788.
598—4. RALPH, b. 1790; d. 1816.
599—5. HUNTER, b. March 1, 1791.
600—6. DELLA, b. 1794; d. 1810.
601—7. ALBERT, b. 1796.
602—8. ISAAC, b. 1800; d. 1834.

603. EUNICE CRANE[5] [219], (Joseph,[4] Joseph,[3] Jonathan,[2] Benjamin[1]), married Comfort Sears, Dec. 18, 1777. He was born March 20, 1751. Settled in Ridgefield, Conn., where he died Dec. 24, 1827. The house stood on " Joe's Hill," named so for her father, who owned a large tract of land there. Children:

1. THIRZA (Sears), b. March 22, 1779.
2. ESTHER (Sears), b. July 29, 1780.
3. DESIRE (Sears), b. May 24, 1782.
4. EUNICE (Sears), b. Feb. 4, 1784.
5. CAMILLA (Sears), b. April 26, 1786.
6. JAMES (Sears), b. Nov. 10, 1788.
7. ALTHA (Sears), b. Dec. 18, 1790.
8. JOSEPH CRANE (Sears), b. Dec. 18, 1792.
9. LEWIS (Sears), b. June 26, 1795.
10. POLLY M. (Sears), b. July 26, 1800.

604. ESTHER CRANE[5] [220], (Joseph,[4] Joseph,[3] Jonathan,[2] Benjamin[1]), married 1st, a Mr. Smith, and lived in or near New Haven, Conn. He died, and she married 2d, Samuel Crane, son

---

* Archives State of New York in Revolution, page 350. Land Bounty Papers, Vol. 14, pages 91, 93, 110, 112.

of Zebulon. Mrs. Barnes says this Esther Crane married her cousin, Samuel Crane, brother of Elijah, and was father to Rev. Samuel R. Crane of Milton, Vt.* Rev. Samuel R. Crane was a resident of Milton, Vt., perhaps a farmer. In 1833 he became a candidate for holy orders, and was ordained deacon by Bishop Hopkins, in Burlington, Vt., May 28, 1834. He officiated at first in Highgate, Sheldon and Fairfax to 1835; ordained priest May 27, 1835, by Bishop Hopkins at Bellows Falls. From Nov., 1835, to Nov., 1836, was in charge of the church at Middlebury, but was, on account of ill health, obliged to resign, and dismissed to the diocese of Ohio. He is said to have died previous to 1840, and buried in the village cemetery at Milton Falls, Vt. He went to Vermont from Connecticut, his aged mother with him. She was alive Jan. 25, 1829; had shock of paralysis in the fall of 1828. Rev. S. R. Crane had a daughter 10 days old Jan. 25, 1829. He travelled (so he wrote in his letter) 1000 miles to find a good place to remove to from Connecticut. His Connecticut friends at that time rather ridiculed Vermont as a country to live in; think he went from near New Haven, Conn., to Vermont. Children:

1. SAMUEL R.
2. A daughter, m. Mr. Keeler. Children:

    1. PHILIP (Keeler).
    2. ESTHER (Keeler), m. —— Mitchell.
    3. ANN (Keeler), m. —— Mason.

605. IRA CRANE[5] [222], (Joseph,[4] Joseph,[3] Jonathan,[2] Benjamin[1]), married Elizabeth Brush, a native of Long Island, and for a time resided in the town of South East, Dutchess County, N. Y.; but subsequently removed to Herkimer, Herkimer County, N. Y. Was drummer in Col. Field's Dutchess County regiment; also private in Col. Jacobus Swartwout's regiment. He died August, 1828. She died at Portage, Allegany County, N. Y., in 1839, at the home of her eldest daughter, Mrs. Moses. Children:

606—1. MARY ANN, b. July 16, 1800.
607—2. JOHN.
608—3. OZELL.
609—4. ELIZA.
610—5. CHARLOTTE.
611—6. CLARISSA.
612—7. FANNY.
613—8. JANE, b. Jan. 27, 1810.
614—9. BRADFORD.
615-10. GILBERT.

---

* There was also Rev. Silas A. Crane, D.D., who officiated in Middlebury, Vt., just before Rev. S. R. Crane. He afterwards kept a school at Burlington, Vt.; last 30 years of his life was passed in Greenwich, R. I. He died in 1872. Silas A. Crane was one of the officiating clergy until 1837 at Trinity Church, Milton, Vt., organized 1832. Samuel R. Crane was one of the delegates to the convention. Do not know that there was any relationship between this Silas and Samuel.

616. DANIEL CRANE[5] [223], (Joseph,[4] Joseph,[3] Jonathan,[2] Benjamin[1]), m. Penelope Hotchkiss. She was born in Green County, N. Y., June 25, 1772, and resided for many years in Durham, Green County, N. Y., where she died Nov. 6, 1830. He died at Jefferson, Schoharie County, Sept. 12, 1848. Children:

617—1. EMMA, b. Oct. 4, 1796.
618—2. DANIEL, b. June 16, 1798.
619—3. CYNTHIA, b. Jan. 12, 1800.
620—4. SUSAN, b. July 1, 1802.
621—5. HIRAM, b. Sept. 16, 1805.
622—6. JOSEPH AUGUSTUS, b. Oct. 20, 1808.

623. JOSIAH NATHAN CRANE[5] [226], (Joseph,[4] Joseph,[3] Jonathan,[2] Benjamin[1]), married Mary Smith, sister to Wm. Smith of Litchfield, Herkimer County, N. Y. Died at sea July, 1797. Children:

624—1. JOSEPH (with American fleet at battle of Plattsburgh), d. at sea.
625—2. AMANDA M.

626. ARZAH CRANE[5] [227], (Joseph,[4] Joseph,[3] Jonathan,[2] Benjamin[1]), married at Burlington, Vt., Dec. 16, 1804, Mandana Holmes, daughter of Peter Holmes, and a native of Hebron, Conn., born Oct. 8, 1778, and became one of the early settlers of Burlington, Vt., where he resided several years. June 5, 1805, he with 10 others petitioned Geo. Robinson, the town clerk, to warn a town meeting of the inhabitants of Burlington for the purpose of forming themselves into a society for social and public worship agreeable to the form and effect of the statute entitled, "An act for the support of the gospel, passed Oct. 26, 1797." He was justice of the peace and held various town offices. He afterwards removed to Chimney Point, Addison County, where he passed the greater portion of his life. He was what might be termed a model farmer, and among the first to introduce improved methods in farming as well as stock breeding. His thoroughbred Durham cattle were among the first kept in that region. He died Feb. 10, 1861, at the home of his son Junius, in Essex County, N. Y., as did also his wife, July 27, 1864. Children:

627—1. A son, b. Dec. 6, 1805; d. Dec. 8, 1805, at Burlington, Vt.
628—2. A son, b. Feb. 29, 1807; d. Feb. 29, 1807, at Burlington, Vt.
629—3. GEORGE ROBINSON, b. May 25, 1808.
630—4. CHARLES HOLMES, b. May 27, 1810; d. April 13, 1832.
631—5. PHEBE BELDEN, b. Jan. 22, 1813; d. Jan. 17, 1814, at Addison, Vt.
632—6. LAURA BELDEN, b. May 16, 1815, at Addison, Vt.
633—7. LUCIEN ARZAH, b. June 23, 1817, at Addison, Vt.
634—8. A daughter, b. and d. Feb. 25, 1819, at Addison, Vt.
635—9. JUNIUS JOSEPH, b. June 24, 1820, at Addison, Vt.
636—10. ELLEN SARAH, b. Sept. 15, 1822.

637. MARY CRANE[5] [231], (Thaddeus,[4] Joseph,[3] Jonathan,[2] Benjamin[1]), married Nathaniel Paddock. He was born Oct. 25, 1744. She died June 30, 1830. Children:

1. ABIGAIL (Paddock), b. Oct. 5, 1774.
2. SARAH (Paddock), b. Sept. 2, 1776.
3. EUNICE (Paddock), b. Oct. 3, 1778.
4. FANNIE (Paddock), b. Aug. 26, 1780; d. Dec. 10, 1864.
5. MARY (Paddock), b. Aug. 17, 1782.
6. THANKFUL (Paddock), b. Sept. 24, 1784.
7. REHEMHAMAH (Paddock), b. Oct. 29, 1786.
8. ELIZABETH (Paddock), b. Nov. 15, 1788.
9. SILAS (Paddock), b. Nov. 15, 1791.
10. MARGARET (Paddock), b. April 15, 1793.
11. BETHIAH (Paddock), b. June 8, 1795.
12. LYDIA (Paddock), b. June, 1797.

638. SARAH CRANE[5] [232], (Thaddeus,[4] Joseph,[3] Jonathan,[2] Benjamin[1]), married Abraham Smith and settled at North Salem, Westchester County, N. Y. She died Oct. 20, 1829. Mr. Smith was a captain and served in the Revolutionary war; was first lieutenant in Col. Samuel Drake's regiment in Revolutionary war. He and his wife were buried at Bolton, Vt. Children:

1. JOHN KEYZAR (Smith), b. Nov. 29, 1785.
2. POLLY (Smith).
3. LYDIA (Smith).
4. SARAH (Smith).
5. BETSY (Smith).
6. THADDEUS (Smith).
7. GERARD (Smith).
8. GEORGE (Smith).
9. ABRAM (Smith).

639. JOHN KEYZAR SMITH [1]; m. Katharine McDonald at Plainfield, Mich., December, 1818. When quite young went to Bolton, Vt.; studied law, and practiced the legal profession at Pottsdam, N. Y., until the war of 1812, when he entered the army, and took part in the battle at Plattsburg. Soon after the close of hostilities he removed to Michigan; held the position of custom house officer, postmaster, justice of the peace, and judge of probate at various times while a resident of Algonac, St. Clair County, Mich., and here he d. in 1855. His wife was b. in Glasgow, Scotland, Oct. 31, 1795; d. at Algonac, Aug. 22, 1881. Katharine, wife of John Keyzar Smith, was dau. of Angus and Jean (Johnston) McDonald; he was a native of Aberdeen, and she of Stirling, Scotland. They were m. at Glasgow, and came to America with their family as members of Lord Thomas Douglas ("Earl of Selkirk's") colony, in 1806, and settled in Beldoon, Canada. He was printer for the colony. In 1812 he purchased a farm on Stromnesse Island, near Algonac, Mich.; was a soldier in the British army, and after the battle of Miami, 1814-1815, was taken prisoner and confined at Detroit. Children:

1. ABRAM (Smith).
2. SARAH CRANE (Smith), b. Dec. 25, 1820.
3. JANE (Smith).

4. ANGUS (Smith).
5. ANNA (Smith).
6. SAMUEL LATTA (Smith).
7. LYDIA REED (Smith)
8. KATHARINE (Smith).
9. FRANCIS GRAY (Smith).
10. MARY BAXTER (Smith), m. Charles J. Johnston.

640. ABRAM SMITH [1]; m. Fidelia Burt, of Algonac, St. Clair County, Mich. Children:

1. BURT (Smith), m. Elizabeth Harris, of Houghton, Mich.
2. CORNELIA DELAY (Smith), m. E. C. Seaman, of New York.
3. JOHN ABRAM (Smith), m. Alvina Schnoor, of Baltimore.
4. ELLA MARIA (Smith), m. W. K. Moore, M.D., of Canada.
5. ANGUS McDONALD (Smith), m. Elizabeth Craddock, of Algonac.

641. SARAH CRANE SMITH [2]; m. Samuel Russell, at Algonac, Mich., Jan. 13, 1841, and d. there Sept. 1, 1887. S. Russell b. in Ireland, 1813; d. Dec. 31, 1879, at Algonac. Children: ·

1. JOHN KEYZAR (Russell), b. Feb. 10, 1842.
2. MARY FRANCES.(Russell), b. Aug. 30, 1844.
3. JANE ELIZABETH (Russell), b. June 8, 1846.
4. KATHARINE MARIA (Russell), b. Sept. 21, 1847.
5. ANNA LYDIA (Russell),   } twins, b. June 27, 1858.
6. SAMUEL LATTA (Russell), }

642. ANGUS SMITH [4]; m. 1st, Maria Peck; 2d, Catherine E. Peck. Children:

1. JESSE HOYT (Smith).

643. SAMUEL LATTA SMITH [6]; m. Eliza Cordelia Seager. Children:

1. DONALD (Smith).
2. KATHARINE (Smith).
3. FRED LATTA (Smith).
4. ANGUS (Smith).
5. MARGARET (Smith).

644. LYDIA REED SMITH [7]; m. 1st, Columbus Colon Douglass in 1856; 2d, Judge E. B. Hinsdale, New York city. Children:

1. JESSE (Douglass).
2. PHŒBE JEAN (Douglass).
3. KATHARINE (Douglass).
4. COURTNEY COLUMBUS (Douglass).

645. KATHARINE SMITH [8]; m. William Rainey. Child:

1. WILLIAM J. (Rainey).

646. MARY FRANCES RUSSELL [2]; m. Horace Brewster Rogers, at Algonac, Mich., Aug. 16, 1871. Children:
1. HORACE BREWSTER (Rogers).
2. KATHARINE SMITH (Rogers) b. Oct. 4, 1873.
3. BEN RUSSELL (Rogers).
4. LAURA SEAGER (Rogers), b. Sept. 10, 1880.
5. DON ANGUS (Rogers).
6. WILSON PARKER (Rogers).
7. FRANK TURNER (Rogers).

647. JANE ELIZABETH RUSSELL [3]; m. Dr. Alfred David, at Algonac, Mich., Dec. 25, 1876. Child:

    1. SARAH ATLANTA (David), b. Dec. 4, 1882.

648. KATHARINE MARIA RUSSELL [4]; m. Shepard Harrison Currie, at Port Huron, Mich., Aug. 5, 1866. Children:

    1. HARRISON SAMUEL (Currie).
    2. WILLIAM RUSSELL (Currie).
    3. CARLOS (Currie).
    4. MARGARET CRANE (Currie), b. 1877.
    5. ARTHUR (Currie).
    6. STEPHEN GRUMMOND (Currie).

649. ANNA LYDIA RUSSELL [5]; m. June 1, 1885, Frank Leslie Vance, at Milwaukee, Wis., at the residence of her uncle, Mr. Angus Smith. F. Vance is son of David and Jane Vance; b. at Sackett's Harbor, N. Y., Sept. 9, 1847. The senior Mr. Vance m. Jane Wilson at Bangor, a suburb of Belfast, Ireland; Mr. Vance was born in 1804. Children:

    1. DAVID (Vance).
    2. WILLIAM (Vance).
    3. CHARLES (Vance).
    4. WILSON (Vance).
    5. JANE (Vance).
    6. LOUIS (Vance).
    7. HATTIE (Vance).
    8. FRANK LESLIE (Vance).

650. KATHARINE SMITH ROGERS [2]; m. William A. Rublee, Oct. 7, 1896, at Milwaukee, Wis., at the residence of Mr. Angus Smith. He was son of Horace and Katharine Hopkins Rublee; was United States consul to Prague about 1890, under the Harrison administration. Horace Rublee was minister to Switzerland under the Grant administration.

651. PETER CRANE[5] [234], (Thaddeus,[4] Joseph,[3] Jonathan,[2] Benjamin[1]), served in Revolutionary war; was private in Capt. Truesdell's company, also in Capt. Lawrence's company; corporal in Capt. Moses St. John's company in Col. Thomas' and Thaddeus Crane's 2d regiment, 1779-80-81. He died Nov. 12, 1818. Children:

652—1. ALFRED.
653—2. PETER.
654—3. NANCY.
655—4. LOCHA; went west.
656—5. THEDA; went west.
657—6. ABBIE.

658. JAMES CRANE[5] [235], (Thaddeus,[4] Joseph,[3] Jonathan,[2] Benjamin[1]), married 1st, Sally Hallock. She was born April 17, 1768, and died March 12, 1802; 2d, June 22, 1803, Clarinda Hallock. She was born Aug. 12, 1781. He removed from North Salem, N. Y., to Richmond, Vt. Two children were the result of first marriage, and eleven by the second. He was a private in the Revolutionary war; served in Telford's, Hunter's, Drake's and Truesdell's companies, Col. Albert Pauling's regiment, 1779; also in Col. Thaddeus Crane's regiment, 1779-80-81; and Col.

William Malcolm's regiment. He died Aug. 17, 1828, at Richmond, Vt. His wife Clarinda died Jan. 20, 1859, at Fort Atkinson, Wis. Children:

659—1. LAURA, b. Dec. 15, 1793.
660—2. THADDEUS, b. July 29, 1795
661—3. SALLY, b. April 26, 1805.
662—4. CLARINDA, b. Feb. 11, 1807.
663—5. BETSEY, b. March 14, 1809; d. July 28, 1842.
664—6. FANNY, b. March 9, 1811.
665—7. JAMES, b. April 13, 1813.
666—8. GERARD, b. March 11, 1815.
667—9. LORETTA, b. Aug. 7, 1817.
668-10. ALEXIS, b. April 27, 1820.
669-11. THOMAS, b. May 12, 1822.
670-12. JANE BAXTER, b. Aug. 1, 1824; d. March 30, 1852.
671-13. MARTHA T., b. May 29, 1828.

672. THADDEUS CRANE[5] [240], (Thaddeus,[4] Joseph,[3] Jonathan,[2] Benjamin[1]), married Dec. 1, 1806, Charlotte Titus, daughter of John Titus, of North Salem, N. Y. She was born Feb. 24, 1781, and died Nov. 16, 1825. He then married Martha Titus, sister of his first wife. She died March 25, 1872. He died Oct. 16, 1849. Children:

1. A son, b. May 17, 1810; d. May 17, 1810.
673—2. LYDIA, } twins, { d. May 4, 1891.
674—3. SALLY, } b. Jan. 9, 1813; { d. Jan. 8, 1879.
675—4. MARY, b. Sept. 5, 1814; d. March 1, 1883.
676—5. CLARISSA, b. Nov. 4, 1816; d. Sept. 16, 1888.

677. FANNY CRANE[5] [241], (Thaddeus,[4] Joseph,[3] Jonathan,[2] Benjamin[1]), married Eli Ganung. She died Jan. 4, 1852.

Children:

1. THERON (Ganung); d. unmarried.
2. THEDA (Ganung); m. Charles Strang. Children:
    1. ELIZABETH (Strang).
    2. ELI (Strang).
    3. GERARD (Strang).
    4. THADDEUS (Strang).

678. LYDIA CRANE[5] [242], (Thaddeus,[4] Joseph,[3] Jonathan,[2] Benjamin[1]), married July 31, 1802, Samuel Banks, M.D. She died Jan. 4, 1852. Children:

1. WILLIAM HENRY (Banks), b. Nov. 19, 1803, at North Salem; d. Aug. 11, 1855.
2. SAMUEL E. (Banks), b. Dec. 3, 1805, at Stamford; d. March 14, 1826.
3. ELI CRANE (Banks), b. Oct. 23, 1807, at Stamford.
4. MARY ANN (Banks), b. Sept. 11, 1809, at New Canaan; d. Dec. 23, 1848.
5. SARAH ELIZABETH (Banks), b. Nov. 4, 1811, at Danbury; d. Feb. 11, 1882.
6. NEMIAH (Banks), b. Nov. 8, 1813, at Danbury; resided at Wallingford, Conn.
7. CHARLES READ (Banks), b. Feb. 25, 1816, at Danbury; d. Aug. 11, 1851.

8. REBECCA (Banks), b. March 21, 1818, at Danbury; m. Henry A.
    Hoyt.
9. THOMAS CRANE (Banks), b. March 10, 1820, at Danbury; lived
    in San Francisco, Cal.
10. LYDIA MARIAH (Banks), b. March 30, 1822, at Danbury; m.
    Chas. Caffray.
11. GEORGE (Banks), b. Feb. 20, 1824, at Danbury; lived in San
    Francisco, Cal.
12. SAMUEL ALBERT (Banks), b. May 9, 1826. at Danbury; d. April
    20, 1881.
13. THADDEUS CRANE (Banks), b. at Danbury; d. Dec. 14, 1881.

679. Hon. THADDEUS CRANE BANKS [13]; m. Margaret Augustus
      Allen, Nov. 13, 1849. He settled in New York, where he re-
      sided for about eighteen years, but previous to 1866 removed
      to Wallingford, Conn. He was business manager of the
      N. Y. *Forest and Stream.* He d. in Brooklyn December, 1882,
      aged 52. Children :

      1. JOHN ALLEN (Banks), b. Feb. 15, 1851.
      2. RACHEL WELLS (Banks), b. May 18, 1855.
      3. MARGARET VISGAR ALLEN (Banks), b. June 10, 1857.
      4. ANNA THOMSON (Banks), b. March 22, 1860.
      5. THADDEUS CRANE (Banks), b. Jan. 8, 1863.
      6. HARKNESS WRAY (Banks), b. April 16, 1866.
      7. HARRY NEMIAH (Banks), ⎫
      8. LIZZIE ALLEN (Banks),   ⎬ twins, b. Aug. 18, 1869.
      9. ALFRED VISGAR (Banks), b. Dec. 29, 1872.

680. JOHN ALLEN BANKS [1]; m. Ellen Julia Hall, dau. of William
      Cook Hall, of Wallingford, Conn., Feb. 3, 1876. Children :

      1. CLAIRE ALLEN (Banks), b. Nov. 8, 1876, in New York.
      2. ANNA HALL (Banks), b. Sept. 17, 1881, in Brooklyn.

681. THEDA CRANE[5] [243], (Thaddeus,[4] Joseph,[3] Jonathan,[2]
Benjamin[1]), married Truman Smith. She died May 17, 1842.
Child :

    1. HARRIET (Smith).

682. GERARD CRANE[5] [245], (Thaddeus,[4] Joseph,[3] Jonathan,[2] Benjamin[1]), a farmer, Canton Falls, N. Y.; married October. 1823, Roxana, daughter of Isaac Purdy, North Salem, N. Y.
She was born June 21, 1805, and died Jan. 24, 1867. Her
mother was a daughter of Lemuel Clift, of Putnam County, N. Y.
His home was styled "Granite Hall." He died Feb. 11, 1872.
Children :

683—1. THADDEUS, b. Sept. 29, 1824.
684—2. LYDIA, b. April 10, 1826; d. July 28, 1844.
685—3. HARRIET, b. March 29, 1829.
686—4. ELLEN, b. Dec. 25, 1832.
687—5. THOMAS, b. March 3, 1835; m. Mary E. Harris, of Parkers-
        burg, W. Va., Dec. 13, 1882.
688—6. MARY, b Oct. 11, 1840.
689—7. GERARD, b. Dec. 7, 1845; m. Mary E. Dawes, of Allegheny,
        Pa., April 4, 1893.

690. SALLY CRANE[5] [246], (Thaddeus,[4] Joseph,[3] Jonathan,[2] Benjamin[1]), married John D. Lounsbury, and is said to have lived in Norwalk, Conn. Children:

1. CAROLINE (Lounsbury), m. Geo. H. Ranelle.
2. SARAH (Lounsbury).

691. ABIGAIL CRANE[5] [251], (Stephen,[4] Joseph,[3] Jonathan,[2] Benjamin[1]), married Joseph Giddings, of Sherman, Conn. They settled in Cooperstown, N. Y. Children:

1. MARY (Giddings); d. February, 1862.
2. SALLY (Giddings).
3. ISAAC (Giddings); lost at sea.
4. STEPHEN (Giddings); lived and d. in Rochester.
5. AMANDA (Giddings); lived in Washington; d. October, 1881.
6. MARILLA (Giddings); d. young.

692. ISAAC CHAPMAN CRANE[5] [252], (Stephen,[4] Joseph,[3] Jonathan,[2] Benjamin[1]), married Rowena Vaughn, and resided in the south part of New Milford, Conn., where they both died of fever in 1800. They were buried in the same grave. Their two children were cared for by relatives. After some years the brother and sister went to Ohio, where the daughter married Mr. Elisha Blake. Children:

693—1. HARMAN.
694—2. MARILLA.

695. STEPHEN CRANE[5] [253], (Stephen,[4] Joseph,[3] Jonathan,[2] Benjamin[1]), married 1st, Hannah Baldwin, Jan. 1, 1792. She died Sept. 3, 1807, and he married 2d, Chloe Averill, at New Preston, Aug. 6, 1808, and resided in New Milford, Conn.; a farmer. He was a justice of the peace for more than thirty years, deciding many important cases. His wife Chloe died Oct. 15, 1856. He died March 21, 1844. Children:

696—1. SUSAN. b. Dec. 8, 1793.
697—2. ANNA BALDWIN, b. May 22, 1795; d. young.
698—3. DAVID, b. July 10, 1797; d. young.
699—4. LAURA, b. Aug. 31, 1799.
700—5. ANNA, b. July 7, 1802.
701—6. HORACE BALDWIN, b. Aug. 8, 1805; d. Jan. 26, 1825.
    Children by 2d wife:
702—7. HEMAN AVERILL, b. Oct. 1, 1809.
703—8. HENRY STEPHEN, b. June 16, 1811.
704—9. HANNAH MARIAH, b. April 16, 1813; d. April 12, 1841, at New Milford, Conn.
705-10. GEORGE ELLIOT, b. June 27, 1815.
706-11. MARY JULIA, b. July 11, 1818; m. Solomon B. Warner, April 10, 1850; a farmer; resided at Brookfield, Conn.; no children.
707-12. CAROLINE MATILDA, b. Oct. 21, 1820.
708-13. JENNETTE, b. March 24, 1823.

709. NOAH CRANE[5] [254], (Stephen,[4] Joseph,[3] Jonathan,[2] Benjamin[1]), married in Litchfield Co., Conn., Rebecca Benjamin,

a native of Windham, Conn. They settled at Elmira, N. Y., also lived in Cooperstown, N. Y. He was a blacksmith by trade. He served in the war of 1812. She died in 1840. He died in 1846. Child:

710—1. EZRA F.

711. JOSEPH CRANE[5] [256], (Stephen,[4] Joseph,[3] Jonathan,[2] Benjamin[1]), married, 1805, Betsey Winegar, of Amenia, N. Y., afterwards settled in Kent, Conn., where he died Sept. 12, 1851. He was a farmer. She died Sept. 25, 1827. Children:

712—1. NELSON, b. Sept. 7, 1806, in Amenia.
713—2. LEONARD, b. 1808, in Amenia.

714. THALIA CRANE[5] [257], (Stephen,[4] Joseph,[3] Jonathan,[2] Benjamin[1]), married James Eggleston, of South East, N. Y., and settled in Catskill. He died October, 1812. She married 2d, Stephen Frost, in 1815, and lived in Bath, where he died.

Children :

1. ALMON (Eggleston), b. 1798.
2. ROANNA (Eggleston), b. 1800.
3. ESTHER (Eggleston), b. 1802.
4. THALIA (Eggleston), b. 1804.
5. MARY (Eggleston), b. 1807.
6. KEZIA (Eggleston), b. 1809.
7. ELIZA (Eggleston), b. 1811.

715. DAVID BALDWIN CRANE[5] [259], (Stephen,[4] Joseph,[3] Jonathan,[2] Benjamin[1]), born at South East, N. Y. He was a Baptist minister and a blacksmith, and preached for a time at Harpersfield, N. Y. He married Dorcas Haskins, a native of Massachusetts, who died at Milwaukee, Wis., in October, 1861. Mr. Crane died at Sidney, Delaware County, N. Y., July 20, 1852. Children:

716—1. OSMOND NOAH, b. July 22, 1807.
717—2. ORSON J., b. 1809.

718. ASHBIL CRANE[5] [272], (John,[4] John,[3] Abraham,[2] Benjamin[1]), married —— ——. First after marriage settled in Worcester, Otsego County, N. Y.; about the year 1796 removed to Cobleskill, Schoharie County, N. Y. Children:

719—1. JOHN, b. March 4, 1793.
720—2. BETSY, b. Sept. 29, 1795.
721—3. CHARLES, b. March 14, 1797.
722—4. LYDIA, b. March 24, 1799.
723—5. HANNAH, b. June 17, 1801.
724—6. ASHIBEL, b. April 10, 1803.
725—7. REBECCA, b. Oct. 3, 1805.
726—8. ABIGAIL, b. April 16, 1808.
727—9. RUTH, b. Oct. 27, 1811.

728. CURTIS CRANE[5] [280], (Curtis,[4] John,[3] Abraham,[2] Benjamin[1]), married, Aug. 28, 1800, Lucy Adams, of Wethersfield, Conn., daughter of John and Mary (Crane) Adams. She

was born Nov. 25, 1777, and died in Angelica, N. Y., May 3, 1867. Their residence was at Wethersfield for a few years, for their daughter Mary was baptized there Oct. 11, 1807. He died at sea Sept. 16, 1810, on the wreck of the schooner *Sally*, which was capsized on Barnegat shoals while bound for the Bermuda Islands, of which he was first mate and supercargo. Child:

729—1. MARY, b. July 25, 1801.

730. HENRY CRANE[5] [282], (Curtis,[4] John,[3] Abraham,[2] Benjamin[1]), married Elizabeth Cassety, and settled in Eaton, N. Y. Children:

731—1. CORDELIA ELIZABETH, b. July 4, 1823.
732—2. CHARLES CURTIS, b. Nov. 29, 1826.
733—3. LYDIA AUGUSTA, b. May 29, 1829.
734—4. NANCY CASSETY, b. July 14, 1831.
735—5. MARY GARDINER, b. May 19, 1835.

736. WILLIAM CRAIN[5] [288], (William,[4] John,[3] Abraham,[2] Benjamin[1]), married Sally Pierson, of Alford, Dec. 31, 1802. Children:

737—1. HARRIET.
738—2. WILLIAM WHITING; is reported to have gone to Michigan, and that he was a Methodist minister.

739. WHITING CRAIN[5] [289], (William,[4] John,[3] Abraham,[2] Benjamin[1]), married Anna Pelton, of Gt. Barrington, Mass., Aug. 8, 1804. He was a wagon-maker. He died about 1809. Children:

740—1. ALBERT LEWIS, b. Jan. 9, 1806.
741—2. AURELIA LOIZA, b. Oct. 17, 1807.

742. Capt. ABRAHAM CRANE[5] [293], (Abraham,[4] Abraham,[3] Abraham,[2] Benjamin[1]), married 1st, Huldah Hanmer, Feb. 9, 1797, at Wethersfield, Conn., where they settled, and where their seven children were baptized Oct. 6, 1811. Mr. Crane was married 2d, to Prudence Wright Treat, March 9, 1834, by Rev. C. J. Tenney. His wife Prudence died Jan. 17, 1861, aged 74. He died Dec. 20, 1842, aged 72. He, with his brother Benjamin, succeeded to his father's tannery business.

743—1. MARY, b. Jan. 27, 1798.
744—2. WILLIAM HANMER, b. Oct. 25, 1799.
745—3. ABRAHAM, b. Nov. 13, 1801; m. Elizabeth Plumer, July 24, 1833, by Rev. Tertius S. Clark.
746—4. MATIA, b. 1803.
747—5. RALPH, b. June 8, 1805.
748—6. EDMUND, b. March 8, 1807.
749—7. ELIZA, b. 1811.

750. BENJAMIN CRANE[5] [295], (Abraham,[4] Abraham,[3] Abraham,[2] Benjamin[1]), married Sarah or Sally Lockwood, Sept. 7, 1794, at Wethersfield, Conn., by pastor of First Church, where

they settled. He, with his brother Abraham, succeeded to the tannery business left by his father He died previous to May 7, 1817, and the estate was administered by his son Benjamin, Jr., who was appointed Jan. 12, 1818. Richard Bruce appointed guardian for John Crane May 7, 1817, Children:

751—1. JOHN, bapt. Aug. 18, 1798.
752—2. BENJAMIN, bapt. Nov. 4, 1798.
753—3. SARAH, bapt. Nov. 4, 1798.
754—4. SAMUEL LOCKWOOD, bapt. Sept. 7, 1800; lived in Pittsfield, Ill. May 8, 1823, appointed guardian of his brothers Ira and Henry.
755—5. JAMES.
756—6. IRA R., bapt. Jan. 17, 1805.
757—7. HENRY, bapt. about 1807.

758. ELIJAH CRANE[5] [303], (Elijah,[4] Abraham,[3] Abraham,[2] Benjamin[1]), a farmer; married Honor Adams, May 20, 1798, at Wethersfield, Conn. She was born there June 13, 1776. He was then of Sandisfield, whither his father had gone. She died in Sheffield, April 22, 1836. He died in Sheffield, March 13, 1863. Children:

759—1. SARAH, b. May 1, 1800.
760—2. HARRIET, b. Aug. 6, 1802.
761—3. CALVIN CAMP, b. Oct. 28, 1805.
762—4. SARAH ADAMS, b. June, 1807.
763—5. GEORGE, b. Feb. 26, 1810; d. April 18, 1850.
764—6. ROYAL, b. May 23, 1812.
765—7. ELIZABETH C., bapt. May 19, 1816.
766—8. MARTHA BUSH, b. Nov. 22, 1820; bapt. July 1, 1821; d. Aug. 15, 1850, at Sheffield.
Children all baptized at Wethersfield, Conn.

767. ELIAS CRANE[5] [304], (Elijah,[4] Abraham,[3] Abraham,[2] Benjamin[1]), married at Bethlehem, Conn., Sept. 17, 1810, Esther Raymond. She was born in Norwalk, Conn., Oct. 19, 1780. He was a farmer, and settled in Sandisfield, Mass., where he died Jan. 22, 1853. She died there April 18, 1849. Child:

768—1. MILO RAYMOND, b. April 27, 1811; lived in Berlin, Conn.

769. SILAS CRANE[5] [306], (Elijah,[4] Abraham,[3] Abraham,[2] Benjamin[1]), married Clarrissa ——, and lived in West Stockbridge, Mass. He died previous to July 6, 1825. Isaac Rees was appointed guardian for Hiram G., son of Silas, deceased, in 1832. He made a will May 29, 1824, in which he names his wife Clarrissa and children as given below. He also named his son Abraham executor; but Abraham declined to accept the trust, and the court appointed, by consent of the heirs, Isaac Rees executor. The estate amounted to $906.12. Children:

770—1. JOHN R.
771—2. STEPHEN D.
772—3. NELSON H.
773—4. ABRAHAM.
774—5. CAROLINE (Thomas).

775—6. LUCINDA (Castle).
776—7. OLIVER.
777—8. HIRAM G.

778. ABRAHAM CRANE[5] [308], (Elijah,[4] Abraham,[3] Abraham,[2] Benjamin[1]), married Betsey Twining, daughter of William and Tabitha (Sparrows) Twining, of Tolland, Conn. Mr. Crane died in Canton, Conn., March 12, 1864. Children:

779—1. WILLIAM.
780—2. ALEXANDER NELSON, b. 1812; Bloomfield, Conn.

781. BENJAMIN ROBBINS CRANE[6] [752], (Benjamin,[5] Abraham,[4] Abraham,[3] Abraham,[2] Benjamin[1]). He is recorded of Berlin, Conn., Oct. 22, 1821, for at that date he sold land in Wethersfield to Abraham Crane of the latter place. It was, perhaps, land he purchased of his mother Sarah (Lockwood) Crane, Dec. 28, 1819.

782. SAMUEL LOCKWOOD CRANE[6] [754], (Benjamin,[5] Abraham,[4] Abraham,[3] Abraham,[2] Benjamin[1]). He went to New Haven, Conn., and while there sold, Nov. 6, 1821, to James H. Hickox and wife, of New Haven, land at Rocky Hill, in Wethersfield, and about six miles from center of said town, bounded east on Abraham Crane's lot. The deed was acknowledged in New Haven.

783. SARAH CRANE[5] [313], (Hezekiah,[4] Abraham,[3] Abraham,[2] Benjamin[1]), married Thomas Harris, at Wethersfield, Conn., Jan. 8, 1797. Mr. Harris died Feb. 2, 1829, aged 58. She died Feb. 7, 1829, aged 56. Children;

1. SALLY (Harris), b. Dec. 25, 1797; m. Sylvester Woodhouse; d. November, 1828. Children:
    1. ELMIRA (Woodhouse); m. Z. Brockway, Supt. of the Reformatory.
    2. Daughter (Woodhouse); in California.
2. THOMAS (Harris), b. Aug 21, 1799; d. September, 1857.
3. MARY (Harris), b. Feb. 21, 1801; d. April 1, 1872.
4. ABIGAIL (Harris), b. Nov. 28, 1802; d. March 8, 1876.
5. HEZEKIAH C. (Harris), b. June 18, 1804; d. June 12, 1812.
6. ELIZA H. (Harris), b. April 10, 1806; m. William Talcott; d. March 31, 1883. Children:
    1. WILLIAM H. (Talcott); at Hartford.
    2. MARSHALL (Talcott); at Chicago.
    3. THOMAS H. (Talcott); at New York City.
    4. ELIZABETH (Talcott); m. J. T. Smith.
    5. CELIA (Talcott); m. George Smith.
    6. ELLA (Talcott); at Wethersfield.
7. EMILY (Harris), b. March 29, 1808; d. Jan. 15, 1809.
8. JANE (Harris), b. Oct. 3, 1810; living January, 1896.
9. HEZEKIAH (Harris), b. July 7, 1814; d. Aug. 9, 1894.
10. CHAUNCEY (Harris), b. Sept. 28, 1816; m. Emeline Welles, and had two sons and three daughters, living in Wethersfield, Conn., January, 1896.

784. SAMUEL CRANE[5] [316], (Hezekiah,[4] Abraham,[3] Abraham,[2] Benjamin[1]), married Dorothy Benton, at Wethersfield,

Conn., March 9, 1799. She died April 29, 1842. He was lost at sea, April 24, 1852. Children:

785—1. NANCY, b. Jan. 15, 1800; d. Aug. 19, 1831.
786—2. LEONARD, b. Sept. 19, 1801; d. June 29, 1801.
787—3. HARRIET, b. June 15, 1803.
788—4. EMILY, b. Nov. 17, 1805.
789—5. MARY, b. Oct. 19, 1807; d. July 15, 1811.
790—6. LEONARD, b. July 5, 1809; lost at sea in 1828.
791—7. SAMUEL, b. July 23, 1813; d. April 24, 1852.
792—8. MARY, b. Oct. 3, 1815; d. May 25, 1819.
793—9. HORACE, b. July 23, 1817; d. young.
794-10. JANE, b. Oct, 19, 1819.

795. HEZEKIAH CRANE[5] [317], (Hezekiah,[4] Abraham,[3] Abraham,[2] Benjamin[1]), married widow Dosha Morley Church; her first husband was Jonathan Church. He died May 19, 1827. She died Nov. 10, 1848, aged 80. Children:

796—1. JANE GREY, b. April 10, 1810.
797—2. JAMES; lost at sea when a young man.

798. REBECCA CRANE[5] [320], (Hezekiah,[4] Abraham,[3] Abraham,[2] Benjamin[1]), married William Robbins. Children:

1. NANCY (Robbins), b. Dec. 29, 1808; d. April 26, 1871.
2. WILLIAM (Robbins), b. Feb. 6, 1811; d. March 15, 1868.
3. FRANCES (Robbins), b. Oct. 15, 1812; living Dec. 26, 1895.
4. MARY (Robbins), b. Sept. 8, 1816.
5. JULIA (Robbins), b. June 20, 1819; d. 1843.
6. REBECCA (Robbins), b. Jan. 9, 1821; d. February, 1888.
7. CELIA (Robbins), b. Oct. 26, 1825.
8. LAWRENCE (Robbins), b. Feb. 20, 1826.
9. LUTHER (Robbins), b. Sept. 13, 1827; m. Eliza Merriman; 4 children. He was living Dec. 26, 1895.

799. EMILY CRANE[5] [321], (Hezekiah,[4] Abraham,[3] Abraham,[2] Benjamin[1]), married March 24, 1815, Ashbel Robertson, of Coventry, Conn. He was a physician, and died Feb. 18, 1847, at Wethersfield, Conn. She died May 13, 1860. Children:

1. JANE ELIZABETH (Robertson), b. Jan. 13, 1816; m. Cornelius Stillman, Nov. 10, 1841; 2 sons and 3 daughters.
2. JULIA (Robertson), b. Sept. 3, 1817.
3. JOHN (Robertson), b. May 18, 1819; m. Clarissa Higley; 5 sons.
4. SUSAN EMILY (Robertson), b. Jan. 20, 1821; m. Wm. H. Hawley; 2 sons and 2 daughters.
5. HARRIET BALDWIN (Robertson), b. Dec. 4, 1822.
6. CHARLES LAFAYETTE (Robertson), b. Dec. 4, 1824; m. Elizabeth Hedden; 2 sons and 4 daughters.
7. AUSTIN JANES (Robertson), b. Nov. 14, 1826.
8. HENRY CLAY, (Robertson), b. Dec. 23, 1828; m. Sophia Bellows; 1 daughter. He d. Jan. 25, 1864.

800. JOSEPH CRANE[5] [326], (Joseph,[4] Abraham,[3] Abraham,[2] Benjamin[1]), married Mary May, at Wethersfield, Conn., Nov. 17, 1803, where they settled. His children had one share in the

distribution of their grandfather's estate, May 7, 1819. He died
Oct. 17, 1805, aged 22. Children:

801—1. JOSEPH, b. March 7, 1804.
802—2. MARY A., bapt. May 4, 1806.

803. GEORGE CRANE⁵ [328], (Joseph,⁴ Abraham,³ Abraham,² Benjamin¹), married Sarah Kelsey, April 19, 1818. He
was a sea captain. He died Nov. 28, 1824, at Bridgeport,
Conn. She died Dec. 13, 1856, at Fairfield, N. Y. Children:

804—1. SARAH SUSAN b. May 20, 1819; d. Dec. 4, 1820.
805—2. EMELINE, b. Jan. 1, 1821; d. Aug. 18, 1888.
806—3. LOUISA MARIA, b. Nov. 4, 1822; d. May 15, 1825.
807—4. GEORGE, b. Oct. 1, 1824; d. March 28, 1825.

808. JUSTUS CRANE⁵ [329], (Joseph,⁴ Abraham,³ Abraham,²
Benjamin¹), married Annah Fordick, of Wethersfield, Conn.,
March 5, 1812. Child:

809—1. ABBY, b. March, 10, 1817.

810. DAVID CRANE⁵ [332], (Joseph,⁴ Abraham,³ Abraham,²
Benjamin¹) married by Rev. Augustus Bolles, pastor of Baptist
Church, Wintonbury, Sept. 25, 1822, Pamelia, daughter of Levi
and Sarah Grant Deming. She died Dec. 28, 1872. Resided
at Wethersfield, Conn., and at time of marriage both were of
that place. Children:

811—1. MARIA, b. Sept. 24, 1823; d. July 20, 1887.
812—2. DAVID, b. March 13, 1826.
813—3. SARAH, b. Oct. 29, 1829.
814—4. JULIETTE, b. July, 1833.
815—5. LEVI D., b. June 26, 1835; d. December, 1847.
816—6. ABIGAIL, b. July 21, 1838; m. Rev. S. D. Jones, who was
preaching in Hackensack, N. J., in 1896.

817. JONATHAN CRANE[6] [339], (Jonathan,[5] Silas,[4] Jonathan,[3] Jonathan,[2] Benjamin[1]), married Mary Morse. They settled in Aylesford County, Nova Scotia. He died previous to Aug. 9, 1820, leaving nine children, five of them daughters, whose names were not given. Children :

818—1. GEORGE C.; d. in Bogota, South America, Jan. 10, 1878.
819—2. WILLIAM J.; d. in Collin County, Texas, March 1, 1879.
820—3. JONATHAN; living in 1879 in New York State.
821—4. CHARLES AMER, b. 1818.

822. Major JAMES NOBLE CRANE[6] [340], (Jonathan,[5] Silas,[4] Jonathan,[3] Jonathan,[2] Benjamin[1]), was born at Grand Pré, Nova Scotia. He married Louisa Charlotte Avery, at that place, Oct. 17, 1815, where he resided. He was a farmer, and a prominent gentleman in the Province, holding a commission as major in the militia. He died at Grand Pré, Aug. 12, 1868. She died at Halifax, N. S., Oct. 3, 1876. Children :

823—1. MARY AVERY, b. Oct. 10. 1816; made her home in Halifax.
824—2. REBECCA ALLISON, b. Dec. 16, 1817; m. Sept. 8, 1855, Geo. H. Starr, President People's Bank, Halifax.
825—3. WILLIAM, b. April 30, 1824.
826—4. JAMES A. Settled in Melbourne, Australia.
827—5. CHARLOTTE L. Settled in Halifax.
828—6. SAMUEL LEONARD, b. 1830. Surgeon-General for British West Indies. Trinidad from 1871. A.M.G.M.D., Pennsylvania; M.R.C.S., England.
829—7. THOMAS A. Settled in Montreal; a merchant, Crane & Baird.
830—8. ELIZABTH. Settled in Halifax.

831. NANCY CRANE[6] [341], (Jonathan,[5] Silas,[4] Jonathan,[3] Jonathan,[2] Benjamin[1]), married Sherman Dennison, and lived in Lower Horton, Nova Scotia. Names of their children as near as could be ascertained :

1. LAVINIA (Dennison).
2. NANCY (Dennison).
3. SOPHIA (Dennison).
4. MARY (Dennison).
5. LOUISA (Dennison).
6. SHERMAN (Dennison).
7. WILLIAM (Dennison).
8. JOSEPH (Dennison).

832. WILLIAM CRANE[6] [342], (Jonathan,[5] Silas,[4] Jonathan,[3] Jonathan,[2] Benjamin[1]), married Susan Dixon Roach, at Fort Lawrence, Nova Scotia, Feb. 2, 1813. She was born Oct. 13,

1795. They settled in Sackville, New Brunswick, where for many years Mr. Crane was a merchant, and of the firm of Crane and Allison. Mr. Crane was a successful business man, and acquired a handsome property. He was active in public affairs, represented Westmoreland County in the Provincial Parliament for many years, and was twice sent as a delegate to England on public business. He was twice Speaker of the House of Assembly, holding that office at the time of his death. For many years he was a member of the Legislative Council. His first wife died Feb. 22, 1830, leaving one child. He married 2d, in London, England, in 1838, Eliza Wood, by whom he had eight children. He died while attending to legislative duties, March 31, 1853, at Fredericton, N. B.

Children:

833—1. RUTH, b. Dec. 7, 1813; m. Edward Cogswell, Jan. 24, 1850.
834—2. MARY SUSAN, b. ——; m. Capt. C. K. Faquharson, late of H. M. 15th Regiment.
835—3. LAURA, b. ——; m. Robert James Sisson, Esq., of North Wales.
836—4. ELIZA EMMA. b. ——; m. Surgeon-General Samuel Leonard Crane, C.M.G.
837—5. MARIAN, b. ——; m. Rear-Admiral Jackson, R. N.
838—6. WILLIAM HENRY, b. ——; residence (1899) London, Eng.
Three other children died in infancy.

839. SILAS HIBERT CRANE[6] [343], (Jonathan,[5] Silas,[4] Jonathan,[3] Jonathan,[2] Benjamin[1]), married Ann Chandler. He was for many years a merchant, and resided at Economy, Colchester County, Nova Scotia, where he died. Children:

840—1. JOSEPH ALLISON, b. July 17, 1824.
841—2. MARIA LOUISA. b. Jan. 12, 1826.
842—3. T. CHANDLER, b. July 19, 1829; a physician in Halifax.
843—4. JONATHAN WILLARD, b. Nov. 12, 1830.
844—5. SUSAN HALIBURTON, b. Aug. 12, 1833.
845—6. ROBERT GRANT, b. ——; d. in childhood.
846—7. ELIZA MARY BLATCHFORD, b. Feb. 27, 1837.
847—8. HELEN GRANT, b. Nov. 22, 1840.

848. REBECCA CRANE[6] [344], (Jonathan,[5] Silas,[4] Jonathan,[3] Jonathan,[2] Benjamin[1]), married Samuel Black, and lived in Halifax, Nova Scotia. Children:

1. JONATHAN (Black).
2. WILLIAM (Black).
3. REBECCA (Black).

849. JOHN CRANE[6] [352], (Benjamin,[5] John,[4] John,[3] Jonathan,[2] Benjamin[1]), married at Bethel, Vt., Catherine ——, May 16, 1792. She was born in Sutton, Mass., Dec. 10, 1772. He died at Lisbon, N. Y., Oct. 31, 1826. She died at Bristol, Vt., Feb. 23, 1830. Children:

850—1. BENJAMIN F., b. Feb. 21, 1793; d. April 6, 1796.
851—2. LEVI, b. Jan. 29, 1795.
852—3. SYLVIA, b. Aug. 13, 1796; d. Jan. 19, 1842, at Bristol, Vt.

853—4. BENJAMIN, b. July 23, 1798; d. Oct. 25, 1823, in Morgan
          County, Ga.
854—5. ELIJAH, b. Nov. 2, 1800.
855—6. JOHN, b. Dec. 11, 1802.
856—7. TRUMAN L., b. May 14, 1805.
857—8. SARAH H., b. April 26, 1808.
858—9. PERMELIA F., b. Jan. 11, 1811; d. Oct. 17, 1816.

859. AMOS CRANE[6] [364], (Elijah,[5] John,[4] John,[3] Jonathan,[2] Benjamin[1]), married Martha Remington, of Suffield,
Conn., Oct..30, 1799, and settled in Washington, Berkshire
County, Mass., where with the exception of two years he passed
his entire life. For thirty-two years he was connected with the
M. E. Church there. He died July 25, 1863, aged 89 years, at
that time being the oldest inhabitant of the town, His wife died
Nov. 16, 1841, in the 65th year of her age; a devoted Christian
woman. Children:

860—1. MARTHA R., b. Feb. 21, 1801.
861—2. AMOS S., b. Nov. 5, 1802.
862—3. SAMUEL R., b. Nov. 27, 1804.
863—4. POLLY, b. Oct. 15, 1806.
864—5. GEORGE, b. April 17, 1808.
865—6. LUCY, b. Sept. 30, 1810.
866—7. JOHN M., b. March 21, 1813.
867—8. WILLIAM H., b. Feb. 12, 1816.

868. JOEL CRANE[6] [366], (Elijah,[5] John,[4] John,[3] Jonathan,[2]
Benjamin[1]), married Sept. 14, 1802, Harriet Sedgwick, of Lenox,
Mass., and settled in Washington, Mass.; a farmer. In the year
1830 he removed to Lysander, Onondaga County, N. Y., where
he died Dec. 20, 1843. Children all born in Washington, Mass.

Children:

869—1. HARRIET, b. Dec. 3, 1803.
870—2. NANCY, b. Feb. 3, 1806.
871—3. JOEL S., b. March 9, 1809.
872—4. EMILY, b. July 15, 1811; d. Feb. 4, 1826.
873—5. EDWIN O., b. March 1, 1814; d. Oct. 5, 1835.

874. ELIJAH CRANE[6] [370], (Elijah,[5] John,[4] John,[3] Jonathan,[2] Benjamin[1]), married Polly Lindsley about the year 1812,
at Madrid, N. Y., where he settled; a farmer. They lived for a
time in Canton. She died Jan. 20, 1875. He died June 20,
1878. Children:

875—1. ELIJAH C., b. June 12, 1815.
876—2. OLVISON W., b. Dec. 6, 1817.
877—3. ORSON N., b. May 16, 1821.
878—4. LESTER, b. July 10, 1823.
879—5. AMOS L., b. Sept. 30, 1825.

880. ABEL CRANE[6] [384], (Samuel,[5] John,[4] John,[3] Jonathan,[2] Benjamin[1]), married Jane ———. She died June 26,
1844. Children:

881—1. SAMUEL; d. in Chicago.
882—2. JAMES; d. in Buffalo, N. Y., leaving a son and two daughters.

883—3. WILLIAM H. Went to Virginia and d. there, leaving two and perhaps more daughters.

884—4. Daughter.

885. ARCHER CRANE[6] [385], (Samuel,[5] John,[4] John,[3] Jonathan,[2] Benjamin[1]), married Dec. 12, 1809, Vilitia Cornish, of Onondaga, N. Y. He was born in Simsbury, Conn. He was a farmer. He removed from New York State to Michigan in 1835. settling in Fredonia, Washtenaw County. She died Dec. 1, 1855. He died Dec. 17, 1855. Both died at Blissfield, Mich.

Children :

886—1. EDWIN D., b. May 14, 1812.
887—2 CHARLES T., b. Sept. 21, 1814.
888—3. JOEL C., b. June 6, 1817.
889—4. CHARITY M., b. July 26, 1819; m. Judah McLean. She d. March 7, 1853, and a few years later her husband and four children died.
890—5. ARCHER H., b. March 30, 1821.
891—6. CELESTIA E., b. June 25, 1824; d. May 24, 1825.

892. AMHERST CRANE[6] [386], (Samuel,[5] John,[4] John,[3] Jonathan,[2] Benjamin[1]), married Polly Brooks, June 1, 1810. They settled in Genesee County, N. Y., and built a log house in the then wilderness. She was born Dec. 24, 1789, and died March 19, 1834. He died June 10, 1861. Children :

893—1. AMBROSE, b. July 17, 1811.
894—2. JANE POLLY, b. Nov. 14, 1812.
895—3. LEORA THEODOSIA, b. Oct. 7, 1814.
896—4. CHARITY MARIA, b. Nov. 28, 1816.
897—5. CLARA FIDELIA, b. Dec. 3, 1818.
898—6. EDMOND D., b. Dec. 23, 1820.
899—7. THIRZA, b. Nov. 11, 1822.
900—8. LUCRETIA L., b. June 30, 1825.
901—9. DIANTHA T., b. Oct. 8, 1827.
902-10. ASA BROOKS, b. June 21, 1830; d. May 21, 1858; unmarried.

903. AMBROSE CRANE[6] [387], (Samuel,[5] John,[4] John,[3] Jonathan,[2] Benjamin[1]), married 1st, Maria Waldron in New York, and went to Florida, where she died, leaving two children. He was engaged in Government business in Tallahassee. After the death of his first wife he went to Galveston, Texas, and married 2d —— ——. He died Oct. 15, 1857. Children :

904—1. ALEXANDER.
905—2. ANNIE.
906—3. AMBROSE BYRON.
907—4. EUGENE.
908—5. BENJAMIN EATON.
909—6. Daughter.
910—7. Daughter.

911. DANIEL COLTON CRANE[6] [388], (Samuel,[5] John,[4] John,[3] Jonathan,[2] Benjamin[1]), married 1st, Thirza Griffin, Jan. 24, 1811. She was born Oct. 21, 1787; died Nov. 26, 1855. He married 2d, Jerusha M. Cott, of Greenfield, Indiana, to which

place he removed at quite an early day in the settlement of that country, where he carried on farming. He removed to Blissfield, Mich., in 1859. He died in Deerfield, Mich., May 5, 1872. In 1818 he was Captain in 170th Regiment, New York Infantry, and had been called for active duty in wars of 1812 and 1814.

Children :

912 —1. THIRZA N., b. March 26, 1812.
913 —2. OLANDO, b. Dec. 9, 1813.
914 —3. JOHN A., b. Feb. 1, 1816.
915 —4. HANNAH A., b. April 21, 1818.
916 —5. SYLVESTER F., b. Sept. 4, 1820; d. Nov. 14, 1821.
917 —6. CHARITY L., b. Aug. 11, 1822.
918 —7. THEODOTIA L., b. Nov. 10, 1825.
919 —8. GEORGE C., b. Oct. 16, 1827; d. April 1, 1855.
920 —9. CHARLOTTE C., b. Nov. 30, 1831; d. April 6, 1847.
921 —10. DANIEL COLTON, b. Sept. 29, 1857.
922 —11. EDWIN S., b. Aug. 15, 1859.
923 —12. THIRZA M., b. April 14, 1862.
924 —13. C. SPENCER, b. March 27, 1864.

925. LUKE CRANE[6] [390], (Samuel,[5] John,[4] John,[3] Jonathan,[2] Benjamin[1]), was born in Onondaga County, N. Y.; married Cynthia Griffin there Dec. 29, 1814, and removed to Genesee County, and later removed to Lansing, Mich., where he died Sept. 4, 1856; by occupation a farmer. She then married 2d, a Mr. Butterfield. She died May 30, 1881. Children :

926 —1. CYNTHIA, b. Feb. 24, 1816; d. June 17, 1834.
927 —2. HIRAM H., b. Aug. 20, 1817.
928 —3. STEPHEN G., b. Jan. 29, 1819.
929 —4. GEORGE W., b. April 30, 1821.
930 —5. MORRIS M., b. Sept. 2, 1822; d. Aug. 17, 1846.
931 —6. LAFAYETTE, b. June 12, 1824.
932 —7. CYRENUS C., b. Jan. 27, 1827; d. Dec. 15, 1887.
933 —8. B. FRANKLIN, b. Dec. 18, 1827.
934 —9. ALBERT T., b. Sept. 2, 1828.
935 —10. CAROLINE, b. April 19, 1831; d. June 20, 1852.

936. SYLVESTER RETURN CRANE[6] [391], (Samuel,[5] John,[4] John,[3] Jonathan,[2] Benjamin[1]), married Abigail P. Austin, at Bennington, Genesee County, N. Y., in the year 1824. She was born in Tyringham, Mass., July 1, 1803. For over forty years he was a resident of Bennington, where he was held in high esteem, having been honored with nearly every public office within the gift of his townsmen. He died there Oct. 26, 1878. Children :

937 —1. HELEN MAR.
938 —2. IRENE ELIZABETH.
939 —3. HANNAH MARIA.
940 —4. SYLVESTER EDGAR.
941 —5. ORIN.

942. ISAAC CRANE[6] [396], (Joshua,[5] Abiah,[4] John,[3] Jonathan,[2] Benjamin[1]), married Polly Brown of Mason, N. H., Nov. 29, 1802. She was born Nov. 18, 1784. Nearly all of the family name in New Hampshire spell it Crain. His youngest

. child, Harriet N., had a guardian appointed by Judge of Probate in 1842. She with the three next older children had a guardian appointed March 16, 1825. Children :

943—1. JONAS B., b. Dec. 30, 1803.
944—2. ORA, b. Oct. 2, 1805; d. June 15, 1812.
945—3. MARIA, b. June 9, 1807; d. Feb. 2, 1809.
946—4. MARIA, b. Oct. 30, 1809.
947—5. RUTH EMELINE, b. Jan. 3, 1812; d. Jan. 26, 1814.
948—6. ORA KIMBALL, b. March 14, 1814; d. Jan. 11, 1815.
949—7. RUTH EMELINE, } twins, } d. July 3, 1818.
950—8. PATTY ADELINE, } b. Feb. 4, 1816 ; }
951—9. CHLOE JULIANA, b. Aug. 15, 1820; d. May, 1839.
952-10. SAMUEL OSWALD, b. Oct. 30, 1822; d. March, 1832.
953-11. HARRIETT NEWELL, b. May 7, 1824.

954. Dr. JOSHUA CRAIN[6] [397], (Joshua,[5] Abiah,[4] John,[3] Jonathan,[2] Benjamin[1]), married Sarah Giddings, a native of Lunenburg, Mass.; born August, 1777. Mr. Crain was reared in Alstead, N. H., but studied medicine with the celebrated Dr. Kittridge of Walpole, N. H., and became a very successful practitioner. He is said to have been a man of high personal character, and that he gained great popularity in his profession. Three students were studying medicine under his direction at his home at the time of his death in Hillsboro, where he located and practiced his profession. He died Feb. 1, 1811. She died in Washington, Oct. 29, 1859. The record of the administration of his estate may be found in Nashua, N. H. Widow Sarah and Elijah Beard were appointed Feb. 19, 1811, to settle it. The widow Sarah was also appointed guardian of her three children June 18, 1811. Children :

955—1. JULIANA, b. Oct. 14, 1803.
956—2. LOUISA R., b. March 24, 1806.
957—3. JOSHUA DARLING, b. Oct. 30, 1809, in Hillsboro.

958. Dr. ELEAZER CRAIN[6] [401], (Joshua,[5] Abiah,[4] John,[3] Jonathan,[2] Benjamin[1]), married Elizabeth ——. He studied medicine, and afterwards settled in Springfield, Vt., where he practiced his profession, and died there. Children :

959—1. SUSANNA.
960—2. DR. HENRY F., m. Helen A. ——; lived in Springfield Vt.; a son, Noble J., lived in Everett, Mass.; druggist.
961—3. MARY ANNE.
962—4. LOVISA.
963—5. NOBLE.
964—6. SARAH.
965—7. FRED.
966—8. PAULINE.
967—9. FRANCIS.
968-10. FRANK.
969-11. CHARLES.

970. DR. SAMUEL CRAIN[6] [402], (Joshua,[5] Abiah,[4] John,[3] Jonathan,[2] Benjamin[1]), married and settled first in Alstead, N.

H., but removed to New Jersey, and afterwards to the State of Pennsylvania. Children:

971—1. SAMUEL.
972—2. ISAAC.
973—3. ELEAZER; was a physician, and went to Pennsylvania before 1837.
974—4. JOSHUA.
975—5. ABNER.
976—6. MARY.
977—7. SARAH.
978—8. RUTH.
979—9. HEZEKIAH.
980-10. MARTHA.

981. POLLY CRAIN[6] [403], (Joshua,[5] Abiah,[4] John,[3] Jonathan,[2] Benjamin[1]), married Jedediah Bacon; settled in Williamstown, Vt. Child:

1. DANIEL (Bacon); residence, Northfield, Vt.

982. EUNICE CRAIN[6] [404], (Joshua,[5] Abiah,[4] John,[3] Jonathan,[2] Benjamin[1]), married June 14, 1812, Amos Goodale of Alstead, N. H. He was born March 12, 1789.

983. JOSIAH CRANE[6] [406], (Isaac,[5] Abiah,[4] John,[3] Jonathan,[2] Benjamin[1]), married the widow Ruth Adams, and settled in Cambria, Niagara County, N. Y. Children:

984—1. BARNEY A.
985—2. MARIAH.
986—3. RHUMAH.
987—4. GRATIA.
988—5. LUCINDA A.
989—6. PHILOTHITA.

990. EUNICE CRANE[6] [407], (Isaac,[5] Abiah,[4] John,[3] Jonathan,[2] Benjamin[1]), married —— Metcalf, and settled in Massachusetts. One report says she died in Brattleboro, Vt. Children:

1. WILLIAM (Metcalf).
2. GEORGE P. (Metcalf).

991. Dr. RUFUS CRAIN[6] [408], (Isaac,[5] Abiah,[4] John,[3] Jonathan,[2] Benjamin[1]), married in 1796 Philotheta Marshall. She was born in Colchester, Conn., April 20, 1778. The marriage took place in Warren, Herkimer County, N. Y,, where the Doctor settled, and remained until his death, Sept. 18, 1846. He studied medicine with Dr. Samuel Ross of Colchester, who gave him a certificate, dated in 1794, attesting his thorough qualification to practice as a physician. Dr. Crain (for he spelled his name with an i) at once removed to Warren, and began the practice of his profession, acquiring the confidence and esteem of the community. For about twenty years, under the administration of various governors, he held the commission of Judge of the Court of Common Pleas for Herkimer County, and in 1828 was presiden-

tial elector for that congressional district, and voted for Andrew Jackson. Children :

992—1. WILLIAM CULLLEN, b. Aug. 31, 1798.
993—2. VIANCY.

994. TIRZAH CRAIN⁶ [411], (Isaac,⁵ Abiah,⁴ John,³ Jonathan,² Benjamin¹), married Augustus Sharp, and settled at Lockport, N. Y. Children :

1. PITT (Sharp); went south.
2. DEWITT (Sharp); settled in Buffalo, N. Y.
3. PHIPPS (Sharp); settled in New York city.
4. ADALINE (Sharp); m. Mr. Alderman and went to Illinois.
5. LEVANCHA (Sharp); m. Mr. Stannard and settled in Buffalo.
6. MARYETTE (Sharp); m. and went west.

995. ASA CRANE⁶ [412], (Isaac,⁵ Abiah,⁴ John,³ Jonathan,² Benjamin¹), married Catharine Lyon, and settled in Hartland, Niagara County, N. Y. Children :

996—1. WILLIAM D.
997—2. CATHARINE; m. a Mr. Webster; no children.
998—3. ELIZA.
999—4. WALTER; m., and was living in Lockport, N. Y.
1000—5. MOSES, d. young.
1001—6. MOSES L.
1002—7. JANE ANN, d. young.
1003—8. VIANCY.
1004—9. HELEN; m. July 2, 1827.
1005-10. FRANCES; m. Jonathan Morris.

1006. AMOS CRANE⁶ [415], (Isaac,⁵ Abiah,⁴ John,³ Jonathan,² Benjamin¹), married 1st, Phebe Filer of Warren, Herkimer County, N. Y., by whom he had two sons; married 2d, Mahala Cooper, Nov. 7, 1819. Mr. Crane served in the war of 1812, and was present at the burning of Buffalo, N. Y., during that period; was a pensioner of that war. Their first child was born at Columbia, Herkimer County, N. Y.; the second and third at Buffalo. In 1821 the family removed to Lockport, where they remained until 1836, when they settled in Rose, Oakland County, Mich., and from there, in 1850, they removed to Greenville, Montcalm County, where Mr. Crane died Dec. 24, 1872. She died Aug. 25, 1857. He was a mechanic, and also a farmer, and was born in Halifax, Windham County, Vt. Children :

1007—1. ISAAC NEWTON, b. July 14, 1814.
1008—2. JOSIAH, b. Nov. 7, 1816.
1009—3. WILLIAM M., b. Sept. 7, 1820.
1010—4. GLEASON P., b. Oct. 17, 1821; d. in infancy.
1011—5. RUFUS C., b. Jan. 9, 1823.
1012—6. LUCINDA, b. Dec. 25, 1825; d. aged 7 years.
1013—7. GEORGE F., b. Sept. 17, 1826; d. in infancy.
1014—8. EPHRAIM, b. Oct. 16, 1827; d. young.
1015—9. EUNICE AMELIA, b. Dec. 17, 1828; d. young.
1016-10. MARYETTE AUGUSTA, b. Dec. 28, 1830.
1017-11. JULIETTE AMELIA, b. Feb. 22, 1832.
1018-12. GEORGE ANDREW, b. Oct. 15, 1834.
1019-13. CYNTHIA GENETTE, b. Feb. 12, 1836.

1020-14. CHARLES EDWIN, b. April 17, 1838; d. young.
1021-15. ANTONETTE PAULINA, b. April 12, 1842; m. Willie Strott; settled in Greenville; no children.

1022. EUNICE CRANE[6] [421], (Abiah,[5] Abiah,[4] John,[3] Jonathan,[2] Benjamin[1]), married in 1810, William Thompson, son of William, Jr., and Patty (Hale) Thompson, who was born in Alstead, N. H., March 12, 1789. She was born at Surrey, N. H., Aug. 28, 1790, and died at Shalersville, Ohio, Aug. 26, 1853.

Children :

,1. WILLIAM (Thompson), b. Feb. 21, 1813, Alstead, N. H.; m. Fanny Peirce.
2. LUCINA (Thompson), b. Aug. 30, 1815, Alstead, N. H.; m. Myron Crane, son of Asa and Theodosia Crane, Feb. 14, 1842. She d. Oct. 10, 1851. Child :
    1. CHARLES H., b. June 8, 1843; d. June 11, 1849.
3. NANCY MARIA (Thompson), b. Jan. 10, 1818, Shalersville, Ohio.
4. JULIAETTE (Thompson), b. March 3, 1823.
5. H. HALE (Thompson), b. Dec. 21, 1831; d. March 21, 1848.

1023. RUTH CRANE[6] [425], (Joseph,[5] Abiah,[4] John,[3] Jonathan,[2] Benjamin[1]), married Welcome Bartlett. They settled in Glover, Vt., where their children were born. Later the family removed to Western, N. Y., where she died. Children :

1. FRANCIS (Bartlett).
2. ALDIS (Bartlett).
2. ELVIRA (Bartlett); m. ——— Flemming.
3. ADALINE (Bartlett); d. at Glover, Vt.

1024. ANNA CRANE[6] [426], (Joseph,[5] Abiah,[4] John,[3] Jonathan,[2] Benjamin[1]), married Paul Cook, of Glover, Vt., and died there. Children :

1. ——— (Cook); m. Miss Simons, of Williamstown, and settled in Glover, Vt.
2. ELSINA (Cook); m. William Drew, of Glover, Vt.
3. LUCY (Cook); m. ——— Jennis; lived in Glover, Vt.
4. LAURA (Cook); d unmarried.

1025. ARIEL CRANE[6] [428], (Joseph,[5] Abiah,[4] John,[3] Jonathan,[2] Benjamin[1]), married Dec. 22, 1820, Mary Herrick, of Randolph, Vt. She was born April 21, 1797. He was a farmer, and spent his days on the farm where he was born. He died Nov. 17, 1876, aged 83. Children :

1026—1. JOSEPH, b. Oct. 24, 1821.
1027—2. MARY, b. Feb. 18, 1823.
1028—3. ELEANOR, b. June 31, 1825; d. Oct. 6, 1827.
1029—4. ARIEL DENISON, b. April 26, 1826; d. Oct. 13, 1827.
1030—5. ELLEN E., b. March 5, 1828.
1031—6. CAROLINE E., b. June 24, 1831.
1032—7. CHARLES, b. Nov. 20, 1834.
1033—8. GEORGE, b. Dec. 12, 1837.

1034. HORATIO CRANE[6] [429], (Joseph,[5] Abiah,[4] John,[3] Jonathan,[2] Benjamin[1]), married Sophia Edson. He was a farmer,

and settled in Williamstown, Vt., where his children were born. About the year 1827 he sold his farm in Williamstown and purchased another in Jericho, Vt., where he was killed, March 10, 1828, while clearing a piece of land. Children:

1035—1. GEORGE H., b. Oct. 6, 1823.
1036—2. SOPHIA, b. January, 1827.

1037. OREN CRANE[6] [430], (Joseph,[5] Abiah,[4] John,[3] Jonathan,[2] Benjamin[1]), born at Williamstown, Vt. He married Lydia Grover, of Brookfield, Vt., April 20, 1820. They settled in Jericho, Vt., where their children were born, and where he died March 26, 1873. She died Jan. 20, 1871. Children:

1038—1. LUCY, b. Jan. 9, 1821.
1039—2. EDWIN, b. Feb. 25, 1822.
1040—3. FRANCIS, b. Aug. 30, 1823; d. March 14, 1882; unmarried.
1041—4. OREN, b. Feb. 1, 1826; m. Martha J. Abbott, March 21, 1852. He d. Feb. 3, 1860; wife also dead.
1042—5. HORATIO DENNISON, b. Sept. 1, 1831.
1043—6. LYDIA, b. Aug. 16, 1838; m. Wm. G. McPherson, Sept. 30, 1880; resides McPherson, Cal.; no children.
1044—7. CHARLES, b. Jan. 24, 1841.

1045. ARBA CRANE[6] [431], (Joseph,[5] Abiah,[4] John,[3] Jonathan,[2] Benjamin[1]), married 1st, Mary Shipman, of Northfield, Vt. They had three sons and two daughters, all born in Northfield, Vt. The family in 1835 removed to the State of Indiana, where his first wife and four of her children died. He married 2d, widow Mary Scott; 3d, Julia Lamphere. He worked in a fulling-mill as a dresser of cloth. He died in 1880.

Children:

1046—1. MARY; d. young in Indiana.
1047—2. SALLIE; d. young in Indiana.
1048—3. JULIUS; d. young in Indiana.
1049—4. ARBA D., b. 1826.
1050—5. CORNELIUS; d. young in Indiana.
1051—6. SAMUEL D., b. Feb. 22, 1843.
1052—7. BENJAMIN F., b. Dec. 19, 1846.
1053—8. ELLA J., b. April 11, 1852.
9. ———; d. in infancy.

1054. LUCINA CRANE[6] [432], (Joseph,[5] Abiah,[4] John,[3] Jonathan,[2] Benjamin[1]), married Dec. 20, 1826, Samuel Bates, of Brookfield, Vt., who was born May 9, 1799, and died Sept. 6, 1861. She died Nov. 5, 1877. Children:

1. LUCINA (Bates), b. Oct. 13, 1828; d. June 5, 1850.
2. THOMAS (Bates), b. July 18, 1830; d. Sept. 16, 1830.
3. SAMUEL LYSANDER (Bates), b. Nov. 11, 1831.
4. ELLEN EFFIGENA (Bates), b. Feb. 18, 1834; d. July 15, 1841.

1055. Rev. SAMUEL LYSANDER BATES [3]; studied for the ministry; graduated at Andover, Mass.; a Congregationalist. He m. Marion Elizabeth Walker, of Vermont, b. Jan. 29, 1843. He

has preached at Newbury, Vt., and was, December, 1896, preaching in Burlington, Vt. Children:

  1. MARY RUSSELL (Bates), b. Sept. 9, 1872.
  2. SAMUEL WALKER (Bates), b. Sept. 9, 1880; d. April 27. 1891.

1056. PORTER CRANE[6] [434], (Joseph,[5] Abiah,[4] John,[3] Jonathan,[2] Benjamin[1]), married Sarah Parkhurst Nelson, of Craftsbury, Vt., born Aug. 30, 1810. They settled in Wolcott, where he was a manufacturer and dresser of cloth. She died there Dec. 6, 1871. He died there Oct. 23, 1880. Children:

1057—1. ARBA NELSON, b. Jan. 11, 1834; lawyer; residence St. Louis, Mo.; unmarried.
1058—2. FRANKLIN, b. Dec. 27, 1835; m. Ella Whitney; residence Kirkhaven, Minn.
1059—3. EDWARD PAYSON, b. Dec. 14, 1837.
1060—4. PORTER, b. Dec. 9, 1839.
1061—5. SARAH E., b. April 17, 1842.
1062—6. FRED E., b. Sept. 12, 1846; d. April 28, 1877.

1063. CHAUNCY CRANE[6] [436], (Joseph,[5] Abiah,[4] John,[3] Jonathan,[2] Benjamin[1]), married September, 1840, at Edgartown, Dukes County, Mass., Clarissa P. Smith, a native of that place. There he settled, on the island of Martha's Vineyard. A farmer. She died Aug. 22, 1890. He died Aug. 16, 1891. Mr. Crane was deeply interested in the genealogy of his branch of the family and rendered valuable assistance in the collection of material for this work. Children:

1064—1. ELLEN B., b. April 7, 1842; m. Leander Mayhew, a native of Chilmark; residence, Edgartown; no children.

1065. CHARLES CRANE[6] [437], (Joseph,[5] Abiah,[4] John,[3] Jonathan,[2] Benjamin[1]), married in Rochester, Mass., Nov. 25, 1841, Miribah Crapo, daughter of Philip and Sally H. Crapo, of Rochester, Mass.; born March 2, 1820. They settled in Fairhaven, now Acushnet, Mass. Child:

1066—1. CHARLES F., b. Oct. 19, 1843. He enlisted as a soldier and went with the 3d Massachusetts Regiment under command of General Foster, and died at Newberne, N. C., Jan. 29, 1863.

1067. EUNICE CRANE[6] [440], (John,[5] Abiah,[4] John,[3] Jonathan,[2] Benjamin[1]), married 1st, Laban Miles, of Dover, N. H., April 5, 1819; 2d, Abner Cobleigh, of Sutton, Vt. All children by first husband. Children:

  1. LYDIA (Miles), b. July, 1820; m. Albert Dwinell, of Glover, Vt.
  2. RUBIN (Miles), b. ——; d. in childhood.
  3. SARAH (Miles), b. October, 1826; m. Lyman Darling; 2 children.
  4. MARY T. (Miles), b. February, 1828; m. Lyman Darling; 2d wife; 9 children.
  5. MARTHA (Miles), b. 1830; m. Wm. Blodgett; 5 children.

1068. SALLY CRANE[6] [441], (John,[5] Abiah,[4] John,[3] Jonathan,[2] Benjamin[1]), married June, 1830, Lyndon Robinson, of

Barton, Vt., where she died April 23, 1872. He died at Newark,
Vt., Aug. 2, 1891, aged 90 years. Children :

1. JOHN PRENTICE (Robinson), b. July 26, 1834; resides at Cam-
   bridgeport, Mass.
2. J. OWEN (Robinson), b. Feb. 6, 1836; resides at Barton, Vt.
3. —— (Robinson), ⎱ twins; d. in infancy.
4. —— (Robinson), ⎰

1069. JOHN CRANE[6] [443], (John,[5] Abiah,[4] John,[3] Jonathan,[2]
Benjamin[1]), married 1st, Nancy Martin, of Williamstown, Vt. ;
2d, Laura Martin.. Child :

1070—1. AARON MARTIN; m. Alida Flint, of Boston, Mass.

1071. NANCY CRANE[6] [444], (John,[5] Abiah,[4] John,[3] Jonathan,[2] Benjamin[1]), married Hezekiah Stellman Bickford; settled
at Glover, Vt. Children :

1. LAURA ANN (Bickford); d. at Glover, Vt.
2. H. PRENTICE (Bickford); m. and resides at Monterey, Cal.
3. SARAH C. (Bickford); m. 1st, Chas. C. Hardy, of Glover, Vt.;
   2d, Elbridge K. Barker, of Milwaukee, Wis.
4. EMILY (Bickford); m. Amos L. Gale, of Swiftwater, N. H.
5. HENRY (Bickford); m. Annie Maria Dickinson; is a physician,
   and resides in Hartford, Conn.
6. LAURA ANN (Bickford); m. George Goldsmith, of Jamaica
   Plain, Mass.

1072. LAURA CRANE[6] [446], (John,[5] Abiah,[4] John,[3] Jonathan,[2] Benjamin[1]), married Clifton Williams in 1836, and died
Oct. 10, 1850. Mr. Williams died Oct. 22, 1894, aged 85. He
was a farmer, and resided in Glover, Vt. Children :

1. AZRO A. (Williams), b. June, 1838.
2. CHARLES C. (Williams), b. September, 1848; d. January, 1864.

1073. AZRO A. WILLIAMS [1]; in 1861 went to the State of Massachusetts; in 1875 m. Adelade M. Paterson, of Milford, Mass., and
returned to the old farm at Glover, Vt., in 1877, and has since
that time resided on the old homestead. Children :

1. PERCY PATERSON (Williams), b. April, 1877; d. October, 1891.
2. EDWIN GRAY (Williams), b. June, 1880.
3. JESSE CLIFTON (Williams), b. 1883.
4. CHARLES AZRO (Williams), b. May, 1890; d. August,
   1890.

1074. PERSIS CRANE[6] [447], (John,[5] Abiah,[4] John,[3] Jonathan,[2] Benjamin[1]), married Olin L. Gray, July 3, 1836. She
died April 19, 1861. He died July 22, 1895, aged 82 years and
7 months. Children :

1. EDWIN S. (Gray), b. May 22, 1838; d. Sept. 19, 1864, at Winchester, W. Va.; soldier in late war; m. Elvira Sanborn,
   May, 1861.
2. ERVIN O. (Gray), b. Aug. 17, 1845; d. Dec. 6, 1853.
3. CHANCEY C. (Gray), b. Oct. 9, 1848; d. Feb. 17, 1851.
4. LAURA VILLA (Gray), b. May 7, 1856.

1075. LAURA VILLA GRAY [4]; m. Albert E. Rich, May 25, 1882; resides at Glover, Vt. Child:

    1. ARTHUR (Rich), b. Oct. 12, 1884.

1076. WILLIAM CRANE[6] [449]; (Elisha,[5] Elisham,[4] John,[3] Jonathan,[2] Benjamin[1]), born in Bolton, Conn.; married March 14, 1801, Hannah Hamilton, and settled in Ellington, Conn., where he died in 1838. She died there in 1861. Children:

1077—1. REBECCA, b. Aug. 28, 1802; d. 1853.
1078—2. HANNAH, b. Nov. 2, 1803; d. in infancy.
1079—3. HANNAH, b. 1806; m. Reuben Pease, of Wilbraham, Mass.; d. Nov. 14, 1864.
1080—4. BETSEY, b. 1809; d. Jan. 17, 1857.
1081—5. WILLIAM, b. 1811; d. March 2, 1829.
1082—6. DARIUS, b. 1816.

1083. DANIEL O. CRANE[6] [450] (Elisha,[5] Elisham,[4] John,[3] Jonathan,[2] Benjamin[1]), married April 20, 1793, at Norwich, Vt., Sarah Reed. She was born in Portsmouth, N. H., July 30, 1776. They settled first in the town where they were married, which was Mr. Crane's birthplace. They removed to Haverhill, N. H., after their children were born, and subsequently lived in Bradford, Newbury and Corinth, Vt. He was a farmer, and died Jan. 21, 1813, of what they called "spotted fever." Mrs. Crane died at Concord, N. H., Dec. 15, 1851. Children:

1084—1. BETSEY PICKERING, b. Aug. 4, 1794; m. Mr. Thompson.
1085—2. LYDIA OWEN, b. Dec. 8, 1795.
1086—3. ABIGAIL SMITH, b. July 10, 1797; d. July 11, 1815.
1087—4. ANDREW MARSH, b. Feb. 2, 1799.
1088—5. SARAH JENKINS, b. Dec. 17, 1800.
1089—6. MARGARET DICKEY, b. Nov. 8, 1802.
1090—7. HEZEKIAH CHARLES PINCKNEY, b. Aug. 27, 1804.
1091—8. WILLIAM REED, b. July 30, 1806; d. July 19, 1819.
1092—9. NANCY P., b April 20, 1808.
1093-10. MAHALA, b. Aug. 7, 1810.
1094-11. DANIEL OWEN, b. June 18, 1812; d. Sept. 17, 1813.

1095. WAREHAM CRANE[6] [455], (Hezekiah,[5] Hezekiah,[4] John,[3] Jonathan,[2] Benjamin[1]), married Eunice Barber at East Windsor, Conn., 1792, and settled in that place; a farmer. He died there Jan. 21, 1835, aged 65 years. She died there Oct. 23, 1854, in the 83d year of her age. Children:

1096—1. CLARISSA, b. July 15, 1792; m. April 19, 1832, Parley Green, and d. April 26, 1867; no children.
1097—2. SIBYL, b. Jan. 2, 1794.
1098—3. EUNICE, b. Jan. 3, 1796.
1099—4. WAREHAM BARBER, b. Jan. 27, 1798; d. May 6, 1842.
1100—5. ANNA, b. Oct. 30, 1799; d., aged 87 years.
1101—6. RUSSELL WILLIS, b. Jan. 31, 1802.
1102—7. SOPHRONIA, b. Feb. 14, 1804.
1103—8. OLIVER ROOT, b. Dec. 6, 1806.
1104—9. ELECTA B., b. Aug. 25, 1809.
1105-10. HEZEKIAH BACKUS, b. Sept. 12, 1811.
1106-11. CHARLES REYNOLDS, b. Feb. 26, 1817; m. Mary West, Oct. 5, 1842; no children.
1107-12. LORENZO BLISS, b. Nov. 21, 1818.

1108.   Joel Crane[6] [456], (Hezekiah,[5] Hezekiah,[4] John,[3] Jonathan,[2] Benjamin[1]), born in East Windsor, Conn.; married Sally Graves in 1796 at Weathersfield, Vt., where they settled; a farmer and a house joiner. Here their children were born. · He died Jan. 14, 1835, at Pharsalia, Chenango County, N. Y. She also died there Oct. 23, 1852, Mr. Crane having removed to that town in 1796.   Children :

1109—1.   Hendrick, b. May 1, 1797.
1110—2.   Luther, b. Sept. 10, 1803.

1111.   Hezekiah Crane[6] [457], (Hezekiah,[5] Hezekiah,[4] John,[3] Jonathan,[2] Benjamin[1]), married Feb. 10, 1797, Prudence Lake, of Rindge, N. H.   Their first three children were born in Weathersfield, Vt., but in 1803 they removed to Eden, Vt.   Children :

1112—1.   Prudence, b. Jan. 16, 1798.
1113—2.   Hezekiah, b. Aug. 25, 1799; d. March 18, 1800.
1114—3.   Gilman, b. June 30, 1801.
1115—4.·   Harriet, b. July 31, 1803.
1116—5.   Sewall L., b. April 13, 1805.
1117—6.   Oberia, b. April 16, 1807; d. May 16, 1807.
1118—7.   Oberia Hill, b. June 26, 1808.

1119.   Abner Crane[6] [459], (Hezekiah,[5] Hezekiah,[4] John,[3] Jonathan,[2] Benjamin[1]), married Roxana Belknap; lived in Springfield, Mass.   He was born in East Windsor, March 15, 1794; guardian was appointed for him by the court, he then being 18 years old; also one for his brother Russell, then 15, at same time; their father being then deceased.   He died Nov. 28, 1846. He lived perhaps some years in Ware; was, April 7, 1828, called of Ware, and an armorer; was also of Ware in 1831.   March 24, 1817, he was of Springfield, and called a yeoman.   Children :

1120—1.   Abner Belknap, b. April 15, 1809.
1121—2.   Amaziah Britto, b. Dec. 20, 1813, in Springfield, Mass.

1122.   Rhoda Crane[6] [460], (Hezekiah,[5] Hezekiah,[4] John,[3] Jonathan,[2] Benjamin[1]), married at East Windsor, Conn., Feb. 2, 1802, Israel Allen, Jr.; born July 6, 1779.   He was a farmer, and died at East Windsor, Nov. 16, 1848 or 1849.   She died there Jan. 18, 1856.   Children :

1.   Israel Edward (Allen), b. April 29, 1803.
2.   ·Rhoda (Allen), b. July 20, 1805; d. Feb. 29, 1808.
3.   Rhoda Emily (Allen), b. Feb. 16, 1808; m. Sampson Dunn.
4.   Sophia Amelia (Allen), b. May 24, 1810; m. Ephraim D. Hodges.
5.   Elvira Lucretia (Allen), b. Aug. 20, 1812; m. Rev. John Caldwell.
6.   Emeret Angeline (Allen), b. Nov. 10, 1815; m. 1st, Marvin Kibbie; 2d, Oscar Kibbie.
7.   Martha Cornelia (Allen), b. April 3, 1819; m. Titus Alcott.
8.   Delina Julietta (Allen), b. May 7, 1822; m. Rev. David K. Merrill.
9.   Rosana Elizabeth (Allen), b. Sept. 6, 1825; m. Nathaniel C. Strong.

1123. RUSSELL WILLIS CRANE[6] [461], (Hezekiah,[5] Hezekiah,[4] John,[3] Jonathan,[2] Benjamin[1]), born in 1779; married Lydia Parnele, of Suffield, Conn. He was a farmer, and resided in South Windsor. He died in East Windsor. She died in Illinois, Nov. 1, 1833. Children :

1124—1. GEORGE R.
1125—2. CAROLINE.
1126—3. WILLIAM WILLIS, b. Jan. 31, 1832.

1127. LUCRETIA CRANE[6] [462], (Hezekiah,[5] Hezekiah,[4] John,[3] Jonathan,[2] Benjamin[1]), married Elnathan Munsell or Murrill. Children :

1. AUSTIN C. (Munsell or Murrill).
2. ALONZO (Munsell or Murrill).
3. ORTENSIA (Munsell or Murrill).
4. LOUISA (Munsell or Murrill).

1128. DAVID CRANE[6] [464], (David,[5] Hezekiah,[4] John,[3] Jonathan,[2] Benjamin[1]), born in the town of East Windsor, Conn., Scantic Parish; married Chloe Loomis. She was born July 1, 1780, and died Nov. 24, 1829. He was a farmer, and died at Oneida Castle, N. Y., Sept. 7, 1851. Their two eldest children were born in East Windsor, Conn.; but after the birth of Franklin L. the family removed to near Ketch Mills, where the other children were born. Franklin Loomis writes that he believes his father was a drummer in the war of 1812. Children :

1129—1. DAVID ORVILLE, b. Oct. 10, 1804.
1130—2. FRANKLIN LOOMIS, b. Jan. 10, 1808.
1131—3. CHLOE PITKIN, b. Aug. 21, 1816.
1132—4. CECILIA A., b. Jan. 20, 1823; d. at McGregor, Iowa, Aug. 27, 1870.

1133. SAMUEL PITKIN CRANE[6] [465], (David,[5] Hezekiah,[4] John,[3] Jonathan,[2] Benjamin[1]), married 1st, Ann Gustin, of Colchester, in 1807. She was born Oct. 17, 1783; died July 15, 1833. He married 2d, Polly Phelps. She was born Nov. 25, ——; died April 16, 1848. He married 3d, Lois Hitchcock. She was born Nov. 4, 1798; died Oct. 24, 1876. He was a farmer. Settled in East Windsor, Conn. He served in the war of 1812 at New London. Mr. Crane died in Springfield, Mass., in 1882. Children :

1134—1. SAMUEL GUSTIN, b. June 12, 1809.
1135—2. SARAH ANN, b. April 10, 1811.
1136—3. JANE C., b. Oct. 4, 1813.
1137—4. ELIZABETH, b. April 9, 1816.
1138—5. DANIEL GILBERT, b. Oct. 31, 1818.
1139—6. SUSAN F., b. May 3, 1821; d. Oct. 11, 1822.

1140. CHAUNCEY CRANE[6] [466], (David,[5] Hezekiah,[4] John,[3] Jonathan,[2] Benjamin[1]), married Phœbe Gustin, Oct. 18, 1809. She died Feb. 25, 1849. He died Jan. 24, 1864. Children :

1141—1. MARY S., b. Aug. 4, 1810.
1142—2. AMANDA, b. May 20, 1812.

1143—3. CHAUNCEY G., b. March 14, 1814.
1144—4. GEORGE C., b. Nov. 9, 1816.
1145—5. ALFRED, b. Dec. 19, 1818; d. Feb. 10, 1819.
1146—6. PURSIS A., b. March 19, 1822.
1147—7. JULIA A., b. March 18, 1827.
1148—8. WALTER G., b. Sept. 17, 1829; d. Nov. 17, 1862; unmarried.

1149. CURTIS CRANE[6] [467], (David,[5] Hezekiah,[4] John,[3] Jonathan,[2] Benjamin[1]), was a carpenter by trade and married Nancy Chapman, at Vernon, Conn., Dec. 25, 1807. She was born May 31, 1789. Oct. 18, 1820, he bought the Silas Holton farm in Springfield. He owned other land there. For a time the family resided in Springfield, Mass., or North Wilbraham, from which place he removed to New Albany, Ind., about 1840. He died Feb. 25, 1862. She died Feb. 21, 1874, at New Albany, Ind. Children:

1150—1. ROSANNAH, b. July 30, 1808.
1151—2. HENRY, b. May 19, 1810.
1152—3. CHARLOTTE, b. July 4, 1812.
1153—4. HARRIETTE, b. Dec. 9, 1814.
1154—5. ELECTA, b. Feb. 24, 1817; m. Capt. E. G. Barry; d. May 22; 1844.
1155—6. LEICESTER FULLER, b. April 25, 1819.
1156—7. MARTIN HALE, b. Sept. 27, 1821.
1157—8. JULIA ANN, b. Dec. 6, 1823.
1158—9. WILLIAM CURTIS, b. June 19, 1826.
1159-10. NANCY MARIA, b. Dec. 3, 1828.
1160-11. JOHN EUGENE, b. Nov. 16, 1832.

1161. LEMUEL CRANE[6] [471], (David,[5] Hezekiah,[4] John,[3] Jonathan,[2] Benjamin[1]), married in October, 1826, Eliza Bull. She was born in 1804, and died May 28, 1857. He died Oct. 20, 1853. Children:

1162—1. MARIA S., b. Aug. 28, 1827.
1163—2. CHARLOTTE E., b. December, 1828.
1164—3. ANNA B., b. April 8, 1831.
1165—4. HATTIE, b. June 3, 1833.
1166—5. JOHN W., b. Sept. 12, 1835.
1167—6. JULIA M., b. Aug. 22, 1837.
1168—7. ELLEN L., b. February, 1840.
1169—8. CHARLES F., b. Aug. 12, 1842.
1170—9. WARREN S., b. Jan. 30, 1844.

1171. BETSEY CRANE[6] [472], (David,[5] Hezekiah,[4] John,[3] Jonathan,[2] Benjamin[1]), married Justus Orlonzo Reed, a farmer. They settled in East Windsor, where he died Sept. 21, 1850, aged 58 years. Children:

1. LEMUEL (Reed), b. Aug. 27, 1817; d. 1879.
2. CHARLOTTE C. (Reed); b. April 9, 1818; d. Aug. 10, 1844 or 1846.
3. JOHN H. (Reed), b. July 15, 1820.
4. MARO S. (Reed), b. May 14, 1822.
5. CELINA (Reed), b. March 22, 1825; d. Nov. 20, 1849.
6. WALDO R. (Reed), b. Oct 22, 1827.

1172. JOHN WASHINGTON CRANE[6] [474], (David,[5] Hezekiah,[4] John,[3] Jonathan,[2] Benjamin[1]), married 1st, Harriette

9

Crane, born Dec. 9, 1814. She died Sept. 8, 1834. He married 2d, Fanny Keown. He married 3d, Mary Pitkin in July, 1840. She was born April 25, 1817, and died ——. He married 4th, Ida Benedict, Oct. 11, 1864. She was born Nov. 10, 1840. Mr. Crane first took a medical course, but immediately turned his attention to dentistry, which latter. profession he practiced in Hartford, Conn. Children:

1173—1. HARRIETTE STELLA, b. Aug. 31, 1834; d. Oct. 11, 1850.
1174—2. FRANCES I., b. 1836; d. 1836.
1175—3. JOHN WASHINGTON, b. Aug. 19, 1837.
1176—4. MARY EMMA, b. 1841; d. 1847.
1177—5. ADELE PLUM, b. 1842.
1178—6. ANNETTE DECOST, b. 1843.
1179—7. HENRY V., b. 1844; d. 1845.
1180—8. GERTRUDE, b. 1846.
1181—9. OTTO F., b. 1848.
1182-10. FRANK, b. 1851.

1183. WARREN SMITH CRANE[6] [475], (David,[5] Hezekiah,[4] John,[3] Jonathan,[2] Benjamin[1]), married 1st, in New York City, Mary Kirtland Crampton, in 1830. She was a native of Madison, Conn., and died July 17, 1835. He then married Julia Bull, who was born June 16, 1811, in Burlington, Conn. He was a dentist and practiced that profession in Hartford, Conn. He died March 11, 1860, at West Hartford. Children:

1184—1. SAMUEL L. G., b. Nov. 12, 1831, in New York City.
1185—2. BURDETTE, b. 1833; d. 1861.
1186—3. MARY, b. 1835.
1187—4. FREDERICK.
1188—5. JULIA.
1189—6. LIZZIE.
1190—7. IDA.
1191—8. WILLIE; d. in infancy.
1192—9. WILLIE.

1193. RUFUS CRANE[6] [477], (Rufus,[5] Hezekiah,[4] John,[3] Jonathan,[2] Benjamin[1]), married June 24, 1811, Wealthy, daughter of Daniel and Submit (Bancroft) Allen, born Sept. 7, 1793. He died Feb. 7, 1851. She died May 22, 1882. His will admitted to probate Feb. 17, 1851, all property given to his wife Wealthy. Wealthy Crane's will probated June 19, 1882. It was dated Nov. 24, 1875, names son Lucius and daughter Frances Nesmuth, balance given to her children and their legal representatives. Children:

1194—1. BETSY ANN, b. Aug. 28, 1811.
1195—2. RUFUS ALLEN, b. Oct. 22, 1813.
1196—3. HENRIETTA, b. Nov. 5, 1815.
1197—4. HENRY, b. Aug. 23, 1818.
1198—5. ELDRIDGE BURT, b. Dec. 22, 1820.
1199—6. HOSEA BURGE, b. July 25, 1823.
1200—7. FRANCES A., b. May 10, 1826.
1201—8. ALMIRA RACHEL, b. Jan. 29, 1829; d. April 14, 1840.
1202—9. LUCIUS H., b. Dec. 26, 1831.
1203-10. ACHSAH MARIA, b. Sept. 2, 1834.

1204–11. LUMAN GRISWOLD, b. June 2, 1837.
1205–12. JEROME, b. Sept. 30, 1839; d. April 14, 1859.

1206. Hon. HOSEA CRANE[6] [481], (Rufus,[5] Hezekiah,[4] John,[3] Jonathan,[2] Benjamin[1]), married Nov. 28, 1827, Laura Ann Hubbard, and lived for a time one-half mile south of Kitch Mills, Scantic Parish, Conn. In the year 1849 he removed to Millbury, Mass., and established the business of manufacturing knit goods. At first it was conducted on a small scale. But with steadily increasing business he in 1857 took as a partner Mr. Samuel Waters, the style of the firm being Crane & Waters. One year later Mr. Horace Waters succeeded to the interest of Samuel Waters, and a large and prosperous business was carried on for many years. It was practically the introduction of the manufacture of knit underwear in this part of the country. Mr. Crane was chosen a director of the Millbury Bank in 1856, and president in 1863, which position he long held. He was also first vice-president of the Millbury Savings Bank. Mr. Crane was a man of strict integrity; and the confidence in which he was held by his fellow-townsmen is shown by the numerous offices of trust and responsibility to which he was called. He was once elected State senator, twice a representative, several times a member of the board of selectmen, and often chosen to other offices of trust and responsibility. He died April 5, 1879. She died April 10, 1883, aged 78 years, 7 months, 25 days.

Children :

1207—1. CARLOS.
1208—2. HOSEA.
1209—3. HENRY H.
1210—4. HELEN E.
1211—5. LAURA.
1212—6. ANNA R.
1213—7. RUFUS R.

1214. POLLY CRAIN[6] [485], (Aaron,[5] Hezekiah,[4] John,[3] Jonathan,[2] Benjamin[1]), married Ebenezer McGregory, of Long-meadow, Mass. He died Oct. 12, 1826, aged 48 years.

Children :

1. POLLY (McGregory), b. Oct. 3, 1802.
2. EBENEZER (McGregory), b. July 13, 1804.
3. JABEZ (McGregory, b. Oct. 17, 1806.
4. EMELINE (McGregory), b. Nov. 17, 1808.

1215. TIMOTHY CRANE[6] [487], (Aaron,[5] Hezekiah,[4] John,[3] Jonathan,[2] Benjamin[1]), married March 10, 1813, at Stafford, Conn., Matilda Needham. She was born in that place Nov. 20, 1790, and died at Windsor Locks, Conn., Dec. 11, 1863. May 5, 1814, purchased land on which stood a carding mill of Jesse Bliss, and was in company with his brother Eli as clothiers. He was a clothier by trade. He died in Russell, Mass., Nov. 27, 1830. Reuben Bradley appointed administrator Dec. 17, 1830.

Children :

1216—1. MATILDA AMELIA, b. Aug. 22, 1814.
1217—2. EDWIN T.; d. Sept. 1, 1852.
1218—3. LYMAN WALBRIDGE; m. Harriet S. Grant. He was a merchant at Stafford Springs, Conn. He d. Nov. 10, 1890. His widow d. May 31, 1895.
1219—4. MARY JANE F.; d. Oct. 6, 1846.
1220—5. CATHARINE C.; living at 40 Beach St., Springfield, Mass., in March, 1897.

1221. ZIBA CRANE⁶ [488], (Aaron,⁵ Hezekiah,⁴ John,³ Jonathan,² Benjamin¹), married Mercy Kibbee, a native of Stafford, Conn., born September, 1787. They settled in Longmeadow, Mass., where he died in 1846. She died there in 1877. He bought land of Aaron Crain, his father, in Longmeadow. He was a farmer. Children :

1222—1. SYLVESTER, b. 1813.
1223—2. ALMIRA; twice married; d. in Springfield, Mass., November, 1883, leaving a daughter Emily.

1224. ELI CRANE⁶ [489], (Aaron,⁵ Hezekiah,⁴ John,³ Jonathan,² Benjamin¹). He was a clothier, and carried on business with his brother Timothy. He was called of Longmeadow, April 13, 1811, and of Wilbraham, April 25, 1812. At this latter date was in company with his brother Timothy. He probably married Sarah ——, for Timothy Crane and Sarah Crane were administrators of his estate.

1225. ELIHU CRAIN⁶ [492], (Aaron,⁵ Hezekiah,⁴ John,³ Jonathan,² Benjamin¹). He lived in Longmeadow, Mass., and sold land there to Aaron Crain, Aug. 22, 1817. Nov. 5, 1816, he was witness to a mortgage made by Timothy his brother.

1226. HEZEKIAH CRANE⁶ [493], (Aaron,⁵ Hezekiah,⁴ John,³ Jonathan,² Benjamin¹), married Mary Heath, Feb. 14, 1817. They lived for a time at Longmeadow, Mass. He died at Albion, Oswego County, N. Y. Children:

1227—1. HEZEKIAH AUGUSTUS, b. Jan. 14, 1818.
1228—2. MARY ABIGAIL, b. Oct. 8, 1819; m. —— Brown. Children:
          1. URIAH (Brown).
          2. AMANDA (Brown).
1229—3. JANE M., b. Oct. 24, 1821; m. John S. Prince; no children. Lived at Salmon River, Oswego Co., N. Y. She d. April 13, 1893.
1230—4. ELI BARBER, b. Sept. 10, 1823.
1231—5. ANTINETT M., b. May 20, 1825; m. and had two sons.
1232—6. MERCY KIBBA, b. May 20, 1827.
1233—7. EUNICE S., b. Jan. 25,-1830.
1234—8. ADALINE L., b. April 26, 1832; m. —— Brown. Children:
          1. ELLA (Brown).
          2. EMMA (Brown).
          3. DORCAS (Brown).
1235—9. GEORGE, b. Jan. 31, 1834. He went to Minnesota. Had a large family of daughters.

1236. EBENEZER CRAIN[6] [497], (Zebulon,[5] Lemuel,[4] John,[3] Jonathan,[2] Benjamin[1]), married Hannah Rice, Feb. 5, 1807. At time of marriage she was of Walpole, N. H., born August, 1779. He was a soldier of the Revolutionary war. She died in 1844. He died in 1863. Children:

1237—1. RHODA, b. Aug. 27, 1807; m. David Cushing, Jr. He d. March 19, 1872. She d. June 30, 1879. One daughter.
1238—2. LEANDER, b. April, 1809.
1239—3. ALBERT, b. June, 1811.
1240—4. GILBERT, b. Aug. 27, 1813.
1241—5. ELISHA, b. February, 1815.
1242—6. EBENEZER, b. Sept. 5, 1819.

1243. RALPH CRANE[6] [505], (Isaac W.,[5] Isaac,[4] Isaac,[3] Jonathan,[2] Benjamin[1]), married Nov. 15, 1826, Clerinda Matson, of South Glastonbury, Conn., born March 31, 1808. Here they resided. He died there April 18, 1872. She died Aug. 11, 1896. Children:

1244—1. Son, b. Aug. 13, 1827; d. Aug. 14, 1827.
1245—2. Son, b. Oct. 12, 1828; d. Oct. 20, 1828.
1246—3. LOUISA MARIA, b. Sept. 12, 1830.
1247—4. LEROY DELOSS, b. May 9, 1833.
1248—5. CLEMENT WESLEY, b. April 21, 1837; d. Dec. 22, 1840.
1249—6. LAURA JANE, b. March 13, 1839.
1250—7. ELTRUDE ALGEVINE, b. July 19, 1842.
1251—8. ADELBERT WADSWORTH, b. Oct. 15, 1846.
1252—9. Daughter, b. and d. May 19, 1851.
1253-10. MONROE WASHBURN, b. Aug. 23, 1853; m. 1st, Alice Rosabel Risley, who d. April 15, 1894; m. 2d, Jennie Maria Dunham, May 22, 1895; live at Rocky Hill, Conn.

1254. HARVEY CRANE[6] [508], (Isaac W.,[5] Isaac,[4] Isaac,[3] Jonathan,[2] Benjamin[1]), married Matilda Burnham, at Hebron, Conn., May 9, 1839. His estate was probated in 1889. Children:

1255—1. Son; living in Hebron, 1881.
1256—2. JULIA MARIA, b. March 28, 1842; d. Dec. 29, 1892; unm.
1257—3. SUSAN VIOLETTE, b. May 25, 1843; m. George Porter Bliss, of Hebron, Conn., and resides in Florence, Mass.

1258. LUCIUS CRAIN[6] [511], (John,[5] Isaac,[4] Isaac,[3] Jonathan,[2] Benjamin[1]), married 1st, Mrs. Parmelia J. Cook (her maiden name was Parmelia J. Smith), February, 1827. She died June 29, 1870, aged 78 years. He married 2d, April 4, 1872, Mary Bailey, of Springfield. He died in Hadley, Mass., June 3, 1887, aged 85 years and 6 months. Children:

1259—1. MARY, b. ——; d. in infancy, Sept. 1, 1827.
1260—2. JOHN LUCIUS, b. April 29, 1829; d. Dec. 25, 1888.
1261—3. DENNIS, b. 1831; d. at the age of 17.
1262—4. MARIA, b. 1834; d. May 29, 1857.
1263—5. ABIGAIL, b. 1836; d. Jan. 15, 1843.

1264. MARY CRAIN[6] [513], (John,[5] Isaac,[4] Isaac,[3] Jonathan,[2] Benjamin[1]), married Anthony Budlong, a carpenter by

trade. They resided in Providence, R. I. She was living in October, 1880. Children:

1. MARY LOUISA (Budlong), b. 1834.
2. ELLEN ANTHONY (Budlong), b. 1837.
   They both died of typhoid fever in 1855..

1265. HARVEY H. CRAIN[6] [514], (John,[5] Isaac,[4] Isaac,[3] Jonathan,[2] Benjamin[1]), born in Abington, Conn.; married (1838) in Pomfret, Dianna Buck, a native of Killingly, born in 1817. He was a farmer, and resided in Pomfret some years. He was living in Thompson when his youngest child was born. Later the family removed to Geneseo, Ill., where they resided in 1879. Children:

1266—1. WILLIAM HENRY, b. April 5, 1840.
1267—2. CHARLES H., b. Nov. 21, 1842.
1268—3. GEORGE, b. May 27, 1851.

1269. JOSEPH CRANE[6] [518], (John,[5] Zebulon,[4] Joseph,[3] Jonathan,[2] Benjamin[1]), married Chloe, daughter of William Hill. She was born in 1767. They settled in Putnam County, N. Y., on the farm which was formerly the home of Deacon Eleazer Hamlin, who settled there in 1740. Mr. Hamlin transferred it to John Carpenter, father of Tamar, wife of Judge John Crane, and Joseph Crane purchased it from the heirs of John Carpenter. Joseph Crane died Dec. 25, 1835, and his wife Chloe died March 12, 1836. The property passed to their son Azor B. Crane, and in 1898 was owned and occupied by his son Ira Crane. This estate has been in the possession of the Crane family four generations, and is consequently one of the oldest homesteads in this section of the country. Mr. Joseph Crane was a most successful farmer, an intelligent, Christian man, public spirited, giving liberally of his time and means to the welfare of both church and State. Children:

1270—1. NOAH HILL, b. November, 1786; physician; m. Mrs. Susan
        Warring; no children; d. May 24, 1836.
1271—2. IRA A., b. Oct. 6, 1788.
1272—3. ADAH, b. April 15, 1791.
1273—4. CORNELIA, b. Oct. 1, 1793.
1274—5. ZILLAH, b. Jan. 29, 1796.
1275—6. BETSEY, b. May 10, 1798.
1276—7. AZOR BELDEN, b. May 25, 1801.
1277—8. CHARLES, b. 1806; d. April 26, 1808.
1278—9. EMELINE, b. May, 1807; m. Reynolds Platt; no children; d.
        April 1, 1889.

1279. ADAH CRANE[6] [519], (John,[5] Zebulon,[4] Joseph,[3] Jonathan,[2] Benjamin[1]), married Moses Fowler, Oct. 18, 1787. She was born April 12, 1765. They settled in Kent, Putnam County, N. Y. She died Dec. 10, 1854. Children:

1. ROSALINDA (Fowler), b. 1791.
2. JAMES HARVEY (Fowler); d. young.

3. JOHN ADDISON (Fowler); m. Deborah Brown, of South East, N. Y. Children:

    1. EDWIN (Fowler); m. Martha Marvin.
    2. ROSALINDA (Fowler); m. Harry Bailey.

1280. EDWIN FOWLER [1]; m. Martha Marvin. Children:

    1. J. ADDISON (Fowler); m. Clara Peck, of Patterson, N. Y.; d. May 26, 1893.
    2. EMMA (Fowler); m. Chester Crosby, of South East, N. Y.; has children; resides in California.
    3. THOMAS B. (Fowler); m. Frances Howes; had one dau., who m. —— Voorhis. Thomas B. d. Sept. 24, 1886, and his wid. m. Edward C. Taylor, of New York City.
    4. HENRY M. (Fowler); official at the Boston "Keeley Institute."

1281. ROSALINDA FOWLER [1]; m. Feb. 23, 1808, Samuel Lyon, of Bedford. He was b. 1789, and settled in North Castle. He d. July 26, 1864. She d. Dec. 19, 1844. Children:

    1. FLORAETTE (Lyon), b. May 24, 1810.
    2. OSMOND C. (Lyon), b. April 28, 1812; d. Jan. 3, 1891.
    3. JOHN A. (Lyon), b. June 29, 1814. d. Aug. 28, 1823.
    4. MARY N. (Lyon). b. July 29, 1816; d. May 17, 1884.
    5. FREDERICK W. (Lyon), b. April 4, 1818; d. April 5, 1818.
    6. ROSALINDA C. (Lyon), b. Feb. 28, 1819; d. Dec. 13, 1891.
    7. SAMUEL A. (Lyon), b. April 24, 1821; d. Feb. 28, 1895.
    8. ANN A. (Lyon), b. Feb. 17, 1823.
    9. HENRIETTA C. (Lyon), b. April 13, 1825; d. Feb. 7, 1895.
    10. JOHN N. (Lyon), b. June 19, 1828; d. April 11, 1885.

1282. FLORAETTE LYON [1]; m. J. Jacob Denicke, and settled in Courtland, Westchester Co., N. Y. She d. Dec. 31, 1880. He d. Sept. 22, 1887. Children:

    1. CAROLINE (Denicke), b. Feb. 14, 1829.
    2. ANTOINETTE (Denicke), b. Aug 1, 1836; m. Stephen Pullen.
    3. SARAH (Denicke), b. July 25, 1835; m. Paul Wessells.
    4. EMMA (Denicke), b. Jan. 5, 1838; m. Elihu Richey.
    5. MARY ELLEN (Denicke), b. March 21, 1840; d. Oct. 6, 1845.
    6. CORNELIA (Denicke), b. July 12, 1843; m. Theo. Lent.
    7. ROSALINDA (Denicke), b. March 1, 1845; m. Amos Nelson; d. Nov. 6, 1896.
    8. GEORGE W. (Denicke), b. Jan. 3, 1847.
    9. JOHN J. (Denicke), b. Oct. 25, 1851; m. Ida Halstead; d. Dec. 6, 1896.
    10. MARY ELLEN (Denicke), b. March 25, 1854; d. 1856.

1283. CAROLINE DENICKE [1]; m. James H. Lent, Jan. 18, 1848. He was born March 14, 1824, and is an auctioneer, while she carries on the millinery business, being at the head of an old established house. Children:

    1. EDWIN B. (Lent), b. Dec. 18, 1848.
    2. ELLA L. (Lent), b. April 24, 1856.
    3. LAURA N. (Lent), b. Nov. 5, 1858.

4. FRANK (Lent), b. March 7, 1862.
5. CORA H. (Lent), b. Sept. 14, 1866.
6. JAMES H. (Lent), b. Nov. 20, 1868.

1284. GEORGE W. DENICKE [8]; m. Mary Louisa Hart, Oct. 21, 1868
He d. Nov. 6, 1896. He was a prosperous dry goods merchant in Peekskill, N. Y., where he was held in much esteem. Children:

1. HARRY HART (Denicke), b. June 4, 1870; m. Grace
   Butterly.
2. LOUIS F. (Denicke), b. April 2, 1872; m. Lillian Maynard.
3. LILLY BELLE (Denicke), b. July 5, 1874; m. John J.
   Yellot.
4. GEORGE CLIFFORD (Denicke), b. Aug. 27, 1886.

1285. STEPHEN CRANE[6] [520], (John,[5] Zebulon,[4] Joseph,[3]
Jonathan,[2] Benjamin[1]), married Sarah Hadden. She was born
Sept. 10, 1769. He settled in New York City, where he died
Sept. 9, 1826. He married 2d, Mrs. Lydia (Hendrickson)
Brower, who was mother of his youngest son. Children:

1286—1. ANNA, b. Jan. 6, 1795.
1287—2. TAMER, b. March 8, 1798.
1288—3. GEORGE LANE, b. July 13, 1800.
1289—4. ANDREWS JAY, b. July 29, 1803.
1290—5. WARD, b. Aug. 2, 1808.
1291—6. JOHN, b. March 31, 1824.

1292. JOHN CRANE[6] [521], (John,[5] Zebulon,[4] Joseph,[3] Jona-
than,[2] Benjamin[1]), married Hannah Gregory, Oct. 29, 1795.
She was born Aug. 10, 1777. Their residence was in Putnam
County, N. Y. He died June 1, 1825. She died Aug. 1, 1853.
Children:

1293—1. SAMUEL HARVEY, b. Dec. 30, 1796.
1294—2. ELIZA, b. June 10, 1798.
1295—3. SALLY BETSEY, b. Dec. 30, 1799.
1296—4. ELIJAH, b. Oct. 25, 1801; d. April 25, 1856; unm.
1297—5. CLORINDA, b. June 16, 1803.
1298—6. NANCY, b. May 9, 1805.
1299—7. MARY ANN, b. Feb. 19, 1807; m. William Monk. She d.
        April 20, 1871. He d. March 28, 1888.
1300—8. HARRIETT, b. Dec. 4, 1808.
1301—9. ALSON BELDEN, b. Dec. 30, 1810; m. Jerusha Shaler; no chil-
        dren; d. Nov, 7, 1888.
1302—10. ADAH, b. April 30, 1813.
1303—11. ANNIS NOBLE, b. May 2, 1816; m. John Monk; d. March 17,
         1843; no children.
1304—12. ROSALINDA LYON, b. May 12, 1818.
1305—13. SUSAN AMELIA, b. April 9, 1820.

1306. ZILLAH CRANE[6] [522], (John,[5] Zebulon,[4] Joseph,[3]
Jonathan,[2] Benjamin[1]), married Nov. 29, 1792, Abraham Knox.
He was born March 4, 1761, and died Dec. 3, 1813. She died
May 31, 1869. Their residence was Red Hook, Dutchess County,
N. Y., and all their children, except the youngest, died there.

Children :

1. LEWIS (Knox), b. March 2, 1795; m. Patience Bailey; no children; d. Feb. 15, 1831.
2. JOHN CRANE (Knox), b. Dec. 31, 1796; d. Aug. 29, 1805.
3. PASCO (Knox), b. March 2, 1799; d. Aug. 27, 1805.
4. PLATT (Knox, b. Aug. 22, 1801; d. Aug. 31, 1805.
5. ARABELLA (Knox), b. Oct. 13, 1803; m. Andrews Joy Crane.
6. ANDREW PASCO (Knox), b. July 12, 1805; d. Dec. 27, 1869; unm.
7. JOHN CRANE (Knox), b. April 4, 1808; d. unm.
8. PLATT (Knox), b. May 9, 1810; d. Feb. 2, 1886; unm.
9. ABRAHAM PHILIP (Knox), b. Sept. 27, 1812; m. Elizabeth Cholwell; d. at Niles, Mich.

1307. NATHANIEL CRANE[6] [523], (John,[5] Zebulon,[4] Joseph,[3] Jonathan,[2] Benjamin[1]) married Martha Ann Townsend, Oct. 3, 1799. She was born Nov. 12, 1783, daughter of Benjamin Townsend, of Mahopac, and died May 1, 1825. He died Sept. 27, 1855. Their home was in Putnam County, N. Y. Children :

1308—1. JOHN ARTHUR, b. July 4, 1800; d. Sept. 9, 1804.
1309—2. TAMAR ANN, b. Jan. 4, 1802; d. Dec. 17, 1825.
1310—3. JAMES TOWNSEND, b. May 3, 1804; d. Dec. 14, 1826.
1311—4. CAROLINE ELIZA, b. June 20, 1806.
1312—5. FREDERICK AUGUSTUS, b. Oct. 17, 1808; d. Dec. 11, 1826.
1313—6. CHARLOTTE LOUISA, b. Dec. 27, 1810.
1314—7. JOSEPH HATFIELD, b. Sept. 11, 1813; m. Ann Eliza Brown, Nov. 1839; d. Feb. 17, 1864.
1315—8. NATHANIEL MORTON, b. Feb. 23, 1816; m. Amelia P. Tabor, May 4, 1844; d. Dec. 25, 1891.
1316—9. MARY ELIZABETH, b. July 29, 1818.
1317—10. AUGUSTA SOPHIA, b. Sept. 12, 1821.
1318—11. BENJAMIN TOWNSEND, b. Jan. 24, 1824.

1319. SARAH CRANE[6] [524], (John,[5] Zebulon,[4] Joseph,[3] Jonathan,[2] Benjamin[1]), married Alvah Trowbridge at Carmel, Putnam County, N. Y., Nov. 30, 1797. She died of measles April 6, 1833. He was born Sept. 4, 1779, and died at South East, N. Y., where he resided, June 10, 1856. Children :

1. PHINEAS BEARDSLEY (Trowbridge), b. Dec. 4, 1798; m. Sally B. Raymond.
2. ADAH ZILLAH (Trowbridge), b. Oct. 18, 1800; m. Levi Knox.
3. ALLERTON MONTGOMERY (Trowbridge), b. Feb. 24, 1803; m. Selina Coe.
4. ARALINDA (Trowbridge), b. Feb. 26, 1805; m. Orrin Richards.
5. WILLIAM CRANE (Trowbridge), b. April 15, 1807; m. Mary E. A. Hobby.
6. CORNELIA ANN (Trowbridge), b. Nov. 8, 1809; m. Reynolds Platt for his 2d wife.
7. ARABELLA CAROLINE (Trowbridge), b. June 28, 1812; m. Reynolds Platt for his 1st wife.
8. SARAH BELDEN (Trowbridge), b. March 21, 1821; m. David B. Rogers.

1320. PHINEAS BEARDSLEY TROWBRIDGE [1]; m. Sally Raymond. Children :

1. EDWIN M., b., Nov. 1, 1824; m. Sarah Marsh, and d. Aug. 29, 1854, leaving a daughter. His widow then m. —— Judd.

2. AMANDA, b. Dec. 5, 1826; d. Aug. 8, 1885.
3. JOHN C., b. Sept. 24, 1828; resides at Wing Station, Dutchess County, N. Y.
4. CORNELIA, b. April 1, 1831; d. Aug. 26, 1848.
5. WILLIAM R., b. May 6, 1833.'
6. GEORGE PLATT, b. July 19, 1840; d. April 15, 1845.

1321 WILLIAM R. TROWBRIDGE [5]; m. Maria W. Shelden. Children:

1. CORA B. (Trowbridge), b. Sept. 20, 1858; m. June 11, 1878, Arthur Dorn.
2. GEORGE A. (Trowbridge), b. Sept. 20, 1861; m. March 19, 1889, Eva Dutcher; reside at Wing Station.
3. ADA (Trowbridge), b. Dec. 27, 1863.
4. ELIZA (Trowbridge), b. April 17, 1866.

1322. ARABELLA CRANE[6] [525], (John,[5] Zebulon,[4] Joseph,[3] Jonathan,[2] Benjamin[1]) married 1st, Eleazer Watrous; 2d, Townsend Winters. They settled near York, Pa. She died July 4, 1854. Children:

1. WILLIAM (Watrous); went to Baltimore, Md.
2. CAROLINE (Winters).
3. EMILY (Winters).

1323. CLORINDA CRANE[6] [526], (John,[5] Zebulon,[4] Joseph,[3] Jonathan,[2] Benjamin[1]), born in Fredericksburg, Dutchess County, N. Y.* Married James Reed, Sept. 23, 1802. He was a farmer, and resided at South East, Putnam County, N. Y. He was born in Norwalk, Conn., March 19, 1780, and died May 23, 1825. She died March 26, 1868. Children:

1. HENRY CRANE (Reed), b. Nov. 21, 1803; m. Abby J. Young.
2. JAMES HARVEY (Reed), b. Aug. 7, 1805.
3. LEWIS AUGUSTUS (Reed), b. April 23, 1807.

1324. HENRY CRANE REED [1]; m. Abby J. Young, Jan. 15, 1834. She was dau. of Nathaniel and Catherine (Carpenter) Young. Children:

1. HENRY CARPENTER (Reed), b. Feb. 14, 1835, in New York city; m. Maria J. Wright; two children; both dead.
2. CATHERINE ANN (Reed), b. Dec. 26, 1844, in New York city; m. C. Ward Varian, Feb. 26, 1868. He served in the civil war.

1325. JAMES HARVEY REED [2]; m. Emily Hazen, April 2, 1826. She was a native of Carmel, N. Y.; b. March 28, 1811, dau. of Thomas and Anna (Smith) Hazen. He was a farmer, and settled in same town. He died Dec. 25, 1888. Children:

1. THOMAS HAZEN (Reed), b. Dec. 27, 1826.
2. HENRY AUGUSTUS (Reed), b. Feb. 11, 1829.
3. JAMES HARVEY (Reed), b. Feb. 6, 1832.
4. JOHN ADDISON (Reed), b. Nov. 23, 1834.
5. WILLIAM BELDEN (Reed), b. Feb. 23, 1838.
6. ABBY JULIA (Reed), b. Dec. 15, 1840.
7. ADELINE AUGUSTA (Reed), b. Sept. 18, 1843.

---

* In 1812 it was changed to Carmel, Putnam County.

8. FRANCIS EDGAR (Reed), b. May 8, 1846.
9. ANSEL HAZEN (Reed), b. July 12, 1848.
10. CHARLES ADRIAN (Reed), b. July 7, 1851.
11. GEORGE EDWARD (Reed), b. Feb. 25, 1854; m. 1st, May 29, 1877, Mary E. Hopkins, dau. of Arvah Hopkins. She d. Feb. 19, 1885; 2d, Oct. 14, 1891, Bessie Crane Foster, granddaughter of Betsey, daughter of Joseph, son of John.

1326. THOMAS HAZEN REED [1]; m. 1st, April 5, 1862, Nancy J. Tillott. She d. Feb. 6, 1855; 2d, Ann Augusta Crosby, Jan. 25, 1860. He was the first representative from Putnam County to the State Normal School at Albany. After graduating from there he taught in public and private schools for a time; then opened a private institution at Carmel, known as the Arcadian High School, erecting a building for that purpose, and employing several assistant teachers. He left the school to establish the Croton River Bank at Brewster in 1855, and was its cashier for a number of years. He was the first Republican Representative to the State Legislature from Putnam County, having been elected in 1862. He served two terms as School Commissioner. He is at present in the employ of the Bishop Gutta Percha Company of New York, and a resident of that city. Children :

1. EMMA PAULINE (Reed), b. March 9, 1861, at Brewster, N. Y.; d. June 9, 1876.
2. BYRON CROSBY (Reed), b. March 8, 1863.
3. EDWARD RADCLIFFE (Reed), b. May 19, 1866; d. Oct. 25, 1894.
4. CARRIE LOUISE (Reed), b. July 17, 1868.
5. BELLE CROSBY (Reed), b. Aug. 31, 1871; d. Nov. 11, 1889.
6. JULIA AUGUSTA (Reed), b. Sept. 10, 1872.
7. PAULINE CROSBY (Reed), b. Aug. 20, 1878; d. Dec. 25, 1878.

1327. HENRY AUGUSTUS REED [2]; m. May 14, 1859, Alice Amelia Boardman; secretary and manager of Bishop Gutta Percha Company, New York city. He learned telegraphy when a young man. In 1849 opened at Croton Falls the first telegraph office on the line of the Harlem Railroad. In 1851 had charge of the office at Hudson, N. Y. In 1852 took charge of the telegraph office at Poughkeepsie, where he assisted Prof. S. F. B. Morse in experiments relating to long distance telegraphy. He had a bookstore in Poughkeepsie for twenty years. Having disposed of his business there, he went in 1879 to New York with the Bishop Gutta Percha Company, and is at present secretary and treasurer of that establishment. He is reliable authority on all kinds of electric cables, and planned the first cables which were successful in carrying high currents under ground in New York, and all cables used by the government in electric buoy work. Children :

1. WILLIAM BOARDMAN (Reed), b. May 27, 1860; graduate Union College 1882.
2. ALICE AUGUSTA (Reed), b. June 22, 1862.
3. HENRY DOUGLASS (Reed), b. Feb. 11, 1869; graduate Stevens Institute Technology, 1872.

4. LOUIS FRANCIS (Reed), b. June 21, 1871; graduate
    Law School, New York city, 1892; lawyer New
    York city.

1328. JAMES HARVEY REED [3]; m. twice; to second wife, Sarah F.
    Griffin, Jan. 25, 1871, at Yorktown, Winchester County,
    N. Y.; lived in New York city 1851 to 1885; since that date
    in Peekskill. Child:

    1. CAROLYN S. (Reed), b. Oct. 24, 1874, in New York
        city.

1329. JOHN ADDISON REED [4]; m. Deborah Hendrickson of New
    York city. Children:

    1. ARTHUR (REED), b. April 6, 1865; business in New
        York city.
    2. HENRY FOREMAN (Reed), b. Jan. 6, 1867; business
        in New York city.
    3. CHARLES EDGAR (Reed), b. Jan. 18, 1869; m. Edith M.
        Robinson, of Battle Creek, Mich. He graduated
        from Jefferson Medical College, Philadelphia, 1895,
        and Oct. 17, 1896, sailed for Canton, China, as
        medical missionary.
    4. ELEANOR ELIZABETH (Reed), b. Oct. 4, 1870; killed
        in railroad accident near Towner's, N. Y. C. &
        H. R. R. R., Aug. 26, 1893.
    5. SUSAN HENDRICKSON (Reed), b. Jan. 14, 1873.
    6. LOUISE ALTHEA (Reed), b. Sept. 18, 1874.

1330. WILLIAM BELDEN REED [5]; m. Nov. 12, 1868, Arietta, dau. of
    Oliver and Maria (Snow) Crane, of Brewster. Children:

    1. WILLIAM BELDEN (Reed), b. Jan. 29, 1876; graduate
        Princeton College, June, 1896; civil engineer,
        employed by Metropolitan Traction Co., New
        York city.
    2. HARRY CRANE (Reed), b. March 2, 1885; d. in infancy.

1331. FRANCIS EDGAR REED [8]; m. Estella J. Sloat, of Carmel, N.
    Y. He d. Dec. 19, 1881; was a carpenter and builder.
    Children:

    1. SAMUEL JAMES (Reed), b. Oct. 6, 1872.
    2. ERASTUS DARWIN (Reed), b. Feb. 1, 1874; graduate
        New York Dental College, June, 1896; practicing
        in New York city.

1332. ANSEL HAZEN REED [9]; m. Margaretta Carson; was head
    of book and stationery department at Wanamaker's, Phila-
    delphia, for eight years; one of the foreign purchasers for
    that establishment. He d. Feb. 7, 1888. Children:

    1. EDITH ADELINE (Reed), b. March 10, 1875, at
        Philadelphia.
    2. HARVEY ANSEL (Reed), b. June 12, 1883, at Phila-
        phia.

1333. CHARLES ADRIAN REED [10]; m. Nov. 26 1882, Ida E. Halstead,
    of New York city. He graduated from the Law School,
    New York City University, 1880. Children:

    1. EMILY HAZEN (Reed), b. April 13, 1884.
    2. GUERNSEY SACKETT (Reed), b. Feb. 4, 1886; d. Aug.
        4, 1887

1334. LEWIS AUGUSTUS REED [3]; m. 1832, Lydia J. Jessup, of
Greenwich, Conn. She d. and he m. 2d, Ann Augusta
Jessup; m. 3d, Ann M. Waring, by whom he had Thomas
Henry. Children:

 1. EMILY AUGUSTA (Reed), b. April 8, 1833.
 2. JOSEPH CRANE (Reed), b. Dec. 30, 1835.
 3. LEWIS AUGUSTUS (Reed), b. Sept. 11, 1838.
 4. AURELIA J. (Reed), b. Aug. 9, 1842; d. Jan. 6, 1847.
 5. SAMUEL J. (Reed), b. Nov. 20, 1844; d. Sept. 18, 1863.
 6. THOMAS HENRY (Reed), b. Sept. 30, 1859; drowned
   Aug. 10, 1881, at Ridgefield, Conn.

1335. BELDEN CRANE[6] [529], (Zebulon,[5] Zebulon,[4] Joseph,[3]
Jonathan,[2] Benjamin[1]), married Jan. 9, 1791, Esther Paddock.
She was born April 7, 1771. They settled in South East, Putnam County, N. Y., but about the year 1832 removed to Tompkins County, whither two of their eldest children had already
located. He died Dec. 2, 1848. She died April 23, 1859.

Children :

1336—1. CLARINDA, b. Nov. 1, 1791.
1337—2. CHARLES, b. March 16, 1793; m. —— ——, 1814; no children; d. May, 1877.
1338—3. ARMINDA, b. Feb. 18, 1795; m. Isaac Pearce; lived in South
   East; no children; d. June 7, 1883.
1339—4. AMANDA, b. Aug. 31, 1797; d. Aug. 26, 1798.
1340—5. ELISHA, b. Oct. 15, 1799.
1341—6. MARY, b. Nov. 26, 1803; m. John Smith; no children; d.
   Oct. 17, 1871.
1342—7. GEORGE BELDEN, b. July 21, 1806.

1343. SAMUEL CRANE[6] [533], (Zebulon,[5] Zebulon,[4] Joseph,[3]
Jonathan,[2] Benjamin[1]), married 1st, Mary Haines; 2d, widow
of Samuel Merrick, whose maiden name was Letitia Weeks.

Children :

1344—1. VIOLETTA, b. 1805; d. 1875.
1345—2. RUTH; d. aged 18 years.
1346—3. JESSE; d. aged 22 years.
1347—4. ABBY JANE; m. Dilazon Thompkins; d. aged 22 years.
1348—5. NORMAN; m. and had eight children; removed to Missouri.
1349—6. JOHN WEEKS, b. April 10, 1819.
1350—7. EMILY, b. May 27, 1822.

Children of Samuel and Letitia (Weeks) Merrick :

 1. NANCY (Merrick).
 2. ORRIN (Merrick).
 3. ELIZA (Merrick).
 4. SAMUEL (Merrick).

1351. ZEBULON CRANE[6] [535], (Zebulon,[5] Zebulon,[4] Joseph,[3]
Jonathan,[2] Benjamin[1]), married Welthan Crane, daughter of
Col. Thaddeus and Lydia (Read) (Baxter) Crane (see page 48),
Rev. Samuel M. Phelps, A.M., performing the ceremony. He
died Aug. 17, 1848. She died Sept. 6, 1860. Children:

1352—1. SARAH MARIA, b. Jan. 28, 1810; d. Dec. 12, 1866; unm.
1353—2. HARRISON, b. April 10, 1817.

1354—3. CHARLOTTE, b. July 4, 1826.
1355—4. ROXANNA, b. April 22, 1831; d. Dec. 9, 1880; unm.

1356. LEWIS CRANE[6] [536], (Zebulon,[5] Zebulon,[4] Joseph,[3] Jonathan,[2] Benjamin[1]), was twice married. By first wife he had a son Nelson. His second wife was Martha Haines.
Children :

1357—1. NELSON.
1358—2. LEONARD BELDEN.
1359—3. MARTHA JANE.
1360—4. REBECCA.
1361—5. RACHAEL.
1362—6. ELIZABETH.

1363. AMZI CRANE[6] [537], (Zebulon,[5] Zebulon,[4] Joseph,[3] Jonathan,[2] Benjamin[1]), married Adilla Hopkins. They removed to Ohio in 1831. Children :

1364 —1. MARY ANN.
1365—2. ALSON BELDEN.
1366—3. ALBACINDA.
1367—4. WASHINGTON.
1368—5. BETSEY.
1369—6. ZEBULON.

1370. MATILDA CRANE[6] [578], (Jonathan,[5] Joseph,[4] Joseph,[3] Jonathan,[2] Benjamin[1]), married Isaac Reed, of South East, Putnam County, N. Y., where they resided, and where she died.
Child :

1. ORVILLE (Reed), who married and resided in New York City.

1371. JOSIAH CRANE[6] [579], (Jonathan,[5] Joseph,[4] Joseph,[3] Jonathan,[2] Benjamin[1]), married Keziah Hall, Nov. 27, 1794. She was born in South East, Putnam County, N. Y., July 26, 1775. He was a farmer, and settled at that place. He died Nov. 28, 1842. She died April 20, 1849. Children :

1372—1. BETSY C., b. Jan. 15, 1796; d. Nov. 14, 1819.
1373—2. PHILANDER, b. April 5, 1797.
1374—3. JOHN, b. March 28, 1799.
1375—4. OLIVER, b. Aug. 3, 1800.
1376—5. STELLA, b. March 24, 1802; d. Feb. 17, 1827.
1377—6. SUSAN, b. Nov. 23, 1803; d. April 26, 1814.
1378—7. WALTER B., b. Dec. 14, 1807; m. Nov. 19, 1833; d. Sept. 5, 1887.
1379—8. DEBORAH A., b. Dec. 9, 1809.
1380—9. CLARRISSA, b. Feb. 12, 1812; d. June 27, 1853.
1381—10. DANIEL T., b. July 2, 1813; d. May 31, 1865.
1382—11. DARIUS P., b. Dec. 28, 1816.
1383—12. SARAH (or SALLY) BETSY, b. Oct. 23, 1818; m. James O. Wood, of Danbury, Conn.; d. Oct. 23, 1893; no children.

1384. DEBORAH CRANE[6] [580], (Jonathan,[5] Joseph,[4] Joseph,[3] Jonathan,[2] Benjamin[1]), married Isaac Meeker, of Reading, Conn., in 1806. He was born March 8, 1768, and died Sept. 14, 1850. Deborah Crane was his second wife. By a former marriage he had two children. Deborah had one.

Child :

1. GEORGE CRANE (Meeker), b. May 24, 1807; d. May 14, 1872; m.
   April 3, 1831, Mary Ann Dobbs, of Danbury, Conn. She was
   b. Aug. 23, 1807; d. Jan. 11, 1890. Children:
   1. ISABELLA (Meeker), b. April 15, 1832; d. Feb. 19, 1886.
   2. AUGUSTA (Meeker), b. Dec. 7, 1833.
   3. HELEN (Meeker), b. Aug. 2, 1835; resides at Danbury,
      Conn.; regent Mary Wooster Chapter, D. A. R.

1385. ISABELLA MEEKER [1]; m. Sept. 16, 1856, Hon. William F. Taylor, of Danbury, Conn. He was b. Oct. 4, 1824, and d. Oct.
   3, 1889. Children:
   1. HOWARD WHEDON (Taylor), b. Aug. 11, 1858.
   2. HELEN MEEKER (Taylor), b. Feb. 13, 1860.
   3. MARY BELLE (Taylor), b. June 20, 1863.

1386. MARY BELLE TAYLOR [3]; m. Dec. 7, 1886, William H. Daniels,
   of Brooklyn, N. Y. Children:
   1. CARRIE BELLE (Daniels), b. Sept. 25, 1890.
   2. WINTHROP TAYLOR (Daniels), b. Aug. 12, 1893.
   3. RICHARD GILBERT (Daniels), b. Dec. 7, 1896.

1387. AUGUSTA MEEKER [2]; m. June 12, 1858, Amos N. Stebbins, of·
   Danbury, Conn. He was b. April 16, 1833, and d. Feb. 5,
   1870. Children:
   1. GEORGE MEEKER (Stebbins), b. Dec. 11, 1861.
   2. FANNY BELLE (Stebbins), b. Oct. 12, 1863.
   3. JULIA LACEY (Stebbins), b. Aug. 28, 1865.
   4. AMOS NEHEMIAH (Stebbins), b. June 24, 1870.

1388. GEORGE MEEKER STEBBINS [1]; m. April 14, 1888, Mary E.
   Hamilton, of Danbury, Conn. Child:
   1. SAMUEL (Stebbins), b. Jan. 15, 1895.

1389. ISAAC CRANE[6] [581], (Jonathan,[5] Joseph,[4] Joseph,[3]
Jonathan,[2] Benjamin[1]), married Mary Ketchum, of South East,
Putnam County, N. Y. Children:

1390—1. RUHAMA; m. 1st, Reuben Tucker; 2d, Charles Avery; lived
   at St. Augustine, Fla.; she d. at South East, N. Y.
1391—2. MATILDA; m. Charles Sawyer, of Colebrook, Conn.; d. in
   Derby, Conn.
1392—3. BERTHA; m. Richard E. Arthur, of Sing Sing, N. Y.; d. in
   Passaic, N. J.; had 1 son and 2 daughters.
1393—4. CHARLOTTE; m. Dr. Albert Roberts, of Sharon, Conn.; had
   a daughter Charlotte Elethea, who m. Abiram Chamberlain, of Meriden, Conn.

1394. ANSON CRANE[6] [582], (Jonathan,[5] Joseph,[4] Joseph,[3]
Jonathan,[2] Benjamin[1]), married Dec. 23, 1806, Experience
Brush, a native of Huntington, Long Island, b. March 13, 1786.
He succeeded to his father's farm in South East, Putnam County,
N. Y., and here he spent his life. The place is now (1898)
owned by Charles C. Fitzhugh, and is known as "Fairview
Manor." The coat of arms used as a frontispiece in Vol. I. of
the Crane Genealogy was preserved in this family, and a sketch
procured from his daughter Miss Kate Eliza Crane. Children:

1395—1. GARRITT BRUSH, b. Sept. 3, 1807; d. Nov. 17, 1892.

1396—2. ESTHER ANN, b. Feb. 1, 1809; d. March 2, 1884; m. Chester
         Crosby; no children.
1397—3. JOHN PLATT, b. Dec. 21, 1811.
1398—4. JAMES LEWIS, b. Oct. 26, 1813.
1399—5. RUFUS ERASTUS, b. June 3, 1815.
1400—6. ISAAC AUGUSTUS, b. Feb. 20, 1817.
1401—7. MARY LOUISE, b. Nov. 26, 1819; d. in Morrisania, Sept. 8,
         1869.
1402—8. ANSON BELDING, b. Nov. 6, 1821; d. June 5, 1865, at Brat-
         tleboro, Vt.
1403—9. VIRGINIA EXPERIENCE, b. May 3, 1824; d. March 24, 1884.
1404-10. KATE ELIZA, b. May 26, 1832; resides (1896) Plainfield, N. J.

1405. ESTHER CRANE[6] [584], (Jonathan,[5] Joseph,[4] Joseph,[3]
Jonathan,[2] Benjamin[1]), married Platt Brush, of South East, N. Y.
She lived and died there.   Children :

     1. ALBERT (Brush); married; lived and d. in South East.
     2. EMILY (Brush); married; lived in New York City; d. young.
     3. JACOB (Brush); d. young.
     4. SUSAN (Brush); d. young.
     5. MATILDA (Brush); married; lived and d. in South East.
     6. SARAH (Brush); married; lived in Reading, Conn.; d.
     7. ALONZO (Brush); married; lived and d. in South East.

1406. CARSO CRANE[6] [588], (Joseph,[5] Joseph,[4] Joseph,[3]
Jonathan,[2] Benjamin[1]), married at South East, N. Y., 1st, Dec.
12, 1821, Emily Young; 2d, March 22, 1848, Mary Ann Crosby.
He settled in Phelps, N. Y.   Children :

     1407—1. ANER B.
     1408—2. JANE A.
     1409—3. JOSEPH.
     1410—4. SARAH.
     1411—5. GERALDINE.
     1412—6. CHARLES.

1413. CHARLOTTE CRANE[6] [590], (Solomon,[5] Joseph,[4] Joseph,[3] Jonathan,[2] Benjamin[1]), married Samuel Field, Jan. 1,
1817.   Children :

     1. CAROLINE (Field), b. Dec. 29, 1817.
     2. SAMUEL AUGUSTUS (Field), b. Aug. 13, 1820; m. Clara Lewis;
         d. Oct. 27, 1866; no children:

1414. CAROLINE FIELD [1]; m. William Taber Rumsey; Oct. 20,
       1842.   Children :

          1. WILLIAM HERBERT (Rumsey), b. Oct. 10, 1843.
          2. ANN AUGUSTA (Rumsey), b. April 6, 1845; d. Oct. 24,
              1845.
          3. FRANCES AMELIA (Rumsey), b. Aug. 23, 1846.
          4. HANNAH TABER (Rumsey), b. Feb. 14, 1848.
          5. SAMUEL PIERSON (Rumsey), b. Dec. 18, 1850.
          6. CHARLOTTE IRENE (Rumsey), b. March 21, 1854.

1415. POLLY CRANE[6] [591], (Solomon,[5] Joseph,[4] Joseph,[3]
Jonathan,[2] Benjamin[1]), married Comfort Field, Jan. 8, 1823.

Child :

1. CHARLOTTE (Field), b. Jan. 16, 1826.

1416. CHARLOTTE FIELD [1]; m. George Kirby Taber, Oct. 13, 1845.
Children :
    1. GILBERT FIELD (Taber), b. Sept. 16, 1846.
    2. HANNAH KIRBY (Taber), b. Jan. 2, 1850; d. Oct. 16,
       1871.
    . MARTHA ANNA (Taber), b. Feb. 15, 1857.
    . ALICIA HOPKINS (Taber), b. April 6, 1859.
    ß. CHARLOTTE FIELD (Taber), b. July 5, 1861; d. Feb.
       23, 1880.

1417. GILBERT FIELD TABER [1]; m. Mary Burr Allen, May 13, 1868.
Children :
    1. HARRIET ALLEN (Taber), b. June 10, 1872.
    2. HANNAH KIRBY (Taber), b. Nov. 26, 1873.
    3. GEORGE KIRBY (Taber), b. Sept. 1, 1875; d. Jan. 17,
       1879.
    4. CHARLOTTE FIELD (Taber), b. July 26, 1880; d. March
       27, 1882.
    5. MARY ALLEN (Taber), b. Jan. 3, 1883.

1418. OLIVER CRANE[6] [593], (Solomon,[5] Joseph,[4] Joseph,[3]
Jonathan,[2] Benjamin[1]), married Laura M. Leach. He was a
farmer, and resided in Patterson, Putnam County, N. Y., on the
homestead left by his father, and where their children were born.
He died about 1835. Children :

1419—1. ROBERT, b June, 1830; d. October, 1859; unm.
1420—2. CHARLOTTE, b. Jan. 23, 1832; lives in Patterson, N. Y.
1421—3. MARY, b. Nov. 21, 1834.

1422. HENRY CRANE[6] [595], (Isaac,[5] Joseph,[4] Joseph,[3]
Jonathan,[2] Benjamin[1]), married Jan. 15, 1805, Amarilla H.
Moses, sister of Dr. Elisha D. Moses, who married Mary Ann
Crane, and daughter of Elisha and Hannah Merrill Moses. She
was born Aug. 1, 1789, and died April 17, 1866. They resided
at Crane's Corners, Litchfield, Herkimer County, N. Y. He died
March, 1876. Children :

1423—1. MOSES, b. May 1, 1809; d. Dec. 23, 1810.
1424—2. SHERBURNE HENRY, b. May 7, 1812.
1425—3. ADDISON MOSES, b. July 2, 1814.
1426—4. SYRENE HANNAH, b. Aug. 26, 1816.
1427—5. DANFORD ELISHA, b. July 22, 1818.
1428—6. IRA MERRILL, b. Sept. 20, 1820; d. Sept. 17, 1837.
1429—7. EMERSON TIMOTHY, b. Oct. 5, 1822.
1430—8. AMELIA PHŒBE, b. Sept. 14, 1824.
1431—9. ALBERT EDMUND, b. Oct. 27, 1826.
1432-10. CHARLES ARDEN, b. Jan. 20, 1829.

1433. SARAH CRANE[6] [596], married William Plumb. She
died 1854.

1434. CHARLES CRANE[6] [597], (Isaac,[5] Joseph,[4] Joseph,[3]
Jonathan,[2] Benjamin[1]), married by Rev. Ezekiel Chapman, of
Lima, Oct. 10, 1811, at Bloomfield, Ontario County, N. Y.,
10

Huldah, daughter of Amos and Lucy Bronson. She was born in Massachusetts, April 30, 1792. He died at East Bloomfield, N. Y., June 2, 1841. She died at Le Roy, N. Y., Feb. 5, 1854. He was a merchant in Weedsport for a time. Children :

1435—1. ALBERT, b. June 22, 1820.
1436—2. WALTER, b. July 13, 1827; for some years was engaged in dry goods trade and as a dealer in real estate in Detroit, Mich. He was commissioned as major and paymaster by Abraham Lincoln, March 11, 1863; and as brevet lieutenant-colonel by A. Johnson, Nov. 15, 1865. Mr. Crane removed from Syracuse, N. Y., to Detroit, in the year 1845. Here he died aged 71 years. At the time of his death (1898) his estate was valued at one million dollars. A considerable portion of this wealth it is said came to him through a claim or title he purchased to the Joe Harvey farm (so called), consisting of about two hundred acres of land, fronting on the river, between Fort Wayne and the copper works, and extending back from the river a mile or more. For many years this claim was in litigation, Mr. Crane finally in 1878 securing a compromise with other claimants and thus acquiring the bulk of this very valuable estate. He left a widow.

1437. HUNTER CRANE[6] [599], (Isaac,[5] Joseph,[4] Joseph,[3] Jonathan,[2] Benjamin[1]), married Maria McMullen, and settled at Sackett's Harbor, Jefferson County, N. Y. He served in the war of 1812 at Sackett's Harbor; was a merchant, and died at Oswego, April, 1859. Children :

1438—1. WILLIAM HUNTER, b. June 14, 1817.
1439—2. ALBERT SEARS.
1440—3. FRANK GREGORY.
1441—4. RICHARD RANKIN.
1442—5. MARY A.
1443—6. CHARLOTTE.
1444—7. JANE E.
1445—8. CASSANDRA B.
1446—9. CLARINDA P.
1447-10. FANNY C.
1448-11. SARAH M.

1449. ALBERT CRANE[6] [601]. (Isaac,[5] Joseph,[4] Joseph,[3] Jonathan,[2] Benjamin[1]), married 1st, Margaret M. Oliver, Feb. 22, 1824. She was born April 29, 1806, in Seneca County, N. Y., and died Dec. 3, 1837, in Auburn, N. Y. He then married Abigail Maynard; was a merchant in Oswego, N. Y., and died Aug. 29, 1847, at Lancaster, Mass. Children :

1450—1. FRANCIS, b. Aug. 29, 1825; d. Sept. 7, 1825.
1451—2. DeWITT CLINTON, b. Nov. 10, 1826; d. Sept. 23, 1880.
1452—3. ARZA, b. Dec. 5, 1828.
1453—4. ANN ELIZA, b. July 4, 1831; m. Frank P. Fisher; no children.
1454—5. ALVIRA, b. Jan. 27, 1834.
1455—6. MARGARET EVELYN, b. July 15, 1837; d. July 28, 1838.

1456. MARY ANN CRANE[6] [606], (Ira,[5] Joseph,[4] Joseph,[3] Jonathan,[2] Benjamin[1]), married Jan. 18, 1821, in Herkimer, N. Y., Dr. Elisha D. Moses, of Rochester, N. Y. He was born

Feb. 12, 1790, in Canton, Hartford County, Conn., and after his marriage he settled in Portage, Allegany County, N. Y., and afterwards removed to Rochester, where he died Oct. 19, 1871. She died there Feb. 28, 1873. Children:

1. ELIZA ANN (Moses), b. Nov. 19, 1821.
2. AMERICA (Moses), b. Sept. 13, 1823.

1457. JOHN CRANE[6] [607], (Ira,[5] Joseph,[4] Joseph,[3] Jonathan,[2] Benjamin[1]), was twice married. Married his 2d wife in Belfast, Canada; was living with one of his daughters at time of his death. Children:

1458—1. BETSEY.
1459—2. RUTH.

1460. FANNY CRANE[6] [612], (Ira,[5] Joseph,[4] Joseph,[3] Jonathan,[2] Benjamin[1]), married 2d, Henry Harrington, of Camillus, Onondaga County, N. Y. By a former marriage to a Mr. Wilson she had a son, who is supposed to have died in California. Children:

1. MARY ANN (Harrington).
2. CLARRISA (Harrington).
3. FRANCES (Harrington).
4. BRADFORD (Harrington).

1461. JANE CRANE[6] [613], (Ira,[5] Joseph,[4] Joseph,[3] Jonathan,[2] Benjamin[1]), married Simon Trask, June 14, 1831. He was born April 5, 1808. She was born Jan. 27, 1810. They removed to the State of Illinois. He died Oct. 31, 1865. She died in Galesburg, March 29, 1886. Children:

1. DELOS R. (Trask), b. Sept. 12, 1832.
2. GILBERT C. (Trask), b. July 14, 1834.
3. OZELL (Trask), b. March 10, 1836.
4. EDWIN W. (Trask). b. July 31, 1838.
5. RIVERUS H. (Trask), b. Sept. 30, 1841.
6. CLARRISA J. (Trask), b. Nov. 30, 1844.

1462. DELOS R. TRASK [1]; m. Mary A. Shafer, Dec. 23, 1862. She was b. March 31, 1842. They reside (1898) at Karoma, Oklahoma. Children:

1, LUELLA JANE (Trask), b. Aug. 10, 1865; m. Sept. 3, 1884, Rollo Constant.
2. RIVERUS EDWIN (Trask), b. Oct. 16, 1870.

1463. OZELL TRASK [3]; m. Cortena A. Forbes, Feb. 11, 1863. Children:

1. GILBERT FORBES (Trask), b. May 22, 1865.
2. BELLE LITTLE (Trask), b. June 10, 1869.
3. GRACIE JANE (Trask), b. Oct. 22, 1875.
4. ISAAC OZELL (Trask), b. May 4, 1877.

1464. EDWIN W. TRASK [4]; m. 1st, Adela C. Hawkins, Oct. 26, 1864; 2d. Emma C. Rapp, June 15, 1881. She was b. Jan. 20, 1861. His first wife d. April 30, 1877, leaving one child. Child:

1. LILLIAN L. (Trask); b. Jan. 24, 1870; residence at Brooklyn, N. Y., 327 State street.

1465. RIVERUS H. TRASK [5]; m. Helen E. Bates, Aug. 22, 1876. She
was b. Dec. 10, 1853. Resides at Ottawa, Ill. Children :

   1. JULIA ESTELLA (Trask), b. March 25, 1878.
   2. HELEN BATES (Trask), b. Jan. 6, 1887.
   3. ODESSA CRANE (Trask), b. Oct. 5, 1889.

1466. CLARRISA J. TRASK [6]; m. 1st, Henry Casner, Jan. 31, 1865;
2d, Tilghman H. Gentry, Oct. 16, 1871. He was b. Oct. 26,
1841. Residence at Galesburg, Ill. Children :

   1. CORA ABBIE (Casner), b. Oct. 3, 1865; m. Henry
      Baker, June 24, 1891.
   2. ADDIE MAY (Gentry), b. Sept. 27, 1874.

1467. LUELLA JANE TRASK [1]; m. Rollo Constant, Sept. 3, 1884.
Children :

   1. GILBERT CLINTON (Constant), b. Aug. 28, 1885.
   2. JOSEPH WILLIAM (Constant), b. Oct. 27, 1887.
   3. MARY ANETA (Constant), b. May 16, 1893.

1468. GILBERT CRANE[6] [615], (Ira,[5] Joseph,[4] Joseph,[3] Jonathan,[2] Benjamin[1]), married Helen Crowner, of Portage, Allegany
County, N. Y., and settled in New York city. After a residence
there of four years they removed to Albany, where for twenty
years their home was on Troy Road. From there the family
went to Lansingburg for five years. Then Mr. Crane purchased
a large property in the city of Rochester, where he remained
until his death, which occurred in the year 1887. She was born
1812, and died in Rochester in 1880. Children :

1469—1. CHARLOTTE AUGUSTA, b. ——; d. at Portage, 1839.
1470—2. HELEN E., b. ——.
1471—3. CHARLOTTE, b. ——; m. Wm. M. Stewart, Rochester.
1472—4. ELIZABETH, b. ——; d. Sept. 25, 1861.
1473—5. GILBERT, b. ——; d. on Troy Road, 1846.

1474. DANIEL CRANE[6] [618], (Daniel,[5] Joseph,[4] Joseph,[3]
Jonathan,[2] Benjamin[1]), married Jan. 6, 1824, Elsie Ann
Demarest at Catskill, Greene County, N. Y., where she was
born July 24, 1801, and where for many years they made their
home. About 1835 they removed to Albany, N. Y., where their
three youngest children were born. Mrs. Crane died in New
York city March 18, 1874. Children :

1475—1. HENRY DEMAREST, b. Feb. 27, 1825.
1476—2. EMMA, b. Aug. 31, 1826; d. Nov. 19, 1826.
1477—3. CHARLES STUART, b. Dec. 14, 1827; d. Feb. 5, 1835.
1478—4. HIRAM AUGUSTUS, b. Aug. 26, 1829.
1479—5. EDWARD PAYSON, b. March 6, 1832.
1480—6. THOMAS SMITH, b. Dec. 13, 1833.
1481—7. WILLIAM NEVINS, b. May 19, 1836.
1482—8. EMMELINE MATILDA, b. July 29, 1838.
1483—9. SARAH ELLEN, b. Nov. 14, 1840.

1484. CYNTHIA CRANE[6] [619], (Daniel,[5] Joseph,[4] Joseph,[3]
Jonathan,[2] Benjamin[1]), married —— Whittlesey. She died
Nov. 3, 1825. Children :

   1. EDWARD N. (Whittlesey), b. May 16, 1823.

2. GILBERT B. (Whittlesey), b. Aug. 9, 1825.
The widow of the latter, Annie Whittlesey, resides at No. 2 Summer Place, Newark, N. J.

1485. SUSAN CRANE[6] [620], (Daniel,[5] Joseph,[4] Joseph,[3] Jonathan,[2] Benjamin[1]), married Henry Pratt, of Stamford, N. Y. Child:

    1. EMILY (Pratt), m. Henry Gilbert. Children:
       -1. FRANK (Gilbert).
       2. EMILY (Gilbert), m. Henry Cook.
       3. SARAH (Gilbert).

1486. HIRAM CRANE[6] [621], (Daniel,[5] Joseph,[4] Joseph,[3] Jonathan,[2] Benjamin[1]), married Emeline Demarest, Nov. 25, 1830, at Catskill, N. Y., of which place she was a native. She was born Aug. 27, 1809, and died in Claverack, N. Y., May 6, 1832. He died in Elmira, May 25, 1853. Child:

    1487—1. THEODORE W., b. Sept. 26, 1831, at Havana, N. Y. He is a coal dealer; resides in Elmira, N. Y.; m. Dec. 7, 1858, Susan Langdon, a native of Spencer; born Feb. 18, 1836.

1488. JOSEPH AUGUSTUS CRANE[6] [622], (Daniel,[5] Joseph,[4] Joseph,[3] Jonathan,[2] Benjamin[1]), married 1st, at Davenport, Delaware County, N. Y., June 25, 1834, Mary Esther Goodrich. She was a native of that place; born Nov. 5, 1812, and died there Jan. 26, 1840; 2d, Sept. 16, 1856, Mary Fisher, daughter of Nahum and Betsy Harrington Fisher, of Westborough, Mass., where she was born Feb. 22, 1825. He was a lumber merchant, having been engaged in that business in Albany, N. Y. and Fall River, Mass. He died at Albany, April 16, 1877. Children:

    1489—1. THEODORE DWIGHT, b. June 9, 1835; d. Aug. 31, 1836.
    1490—2. ELLEN CORNELIA, b. May 26, 1837.
    1491—3. HENRY MARTYN, b. Feb. 24, 1859; d. Oct. 4, 1859, at Fall River.
    1492—4. MARY FISHER, b. Feb. 22, 1861.

1493. AMANDA M. CRANE[6] [625], (Josiah N.[5] Joseph,[4] Joseph,[3] Jonathan,[2] Benjamin[1]), married William Mervine in 1815. He was rear admiral in the United States navy. Died at Utica, N. Y., in 1868, in the 78th year of his age. She died in May, 1874, aged 78 years. Children:

    1. WILLIAM C. (Mervine), m. Martha Sawyer.
    2. CHARLES H. (Mervine), m. Helen McDonald.
    3. EMILY M. (Mervine), m. Leander M. Drury.
    4. HENRY G. (Mervine), m. Eliza Fairman.
    5. MARY A. (Mervine), m. Edward Sturgis.
    6. CASSARINUS B. (Mervine), captain in Union army; d. at City Point Hospital, Aug. 17, 1864.

1494. GEORGE ROBINSON CRANE[6] [629], (Arzah,[5] Joseph,[4] Joseph,[3] Jonathan,[2] Benjamin[1]), married 1st, Lily Sweet, of Troy, N. Y. She died leaving no issue. Married 2d, Mary Louisa, daughter of Daniel and Sarah Margaret (Prout) Taylor; settled in Troy; but about 1851 removed to Addison, Vt., where

he remained a few years.   January, 1856, found the family again in Troy, N. Y.   Children :

1495—1. JUNIUS, d. in infancy.
1496—2. ALBERT, d. in infancy.
1497—3. LILLEIS ALBERTINE, b. Aug. 8, 1849.
1498—4. SARAH ELLEN, b. Oct. 10, 1851.
1499—5. IDA, b. March 6, 1852.
1500—6. CHARLES EDGAR, b. Dec. 20, 1854.
1501—7. FRANCES ANN, b. Jan. 29, 1856.

1502. LAURA BELDEN CRANE[6] [632], (Arzah,[5] Joseph,[4] Joseph,[3] Jonathan,[2] Benjamin[1]), married Nov. 15, 1841, in St. Stephen's Church, Middlebury, Vt. Rev. Henry More Davis, Rev. J. W. Diller performing the ceremony. She died Jan. 4, 1845, in the house where she was born.   Child :

1. LAURA ELIZABETH (Davis), b. Sept. 10, 1842, at Vergennes, Vt.; m. June 18, 1866, Albert Kendall Broughton in St. Paul's Church, Salem, Washington County, N. Y., her father officiating. Children :

    1. LAURA ELIZABETH (Broughton), b. June 12, 1867, at Salem.
    2. ALICE HARRIET (Broughton), b. Dec. 17, 1868, at Salem.
    3. HENRIETTA (Broughton), b. Oct. 3, 1870, at Salem.
    4. ALBERT DAVIS (Broughton), b. July 14, 1872, at Salem.
    5. CHARLES DUBOIS (Broughton), b. Oct. 17, 1874, at Salem.
    6. LYDIA (Broughton), b. Sept. 14, 1883; d. Sept. 17, 1883.
    7. ANNA B. (Broughton), b. Sept. 9, 1885, at Salem.

1503. LAURA ELIZABETH BROUGHTON [1]; m. Harry Evans Cole in St. Paul's Church, Salem, Oct. 2, 1889, by Rev. John Henry Houghton. Children :

    1. MARGARET BROUGHTON (Cole), b. Oct. 14, 1892, at Greenbush, N. Y.
    2. HUGH BROUGHTON (Cole), b. May 29, 1896, at New York city.

1504. ALICE HARRIET BROUGHTON [2]; m. June 25, 1891, Clarence Houghton in St. Paul's Church, Salem, N. Y., Rev. John Henry Houghton officiating. Children :

    1. LAURA ELIZABETH (Houghton), } twins, b. Jan. 17,
                                   } 1895, at Green-
    2. FRANCES MILDRED (Houghton), } bush, N. Y.

1505. HENRIETTA BROUGHTON [3]; married Walter Graham Murphy, June 30, 1892, in St. Paul's Church, Salem, N. Y., by Rev. John Henry Houghton, rector of St. Paul's School, Salem, and Rev. Harris Cox Rush, rector of St. Paul's Church, and settled at East Hartford, Conn. Children :

    1. ELINOR DAVIS (Murphy), b. Sept. 3, 1893.
    2. FRANCES BROUGHTON (Murphy), b. March 30, 1895.

1506. ELLEN SARAH CRANE[6] [636], (Arzah,[5] Joseph,[4] Joseph,[3] Jonathan,[2] Benjamin[1]), married Asahel Barnes, Jr., at Addison, Vt., Nov. 15, 1849. He was a native of Bristol, Conn.; born Jan. 18, 1810; by occupation a farmer, but called

to fill various public offices; was justice of the peace, and for about forty years held the office of postmaster. He died in Addison, Oct. 28, 1886. Children:

1. ALICE ADELAIDE (Barnes), b. Feb. 1, 1851; d. Nov. 11, 1853.
2. ALBERT CRANE (Barnes), b. June 28, 1853; m. 1st, Carrie E. Smith, Feb. 24, 1885; she d. Aug. 30, 1891; m. 2d, Jessie Griswold, May 25, 1895. He is a lawyer in Chicago, Ill.
3. ELLA SALINA (Barnes), b. Sept. 19, 1854.
4. MILLARD FILLMORE (Barnes), b. Aug. 21, 1856.

1507. ELLA SALINA BARNES [3]; m. Sept. 23, 1879, Hon. Winslow C. Watson, a native of Plattsburgh, Clinton County, N. Y.; b. Jan. 19, 1832; a lawyer by profession; graduate of University of Vermont, 1854. He was school commissioner for Essex County in 1857–1860; county judge and surrogate for Clinton County, N. Y., 1876–1882. Residence in Plattsburgh. She is a graduate of Mount Holyoke Seminary. Children:

1. WINSLOW BARNES (Watson), b. Aug. 28, 1880.
2. RICHARD PIERREPOINT (Watson), b. April 12, 1883.
3. MARK SKINNER (Watson), b. June 24, 1887.
4. ELLEN FRANCES (Watson), b. Nov. 12, 1893.

1508. MILLARD FILLMORE BARNES [4]; was elected in 1896 to represent the town of Addison in the Vermont legislature. He is also one of the judges of the Addison County court In whatever station he has been called to act, the public have not been disappointed in his ability to meet all questions, whether of a public .or private nature, in an intelligent, broad and manly way.

1509. ALFRED CRANE[6] [652], (Peter[5] Thaddeus,[4] Joseph,[3] Jonathan,[2] Benjamin[1]), married Phena Robbins. Children:

1510—1. PETER.
1511—2. WYRAM, b. April 17, 1828.
1512—3. JACKSON, m. Ruth Croft.

1513. PETER CRANE[6] [653], (Peter,[5] Thaddeus,[4] Joseph,[3] Jonathan,[2] Benjamin[1]), married Phena Bennett. Settled in Richmond, Vt. Children:

1514—1. ALFRED, went west.
1515—2. SARAH ANN.
1516—3. EDWIN, m. Lauraette Chatfield..

1517. NANCY CRANE[6] [654], (Peter,[5] Thaddeus,[4] Joseph,[3] Jonathan,[2] Benjamin[1]), married Charles Stevens, and lived in Richmond, Vt. Children:

1. RUFUS (Stevens).
2. ALEXIS (Stevens).
3. ALMIRA (Stevens).
4. CLAMANA (Stevens).
5. FANNIE (Stevens).

1518. RUFUS STEVENS [1]; m. Anna Jones. Children:

1. CHARLES C. (Stevens).
2. EDWARD J. (Stevens).
3. EZRA (Stevens).

  4. EURETTA (Stevens).
  5. MILTON (Stevens).
  6. CHARLOTTE (Stevens), m. D. E. Slater.

1519. CHARLES C. STEVENS [1]; m. Hannah Towne. Children:

  1. FLORENCE M. (Stevens).
  2. EDWARD M. (Stevens).
  3. ALBERT T. (Stevens).

1520. EDWARD J. STEVENS [2]; m. Calista Welch. Children:

  1. LAURA (Stevens).
  2. MENNIE (Stevens).

1521. EZRA STEVENS [3]; m. Susan L. Wheeler. He d. November, 1897. Children:

  1. CHARLES E. (Stevens).
  2. THAD L. (Stevens).
  3. CARRIE M. (Stevens).
  4. JOHN M. (Stevens).
  5. FANNIE J. (Stevens).

1522. EURETA STEVENS [4]; m. A. C. Robinson. Children:

  1. GEORGE C. (Stevens).
  2. MORTIMER C. (Stevens).
  3. ADELLA (Stevens).
  4. MINNIE (Stevens).
  5. BERNIE (Stevens).
  6. BERTHA (Stevens).

1523. MILTON STEVENS [5]; m. Marion Shedd. Child:

  1. INA (Stevens).

1524. ABBIE CRANE[6] [657], (Peter,[5] Thaddeus,[4] Joseph,[3] Jonathan,[2] Benjamin[1]), married Thomas Cutler. Children:

  1. OLIVER (Cutler).
  2. ALEXIS (Cutler), went west; m. and d., leaving a son, Alexis.
  3. SAMUEL (Cutler), m. Emily Barber; had a son, Elber; d. young.
  4. HORACE (Cutler).
  5. LUCY (Cutler), m. Samuel Wyman; both d.
  6. JANE (Cutler).

1525. OLIVER CUTLER [1]; m. 1st, Jane Barber; 2d, Rhoda Hildreth. Children:

  1. MINNIE (Cutler), d. aged 16.
  2. THOMAS (Cutler).
  3. ABBIE (Cutler).
  4. HYMAN (Cutler), d. when a young man.

1526. THOMAS CUTLER [2]; m. L. Fitzsimmonds. He d. Children:

  1. MINNIE (Cutler)).
  2. FREDDIE (Cutler).
  3. HYMAN (Cutler).

1527. ABBIE CUTLER [3]; m. Ransom Conant, and d. Children:

  1. FAY (Conant), d. in infancy.
  2. LEVY CUTLER (Conant), b. 1886.

1528. HORACE CUTLER [4]; m. Cordelia Ross. Children:

  1. DORA (Cutler).
  2. CHESTER (Cutler).

1529. DORA CUTLER [1]; m. Ed. Olmstead. Children:
    1. MINNIE (Olmstead), d. young.
    2. MILLISSA (Olmstead).

1530. JANE CUTLER [6]; m. E. M. Irish. Child:
    1. ADDIE (Irish), m. Will Harlowe. She d. Child:
        1. HELEN (Harlowe).

1531. LAURA CRANE[6] [659], (James,[5] Thaddeus,[4] Joseph,[3] Jonathan,[2] Benjamin[1]), married Charles Brewster. He was born March 18, 1794, and died Dec. 30, 1867. Children:
    1. HENRY (Brewster), b. Oct. 16, 1824; m. Mary Eddy, b. July 22, 1827.
    2. BYRON (Brewster), b. March 15, 1829; m. Annette Mix, b. May 12, 1845.
    3. FANNY (Brewster), b. Feb. 12, 1831.

1532. FANNY BREWSTER [3]; m. George H. Lewis, who was b. March 17, 1825. Children:
    1. IDA B. (Lewis), b. April 24, 1853.
    2. CHARLIE (Lewis), b. Aug. 23, 1855.
    3. ANNABEL (Lewis), b. Sept. 10, 1859.

1533. IDA LEWIS [1]; m. Benona Sprague, b. May 15, 1852. He d. Dec. 13, 1895. Children:
    1. WILLIE (Sprague), b. June 14, 1874; m. Effie Phillips, b. March 31, 1880. Child:
        1. BENONI (Sprague), b. July 15, 1897.

1534. ANNABEL LEWIS [3]; m. Smilie Kenyon, b. Aug. 15, 1853. Child:
    1. DAISEY M. (Kenyon), b. May 22, 1883.

1535. THADDEUS CRANE[6] [660], (James,[5] Thaddeus,[4] Joseph,[3] Jonathan,[2] Benjamin[1]), married Ruth Seely, Dec. 13, 1825. She was born June 24, 1800. Settled in Richmond, Vt.; was an active business man and a prominent citizen. He died Nov. 28, 1842. She died March 21, 1868. Children:
1536—1. ANSON J., b. Dec. 6, 1826.
1537—2. MARY MARIA, b. Sept. 15, 1828; d. April 17, 1829.
1538—3. MARY MARIA, b. July 8, 1831.
1539—4. JAMES GERARD, b. Nov. 2, 1840; d. Aug. 27, 1856.

1540. SALLY CRANE[6] [661], (James,[5] Thaddeus,[4] Joseph,[3] Jonathan,[2] Benjamin[1]), married Miles Jones, April 4, 1832; settled at Fort Atkinson, Wis. She died June 28, 1871. He died Nov. 17, 1893, at Fort Atkinson. He was government surveyor in Wisconsin in 1835. Children:
    1. NEWTON (Jones), b. Dec. 15, 1833.
    2. AMELIA MARIA (Jones), b. Jan. 16, 1835; m. Edward Rankin.
    3. FANNY CAROLINE (Jones), b. Nov. 2, 1840; m. William Talcott, Sept. 25, 1862.
    4. EDWARD MILTON (Jones), b. Aug. 3, 1842; d. Nov. 14, 1863.
    5. ANSON (Jones), b. Feb. 15, 1844; d. Jan. 17, 1845.
    6. GEORGE WASHINGTON (Jones), b. Feb. 9, 1847; d. May 23, 1849.
    7. MILO CORNELIUS (Jones),   { twins,
    8. MELVIN AUGUSTUS (Jones), { b. Feb. 14, } m. Mary Francis
                                { 1849;   } Cole, Oct. 26, 1870.

1541. NEWTON JONES [1]; m. Oct 2, 1865, Phedora Turner. Children :

    1. LILLIAN POWELL (Jones), b. April 20, 1871.
    2. FRANKLIN TURNER (Jones), b. Nov. 13, 1874.

1542. AMELIA MARIA JONES [2]; m. Edward Rankin, Oct. 16, 1856. Child :

    1. WARNER H. (Rankin), b. May 19, 1858, at Jefferson, Wis., who m. Nellie Peirce, b. April 10, 1859, at Kenosha. Child :

        1. EDWARD IRA (Rankin), b. Oct. 6, 1886, at Fort Atkinson, Wis.

1543. FANNIE CAROLINE JONES [3]; m. at Fort Atkinson, Wis., Sept. 25, 1862, William A. Talcott, of Rockford, Ill., where they reside. Children :

    1. AMELIA (Talcott), b. Nov. 28, 1863; d. Aug 1, 1866.
    2. WAIT (Talcott), b. May 6, 1866.
    3. FREDERICK (Talcott), b. Nov. 10, 1868; d. Sept. 20, 1869.
    4. WILLIAM A. (Talcott), b. Feb. 25, 1870; graduate of Amherst College, 1893, and Harvard Law School, 1896, and soon began the practice of law in New York city. At the call for soldiers to serve in the war with Spain he enlisted as private in company M, 71st New York Volunteers, and was promoted to corporal for gallant conduct in the charge before Santiago, Cuba, having received favorable mention by his superior officers. On his return from Cuba he arrived at Camp Wikoff, Aug. 23, 1898, sick with malarial fever. Three days later he was removed to the Larkin House, Watch Hill, R. I., and for a few days gave signs of improvement, but d. Aug. 1; buried at Rockford, Ill.
    5. ELIZABETH (Talcott), b. Sept. 10, 1872; d. Aug. 20, 1873.
    6. FANNY (Talcott), b. April 13, 1878; d. Jan. 24, 1885.

1544. CLARINDA CRANE[6] [662], (James,[5] Thaddeus,[4] Joseph,[3] Jonathan,[2] Benjamin[1]), married Hiram Brewster in 1828, and lived in Huntington, Vt. Children :

    1. MAHALA (Brewster), b. 1831; d. 1832.
    2. MARILLA (Brewster), b. 1832.
    3. WYRAM (Brewster), b. 1835.
    4. WESLEY (Brewster), b. 1838.
    5. HARRISON (Brewster), b. 1840.
    6. GEORGE (Brewster), b. 1845.
    7. ELLEN (Brewster), b. 1848.

1545. MARILLA BREWSTER [2]; m. Alfred Bates in 1860.

1546. WYRAM BREWSTER [3]; m. Annette Remington. Children :

    1. HIRAM (Brewster).
    2. HENRY (Brewster).
    3. LAURA (Brewster).

1547. WESLEY BREWSTER [4]; m. Emma Sherman. Children:

    1. FRANK (Brewster).
    2. CARLOS (Brewster).
    3. LENA (Brewster).
    4. CLINTON (Brewster).

1548. HARRISON BREWSTER [5]; m. Ella Eddy. Child :

    1. MORTON (Brewster).

1549. GEORGE BREWSTER [6]; m. Alma Sweet. Children.·

    1. CLARINDA (Brewster).
    2. GEORGIE (Brewster).

1550. ELLEN BREWSTER [7]; m. Amos Small. Children:

    1. MELVIN (Small).
    2. HERBERT (Small).
    3. FAY (Small).

1551. FANNY CRANE[6] [664], (James,[5] Thaddeus,[4] Joseph,[3] Jonathan,[2] Benjamin[1]), married Horace Bailey, Esq., Oct. 12, 1831, at Somers, N. Y., and settled there. He was born June 8, 1790, and died July 29, 1874. She died May 1, 1886. Child:

    1. CLARINDA (Bailey), b. Feb. 4, 1833; d. Jan. 22, 1896.

1552. JAMES CRANE[6] [665], (James,[5] Thaddeus,[4] (Joseph,[3] Jonathan,[2] Benjamin[1]) married Lydia Barber, and lived at Fort Atkinson, Wis., where their two eldest children were born. Ada M. was born in Oakland, Wis., but George A. was born at Fort Atkinson. He afterwards went to Kansas, and settled at Neosho Falls, where he died March 30, 1897.* Children:

1553—1. LAURA, b. Oct. 6, 1842; d. at Neosho Falls, July 29, 1858.
1554—2. THADDEUS, b. Feb. 26, 1845.
1555—3. ADA MARY, b. July 10, 1849.
1556—4. GEORGE ALLEN, b. May 4, 1850; lived (1897) at St. Louis, Mo.

1557. GERARD CRANE[6] [666], (James,[5] Thaddeus,[4] Joseph,[3] Jonathan,[2] Benjamin[1]), married Sarah Ellen Roberts, June 14, 1840. He died Dec. 16, 1880. Children:

1558—1. ROXANA ELLEN, b. Sept. 6, 1841.
1559—2. LAURA CYLENA, b. Jan. 13, 1843; d. March 8, 1843.
1560—3. MARY KETURAH, b. Sept. 19, 1844; d. Feb. 5, 1845.
1561—4. SARAH JANET, b. July 29, 1855; d. June 5, 1865.
1562—5. MABEL, b. Jan. 13, 1866; m. Mason D. Pratt, March, 1889; reside at Steelton, Pa.

1563. LORETTA CRANE[6] [667], (James,[5] Thaddeus,[4] Joseph,[3] Jonathan,[2] Benjamin[1]), married Charles Farnsworth, May 19,

---

* James Crane, Neosho Falls, enlisted Oct. 26, 1861. Promoted 2d Lieutenant of Company H, May 28, 1862; 1st Lieutenant, March 17, 1863. Mustered out Jan. 16, 1865, at Devall's Bluff, Ark. Also Thaddeus Crane, residence Neosho Falls, enlisted Oct. 26, 1861. Mustered out at same place in Arkansas, Jan. 16, 1865. Probably the above were father and son.

1840. They had two children; only one of them lived to grow
up. She died Sept. 20, 1845. Child:

    1. LOUISA (Farnsworth).

1564. ALEXIS CRANE[6] [668], (James,[5] Thaddeus,[4] Joseph,[3]
Jonathan,[2] Benjamin[1]), married Jane A. Gilbert. He died.
Children:

    1565—1. JUDSON G. b. 1857.
    1566—2. ALEXIS.
    1567—3. CLARA.
    1568—4. EMILY.

1569. THOMAS CRANE[6] [669], (James,[5] Thaddeus,[4] Joseph,[3]
Jonathan,[2] Benjamin[1]), married 1st, Olive Ives, Nov. 24, 1845.
She was born June 18, 1822, and died Sept. 11, 1846. He then
married 2d, Deborah Eliza Colton, April 20, 1848. She was
born in Waitsfield, Vt., and died Feb. 23, 1881. He then went
to Fort Atkinson, Wis., and now (1897) resides there. Children:

    1570—1. BESSIE EVILYN, b. April 7, 1849.
    1571—2. OLIVE IVES, b. Nov. 21, 1850.
    1572—3. ALICE FRANCES, b. July 13, 1852.
    1573—4. MATILDA ABBIE, b. July 12, 1854.
    1574—5. JENNIE MARIA, b. Dec. 18, 1858.
    1575—6. CLARA AMELIA, b. Feb. 22, 1861.

1576. JANE BAXTER CRANE[6] [670], (James,[5] Thaddeus,[4]
Joseph,[3] Jonathan,[2] Benjamin[1]), married Alexander Hart, Nov.
22, 1843, and removed to Fort Atkinson, Wis. Children:

    1. LORETTA (Hart), m. Rev. Albert B. Irwin, and settled at
       Beatrice, Neb.; now (1897) residing in Highland, Kan.
    2. ALEXIS (Hart), d.
    3. WYMAN ALEXANDER (Hart), b. March 13, 1852. The mother
       d. April 17, 1852, and he was placed with her brother Gerard
       and Sarah E. (Roberts) Crane to bring up, and when he
       became of age changed his name to Wynam Alex. Crane, and
       he is now (1897) living in Portland, Chautauqua County,
       N. Y. He m. Annie Taylor, Sept. 4, 1878.

1577. MARTHA T. CRANE[6] [671], (James,[5] Thaddeus,[4] Joseph,[3]
Jonathan,[2] Benjamin[1]), married Martin Luther Bates, April 20,
1848, and removed to Fort Atkinson, Wis. Children:

    1. CLARA (Bates).
    2. MILO (Bates).

1578. LYDIA CRANE[6] [673], (Thaddeus,[5] Thaddeus,[4] Joseph,[3] Jonathan,[2] Benjamin[1]), married 1st, Oliver Field, who
was born Sept. 28, 1808, and died in 1840, leaving three children. She married 2d, John Dickenson, a farmer. He was
born Aug. 24, 1811, and died April 12, 1893. She died May 4,
1891. Children:

    1. THADDEUS (Field); a merchant; resides in St. Paul, Minn.; m.
       Julia Ingersol.
    2. ELBERT (Field); a farmer; m. Lydia Howe.

3. Sibylla (Field).
4. John W. (Dickenson), b. May 21, 1857; d. Aug. 28, 1859.

1579. Sally Crane[6] [674], (Thaddeus,[5] Thaddeus,[4] Joseph,[3] Jonathan,[2] Benjamin[1]), married at Somers, N. Y., Jabez Jones, a farmer, and a native of Richmond, Vt. He was born Nov. 15, 1811, and died May 26, 1883. She died Jan. 8, 1879. Their residence was Somers, N. Y. Children :

1. Edward (Jones), born July 16, 1839; was major in late war in 6th New York Heavy Artillery; d. Oct. 30, 1864, from wounds received at the battle of Cedar Creek, Oct. 19.
2. Oliver F. (Jones), b. May 10, 1841; m. Henrietta Griffin, Oct. 15, 1863; d. July 13, 1894.
3. Charlotte C. (Jones), b. Aug. 14, 1842; d. May 5, 1867.
4. Thaddeus C. (Jones), b. July 31, 1845; m. Carrie V. Kountz, Nov. 6, 1878; residence St. Paul.
 . Thomas (Jones), b. May 13, 1849.
5. Mary C. (Jones), b. Oct. 1, 1852; m. Isaac C. Wight; residence Somers, N. Y.

1580. Oliver F. Jones [2]; m. Henrietta Griffin. Children :

1. Edward (Jones), b. Jan. 15, 1865; residence St. Paul, Minn.
2. Fred J. (Jones), b. Aug. 30, 1866; residence Peekskill, N. Y.
3. Charlotte W. (Jones), b. Oct. 28, 1867; residence Peekskill, N. Y.
4. Fannie G. (Jones), b. Aug. 11, 1870; residence Peekskill, N. Y.
5. Sally (Jones), b. May 28, 1877; d. Feb. 11, 1882.
7. John R. (Jones), b. Nov. 27, 1878; residence Peekskill, N. Y.

1581. Charlotte C. Jones [3]; m. Dec. 18, 1861, Isaac C. Wright. Child :

1. Charles (Wright), b. Nov. 21, 1862, at St. Paul, Minn.

1582. Thomas Jones [5]; m. M. Louise Mead, May 19, 1871, at Somers, N. Y. A farmer. Children :

1. Clara S. (Jones), b. Nov. 8, 1871.
2. M. Louise (Jones), b. June 23, 1873; m. Oscar E. . McBride, Dec. 7, 1892.
3. Ella L. (Jones), b. Dec. 25, 1879.

1583. Clara S. Jones [1]; m. John W. Palmer, March 14, 1894, at Somers, N. Y. Child :

1. John Wetherill (Palmer), b. Jan. 1, 1895.

1584. Clarissa (or Clara) Crane[6] [676], (Thaddeus,[5] Thaddeus[4] Joseph,[3] Jonathan,[2] Benjamin[1]), married Morgan Smith, a farmer. He was born in 1808, and died March 18, 1892. Children :

1. Anna (Smith).
2. Clara (Smith).

1585. Thaddeus Crane[6] [683], (Gerard,[5] Thaddeus,[4] Joseph,[3] Jonathan,[2] Benjamin[1]), married Clarinda Bailey, of

Somers, N. Y., June 8, 1854. She was born Feb. 4, 1833, and died Jan. 22, 1896. He was a graduate of Trinity College 1845. A farmer. Children:

1586—1. GERARD, b. March 15, 1855; d. Sept, 23, 1856.
1587—2. WILLIAM (Bailey), b. March 27, 1858; d. June 7, 1873.
1588—3. FANNY (Bailey), b. Feb. 12, 1860; d. Dec. 24, 1861.
1589—4. THADDEUS (Bailey), b. Sept. 29, 1862.
1590—5. ELLEN (Bailey), b. Oct. 6, 1864.
1591—6. CLARINDA (Bailey), b. Dec. 25, 1869; d. Nov. 11, 1873.
1592—7. JAMES B. (Bailey), b. Aug. 17, 1871.
1593—8. CHARLES S. Bailey), b. Jan. 29, 1876.

1594. HARRIET CRANE[6] [685], (Gerard,[5] Thaddeus,[4] Joseph,[3] Jonathan,[2] Benjamin[1]), married William Coffin, at Somers, N. Y., June, 1854. She died Dec. 9, 1857. Children:

1. LYDIA (Coffin), b. May 4, 1855; d. April 22, 1858.
2. WILLIAM H. (Coffin), b. June 29, 1857; d. Dec. 13, 1858.

1595. ELLEN CRANE[6] [686], (Gerard,[5] Thaddeus,[4] Joseph,[3] Jonathan,[2] Benjamin[1]), married Andrew C. Scott, at Somers, N. Y. Children:

1. GERARD C. (Scott), b. July 14, 1860.
2. WILLIAM H. (Scott), b. Aug. 29, 1862.
3. LILLIAN C. (Scott), b. June 14, 1865.
4. HOBART (Scott), b. Aug. 22, 1873.

1596. MARY CRANE[6] [688], (Gerard,[5] Thaddeus,[4] Joseph,[3] Jonathan,[2] Benjamin[1]), married in 1866 Dr. Charles E. Lee, at Somers, N.Y., where for a few years they resided, then removed to St. Paul, Minn., where he is practicing his profession. Dr. Lee is a graduate of Lafayette College, Easton, Pa. Children:

1. MARY RANKIN (Lee), b. May 1, 1867.
2. BESSIE STUART (Lee), b. Dec. 18, 1868.
3. MARGARET GUION (Lee), b. Feb. 13, 1871.
4. HENRY THOMAS (Lee), b. July 29, 1872; student January, 1897, at College of Physicians and Surgeons, New York city.

1597. BESSIE STUART (Lee) [2]; m. Thomas T. Fauntleroy, a lawyer. They reside at St. Louis, Mo. Child:

1. MARY LEE (Fauntleroy), b. March 16, 1892.

1598. MARILLA CRANE[6] [694], (Isaac Chapman,[5] Stephen,[4] Joseph,[3] Jonathan,[2] Benjamin[1]), married in 1811 Elisha Blake, son of Samuel and Margaret (Johnson) Blake. Samuel was born July 22, 1747, and married Margaret Johnson in 1785. Stephen Blake, father of Samuel, was born in Middletown, Conn., July 16, 1687, and married 1st, Hannah Cole; 2d, Abigail Hubbard; and 3d, Anna Lucas. The latter was mother of the above Samuel. Children:

1. WILLIAM ISAAC (Blake), b. Sept. 12, 1812; m. Mary, dau. of Major Butler, of Pittsburg, in 1835; no children; d. 1837.
2. ERASTUS HARMAN (Blake), b. Nov. 25, 1814; d. 1815.
3. MALISSA ROWENA (Blake), b. Oct. 16, 1816; m. Timothy Newton; had son and daughter; d. 1877.

COMMODORE HOMER CRANE BLAKE.

4. HARRIET AMANDA (Blake), b. June, 1820; d. 1829.
5. HOMER CRANE (Blake), b. Feb. 1, 1822.
6. HENRY SAMUEL (Blake), b. June 25, 1823; d. 1829.
7. CHARLES VAUGHN (Blake), b. April 10, 1828; d. 1846.

1599. Commodore HOMER CRANE BLAKE [5], was born in Dutchess
County, N. Y. When about a year old his parents removed
to Ohio, and settled on what was called the Western Reserve,
where Homer passed his boyhood days. At the age of
eighteen he entered the United States Navy as a midship-
man. Date of the appointment being March 2, 1840. He
was soon assigned to duty on board the *Constellation* frigate,
which set sail for a voyage lasting over three years, and en-
circling the globe. During this trip, while the *Constellation*
was anchored off Canton, China, Blake was assigned the
hazardous task of maintaining communication between the
vessel and Canton, which he successfully accomplished in an
open boat with but twelve men, at a time, too, when in China
an Englishman's head was worth one thousand dollars, and it
was not an easy matter to distinguish between the head of an
American and an Englishman. After reaching home in 1844
and spending a short furlough visiting relatives and friends,
he was ordered to join the sloop-of-war *Preble* and served a
year on the coast of Africa suppressing the slave trade. Returning to the United States he entered the Naval Academy,
at Annapolis. From here he graduated in 1846 as passed mid-
shipman. As war with Mexico seemed inevitable, Blake applied for active service and was attached to his old vessel, the
sloop-of-war *Preble*, and sent to the coast of California. In
1848 the *Preble* was ordered to the East Indies. On reaching
Canton, China, Blake was so ill as to be unfit for duty, and
permitted to return home for the purpose of recovering his
health. For a short period he was engaged on shore in the
coast survey. In 1850, he again appears bound for the
Pacific on board the frigate *Raritan*, but was transferred
from this vessel to the sloop-of-war *St. Mary's* and proceeded
to the China Seas and home by the Cape of Good Hope, thus
making in about nine years three voyages around the world.
In 1856, he again joined the *Raritan* frigate and repaired to
the coast of Brazil. Returning to the United States in 1857,
he was employed for a time on shore, and again sent to the
coast of Africa to return the following year. With the
breaking out of our Civil War, Blake applied for active duty,
for the purpose of defending the flag that had been his protection in almost every prominent harbor of the world.
He was ordered to the *Sabine* and employed on the coast of
South Carolina, but when this vessel was assigned to recruiting duty he asked to be detached from her and given a place
nearer the post of danger. He was then assigned to command the *R. R. Cuyler;* soon, however, transferred to the
command of the *Hatteras*. She was originally built as a passenger boat to run between New Orleans and Galveston, but
suddenly transformed into a substitute man-of-war by the
help of a few pine plank to strengthen her decks, that they
might support the few small guns she was chosen to carry,
and removing her after cabin. Thus equipped she was of
suitable strength to perform ordinary blockading duty, to
which service she was assigned off Galveston, Texas, Commander Blake having been sent there from New Orleans
with the *Hatteras* and a few other vessels to attempt the re-
taking of that place, arriving Jan. 10, 1863.

About 3 P. M. the following day a strange vessel appeared off the port. Supposing it to be a blockade-runner the *Hatteras* was signaled to give chase, and Commander Blake was soon in pursuit. The stranger proved to be no less than the Confederate steamer *Alabama*, Capt. Semmes in command. The *Hatteras* was no even match for the *Alabama*, not being able to hurl in a single broadside one-quarter the weight in metal that the latter could, and Blake found himself in a position where he must either attempt to run away or fight. He chose the latter, and gave the order to clear the *Hatteras* for action, resolving at the same moment to bring the vessels into close quarter, if possible, and attempt to carry his foe by boarding. As the *Hatteras* steamed on for the encounter, the *Alabama* was lying to, broadside on, waiting for the struggle soon to come. With the discharge of a broadside from the *Alabama* the battle was begun. Every nerve on both vessels was strained to the utmost tension. The superior speed of the *Alabama* enabled Semmes to thwart all attempts made for boarding by Commodore Blake, although the vessels were within thirty yards of each other. For twenty minutes the frail *Hatteras* was exposed to the tremendous pounding of shot and shell, the latter starting a fire, which was raging fiercely and rapidly working towards the magazine, which was composed above the water line of light pine plank. The men at the magazine remained at their post as long as powder could be passed up without exploding. The flames had reached the two-inch plank partition separating it from the magazine and the vessel was fast sinking, but not a man flinched nor left his gun. The *Hatteras* was so torn and disabled that not one of her guns could now be brought to bear on the *Alabama*, and Blake feeling he had no right to sacrifice uselessly the brave men under his command, reluctantly gave orders to fire a lee-gun in token of surrender. With the aid of the boats from both vessels the men of the *Hatteras* were soon placed on board the *Alabama*, and within ten minutes the *Hatteras* went to the bottom of the ocean with her pennant still flying at the masthead, Semmes gaining a fruitless victory. The *Alabama* was severely damaged by the encounter and at once proceeded to Kingston, in Jamaica, where she remained thirteen days for repairs, which cost eighty-six thousand dollars in gold. Commander Blake and his crew in due time reached New York via Key West. These men, who fought under Blake, held him in such high esteem that they petitioned the Navy Department to give their commander the steamer *Eutaw*, and that they might be allowed to join him in a cruise for the *Alabama*, believing they could either sink or capture that formidable enemy. The *Eutaw* was given Blake, but he was stationed at the James River, where he rendered valuable service. In the latter part of 1863 a desperate movement was announced soon to take place on the side of the Confederates. Jan. 24, 1864, the attempt was made, and had not the two rebel rams got aground the result might have been much more disastrous, for the Union Naval Commander instead of protecting his defences from the attack of the Confederate fleet under command of Semmes, who had been working down the James River, retired and thus allowed the channel to be opened. The night following, at high water, the second attempt was to be made. Commander Blake had been stationed on the east side, at Deep Bottom, to protect

the right of the Army of the James. On the morning of the twenty-fifth, the commander of the naval division having been removed for his conduct the previous day, Blake was placed in command of the ironclad fleet, torpedo and picket boats. On going on board the *Onondaga* he found her port propeller disabled; yet, with her in this condition and only a few small gunboats, he was able to contend with the Confederate fleet and caused it to retreat back to Richmond. A false step or a moment's hesitation at that time would have endangered the safety of the Union armies. Against the advice of nearly all the officers, he got the *Onondaga*, with the assistance of tugs, close to the obstructions, and directly under the fire of the Confederate batteries, and in such a position that if she was sunk, either by the rams or torpedo boats, as he expected, she would take the place of the removed obstructions. This action prevented a second attempt, as he was afterward informed by one of the officers who was then attached to the Confederate fleet. Admiral Porter wrote Blake, "Had your predecessor done as well, we should now be in possession of the entire rebel navy and on our way to Richmond."

Blake was continued in command of the ironclads and naval picket line, and took part in the engagement which caused the fall of Richmond. In 1867 he was head of the Bureau of Navigation, at Portsmouth, N. H. But the order soon came to proceed again to the Chinese waters. This time under the fighting Admiral John Rogers. Capt. Blake was sent up the Han River, in Korea, in command of an expedition to punish the Koreans for a treacherous attack upon an American force sent to inquire into the loss of the crew of the schooner *General Sherman* in August, 1866, and to arrange for a treaty between the United States and Korea. Although this sudden attack was planned by the Koreans with the intention of annihilating the Americans, it resulted in comparatively little damage. Admiral Rogers gave them ten days in which to make an apology. None came, and the expedition, with 759 men in all, under Capt. Blake, was dispatched to punish the treacherous Koreans. June 10, 1868, the men landed and with the help of the gunboats *Monocacy* and *Colorado* captured the first fort. The following day the men proceeded on up the heights capturing the second line of fortifications. But the third and main fortification, located on a high rocky hill, garrisoned by a vastly superior force in numbers, was yet to be taken. It was a severe and hazardous undertaking. Many of the Americans were overcome with heat. But the word was given, and up our men climbed the steep hill in the face of deadly missiles, and made a desperate hand-to-hand encounter, with this result: about 350 Koreans were killed and 20 taken prisoners. The Americans had three men killed and ten wounded. Five forts, with fifty flags, and a considerable number of large and small guns were captured during the two days.

His extended service along the coast of China and exposure to the malaria of that region completely shattered his constitution, and for some years after his return home he suffered severely in bodily health. He died at his home in New York City, Jan. 27, 1880, at the age of 58 years, just after receiving his well-earned commission as Commodore in the United States Navy. He was a warm-hearted, courteous, considerate, Christian gentleman. When he was on

11

his way to Galveston, Texas, just prior to the engagement with the *Alabama*, in a private letter, written to a friend, he said: "I have much to live for, but I could not be happy to purchase my life with any neglect of the duty I owe to my country. I shall not seek danger; but if it comes I shall take it in the line of my duty, and endeavor to do credit to myself, family and State." Several officers of the United States Navy, who have rendered signal service to their country during the late war with Spain, served under Blake in that memorable Korean expedition. Among them, Commodores J. C. Watson, W. S. Schley, Rear-Admiral L. A. Kimberly, Captain C. M. Chester, and Commander Albion V. Wadhams, all of whom speak in the highest terms that he was an officer of great ability, ceaseless energy, indomitable courage and an excellent seaman.

He married Mary, daughter of Judge James Flanagan. Children:

1. HOMER K. F. (Blake), b. 1854; d. 1877.
2. MARY E. M. (Blake), b. 1855.

1600. SUSAN CRANE[6] [696], (Stephen,[5] Stephen,[4] Joseph,[3] Jonathan,[2] Benjamin[1]), married Oct. 21, 1811, Homer Dakin, of North East, N. Y., who was born Jan. 10, 1785. He was a carpenter by trade, and removed to Ohio. He died Feb. 14, 1855. She died March 26, 1863. Children:

1. MARY STODDARD (Dakin), b. Aug. 25, 1812; m. 1st, Andrew Dickson; 2d, Asa Baldwin, March 1, 1876.
2. PHEBE (Dakin), b. Oct. 31, 1814; m. 1st, Jan. 2, 1834, Aliram Squiers, d. Oct. 19, 1855; 2d, June 10, 1856, Rueben Howes.
. HARRIET ANN (Dakin), b. Sept. 10, 1816; m. Moses Spaulding, Oct. 8, 1834.
4. CAROLINE (Dakin), b. Dec. 25, 1818; m. John K. Stout, June 8, 1853. She d. March 26, 1873.
. CHARLOTTE BALDWIN (Dakin) b. Oct. 13, 1820; d. Aug. 16, 1849.
5. ALBERT (Dakin), b. Oct. 22, 1822; m. 1st, Jerusha Wells, Nov. 13, 1850, d. March 4, 1860; 2d, Amelia Tow, May 2, 1861.
7. STEPHEN CRANE (Dakin), b. Sept. 3, 1824; m. Oct. 8, 1855, Adda J. Porlious. He d. Aug. 28, 1865.
8. LAURA SHERMAN (Dakin) b. Sept. 6, 1826; m. Fowler Bryant, Nov. 29, 1850. She d. Aug. 9, 1860.
9. SUSAN AMELIA (Dakin), b. Feb. 4, 1829; d. March 16, 1846.
10. HORACE EDWIN (Dakin), b. Jan. 1, 1831; m. Elizabeth Tibbets, April 23, 1857.
11. JAMES RUTHVAN (Dakin), b. and d. March 5, 1834.
12. HENRY MARTIN (Dakin), b. Sept. 6, 1835; m. Harriet Stevens, Aug. 17, 1861; lived in Cleveland, Ohio.

1601. LAURA CRANE[6] [699], (Stephen,[5] Stephen,[4] Joseph,[3] Jonathan,[2] Benjamin[1]), married December, 1818, Homer B. Sherman, of New Milford, Conn. She died July 2, 1826.

Children:

1. FREDERICK (Sherman), b. Nov. 18, 1819.
2. MARY J. (Sherman), b. Nov. 10, 1821; m. Stephen Wills; have 2 daughters; live in New Milford, Conn.
3. GEORGE F. (Sherman), b. Feb. 10, 1824; m. Mary Robbins, of Cold Spring, N. Y.; have a daughter.
4. LAURA C. (Sherman), b. June 15, 1826; unm.

1602. FREDERICK SHERMAN [1.]; was in active service during the late war, distinguishing himself in various positions. He married Lydia Bishop, of Washington, Conn., Nov. 16, 1843. Children:

    1. HOMER W. (Sherman), b. June 17, 1846; d. April 20, 1870.
    2. HORACE M. (Sherman), b. July 6, 1847; lived in New York City.

1603. ANNA CRANE[6] [700], (Stephen,[5] Stephen,[4] Joseph,[3] Jonathan,[2] Benjamin[1]), married Joseph Sanford. She died Aug. 6, 1825. Child:

    1. HARRIET ELIZA (Sanford); d. at 2½ years of age.

1604. HEMAN AVERILL CRANE[6] [702], (Stephen,[5] Stephen,[4] Joseph,[3] Jonathan,[2] Benjamin[1]), left home when quite young to learn the mercantile business, first finding a place in his native town, New Milford, Conn. Later he went to Hartford or New Haven. In 1830 he went to Darien, Georgia, where he engaged in business under the firm name of Rogers, Crane & Shackelford, merchants, and agents for a line of steamers between Savannah and that port. Nov. 18, 1835, he married Julia R. Underwood, a native of St. Mary's, Ga. In 1843, he removed to Savannah and entered the firm of O. G. Sparks & Co., wholesale grocers and commission merchants. They were succeeded by H. A. Crane & Co., and later by Crane & Holcombe, Crane, Johnson & Co., and Crane & Graybill. In 1870, he entered into partnership with his son Horace A. Crane. After an experience of three years, the son retired for the purpose of engaging in the banking business, leaving the father to continue the commission trade. Mr. Crane was of a retiring disposition, devoting his time chiefly to his domestic and private business. He, however, served one term as alderman in his city with great acceptability. He was also a member of the Board of Commissioners of Pilotage and of the Savannah Benevolent Association.

Mr. Crane was an active member of the First Presbyterian Church, in which he held the office of elder, and was also superintendent of the Sunday-school. A man of strict integrity and purity of life. At the time of his death he was the oldest member of the First Presbyterian Church, having joined it March 15, 1844. He died May 26, 1879, greatly lamented by all who knew him. Children:

1605—1. JULIA CATHERINE, b. July 25, 1837.
1606—2. WILLIAM HENRY, b. Oct. 31, 1839; killed at Manassas, July 21, 1861, while serving his State.
1607—3. HORACE AVERILL, b. Sept. 25, 1841.

1608. HENRY STEPHEN CRANE[6] [703], (Stephen,[5] Stephen,[4] Joseph,[3] Jonathan,[2] Benjamin[1]), married Oct. 14, 1833, Betsey J. ——, at New Milford, Conn., where she was born July 19,

1810. He was a farmer, and later resided in **Woodbury, Conn.**, where he died April 23, 1858. Children:

1609—1. HORACE B., b. Aug. 5, 1834; d. April 13, 1855, at Woodbury.
1610—2. GEORGE P., b. Jan. 14, 1837.
1611—3. STEPHEN H., b. Sept. 6, 1843.

1612. GEORGE ELLIOT CRANE[6] [705], (Stephen,[5] Stephen,[4] Joseph,[3] Jonathan,[2] Benjamin[1]), married Sept. 25, 1839, Emily A. Clark, at North East, N. Y., where she was born June 25, 1816. He was a farmer; residence Millerton, N. Y.

Children:

1613—1. HATTIE M, b. Jan. 29, 1842.
1614—2. MOSES C., b. Feb. 24, 1843.
1615—3. MARY E., b. March 30, 1844.
1616—4. JULIA E., b. Nov. 15, 1846.
1617—5. GEORGE H., b. Oct. 15, 1852.
1618—6. BLANCHE A., b. Dec. 21, 1861.

1619. CAROLINE MATILDA CRANE[6] [707], (Stephen,[5] Stephen,[4] Joseph,[3] Jonathan,[2] Benjamin[1]), married at New Milford, Conn., in 1845, Hiram R. Snyder. He was a native of Bridgeport, and born in 1814. He was an artist. They resided at Hoosick, N. Y. She was divorced from him in 1851, and married second, Capt. Barlow Russell, in 1862, a native of Southbury, born in 1799. He was a farmer, and resided in Woodbury, Conn., where he died Sept. 28, 1870. Children:

1. AUGUSTA CAROLINE (Snyder), b. 1845; m. at Woodbury, Conn., in 1865, George Morse Allen, a native of that place, b. in 1845. He is a merchant there. Children:

    1. CATHARINE MARIA (Allen), b. Jan. 8, 1866.
    2. GEORGE HEMAN (Allen), b. Nov. 5, 1868.
    3. WILLIAM HENRY (Allen), b. Sept. 11, 1870.
    4. GIDEON MORSE (Allen), }
    5. ALTHA AVERILL (Allen), } twins, b. Nov. 16, 1873.
    6. FRANK MORRIS (Allen), b. May 19, 1877.
    7. HOWARD SHERWOOD (Allen), }
    8. HORACE CRANE (Allen), } twins, b. June 15, 1880.

1620. JENNETTE CRANE[6] [708], (Stephen,[5] Stephen,[4] Joseph,[3] Jonathan,[2] Benjamin[1]), married George Miner Allen, at New Milford, Conn. He was born there Nov 27, 1824. His occupation a builder. He died in New Milford, Conn., Aug. 28, 1870. She died there May 8, 1878. Children:

1. WILLIAM MYGATT (Allen), b. Oct. 13, 1851.
2. HENRY PERRY (Allen), b. April 17, 1855.
3. SARAH ELIZABETH (Allen), b. May 7, 1858.
4. HORACE AVERILL (Allen), b. Feb. 12, 1863.

1621. WILLIAM MYGATT ALLEN [1]; m. Caroline Elmer Weaver, at Washington, Conn., Oct. 10, 1878. He is a farmer and resides at New Milford, Conn. Child:

1. GEORGE HENRY (Allen), b. August, 1879.

1622. Rev. EZRA F. CRANE[6] [710], (Noah,[5] Stephen,[4] Joseph,[3] Jonathan,[2] Benjamin[1]), married in Burlington, N. Y., in 1830, Sallie Fairman, a native of Richfield, N. Y. She died April, 1870, and he married 2d, Elvira Babcock. ·She was born in Massachusetts. Mr. Crane graduated from the Fairfield College of Physicians. He enlisted May, 1861, in the 23d New York Vols., serving as chaplain. He served as postmaster under President Polk. Residence at Corry, Pa.; occupation a clergyman. Children :

1623—1. A. D. W.
1624—2. AMANDA·M.
1625—3. SARAH W.
1626—4. E. C.
1627—5. FRANKIE.
1628—6. EMMA.
1629—7. HARRY.
1630—8. FANNIE L.

1631. NELSON CRANE[6] [712], (Joseph,[5] Stephen,[4] Joseph,[3] Jonathan,[2] Benjamin[1]), married June 3, 1830, at Kent, Catharine Hall, a native of Greenfield, Conn., and born April 3, 1808. For a time they resided in Kent, but of late they have lived in Danbury, Conn. Children :

1632—1. BETSEY, b. June 23, 1831; d. in Kent Nov. 5, 1843.
1633—2. LOIS B., b. July 25, 1833.

1634. LEONARD CRANE[6] [713], (Joseph,[5] Stephen,[4] Joseph,[3] Jonathan,[2] Benjamin[1]), married Lucy Jane Hatch, a native of Kent, born in 1814. She died Oct. 1, 1839. He died Oct. 11, 1842. Both died in Kent. Child :

1635—1. JOSEPH WILLARD. b. April 25, 1839; enlisted in the late war and d. in a southern hospital.

1636. OSMOND NOAH CRANE[6] [716], (David B.,[5] Stephen,[4] Joseph,[3] Jonathan,[2] Benjamin[1]), was born at North East, Dutchess County, N. Y. He was a farmer. He was married at Monroe, Fairfield County, Conn., Jan. 3, 1832, to Mary Hubbell, and for a time resided there, but removed to Unadilla, N. Y.

Children :

1637—1. SARAH ANN, b. April 6, 1834.
1638 —2. MARY ANN, b. July 15, 1837.
1639—3. WILLIAM HUBBELL, b. Aug. 20, 1839.
1640—4. SUSAN EMILY, b. June 30, 1842.
1641—5. CORNELIA MARIA, b. April 6, 1845.
1642—6. LAURA SHERMAN, b. July 1, 1846; d. Oct. 18, 1861.

1643. ORSON J. CRANE[6] [717], (David B.,[5] Stephen,[4] Joseph,[3] Jonathan,[2] Benjamin[1]), married 1st, Sarah Ann Wright, Feb. 5, 1837, at Hartwick, Otsego County, N. Y.; 2d, Ann Van Inwegen, Oct. 24, 1848, in Sullivan County. Educated at Westford, Otsego County. An eclectic physician; residence Newtown, Ind. He had three children by first marriage, all died young.

By second marriage eight children, five living, three daughters and two sons. One daughter:

1644—1. FRANCES JEWELL; m. ——— Stephens.

1645. CHARLES CRANE[6] [721], (Ashbil,[5] John,[4] John,[3] Abraham,[2] Benjamin[1]), married Lydia Fuller. Their first seven children were born in Cobbleskill, Schoharie County, N. Y. The last three in La Grange, Lorain County, Ohio, whither he removed with his family in 1835. Children:

1646—1. EMILY, b. July 3, 1820.
1647—2. LYMAN, b. May 27, 1822.
1648—3. ASHBIL, b. Aug. 1, 1824.
1649—4. LEWIS, b. Aug. 14, 1826.
1650—5. ELMIRA, b. Aug. 9, 1829.
1651—6. HANNAH, b. March 12, 1831.
1652—7. WALTER C., b. Dec. 10, 1832.
1653—8. ABIGAIL, b. March 17, 1836.
1654—9. JOHN, b. Sept. 18, 1838; wounded in the face at battle of Stone River, Feb. 11, 1863; d. at Nashville, Tenn.
1655-10. SARAH J., b. Dec. 21, 1842.

1656. MARY CRANE[6] [729], (Curtis,[5] Curtis,[4] John,[3] Abraham,[2] Benjamin[1]), married Jan. 22, 1822, Lyman Gardiner, son of David D. and Eunice (Otis) Gardiner, at Eaton, N. Y. He was born in Colchester, Conn., July 25, 1798, and died in Nunda, N. Y., Dec. 7, 1849. She died at Angelica, April 29, 1844. Children:

1. CURTIS CRANE (Gardiner), b. Dec. 1, 1822. Served in the late war and is (1881) a prominent lawyer in St. Louis, Mo., and the author of the "Gardiner Family History," which gives eight generations of the descendants of Lion Gardiner, the first European resident proprietor of Gardiner's Island, N. Y. Besides containing a genealogy of the family the book is filled with considerable valuable historical matter.
2. DANIEL DENISON (Gardiner).
3. EMILY FOOTE (Gardiner).
4. LYMAN (Gardiner).
5. MARY JANE (Gardiner).
6. HARRIET MORSE (Gardiner).
7. HIRAM TYRIAN (Gardiner).
8. DEWITT CLINTON (Gardiner).
9. BELINDA ATKLINE (Gardiner).
10. FRANK HAMILTON (Gardiner).
11. EUNICE ATKLINE (Gardiner).
12. CORNELIA RAYMOND (Gardiner).
13. LUCY ELIZABETH (Gardiner).

1657.. ALBERT LEWIS CRAIN[6] [740], (Whiting,[5] William,[4] John,[3] Abraham,[2] Benjamin[1]), married in Great Barrington, ·Mass., Margaret L. Hogg, born July 15, 1815, in the parish of Ettreck, Scotland, and settled in East Maine, Broome County, N. Y.; a farmer. He died there Jan. 7, 1870. Children:

1658—1. ROBERT W., b. Aug. 25, 1840.
1659—2. WILLIAM H., b. June 14, 1842; served in United States army 18 months, and d. 1865.

1660—3. ELIZABETH, b. Dec. 2, 1844.
1661—4. WALLACE S., b. Aug. 10, 1847.; lived at Binghamton, N. Y.
1662—5. GEORGIA A., b. May 12, 1850.
1663—6. MABEL I., b. May 13, 1856.
1664—7. SARAH A., b. April 20, 1859.

1665. AURELIA LOIZA CRAIN[6] [741], (Whiting,[5] William,[4] John,[3] Abraham,[2] Benjamin[1]), married July 22, 1832, Russell L. Chauncey. He was born Nov. 18, 1810. She died Oct. 26, 1873. Settled in East Maine, Broome County, N. Y. Children :

1. JOSEPH W. (Chauncey), b. May 16, 1833.
2. JANE S. (Chauncey), b. Oct. 1, 1836.
3. BESSIE A. (Chauncey), b. July 16, 1839 ; m. Benj. R. Russell, Oct. 11, 1865.
4. EMILISSA (Chauncey), b. Aug. 22, 1841.
5. RUSSELL F. (Chauncey), b. Feb. 14, 1844.
6. AURELIA L. (Chauncey), b. Feb. 22, 1846.
7. ROSEPHA C. (Chauncey), b. Jan. 23, 1848.
8. WILLIA D. (Chauncey), b. Sept. 19, 1850 ; d. Nov. 21, 1850.

1666. JOSEPH W. CHAUNCEY [1] ; m. Oct. 28, 1856, Olive West. He d. Feb. 22, 1872. Child :

1. MIMMIE (Chauncey), b. May 27, 1862.

1667. JANE S. CHAUNCEY [2] ; m. Feb. 21, 1856, Franklin Updegrave. Child :

1. HATTIE E. (Updegrave), b. July 1, 1860.

1668. EMILISSA CHAUNCEY [4] ; m. Oct. 15, 1861, Albert Greene. Children :

1. FERNANDO (Greene), b. Dec. 17, 1862.
2. MELAIN (Greene), b. Nov. 16, 1867.
3. ELLA B. (Greene), b. Jan. 17, 1879.

1669. RUSSELL F. CHAUNCEY [5] ; m. Louisa Russell, Oct. 12, 1865. Children :

1. JAMES R. (Chauncey), b. Aug. 5, 1866.
2. FANNIE (Chauncey), b. July 13, 1868.
3. LINDA (Chauncey), b. Feb. 19, 1872.
4. CHARLES L. (Chauncey), b. Aug. 19, 1874.
5: ISRAEL C. (Chauncey), b. March 17, 1879.

1670. AURELIA L. CHAUNCEY [6] ; m. Sept. 29, 1874, Joseph Johnson. Child :

1. ERNEST (Johnson), b. June 26, 1875.

1671. ROSEPHA C. CHAUNCEY [7] ; m. May 8, 1873, James McGregor Child :

1. ROB ROY (McGregor), b. Feb. 22, 1878.

1672. EDMUND CRANE[6] [748], (Abraham,[5] Abraham,[4] Abraham,[3] Abraham,[2] Benjamin[1]), married Amelia Johnson, Oct. 8, 1849. She was born in Middletown, Conn., April 11, 1808. He was a farmer. · She died in Manchester, Conn., Feb. ·12, 1865. Child :

1673—1. EDMUND J., b. April 30, 1851 ; prison officer, Hartford, Conn.

1674. IRA R. CRANE[6] [756], (Benjamin.[5] Abraham,[4] Abraham,[3] Abraham,[2] Benjamin[1]), married Lucy B. Rawdon, of

Tolland, Conn. He was a shoe dealer in West Farmington, Ohio, although he had resided in both Warren and Bristol in that State. Children :

1675—1. JAMES, b. Aug. 6, 1830.
1676—2. HENRIETTA, d. in Bristol.
1677—3. HORACE.

1678. HARRIET CRANE[6] [760], (Elijah,[5] Elijah[4], Abraham,[3] Abraham,[2] Benjamin[1]), married Josiah Robbins, Feb. 24, 1826, at Wethersfield, Conn. Children :

. ROSSITER (Robbins), b. Dec. 14, 1827.
. GURDON (Robbins), b. Oct. 26, 1829.
. LUCY ANN S. (Robbins), b. April 22, 1832.
⅃. FRANCES CORNELIA (Robbins), b. July 11, 1835.

1679. CALVIN CAMP CRANE[6] [761], (Elijah,[5] Elijah,[4] Abraham,[3] Abraham,[2] Benjamin[1]), was born in Sandisfield, Mass., and married Lucretia Wolf at New Marlboro, Mass., Jan. 31, 1828. She was a native of New York, born 1803, and died Nov. 26 (another report says d. March 28), 1874. He died April 21, 1881. He was a carpenter by trade, and was deputy sheriff for Berkshire County 1842 to 1850. Residence at Great Barrington. Children :

1680—1. CHARLOTTE JANE, b. Feb. 3, 1829, in Sheffield, Mass.; m. Martin Isaac Lee.
1681—2. CAROLINE M., b. Feb. 11, 1830, in Sheffield, Mass.; m. Albert Winchell.
1682—3. EMILY, b. June 15, 1831, in Sheffield, Mass.; d. Oct. 15. 1835.
1683—4. HENRY JAMES, b. June 11, 1833, in Sheffield, Mass.

1684. ROYAL CRANE[6] [764], (Elijah,[5] Elijah,[4] Abraham,[3] Abraham,[2] Benjamin[1]), married Mary A. Beach, of Springfield, Mass., at Sheffield, Dec. 27, 1843 ; a farmer; residence at Mantorville, Dodge County, Minn. Was a member of the legislature 1864 and 1865. He died about 1890. Children :

1685—1. ROYAL, served in Co. I, 10th Regt. Minn. Vol. Infantry; lives in Mantorville; no children.
1686—2. GEORGE E.
1687—3. CLARA L.
1688—4. MARTHA J.
1689—5. MARY A.

1690. MILO R. CRANE[6] [768], (Elias,[5] Elijah,[4] Abraham,[3] Abraham,[2] Benjamin[1]), married Cordelia S. Vaugh, in Torrington, Conn., Oct. 8, 1839. She was a native of Morris, Conn., born Sept. 11, 1815; a farmer; residence at Berlin, Conn. Children :

1691—1. CHARLES W., b. July 26, 1845; m. Eva S. Moore, July 1, 1875; is superintendent of Union Chair Co. Works, Robertsville, Conn.
1692—2. FREDERICK H., b. April 13, 1847 ; a merchant.

1693. ALEXANDER NELSON CRANE[6] [780], (Abraham,[5] Elijah,[4] Abraham,[3] Abraham,[2] Benjamin[1]), married 1st, Sarah

Ann Shepard, of Hartford, Conn., Oct. 14, 1835. She died Jan. 30, 1866, aged 49; 2d, widow Sarah Marshall, of Collinsville, Conn. He was a farmer; residence at Bloomfield, Conn. Children :

1694—1. NELSON ALEXANDER, b. July 16, 1843.
1695—2. SARAH MARIA, b. June 16, 1850; d. April 25, 1851.
1696—3. ELLA RISSA, b. June 3, 1853; d. Sept. 15, 1853.
1697—4. NELSON W., b. 1868.

1698. NANCY CRANE[6] [785], (Samuel,[5] Hezekiah,[4] Abraham,[3] Abraham,[2] Benjamin[1]), married Royal Treat, March 6, 1828. She died Aug. 19, 1831. Child:

1 NANCY EMILY (Treat), b. Jan. 5, 1829.

1699. HARRIET CRANE[6] [787], (Samuel,[5] Hezekiah,[4] Abraham,[3] Abraham,[2] Benjamin[1]), married 1st, —— Vail; 2d, —— Hathaway.

1700. EMILY CRANE[6] [788], (Samuel,[5] Hezekiah,[4] Abraham,[3] Abraham,[2] Benjamin[1]), married Sylvester Woodhouse for his second wife. She died Jan. 15, 1890. Children:

1. NANCY EMILY (Woodhouse).
2. SYLVESTER (Woodhouse).

1701. JANE CRANE[6] [794], (Samuel,[5] Hezekiah,[4] Abraham,[3] Abraham,[2] Benjamin[1]), married Dr. John Charles Austin, of Fenton, England, May 4, 1840, and for a few years resided in Jersey City. They then removed to Albany, N. Y., where Dr. Austin practiced his profession until his death. He died Oct. 23, 1881. She died Nov. 6, 1895. Children:

1. CHARLES SAMUEL (Austin), b. Aug. 6, 1841; d. Feb. 7, 1842.
2. JOSEPHINE AMELIA (Austin), b. Nov. 1, 1842.
3. JOHN SAMUEL (Austin), b. June 23, 1845; d. March 19, 1848.
4. ELIZABETH JANE (Austin), b. Nov. 27, 1847; d. July 31, 1849.
5. THOMAS A. (Austin), b. Dec. 20, 1848.
6. EMMA JANE (Austin), b. Sept. 23, 1856.
7. FLORENCE (Austin), b. June 27, 1863.

1702. JOSEPHINE AMELIA AUSTIN [2]; m. John A. Baker, Feb. 7, 1865. She d. Dec. 19, 1894. Child:

1. CHARLES ALBERT (Baker), b. Nov. 18, 1868.

1703. THOMAS A. AUSTIN [5]; m. Anna Lansing Lemon, Nov. 17, 1870. Children:

1. WILLIAM LACY (Austin), b. Sept. 1, 1872.
2. BLANCHE CRANE (Austin), b. Aug. 15, 1875.

1704. EMMA JANE AUSTIN [6]; m. James Hilton Manning, Oct. 22, 1879; residence, January, 1897, Albany, N. Y. Child:

1. BEATRICE AUSTIN (Manning), b. Aug. 15, 1880.

1705. FLORENCE AUSTIN [7]; m Charles M. Adams, March 17, 1885. Child:

1. HAROLD MANNING (Adams), b. Nov. 10, 1892.

1706. JANE GREY CRANE[6] [796], (Hezekiah,[5] Hezekiah,[4] Abraham,[3] Abraham,[2] Benjamin[1]), married Martin Porter, Aug. 14, 1837. Children :

1. EDWARD ROMANTA (Porter), b. Oct. 22, 1838; residence at Hartford.
2. CARISSA JANE (Porter), b. Dec., 1848; d. young.
3. NELLIE WEBSTER (Porter), b. Aug. 22, 1852; residence at Unionville.

1707. JOSEPH CRANE[6] [801], (Joseph,[5] Joseph,[4] Abraham,[3] Abraham,[2] Benjamin[1]), married Sarah Bushnell, of Saybrook, Conn., in 1828, and settled in Norway, N. Y., where he was killed while sliding down hill, Feb. 21, 1859. His father died when he was less than two years of age, and March 10, 1813, Benj. S. Kelsey, of Fairfield, Herkimer County, N. Y., was appointed by the court in Connecticut guardian of Chauncey, as he was then called in the record, and his sister Mary. He was then about nine years old, and Mary about seven years. Benj. S. Kelsey appeared and gave bonds. Children :

1708—1. FRANCES E., b. May 17, 1829.
1709—2. SARAH, b. Feb. 8, 1832; d. Feb. 24, 1832.
1710—3. JOSEPH, b. Aug. 10, 1837; d. Aug. 28, 1837.

1711. MARY A. CRANE[6] [802], (Joseph,[5] Joseph,[4] Abraham,[3] Abraham,[2] Benjamin[1]), married James Wright, and removed to Indiana about 1850. Children :

1. MARTHA A. (Wright).
2. RUSSELL (Wright).
3. JOSEPH C. (Wright).
4. HAMILTON (Wright).

1712. EMELINE CRANE[6] [805], (George,[5] Joseph,[4] Abraham,[3] Abraham,[2] Benjamin[1]), married James L. Morehouse, Dec. 26, 1844, at Fairfield, Herkimer County, N. Y. She died Aug. 18, 1888. Both were teachers. He died near Minetto, Oswego County, N. Y., Nov. 30, 1860. Children :

1. ALMIRA U. (Morehouse), b. and d. 1845.
2. GEORGE CRANE (Morehouse), b. May 14, 1846.
3. JAMES L., Jr. (Morehouse), b. Jan. 16, 1853; d. Feb. 9, 1854.
4. EDWARD L. (Morehouse), b. June 2, 1855.

1712½. GEORGE CRANE MOREHOUSE [2]; m. Eugenia M. Miller at Trenton, Oneida County, N. Y., Dec. 25, 1877. She d. Nov. 19, 1879, leaving one child. He m. 2d, Mary Breen at Trenton, N. Y., July 2, 1888, and had three children by her. He is a graduate of Cornell University, class of 1873; LL.B. Hamilton College, class of 1875; a lawyer; and city judge of Utica, N. Y., 1892 to 1896. Children :

1. FLORENCE (Morehouse), b. Sept. 22, 1878; d. Dec. 7, 1881.
2. LAWRENCE (Morehouse), b. Feb. 24, 1889.
3. MERWIN (Morehouse), b. April 20, 1890.
4. RUSSEL (Morehouse), b. Nov. 6, 1891.

1713. ABBY CRANE[6] [809], (Justus,[5] Joseph,[4] Abraham,[3] Abraham,[2] Benjamin[1]), married Oct. 12, 1834, William Bradford Douglas. Children :

1. ANNA LOUISA (Douglas), b. May 18, 1837 ; d. 1839.
2. HORACE BEDFORD (Douglas), b. April 22, 1840.
3. WILLIAM CRANE (Douglas), b. July 21, 1843.
4. THEODORE WHITFIELD (Douglas), b. June 18, 1847:
5. EMMA CAROLINE (Douglas), b. Sept. 5, 1850.

1714. DAVID CRANE[6] [812], (David,[5] Joseph,[4] Abraham,[3] Abraham,[2] Benjamin[1]) married Katharine Callahan, Feb. 13, 1861. Residence at Wethersfield, Conn. She died February, 1875. Children :

1715—1. GEORGE, b. Sept. 8, 1863.
1716—2. EDITH A., b. April 14, 1866.
1717—3. HARRY W., b. Dec. 11, 1868; lives in Wethersfield, Conn.

1718. CHARLES AMER CRANE[7] [821], (Jonathan,[6] Jonathan.[5] Silas,[4] Jonathan,[3] Jonathan,[2] Benjamin[1]), was born in Aylesford County, Nová Scotia. He served three and a half years in the confederate army; was at Vicksburg and other places in the States of Mississippi and Louisiana. He married Julia B. Wills, a native of Jackson, La., Jan. 7, 1873, at that place; and in 1879 was keeper of a livery stable at Clinton, La. Children:

1719—1. KATIE AMELIA.
1720—2. CHARLES DAVID.

1721. WILLIAM CRANE[7] [825], (James N.,[6] Jonathan,[5] Silas,[4] Jonathan,[3] Jonathan,[2] Benjamin[1]), a farmer, and resided at Grand Pré, his residence being near where the old French chapel stood described in Longfellow's poem, "Evangeline." He took considerable interest in the history of the family; owned the coat of arms used by his grandfather, Jonathan Crane, and sent it to the compiler of this family history that he might copy it. He married at Louisburg, Cape Breton, July 12, 1849, Catherine M. McAlpine, born Dec. 4, 1827. The last few years of his life he was not in robust health, and visited Florida to avoid severe weather. He died Nov. 11, 1884. The estate was settled by his widow as administratrix, and his son, James Noble, administrator. Children:

1722—1. CHARLES L.
1723—2. HENRIETTA L.
1724—3. JAMES NOBLE.
1725—4. LAURA A.
1726—5. WILLIAM A.
1727—6. EDITH M.
1728—7. FREDERICK H.

1729. TRUMAN L. CRANE[7] [856], (John,[6] Benjamin,[5] John,[4] John,[3] Jonathan,[2] Benjamin[1]), married Lucy Rathburn, Oct. 23, 1828, at Bristol, Vt. He died there Feb. 22, 1876. She died there Oct. 9, 1891. Children, all born at Bristol:

1730—1. HORACE ALONZO, b. Feb. 16, 1830.
1731—2. ROSINA L., b. Sept. 12, 1831; m. Judson L. Scott; residence Highgate Springs, Vt.
1732—3. CALISTA R., b. July 4, 1833; m. Noble Varney.
1733—4. CYLENA D., b. June 19, 1836; m. Joshua Rockwood.
1734—5. JULIA M., b. July 22, 1842; m. Reuben Parker.

1735. MARTHA R. CRANE[7] [860], (Amos,[6] Elijah,[5] John,[4] John,[3] Jonathan[2], Benjamin[1]), was born in Washington, Mass.;

married Daniel Sibley, of that town, Oct. 29, 1818, and resided there until the year 1870, when they removed to Minneapolis, Minn. She died there June 14, 1882, aged 81 years.

Children :

1. MARTHA A. (Sibley), b. Oct. 26, 1819; m. Hiram Merriam, Jan. 1, 1839; d. June 30, 1839.
2. MARY (Sibley), b. April 8, 1821; m. 1st, Henry Deary, Aug. 7, 1845; 2d, Peter Mabies. Sept. 2, 1875.
3. PHEBE M. (Sibley), b. Dec. 5, 1822; m. William Fowler, April 28, 1840; d. March 2, 1868.
4. AMANDA (Sibley), b. Sept. 11, 1824; d. Sept. 26, 1826.
5. CORNELIA A. (Sibley), b. Sept. 6, 1826; m. Absalom Mallison, June 29, 1848.
6. LOUISA A. (Sibley), b. Oct. 5, 1828; m. Horace L. Savery, Feb. 6, 1851.
7. NANCY A. (Sibley), b. Dec. 2, 1830; m. Jonathan Peirce, Sept. 1, 1847; d. July 10, 1883, at Derby, Conn.
8. LUCY (Sibley), b. March 31, 1833; m. Solomon Wring. June 8, 1852.
9. DANIEL M. (Sibley), b. June 19, 1835; m. Maria A. Buck, July 3, 1856.
10. Infant son (Sibley), b. Aug. 1, 1837, d. Aug. 27, 1837.
11. Infant son (Sibley), b. Aug. 7, and d. Nov. 21, 1838.
12. HARRIET P. (Sibley), b. Sept. 18, 1840.
13. WILLIAM F. (Sibley), b. March 6, 1843; m. Mary E. Morgan, Aug. 22, 1872.

1736. AMOS S. CRANE[7] [861], (Amos,[6] Elijah,[5] John,[4] John,[3] Jonathan,[2] Benjamin[1]), was born in Washington, Mass.; married Fanny Lewis, of Suffield, Conn., Sept. 26, 1828, and settled in Washington, a farmer, where he remained until 1847, when he removed to Suffield, Conn., continuing his vocation as a farmer. He was an influential citizen; a member of the Massachusetts Legislature in 1842, and also a member of the Connecticut Legislature in 1853. Children :

1737—1. JOHN L., b. Sept. 9, 1829; m. Mary A. Hill, of North Brookfield, Mass., Sept. 15, 1858. He went to Kansas and was actively engaged with John Brown in excluding slaveholders from that State. He was killed during the massacre at Lawrence, by Quantrell's bands of raiders, on the morning of Aug. 21, 1863, when they called him from his bed to the door and shot him down on his own doorstep. His widow died Oct. 16, 1880, aged 74 years.
1738—2. GEORGE S., b. Aug. 27, 1831.
1739—3. ELLEN M., b. Jan. 3, 1833.
1740—4. LUTHER K., b. March 31, 1835.
1741—5. JAMES P., b. July 22, 1840.

1742. SAMUEL R. CRANE[7] [862], (Amos,[6] Elijah,[5] John,[4] John,[3] Jonathan,[2] Benjamin[1]), was born in Washington, Mass.; married Mary W. Butler, of Pittsfield, Mass., May 11, 1836. He spent most of his married life in Springfield, where he was employed in the United States Armory, and at time of his death was one of the employés who had given the longest service in that institution. He died in Springfield, Oct. 5, 1879. He was

admitted a member of Hampden Lodge of Odd Fellows, Feb. 6, 1846, and into Agawam Encampment, Oct. 22, 1847. After filling nearly all the minor offices he was advanced to the highest offices in the gift of the two bodies. All of these positions he filled with great credit to himself and the order, to which he was most devotedly attached. Mr. Crane's funeral was largely attended by the fraternity. His remains were carried to the grave by his three sons (Samuel H., Merritt B. and Frank S.) and his son-in-law, Charles E. Brown, of West, Stone & Co., this being the father's request. The late Mr. Crane was a member of Class A of the Odd Fellows' Mutual Relief Association.

The following notice of his death appeared in the *New England Homestead*, a newspaper published in that city:

" It is with sadness that we record the death of that good man, Past Grand and Past Chief Patriarch Samuel R. Crane, which occurred at his residence on Walnut Street last Sunday. His health has been failing for more than a year, but he was confined to his bed only a few days. He had reached the good old age of 74 years and 11 months. Mr. Crane leaves a wife, one daughter and three sons, who deeply mourn their loss, for he was loved and respected by all who knew him as a considerate neighbor, kind husband and affectionate parent. He had resided in Springfield 43 years, having been employed most of the time in the armory, so that he was one of the oldest armorers in the city."

Children :

1743—1. SAMUEL H., b. Nov. 9, 1839.
1744—2. MARY E., b. Oct, 6, 1841.
1745—3. JOHN R., b. May 12, 1844 ; d. June 15, 1862.
1746—4. MARTHA W., b. April 15, 1845 ; d. Aug. 17, 1845.
1747—5. MERRITT B., b. Jan. 14, 1847, m. Mary E. Davis, of Springfield, Nov. 25, 1868.
1748—6. FRANK S., b. Jan. 11, 1850 ; m. Emma Mills, of Springfield, Oct. 22, 1873.

1749. POLLY CRANE[7] [863], (Amos,[6] Elijah,[5] John,[4] John,[3] Jonathan,[2] Benjamin[1]), was born in Washington, Mass. ; married William Hamilton, of Chester, Mass., Oct. 11, 1832. She died in Southwick, April 7, 1859. Children :

1. GEORGE W. (Hamilton), b. March 12, 1834, in Chester.
2. MARTHA (Hamilton), b. April 17, 1839, in Middlefield, Mass.

1750. GEORGE W. HAMILTON [1] ; m. Mary E. Gillette, of Southwick, Oct. 6, 1857, where they settled. Children :

1. WILLIAM A. (Hamilton), b. Oct. 18, 1858.
2. JESSIE S. (Hamilton), b. Oct. 15, 1860.
3. FRANK S. (Hamilton), b. July 24, 1864.

1751. MARTHA HAMILTON [2] ; m. Frank G. Fox, of Bethel, Conn., April 6, 1864. He died before July, 1882, and she m. 2d, Andrew Bryson, of Springfield, Mass., and removed to Worcester. Child :

1. FRANK G. (Fox), b. Jan. 15, 1865, at Suffield, Conn.

1752. GEORGE CRANE[7] [864], (Amos,[6] Elijah,[5] John,[4] John,[3] Jonathan,[2] Benjamin[1]), was born in Washington, Mass. ; married Amanda Pease, of Middlefield, Mass., Oct. 20, 1841, and settled in Washington as a farmer. About the year 1850 he removed to Chester. After the death of his first wife he married Lucy M. Tucker, of Chicopee, Dec. 11, 1855. Children :

1753—1. GEORGE P., b. Dec. 16, 1842; d. Aug. 7, 1851.
1754—2. CHARLES E., b. Jan. 28, 1845.
1755—3. AMOS S., b. Nov. 12, 1846.
1756—4. MYRON L., b. Sept. 26, 1850.
1757—5. WILLIAM G., b. Aug. 7, 1852.
1758—6. ISABELLA A., b. Jan. 1, 1857; m. Amos Belcher, of Chester, Mass., Nov. 28, 1877.
1759—7. JAMES E., b. July 3, 1858.
1760—8. JENNY L., b. Nov. 9, 1862.

1761. JOHN M. CRANE[7] [866], (Amos,[6] Elijah,[5] John,[4] John,[3] Jonathan,[2] Benjamin[1]), was born in Washington, Mass. ; married 1st, Sarah M. Joy; 2d, Mary C. Wright, of Middlefield, May 20, 1846. He settled in Washington; a farmer, tilling a portion of the ancestral farm, and the last of the name of this large family to retain a residence in the old home of their birth. His wife Mary C. died Feb. 5, 1880. Children :

1762—1. JOHN W., b. May 23, 1847.
1763—2. DELIA M., b. May 1, 1849.
1764—3. MYRA C., b. Oct. 15, 1850.
1765—4. LESTER M., b. Dec. 31, 1852.

1766. NANCY CRANE[7] [870], (Joel,[6] Elijah,[5] John,[4] John,[3] Jonathan,[2] Benjamin[1]), married Daniel Kelly, of Lysander, Onondaga County, N. Y., Aug. 25, 1830, and that place became their home. She died there Feb. 4, 1864. Children :

1. ALBERT O. (Kelly), b. Aug. 27, 1831.
2. EDWIN O. (Kelly), b. Nov. 4, 1833.
3. EMILY J. (Kelly), b. Sept. 5, 1835.
4. JOEL F. (Kelly), b. July 23, 1837.
5. HENRY T. (Kelly), b. April 25, 1839.
6. CELESTIA (Kelly), b. May 15, 1842.
7. MARION (Kelly), b. March 7, 1844.
8. HARRIET (Kelly), b. Nov. 6, 1845.
9. THERON D. (Kelly), b. Aug. 7, 1848.

1767. JOEL S. CRANE[7] [871], (Joel,[6] Elijah,[5] John,[4] John,[3] Jonathan,[2] Benjamin[1]). In the year 1826, when but seventeen years of age, he removed to the State of New York, where he married Dec. 30, 1833, Polly McCabe, and settled in the town of Lysander, Onondaga County. He was a farmer, and with the exception of three years his subsequent life was passed on the farm where he first located. He died March 20, 1868, after a long illness. Children :

1768—1. ALFRED E., b. April 21, 1835.
1769—2. LUCY A., b. May 1, 1840; m. Charles E. Crane.

"Our deceased brother, Mr. Joel S. Crane, in 1832, experienced religion, we believe, under the ministration of Father

Young, of blessed memory, and soon after joined the Methodist Episcopal Church, in which communion he remained until his death. He held the office of Class Leader from the period of his first introduction into the Church until his infirmities prevented him from farther engaging in the active duties of the position. He also acted as Superintendent of the Sabbath School for a great portion of the time; and all that appertained to his official position was always well and faithfully done. In all the relations of life, Mr. Crane was ever respected and esteemed. As a neighbor he was kind and obliging; as a friend true as the needle to the pole; as a citizen loyal and patriotic. But it was in his own family and in the Church of Christ where his many excellent qualities shone forth most conspicuously. To the loving, devoted husband and the watchful and affectionate father, he joined the character of the humble, self-denying, earnest, working Christian. To toil in the vineyard of his Master was to him a labor of love. In this regard he seemed to count all else but loss so that ' he might attain unto the excellency of the knowledge which is in Christ Jesus our Lord.' Brother Crane not only adorned his profession in the way we have . just indicated, but he was likewise equally ready to contribute of his money, generously too, to support the good cause he loved so well. His house was always open, and no man ever came to it hungry, but that he fed him; thirsty, but that he gave him drink; naked, and he clothed him; sick, and he ministered unto him. Thus in his charities he seemed to be actuated by the principle, that ' inasmuch as ye have done it unto one of the least of these, my brethren, ye have done it unto me.' Mr. Crane, too, was a man of more than ordinary intellect, well posted on all the prominent topics of the day, and his opinions in relation to them were always characterized with intelligence and good sense. He was likewise one of the most genial and pleasant companions with whom to converse that can be found in any community, and this particular element in his constitutional make-up caused his society to be eagerly sought both by young and old. Mr. Crane was also a very successful farmer and left a fine estate to be inherited by his widow and children. One other thing we must not forget to mention, and that is the fortitude, resignation and cheerfulness, which he exhibited all through his protracted and painful illness. No words of complaint or murmuring ever escaped him. In fact, he would not unfrequently raise the spirits of his own family and friends by perpetrating some little pleasantry, or by throwing into the conversation a spicy remark, which would serve to drive away all gloom and melancholy. Indeed, it is our opinion that this cheerfulness and the stir and ambition with which he was naturally endowed, added months if not years to his life."

1770. ELIJAH C. CRANE[7] [875], (Elijah,[6] Elijah,[5] John,[4] John,[3] Jonathan,[2] Benjamin[1]), was born in Madrid, N. Y.; mar-

ried at Potsdam, N. Y., in 1837, Julia Bird. She was born in Potsdam in 1819. For many years their residence was Canton, N. Y. He was a carpenter by trade. In 1860, he was living in Sterling, Wis., but later removed to Burlington, Iowa.

Children :

1771—1. RHODA, b. at Canton.
1772—2. MARY, b. at Canton.
1773—3. ROSINA, b. at Canton.
1774—4. WRIGHT S., b. 1850, at Canton.
1775—5. GEORGE V., b. Sept. 2. 1853, at Canton.
1776—6. THERON E., b. at Canton; d. March, 1868.
1777—7. CARLOS O., b. Nov. 12, 1860, at Sterling, Wis.

1778. OLVISON W. CRANE[7] [876], (Elijah,[6] Elijah,[5] John,[4] John,[3] Jonathan,[2] Benjamin[1]), was born in Madrid, N. Y.; married at Canton, N. Y., Nov. 7, 1847, Emily R. Emerson, a native of Colebrook, Vt. She was born Sept. 26, 1826. He is a farmer, and resided in Canton, N. Y., for many years, but late in life removed to Minnesota. Children :

1779—1. CYRUS M., b. Sept. 6, 1848; unm.
1780—2. MATILDA A., b. Jan. 19, 1850; d. Mch. 5, 1861.
1781—3. GEORGE W., b. Aug. 4, 1854.
1782—4. RALPH E., b. April 22, 1858; school teacher, Canton, N. Y., but late residence at Austin, Minn.
1783—5. FIDELIA R., b. June 2, 1860; d. Dec. 7, 1861.
1784—6. WADE O., b. June 13, 1862.
1785—7. LUCY A., b. Sept. 25, 1864.
1786—8. EMMA M., b. Dec. 22, 1866; d. Feb. 9, 1867.
1787—9. MINA L., b. Feb. 14, 1871.

1788. ORSON N. CRANE[7] [877], (Elijah,[6] Elijah,[5] John,[4] John,[3] Jonathan,[2] Benjamin[1]), was born at Madrid, N. Y.; married there April 5, 1847, to Lavina L. Chamberlain. He was a farmer, and resided in his native town, She was born in Madrid, Feb. 5, 1826. He died Oct. 16, 1893. She died Jan. 28, 1897. Child :

1789—1. WALTER O., b. July 16, 1860; a farmer at Madrid, N. Y.

1790. LESTER CRANE[7] [878], (Elijah,[6] Elijah,[5] John,[4] John,[3] Jonathan,[2] Benjamin[1]), was a native of Madrid, N. Y.; married in Canton, about 1848, Ann Cole. He removed to Lansing, Iowa, where he is engaged in fruit raising. Children :

1791—1. GILBERT E., b. Mch. 24, 1854, at Canton; d. Sept. 24, 1868.
1792—2. STELLA E., b. June 3, 1858, at Canton.
1793—3. SUMNER L., b. Mch. 28, 1861, at Canton.
1794—4. CLINTON L., b. Nov. 26, 1869, at Sterling, Wis.
1795—5. ARTHUR L., b. Mch. 21, 1875, at Lansing, Iowa.

1796. AMOS L. CRANE[7] [879], (Elijah,[6] Elijah,[5] John,[4] John,[3] Jonathan,[2] Benjamin[1]), was a native of Madrid, N. Y.; married at Canton, May 9, 1853, Laura P. Fish. She was born Sept. 24, 1828. His children were born in Canton. Children :

1797—1. EDGAR A., b. July 6, 1856.
1798—2. CARRIE A., b. July 14, 1860.

12

1799. EDWIN D. CRANE[7] [886], (Archer,[6] Samuel,[5] John,[4] John,[3] Jonathan,[2] Benjamin[1]), married June, 1831, Sarah B. Keyes, of Sodus, N. Y., In August, 1837, he removed to Michigan, and settled in Blissfield in 1842; a farmer. He died Feb. 14, 1867. She died June 20, 1884. Children :

1800—1. MAHLON D., b. April 6, 1832.
1801—2. JAMES K., b. March 8, 1834.
1802—3. CHARLES E., b. Feb. 14, 1836.
1803—4. HELEN M., b. July 14, 1845.

1804. CHARLES T. CRANE[7] [887], (Archer,[6] Samuel,[5] John,[4] John,[3] Jonathan,[2] Benjamin[1]), married Amyrillis Judd, Nov. 22, 1837. He died March 20, 1886. Children :

1805—1. CELESTIA C., b. Aug. 5, 1842.
1806—2. EDITH A., b. May 15, 1849.
1807—3. CLARENCE O., b. March 27, 1853.
1808—4. IDA M., b. March 10, 1856; m. Elroy Zimmerman, Nov. 23, 1881.
1809—5. ARCHER G., b. Dec. 3, 1858.
1810—6. C. LYLE, b. September, 1864.

1811. JOEL C. CRANE[7] [888], (Archer,[6] Samuel,[5] John,[4] John,[3] Jonathan,[2] Benjamin[1]), married Catharine Lawrence, Oct. 16, 1845. He died in Marcellus, N. Y., about 1866.
Child :

1812—1. MARIE.

1813. ARCHER H. CRANE[7] [890], (Archer,[6] Samuel,[5] John,[4] John,[3] Jonathan,[2] Benjamin[1]), was married four times. 1st, Helen M. Wood, March 8, 1846; 2d, Helen F. Rowe; 3d, Sally A. Barrett; 4th, Julia E. Robinson. For many years he was a supervisor of his township. Also a member of the Legislature. Children :

1814—1. CLARA A., b. July 25, 1854.
1815—2. MYRTIE M., b. Sept. 21, 1857; d. July 23, 1870.
1816—3. HELEN, b. May, 1883.

1817. DANIEL COLTON CRANE[7] [921], (Daniel C,[6] Samuel,[5] John,[4] John,[3] Jonathan,[2] Benjamin[1]), born in Greenfield, Ind.; married Dec. 24, 1891, in Deerfield, Mich., Alice C. Baker. She was a native of Canada, and born July 27, 1870. He is a farmer, and lives in Deerfield, Mich.; have an adopted child.
Child :

1818—1. LESLIE J., b. March 4, 1893.

1819. EDWIN S. CRANE[7] [922], (Daniel C.,[6] Samuel,[5] John,[4] John,[3] Jonathan,[2] Benjamin[1]), married Arvilla E. Burton, Nov. 27, 1881. She was born Oct. 5, 1862. Children :

1820—1. ETHEL J., b. Aug. 30, 1882.
1821—2. EARL E., b. Oct. 25, 1883.
1822—3. D. CARLTON, b. March 5, 1886.
1823—4. ROBERT R., b. June 30, 1889.

1824—5. LLOYD M., b. May 13, 1892.
1825—6. FRANK, b. Sept. 21, 1896; d. March 11, 1897.

1826. THIRZA M. CRANE[7] [923], (Daniel C,[6] Samuel,[5] John,[4] John,[3] Jonathan,[2] Benjamin[1]), married William Thompson, Aug. 18, 1886. She died March 10, 1893. Children:

1. VIOLET (Thompson), b. March 9, 1888.
2. RUSSEL (Thompson), b. Dec. 18, 1890; d. May 28, 1894.
3. LESLIE J. (Thompson), b. March 4, 1893. *(See* Daniel Colton Crane).

1827. LAFAYETTE CRANE[7] [931], (Luke,[6] Samuel,[5] John,[4] John,[3] Jonathan,[2] Benjamin[1]), born in Genesee County, N. Y.; married in ——, Mich., Sept. 10, 1850, Mary A. Van Nest; settled in La Porte, Ind.; a hardware merchant. Child:

1828—1. KATHARINE, b. April 30, 1870.

1829. B. FRANKLIN CRANE[7] [933], (Luke,[6] Samuel,[5] John,[4] John,[3] Jonathan,[2] Benjamin[1]), married 1st, Dec. 24, 1857, Amanda E. Bryant; 2d, Margaret Ann Richards. Both wives were of La Porte, Ind. He died September, 1898. Children:*

1830—1. ADDIE MAY.
1831—2. CLARA MAUDE.
1832—3. AMANDA E.
1833—4. CLARA E.

1834. Dr. JONAS B. CRANE[7]. [943], (Isaac,[6] Joshua,[5] Abiah,[4] John,[3] Jonathan,[2] Benjamin[1]), married in 1834 Mary Chandler; settled in Halifax, Pa. He died May 8, 1849, in Plain Grove, Mercer County, Pa. Was tall and of slim build, of light complexion, and had the reputation of being a good physician. Children:

1835—1. EMILY, b. Nov. 8, 1835; d. 1840.
1836—2. Son; d. in infancy.
1837—3. FRANCES MARIA, b. March 8, 1839; m. Wm. Maybury.
1838—4. JULIA EMMA, b. April 22, 1842; m. Wm. McCarnes.

1839. MARIA CRANE[7] [946], (Isaac,[6] Joshua,[5] Abiah,[4] John,[3] Jonathan,[2] Benjamin[1]), married Jan. 13, 1831, Elisha Kingsbury. Children:

1. CYRUS ASWELL (Kingsbury), b. Jan. 1, 1832.
2. MARTHA ADELINE (Kingsbury), b. June, 1844.
3. MILTON (Kingsbury), } twins, b. 1848; { d. 1872.
4. MARY (Kingsbury), } { d. 1849.
5. HARRIETT (Kingsbury), b. 1851; m. James Wilson, and resides at Slippery Rock township, Butler County, Pa.

1840. PATTY ADELINE CRANE[7] [950], (Isaac,[6] Joshua,[5] Abiah,[4] John,[3] Jonathan,[2] Benjamin[1]), married March 20, 1838, William Marvin, Jr. He was born in Springfield, Vt., May, 1811, and died September, 1861; she died September, 1871. Children:

1. OSROW (Marvin), b. July 30, 1841.

———

* Records very confusing; not sure of this family.

2. BYRON (Marvin), b. Sept. 13, 1843.
3. ELLA (Marvin), b. May 13, 1845.
4. ORA (Marvin), b. May 17, 1849.
5. NORMAN (Marvin), b. June 26, 1851.
6. NOBLE (Marvin), b. July 30, 1854.

1841. HARRIETT NEWELL CRANE[7] [953], (Isaac,[6] Joshua,[5] Abiah,[4] John,[3] Jonathan,[2] Benjamin[1]), married Jackson Marvin, of Alstead, N. H., son of William and Mercy Marvin. Residence at Alstead, where their eldest son is town clerk. Children:

1. FRED T. (Marvin), b. Dec. 4, 1854.
2. BELLE H. (Marvin), b. Dec. 25, 1856.

1842. JULIANA CRAIN[7] [955], (Joshua,[6] Joshua,[5] Abiah,[4] John,[3] Jonathan,[2] Benjamin[1]), married Hon. Hiram Monroe, Nov. 29 (Thanksgiving day), 1827. Children:

1. SARAH CRAIN (Monroe), b. Feb. 5, 1829; d. Nov. 27, 1854.
2. LAVINA (Monroe), b. June 15, 1830.
3. HARVEY H. (Monroe), b. Feb. 27, 1832.

1843. LAVINA MONROE [2]; m. Charles Morgan, May 9, 1854. Child:

1. CHARLES H. (Morgan), b. April 8, 1855.

1844. HARVEY H. MONROE [3]; m. September, 1860, Anna Griffin, of Gloucester, Mass. He graduated at Dartmouth in 1858, and from the Medical School the year following, and commenced the practice of medicine at East Washington, N. H., in May, 1860, and d. May 2, 1863. His widow practiced medicine after the death of her husband, and d. some years later in Boston, Mass. Children:

1. LIZZIE (Monroe), b. Sept. 15, 1861; d. June 20, 1863.
2. ANNA HARVEY (Monroe), b. May 1, 1863; d. Aug. 9, 1863.

1845. LOUISA R. CRAIN[7] [956], (Joshua,[6] Joshua,[5] Abiah,[4] John,[3] Jonathan,[2] Benjamin[1]), married James Dwinels, Feb. 22, 1832, and settled in Canaan, N. H., where she died Oct. 18, 1851. Children:

1. JULIANA CRAIN (Dwinels), b. Feb. 23, 1833.
2. CHARLES (Dwinels), b. Aug. 25, 1834.
3. GEORGE (Dwinels), b. Dec. 18, 1835; d. Feb. 25, 1840.
4. SARAH C. (Dwinels), b. March 29, 1837; d. June 28, 1868.
5. CATHARINE M. (Dwinels), b. June 10, 1843; d. June 18, 1843.

1846. JULIANA CRAIN DWINELS [1]; m. Moses Withington, April 21, 1859. Child:

1. J. FRANK (Withington), b. Jan. 8, 1861.

1847. CHARLES DWINELS [2]; m. 1st, Albina L. Richardson, Jan. 16, 1861; she d. Nov. 25, 1874; m. 2d, Mrs. Julia A. Richardson, April 3, 1876. Children:

1. CORA B. (Dwinels), b. Nov. 20, 1866; d. April 25, 1875.
2. DAISY D. (Dwinels), b. Jan. 30, 1872.

1848. JOSHUA D. CRAIN[7] [957], (Joshua,[6] Joshua,[5] Abiah,[4] John,[3] Jonathan,[2] Benjamin[1]), born in Hillsboro, N. H.; married

Elizabeth Minott, Feb. 21, 1837. She was a native of that place, and born Jan. 26, 1815. They settled in Washington, N. H., where he carried on farming, and where he died Aug. 4, 1870. She died April 5, 1884. Children:

1849—1. SYLVANUS ORLANDO, b. May 2, 1840; d. Feb. 16, 1841.
1850—2. SARAH EGLENTINE, b. June 20, 1842.

1852. SAMUEL CRAIN[7] [971], (Samuel,[6] Joshua,[5] Abiah,[4] John,[3] Jonathan,[2] Benjamin[1]), was born in Alstead, N. H.; married Nancy Richardson, of New Hampshire, and removed to New Jersey about the year 1817, where he taught school many years. His home was for a time in Newark, but he died in Elizabeth, N. J., in 1847. His widow died May 20, 1879.
Children:

1853—1. SAMUEL O., b. about 1814.
1854—2. OSCAR V., b. July, 1816.
1855—3. OZRO A.,   } twins, b. 1821.
1856—4. AMANDA ESTHER, }

1857. WILLIAM CULLEN CRAIN[7] [992], (Rufus,[6] Isaac,[5] Abiah,[4] John,[3] Jonathan,[2] Benjamin[1]), was born in Warren, Herkimer County, N. Y.: married June, 1826, Perses Narina Tunnicliff, a native of Warren, born in 1808. He was a member of the Legislature of New York, in 1831, 1845 and 1846, the latter year being Speaker of the House. He died March 16, 1865.
Children:

1858—1. PHILOTHETA M., b. March 3, 1827.
1859—2. RUFUS WILLIAM, b. Jan. 14, 1829; d. May 7, 1863.
1860—3. DUNHAM JONES, b. Feb. 28, 1831.
1861—4. RICHARD T., b. April 30, 1833, at Cullenwood; d. Oct. 26, 1895. From 1878 to 1894 he resided at Port-au-Prince, Hayti, where he had business interests. He was on most friendly terms with Presidents Solomon, Legitime and Hippolite, and was conspicuous for his generous hospitality to Americans visiting Hayti.
1862—5. CHARLOTTE R., b. July 4, 1835.
1863—6. WILLIAM BAKER, b. April 20, 1838. This well-known physician was born at Cullenwood, the family homestead. Having graduated at the Medical University of Pennsylvania just as the War of the Rebellion was opening, he was soon placed in charge of the United States Military Hospital at Washington, D. C. Subsequently he was assigned to the charge of the United States Hospital, at New Creek, Va. He was also commissioned as Surgeon, with the rank of Major, in a regiment of Maryland Cavalry. He was present at Antietam and other battles. At the close of the war he began the practice of medicine at Richfield Springs, N. Y., where he still resides.
1864—7. BIANCA LOUISA, b. March 16, 1841; d. July 10, 1846.

1865. VIANCY CRAIN[7] [993], (Rufus,[6] Isaac,[5] Abiah,[4] John,[3] Jonathan,[2] Benjamin[1]), married William Baker. Child:

1. RUFUS (Baker); settled in Utica, N. Y.

1866. WILLIAM D. CRANE[7] [996], (Asa,[6] Isaac,[5] Abiah,[4] John,[3] Jonathan,[2] Benjamin[1]), married Louisa E. Dunning. Children :

1867—1. JAMES D., b. Jan. 19, 1835.
1868—2. ANN M., b. June 29, 1837; m. E. N. White; d. Dec. 1, 1884; no children.
1869—3. ALBERT, b. Nov. 1, 1839; d. Nov. 14, 1867.
1870—4. MARY L., b. Oct. 22, 1841; m. Orris Pratt; residence Spring Prairie, Wis.; no children.
1871—5. FRANCES D., b. Aug. 3, 1843; m. Wilson R. Law; d. May 6, 1886.
1872—6. WALTER L., b. July 25, 1845; d. April, 1870.
1873—7. WILLIAM HENRY, b. Dec. 2, 1847.
1874—8. AMARYLLIS D., b. June 23, 1850; m. Walter J. Thompson; residence Palo Alto, Cal.
1875—9. APHIA M., b. Dec. 10, 1852; residence Colorado Springs, Col.

1876. ELIZA CRANE[7] [998], (Asa,[6] Isaac,[5] Abiah,[4] John,[3] Jonathan,[2] Benjamin[1]), married Ichabod Marshall. Children :

1. HELEN (Marshall).
2. RICHARD (Marshall).

1877. MOSES L. CRANE[7] [1001], (Asa,[6] Isaac,[5] Abiah,[4] John,[3] Jonathan,[2] Benjamin[1]), married Sept. 5, 1849, Susan P. Chase. She was born Dec. 2, 1824. Children :

1878—1. CHARLES D., b. July 6, 1850.
1879—2. WILLIS E., b. July 22, 1855; Wilmette, Ill.

1880. HELEN M. CRANE[7] [1004], (Asa,[6] Isaac,[5] Abiah,[4] John,[3] Jonathan,[2] Benjamin[1]), married Feb. 2, 1848, Cantine Garrison. He was born Aug. 26, 1822. Children :

1. MARSHALL (Garrison), b. July 24, 1849; residence Evanston, Ill.
2. CATHARINE (Garrison), b. Oct. 22, 1851; m. C. W. Wood; Madison, So. Dakota.
3. FLORENCE (Garrison), b. Nov. 7, 1854; d. Oct. 22, 1855.
4. CLARENCE (Garrison), b. April 8, 1855; d. Aug. 2, 1857.
5. BERNICE (Garrison), b. Dec. 29, 1857; m. J. D. Frazer; Lockport, Ill.
6. BLANCHE (Garrison), b. Oct. 10, 1860; d. April 24, 1885.
7. HANSERD K. (Garrison), b. March 9, 1863.
8. GLADYS E. (Garrison), b. Aug. 19, 1865; m. Chas. W. Williams; lives at Sioux City, Ia.

1881. ISAAC NEWTON CRAIN[7] [1007], (Amos,[6] Isaac,[5] Abiah,[4] John,[3] Jonathan,[2] Benjamin[1]), married June 31, 1842, Synthia Amanda Holmes. At the age of fourteen he went to learn the tailor's trade at Lockport, N. Y. He settled in Michigan, first living in Niles about five years; then in Caro, where he was engaged in farming about six years. From there he removed to Saginaw, where he manufactured shingles for nine years. He was engaged sixteen years as sexton of St. Paul's Episcopal church there. Now (December, 1896), 83 years old.

Children :

1882—1. DE WITT W., b. April 6, 1843; d. Nov. 2, 1864, in East
Saginaw.
1883—2. PHEBE E., b. May 24, 1846.
1884—3. CHARLES J., b. Oct. 31, 1850; d. March 29, 1882, in East
Saginaw.
1885—4. MARY E., b. Nov. 27, 1853.
1886—5. LEWIS C., b. April 3, 1855.
1887—6. SILVEA D., b. Feb. 6, 1860.

1888. WILLIAM M. CRANE[7] [1009], (Amos,[6] Isaac,[5] Abiah,[4]
John,[3] Jonathan,[2] Benjamin[1]), married in Niles, Mich., Sept.
18, 1849, Sarah Elizabeth Griffith. She was born at Cedar
Creek, Sussex County, Delaware, Aug. 21, 1830. He was educated at Albion Seminary, Michigan, graduating in class of
1846-7. He resided for many years in Greenville, Montcalm
County, Mich., engaged in the real estate and insurance business.
Their eldest child was born in Niles, the other children in Greenville. Children :

1889—1. MORTIMER E., b. July 10, 1850; m. June 11, 1874, Mary
Louise Smith, at Marion, Iowa, where they reside.
1890—2. EMMA G., b. Sept. 2, 1853; m. Chas. G. Godfrey, Dec. 18,
1877. She is a graduate of Ladies' Seminary, Glens
Falls, N. Y.
1891—3. LILLIE, F., b. June 6. 1857.

1892. RUFUS C. CRANE[7] [1011], (Amos,[6] Isaac,[5] Abiah,[4]
John,[3] Jonathan,[2] Benjamin[1]), married 1st, Minerva Hickey,
September, 1849; 2d, Mary A. Lathrop, of Lansing, Mich.
He is a Methodist minister, and for many years resided at
Greenville, Mich. Children :

1893—1. MENERVIA ANN, b. Oct. 30, 1853.
1894—2. AMOS AMES, b. Sept. 26, 1856.
1895—3. IDA E., b. July 7, 1860.
1896—4. MARY VIOLA, b. Jan. 31, 1863; d. in infancy.
1897—5. HENRY.

1898. MARYETTE AUGUSTA CRANE[7] [1016], (Amos,[6] Isaac,[5]
Abiah,[4] John,[3] Jonathan,[2] Benjamin[1]), married —— Hart, and
removed to Illinois. Children :

1. WARREN (Hart).
2. ANDREW (Hart).
3. METCALF (Hart).

1899. JULIETTE AMELIA CRANE[7] [1017], (Amos,[6] Isaac,[5]
Abiah,[4] John,[3] Jonathan,[2] Benjamin[1]), married Orlando Loncks,
and settled in Marshall County, Iowa. Children :

1. DOLLY (Loncks).
2. EMMA (Loncks).
3. FRANK (Loncks).
4. EVA (Loncks).

1900. GEORGE ANDREW CRANE[7] [1018], (Amos,[6] Isaac,[5] Abiah,[4] John,[3] Jonathan,[2] Benjamin[1]), married 1st, Sylvia Pierce. She died about 1871 and he married 2d, Mrs. Maggie ——. Children:

1901—1. ANDREW.
1902—2. MARY.
1903—3. EBEN.
1904—4. ——; d. 2 years old.
1905—5. FRANK, } twins.
1906—6. FRED, }

1907. CYNTHIA GENETTE CRANE[7] [1019], (Amos,[6] Isaac,[5] Abiah,[4] John,[3] Jonathan,[2] Benjamin[1]), married Rev. Henry Carlton, a Methodist minister. He enlisted in the late war in an Iowa regiment, and was killed while serving as captain. His widow resides in Iowa City, Iowa. Children:

1. ELLA (Carlton).
2. HATTIE M. (Carlton).
3. HENRY (Carlton); d. in infancy.

1908. JOSEPH CRANE[7] [1026], (Ariel,[6] Joseph,[5] Abiah,[4] John,[3] Jonathan,[2] Benjamin[1]), married April 20, 1848, Mary Ann Smith, of Williamstown, Vt., where he resided. She was born Sept. 23, 1825. He was a farmer. He died April 18, 1863, aged 42 years. Children:

1909—1. EDWARD ARIEL, b. March 14, 1849.
1910—2. WILLIAM SMITH, b. Oct, 14, 1852; vice-consul to U. S. Colombia, S. A., 1880 to 1884; m. Mercy Joy, dau. of Capt. Joy, president of the steamship company there. Their home is in U. S. Colombia, S. A.
1911—3. MARY ISABELLA, b. Sept. 21, 1854; m. Dec. 27, 1883, A. B. Munson.
1912—4. KATHERINE HELEN, b. June 11, 1857.

1913. MARY CRANE[7] [1027], (Ariel,[6] Joseph,[5] Abiah,[4] John,[3] Jonathan,[2] Benjamin[1]), married John Lamson, of Brookfield, Vt. She died, and he married widow Lyman, sister of his first wife. He was a farmer. Children:

1. CAROLINE (Lamson), b. 1844.
2. MARY ELIZABETH (Lamson).
3. ANNETTE (Lamson).
4. ADELINE (Lamson).
5. FRANKLIN P. (Lamson).
6. GEORGE (Lamson).
7. WILLIAM (Lamson).

1914. ELLEN E. CRANE[7] [1030], (Ariel,[6] Joseph,[5] Abiah,[4] John,[3] Jonathan,[2] Benjamin[1]), married 1st, Julius Lyman, of Brookfield, Vt. He died, and she became second wife of John Lamson, of Brookfield, Vt. Children:

1. LUCIA (Lyman).
2. LOUISA (Lyman).
3. CHARLES (Lyman), d. in infancy.
4. ARTHUR (Lyman).
5. JULIUS B. (Lyman).

1915. CAROLINE E. CRANE[7] [1031], (Ariel,[6] Joseph,[5] Abiah,[4] John,[3] Jonathan,[2] Benjamin[1]), married Zenas Upham, of Brookfield, Vt. Children:

1. LUCY (Upham).
2. MARY (Upham).

1916. CHARLES CRANE[7] [1032], (Ariel,[6] Joseph,[5] Abiah,[4] John,[3] Jonathan,[2] Benjamin[1]), married 1st, Dec. 25, 1860, Susan M. Blair, of Goliad, Texas. She was born Nov. 24, 1834, and died Nov. 13, 1874. April 6, 1876, he married 2d, Achsah A. Marshall, of Blufftown, Ohio. She was born June 15, 1839. Mr. Crane is a graduate of the University at Burlington, Vt., and became a teacher, first settling in Texas, but later removed to Iowa. Children:

1917—1. MARY P., b. Oct. 20, 1861, in Goliad, Texas.
1918—2. ELLEN D. M., b. Jan. 12, 1864, in Goliad, Texas; m. Prof. Homer R. Miller, July 5, 1894.
1919—3. CHARLES BLAIR, b. Sept. 2, 1867, in Kossuth, Iowa.
1920—4. GEORGE ARIEL, b. Sept. 12, 1870, in Dexter, Iowa; m. Mabel Dean, Dec. 24, 1894.
1921—5. RALPH M., b. April 2, 1877, in Dexter, Iowa.
1922—6. CARRIE L., b. Sept. 11, 1878, in Dexter, Iowa; d. Dec. 27, 1878.
1923—7. CARROLL F., b. Jan. 1, 1880; d. Nov. 3, 1880.
1924—8. ERNEST B., b. March 15, 1882.

1925. GEORGE CRANE[7] [1033], (Ariel,[6] Joseph,[5] Abiah,[4] John,[3] Jonathan,[2] Benjamin[1]), married Dec. 25, 1860, Ann Simons, of Williamstown, Vt., born March 18, 1838, and resides on the old homestead; a farmer. She is the daughter of Porter and Eliza (Smith) Simons. Mr. Crane served as a member of the Vermont legislature in 1876 and 1877. Post-Office address, Brookfield, Vt. Children:

1926—1. LESLIE, b. May 11, 1866.
1927—2. CHARLES CARROL, b. May 3, 1871.

1928. GEORGE HENRY CRANE[7] [1035], (Horatio,[6] Joseph,[5] Abiah,[4] John,[3] Jonathan,[2] Benjamin[1]), married Sarah Denny, of Northfield, Vt., Feb. 1, 1847. She was daughter of Adolphus Denny, born June 25, 1827.. Mr. Crane was a merchant at Northfield. He died Jan. 26, 1890. Children:

1929—1. EMMA TAMAR, b. Jan. 19, 1848.
1930—2. LUCIA S., b. Feb. 13, 1850.
1931—3. SARAH ELIZABETH, b. Feb. 22, 1852; m. Edward Stephen Rice, Sept. 12, 1894.
1932—4. ALICE ELIZA, b. June 1, 1855.

1933. SOPHIA CRANE[7] [1036], (Horatio,[6] Joseph,[5] Abiah,[4] John,[3] Jonathan,[2] Benjamin[1]), married John Reed, of Brookfield, Vt., a farmer, and had two daughters. One:

1. MARY (Reed), m. John McDermot.

1934. LUCY CRANE[7] [1038], (Oren,[6] Joseph,[5] Abiah,[4] John,[3] Jonathan,[2] Benjamin[1]), married John Johnson, of Jericho, Vt., Oct. 14, 1849. Settled in Williston, Vt. Children :

1. LUCIA BATES (Johnson), b. July 4, 1852.
2. CHARLES FRANCIS (Johnson), b. Sept. 4, 1859.
3. BYRON CRANE (Johnson), b. Aug. 14, 1861.

1935. LUCIA JOHNSON [1]; m. M. W. Chapman, and d. Oct. 31, 1885. Child :

1. PAUL L. (Chapman), b. Oct. 31, 1885.

1936. CHARLES FRANCIS JOHNSON [2]; m. 1st, Obi M. Walston; 2d, Ella A. Patten; 3d, Katherine L. Patten. Resides at Williston. Vt.; a farmer. Children :

1. SETH PATTEN (Johnson), b. Jan. 24, 1892, by 2d wife.
2. ELLA (Johnson), b. April 28, 1896, by 3d wife.

1937. BYRON CRANE JOHNSON [3]; m. Mary A. Courtney. Child :

1. JESSIE (Johnson), b. June 1, 1892.

1938. EDWIN CRAN$_E$[7] [1039], (Oren,[6] Joseph,[5] Abiah,[4], John,[3] Jonathan,[2] Benjamin[1]), married Minora Smith, of Williamstown, Vt. Children :

1939—1. EDWIN.
1940—2. JOSIE, } twins; d.
1941—3. JESSIE, }
1942—4. JOSIE.
1943—5. CLARA; m. Curtis Kent, Oct. 15, 1896; lives at Baltimore, Md.

1944. HORATIO DENNISON CRANE[7] [1042], (Oren,[6] Joseph,[5] Abiah,[4] John,[3] Jonathan,[2] Benjamin[1]), married Feb. 9, 1854, Mary A. Brown, a native of Williston, Vt.; born July 4, 1832. For a few years they lived in Jericho. August, 1861, found them residing in Williston. She died April 17, 1887. He died Oct. 14, 1889. Children :

1945—1. CARL H., b. Aug. 25, 1855; m. Mattie Christian, of San Francisco, Cal., and reside there.
1946—2. FRANK L., b. Nov. 6, 1858; m. Laura Estey, of Pasadena, Cal., his home.
1947—3. JOSIE, b. Sept. 6, 1860; d. Oct. 22, 1860.
1948—4. ELMER E., b. Aug. 22, 1861.
1949—5. ANGIE M., b. April 15, 1863; d. March 5, 1865.
1950—6. W. GRANT, b. April 10, 1866; m. and d. May 30, 1896, at Los Angeles, Cal.
1951—7. VERNON E., b. July 31, 1868; m. Carrie Wooley. Reside in Whitesboro, N. Y.

1952. CHARLES CRANE[7] [1044], (Oren,[6] Joseph,[5] Abiah,[4] John,[3] Jonathan,[2] Benjamin[1]), married Ellen Van Vlirt, June 13, 1877. He died Feb. 17, 1883. His widow and children reside (1897) in Orange, Cal. Children :

1953—1. FRED, b. July 4, 1880.
1954—2. WALTER V., b. Sept. 13, 1881.

1955. ARBA D. CRANE[7] [1049], (Arba,[6] Joseph,[5] Abiah,[4] John,[3] Jonathan,[2] Benjamin[1]), married Melinda Van Alstine. The family removed to Oregon in 1885, and located at Spring Water, Clackamas County, where she died Dec. 5, 1891. The daughters are married and reside in Michigan. Children:

1956—1. OLIVE, b. Nov. 16, 1852.
1957—2. WALTER, b. Jan. 17, 1856.
1958—3. WILLIAM, b. Aug. 1, 1860.
1959—4. IDA, b. Sept. 25, 1863.
1960—5. DELOSS, b. June 15, 1872.

1961. SAMUEL D. CRANE[7] [1051], (Arba,[6] Joseph,[5] Abiah,[4] John,[3] Jonathan,[2] Benjamin[1]), graduated from Hillsdale College in 1873, and has been for many years a teacher and superintendent of schools. For the past six years he has been connected with a Business College at Conway Springs, Kas.; at present (February, 1897) one of the clerks in the legislature at Guthrie, Oklahoma. Married 1st, Imogene Nichols in 1869; 2d, Asenath Grimes, a teacher, from Fredonia, N. Y. His first wife died at Lagrange, Ind., March 12, 1876. Children:

1962—1. CLAIR, b. June 5, 1870; a printer.
1963—2. CHARLES, b. May 10, 1873; stenographer at Land Office, Oklahoma City.
1964—3. ROBERT, b. Oct. 10, 1875; a teacher.
1965—4. CARRIE, b. Oct. 10, 1890.

1966. BENJAMIN F. CRANE[7] [1052], (Arba,[6] Joseph,[5] Abiah,[4] John,[3] Jonathan,[2] Benjamin[1]), married Sarah Ann Dunn; a farmer at Fawn River, Mich. She was a teacher. Children:

1967—1. JENNIE MAY, b. Sept. 9, 1873; a teacher.
1968—2. ROLLIN, b. Dec. 21, 1875.
1969—3. ELLA, b. Nov. 10, 1880.
1970—4. GLEN, b. March 28, 1882.
1971—5. MABEL, b. May 6, 1885.

1972. ELLA J. CRANE[7] [1053], (Arba,[6] Joseph,[5] Abiah,[4] John,[3] Jonathan,[2] Benjamin[1]), married May 8, 1879, Jacob Yeagla, a hardware merchant. They reside in Lima, Ind. Enlisted Sept. 15, 1861, in Company C, 111th Pennsylvania Infantry; wounded May, 1864, at Dallas, Ga.; honorably discharged Feb. 8, 1865. Child:

1. MAY ETHEL (Yeagla), b. May 17, 1883.

1973. EDWARD PAYSON CRANE[7] [1059], (Porter,[6] Joseph,[5] Abiah,[4] John,[3] Jonathan,[2] Benjamin[1]), married Sept. 29, 1861, at St. Anthony, Ellen M. Stiles, of Minneapolis, Minn., daughter of Martin and Margaret (Scott) Stiles. Mr. Crane went to Minnesota in 1858, and settled there. Residence at Minneapolis. Children:

1974—1. EMORY PARKHURST, b. Aug. 2, 1863; d. April 7, 1866.
1975—2. EDITH MAY, b. March 7, 1866; m. May 24, 1888, Joseph S. Bailey, at Wolcott, Vt. He d. Oct. 25, 1893.

1976—3. EDWARD MARTIN, b. July 30, 1868.
1977—4. SARAH AGNES, b. Aug. 19, 1872.
1978—5. FRED BENSON, b. Sept. 6, 1875.

1979. Capt. PORTER CRANE[7] [1060], (Porter,[6] Joseph,[5] Abiah,[4] John,[3] Jonathan,[2] Benjamin[1]), married Louise Bundy, daughter of Rev. Horace Bundy, of Lake Village (now Lakeport), N. H., Jan. 11, 1864. She was born Feb. 10, 1845. He enlisted in August, 1861, and was mustered into service in October following, in Company H, 6th Vermont Volunteers, as 5th sergeant. In December he was promoted to 1st sergeant; February, 1862, to 2d lieutenant; July to 1st lieutenant; and May, 1863, to captain. He was severely wounded at Fredericksburg, May 4, 1863; mustered out Oct. 15, 1864. Resides at Concord, N. H. Children:

1980—1. CRESSY, b. Dec. 9, 1866; d. Dec. 14, 1866.
1981—2. BERTRAM H., b. May 6, 1868; d. Sept. 29, 1868.
1982—3. EDNA L., b. March 13, 1871; d. May 29, 1871.
1983—4. STELLA B., b. Feb. 6, 1879.

1984. SARAH E. CRANE[7] [1061], (Porter,[6] Joseph,[5] Abiah,[4] John,[3] Jonathan,[2] Benjamin[1]), married in 1863 Miltimore Conant, of Hardwick, Vt., and reside on the homestead at Wolcott, Vt. Child:

1. MABEL (Conant), b. Dec. 5, 1873; m. W. L. Tillotson, of Wolcott. They reside in Morrisville, Vt.

1985. Hon. DARIUS CRANE[7] [1082], (William,[6] Elisha,[5] Elisham,[4] John,[3] Jonathan,[2] Benjamin[1]), born in Ellington, Conn. Married in 1845 Permelia Phillips, a native of Somers, Conn., born 1822. He was a farmer, justice of the peace, selectman, representative, and Senator, spending his life in the town where he was born. Children:

1986—1. WILLIAM, b. November, 1847.
1987—2. ELLEN B., b. November, 1849.
1988—3. JOSEPHINE, b. Feb. 8, 1850.
1989—4. CHARLES, b. Feb. 23, 1861; d. May 19, 1879.

1990. LYDIA OWEN CRAIN[7] [1085], (Daniel O.,[6] Elisha,[5] Elisham,[4] John,[3] Jonathan,[2] Benjamin[1]), born in Bradford, Vt. Married Jonathan Tenney, a native of Corinth, Vt., Nov. 21, 1816; a farmer. The family have resided in Corinth, Bradford, Marshfield and Newbury. Mr. Tenney died at Boscawen, N. H., June 19, 1865. Mrs. Tenney enjoyed her centennial birthday Dec. 8, 1896, at the home of her son, Daniel C. Tenney, whose farmhouse stands near the shore of Penacook Lake, West Concord, N. H. She was then in comparatively good health, having enjoyed that comfort throughout her long and busy life, very little sickness having fallen to her lot. She was then able to use her needle and attend to work about the house, and continued remarkably well and active for a person of her years up to the very moment of her death, which occurred Dec. 18, 1898, at the

LYDIA OWEN CRAIN TENNEY.

From a photograph taken January 10, 1896. She was then 100 years, 1 month and 2 days old.

ripe old age of 103 years and 10 days. She was sitting in her chair conversing with her son's wife, when suddenly she paused, and in a moment life was gone; she passed away so peacefully that it was some moments before the family realized she had fallen into that deep sleep that knows no waking. She was what might be termed an observing woman, and was always equipped with a good supply of general information, and greatly beloved by her family. Children :

1. JONATHAN (Tenney), b. Sept. 14, 1817, at Corinth, Vt.
2. DANIEL C. (Tenney), b. Nov. 9,.1819, at Corinth, Vt.; d. Jan. 6, 1899.
3. ASA P. (Tenney), b. Dec. 4, 1821, at Bradford, Vt.
4. JOHN ELLIS (Tenney), b. April 22, 1824, at Marshfield, Vt.
5. JAMES GREGG (Tenney), b. Feb. 25, 1827, at Marshfield, Vt.
6. JAMES GREGG (Tenney), b. July 2, 1829, at Bradford, Vt.
7. LYDIA ANN (Tenney), b. Feb. 8, 1832, at Bradford, Vt.
8. ANDREW P. F. (Tenney), b. March 12, 1834, at Newbury, Vt.
9. JUDITH ANN.(Tenney), b. July 12, 1836, at Newbury, Vt.

1991. ANDREW M. CRANE[7] [1087], (Daniel O.,[6] Elisha,[5] Elisham,[4] John,[3] Jonathan,[2] Benjamin[1]), was born in Bradford, Orange County, Vt.; married in Grafton, Mass., April 15, 1831, Eliza Kelly. She was born in Grafton Aug. 6, 1811. He was by trade a shoemaker and settled in Bradford, Vt. He served in the late war. She died Oct. 3, 1874. He died Jan. 29, 1893, aged 93 years, 11 months, 29 days. Children :

1002—1. ELLEN M.
1003—2. LYDIA A. T.
1994—3. MARIA T., b. 1842, in Bradford, Vt.
1995—4. ANDREW J.
1996—5. SARAH M. A.
1097—6. DANIEL F., b. Nov. 4, 1840.

1998. SIBYL CRANE[7] [1097], (Wareham,[6] Hezekiah,[5] Hezekiah,[4] John,[3] Jonathan,[2] Benjamin[1]), married James Rockwell, March 26, 1816, and removed with several of her brothers and sisters to the Western country. They had a son who became a minister. Mrs. Rockwell died in Michigan some years ago.

1999. EUNICE CRANE[7] [1098], (Wareham,[6] Hezekiah,[5] Hezekiah,[4] John,[3] Jonathan,[2] Benjamin[1]), married Joshua Wells, of East Windsor, Conn., Oct. 2, 1814. She died October, 1854.

Children :

1. HENRY (Wells).
2. DAVID (Wells).
3. HULDAH (Wells).
4. JULIA (Wells).
5. NEWTON (Wells).
6. JULIA ANN (Wells).
7. HORACE (Wells).
8. JOHN (Wells).

2000. JULIA ANN WELLS [6]; m. Roger Griswold, of Lyme, Conn.,
Jan. 1, 1856. Children:

    1. HENRY (Griswold), b. Jan. 27, 1858.
    2. EDWARD (Griswold), b. April 7, 1861.
    3. LILIAN (Griswold), b. Oct. 28, 1865.

2001. RUSSELL WILLIS CRANE[7] [1101], (Wareham,[6] Hezekiah,[5] Hezekiah,[4] John,[3] Jonathan,[2] Benjamin[1]), married Lydia
Parmle, of Suffield, at East Windsor, Conn., July 3, 1825. He
was a farmer. He died in East Windsor, Dec. 13, 1842. She
died Nov. 1, 1833, in Illinois. Children:

2002—1. GEORGE R.
2003—2. CAROLINE E.; m. —— Ayres.
2004—3. WILLIAM WILLIS, b. Jan. 31, 1832.

2005. SOPHRONIA CRANE[7] [1102], (Wareham,[6] Hezekiah,[5]
Hezekiah,[4] John,[3] Jonathan,[2] Benjamin[1]), married Hiram Wolcott, of East Windsor, Conn., Sept. 23, 1824. She died Nov.
20, 1878. Children:

    1. SOPHRONIA MARIA (Wolcott), b. March 7, 1826; d. Feb. 14, 1880.
    2. HIRAM HENRY (Wolcott), b. Jan. 1, 1829.
    3. EMILY LUCINDA (Wolcott), b. Nov. 5, 1830.
    4. JAMES MUNROE (Wolcott), } twins, { m. Nancy Ward;
                                                      d. Sept. 12, 1878.
    5. JANE MARILLA (Wolcott), } b. Oct. 7, 1833; { d. Dec. 16, 1891.
    6. JULIA MARANDA (Wolcott), } twins, b. { m. Benj. Parker;
                                                       June 19, 1840; d. Sept. 17, 1864.
    7. JULIUS MARO (Wolcott),
    8. FRANCIS NEWTON (Wolcott), b. Dec. 10, 1843.

2006. SOPHRONIA MARIA WOLCOTT [1]; m. Lewis T. Skinner, Nov.
27, 1845. She d. Feb. 14, 1881. Children:

    1. CHARLES ALBERT (Skinner), b. April 3, 1848; d. Sept.
        19, 1848.
    2. CALVIN LEWIS (Skinner), b. Oct. 21. 1849.
    3. ELLEN MARIA (Skinner), b. April 28, 1854.
    4. GEORGE NELSON (Skinner), b. Dec. 10, 1858.

2007. HIRAM HENRY WOLCOTT [2]; m. Dolly Kibbe, March 17, 1852.
She d. Sept. 21, 1885, aged 57 years. Children:

    1. ALICE G. (Wolcott), b. March 19, 1853; d. March 28,
        1872.
    2. ADA J. (Wolcott), b. July 15, 1855.
    3. ETTA L. (Wolcott), b. Nov. 2, 1857.
    4. JENNIE E. (Wolcott), b. Oct. 1, 1860.
    5. WARREN H. (Wolcott), b. Aug. 13, 1863; d. Sept. 5,
        1866.
    6. ANGIE S. (Wolcott), b. Aug. 20, 1868.
    7. HATTIE S. (Wolcott), b. Sept. 24, 1872.

2008. EMILY LUCINDA WOLCOTT [3]; m. William C. Covill, Nov. 26,
1857. Mr. Covill enlisted for the war Aug. 9, 1862, and left
Hartford Aug. 28; discharged June 1, 1865. He d. Dec. 25,
1896. Children:

    1. ELLA M. (Covill), b. Sept. 11, 1862.
    2. WILLIE C. (Covill), b. July 28, 1866; d. Nov. 8, 1866.
    3. CHARLES W. (Covill), b. Sept. 26, 1867.

2009. JANE MARILLA WOLCOTT [5]; m. 1st, Geo. H. Fielding, July 5, 1871. He d. Oct. 5, 1872. She then m. 2d, Wilson C. Shaw, April 29, 1875. He d. June 3, 1878, and she m. 3d, William J. Ladd, April, 1879. She d. Dec. 16, 1891.

2010. JULIUS M. WOLCOTT [7]; m. Eunice M. Spencer, Nov. 11, 1872. Children:

    1. FRANCIS EUGENE (Wolcott), b. Nov. 26, 1875.
    2. JULIA MABEL (Wolcott), b. March 26, 1877.

2011. FRANCIS NEWTON WOLCOTT [8]; m. Anna Maria Bishop, May 12, 1877. Children:

    1. BERTIE EDSON (Wolcott), b. Oct. 29, 1878.
    2. EDNA ADELE (Wolcott), b. Sept. 17, 1880; d. in infancy.

2012. OLIVER ROOT CRANE[7] [1103], (Wareham,[6] Hezekiah,[5] Hezekiah,[4] John,[3] Jonathan,[2] Benjamin[1]), married Annie Rebecca Lewis, March 14, 1840; died at Waterford, Conn., Nov. 17, 1870. Children:

2013—1. GEORGE OLIVER, b. Oct. 26, 1842; d. April 26, 1892.
2014—2. DAVID LEWIS, b. Nov. 13, 1844.
2015—3. WILLIAM SIMEON b. April 14, 1847; d. April 1, 1851.
2016—4. ANNIE REBECCA, b. Aug. 30, 1850.
2017—5. ABBY ELEANOR, b. June 22, 1856.
2018—6. HERBERT WALLACE, b. June 27, 1860; d. March 1, 1865.
2019—7. MARY EMMA, } twins, { d. Dec. 3, 1865.
2020—8. MARY ELLEN, } b. May 27, 1864; { d. May 7, 1885.

2021. ELECTA B. CRANE[7] [1104], (Wareham,[6] Hezekiah,[5] Hezekiah,[4] John,[3] Jonathan,[2] Benjamin[1]), married Elisha W. Hickerson, July 17, 1834. Resides in Detroit, Illinois. March 5, 1897, she was in her 88th year and in comfortable health. Children:

    1. SARAH EUNICE (Hickerson), b. April 21, 1835.
    2. OSCAR MONROE (Hickerson), b. Nov. 21, 1836.
    3. ELIZABETH ANN (Hickerson), b. Dec. 21, 1837.
    4. MARY JANE (Hickerson), b. March 1, 1840.
    5. JOSEPHINE MARIA (Hickerson), b. Jan. 26, 1842.
    6. HULDAH CRANE (Hickerson), b. March 12, 1851.

2022. HEZEKIAH BACKUS CRANE[7] [1105], (Wareham,[6] Hezekiah,[5] Hezekiah,[4] John,[3] Jonathan,[2] Benjamin[1]), married Angeline Gowdy, May, 1838. Child:

2023—1. ROMAN A., b. Feb. 19, 1842.

2024. LORENZO BLISS CRANE[7] [1107], (Wareham,[6] Hezekiah,[5] Hezekiah,[4] John,[3] Jonathan,[2] Benjamin[1]), married April 5, 1843, Emeline Gowdy, a native of Somers, born Dec. 7, 1820. He was a farmer, and resided at South Windsor, Conn. He died at Manchester, Conn., Nov. 6, 1892. Children:

2025—1. CURTIS L., b. March 22, 1845.
2026—2. ORSON W., b. Sept. 24, 1849.

2027. HENDRICK CRAIN[7] [1109], (Joel,[6] Hezekiah,[5] Hezekiah,[4] John,[3] Jonathan,[2] Benjamin[1]), was born in Wethersfield,

Vt.; married at Pharsalia, N. Y., Sept. 25, 1832, Mary Dye. She was a native of Pitcher, N. Y.; born Aug. 11, 1811. Mr. Crane was a brigadier-general of infantry, and a prominent business man, being a merchant in Pharsalia, N. Y., where he passed a long and active life. He died April 16, 1881. Children:

2028--1. USTACIA, b. Dec. 21, 1832.
2029--2. ANN ELIZA, b. Feb. 21, 1834; d. April 9, 1834.
2030--3. VAN BUREN, b. May 6, 1835.
2031--4. JOHN RANDOLPH, b. Jan. 27, 1837; d. Sept. 6, 1855, in Norwich, N. Y.
2032--5. MARQUIS DE LAFAYETTE, b. April 1, 1841.
2033--6. GEORGE HENDRICK, b. March 20, 1846; m. Helen Mary Wood, Dec. 25, 1866; residence St. Louis, Mo.

2034. LUTHER CRANE[7] [1110], (Joel,[6] Hezekiah,[5] Hezekiah,[4] John,[3] Jonathan,[2] Benjamin[1]), married Jan. 30, 1834, at Utica, N. Y., Harriet Brown. She was born in Pharsalia, N. Y., Sept. 24, 1812. He was an innkeeper at Pharsalia and died there Feb. 11, 1850. Child:

2035--1. CURTIS, b. March 23, 1842.

2036. PRUDENCE CRANE[7] [1112], (Hezekiah,[6] Hezekiah,[5] Hezekiah,[4] John,[3] Jonathan,[2] Benjamin[1]), married Thomas Davis. She was born May 27, 1795, and died Jan. 8, 1853.

Children:

1. ABBY L. (Davis).
2. WILLIAM E. (Davis).
3. EDWARD E. (Davis).
4. SARAH (Davis).

2037. GILMAN CRANE[7] [1114], (Hezekiah,[6] Hezekiah,[5] Hezekiah,[4] John,[3] Jonathan,[2] Benjamin[1]), married 1st, Aug. 15, 1824, Roselinda Ginn, of Orland, Me. She was born April 1, 1803, and died Feb. 16, 1864. He then married 2d, Mrs. Eliza A. Dix, of Salem, Mass., Aug. 23, 1867. He died in Orland, Me., July 21, 1888. Children:

2038--1. HEZEKIAH, b. July 15, 1825, at Prospect, Me.; d. Sept. 18, 1827, at Bucksport.
2039--2. HARRIET, b. Jan. 22, 1827, at Bucksport.
2040--3. HEZEKIAH, b. Jan. 13, 1829, at Bucksport; d. June 20, 1850.
2041--4. PRUDENCE JANE, b. May 15, 1831, at Orland.
2042--5. ROSELINDA, b. Nov. 17, 1833, at Orland.
2043--6. GILMAN CHARLES, b. Oct. 2, 1835, at Orland.
2044--7. CATHERINE JOHNSTON, b. Dec. 7, 1837, at Orland.
2045--8. ALPHEUS AUGUSTINE, b. June 6, 1842, at Orland; d. Feb. 21, 1892.
2046--9. LAURA ELLEN, b. Dec. 15, 1844, at Orland.

2047. HARRIET CRANE[7] [1115], (Hezekiah,[6] Hezekiah,[5] Hezekiah,[4] John,[3] Jonathan,[2] Benjamin[1]), was born in Eden, Vt.; married Benjamin C. Choate, who was born July 29, 1800, and died Aug. 28, 1858. Children:

1. HARRIET JANE (Choate), b. Aug. 13, 1828; d. 1834.

2. EDWARD H. (Choate), b. July 6, 1830.
3. M. MARIA (Choate), b. Oct. 22, 1832.
4. HARRIETT J. (Choate), b. July 30, 1834; d. May 26, 1851.
5. SARAH P. (Choate), b. Sept. 17, 1837.

2048. SEWALL L. CRANE[7] [1116], (Hezekiah,[6] Hezekiah,[5] Hezekiah,[4] John,[3] Jonathan,[2] Benjamin[1]), married April 6, 1827, Eliza L. Hows, who was born June 15, 1805.
Children :

2049—1. PARKER C., b. Nov. 16, 1829.
2050—2. CHARLES L., b. May 27, 1832; m. Nov. 25, 1852, Phebe A. Saunders.
2051—3. JOSHUA R., b. June 14, 1834; m. Elizabeth Marlow.
2052—4. SARAH J., b. Oct. 20, 1836; m. Gilman Campbell.
2053—5. SEWALL H., b. Jan. (or June) 18, 1838.
2054—6. CAROLINE E., b. Nov. 27, 1840; m. Thomas Heuston.
2055—7. ALBERT A., b. Jan. 2, 1843.
2056—8. MARCIA L., b. May 9, 1845; m. Willard Dillaway, May, 1864.
2057—9. GEORGE D., b. Aug. 19, 1848.
2058-10. ELLEN R., b. March 19, 1850; d. March 22, 1864.

2059. OBERIA HILL CRANE[7] [1118], (Hezekiah,[6] Hezekiah,[5] Hezekiah,[4] John,[3] Jonathan,[2] Benjamin[1]), married in 1835 Calvin L. Saulsbury. She died Sept. 1, 1854, in South Reading, Mass.
Children :

1. FRANCIS (Saulsbury), b. Jan. 24, 1842.
2. LAURA (Saulsbury), b. June 23, 1845.

2060. ABNER BELKNAP CRANE[7] [1120], (Abner,[6] Hezekiah,[5] Hezekiah,[4] John,[3] Jonathan,[2] Benjamin[1]). His intention to marry Almira Holmes, both of Springfield, Mass., was published there Nov. 1, 1832. He died May 13, 1842. June, 1843, his estate was probated, at which time the widow Almira and one child, then five years old, were reported in feeble health.

2061. AMAZIAH BRITTO CRANE[7] [1121], (Abner,[6] Hezekiah,[5] Hezekiah,[4] John,[3] Jonathan,[2], Benjamin[1]). He married Aug. 20, 1837, Elizabeth Sanderson, of Springfield, Mass., and Dec. 21, 1843, m. 2d, Mary S. Masters, of Chester. Mr. Crane was born in Springfield, and after marriage settled there. He subsequently removed to Leicester, Worcester and Boston, and died at Auburndale, April 18, 1880. Children :

2062—1. FRANK E., b. July 9, 1840, in Springfield; d. March 29, 1896.
2063—2. WILLIAM HENRY, b. April 30, 1845, in Leicester. He is the popular comedian who has charmed audiences in nearly every city of considerable size in the United States, by his brilliant acting, achieving remarkable success in his well known play " The Senator," as well as other plays that have been written at his solicitation, all of which are of high order.
2064—3. MARY JANE, b. May 25, 1847, in Worcester.
2065—4. HELEN MARIA, b. April 7, 1851, in Newton.

2066. DAVID ORVILLE CRANE[7] [1129], (David,[6] David,[5] Hezekiah,[4] John,[3] Jonathan,[2] Benjamin[1]), married Clarissa
13

Cooley in Springfield, Mass. He learned to make joiners' tools of Leonard Kennedy in Hartford, Conn., and after his marriage removed to New Hartford, south of Utica, N. Y.; studied dental surgery, and practiced it in Geneva, N. Y. After some years he removed to Rochester, and there practiced dentistry. She died in St. Louis, Mo., January, 1879. Children:

2067—1. EDWARD A., practiced dentistry in St. Louis, Mo.; d. Aug. 26, 1874, at Topeka, Kan.
2068—2. HELEN M.
2069—3. FRANKLIN ORVILLE, residence in Shawnee County, Kan.

2070. FRANKLIN LOOMIS CRANE[7] .[1130], David,[6] David,[5] Hezekiah,[4] John,[3] Jonathan,[2] Benjamin[1]), married Oct. 16, 1838, at Easton, Pa., Mary Elizabeth Howell. She was born there Sept. 18, 1820, and there they established their home. She died May 20, 1845. He was born at East Windsor, Hartford County, Conn., on an old manor that had been handed down from father to son for generations before the Revolution. In that dark and desperate struggle his grandfather, David Crane, did good service under the immediate command of Gen. Washington.

The home training of young Crane was in the strict Puritan style. His school days did not differ materially from those of other boys similarly situated; attended the common school, where he paid his own way. Receiving a certificate of qualification to teach the common English branches, he soon began teaching in Vernon, Conn.; in a short time however he accepted an invitation from his uncle, Dr. John W. Crane, a practicing physician of Hartford, to commence the study of medicine and dental surgery in his office. After thoroughly preparing himself, he opened an office in Easton, Pa., where he conducted a successful business for 22 years.

In October, 1854, he emigrated to Kansas, and settled on the present site of Topeka. As a member of the town company he took an active part in everything that pertained to the upbuilding of the city. Town lots were donated to all who would erect houses and live on the town site, and also to churches and societies of all kinds that were ready to take advantage of the generous offer. Dr. Crane was appointed to the difficult task of making selections for incomers, societies and churches. Many persons are still living in Topeka who remember with what zeal he pointed out the advantages of this or that particular locality. His language on such occasions proved prophetic in many instances.

He was active in the formation of the Kansas Free State party. In 1857 the St. Joseph & Topeka Railroad Company was organized, and he was chosen treasurer. Little actual work was ever done on this route, although he expended much time and money in making it a living institution by securing the payment of 10 per cent. of capital stock. This planning and managing

DR. FRANKLIN LOOMIS CRANE

Born, East Windsor, Connecticut, January 10, 1808.
Died, Carthage, New Mexico, November 21, 1884.
Married Mary Elizabeth Howell, October, 1838,
who died May 22, 1845.

FRANKLIN LOOMIS CRANE, JR.

2d Son of DR. F. L. CRANE.
Born, Easton, Pennsylvania, August 23, 1841.
Died, Fort Larned, Kansas, June 17, 1864.

JESSE HOWELL CRANE

Eldest Son of DR. F. L. CRANE.
Born, Easton, Pennsylvania, June 8, 1839.
Married Clara R. Dodds, June 15, 1865.
Clara R. Crane died March 5, 1889.

HARRY J. CRANE

Son of JESSE H. CRANE.
Born, Topeka, Kansas, January 5, 1872.
Died, Hillsboro, New Mexico, January 14, 1899.

finally resulted in the construction of the Atchison, Topeka & Santa Fé Railroad.

In 1859, there being no permanent place in Topeka for the interment of the dead, and having failed in several efforts to organize a cemetery company, Dr. Crane made the venture at his own expense, and laid out, in a very tasty and artistic manner, a large plot of ground about a mile east of the city. For this act of generosity, if for nothing else, he will ever be remembered kindly by the citizens of Topeka. In the same year he became mayor of the city, on the death of the mayor-elect, by virtue of his office of president of the city council. This was just at the time when the permanent location of the State capital by a direct vote of the people was being agitated. Mainly through the wish and prompt action of the acting mayor and city council Topeka was made the permanent seat of government at that election. The first bridge over the Kansas River was built in 1857–8, largely through his influence and exertions. This bridge was swept away by a freshet July 19, 1858, and was replaced by a temporary pontoon, that served the purpose until the present iron structure was erected by Mortimer Cook, Dr. Crane and others.

On the breaking out of the rebellion he and two of his sons enlisted for the war. His knowledge of medicine, kindness of heart and generosity peculiarly fitted him to take care of the sick, and he was made a hospital steward, and on several occasions established and conducted general hospitals by order of the medical directory. This branch of service was in accord with his sympathetic nature, and he was enabled to make it a perfect success.

On his return from the camp he was chosen president of the board of education. Under his administration several large * school-houses were erected, among them the Lincoln School building. He has ever been liberal and foremost in advocating the interests of education, assisting all societies and efforts in every move to harmonize and liberalize society. From the rigid church discipline under which he was reared he gradually became more liberal in his views, until he found himself a willing and confirmed disciple of ancient and modern Spiritualism, and in all his relations with his fellows he carried into his daily practice the firm belief that there is ever by his side an immortal spirit that is cognizant of his every act, whether good or evil; one that mourns over his wrong doings and rejoices in every good deed, and under certain conditions is able, as in the old biblical times, to make its presence manifest by words and signs, and to give admonition of coming events.* He died Nov. 21, 1884, at the home of his eldest son in Carthage, New Mexico, whither he had gone for a visit. Funeral services were at Topeka, Kan. Children :

2071—1. JESSE HOWELL, b. June 23, 1839.

---

* From the *Topeka Daily Capital* of Nov. 22, 1884

2072—2. FRANKLIN LOOMIS, b. Aug. 8, 1840.
2073—3. DAVID ORVILLE, b. Feb. 12, 1842.
2074—4. GEORGE WOOLSEY, b. Aug. 25, 1843.

2075. CHLOE PITKIN CRANE[7] [1131], (David,[6] David,[5] Hezekiah,[4] John,[3] Jonathan,[2] Benjamin[1]), married John Phelps at Stockbridge, Madison County, N. Y., and settled in Oneida Castle. Children:

1. ELLEN MEROE (Phelps), b. Dec. 18, 1841.
2. SUSAN ANNETTE (Phelps), b. March 18, 1844; m. Eugene Smith.
3. JOHN ALLISON (Phelps), b. Feb. 22, 1846; d. Feb. 27, 1868.
4. FRANK CRANE (Phelps), b. Jan. 10, 1851; d. Dec. 10, 1860.
5. EDMUND ORVILLE (Phelps), b. June 15, 1853; d. Dec. 12, 1857.

2076. DANIEL GILBERT CRANE[7] [1138], (Samuel P.,[6] David,[5] Hezekiah,[4] John,[3] Jonathan,[2] Benjamin[1]), born at East Windsor, Conn. Married Oct. 24, 1844, Mary A. Taft. She was born in West Mendon, Monroe County, N. Y., Feb. 28, 1825. He is a merchant at Rochester, N. Y. Children:

2077—1. HENRY P., b. in Rochester. N. Y.; d. 1847.
2078—2. ALICE, b. in Springfield, Mass.
2079—3. GEORGE D., b. in Rochester, N. Y.; 1872.
2080—4. HATTIE E., b. in Lockport, N. Y.
2081—5. CORA, b. in Rochester, N. Y.

2082. ROSANNAH CRANE[7] [1150], (Curtis,[6] David,[5] Hezekiah,[4] John,[3] Jonathan,[2] Benjamin[1]), married March 4, 1833, Moses Church Browning. Children:

1. HARRIET MARIA (Browning), b. March 2, 1834.
2. EMILY PYNCHON (Browning), b. May 24, 1841.

2083. HARRIET MARIA BROWNING [1]; m. William Heber Daniel. Children:

1. EMILY MAY (Daniel), m. Thomas Calterson; d. August, 1893. Child:
   1. SHIRLEY (Calterson).
2. ELLA (Daniel), m. William James. Children:
   1. GEORGE (James).
   2. HEBER (James).
   3. ALLEN (James).
3. HENRY M. (Daniel); m. Nannie Fisher.

2084. EMILY PYNCHON BROWNING [2]; m. Robert Ralston Lynd. Children:

1. STOUGHTON BROWNING (Lynd), b. Oct. 30, 1867.
2. CURTIS CRANE (Lynd), b. Aug. 14, 1872.

2085. STOUGHTON BROWNING LYND [1]; m. Nelly Day, Oct. 10, 1888. Children:

1. VIRGINIA (Lynd), b. 1889.
2. ROBERT (Lynd), b. September, 1892.

2086. HENRY CRANE[7] [1151], (Curtis,[6] David,[5] Hezekiah,[4] John,[3] Jonathan,[2] Benjamin[1]), married Zervey Hanks. He was a dentist, and lived in Brooklyn, N. Y. Children:

2087—1. LOUISE; m. J. N. Green; lives West. Children:
   1. JOHN N. (Green).
   2. LULA C. (Green).

2088—2. MARIA; m. —— Beach.
2089—3. BELLE; m. Henry J. Schenk.
2090—4. ELLA; m. Alfred Nickolds.
2091—5. JOHN N.; m. Lizzie D. Deckins. Children:
    1. CHARLES.
    2. MARGARETTA.
2092—6. LILLY.
2093—7. GEORGE A.; m. Mary Perry, of South Windsor, Conn.

2094. CHARLOTTE CRANE[7] [1152], (Curtis,[6] David,[5] Hezekiah,[4] John,[3] Jonathan,[2] Benjamin[1]), married 1st, April 27, 1831, in Springfield, Mass., Samuel King, who died in New Albany, Ind., Jan. 5, 1862. She married 2d, John Gordon, March 26, 1867. He died May 5, 1880, at Goodland, Ind.
Children:

1. HELEN L. (King), b. June 23, 1839, in Piqua, Ohio.
2. ELIZA A. (King), b. June 18, 1841, in Piqua, Ohio; d. June 29, 1841.
3. HORACE C. (King), b. Oct. 25, 1844, in Piqua, Ohio; m. and d. Nov. 29, 1897.
4. EMMA A. (King), b. March 10, 1849, in College Hill, Ohio; d. Oct. 4, 1853.

2095. HELEN L. KING [1]; m. John Gordon, Jr., July 1, 1858, at New Albany, Ind. Children:

1. CHARLOTTE E. (Gordon), b. May 29, 1859; m. George R. Brewster, Sept. 24, 1878.
2. GEORGE B. (Gordon), b. June 14, 1861; m. Jessie A. Stevens, Sept. 25, 1887.
3. HENRY L. (Gordon), b. Dec. 8, 1863; d. Jan. 1, 1864.
4. STELLA M. (Gordon), b. July 11, 1865; m. Marcellus Waltz, June 10, 1884.
5. CHARLES H. (Gordon), b. Oct. 11, 1867; d. Oct. 12, 1867.
6. HORACE K. (Gordon), b. Sept. 16, 1869, in Goodland, Ind.
7. MARY L. (Gordon), b. Aug. 7, 1871, in Goodland, Ind.; m. Samuel C. Miller, April 7, 1896.
8. ARTHUR K. (Gordon), b. Jan. 4, 1874, in Goodland, Ind.; d. same day.
9. ROLLIN J. (Gordon), b. March 30, 1879, in Goodland, Ind.

2096. MARTIN HALE CRANE[7] [1156], (Curtis,[6] David,[5] Hezekiah,[4] John,[3] Jonathan,[2] Benjamin[1]), was born in Springfield, Mass.; married in Cincinnati, Ohio, June 29, 1852, Sallie Phillips Davis. She was born in Dayton, Ohio, May 31, 1822. He was of the firm of Crane & Breed Manufacturing Co., Cincinnati. He settled in that city. He was a foundryman, but later engaged in furnishing appliances for heating by steam and hot water.
Children:

2097—1. HARRIE D., b. Sept. 26, 1853.
2098—2. IDA M., b. Jan. 9, 1857.

2099. JULIA ANN CRANE[7] [1157], (Curtis,[6] David,[5] Hezekiah,[4] John,[3] Jonathan,[2] Benjamin[1]), married Perry Tuttle. She lives in Indianapolis, Ind. Children:

1. HATTIE (Tuttle).

    2. MILLIE (Tuttle).
    3. LOTTIE (Tuttle).
    4. ZEROCY (Tuttle).
    5. —— (Tuttle).
    6. —— (Tuttle).
    7. —— (Tuttle).

2100. WILLIAM CURTIS CRANE[7] [1158], (Curtis,[6] David,[5] Hezekiah,[4] John,[3] Jonathan,[2] Benjamin[1]), married Mary E. Shields. He settled in New Albany, Ind., and served about there in 1862, during the rebellion. He died Jan. 6, 1899, at his residence in New Albany, Ind. Children:

    2101—1. CHARLES EUGENE, b. Dec. 14, 1853.
    2102—2. WILLIAM FRANKLIN, b. Feb. 3, 1856.
    2103—3. EDGAR SHIELDS, b. June 17, 1858.
    2104—4. ALBERT CURTIS, b. 1860; d. at one year of age.
    2105—5. ARTHUR CLEMENT, b. Oct. 13, 1863; m. Oct. 29, 1890, Emily P. Hare, at New Albany, Ind.; resides in Louisville, Ky.
    2106—6. EMMA LOUISE, b. Nov. 5, 1865.
    2107—7. JULIA ADALINE,   } twins, b. May 10, 1870.
    2108—8. MARTIN BURDETTE,   }
    2109—9. MARY BESSIE; d. in infancy.

2110. NANCY MARIA CRANE[7] [1159], (Curtis,[6] David,[5] Hezekiah,[4] John,[3] Jonathan,[2] Benjamin[1]), married 1st, Ca'pt. Elijah Gore Barney, of Henderson, N. Y. She died in Shelby Springs, Ala., July 21, 1864, and was buried in Spring Grove, Cincinnati, Ohio. He married 2d, Mary Batersby Reader, in 1865. He died in Eatonton, Ga., at the home of his eldest son, of black cholera. He was sick only twenty-four hours, having contracted the disease on board steamer and just having returned from South America. Children:

    1. HENRY CRANE (Barney), b. Dec. 8, 1847, at Dayton, Ohio.
    2. CHARLES CURTIS (Barney); d. aged 14 months at Oxford, Miss.
    3. WILLIAM ALBERT (Barney), b. at Holly Springs, Miss., 1859.
    4. EDWARD NORTON (Barney), b. at Holly Springs, Miss., 1861.
    5. EARNEST EUGENE (Barney); by second wife.

2111. HENRY CRANE BARNEY [1]; m. 1st, Julia Marrium, of Rome, Ga., April 12, 1870; 2d, Mary J. Luther, of Eatonton, Ga., Jan. 24, 1873. Child:

    1. CLARENCE LUTHER (Barney), b. March 6, 1874, at Plainville, Ga.

2112. WILLIAM ALBERT BARNEY [3]; m. a Spanish woman in South America. He has eight children. The names of two are:

    1. NANCY MARIA (Barney).
    2. E. G. (Barney).

2113. EDWARD MARTIN BARNEY [4]; m. Anna ——, of Dayton, Ohio. Children:

    1. CHARLES (Barney).
    2. WILLIAM HENRY (Barney).

2114. EARNEST EUGENE BARNEY [5]; m. Edna Hall   Child:

    1. GLEN VIOLET (Barney).

2115. JOHN EUGENE CRANE[7] [1160], (Curtis,[6] David,[5] Hezekiah,[4] John,[3] Jonathan,[2] Benjamin[1]), married April 25, 1857, Elizabeth Jane Lee Crane, at New Albany, Ind., where she was born Sept. 3, 1836. Her father was from New Jersey. She was a daughter of David and Charlotte (Stewart) Crane. Mrs. Crane is the seventh generation in descent from Stephen Crane, one of the founders of Elizabethtown, N. J. Children, all born in New Albany:

2116—1. LOTTIE STEWART, b. Sept. 11, 1858.
2117—2. NANNIE MONTGOMERY, b. June 28, 1861.
2118—3. JESSIE BROWN, b. Sept. 21, 1863; d. Aug. 4, 1864.
2119—4. LOUISE BARNEY, b. Jan. 2, 1866.
2120—5. JENNIE LEE, b. Dec. 16, 1868.
2121—6. STELLA BROWN, b. March 29, 1872.

2122. JOHN WASHINGTON CRANE[7] [1175], (John W.,[6] David,[5] Hezekiah,[4] John,[3] Jonathan,[2] Benjamin[1]), was born at No. 5, Park Place, New York city, and graduated at New York University in 1855. He studied dentistry, and for many years practiced that profession in Paris, France. His address 7 Rue Scribe, that city. He married Nov. 27, 1867, Josiephene Daniell Leavitt, a native of New Orleans, b. May 1, 1847. Mr. Crane has always been greatly interested in the history of the Crane family, and in 1898 secured through a Mr. Strangman, also a descendant of the Crane family, an engraved portrait of Sir Francis Crane Stoke Park; also some coin (farthings) struck off by him.
Children:

2123—1. JOSEPHENE LEAVITT, b. June 16, 1870, in Paris, France; d. there Dec. 29, 1888.
2124—2. JOHN WELLS, b. May 31, 1874, in Paris, France; d. Nov. 2, 1887, at his school, Eastbourne, Eng.
2125—3. MARY EMMA, b. May 27, 1878, in Paris, France.

2126. SAMUEL L. G. CRANE[7] [1184], (Warren S.,[6] David,[5] Hezekiah,[4] John,[3] Jonathan,[2] Benjamin[1]), was born in New York city; married 1st, Harriet Augusta Ellis, of Hartford, Conn., April, 1853. She was born in 1834, and died September, 1861. He then married 2d, Oct. 21, 1862, Susan J. Underwood, of Enfield, born Oct. 21, 1837. Mr. Crane was a dentist and resided in Hartford, Conn., where he practiced his profession.

2127—1. HATTIE E., b. Nov. 11, 1858.
2128—2. ROSWELL U., b. Dec. 21, 1870; d. Jan. 15, 1873.
2129—3. FRANCIS B., b. Dec. 23, 1874.

2130. BETSY ANN CRANE[7] [1194], (Rufus,[6] Rufus,[5] Hezekiah,[4] John,[3] Jonathan,[2] Benjamin[1]), married Joshua Risley.
Children:

1. JOSHUA ALLEN (Risley), b. April 20, 1830.
2. ANN ELIZABETH (Risley), b. Feb. 4, 1832.
3. ESTHER McCLOUD (Risley), b. Feb. 1, 1834; d. Aug. 13, 1856.
4. ELLEN JANE (Risley), b. March 7, 1836; d. Oct. 2, 1891.
5. EMERETT ALLEN (Risley), b. April 4, 1838.

6. ALBERT GRIFFIN (Risley), b. April 3, 1840; d. Nov. 23, 1895.
7. HENRY GILBERT (Risley), b. March 20, 1842.
8. ANSON BISSELL (Risley), b. May 2, 1844; d. Jan. 16, 1846.
9. ELVIRA WEALTHY (Risley), b. Aug. 1, 1847; d. Aug. 20, 1848.
10. EVELINE WEALTHY (Risley), b. Aug. 5, 1849.
11. ERASTUS EDWARD (Risley), b. July 1, 1851.
12. WELLIE (Risley), b. July 7, 1853; d. Oct. 7, 1853.
13. BENNET TYLER (Risley), b. Sept. 23, 1855.

2131. RUFUS ALLEN CRANE[7] [1195], (Rufus,[6] Rufus,[5] Hezekiah,[4] John,[3] Jonathan,[2] Benjamin[1]), married Louisa Wolcott, Dec. 2, 1846. She was born Nov. 18, 1818. He died April 30, 1869. She died Nov. 20, 1887. Children:

2132—1. EMMA L., b. May 21, 1849; m. Dwight Goodale, Sept. 29, 1869.
2133—2. ELLA F., b. June 17, 1853; d. Aug. 7, 1856.
2134—3. ELROY A., b. May 2, 1857; m. Carrie Talcott, March 12, 1888.
2135—4. GEORGE H., b. Dec. 14, 1862; m. Mary J. Hurd, Dec. 2, 1885.
2136—5. EDWIN L., b. Aug. 9, 1866; d. May 26, 1867.

2137. HENRIETTA CRANE[7] [1196], (Rufus,[6] Rufus,[5] Hezekiah,[4] John,[3] Jonathan,[2] Benjamin[1]), married Merrit Doane. She died Oct. 13, 1890. Children:

1. JULIA H. (Doane), b. Sept. 3, 1840; d. Dec. 7, 1843.
2. JANE A. (Doane), b. Aug. 20, 1842.
3. MERRIT (Doane), b. Aug. 30, 1844.
4. MARTIN (Doane), b. May 6, 1846.
5. MARCUS (Doane), b. Aug. 2, 1848; d. Nov. 9, 1848.
6. MARSHALL (Doane), b. Jan. 7, 1850; d. June 24, 1858.
7. SUMNER L. (Doane), b. April 16, 1852.
8. CARLOS (Doane), b. April 29, 1855.
9. Infant son (Doane), b. and d. May 10, 1857.
10. EBENEZER S. (Doane), b. April 26, 1859.

2138. HENRY CRANE[7] [1197], (Rufus,[6] Rufus,[5] Hezekiah,[4] John,[3] Jonathan,[2] Benjamin[1]), married Harriet M. Taylor, who was born Dec. 11, 1825. She died Dec. 27, 1867. Children:

2139—1. EDWARD H., b. Feb. 22, 1845; d. Jan. 12, 1887.
2140—2. ANNAH H., b. Jan. 1, 1847; d. March 5, 1858.
2141—3. FREDERICK TAYLOR, b. June 1, 1850; d. 1893.
2142—4. WILLIAM F., b. July 15, 1852.
2143—5. LIZZIE A., b. Jan. 5, 1854; m. Frank Craw, Jan. 1, 1872.

2144. ELDRIDGE BURT CRANE[7] [1198], (Rufus,[6] Rufus,[5] Hezekiah,[4] John,[3] Jonathan,[2] Benjamin[1]), married Sarah Farrell. Children:

2145—1. CHARLOTTE ELLEN, b. March 8, 1851.
2146—2. FLORENCE ISABELLE, b. Oct. 14, 1856.
2147—3. CHARLIE ELDRIDGE, b. March 15, 1858.

2148. HOSEA BURGE CRANE[7] [1199], (Rufus,[6] Rufus,[5] Hezekiah,[4] John,[3] Jonathan,[2] Benjamin[1]), married Sarah Janes. Children:

2149—1. FRANKLIN H.

2150—2. THOMAS.
2151—3. ELIZABETH, b. Feb. 22, 1854; d.
2152—4. CORA E., b. June 5, 1856.

2153. FRANCES A. CRANE[7] [1200], (Rufus,[6] Rufus,[5] Hezekiah,[4] John,[3] Jonathan,[2] Benjamin[1]), married Thomas Nesmith, Jr., of Windham, N. H. She was born July 25, 1822, and died Aug. 27, 1895. Children:

1. FRANKLIN ELLSWORTH (Nesmith), b. Nov. 9, 1861.
2. HENRY IRVING (Nesmith), b. Aug. 24, 1864.
3. ELIZABETH FRANCES (Nesmith), b. July 19, 1866; m. June 6, 1888, Amasa Harrington, of Waltham, Mass.

2154. HENRY IRVING NESMITH [2]; m. Oct. 14, 1885, Ella Elvena Olney, of Lowell, Mass. They now (1897) reside in Lynn, where Mr. Nesmith is treasurer and manager of the Lynn Box Company, manufacturers of wood and paper boxes. Children:

1. ESTELLA MAY (Nesmith), b. Sept. 12, 1886; d. Oct. 7, 1887.
2. ROBERT IRVING (Nesmith), b. Sept. 16, 1891.

2155. LUCIUS H. CRANE[7] [1202], (Rufus,[6] Rufus,[5] Hezekiah,[4] John,[3] Jonathan,[2] Benjamin[1]), married May 1, 1866, Margaret H. Bartlett, who was born 1839, and died Oct. 4, 1869, at Ellington. He served in the late war in company G, 25th regiment Connecticut Volunteers, in 1863. Settled at East Windsor, Conn. Child:

2156—1. MAGGIE B., b. Aug. 29, 1868.

2157. ACHSAH M. CRANE[7] [1203], (Rufus,[6] Rufus,[5] Hezekiah,[4] John,[3] Jonathan,[2] Benjamin[1]), married George H. Sloan, Jan. 1, 1855. Reside at Windsorville, Conn. She has been much interested in securing records of her branch of the family, thereby rendering material help to the compiler. Children:

1. LEON HENRY (Sloan), b. Feb. 7, 1859; m. Fannie J. Parson, June 10, 1885; have one child.
2. JEROME HERBERT (Sloan), b. Nov. 27, 1860.
3. ELBERT HOSEA (Sloan), b. March 11, 1866; m. Clara Tenzler, July 18, 1890; have two children.
4. JULIA MARY (Sloan), b. Dec. 3, 1867.
5. ELLERY GEORGE (Sloan), b. Jan. 19, 1874; d. Sept. 16, 1874.
6. BURDETT HOWARD (Sloan), b. Dec. 22, 1876.

2158. LUMAN GRISWOLD CRANE[7] [1204], (Rufus,[6] Rufus,[5] Hezekiah,[4] John,[3] Jonathan,[2] Benjamin[1]), married Abbie R. Osborn. She was born Dec. 11, 1843. Children:

2159—1. ADDIE FRANCES, b. Oct. 19, 1865.
2160—2. LOUIS GILBERT, b. April 9, 1877; d. July 14, 1886.
2161—3. FRANK EDWARD, b. Jan. 1, 1879.

2162. HELEN E. CRANE[7] [1210], (Hosea,[6] Rufus,[5] Hezekiah,[4] John,[3] Jonathan,[2] Benjamin[1]), married G. Buzzell. Child:

1. LIZZIE (Buzzell).

2163. ANNA R. CRANE[7] [1212], (Hosea,[6] Rufus,[5] Hezekiah,[4] John,[3] Jonathan,[2] Benjamin[1]), married L. L. Whitney, of Millbury, Mass. Children :

1. WALTER (Whitney).
2. MINNIE (Whitney).
3. LAURA (Whitney), m. Wm. Carter.
4. MAUD (Whitney).

2164. WALTER WHITNEY [1] ; m. Martha Atwood. Children :

1. MARION (Whitney).
2. WALTER (Whitney).

2165. RUFUS R. CRANE[7] [1213], Hosea,[6] Rufus,[5] Hezekiah,[4] John,[3] Jonathan,[2] Benjamin[1]), married Josie Sutton. Settled in Millbury, Mass. Children :

2166—1. FLORENCE.
2167—2. HOSIA.

2168. MATILDA AMELIA CRANE[7] [1216], (Timothy,[6] Aaron,[5] Hezekiah,[4] John,[3] Jonathan,[2] Benjamin[1]), married William Pitt Mowry, April 17, 1836. Resided at Windsor Locks, Conn. Children :

1. CAROLINE MATILDA (Mowry), b. April 23, 1837 ; d. Jan. 2, 1839.
2. JAMES WILLIAM (Mowry), b. Nov. 9, 1839 ; d. Oct. 21, 1860.
3. LOUISA AMELIA (Mowry), b. Jan. 2, 1843.
4. MARY JANE (Mowry), b. Nov. 25, 1849.

2169. SYLVESTER CRANE[7] [1222], Ziba,[6] Aaron,[5] Hezekiah,[4] John,[3] Jonathan,[2] Benjamin[1]), married at Springfield, Mass., in 1840, Mary Ann Alden, of Wilbraham, born in 1818, and settled in Longmeadow ; a farmer. He died there June 20, 1890. Children :

2170—1. SYLVESTER, b. 1842, m. 1st, Clarinda J. Allen, March 8, 1866 ; 2d, Laura Hancock, 1895 ; no children.
2171—2. MARGARETT, b. 1846.
2172—3. ELSIE A., b. 1848.
2173—4. HENRY, b. 1851 ; salesman ; d. February, 1883, at Wilbraham.
2174—5. MARY E., b. 1856 ; d. at East Longmeadow, May, 1889.
2175—6. ELLEN J., b. 1858 ; d. at East Longmeadow, Oct., 1882.

2176. HEZEKIAH AUGUSTUS CRANE[7] [1227], (Hezekiah,[6] Aaron,[5] Hezekiah,[4] John,[3] Jonathan,[2] Benjamin[1]), married Susan C. Thompson, Oct. 22, 1845. She was born Aug. 11, 1828, and died in Cheshire, Mass., Dec. 31, 1876. He was a farmer in Becket, Mass. He died Jan. 15, 1875. Children :

2177—1. LUCY AUGUSTA, b. Dec. 9, 1847.
2178—2. DAVID AUGUSTUS, b. July 21, 1849 ; lives in Sheffield, Mass. ; farmer.
2179—3. KATIE JANE, b. Jan. 16, 1855.
2180—4. WALTER LEON, b. Sept. 19, 1858 ; lives in Dalton, Mass.
2181—5. BERDELLA J., b. Jan. 4, 1866 ; d. at Springfield, Mass.
2182—6. ADALINE, b. Jan. 26, 1870.

2183. ELI BARBER CRANE[7] [1230], (Hezekiah,[6] Aaron,[5] Hezekiah,[4] John,[3] Jonathan,[2] Benjamin[1]), married Adelaide Jaquith at Albion, Oswego County, N. Y. Enlisted in company K, 81st New York, Nov. 10, 1861, and served in the late war, battles at Yorktown, Fair Oaks and Cold Harbor. Killed at last named place June 3, 1864. Child:

2184—1. WILLIS J., b. Dec. 29, 1856, at Sand Bank, Oswego County, N. Y.

2185. LEANDER CRANE[7] [1238], (Ebenezer,[6] Zebulon,[5] Lemuel,[4] John,[3] Jonathan,[2] Benjamin[1]), married Hannah Pollard, of Surry, N. H. She was born in 1815. Removed to Belle Plain, Wis. Children:

2186—1. HARRIETT M., b. May, 1835.
2187—2. ELEANOR A., b. 1837.
2188—3. MARTHA, b. September, 1841.
2189—4. SARAH, b. 1847.
2190—5. HELEN, b. 1849.

2191. ALBERT CRANE[7] [1239], [Ebenezer,[6] Zebulon,[5] Lemuel,[4] John,[3] Jonathan,[2] Benjamin[1]), married Ann Colman, of Leominster, Mass. She died in January, 1857, and he married Kate Hervey. Lived at Belle Plain, Wis. He died in August, 1863, leaving a daughter by second wife. His widow again married, and settled in Leominster, Mass. Child:

2192—1. KATE, b. March, 1858.

2193. GILBERT CRAIN[7] [1240], (Ebenezer,[6] Zebulon,[5] Lemuel,[4] John,[3] Jonathan,[2] Benjamin[1]), married Sept. 29, 1842, Harriet N. Thomas, daughter of Philip and Ruth (Fish) Thomas, of Surry, N. H. She was born Oct. 10, 1820. Settled in Surry, N. H. He died leaving a will, dated Aug. 3, 1882, in which he names his wife Harriet, and children, Jane H., Chas. G., Frederick R., Frank P., and Mary L. Nesmith. Children:

2194—1. HARRIETT, b. Oct. 27, 1843.
2195—2. CHARLES GILBERT, b. May 15, 1845; m. Stella Hayward; no children.
2196—3. FREDERICK R., b. May 23, 1847.
2197—4. FRANK P., b. June 27, 1849.
2198—5. MARY LOUISE, b. Aug. 26, 1851; m. Frank E. Nesmith; no children.
2199—6. EBENEZER, b. Aug. 28, 1853.
2200—7. GEORGE, b. 1861.

2201. ELISHA CRANE[7] [1241], (Ebenezer,[6] Zebulon,[5] Lemuel,[4] John,[3] Jonathan,[2] Benjamin[1]), married Abigail Stone, of Chesterfield, N. H. She was born in 1818, and settled in San Francisco, Cal. Children:

2202—1. ELIZA.
2203—2. GEORGE.
2204—3. FRANCIS.
2205—4. ELLEN.
2206—5. VELMA.

2207. EBENEZER CRANE[7] [1242], (Ebenezer,[6] Zebulon,[5] Lemuel,[4] John,[3] Jonathan,[2] Benjamin[1]), married Calista Coburn, of Chesterfield, N. H. She was born in March, 1824. Settled in the northern part of the State of Iowa. Children :

2208—1. JULIA, b. 1841.
2209—2. HANNAH.
2210—3. ALBERT.
2211—4. LOVISA.
2212—5. LAURA.
2213—6. ELVA.
2214—7. ARTHUR.
2215—8. ALICE.
2216—9. AYRES.
2217-10. EMMA.

2218. LEROY DELOSS CRANE[7] [1247], (Ralph,[6] Isaac,[5] Isaac,[4] Isaac,[3] Jonathan,[2] Benjamin[1]), married 1st, Sept. 12, 1855, Jane Broughton Whipple, of North Stonington, Conn.; born May 7, 1838, and settled in Groton, Conn. She died April 18, 1863, and he married 2d, Mary Jane Faulkner, of Yantic. She was born March 22, 1848. Children :

2219—1. EVERETT LEROY, b. Aug. 12, 1856.
2220—2. ELLA JENNY, b. Aug. 10, 1858; d. Jan. 18, 1862.

2221. ADELBERT WADSWORTH CRANE[7] [1251], (Ralph,[6] Isaac,[5] Isaac,[4] Isaac,[3] Jonathan[2], Benjamin[1]), married Sept. 12, 1876, Margaret Eliza Goodrich, of South Glastonbury, Conn. She was born July 5, 1835.

2222. IRA A. CRANE[7] [1271], (Joseph,[6] John,[5] Zebulon,[4] Joseph,[3] Jonathan,[2] Benjamin[1]), married 1st, Hannah Hopkins. She was born Jan. 14, 1791, and died March 2, 1839. He married 2d, Zillah Hazen ; 3d, Polly Foster. He removed to Barrington, Yates County, N. Y., where he died April 4, 1860. Children :

2223—1. JOHN J., b. Dec. 6, 1810; d. March 29, 1825.
2224—2. WILLIAM EGBERT, b. Feb. 5, 1813.
2225—3. EMILY, b. May 17, 1815.
2226—4. ABRAHAM H., b. Sept. 11, 1817.
2227—5. JOSEPH N., b. Sept. 29, 1820; m. Helena A. Mitchell; lived in Geneva, N. Y., in 1897.
2228—6. JOHN, b. Nov. 5, 1827.
2229—7. ARZOR BELDEN, b. April 25, 1830; d. unm. March 6, 1894.
2230—8. EMELINE, b. August, 1833; d. Jan. 13, 1848.
2231—9. GEORGE W., b. Jan. 24, 1835; d. April 16, 1849.

2232. ADAH CRANE[7] [1272], (Joseph,[6] John,[5] Zebulon,[4] Joseph,[3] Jonathan[2] Benjamin[1]), married James Baldwin. She died Sept. 9, 1855. Children :

1. NOAH C. (Baldwin), b. 1816.
2. JAMES E. (Baldwin), b. 1818; m. Sarah Adams; son William lives in Peekskill.

2233. NOAH C. BALDWIN [1]; m. Martha P. Burhuss. He died Oct. 21, 1879. She died May 18, 1889. Children:

1. LEWIS G. (Baldwin), b. 1844; m. —— Pierce, and d. about 1893.
2. ADAH A. (Baldwin); m. Cornelius Pierce, brother of above; lives in Michigan.
3. EMMA A. (Baldwin), b. 1856; d. Sept. 28, 1872.

2234. CORNELIA CRANE[7] [1273], (Joseph,[6] John,[5] Zebulon,[4] Joseph,[3] Jonathan,[2] Benjamin[1]), married Lewis Crosby, a son of Enoch Crosby, who figures in history as "Harvey Birch the Spy," Cooper. She died Dec. 3, 1857. Children:

1. EDWARD (Crosby), b. June 22, 1812; m. 1st, Rachel Hasbrouck; 2d, Rachel Duel; 3d, Nancy Brundage; d. Oct. 1, 1890; he was an M.D.
2. JOSEPH (Crosby).
3. ZILLAH (Crosby).
4. IRA (Crosby).
5. BENJAMIN (Crosby), b. 1826; m. Laura Ketcham and d. March 22, 1886.
6. CHARLES (Crosby); d. when about 18 years of age.
7. HENRY (Crosby), b. 1834; m. Susan Lounsbury. She d. Oct. 30, 1873. He d. March 16, 1887. Children:
    1. CORNELIA (Crosby); d. young.
    2. LEWIS (Crosby); resides in New London, Conn.
    3. EUGENE (Crosby); resides in Fishkill on the Hudson.
    4. CARRIE (Crosby); d. March 12, 1889.

2235. ZILLAH CRANE[7] [1274], (Joseph,[6] John,[5] Zebulon,[4] Joseph,[3] Jonathan,[2] Benjamin[1]), married Gilbert H. Travis. She died Jan. 17, 1833. Child:

1. EMELINE C. (Travis), b. July 14, 1820; m. Oct. 10, 1843, George Ludington, a son of Col. Henry Ludington of Revolutionary fame. He d. April 11, 1874. She d. May 4, 1887. Children:
    1. GILBERT T. (Ludington), b. July 12, 1847; m. Mary Barker.
    2. JOSEPH (Ludington), b. 1849.
    3. EMILY F. (Ludington), b. December, 1850; m. Rev. Walter A. Chadwick. Children:
        1. ELSIE (Chadwick).
        2. GEORGE (Chadwick).
        3. ALBERT (Chadwick).
        4. HAROLD (Chadwick).
    4. NELSON E. (Ludington), b. 1852.
    5. THOMAS EDWARD (Ludington), b. Sept. 19, 1854; m. and resides in St. Paul, Minn.
    6. GEORGIA (Ludington), b. April 22, 1861.

2236. BETSEY CRANE[7] [1275], (Joseph,[6] John,[5] Zebulon,[4] Joseph,[3] Jonathan,[2] Benjamin[1]), married Thomas Foster. She died June 27, 1825. Children:

1. JOSEPH C. (Foster), b. about 1822; was a Presbyterian minister; m. Mrs. Hannah (Pierce) Jackson; d. 1860. She d. May 8, 1891.
2. WILLIAM H. (Foster), b. May, 1824; m. Rachel Chapman. Children:
    1. EMMA J. (Foster), b. Dec. 26, 1853.

2. MARILLA C. (Foster), b. Aug. 2, 1859.
3. BESSIE C. (Foster), b. Nov. 23, 1863; m. Geo. E. Reed,
    Oct. 14, 1891.

2237. AZOR BELDEN CRANE[7] [1276], (Joseph,[6] John,[5] Zebu-
lon,[4] Joseph,[3] Jonathan,[2] Benjamin[1]), married Aurelia Doane.
She was born Feb. 21, 1814, and died Oct. 22, 1859. He died
Oct. 14, 1864. Children:

2238—1. BENJAMIN D., b. Sept. 6, 1832.
2239—2. IRA, b. Aug. 13, 1834.
2240—3. AZOR B., b. May 15, 1838; d. Sept. 9, 1841.
2241—4. GEORGE T., b. Feb. 28, 1840; d. March 2, 1841.
2242—5. GEORGE B., b. Aug. 3, 1845; d. June 19, 1848.
2243—6. JOSEPH HENRY, b. Dec. 12, 1850; lives at Mt. Kisco, N. Y.

2244. GEORGE LANE CRANE[7] [1288], (Stephen,[6] John,[5] Zebulon,[4] Joseph,[3] Jonathan,[2] Benjamin[1]), married March, 1823, in
New York city, Helena Brewer. She was from Monmouth
County, N. J., born July 9, 1803. He was a builder. He resided in New York city and Red Hook, but died in Dayton, Ohio,
in 1839. She died in Brooklyn, N. Y., Feb. 23, 1879.
    Children:

2245—1. STEPHEN.
2246—2. ARRABELLA.
2247—3. EDWARD M., b. Dec. 23, 1831.
2248—4. LYDIA HELLEN.
2249—5. GEORGE L., b. Sept. 9, 1836; m. Helen M. Dow, Nov. 5,
         1865; no children. He served in late war, 1861 to 1864,
         mostly in Virginia. In New York Custom House 1866,
         1867 and 1868.

2250. ANDREWS JAY CRANE[7] [1289], (Stephen,[6] John,[5] Zebulon,[4] Joseph,[3] Jonathan,[2] Benjamin[1]), married Arabella Knox,
in 1825, at Carmel, N. Y. She was born in Somers, Westchester County, N. Y., Oct. 3, 1803, and died in Red Hook, Jan. 24,
1857. Children:

2251—1. SARAH, b. and d. 1826, in New York.
2252—2. SARAH HADDEN, b. 1830, in New York.
2253—3. JOHN KNOX, b. 1835, in Red Hook; d. 1837.
2254—4. ZILLA KNOX, b. 1841, in Red Hook.

2255. SAMUEL HARVEY CRANE[7] [1293], (John,[6] John,[5] Zebulon,[4] Joseph,[3] Jonathan,[2] Benjamin[1]), married Elizabeth Webb.
He went to Seneca County, N. Y. Children:

2256—1. JOHN; d. 1894.
2257—2. HARVEY.
2258—3. EMELINE.

2259. ELIZA CRANE[7] [1294], (John,[6] John,[5] Zebulon,[4] Joseph,[3] Jonathan,[2] Benjamin[1]), married Stephen Knapp.
    Children:

1. GEORGE (Knapp); a Methodist minister.
2. CORNELIA (Knapp).
3. CATHARINE (Knapp).

Azor B Crane

Was in 1843 appointed judge of Court of Common Pleas and was the first County judge and surrogate under the new constitution.

During his life one of the most prominent citizens of Putnam County, N. Y.

4. MARY ANN (Knapp).
5. HARRISON B. (Knapp).
6. BENJAMIN (Knapp).

2260. SALLY BETSEY CRANE[7] [1295], (John,[6] John,[5] Zebulon,[4] Joseph,[3] Jonathan,[2] Benjamin[1]), married Gilbert Ganong. She died Oct. 9, 1889. Children:

1. GEORGE (Ganong).
2. SARAH (Ganong).
3. GILBERT (Ganong).

2261. GEORGE GANONG [1]; m. Emma A. Carver. Children:

1. EDWARD (Ganong).
2. ADILE E. (Ganong).

2262. CLORINDA CRANE[7] [1297], (John,[6] John,[5] Zebulon,[4] Joseph,[3] Jonathan,[2] Benjamin[1]), married Stephen Monk. He died March 15, 1859. Children:

1. MARY ANN (Monk), b. Sept. 8, 1829; m. James M. Ganun (or Ganong).
2. STEPHEN WALLACE (Monk), b. Feb. 5, 1831; m. Josaphine Moses.
3. EMMA CAROLINE (Monk), b. Aug. 29, 1832; m. J. H. Ferris.
4. SARAH JOSAPHINE (Monk), b. July 18, 1834; m. Wm. H. Storms.
5. WILLIAM W. (Monk), b. June 3, 1836; m. Mary A. Starr.
6. GEORGE H. (Monk), b. Jan. 18, 1838.
7. ROSELINDA G. (Monk), b. March 22, 1839; m. Walter R. Jones.
8. CLORINDA (Monk), b. March 18, 1840; d. at the age of 13 years.

2263. MARY ANN MONK [1]; m. James M. Ganun. Children:

1. E. ISABEL (Ganun).
2. STEPHEN MONK (Ganun).
3. JOHN J. (Ganun).
4. SARAH JOSAPHINE (Ganun).

2264. STEPHEN WALLACE MONK [2]; m. Josaphine Moses. Children:

1. LOUISA (Monk).
2. ELENOR (Monk).

2265. EMMA CAROLINE MONK [3]; m. James Henry Ferris. Child:

1. CARRIE JANE (Ferris); d. at age of 3 years.

2266. SARAH JOSAPHINE MONK [4]; m. William H. Storms. Child:

1. GEORGE WOODWARD (Storms); d. in infancy.

2267. WILLIAM W. MONK [5]; m. Mary A. Starr. Children:

1. DELIA H. (Monk); d.
2. FLORENCE A. (Monk).
3. GEORGE L. (Monk).
4. BLANCH A. (Monk).
5. WILLIAM W. (Monk).
6. GRACE,   } twins.
7. EDGAR, d.   }

2268. ROSELINDA G. MONK [7]; m. Walter Richard Jones. Child:

1. CHARLOTTE OPHELIA (Jones); m. Frederick Gilbert Lockwood.

2269.   NANCY CRANE[7] [1298], (John,[6] John,[5] Zebulon,[4] Joseph,[3] Jonathan,[2] Benjamin[1]), married Elias Newman, Oct. 20, 1824.   He was born Dec. 30, 1798, and died Oct. 16, 1886. She died Aug. 31, 1835.   In the family record kept by Mr. Newman her birth is recorded May 8, 1805.   Children :

1. SARAH ELIZABETH (Newman), b. Jan. 3, 1829.
2. JULIA ANN (Newman), b. Oct. 11, 1832.

2270.   SARAH ELIZABETH NEWMAN [1] ; m. Jonathan Kenyon in 1847.
     Children :

1. MARY (Kenyon).
2. HATTIE R. (Kenyon).

2271.   JULIA ANN NEWMAN [2] ; m. Niles Kenyon, Jan. 2, 1852.
     Children.:

1. FRED D. (Kenyon).
2. ELLA N. (Kenyon).
3. EDWARD N. (Kenyon).

2272.   HARRIETT CRANE[7] [1300], (John,[6] John,[5] Zebulon,[4] Joseph,[3] Jonathan,[2] Benjamin[1]), m. 1st, —— Horton ; 2d, Palmer Hayden ; 3d, Isaac Newman, Nov. 29, 1833.   She died Oct. 13, 1875.   Mr. Newman died March 31, 1890.   Children :

1. JULIA (Hayden), b. Sept. 29, 1829 ; m. Peter Reynolds ; residence Whitney's Point, N. Y.
2. JOHN P. (Hayden) ; b. July 26, 1832.
3. STEPHEN (Newman), b. Feb. 24, 1835 ; residence Binghamton, N. Y.
4. ISAAC N. (Newman), b. March 15, 1837 ; residence Moravia, N. Y.
5. HANNAH E. (Newman), b. March 14, 1839 ; residence Whitney's Point. N. Y.
6. HENRY W. (Newman), b. Oct. 6, 1841 ; d. Nov. 12, 1846.
7. IRA A. (Newman), b. Sept. 12, 1848 ; residence Itaska, N. Y.

2273.   ADAH CRANE[7] [1302], (John,[6] John,[5] Zebulon,[4] Joseph,[3] Jonathan,[2] Benjamin[1]), married Benjamin Mead.
     Child :

1. ANNIS (Mead).

2274.   ROSALINDA LYON CRANE[7] [1304], (John,[6] John,[5] Zebulon,[4] Joseph,[3] Jonathan,[2] Benjamin[1]), married Henry Adolphus Gahn, of New York city.   Mr. Gahn's father was a Swedish consul.   Mr. Gahn died June, 1863.   She died April 2, 1889.
     Children :

1. HENRIETTA MAGDALENA (Gahn), b. January, 1841.
2. MARY DEVEN (Gahn), b. October, 1842.
3. JANE F. (Gahn), b. October, 1844.
4. JULIA F. (Gahn), b. Feb. 23, 1847.
5. HENRY A. (Gahn), b. November, 1850 ; m. Lillian Wright.
6. WILLIAM E. (Gahn), b. October, 1852.
7. AMELIA B. (Gahn), b. September, 1855 ; m. John B. Frost ; 2 children.

2275. HENRIETTA MAGDALENA GAHN [1]; m. in 1862 to Henry Horton. Children:

1. EDWARD GAHN (Horton).
2. MARY L. (Horton).
3. HARRY (Horton).
4. CLARENCE (Horton).
5. JENNIE (Horton).

2276. MARY DEVEN GAHN [2]; m. George Quimby. She d. April 14, 1875. Children:

1. MABEL (Quimby).
2. ETHEL (Quimby).

2277. SUSAN AMELIA CRANE[7] [1305], (John,[6] John,[5] Zebulon,[4] Joseph,[3] Jonathan,[2] Benjamin[1]), married Lewis Hutchings. She died July 27, 1858. He died Jan. 21, 1864. Children:

1. HELEN (Hutchings); d. young.
2. BLEEKER (Hutchings); d. young.
3. LEWIS (Hutchings); d. young.
4. ISABEL (Hutchings); m. —— Ferris.

2278. CAROLINE ELIZA CRANE[7] [1311], (Nathaniel,[6] John,[5] Zebulon,[4] Joseph,[3] Jonathan,[2] Benjamin[1]), married December, 1826, Pierce Pinckney. She died Feb. 16, 1839. Children:

1. JAMES HENRY (Pinckney).
2. FREDERICK (Pinckney); d. January, 1892.
3. MARTHA ANN (Pinckney).
4. NATHANIEL (Pinckney); d. young.

2279. CHARLOTTE LOUISA CRANE[7] [1313], (Nathaniel,[6] John,[5] Zebulon,[4] Joseph,[3] Jonathan,[2] Benjamin[1]), married May 9, 1832, Ammon Fowler. He was born Sept. 9, 1809, and died June 5, 1885. She died Oct. 5, 1867. Children:

1. JAMES GILBERT (Fowler); d. 1861.
2. CHARLES EDGAR (Fowler), b. April, 1841; m. in 1869, Charlotte Louise Richards. Children:

    1. CHARLES; d. young.
    2. CHARLOTTE LOUISE.

2280. MARY ELIZABETH CRANE[7] [1316], (Nathaniel,[6] John,[5] Zebulon,[4] Joseph,[3] Jonathan,[2] Benjamin[1]), married Jan. 23, 1837, Thomas Wright. She died Jan. 28, 1897. Children:

1. BENJAMIN T. (Wright), b. Feb. 28, 1838.
2. SACKETT L. (Wright), b. April 19, 1841.
3. REUBEN A. (Wright), b. Dec. 24, 1843.
4. MARY AUGUSTA (Wright), b. Dec. 17, 1846.
5. MORTON C. (Wright), b. Dec. 15, 1850.
6. AMELIA P. (Wright), b. May 18, 1852.
7. FREDERICK K. (Wright), b. Oct. 31, 1855.
8. SOPHIA E. (Wright), b. June 6, 1860.

2281. BENJAMIN T. WRIGHT [1]; m. May 9, 1866, Mary A. Howland, at Lyle, N. Y. Children:

1. MARY LIDA (Wright), b. Dec. 8, 1868.
2. ELIZABETH LINNELL (Wright), b. May 9, 1872.
3. MARGARET SQUIRES (Wright), b. June 20, 1874.

14

2282. SACKETT L. WRIGHT [2]; m. May 8, 1867, Priscilla Longman, of Brooklyn, N. Y. Children:

    1. CARRIETTA P. (Wright), b. Aug. 26, 1868; m. Frank Hibbard, May 4, 1891; no children.
    2. GEORGIA LULU (Wright), b. Nov. 13, 1870; m. Robert H. Steed, April 3, 1894. Child:
        1. ROBERT L. (Steed), b. June 5, 1895.
    3. ANNIE LOUISE (Wright), b. Dec. 31, 1872; m. Charles Bowen, Nov. 19, 1893. Child:
        1. CLARENCE S. (Bowen), b. April, 1895.
    4. RALPH EUGENE (Wright), b. Sept. 30, 1875.

2283. REUBEN A. WRIGHT [3]; m. 1st, Dec. 24, 1868, Lida P. Howland; 2d, June 23, 1871, Ella Willis; 3d, Jan. 7, 1891, Fannie Middaugh. First wife had no children. Child by 2d wife:

    1. LENA P. (Wright), b. Sept. 13, 1873; m. Ralph W. Mitchell, in 1890. Children:
        1. DOROTHY F. (Mitchell).
        2. HELEN R. (Mitchell).
        3. EDITH (Mitchell).
Children by 3d wife:
    2. EDWARD TAYLOR (Wright), b. Aug. 28, 1893.
    3. MARY ELIZABETH (Wright), b. Nov. 17, 1895.

2284. MORTON C. WRIGHT [5]; m. Dec. 4, 1877, Jennie Hitchcock. He d. at Rome, N. Y., May 8, 1895. Child:

    1. EARL HITCHCOCK (Wright), b. April 6, 1879.

2285. AMELIA P. WRIGHT [6]; m. Dec. 4, 1877, Nelson H. Ripley. Children:

    1. AUGUSTA S. (Ripley), b. June 8, 1880.
    2. JESSE A. (Ripley), b. Feb. 27, 1882.
    3. CLARENCE L. (Ripley), b. Jan. 20, 1885.
    4. REUBEN W. (Ripley), b. Dec. 20, 1887.
    5. WILLIAM N. (Ripley), b. July 4, 1893.

2286. FREDERICK K. WRIGHT [7]; m. Oct. 11, 1877, Mary A. Reilly. Children:

    1. FREDERICK FRANCIS (Wright), b. Nov. 23, 1878.
    2. BERTHA MARY (Wright), b. Aug. 4, 1880.

2287. SOPHIA E. WRIGHT [8]; m. Aug. 4, 1880, Will P. Haynes. She d. Jan. 4, 1884. Child:

    1. HARRY NICHOLAS (Haynes), b. May 4, 1882.

2288. AUGUSTA SOPHIA CRANE[7] [1317], (Nathaniel,[6] John,[5] Zebulon,[4] Joseph,[3] Jonathan,[2] Benjamin[1]), married April 23, 1844, Reuben Kirkham. He was born April 23, 1818. They settled in South East, N. Y. She died Jan. 7, 1888. He died Sept. 17, 1897. Children:

    1. CAROLINE AMELIA (Kirkham), b. July 6, 1845.
    2. PETER ZOPHER (Kirkham), b. March 30, 1847.
    3. MORTON EUGENE (Kirkham), b. Dec. 8, 1848; d. July 17, 1871.
    4. ESTELLA AUGUSTA (Kirkham), b. June 13, 1851.
    5. CHARLOTTE ELIZABETH (Kirkham), b. April 19, 1854.
    6. BENJAMIN CRANE (Kirkham), b. July 14, 1857; d. April 12, 1860.
    7. FREDERICK NATHANIEL (Kirkham), b. Feb. 17, 1859; d. Oct. 1, 1860.
    8. MATTIE A. (Kirkham), b. April 15, 1861; d. April 6, 1863.

Truly C B Crane

For sketch see page 233.

2289. CAROLINE AMELIA KIRKHAM [1]; m. 1868, Samuel Kelley. He
d. April 20, 1894. Children:

1. WALLACE H. (Kelley), b. Oct. 9, 1869.
2. ARTHUR D. (Kelley), b. July 29, 1871.

2290. PETER Z. KIRKHAM [2]; m. Henrietta Kelley, who d. Sept. 2,
1894. Child:

1. NELLIE (Kirkham), b. Feb. 26, 1876.

2291. ESTELLA A. KIRKHAM [4]; m. Starr Ga Nong. Children:

1. CHARLES E. (Ga Nong), b. April 10, 1877; d. Feb. 16,
1894, aged 17 years.
2. REUBEN K. (Ga Nong), b. Aug. 1, 1879.
3. AUGUSTA (Ga Nong), b. Oct. 27, 1885.

2292. BENJAMIN TOWNSEND CRANE[7] [1318], (Nathaniel,[6]
John,[5] Zebulon,[4] Joseph,[3] Jonathan,[2] Benjamin[1]), married Jan.
11, 1860, Emma Augusta Washburn. She was born May 10,
1837, and died Dec. 21, 1883. Children:

2293—1. AURELIA, b. Dec. 29, 1860.
2294—2. LAURA, b. July 29, 1863; d. Feb. 20, 1865.
2295—3. JOHN, b. Nov. 12, 1865; d. Dec. 10, 1865.
2296—4. SAMUEL BELDEN, b. Nov. 16, 1867.
2297—5. GERTRUDE, b. March 25, 1869.
2298—6. NATHANIEL MORTON, b. Dec. 3, 1871.
2299—7. BENJAMIN TOWNSEND, b. Oct. 11, 1874.

2300. CLARINDA CRANE[7] [1336], (Belden,[6] Zebulon,[5] Zebulon,[4] Joseph,[3] Jonathan,[2] Benjamin[1]), married Philip Smith.
She died Feb. 9, 1875. Children:

1. BELDEN CRANE (Smith).
2. ALEXANDER (Smith).

2301. Dr. GEORGE BELDEN CRANE[7] [1342], (Belden,[6] Zebulon,[5] Zebulon,[4] Joseph,[3] Jonathan,[2] Benjamin[1]), studied medicine and received the title of M.D. He married 1st, Maria
Young; 2d, Mrs. Fannie Grayson. Since 1853 he has resided
in California. In 1896 his home was at St. Helena, where he
owned a large and flourishing vineyard, and although 90 years
of age was quite active. Child:

2302—1. MARY; m. —— McPike; d. a few years since, leaving
several children.

2303. JOHN WEEKS CRANE[7] [1349], (Samuel,[6] Zebulon,[5]
Zebulon,[4] Joseph,[3] Jonathan,[2] Benjamin[1]), married Jan. 1, 1851,
Elmira Bogart Miller, of Pound Ridge, near New Canaan, Conn.
He died May 1, 1892. Children, born in Danbury, Conn.:

2304—1. MARY ESTHER, b. Nov. 31, 1851; d. Oct. 13, 1853.
2305—2. LYDIA JOSEPHINE, b. Jan. 23, 1853.
2306—3. LETITIA, b. April 3, 1855.
2307—4. LILLIE ELIZABETH, b. March 30, 1861; m. Edwin Moore, of
Bridgeport; residence, Danbury, Conn.
2308—5. LENA EMILY, b. Oct. 7, 1866; d. Feb. 7, 1868.
2309—6. MINNIE ELIZA, b. Aug. 5, 1867.

2310. HARRISON CRANE[7] [1353], (Zebulon,[6] Zebulon,[5] Zebulon,[4] Joseph,[3] Jonathan,[2] Benjamin[1]), married at Patterson, N. Y., by Rev. E. P. Benedict, Oct. 17, 1854, Ann Jane Pepper, daughter of Nehemiah and Minerva (Peet) Pepper. She was born in Danbury, Conn., Jan. 9, 1829. They settled in New Fairfield, Conn. He died Oct. 15, 1880. Children:

2311—1. MARY MINERVA, b. Oct. 7, 1855.
2312—2. JAMES NEHEMIAH, b. Sept. 25, 1857.
2313—3. CARRIE MARIA, b. March 12, 1860; resides at Patterson, Putnam Co., N. Y.

2314. CHARLOTTE CRANE[7] [1354], (Zebulon,[6] Zebulon,[5] Zebulon,[4] Joseph,[3] Jonathan,[2] Benjamin[1]), married in 1848, Levi Wakeman, son of Hall and Amy (Banks) Wakeman. He was born March 17, 1815. Children:

1. MARTHA CRANE (Wakeman), b. Jan. 1, 1849.
2. GEORGE MILES (Wakeman), b. Feb. 19, 1851.
3. WILLIAM ALONZO (Wakeman), b. Oct. 31, 1856.
4. THADDEUS CRANE (Wakeman), b. May 23, 1860; m. Lillian Halliwell, of Wappinger's Falls, N. Y., June 5, 1883. She d. in 1886.

2315. MARTHA CRANE WAKEMAN [1]; m. Nov. 16, 1870, James Wright Palmer, son of Dennis and Millison (Towner) Palmer. He was born Dec. 31, 1847. Children:

1. WILLIAM GERARD (Palmer), b. Dec. 28, 1872.

2316. GEORGE MILES WAKEMAN [2]; m. Sept. 20, 1876, Calvina Vosburgh, of Hillsdale, Columbia Co., N. Y. Children:

1. CHARLOTTE JULIA (Wakeman), b. August, 1877.
2. JEAN ROMER (Wakeman), b. Jan. 19, 1885.

2317. PHILANDER CRANE[7] [1373], (Josiah,[6] Jonathan,[5] Joseph,[4] Joseph,[3] Jonathan,[2] Benjamin[1]), married Dec. 5, 1822, Delight Field. She died June 2, 1847. He died Oct. 5, 1875. Children:

2318—1. GEORGE PROVOST, b. Feb. 9, 1824.
2319—2. ELBERT, b. July 27, 1841.

2320. JOHN CRANE[7] [1374], (Josiah,[6] Jonathan,[5] Joseph,[4] Joseph,[3] Jonathan,[2] Benjamin[1]), married March 11, 1824, Betsey Wakefield. She was born in 1801 near New Haven, Conn., and died in 1853. For several years they resided in South East, Putnam County, N. Y. They removed to Seneca County, where they remained fifteen years. From there they went to Orleans County, where they died. He died April 28, 1860. Children:

2321—1. STELLA ANN, b. March 23, 1827; d. May 20, 1845.
2322—2. SARAH E., b. April 14. 1828; m. —— Baker.
2323—3. CRISTOPHER COLUMBUS. b. March 29, 1829.
2324—4. HANNAH, b. Sept. 24, 1830; m. —— Sandhouse; living 1896.
2325—5. JOSEPHUS; d. in the army in 1863, aged 31 years.
2326—6. CHARLES F., b. 1832.
2327—7. ORRIN BALDWIN, b. April 2, 1835
2328—8. FRANCES A., b. Feb. 8, 1836.

2329—9.   CARSO, b. July 22, 1837.
2330-10.   EMILY, b. May 22, 1839.
2331-11.   WILLIAM H. H., b. Oct. 23, 1840; d. aged 23, of consumption.
2332-12.   ISABELLA S., b. March 24, 1845; residence 1899, Anamosa,
     Iowa; unm.

2333.   OLIVER CRANE[7] [1375], (Josiah,[6] Jonathan,[5] Joseph,[4]
Joseph,[3] Jonathan,[2] Benjamin[1]), married March 1, 1832, Maria
Snow, of South East, Putnam County, N. Y. She was born
Sept. 14, 1808. He died Nov. 18, 1888. Child:

2334—1.   WILLIAM SNOW, b. Jan. 16, 1835.

2335.   DARIUS P. CRANE[7] [1382], (Josiah,[6] Jonathan,[5]
Joseph,[4] Joseph,[3] Jonathan,[2] Benjamin[1]), married Hannah
Forbes, Sept. 28, 1837, at Galen, Wayne County, N. Y. She
was born in Corfu, Greece, in November, 1819. Removed to
Hillsdale, Mich. He was a farmer. He died Aug. 5, 1890.
Children:

2336—1.   EMILY R., b. September, 1838.
2337—2.   KATE H.
2338—3.   ANNA E.
2339—4.   ALBERT A.
2340—5.   AMBROSE W., b. July, 1848.
2341—6.   MARK D.
2342—7.   ELLA L.
2343—8.   LON A.

2344.   JOHN PLATT CRANE[7] [1397], (Anson,[6] Jonathan,[5]
Joseph,[4] Joseph,[3] Jonathan,[2] Benjamin[1]), married Catharine
DeForrest.

2345.   RUFUS ERASTUS CRANE[7] [1399], (Anson,[6] Jonathan,[5]
Joseph,[4] Joseph,[3] Jonathan,[2] Benjamin[1]), married Annie Ridley
in New York city June 10, 1850. He died in New York city
Sept. 5, 1865. Children:

2346—1.   ANNIE RIDLEY, b. March 6, 1851; m. Edward L. Finch.
2347—2.   LOUISE ADELAIDE, b. July 1, 1853; d. Sept. 12, 1897.

2348.   ISAAC AUGUSTUS CRANE[7] [1400], (Anson,[6] Jonathan,[5]
Joseph,[4] Jonathan,[3] Jonathan,[2] Benjamin[1]), married Marie
Hill, of Chicago, Ill., where he died May 12, 1892 or 1893.
Children:

2349—1.   ADDIE MARIE, b. in Chicago, April 7, ——; d. young.
2350—2.   MARY VIRGINIA, b. in South East, Putnam County, N. Y.,
     Dec. 20, 1865; d. young.

2351.   MARY CRANE[7] [1421], (Oliver,[6] Solomon,[5] Joseph,[4]
Joseph,[3] Jonathan,[2] Benjamin[1]), married Francis B. Lane, Feb.
13, 1856, and settled in New York city, which has practically
been the home of the family.   Children:

   1.   FRANCES JOSEPHINE (Lane), b. April 18, 1857; m. Sept. 30, 1879,
     Spencer W. Lewis. Children:
       1.   MAUDE SPENCER (Lewis), } twins, { d. July 3, 1884.
                                    } b. Sept. 14, {
       2.   GRACE CRANE (Lewis),   } 1880;   {

3. BEATRICE LOEW (Lewis),   } twins, b. May 26, 1883.
4. BLANCHE BROWNING (Lewis), }

2352. ADDISON MOSES CRANE[7] [1425], (Henry,[6] Isaac,[5] Joseph,[4] Joseph,[3] Jonathan,[2] Benjamin[1]), married at Catskill, N. Y., Oct. 21, 1839, Gertrude Ashley. She was born at that place June 15, 1820. Their two eldest children were born in Nunda, N. Y., after which they removed to Lafayette, Ind., where they resided until after 1851. Subsequent to that date they removed to Alameda County, Cal., where they were residing in April, 1855. He died in Oakland, Alameda County, Cal., Oct. 20, 1889. Children:

2353—1. CATHERINE AUGUSTA, b. Oct. 12, 1840.
2354—2. LAUREN ELLIOT, b. July 18, 1842; d. February, 1897.
2355—3. ANNA FRANCES, b. May 18, 1845.
2356—4. MARY GERTRUDE, b. March 8. 1847; d. Jan. 2, 1856.
2357—5. ASLEY ADDISON, b. May 18, 1849; d. at sea, October, 1871.
2358—6. ALBERT EMERSON, b. June 7, 1851; d. May, 1859.
2359—7. HELEN ELIZA. b.-April 1, 1855; d. March, 1858.
2360—8. GERTRUDE ASHLEY, b. Sept. 24, 1857.
2361—9. MARIA DUBOIS, b. Oct. 27, 1859.

2362. ALBERT CRANE[7] [1435], (Charles,[6] Isaac,[5] Joseph,[4] Joseph,[3] Jonathan,[2] Benjamin[1]), born in East Bloomfield, N. Y. Studied law and graduated from the law department, Harvard University, in 1842. Married at New Bedford, Mass., Aug. 13, 1846, Anna Waterman. She was born in South America, Feb. 22, 1828. Their eldest child was born in New Bedford, Mass. They soon removed to Detroit, Mich., where the second child was born. Here they remained until about the year 1866, when they removed to Chicago, where he, in addition to the practice of his profession, became a dealer in real estate. Children:

2363—1. DANIEL WATERMAN, b. July 22, 1847.
2364—2. ALICE BRUNSON, b. March 13, 1849; d. Feb. 24, 1850.
2365—3. ALBERT HUNTER, b. Dec. 17, 1850; d. April 10, 1852.
2366—4. CHARLES ALBERT, b. April 27, 1853.
2367—5. ARCH MCLEAN, b. July 29, 1855, at Pittsfield, Mass.
2368—6. GEORGE WRIGHT,   } twins, b. June 27, 1857.
2369—7. ANNA WATERMAN, }
2370—8. WALTER, b. May 28, 1865.
2371—9. ESTHER WATERMAN, b. Feb. 27, 1867.

2372. WILLIAM HUNTER CRANE[7] [1438], (Hunter,[6] Isaac,[5] Joseph,[4] Joseph,[3] Jonathan,[2] Benjamin[1]), born at Sackett's Harbor, N. Y. Married Jane C. Brothers, Sept. 15, 1853, at Danville, Ill. In 1864 he enlisted at Chicago in the 1st Regt. Illinois Light Artillery, Battery A, and served until the battery was mustered out in July, 1865. In July, 1879, was residing in St. Louis, Mo. Children:

2373—1. WILLIAM HUNTER, b. Sept. 1, 1864, at Danville, Ill.
2374—2. ADA, m.; lives in Paris, Ill.

2375. ARZA CRANE[7] [1452], (Albert,[6] Isaac,[5] Joseph,[4] Joseph,[3] Jonathan,[2] Benjamin[1]), married Laura Belle Wilk, Aug.

Very Truly Yours
A. M. Crane

For sketch see page 235.

30, 1871. She was born in Cincinnati, Ohio, Nov. 12, 1848. Settled in Chicago, where he was engaged in the real estate business. · Children :

2376—1. GRACE EDITH, b. Aug. 22, 1872.
2377—2. RAYSTON MAYNARD, b. June 12, 1876.

2378. ALVIRA CRANE[7] [1454], (Albert,[6] Isaac,[5] Joseph,[4] Joseph,[3] Jonathan,[2] Benjamin[1]), married George Beals Sloan, Sept. 2, 1856, at Oswego, N. Y., where he was born June 20, 1831. Mr. Sloan has enjoyed the confidence and esteem of his fellow-citizens in various complimentary ways, having been called to represent them in the Assembly and State Senate; was chosen Speaker of the Legislature, and also a Presidential Elector. Engaged in banking business in Oswego. Children :

1. HELEN LAFLIN (Sloan), b. July 28, 1857.
2. ROBERT SAGE (Sloan), b. Oct. 23, 1859.
3. GEORGE BEALS (Sloan), b. March 23, 1865.

2379. HELEN LAFLIN SLOAN (1); m. Lieut. John Wilson Danenhower, of the United States Navy, who was a member of the Arctic exploring expedition in the *Jeannette* under command of Capt. DeLong. Children :

1. SLOAN (Danenhower), b. Jan. 26, 1885.
2. RUTH (Danenhower), b. Feb. 14, 1887.

2380. ROBERT SAGE SLOAN [2]; m. Ethel Donaldson, June 13, 1883, at Elk Ridge, Md. He is a graduate of the United States Naval Academy, class of 1879; served in United States Navy from 1875 to 1882. Resides at Oswego, N. Y. Children :

1. DONALDSON (Sloan), b. April 21, 1884.
2. ETHEL DONALDSON (Sloan), b. Aug. 25, 1886.

2381. HELEN E. CRANE[7] [1470], (Gilbert,[6] Ira,[5] Joseph,[4] Joseph,[3] Jonathan,[2] Benjamin[1]), married Sept. 20, 1864, A. Frank Waters. He was born at Little Falls, Herkimer County, N. Y., in 1841, and settled in Buffalo, where he died Oct. 27, 1874. Children :

1. FRANKLIN (Waters), was about 1897 living in Boston.
2. —— (Waters).

2382. HENRY DEMAREST CRANE[7] [1475], (Daniel,[6] Daniel,[5] Joseph,[4] Joseph,[3] Jonathan,[2] Benjamin[1]), married Feb. 6, 1850, at Albany, N. Y., Julia M. Seymour. She was a native of that city, and born Oct. 28, 1824. Mr. Crane succeeded his father in the lumber trade in New York city. Children :

2383—1. FREDERICK BARNARD, b. Jan. 5, 1851, in New York city.
2384—2. CHARLES SEYMOUR, b. Nov. 22, 1852, in New York city.
2385—3. ARTHUR DEMAREST, b. Nov. 7, 1854, in New York city.
2386—4. ELSIE DEMAREST, b. Sept. 20, 1856, in New York city.
2387—5. JULIA SEYMOUR, b. Dec. 22, 1858, in New York city.
2388—6. JAMES RUTHORN, b. Jan. 16, 1861, in New York city.
2389—7. HENRY MARTYN, b. April 4, 1863, in New York city.
2390—8. WILLIAM SEYMOUR, b. Feb. 1°, 1866, at Greenbush, Westchester County, N. Y.

2391. HIRAM AUGUSTUS CRANE[7] [1478], (Daniel,[6] Daniel,[5] Joseph,[4] Joseph,[3] Jonathan,[2] Benjamin[1]), married Sept. 18, 1866, in New York city, Elizabeth S. Clark. She was born in that city Nov. 1, 1829. Mr. Crane was born in Jefferson, Green County, N. Y., and with his brother became a lumber merchant in New York city, where his children were born. Children:

2392—1. ELSIE, b. Sept. 25, 1857.
2393—2. AUGUSTA JANE, b. Oct. 7, 1859.
2394—3. ELIZABETH CLARK, b. Jan. 3, 1862.
2395—4. WILLIAM FORBES, b. Nov. 21, 1863.
2396—5. ELLEN CLARK, b. Aug. 6, 1868.
2397—6. MARY DARROW, b. Nov. 21, 1875.

2398. WILLIAM NEVINS CRANE[7] [1481], (Daniel,[6] Daniel,[5] Joseph,[4] Joseph,[3] Jonathan,[2] Benjamin[1]), was born in Albany, N. Y., and married in New York city, Oct. 16, 1861, Sarah Ann Ivison, who died in that city Nov. 29, 1863. He married 2d, Caroline Abby Merriam at Passaic, N. J., Nov. 2, 1870. Residence in New York city; occupation, publisher. Child:

1. HENRIETTA IVISON, b. April 22, 1863; d. Sept. 3, 1863.

2399. ELLEN CORNELIA CRANE[7] [1490], (Joseph A.,[6] Daniel,[5] Joseph,[4] Joseph,[3] Jonathan,[2] Benjamin[1]), married at Fall River, Mass., March 8, 1864, George Woods, a native of Yarmouth, Me., a graduate of Bowdoin College. She was educated at Ipswich Seminary in 1856. Present residence at Sewickley, Pa. Children:

1. EDWARD AUGUSTUS (Woods), b. Jan. 1, 1865, at Pittsburg, Pa.
2. CHARLES ALBERT (Woods), b. Aug. 21, 1868, at Pittsburg, Pa.; graduate of Princeton in 1890; attorney-at-law.
3. LAWRENCE CRANE (Woods), b. Dec. 22, 1869, at Pittsburg, Pa.; graduate of Princeton in 1891; secretary of West Pennsylvania Agency of Equitable Life Assurance Society.

2400. EDWARD AUGUSTUS WOODS [1]; m. Gertrude Macrum, May 28, 1891, at Sewickley. He is manager of the Equitable Life Assurance Society. Residence at Sewickley. Child:

1. MARJORY (Woods), b. Aug. 8, 1892.

2401. LILLIES ALBERTINE CRANE[7] [1497], (George R.,[6] Arzah,[5] Joseph,[4] Joseph,[3] Jonathan,[2] Benjamin[1]), married John Atkinson, of Cohoes, N. Y. He died. His widow resides in New York city. Children:

1. LILLIES JOSEPHINE ELLA (Atkinson).
2. MARY IDA (Atkinson).

2402. SARAH ELLEN CRANE[7] [1498], (George R.,[6] Arzah,[5] Joseph,[4] Joseph,[3] Jonathan,[2] Benjamin[1]), married Joseph Brownell Wilkinson, Jr. Children:

1. JOSEPH PARDO (Wilkinson), b. March 12, 1876; d. March 19, 1881, at Troy, N. Y.
2. SARAH BELDING (Wilkinson), b. March 12, 1880, in Troy, N. Y.
3. ALCE DEFOREST (Wilkinson), b. Jan. 30, 1882, in Troy, N. Y.

4. RUTH HOPKINS (Wilkinson), b. Sept. 6, 1884, in Troy, N. Y.
5. JOSEPH BROWNELL (Wilkinson), b. Aug. 15, 1887, in Johnson-·ville, N. Y.
6. A Daughter (Wilkinson), d. in infancy.

2403. IDA CRANE[7] [1499], (George R.,[6] Arzah,[5] Joseph,[4] Joseph,[3] Jonathan,[2] Benjamin[1]), married Leicester LeRoy. Reside in Chicago, Ill.

2404. CHARLES EDGAR CRANE[7] [1500], (George R.,[6] Arzah,[5] Joseph,[4] Joseph,[3] Jonathan,[2] Benjamin[1]), married. Reside in Chicago, Ill.

2405. PETER CRANE[7] [1510], (Alfred,[6] Peter,[5] Thaddeus,[4] Joseph,[3] Jonathan,[2] Benjamin[1]), married Lucy Wyman. Children :

2406—1. ALBERT.
2407—2. LILLA.
2408—3. GERARD.

2409. WYRAM CRANE[7] [1511], (Alfred,[6] Peter,[5], Thaddeus,[4] Joseph,[3] Jonathan,[2] Benjamin[1]), married Helen Rhodes. She was born Jan. 4, 1830. Children :

2409¼—1. EVA L., b. June 18, 1852.
2409¾—2. NETTIE, b. May 3, 1854.

2410. ANSON J. CRANE[7] [1536], (Thaddeus,[6] James,[5] Thaddeus,[4] Joseph,[3] Jonathan,[2] Benjamin[1]), married Marilla E. Derby, Oct. 13, 1847. He died May 30, 1881. Children :

2411—1. THADDEUS DERBY, b. Dec. 31, 1848 ; d. March 4, 1862.
2412—2. GEORGE E., b. Sept. 3, 1857.
2413—3. BUEL D., b. Jan. 15, 1860.
2414—4. JESSIE MAY, b. Aug. 15, 1865.

2415. MARY MARIA CRANE[7] [1537], (Thaddeus,[6] James,[5] Thaddeus,[4] Joseph,[3] Jonathan,[2] Benjamin[1]), married George R. Wyman. He was born July 29, 1824, and died Sept. 11, 1888. Mrs. Wyman resides in Huntington, Vt., and made special effort to secure records of her branch of the family tree.
Child :

1. CLARENCE L. (Wyman), b. May 5, 1859 ; m. June 25, 1896, Alice I. Adams, who was b. Jan. 21, 1862.

2416. THADDEUS CRANE[7] [1554], (James,[6] James,[5] Thaddeus,[4] Joseph,[3] Jonathan,[2] Benjamin[1]), was born at Fort Atkinson, Wis. ; married Mollie Cutright, Oct. 3, 1869, and settled at Neosho Falls, Kansas. Children :

2417—1. FRANK BOYLE, b. June 26, 1870.
2418—2. FANNY, b. Aug. 4, 1877.

2419. ADA MARY CRANE[7] [1555], (James,[6] James,[5] Thaddeus,[4] Joseph,[3] Jonathan,[2] Benjamin[1]), was born at Oakland,

Wis.; married Capt. W. J. Haughawout, March 7, 1867. They lived for a time at Neosho Falls, Kansas, where their daughter was born. In 1897 they resided in Los Angeles, California.
Child :

   1. LOLLIE CRANE (Haughawout), b. Feb. 7, 1869; m. Charles Lee Powell, Jan. 2o, 1893.

2420. ROXANA ELLEN CRANE[7] [1558], (Gerard,[6] James,[5] Thaddeus,[4] Joseph,[3] Jonathan,[2] Benjamin[1]), married Byron A. Barlow, Nov. 22, 1860. They reside in Jamestown, N. Y.
Children :

   1. BELLE (Barlow), b. Sept. 5, 1861.
   . JESSIE (Barlow), b. Dec. 8, 1862; d. Oct. 3, 1863.
   . EDITH (Barlow), b. Aug. 30, 1864.
   4. KARL DEANE (Barlow), b. Sept. 29, 1866; d. Sept. 27, 1867.
   5. BYRON ABNER (Barlow), b. June 8, 1869.
   6. GERALD BRUCE (Barlow), b. July 25, 1875; d. Sept. 18, 1875.

2421. MABEL CRANE[7] [1562], (Gerard,[6] James,[5] Thaddeus,[4] Joseph,[3] Jonathan,[2] Benjamin[1]), married Mason Delano Pratt, March 14, 1889. He was born Jan. 23, 1865. Residence at Steelton, Pa. Children :

   1. SARAH (Pratt), b. May 24, 1890.
   2. RICHARD HENRY (Pratt), b. Dec. 2, 1891.
   3. ROXANA MABEL (Pratt), b. Jan. 18, 1893.
   4. MARION (Pratt), b. July 23, 1894.

2422. JUDSON GILBERT CRANE[7] [1565], (Alexis,[6] James,[5] Thaddeus,[4] Joseph,[3] Jonathan,[2] Benjamin[1]), married Kitty (or Catherine) R. Muntz, at Butler, Pa., May 10, 1877. He died Feb. 5, 1891. Children :

2423—1. MARY GEORGIANA, b. Feb. 9, 1878.
2424—2. ADELAIDE MUNTZ, b. Oct. 2, 1882.
2425—3. CLIFFORD, b. Sept. 25, 1884; d. Oct. 19, 1884.

2426. ALEXIS CRANE[7] [1566], (Alexis,[6] James,[5] Thaddeus,[4] Joseph,[3] Jonathan,[2] Benjamin[1]), married July, 1880, Emily Harrington, born 1859. Child :

2427—1. IMOGENE, b. May 12, 1887.

2428. CLARA CRANE[7] [1567], (Alexis,[6] James,[5] Thaddeus,[4] Joseph,[3] Jonathan,[2] Benjamin[1]), married Wheeler C. Whicoff, at Jamestown, N. Y., Nov. 7, 1889.

2429. ALICE FRANCES CRANE[7] [1572], (Thomas,[6] James,[5] Thaddeus,[4] Joseph,[3] Jonathan,[2] Benjamin[1]), married William J. Hoare, June 2, 1873. Residence at Parkston, South Dakota.
Children :

   1. ELTON WILLIAM (Hoare), b. March 20, 1873.
   2. FANNIE ELIZABETH (Hoare), b. April 23, 1875.
   3. OLIVE EVELYN (Hoare), b. April 15, 1879.
   4. BETH FRANCES (Hoare), b. April 8, 1887.
   5. WILLIAM JOHN (Hoare), } twins, b. April 22, 1895.
   6. WILBER WOOLCOX (Hoare), }

2430. MATILDA ABBIE CRANE[7] [1573], (Thomas,[6] James,[5] Thaddeus,[4] Joseph,[3] Jonathan,[2] Benjamin[1]), married Jan. 5, 1878, Charlie H. Hurd. Resides in Kenosha, Wis. Children :

1. RUTH IMOGENE (Hurd), b. Nov. 3, 1878.
2. BESSIE CELESTIA (Hurd), b. Sept. 21, 1880.
3. RAYMOND CRANE (Hurd), b. March 20, 1882.

2431. JENNIE MARIA CRANE[7] [1574], (Thomas,[6] James,[5] Thaddeus,[4] Joseph,[3] Jonathan,[2] Benjamin[1]), married 1st, Foster Keen, Dec. 27, 1884. He died Sept. 24, 1890. She married 2d, Dec. 30, 1892; John M. Gray. Residence Parkston, South Dakota. Children :

1. ROBIN COLTON (Keen), b. June 2, 1886.
2. HALLOCK FOSTER (Gray), b. April 4, 1895.

2432. THADDEUS BAILEY CRANE[7] [1589], (Thaddeus,[6] Gerard,[5] Thaddeus,[4] Joseph,[3] Jonathan,[2] Benjamin[1]), married at Somers, N. Y., Oct. 28, 1891, Mary L. Brown, of that place. She was born Aug. 30, 1866. Children :

2433—1. DOROTHY D., b. Aug. 22, 1892.
2434—2. WILLIAM B., h. Feb. 15, 1894.
2435—3. ELLEN S., b. Dec. 22, 1895.

2436. JULIA CATHERINE CRANE[7] [1605], (Heman A.,[6] Stephen,[5] Stephen,[4] Joseph,[3] Jonathan,[2] Benjamin[1]), married March 5, 1860, Dr. Thomas J. Charlton. Residence Savannah, Ga. Children :

1. W. HALES (Charlton), b. Dec. 8, 1860; d. Oct. 8, 1862.
2. THOMAS J. (Charlton), b. Nov. 3, 1863.
3. HEMAN H. (Charlton), b. July 20, 1866.
4. JULIA (Charlton), b. July 31, 1868.
5. ELLEN H. (Charlton), b. July 30, 1870.
6. SALLIE W. (Charlton), b. March 31, 1872.
7. JOSIAH T. (Charlton), b. Feb. 21, 1874.
8. EMILY W. (Charlton), b. Jan. 26, 1876.
9. GEORGIA H. (Charlton), b. Dec. 2, 1878.

2437. HORACE AVERILL CRANE[7] [1607], (Heman A.,[6] Stephen,[5] Stephen,[4] Joseph,[3] Jonathan,[2] Benjamin[1]). At the close of the late war Mr. Crane returned to Savannah, Ga., and entered into business with his father, where he remained until 1873, when he withdrew to accept a position in the Southern Bank of Georgia, where in 1882 he was still engaged. Mr. Crane served in the southern army during the late war, and was wounded at the battle of Chickamauga. He had so far recovered as to be serving in the invalid corps, at Fort McAllister, when Sherman's army entered Savannah. He was then taken prisoner to Fort Delaware and released at close of the war. Feb. 25, 1866, he married Georgia Anderson, of Savannah. She died April 2, 1880. Children :

2438—1. WILLIAM HENRY, b. Nov. 22, 1867.
2439—2. HORACE AVERILL, b. March 27, 1873.

2440—3. EDWARD ANDERSON, b. June 16, 1876.
2441—4. NINA ANDERSON, b. April 14, 1879.

2442. GEORGE P. CRANE[7] [1610], (Henry S.,[6] Stephen,[5] Stephen,[4] Joseph,[3] Jonathan,[2] Benjamin[1]), married in Woodbury, Conn., Jan. 15, 1861, S. Cordelia Root. She was born there Feb. 20, 1838. He is a farmer, and resides in Woodbury, Conn. He was a member of the Assembly for Connecticut in 1870. Children:

2443—1. HENRY R., b. Aug. 14, 1863.
2444—2. GEORGE H., b. April 15, 1869.
2445—3. STEPHEN T., b. Sept. 15, 1872.

2446. STEPHEN H. CRANE[7] [1611], (Henry S.,[6] Stephen,[5] Stephen,[4] Joseph,[3] Jonathan,[2] Benjamin[1]), married Emma B. Stone, May 25, 1865, at Woodbury, Conn., where they resided some years and then removed to California. Children:

2447—1. CARRIE, b. March 8, 1866.
2448—2. HORACE, b. May 31, 1870.

2449. LOIS B. CRANE[7] [1633], (Nelson,[6] Joseph,[5] Stephen,[4] Joseph,[3] Jonathan,[2] Benjamin[1]), married Nov. 10, 1858, at Newtown, Conn., Charles A. Cornwall. He was born Oct. 8, 1833. They settled in Danbury, Conn. Children:

1. HELEN M. (Cornwall), b. Aug. 29, 1859.
2. JENNIE C. (Cornwall), b. March 9, 1861.
3. ALICE S. (Cornwall), b. Sept. 22, 1862.
4. LEWIS N. (Cornwall), b. June 4, 1864.

2450. EMILY CRANE[7] [1646], (Charles A.,[6] Ashbel,[5] John,[4] John,[3] Abraham,[2] Benjamin[1]), married Noah Holcomb in 1836. Residence La Grange, Lorain County, Ohio. Children:

1. RUFUS (Holcomb).
2. JANE (Holcomb).
3. ELLEN (Holcomb).
4. MELVIN (Holcomb).
5. CHARLES (Holcomb).
6. SCOTT (Holcomb).
7. ANDREW (Holcomb).
8. ESTHER (Holcomb).

2451. LYMAN CRANE[7] [1647], (Charles A.,[6] Ashbil,[5] John,[4] John,[3] Abraham,[2] Benjamin[1]), married Dianna S. Hastings, a native of New York. Residence Chatham, Medina County, Ohio. Children:

2452—1. DIANNA S.; d. young.
2453—2. MARY K.
2454—3. CHESTER C.; m. and d. leaving son:
    1. CLARENCE.
2455—4. ERNEST H.; d. young.

2456. ASHBIL CRANE[7] [1648], (Charles A.,[6] Ashbil,[5] John,[4] John,[3] Abraham,[2] Benjamin[1]), married Nancy Caldwell.

Children :

2457—1. ALICE, b. Oct. 15, 1847; d. Aug. 10, 1870, leaving children :
    1. GEORGE (Smith).
    2. BLANCH (Smith).
2458—2. LUELLA; m. Walter Helman; residence Wellington, Ohio.

2459. LEWIS CRANE[7] [1649], (Charles A.,[6] Ashbil,[5] John,[4] John,[3] Abraham,[2] Benjamin[1]), married Zilpha Townsend. Children :

2460—1. LUCY.
2461—2. CHARLES.
2462—3. LIZZIE.

2463. ELMIRA CRANE[7] [1650], (Charles A.,[6] Ashbil,[5] John,[4] John,[3] Abraham,[2] Benjamin,[1]), married Josiah Richardson, at La Grange, Lorain County, Ohio, Dec. 5, 1844, and settled in Grafton, where their two eldest children were born. Children :

    1. MALESSA J. (Richardson), b. Feb. 20, 1846; d. March 10, 1846.
    2. ORIN S. (Richardson), b. Nov. 28, 1848; d. March 25, 1865, in army.
    3. ANN ADELLE (Richardson), b. June 5, 1861, in Perry, Ohio.
    4. ELLA MAY (Richardson), b. May 13, 1865, in Fostoria, Ohio; d. July 13, 1865.
    5. HERBERT O. (Richardson), b. Oct. 29, 1873, in Perry, Ohio.

2464. HANNAH CRANE[7] [1651], (Charles A.,[6] Ashbil,[5] John,[4] John,[3] Abraham,[2] Benjamin[1]), married Goodrich Hastings. They resided in La Grange, Ohio. She died some years ago. Children :

    1. SUSAN (Hastings).
    2. GEORGE (Hastings).
    3. EVELINE (Hastings).

2465. WALTER C. CRANE[7] [1652], (Charles A.,[6] Ashbil,[5] John,[4] John,[3] Abraham,[2] Benjamin[1]), was born in Cobleskill, Schoharie County, N. Y. In 1835, when a child, he went with his parents to La Grange, Lorain County, Ohio. He married 1st, Oct. 10, 1857, at Penfield, Ohio, Mariah Newton, and their eldest child was born in that town. The other children were born in Wellington, which is now his home, and where his wife died Aug. 19, 1877. He married 2d, March 31, 1887. He is in the employ of the Big 4 R. R., or the Cleveland, Cincinnati, Chicago, and St. Louis Railway. Children :

2466—1. HARRIS W., b. Sept. 7, 1859.
2467—2. CHARLES A., b. June 13, 1861; d. June 4, 1890.
2468—3. HARRY E., b. May 18, 1865; d. July 25, 1886.

2469. ABIGAIL CRANE[7] [1653], (Charles A.,[6] Ashbil,[5] John,[4] John,[3] Abraham,[2] Benjamin[1]), married Horace Seeley. She died, leaving a son, who was born in Toledo, Ohio. Child :

    1. MYRON (Seeley), b. Oct. 25, 1856.

2470. SARAH J. CRANE[7] [1655], (Charles A.,[6] Ashbil,[5] John,[4] John,[3] Abraham,[2] Benjamin[1]), married Daniel P. Shel-

don, April 3, 1861, at Penfield, Lorain County, Ohio, where for a time they lived. They also resided in Wellington, Ohio. Now (1898) their home is in Vermillion, Clay County, South Dakota. Children :

1. ELMER OWEN (Sheldon), b. March 3, 1862.
2. CHARLES MUNSON (Sheldon), b. May 23, 1867.
3. JOHN LERO (Sheldon), b. April 18, 1869.
4. AMY ELIDA (Sheldon), b. May 25, 1872.
5. NELLIE LILLIAN (Sheldon), b. Feb. 1, 1883.

2471. ROBÈRT WHITING CRAIN[7] [1658], (Albert L.,[6] Whiting,[5] William,[4] John,[3] Abraham,[2] Benjamin[1]), married Lucy Isabel Moores, Dec. 12, 1866, at Maine, N. Y. He served four years and six days in the civil war. Children :

2472—1. LOTTY ISABEL, b. Jan. 3, 1868.
2473—2. GEORGIA ADELIA, b. Feb. 13, 1874; d. June 8, 1877.
2474—3. VIRGIA ALMA, b. Oct. 23, 1878.

2475. JAMES CRANE[7] [1675], (Ira R.,[6] Benjamin,[5] Abraham,[4] Abraham,[3] Abraham,[2] Benjamin[1]), was born in Warren, Ohio, and married at Farmington in 1855, Amelia E. Lewis, of that place. From 1861 to 1864 he was Captain of Battery E, 5th N. Y. V. Artillery, serving in the Army of the Potomac. He is now a merchant. Children :

2476—1. WILLIE, b. June 6, 1856; d. 1857.
2477—2. MINNIE L., b. July 11, 1861.
2478—3. JAY D., b. March 6, 1868.

2479. HENRY JAMES CRANE[7] [1683], (Calvin C.,[6] Elijah,[5] Elijah,[4] Abraham,[3] Abraham,[2] Benjamin[1]), married 1st, at Rockford, Ill., Dec. 24, 1857, Emma Kilborn, a native of Great Barrington, Mass. She died May 4, 1867. He married 2d, at Alton, Ill., June 12, 1872, Carrie E. Pierce, of Woodstock, Vt. He was for many years from April 1, 1866, Deputy U. S. Collector of Internal Revenue at Alton, Ill. Children :

2480—1. HARRY LEE, b. Dec. 29, 1864; d. July 3, 1865.
2481—2. HARRY KILBORN, } twins, { d. July 10, 1867.
2482—3. CARRIE EMMA, } b. May 4, 1867; { d. Aug. 9, 1867.
2483—4. WILLIAM PIERCE, b. Nov. 26, 1877.
2484—5. BYRON WOLF, b. Sept. 13, 1881.
2485—6. LUCRETIA CHARLOTTE, b. June 21, 1885.

2486. NELSON ALEXANDER CRANE[7] [1694], (Alexander N.,[6] Abraham,[5] Elijah,[4] Abraham,[3] Abraham,[2] Benjamin[1]), married Oct. 1, 1865, Mary Potts, of Bloomfield, Conn. Settled at Bristol, where he is a manufacturer.

2487. FRANCES E. CRANE[7] [1708], (Joseph,[6] Joseph,[5] Joseph.[4] Abraham,[3] Abraham,[2] Benjamin[1]), married at Norway, N. Y., Jan. 25, 1853, George Randall. About the year 1870

they removed from Norway to Piper City, Ill., where they now (1896) reside.   Children :

1. HENRY (Randall), b. Dec. 31, 1853; m. Gertie Hobbies, Feb. 13, 1877.
2. CORA E. (Randall), b. March 10, 1858; m. G. Reeder, Nov. 29, 1888.
3. JOSEPH C. (Randall),   } twins, b.   { d. Sept. 28, 1860.
4. G. CHAUNCEY (Randall), } July 20, 1860; { m. Minnie Balloo, Sept. 6, 1888.
5. ESTELLE S. (Randall), b. March 25, 1865; d. April 20, 1866.

2488. HORACE ALONZO CRANE[8] [1730], (Truman L.,[7] John,[6] Benjamin,[5] John,[4] John,[3] Jonathan,[2] Benjamin[1]), a farmer. Resided in Bristol, Vt. Married Philomelia L. Wright at New Haven, Vt., Nov. 4, 1857. He died at Bristol, May 30, 1858. She died at New Haven, March 25, 1888. Child:

2489.—1. HORACE ALONZO, b. Feb. 13, 1859.

2490. GEORGE S. CRANE[8] [1738], (Amos S.,[7] Amos,[6] Elijah,[5] John,[4] John,[3] Jonathan,[2] Benjamin[1]), married Jennette D. Owen, of Suffield, Conn., March 23, 1859, and there they settled. He is a farmer and dealer in agricultural implements. Children :

2491—1. FANNY, b. March 3, 1862; d. Aug. 20, 1863.
2492—2. CHESTER, b. Aug. 15, 1864; d. Nov. 15, 1864.
2493—3. CLARA E., b. Nov. 8, 1865.
2494—4. AMOS B., b. Feb. 13, 1868.
2495—5. NELLY O., b. July 27, 1871.
2496—6. JOHN S., b. July 21, 1878.

2497. ELLEN M. CRANE[8] [1739], (Amos S.,[7] Amos,[6] Elijah,[5] John,[4] John,[3] Jonathan,[2] Benjamin[1]), married Gurdon Grosvenor at Suffield, Conn., Oct. 28, 1852. They removed to Lawrence, Kan., Oct. 1, 1857, where he died April 6, 1869. Children :

1. CHARLES P. (Grosvenor), b. Aug. 25, 1855.
2. JOHN C. (Grosvenor), b. May 9, 1863; d. June 19, 1865.
3. FANNY M. (Grosvenor), b. Oct. 7, 1865; d. Sept. 27, 1872.

2498. LUTHER K. CRANE[8] [1740], (Amos S.,[7] Amos,[6] Elijah,[5] John,[4] John,[3] Jonathan,[2] Benjamin[1]), married the widow of his brother, John L., at North Brookfield, Mass., June 11, 1868. He enlisted in the fall of 1862 in 2d Colorado Infantry; was in the battles of Elm Creek, Honey Springs and Camden Point, Mo., where he was severely wounded; mustered out in March, 1865. His home is at Leadville, Col. Adopted children :

2499—1. FRANK, b. Nov. 1, 1873, in Boston, Mass.
2500—2. CORA, b. Feb. 9, 1877, in Denver, Col.

2501. JAMES P. CRANE[8] [1741], (Amos S.,[7] Amos,[6] Elijah,[5] John,[4] John,[3] Jonathan,[2] Benjamin[1]), married Cyrena Sykes, of Suffield, Conn., Nov. 29, 1865, and settled there as a farmer. In the spring of 1868 he went to Lawrence, Kan., and engaged in the freighting business. In June, 1871, he went to Garnett, and engaged in the lumber business. In April the following year

he was elected mayor, and reëlected in 1873, and a member of
the city council in 1875. In 1878 he returned to Lawrence, and
was employed by a firm in St. Louis as a commercial traveller
during the summer. In November of that year he removed to
Suffield, Conn.; but the year 1880 found him again in Kansas as
a farmer. He enlisted in August, 1862, as private in company
G, 22d Regt. Connecticut Volunteers, a nine months regiment,
although they served nearly eleven months. Children:

2502—1. CYRUS S., b. Oct. 4, 1866, at Suffield, Conn.
2503—2. LEWIS, b. Sept. 4, 1871, at Garnett, Kan.

2504. SAMUEL H. CRANE[8] [1743], (Samuel R.,[7] Amos,[6]
Elijah,[5] John,[4] John,[3] Jonathan,[2] Benjamin[1]), was born in
Springfield, Mass. Married in Newtown, Md., April 14, 1869,
Ellen Louisa Barnes, a native of Fair Haven, Conn. She was
born Oct. 8, 1846. He was a popular hotel keeper in New
Haven, Conn., for several years, proprietor of the Elliot House.
Children:

2505—1. MARY LOUISE, b. July 14, 1874.
2506—2. A son, b. Oct. 19, 1880.

2507. MARY E. CRANE[8] [1744], (Samuel R.,[7] Amos,[6] Elijah,[5]
John,[4] John,[3] Jonathan,[2] Benjamin[1]), married Charles E.
Brown, of Springfield, Mass., Oct. 26, 1864. Settled in Spring-
field. Children:

1. FRED R. (Brown), b. Dec. 29, 1868.
2. ALICE (Brown), b. Nov. 22, 1883.

2508. CHARLES E. CRANE[8] [1754], (George,[7] Amos,[6] Elijah,[5]
John,[4] John,[3] Jonathan,[2] Benjamin[1]), married Lucy A. Crane,
of Lysander, Onondaga County, N. Y., March 30, 1871, a third
cousin, and settled there as a farmer. In March, 1878, he removed to Cambria Mills, Hillsdale County, Mich., continuing the
occupation of farmer. Children:

2509—1. ADDIE S., b. Nov. 8, 1872.
2510—2. HATTIE A., b. May 18, 1875.
2511—3. LELAND J., b. Sept. 26, 1876.
2512—4. GEORGE A., b. Aug. 25, 1878.
2513—5. CLARA L., b. Sept. 5, 1880.

2514. AMOS S. CRANE[8] [1755], (George,[7] Amos,[6] Elijah,[5]
John,[4] John,[3] Jonathan,[2] Benjamin[1]), married Clara E. Stiles, of
Suffield, Conn., Nov. 1, 1875. Settled in Westfield, Mass., in
the manufacture of cigars. October, 1877, he removed to Chicago, Ill., where he was agent for the South Shore Line of
Freight. May 1, 1880, he located in Boston, Mass., as agent for
the above line. Children:

2515—1. ROBERT STILES, b. Aug. 7, 1876, at Suffield, Mass.
2516—2. PHILLIP BAXTER, b. Aug. 11, 1878, at Chicago, Ill.

2517. JOHN W. CRANE[8] [1762], (John M.,[7] Amos,[6] Elijah,[5]
John,[4] John,[3] Jonathan,[2] Benjamin[1]), married Harriet Church,

15

of Middlefield, Mass., Nov. 4, 1875, and settled there as a merchant. Children :

2518—1. A son, b. April 15, 1877; d. in infancy.
2519—2. ALFRED S., b. January, 1880.

2520. ALFRED E. CRANE[8] [1768], (Joel S.,[7] Joel,[6] Elijah,[5] John,[4] John,[3] Jonathan,[2] Benjamin[1]), married Adaline Vanderveer, May 27, 1857, and settled in Lysander, N. Y.; a farmer. Children :

2521—1. EDWIN JOEL, b. June 4, 1859; d. June 14, 1860.
2522—2. CLARENCE J., b. May 27, 1863; d. Feb. 5, 1864.

2523. GEORGE W. CRANE[8] [1781], (Olvison W.,[7] Elijah,[6] Elijah,[5] John,[4] John,[3] Jonathan,[2] Benjamin[1]), married March 7, 1872, Elenor Clark, at Hermon, N. Y., and settled at Canton ; a farmer. Children :

2524—1. EUGENE G., b. Jan. 26, 1874.
2525—2. CARRIE A., b. April 17, 1876.
2526—3. LILLIAN M., b. July 1, 1877.
2527—4. EMILY E., b. Jan. 12, 1879.

2528. MAHLON D. CRANE[8] [1800], (Edwin D.,[7] Archer,[6] Samuel,[5] John,[4] John,[3] Jonathan,[2] Benjamin[1]), married Emily House, a native of Greenville, Park County, Ohio, Sept. 4, 1851, by Rev. Jesse Pryor, in Blissfield, Mich. She was born Jan. 18, 1833. For several years he carried on farming in South Dakota. Late residence at La Porte, Ind. Children :

2529—1. EDWIN C., b. Sept. 14, 1852.
2530—2. SARAH L., b. Nov. 12, 1854.

2531. JAMES K. CRANE[8] [1801], (Edwin D.,[7] Archer,[6] Samuel,[5] John,[4] John,[3] Jonathan,[2] Benjamin[1]), served three years as a soldier in the late war. Enlisted in company F, Michigan Infantry, Aug. 13, 1862. December 12th the regiment left camp in Jackson for Washington, D. C. From there was ordered to Union Mills near Bull Run, and thence to Alexandria, Va. Oct. 4, 1864, he was commissioned first lieutenant in Co. A, U. S. C. T., unassigned; the company was sent to Accotink, Va., on the picket-line, where they saw continuous service, scouting on picket and capturing guerillas, which were sent to Alexandria. He is a prosperous and well-to-do farmer, and resides in Blissfield, Mich. Married March 27, 1856, Cynthia A. Sperry, who died of pneumonia Feb. 20, 1899, after being confined to her bed but four days. Children :

2532—1. DWIGHT H., b. April 1, 1857.
2533—2. CYNTHIA A., b. May 2, 1859.
2534—3. MYRA A., b. March 18, 1861; m. Adam Goetz, Nov. 11, 1897.
2535—4. ALFRED J., b. Sept. 16, 1863.
2536—5. EDMUND B., b. June 19, 1866; d. Feb. 19, 1891.
2537—6. HELEN A., b. Jan. 20, 1870; m. Geo. W. Goetz, Oct. 9, 1897.

2538. CHARLES E. CRANE[8] [1802], (Edwin D.,[7] Archer,[6] Samuel,[5] John,[4] John,[3] Jonathan,[2] Benjamin[1]), married Amanda E. Seoy, of Wilson County, Tenn., May 2, 1861; a lawyer and farmer. He died June 16, 1887, at Sandborn, Ind. Child:

2539—1. CHARLES J., b. Aug. 28, 1862.

2540. CELESTIA C. CRANE[8] [1805], (Charles T.,[7] Archer,[6] Samuel,[5] John,[4] John,[3] Jonathan,[2] Benjamin[1]), married Calvin Lazell, March 22, 1864. He is a farmer, and lives in the township of Napoleon, Jackson County, Mich. Children:

1. LLOYD (Lazell), b. June 10, 1865.
2. CHARLES T. (Lazell), b. Nov. 8, 1868.
3. IDA M. (Lazell), b. April 5, 1872.
4. PEARL (Lazell), b. Dec. 16, 1879.

2541. EDITH A. CRANE[8] [1806], (Charles T.,[7] Archer,[6] Samuel,[5] John,[4] John,[3] Jonathan,[2] Benjamin[1]), married Erastus Walter, Dec. 28, 1871. He was a member of the 4th Michigan Infantry, and served over four years in the civil war. Children:

1. GUY L. (Walter), b. Nov. 22, 1872.
2. MINNIE (Walter), b. May 14, 1875.

2542. CLARENCE O. CRANE[8] [1807], (Charles T.,[7] Archer,[6] Samuel,[5] John,[4] John,[3] Jonathan,[2] Benjamin[1]), married Hattie Hibbard, October, 1886. He is a prosperous farmer, residing near Oakley, Saginaw County, Mich. Children:

2543—1. ALMA, b. April 6, 1889.
2544—2. HAZEL, b. Feb. 11, 1894.

2545. ARCHER G. CRANE[8] [1809], (Charles T.,[7] Archer,[6] Samuel,[5] John,[4] John,[3] Jonathan,[2] Benjamin[1]), married Annie B. Kinney, Jan. 26, 1887. She died Nov. 24, 1895. He taught school a number of years; now a farmer, living near Clinton, Mich. Child:

2546—1. CHARLES, b. July 1, 1892.

2547. C. LYLE CRANE[8] [1810], (Charles T.,[7] Archer,[6] Samuel,[5] John,[4] John,[3] Jonathan,[2] Benjamin[1]), married Minnie Martin, of Clinton, Mich. He has been a school teacher; now a farmer. Children:

2548—1. E. IRENE, b. Jan. 27, 1891.
2549—2. DON C., b. March 27, 1896.

2550. CLARA A. CRANE[8] [1814], (Archer H.,[7] Archer,[6] Samuel,[5] John,[4] John,[3] Jonathan,[2] Benjamin[1]), married J. J. Nachtrieb, Feb. 15, 1877. He is a farmer; lived near Hudson, Mich. Children:

1. ARCHER C. (Nachtrieb), b. Jan. 26, 1878.
2. AMBROSE W. (Nachtrieb), b. Jan. 17, 1880.
3. LOUISE (Nachtrieb), b. March 18, 1882.
4. ALICE M. (Nachtrieb), b. April 14, 1884.

5. FLORENCE H. (Nachtrieb), b. Oct. 9, 1889.
6. CLARENCE (Nachtrieb), b. April 28, 1895.

2551. DUNHAM JONES CRAIN[8] [1860], (William C.,[7] Rufus,[6] Isaac,[5] Abiah,[4] John,[3] Jonathan,[2] Benjamin[1]), was born in the town of Warren, Herkimer County, N. Y.; graduate of Union College, and a lawyer by profession. Was member of the legislature of New York in 1858; United States consul at Milan from 1877 to 1884. Married April 25, 1859, in New York city, Hannah Ann Crocker, daughter of David and Eliza C. Crocker. She was born in that city Jan. 21, 1837, and where for many years they have made their home. Children:

2552—1. THOMAS C. T:, b. May 25, 1860.
2553—2. SARAH N. ELIZA, b. Sept. 29, 1862; d. Jan. 31, 1866.
2554—3. HANNAH ANN, b. Oct. 5, 1864.
2555—4. CHRISTOBELLE, b. April 3, 1867.
2556—5. DUNHAM JONES, b. July 12, 1869; d. Oct. 8, 1870.
2557—6. DAVEDA CROCKER, b. Jan. 25, 1872.
2558—7. EDITH RANTZAN, b. Oct. 14, 1874; d. Sept. 30, 1877.

2559. JAMES D. CRANE[8] [1867], (William D.,[7] Asa,[6] Isaac,[5] Abiah,[4] John,[3] Jonathan,[2] Benjamin[1]), married Anna M. Steele, of Clinton, N. Y. Now (February, 1897), residing in San Diego, Cal. Child:

2560—1. JULIA LOUISA, b. Aug. 17, 1880, at Ouray, Colorado.

2561. WILLIAM HENRY CRANE[8] [1873], (William D.,[7] Asa,[6] Isaac,[5] Abiah,[4] John,[3] Jonathan,[2] Benjamin[1]), married Nellie Hogan. Children:

2562—1. WILLIE D.
2563—2. AMARYLLIS.
2564—3. FLORENCE.
2565—4. MABEL.
2566—5. ROLAND RODIRICK.
2567—6. RALPH.

2568. CHARLES D. CRANE[8] [1878], (Moses L.,[7] Asa,[6] Isaac,[5] Abiah,[4] John,[3] Jonathan,[2] Benjamin[1]), married Jan. 10, 1884, Belle M. Parker. She was born June 24, 1859. Residence at Milwaukee, Wis. Mr. Crane is a member of the firm of Crane & Barkhausen, architects and superintendents. Children:

2569—1. STANLEY P., b. Sept. 29, 1885.

2570. PHEBE E. CRANE[8] [1883], (Isaac N.,[7] Amos,[6] Isaac,[5] Abiah,[4] John,[3] Jonathan,[2] Benjamin[1]), married —— Good. Children:

1. MARY CECILIA (Good), b. Jan. 9, 1872.
2. ETHELL EDNA (Good), b. Oct. 29, 1875.

2571. MARY E. CRANE[8] [1885], (Isaac N.,[7] Amos,[6] Isaac,[5] Abiah,[4] John,[3] Jonathan,[2] Benjamin[1]), married —— Annis. Children:

1. WILLIAM McCLINTOCK (Annis), b. Sept. 28, 1879.
2. CHESTER HOLMES (Annis), b. Oct. 30, 1885.

2572. SILVEA D. CRANE[8] [1887], (Isaac N.,[7] Amos,[6] Isaac,[5] Abiah,[4] John,[3] Jonathan,[2] Benjamin[1]), married —— Avery. Child:

1. ROY B. (Avery), b. Feb. 7, 1884.

2573. EDWARD ARIEL CRANE[8] [1909], (Joseph,[7] Ariel,[6] Joseph,[5] Abiah,[4] John,[3] Jonathan,[2] Benjamin[1]), married Lizzie Backley at Brookfield, Vt., Dec. 25, 1876. Is a railway mail clerk, and resides (1897) at Omaha, Neb. His first wife died in September, 1884, and ·he married 2d, Nellie B. Fitch, of Mooresville, Vt. Child:

2574—1. MINNIE WORTH, b. Jan. 28, 1877; graduate of the Omaha High School, and at present (1897) at Mt. Holyoke College.

2575. MARY P. CRANE[8] [1917], (Charles,[7] Ariel,[6] Joseph,[5] Abiah,[4] John,[3] Jonathan,[2] Benjamin[1]), married April 15, 1890, Rev. J. Ross Lee. He was born April 15, 1859, and died Feb. 14, 1893. Child:

1. MARY CRANE (Lee), b. Jan. 28, 1891; d. May 16, 1892.

2576. CHARLES BLAIR CRANE[8] [1919], (Charles,[7] Ariel,[6] Joseph,[5] Abiah,[4] John,[3] Jonathan,[2] Benjamin[1]), married Sept. 2, 1890, at Dexter, Iowa, Cora B. Clark, born Jan. 22, 1870. Children:

2577—1. CHARLES A., b. June 18, 1891, at Dexter, Iowa.
2578—2. BERNICE, b. July 1, 1893, at Hooperston, Ill.

2579. EMMA TAMAR CRANE[8] [1929], (George H.,[7] Horatio,[6] Joseph,[5] Abiah,[4] John,[3] Jonathan,[2] Benjamin[1]), married Dec. 27, 1880, Frederick Louis Small. She died April 26, 1886. Children:

1. ALICE EMMA (Small), b. July 25, 1882.
2. LUCY ELIZABETH (Small), b. Dec. 20, 1883.
3. LOUIE MAY (Small), b. Dec. 26, 1885.

2580. ALICE ELIZA CRANE[8] [1932], (George H.,[7] Horatio,[6] Joseph,[5] Abiah,[4] John,[3] Jonathan,[2] Benjamin[1]), married Aug. 23, 1882, Leland Ellis Tupper. Child:

1. LELIA EVELYN (Tupper), b. Oct. 5, 1892.

2581. ELMER E. CRANE[8] [1948], (Horatio D.,[7] Oren,[6] Joseph,[5] Abiah,[4] John,[3] Jonathan,[2] Benjamin[1]), married Jennie M. Draper, April 19, 1883. They reside in Whitesboro, N. Y. Child:

2582—1. RAYMER D., b. March 3, 1888.

2583. EDWARD MARTIN CRANE[8] [1976], (Edward P.,[7] Porter,[6] Joseph,[5] Abiah,[4] John,[3] Jonathan,[2] Benjamin[1]), married May 10, 1892, Carrie E. Fairman, of Hardwick, Vt. Child:

2584—1. EDWARD FAIRMAN, b. Feb. 26, 1893.

2585. MARIA T. CRANE[8] [1994], (Andrew M.,[7] Daniel O.,[6] Elisha,[5] Elisham,[4] John,[3] Jonathan;[2] Benjamin[1]), married 1st, Daniel W. Stevens, in 1857; 2d, Ishmael M. Cole, July 23, 1884. Resides in Lake Crystal, Minn. Children:

1. ORLANDO M. (Stevens), b. Dec. 19, 1858.
2. ANNA M. (Stevens), b. April 6, 1861.
3. HARRIET M. (Stevens), b. Oct. 30, 1862.
4. EVA M. (Stevens), b. Jan. 30, 1866.
5. MASON W. (Stevens), b. Dec. 7, 1868.
6. ELMER E. (Stevens), b. April 28, 1870.
7. LESTER K. (Stevens), b. Sept. 22, 1872.
8. ROY (Stevens), b. Aug. 8, 1875.
9. LOTTY E. (Stevens), b. July 23, 1877.

2586. WILLIAM WILLIS CRANE[8] [2004], (Russell W.,[7] Wareham,[6] Hezekiah,[5] Hezekiah,[4] John,[3] Jonathan,[2] Benjamin[1]), married Elizabeth Spencer, of East Hartford, Conn., where she was born July 20, 1821. He is engaged in the manufacture of sash, doors and blinds at Plainville, Conn. Children:

2587—1. ALLICE LYDIA, b. Jan. 26, 1858, in Hartford.
2588—2. WILLICE SPENCER, b. Sept. 15, 1863, in Hartford.

2589. DAVID LEWIS CRANE[8] [2014], (Oliver R.,[7] Wareham,[6] Hezekiah,[5] Hezekiah,[4] John,[3] Jonathan,[2] Benjamin[1]), married 1st, Harriet Watrous, by whom he had a son. After her death, he married 2d, Nellie Watrous, a sister of his first wife. Residence New London, Conn. Child:

2590—1. LEWIS.

2591. ANNIE REBECCA CRANE[8] [2016], (Oliver R.,[7] Wareham,[6] Hezekiah,[5] Hezekiah,[4] John,[3] Jonathan,[2] Benjamin,[1]), married Edwin John Archer, Aug. 15, 1872, and resides in New London, Conn. Children:

1. MARY ABBIE (Archer), b. Feb. 7, 1874.
2. EMMA LOUESA (Archer), b. March 23, 1876.
3. ANNIE FLORENCE (Archer), b. Oct. 11, 1877.
4. ELIZABETH MATILDA (Archer), b. Aug. 18, 1879; d. Sept. 14, 1879.
5. GEORGIA CRANE (Archer), b. May 12, 1881; d. Aug. 7, 1881.
6. GEORGIA (Archer), b. June 19, 1882; d. March 14, 1883.
7. FRANK EDWIN (Archer), b. Aug. 8, 1883; d. Aug. 28, 1883.

2592. ABBY ELEANOR CRANE[8] [2017], (Oliver R.,[7] Wareham,[6] Hezekiah,[5] Hezekiah,[4] John,[3] Jonathan,[2] Benjamin[1]), married 1st, William Maloney. He died, and she married 2d, Frederick Douglass. Children:

1. PHEBE CRANE (Douglass), b. June 18, 1883.
2. CHARLES FREDERICK (Douglass), b. Dec. 17, 1885.
3. MARION (Douglass), b. March 10, 1893.

2593. CURTIS L. CRANE[8] [2025], (Lorenzo B.,[7] Wareham,[6] Hezekiah,[5] Hezekiah,[4] John,[3] Jonathan,[2] Benjamin[1]), married Celia ——, b. 1844. Children:

2594—1. CORA M., b. 1865.

2595—2. MINNIE V., b. 1866; m. Lucus Moore, 1893.
2596—3. EVA E., b. 1868; m. Myron Ludington, 1892.
2597—4. WILLIE C., b. 1868; m. Ora H. House, 1892.
2598—5. ALICE MAY, b. 1873; m. Frank V. Pinkham, 1891.
2599—6. IRVING H., b. 1877.
2600—7. EMMA L., b. 1878.
2601—8. ROSE L., b. 1886.

2602. ORSON W. CRANE[8] [2026], (Lorenzo B.,[7] Wareham,[6] Hezekiah,[5] Hezekiah,[4] John,[3] Jonathan,[2] Benjamin[1]), married Hattie E. Collins. She was born 1851. Children:

2603—1. EDWARD E., b. 1872; m. Ida Pearle, 1892.
2604—2. ARCHE, b. and d. 1873.
2605—3. Twin boys, b. 1877.
2606—4. HATTIE E., b. 1884.
2607—5. RAZMON, b. 1888.

2608. USTACIA CRAIN[8] [2028], (Hendrick,[7] Joel,[6] Hezekiah,[5] Hezekiah,[4] John,[3] Jonathan,[2] Benjamin[1]), married William A. Raymond, Oct. 15, 1867, in Norwich, N. Y., where they now (1882) reside. Children:

1. WILLIAM CRAIN (Raymond), b. Feb. 9, 1869.
2. MARY ELIZABETH (Raymond), b. Oct. 2, 1872.
3. HARRY RANDOLPH (Raymond), b. Nov. 8, 1874.

2609. VAN BUREN CRANE[8] [2030], (Hendrick,[7] Joel,[6] Hezekiah,[5] Hezekiah,[4] John,[3] Jonathan,[2] Benjamin[1]), married Phebe Ackley, Sept. 8, 1862. Residence (1882) at Norwich, N. Y. Children:

2610—1. GEORGE AMAZIAH, b. Aug. 20, 1868.
2611—2. KITTIE LOTTIE, b. Oct. 3, 1871.

2612. MARQUIS DE LAFAYETTE CRAIN[8] [2032], (Hendrick,[7] Joel,[6] Hezekiah,[5] Hezekiah,[4] John,[3] Jonathan,[2] Benjamin[1]), married Isabella Guerin, Nov. 19, 1864, in St. Louis, Mo., and settled there. Children:

2613—1. MARY ISABELLA, b. Feb. 10, 1866.
2614—2. HENRY VAN BUREN, b. Oct. 6, 1867.
2615—3. USTACIA, b. Aug. 7, 1870.
2616—4. EMMA E., b. May 20, 1872.
2617—5. MARQUIS D. L., b. March 4, 1874.
2618—6. ROSITA M., b. Sept. 20, 1876.
2619—7. DAVIE ELLA, b. Oct. 26, 1878.

2620. CURTIS CRANE[8] [2035], (Luther,[7] Joel,[6] Hezekiah,[5] Hezekiah,[4] John,[3] Jonathan,[2] Benjamin[1]), married Elsie B. Spencer, Jan. 16, 1873, at Scranton, Pa., where she was born April 25, 1853. They settled in Des Moines, Ia., where he is a merchant. Children:

2621—1. CHARLES S., b. Oct. 5, 1874.
2622—2. HARRIET A., b. April 23, 1877.

2623. HARRIET CRANE[8] [2039], (Gilman,[7] Hezekiah,[6] Hezekiah,[5] Hezekiah,[4] John,[3] Jonathan,[2] Benjamin[1]), married Elisha

G. Hatch, Aug. 6, 1865. The ceremony was performed by Rev. E. W. Hutchingson, of Bucksport, at the home of her father in Orland, Me. Children :

1. ARTHUR DELMONT (Hatch), b. July 26, 1866.
2. GILMAN GRINDLE (Hatch), b. Jan. 5, 1868.
3. ALENIA ROSE (Hatch), b. and d. Dec. 8, 1869.

2624. ARTHUR DELMONT HATCH [1]; m. in Surry, Me., by Rev. A. Gray, Abbie D. Carter, of that town, April 14, 1889. Children :

    1. RALPH WALTER (Hatch), b. April 12, 1890, in Orland.
    2. JENNIE A. (Hatch), b. March 15, 1893.
    3. ROY CLYDE (Hatch), b. July 18, 1896, in Sedgwick.

2625. GILMAN GRINDLE HATCH [2]; m. in Bucksport, Me., by Rev. E. H. Boynton, Nov. 29, 1894, Ursula F. Trundy, of Blue Hill, Me. Children :

    1. MERLE PRESTON (Hatch), b. Dec. 11, 1895, in North Penobscot.
    2. LILIAN FRANCES (Hatch), b. and d. Nov. 8, 1896.

2626. PRUDENCE JANE CRANE[8] [2041], (Gilman,[7] Hezekiah,[6] Hezekiah,[5] Hezekiah,[4] John.[3] Jonathan,[2] Benjamin[1]), married Capt. Epps G. Gilley in Bucksport, Me., Oct. 2, 1852. He was son of Francis and Ruth (Gott) Gilley, and born in Fremont, on the Island of Placentia, May 6, 1831. He died March 29, 1897. Children :

1. ARTHUR (Gilley), b. May 5, 1854.
2. WILLIS H. (Gilley), b. April 3, 1857; lost at sea, near Cape Good Hope, Nov. 18, 1876, from ship *N. T. Hill*.
3. HARRY F. (Gilley), b. March 10, 1862; d. April 10, 1862.
4. GEORGE D. (Gilley), b. May 12, 1865; d. Aug. 12, 1865.

2627. ARTHUR GILLEY [1]; m. in Orland, Me., May 9, 1877, Helen L. Dorr. She was b. May 13, 1857, and dau. of G. M. and Susan Keyes Dorr, of Orland, Me. Children :

    1. EPPS HOWARD (Gilley), b. April 2, 1878.
    2. FLORENCE L. (Gilley), b. Dec. 6, 1886.
    3. GLADYS M. (Gilley), b. May 5, 1888.

2628. ROSELINDA CRANE[8] [2042], (Gilman,[7] Hezekiah,[6] Hezekiah,[5] Hezekiah,[4] John,[3] Jonathan,[2] Benjamin[1]), married, by Rev. Enoch M. Fowler, in Orland, Me., April 23, 1852, Rufus Leach, of Penobscot, Me. He was born July 23, 1829. She died in Bangor, Me. July 12, 1887. Children :

1. FRED M. (Leach), b. Aug. 13, 1853.
2. CARO H. (Leach), b. Nov. 18, 1855.
3. SEWALL B. (Leach), b. Jan. 7, 1859.
4. EPPS G. (Leach), b. June 11, 1862; m. Helen Malcom, March 19, 1884, and d. at Bangor, December, 1886.
5. LAURA BELLE (Leach), b. July 19, 1869; m. Mr. Richards, Aug. 19, 1887.

2629. FRED M. LEACH [1]; m. Vine Hamilton, and settled in Orland, but now of Brewer, Me. Children :

    1. ADDIE H. (Leach), b. Oct. 1, 1877.
    2. WILLIS (Leach), b. Aug. 29, 1881.

2630. CARO H. LEACH [2] ; m. Albion C. Batchelder, of Bangor, Me.
She d. Aug. 19, 1887. Children.:

   1. LETA MARIE (Batchelder).
   2. RENA LOUISE (Batchelder).

2631. GILMAN CHARLES CRANE[8] [2043], (Gilman,[7] Hezekiah,[6]
Hezekiah,[5] Hezekiah,[4] John,[3] Jonathan,[2] Benjamin[1]), married
1st, January 1, 1867, Mary Jane Page, of Bucksport, Me. She
died without issue April 21, 1868. He then married Ella E.
Cobburn, who was born in Bangor, Nov. 1, 1850. Children :

2632—1. ALICE M., b. Nov. 18, 1873, in Bangor.
2633—2. HELEN F., b. Jan. 6, 1876, in Orland.

2634. CATHERINE JOHNSTON CRANE[8] [2044], (Gilman,[7] Hezekiah,[6] Hezekiah,[5] Hezekiah,[4] John,[3] Jonathan,[2] Benjamin[1]),
married Elisha D. Lowell, Dec. 4, 1861, by Rev. Edwin Parker.
She died in Verona, Me., April 3, 1878. Mr. Lowell was born
Aug. 17, 1840, and son of Abner and Olive C. Lowell, of Bucksport. Children :

   1. HARVEY A. (Lowell), b. March 5, 1863; d. July 6, 1863.
   2. EDWARD G. (Lowell), b. Oct. 29, 1865; d. March 7, 1868.
   3. OLIVE B. (Lowell), b. Dec. 1, 1868.
   4. ABBIE L. (Lowell), b. April 26, 1872.
   5. MARIA L. (Lowell), b. March 10, 1874.

2635. OLIVE B. LOWELL [3] ; m. Sept. 22, 1888, Austin D. Abbott, at
Bucksport, Me., by Rev. Wm. Forsyth. He is son of Dudley
A. and Arvilla J. Abbott, of Verona. Children :

   1. ROLAND L. (Abbott), b. June 18, 1889.
   2. MILDRED L. (Abbott), b. May 29, 1896.

2636. ABBIE L. LOWELL [4] ; m. May 17, 1894, Albert L. Avery, at
Ellsworth, Me., by Rev. G. W. Avery. Mr. Avery was b.
May 27, 1869, son of Edward and Marion M. Avery, of Pros-
pect. Children :

   1. FRANCIS E. (Avery), b. and d. July 31, 1894.
   2. CORA F. (Avery), b. Aug. 21, 1896.

2637. LAURA ELLEN CRANE[8] [2046], (Gilman,[7] Hezekiah,[6]
Hezekiah,[5] Hezekiah,[4] John,[3] Jonathan,[2] Benjamin[1]), married
Edward Narbis, of Malaga, Spain, March 11, 1864. He was
born Oct. 7, 1845, and settled in Orland, Me. Children :

   1. MARCIA E. (Narbis), b. May 29, 1866.
   2. MABEL IMOGENE (Narbis), b. Sept. 18, 1867; m. Geo. A. Dingle.
   3. ALBERT F. (Narbis), b. June 6, 1869.
   4. JOSEPHINE C. (Narbis), b. July 25, 1871; d. April 14, 1884.
   5. AGNES L. (Narbis), b. Nov. 13, 1873.
   6. LAURA L. (Narbis), b. June 22, 1877.
   7. EDWARD L. (Narbis), b. March 5, 1880.

2638. MARCIA E. NARBIS [1] ; m. Clarence S. York, of Weld, Me.,
Oct. 23, 1889, in Orland, by Rev. H. W. Norton. Child :

   1. HELEN S. (York), b. Jan. 15, 1892, in Bethel.

2639. ALBERT F. NARBIS [3]; m. Annie M. Aiken, of Dedham, Me., Nov. 10, 1892, by Rev. T. S. Ross. Residence at Salem, Mass. Children:

    1. FRANK A. (Narbis), b. Nov. 5, 1894, in Salem, Mass.
    2. ERNESTINE (Narbis), b. Nov. 2, 1896, in Salem, Mass.

2640. PARKER C. CRANE[8] [2049], (Sewall L.,[7] Hezekiah,[6] Hezekiah,[5] Hezekiah,[4] John,[3] Jonathan,[2] Benjamin[1]), married Dec. 31, 1856, Lorana Brown, who was born April 6, 1840. Child:

2641—1. LEWEY, b. June 25, 1858.

2642. SEWALL H. CRANE[8] [2053], (Sewall L.,[7] Hezekiah,[6] Hezekiah,[5] Hezekiah,[4] John,[3] Jonathan,[2] Benjamin[1]), married June, 1861, Emma Folsom. Children:

2643—1. NETTIE.
2644—2. WILLIAM.
2645—3. CAROLINE.
2646—4. SEWALL.

2647. HELEN M. CRANE[8] [2068], (David O.,[7] David,[6] David,[5] Hezekiah,[4] John,[3] Jonathan,[2] Benjamin[1]), married George Hoffman; a dentist. Residence at St. Louis, Mo. Children:

    1. MINNIE (Hoffman).
    2. GEORGIE (Hoffman).

2648. JESSE HOWELL CRANE[8] [2071], (Franklin L.,[7] David,[6] David,[5] Hezekiah,[4] John,[3] Jonathan,[2] Benjamin[1]), married at Fort Larned, Kan., May 22, 1865, Clara R. Dodds, a native of Dayton, Ohio. She was born Nov. 25, 1844. He was born in Easton, Pa., and educated there, passing two years at LaFayette College. During the late war he was sutler at Fort Larned. Of late years he has resided in San Francisco, Cal., where he is a merchant. Child:

2649—1. HARRY JESSE, b. Jan. 21, 1872, at Topeka, Kan.

2650. DAVID ORVILLE CRANE[8] [2073], (Franklin L.,[7] David,[6] David,[5] Hezekiah,[4] John,[3] Jonathan,[2] Benjamin[1]), born at Easton, Pa., and educated in the common schools there. He enlisted with his brother, Franklin L., May 4, 1861, and continued in service during the war. They were both at the hard-fought battle of Springfield, Mo., and were witnesses to the killing of Gen. Lyon, and the wounding of Col. Robert B. Mitchell about the same time. In 1861 he was musician in 2d Regt. Kansas Volunteer Infantry, and veteran in 5th Cavalry, and saw severe service. He is clerk at Osage City, Kan., where they reside. Children:

2651—1. ELIZABETH ALICE, b. Nov. 22, 1870; d. September, 1871.
2652—2. MARY ELIZABETH, b. Dec. 7, 1871.
2653—3. ANNA SOPHIA, b. March 16, 1873.
2654—4. FRANKLIN LOOMIS, b. Oct. 4, 1878.

DAVID ORVILLE CRANE

3d Son of Dr. F. L. Crane.
Born, Easton, Pennsylvania, February 12, 1842.
Married to Anna S. Kay, March 3, 1869.

CHILDREN OF D. O. CRANE

CRANE	ANNA S. CRANE	FRANKLIN LOOMIS CRANE, 3d.
nsas,	Born, Topeka, Kansas,	Born, Topeka, Kansas, October 4, 1878
71.	March 16, 1873.	Married Harriett Maude Dallas,
adcliff,		Cincinnati, October 4, 1899.

GEORGE WOOLSEY CRANE

4th Son of Dr. F. L. Crane.
Born, Easton, Pennsylvania, August 25, 1843.
Married Ella Rain, June 15, 1870,
who died April 17, 1881.
Married Fannie Kiblinger, November 7, 1882.

CHILDREN OF GEORGE W. CRANE

FRANK SNOW CRANE

orn, Topeka, Kansas, February 7, 1871.
·ried Mary Gertrude Smith, October 3, 1894.

EDNA C

Born, Topeka, Kansas, Dec

CHARLES EUGENE CRANE.

2655. GEORGE WOOLSEY CRANE[8] [2074], (Franklin L.,[7] David,[6] David,[5] Hezekiah,[4] John,[3] Jonathan,[2] Benjamin[1]), was born in Easton, Pa. Educated at Hamilton (C.W.) University, 1863. He married June 29, 1870, at East Topeka, Kansas, Ella Rain, a native of Elkhart, Ind., born Jan. 28, 1853. He is a printer and binder. Resides in Topeka, Kansas.
Children :

2656—1. FRANK S., b. March 29, 1871.
2657—2. EDNA, b. Dec. 10, 1875.

2658. HARRIE D. CRANE[8] [2097], (Martin H.,[7] Curtis,[6] David,[5] Hezekiah,[4] John,[3] Jonathan,[2] Benjamin[1]), married Laura Alace Mills, who was born July 24, 1856. Child:

2659—1. IDA MAE, b. July 12, 1876.

2660. CHARLES EUGENE CRANE[8] [2101], (William C.,[7] Curtis,[6] David,[5] Hezekiah,[4] John,[3] Jonathan,[2] Benjamin[1]), married June 2, 1880, Alice Elizabeth, daughter of Munson and Ann Augusta Hinman, in Hallock, Peoria Co., Ill., she was born Oct. 25, 1858. He was educated in the common schools and at Morse Academy of New Albany, Ind. and learned the hardware business with his uncle and father, he afterwards was in the employ of Rankins-Snyder Hardware Co., of Louisville, Ky., where he remained up to July 1, 1881, in the capacity of clerk and travelling-man. After travelling for the Louisville firm for one year, he removed to Yazoo City, Mississippi, where he clerked for Nierman & Doherty for eighteen months, when he organized the firm of Crane, Nierman & Co., which was changed Aug. 1, 1883, to Crane Bros. & Co., his brother Edgar being associated with him in the management of the firm. A general hardware business was carried on by them until July 1, 1891, when he withdrew from the firm and removed to Seattle, Washington. After a year's residence there he organized the Diamond Ice and Storage Co. and became its president and general manager and is still (1899) acting in that capacity. He is also the president of the Co-operative Mining Syndicate, and vice-president of the Equitable Building Loan and Investment Association, a trustee of the Chamber of Commerce and a member of the First Presbyterian Church of that city. Children :

2661—1. JULIA HINMAN, b. March 30, 1881, in New Albany, Ind.
2662—2. BESSIE SHIELD, b. Feb. 8, 1883, in Yazoo City, Miss.
2663—3. HARRY STEWART, b. Nov. 6, 1886, in Yazoo City, Miss.
2664—4. ALINE TERRELL, b. Nov. 14, 1890, in Yazoo City, Miss.; d. Jan. 12, 1891.
2665—5. BONNIE MARGUERITE, b. Dec. 3, 1891, in Seattle, Wash.
2666—6. CHARLES LESLIE, b. Jan. 8, 1898.

2667. WILLIAM FRANKLIN CRANE[8] [2102], (William C.,[7] Curtis,[6] David,[5] Hezekiah,[4] John,[3] Jonathan,[2] Benjamin[1]), married Dec. 16, 1885, Lillie May Hammond, who was born July 24, 1866. He is a member of the firm of Lampton, Crane &

Ramey Co., Louisville, Ky., dealers in paints, oils, window-glass, etc. Resides in Clinton, Miss. Child:

2668—1. HUBERT HAMMOND, b. April 25, 1893.

2669. EDGAR SHIELDS CRANE[8] [2103], (William C.,[7] Curtis,[6] David,[5] Hezekiah,[4] John,[3] Jonathan,[2] Benjamin[1]), married Oct. 18, 1883. Elizabeth Letitia Gebhart, a native of New Albany, Ind., born Sept. 26, 1861. They reside in Yazoo City, Miss., where Mr. Crane is engaged in the hardware trade, also stoves, paints, &c., under style of Crane-Hinman Hardware Co.
Children, all born in Yazoo City, Miss.:

2670—1. JANET, b. July 23, 1885.
2671—2. JOHN CURTIS, b. Feb. 25, 1888.
2672—3. PAUL SACKETT, b. Feb. 4, 1889.

2673. EMMA LOUISE CRANE[8] [2106], (William C.,[7] Curtis,[6] David,[5] Hezekiah,[4] John,[3] Jonathan,[2] Benjamin[1]), married Stephen E. Barnwell, of Yazoo City, Miss. Children:

1. BESSIE (Barnwell).
2. LOUSIE (Barnwell).
3. STEPHEN (Barnwell).

2674. JULIA ADALINE CRANE[8] [2107], (William C.,[7] Curtis,[6] David,[5] Hezekiah,[4] John,[3] Jonathan,[2] Benjamin[1]), married Allen E. Wright, of New Albany, Ind. Child:

1. BURDETTE (Wright).

2675. LOTTIE STEWART CRANE[8] [2116], (John E.,[7] Curtis,[6] David,[5] Hezekiah,[4] John,[3] Jonathan,[2] Benjamin[1]), married in New Albany, Ind., Oct. 6, 1881, Frank C. Nunemacher. Residence Louisville, Ky. Child:

1. STEWART (Nunemacher), b. Feb. 8, 1886.

2676. NANNIE MONTGOMERY CRANE[8] [2117], (John E.,[7] Curtis,[6] David,[5] Hezekiah,[4] John,[3] Jonathan,[2] Benjamin[1]), married Nov. 6, 1885, Horace C. Kent, at New Albany, Ind. They settled in Louisville, Ky., but returned to New Albany, Ind., previous to June 20, 1890, and now reside there. Children:

1. MILLARD CRANE (Kent), b. Jan. 30, 1887.
2. ELIZABETH GERTRUDE (Kent), b. Jan. 6, 1888; d. June 20, 1888.
3. RONALD WILSON (Kent), b. June 20, 1890.

2677. STELLA BROWN CRANE[3] [2121], (John E.,[7] Curtis,[6] David,[5] Hezekiah,[4] John,[3] Jonathan,[2] Benjamin[1]), married Oct. 6, 1892, at New Albany, Ind., Wilson Warmon Godfrey, where they reside. Child:

1. VIRGINIA LEE (Godfrey), b. Sept. 23, 1895.

2678. WILLIS JAQUITH CRANE[8] [2184], (Eli B.,[7] Hezekiah,[6] Aaron,[5] Hezekiah,[4] John,[3] Jonathan,[2] Benjamin[1]). His father having been killed in the battle of Cold Harbor, June 3, 1864, the death of his mother by pneumonia a few years later, left

Willis J., a very small boy, to be cared for by relatives on his mother's side. They removed to Neenah, Wis., in 1866, where he was married 1st, in 1880, to Frankie Ohorn, of that place. The following year he removed to Manistee, Mich., and in May, 1883, removed to Ordway, South Dakota, where she died in November. In September, 1884, he settled in Chippewa Falls, Wis., and July 5, 1886, removed to Negaunee, Mich., where he has since resided. Nov. 30, 1887, he was married 2d, to Philomene Cyr.

Children:

2679--1. WILLIS JAQUITH, b. Sept. 9, 1881.
2680—2. FRANKIE, b. November, 1883; d. 1884.
2681—3. FLORENCE ADALAID, b. Aug. 12, 1888.
2682—4. HELEN BEATRICE, b. March 7, 1890.
2683—5. SHELDON CYR, b. Aug. 15, 1892.
2684—6. KATHARINE BARNES, b. Feb. 13, 1894.
2685—7. EDNA LOUISE, b. Feb. 4, 1897.

2686. FREDERICK R. CRANE[8] [2196], (Gilbert,[7] Ebenezer,[6] Zebulon,[5] Lemuel,[4] John,[3] Jonathan,[2] Benjamin[1]), married April, 1867, Melissa G. Wilber, who was born in Westmoreland in 1849.

Children:

2687—1. HERBERT, b. May, 1868.
2688—2. BESSIE, b. December, 1873.
2689—3. JESSIE, b. February, 1876.

2690. EVERETT LEROY CRANE[8] [2219], (Leroy D.,[7] Ralph,[6] Isaac,[5] Isaac,[4] Isaac,[3] Jonathan,[2] Benjamin[1]), married May 1, 1879, Berther Wilson Chapman, a native of Groton, Conn., born March 20, 1861. Resides at Poquonock Bridge. Children:

2691—1. RALPH WILLIAM, b. June 28, 1881.
2692—2. CASSIE LOUISE, b. June 15, 1889.

2693. WILLIAM EGBERT CRANE[8] [2224], (Ira A.,[7] Joseph,[6] John,[5] Zebulon,[4] Joseph,[3] Jonathan,[2] Benjamin[1]), married Hannah Morse. She died March 28, 1889. He died in 1890. Child:

2694—1. GEORGIA.

2695. EMILY CRANE[8] [2225], (Ira A.,[7] Joseph,[6] John,[5] Zebulon,[4] Joseph,[3] Jonathan,[2] Benjamin[1]), married William S. Knapp. Children:

1. IRA (Knapp). Enlisted in late war and died from effects of exposure in southern prison.
2. BELDEN (Knapp). Enlisted in late war and marched with Sherman, and died before reaching the sea.
3. EMILY AUGUSTA (Knapp); m. and d.
4. WILLIAM E. (Knapp).
5. HELEN AURELIA (Knapp).

2696. ABRAHAM H. CRANE[8] [2226], (Ira A.,[7] Joseph,[6] John,[5] Zebulon,[4] Joseph,[3] Jonathan,[2] Benjamin[1]), married Abigail Richards. He died Oct. 4, 1864. She died January, 1895.

Children:

2697—1. CHARLES B.
2698—2. HARRIET.

2699. JOHN CRANE[8] [2228], (Ira A.,[7] Joseph,[6] John,[5] Zebulon,[4] Joseph,[3] Jonathan,[2] Benjamin[1]), married Elizabeth Clark. He died Dec. 9, 1874.   Children :

2700—1. GEORGE.
2701—2. ESTELLA.

2702. IRA CRANE[8] [2239], (Azor B.,[7] Joseph,[6] John,[5] Zebulon,[4] Joseph,[3] Jonathan,[2] Benjamin[1]), married Louise E. Strang, daughter of Martin Strang.   Children :

2703—1. AZOR B., b. Oct. 8, 1884.
2704—2. BESSIE AURELIA, b. March 20, 1886; d. Nov. 11, 1888.
2705—3. MARY AURELIA, b. Sept. 22, 1887.
2706—4. LOUISA STRANG, b. Jan. 14, 1891.

2707. JOSEPH HENRY CRANE[8] [2243], (Azor B.,[7] Joseph,[6] John,[5] Zebulon,[4] Joseph,[3] Jonathan,[2] Benjamin[1]), married Julia Gorham, daughter of Fletcher Gorham, of Mount Kisco, Westchester County, N. Y.   Children :

2708—1. LEWIS BELDEN.
2709—2. HAROLD.
2710—3. BESSIE AURELIA.
2711—4. FLETCHER GORHAM.

2712. EDWARD M. CRANE[8] [2247], (George L.,[7] Stephen,[6] John,[5] Zebulon,[4] Joseph,[3] Jonathan,[2] Benjamin[1]), married in Brooklyn, N. Y., where they now reside, September, 1865, Esther C. Watson.   She was a native of New York State, and born March 30, 1836.   He is a type finisher.   Children :

2713—1. CARRILENA.
2714—2. GEORGE.
2715—3. EDWARD.

2716. LYDIA JOSEPHINE CRANE[8] [2305], (John W.,[7] Samuel,[6] Zebulon,[5] Zebulon,[4] Joseph,[3] Jonathan,[2] Benjamin[1]), married David W. Whaley, of New Canaan, Conn., June 11, 1875. Children :

1. HATTIE (Whaley), d. in infancy.
2. PEARL (Whaley); residence Southville, Conn.
3. SAMUEL (Whaley), d. in infancy.

2717. LETITIA CRANE[8] [2306], (John W.,[7] Samuel,[6] Zebulon,[5] Zebulon,[4] Joseph,[3] Jonathan,[2] Benjamin[1]), married July 4, 1874, James Andrew.   They settled in Danbury, Conn.   Children :

1. HATTIE (Andrew), b. March 30, 1875; m. Alfred Doyle; residence Danbury.
2. JOHN WILLIAM (Andrew), b. Jan. 23, 1877; residence Danbury.
3. ALFRED A. (Andrew), b. July 21, 1883; residence Danbury.
4. JAMES (Andrew), b. June 22, 1889; d. May 5, 1890.

2718. MINNIE ELIZA CRANE[8] [2309], (John W.,[7] Samuel,[6] Zebulon,[5] Zebulon,[4] Joseph,[3] Jonathan,[2] Benjamin[1]), married

Residence: " Old Crane Homestead," at Carmel, Putnam County, N. Y.

June 24, 1891, George Adelbert Washburn, of Danbury, Conn., where they reside. Child :

1. NINA ELMIRA (Washburn), b. Aug. 22, 1892.

2719. MARY MINERVA CRANE[8] [2311], (Harrison,[7] Zebulon,[6] Zebulon,[5] Zebulon,[4] Joseph,[3] Jonathan,[2] Benjamin[1]), married Charles Henry Peet, son of Henry and Laura A. (Wheelock) Peet, at New Fairfield, Conn., Sept. 18, 1894, Rev. Edward Payson Herrick, pastor of Congregational Church, Tampa, Florida, performing the ceremony. Mr. Peet was born Jan. 8, 1856, in Danbury, Conn. Child :

1. MARY BELL (Peet), b. Nov. 15, 1895.

2720. JAMES NEHEMIAH CRANE[8] [2312], (Harrison,[7] Zebulon,[6] Zebulon,[5] Zebulon,[4] Joseph,[3] Jonathan,[2] Benjamin[1]), married June 21, 1881, Fannie, daughter of John and Amanda (White) Paget, in Pawling, N. Y., Rev. Burroughs S. Fauton officiating. She was born Dec. 22, 1863, in South East, N. Y. Child :

2721—1. NELLIE ANN, b. Aug. 19, 1885.

2722. GEORGE PROVOST CRANE[8] [2318], (Philander,[7] Josiah,[6] Jonathan,[5] Joseph,[4] Joseph,[3] Jonathan,[2] Benjamin[1]), married March 16, 1846, Ann Jennette Smith, who was born Feb. 28, 1825. Children :

2723—1. HARRIET ESTELLE, b. Nov. 25, 1848; m. Jan. 13, 1876.
2724—2. ANNA DELIGHT, b. Nov. 2, 1850; m. Nov. 16, 1871; d. Dec. 16, 1889.
2725—3. SARAH JANNETTE, b. June 2, 1856; m. May 23, 1878; d. Nov. 24, 1894.
2726—4. EUGENIA SMITH, b. May 11, 1863; d. May 2, 1869.
2727—5. LILLIE IRENE, b. Dec. 27, 1868; d. Jan. 3, 1875.

2728. ELBERT CRANE[8] [2319], (Philander,[7] Josiah,[6] Jonathan,[5] Joseph,[4] Joseph,[3] Jonathan,[2] Benjamin[1]), married Margaret Porce, in 1862. He died Jan. 27, 1865. Child :

2729—1. PHILANDER, b. Oct. 4, 1863; d. March 23, 1865.

2730. SARAH E. CRANE[8] [2322], (John,[7] Josiah,[6] Jonathan,[5] Joseph,[4] Joseph,[3] Jonathan,[2] Benjamin[1]), married John Baker, of Albion, N. Y. Children :

1. JOHN C. (Baker).
2. ADELLA (Baker).
3. EMMA (Baker).
4. CHARLES (Baker).

2731. CHRISTOPHER COLUMBUS CRANE[8] [2323], (John,[7] Josiah,[6] Jonathan,[5] Joseph,[4] Joseph,[3] Jonathan,[2] Benjamin[1]), married Evaline Kuck. He died in his 27th year, of consumption. Child :

2732—1. CARRIE E.

2333. HANNAH CRANE[8] [2324], (John,[7] Josiah,[6] Jonathan,[5] Joseph,[4] Joseph,[3] Jonathan,[2] Benjamin[1]), married Harmon Sandhouse. Children :

   1. ADELBERT (Sandhouse).
   2. HARRY (Sandhouse).
   3. JENNY (Sandhouse).
   .4. WILLIAM (Sandhouse).
   5. CORA (Sandhouse).

2734. CHARLES F. CRANE[8] [2326], (John,[7] Josiah,[6] Jonathan,[5] Joseph,[4] Joseph,[3] Jonathan,[2] Benjamin[1]), married in 1859, Lucy A. Battles, a native of Massachusetts, born in 1842. He was a farmer and resided for a time in Monticello, Iowa, but about 1888 went to California and settled at Fall Brook. Children :

   2735—1. EVA D., b. 1861.
   2736—2. WILLIE E., b. 1863.
   2737—3. IDA M., b. 1865.
   2738—4. FLORA B., b. 1867.
   2739—5. FRANK S., b. 1869.
   2740—6. CHARLIE F., b. 1873.
   2741—7. ORRIN B., b. 1878.

2742. ORRIN BALDWIN CRANE[8] [2327], (John,[7] Josiah,[6] Jonathan,[5] Joseph,[4] Joseph,[3] Jonathan,[2] Benjamin[1]), married Jennie Burlingame, of Cleveland, Ohio. He died at the age of 42 years, of consumption. Children :

   2743—1. CORA.
   2744—2. DE FORREST.

2745. FRANCES A. CRANE[8] [2328], (John,[7] Josiah,[6] Jonathan,[5] Joseph,[4] Joseph,[3] Jonathan,[2] Benjamin[1]), married John D. Walworth. She died aged 34 years, of consumption. Children :

   1. CLARA A. (Walworth); m. Lon B. Griffin, of Kirkville, Mo.
   2. CARRIE (Walworth); d. in infancy.

2746. CARSO CRANE[8] [2329], (John,[7] Josiah,[6] Jonathan,[5] Joseph,[4] Joseph,[3] Jonathan,[2] Benjamin[1]), married Electa L. Glidden. He was a captain in the late civil war, and went from Iowa. Now (1899) resides in Anamosa. Children :

   2747—1. FRED G.; m. Minnie Austin; residence Sumner, Iowa.
   2748—2. LIZZIE A.; m. Fred A. Brainard; residence Anamosa, Iowa.

2749. EMILY CRANE[8] [2330], (John,[7] Josiah,[6] Jonathan,[5] Joseph,[4] Joseph,[3] Jonathan,[2] Benjamin[1]), married William G. Condit. She died aged 52 years, of consumption. Children :

   1. LALIA (Condit).
   2. WILLIAM C. (Condit); m. Sylvia Walker; residence Ames, Neb.
   3. ERNEST D. (Condit); residence Anamosa, Iowa.
   4. BESSIE (Condit); residence Anamosa, Iowa.
   5. ORRIN (Condit); residence Ames, Neb.

The material from which the following sketches were drawn was furnished the compiler after the family record had been arranged.

[See opposite page, No. 2746.]

CARSO CRANE[8] married Electa L. Glidden. He served in the late war. Enlisted as a private from Jones County, Iowa, in July, 1861, elected 2d Lieutenant, ordered into camp at Dubuque, and mustered into the United States service Sept. 2, in Co. D, 9th Regt. Iowa Infantry. Then proceeded via. St. Louis, Mo., to Pacific City, and with Gen. Curtis in command, the army of the South West started after the enemy under General Price, came up with the rear of the enemy before reaching Springfield, but could not bring on an engagement until Price had formed a junction with Van Dorn, when with a force of 35,000 they turned upon Curtis with his 10,000 men. In a skirmish at Nubben Ridge the casualties were light, but at Pea Ridge, where they fought March 6 and 7, 1861, the company of which he was then in command went into the engagement with 55 men, had 2 killed, 2 taken prisoners, and 29 wounded. Company C, having lost its officers, was attached to Mr. Crane's company on the afternoon of the 6th, and continued there throughout that action. Afterwards they marched through Arkansas to Helena, in August; remained there until December; made an attack on Chickasaw Bayou and were repulsed; returned to Arkansas and captured Arkansas Post; returned to Vicksburg and worked in the famous cut-off canal. Here Mr. Crane became prostrated by the effects of a sunstroke in connection with chronic diarrhœa and resigned in March, 1863, on a surgeon's certificate. He was made 1st Lieutenant in September, 1862, and Captain in February, 1863. While in camp at Helena, he served several months on the staff of Gen. Vandevers. Now (1899) resides in Anamosa, Iowa. Children:

[See page 203, No. 2301.]

" Dr. George Belden Crane was born July 31, 1806, in the State of New York, Dutchess County, now Putnam, and died Monday, May 9, 1898. His first school-days were spent in a little shanty near his father's sawmill on the Croton river. Like other boys in those days, he worked on the farm in the summer and went to school in the winter. When sixteen years old he secured a certificate and commenced teaching school, receiving therefor about $12 per month and board. Four years later he entered the medical department of the State University in New York City, graduating in 1832. He soon turned his face westward, travelling from Albany to Schenectady on the first passenger railroad in the United States. He continued his journey on

16

a canal-boat to Buffalo, and by steamer from there to Cleveland, Ohio, thence to the Great Scioto river. Here he settled and practiced medicine for nearly five years, marrying, meantime, Maria, eldest daughter of Dan Young, a pioneer from New Hampshire. The health of his wife demanding a change of climate, he in 1836 removed to Northern Alabama, where he continued the practice of his profession until he found his constitution was being undermined by hard labor in what was then not only a hot but a malarious section. From here he went to Pike county, Missouri, a place made conspicuous by California emigration. It was here that in 1848 he had, unsolicited, the honor of being one of two or three physicians of that State on whom the medical department of the University of Missouri conferred the honorary degree of M. D. In January, 1853, Dr. Crane, with family, started by sailing vessel for California via the Horn. On the 3rd of May, 1853, he left San Francisco by steamer for Alviso, and thence to San Jose by stage. Here he lived and prospered for four years, when the continued ill health of his wife, caused him to relinquish charge of the city and county hospital and a large private practice and remove to Napa. Having studied viticulture as followed in France and Germany, and comparing the soil of this valley with that of other countries, he decided to engage in that industry and at once purchased nearly 400 acres of land near the little hamlet of St. Helena, paying therefor an average of between $6 and $7 per acre. He procured Mission cuttings from San Jose, there being no foreign ones in the country, and planted about twelve acres in February, 1859, a portion of which grew well. The planting was continued, and in ten years he possessed a vineyard of one hundred acres. He encountered all the vicissitudes usual to pioneers in any movement, but ultimately achieved success. It was not long after his acres of wilderness had been converted into a fruitful and beautiful home that his first wife died, and in 1872 he married the widow of A. J. Grayson, the ornithologist who lost his life while painting the ornithology of Central America. The doctor saw the little hamlet of redwood shanties near his home grow to a substantial and thrifty town with comfortable homes established so close together that stations along the line of railroad had to be placed a mile or two apart for the convenience of residents. For many years deceased lived quietly, always extending a hearty welcome to the visitor who crossed the threshold of his hospitable home. He passed considerable time in reading and writing. His articles for the press were many, and he was always pleased when new thoughts were brought out. In 1885, when 79 years old, he wrote his life history, together with incidents, experiences and comments on a variety of topics. This he caused to be published for distribution among his relatives and friends. And now that its author has gone, we quote from its pages a few of his thoughts on death: 'But why regard the day of death as an "evil day"? It is an

event as natural as that of our birth.   Our birth was for a purpose.   We are compelled to believe, from an analogical reason-
ing, that there is a purpose in so called death.   The apparent
difference between birth and death is not real.   The first is to
people earth with rudimental intelligences, the next to translate
those intelligences to a higher sphere of existence.   Progress is
the rule of nature.'   What better can be said of him than that
the ninety-two years of his earthly existence were spent in well-
directed efforts for the benefit of mankind!   He possessed a
noble character, was a kind friend and a good citizen.

Child :

2302—1.   MARY; m. John McPike.   She d. a few years since, leaving
four sons and a daughter, who together with their
children number five grandchildren and six great-grandchildren that Dr. Crane left at his decease.

[See page 206, No. 2352.]

Judge ADDISON MOSES CRANE was born in Litchfield, Herki-
mer County, N. Y., July 2, 1814.   He served at Buffalo, N.
Y., in the Navy Island rebellion during the months of June
and September, 1838.   He married in Catskill, Greene County,
Oct. 21, 1839, Gertrude Ashley, who was born at Catskill, June
20, 1820.   They settled at Nunda, Livingston County, where
their two eldest children were born.   About 1844 he removed to
La Fayette, Ind., where he served as judge from 1848 to 1852.
In 1853 he removed to California, making the trip around Cape
Horn, and settled in Alameda County.   Here he purchased twelve
acres of land, extending from Buena Vista avenue back to the
Canal and from Oak to Walnut streets, in Oakland, where he lived.
He was the first judge for Alameda County, 1853 to 1857, and
represented Alameda County in the State Senate, 1862 and 1863,
and was also a railroad commissioner.   His death occurred Oct.
20, 1887, and the following memorial so plainly shows with what
high esteem he was held by those who knew him best, that we
cannot refrain from printing it in full :

" IN MEMORIAM.

To the Hon. Superior Court of Alameda Co., Cal.

The committee heretofore appointed by this court to draft
suitable resolutions respecting the death of the late Addison M.
Crane report the following Preamble and Resolutions :

Whereas, We having learned with sincere regret of the death
of Hon. Addison M. Crane, for many years a resident of this
county, a member of the Bar of the State, and late Judge of this
Court, which occurrence took place at his residence in the city
of Oakland, on the 20th day of October, 1887 ; and

Whereas, We, as members of the Bar, have known him long
and intimately, as well in private and social life, as in the worry-
ing and harassing duties of his profession — ever finding him a

conscientious, upright and faithful lawyer, an impartial and wise Judge, and an honest man, distinguished alike for his gentleness of manner and kindness of disposition, and in all the relations of life for strict fidelity and integrity—faithful and capable in the discharge of the duties devolving upon him as a lawyer and a Judge, truthful and trustworthy as a man, reliable and able in the discharge of the duties devolving upon him in the many official positions held by him—his character was always above reproach, without stain, and without blemish. Therefore,

Resolved, That in the death of Hon. Addison M. Crane society has lost a useful citizen and an influential man, and the Bar a faithful, capable and earnest member, and the County and State an old and respected citizen.

Resolved, That we tender to his surviving widow, his family and friends our heartfelt sympathy in their bereavement.

Resolved, That a copy of these resolutions be presented to the family of the deceased, and also spread upon the minutes of this Court.

R. A. REDMAN,
JAMES C. MARTIN,
A. M. ROSBOROUGH,
A. A. MOORE,
JOHN R. GLASCOCK,
Committee."

A son of Judge Addison Moses Crane.

2354—2. LAUREN ELLIOTT, b. July 18, 1842; d. February, 1897, of paralysis of the heart, in San Francisco. He was a bright, ambitious youth, became highly educated and a linguist; was a successful writer of both prose and verse, and gained thereby considerable distinction; was on the staff of the old *Overland Monthly, Post and Chronicle* of San Francisco; also assistant editor of the Sacramento *Record-Union.* He arranged and threw open for circulation books of the Free Public Library of San Francisco. Among various stories from his pen, perhaps he is best known by his "Newton Booth of California." He acted as Governor Booth's private secretary, and he was also secretary for Governor Pacheco. "Dick Doone a California gambler," a dialect poem, also his poem "Juanita," attracted no small degree of attention. He was of fine physique, and a person of rare personality.

2750. WILLIAM SNOW CRANE[8] [2334], (Oliver,[7] Josiah,[6] Jonathan,[5] Joseph,[4] Joseph,[3] Jonathan,[2] Benjamin[1]), married Dec. 3, 1856, in New York city, Eleanor Frances Collin. She was born in that city Dec. 12, 1837, and there they have resided. He is engaged in the dry goods business. Children:

2751—1. CARRIE ELLA, b. March 31, 1858.
2752—2. EDNA ELIZABETH, b. Oct. 21, 1862; d. Oct. 7, 1865.

2753. Eva L. Crane[8] [2409½], (Wyram,[7] Alfred,[6] Peter,[5] Thaddeus,[4] Joseph,[3] Jonathan,[2] Benjamin[1]), married Geo. W. Sayles, born Nov. 1, 1841. Children :

   1. Kathleen A. (Sayles), b. Oct. 14, 1880.

2754. Nettie Crane[8] [2409¾], (Wyram,[7] Alfred,[6] Peter,[5] Thaddeus,[4] Joseph,[3] Jonathan,[2] Benjamin[1]), married Ovett Morrill, born Aug. 23, 1856. Children :

   1. Earl Crane (Morrill), b. Jan. 22, 1883.
   2. Julia H. (Morrill), b. Sept. 12, 1888.

2755. Frank Boyle Crane[8] [2417], (Thaddeus,[7] James,[6] James,[5] Thaddeus,[4] Joseph,[3] Jonathan,[2] Benjamin[1]), was born in Neosho Falls, Kansas ; married Nov. 12, 1891, Clella Jackson. Child :

   2756—1. James Jackson, b. May 17, 1894, at Vernon, Kan.

2757. Mary K. Crane[8] [2453], (Lyman,[7] Charles A.,[6] Ashbil,[5] John,[4] John,[3] Abraham,[2] Benjamin[1]), married Edward Goodyear. They settled in Chatham, Medina County, Ohio. Children :

   1. Charles E. (Goodyear).
   2. George R. (Goodyear).
   3. Edna D. (Goodyear).

2758. Charles E. Goodyear · [1]; m. and settled in Litchfield, Ohio. Children :

   1. Florance (Goodyear).
   2. Lola (Goodyear).

2759. Harris W. Crane[8] [2466], (Walter C.,[7] Charles A.,[6] Ashbil,[5] John,[4] John,[3] Abraham,[2] Benjamin[1]), married Abbie Hales, of Mount Gilead, Ohio, Jan. 3, 1822. He is an engineer on Big 4 R. R., or the Cleveland, Cincinnati, Chicago, and St. Louis Railway. Children :

   2760—1. Louretta.
   2761—2. Charles Arthur.
   2762—3. George Walter.

2763. Rev. HORACE ALONZO CRANE,[9] .M.A., [2489], (Horace A.,[8] Truman,[7] John,[6] Benjamin[5], John,[4] John,[3] Jonathan,[2] Benjamin[1]), born at New Haven, Vt.; a Methodist minister. Graduated at Syracuse, N. Y., 1885; spent several years in missionary work. Was in India in 1896 and 1897, and presiding elder of the Bombay district. Since his return to America he has given several lectures on life in India, its people, their manners and customs, etc. He is at present (1899) pastor of the Methodist Episcopal Church at Lima, N. Y. A man of scholarly attainments; an eloquent and forcible speaker. June 17, 1885, he married Julia Farr at Middlebury, Vt. She was born at Lincoln, Vt., Jan. 21, 1860. Children:

2764—1. GEORGIANA A., b. June 5, 1886, at Central City, Neb.
2765—2. PHILA LUELLA, b. Oct. 23, 1891, at Omaha.

2766. EDWIN C. CRANE[9] [2529], (Mahlon D.,[8] Edwin D.,[7] Archer,[6] Samuel,[5] John,[4] John,[3] Jonathan,[2] Benjamin[1]), married Augusta L. Boyd, of La Porte, Ind., Oct. 19, 1882. He was for several years telegraph operator for the L. S. & M. S. R. R.; now (1898) railroad ticket agent at La Porte, Ind. Children:

2767—1. EMILY L., b. Aug. 21, 1883.
2768—2. MAHLON B., b. May 2, 1887.
2769—3. GLADYS VIRGINIA, b. Aug. 28, 1889.

2770. SARAH L. CRANE[9] [2530], (Mahlon D.,[8] Edwin D.,[7] Archer,[6] Samuel,[5] John,[4] John,[3] Jonathan,[2] Benjamin[1]), married Arthur L. Williams, Jan. 2, 1873. He was born at Blissfield, Mich., Sept. 4, 1852. For some years he was a merchant in Blissfield. In the year 1882 he went to South Dakota, and was engaged in farming for a few years; now (1898) resides in Chicago, Ill. Children:

1. EDWIN F. (Williams), b. June 23, 1874; d. September, 1874.
2. CLARA L. (Williams), b. Feb. 27, 1878.
3. J. STANLEY (Williams), b. Dec. 25, 1892; d. Aug. 5, 1893.

2771. DWIGHT H. CRANE[9] [2532], (James K.,[8] Edwin D.,[7] Archer,[6] Samuel,[5] John,[4] John,[3] Jonathan,[2] Benjamin[1]), went to California, and worked in the silver mines some five years. Was also in the service of the Street Railway Company in the city of San Francisco about five years. Returned to Michigan, and settled at Deerfield; a farmer.

Rev. HORACE ALONZO CRANE, M. A.

2772. CYNTHIA A. CRANE[9] [2533], (James K.,[8] Edwin D.,[7] Archer,[6] Samuel,[5] John,[4] John,[3] Jonathan,[2] Benjamin[1]), married Lucy P. Wilson, Jan. 16, 1881. Child:

  1. ADALINE E. (Wilson).

2773. ALFRED J. CRANE[9] [2535], (James K.,[8] Edwin D.,[7] Archer,[6] Samuel,[5] John,[4] John,[3] Jonathan,[2] Benjamin[1]), married Hattie A. Goodrich, Nov. 20, 1884, daughter of Lyman E. and Mary —— Goodrich. She was born Feb. 23, 1863. He is agent for the L. S. & M. S. R. R., at Riga, Mich. Children:

  2774—1. EDNA B.
  2775—2. HAZEL.
  2776—3. IVA G.
  2777—4. HEROLD ALFRED, b. Oct. 19, 1898.

2778. CHARLES J. CRANE[9] [2539], (Charles E.,[8] Edwin D.,[7] Archer,[6] Samuel,[5] John,[4] John,[3] Jonathan,[2] Benjamin[1]), married Lillie Curry, July 30, 1884. She was born Oct. 31, 1860, at Vincennes, Ind. For several years he has been ticket agent for the Pennsylvania Railroad lines at Indianapolis, Ind. Children:

  2779—1. CHARLES E., b. May 3, 1885.
  2780—2. PERRY CURRY, b. Sept. 19, 1886.
  2781—3. HENRY BARTON, b. July 15, 1888.
  2782—4. GEORGE F., b. March 4, 1891.
  2783—5. HELEN, b. Jan. 19, 1898.

JOHN CRANE, OF COVENTRY, CONNECTICUT,
AND HIS DESCENDANTS.

Mr. William L. Weaver, then editor of the *Willimantic Journal*, began Oct. 10, 1862, to publish in that paper data relating to the history of Windham County, Conn., and gave considerable attention to genealogies of the families that were early settlers there. Among them were some of the descendants of Jonathan Crane, of Windham, and John Crane, of Coventry. For reasons best known to himself, the publication of the history was abandoned, although the publication of the genealogies was continued in the *Journal* for some time: and the following is copied from that paper, issued under date of Oct. 20, 1864, and from the pen of Mr. Weaver:—

"John Crane, an early settler of Coventry, was the common ancestor of the Mansfield Cranes. We have made considerable effort to trace his ancestry, and to connect him with some of the early Crane families in New England; but without success. He was certainly one of the very early settlers of Coventry, where he was living in 1708, where he had land deeded to him. He was not a descendant from Jonathan, of Windham, and we cannot find that he was the son of either of the brothers of Jonathan, of Wethersfield; but we strongly suspect there was a connection between the families. The fact that John Crane, of Windham, settled in Coventry while John Crane, the Coventry settler, was living there; the similar family names and traditions among some branches of the Cranes, lend color to the suspicion. The early settlers of Coventry were mostly from the towns of the Connecticut River valley, including some families from Wethersfield; and we consider it not at all impossible that John Crane, the Coventry settler, was a son of the Wethersfield Cranes, though no record of his birth has been found there. John Crane was one of the accepted inhabitants of Coventry in 1730, when the first list of

17

freemen was made; and, of course, a resident of the town at that time. He subsequently removed to Mansfield, but at what time is not ascertained. It is supposed that he lived near the Willimantic River, and that his removal to Mansfield was only across the stream, the dividing line between the towns. Descendants say he was buried in the Willimantic burying-ground above Eagleville, in Mansfield. We have not ascertained in regard to the church relations of John Crane; but from what we have been able to gather, judge that both he and his wife were pious and respectable people in comfortable circumstances. He is called *Mr.* in the Mansfield records,—then a special mark of respect.

John Crane's will names his " wife Abigail; children, Hezekiah, Ebenezer, John; three grandchildren of my daughter Abigail Barrows; daughter Mary Allen, wife of Samuel; and children of my daughter Ruth Paddock, deceased." Mrs. Crane also names the same children in her will. After careful investigation, with records of the various lines in view, the *suspicion* still remains, with accumulated strength, even bordering on *belief*, that John Crane, of Coventry, was a descendant of Benjamin, senior, of Wethersfield. From the birth of this John, of Coventry, in 1689 or 1690, to his death, in 1765, there were no less than seven John Cranes living within a radius of twenty-five or thirty miles from Wethersfield: John, son of Benjamin, b. 1663; John, son of Jonathan, b. 1687; John, son of Abraham, b. 1700; John, son of John of Jonathan, b. 1709; John, son of John of Coventry, b. 1716; John, son of John of Abraham, b. 1739; and John, son of John, of Coventry, b. 1743. It is, therefore, apparent that John was a popular name with the Crane family at that time, and great care has been exercised in arranging their children in their proper lines.

The question arises: If this John was grandson of Benjamin, senior, of Wethersfield, whose son was he? Most likely he was son of John, who went among the first settlers to Windham with his brother Jonathan. He is reported as having been by trade a blacksmith, and the record fixes his death Oct. 21, 1694, at the age of 31 years. He married Abigail Butler, by whom he had one child, Josiah, b. March 22, 1694. This marriage with Abigail Butler took place Oct. 27, 1692, he being then twenty-nine years and six months old. With the laws of the colony encouraging, and almost compelling, early marriages, it is not unlikely that this was his second marriage. and that, while in Windham,

by a former wife, who had died, he had a son John. If not, why did he not follow the custom and name Abigail's child John? Of course, this is theory; no records have been found to confirm beyond doubt the position here taken. He may have been the son of Jacob, but that is rather doubtful.

John Crane, supposed to be this ancestor of the Mansfield Cranes, purchased land of Samuel Burnham, of Windsor, Conn., in 1708, which he sold in 1711 to Benjamin Jones. He then purchased home lot No. 68.

Rev. Jonathan Crane, for forty years a minister at Middletown, N. Y., who gave much time to investigating the history of his immediate family, entertained the same opinion, that this John, of Coventry, was grandson of Benjamin, of Wethersfield.

FIRST GENERATION.

FROM RECORDS OF COVENTRY, CONN., MOSTLY OBTAINED FROM MANUSCRIPTS OF MR. WM. L. WEAVER, BY E. B. CRANE IN 1879.

1. JOHN CRANE was one of the early settlers of Coventry, Conn., born 1689 or 1690, married Abigail Cross, Oct. 29, 1712, she was daughter of Peter Cross of Mansfield, and Mary, his wife. She was born in Windham, June 23, 1694. October, 1743, John Crane of Mansfield, and Wm. Williams with others asked the Assembly to fix site for Second Society Meeting-house. John Crane's will is dated May 31, 1764, proved March 16, 1765, probated March 19, 1765. (Invo. £146-17-6). Will mentions wife Abigail, children Hezekiah, Ebenezer, John, and Mary Allen, three grandchildren of his daughter Abigail Barrows, and three grandchildren of daughter Ruth Paddock. Mrs. Crane's will was dated July 6, 1765, proved Sept. 25, 1765, probated Oct., 1765. He died in Mansfield, March 1, 1765, aged 75. She died Sept. 1, 1765, aged 71.

In what has been known as the Gurley burial-ground, situated about a mile and a half northwest from the meeting-house in North Mansfield, John Crane and his wife Abigail were buried, and their grave-stones were standing in 1868, bearing the following inscriptions: "In memory of Mr. John Craine who died March y^e —— 1765 in ye 76 year of his age," "In memory of Mrs Abigail ye wife of Mr. John Craine, who died Sept y^e —— 1765, in y^e —— year of her age." Children:

2—1. JOHN, b. Sept. 8, 1713; d. Sept. 20, 1713.
3—2. ABIGAIL, b. Oct. 20, 1714.
4—3. JOHN, b. Oct. 25, 1716.
5—4. EBENEZER, b. July 4, 1720.
6—5. MARY, b. May 22, 1722; m. Samuel Allen, and had three or four children.
7—6. SAMUEL, b. April 23, 1724.
8—7. HEZEKIAH, b. Oct. 10, 1725.
9—8. DEBORAH, b. Aug. 1, 1727; probably died young.
10—9. DANIEL, b. Jan. 29, 1728-9; died young (Jan. 4, 1739).
11—10. RUTH, b. Dec. 22, 1730; m. —— Paddock and d. before 1764.

12. ABIGAIL CRANE^2 [3], (John^1), married Lieut. Thomas Barrows for his second wife Feb. 2, 1743-4, she died Aug. 9, 1750. Lieut. Barrows married for his first wife Mehitable Porter, and after the death of Abigail Crane, married Elizabeth Turner for a third wife, by whom he had several children, names not given.

1. ABIGAIL (Barrows), b. Nov. 5, 1744; m. Nathan Palmer.
2. MEHITABLE (Barrows), b. Jan. 7, 1745-6; m. Thos. Swift, Jr.
3. THOMAS (Barrows), b. May 24, 1748; d. Mar. 15, 1749.
4. THOMAS (Barrows), b. July 27, 1750.

SECOND GENERATION.

13.   JOHN CRANE[2] [4], (John[1]), married Sarah Chamberlain, May 18, 1738. She was daughter of Edmund. Mr. Crane settled first in Mansfield, Conn., where his children were born. He afterwards removed to Becket, Mass.

14—1.   SARAH, } twins; b. April 20, 1739. { d. Nov. 18, 1744.
15—2.   DEBORAH. }
16—3.   ANNA, b. May 18, 1741.
17—4.   JOHN, } twins; b. March 4, 1743.
18—5.   THANKFUL, }
19—6.   CATHERINE, b. Oct. 3, 1744.
20—7.   STEPHEN, b. Jan. 10, 1747.
21—8.   SAMUEL, b. July 4, 1749.
22—9.   SOLOMON, b. July 15, 1754.

23.   EBENEZER CRANE[2] [5], (John [1]), married Sarah, daughter of Jonathan Curtis, June 21, 1744. Settled first in Mansfield, Conn., but was of Lebanon in 1765, when in April of that year he declined to act with his brother Hezekiah as one of the executors of his father's will. ·He could not have long been a resident of Lebanon, for he was of Mansfield in 1762 and again in 1770. It is supposed the family removed from the town, as no records of his descendants are to be found at Mansfield where his children were born. It appears that he was twice married, for his grandson Edmund Franklin Craine, says he married a Welsh lady by name of Mary Neff.   Children:

24—1.   ABIGAIL. b. Oct. 1, 1745.
25—2.   EBENEZER, b. July 26, 1747.
26—3.   ELIZABETH, b. Oct. 14, 1749.
27—4.   DEBORAH, b. Aug. 11, 1751.
28—5.   REBECKAH, b. Sept. 7, 1753; d. Oct. 7, 1753.
29—6.   REBECKAH, b. Sept 11, 1755.
30—7.   JONATHAN, b. Aug. 20, 1757.
31—8.   AMARIAH, b. Oct. 16, 1759.
32—9.   ROGER, b. May 4, 1762.
33—10.   SARAH, b. Sept 4, 1770.

34.   HEZEKIAH CRANE[2] [8], (John[1]), married Tamesin, daughter of Elisha Eldridge of Mansfield, Conn., June 6, 1749. She died March 15, 1771. He died Jan. 8, 1795, aged 68. Mr. Crane lived and died in Mansfield, Conn.; he was executor of his father's will, and it is supposed from the records that he lived on the Crane homestead, and that his father and mother spent their last days with him.   Children:

35—1.   HEZEKIAH, b. March 4, 1751.
36—2.   DANIEL, b. April 14, 1752.

37—3. RUTH, b. May 1, 1753; m. ——— Clark of Ellington, Conn.
38—4. ELISHA, b. July 13, 1754; m. ——— Hanks.
39—5. TAMESIN, b. Feb. 16, 1755; m. Elijah Field, Jan. 26, 1774. He was b. April 20, 1756, son of Bennett Field who was son of John of Deerfield, Mass. The latter's wife was taken captive by the Indians, 1704, and returned 1706, and son Bennett was born afterwards, 1709. Elijah Field after marriage removed from Woodstock, Vt., and from there to Houndsville, N. Y., where he d. Oct., 1828. He was a drummer through the Revolutionary war.
40—6. DORCAS, b. Aug. 28, 1757; m. ——— Howard.
41—7. PHILLIP, b. July 3, 1759; a fifer in the Revolutionary war; d. while in army at E. Chester, N. Y., Oct. 9, 1776.
42—8. JEMIMA, b. Oct. 25, 1761.
43—9. DAVID E., b. Dec. 16, 1763; removed to Dorset, Vt.
44-10. ANNE, b. Dec. 20, 1766; m. Constad Constanse Balcom.
45-11. ZERVIAH, b. May 28, 1769; m. Chester Southworth, May 4, 1786.

THIRD GENERATION.

46. JOHN CRANE[3] [17], (John,[2] John[1]), born March 4, 1743. Married Sarah ——. Think this is the John Crain, yeoman, who purchased his farm of one hundred acres in Wilbraham, Mass., of Stephen Bliss, Oct. 23, 1765. Nov. 24, 1775, he sold this farm with the buildings on it to his son, Stephen Crain, for £200. He died 1798, and Aug. 28, 1798, the court appointed Simeon Graves of Palmer administrator; Gideon Ring, Theophilus Knight and Daniel Newell appraisers. Sept. 4, 1798, they presented their inventory, amounting to $286.74; to this was added for interest $14.62, making the total amount $301.36. The estate was settled June 25, 1799, at which time the son Stephen was deceased, and his widow Mary was given $8.44. Widow Sarah had $74.96. The children of Stephen, deceased, had $24.98, and the sisters of Stephen received a like amount; also John and Cyrus, children of Stephen. Children, their names being given in settlement of the estate:

47—1. STEPHEN.
48—2. SARAH, m. —— Conant.
49—3. ANNA, m. —— Heth.
50—4. CATY, m. —— Graves.
51—5. MARY, m. —— Colton.
52—6. RHODA, m. —— Caldwell.

53. EBENEZER CRANE[3] [25], (Ebenezer,[2] John[1]). An Ebenezer Crane died in Alstead, N. H., April 9, 1777, who is supposed to have been the above Ebenezer, who, with his wife, Thankful Bickmore, resided at that place. Children:

54—1. EBENEZER, b. April, 1770.
55—2. ROBERT, m. Polly Child.
56—3. WILLIAM, m. Susan Dutton, Jan. 23, 1805, at Alstead, N. H.
57—4. BETSEY or POLLY.

58. JONATHAN CRAINE[3] [30], (Ebenezer,[2] John,[1]), enlisted May 6th, and discharged Dec. 16, 1775. Was private in 5th Co., Capt. Thomas Knowlton, of Ashford, 3d Regt. Vols., Gen. Putnam; served in and about Boston. Enlisted again May 22, 1777, for three years; discharged May 22. 1780. Was private in Capt. Willis Clift's Co., of Plainfield, 3d Regt., Connecticut Line, Col. Samuel Wyllys, of Hartford. This regiment served in New York and along the Hudson River, at Stony Point, and the raid on Danbury. Was in the battle of Trenton. Granted a pension in 1819. Married Sybil Ranney, daughter of Elijah Ranney, of Blandford, Mass. In the record at Spring-

field, Mass., it is spelled Sibbel. Jan. 26, 1797, they sold land
in Blandford, which Sibbel received from her father's estate, to
Noah Warren, of Blandford, for $100, and about that time
removed to Chenango Co., N. Y., where he kept a hotel. He
died in Plymouth, Chenango Co., N. Y., April 13, 1820. She
died in 1842. Children :

59—1. SYLVESTER, b. Aug. 2, 1785, in Blandford, Mass.
60—2. EBENEZER, b. July 27, 1787, in Blandford, Mass.
61—3. SALLY, b. 1789 or 1790, in Blandford, Mass.
62—4. MARY or POLLY, b. Oct. 19, 1792, in Blandford, Mass.
63—5. ABIGAIL, b. April 8, 1794, in Blandford, Mass.
64—6. MARTHA (PATTY), b. Aug. 12, 1797.
65—7. ROXANA, b. 1798, in Chenango Co., N. Y.
66—8. RHODA, b. 1799, in Chenango Co., N. Y.; d. in infancy.
67—9. JONATHAN, b. June 18, 1801, in Plymouth, Chenango Co., N. Y.
68-10. SYBIL ANN, b. 1803, in Plymouth, Chenango Co., N. Y.; d.
        May, 1835.
69–11. RACHEL, b. June 4, 1805, at Plymouth, Chenango Co., N. Y.

70. AMARIAH CRANE[3] [31], (Ebenezer,[2] John[1]), married
Tryphena —— Settled on Ware River, Mass. Was a soldier
in the Revolutionary war. Enlisted in Capt. Benj. Throop's Co.
May 12, 1777, for three years, at 18 years of age. Promoted as
fifer May 18. Discharged May 12, 1780. Served in Col.
Jedediah Huntington's 1st Regt., Conn. Line. Was a carpenter
and joiner by trade. He was recorded as a pensioner in 1818,
and was then living in N. Y. State. He sold property in Ware,
Mass., March 10, 1809, for $2500, to John Shaw, Jr.; April 18th
another piece to Joseph Field for $2000; Sept. 9th still another
piece for $1000. Children, all born in Ware, Mass.:

71—1. ABIGAIL, b. May 24, 1790.
72—2. AMARIAH, b. Oct. 17, 1792.
73—3. TRYPHENA, b. June 12, 1794.
74—4. EUNICE, b. Sept. 29, 1796.
75—5. MARY, b. April 17, 1798.
76—6. SARAH, b. March 28, 1800.
77—7. SOPHIA, b. Jan. 3, 1802.

78. ROGER CRAINE[3] [32], (Ebenezer,[2] John[1]), married in
Ashford, Conn., May 20, 1784, Sarah Whiting, who was born in
Ashford, Conn., Oct. 26, 1764. He served in the Revolutionary
war six years, and his granddaughter says he was with Washington at Valley Forge through the winter; also that he was one of
forty men under Col. Barton who surprised and captured Major-
Gen. Prescott in his own quarters at night, and who was
exchanged for Gen. Lee. In *Massachusetts Soldiers and Sailors
in the War of the Revolution* will be found on page 75, vol. 4,
Roger Crain served for Medway, enlisting for three years as
private in Capt. John Fuller's Co., Col. Wm. Shepard's (4th)
Regt. Served along the Hudson River. Was at West Point,
February, 1782. He receipted for his bounty paid him by the
town committee, May 30, 1781. His time began June 1st. He
was a farmer, and for many years lived in Groton, N. Y. He

died in Painesville, Ohio, June 3, 1841. She died in Groton, N. Y., Jan. 21, 1854. Children:

79—1. ABIGAIL, b. 1786.
80—2. SAMUEL, b. July 28, 1788.
81—3. CYRUS.
82—4. AHIRA, b. Sept. 12, 1794.
83—5. ELEAZER WHITING, b. May 22, 1796.
84—6. TOWER WHITING, b. June 4, 1799.
85—7. HORACE.
86—8. ALVIN, b. July 23, 1803.
87—9. ALEXIS.

88. HEZEKIAH CRANE[3] [35], (Hezekiah,[2] John[1]), married Rachel, daughter of Isaac Hall, April 14, 1774. She was born June 1, 1751. Lived in Mansfield, Conn. Was a farmer and dealer in stock. One informant says he went to Dorset, Vt., another says he died in Mansfield. His grandson Charles, son of Jesse, says this Hezekiah Crane was a trooper in the Revolutionary war. He died of fever at Canton, St. Lawrence Co., N. Y., in 1813. His brother David E. falling a victim to the then prevailing epidemic in the form of a fever. Children:

89—1. ISAAC, b. Feb. 20, 1775; m. Sarah Leonard.
90—2. JOHN, b. May 16, 1776; is said to have settled East Hartford, Conn. There was a John Crane of Hartford, d. insolvent. Estate settled Oct. 27, 1820, Elizabeth Crane, administratrix. The estate was reported to the Court Oct. 30, 1819.
91—3. JESSE, b. May 9, 1779; m. Rhoda Abbe.
92—4. ASA, b. April 27, 1781.
93—5. AMASA, b. July 27, 1782; settled in N. Y. State.
94—6. ABIGAIL, b. June 11, 1784.
95—7. DANIEL, b. July 26, 1786.
96—8. ZERVIAH, b. April 3, 1789; m. Thos. Baldwin.
97—9. ANNA, b. Aug. 21, 1792.

98. DANIEL CRAIN[3] [36], (Hezekiah,[2] John[1]), married Esther Fuller, Jan. 31, 1776. He died 1832, aged 80. Settled in Mansfield, Conn. Esther Fuller was daughter of Dr. Jonathan Fuller and was born in 1755. Mr. Bela Crane stated that his father served during the war of the Revolution; was one of Washington's body-guard, and was present at the execution of Maj. Andre. Was private in 2d Co., Capt. Experience Storrs of Mansfield, in Gen. Putnam's regiment, from May 17 to Dec. 1, 1775; served in and around Boston, and part of this regiment was engaged in the battle of Bunker Hill.* The Bureau of Pensions at Washington, D. C., gives the following: Aug. 11, 1832, Daniel Crain, a soldier of the Revolutionary war, made application for a pension, at which time he was eighty years old, and residing in Mansfield, Conn., and his pension was allowed for nine months' actual service as a private in the Connecticut troops, Revolutionary war. A part of the time he served under Col. Experience Storrs and Gen. Putnam. He enlisted at Mansfield. Children:

99—1. DANIEL, b. Aug. 15, 1778; m. Clarissa Whitman.

*Connecticut Records.

100—2. MEHITABEL, b. Aug. 20, 1780; d. Feb. 20, 1789.
101—3. CLARISSA, b. Nov. 4, 1781; m. ——— Eldridge; lives (1864)
      Willington, Conn.
102—4. CORDIAL S., b. Nov. 9, 1783.
103—5. SYBIL, b. April 22, 1785; m. Parley Kendall, June 22, 1805;
      m. Lyman Randall; lives (1864) Whitewater, Wis.
104—6. LUCY, b. May 7, 1787.
105—7. JONATHAN, b. Feb. 5, 1790; m. Orpha Barrows.
106—8. BELA, b. March 6, 1792; m. Deborah Aylsworth.
107—9. MEHITABLE, b. May 26, 1793.

108.   ELISHA CRANE[3] [38], (Hezekiah[2], John[1]); m. Irene
Hanks, Dec. 6, 1776, and settled first in Mansfield; after 1802 he
removed to Orleans, N. Y.   Was at the battle of Bunker Hill,
and served through the Revolutionary war.   Children :

109—1. LIBBEUS, b. April 25, 1777.
110—2. PHILLIP, b. April 1, 1779.
111—3. ZILPHA (dau.), b. Oct. 12, 1781.
112—4. LUCINDA, b. Oct. 3, 1783.
113—5. CHESTER, b. Dec. 6, 1786.
114—6. PHILENA, b. Jan. 27, 1793.
115—7. POLLY, b. Jan. 29, 1795.
116—8. JULIA, b. Aug. 29, 1799.
117—9. LUCIUS, b. July 3, 1802.

118.   DAVID ELDRIDGE CRAIN[3] [43], (Hezekiah,[2] John[1]),
m. 1st Phebe Sargeant, April 3 or 21, 1785; 2d Rachel Baldwin,
Jan. 30, 1798, Dorset, Vt.   Phebe Sargeant was born in Mansfield, Conn., Nov. 15, 1768, and died in Dorset, Vt., March 2,
1797.   Rachel Baldwin, his second wife, was born in Oblong,
Dutchess Co., N. Y., Sept. 24, 1769, and died at East Poultney,
May 6, 1836.   Mr. Crane served in the war of the Revolution;
was a teamster under Gen. Lafayette.   He died at Canton, St.
Lawrence Co., N. Y., of fever, Feb. 16, 1813, as also did his
brother Hezekiah.   Both were buried side by side at the head of
Wm. Farewel's grave.   Children :

119—1. NATHAN, b. Feb. 15, 1787.
120—2. PHEBE, b. Jan. 17, 1789.
121—3. DAVID ELDRIDGE, b. May 6, 1791; was voted to be credited
      by State Treasurer of Vermont, Nov. 6, 1819, according
      to sum mentioned in the act.   Nov. 8, 1820, an act was
      passed directing Treasurer of Vermont to pay David
      Crane.
122—4. LAURETTA, b. Nov. 1, 1794.
123—5. HEZEKIAH, b. Feb. 3, 1797.
124—6. BENJAMIN BALDWIN, b. Dec. 10, 1798.
125—7. RACHAEL BALDWIN, b. Dec. 12, 1800.
126—8. PHILIP PADDOCK, b. Oct. 23, 1802.
127—9. ARDELIA, b. Oct. 7, 1804.
128—10. RUTH BALDWIN, b. July 5, 1806.
129—11. TAMESIN ELDRIDGE, b. Jan. 2, 1809.
130—12. HIRAM ABIFF, b. May 19, 1811.

131.   ZERVIAH CRANE[3] [45], (Hezekiah,[2] John[1]); married
Chester Southworth and was the mother of nine children, all
born in Dorset and Pawlett, Vt.   After her death Mr. South-

worth married 2d, widow Potter, by whom he had two children, Ralph and a daughter whose name was not given. Children:

1. TAMESIN (Southworth); m. David Dunton.
2. IRENE (Southworth), b. Nov. 22, 1788.
3. POLLY (Southworth); m. Anson Richardson.
4. CHESTER (Southworth); m. Miss Church.
5. LEMUEL (Southworth); m. Marcia Clark.
6. ORIGIN (Southworth); m. Miss Clark, sister of above.
7. ZERVIAH (Southworth); m. Nathan White.
8. LUTHER (Southworth); m. Sarah Graham.
9. EMILY (Southworth); m. Robert Dubois.

132. IRENE SOUTHWORTH [2]; m. Hugh Montgomery a native of Londonderry, Vt., b. Aug. 12, 1785. They were married at South Canton, St. Lawrence Co., N. Y., and here they resided until their death. Children:
    1. CHESTER (Montgomery), b. Sept. 1, 1809.
    2. HANNAH (Montgomery), b. Sept. 10, 1811.
    3. CHARLES (Montgomery. b. May 5, 1814.
    4. MACK (Montgomery), b. Dec. 31, 1815.
    5. PORTER (Montgomery), b. July 11, 1818.
    6. ALTHA B. (Montgomery), b. Nov. 12, 1821.
    7. JOHN C. (Montgomery), b. Sept. 28, 1824.
    8. ELIZA A. (Montgomery), b. Oct. 31, 1827.
    9. LORENA M. (Montgomery), b. Dec. 24, 1829.
    10. WILLIAM (Montgomery), b. April 2, 1833.

133. MACK MONTGOMERY [4]; m. Jane Elizabeth Warren, dau. of Rev. Augustus Warren. Children:
    1. FRANK WARREN (Montgomery), b. Sept. 19, 1850, at Silver Creek, Chautauqua Co., N. Y.
    2. NELLIE MARIE (Montgomery), b. Sept. 30, 1856, at Silver Creek, Chautauqua Co., N. Y.

FRANK WARREN MONTGOMERY [1]; m. Alice Brooks Norris, who was born in Milwaukee, Wis., Sept. 11, 1852, dau. of Greenleaf Dudley Norris, and following children born in Milwaukee, although he is now (1896) resident of New York City. Children:
    1. ALICE NORRIS (Montgomery), b. Dec. 1, 1879
    2. WARREN (Montgomery), b. Nov. 9, 1881.
    3. DUDLEY (Montgomery), b. Aug. 20, 1883.
    4. HUGH (Montgomery), b. March 8, 1890.

FOURTH GENERATION.

134. STEPHEN CRANE[4] [47], (John,[3] John,[2] John[1]). He purchased the farm, with the buildings thereon, of his father John Crane, Nov. 24, 1775, for £200. This farm contained one hundred acres, and was the same land his father bought of Stephen Bliss, Oct. 23, 1765, in Wilbraham; witnessed by Isaac Conant and Rhoda Crane. June 7, 1785, Stephen mortgaged this farm to Oliver Bliss for £46 13s., at which time his father John Crane was living. He married widow Mary (Miner) Wheeler. He died prior to Aug. 28, 1798, and his widow Mary received $8.44 from his father John Crane's estate. Sept. 28, 1805, Mary Crane, the widow of Stephen Crane, mortgaged land on which she then lived to her son Joseph Wheeler, of Wilbraham. Nov. 6, 1812, widow Mary Crane paid John Crane, son of her late husband, Stephen Crane, $150 to release his right or interest in a certain piece of land to her own use. Children:

135—1. JOHN, b. about 1786.
136—2. CYRUS, b. March 26, 1788.

137. EBENEZER CRANE[4] [54], (Ebenezer,[3] Ebenezer,[2] John[1]), married Rhoda Towne of Ipswich, Mass. She was born in 1776. They were married in 1794 in Alstead, N. H., where they settled. His mother is said to have lived in his family for some years, and died there between 1809 and 1812. Children:

138—1. EBENEZER, b. April 12, 1795, in Alstead, N. H.
139—2. RHODA, b. Aug. 23, 1797; d. July 3, 1815.
140—3. ELIZA, b. Dec. 12, 1799; d. July 9, 1815.
141—4. SAPHRONIA, b. Sept. 10, 1802; m. Calvin Carpenter, of Walpole, N. H.; she d. in Alstead, N. H.
142—5. EZRA T., b. June 10, 1806; lived in Claremont, N. H., also at Keene in 1862, and Boston, Mass., and d. in Illinois; m. 1st, Betsy Wilder; m. 2d, Fanny Wilder.
143—6. MERCY, b. July 7, 1809; d. Sept. 2, 1862, in Alstead, N. H.
144—7. GEORGE W., b. Oct. 14, 1812, at Nunda, N. Y.; m. Mary Day, of Gilsum, N. H. He d. in 1882.
145—8. FRANKLIN, b. Aug. 20, 1814; d. March 23, 1846, in Alstead, N. H.
146—9. JERRY, b. March 21, 1818; d. Feb. 29, 1835, in Alstead, N. H.

147. ROBERT CRANE[4] [55], (Ebenezer,[3] Ebenezer,[2] John,[1]), married Polly Child, Jan. 31, 1804, at Alstead, N. H. It is reported that his family lived among the Shakers; but they lived in Dalton, N. H., for a time. Children:

148—1. JULIANA, b. Nov. 8, 1804.

149—2. MARYANA, b. Aug. 4, 1806.
150—3. EDWARD L., b. Nov. 1, 1808.
151—4. ROBERT, b. July 29, 1810.

152. SYLVESTER CRAIN[4] [59], (Jonathan,[3] Ebenezer,[2] John[1]), married Sally Chapman, June 9, 1808, at Plainfield, N. Y. She was born Jan. 27, 1785, in Lyme, Conn., and died Aug. 20, 1850. He died in Courtlandville, N. Y., May 21, 1847.
Children :

153—1. SYLVESTER, b. July 4, 1810, in Cortland, Cortland Co., N. Y.
154—2. JONATHAN G., b. Oct. 27, 1811, in Plymouth, Chenango Co., N. Y. ·
155—3. SALLY, b. June 24, 1813, in Cortland Co., N. Y.
156—4. NELSON, b. March 26, 1815, in Cortland Co., N. Y.
157—5. CERNAH, b. April 6, 1817, in Cortland, Cortland Co.; d. 1818.
158—6. ELIJAH, b. Dec. 25, 1821, in Cortland; d. 1823.
159—7. ELIZA, b. Dec. 25, 1821, in Cortland; d. Oct. 4, 1851.
160—8. NANCY, b. Feb. 16, 1824, in Cortland; m. Reuben Davis; d. Nov. 3, 1846.
161—9. LORENZO, b. Jan. 2, 1827, in Cortland; d. in 1828.
162-10. LORINDA, b. Jan. 2, 1827, in Cortland.

163. EBENEZER CRAIN[4] [60], (Jonathan,[3] Ebenezer,[2] John[1]), married, Aug. 29, 1800, Hannah Geer. She was born in Massachusetts, Sept. 14, 1787, and died in 1856 at Earlville, N. Y. He died there in 1867. Children :

164—1. BETSEY, b. Dec. 28, 1810; d. Jan. 4, 1811.
165—2. BETSEY ANN, b. Aug. 31, 1813, in Earlville, N. Y.
166—3. CHARLES, b. April 13, 1815; d. Feb. 21, 1820.
167—4. SILAS HARVEY, b. Sept. 24, 1816, in Earlville, N. Y.
168—5. EMMELINE F., b. May 18, 1823, in Earlville, N. Y.
169—6. MIRANDA, b. April 14, 1826, in Earlville, N. Y.

170. SALLY CRAIN[4] [61], (Jonathan,[3] Ebenezer,[2] John[1]), married George Wales, Feb. 20, 1808. He was born Feb. 20, 1780. They settled in Plymouth, Chenango County, N. Y., where she died Feb. 9, 1832. He then married her sister Rachel Crain, and died July 29, 1844. (See page 262). Children :

1. SALLY (Wales), b. 1808; d. 1809.
2. ALMIREN (Wales), b. July 16, 1809; d. 1813.
3. LAWRENCE (Wales), b. June 6, 1813.
4. FREDERICK (Wales), b. Dec. 12, 1814.
5. EBEN VINE (Wales), b. Aug. 29, 1816.
6. CHARLES (Wales), b. Oct. 22, 1818.
7. JONATHAN (Wales), b. June 16, 1820; d. 1821.
8. GEORGE (Wales), b. March 21, 1822.
9. RICHMOND (Wales), b. March 29, 1824; d. 1831.
10. SMITH (Wales), b. Feb. 8, 1832; d. 1832.

171. LAWRENCE WALES [3]; m. 1st, Annie M. Fox, July 19, 1853; b. May 22, 1819; d. Nov. 10, 1860; 2d, Elvira Rosseter, Nov. 8, 1866; she d. 1879. Settled in Plymouth, N. Y., and d. there Feb. 7, 1880. Children :
1. ADDISON (Wales), b. April 29, 1854.
2. BURT (Wales), b. May 29, 1858.
3. MARY (Wales), b. May 6, 1860; d. June 2, 1863.

ADDISON WALES [1]; m. A. Nightingale, Dec. 24, 1874. · Settled in Plymouth, Chenango County, N. Y. Child:
1. MERTON (Wales), b. Feb. 11, 1877.

BERT WALES [2]; m. Clara Aldrich, March 1, 1882, at Plymouth, N. Y. Settled there. Children:
1. FLOYD CHARLES (Wales), b. 1889; d. May 30, 1889.
2. LEON D. (Wales), b. March 9, 1891.
3. HERMON MORELL (Wales), b. Sept. 21, 1893.

172. FREDERICK WALES [4]; m. March 7, 1843, Laura Shoals; b. Aug. 18, 1816. She d. Jan. 1, 1883, in North Genoa, Wis. He d. in Elkhorn, Wis., 1889. Children, born in Plymouth, N. Y. Children:
1. GENORA (Wales), b. Dec. 7, 1844.
2. EDGAR (Wales), b. April 18, 1846.
3. ADARESTA (Wales), b. Sept. 22, 1847.
4. ELTON (Wales), b. April 17, 1849; d. May 7, 1864.
5. ELI (Wales), b. Oct. 23, 1850.
6. ALICE (Wales), b. Dec. 3, 1852.
7. WALTER (Wales), b. April 4, 1855.
8. ARTHUR (Wales), b. April 12, 1857.

GENORA WALES [1]; m. Thomas Morefield in Elkhorn, Wis., March 18, 1871. He was b. in Gloucester, Eng., March 18, 1850. Settled in Elkhorn. Children:
1. ALICE GENORA (Morefield), b. Feb. 20, 1872.
2. ROSA LAURA (Morefield), b. Feb. 11, 1875.
3. OLIVE MAY (Morefield), b. July 8, 1878.
4. MABEL (Morefield), b. Dec. 16, 1882.

EDGAR WALES [2]; m. March 4, 1874, Ellen A. Shepard. She was b. March 14, 1850. Settled in Elkhorn, Wis. Children:
1. LUELLA (Wales), b. Jan. 12, 1879; d. Feb. 9, 1879.
2. CHARLES E. (Wales), b. Sept. 24, 1880.
3. HENRY S. (Wales), b. Sept. 25, 1884.

ADARESTA WALES [3]; m. in Elkhorn, Wis., Nov. 30, 1871, John W. Farrar. He was b. in Ogdensburg, N. Y., May 5, 1847. She lives in Elkhorn. Children, b. in Delavan, Wis.:
1. HILA (Farrar), b. March 18, 1874.
2. LAURA A. (Farrar), b. Aug. 3, 1878.
3. HARRISON (Farrar), b. Oct. 8, 1888.

ELI WALES [5]; m. Sarah Ellen Baker, Feb. 22, 1875. Lives in Aurora, Kan. Children:
1. FREDERICK E. (Wales), b. March 22, 1878, in Madison County, Iowa.
2. JOHN LEROY (Wales), b. Dec. 9, 1879, in Walworth County, Wis.

ALICE WALES [6]; m. George B. Dunlap, May 6, 1885, at Elkhorn, Wis. Lives in Stevens Point, Wis. Children:
1. NELLIE (Wales), b. May 17, 1886, in Barabo, Wis.
2. EARL B. (Wales), b. July 26, 1893, in Waukesha, Wis.

WALTER WALES [7]; m. 1st, Julia Goodspeed, Sept. 15, 1881. She d. Dec. 25, 1882, and he m. 2d, Frank Montgomery, 1886, in Elkhorn, Wis., where he lives. Children:
1. MERTON (Wales), b. Dec. 25, 1882.
2. HARLEY (Wales), b. Feb. 24, 1887.
3. NETTIE IRENE (Wales), b. Oct. 24, 1889.
4. RISPAH MAY (Wales), b. May 20, 1892.

ARTHUR WALES [8]; m. Rita Isham, April 13, 1883. She was
b. Sept. 18, 1861. Live in Elkhorn, Wis. Children:
1. LULU (Wales), b. Sept. 7, 1884.
2. HERBERT (Wales), b. March 29, 1889.

173. EBEN VINE WALES [5]; m. Sept. 18, 1849, Helen M. Comstock.
She was born April 10, 1828. He was a Presbyterian minister, and d. June 28, 1878, at Oneonta, N. Y. She d. at Spra-
kers, Dec. 12, 1891. Children:
1. HELEN MARIA (Wales), b. June 20, 1850, at Laurens, N.
Y.; m. Clinton Ford, Sept. 30, 1875; lives at Oneonta,
N. Y.
2. EBEN VINE (Wales), b. Aug. 6, 1855; d. Nov. 2, 1863.

174. CHARLES WALES [6]; m. 1st, in Cortland, N. Y., Eliza Ann
Crandall, Oct. 26, 1848. She d. April 6, 1868, and he m. 2d,
Lorahama Butler, Dec. 20, 1869; lives at Elkhorn, Wis.
(1899). Children:
1. RUTH ELIZA (Wales), b. Sept. 20, 1849, at North
Geneva, Wis.; m. Fred W. Isham, June 1, 1893;
lives at Elkhorn, Wis.
2. ROSA PHILINDA (Wales), b. Aug. 3, 1851; m. Feb. 14,
1882, H. A. Newton; d. May 10, 1884.
3. RICHMOND (Wales), b. 1855; d. 1855.
4. BELLE BETHANIA (Wales), b. May 12, 1859, at North
Geneva; m. Clinton D. Dewing, Jan. 30. 1881.
5. CHARLES MARSHALL (Wales), b. May 2, 1862.
6. JANET (Wales), b. Oct. 26, 1880, at Elkhorn, Wis.; d.
Jan. 11, 1882.

CHARLES MARSHALL WALES [5]; married Katharine Gillet.
April 4. 1894, at Addison, N. Y.; lives (1899), 256 West 85th
street, New York City. Child:
1. KATHARINE ELIZA (Wales), b. July 15, 1898, at Addison,
N. Y.

175. GEORGE WALES [8]; m. 1st Eunice Catharine Ramsdell, May 4,
1842, in Plymouth, N. Y. She was b. Aug. 24, 1823. She d.
May 15, 1860. He then m. Mrs. Priscilla Annie Washburn
Scott, April 13, 1865. She was b. Aug. 11, 1839, in Merrimac, Mo. She d. Oct. 22, 1880, in Delavan, Wis. He d. in
North Geneva, March 17, 1895. Children:
1. MERCY LOVINIA (Wales), b. March 14, 1844, at Plymouth, N. Y.
2. SALLY AMELIA (Wales), b. Jan. 28, 1852, at Plymouth,
N. Y.; d. Feb. 12, 1852.
3. GEORGE (Wales), b. Jan. 25, 1867, at North Geneva,
Wis.
4. EUDORA FRANCES (Wales), b. Aug. 17, 1869, at Delavan, Wis.

MERCY LOVINIA WALES [1]; m. A. Wallace Wilcox, Oct. 5,
1862, at Plymouth, N. Y. She d. Jan. 17, 1883. Children:
1. CLARA LOVINIA (Wilcox), b. Aug. 1, 1864; m. Feb. 3,
1881, Henry E. Sabin.
2. GEORGE W. (Wilcox), b. Sept. 9, 1866; m. Susan Stone,
Sept. 27, 1894.
3. BERTHA L. (Wilcox), b. June 30, 1874.

176. MARY or POLLY CRAIN[4] [62], (Jonathan,[3] Ebenezer,[2]
ohn[1]), married James Swain, May 12, 1812. He was born in

Vermont, March, 15, 1785, and died June 6, 1853, at Cortland, N. Y. She died May 14, 1872, at Toledo, Ohio. Children:

1. MARY POLLY (Swain), b. Oct. 9, 1813, at Plymouth, N. Y.; d. Oct. 13, 1813.
2. IRVIN (Swain), b. April 13, 1815.
3. JAMES PERRY (Swain), b. June 30, 1817; d. March 28, 1843, in South Carolina.
4. RICHARD W. (Swain), b. July 2, 1819, in Cortlandville, N. Y.
5. CHARLES HARVEY (Swain), b. Feb. 28, 1822; d. Nov. 20, 1877, at Salt Lake City.
6. MARY ELVIRA (Swain), b. Aug. 23, 1826, at Plymouth, N. Y.
7. ALLEN (Swain), b. Sept. 11, 1831, at Cortland.

177. IRVIN SWAIN [2]; m. Rebecca Pike, Feb. 7, 1841. She was b. Jan. 31, 1816. He d. June 21, 1877, at Toledo, Ohio. She d. Sept. 24, 1897, at the same place. Children:
  1. FRANCES (Swain), b. July 25, 1845, in Cortland, N. Y.; d. Jan. 30, 1846.
  2. RANSOM P. (Swain), b. Aug. 31, 1847, in Cortland, N. Y.
  3. LUELLA (Swain), b. Dec. 2, 1849, in Cortland, N. Y.; d. Sept. 3, 1857.
  4. CHLOE FRANCES (Swain), b. Aug. 11, 1855, in Cortland.

RANSOM P. SWAIN [2]; m. Mary Brigham Dec. 28, 1876. She was b. June 17, 1855; living (1899) in Toledo, Ohio. Children:
  1. MAUD (Swain). b. Nov. 11, 1877.
  2. NETTIE (Swain), b. Nov. 16, 1879.
  3. IRVIN (Swain), b. Apr. 20, 1855.
  4. MILDRED (Swain), b. Dec 14, 1891.

CHLOE FRANCES SWAIN [4]; m. Peter C. Lowe April 15, 1882; lives (1899) in Toledo, Ohio. Children:
  1. EDNA (Lowe), b. July 6, 1883.
  2. GRACE (Lowe), b. Sept. 30, 1884.
  3. RUTH (Lowe), b. March 9, 1887.
  4. RALPH (Lowe), b. March 22, 1891.

178. RICHARD W. SWAIN [4]; m. in Charleston, S. C., Martha J. Cameron, May 9, 1850. She was b. Nov. 11. 1826. He d. May 1, 1891, in Toledo, Ohio, where his widow now (1899) resides. Children:
  1. JAMES PERRY (Swain), b. Apr. 3, 1851, at Charleston, S. C.; m. 1st, Feb. 8, 1876, Anna Mathews. She d. Apr., 1881; m. 2d, Dec. 7, 1887, Sadie Thompson. Resides in Cleveland, Ohio.
  2. CHARLES HARVEY (Swain), b. Jan, 16, 1853, in Cortland, N. Y.; d. Dec. 3, 1873.
  3. FRANCES JULIA (Swain), b. Jan. 15, 1855, in Toledo, Ohio; d. May 22, 1860.
  4. ARTHUR CAMERON (Swain), b. Dec. 3, 1856.
  5. LUELLA LOGAN (Swain), b. June 12, 1860.
ARTHUR CAMERON SWAIN [4]; m. Estella Robinson, May 25, 1886; lives (1899) Toledo, Ohio. Children:
  1. MARTHA (Swain), b. July 22, 1894.
  2. MARION (Swain), b. Jan. 17, 1897.

LUELLA LOGAN SWAIN [5]; m. William L. Schaefer Jan. 10, 1883. Residence, Toledo, O. Children:
  1. OTTO H. (Schaefer), b. March 17, 1885.

2. CHARLES H. (Schaefer), b. Déc. 12, 1886; d. Aug. 18, 1887.
3. CLARENCE (Schaefer), b. Sept. 28, 1889.

179. MARY ELVIRA SWAIN [6]; m. Richard D. Logan, Nov. 11, 1858, in Washington, Ark. She d. May 4, 1892, in Rogers, Ark., where the family reside.
  1. LILLIAN L. (Logan), b. Nov. 24, 1862, at Bethel, Owen Co., Ky.; lives (1899) at St. Louis, Mo.
  2. GERTRUDE N. (Logan), b. Dec. 20, 1864, in Toledo, Ohio; lives at St. Louis, Mo.
  3. SYDNOR M. (Logan), b. Sept. 2, 1868, in Jeffersonville, Ind.

SYDNOR M. LOGAN [3]; m. Bertha Chambers, Nov. 20, 1892, in Fort Smith, Ark., and d. July 26, 1894, at Rogers, Ark.
Child:
  1. EARL MARCELLUS (Logan), b. July 26, 1893, in Rogers. Ark.

180. ALLEN SWAIN [7]; m. Clara Partridge, Sept. 28, 1870; residence, St. Paul, Minn. Children:
  1. ALBERT (Swain), b. Dec. 19, 1871; d. Oct. 15, 1882.
  2. CHARLES (Swain), b. June 6, 1874; d. Jan. 8, 1874.
  3. EDWARD (Swain), b. Dec. 17, 1876.
  4. WALTER (Swain), b. Aug. 1, 1883.

181. ABIGAIL CRAIN[4] [63], (Jonathan,[3] Ebenezer,[2] John[1]), married 1st, Elisha Ransom. He died, leaving one child. She married 2d, Richard Crandall in 1817. He died in Elkhorn, Wis., in 1865. She died June 3, 1877, in Cortland, N. Y.
  Children:

  1. ELISHA DARWIN (Ransom).
  2. HIRAM (Crandall), b. May 14, 1818, in Plymouth, N. Y.
  3. RICHARD O. (Crandall), b. Aug. 12, 1820, in Norwich, N. Y.
  4. PHILINDA (Crandall), b. Sept. 10, 1822, in Norwich, N. Y.
  5. ELIZA ANN (Crandall), b. March 21, 1827, in Norwich, N. Y.
  6. ABBA MARIA (Crandall), b. Dec. 21, 1827; d. Aug. 28, 1829.
  7. BETHANIA (Crandall), b. Dec. 28, 1829, in Burdette, Tompkins Co., N. Y.
  8. ALBERT (Crandall), b. Aug. 8, 1835; d. Feb. 14, 1875, at North Geneva, Wis.
  9. EDWARD (Crandall), b. Dec. 3, 1838; d. March 16, 1839.

182. ELISHA DARWIN RANSOM [1]; m. 1st, Nancy Gifford in 1840. She d. and he m. 2d, Olive Courtwright, April 15, 1847. He d. Dec. 17, 1891, in Cortland, N. Y. His widow lives (1899) in Ithaca, N. Y. Children:
  1. JAMES ORVILLE (Ransom), b. July 29, 1841; d. Sept. 14, 1841.
  2. FRANK EATON (Ransom), b. April 30, 1848; d. Jan. 9, 1853.
  3. HARRIET EUDORA (Ransom), b. July 28, 1852; d. Jan. 1, 1860.

HIRAM CRANDALL [2]; m. 1st, Wilhelmena Sanders, Feb. 6, 1861, in Cortland, N. Y. She d. March 30, 1867, and he m. 2d, Jennie Barnes. He d. Aug. 31, 1881, in Cortland, N. Y.
Children:
  1. KATHARINE (Crandall), b. Dec. 29, 1863.
  2. RICHARD S. (Crandall), b. March 17, 1867; d. Feb. 10, 1881.

19

KATHARINE CRANDALL [1]; m. Sept. 2, 1885, Chicago, Ill.,
Charles B. Ver Nory, who was born in Accord, N. Y., Sept.
7, 1860. Residence (1899) Chicago. Child:
    1. WINIFRED (Ver Nory), b. July 14, 1891.

183. RICHARD O. CRANDALL [3]; m. in 1849, Mrs. Maria Cushman
Curtis, in Flint, Mich. She was b. June 13, 1818, in Toronto,
Can. He d. Jan. 30, 1893, in La Porte, Ind. She d. Sept. 1,
1894. He was a physician. Children:
    1. CHARLES SPENCER (Crandall), b. Oct. 12, 1852, in
       Waverly, N. Y.
    2. HIRAM MENDEZ (Crandall), b. Oct. 27, 1855, in
       Waverly, N. Y.; d. March, 1861, in La Porte, Ind.
    3. CLARA MARY (Crandall), b. May 1, 1857, in Oswego,
       N. Y.

CHARLES SPENCER CRANDALL [1]; m. 1st, Lina Ocoboch, April
28, 1879, in Harbor Springs, Mich. She was b. Jan. 20, 1852,
in Medina, N. Y., and d. Jan. 13, 1892. June 9, 1897, m. 2d, at
Fort Collins, Col., Maud Bell. She was b. Oct. 8, 1859, in
New York city. He is Professor of Plant Diseases in Agricultural College, Colorado. Child:
    1. LINETA (Crandall), b. April 19, 1882, in Harbor
       Springs, Mich.

CLARA MARY CRANDALL [3]; m. James A. Hughston, Jan. 9,
1892, at La Porte, Ind. He was b. April 18, 1845, at Unadilla, N. Y. Residence at La Porte, Ind. (1899).

PHILINDA CRANDALL [4]; m. David Flack, Jan. 24, 1852, at
Elkhorn, Wis., and d. Jan. 20, 1872. He d. there April 20,
1893. Children:
    1. HIRAM C. (Flack), b. March 23, 1855.
    2. MARY A. (Flack), b. Nov. 25, 1857.

HIRAM C. FLACK [1]; m. Amanda Bulkley, Oct. 26, 1881, in
Elkhorn, Wis. She was b. April 5, 1861. Residence at
Perry, Iowa. Child:
    1. FRANK W. (Flack), b. June 20, 1889.

184. BERTHANIA CRANDALL [7]; m. Charles Dunlap, Dec. 1, 1853.
Residence at Elkhorn, Wis. Children:
    1. GEORGE B. (Dunlap), b. June 4, 1856; m. Alice Wales,
       May 6, 1885.
    2. HORATIO S. (Dunlap), b. April 25, 1859.
    3. ALICE M. (Dunlap), b. Dec. 9, 1862; d. May 9, 1867.
    4. MARK C. (Dunlap), b. May 26, 1866.
    5. DORA H. (Dunlap), b. Sept. 25, 1868.
    6. WILLIAM P. (Dunlap), b. Feb. 6, 1871.
    7. CHARLES K. (Dunlap), b. Oct. 5, 1872.

185. HORATIO S. DUNLAP [2]; m. Julia Amos, Sept. 19, 1883. Residence (1899) Soulsbyville, Cal. Child:
    1. CHARLES K. (Dunlap), b. July 14, 1884.

MARK C. DUNLAP [4]; m. Laura Loyd, March 26, 1890, at
Janesville, Wis., where she was b. April 16, 1869. Residence
(1899) at Milwaukee. Children:
    1. LESTER (Dunlap), b. Jan. 21, 1891, in Elkhorn, Wis.
    2. LOYD K. (Dunlap), b. Nov. 13, 1894, in Janesville, Wis.;
       d. Dec. 16, 1894.

DORA H. DUNLAP [5]; m. Clinton Bennett, Oct. 10, 1894. Residence at Doon, Iowa. Child:
    1. CLIFFORD (Bennett), b. May 23, 1897.

WILLIAM P. DUNLAP [6]; m. Oct. 14, 1891, Lessie Dunbar.
Residence (1899) at Elkhorn, Wis. Children:
1. LEO D. (Dunlap), b. Aug. 24, 1892.
2. CLIFFORD C. (Dunlap), b. Nov. 28, 1894.

186. MARTHA CRAIN[4] [64], (Jonathan,[3] Ebenezer,[2] John[1]),
married Solomon Burrell Aldrich, April 4, 1822. He died June
11, 1872, at Warsaw, Minn. She was familiarly called Patty.
She died at Morristown, Minn., Aug. 24, 1881. Children:
1. MARTHA ANN (Aldrich), b. Jan. 24, 1823, in Virgil, Cortland
County, N. Y.
2. LEVI (Aldrich), b. Oct. 1, 1833, in Norwich, N. Y.
3. POLLY ANGELINA (Aldrich), b. May 24, 1835, in Virgil, N. Y.
4. GEORGE W. (Aldrich), b. Sept. 19, 1836, in Virgil, N. Y.
5. CURTIS P. (Aldrich), b. Jan. 10, 1838, in Virgil, N. Y.; d. Jan.
11, 1838.
6. IRA C. (Aldrich), b. May 9, 1839, in Virgil, N. Y.

MARTHA ANN ALDRICH [1]; m. Levi T. Brook, Oct. 2, 1846;
d. May 10, 1886, in Morristown, Minn. She d. Dec. 2, 1891.
Children:
1. WILLIAM E. (Brook), b. July 19, 1854, in Plymouth,
N. Y.

187. WILLIAM E. BROOK [1]; m. Ellen D. Moshier, May 16, 1880.
Lives (1899) in Rice County, Minn. Children:
1. ELMER F. (Brook), b. July 5, 1881.
2. CHARLES (Brook), b. Sept. 26, 1883.
3. ANNA M. (Brook), b. Oct. 3, 1885.
4. WALTER (Brook), b. Oct. 1, 1887; d. July 1, 1888.
5. CLARENCE (Brook), b. April 21, 1891.
6. MARTHA A. (Brook), b. Oct. 17, 1894.
7. HARRY (Brook), b. March 26, 1897; d. Sept. 8, 1897.

188. LEVI ALDRICH [2]; m. Eliza Wait, July 29, 1859, in Warsaw,
Minn., and d. Jan. 11, 1896, at Pipestone, Minn., where his
widow (1899) resides. Children:
1. ELMER E. (Aldrich), b. Aug. 7, 1861; d. Aug. 25, 1879.
2. MAYBELL E. (Aldrich), b. June 8, 1866.
3. RUTH C. (Aldrich), b. Feb. 2, 1869; d. Aug. 27, 1879.
4. OLIVIA L. (Aldrich), b. Aug. 19, 1871.
5. CLARENCE H. (Aldrich), b. June 2, 1881.

MAYBELL ALDRICH [2]; m. Lyman Taylor, Nov. 28, 1888. Residence at Rochester, N. Y. Children:
1. RUTH (Taylor), b. Dec. 16, 1889.
2. ELBERT (Taylor), b. Aug. 27, 1891.
3. ALLISON (Taylor), b. June 2, 1895.

OLIVIA L. ALDRICH [4]; m. John W. Kufus, Oct. 30, 1890. Residence at Pipestone, Minn. Children:
1. FLOYD (Kufus), b. Sept. 2, 1891.
2. MOLLY (Kufus), b. Jan. 11, 1893.
3. VERA (Kufus), b. Aug. 7, 1894.
4. ALMA (Kufus), b. May 17, 1896.

189. POLLY ANGELINA ALDRICH [3]; m. 1st, Alxander Evans, Feb.
13, 1853, at Plymouth, N. Y. He d. Jan. 11, 1891, and she m.
2d, Benjamin Clemons, July 26, 1894, at Morristown, Minn.
Residence at Warsaw, Rice County, Minn. Children:
1. FRANCIS A. (Evans), b. Aug. 12, 1854, in Plymouth, N.
Y.; m. Margaret Shaffer, Sept. 30, 1884.

  2. IDA M. (Evans), b. Sept. 23, 1856, in Plymouth, N. Y.
  3. ELMER E. (Evans), b. Sept. 21, 1861, in Preston, N. Y.
  4. ALICE MAY (Evans), b. Feb. 11, 1869; d. Jan. 4, 1873.

IDA M. EVANS [2]; m. William Griffith, July 4, 1877, at Warsaw, Minn. Children:
  1. EDITH F. (Griffith), b. Aug. 23, 1878.
  2. EARNEST (Griffith), b. June 23, 1880.
  3. BESSIE (Griffith), b. June 31, 1884.

ELMER E. EVANS [3]; m. Julia Sweeney, June 11, 1885. Lives in Rice County, Minn. Children:
  1. ALICE MAY (Evans), b. March 28, 1886; d. Feb. 24, 1888.
  2. GEORGE (Evans), b. June 3, 1889; d. Oct. 8, 1889.

190. GEORGE W. ALDRICH [4]; m. Margaret J. Gilhousen, June 5, 1860. Residence (1899) at Warsaw, Minn. Children:
  1. ROMANZO E. (Aldrich), b. April 7, 1861; d. Oct. 31, 1863.
  2. JAMES M. (Aldrich), b. Nov. 11, 1864.
  3. WILLIAM R. (Aldrich), b. Sept. 5, 1869.
  4. OTIS W. (Aldrich), b. July 26, 1873.
  5. GEORGE F. (Aldrich), b. Feb. 6, 1876; d. Feb. 8, 1896.
  6. CURTIS I. (Aldrich), b. March 28, 1880.
  7. ROY C. (Aldrich), b. Oct. 15, 1883.

191. JAMES M. ALDRICH [2]; m. Cora Wales, Oct. 25, 1884. Residence at Warsaw, Rice County, Minn. Children:
  1. MARTON (Aldrich), b. Aug. 21, 1885.
  2. FLOYD (Aldrich), b. Dec. 15, 1887.
  3. PEARL (Aldrich), b. Nov. 28, 1889.
  4. MAUD (Aldrich), b. Dec. 5, 1891.
  5. CLIFFORD (Aldrich), b. April 8, 1894.
  6. JAMES (Aldrich), b. Oct. 21, 1897.

WILLIAM R. ALDRICH [3]; m. Edna Dowe, July 19, 1890. Residence at Morristown, Rice County, Minn. Child:
  1. ARCHIE (Aldrich), b. April 4, 1892.

192. OTIS W. ALDRICH [4]; m. Maud Baker, Dec. 25, 1896. Residence at Warsaw, Minn. Child:
  1. HAZEL (Aldrich), b. Nov. 21, 1897.

193. IRA C. ALDRICH [6]; m. 1st, Laura I. Snyder, Jan. 1, 1866, at Fairbault, Minn. She d. April 14, 1891, and he m. Ida A. Clemons, July 26, 1894, at Morristown, Minn. Residence (1899) at Fairbault. Children:
  1. LLOYD B. (Aldrich), b. Oct. 5, 1866.
  2. INEZ V. (Aldrich), b. Dec. 16, 1871; d. April 8, 1892.

LLOYD B. ALDRICH [1]; m. Lizzie Doweney, April 27, 1892. Residence (1899) at Owatonna, Minn. Child:
  1. CATHERINE (Aldrich), b. May 8, 1893.

194. ROXANA CRAINE[4] [65], (Jonathan,[3] Ebenezer,[2] John[1]), married Taft Aldrich, in Chenango County, N. Y., in 1830, cousin to Solomon B. Aldrich, who married her sister, Martha Craine. He was born in Providence, R. I., April 27, 1804, and died Feb. 21, 1866, in Illinois. She died in Cortland, N. Y., in 1839. Children:
  1. CYRUS C. (Aldrich), b. Aug. 5, 1833.
  2. AMBROSE (Aldrich), b. May 14, 1838; wounded at battle of Pea Ridge, Ark.; d. April 1, 1862.
  3. HARRIET (Aldrich), b. June 20, 1839; d. April 11, 1840.

195. CYRUS C. ALDRICH [1]; m. Amánda Chapin, Feb. 18, 1854. She d. June 29, 1897. He lives in Elsinore, Cal. Children:

1. CHARLES C. (Aldrich), b. August, 1854, at Cincinnatus, N. Y.; d. 1854.
2. HERBERT C. (Aldrich), b. Sept. 13, 1858, at Warsaw, Rice Co., Minn.
3. LUELLA E. (Aldrich), b. June 5, 1860, at Morristown, Rice Co., Minn.
4. VICTOR L. (Aldrich), b. Sept. 11, 1864, at Morristown, Rice Co., Minn.
5. JESSE A. (Aldrich), b. July 24, 1876, at Morristown, Rice Co., Minn.
6. ARTHUR A. (Aldrich), b. 1879; lives in Elsinore, Cal.

HERBERT C. ALDRICH [2]; m. Mary J. Chapman, April 16, 1882, at Rochester, Minn. He lives in Moose, Beltrami Co., Minn. Children:

1. HARRY C. (Aldrich), b. Feb. 7, 1884, at Morristown, Minn.
2. CLARA M. (Aldrich), b. Dec. 16, 1887, at Maine, Minn.
3. JAMES C. (Aldrich), b. April 5, 1891, at Maine, Minn.
4. MAUD R. (Aldrich), b. Sept. 19, 1895, at Moose, Beltrami Co., Minn.
5. WALLACE (Aldrich), b. Aug. 29, 1896.

LUELLA EDITH ALDRICH [3]; m. Orange Bennett, Dec. 25, 1879, at Morristown, Minn. Children:

1. LILLIE P. (Bennett), b. Sept. 18, 1880; m. Mathew Bauer, April 8, 1896.
2. MABEL F. (Bennett), b. Oct. 22, 1882; lives in Morristown, Minn. ·

VICTOR L. ALDRICH [4]; m. Jennie Birch, in 1886, at Morristown, Minn. She was b. Sept. 3, 1868, at Fairbault, Minn. Children:

1. CHARLES R. (Aldrich), b. June 26, 1887, at Morristown.
2. ALFRED A. (Aldrich), b. Aug. 18, 1889, at Brownsville.
3. GRACE E. (Aldrich), b. Feb. 22, 1891, at Brownsville.
4. LESLIE J. (Aldrich), b. Jan. 21, 1894, at Brownsville.
5. CLAUD F. (Aldrich), b. Oct. 20, 1896, at Brownsville.

196. JONATHAN CRAINE[4] [67], (Jonathan,[3] Ebenezer,[2] John[1]), married Aug. 7, 1825, Susan Tiley Wales, at Plymouth, Chenango Co., N. Y. She was born Aug. 16, 1804, at Saybrook, Conn. He died Dec. 4, 1848, at Oriskany Falls, N. Y. She married 2d, Calvin Bently, March 29, 1856, and died March 28, 1876, in Clinton, N. Y. Children:

197—1. IRA, b. Oct. 24, 1828, at Plymouth; d. 1833.
198—2. CHARLES RICHARD, b. Feb. 15, 1831, at Cortland, N. Y.
199—3. SMITH WALES, b. April 5, 1833, at Cortland. N. Y.
200—4. ANTOINETTE, b. Nov. 12, 1835, at Oriskany Falls, N. Y.
201—5. LYMAN CURTIS, b. July 4, 1838, at Oriskany Falls, N. Y.; d. May 15, 1881, from result of confinement in Libby Prison.
202—6. FRANCES ADELAID, b. Aug. 25, 1841, at Oriskany Falls, N. Y.; d. March 2, 1843.
203—7. JAMES PERRY, b. May 17, 1844.
204—8. MARY ADELAIDE, b. June 20, 1847, at Hamilton, N. Y.

205. RACHEL CRAIN[4] [69], (Jonathan,[3] Ebenezer,[2] John[1]), married George Wales, at Plymouth, Chenango Co., N. Y., in

1834. His first wife was Rachel's sister, Sally Crain. She died Jan. 20, 1870, at North Geneva, Wisconsin. He died July 29, 1844, at Plymouth, N. Y. Children :

1. ALMIRA (Wales), b. Jan. 1, 1836, at Plymouth, N. Y.; resides in Elkhorn, Wis.
2. ELISHA CLARK (Wales), b. Nov. 2, 1839.
3. WILLIAM DWIGHT (Wales), b. Oct. 2, 1841.

ELISHA CLARK WALES [2]; m. Laura Rider. March 26, 1867, at Plymouth, N. Y. He d. Jan. 24, 1878, at Parkersburg, Kansas. She d. Child :

1. ALBERT (Wales), b. Oct. 18, 1870; d. March 28, 1888, at Parkersburg, Kan.

WILLIAM DWIGHT WALES [3]; m. Eva Hand, May 28, 1891, at Elkhorn, Wis. Reside in Springfield, Wis. Child :

1. DWIGHT HOWARD (Wales), b. Sept. 15, 1894; d. Dec. 13, 1894.

206. AMARIAH CRAIN[4] [72], (Amariah,[3] Ebenezer,[2] John[1]), married Betsey Hakes, born May 3, 1796, in New York State. They were married in Rensselaer County. He was a farmer. Removed to Indiana, where he died in September, 1854; she died there in 1863. Children :

207—1. GEORGE S., born July 31, 1820, in Montgomery Co., N. Y.
208—2. ORRIN.
209—3. JUDSON W.
210—4. ALFRED, b. 1827.
It is reported that another son lived in Michigan, but no name given.

211. ABIGAIL CRAINE[4] [79], (Roger,[3] Ebenezer,[2] John[1]), married Nov. 11, 1813, David Hopkins, at Groton, Tompkins Co , N. Y. She died Sept. 13, 1833, aged 47 years. Nine of their children lived to mature age, married, and had families. In furnishing the data for this family record, their daughter, Phebe Ann (Hopkins) Sullivan, of Geneva, Ohio, wrote, Jan. 13, 1898: "I will say, as Washington said of his mother, she was the nearest Heaven of all on earth I knew, and all but adoration was her due." Children :

1. ALFRED (Hopkins).
2. LAURA (Hopkins).
3. WARNER W. (Hopkins).
4. NANCY JANE (Hopkins).
5. MARY ABIGAIL (Hopkins), b. Nov. 11, 1819; m. —— Alden; resided at Coldwater, Mich.
6. HARRIETT (Hopkins).
7. DAVID (Hopkins).
8. PHEBE ANN (Hopkins), b. June 4, 1824; m. Josiah Sullivan; she d. at her home, N. Geneva, Ohio, May 13, 1899.
9. CHARLES M. (Hopkins).
10. HANNAH (Hopkins); d. in infancy.

212. SAMUEL CRAINE[4] [80], (Roger,[3] Ebenezer,[2] John[1]), married Theodora Thirston, Dec. 26, 1809, at Cincinnatus, N. Y. He died in Michigan, June 15, 1872. Child :

213—1. LOVINA; m. —— Oakley; no children.

214. CYRUS CRAINE[4] [81], (Roger,[3] Ebenezer,[2] John[1]), married Sarah Snow. Children:

215—1. EDGAR, b. Aug. 15, 1813; went to Tennessee; m. and had family.
216—2. SARAH ANN, b. March 25, 1815; m.
217—3. MARY, b. March 27, 1817; d. Feb. 14, 1844.
218—4. CAMILLA, b. Dec. 27, 1818.
219—5. SYBIL MARILLA, b. May 29, 1821; d.
220—6. RUTH MARILLA, b. Aug. 22, 1823; d.
221—7. CYRUS S., b. May 23, 1825.
222—8. ROSANNA. b. March 26, 1827.
223—9. HENRY MARTYN, b. April 13, 1829; m. Maggie Howe.

224. AHIRA CRAINE[4] [82], (Roger,[3] Ebenezer,[2] John[1]), married —— ——. He died April 3, 1874, at the home of his son, Lewis S. Craine, Traverse City, Mich. Children:

225—1. AHIRA B., b. May 7, 1823.
226—2. ESTHER, b. July 23, 1824.
227—3. LEWIS S., b. March 15, 1826.
228—4. ABIGAIL, b. Oct. 21, 1827.
229—5. MILTON W., b. Sept. 6, 1830.
230—6. CYRUS R., b. May 7, 1833.
231—7. SAMUEL E., b. Oct. 31, 1835.

232. Dr. ELEAZER WHITING CRAINE[4] [83], (Roger,[3] Ebenezer,[2] John[1]), married 1st, Lydia Willoughby, April 25, 1815. She was born July 7, 1796, and died Jan. 7, 1840. For a time they resided in Groton, N. Y. He married 2d, Ruby Ann Demmon. They removed to Kent, Ohio, in 1843. He practiced his profession as a physician both in Groton and in Kent. He died March 4, 1866. Children:

233—1. EDMUND F., b. Jan. 14, 1816; d. June 27, 1832.
234—2. LAURETTA E., b. April 16, 1818; d. July 10, 1822.
235—3. JOSIAH WILLOUGHBY, b. Oct. 5, 1820.
236—4. A son, b. April 10, 1823; d. June 5, 1823.
237—5. HENRY C., b. March 4, 1825; d. Sept. 12, 1825.
238—6. LYDIA O. E., b. July 5, 1827.
239—7. SARAH M., b. Aug. 8, 1833.
240—8. EMMA W., b. April 27, 1836.
241—9. GEO. BYRON, b. May 19, 1841; d. 1861.
242-10. LEWIS CASS, b. October, 1847; m. Minnie Smith, at West Haven, Conn.; killed in Ashtabula disaster, December, 1876.
243-11. WALTER S., b. ——, at Groton, N. Y.
244-12. FRANK D., b. July 20, 1853.
245-13. EVALINE; said to have m. —— Dean, at Goshen, Ind

246. TOWER WHITING CRAINE[4] [84], (Roger,[3] Ebenezer,[2] John[1]), married 1st, Nov. 6, 1822, at Marcellus, N. Y., Nancy Anna Whiting, born at Ashford, Conn., March 1, 1802; died at Mentor, Ohio, in 1856. He married 2d, Jan. 28, 1857, Ann S. Grey, at Madison, Ohio, born in Massachusetts. He married 3d, Jan. 3, 1875, Marinda A. Griswold, at Painesville, Ohio, born June 9, 1825, at Mentor, Ohio. Painesville, Ohio, has been his

home since 1832, having previously resided in Genoa and Groton, N. Y. He was a farmer and shoemaker. Children:

247—1. GILES W., b. Sept. 29, 1823, at Genoa, N. Y.
248—2. LOUISA J., b. April 4, 1825, at Groton, N. Y.; d. Oct. 30, 1849.
249—3. CHARLES M., b. March 27, 1829, at Perry, Ohio.
250—4. HENRY W., b. Oct. 19, 1830.
251—5. LORETTA A., b. Nov 17, 1832, at Painesville, Ohio; d. Feb. 2, 1834.
252—6. SAMUEL T., b. Aug. 12, 1834; d. Sept. 12, 1835.
253—7. CHARLOTTE E., b. May 25, 1836.
254—8. JARED W., b. Jan. 4, 1838; d. March 4, 1839.
255—9. HARLAN P., b. April 27, 1840; d. March 20, 1862.
256—10. FRANKLIN E., b. April 29, 1844.

257. ALVIN CRAINE[4] [86], (Roger,[3] Ebenezer,[2] John[1]), was born in Genoa, Cayuga Co., N. Y. He was twice married. His first wife was the widow Castle, whose maiden name was Lydia Niles. She died June, 1824, leaving children by Mr. Castle, but only one by marriage with Mr. Craine, a daughter. He married 2d, Feb. 8, 1827, Tamzen Seaton, a native of the same place. Occupation, clock-maker. Justice of the peace, twelve years. Last residence, Brownsville, Houston Co., Minn. Children:

258—1. CORDELIA, b. June 2, 1824; m. Norman Perry, 1842; d. Sept., 1879.
259—2. FREDERICK WILLIAM AUGUSTUS, b. 1827; m. Martha Lowell, 1853, at Baraboo, Wis.; is a silversmith and resides at Brownsville, Minn. Served in late war; was corporal in 27th Iowa Volunteers.
260—3. MARY MELISSA.
261—4. EDMUND FRANKLIN, b. May 20, 1830; served in Civil War.
262—5. SARAH JANE.
263—6. HORACE NEWTON. Watchmaker and jeweler; m. T. P. Longfellow, Minneapolis, Minn.
264—7. JOSEPHINE LOVINIA.
265—8. ELEAZER WHITING. Served in Civil War.

266. ALEXIS CRAINE[4] [87], (Roger,[3] Ebenezer,[2] John[1]), married Elizabeth Clark. He died at his home in Winfield, Cowley Co., Kansas, Dec. 25, 1890, at the age of 83. She died April 21, 1893, aged 85. Five of their sons served in the Union army in the Civil War. Children:

267—1. JAMES ALEXIS; lives in Kansas City.
268—2. ELIJAH EVANS; lives in Kansas City.
269—3. ISAAC CLARK; d. Oklahoma, 1897.
270—4. DAVID C; d. in Arkansas, 1898.
271—5. ANNE B.; m. A. B. Knight; lives in New Salem, Kan.
272—6. SARAH SOPHIA; m. Chas. Everett; lives in Winfield, Kan.
273—7. JOHN; lives in Winfield, Kan.
274—8. RICHARD HENRY; m.; lives in Kansas City.
275—9. MARTIN ROGER; m. and has three sons; lives in Oklahoma.
276—10. CHARLES AUGUSTUS; m. and lives in Kankakee, Ill.

277. ISAAC CRANE[4] [89], [Hezekiah,[3] Hezekiah[2], John[1]), married Jan. 19, 1795, widow Sarah Leonard, daughter of Solo-

mon Abbe, Jr., and settled in that part of Mansfield now called Atwoodville. Was a weaver and manufacturer of carpets, mats, robes, etc., also had a carding factory. Children:

278—1. HEZEKIAH, b. Dec. 25, 1795.
279—2. JESSE, b. June 7, 1797.
280—3. HARRY, b. May 10, 1799.
281—4. SOPHIA, b. June 1, 1802; m. Westhorp Geer; lives in Ill.
282—5. ANNA, b. March 30, 1806; m. E. Chapman Moulton.
283—6. CAROLINE, b. Jan. 14, 1808; m. Alvin Moulton of Chaplin.
284—7. AMANDA, b. April 6, 1809; m. Azariah Freeman; lives in Valparaiso, Ind.
285—8. SARAH ABBE, b. March 24, 1811; m. Aaron Geer; lives in Willimantic.
286—9. MARTHA, b. June 21, 1815; m. Manning F. Hunt of Chaplin.

287. JESSE Crane[4] [91], (Hezekiah,[3] Hezekiah,[2] John[1]), married Sept. 16, 1798, Rhoda Abbe, daughter of Solomon A., Jr., and Lucy (Johnson) Abbe, b. March 2, 1781. He was a farmer, and lived in Mansfield, Conn. He died April 7, 1862, aged 83. Children:

288—1. CHARLES, b. Feb. 5, 1799.
289—2. MILLEN, b. Dec. 19. 1802.
290—3. ORIGEN, b. July 25, 1804.
291—4. ABBY ANN, b. Feb. 19, 1810; m. Eleazer Freeman.
292—5. MARY ANN, b. May 30, 1813; m. Enoch Freeman; 2d, Thos. Alexander.
293—6. MARILLA; m. Albert Storrs.

294. ASA CRAIN[4] [92], (Hezekiah,[3] Hezekiah,[2] John[1]), married 1st, Welthy, daughter of Timothy Babcock, Nov. 28, 1805, at Ashford, Conn., where she was born May 27, 1785. She died there, Aug. 22, 1823. Married 2d, Mary B. Balch, Oct. 26, 1823. She was born July 20, 1797. He died in Cicero, N. Y., Oct. 2, 1844. Children:

295—1. ALMYRON W., b. Jan. 17, 1807, in Ashford, Conn.
296—2. GEORGE S. B., b. Oct. 6, 1808, in Ashford, Conn.
297—3. ACHSAH BABCOCK, b. Sept. 22, 1811, in Ware, Mass.; m. Ebenezer G. Lamb, Cicero, N. Y.; d. leaving 2 children, in Clinton, Mich.
298—4. TIMOTHY B., b. Aug. 25, 1814, in Ashford, Conn.
299—5. ARCHIBALD B., b. Aug. 2, 1817, in Mansfield, Conn.
300—6. ROSETTA, b. Oct. 27, 1819, in Mansfield, Conn.
301—7. WELTHY. E., b. Dec. 2, 1822, in Ashford; d. July 10, 1823.
302—8. WELTHY, b. Sept. 16, 1824, in Mansfield; d. May 10, 1840.
303—9. SOPHIA, b. Aug. 6, 1829, in Cicero, N. Y.
304—10. ISAAC, b. March 11, 1832.
305—11. HARRIETT AMANDA, b. March 7, 1834.
306—12. MARYETTE, b. Aug. 2, 1837; m. Geo. W. Ward; living (1866) in Fulton, N. Y. 2 children.
307—13. CAROLINE ELIZABETH, b. Dec. 30, 1839.

308. AMASA CRAIN[4] [93], [Hezekiah,[3] Hezekiah,[2] John[1]), married Elizabeth Bugsby. She was born Dec. 17, 1787. He died June 11, 1832. She died April, 1872. Soon after marriage they removed from Connecticut, to Thompson Township, Sulli-

20

van Co., N. Y., at which time the country was a wilderness.
Had a number of children who died young.   Children :

309—1. RALPH, 2. HEZEKIAH, 3. JOSIAH, 4. LESTER. d. young.
310—5. AUSTIN BUGSBY, b. April 9, 1816.

311. DANIEL CRAIN[4] [95], (Hezekiah[3], Hezekiah[2], John[1]),
married Eunice Conant, born about 1801.   He had two sons
and a daughter; only one son living in 1864.   Child :

312—1. EDMUND; residence, Willimantic (1887).

313. ZERVIAH CRANE[4] [96], (Hezekiah,[3] Hezekiah,[2] John[1]),
married Thomas Baldwin, of Mansfield, Conn., about 1825, and
removed to New York State.   Children :

1. ANNA (Baldwin); m. Wm. V. Johnson, of Mansfield.
2. EBENEZER (Baldwin).
3. DANIEL (Baldwin).
4. MANSFIELD (Baldwin).
5. WINDHAM (Baldwin).
      And perhaps others.

314. ANNA CRANE[4] [97], (Hezekiah,[3] Hezekiah,[2] John[1]),
married Simeon Abbe, of Mansfield, Conn.   She died October
5, 1822.   He then married Lydia Nichols, by whom he had
eight children.   Children :

1. LUCY (Abbe), b. May 25, 1810.
2. FEARING (Abbe), b. Nov. 8, 1811; m. Julia A. Thompson.
3. AUSTIN (Abbe), b. May 5, 1813; m. Clarissa Gordon.
4. LUCY ANN (Abbe), b. July 26, 1820; m. Joseph Woodward and
      settled in Mansfield, and have three children.

315. DANIEL CRANE[4] [99], (Daniel,[3] Hezekiah,[2] John[1]),
married in 1807, Clarissa Whitman, of Williamsburg, Mass.   He
died in Lisle, N. Y.   Children :

316—1. ESTHER FULLER; m. Wm. Butterfield, of Syracuse, N. Y.
317—2. ELECTA; m. Amos Hoadley.
318—3. LUCIAN E.; m. Hannah Jenning.
319—4. SHEPHERD P., b. May 29, 1813; m. Almira Bosworth.
320—5. ABBY ANN; m. Henry Williams.
321—6. HARRIET; m. William Burnham.
322—7. HANNAH; m. Niles Woodworth, of Franklin, N. Y.
323—8. CHARLES B.; m. Speedy Dexter, of Fayette, N. Y.

324. CLARISSA CRANE[4] [101], (Daniel,[3] Hezekiah,[2] John[1]),
married Elijah Eldridge, Dec. 31, 1806.   She died Oct. 22, 1809.
He married 2d, June 21, 1810, Sally Hunt, by whom he had eight
children.   She was living (1864) at Willington, Conn.   Children :

1. CLARISSA (Eldridge), b. Feb. 24, 1808.
2. ESTHER (Eldridge), b. May 5, 1809.

325. CORDIAL S. CRANE[4] [102], (Daniel,[3] Hezekiah,[2] John[1]),
married 1st, Mary Cross in 1808; 2d, Mary Wheeler, June 10,
1822; 3d, Lucy Rising, who died May 29, 1863.   Lived in
Mansfield until after second marriage, when he removed to

Willimantic. After the death of second wife he returned to Mansfield, and in 1864 was living with his son Harvey. Children :

326—1. HARVEY L., b. Oct. 5, 1810.
327—2. WILLIAM H., b. Aug. 31, 1812.
328—3. JEHIEL W., b. Nov. 20, 1814; d. 1815.
329—4. MARY B., b. May 7, 1816.

330. SYBIL CRANE[4] [103], (Daniel,[3] Hezekiah,[2] John[1]), married Parley Kendall, June 22, 1805. Living (1864) in Whitewater, Wis. Parley Kendall settled on a farm near Springfield, Mass., but in 1833 he removed to Cortland, N. Y., where he died in 1838. About the year 1842 the family removed to Whitewater, Wis. She married 2d, Lyman Randall and died in 1868. Her son Albert's children reside at or near that place. Children :

1. HANNAH (Kendall), b. March 2, 1808; m. Mr. Fales, and d. 1831 at South Dedham.
2. LYMAN (Kendall), b. Dec. 3, 1809; m. Helen Chamberlin in Cortland, N. Y., 1838; lived and d. at Kalamazoo, Mich., 1843.
3. MARIA (Kendall), b. 1813; m. Benj. Freeman, and d. at Whitewater, Wis., 1850.
4. LUCIUS BOLES (Kendall), b. 1816; d. at Cortland, N. Y., 1836.
5. CLARISSA Kendall), b. 1818; m. Benj. Freeman; d. at Whitewater, Wis., 1840.
6. ALBERT (Kendall), b. 1820; m. 1st, Martha P. Woodbury; 2d, Jane Pratt. He d. 1877 in Whitewater, Wis.

331. JONATHAN CRANE[4] [105], (Daniel,[3] Hezekiah,[2] John[1]), married Orpha Barrows, May 10, 1810. She was born in Mansfield, Conn., Dec. 27, 1788, daughter of Ethan. She died in 1824. He then married 2d, Azubah Hamilton, of Brookfield, Mass. He was born in North Mansfield, Conn., where he passed his boyhood days, receiving his early education in the country schools. At the age of eighteen he left home and located at Newburgh, N. Y. In 1814 Mr. Crane removed to Schenectady, which place he afterwards made his home. In 1819 he purchased a large tract of land, and erected factories that have since continued to be among the chief industries of the place. The first passenger railway built from Albany to Schenectady passed near his factories, attracting his interest in railway construction, and, with the use of inventions of his own, assisted in the building of the Hartford & New Haven, Providence & Stonington, Boston & Providence, Boston & Albany, and Boston & Maine railways. For many years he carried on the manufacture of screws, and was a man of much financial ability and business energy, with a true Christian character. He served as alderman for Schenectady. He died Oct. 9, 1870. Children :

332—1. ETHAN B., b. July 11, 1811.
333—2. JONATHAN, b. March, 1814.
334—3. EDWARD, b. 1816.
335—4. CORDIAL S., b. 1819.

336—5. ELIZA, b. March 24, 1820; m. J. R. Hayward. Residence
 (1842) at Hannibal, Mo.
337—6. DAVID; d. in infancy.
338—7. CATHARINE HAMILTON, b. 1825; d. Sept. 5, 1841.
339—8. LUCINDA, b. 1827.
340—9. HENRY MARTYN, b. 1828.
341-10. MARTHA O., b. 1834.

342.   BELA CRANE[4] [106], (Daniel,[3] Hezekiah,[2] John[1]), married Sept. 28, 1816. at Half Moon (now Orange), Saratoga Co.,
N. Y., Deborah Aylworth. She was born there March 27. 1794.
Mr. Crane served six months at Sackett's Harbor in 1812, and
four months in New York city in 1814; was a musician in both
campaigns. Mr. Crane has resided in Mansfield, Conn., where
five generations of Cranes have been born and lived on the
old homestead, which has been in the possession of the family
two hundred years. He has also lived in Schenectady, Troy, N.
Y., Saratoga Co., Delaware Co.. N. Y., Luzerne Co., Pa. ; but
in December, 1879, was residing in Middletown, Orange Co., N.
Y. Has held the office of school director and supervisor in Delaware Co., N. Y. By occupation has been a farmer, raftsman
and ropemaker. Children :

343—1. MELISSA CATHARINE, b. July 20, 1817, in Schenectady, N. Y.
344—2. MELANCTHON CRYDENWISE, b. July 26, 1824, in Delaware
  · Co., N. Y.

345.   LIBBEUS CRAIN[4] [109], (Elisha,[3] Hezekiah,[2] John[1]),
married Sally Dimick, Nov. 9, 1800. He was a blacksmith, and
died at Cassville, Oneida Co., N. Y., Nov. 25, 1858. Child :

346—1. LAFAYETTE, b. July 27, 1824.

347.   NATHAN CRAIN[4] [119], (David E.,[3] Hezekiah,[2] John,[1]),
married Mary Choate. She was born in Leicester, Mass., Nov.
15, 1787. He died at Evans Mills, Jefferson Co., N. Y., May
4, 1837. She died at same place May 27, 1830. Children :

348 —1. ISAAC S., b. June 3, 1810, in Canton, St. Lawrence Co., N. Y.
349—2. PHEBE A., b. June 26, 1812, in Dorset, Vt.; d. Nov. 18, 1857.
350—3. GEORGE W., b. Sept. 13, 1814, in Rutland, Vt; d. in Grinnell,
  Iowa.
351—4. MARIANN, b. Sept. 5, 1816, in Felt's Mills.
352—5. CHARLES E., b. June 26, 1819, in Le Roy; d. May 14, 1824.
353—6. BETSEY M., b. Sept. 3, 1822.
354—7. OLIVE W., b. Jan. 5, 1824.
355—8. RUTH K., b. Nov. 25, 1826.
356—9. EVELINE W., b. March 8, 1828.

357.   DAVID ELDRIDGE CRAIN[4] [121], (David E,[3] Hezekiah,[2]
John[1]), married 1st, ——; 2d, Mary Pepper at Ogdensburg, N.
Y., in 1829. She was born Feb. 4, 1805, in Enniscorthy,
County of Wexford, Ireland. He died at Maitland, Ontario,
Canada, May 8, 1849. She died at Brockville, Ontaria, Oct.
31, 1889. First three children, born in Canton, St. Lawrence
Co., N. Y., were by his first wife, who died at that place;

all the other children were born in Maitland, Ontario, Canada.
Children :

358—1. LORETTA.
359—2. SARIAH MORIAH.
360—3. MALISSA.
361—4. ELIZA J., b. May 7, 1830.
362—5. HIRAM ABIFF, b. Sept. 8, 1832.
363—6. ROBERT, b. Oct. 14, 1834.
364—7. LEVI, b. July 13, 1836.
365—8. JOHN, b. April 16, 1838; d. at Manteno, Ill., Feb., 1856.
366—9. GEORGE, b. March 29, 1841; m. 1st, Feb. 15, 1871, Emma
Elizabeth Aylsworth, of Bath, Ontario, Canada. She d.
May 9, 1872, and he m. Aug. 2, 1876, Adeline Church
Leggo, of Ottawa; no children. He is an architect and
builder; also a manufacturer of woolen goods.
367-10. MARY ANN, b. Oct. 14, 1844.

368. RACHEL BALDWIN CRAIN[4] [125], (David E.,[3] Hezekiah,[2] John[1]), married, in 1833, Allin Grover, of Wells, Vt.; born
1802. She died Sept. 3, 1887. He was a merchant there, and
represented his town in the Vermont legislature, 1838, and died
in 1865. She, by her first husband, had a daughter, Luthera
Cornelia (Harnden), born in Poultney, Vt., Dec. 7, 1824, who
married Rev. William H. Hull, minister of the Methodist Episcopal Church. Mrs. Hull died Jan. 14, 1885, leaving no children.
Children :

1. ALLIN CRAIN (Grover), b. March 31, 1837, in Wells, Vt.
2. MARCUS DELETT (Grover), b. June 18, 1841, in Wells, Vt.

369. Dr. ALLIN CRAIN GROVER [1]; m. Corinthia Vandermarker.
She was b. in Chester, Warren Co., N. Y., in 1848. They
were m. there Dec. 24, 1874, and settled at Wells, Vt., where
he has carried on a farm and practiced his profession, he
being a graduate of the Albany Medical College in 1866. Was
selectman for Wells in the years 1872, 1873 and 1874. In
1884 he removed to Port Henry, N. Y., where he now (1897)
resides and practices his profession. Children :
1. MARCUS ALLIN (Grover), b. Aug. 7, 1876, in Wells, Vt.
2. ANNIS LUTHERA (Grover), b. Sept. 3, 1878, in Wells,
Vt.
3. ADRAIN CRAIN (Grover), b. Dec. 20, 1880, in Wells, Vt.
4. SCOTT VANDERMARKER (Grover), b. Nov. 14, 1884; d.
at Port Henry, N. Y., Sept. 1, 1885.

370. MARCUS DELETT GROVER [2]; m. Virginia A. Townsend, of
Jordan, Onondaga Co., N. Y., October, 1869. He is a lawyer
of considerable prominence. He now (1897) resides at St.
Paul, Minn., and is general soclicitor for the Great Northern
Railroad. Children :
1. VINNIE LUTHERA (Grover), b. April 3, 1871, in Wells,
Vt.
2. MYRA ELECTA (Grover), b. May 5, 1876, in Port
Henry, N. Y.

371. RUTH BALDWIN CRAIN[4] [128], (David E,[3] Hezekiah,[2]
John[1]), born in Dorset, Vt. Married at Poultney, July 6, 1824,
Chester Whitney, a native of Poultney, born May 22, 1798. He

was a farmer, and died in the town where he was born Aug. 6, 1845. She died there July 29, 1845. Children :

1. RACHEL E. (Whitney), b. July 29, 1825 ; m. Sept. 12, 1846.
2. JOHN (Whitney), b. Jan. 16, 1827 ; m. July 3, 1851 ; d. Jan., 1864, in San Francisco, Cal.
3. SARAH (Whitney), b. May 5, 1829 ; m. May 7, 1857.
4. HIRAM (Whitney), b. 1831 ; d. aged 10 months.
5. MINERVA (Whitney), b. 1834 ; d. aged 18 months.
6. ANN W. (Whitney), b. Sept. 1, 1835 ; m. Jan., 1852, at Wells, Vt.

372. TAMESIN ELDRIDGE CRAIN[4] [129], (David E.,[3] Hezekiah,[2] John,[1]), married Feb. 21, 1828, in Poultney, Vt., John K. Webster, of Hampton, Washington Co., N. Y., at which place their eldest child was born. He died Feb. 15, 1856. She was living Nov. 4, 1897, with her son Hiram D., in Jefferson, Allen Co., Ind., the only survivor of her father's family, aged 89. Children :

1. BUEL CRAIN (Webster), b. May 5, 1829, in Warsaw, Wyoming Co., N. Y.
2. EARLINE A. (Webster), b. May 6, 1832.
3. HIRAM D. (Webster), b. Feb. 22, 1835, in Huron, Erie Co., Ohio.
4. FANNIE M. (Webster), b. Oct. 31, 1837.
5. MARY L. (Webster), b. June 15, 1840.
6. JOHN W. (Webster), b. March 29, 1842.

HIRAM D. WEBSTER [3]; m. Jan. 1, 1860, Sophia Miller, of Unity, Columbiana Co., Ohio. She was b. Dec. 25, 1840, and settled in Jefferson, Allen Co., Ind. Children :
1. NATHAN CRAIN (Webster).
2. MARTHA M. (Webster), b. Jan. 11, 1863 ; d. Feb. 22, 1871.
3. JOHN W. (Webster), b. March 23, 1865.
4. WARREN B. (Webster), b. Dec. 25, 1866.
5. DELETT GROVER (Webster), b. July 16, 1869.
6. IDA J. (Webster), b. June 21, 1872.
7. HIRAM D. (Webster), b. April 13, 1875.
8. ELMA L. (Webster), b. and d. April 28, 1878.
9. MYRA E. (Webster), b. June 6, 1880.

NATHAN CRAIN WEBSTER [1]; m. Sept. 9, 1884, Addie J. Brandlier. She was b. in Jefferson, Allen Co., Ind., Oct. 15, 1861. Children :
1. JULIA A. (Webster), b. Aug. 5, 1885.
2. WILLARD H. (Webster), b. Feb. 21, 1888 ; d. March 17, 1888.
3. HIRAM D. (Webster), b. June 15, 1890.
4. MABEL M. (Webster), b. April 9, 1892.
5. HOWARD E. (Webster), b. Jan. 12, 1895.
6. WILMUR E. (Webster), b. March 29, 1897.

FIFTH GENERATION.

373. JOHN CRANE[5] [135], (Stephen,[4] John,[3] John,[2] John[1]), married Sarah Burke. Oct. 4, 1811, he sold for $120 his interest in the same lot of. land that his father Stephen Crane mortgaged to Oliver Bliss, to his brother Cyrus Crane, housewright. There were several transfers back and forth between the brothers John and Cyrus, and the widow Mary Crane. About the year 1816 Mr. Crane removed from Wilbraham, Mass., to Cortland, Cortland Co., N. Y., and from there John Crane and his family removed to Addison, Steuben Co., N. Y. Oct. 24, 1811, he sold land in Wilbraham to William Rindge for $560. He sold land in Wilbraham for $275, Dec. 2, 1815, and again to John Bliss for $400, July 9, 1816. Children:

374—1. STEPHEN; killed by lightning, aged 12 years.
375—2. CYRUS LYMAN.
376—3. JOHN M., b. Dec. 19, 1812.
377—4. WILLIAM E.
378—5. ANSON; m. Mary Jane Hutchinson; no children.
379—6. ALONZO G.
380—7. EGBERT L.
381—8. LETTICE MARIA, b. May 15, 1810; m.
382—9. MARY A.
383-10. SARAH; m. R. Jones.

384. CYRUS CRANE[5] [136], (Stephen,[4] John,[3] John,[2] John[1]), married Mary Chapin, July 20, 1809. She was a daughter of Abner and Rhoda (Kibbe) Chapin, born April 7, 1789. Abner Chapin was private in Capt. Paul Langdon's company of minutemen (Wilbraham company), marched in response to the alarm April 19, 1775, April 20, served nine days. Enlisted April 29, 1775, in the army in same company, Col. Timothy Danielson's regiment, muster-roll dated Aug. 1, 1775; in service Oct. 6, 1775, and also Dec. 25, same year. Probably the same Abner who was corporal, Capt. James Shaw's company detached from Col. Chas. Pynchon's regiment, entered service Sept. 24, 1777, discharged Oct. 18, 1777, ordered to join army under General Gates. Cyrus Crane was of rather a wild, restless disposition. Left home (so his son Rollin writes) when he was very young, that he was a soldier in War of 1812, and was drowned in New York State, July 20, 1832. Cyrus Crane, Oct. 14, 1811, sold his interest in the home estate to his brother John Crane for $250, and must have left Wilbraham soon afterward, for his son Rollin was not old enough to remember him. She died Jan. 4, 1864.

Children :

385—1. ROLLIN C., b. May 8, 1811.
386—2. JULIA A., b. Nov. 5, 1813.

387. EBENEZER CRANE[5] [138], (Ebenezer,[4] Ebenezer,[3] Ebenezer,[2] John[1]), m. January, 1822, Rebecca Gordon Russell, daughter of John Russell. She was born at Dublin, N. H., April 19, 1801. He first went to Dalton, N. H., in 1815, and worked one season for his uncle Robert Crane on the same farm he afterwards made his home and what is now known as the "Crane Farm." That year, 1815, he excavated the cellar for the house, now the homestead, the house having been completed in 1816. He received a deed of this place from his father, and went there to live in 1819, taking his bride there in January, 1822. The father of Mrs Crane was a soldier in the Revolutionary war, born June, 1760; died 1829. John Russell married Abigail Gordon of Rindge, N. H., born in 1780. He was born in Harvard, Mass. Mr. Crane was a man of great energy, and for many years carried on farming on a large scale, having as many as three farms under cultivation at one time. He died at Dalton, Oct. 5, 1867.
Children :

388—1. ABBY ELIZA, b. Nov. 11, 1822.
389—2. RHODA R., b. June 1, 1824; d. Nov. 2, 1892.
390—3. GEORGE EBEN, b. March 31, 1826.
391—4. SAPHRONIA M., b. March 18, 1828; d. July 4, 1855.
392—5. FRANK R., b. July 31, 1831.
393—6. CHARLES ALBERT, b. Feb. 26, 1833.
394—7. FRANCIS J., b. April 19, 1835.
395—8. Infant son, b. and d. March, 1837.
396—9. LOUISA M., b. June 11, 1839.
397-10. M. ELIZABETH, b. Dec. 25, 1843.
398-11. ELBRIDGE G., b. Nov. 25, 1845; d. Oct. 27, 1890.

399. SYLVESTER CRAIN[5] [153], (Sylvester,[4] Jonathan,[3] Ebenezer,[2] John[1]), married Mary A. Goodell, Nov. 5, 1833, at Cortland, N. Y. She was born Aug. 11, 1813; d. May 14, 1883. He died April 22, 1878, at Virgil, Cortland Co., N. Y.
Children :

400—1. SYLVESTER, b. Jan. 20, 1835.
401—2. MARY M., b. Feb. 15, 1837.
402—3. EDWARD A., b. Aug. 5, 1838.
403—4. SAMANTHA E., b. Jan. 10, 1839.

404. JONATHAN G. CRAIN[5] [154], (Sylvester,[4] Jonathan,[3] Ebenezer,[2] John[1]), married Nancy Pettis, Nov. 14, 1839, at Groton, N. Y. He died Aug. 8, 1896, at Cortlandville, N. Y. She was born April 29, 1816, at Groton, and was living in 1899 at South Cortland, N. Y. Children :

405—1. MARY, b. Oct. 31, 1855.
406—2. WILBER C., b. Aug. 11, 1858.

407. SALLY CRAIN[5] [155], (Sylvester,[4] Jonathan,[3] Ebenezer,[2] John[1]), married Edward Adriance, Oct. 10, 1839. He was born April 18, 1814, in Dutchess County, N. Y. She died Oct. 19, 1844, at Scipio, Cayuga Co., N. Y. He died Jan. 16, 1884, at Delhi, Ohio.

Child:

1. ELLEN (Adriance), b. Nov. 27, 1840, at Scipio, N. Y.; m. George
D. Mercereau, Jan. 22, 1867; residence Shortsville, Ontario
Co., N. Y. Children:
    1. MARY ELIZA (Mercereau), b. Sept. 7, 1869, at Flint,
    Mich.
    2. CAROLINE ISABEL (Mercereau), b. July 20, 1871, at Flint,
    Mich.
    3. MABEL EDNA (Mercereau), b. May 3, 1877, at Farming-
    ton, N. Y.

408. NELSON CRAIN[5] [156], (Sylvester,[4] Jonathan,[3] Ebenezer,[2] John[1]), married Orinda Barber, Oct. 4, 1840, in Cortland
Co., N. Y.; where he d. Dec. 17, 1847; she d. 1861. Children:

409—1. OLIVE, b. July 11, 1841.
410—2. CARLTON, b. Nov. 13, 1842.
411—3. THEODORE, b. Jan. 6, 1845; d. May 8, 1870. Said to have
left Child:
    1. BERT, b. May 10, 1869.
412—4. CHARLES, b. July 30, 1846.

413. LORINDA CRAIN[5] [162], (Sylvester,[4] Jonathan,[3] Ebenezer,[2] John1), married Reuben Davis, widower of her sister Nancy
Crain, at Cortland, N. Y., and died May 5, 1886. He died June
29, 1888. Child:

1. CLARA (Davis), b. 1851; d. aged 9 years.

415. BETSEY ANN CRAIN[5] [165], (Ebenezer,[4] Jonathan,[3]
Ebenezer,[2] John[1]), married Aug. 20, 1837, Oranel Livermore.
He was a physician, and died March 18, 1872. She died Nov.
3, 1880. They resided at Deansville, N. Y. Children:

1. EUDORA M. (Livermore), b. Dec. 6, 1839; d. Nov. 9, 1896.
2. MORTIMER C. (Livermore); m. Docia Churchill.
3. SILAS WRIGHT (Livermore), b. March 24, 1844.
4. LESLIE (Livermore), b. December, 1846.
5. HARVEY CRAIN (Livermore), b. July 21, 1850.
6. ARTHUR (Livermore), b. Nov. 29, 1854; d. Feb. 3, 1871.

SILAS WRIGHT LIVERMORE [3]; m. Anna Churchill, Jan. 27, 1865.
She was sister to Mortimer Livermore's wife. Residence
Bridgewater, N. Y. Children:

    1. ZAYDA C. (Livermore), b. March 31, 1866, at Sanger-
    field, N. Y.; m. Harvey M. Hull, Oct. 11, 1894.
    2. MAUD E. (Livermore), b. Dec. 16, 1868, at Glenmore,
    N. Y.
    3. VIRGINIA S. (Livermore), b. March 8, 1871, at Willow
    Springs. Kan.; m. Wm. H. Briggs, June 20, 1898.
    4. IRA J. (Livermore), b. March 16, 1873, at Willow
    Springs, Kan.
    5. WILLIAM H. (Livermore), b. July 11, 1877, at Bridge-
    water, N. Y.
    6. GRACE B. (Livermore), b. Jan. 2, 1882, at Bridgewater,
    N. Y.
    7. LELAND W. (Livermore), b. Sept. 10, 1883, at Bridge-
    water, N. Y.

21

HARVEY CRAIN LIVERMORE [5]; m. Genoa Burton in 1874. Residence Olathe, Kansas. Children:

1. HARVEY (Livermore), b. 1874.
2. ETTA B. (Livermore), b. 1876.

416. SILAS HARVEY CRAIN[5] [167], (Ebenezer,[4] Jonathan,[3] Ebenezer,[2] John[1]), married Roxana Cory in 1853, and died in 1857. She died in 1871. Child:

417—1. EDWIN HARVEY, b. March 23, 1860.

418. EMMELINE F. CRAIN[5] [168], (Ebenezer,[4] Jonathan,[3] Ebenezer,[2] John[1]), married Lafayette Slocum in 1848. He died in 1893. She resides (1899) at Earlville, N. Y. Child:

1. FRANCES E. (Slocum), b. Feb. 1, 1851; d. Jan. 27, 1858.

419. CHARLES RICHARD CRAINE[5] [198], (Jonathan,[4] Jonathan,[3] Ebenezer,[2] John[1]), married May 30, 1864, Louisa Bradt, in Oswego, N. Y., and removed to Detroit, Mich. She died Aug. 3, 1865. He married 2d, Lucinda M. Stevens, of Roseville, Mich., Dec. 31, 1867, in Detroit. She was born Nov. 2, 1847. Child:

420—1. WINEFRID ROOS, b. Sept. 1, 1873, in Detroit, Mich. Residence (1899), Detroit, Mich.

421. SMITH WALES CRAINE[5] [199], (Jonathan,[4] Jonathan[3], Ebenezer,[2] John[1]), married Mary S. Clark, July 19, 1864, in Mount Pleasant, Iowa. She was born Dec. 10, 1845. Residence (1899), Buffalo, N. Y. Children:

422—1. GEORGE BENJAMIN, b. July 1, 1866, in Mt. Pleasant, Iowa; d. Aug. 6, 1883.
423—2. LAURA ALICE, b. April 3, 1868, in Mt. Pleasant, Iowa; d. April 12, 1870, in Buffalo, N. Y.
424—3. CHARLES ROLLEN, b. June 12, 1876, in Buffalo, N. Y.

425. ANTOINETTE CRAINE[5] [200], (Jonathan,[4] Jonathan,[3] Ebenezer,[2] John[1]), married Berthier David Bancroft, Dec. 29, 1858, at New Hartford, N. Y. He was born March 22, 1828, in Sangerfield, N. Y., and died April 4, 1884, at Clinton, N. Y. She is living (1889) in the latter place. Children:

1. VERNON FERMER (Bancroft), b. Nov. 6, 1859, in Oriskany Falls, N. Y.; d. March 1, 1884, at Clinton.
2. CHARLES PRATT (Bancroft), b. Jan. 24, 1861, at Oriskany Falls; d. March 26, 1864, at Waterville, N. Y.
3. FRED SEYMOUR (Bancroft), b. May 23, 1863; d. April 29, 1898, in Clinton.
4. JAMES PERRY (Bancroft), b. June 22, 1865; d. June 13, 1889, in Clinton.
5. SUSAN ESTELLA (Bancroft), b. Sept. 1, 1869; d. July 26, 1871, in Clinton.
6. NELLIE MAY (Bancroft), b. Jan. 12, 1872, in Clinton.
7. JESSIE ALICE (Bancroft), b. Oct. 13, 1874, in Clinton.

426. JAMES PERRY CRAINE[5] [203], [Jonathan,[4] Jonathan,[3]

Ebenezer,[2] John[1]), married Georgiana Barker, Oct. 22, 1873, at Deansville, N. Y. She was born Feb. 22, 1852. Children:

427—1. WILLIAM ELMER, b. Sept. 21, 1874, at Deansville, N. Y.
428—2. EDDANEVA MAY, b. Aug. 2, 1877, at Deansville, N. Y.

429. MARY ADELAIDE CRAINE[5] [204], (Jonathan,[4] Jonathan,[3] Ebenezer,[2] John[1]), married June 21, 1866, David Austin, at New Hartford, N. Y. He was born Nov. 4, 1840. Residence (1899), Clinton, Oneida Co., N. Y.

1. NORMAN JOHN (Austin), b. Nov. 1, 1867; m. Olive J. Loomis, Jan. 8, 1887, in Clinton, N. Y.
2. ELMER CHARLES (Austin), b. March 11, 1871.
3. EDITH ELLA (Austin), b. Aug. 19, 1879.

430. GEORGE S. CRAIN,[5] [207], (Amariah,[4] Amariah,[3] Ebenezer,[2] John[1]), was born in Montgomery Co., N. Y., and removed with his father to the State of Indiana, where he married Lucinda Barton, and settled in Elkhart Co.; a farmer. Here four of his children were born. In 1858 or 1859 he removed to Kansas, settling in Franklin Co. Children:

431—1. MARY J., b. Aug. 17, 1852; m. March 21, 1871.
432—2. DAVID, b. Oct. 11, 1854; d. Sept. 9, 1855.
433—3. CYNTHA E., b. Sept. 24, 1856; m. Feb. 18, 1875.
434—4. OLIVER C. b. March 8, 1858.
435—5. LEWIS M., b. Jan. 29, 1860.
436—6. BETSEY D., b. Sept. 1, 1862.
437—7. JUDSON W., b. Dec. 13, 1864; d. Apr. 14, 1869.
438—8. MATTIE A., b. Feb. 18, 1866.
439—9. ROSETTA A., b. Dec. 15, 1868.
440-10. ALICE D., b. July 2, 1871.
441-11. EDA M., b. Feb. 17, 1874.

442. ALFRED CRAIN[5] [210], (Amariah,[4] Amariah,[3] Ebenezer,[2] John[1]), married Fanny Barton, in Indiana, Oct. 25, 1857. She was born there Oct. 1, 1835; settled in Franklin County, Kansas; a farmer. Children:

443—1. MARTHA R., b. May 5, 1858.
444—2. CHARLES, b., July 27, 1860.
445—3. WILLIAM W., b. Jan. 16, 1862.
446—4. MARY A., b. Feb. 26, 1864.
447—5. GRANT, b. April 8, 1866.
448—6. EDWIN, b. March 26, 1868.
449—7. FLORA, b. Jan. 30, 1870.
450—8. IDA, b. Aug. 11, 1872.
451—9. JOHN A., b. April 14, 1875.
452-10. CALVIN, b. Nov. 24, 1877.

453. SARAH ANN CRAIN[5] [216], (Cyrus,[4] Roger,[3] Ebenezer,[2] John[1]), married Luman Burtch, and lived in Groton, N. Y. She died in Auburn, N. Y., Jan. 18, 1899. Child:

1. WILLARD (Burtch), b. 1848; d. Dec. 22, 1898, leaving a daughter, Bertie.

454. CAMILLA CRAIN[5] [218], (Cyrus,[4] Roger,[3] Ebenezer,[2] John[1]), married E. Burtch. She died Oct. 31, 1848, leaving two daughters. Children:

1. EMOGENE (Burtch); m. and has: 1. MILLIE and 2. JENNIE.
2. JENNIE (Burtch).

455. CYRUS SNOW CRAIN[5] [221], (Cyrus,[4] Roger,[3] Ebenezer,[2] John[1]), married Merab Evaline Yale. He was a Baptist minister, and lived in Delphi, Onondaga Co., N. Y. He enlisted in the Union army in the fall of 1862, and served twenty months. She died in June, 1862, leaving two sons. He married 2d, Mary A. Lee. He died July 10, 1895. Children:

456—1. HERMANN LESLIE, b. May 15, 1850, at Groton, Tompkins Co.
457—2. STEPHEN B., b. April 7, 1854.
458—3. JESSIE A., b. June 29, 1865.
459—4. J. HENRY, b. Jan. 22, 1870.

460. ROSANNA CRAIN[5], [222], (Cyrus,[4] Roger,[3] Ebenezer,[2] John[1]), married David Adams. She died leaving two daughters. Children:

1. MARY (Adams), b. 1850; m. S. L. Peer.
2. NETTIE (Adams), b. 1852; d. young.

461. AHIRA B. CRAINE[5] [225], (Ahira,[4] Roger,[3] Ebenezer,[2] John[1]), married Laura Churchill, and settled in Traverse City, Mich. Children:

462—1. EARNEST; m. Eva Weller.
463—2. ELMER; m. Hattie Jewell.
464—3. BURNET; m. May Crain.
465—4. DEAN; m. Hattie Chase.
466—5. KATIE; m. Joseph Jewell.
467—6. EMOGENE; m. John Zimmerman.

468. ESTHER CRAIN[5] [226], (Ahira,[4] Roger,[3] Ebenezer,[2] John[1]), married Archibald Houghtaling. Settled near Monroe Centre, Mich. He died about 1872. She died about 1874.

1. TOBIAS (Houghtaling); d. Aug., 1862.
2. CLORINDA ANN (Houghtaling).
3. ELI (Houghtaling).
4. OLIVE (Houghtaling).
5. SAMUEL (Houghtaling).

469. LEWIS S. CRAINE[5] [227], (Ahira,[4] Roger,[3] Ebenezer,[2] John[1]), married Sally Fish, in 1845. She died in 1858, and in 1862 he married Mary E. Butler. Mr. Craine was born in Livingston Co., N. Y., March 15, 1826, and two years later removed with his parents to Ohio, where he was bound out to work on a farm until of age. After eight years of service he ran away, and returned to the State of New York, Onondaga Co., and lived with a half-brother until he married. He then settled at Mentor, Lake County, Ohio, in 1852. In 1860, he removed to Traverse City, Mich.

470—1. MARY M., b. 1846.

471—2. SYLVESTER E., b. May 12, 1848.
472—3. VILES LESLIE, b. Dec. 6, 1851.
473—4. ROSANNAH, b. July 14, 1855.
474—5. JOSEPHINE, b. April 22, 1862.
475—6. NETTIE, b. Dec. 26, 1865.

476. ABIGAIL CRAINE[5] [228], (Ahira,[4] Roger,[3] Ebenezer,[2] John[1]), married Smith Weller, by whom she had all her children; married 2d, Addison White. Settled in Almira, Benzie Co., Mich. Children:

1. WILLIAM W. (Weller); m. Irene Palmer.
2. HARLAND (Weller); m. Sarah Palmer.
3. SALINA ADELL (Weller); m. John Grelish.
4. ALMIRA (Weller); m. Samuel Martin.
5. EVA JANE (Weller); m. Earnest Crain.
6. VICTORIA (Weller); m. Julius Chase.

477. CYRUS R. CRAINE[5] [230], (Ahira,[4] Roger,[3] Ebenezer,[2] John[1]), married ——. Lives in Traverse City, Mich. Children:

478—1. GILBERT.
479—2. BYRON.
480—3. MARY.

481. JOSIAH WILLOUGHBY CRAIN[5] [235], (Eleazer W.,[4] Roger,[3] Ebenezer,[2] John[1]), married Cornelia Emery at Novi, Mich., June 10, 1847. He was a major in the late war, and was killed at the battle of Shiloh. Children:

482—1. FRANK WILLOUGHBY, b. May 25, 1848.
483—2. CHARLES EMERY, b. March 22, 1850.
484—3. MARY HELEN, b. Sept. 27, 1852.
485—4. GEORGE EDMOND, b. Oct. 26, 1854.
486—5. JARED WALTER, b. April 25, 1857.

487. LYDIA O. E. CRAIN[5] [238], (Eleazer, W.,[4] Roger,[3] Ebenezer,[2] John[1]), married Lathrop Wells Root, June 2, 1844. He died Jan. 8, 1887. Children:

1. WELLS JOSIAH (Root), b. July 17, 1845. Served in 42d Ohio Vols. under Garfield. Came home at close of the war, and d. Jan. 19. 1865.
2. CHARLES WILLOUGHBY (Root), b. Jan. 14, 1847; d. April 1, 1847.
3. FRANK WILLOUGHBY (Root), b. April 20, 1849.
4. CHARLES HAMILTON (Root), b. Sept. 11, 1855.
5. HELEN LOUISE (Root), b. May 26, 1860.
6. LOUIS BURTON (Root), b. May 4, 1865.
7. DEWITT CLINTON (Root), b. April 25, 1868.

FRANK WILLOUGHBY ROOT [3]; m. Olie Perdue in 1878. Child:
   1. CORNELIA VIOLA (Root), b. Aug. 1, 1879.

CHARLES HAMILTON ROOT [4]; m. Mary Vickers in 1884. He resides in St. Louis, Mo. Children:
   1. LATHROP WILLS (Root).
   2. CHARLES HAROLD (Root).
   3. HELEN (Root).
   4. NELLIE OLIVIA (Root).
   5. LAURA MAY (Root).

HELEN LOUISE ROOT [5]; m. Edward A. Sheets in 1883
    Child:
    1. EMMA LORA (Sheets), o. June 30, 1884.

488. SARAH M. CRAIN[5] [239], (Eleazer W.,[4] Roger,[3] Ebenezer,[2] John[1]), married Samuel B. Howe, July 15, 1862. She
died Jan. 19, 1889, leaving three children. He then, March 17,
1890, at Groton, N. Y., married 2d, Emma W. Crain, a sister
of his first wife. Residence at Schenectady, N. Y., where Mr.
Howe has for thirty years been the superintendent of schools.
His long tenure of that office tells more plainly than words his
efficiency for the position. Children:

    1. ROSEDELLE (Howe), b. April 2, 1865.
    2. MATHER CRAIN (Howe), b. June 19, 1867.
    3. SAMUEL B., Jr. (Howe), b. July 15, 1879.

    ROSEDELLE HOWE [1]; m. William Beattie Jameson in Philadel-
        phia. Pa., April 2, 1893, where they reside, and are both
        practicing physicians.

    MATHER CRAIN HOWE [2]; m. Belle Gertrude Smith in Groton,
        N. Y., Feb. 7, 1891. He is a teacher at Oneida Castle.
    Children:
        1. SMITH BURNETT (Howe), b. Nov. 18, 1892.
        2. SARAH LOUISE (Howe), b. Oct. 3, 1894.
        3. ROSE BELLE (Howe), b. Nov. 27, 1896.

489. FRANK D. CRAIN[5] [244], (Eleazer W.,[4] Roger,[3] Ebenezer,[2] John[1]), married Jan. 26, 1878, Lillie A. Kenyon. Residence at Maumee, Ohio. Editor of *The New Era*. Children
all born there. Children:

    490—1. ROY K., b. Oct. 31, 1878.
    491—2. EVA E., b. Nov. 18, 1879.
    492—3. HARRY F., b. Sept. 5, 1881; d. Sept. 30, 1881.
    493—4. GUY H., b. Oct. 7, 1885.
    494—5. RUBY B., b. Aug. 4, 1889.
    495—6. MAY, b. and d. May 20, 1890.
    496—7. LEE D., b. May 19, 1892.
    497—8. HAROLD, } twins, b. May 9, 1895; { d. Aug. 27, 1895.
    498—9. HELEN,

499. GILES W. CRAINE[5] [247], (Tower W.,[4] Roger,[3] Ebenezer,[2] John[1]), was born in Groton, Tompkins Co., N. Y. He
married at Painesville, Ohio, April 16, 1846, Eliza A. Holden, a
native of Parishville, St. Lawrence Co., N. Y. She was born
Aug. 15, 1828. They removed to Marengo, Ill., where four of
their children were born. The two youngest were born in
Winona, Minn. Late residence, Mankato. He is by trade a
blacksmith. Children:

    500—1. WALTER E., b. Jan. 19, 1848.
    501—2. ARTHUR E., b. Aug. 22. 1851.
    502—3. FRANK H., b. July 8, 1856.
    503—4. ADDIE M., b. Aug. 20, 1862.
    504—5. LINCOLN E., b. Nov. 8, 1864.

505.   CHARLES M. CRAINE,[5] [249], (Tower W.,[4] Roger,[3] Ebenezer,[2] John[1]), was born in Perry, Ohio.   He married, July 16, 1859, Adaline H. Barrett, who was born July 29, 1836. He died July 21, 1889, at Mentor, Lake Co., Ohio, leaving the record of a Christian, a man loved and respected by all who knew him.   Children :

506—1. GEORGE GILES, b. Jan. 27, 1864.
507—2. LOUISA ANNA, b. Nov. 2, 1865.
508—3. ADDIE LILLIAN, b. March 1, 1870.
509—4. LENA EMMA, b. June 9, 1872.

510.   CHARLOTTE E. CRAINE[5] [253], (Tower W.,[4] Roger,[3] Ebenezer,[2] John[1]), married Jan. 29, 1857, at Mentor, Ohio, Asa V. Churchill.   He was a soldier in the late war, enlisting in Mich. Vol. Infantry, Aug. 14, 1862, joining Capt. Holden's Co. ''Lake Shore Tigers,'' and served until July 5, 1865, a portion of the time as hospital nurse.   He was discharged July 5, 1865, and returned home with a broken elbow and a shattered constitution.   In the spring of 1869, the family removed from Michigan to Iowa.   In March, 1880, Mr. Churchill went to Minnesota, where he for a time seemed to enjoy life, but the seeds of disease had been sown, and the result was insanity, and for about a year he was confined in the hospital in St. Peters, Minn., where he died.   Just before his death, notice had been received that he had been allowed a pension, dating July, 1865, which brought help and comfort to the widow's aching heart, and from which she is still enjoying a remittance of twelve dollars a month.   Late residence, Plainfield, Iowa (Aug., 1897).
Children :

1. MARY L. (Churchill), b. Jan. 18, 1858, at Mentor; m. Feb. 13, 1882, Arza W. Swayne, of Bartlett, Washington Co., Ohio.
2. ALBERT (Churchill), b. Oct. 17, 1860, at Chardon; m. Esther Stowell.
3. JESSIE, b. May 21, 1866, at Traverse City, Mich.; m. at Preston, Minn., July 30, 1886, George McMarron, of Chatfield, and resides at Stewartville, Minn.
4. FRANK (Churchill), b. Oct. 15, 1867, at Traverse City Mich.
5. WINFLORA GERTRUDE (Churchill), b. Oct. 25, 1869, at Plainfield, Iowa; m. Feb. 15, 1893, Sherman U. Foster, of Horton, P. O. address, Plainfield, Iowa.

511.   FRANKLIN E. CRAINE[5] [256], (Tower W.,[4] Roger,[3] Ebenezer,[2] John[1]), married Philena Perry, of Perry, Ohio, Sept. 20, 1868.   She was born there, July 3, 1842.   He is a painter and a harness-maker.   Settled in Perry.   Children :

512—1. PAGE, b. Jan. 14, 1871. Has spent two years in Klondike region, with considerable pecuniary profit. Residence at or near Dawson.
513—2. EARL, b. Sept. 4, 1872.
514—3. MAX J., b. Sept. 18, 1874.

515.   HEZEKIAH CRANE[5] [278], (Isaac,[4] Hezekiah,[3] Hezekiah,[2] John[1]), married Elizabeth Fenton.   Lived in Killawog, Broome Co., N. Y.

516. JESSE CRANE[5] [279], (Isaac,[4] Hezekiah,[3] Hezekiah,[2] John[1]), married Joanna P. Hall, Nov. 25, 1818. He died in Indiana, and his widow married Horace Lee. Children:

517—1. MARY ANN, b. Jan. 18, 1819.
518—2. LESTER, b. March 20, 1822.

519. HARRY CRANE[5] [280], (Isaac,[4] Hezekiah,[3] Hezekiah,[2] John[1]), married Martha Barrows, and lived on the Crane homestead. She died Jan. 15, 1892, aged 87. He died Oct. 13, 1873, aged 73. Children:

520—1. SOPHRONIA M., b. Dec. 7, 1831.
521—2. CAROLINE M., b. July 29, 1833.
522—3. CHARLES B., b. Feb. 29, 1835.
523—4. ISAAC T., b. March 27, 1836.
524—5. SARAH S., b. Dec. 2, 1837.
525—6. CORNELIA S., b. March 15, 1840
526—7. WILLIAM H., b. Oct. 24, 1841.
527—8. CHARLES T., b. April 29, 1843.
528—9. GEORGE A., b. March 23, 1849.

529. CHARLES CRANE[5] [288], (Jesse,[4] Hezekiah,[3] Hezekiah,[2] John[1]), married Theoda Bennett of Mansfield, Conn., in 1821. A farmer. P. O. address, Eagleville, Tolland Co., Conn.

530—1. WILLIAM B.; lived in Mansfield, Conn.
531—2. ALBERT J.
532—3. AUSTIN.
533—4. AMELIA.
534—5. HARRIET.
535—6. ANNA.

536. Deacon MILLEN CRANE[5] [289], (Jesse,[4] Hezekiah,[3] Hezekiah,[2] John[1]), married March 3, 1824, Sarah Bennett, only child of Eleazer and Deborah (Hall) Bennett. He settled in that part of Mansfield, Conn., called Chestnut Hill; was a respected and esteemed citizen of that town. A member of the Connecticut Legislature in 1843; was deacon of the Baptist Church; by occupation a farmer. He made a visit to his son then in the army, stationed at Fortress Monroe, and died Oct. 20, 1863, soon after returning home. Children:

537—1. SARAH CORDELIA; m. Don F. Johnson; lived in Willimantic.
538—2. DEBORAH BENNETT.
539—3. ABBY ANN.
540—4. ELEAZER BENNETT, b. Sept. 10, 1834.
541—5. ALVIN M.; b. Aug. 3, 1839.

542. Rev. ORIGEN CRANE[5] [290], (Jesse,[4] Hezekiah,[3] Hezekiah,[2] John[1]), married Bridget T. Greene, who was born in Richmond, R. I., July 29, 1804. Mr. Crane was educated at the Newton Theological Institution, in Massachusetts, and preached in Weston and Grafton, Mass. He was a Baptist minister. He often had children placed in his care to be educated, and at one time had a daughter of Ex-Governor Fenton of New York State at his home for that purpose. On a certain

occasion the Governor came to New England Village, Grafton, to visit with his daughter at Mr. Crane's home. They were out in the yard enjoying a little exercise at the swing. The Governor sat in the swing while Mr. Crane gave him a vigorous push or two, and immediately fell on his face and died April 20, 1860.

Children :

543—1. ORIGEN CLARK, b. Oct. 21, 1830.
544—2. EMMA.
545—3. FRANK.

546. ALMYRON W. CRAIN[5] [295], (Asa,[4] Hezekiah,[3] Hezekiah,[2] John[1]), removed to the State of New York, and married Jan. 12, 1832, at Fabins, Lucy Penoyer. She was the daughter of Truman Penoyer, a native of that place, born May 3, 1810. He died at Truxton, Cortland Co., N. Y., June 15, 1876. In 1866 he was of a woolen manufacturing firm, A. W. Crain & Son, in Truxton. Perry P. and Wyatt were associated with their father in this manufacture of woolens. Children :

547—1. PERRY P., b. Feb. 28, 1833, at Pompey, N. Y.
548—2. WYATT ASA, b. Dec. 10, 1837; m. Sarah M. Dunham, Jan. 23, 1862, at Truxton; d. June 20, 1862.
549—3. SARAH DELUCIA, b. Oct. 5, 1842, at Truxton.

550. GEORGE S. B. CRAIN[5] [296], (Asa,[4] Hezekiah,[3] Hezekiah,[2] John[1]), married Esther Close, June 28, 1842, and died in Fayetteville, N. Y., Aug. 19, 1854. Children :

551—1. CHARLES H., b. April 22, 1843. Enlisted in 122d Regt. N. Y. Vol.; taken sick; was discharged, and d. at home Aug. 17, 1864, of consumption.
552—2. WELTHY, b. Jan. 4, 1845; d. Oct. 12, 1847.
553—3. MARY L., b. June 13, 1848.
554—4. GEORGE A., b. Oct. 12, 1850.

555. TIMOTHY B. CRAIN[5] [298], (Asa,[4] Hezekiah,[3] Hezekiah,[2] John[1]), married Jan. 17, 1839, Mary Ann McGebany. She was·born May 9, 1822. He died Dec. 14, 1862. Children :

556—1. MERRITT, b. March 20, 1840.
557—2. MILO T., b. Jan. 13, 1842.
558—3. MARGARET A., b. March 2, 1846; m. Myron Clark, Dec. 1, 1863, at Clay, N. Y.

559. ARCHIBALD B. CRAIN[5] [299], (Asa,[4] Hezekiah,[3] Hezekiah,[2] John[1]), married Sarah Lane. Was for many years constable and collector at Cicero, N. Y. He died May 12, 1860. No children.

560. ROSETTA CRAIN[5] [300], (Asa,[4] Hezekiah,[3] Hezekiah,[2] John1), married Horace Holmes, of Truxton, N. Y. Living in 1866 in Monmouth, Iowa. Children :

1. ELLEN M. (Holmes). b. March 18, 1848.
2. LUTHER ALMIRON (Holmes), b. July, 1859; d. Jan. 1, 1865.

22

561. SOPHIA CRAIN[5] [303], (Asa,[4] Hezekiah,[3] Hezekiah,[2] John[1]), married George W. Ward, Jan. 22, 1845. She died Sept. 12, 1859. Children :

    1. CORREL ASA (Ward), b. Aug. 28, 1846.
    2. MARY ELIZABETH (Ward), b. May, 1849; d. April, 1860.

562. ISAAC CRAIN[5] [304], (Asa,[4] Hezekiah,[3] Hezekiah,[2] John[1]), married Sarah Kipley. She was born Nov. 22, 1840. He resided in Clay, N. Y. Was a farmer and gardener. Children :

    563—1. WILBARD H., b. Dec. 18, 1856.
    564—2. WALTER A., b. March 2, 1858.
    565—3. SOPHIA E., b. Oct. 20, 1859.
    566—4. FRANKLIN J., b. Aug. 16, 1862.
    567—5. ELLA MAY, b. Dec. 26, 1864.

568. HARRIET AMANDA CRAIN[5] [305], (Asa,[4] Hezekiah,[3] Hezekiah,[2] John[1]), married March 7, 1854, Homer Dunham, a farmer, in Clay, N. Y. She died about 1869. Children :

    1. CORA ESTHER (Dunham), b. Oct. 25, 1857.
    2. MILTON ASA (Dunham), b. Dec. 13, 1864; d. Feb. 23, 1865.

        CORA ESTHER DUNHAM [1]; m. Moses Welton Newcomb about
        the year 1880. Residence at N. Syracuse, N. Y. Children :
            1. HOMER DUNHAM (Newcomb).
            2. BELLE EVELYN (Newcomb), d.
            3. ALVA ALLEN (Newcomb), d.

569. CAROLINE ELIZABETH CRAIN[5] [307], (Asa,[4] Hezekiah,[3] Hezekiah,[2] John[1]), married R. E. B. Wilcox, Nov. 10, 1859, and settled in Auburn, N. Y., but removed about 1864 to Fremont, Minn. Was living in April, 1899, in Minnesota City. Children :

    1. FLORA MAY (Wilcox), b. Sept. 17, 1860; d. Oct. 3, 1860.
    2. JENNIE AMANDA (Wilcox), b. Nov. 28, 1861.
    3. WILLARD B. (Wilcox), b. Feb. 9, 1865.
    4. CORA R. (Wilcox), b. Oct. 27, 1868.
    5. BYRON H. (Wilcox), b. June 7, 1871.
    6. MYRON H. (Wilcox), b. June 7, 1871; d. Aug. 26, 1871.
    7. ALMIRON H. (Wilcox), b. March 30, 1873.

570. AUSTIN BUGSBY CRAIN[5] [310], (Amasa,[4] Hezekiah,[3] Hezekiah,[2] John[1]), married Mahetabel, daughter of Constant Lindsley. She was born Sept. 4, 1810,.and died April 4, 1866. He died March 17, 1876. Children :

    571—1. ALPHEUS AMASA, b. May 15, 1835.
    572—2. ELIZABETH BUGSBY, b. Dec. 31, 1838.

573. SHEPHARD P. CRAIN[5] [319], (Daniel,[4] Daniel,[3] Hezekiah,[2] John[1]), married Almira Bosworth, June 8, 1837. She was born April 9, 1815, at Killawog, Broome Co., N. Y. She was a school teacher. He was a carpenter by trade, and was

living in 1848 in Middlebury, Elkhart Co., Ind. He died in 1850. Children:

574—1. FRANCES B., b. June 26, 1842; d. July 14, 1846.
575—2. DANIEL S., b. Sept. 24, 1848.

576. HARVEY L. CRANE[5] [326], (Cordial S.,[4] Daniel,[3] Hezekiah,[2] John[1]), married March 13, 1838, Eliza Weed. Was engaged in silk manufacture. Residence (1864) at Mansfield, Conn. Children:

577—1. MARY E., b. Sept. 20, 1839.
578—2. JOSEPH H:, b. June 1, 1841; d. 1843.
579—3. MARTHA T., b. Nov. 4, 1844.
580—4. NANCY W., b. Feb. 13, 1849.
581.-5: CORDIAL S., b. Jan. 11, 1857.

582. WILLIAM H. CRANE[5] [327], (Cordial S.,[4] Daniel,[3] Hezekiah,[2] John[1]), married May 29, 1836, Mrs. Fanny (Bishop) Fish, of Seekonk, Mass. He died at Dorchester, Mass., 1858. Children:

583—1. WILLIAM H., b. April 24, 1837; d. 1852.
584—2. JONATHAN, b. Oct. 9, 1838; d. 1838.
585—3. EDWARD H., b. Sept. 18, 1839; d. 1858.
586—4. FANNY E., b. Sept. 2, 1841; d. 1844.
587—5. JOSEPH.
588—6. EBENEZER B., b. March 24, 1844.
589—7. CORDIAL S. J., b. Nov. 15, 1845.

590. MARY B. CRANE[5] [329], (Cordial S.,[4] Daniel,[3] Hezekiah,[2] John[1]), married in 1838 James Walker, Jr. Children:

1. EDWARD (Walker).
2. LILLIE (Walker).
3. MARY C. (Walker), b. Jan. 6, 1847.

591. REV. ETHAN B. CRANE[5] [332], (Jonathan,[4] Daniel,[3] Hezekiah,[2] John[1]), was born in West Troy, N. Y. He graduated in Union College, class 1832. He studied Theology in Auburn Seminary. Married in 1839, Deborah Pratt. He was installed pastor of the Congregational Church, Old Saybrook, Conn., June 27, 1838, where he preached about thirteen years, when his health compelled him to rest from his labors. He spent a year in Europe, on his return was dismissed, and, as his health would allow, has preached some since. His late home was in Brooklyn, N. Y. Children:

592—1. FREDERICK WM. HOTCHKISS, b. Nov 4, 1840.
593—2. CATHERINE HAMILTON, b. Dec. 12, 1841.

594. REV. JONATHAN CRANE[5] [333], (Jonathan,[4] Daniel,[3] Hezekiah,[2] John[1]), married Anna Hannah Sanford, daughter of Hannah Crane, who was in the fifth generation in descent from Jasper Crane, of New Haven, Conn., and Newark, N. J. She was a daughter of John, great grandson of Jasper. Her mother was Rhoda Lyon. He was born in Schenectady, N. Y., gradu-

ated at Union College, and Auburn Theological Seminary. He preached in Attleboro, Mass., New York city, St. Joseph, Mo., and Kalamazoo, Mich. He was ordained, Oct. 20, 1836, and was minister at Middletown, N. Y., for forty years, a Congregationalist. He died of appoplexy Dec. 25, 1877. He took great interest in the genealogy of the family of Crane, and had written considerable upon it. Children :

595—1. ANNA E., b. June 26, 1838.
596—2. MARY B., b. Nov. 15, 1839.
597—3. NATHANIEL WHITING S., b. April 19, 1843; m. Helen M. Shepherd; lived in Kalamazoo, Mich.
598—4. EMMA H., b. Jan. 5, 1846; d. May 2, 1854.
599—5. JONATHAN, b. Oct. 14, 1847.
600—6. FRANCIS P. J., b. May 27, 1857.

601. EDWARD CRANE⁵ [334], (Jonathan,⁴ Daniel,³ Hezekiah,² John¹), was for some time connected with the prominent railroads in New England. He married in 1841, Anna S. Farrar, and for some years lived in Dorchester, Mass. He was an extensive railroad builder. Children :

602—1. TIMOTHY FARRAR, b. Feb., 1843; d. Nov., 1866.
603—2. MARY ORPAH, b. Oct. 27, 1844; m. Geo. S. Jackson, Oct. 15, 1867; lived in Dorchester.
604—3. EDWARD BARROWS, D. May 8, 1849.

605. CORDIAL CRANE⁵ [335], (Jonathan,⁴ Daniel,³ Hezekiah,² John¹), married June 8, 1842, Emily S. Phelps, and lived in Boston, Mass. Children :·

606—1. AUSTIN H., b. Nov. 23, 1843.
607—2. ELIZA FORBES, b. April 29, 1847.
608—3. EMILY AZUBAH, b. July 28, 1855; d. April, 1856.

609. ELIZA CRANE⁵ [336], (Jonathan,⁴ Daniel,³ Hezekiah,² John¹); married in 1842, John T. R. Hayward. Children :

1. CATHARINE (Hayward), b. April 22, 1843.
2. JONATHAN K. (Hayward), b. Nov. 17, 1845.
3. ELIZA CRANE (Hayward), b. Oct., 1847; d. Oct., 1849.
4. ELIZABETH (Hayward), b. 1850; d. 1851.
5. JAMES (Hayward), b. Aug. 28, 1856.
6. EDWARD CRANE (Hayward), b. Oct. 21, 1863.

610. LUCINDA CRANE⁵ [339], (Jonathan,⁴ Daniel,³ Hezekiah,² John¹), married June 14, 1853, Rev. Thos. E. Bliss, and died in Hancock, Mich., 1863. Children :

1. CATHARINE CRANE (Bliss), b. May 2, 1854.
2. ADELIA PHILLIPS (Bliss), b. July 14, 1858; d. Jan. 6, 1863.
3. CHARLES HAMILTON (Bliss), b. Oct., 1860; d. Jan. 4, 1863.

611. HENRY MARTYN CRANE⁵ [340], (Jonathan,⁴ Daniel,³ Hezekiah,² John¹), married, 1848, Elizabeth Griswold. Residence near Schnectady, N. Y. Children :

612—1. HENRY, b. 1851.
613—2. EDWARD E.

614—3. JONATHAN.
615—4. JASPER.
616—5. HERMAN G., b. 1860.
617—6. ELIZABETH.

618. MARTHA ORPHA CRANE[5] [341], (Jonathan,[4] Daniel,[3] Hezekiah,[2] John[1]), married Edward Cartledge; settled in Hannibal, Mo. Children:

1. EDWARD (Cartledge).
2. MARTHA HAMILTON (Cartledge).
3. ELIZA HAYWARD (Cartledge.)
4. ABIA E. (Cartledge).
5. CHARLES (Cartledge).

619. MELISSA CATHARINE CRANE[5] [343], (Bela,[4] Daniel,[3] Hezekiah,[2] John[1]), married Rev. William Case, June, 1843, at Plymouth, Luz Co., Pa. Children:

1. DEBORAH ALBERTINE (Case).
2. CATHARINE E. (Case).
3. ANNA JOSEPHINE (Case).
4. EVALINE CLEMENTINE (Case).
5. WILLIAM MALANCTHON (Case).

620. LAFAYETTE CRAIN[5] [346], [Libbeus,[4] Elisha,[3] Hezekiah,[2] John[1]), married April 7, 1846, Martha Jane McConnell, who was born Dec. 16, 1821; resides at Alamo, Mich.; is a farmer. Children:

621—1. CHARLES F., b. Oct. 22, 1853; m. March 22, 1876, at Otsego, Mich.
622—2. MARTHA JENNIE, b. April 22, 1856; m. Oct. 1, 1879, at Kalamazoo, Mich.

623. ISAAC S. CRAIN[5] [348], (Nathan,[4] David E.,[3] Hezekiah,[2] John[1]), was born in Canton, St. Lawrence Co., N. Y. He married at Evans Mills, Dec. 29, 1834, Myrtilla Root, who was born in Russia, Herkimer Co., April 9, 1811. He was a plasterer, brick and stone mason by trade, as was his father before him, and was, in 1879, residing in Carthage, N. Y., although all his children were born at Evans Mills. Children:

624—1. SARAH LOUISA, b. Oct. 12, 1835; lived at Oxbow, Jefferson Co., N. Y.; m. —— Overton.
625—2. ELIZABETH GREEN, b. March 15, 1837.
626—3. CHARLES BOWEN, b. Aug. 12, 1838; d. Aug. 25, 1839.
627—4. MARY AMELIA, b. Jan. 13, 1840; m. —— Gates, Carthage.
628—5. AARON ROOT, b. May 14, 1841.
629—6. EMILY MYRTILLA, b. April 4, 1843.
630—7. GEORGE BOWEN, b. Sept. 12, 1844.
631—8. HARRIET FRANCES, b. Oct. 4, 1846.
632—9. CAROLINE OAKS, b. Nov. 13, 1847; m. —— Lewis, Carthage, N. Y.
633-10. WILLIE, b. Aug. 18, 1850; d. June 25, 1852.

634. ROBERT CRAIN[5] [363], (David E.,[4] David E.,[3] Hezekiah,[2] John[1]), was born in Maitland, Ontario, Canada. He married at Algonquin, Ontario, Canada, March 12, 1857, Per-

milla Ann Earl. She was a native of that place, and was born Sept. 22, 1834. She died in Ottawa, Nov. 21, 1865. He then married Dec. 30, 1867, at Ottawa, Martha Ann Davies, who was born at Bytown, now Ottawa, April 17, 1847. Mr. Crain was a contractor and builder, having carried on that business in Ottawa for many years. He died there Sept. 23, 1893.

Children :

635—1. NELLY, b. May 7, 1858, at Algonquin.
636—2. CORODAN ELDRIDGE, b. Jan. 27, 1861, at Algonquin; d. Feb. 28, 1865.
637—3. EDGERTON RUFUS, b. Sept. 20, 1863, at Algonquin; d. Feb. 26, 1865.
638—4. ARTHUR HERBERT, b. Feb. 3, 1869, at Ottawa.
639—5. GEORGE ALBERT, b. Feb. 20, 1872.
640—6. FREDERICK HIRAM, b. July 7, 1874.
641—7. GERTRUDE MIRA, b. Jan. 3, 1876.
642—8. ROBERT HUGH, b. Feb. 27, 1879.
643—9. LILLIAN EMMA, b. Apr. 16, 1888.

644. LEVI CRAIN[5] [364], (David E.,[4] David E.,[3] Hezekiah,[2] John1), was born in Maitland, Ontario, Canada. He married in Augusta, Jan. 10, 1866, Henrietta M. Dake. She died Feb. 25, 1878, at Ottawa, where he is a contractor and builder.

Children :

645—1. LILLIE VERGILLIA, b. May 25, 1870, at Augusta; d. Sept. 7, 1870.
646—2. WILLIE ELDRIDGE, b. July 21, 1871, at Augusta.
647—3. ETHEL LENA, b. July 19, 1875, at Ottawa.

SIXTH GENERATION.

648. CYRUS LYMAN CRANE[6] [375], (John,[5] Stephen,[4] John,[3] John,[2] John[1]), married Charlotte Howe. Children:

649—1. FRANCES L.
650—2. EDMOND D.; served in Civil War.
651—3. EMET.
652—4. MANLY.
653—5. JOHN FERRAL.
654—6. NANCY.
655—7. CLARA.
656—8. LOUIS.
657—9. MATILDA A.; m. Wm. Anson Benedict.

658. JOHN M. CRANE[6] [376], (John,[5] Stephen,[4] John,[3] John,[2] John[1]), married, in 1836, Lorenda Hutchinson. She died Dec. 17, 1862. He died Dec. 27, 1876. About the year 1857 he became interested in the cure of cancers, studied medicine, passed examination, and was admitted to practice pursuant to the laws of New York State. He established an infirmary for the cure of cancers on South Street, in Addison, and soon gained a widespread reputation as a successful practitioner in his chosen profession. His highest ambition seemed to be to relieve the sufferings of the human family in so far as it came within his power and skill. He gained the reputation of being a generous, kind-hearted, honorable gentleman. Children:

659—1. GEORGE, b. 1840; m. 1st, Mary E. Orr, who d. leaving four children; 2d. Lida Montgomery. He served four years in U. S. A. during Civil War. After the death of his father he continued the treatment of cancers until 1880, when Dr. Rush P. Brown became associated with him at the institution established by his father, Dr. John M. Crane. Children:

    1. MINNIE; m. S. C. Erwin.
    2. HOWARD.
    3. HORACE.
    4. JOHN M.
    5. MARY E.
    6. CARLTON.

660—2. HARRISON.
661—3. ALBERT.
662—4. CHARLES.
663—5. SUSAN.
664—6. MARY.
665—7. SARAH.
666—8. JANE.

667. WILLIAM E. CRANE[6] [377], (John,[5] Stephen,[4] John,[3] John,[2] John[1]), married Jane Adams, of Tioga, Pa., and settled in Williamsport. Children :

668—1. UTLEY.
669—2. JULIA.

670. ALONZO G. CRANE[6] [379], (John,[5] Stephen,[4] John,[3] John,[2] John[1]), married Nancy Ruff, of Tioga, Pa., and settled at Lawrenceville ; had several children, among them the following :

671—1. LEWIS.
672—2. ELLA.

673. EGBERT L. CRANE[6] [380], (John,[5] Stephen,[4] John,[3] John,[2] John[1]) m. Frances L. Williams, of Woodhull, N. Y., and settled at Addison. Served in the Civil War. Enlisted in Co. B, 86th Regiment, N. Y. Vol. Inf., Aug. 14, 1861; appointed orderly sergeant Nov. 15 ; elected first lieutenant, receiving his commission Nov. 22 ; served until March 23, 1863, when he was discharged on surgeon's certificate. Was at second Bull Run, Aug. 30, 1862, and battle of Fredericksburg, Dec. 11 to 16, 1862. Six of his nephews were in the union army during the war. Child :

674—1. WILLIE D.; m. Emma Mourhess; residence Addison, N. Y.
        Children :
            1. LEILAH BELLE.
            2. FRANCES LEONE.

675. LETTICE MARIA CRANE[6] [381], (John,[5] Stephen,[4] John,[3] John,[2] John[1]), married June 14, 1835, Luke Wadsworth Benedict, of Cortland, N. Y. She is deceased. Children :

    1. LESTER HERBERT (Benedict), b. May 21, 1836; served in war,
        and d. at Yorktown, Va.
    2. WILLIAM ANSON (Benedict), b. Dec. 10, 1838; m. Matilda A.
        Crane; residence Elmira, N. Y.
    3. HENRY H. (Benedict), b. Aug. 29, 1840; d. 1840.
    4. SARAH A. (Benedict), b. Aug. 16, 1844; d. 1850.
    5. JOHN LEROY (Benedict), b. June 27, 1848; d.

676. MARY A. CRANE[6] [382], (John,[5] Stephen,[4] John,[3] John,[2] John[1]), married William Morton, of Woodhull, N. Y. She is deceased. Child :

    1. WILLIAM O. (Morton), of Cameron Mills, N. Y.

677. ROLLIN C. CRANE[6] [385], (Cyrus,[5] Stephen,[4] John,[3] John,[2] John[1]), left home at the age of fourteen to care for himself. Went to sea. Served three and a half years in the United States Navy; also in the United States Army. Was in the battles of South Mountain, Antietam and Fredericksburg. Went to California via Cape Horn in the early days of gold excitement there, and has visited that State three different times since. By trade a house joiner, an occupation he followed many years. Made his will Aug. 19, 1893; Oct. 4, 1893, it was

admitted to probate at East Windsor, Conn. He married Elizabeth Blodget, of East Windsor, Conn., Feb. 28, 1839. Child :

678—1. ELIZABETH ; m. —— Fengar, and had Ella, who was mentioned in the will as his granddaughter.

679. SYLVESTER CRAIN[6] [400], (Sylvester,[5] Sylvester,[4] Jonathan,[3] Ebenezer,[2] John[1]), married in 1859 Maria Ryan. He died June 7, 1870, at Virgil, N. Y. His widow resides at Lyons, N. Y.; also her son. Child :

680—1. MARVIN, b. Jan. 10, 1862, at Virgil.

681. MARY M. CRAIN[6] [401], (Sylvester,[5] Sylvester,[4] Jonathan,[3] Ebenezer,[2] John[1]), married 1st, George Ladd, Oct. 2, 1853, at Virgil, Cortland Co., N. Y. He died Jan. 16, 1889, and she married 2d, Harvey Yeager, Feb. 24, 1891, at Virgil, where they reside (1899), and where her children were born. Children :

1. EVA (Ladd), b. Sept. 7, 1854; d. Nov. 20, 1859.
2. RAY (Ladd), b. Sept. 5, 1879; d. April 11, 1881.

682. EDWARD A. CRAIN[6] [402], (Sylvester,[5] Sylvester,[4] Jonathan,[3] Ebenezer,[2] John[1]), married Sally Watrous, Sept. 6, 1857, in Virgil, Cortland Co., N. Y. He died May 15, 1898. His widow lives (1899) in Virgil, N. Y. Children :

683—1. FRANK, b. Dec. 10, 1862; d. March 6, 1865.
684—2. EDDIE, b. Nov. 15, 1866; d. April 25, 1867.
685—3. MARY, b. March 10, 1872.
686—4. MINNIE E., b. March 10, 1872; d. Jan. 28, 1885.
687—5. SUSIE, b. July 4, 1876.

688. MARY CRAIN [3]; m. Harry Ingraham. Dec. 25, 1888. Lives in Dryden, Tompkins Co., N. Y. Children :
1. FOSSIE (Ingraham), b. March 3, 1891, in Virgil, N. Y.
2. MARIE (Ingraham), b. Sept. 25, 1895, in Virgil, N. Y.
3. CECIL (Ingraham), b. July 7, 1896, in Dryden, N. Y.
4. WEBSTER (Ingraham), b. Dec. 22, 1898, in Dryden, N. Y.

689. SUSIE CRAIN [5]; m. A. V. Rounds, Aug. 11, 1892. Settled in Virgil, Cortland Co., N. Y. Child :
1. LENORA (Rounds), b. June 16, 1894.

690. SAMANTHA E. CRAIN[6] [403]. (Sylvester,[5] Sylvester,[4] Jonathan,[3] Ebenezer,[2] John[1]), married Cornelius Chaplin, Sept. 16, 1856. She died Nov. 7, 1880, in Stockton, Cal. He also deceased. Children :

1. HENRY A. (Chaplin).
2. MARK H. (Chaplin).

691. MARY CRAIN[6] [405], (Jonathan G.,[5] Sylvester,[4] Jonathan,[3] Ebenezer,[2] John[1]), married William Hamilton, Dec. 25, 1873. Settled in Cortland, N. Y. Children :

1. ALBERT J. (Hamilton), b. July 14, 1875.
2. GEORGE H. (Hamilton), b. April 6, 1877.

23

692. WILBER C. CRAIN[6] [406], (Jonathan G.,[5] Sylvester,[4] Jonathan,[3] Ebenezer,[2] John[1]), married Laura Gibson, of Etna, N. Y., Oct. 17, 1883. Settled in Gracie, Cortland Co., N. Y. Child:

693—1. OLIN B., b. July 1, 1885.

694. OLIVE CRAIN[6] [409], (Nelson,[5] Sylvester,[4] Jonathan,[3] Ebenezer,[2] John[1]), married Benjamin B. Logue, June 7, 1860, at Sinnamahoning, Pa. Died Nov. 13, 1886, at that place. Children:

  1. ELIZABETH (Logue), b. Sept. 16, 1861; m. John M. Russell.
  2. LUCINA M. (Logue), b. April 19, 1863; d. Sept. 25, 1870.
  3. GRANT (Logue), b. March 20, 1865; m. Carrie Sones.
  4. MARY (Logue), b. May 15, 1867.
  5. JULIA (Logue), b. Oct. 9, 1869; m. Edward Beldin.
  6. EDWARD (Logue), b. Oct. 9, 1871.
  7. CARLTON (Logue), b. March 22, 1874.
  8. OLIVE (Logue), b. Aug. 11, 1876; m. James Hurley.
  9. LAFAYETTE (Logue), b. March 7, 1879.
 10. THOMAS (Logue), b. July 13, 1881.

  ELIZABETH LOGUE [1]; m. John M. Russell, at Sinnamahoning, Pa. She d. July 10, 1891, at Quinton, McKean Co., Pa. His residence 1899, at Straight. Children:
      1. FREDERICK, d.
      2. RAYMOND.
      3. VOYLE, d.
      4. ELLEN.
      5. BENJAMIN.

  GRANT LOGUE [3]; m. Carrie Sones. Children:
      1. MILDRED, b. Aug. 11, 1896, at Wheaton, Potter Co., Pa.
      2. MABEL, b. June 13, 1898, at Beaver Lake, Lycoming Co., Pa.

  JULIA LOGUE [5]; m. Edward Beldin. Children:
      1. CHARLES, b. Feb. 6, 1895, at Sinnamahoning, Pa.
      2. LUCIUS, b. Nov. 12, 1896, at Sinnamahoning, Pa.
      3. CLAUDE, b. Nov. 6, 1898, at Sinnamahoning, Pa.

  OLIVE LOGUE [8]; m. James Hurley. Children:
      1. HELEN, b. Nov. 13, 1897, at Wheaton, Potter Co., Pa.
      2. RALPH, b. April 30, 1899, at Wheaton, Potter Co., Pa.

695. CARLTON CRAIN[6] [410], (Nelson,[5] Sylvester,[4] Jonathan,[3] Ebenezer,[2] John[1]), married 1st, Elizabeth Busambarg, in 1870. She died 1873, and he married 2d, Elsie Busambarg, cousin of his first wife, in 1875. Residence Sonora, Steuben Co., N. Y. Child:

696—1. BERTHA M., b. June 16, 1878.

697. CHARLES CRAIN[6] [412], (Nelson,[5] Sylvester,[4] Jonathan,[3] Ebenezer,[2] John[1]), married Harriet Johnson, July 4, 1871, at Philipsburg, Pa. Lives at Sinnamahoning. Child:

698—1. WILLIAM, b. March 26, 1876.

699. HERMANN LESLIE CRAIN[6] [456], (Cyrus S.,[5] Cyrus,[4] Roger,[3] Ebenezer,[2] John[1]), married Olive Marion Covey, May 1, 1876. She was born at Bainbridge, Chenango Co., N. Y., Oct. 27, 1858. They reside at Mt. Upton, where he is a dealer in sash and blinds, lumber, lime, cement, brick, and a general line of building materials. She died leaving a son. Child:

700—1. FRANK HOWARD, b. Nov. 13, 1878.

701. STEPHEN B. CRAIN[6] [457], (Cyrus S.,[5] Cyrus,[4] Roger,[3] Ebenezer,[2] John[1]), married Libbie Bailey. Children:

702—1. JESSIE.
703—2. ELSIE.

704. SYLVESTER E. CRAINE[6] [471], (Lewis S.,[5] Ahira,[4] Roger,[3] Ebenezer,[2] John[1]), married Oct. 20, 1867, Eliza J. Chapman. He is a carpenter, and resides at Traverse City, Mich. Children:

705—1. EDWIN A., b. 1868.
706—2. LEWIS J., b. 1870.
707—3. HERBERT E., b. 1872.
708—4. ARTHUR, b. 1874.
709—5. LESLIE, b. 1877.
710—6. JOHN W., b. 1880.
711—7. REUBEN, b. 1882.
712—8. SYLVESTER, b. 1885; d.
713—9. OTTO, b. 1887.

714. VILES LESLIE CRAINE[6] [472], (Lewis S.,[5] Ahira,[4] Roger,[3] Ebenezer,[2] John[1]), married 1st, Rebecca Chapman in 1876; 2d, Jennie Vorhies in 1879. Children:

715—1. ALMOND; d.
716—2. ETHEL.
717—3. NINA.
718—4. WALLACE.
719—5. MAKINLY.

720. ROSANNAH CRAINE[6] [473], (Lewis S.,[5] Ahira,[4] Roger,[3] Ebenezer,[2] John·), married Joseph M. Seaton in 1874. She died May 4, 1878. Child:

1. MAY (Seaton).

721. GEORGE GILES CRAINE[6] [506], (Charles M.,[5] Tower W.,[4] Roger,[3] Ebenezer,[2] John[1]), married Alta L. Smith, Oct. 28, 1893, at Enterprise, Whatcom Co., Washington. Child:

722—1. EARL CHARLES, b. Sept. 1, 1894, at Ferndale.

723. MAX J. CRAINE[6] [514], (Franklin E.,[5] Tower W.,[4] Roger,[3] Ebenezer,[2] John[1]), married Dec. 29, 1896, Lucy M. Abbott, at Perry, Ohio.

724. CHARLES T. CRANE[6] [527], (Harry,[5] Isaac,[4] Hezekiah,[3] Hezekiah,[2] John[1]), married June 14, 1868, Vilura F. Parker, of Mansfield. She was born Nov. 18, 1844. He has been honored

by his fellow townsmen, having held the positions of constable, collector, and representative of Mansfield in the General Assembly for Connecticut, 1897 and 1898.   Children:

725—1. ANNIE G., b. April 2, 1872; d. Sept. 9, 1873.
726—2. EUGENIE M., b. Sept. 16, 1875; m. Fred W. Gerrick, Rockville.
727—3. ANNIE E., b. Dec. 6, 1880.

728. ELEAZER BENNETT CRANE[6] [540], (Millen,[5] Jesse,[4] Hezekiah,[3] Hezekiah,[2] John[1]), was born in Mansfield, Conn.; married there Oct. 5, 1859, Clara A. Barrows, daughter of Robert A. Barrows. She was born July 30, 1840. He is a farmer and settled on the homestead.   Children:

729—1. WINNIE S., b. June 13, 1862.
730—2. ALICE M., b. Sept. 9, 1867.
731—3. GERTRUDE B., b. Oct. 12, 1873.

732.   Rev. ALVIN M. CRANE[6] [541], (Millen,[5] Jesse,[4] Hezekiah,[3] Hezekiah,[2] John[1]), graduated from Brown University 1869, Newton Theological Seminary 1872, and for some years settled as a clergyman at West Boylston and Shelburne Falls, Mass. He was a soldier in the Civil War, serving three years in Virginia. Enlisted in 1862 in Co. D, 21st Regt., appointed Lieutenant, promoted to Captain in place of Capt. F. S. Long, who was killed before Petersburg; this commission he held the last year of his service.   Elected a member of the Connecticut Legislature in 1866.   He married July 13, 1869, at Mansfield, Conn., Sarah G. Adams. She was a native of Gosnold, born July 15, 1844.
Child:

733—1. JUDSON ADAMS, b. 1884.

734.   ORIGEN CLARK CRANE[6] [543], (Origen,[5] Jesse,[4] Hezekiah,[3] Hezekiah,[2] John[1]), was born in Mansfield, Conn.; married Oct. 31, 1853, at New England Village, Grafton, Mass., Caroline M. Gove, a native of Amesbury, Mass., born Sept. 27, 1830. She died Oct. 10, 1876. He is a machinist, and after conducting that business a few years in New England Village, removed soon after 1859 to New York city, and was employed on the Brooklyn Bridge.   Children:

735—1. HELEN A., b. March 16, 1855; d. Dec. 8, 1872.
736—2. THOMAS E., b. Oct. 14, 1856.
737—3. ANNA G., b. Aug. 11, 1859.
738—4. HARRY L., b. Feb. 27, 1862.

739.   PERRY P. CRAIN[6] [547], (Almyron W.,[5] ASA,[4] Hezekiah,[3] Hezekiah,[2] John[1]), was born in Pompey, N. Y.   He married at Otselic, Nov. 10, 1859, Annah, daughter of Eli Church, native of Columbus, born Nov. 21, 1836. He settled in Truxton; a woolen manufacturer, and was honored with office of magistrate,   Children:

740—1. NELLIE, b. Dec. 29, 1862; d. Jan. 30, 1864.
741—2. HATTIE, b. Jan. 28, 1865.
742—3. ALMYRON P, b. May 28, 1868.

743. SARAH DELUCIA CRAIN[6] [549], (Almyron W.,[5] Asa,[4] Hezekiah,[3] Hezekiah,[2] John[1]), married Charles A. Pierce, a farmer in Truxton, N. Y. Children:

1 NORA (Pierce). b. Nov. 16, 1863.
2. WILLIAM WYATT (Pierce), b. June 8, 1865.

744. MARY L. CRAIN[6] [553], (George S. B.,[5] Asa,[4] Hezekiah,[3] Hezekiah,[2] John[1]), married Joseph L. Butler, March 23, 1864. He settled in Fayetteville, N. Y. Children:

1. CHARLES A. L. (Butler), b. April, 1865.
2. GEORGE (Butler).

745. MERRITT CRAIN[6] [556], (Timothy B.,[5] Asa,[4] Hezekiah,[3] Hezekiah,[2] John[1]), married Barbara Bard. Children:

746—1. ADDIE; m. Arthur Collins; has three boys and lived in Buffalo, N. Y.
747—2. MYRON.

748. MILO T. CRAIN[6] [557], (Timothy B.,[5] Asa,[4] Hezekiah,[3] Hezekiah,[2] John[1]), married Caroline Walton. Children:

749—1. EDNA.
750—2. GENIVIE.

751. ALPHIUS AMASA CRAIN[6] [571], (Austin B.,[5] Amasa,[4] Hezekiah,[3] Hezekiah,[2] John[1]), married Francés M., daughter of M. P. Lindsley, and resides at Monticello, N. Y. Children:

752—1. IDA LINCOLN, b. Aug. 16, 1861.
753—2. FREDERICK MERVIN, b. Sept. 9, 1867.

754. ELIZABETH BUGSBY CRANE [572], (Austin B.,[5] Amasa,[4] Hezekiah,[3] Hezekiah,[2] John[1]), married R. B. Cooper, of Liberty, Sullivan Co., New York State, where they reside. Children:

1. FRANK (Cooper), b. June 21, 1869.
2. FREDERICK (Cooper), b. 1877.

755. ELIZABETH GREEN CRAIN[6] [625], (Isaac S.,[5] Nathan,[4] David E.,[3] Hezekiah,[2] John[1]), married Oliver P. V. Root, June 24, 1858; settled near Norway, N. Y.; resides on the old homestead farm. Children:

1. JOHN C. H. (Root), adopted, b. Oct. 15, 1858.
2. HATTIE LIZZIE (Root), b. Nov. 6, 1861.
3. FANNIE MYRTILLA (Root), b. Dec. 15, 1863.
4. ROSELL BOWEN (Root), b. May 26, 1866.
5. SARAH ROSELIA (Root), b. July 5, 1868.

756. AARON R. CRAIN[6] [628], (Isaac S.[5] Nathan,[4] David E.,[3] Hezekiah,[2] John[1]), married 1st, Dec. 30, 1863, Maria L. Gates. She died July 4, 1866, having had two children who died in infancy. He than married at Deer River, Lewis Co., N. Y., April 9, 1867, Emma B. Sammons, native of that place, born June 6, 1846. Mr. Crain is a mason by trade, and has

conducted business in Carthage, N. Y., but removed Aug., 1878, to Norway, Herkimer Co. Children:

757—1. CHARLES H., b. July 24, 1869.
758—2. MYRTILLA M., b. Dec. 12, 1871.
759—3. SARAH FRANCES, b. June 1, 1875.

760. GEORGE BOWEN CRAIN[6] [630], (Isaac S.,[5] Nathan,[4] David E.,[3] Hezekiah,[2] John[1]), served in 20th N. Y. Cavalry, in Civil War. He married at Carthage, N. Y., Dec. 14, 1870, Carrie C. Hurd, who was born in Montezuma, Jan. 19, 1844. He is a mason by trade, and removed from Carthage to Lapeer, Mich. Children:

761—1. GEORGE J., b. July 30, 1873, at Lapeer.
762—2. NORMAN, b. June 3, 1877, at Lapeer.

JASPER CRANE OF NEW HAVEN, CONN., ALSO, NEWARK, N. J., AND HIS DESCENDANTS.

FIRST GENERATION.

1. JASPER CRANE[1] was one of the original settlers of the New Haven Colony, June 4, 1639, and signed the first agreement at a general meeting of all the free planters held in Mr. Newman's barn. He took the oath of fidelity at the organization of the government, with Campfield, Pennington, Gov. Eaton and others. In 1644 he was "freed from watching and trayning in his own person because of his weakness, but to find one for his turn." Was a member (with Treat) of the General Court, and many years a magistrate. Was interested in a bog-ore furnace at East Haven in 1651. He removed to Branford in 1652. He was elected a magistrate in 1658, and held the office of deputy for some years previous to that date.

In a note-book kept by Thomas Lechford, Esq., a lawyer in Boston, Massachusetts Bay, from June 27, 1638, to July 29, 1641, we find the following: "Samuel Searle of Quinapeage Planter in behalfe of Jasper Crane of the same Agent or Attorney for Mr. Roe Citizen of London Demiseth unto Henry Dawson and John Search of the Same one house and house Iott and three acres of land lying in Boston wherein William Herricke now dwelleth from 29 Sept. next for five years four pounds ten shillings rent half yearly, to fence to the value four pounds ten shillings, to repaire 21-6-1640."

This transaction, showing his connection with a gentleman of London, England, would lead one to think that he certainly was known there, and might have lived there. Whether or not the above record furnished the foundation for the tradition that he came from London to America, we do not know. But such a tradition has been cherished by some of his descendants. Extensive research among the record offices in London has thus far failed however of finding any trace of him there. It is also said that he came over from England with Winthrop in the ship *Arbella*.

But the date of Jasper Crane's birth, or the place in which he was born, have not been fixed. Whether he came from parents occupying high or middle stations in life can as yet only be determined by the records revealed to us. He assuredly was one of the staunch and active men among the first settlers of the New Haven Colony as well as one of the fathers of the new settlement in New Jersey. He, with Capt. Robert Treat, seemed to have a large share of the weight of responsibility of that young colony upon their shoulders, and its success at heart. Mr.

Crane did not go, it is said, with the first company to " Milford,"
as the first settlement at Newark, N. J., was called, but signed,
with twenty-two others, the first contract in 1665. Jan. 20,
1667, he headed the list of signers and church members of the
first Church at Newark, and became one of the most influential
and active men of the new colony. Jasper Crane and Robert
Treat were the first magistrates in Newark. It is said that Mr.
Crane was dissatisfied at the New Haven Colony becoming united
with the Connecticut Colony; he preferred to have the New Haven
Colony remain separate.

He was a surveyor and merchant, as well as a magistrate, and
with Mr. Myles laid out the most of the New Haven town plot,
located grants, established division lines, and settled disputed
titles. It is said that he was steward of Rev. John Davenport's
property in 1639. In March, 1641, he received a grant of 100
acres of land in the East Meadow. He was one of the New
Haven Company concerned in the settlement on the Delaware
River in 1642, who were so roughly handled by the Dutch. In
1643 his estate was voted at £480, with three persons in his
family,—self, wife and son John. In 1644–45 he received a
grant of 16 acres of upland, situated in East Haven, upon which he
built a house, in which his son Joseph was born. While residing
at this place he was in trade as a merchant, but not being satisfied
with the location he sold this place Sept. 7, 1652, and became
one of the first planters of Branford, Conn., a new settlement
then just being instituted by families from Wethersfield, Conn.,
under the leadership of Mr. Swayne, and a few from Southampton, L. I.

Jasper Crane, Esq., and Mr. Wm. Swayne were the first deputies to the General Court of Electors from Branford in May,
1653, Mr. Crane being returned during the four succeeding years.
In May, 1658, he was chosen one of four magistrates for the New
Haven Colony and held the office by appointment until 1663;
also one of the magistrates called together by the Governor, at
Hartford, in 1665–67. In the union of the Colonies he· was
chosen one of the assistants, was also Trustee of County Court,
New Haven, 1644. His house lot in New Haven was located on
what is now Elm Street, at the corner of Orange Street, the same
now occupied by the Church of St. Thomas.

The first Church of Newark was founded in 1667, and a building erected, about 1714 or 1716, a second meeting-house was
built, and the third erected about 1787 to 1791. The people of
Orange, Bloomfield and Montclair communed with the Newark
Church until about 1716. In fact, for considerably more than a
hundred years after the founding of Newark the crest of the first
mountain was the western boundary of the town, and until the
year 1806 the town of Newark was divided into three wards:
Newark Ward, Orange Ward, and Bloomfield Ward. That year
Orange became a separate town, and six years later Bloomfield
Ward became the town of Bloomfield. This part of Newark took

in the territory from the Passaic on the east to the crest of the first mountain on the west, and as this section was so thoroughly occupied by the descendants of Jasper Crane it was early called Cranetown.

Jasper Crane senior was one of the purchasers of the "Kingsland Farms," an immense estate near Newark, now known as Belleville.

The exact date that Jasper senior took his leave of Branford has not been definitely fixed. In the spring of 1666 the people of Branford, becoming dissatisfied about the union of the New Haven and Connecticut Colonies, and particularly on account of granting the right of suffrage to the inhabitants not members of the ᵕhurch, resolved at once to remove to New Jersey, as agents, who had been sent thither, came back bringing favorable reports of the new country. In October, after adopting a code of laws for their government, Mr. Pierson with a portion of his congregation left Branford for their future home, Newark, N. J.· Jasper senior although one of the original twenty-three who signed the first contract in 1665, still was active in public affairs in Branford, holding the office of assistant magistrate in 1666 and 1667. But Jan. 30, 1667, he headed the list of signers to a new covenant and disposing of his property at Branford that year took up his permanent home at Newark and became very prominent in all transactions of the town, especially during the first fourteen years of its growth and development. He was the first president of the town court, and first on the list of deputies to the General Assembly of New Jersey for several years. At the drawing of Home Lots, Feb. 6, 1667, Lot 49 fell to the senior Jasper Crane, No. 40 to Deliverance Crane, and No. 62 to John Crane, they being his two eldest sons.

At a town meeting of Newark, held January, 1668, Jasper Crane, with Robert Treat, were chosen magistrates for the year ensuing, and also deputies or burgesses for the General Assembly for the same year. This Robert Treat was the first recorder or town clerk for Newark, and was exceedingly prominent in all public matters while he remained in the settlement. But in 1671 he returned to Connecticut, where he was held in high esteem, and for several years was Governor of that Colony, proving a faithful and conscientious worker for the interest of the inhabitants under his charge. From January, 1668, until his death, Jasper Crane senior was given a prominent part to perform in the settlement of Newark. May 20, 1668, he as one of a committee signed an agreement fixing the dividing line between Newark Town and Elizabeth Town. July 28, 1669, he with Robert Treat was chosen by the town to take first opportunity " to go to ' *York* ' to advise with Col. Lovelace concerning our standing. Whether we are designed to be a part of the Duke's Colony or not, and about the Neck, and liberty of purchasing lands up the river, that the Town would petition for." Re·elected magistrate January, 1669, " and Deputy to the General Assembly

24

if there shall be any." He with Robert Treat were chosen to be moderators of town meetings for the year ensuing. Jan. 2, 1670, again chosen magistrate and deputy, serving in latter capacity annually until 1674, and at the town meeting Feb. 20, it was voted that the governor be requested to confirm Jasper Crane and Robert Treat magistrates or justices of the peace. The same honors were conferred in 1671. and in addition it was voted Jan. 22, 1671, that "every man should bring his half bushel to Henry Lyon & Joseph Waters and have it tried and sealed when made fit with Mr. Crane's, which for the present is the standard." Mr. Crane was also one of a committee to see to burning the woods for a year. May 13, 1672, Mr. Crane and Lieut. Swain were chosen representatives for the town to consult with other representatives of the country to order matters for the safety for the country. June 17, 1672, Mr. Crane was again chosen magistrate, and also chosen "President of the Quarterly Court to be held in Newark to begin September next." He was also given "liberty to sell liquors in the town till the country order alter it."

At a town meeting July 1, 1673, Mr. Crane was chosen to serve on a committee, with Mr. Bond, Mr. Swain, Mr. Kitchell and Mr. Lyon, to consider with messengers from other towns about sending a petition to the Lords Proprietors in England for the removal of grievances; and July 5th the town agreed to pay for sending the messenger to England, as the above committee had agreed with Mr. Delevall about money to cover that expense.

August 4th the town chose Mr. Crane, Mr. Bond, Lieut. Swain and Sergeant John Ward deputies to treat with the generals about having a privileged county between the two rivers Passaic and Araritine. August 12th again chosen magistrate; September 6th, on committee to try and secure the "Neck" to add to the possessions of Newark; and September 16th instructed by the town to "treat with the generals, and, if they can, to buy it." It would seem the committee were successful, for October 25th Mr. Crane, Mr. Molyns and Mr. Hopkins were chosen to look after the confirmation of the purchase of the Neck and sue for further easement in respect to pay. November 17th Capt. Swain and Mr. Crane were chosen to continue the trade for the Neck. The following year (June 29, 1674,) the town voted to have Mr. Crane and Mr. Pierson, Jr., carry the petition and present it to the Governor and Council at North Orange to "obtain confirmation of their bought and paid for lands." August 10, 1674, was again chosen magistrate. Mr. Crane was now becoming quite advanced in years, and the important and exacting services required of him by the town must have proved a heavy tax upon his strength, for he now dropped out of political office, while his sons, John, Azariah and Jasper, Jr., began to work in. Feb. 19, 1678–9, it having been discovered that many of the settlers had taken up lands contrary to a town agreement, Mr. Crane stated

at town meeting that he would lay down all lands so taken if others would, and March 10th following he was chosen, with Robert Dalglesh and Jasper Crane, Jr., to lay out Samuel Potter's lot again. This entry, so far as the public records of Newark shows, closes the public life of the senior Jasper Crane.

If we may judge from the entries upon the Newark Town Records we should say that, next to Robert Treat, Jasper Crane was the most prominent figure in the early settlement of that town. After Treat returned to Connecticut, Jasper Crane's name came first in the filling by popular vote the highest and most responsible positions of public trust in the settlement. That he held the confidence of the people is clearly manifested by their returning him annually for so many years, and until the infirmities of age unfitted him for further public service. But the family name and traits of character were appreciated, for no sooner than the name of Jasper senior disappears from the proceedings of the town meetings than the names of John, Azariah and Jasper, Jr., are brought into recognition. The patents for land in Newark to Jasper Crane, Aug. 25, 1675, covering one hundred and sixty-eight acres, are as follows: "House; lot 14 acres, 17 a. his first division on Great Neck, 11 a. in part for his second division on said Neck, 6 a. on said Neck, 4 a. at bottom of the Neck, 20 a. for his second division by Two Mile Brook, 26 a. his third division by head of Mile Brook, 20 a. for his third division at the head of the branch of Second River, 14 a. of meadow for his first division at Great Island, 12 a. of meadow for his second division by the Great Pond, 14 a. for proportion of bogs, 5 a. of meadow near the Great Island, 1 a. of meadow at Beef Point, 4 a. of meadow near Wheeler's Point, yealding ½ penny lawful money of England, or in such pay as the country doth produce at merchants' price, for every one of the said acres, the first payment to begin the 25th of March, which was in the year 1670." These lands were taken up and occupied some time prior to date of the patents. Another warrant seems to have been issued to Jasper Crane, May 1, 1675, for 103 acres of land in Newark.

At a town meeting held Aug. 24, 1670, an agreement was made with Mr. Robert Treat and Sergt. Richard Harrison to build and maintain a sufficient corn-mill upon the brook called Mill Brook. They were given sole privilege of this brook, with all the town grists, and all stone within the town limits suitable for millstones, with all the timber that was prepared by Joseph Horton for the mill, and two days' work of every man and woman that holds an allotment in the town, with all the lands formerly granted to Joseph Horton. They were to hold this land as their own so long as they held and maintained the mill, and not to dispose of the mill without consent of the town. The town was also to give thirty pounds in good wheat, pork, beef, or one-fourth in good Indian corn, at such prices as would enable them to exchange it for or procure iron, millstones, or the work-

man's wages, &c. : Winter wheat 5 shillings per bushel; summer wheat 4s. 5d.; pork 3d. per lb.; beef 2d.; Indian corn 2s. 6d. per bushel. As Mr. Treat was to return to Connecticut, Jasper Crane assumed his portion of the contract.

From Jasper Crane we have a large number of descendants— one branch of them located westward of Newark, and five or six miles distant, calling the place Cranetown. Some of his descendants located four miles southward of Newark, at a place called Elizabeth Town. Among those who settled here was Stephen Crane, who there is good reason to believe was an elder son of Jasper, born in England about 1630.

From these points members of the family pressed their way further westward, crossing the Passaic River, settling Morris County. They were all remarkable for frugality, honesty and piety, and were mostly Presbyterians. It has been said by one, not a member of the family, "no more respectable people, no better citizens, are found in our communities than those who bear Crane blood in them."

Oct. 30, 1666, at a meeting in Branford, Conn., the preliminary agreement outlining the conduct of the proposed new settlement upon the "Passiack River in the Province of New Jersey" was signed by many Branford people, among them Jasper Crane senior and his sons John and Delivered.* These three names appear among the first proprietors of the town of Newark, and at the town meeting held Feb. 6, 1667, Mr. Jasper Crane, John and Deliverance* appear to have been present. Thenceforth for more than a century the name of Crane occupied a conspicuous place in the annals of the town, and scarcely a town meeting was held during a period of one hundred years that there was not a Crane chosen to fill some town office, and it was not unusual to elect to public positions several of the name at one meeting. But March 13, 1759, the family seemed to have reached the zenith of its popularity, for at that meeting by vote of the town eight different offices were filled by Cranes. As it appears, however, that John Crane was chosen collector and John Crane to serve on a committee to settle a line in the parsonage land, it may have required but seven Cranes to fill the eight positions; so that the election held this day exceeded but a trifle that held March 12, 1754, when six Cranes were elected to fill seven public positions. Their names were: John, for collector; Timothy and Ezekiel, surveyors of highways; Elijah and William, overseers of the poor; John, clerk of strays; Noah, on committee to settle the line between the towns of Newark and Elizabethtown.

Jasper Crane's will, dated 1678, named children John, Azariah, Jasper, and Hannah Huntington, and granddaughter Hannah Huntington; John to have his "silver bole." Mr.

---

* This name is spelled both ways.

Crane was probably born about 1605, and died 1681, his will having been proved that year, and names wife Alice. Children of Jasper Crane, 1st, and wife Alice:

2—1. JOHN, b. about 1635.
3—2. HANNAH, b. about 1639.
4—3. DELIVERED, b. July 12, 1642; settled at Newark, N. J.; left no children. On map published 1806 his house lot appears on High street, near the northerly end.
5—4. MERCY (or MARY), bapt. March 1, 1645.
6—5. MICAH. bapt. Nov. 3, 1647.
7—6. AZARIAH, b. 1649.
8—7. JASPER, b. April 2, 1651.

SECOND GENERATION.

9. JOHN CRANE[2] [2], (Jasper[1]). Rev. Stephen Dodd says he married Elizabeth Foote, a sister of Nathaniel Foote, of Wethersfield, Conn., and settled in Branford, Conn., in 1663, signing the Branford agreement with his father. He with his brothers Delivered and Jasper were among the first to remove to the settlement of Newark, N. J., in the spring of 1666. The first town meeting was held in Newark, May 21, 1666. He died in 1694, aged 59. He was first elected to public office there as fence viewer, Jan. 2, 1670-1, and he soon became prominent in public affairs. He had a seat in the first meeting-house in Newark. Was among the deputies to the General Assembly of New Jersey, 1671-5. In 1674, he was chosen by vote of the town to warn the people, at his end of the town, of town meetings. He was chosen grand juryman for 1677, and select-man in 1683. His house lot plated on the map of Newark, published in 1806, places it on Broad Street, northerly from Trinity Episcopal Church and the upper Common, and extending to the Passaic River. He was to have the "silver bole," and at his death, the bowl evidently went to his brother Azariah, although it may have passed through the hands of Delivered. A warrant was issued under date, April 27, 1694, to him for seventy-three acres of land, in eight parcels, the fifth by Maple Island. His will, dated, 1694, proved Jan. 6, 1695, names wife Hannah. She was his 2d wife. Children:

10—1. JOHN, b. 167Ī.
11—2. JASPER, b. 1679.
12—3. DANIEL, b. 1684.
13—4. SARAH.

14. HANNAH CRANE[2] [3], (Jasper[1]), married Thomas Huntington, who was son of that Simon who died on the passage from England to Boston, in 1633. Thomas had two brothers, Simon and Christopher. Margaret, mother of Thomas, lived for a time in Roxbury, Mass. Married for 2d husband, Thos. Stoughton, of Dorchester, Mass., and removed to Windsor, Conn. Thomas Huntington was freeman in Connecticut, in 1657; settled in Branford, in 1663, and died after 1684. She married 2d, John Ward senior, of Branford, and was his 2d wife. Children:

15—1. SAMUEL.
16—2. HANNAH.

17. MERCY (or MARY) CRANE[2] [5], (Jasper[1]), married Jonathan Bell of Stamford, Conn., Aug. 22, 1662. He was the first white child born in that town. She died Oct. 26, 1671, leaving three children. Mr. Bell, Oct. 31, 1672, married Susanna Pierson of Branford, Conn. Children:

1. JONATHAN (Bell), b. Feb. 14, 1663.
2. HANNAH (Bell), b. Aug. 29, 1665.
3. REBECCA (Bell), b. Dec. 6, 1667.
4. ABIGAIL (Bell), b. Dec. 23, 1673.
5. ABRAHAM (Bell), b. June 22, 1675.
6. MERCY (Bell), b. Nov. 5, 1678.
7. JOHN (Bell), b. Jan. 16, 1681.
8. A daughter, b. Aug. 3, 1683.
9. JAMES (Bell), b. Dec. 11, 1684.
10. SUSANNAH (Bell), b. Dec. 25, 1686.
11. MARY (Bell), b. Sept. 29, 1689.

18. Deacon AZARIAH CRANE[2] [7], (Jasper[1]), married Mary daughter of Capt. Robert Treat. She was born 1649, died Nov. 12, 1704, aged 55; he died Nov. 5, 1730, in his 83d year. In the overturn of the government by the Dutch, etc., he was betrusted with the concerns of his father-in-law, Mr. Robert Treat, who was Governor of Connecticut during the Charter Oak affair. Azariah appears to have outlived all the original settlers and left his silver bowl to be used forever in the 1st Presbyterian Church in Newark, where he was a deacon from 1690 until his death. He held many offices of public trust in the town: in 1690, on committee of safety; in 1691, chosen to care for the poor of the town; in 1692, to treat with Rev. John Pruden to become the minister; Jan. 1693-4, deputy to Provincial Assembly, also deputy in 1695; selectman in 1676, 1683 and 1694; also as constable, grand juryman, pound-keeper; to look after the young people of the town, to lay out highways, view children's estates, overseer of the poor, etc.

As early as 1715, he was living on his home place at the Mountain, and it is almost certain that he located there many years prior to that date, for we find in the early town records the following: "By warrant, April 27, 1694, there was laid out by John Gardner a tract of land at the foot of the Mountain, having Azariah Crane on the northeast, and Jasper Crane on the southwest."

June 9, 1679, warrants were issued to him for 136 acres in nine parcels, the sixth was fifty acres on branches of the Elizabeth River, April 27, 1694, 100 acres in three parcels. April 19, 1698, the town voted that a committee of five should view whether Azariah Crane should be given land out of the Common for a tanyard at the front of John Plum's home lot; on committee in 1706, to treat with Rev. Samuel Whittlesey, to settle in work of the ministry. They must have had some little trouble in securing the right man, for March 21, 1708, he was on a committee to instruct Mr. Pearson, who was going to New England, to endeavor to procure a minister. He secured

Nathaniel Bowers, who remained with the people there until his death, Aug 30, 1716, and again Mr. Crane was on committee to secure a new minister.

There was apparently some hitch in the arrangement for the tannery before referred to, for Azariah soon after that date removed to a place near the mountain, and formed a settlement known as Cranetown (Montclair), six miles from Newark. Jan. 13, 1719, there was organized a Church called "The Society at the Mountain," now Orange, two miles west of Newark, and during that year land was purchased for a meeting-house plot of Thomas Gardner, and soon a small church edifice was erected. Azariah Crane became a prominent actor in the society, and for many years was a deacon there, living to the age of seventy-four years.

His sons, Nathaniel, Noah, Azariah and William, also in their turn, took leading positions in this society, aiding materially with funds in building the church edifice.   William succeeded his father Azariah as deacon in that Church.   Oct., 1785, this mountain "Society at the Mountain" was first called "Orange Dale," and two years later the "Dale" was omitted, and thenceforth known as Orange.

In June, 1798, Joseph Crane, son of Noah, was deacon of this Church.   He was then a resident of Cranetown, and afterwards became elder in the Church at Bloomfield.   Of the elders in that Church by the name of Crane, we may name Lewis, who died in 1777, aged 59 ; Noah in office, 1776, died June 8, 1800, aged 81 ; Joseph, mentioned above, in office, 1794-98, died Oct. 11, 1832, aged 81.   Children :

19—1. HANNAH; m. John Plum, of Milford, Conn., and had MARY, who m. Mr. Dickenson.
20—2. NATHANIEL, b. about 1680.
21—3. AZARIAH, b. 1682.
22—4. ROBERT, b. 1684.
23—5. JANE, b. 1686.
24—6. MARY, b. 1693; m. Mr. Baldwin.
25—7. JOHN, b. 1695.
26—8. RICHARD; d. in infancy.
27—9. JASPER; d. in infancy.

28. JASPER CRANE[2] [8], (Jasper[1]), married Joanna Swaine, born 1651, daughter of Capt. Samuel and Joannah Swaine. She died Sept. 16, 1720, aged 69.   He was born at East Haven, Conn., and removed with his parents to New Jersey.   In 1684, he purchased the property of Robert Lyman, who had returned to England.   He was a member of the Assembly in 1704, in Cornbury's time, and also a magistrate.

He with his brothers John and Deliverance, owned seats in the first Church in Newark.   Jasper, Jr., was given his share of public honors, having been chosen by popular vote to fill the various offices of fence viewer, surveyor of highways, constable, and selectman, as well as committeeman, deputy to the Provincial

Assembly in 1697-1702, and to see about settling the minister, and the boundary controversy between Newark and Elizabeth-town, etc. He received two warrants for land, one, April 27, 1694, and the other, April 10, 1696, aggregating 120 acres, located on branches of the Elizabethtown River.

Jasper Crane has a house lot located on the map of Newark, published in 1806, at the corner of High and Market Streets; whether this was meant for senior or junior does not appear.

It is quite certain that he located in that part of Newark called Cranetown, afterwards West Bloomfield, now Montclair. Soon after the year 1681, at which time the town of Newark ordered the laying out of a highway as far as the mountain, which act no doubt was for the accommodation of settlers in that portion of the town, and where in the year, 1694, the town records give him a location, and it is said that his descendants, and those of his brother Azariah, occupied nearly, if not quite, all the westerly side of the town. He died March 6, 1712, aged 62. His tombstone stood in the Presbyterian churchyard on Broad Street, Newark. According to his will he had the follow-ing children :

29—1. JOSEPH, b. 1676.
30—2. ELIHU, b. 1689.
31—3. DAVID, b. 1693.
32—4. JONATHAN, b. 1678.
33—5. SARAH, b. 1683; m. Joseph Wheeler.
34—6. HANNAH, b. 1690; m. Robt. Ogden, Esq.

25

THIRD GENERATION.

35. JOHN CRANE[3] [10], (John[2], Jasper[1]), in 1719, was chosen assessor and collector of taxes, and served as such several years. He was overseer of the poor in 1725, and sheep-master same year, and in 1736, to record strays. For many years he was assessor and rate maker; tithingman in 1735; and chosen on committee to agree with Rev. Aaron Burr, Nov., 1736. He removed to Whippany; died Feb. 22, 1739, aged 68, buried at Whippany. His will, dated Jan. 2, 1734, proved May, 1739, names the following children:

36—1. JOHN.
37—2. EDMOND, b. about 1692.
38—3. AMOS; m. Elizabeth ———; lived at Whippany. She d. Sept. 1, 1736.
39—4. MARY; m. ——— Hamilton.
40—5. ABIGAIL; m. Stephen Ward.
41—6. KEZIAH; m. ——— Canfield.

42. JASPER CRANE[3] [11], (John,[2] Jasper[1]), married Ann ———; died 1749 (or 1769); will names children:

43—1. DAVID.
44—2. JOSEPH, b. about 1722.
45—3. SOLOMON, b. about 1725; elected overseer of highways, March 13, 1759, and March 8, 1768; d. Jan. 9, 1784.
46—4. SARAH; m. ——— Barber.
47—5. HANNAH; m. ——— Kingsland.

48. DANIEL CRANE[3] [12], (John,[2] Jasper[1]), married Phebe, supposed to have been daughter of Nathaniel Ward. He died Sept. 8, 1747, aged 63 years, and was buried at Newark, N. J. Children:

49—1. PHEBE, b. 1711; d. Jan. 8, 1732, aged 21.
50—2. THOMAS, b. 1713; d. Nov. 10, 1736, aged 23.
51—3. JAMES, b. 1723; m. Lydia ———; she joined First Presbyterian Church at Newark; d. March, 1750, aged 27.
52—4. DANIEL, b. 1721; d. Jan. 15, 1748-9, aged 28.
53—5. JOSHUA, b. 1725,; d. Jan. 14, 1748-9, aged 23.
54—6. MOSES, b. 1715; d. Nov. 16, 1736, aged 21.
55—7. PHINEAS, b. 1730; d. Nov. 13, 1759, aged 29.
56—8. JEREMIAH.
57—9. PATIENCE, b. 1733; m. Joseph Crane, perhaps a son of Lt. David,[3] Jasper;[2] d. March 1, 1760, aged 27.
58-10. JOANNA; m. Stephen Young.
59-11. LYDIA.

60. Major NATHANIEL CRANE[3] [20], (Azariah,[2] Jasper[1]), married Elizabeth Gibson. He settled near a spring at West

Bloomfield on the place which was afterwards occupied by Cyrus Pierson as late as 1851. The spring near which he lived is located near the railway depot in Montclair, N. J. He was chosen to record strays March, 1744. He died in 1760, aged about 80 years. The will (1760) names the children.

About the year 1716 the people in and about Cranetown formed what for some years was known as the "Mountain Society" and later became the "Second Church of Newark," now the "First Presbyterian Church of Orange." He, in 1753, was one of the subscribers to build the second meeting-house. His son Nathaniel, Jr., was also a subscriber with the following Cranes: Caleb, William, Job, Gamaliel, Noah, Stephen, Jedediah, Louis, Elihu and Ezekiel. Their subscriptions amounting to 56–16–6. Dec. 7, 1796, a resolution was passed by the congregation and trustees assuming the title of "The Presbyterian Church of Bloomfield," and the following Cranes contributed to hire a minister for six months: Oliver, Stephen, William, Job, Simeon, Widow Susanna, Phineas, Noah, Noah, Jr., Joseph, Israel, Aaron, Nathaniel, Benjamin, Eleakim, Widow Jane and Iddok (probably meant for Zadock). Children:

61—1. WILLIAM.
62—2. NOAH, b. 1719.
63—3. NATHANIEL; never married.
64—4. ELIZABETH; m. —— Young.
65—5. JANE; m. —— Smith.
66—6. MEHITABEL.

67. AZARIAH CRANE[3] [21], (Azariah,[2] Jasper[1]). Azariah, Jr., had wife Rebecca. In 1733 he granted three acres at the mountain plantation to his well beloved son-in-law Zachariah Baldwin. He settled at West Bloomfield, N. J., near his brother Nathaniel. Elias B. Crane lived on the place in 1851. She died June 15, 1739, aged 48, and he married again. He with his brother Nathaniel were the promoters of (Cranetown) Montclair, locating their home places near the spring which was a few years ago, and possibly at present time may be seen near the railroad depot at Montclair, N. J. In 1753 Azariah conveyed to his son Azariah a tract of land extending to the top of the mountain. He was a subscriber to the fund for erecting a parsonage at Montclair, and also the meeting-house. He was not without his honors at the hands of his fellow-townsmen; as early as Nov. 2, 1703, he was chosen one of the pounders. Children:

68—1. REBECCA, b. Sept. 6, 1707.
69—2. AZARIAH.
70—3. JOB.
71—4. GAMALIEL, b. 17—.
72—5. EZEKIEL.
73—6. JOSIAH.
74—7. MOSES, b. 1731.
75—8. STEPHEN.

76. ROBERT CRANE[3] [22], (Azariah,[2] Jasper[1]), married Phebe ——. She died May 13, 1759. He died July 14, 1755, aged 71. His will named children as given below. He is said to have lived in a stone house in Newark, N. J. It seems quite certain that having been named for his grandfather Robert Treat he inherited a part of the land in Newark once the property of this grandfather, located on Market Street, between Broad and Mulberry Streets, and back of the old meeting-house through to Washington Street. In 1806 the Presbyterian Church stood on what was once a portion of this estate. Mr. Isaac Watts Crane says Mulberry Street was formerly called Baldwin's Lane. He also writes that on this above-mentioned tract of land, meaning the Robert Treat estate, he could recall among those who had occupied it "John Crane, Isaac, Timothy, Obadiah, & Azariah." They were doubtless all of them descendants of Deacon Azariah Crane, father of this Robert. March 11, 1718, he was chosen pounder, and surveyor of highways in 1736 and 1737, and fence viewer in 1740. Children:

77—1. EUNICE, b. 1720; m. David Johnson.
78—2. TIMOTHY, b. 1726.
79—3. ISAAC.
80—4. JOSIAH, b. 1732.
81—5. MARY, b. 1735; m. David Hayes.
82—6. PHEBE.
83—7. LYDIA; m. Timothy Bruen.

84. JANE CRANE[3] [23], (Azariah,[2] Jasper[1]), married John Richards, and settled at Newark, N. J. She was his first wife. She died Sept. 12, 1741, aged 55. He died March 16, 1748, aged 61. Children:

1. MOSES (Richards), ⎫ twins, ⎰ d. March 14, 1745.
2. AARON (Richards), ⎬ b. ⎱ grad. Yale 1745; m. Susan Smith;
                     ⎭ 1718; ⎰ 45 years in ministry; d. May, 1793.
3. DAVID (Richards); m. Edus Crane.

DAVID RICHARDS [3]; m. Edus Crane, of Bloomfield, N. J., and for several years resided in Newark. He then purchased a farm in Columbia, Morris County, where they lived and died; he in the year 1773 or 1774, she in 1781. Children:

1. JOHN (Richards), b. 1751; d. Aug. 20, 1752, aged 13 mos.
2. AARON (Richards); m. —— Bonnell.
3. SAMUEL (Richards), b. 1755; killed at battle of Springfield, Jan. 23, 1780.
 . ABIGAIL (Richards); m. Abram Corey.
5. HANNAH (Richards); m. Col. Daniel Corey.
6. JEMIMA (Richards); m. Reuben Chadwick.
7. NANCY (Richards); d. unmarried.
8. THOMAS (Richards), b. 1769; d. Nov. 3, 1816.
9. JONATHAN (Richards), b. 1771; d. June 21, 1859.

85. JOHN CRANE[3] [25], (Azariah,[2] Jasper[1]), m. 1st, Abigail ——, about 1717. She was b. 1700; she d. June 25, 1744. 2d, Rebecca ——. He d. Sept. 5, 1776, aged 81. Will names children: Jonas, a minor, named for a son who died Jan. 24,

1745, aged 27 years. This Jonas was father of Rufus, and this Rufus was father of William, of Baltimore, Md. He lived on the east side of Broad Street, on a part of the home lot inherited by his mother from her father Robert Treat; was a very active and influential man in the town. He was chosen in 1740 recorder for strays as well as assessor of taxes. These duties he performed many years; also serving on many important town committees, such as looking after the parsonage, collecting for the parsonage and burying-ground, etc.; a freeholder 1757. Obadiah and Jonas were children by second wife. Children:

86—1. Jonas, b. 1718.
87—2. Samuel, b. 1723.
88—3. Abigail, b. 1725; d. Oct. 29, 1736, aged 11 years.
89—4. John.
90—5. Eliakim.
91—6. Elias.
92—7. Matthias; graduated at Yale, 1747; chosen pound-keeper, March 11, 1766; d. about 1777.
93—8. Benjamin, b. 1740.
94—9. Obadiah, b. 1741; d. Sept. 28, 1784, aged 43; lived in the stone house, Broad Street; m. Azariah Crane; probably served in Capt. Squiers' Co., 2d Regt., Essex Co., in Revolution.
95-10. Jonas, b. 1747.

96. Joseph Crane,[3] Esq. [29], (Jasper,[2] Jasper[1]), married Abigail Lyon, daughter of Joseph Lyon. He died 1726, aged 50. His will names children given below. Was magistrate of the county for many years. Served the town in 1721 as freeholder. His name appears among the charter members in the patent of incorporation for the town of Newark, N. J., issued by the province of New Jersey, April 27, 1713. March 28, 1719, he received a deed of warrant of 92 acres of land located in Newark, from the New Jersey Society. April 20, 1720, from same source, a warrant for 120 acres; and again, Feb. 27, 1724, 21¼ acres; also, Dec. 18, 1724, 120 acres. These tracts of land came to him from the New Jersey Society as heir to the right of his father. He was chosen surveyor of highways March 8, 1720. Children:

97—1. Benjamin, b. Nov. 27, 1705; d. 1777.
98—2. Isaac, b. Oct. 8, 1709.
99—3. Ezekiel, b. May 8, 1711.
100—4. Israel, b. Jan. 2, 1713; d. Aug. 1, 1785.
101—5. Josiah, b. Jan. 2, 1716.
102—6. Joseph, b. Dec. 28, 1717; m. Elizabeth Johnson.
103—7. Joanna, b. Sept. 8, 1718; m. Samuel Conger.
104—8. Abigail, b. April 1, 1727.

105. Elihu Crane[3] [30], (Jasper,[2] Jasper[1]), married Mary Plum. She afterwards married Rev. Jonathan Dickenson, one of the first presidents of Princeton College. He died in Newark, N. J., April 27, 1732, aged 43. His will names children. She died Aug. 30, 1762, in the 68th year of her age. He served the

town as overseer of the poor in 1725, and collector of taxes in
1728–1730. Children:

106—1. LEWIS, b. 1718.
107—2. CHRISTOPHER, b. 1720; d. April 17, 1750, without issue.
108—3. CHARLES, b. 1724; d. April 22, 1758, without issue.
109—4. ELIHU, b. 1726.
110—5. ISAAC; d. without issue.
111—6. HANNAH.
112—7. PHEBE.

113. DAVID CRANE[3] [31], (Jasper,[2] Jasper[1]), married Mary
——. Lieut. David,[3] died May 16, 1750, aged 57. His will
names children given below. He served the town in 1742 as
collector of taxes, and March 11, 1745–6, was chosen on a committee to prosecute any person or persons for cutting wood or
timber on the parsonage within the space of seven years from
that date, and the following year was chosen on a committee to
have charge of the parsonage lands in addition of the power to
prosecute offenders. Children:

114—1. JEDEDIAH, b. about 1716.
115—2. DAVID, b. about 1721.
116—3. JOSEPH, b. about 1732.
117—4. ABIGAIL; m. —— Johnston.
118—5. PHEBE; m. —— Lawrence.
119—6. MARY; m. —— Alling.
120—7. DORCAS.
121—8. SARAH, b. Aug. 24, 1734; perhaps, if so, she m. March, 1762,
 Isaac Plume, b. Oct. 1, 1734. He d. Nov. 19, 1799; she d.
 Nov. 24, 1779, at Newark, N. J.

122. JONATHAN CRAINE,[3] Esq. [32], (Jasper,[2] Jasper[1]),
married Sarah Treat, daughter of Major John Treat, and granddaughter of Capt. Robert Treat. For nearly thirty years he was
active in the public life of Newark. April 12, 1714, he was
ushered into service, when "Lieut. Jonathan Crane," was
elected on the "Prudentiall" Committee to attend to matters at
the Neck; Aug. 30, 1716, on committee to procure a minister;
March, 1717, surveyor of highways; Nov. 20, 1719, chosen to
inspect account of debts and give the account to the assessors,
with rate to be made; March 8, 1725, chosen collector for the
provincial tax; and for many years he was continued in this
office, adding in 1736 the duty of serving on committee to secure
the services of Rev. Aaron Burr and agree with him in the work
of the ministry in Newark. This Rev. Aaron Burr was the first
president of Princeton College, and also father of Aaron Burr,
born in the parsonage of the First Church at Newark, Feb. 6,
1756, who became the famous Col. Burr, of Revolutionary fame,
the political rival of General Hamilton, and his slayer in a duel.
In 1739 Jonathan Crane, Esq., was chosen on a committee to
treat with the people of Elizabethtown about settling the boundary line between the two towns; from 1740 to 1743 he was
assessor; and for about twenty-five years held the office of judge

of Essex County Court of Common Pleas. He died June 25, 1744, aged 66 years and 7 months. His will names children. Children :

123—1. SAMUEL, b. about 1712.
124—2. CALEB, b. about 1713.
125—3. ELIJAH, b. about 1716.
126—4. NEHEMIAH, b. about 1719.
127—5. JOHN TREAT.
128—6. MARY; m. —— Johnson.
129—7. EUNICE.

130. HANNAH CRANE[3] [34], (Jasper,[2] Jasper[1]), married about 1712 Robert Ogden, of Elizabethtown, N. J., son of Jonathan and Rebecca Ogden, from whom it is said descended Governor Aaron Ogden, son of Robert and Phebe (Hatfield) Ogden; also governor, afterwards judge, Haines. Children :

1. HANNAH (Ogden), b. 1714; m. Samuel Winans; d. March 14, 1783; had 12 children.
2. ROBERT (Ogden), b. Oct. 7, 1716; m. Phebe Hatfield; d. Jan. 21, 1789.
. PHEBE (Ogden), b. 1718; d. Oct. 14, 1735.
. MOSES (Ogden), b. 1722; m. Mary Cozzens; d. 1768.
. ELIHU (Ogden).
3. DAVID (Ogden), b. Oct. 26, 1726; m. Hannah Woodruff; d. Nov. 28, 1801.

131. EDMOND (or EDMUND) CRANE[4] [37], (John,[3] John,[2] Jasper[1]), married Abigail Kitchell. She was born Nov., 1717, and died Aug. 20, 1801. He died about 1761. His will is dated 1761; proved Jan. 30, 1762. He lived between Madison and Morristown, N. J., at what was called the "Hummock." Was a farmer, and his grandson Loyal Crane, born 1813, says his grandfather Edmund served in the Revolutionary war. It appears that two of his sons, Josiah and Ezekiel, were captains in the service. Names and dates of births of their children were furnished by Dorothy N. Law, of Dixon, Ill., a descendant of the family. She copied them from the family Bible.

Children:

132—1. STEPHEN, b. June 23, 1735.
133—2. EUNICE, b. Sept. 15, 1738.
134—3. AFFIE, b. July 15, 1740.
135—4. PHOEBY, b. April 13, 1743.
136—5. JOSIAH, b. June 25, 1745.
137—6. EZEKIEL, b. Oct. 29, 1747
138—7. JOHN, b. Jan. 24, 1749.
139—8. ABIGAIL, b. May 28, 1752.
140—9. JAMES, b. July 27, 1754.
141-10. DAVID, b. Dec. 24, 1756; probably served in Revolutionary war from Morris Co., N. J
142-11. BENONIE, b. June 27, 1761.

143. JOSEPH CRANE[4] [44], (Jasper,[3] John,[2] Jasper[1]), married Eunice Dodd, daughter of Thomas Dodd, for his 2d wife; lived in or near Bloomfield, N. J. Will dated 1807. He died in or near Bloomfield, Sept. 20, 1807, aged 85. She died Jan. or Feb. 20, 1822, aged 80. His grandson, Nathan J. Crane, reports that this Joseph Crane served in the French and Indian wars, and died in Bloomfield. Mr. Kimball says he lived and died in Belleville, N. J. March 14, 1758, he was chosen one of the overseers of highways for the town of Newark.

Children:

144—1. JOSEPH, b. 1767.
145—2. MOSES.
146—3. DANIEL.
147—4. AARON; said to have lived and died at Caldwell, N. J.
148—5. HANNAH; m. Samuel Mun, a farmer of Caldwell, N. J.; had twelve children; a granddaughter, Eunice Taylor, m.——— Ward and lived in Newark.

149. JEREMIAH CRANE[4] [56], (Daniel,[3] John,[2] Jasper[1]), was born about 1717, and married about 1764. He was the only son

ANCIENT CRANE HOMESTEAD,

Montclair, N. J.

Occupied several weeks during the Revolutionary War by General George Washington and the Marquis de Lafayette as their Headquarters. And now (1899) the
property of Mr. Alfred J. Crane, No. 1024, page 363. It has been the birthplace of
four generations of Cranes: Nathaniel, William, Oliver and Amos.

of Daniel[3] who married. Will was dated Aug. 17, 1785, and names the following children :

150—1. REBECKAH, b. about 1765.
151—2. ELEANOR, b. about 1772; d. young, unmarried.
152—3. WILLIAM, b. about 1775.
    Also a niece, widow Martha of John Gifford; "my nephew Moses Newel Combs."

153. LYDIA CRANE[4] [59], (Daniel,[3] John,[2] Jasper[1]), married —— Combs. Child :

1. MOSES NEWELL (Combs), b. Jan. 2, 1754, who m. Mary, dau. of David and Mary (Crane) Hayes (see No. 246), who was b. June 22, 1760, and d. Feb. 10, 1816. He d. April 12, 1834. Children :
    1. SALLY (Combs).
    2. POLLY (Combs).
    3. MARY (Combs).
    4. RICHARD N. (Combs).
    5. DAVID (Combs); m. —— Richards. Children :
        1. PETER W. (Combs); m. and had ERNEST B. (Combs), of Morristown, N. J.
        2. ISAAC (Combs).
        3. CHARLES (Combs).
        4. MARY (Combs).
        5. JULIA (Combs).
        6. ANN (Combs).
        7. SALLY (Combs).
    6. PHEBE (Combs).
    7. ISAAC (Combs).
    8. PHEBE H. (Combs).
    9. HANNAH (Combs).
    10. LYDIA (Combs).
    11. DEBORAH (Combs).
    12. AARON (Combs).
    13. RACHEL (Combs).

154. WILLIAM CRANE[4] [61], (Nathaniel,[3] Azariah,[2] Jasper[1]), married 1st, —— Wheeler, of Newark; 2d, Mary (or Mercy) ——. He resided in that part of Newark called for many years Crane-town, then West Bloomfield, now Mont Clair, N. J., and was a subscriber for the purpose of hiring a minister to preach the Gospel there. He was overseer of the poor from 1753 to 1756 inclusive, and of highways from 1760 to 1764; freeholder, 1767. He may have inherited property here from his father, and possibly succeeded to the home estate; of that, however, we are not certain, but the notable Crane mansion occupied by him or his family during the period of the war of the Revolution, still standing at the junction of Valley road and Clairmont avenue, was his home, and occupied about three weeks by Gen. Washington as his headquarters, Gen. Lafayette being with him. The time of occupation doubtless being from the latter week in October to about the middle of November, 1780. While those two great generals were making Mr. Crane's house their home, he with four if not five of his sons were performing soldiers' duties in the army of which they were the commanders. It is related by Rev. Oliver

26

Crane, D.D., LL.D., that on the arrival of Gen. Washington at
the house, Mercy Crane then in charge, and causing supper to be
prepared, discovered she had no tea to serve, and becoming
quite disturbed about it offered an apology to the General for
the lack of what might seem to him an important feature of his
repast. " Never mind, my good lady," replied His Excellency,
" please have a crust of bread toasted and use it for tea, that is
good enough for me." Mrs. Crane's anxiety was thus dispelled,
and supper was served. Night came on, and the capacity of the
house for beds was overtaxed, the lower back room selected by
the two generals for their use, had been used for the dining-room,
the deficiency of beds then was thereupon made known to the
General, who rejoined, " But there is plenty of straw in the barn,
is there not? " The straw was soon brought in and spread in one
corner of the room, and the two famous generals retired to rest,
wrapped in their army blankets, on that bundle of straw.

Children :

155—1. RACHEL; m. Simeon Baldwin.
156—2. HANNAH; m. Major Nathaniel Crane.
157—3. MATTHIAS.
158—4. JONATHAN.
159—5. JONAS, b. 1750.
160—6. SARAH, b. 1755; m. Stephen Fordham; d. 1825.
161—7. JAMES; d. unmarried.
162—8. ZADOC, b. 1758; m.; no children; d. 1841. Gen. Washington had an old gray horse which was almost as well known
as its rider. Zadoc Crane, one of the Revolutionary
Fathers, took care of the old gray when Washington was
at Cranetown, in New Jersey. While Zadoc took care of
the horse, the family entertained Washington, and waited
upon him with a finely Japanned server. This server,
though the Japanning is all worn off, was brought to the
Fair to exhibit in Bric-a-brac, by Mrs. Emma Fasshaber,
whose father was Zadoc Crane's uncle. Those were times
famous for having tried men's souls, and it was absolutely
necessary to exercise the greatest care and vigilance. The
oats fed to Washington's horse were kept concealed under
a stack of hay, and every time Zadoc got a mess from
under it he replaced the hay nicely, and after feeding, he
carefully picked up every scattered straw for fear the
British might nose the oats and " cabbage " them.
During the time Washington was occupying "Cranetown
Gap," as he styled it, the alarm came that the British were
about to make an attempt on the American lines in their
somewhat insecure position, and desiring to be in readi-
ness to meet such a movement should it be made, and not
feeling at this critical moment that he had a man to spare
from the ranks, he called for volunteers outside of those
in the service to act as couriers to warn the minute-men
living beyond the so called " first and second mountains,"
covering the region between the Passaic River and the
second mountain, including Horseneck, Pine Brook, Swine-
field, etc. Zadoc, a son of William, who had been lame
from boyhood, offered to assume the difficult and perilous
undertaking. Although lame, one leg being shorter than

the other, was well able to ride on horseback, and soon appeared mounted on his own spirited horse, and armed with a heavy cutlass, this being his only weapon; just as the sun was disappearing behind the mountains, under special orders from the General, he set out on his important errand. It was a ride for the night, calling at every house and routing them from their slumbers. As the gray of the morning began to show itself, he was marching his men toward the Crane mansion, and just at daybreak drew up his squad in front of the doorstep, on which stood Gen. Washington for the purpose of inspecting them. "Well done, my man," was the salute of His Excellency. "Now come in and take a horn of whiskey, for you must need it."

163—9. WILLIAM, b. 1759.
164-10. OLIVER, b. Sept. 29, 1765.

165. NOAH CRANE[4] [62], (Nathaniel,[3] Azariah,[2] Jasper[1]), married Mary Baldwin, daughter of Samuel. He died June 8, 1800, aged 81 years. She died May 18, 1805, aged 81 years. Lived in Cranetown, 1779; at town meeting at Newark, March 12, 1754, chosen one of the overseers of highways; March 12, 1765, again chosen at town meeting one of the overseers of highways. In 1776 was one of the officers of the Church at Bloomfield. Children:

166—1. SAMUEL, b. Oct. 29, 1747.
167—2. ESTHER; m. Joseph Baldwin.
168—3. JOSEPH, b. 1751.
169—4. ELIZABETH, b. April 13, 1753; m. John R. Crane.
170—5. CALEB; d. unmarried.
171—6. NATHANIEL; d. 1758.
172—7. NEHEMIAH; d. in infancy.
173—8. MEHITABLE; m. Gen. Wm. Gould.
174—9. MARY.
175-10. NEHEMIAH.
176-11. STEPHEN.

177. MEHITABLE CRANE[4] [66], (Nathaniel,[3] Azariah,[2] Jasper[1]), married Thomas Richards. He died, leaving a will dated 1758. Children:

1. THOMAS (Richards), b. 1741; d. April 14, 1788, at Newark, N. J.
2. NATHANIEL (Richards); he was a loyalist during the Revolutionary war, and his estate was confiscated, valued at £482 2s.
3. MARY (Richards).
4. ABIGAIL (Richards).

178. REBECCA CRANE[4] [68], (Azariah,[3] Azariah,[2] Jasper[1]), married Zachariah Baldwin, and settled at Parsippany, where she was buried in the old churchyard June 15, 1791, aged 84. He was born in Milford, Conn., Sept. 6, 1709. He removed to Hanover with his brother Abraham. Azariah Crane, father of Mrs. Baldwin, gave " three acres of mountain plantation to his beloved son-in-law Zachariah Baldwin." The following children are found accredited to them, and they may have had others. Children:

1. JACOB (Baldwin), b. about 1733.

2. JOB (Baldwin), b. about 1738.
3. SILAS (Baldwin), b. about 1749; m. and had Ephraim, whose son Amos m. Rachel, daughter of Deacon Oliver Crane, of Cranetown, N. J.

179. AZARIAH CRANE[4] [69], (Azariah,[3] Azariah,[2] Jasper[1]), married ——. He died 1752. His will names the following children:

180—1. SILAS.
181—2. DANIEL.
182—3. CALEB.
183—4. SARAH.
184—5. REBECCA.

185. JOB CRANE[4] [70], (Azariah,[3] Azariah,[2] Jasper[1]), married Abigail Dodd, daughter of John and Elizabeth Lampson (or Sampson) Dodd. Settled in Cranetown, now Mont Clair, N. J. Children:

186—1. TIMOTHY; no children.
187—2. AARON, b. March 5, 1750; d. Feb. 7, 1836, at Mont Clair.
188—3. THOMAS; killed on eve of marriage by the falling of a tree.
189—4. BETSY; m. Matthias Crane.

190. GAMALIEL CRANE[4] [71], (Azariah,[3] Azariah,[2] Jasper[1]). He may have married 1st, a Miss Brown, who died. He lived in Cranetown, N. J. Married Susanna Dodd, who was born at that place in 1747. She died in Williamson, Wayne Co., N. Y., February, 1824. Children:

191—1. JANE; m. Parmenas Dodd.
192—2. SIMEON.
193—3. MOSES.
194—4. JACOB.
195—5. CALEB.
196—6. ZEBINA, b. April 25, 1772.
197—7. ELIZABETH.
198—8. OBEDIAH, b. 1786.

199. EZEKIEL CRANE[4] [72], (Azariah,[3] Azariah,[2] Jasper[1]), married Elizabeth Halloway, of Southold, L. I. She married 2d, John Range, Esq. Served in Col. Schuyler's Regiment, Jersey Blues. Was taken prisoner by the French at Oswego in 1758, and died in Canada. Chosen March 12, 1754, surveyor of highways. Children:

200—1. JOHN R.; m. Elizabeth, daughter of Noah Crane.
201—2. JOSEPH; m. —— Baldwin.
202—3. LOIS, b. March 26, 1754; m. Moses Dodd.
203—4. BETTY; m. Enos Tompkins, and had six children.
204—5. DEBORAH; m. Ebenezer Dodd.

205. JOSIAH CRANE[4] [73], (Azariah,[3] Azariah,[2] Jasper[1]), married Joanna ——. Settled at Parsippany, where he with his wife and child Samuel were baptized into the First Presbyterian Church by the Rev. Timothy Johnes. Children:

206—1. SAMUEL; baptized Oct. 11, 1747; first postmaster for Chatham, Morris Co., N. J.

207—2. ELIJAH; baptized March 17, 1851.
208—3. HANNAH; baptized July 29, 1753.
209—4. MARY; baptized Dec. 21, 1755.

210. MOSES CRANE[4] [74], (Azariah,[3] Azariah,[2] Jasper[1]), married 1st, Susannah Brant. She died Aug. 14, 1776, aged 46; 2d, widow Rogers, with six children, her maiden name was Catharine Littell, of Littleton. Settled at Parsippany and died there, Feb. 12, 1795, aged 64. Married by the Rev. Timothy Johnes, first pastor of the First Presbyterian Church at Morristown, N. J., March 1, 1750. He was then called of Hanover. He was probably the Moses Crane, who served in the Revolutionary war from Morris Co., N. J. Children:

211—1. AMOS.
212—2. STEPHEN.
213—3. DANIEL PRINCE; baptized Sept. 15, 1751; m. Phebe Burnet.
214—4. EZEKIEL.
215—5. RACHEL, b. July 30, 1757; m. Ralph Burnett, and had four children.

By 2d wife:

216—6. JOSIAH; m. 1st, Rachel ——; went to Seneca Falls, N. Y. about the year 1800; she d. and he m. 2d, Philomelia Parks, a widow. He d. about 1824; no children.
217—7. JONAS; lived and d. at Junius, N. Y.
218—8. PHEBE. b. Feb. 22, 1783.
219—9. ELIZABETH, b. Feb. 6, 1787; m. Caleb Woodworth; went to New York State, 1804, and d. in 1829.

220. STEPHEN CRANE[4] [75], (Azariah,[3] Azariah,[2] Jasper[1]), married Rhoda Holloway. Settled at West Bloomfield, N. J. He died, 1794. March 14, 1758, was chosen one of the overseers of highways. His will also names his "poor son Bradford." Children:

221—1. BENJAMIN, b. 1753.
222—2. STEPHEN, b. Sept. 1, 1787; was the father of Benjamin.
223—3. AZARIAH, b. 1754; m. —— Tucker.
224—4. JEREMIAH.
225—5. LOIS; baptized May 11, 1760; m. Justice Burnet.
226—6. POLLY; m. Dr. Bone.
227—7. RHODA, b. about 1760; m. Linus Baldwin.
228—8. ABIGAIL; m. Caleb Martin.
229—9. KETURAH; m. Ira Williams; went to New York State; had a large family.
230—10. SARAH; m. Nehemiah Baldwin.
231—11. BRADFORD.

232. TIMOTHY CRANE[4] [78], (Robert,[3] Azariah,[2] Jasper[1]), married Sarah ——. She died Jan. 1, 1752, aged 25. He died Feb. 22, 1786, aged 60. His will names child Timothy of brother Isaac; also names Sayres, child of brother Josiah. There was a Timothy Crane, uncle to Samuel Curry, whose will in 1786 mentions him as uncle Timothy Crane. March 12, 1754, was chosen one of the surveyors of highways, and again March 8, 1763. In 1737 he was one of the pounders for the Great Neck,

and to perform same duties in company with Jonas Crane in 1739-40. He was probably the Timothy who served in the Revolutionary war from Essex Co., N. J.

233. ISAAC CRANE[4] [79], (Robert,[3] Azariah,[2] Jasper[1]), married Hannah ——. Was surveyor of highways, March 10, 1772. He perhaps was the Isaac Crane who served in the Revolutionary war from Essex Co., N. J. Children :

234—1. JOHANNA, b. March 29, 1760.
235—2. MARY, b. June 6, 1762.
236—3. DORCAS, b. Nov. 25, 1764.
237—4. PHEBE, b. Nov. 6, 1767.
238—5. TIMOTHY, b. March 28, 1770.
239—6. ISAAC, b. March 28, 1770.

240. JOSIAH CRANE[4] [80], (Robert,[3] Azariah,[2] Jasper[1]). Mr. Isaac Watts Crane thinks he married Hannah Pennington. He died Jan. 18, 1774, aged 42. Children :

241—1. SAYRES; d. May 5, 1795, aged 34. Buried in First Church yard, Newark. In his will he left $1000 to his sister Hannah, and remembers also Comfort and Phebe.
242—2. HANNAH.
243—3. COMFORT: m. Garret Jacobs.
244—4. PHEBE; m. John Day.
245—5. ABIGAIL; m. Moses Vertoot.

246. MARY CRANE[4] [81], (Robert,[3] Azariah,[2] Jasper[1]), married David Hayes. He was born about 1732. He died Jan. 28, 1811, aged 79. She died Dec. 18, 1817, aged 82. Children :

1. ROBERT (Hayes).
2. DAVID (Hayes).
3. JOSEPH (Hayes).
4. MARY (Hayes); m. —— Combs.
5. ABIGAIL (Hayes); m. —— Pike.
6. LYDIA (Hayes); m. —— Drake.
7. ELIZABETH (Hayes); m. —— Congar.
8. RACHEL (Hayes).

247. PHEBE CRANE[4] [82], (Robert,[3] Azariah,[2] Jasper[1]), married 1st, —— Lawrence. Perhaps married 2d, David Bruen for his second wife. Children :

1. BENJAMIN (Lawrence).
2. JONATHAN (Lawrence).
3. BARNABAS (Lawrence).

248. LYDIA CRANE[4] [83], (Robert,[3] Azariah,[2] Jasper[1]), married Timothy Bruen. His will, 1798, names children :

1. THADDEUS (Bruen).
2. NATHANIEL (Bruen).
3. JOSIAH (Bruen).
4. JOSEPHUS (Bruen).
5. PHEBE (Bruen).
6. CHARLOTTE (Bruen); m. —— Farrand.
7. CATHARINE (Bruen); m. —— Crane.

249. EUNICE CRANE[4] [77], (Robert,[3] Azariah,[2] Jasper[1]), married David Johnson at Newark, N. J. He had 2d wife, Hannah ——. She died Oct. 22, 1776, aged 56. Children:

1. NATHANIEL (Johnson).
2. DAVID (Johnson).
3. JOTHAM (Johnson).
4. JABEZ (Johnson).
5. TIMOTHY C. (Johnson).
6. PHEBE (Johnson); m. Daniel Johnson.
7. MARTHA (Johnson); m. Aaron Day.

250. JONAS CRANE[4] [86], (John,[3] Azariah,[2] Jasper[1]), married Hannah Lyon, daughter of Benjamin Lyon, and lived in Newark, N. J., on east side of Broad Street, on part of the house lot given his mother by Robert Treat, her father, and died there Jan. 24, 1745, aged 27 years. His wife also died the same day, and they were buried together. They left one child about a year old named Rufus, who was taken to live with his grandfather, John Crane. Was chosen pounder for the Great Neck in 1740. March 5, 1743–4 was chosen one of the assessors for the town.
Child:

251—1. RUFUS, b. 1744.

252. SAMUEL CRANE[4] [87], (John,[3] Azariah,[2] Jasper[1]), married Keziah, daughter of Nathaniel Baldwin, of Newark. She was born about 1722, and died Sept. 24, 1779, aged 56. March 3, 1755, he was chosen one of the assessors for the town of Newark. He died July 2, 1796, aged 73. During the Revolutionary war he lived in Newark, was taken prisoner by the British, and had his feet frozen from exposure. He lived in a stone house, with quite a large lot of land surrounding it, situated on —— Street, in Newark, N. J. His youngest daughter Abigail inherited the estate, and resided there for many years, refusing to part with the land, although urged to do so by persons needing it for the site of stores and for other business purposes. In 1836 she was residing there; but a few years later she was persuaded to relinquish the place and secure a home in another portion of the city. It is said she had previously refused $10,000 in money and a lot with a much better house upon it in exchange for her home. But now she was far advanced in years and by force of circumstances obliged to yield to the onward march of improvements. She died about 1844, soon after leaving her old home. This stone house had over the door the figures 1760. Mr. Edwin Crane thinks that may have been the date of its construction. Children:

253—1. SAMUEL; may have gone to Amsterdam, N. Y.; conveyed a lot in Newark in 1796.
254—2. TIMOTHY, b. May 27, 1760.
255—3. ESTHER; m. Cyrenus Riggs.
256—4. HANNAH; d. young.
257—5. ABIGAIL; d. in Newark 1804 or 1805; unmarried.

258. JOHN CRANE[4] [89], (John,[3] Azariah,[2] Jasper[1]), married 1st, Hannah Johnson, who died in 1779, aged 46; 2d, Rhoda Lyon, the widow of James Wheeler. He died about 1790. May have been the John Crane who served in Capt. Abraham Lyons' Co., 2d Regt., from Essex Co., N. J. Children:

259—1. SAYERS.
260—2. AZARIAH; d. in Philadelphia about 1812, leaving a wife and daughter.
261—3. MATTHIAS, b. 1765.
262—4. MARTHA, b. May 12, 1759.
263—5. REBECCA; m. David E. Crane.
264—6. HANNAH, b. 1772; d. 1776.
265—7. HANNAH, b. 1784; m. —— Sanford.

266. ELIAKIM CRANE[4] [90], (John,[3] Azariah,[2] Jasper[1]), married Joanna ——. Lived between Orange and West Bloomfield. He died about 1811. March 14, 1758, he was chosen one of the overseers of highways. Probably served in the Revolutionary war from Essex Co., N. J. Children:

267—1. JOHN.
268—2. JOSIAH.
269—3. ELIAKIM; April 8, 1793, and 1797, chosen overseer of highways at Newark town meeting; probably served in War of 1812.
270—4. CATHARINE; m. Stephen Ward.
271—5. MARGARET; baptized Sept. 19, 1756; m. Samuel J. Ward.

272. ELIAS CRANE[4] [91], (John,[3] Azariah,[2] Jasper[1]). He died 1789; his will, Jan. 4, 1789, proved August following, names Sayers Crane, son of his brother John Crane, and his son David executors; and besides his four children mentions Abigail and Mary, daughters of his daughter Mary Smith. March 10, 1761, he was chosen overseer of highways and pounder for the Neck. March 9, 1762, he with David Rogers and Joseph Ball were chosen pounders to take care of the Neck. He was, we presume, the Elias Crane who served in Capt. Josiah Pierson's Co., 2d Regt., from Essex. Children:

273—1. DAVID.
274—2. SARAH; m. —— Tichnor.
275—3. PHEBE; m. —— Cadmus.
276—4. MARY; m. —— Smith.

277. BENJAMIN CRANE[4] [93], (John,[3] Azariah,[2] Jasper[1]), married Phebe Meeker, and moved to Amsterdam, N. Y., early in the history of that place, probably about 1790. He was a blacksmith. Was buried near Craneville, Montgomery Co., N. Y. She died on the Ohio River while making the journey west with her son Jonas and his family. Children:

278—1. JONAS, b. May 20, 1766.
279—2. OBEDIAH M., b. 1780.
280—3. BENJAMIN.
281—4. ISAAC B.; settled in New York city.
282—5. DAVID.

283—6. CALEB C..
284—7. PHEBE.

285. JONAS CRANE[4] [95], (John,[3] Azariah,[2] Jasper[1]), married
Sarah, daughter of Josiah Beach. She died Sept. 8, 1785, aged
37. He was mortally wounded near Fort Delancy, the enemy's
post on Newark Bay, and died April 4, 1782. He served in the.
Revolutionary war from Essex Co. Children:

286—1. JOHN HOYT, b. 1773; d. April 13, 1785.
287—2. REBECCA; m. 1st, James Campbell, who d. 1804; m. 2d, Mr.
　　　　Hawley..
288—3. PAUL.

289. BENJAMIN CRANE[4] [97], (Joseph,[3] Jasper,[2] Jasper[1]),
lived in Elizabeth, N. J., and died there July 14, 1777, at the
age of 72 years, and was designated as Benjamin Crane senior.
Sarah ——, his wife, was born Aug. 11, 1709. Children:

290—1. HANNAH, b. Nov. 20, 1729.
291—2. ABIGAIL, b. Dec. 20, 1731; m. Mr. Beach.
292—3. STEPHEN, b. Oct. 9, 1733.
293—4. SARAH, b. 1735; m. Mr. Hayes.
294—5. JOSIAH, b. Jan. 16, 1738.
295—6. BENJAMIN, } twins. b. Feb. 4, 1740.
296—7. ELIZABETH, }

297. EZEKIEL CRANE[4] [99], (Joseph,[3] Jasper,[2] Jasper[1]),
lived in that part of Newark called Lyons Farms. March 12,
1754, he was chosen one of the surveyors of highways in
Newark. He died about 1794. His will, dated 1787, names the
following children:

298—1. JOSEPH.
299—2. ELIAS, b. April 10, 1753.
300—3. JOANNA; m. Mr. Plume.
301—4. RACHAEL; m. Joseph Lyon, Nov. 19, 1766, and were of Lyons
　　　　Farms, N. J.
302—5. PHEBE, b. 1740.
303—6. SARAH.

304. ISAAC CRANE[4] [98], (Joseph,[3] Jasper,[2] Jasper[1]). He is
reported to have been the printer of Newark, N. J. Children:

305—1. ISAAC.
306—2. DAVID.
307—3. UZAL; m. Sarah Pierson, Nov. 4, 1778.
308—4. MARY.
309—5. PHEBE; m. Jonathan Clark.
310—6. ABIGAIL; m. John Swain.
311—7. MARTHA; m. James Webster; may have had Keturah, who
　　　　m. Caleb Harrison.

312. ISRAEL CRANE[4] [100], (Joseph,[3] Jasper,[2] Jasper[1]),
lived between Camptown and Connecticut Farms, N. J. At town
meeting March 9, 1762, he was chosen one of the overseers of
highways. March 12, 1776, he was chosen on committee for
raising money for the poor of the town of Newark. He died
Aug. 1, 1785, aged 73. His will names the following children:

313—1. ISRAEL, b. about 1755.
27

314—2. RACHEL.
315—3. MARY; m. —— Woodruff.
316—4. LUCY; m. James Clisba.
317—5. ESTHER; m. —— Eagles.

318. JOSIAH CRANE[4] [101], (Joseph,[3] Jasper,[2] Jasper[1]), married Phebe ——. Will, 1786, names children and wife Phebe. From the headstone at his grave we learn that he died Dec. 15, 1785, in the 67th year of his age, and that he was known as Captain Josiah Crane; also that his wife's name was Jerusha; that she died Oct. 10, 1777, in the 55th year of her age. The writer has not been able to learn whether Captain Josiah lived at Connecticut Farms or not, although his son Josiah did; therefore it is uncertain which one of these two Josiahs is referred to in the town records, March 8, 1768, where it reads: "Josiah Crane, at the Farms, chosen one of the overseers of highways." At this time there were no less than four Josiah Cranes, of suitable age to serve in public office; hence the difficulty of proper designation. Children:

319—1. OBEDIAH, b. 1755.
320—2. JOSIAH.
321—3. ELIAS; served as overseer of highways, 1798.
322—4. LOIS; m. Mr. Hinman.
323—5. BETSY; m. Mr. Pool.
324—6. MARY; m. Mr. Harrison.
325—7. JOANNA; m. Mr. Heard.
326—8. JERUSHA; m. Mr. Brown.

327. JOSEPH CRANE[4] [102], (Joseph,[3] Jasper,[2] Jasper[1]); married Elizabeth Johnson. She was born Oct. 3, 1729. Mr. Burnet writes that most of the Cranes in the line of Joseph, lived during the last century, between Newark and South Orange, N. J., in and about Springfield, and at North Farms, now Middleville. March 8, 1757, was chosen one of the overseers of highways. She was left a widow, and married Paul Day, and her will, dated 1785, names the following children:

328—1. ABIGAIL, b. April 1, 1750.
329—2. JOHN, b. Feb. 12, 1754.
330—3. DAVID, b. March 12, 1756.
331—4. PHEBE, b. March 26, 1758; said to have married —— Pribby, and settled at Cincinnati, Ohio.
332—5. ELIZABETH, b. March 4, 1760.
333—6. BENJAMIN, b. Feb. 6, 1762.
334—7. SARAH, b. Feb. 6, 1762; m. Mr. Thompson, and lived in Mendham, Morris Co., N. J.
335—8. JOSEPH, b. March 6, 1764.
336—9. ISAAC, b. Feb., 1766.

337. JOANNA CRANE[4] [103], (Joseph,[3] Jasper,[2] Jasper[1]), married Samuel Conger. He died Dec. 14, 1752, aged 37 years. She then married Joseph Camp. Children:

1. DAVID (Conger).
2. JONATHAN (Conger).
3. STEPHEN (Conger).

 4. SAMUEL (Conger).
 5. JOANNA (Camp).

 338. LEWIS CRANE[4] [106], (Elihu,[3] Jasper,[2] Jasper[1]), married Mary Burr; settled at Orange, N. J.; lived and died on the place opposite Phineas Crane's, on the Orange road to Crane-town. She was sister to Rev. Aaron Burr, of Newark, N. J., who was son of Daniel Burr, Esq.; of Fairfield Street, first president of Princeton College, who married Esther Edwards, daughter of Rev. Jonathan Edwards, of Stockbridge, Mass., father of Col. Aaron Burr, who killed Alexander Hamilton in a duel. March 12, 1776, he was chosen one out of a committee of thirty-seven to oversee the highways in the town of Newark. This would seem as if they were putting things in order for the transportation of armies. It certainly shows that the roads about Newark needed a vast amount of attention. She died in 1781, aged 59. He died July 14, 1777, aged 59. Date of will 1776, named children given below:

 339—1. ISAAC, b. 1746.
 340—2. MARY; m. John Ward; no children.
 341—3. JOANNA; never m.
 342—4. CHARLES; d. at Lebanon Springs, 1804, leaving two children.
 343—5. PHEBE.

 344. ELIHU CRANE[4] [109], (Elihu,[3] Jasper,[2] Jasper[1]), married Hannah, daughter of Dr. Timothy Mix, of New Haven. Settled in Newark, N. J. He died Feb. 4, 1786, aged 60, "an elder in the Christian Church." He was overseer of highways in 1756 and 1765. Children:

 345—1. MARY; m. Cornelius Davis.
 346—2. MARTHA, b. Sept. 19, 1762; m. Rev. John Cross, afterwards bishop.
 347—3. SARAH; m. Joseph Lyon, A. M., of Lyons Farms; d. at Bloomfield, 1841, aged 77.
 348—4. HETTY; d. when 10 years old.
 349—5. ANNA; m. Joseph Davis, Esq., of Bloomfield.
 350—6. ELIHU, b. 1771; lived in Bloomfield, N. J.; was constable in 1801; overseer of highways in 1805 and 1811. A stone marking his resting-place bears the following: "In memory of Elihu Crane, son of Elihu the son of Elihu Yale, & grandson of Jasper Crane, 2d, who died Jany 30 1847 aged 76."
 351—7. ISAAC WATTS; lived in Orange. (Made this record, Nov. 2, 1850).
 352—8. HANNAH; died in infancy.
 353—9. JOHN AUSTIN; went to the west in 1823; not heard from for 26 years (now 1850).

 354. HANNAH CRANE[4] [111], (Elihu,[3] Jasper,[2] Jasper[1]). Mr. Burnet says she married 1st, Mr. Johnson, and had Anna (Johnson), who married Dr. Moses Scott of New Brunswick; married 2d, Peter Paine; settled at Hopewell, Hunterdon Co., and had Elihu (Paine).

355. PHEBE CRANE[4] [112], (Elihu,[3] Jasper,[2] Jasper[1]). Mr. Burnet says she married Rev. Mr. Carmichael, of Brandywine, and was related to the Carmichaels of Queen Ann Co., Md.
Child :

    1. Dr. JOHN FLAVEL (Carmichael) ; d. previous to 1851, at Pinkney-ville, Miss.

356. JEDEDIAH CRANE[4] [114], (David,[3] Jasper,[2] Jasper[1]), married Elizabeth ———. He was, we presume, twice married, for Mary Crane, wife of Jedediah Crane, joined the first Presbyterian Church, in Newark. In 1756, he was chosen one of the overseers of highways, also the following year, and for several years afterwards, even as late as 1771. He died Sept. 10, 1785, aged 69 ; will names no children.

357. DAVID CRANE[4] [115], (David,[3] Jasper,[2] Jasper[1]), married 1st, Sarah A. Dodd, born 1734. She died March 6, 1772, aged 38 years. He married Abigail Ogden for his 2d wife. She was daughter of Justice John Ogden, and sister to Mrs. Caldwell, wife of Rev. James Caldwell, of Elizabeth, from whom the township received its name *Caldwell*. He died March 6, 1794, aged 73. March 13, 1753, Mr. Crane was chosen one of the surveyors of highways, and 1755 one of the overseers of highways. March 10, 1778, chosen one of the surveyors for the town, and the following year, pound-master. Looking after the highways and strays seemed to demand the principal or chief attention of the settlers of Newark about this time. Will names children :

    358—1. STEPHEN.
    359—2. JEDEDIAH ; April 12, 1802, chosen constable for Newark ; 1815 and 1819, overseer of highways.
    360—3. JOSEPH.
    361—4. AARON.
    362—5. DAVID D., b. Sept. 19, 1763.
    363—6. PHEBE ; m. Mr. Davis.
    364—7. ANNA ; m. Joseph Davis, of Bloomfield, N. J.

365. JOSEPH CRANE[4] [116], (David,[3] Jasper,[2] Jasper[1]). It is said he married Patience Crane. He died Nov. 21, 1789, aged 57. He was chosen Constable, March 10, 1778. Will names children :

    366—1. PHINEAS ; perhaps served in War of 1812, from Cranetown.
    367—2. JAMES.
    368—3. JOHN.
    369—4. SARAH.
    370—5. HANNAH ; m. John Gifford. She was mother to late Archer Gifford.
    371—6. ABIGAIL ; m. Uriah James.
    372—7. MARY ; m. John Baldwin.

373. SAMUEL CRANE, Esq.[4] [123], (Jonathan,[3] Jasper,[2] Jas-

perl), married Ann ——; died Dec. 28, 1746, aged 34 years. Will mentions these children:

374—1. SARAH.
375—2. ELIZABETH.
376—3. MARGARET.

377. CALEB CRANE, Esq.[4] [124], (Jonathan,[3] Jasper,[2] Jasper[1]), married Phebe Farrand; died July 16, 1793, aged 80. He was born and buried at Orange, N. J. Will names children:

378—1. SAMUEL; was mortally wounded in a skirmish near Belleville, and d. Sept., 1777, aged 23. He left a son Dr. Caleb, who d. 1842, aged 68.
379—2. JOHN CALEB.
380—3. SARAH.
381—4. HANNAH.
382—5. PHEBE; m. Benjamin Williams.
383—6. SILAS; d. in Indiana.
384—7. CALEB; had in Allegheny Co., Pa., children:
    1. DANIEL, b. 1808.
    2. JOHN.
    3. STEPHEN.
    4. CALEB.
    5. EZRA.
    6. SILAS.

385. DANIEL CRANE [1]; had children;

    1. JOHN, b. about 1836; settled in Exira, Iowa.
    2. VAN BUREN; edited *The Pilot*, Jackson, Minn.

386. ELIJAH CRANE[4] [125], (Jonathan,[3] Jasper,[2] Jasper[1]), married Rachel Beach, and died April 24, 1790, aged 74. At town meeting, March 13, 1759, he was chosen collector of taxes, serving several years in that capacity. In 1764, he was chosen town clerk, collector, and bookkeeper for strays. March 12, 1774-5, pursuant to act of the Assembly, Elijah Crane was chosen assessor for the county and poor-rates. He served as town clerk for Newark, several years, 1764 to 1769. Will names children:

387—1. ELIJAH.
388—2. JONATHAN; d. at Newark; unmarried.
389—3. REBECCA; d. at Newark; unmarried.
390—4. LUCY; d. May 19, 1806, age 36.
391—5. PHEBE; m. Zephaniah Grant.
392—6. RACHEL; m. —— Sickels.
393—7. HANNAH; m. —— Baldwin.
394—8. ABIGAIL; m. —— Spinning.
395—9. ANNIS; m. —— Whittemore.
    10. —— ——, who m. a Dr. Browne, son of loyal Rev. Isaac Browne, of Trinity Church, Newark, N. J.

396. NEHEMIAH CRANE[4] [126], (Jonathan,[3] Jasper,[2] Jasperl), died Aug. 11, 1751, aged 32, in Newark, N. J. Child:

397—1. JONATHAN, b. March 17, 1743.

398. JOHN TREAT CRANE[4] [127], (Jonathan,[3] Jasper,[2] Jasper[1]), married Elizabeth Baldwin. She died May 4, 1806. He was chosen surveyor of highways, March 13, 1759. Isaac Watts Crane says this John Treat Crane built a house down near Chestnut Street, and nearly opposite Dr. Barnet's, where Van Berker lived, and where Samuel Pennington died. The house was then (1850) standing. Child:

399—1. AARON TREAT; d. at St. Louis, Sept. 26, 1819, where he was postmaster.

FIFTH GENERATION.

400. STEPHEN CRANE[5] [132], (Edmund,[4] John,[3] John,[2] Jasper[1]). Quite recently we have been furnished data which, to the best of our judgment, after careful investigation, belongs here. And being unable to perfect the line before the arrangement of other families was made, the full line is entered at this point. The above Stephen Crane was a cooper by trade, and lived in Elizabeth, N. J. Subsequently he removed to Goshen, N. Y. Married ———, and the following, with record of his descendants, has been furnished by Rev. Floyd N. Crane, of Goshen, son of John Sears Crane:

In a bond of indemnity by Nathaniel Ball, of Newark, N. J., to Stephen Crane, dated April 22, 1761, Josiah Crane was a witness.

In a deed of 59 acres to Stephen Crane by Elkanah Fuller, Stephen C. is said to be "of late from East New Jersey."

In an old bond of my grandfather, John Crane, to his brother, Stephen, Jr., the time of payment is thus worded: "the same to be paid six months after the death of Stephen Crane, the father of the said Stephen Crane, Jun'."

In a deed made "May 20, 1757, in the 30th yr of his Majesties Reign King George the Second of Great Brittain, Between Josiah Woodruff of Borough of Elizabeth in the County of Essex & Eastern Division of the Province of N. J. & Stephen Crane of the Borough aforesaid." Consideration, "110 pounds at 8 shillings the ounce & all one certain Messuage & in the Borough of Elizabeth, 3½ acres with House, &c."

Children:

401—1. STEPHEN; supposed to have m. Oct. 11, 1781, Mary Arnout.
402—2. WILLIAM.
403—3. JOHN, b. Aug. 24, 1766; m. Abigail Sears.
404—4. BENJAMIN.
405—5. LETTY; m. Thomas Bronson.
406—6. SARAH; m. Samuel Bronson, Nov. 21, 1790.

WILLIAM CRANE [2]; m., it is said, Mary Cooley, March 16, 1788. He d. of dysentery, Sept. 26, 1827, and she d. of the same disease in the forenoon of the following day. Both were buried in the same grave, Webb Cemetery, in Goshen, N. Y. Children:

407—1. STEPHEN NELSON, b. May 27, 1799; d. Feb. 1, 1875.
408—2. OLIVER; d. at Goshen, Ind.
409—3. DANIEL.

410. STEPHEN NELSON CRANE [1]; m. Mary E. Crane, a cousin. She was b. Sept. 20, 1799, and d. Nov. 20, 1873. He d. Feb. 1, 1875. Children:

1. MARY E.; d. June 10, 1835.

2. MARY E.; d. June 17, 1850.
3. ALFRED; d. Sept. 15, 1875.
4. FANNIE A.; d. Dec. 23, 1882.
5. SARAH F.; d. April 27, 1876.
6. CARRIE; m. George C. Baldwin; had Alfred H.
7. STEPHEN NEWTON; m. Helen V. Sawyer; had Benjamin, Frank, Mary Louisa.
8. G. D. F.

As Stephen senior mentions in his will a grandson, John Nelson Crane, we infer he was son of Stephen Nelson.

JOHN CRANE [3]; m. Abigail Sears. She was b. July 24, 1774. He resided in Goshen, N. Y., where he was a farmer and cooper. He d. Oct. 1, 1824. She d. July 22, 1860. They had one child:

411—1. JOHN SEARS, b. Aug. 3, 1795; m. Sarah Smith, April 18, 1822. She was b. March 17, 1802. He d. Jan. 1, 1875. She d. March 8, 1879. Both lived and died in Goshen, N. Y. He was an M. D. Children:
   1. FANNIE E.
   2. ANN ELIZA, b. May 18, 1825; d. Dec. 1, 1826.
   3. IRA SMITH, b. Jan. 27, 1828; d. July 24, 1846.
412—4. ALBERT GALATIN, b. Sept. 15, 1829; m. Julia Ayrault Holden. Children:
   1. FLOYD HOLDEN, b. July 22, 1866.
   2. ALBERT SMITH.
   3. ANNA LOUISE, b. Feb. 10, 1870; m. Burton G. Winton; had Robert McB. (Winton); d. Nov. 12, 1896.
   4. EDESH A., b. Dec. 7, 1872.
   5. MABEL.
413—5. WILLIAM HENRY, b. Sept. 25, 1831; d.
414—6. FLOYD AUGUSTUS, b. Sept. 28, 1835; m. June 15, 1858, Melissa A. Jennings, who was b. July 5, 1833. He is a graduate of Princeton College, class 1855, and from Princeton Seminary, 1858. A clergyman; settled at Goshen, where he was born. Child:

    1. MELISSA JENNINGS, b. Aug. 23, 1859, at Goshen, Orange Co., N. Y.; m. Oct. 12, 1881, Edgar Batterson Redfield, who was b. July 4, 1859. Child:

       1. FLORENCE JENNINGS (Redfield), b. Nov. 15, 1884; d. Jan. 6, 1889.

BENJAMIN CRANE [4]: m. 1st, Dec. 22, 1791, it is said, Asunath Pellet. She d. May 3, 1807, and he m. 2d, Sally Lusk, April 7, 1810, and possibly 3d, Eve ———, who withdrew from the Church, Oct. 29, 1831, and removed from Goshen. Children:

415—1. MARY E.; m. Stephen Nelson Crane; d. Nov., 1873.
416—2. ELLEN; m. G. D. Smith; had Benjamin and Moses.
417—3. SALLIE; m. ——— Slaughter.
418—4. HORACE; m. Maria Lusk. Children:
419—1. MARY E.; m. Jack Harrison.
420—2. ELLEN; m. Merrit C. Owen.
421—3. SARAH F.; m. Harlan Hall.
422—4. FANNIE; m. John Kimber.
423—5. ANNA; m. James V. Brown.

424. Capt. JOSIAH CRANE[5] [136], (Edmund,[4] John,[3] John,[2] Jasper[1]), married Abigail Hathaway, March 28, 1768. She was

daughter of Dr. Benjamin Hathaway, of Morristown, N. J., born Oct. 6, 1746; she died April 19, 1792.

Mrs. D. H. Law, a descendant who has given much time to investigation, writes that he entered into covenant in the Presbyterian Church of Morristown, Nov. 4, 1764; that he served as lieutenant in Captain Halsey's Company, Eastern Battalion, Morris Co., N. J. Militia, during August and September, 1776, and as captain from September until the close of the Revolutionary war. In the spring of 1784, he removed to Goshen, N. Y., with his three sons, and purchased three hundred acres of land in Orange Co., giving each of them a farm there. Some of his descendants still (1897) reside on a portion of that original tract of land. By trade he was a hatter, and before removing to New York State, kept a store in Morristown, N. J. He was a large man, weighing about 250 pounds. Is said to have married three times, one wife being a Kitchell, of Rockaway Neck, N. J., but all his children were by his first wife. He died July 14, 1822, aged 77. He was a man of good repute, and enjoyed the confidence and respect of all who knew him. His last wife survived him. Children:

425—1. BENJAMIN, b. Feb. 12, 1769.
426—2. ABRAHAM, b. Dec. 25, 1774.
427—3. AFFA (or ALPHIA), b. July 19, 1777; m. William Morrison, May 28, 1796.
428—4. STEPHEN, b. May 5, 1780.
429—5. ELIZABETH, b. Feb. 7, 17—; m. —— Robbins.

430. Capt. EZEKIEL CRANE[5] [137], (Edmund,[4] John,[3] John,[2] Jasper[1]), married Eunice Hayward, Sept. 23 (or Oct. 10), 1770. She was probably daughter of Shadrack Hayward. She was baptized April 1, 1754. He was a house-builder, and at one time owned and operated the Hoboken ferry, at which time he resided in New Jersey, opposite New York city. He was a schoolmate of Martin Van Buren and DeWitt Clinton. Was also a surveyor, and became one of the first settlers of Mentz, Cayuga Co., N. Y. Was the first supervisor of the town of Aurelius when it embraced nearly one-half of the present territory of Cayuga Co. Was appointed justice of the peace and associate justice of the court of common pleas by Gov. John Jay, March 9, 1796. He left Morristown Church March 2, 1775. Church records mention him as "captain" in Nov., 1783. He died suddenly March 15, 1813. She died May 28, 1816. Both were buried in an ancient cemetery on the farm occupied by them, seven miles northwest of Auburn. He was a soldier in the Revolutionary war, serving at Valley Forge, and later became a captain in the western battalion State troops. Children:

431—1. SHADRACK, b. May 24, 1773.
432—2. ABIGAIL, b. July 21, 1776.
433—3. SILAS, b. Jan. 30, 1780.
434—4. ANN, b. July 14, 1783; d. Sept. 12, 1784.
435—5. ANN KIMBALL, b. Feb. 28, 1785.
436—6. NANCY; d. young.
28

437.　As the brothers whose names are given below were cousins of the above Shadrack Crane, we give here what we have been able to obtain concerning their descendants. The name of their father seems not to have been made clear. Whether it was Stephen or John (uncles to Shadrack) we do not know, although that would seem probable, or it may have been Aaron. Alexander Dallas Crane gave the latter as his grandfather's name, and at the same time said his own father Stephen was cousin to Shadrach Crane, who married Hannah Palmer. A daughter of Martin L. Crane writes: " Aaron was half brother to Stephen, I think. I never heard his name mentioned in connection with the Cranes but once or twice, and then I asked my father who Aaron was; he said to me he was ' an odd sheep' and they never paid any attention to him. That is all I know of the said Aaron."

- 1.　STEPHEN CRANE, b. June 1, 1781, in Hanover, Morris Co., N. J.
- 2.　DANIEL CRANE, who lived at or near Port Byron, Cayuga Co., N. Y. About 1840 he removed to the State of Michigan, and located near Lansing; d. about 1860.

438.　STEPHEN CRANE [1]; m. April 5, 1804, Katurah, dau. of Simon H. and Mary Topping, and lived in Mentz, Cayuga Co., N. Y., where he d. June 19, 1813. Katurah Topping was b. in Hanover, Morris Co., N. J., July 2, 1786, and d. at Montezuma, N. Y., March 5, 1824. Children:
- 1.　JOANNA, b. March 1, 1805; d. at Lima, Mich., July 10, 1868.
- 2.　ELIZABETH, b. July 12, 1807; m. —— Fox; lived at Redwood, Cal., with her son, George Fox.
- 3.　ALEXANDER DALLAS, b. Oct. 5, 1809.
- 4.　MARTIN L., b. Feb. 22, 1812.

439.　Hon. ALEXANDER DALLAS CRANE [3]; was b. in Mentz or Montezuma, N. Y., the son of a farmer. Learned the trade of a blacksmith. In the year 1827 he removed to Michigan, arriving there Nov. 24, stopping at Ann Arbor. Three years later he located at Dexter, continuing to work at his trade until 1832, when he began the study of law. Was soon elected constable; and subsequently was deputy sheriff and collector of taxes, continuing in the latter position ten years. He tried merchandising for a year and a half, when, in 1843, he was admitted to the bar, and learned to practice in the legal profession. In 1849 President Fillmore appointed him postmaster at Dexter; also served as justice of the peace. At the close of the year 1853 he resigned the postmastership to accept the office of prosecuting attorney of Washtenaw Co., 1854 to 1865. Four times in succession he was called upon to preside over the circuit court as its judge, and in 1873 he was appointed judge of the fourth judicial district of Michigan, embracing the counties of Jackson, Ingham and Washtenaw, which seat he filled with credit and honor for three years. At the close of his judgeship he formed a copartnership with A. J. Sawyer at Ann Arbor. Little later he returned to Dexter, where he continued his law practice, adding the insurance business, and continuing it until failing health compelled the relinquishment of all care. Mr. Crane was appointed colonel of the 7th Regt., 4th Brigade, 2d division of Michigan State Militia, by Governor S. T. Mason, March 30,

1832. April 29, 1842, he was appointed brigadier-general by Governor E. Ransom. and by Governor K. S. Bingham major-general of the 2d division. In 1861 he raised a company of 101 men, and entered the service of the United States, May 29, 1861, as captain of Co. K, 4th Regt., Michigan Infantry. Ill health from exposure and service soon compelled him to resign, much to his regret. Feb. 6, 1830, Mr. Crane married in Redford, Mich., Nancy Smith, a native of Meadville, Pa., b. June 9, 1807, by whom he had six children. She d. Sept. 13, 1842, and he m. May 11, 1843, Julia Ann Heller at Ann Arbor. She was b. in Germany, and d. June 21, 1862, at Dexter. He m. 3d, Feb. 8, 1863, Helen L. Palmer. She was b. in Queensbury, N. Y., April 16, 1823. He d. Aug. 14, 1893, at Dexter, Mich. Children, all b. in Dexter:

1. JAMES M., b. July 1, 1832.
2. HELEN M., b. May 31, 1834; d. June 6, 1839.
3. NANCY LOISA, b. May 31, 1836; d. Aug. 7, 1836.
4. JOANNA, b. Nov. 8, 1837; d. Nov. 12, 1837.
5. HENRY CLAY, b. Dec. 9, 1838; d. Jan. 30, 1860.
6. JOSEPHINE, b. Jan. 27, 1841; d. July 3, 1842.
7. CHARLES FOX, b. Dec. 28, 1863.
8. GEORGE D., }
9. STEPHEN, } twins, b. Dec. 28, 1865.

440. MARTIN L. CRANE [4]; m. 1st, Phebe Kendrick; 2d, Louisa Curtis, both natives of New York State. Settled in Novi, Mich., where he died July 15, 1896, having had two sons by first marriage and two daughters by the second. Children:

1. GEORGE NEWTON; was with Sherman's army, and killed on the march to the sea.
2. ALEXANDER BARTON; d. in Jackson, Mich.
3. FRANCES JOAN.
4. ELIZABETH.

FRANCES JOAN CRANE [3]; m. Philip McCrumb. Lives in Novi, Mich. Children:

1. EVA L. (McCrumb).
2. AGGIE MAY (McCrumb).
3. MARSHALL (McCrumb); drowned June 17, 1888.

ELIZABETH CRANE [4]; m. Miles Hodges. Residence at Vanderbilt, Otsego Co., Mich. Children:

1. EDWIN J. (Hodges).
2. CLARENCE A. (Hodges).
3. CORA (Hodges); d., aged 5 years.

441. JAMES CRANE[5] [140], (Edmund,[4] John,[3] John,[2] Jasper[1]). He was born May 20, 1786. He married Sally Palmer, by whom he had three children; 2d, Polly Southwell, by whom he had two children; 3d, Mary Ann Brush. He was a farmer. Served in the War of 1812 in western New York, and died Sept. 27, 1868. Thus it is given by James M. Crane, of Paw Paw, Mich., the grandson.* Children:

442—1. A. LANSON.
443—2. HARRY.

---

* There was, we presume, another James,[6] son of James,[5] who was father of the above five children; for Mr. Crane says his grandfather James was born 1786, while James,[5] was born 1754, and served in the Revolutionary war from Morris Co., N. J.

444—3. LOYAL, b. April 14, 1813.
445—4. ALONZO.
446—5. JAMES M.

447. PHOEBY CRANE[5] [135], (Edmund,[4] John,[3] John,[2] Jasper[1]), supposed to have married Isaac Pierson, Nov. 4, 1759. She died ——. He married 2d, Mary ——. He died Aug. 24, 1790. Children :

   1. JACOB, } twins; bapt. Nov. 14, 1762.
   2. TOPENA, }
   3. ASA; bapt. Nov. 1, 1764.
   4. CYRUS; bapt. Jan. 11, 1767.
   5. EUNICE, b. Feb. 10, 1770.
   6. PHEBE, b. Sept. 3, 1772.
   7. JACOB, b. Aug. 28, 1774.
   8. JOHN, b. May 16, 1779.
   9. ABRAHAM, b. March 6, 1781.
  10. ELIZA M., b. Dec. 26, 1785, by wife Mary.

448. JOSEPH CRANE[5] [144], (Joseph,[4] Jasper,[3] John,[2] Jasper[1]), married Sarah Jones, of Orange, Jan. 21, 1796. Lived in Bloomfield, N. J.; a farmer. Served in the " whiskey war " in Pennsylvania. He died Sept. 27, 1832, at Bloomfield, aged 65. She died June 7, 1846, aged 73 years, 5 months and 22 days. On his tombstone you may read: " Pause, reader, and reflect that thou, too, art mortal." Children :

449—1. PHEBE.
450—2. RACHEL.
451—3. NATHANIEL J.
452—4. HANNAH.
453—5. EUNICE.

454. MOSES CRANE[5] [145], (Joseph,[4] Jasper,[3] John,[2] Jasper[1]), married ——. Presume this Moses Crane served as overseer of highways in 1808. Children :

455—1. ROBERT.
456—2. HARRY.
457—3. LOUISA.
458—4. PHEBE.
459—5. JANE.

460. DANIEL CRANE[5] [146], (Joseph,[4] Jasper,[3] John,[2] Jasper[1]), said to have died in Jersey City, April 26, 1863   Children :

461—1. AARON; m. Henrietta ——; had 5 children.
462—2. WALTER; drowned at sea.
463—3. SARAH; m. Isaac Seaman; he was killed on railroad.
464—4. ANN; m.; lived in Pennsylvania.
465—5. MARY; m. Methodist minister.
466—6. EDIE.
467—7. JANE; m. a brother of her brother Aaron's wife, and lived near Jersey City.

468. REBECKAH CRANE[5] [150], (Jeremiah,[4] Daniel,[3] John,[2]

Jasper[1]), married Joseph Davis in 1790. He was captain of Washington's Life Guard. Children :

1. WILLIAM (Davis), b. July 4, 1791.
2. JAMES (Davis).
3. JOHN (Davis).

469. WILLIAM DAVIS [1]; m. Catharine Kingsland, who was b. Oct. 28, 1806, and d. Dec. 7, 1880. He d. Oct., 1856. Children :
  1. WILLIAM H. (Davis), b. July 22, 1828; d. Sept. 7, 1837.
  2. SAMUEL STEPHEN (Davis), b. Oct. 17, 1830.
  3. CATHARINE MARY (Davis), b. Dec. 9, 1835.
  4. ELEANOR E. (Davis), b. Aug. 25, 1837.
  5. WILLIAM TYLER (Davis), b. March 20, 1841; d. July 17, 1846.
  6. ERASTUS (Davis), b. June 30, 1842; d. Aug. 26, 1848.

470. SAMUEL STEPHEN DAVIS [2]; m. Charlotte Ann Scott. Children :
  1. SAMUEL S. (Davis).
  2. CATHARINE (Davis).
  3. ADALINE (Davis).
  4. WILLIAM SCOTT (Davis).
  5. JOHN CRAWFORD (Davis)

471. CATHARINE MARY DAVIS [3]; m. James O. Haulenbeck, Feb. 17, 1850. Children :
  1. WILLIAM (Haulenbeck), b. Nov. 11, 1850; d. Jan. 28. 1880.
  2. FRANKLIN (Haulenbeck), b. Aug. 5, 1853.
  3. JAMES (Haulenbeck), b. Sept. 20, 1856.
  4. CHARLES (Haulenbeck), b. March 5, 1859.

472. ELEANOR E. DAVIS [4]; m. Charles L. Fithian, Dec. 28, 1858. Children :
  1. WILLIAM H. (Fithian), b. Dec. 27, 1859; d.
  2. KATIE E. (Fithian), b. Aug. 31, 1862.
  3. THOMAS (Fithian), b. Nov. 20, 1864; d.
  4. WILLIAM H. (Fithian), b. Sept. 16, 1866; d.
  5. EMMA (Fithian), b. Apr. 8, 1869.

473. WILLIAM CRAIN[5] [152], (Jeremiah,[4] Daniel,[3] John,[2] Jasper[1]). He spelled his name Crain; supposed to have been born at Newburgh, Orange Co., N. Y.; married Phebe, daughter of Lieutenant Thos. Nicholson. Her grandfather Nicholson settled at Little Britain, in 1730, with Chas. Clinton.

Children :

474—1. MARIA, b. about 1805.
475—2. AMANDA; d. young.
476—3. ACHILLES RAINER, b. March 3, 1810. at Newburgh, N. Y.
477—4. JOSEPHUS NICHOLSON, b. 1812; m. Frances E. Guinness.
478—5. SUSAN; m. Dennis Gahagan.
479—6. WILLIAM DAVIS, b. April 10, 1819; m. Emily Matilda Blake.
480—7. HECTOR; d. young.

481. MATTHIAS CRANE[5] [157], (William,[4] Nathaniel,[3] Azariah,[2] Jasper[1]), married Elizabeth Crane, daughter of Job Crane. She was born, 1744. Probably was the Matthias Crane who served in the Revolutionary war, Morris Co. He died Sept. 14, 1786, aged 43 years, 2 days. Children :

482—1. ISRAEL, b. 1774; m. Fannie Peirson.
483—2. ABIGAIL; m. Hugh Holmes.

484. JONATHAN CRANE[5] [158], (William,[4] Nathaniel,[3] Azariah,[2] Jasper[1]), married Mary Ward. She died Nov. 4, 1820. The silver tankard which was an heirloom in the Crane family, was, so says Henry A. Crane, grandson of Jonathan, in possession of "grandmother Mary Ward Crane, and destroyed at the burning of Uncle Timothy Crane's house at Caldwell, N. J., in 1824." One record says he died Aug. 1, 1801; another says he died in Caldwell, N. J., 1805. March 12, 1776, chosen surveyor of highways. Children:

485—1. ABIJAH, b. June 11, 1765.
486—2. UZEAL.
487—3. TIMOTHY.

488. JONAS CRANE[5] [159], (William,[4] Nathaniel,[3] Azariah,[2] Jasper[1]), married. He died in Caldwell, N. J., Oct. 17, 1806, aged 56. Children:

489—1. AMOS.
490—2. WILLIAM.
491—3. CALVIN SMITH, b. Jan. 20, 1795.
492—4. BETHUEL, b. 1780
493—5. LYDIA.
494—6. RACHEL.
495—7. PHEBE.
496—8. ABIGAIL.

497. WILLIAM CRANE[5] [163], (William,[4] Nathaniel,[3] Azariah,[2] Jasper[1]), married Lydia Baldwin, daughter of Joshua. His granddaughter Hester says he was a lieutenant and captain in the war of the Revolution, and was in the War of 1812. He was a farmer and lived in Cranetown, N. J. Subscribed £22 toward building the church in 1794. She died in Cranetown, N. J., where they lived, June 22, 1832. He died there Nov. 16, 1832. Children:

498—1. HENRY; d. young.
499—2. ELISHA; d. young.
500—3. ———; d. young.
501—4. HANNAH, b. about 1781.
502—5. SARAH.
503—6. JOSIAH W., b. 1786.
504—7. WILLIAM, b. 1788.
505—8. MARY, b. 1791; m. Joseph Harrison, Jr., of Caldwell, N. J. She died in Delaware, Ohio, Aug. 5, 1827.
506—9. LUCY; m. Lewis Pierson, of Orange, N. J.
507—10. JOSHUA, b. 1797.
508—11. PRUDENCE; m. Z. Baldwin, Bloomfield, N. J.

509. OLIVER CRANE[5] [164], (William,[4] Nathaniel,[3] Azariah,[2] Jasper[1]), married Susannah, daughter of David Baldwin, of Bloomfield, N. J., and lived in the stone house built by his father in Cranetown now Montclair; was overseer of highways for 1797. He subscribed £25 toward building the church, 1794. He was killed by a horse kicking him on the Sabbath day, Aug. 31, 1817, while getting ready to go to Church. He was 51

years of age at the time of his death. She died Nov. 11, 1838, aged 70. He was in the War of 1812. Children :

510—1. SARAH, b. June 3, 1787; d. Dec. 27, 1835.
511—2. LYDIA, b. Feb. 5, 1789.
512—3. STEPHEN FORDHAM, b. Dec. 27, 1791.
513—4. RACHEL, b. Oct. 16, 1794.
514—5. AMOS, b. Jan. 20, 1799.
515—6. ZOPHAR BALDWIN, b. June 14, 1803.
516—7. NATHANIEL MARCUS, b. Dec. 12, 1805.
517—8. ISAAC WHEELER, b. July 8, 1808.

518. SAMUEL ·CRANE[5] [166], (Noah[4], Nathaniel,[3] Azariah,[2] Jasper[1]), married Mary, daughter of John and Elizabeth Baldwin. He was a farmer; born in Cranetown, and lived in Caldwell, N. J., where he died Feb. 28, 1811. She died Jan. 26, 1817. Dec. 3, 1784, Church was organized at Caldwell; his name appears in the first list, with Mary and Phebe Crane. He was elected deacon, 1784. Children :

519—1. CALEB, b. Aug. 28, 1769.
520—2. ZENAS, b. 1772.
521—3. CYRUS; d. in infancy.
522—4. DORCAS, b. 1777; m. Timothy Crane. She d. 1805.
523—5. CYRUS, b. 1779.
524—6. ELIZABETH, b. 1781.
525—7. MARY, b. 1784.
526—8. NATHANIEL S., b. Feb. 24, 1789.

527. Deacon JOSEPH CRANE[5] [168], (Noah,[4] Nathaniel,[3] Azariah,[2] Jasper[1]), married Hannah Sampson; resided in West Bloomfield, N. J. Held office in the Church, 1794 to 1798, and subscribed £60 toward building the church in 1794; served in the War of 1812. He doubtless served his turn as overseer of highways in 1806. He died Oct. 11, 1832. Children :

528—1. ELEAZER; bapt. Dec. 21, 1783; was overseer of highways in 1807 and 1809; d. at Mont Clair, N. J., May 24, 1865, aged 39; no children.
529—2. Rev. DANIEL; m. H. Crane, dau. of Aaron and Tabatha.
530—3. Rev. NOAH; m. —— Grover.
531—4. NATHANIEL; bapt. Dec. 21, 1783.
532—5. HARRISON.
533—6. SARAH.
534—7. JANE; m. Oct. 24, 1806, Amzi L., son of Deacon Samuel Ball; lived many years in Orange Co., N. Y., where he was sheriff. Subsequently returned to New Jersey. He died in Mont Clair, Sept. 26, 1860. She d. Feb. 9, 1864.
535—8. MARY.
536—9. RHODA.
Peter Doremus m. one of these last two daughters.

537. ELIZABETH CRANE[5] [169], (Noah,[4] Nathaniel,[3] Azariah,[2] Jasper[1]), married John R. Crane. Children :

1. MARY.
2. NEHEMIAH.
3. HENRY.
4. SARAH.
5. HETTY.
6. ˴NATHANIEL.

538. Major Nathaniel Crane[5] [171], (Noah,[4] Nathaniel,[3] Azariah,[2] Jasper[1]), married Hannah, daughter of William Crane, son of Nathaniel. Had no children. He was in the battle of Long Island, Sept. 15, 1776. He died in 1833, aged 75. He was in the War of 1812. He gave the bulk of his property for the support of the Presbyterian ministry in the town where he had lived. Served as overseer of highways in 1795 and 1796, and also on the town committee for the years 1799 and 1800. He is supposed to be the Nathaniel Crane who subscribed £100 towards building the church in 1794.

539. Mehitable Crane[5] [173], (Noah,[4] Nathaniel,[3] Azariah,[2] Jasper[1]), married General William Gould. She died Dec. 4, 1843, aged 79 years. Children :

1. Mary (Gould); m. Robert Baldwin.
2. Johnson N. (Gould); m. Elizabeth Reeves.
3. Phebe (Gould).
4. Betsey (Gould) ; m. Dr. Abner Reeves.
5. Stephen (Gould); d. young.
6. Emily (Gould).
7. Charlotte (Gould); m. Joseph Harrison.
8. Nathaniel (Gould); m. Mary Ward.
9. Harriet (Gould).
10. William (Gould); m. Charlotte Ward.
11. Stephen (Gould); m. Sarah ——.

540. Aaron Crane[5] [187], (Job,[4] Azariah,[3] Azariah,[2] Jasper[1]), married Tabatha Baldwin, of Orange, N. J. Settled in Mont Clair, N. J. The place was formerly called Cranetown. He was a farmer. Served in the Revolutionary war, so says his son Zenas S. He subscribed £90 towards building the church in 1794. Was in the War of 1812. He died Feb. 7, 1836. Children :

541—1. Nancy, b. Sept. 1, 1775.
542—2. Thomas, b. Sept. 8, 1778; at town meeting in Newark, April 8, 1805, was chosen overseer of highways, and constable in 1809.
543—3. Jeptha, b. July 17, 1780.
544—4. Hannah, b. Aug. 27, 1782.
545—5. Abigail, b. June 18, 1785.
546—6. Timothy A., b. June 17, 1787.
547—7. Elias B., b. Dec. 17, 1789.
548—8. Zenas Squier, b. Oct. 20, 1793.
549—9. Polly, b. March 19, 1797.

550. Jane Crane[5] [191], (Gamaliel,[4] Azariah,[3] Azariah,[2] Jasper[1]), married Parmenas Dodd, son of Nathaniel and Ruth (Condit) Dodd. Children :

1. Thaddeus (Dodd), b. March 8, 1784; m. Lucy Rice
2. Nathaniel (Dodd), b. Jan. 17, 1787.
3. Stephen (Dodd), b. March 18, 1789; m. Mary Riker
4. Jeptha (Dodd), b. Oct. 15, 1791; m. Polly Hinkman.
5. Daniel (Dodd), b. 1793.
6. Albert (Dodd), b. March, 1797; d. Sept. 13, 1846.
7. Matthew (Dodd), b. Nov. 4, 1800.

8. ABNER (Dodd); m., and went to Canada West.
9. REUBEN (Dodd).
18. ISAAC (Dodd), b. May 9, 1806; went to Williamsport, Md.

551. SIMEON CRANE[5] [192], (Gamaliel,[4] Azariah,[3] Azariah,[2] Jasper[1]), married Eunice Baldwin. Lived at the top of the mountain in Cranetown, now Mont Clair, N. J. He attended town meeting in Newark, N. J., April 14, 1800, and was elected overseer of highways for Bloomfield. All went to New York State and Michigan. Children:

552—1. AMBROSE; d. young.
553—2. LYDIA.
554—3. DAVID.
555—4. ISAAC.
556—5. CALEB.
557—6. HARRIET.
558—7. JANE.
559—8. ELIZABETH.
560—9. MARIA.
561-10. MARK.
562-11. LEWIS DODD.
563-12. AMBROSE.

564. JACOB CRANE[5] [194], (Gamaliel,[4] Azariah,[3] Azariah,[2] Jasper[1]), probably married Anna Pennington. Children:

565—1. SOPHIA, b. Sept. 4, 1785; residence, 1870, at Greenfield, Mass.
566—2. SARAH.
567—3. GEORGE W.; d. Nov. 1, 1807.

568. ZEBINA CRANE[5] [196], (Gamaliel,[4] Azariah,[3] Azariah,[2] Jasper[1]), married Jan. 8, 1793, Anna Gould. When a small boy he was bound out by an older brother to a teamster who lived near the family home. The boy was so harshly treated that he ran away, and while travelling barefooted and ragged, without food, he came upon a woman milking a cow, and asked her for food and lodging. He stayed with this family a number of years, who treated him very kindly, and gave him some schooling; but he finally became homesick, and returned to his old home. About the year 1807 or 1808 he left the State of New Jersey, and sought to better his fortune in what was then the wilderness of Central New York, and settled in the town of Genoa, Cayuga County. He stayed there until the 6th of May, 1810, when he moved to what is now the town of Marion, Wayne County, about one-half mile from the pleasant little village of Marion. His house was made of logs, with bark roof, stone fireplace, and blankets for doors. In this house he lived about two years, clearing his land and turning his hand to anything by which he might earn an honest penny. He built the first blacksmith shop in town. He was also a famous shingle-maker; could do a fair job at mason-work or carpentering. In the War of 1812 he went to the defence of Pultneyville, and afterwards volunteered for six months on Niagara frontier, serving most of the time on detached duty, building barracks and other mechanical work; was taken

29

sick near Black Rock, and offered a discharge, but only accepted
a furlough that he might come home for medicine.   He never was
quite well afterwards, although a great worker.   He built a frame
house, barn and corn-house on his farm, and lived there until his
death, which occurred on the 11th of September, 1823.   Children :

569—1.   JACOB G., b. April 5, 1795.
570—2.   SUSANNAH, b. Nov. 22, 1796.
571—3.   ELIZABETH. b. Oct. 28, 1798.
572—4.   CALEB, b. July 1, 1801; d. May 26, 1822.
573—5.   HANNAH, b. March 12, 1804.
574—6.   DAVID, b. June 9, 1806.
575—7.   OBEDIAH, b. June 8, 1808.
576—8.   SARAH ANN, b. Aug. 1, 1810.
577—9.   ZEBINA, b. Nov. 21, 1812; d. March 14, 1813.
578-10. RACHEL, b. May 6, 1814.
579-11. ANNA, b. Nov. 28, 1815.

580.   OBEDIAH CRANE[5] [198], (Gamaliel,[4] Azariah,[3] Azariah,[2]
Jasper[1]), married April 10, 1811, Charlotte Osborn, daughter of
Ichabod Osborn, who was a soldier in the Revolutionary war,
and lived at Chatham, N. J.; also at Bottle Hill; all but the
eldest and youngest of their children named were born at the
latter place. He died at Goshen, Orange Co., N. Y., Nov. 6,
1843. . She was born at Orange, N. J., Oct. 12, 1786, and died
at Middletown, N. J., Aug. 3, 1859.   Ichabod Osborn was born
in Cranetown, N. J., 1760, and died at Springfield in 1826.   His
wife Eliza Grummon was born in Orange in 1763, and died in
1790.   He was a sergeant in the War of 1812.   Children :

581—1.   ELMIRA, b. Jan. 23, 1812; m. Philetus Phillips; he d. Aug.
           30, 1881; she d. Sept. 17, 1884.
582—2.   AARON G., b. June 17, 1814, at ("Bottle Hill") Madison,
           N. J.
583—3.   ELIZA G., b. Jan. 29, 1817.
584—4.   RACHEL H., b. April 14, 1818; d. Dec. 3, 1861, at Trenton,
           N. J.
585—5.   CHARLOTTE O., b. Oct. 14, 1820.
586—6.   SARAH, b. Aug. 22, 1822; d. Sept. 28, 1822.
587—7.   TIMOTHY DWIGHT, b. Oct. 12, 1824; d. July 15, 1825.
588—8.   TIMOTHY DWIGHT, b. Oct. 14, 1826.

589.   JOHN R. CRANE[5] [200], (Ezekiel,[4] Azariah,[3] Azariah,[2]
Jasper[1]), was called of Cranetown, afterwards known as Mont
Clair, married Elizabeth, daughter of Noah Crane. His grandson Noah H. Crane, of Bloomfield, N. J., says he was a lieutenant in the Revolutionary war, and died in 1821. His wife died
in 1831.   She was born April 13, 1753.   Children :

590—1.   MARY called POLLY.
591—2.   JOHN.
592—3.   NEHEMIAH, b. May 6, 1778.
593—4.   HENRY.
594—5.   MEHITABLE.
595—6.   NATHANIEL.
596—7.   SALLY.
597—8.   WILLIAM.

598. JOSEPH CRANE[5] [201], (Ezekiel,[4] Azariah,[3] Azariah,[2] Jasper[1]), married —— Baldwin. Children:

599—1. JOSEPH; died young.
600—2. JOSEPH.

601. LOIS CRANE[5] [202], (Ezekiel,[4] Azariah,[3] Azariah,[2] Jasper[1]), married Moses Dodd, July 3, 1775. He was son of Isaac Dodd of Bloomfield, N. J. She died Oct. 17, 1818. He died Dec. 6, 1839, aged 84. Children:

1. STEPHEN (Dodd), b. March 8, 1777; was Congregational minister, and died Feb. 5, 1856, at East Haven, Ct.
2. HIRAM (Dodd), b. Nov. 22, 1779.
3. ABIGAIL (Dodd), b. Jan. 20, 1782.
4. BETSEY (Dodd), b. May 3, 1784.
5. IRA (Dodd), b. June 22, 1786.
6. FANNY (Dodd), b. April 25, 1791.

602. DEBORAH CRANE[5] [204], (Ezekiel,[4] Azariah,[3] Azariah,[2] Jasper[1]), married Ebenezer, son of Joseph Dodd, and settled first at Bloomfield, N. J. Children:

1. BETSEY (Dodd), b. March, 1779; m. Wm. Early and d. 1811.
2. MARY (Dodd), b. Sept., 1781; m. 1st, Henry Carpenter; 2d, Oliver Tuttle.
3. EZRA BUEL (Dodd), b. July, 1784.
4. NANCY (Dodd), b. about 1785.
5. LOIS (Dodd), b. about 1787.
6. EBENEZER LINDLEY (Dodd), b. about 1790, at Caldwell, N. J.
7. ——— } twins; d. young.
8. ———
9. JOSHUA HORTON (Dodd), b. 1794, at Paterson, N. J.
10. JOSEPH (Dodd), b. 1796, at Cranetown, N. J.
11. JOHN (Dodd), b. about 1799, at Remsen, Oneida Co., N. Y.
12. VALERIA (Dodd), b. 1802, at Utica, N. Y.

603. AMOS CRANE[5] [211], (Moses,[4] Azariah,[3] Azariah,[2] Jasper[1]), about the year 1790 removed to Ohio, and settled in what was then called the "Miami Country," where a short time afterwards he was thrown from his horse and killed. This is probably the Amos Crane who served in Capt. Baldwin's Co., Eastern Battalion, Morris Co.; also Continental army. Children:

604—1. SAMUEL, b. about 1770.
605—2. DANIEL; lived near Cincinnati, in Warren Co., where his father settled, and is reported to have been, in 1860, the only survivor of his father's family, and at that time was a member of the Ohio State Legislature. He died previous to 1882.

606. STEPHEN CRANE[5] [212], (Moses,[4] Azariah,[3] Azariah,[2] Jasper[1]), married 1st, Polly Masco; 2d, Agnes DeGormo; 3d, ———. He settled first in Morris Co., N. J., where his two eldest children were born. Previous to 1797 or during that year, he removed to Seneca Co., N. Y. He was a farmer; served in wars of the Revolution, and of 1812, and he, with his

brother Ezekiel, was with Gen. Sullivan's army during his famous march against the Indians, in 1779, at which time they saw the land which they afterwards settled upon. He died Jan. 24, 1834, in Tyre, Seneca Co. His wife, Agnes, died there Jan., 1812. Children:

607—1. MOSES MASCO, b. 1786.
608—2. STEPHEN BRANDT, b. 1795.
609—3. POLLY, b. 1797.
610—4. DANIEL PRINCE. b. 1800; d. 1870; was an evangelist, and at one time owned Congress Spring and Hall, Saratoga, N.Y.
611—5. ELIZABETH, b. 1802.
612—6. RACHEL. b. 1804.
613—7. JOHN, b. March, 1808.
614—8. CHARLES, b. March, 1810.

615. DANIEL PRINCE CRANE[5] [213], (Moses,[4] Azariah,[3] Azariah,[2] Jasper[1]), married Phebe Burnet, Nov. 29, 1774. Child:

616—1. JOHN, who had DAVID B., of Newark, who m. Esther Miller. Children:
  1. MARY.
  2. MENTOR.
  3. ASENATH.
  4. MOSES.
  5. WILLIAM.

617. EZEKIEL CRANE[5] [214], (Moses,[4] Azariah,[3] Azariah,[2] Jasper[1]), served in the Revolutionary war, and, with Sullivan's army, marched through the "Lake Country," State of New York. He was so delighted with the country that after the close of the war, his wife having died, he returned to New York, purchased a home there, and married Abby ——, by whom it is said he had five children, names of four of whom we have not been able to obtain in connection with the record of this Ezekiel, although some of them may be found in the book. Reports seem to indicate that he was twice married, but have nothing to prove the statement. Dec. 12, 1803, he was shot by John, a Delaware Indian, who was arraigned in Court, pleaded guilty and was hanged, Aug. 17, 1804. As this was the first murder trial held in Cayuga Co., it may be interesting to give account of it, taken from records of the Court. The murder was committed in Junius, then in that County, but now in Seneca County. The trial was held in June, 1804, at Aurora, then the County seat. Judge Ambrose Spencer, of the Supreme Court, presided, assisted by Seth Phelps, John Tillotson, Joseph Annin, and Joseph Beardsly, "Justices of Oyer and Terminer." William Stuart was district attorney, and Samuel Buel, sheriff. The indictment is as follows:

Cayuga County, ss.
The jurors for the people of the State of New York, in and for the body of the county of Cayuga, upon their oath, present that John, a Delaware Indian. otherwise called Delaware John, late of the town of Junius, in the county of Cayuga. laborer, not having the fear of God before his eyes, but being moved and seduced by the instigation of the devil, on the 12th day of December, in the year of our Lord 1803, with

force and arms, at the town of Junius aforesaid, in the county aforesaid, in and upon one Ezekiel Crane, in the peace of God, and of the people of the State of New York, then and there, being feloniously. willfully,
and of his malice aforethought, did make an assault; and that the
said John, a Delaware Indian, otherwise called Delaware John, a certain rifle gun, of the value of $15, then and there loaded and charged
with gunpowder and one leaden bullet, which rifle gun he, the said
John, a Delaware Indian, otherwise called Delaware John, in his right
hand, then and there, had and held to, against and upon the said
Ezekiel Crane, then and there feloniously, willfully, and of his malice
aforethought, did shoot and discharge, and that the said John, a
Delaware Indian, otherwise called Delaware John, with the leaden
bullet aforesaid, out of the rifle gun aforesaid, then and there by force
of the gunpowder, shot and sent forth as aforesaid, the aforesaid
Ezekiel Crane in and upon the right breast of him the said Ezekiel
Crane, a little above the right pap of him the said Ezekiel Crane, then
and there with the leaden bullet aforesaid, out of the rifle gun aforesaid, by the said John, a Delaware Indian, otherwise called Delaware
John, so as aforesaid shot, discharged and sent forth, feloniously, willfully. and of his malice aforethought, did strike, penetrate and wound,
giving to the said Ezekiel Crane, then and there, with the leaden bullet
aforesaid, so as aforesaid shot discharged and sent forth out of the
rifle gun aforesaid, by the said John, a Delaware Indian. otherwise
called Delaware John, in and upon the said right breast of him, the
said Ezekiel Crane, a little above the right pap of him, the said Ezekiel
Crane, one mortal wound of the depth of six inches, and of the
breadth of one inch, of which said mortal wound the aforesaid Ezekiel
Crane from the said 12th day of December, in the year of our Lord,
1803, until the 17th day of the said month of December, in the year
aforesaid, did languish, and languishing did live, on which 17th day of
December, in the year of our Lord 1803 aforesaid, at the town aforesaid, in the town aforesaid, in the county aforesaid, he the said Ezekiel
Crane, of the mortal wound aforesaid died: And so the jurors aforesaid, upon their oath aforesaid, do say that the said John, a Delaware
Indian, otherwise called Delaware John, him, the said Ezekiel Crane,
in manner and form aforesaid, feloniously, willfully, and of his malice
aforethought, did kill and murder against the peace of the people of
the State of New York and their dignity.

The People vs. Delaware John:

The prisoner being arraigned on his indictment, pleaded guilty of the
felony whereof he stands indicted. It is thereupon ordered and
adjudged by the Court that the said John, a Delaware Indian, otherwise called Delaware John for the felony aforesaid be hung by the neck
until he is dead, by the sheriff of this county on Friday, the 17th day of
August next, between the hours of one and three in the afternoon of
that same day. And further that the body of the said John be
delivered over by the said sheriff after the said execution to Frederick
Delano, a surgeon, for dissection.

Mr. Crane was foreman of the grand jury, at a term of Court
held there in 1798. Samuel Buel afterwards sheriff was also a
member of that jury when Mr. Crane was foreman. Child:

618—1. Jonas, b. April 17, 1803.

619. Phebe Crane[5] [218], (Moses,[4] Azariah,[3] Azariah,[2]
Jasper[1]), married Edward Compson, at Parsippany, N. J., in
1800, and removed at once to western New York. Children:

1. Hannah (Compson), b. Dec. 22, 1800.
2. Maria (Compson), b. June 14, 1803.

- CHARLES CRANE (Compson). b. 1805.
4. CAROLINE AMELIA (Compson), b. June 24, 1810; m. Charles
    Crane, son of Stephen [116].
5. JULIA (Compson), b. April 13, 1812.
6. JONAS WARD (Compson), b. April 2, 1814.
7. EDWARD SANFORD (Compson), b. 1815.
8. STEPHEN (Compson), b. 1817.
9. THOMAS WILBER (Compson), b. 1820.

620. BENJAMIN CRANE[5] [221], (Stephen[4], Azariah,[3] Azariah,[2] Jasper[1]), married Mehitable Dunning, of Florida, N. Y.,
at Bloomfield, N. J. April 13, 1801, he was chosen at town
meeting overseer of highways for Bloomfield. Probably served
in the war of 1812. He died 1819, aged 66 years.
   Children :

   621—1. JULIA.
   622—2. BENJAMIN.
   623—3. HATTY; m. John Farrand; settled in New York State.
   624—4. BARSHEBA or SHIBBY.
   625—5. JEREMIAH.
   626—6. AMZI L.
   627—7. JOHN.

628. STEPHEN CRANE[5] [222], (Stephen,[4] Azariah,[3] Azariah,[2]
Jasper[1]), in the year 1786, and again April 28, 1788, chosen at
town meeting, Newark, N. J., one of the numerous surveyors of
highways. Perhaps had :

   629—1. BENJAMIN, b. Sept. 1, 1787.
   630—2. AZARIAH.
   631—3. BETSEY.
   632—4. RHODA.
   633—5. LOUISA.
   634—6. CHARLES.
   635—7. ELISHA.
   636—8. ISAAC.
   637—9. HANNAH.
   638-10. PHEBE.

639. AZARIAH CRANE[5] [223], (Stephen,[4] Azariah,[3] Azariah,[2] Jasper[1]), married —— Tucker; settled in Caldwell, N. J.,
where he died March 15, 1814, aged 60. Children :

   640—1. IRA.
   641—2. BETSEY.
   642—3. BENJAMIN.

643. JEREMIAH CRANE[5] [224], (Stephen,[4] Azariah,[3] Aza-
riah,[2] Jasper[1]), married Hannah Corly, daughter of William
Corly, of Vernon; settled in Bloomfield, N. J. He died at
West Bloomfield, Dec. 21, 1829. Children :

   644—1. WILLIAM, b. March 27, 1797.
   645—2. STEPHEN; never married; d. Dec. 11, 1836.
   646—3. LINUS; m. Peggy Yorks. He was a constable.
   647—4. ISRAEL; d. March 11, 1832.
   648—5. IRA, b. May 24, 1808.
   649—6. RHODA.
   650—7. JULIA.

651—8. HANNAH.
652—9. ELIZA.
653-10. MARY.
654-11. MARTHA.
655-12. PARTHENIA.

656. LOIS CRANE[5] [225], (Stephen,[4] Azariah,[3] Azariah,[2] Jasper[1]), married Justice Burnet, who died 1826. She died Nov. 7, 1831, aged 64; buried at Hanover, N. J. Children:

1. LINUS (Burnet).
2. WILLIAM (Burnet).
3. GROVER (Burnet).
4. RHODA (Burnet); m. D. Harrison.
5. SALLY (Burnet).
6. HANNAH (Burnet).
And perhaps other sons.

657. POLLY CRANE[5] [226], (Stephen,[4] Azariah,[3] Azariah,[2] Jasper[1]), married Dr. —— Bone. Children:

1. BENJAMIN H. (Bone).
2. LOT (Bone); m. —— Ricker.
3. ISABELLA (Bone); m. John Wells.
4. JULIA (Bone); m. Israel Corby.

658. RHODA CRANE[5] [227], (Stephen,[4] Azariah,[3] Azariah,[2] Jasper[1]), married Linus Baldwin. Children:

1. RHODA (Baldwin).
2. JOSEPH (Baldwin).
3. JUSTICE (Baldwin).
4. ROBERT (Baldwin).
5. ELIJAH (Baldwin).
6. LINUS (Baldwin).
7. MATTHIAS (Baldwin).

659. ABIGAIL CRANE[5] [228], (Stephen,[4] Azariah,[3] Azariah,[2] Jasper[1]), married Caleb Martin. Children:

1. STEPHEN (Martin).
One daughter m. —— Bumstead.

660. RUFUS CRANE[5] [251], (Jonas,[4] John,[3] Azariah,[2] Jasper[1]), married 1st, —— Lyon; 2d, Charity Campbell, 1779, daughter of John. She was born 1760, and died in 1829. He was born in Newark, N. J., 1744; served in the Revolutionary war, in McDougall's New Jersey Brigade, Continental Army; private, Capt. Henry Squires Co., 2d Essex Regiment, New Jersey Militia, Col. Philip Van Courtlandt. He died in Newark, in 1814; was precentor of the music in the 1st Presbyterian Church, Newark. Charity was daughter of John and Rebecca (Baldwin) Campbell. Children:

661—1. JONAS, b. April 22, 1780.
662—2. BETSEY, b. Sept. 9, 1782.
663—3. ABIGAIL, b. March 5, 1785; d. in infancy.
664—4. ABIGAIL, b. July 19, 1787.
665—5. WILLIAM, b. May 6, 1790.
666—6. IRA, b. Oct. 29, 1792; d. young.

667—7. REBECKAH, b. Aug. 6, 1794.
668—8. RICHARD MONTGOMERY, b. July 10, 1797.
669—9. JAMES CAMPBELL, b. Sept. 7, 1803.

670. SAMUEL CRANE[5] [253], (Samuel,[4] John[3], Azariah,[2] Jasper[1]), married ——; removed to Amsterdam, Montgomery Co., N. Y., about 1791, and removed to Ohio, about 1806, and settled in Cincinnati; died. Child:

671—1. CAROLINE, b. 1800; m. —— Harris.

672. TIMOTHY CRANE[5] [254], (Samuel,[4] John,[3] Azariah,[2] Jasper[1]), married Esther Bruen in 1782, at Newark, N. J., where his three eldest children were born. They removed in the year 1791, to Charlton, Saratoga Co., N. Y., where he died May 3, 1836, aged 76. He served in the Revolutionary war, and during the last six years of his life drew a pension for such service. She was born in Dec., 1763, and died in Jan., 1824. Children:

673—1. AARON, b. Oct. 13, 1782; not m.; d. Jan. 23, 1860.
674—2. SARAH, b. Sept. 28, 1784.
675—3. MARY, b. Nov. 27, 1786.
676—4. PIERSON, b. Nov. 16, 1792.
677—5. JONAS, b. Dec. 20, 1794.
678—6. JOHN B., b. March 24, 1800; not m.; d. March 18, 1877.
679—7. EDWIN, } twins, b. Sept. 26, 1804; { d. May, 1807.
680—8. ELIZA, }

681. ESTHER CRANE[5] [255], (Samuel,[4] John,[3] Azariah,[2] Jasper[1]), married Cyrenus Riggs, and removed to Amsterdam, Montgomery Co., N. Y., about 1791, with his brother Samuel. Child:

1. ISAAC (Riggs); settled the estate of his Aunt Abigail, daughter of Samuel Crane.

682. SAYERS CRANE[5] [259], (John,[4] John,[3] Azariah,[2] Jasper[1]), married Widow Baldwin, who had at the time of this marriage two sons, Joseph and Moses, also a daughter Maria. Mr. Crane died suddenly in Newark, N. J. Child:

683—1. SALLY.

684. MATTHIAS CRANE[5] [261], (John,[4] John,[3] Azariah,[2] Jasper[1]), married Jane Ferris, and died in Fayette Co., Pa., in 1838, aged 73. He was one of the ruling elders in the first Church in Morristown, N. J., Jan. 2, 1792, and dismissed from there to Union Town, Pa., Jan. 7, 1825. Was dismissed from first Church in New Jersey, whither he went in 1805, to this Church. His wife Jane with him. She, Jane Ferris, migrated from Holland with her parents and a sister Margaret, who married Michael Flagg, father of the late Rev. Dr. Flagg, of New York. He probably served in the War of 1812. Children:

685—1. DEBORAH FERRIS, b. 1792.

686—2. JAMES COGGSWELL, b. Jan. 11, 1794; appointed May, 1825, secretary of the United Foreign Missionary Society; d. in New York, Jan. 12, 1826.
687—3. HANNAH JOHNSON, b. 1796; d. 1813.
688—4. JOSIAH FERRIS, b. 1797; d. 1834, in New York.
689—5. JOHN, b. April 16, 1799.
689½-6. ALETTA.

690. MARTHA CRANE[5] [262], (John,[4] John,[3] Azariah,[2] Jasper1), married Jotham Baldwin, a widower with two sons, Rev. Ely and Micah. In 1819, they lived near Newark, N. J. She died May 29, 1820. Children:

1. CYRUS (Baldwin), b. May 10, 1796; a watchmaker; d. Feb. 24, 1800.
2. RHODA (Baldwin), b. Sept. 7, 1799.
3. JOHN (Baldwin), b. Jan. 20, 1802; a minister.
4. MARIANNA (Baldwin), b. Feb. 25, 1804; d. Jan. 24, 1837.

691. REBECCA CRANE[5] [263], (John,[4] John,[3] Azariah,[2] Jasper1), married David E. Crane, and died about 1820. Children:

692—1. ICHABOD.
693—2. ELIAS.
694—3. RHODA.
695—4. LOUISA.
696—5. MATILDA.
697—6. HESTER.

698. HANNAH CRANE[5] [264], (John,[4] John,[3] Azariah,[2] Jasper1), married —— Sanford, and died in Middletown, N. Y., Aug. 24, 1862, aged 78 years. Children:

1. FRANCES PHILO (Sanford); d. suddenly in Orange, N. J., July 12, 1862.
2. ANNA HANNAH (Sanford).

699. JOHN CRANE[5] [267], (Eliakim,[4] John,[3] Azariah,[2] Jasper1). From the best information at hand, it is believed that he is the John Crane born Dec. 1, 1759, married Cornelia Catharine Brewen. He was born and married in Orange, N. J He died May 9, 1838, aged 78 years, 5 months and 9 days. Children:

700—1. ABRAHAM.
701—2. JOANNA; m. Ogden Riggs.

ABRAHAM CRANE [1]; m. Rachel H. Hannold Welling, a widow. He d. in his 93d year. Children:
1. T. H. BENTON; cashier First National Bank, Amsterdam, N. J., where he resides.
2. CORNELIA C.; m. William Bolster. Child:
1. FRANK J. (Bolster).

702. JOSIAH CRANE[5] [268], (Eliakim,[4] John,[3] Azariah,[2] Jasper1), baptized Dec. 3, 1758; married Lydia Crane, daughter of Oliver. Children:

703—1. EDWARD AMES.
704—2. LYMAN MARK.
705—3. JASON.
706—4. CHARLES OLIVER.
30

707. JONAS CRANE[5] [278], (Benjamin,[4] John,[3] Azariah,[2] Jasper[1]), married 1st, ———; 2d, Jan. 22, 1795, Abigail Kitchell; went west, settling first at Harrison, Ohio; from there he removed to Seymour, Jackson Co., Ind., and died near that place about 1840. His mother, then quite an old lady, died on the Ohio River, while making the journey west. His wife Abigail died Jan. 18, 1836. Children:

708—1. JABEZ, b. Nov. 16, 1795; m. Olive Olds; d. May, 1829.
709—2. ASA, b. Jan. 18, 1797.
710—3. DAVID, b. Nov. 4, 1799; m. Harriet Crabb; d. March, 1824.
711—4. JOSEPH, b. Feb. 6, 1802.
712—5. PHEBE, b. July 14, 1805.
713—6. JAMES, b. Dec. 2, 1807.
714—7. JONAS, b. May 2, 1810; m. Sedarey Ann Salmon; d. in Texas, after the war.
715—8. WYCLIFF, b. Nov. 18, 1811; m. Athia Douglass; d. Jan. 16, 1842.
716—9. RHODA ANN KITCHELL, b. March 22, 1816.

717. OBEDIAH M. CRANE[5] [279], (Benjamin,[4] John,[3] Azariah,[2] Jasper[1]), married Feb. 26, 1804, Elizabeth Schuler. She was born Feb. 3, 1778, in the State of New York, near Amsterdam. He was a farmer, and moved to Ohio, previous to 1819, and then to Indiana; was a member of the Legislature there in 1825. He died at Keokuk, Iowa, 1852. She died at Brownstown, Ind., 1844. Children:

718—1. JOHN SCHULER, b. Aug. 20, 1805; d. 1867, Amsterdam, N. Y.
719—2. PHEBE, b. Sept. 4, 1807; d. 1854, Columbus, Ind.
720—3. ISAAC B., b. Dec. 5, 1808; d. 1851.
721—4. GEORGE CLINTON, b. March 21, 1810; d. Aug., 1881, Carroll Co., Mo.
722—5. JAMES, b. Jan. 16, 1812; d. 1848, in Indiana.
723—6. FREDERICK, b. May 10, 1813; d. 1839, in Indiana.
724—7. OBEDIAH MEEKER, b. Oct. 30, 1814; living in 1882, Los Angeles, Cal.
725—8. MARY ANN, b. Nov. 5, 1816.
726—9. JABEZ TUNIS, b. Jan. 11, 1819.
727-10. ELIZABETH, b. March 20, 1821; d. 1850, Columbus, Indiana.

728. DAVID CRANE[5] [282], (Benjamin,[4] John,[3] Azariah,[2] Jasper[1]), married Electa Riggs, Dec. 4, 1797; settled at what was afterwards called Crane Village, about the year 1791. Children:

729—1. JOHN S., b. Oct. 20, 1799.
730—2. EXPERIENCE, b. Feb. 9, 1801.
731—3. JAMES, b. June 17, 1802.
732—4. OGDEN RIGGS, b. Nov. 17, 1804.
733—5. ISAAC, b. Dec. 17, 1806.
734—6. ABRAM RIGGS, b. Feb. 4, 1809.
735—7. ELECTA, b. Jan. 2, 1811.
736—8. MARIE, b. Oct. 15, 1812.
737—9. DAVID, b. April 22, 1815.
738-10. CATHARINE, b. May 10, 1818.

739. CALEB CAMP CRANE[5] [283], (Benjamin,[4] John,[3] Azariah,[2] Jasper[1]), was born Aug. 27, 1768. He married 1st,

Elizabeth Ostrander, who died leaving one child. He then married Mary Steel, who was born June 24, 1778. They resided in Amsterdam, N. Y. The locality where he settled was called Crane's Hollow for him. He died in the summer of 1845.

Children:

740—1. JABEZ, b. June 24, 1797.
741—2. OBEDIAH MEEKER, b. Nov. 2, 1800
742—3. CALEB CAMP, b. Nov. 25, 1801.
743—4. EDWARD S., b. March 12, 1803.
744—5. PHEBE M., b. Dec. 17; 1804.
745—6. ANN, b. Oct. 21, 1806.
746—7. JAMES W., b. May 21, 1808.
747—8. MARY C., b. Jan. 27, 1810.
748—9. JONAS HALSTED, b. April 21, 1812; lived in Schnectady, N Y.; no children.
749-10. ELECTY Z., b. May 12, 1815.
750-11. PETER OSTRANDER, b. Sept. 1, 1816; d. Feb. 6, 1842; unm.
751-12. ARCHIBALD M., b. Aug. 22, 1818.
752-13. MARGARET R., b. Jan. 9, 1820.
753-14. JANE DAWSON, b. July 8, 1822.

754. PHEBE CRANE[5] [284], (Benjamin,[4] John,[3] Azariah,[2] Jasper[1]), married John French, of Florida, Montgomery Co., N. Y. Children:

1. SAMUEL (French).
2. DAVID (French).
3. BENJAMIN (French).

755. BENJAMIN CRANE[5] [295], (Benjamin,[4] Joseph,[3] Jasper,[2] Jasper[1]), married 1st, Elizabeth Headly, by whom he had one son; 2d, Rachel, daughter of Timothy Ball. He removed to the State of New York, near Gallaway, where he lived some years. About 1812, he went to Ohio, and died in Bethel, Clermont Co., Feb., 1811, aged 70 years. Wife Rachel died 1824, age 74.

Children:

756—1. ABNER, b. March 4, 1768.
757—2. TIMOTHY, b. Sept. 9, 1771.
758—3. HANNAH, b. Jan. 29, 1774; m. 1st, Silas Seymore, and had three children: 1. SILLICK (Seymore); lived, 1849, Cold Water, Branch Co., Mich.; 2d, Oliver Phelps; 1 child; d. young; 3rd, William Easterly; d. 1848; 1 child; d. young.
759—4. PHEBE, b. Oct. 4, 1776; m. Flavel Bartlet, a tanner; she d. 1847, leaving five children; a son living, 1849, in Mayfield, Fulton Co., N. Y.
760—5. ESTHER, b. April 24, 1778; m. David Hinman.
761—6. SEARS; Baptist minister; d. in Illinois.
762—7. LUTHER.
763—8. SARAH, b. March 12, 1783.
764—9. DAVIS, b. March 10, 1788.
765-10. OLIVER.

766. ELIAS CRANE[5] [299], (Ezekiel,[4] Joseph,[3] Jasper,[2] Jasper[1]), married Phebe Brown, who was born Feb 12, 1758. Mr. Crane was born April 10, 1753, and died March 13, 1809. She died Dec. 22, 1828. He purchased for 40 pounds, April 23, 1778, $7\frac{40}{100}$ acres of land within the bounds of Elizabethtown, of

his father Ezekiel, and the deed was witnessed by his brother
Joseph, all of Newark at that time. Was he the private in
Capt. Josiah Pierson's Company, 2d Regiment, Essex Co.?
   Children :

767—1.   DAVID, b. Aug. 7, 1776; d. Dec. 15, 1782.
768—2.   STEPHEN, b. March 6, 1778.
769—3.   MOSES, b. Aug. 31, 1779.
770—4.   EUNICE, b. July 17, 1781; d. Oct. 21, 1781.
771—5.   MARY, b. May 13, 1783.
772—6.   JONATHAN, b. Aug. 28, 1784; d. Aug. 17, 1785.
773—7.   DAVID B., b. Dec. 22, 1785.
774—8.   RACHEL, b. Jan. 11, 1789; d. April 19, 1814.
775—9.   JABEZ, b. Aug. 25, 1790; d. Aug. 9, 1811.
776-10. CYRUS, b. Oct. 6, 1791; d. Nov. 1, 1809.
777-11. ABIGAIL, b. May 11, 1794; d. Sept. 12, 1836.
778-12. WILLIAM, b. Nov. 7, 1799.

779. JOANNA CRANE[5] [300], (Ezekiel,[4] Joseph,[3] Jasper,[2]
Jasper[1]), married John Plum, said to be son of Mary Plum.
Had the following, and perhaps other children :

   1. ISAAC (Plum), he or his son were first to put the letter *e* to their
       names.

780. PHEBE CRANE[5] [302], (Ezekiel,[4] Joseph,[3] Jasper,[2]
Jasper[1]), married Deacon John Ball of Parsippany. She was
his first wife, and died 1781, aged 41. The family removed to
Ohio. Children :

   1. CALVIN (Ball).
   2. LUTHER (Ball).
   3. PHEBE (Ball).

781. ISAAC CRANE[5] [305], (Isaac,[4] Joseph,[3] Jasper,[2] Jas-
per1), lived in Newark, N. J.; was a printer, and at one time
published the *Centinel of Freedom* at that place. His sons
were also printers. Children :

782—1.   ISAAC.
783—2.   TIMOTHY.
784—3.   ABIJAH.
785—4.   JAMES.

786. MARY CRANE[5] [308], (Isaac,[4] Joseph,[3] Jasper,[2] Jas-
per1), married Thomas Ball. Child :

   1. ABNER (Ball); grandfather of J. R. Burnett, on his maternal
       side.

787. ISRAEL CRANE[5] [313], (Israel,[4] Joseph,[3] Jasper,[2] Jas-
per1), married Mary ——. After the death of Mr. Crane, Aug.
2, 1795, aged 40, she married Captain —— Meeker. She died
Feb. 25, 1831, aged 71 years. Both were buried at Lyons
Farms, N. J. April 27, 1789, he was chosen one of the overseers of highways, and again in 1792. He subscribed £100
towards building the church in 1794. Child :

788—1.   ISRAEL C.

789. RACHEL CRANE[5] [314], (Israel,[4] Joseph,[3] Jasper,[2] Jasper[1]), married Nathaniel Camp. He died June 22, 1827, aged 87 years. Children :

1. Dr. STEPHEN (Camp).
2. JOHN (Camp).
3. WILLIAM (Camp).
4. AARON (Camp); lived in Newark, N. J.
5. PHEBE WHITE (Camp).
6. ELIZABETH HINSDALE (Camp).
7. HANNAH TUTTLE (Camp).
8. RACHEL BRUEN (Camp).
9. ABBY (Camp); m. Joseph Beach.
10. MARY (Camp); m. Cyrenus Beach.

790. OBEDIAH CRANE[5] [319], (Josiah,[4] Joseph,[3] Jasper,[2] Jasper[1]), married Martha ——, who died Jan. 16, 1802, in the 49th year of her age. He was chosen, April, 1788, surveyor of highways, also in 1799, 1801, and 1806, for Cranetown and North Farms. He died April 11, 1833. Children :

791—1. SUSANA B.; d. Dec. 7, 1783, aged 1 year, 11 months, 17 days
792—2. PHEBE S.; d. Dec. 6, 1801, aged 7 years, 11 months, 23 days.
793—3. PHEBE P.; d. Sept. 6, 1805, aged 1 year, 7 months, 21 days.

794. JOSIAH CRANE[5] [320], (Josiah,[4] Joseph,[3] Jasper,[2] Jasper[1]), m. Abigail ——* Residence, Lyons Farms, N. J. A grandson, Mr. John J. Crane, of New York city, says of this Josiah that he was a soldier in the Jersey Blues during the Revolutionary war; was with Washington and Lafayette in the battles fought in New Jersey, including Trenton, Monmouth, and Brandywine. After the close of the war, about 1785, he died while on a journey to the new country, as Kentucky was then called, to visit his brother, who was living in that section. Children :

795—1. JOHN JOSIAH, b. March 8, 1767; d. 1808.
796—2. BENJAMIN, b. Feb. 18, 1783; d. in New York, in 1832.

797. DAVID CRANE[5] [330], (Joseph,[4] Joseph,[3] Jasper,[2] Jasper[1]), married Hannah Wade, who was born at Connecticut Farms, N. J. He died and his widow married —— Tichnor, by whom she had seven children. Children :

798—1. PHEBE, b. Nov. 3, 1778.
799—2. ELIZA, b. 1780.

800. Col. ISAAC CRANE[5] [339], (Lewis,[4] Elihu,[3] Jasper,[2] Jasper[1]), married Joanna Ogden. Lived on the Crane place on the hill, near Williamsville, N. J., where he died in 1815, aged 69 years. Children :

801—1. KATURAH, b. May 6, 1769.
802—2. ABIGAIL, b. Feb. 13, 1771.

---

*Josiah Crane married Abigail Hathaway, March 28, 1768, *Morristown church records*. They were of Lyons Farms district. This may have been the above.

803—3. HANNAH, b. Aug. 4, 1773; d. May 4, 1813.
804—4. MARY, b. Oct. 17, 1775; d. Sept. 1, 1794.
805—5. SARAH, b. June 6, 1778.
806—6. ISAAC, b. June 10, 1781; d. Oct., 1782.
807—7. PHEBE, b. Oct. 10, 1783; d. Nov., 1783.
808—8. PHEBE, b. Feb. 21, 1785.
809—9. LEWIS, b. June 26, 1787.
810-10. CHARLOTTE, b. Oct. 19, 1789.

811. PHEBE CRANE[5] [343], (Lewis,[4] Elihu,[3] Jasper,[2] Jasper[1]),
married Major Aaron Harrison. He was son of Mathew and
Martha Dodd Harrison. He was born in 1753, and died in 1837.
Major Harrison's first wife was Jemima Condit, daughter of
Daniel and Ruth Williams Condit; she left no children. She
died 1834. Major Harrison was distinguished as a cavalry officer.
Children :

1. SAMUEL A. (Harrison), b. 1783.
2. JEMIMA (Harrison), b. 1784.
3. CHARLES (Harrison), b. 1786.
4. MATILDA (Harrison), b. 1788.
5. PHOEBE (Harrison); d.
6. IRA (Harrison), b. 1795.
7. AARON BURR (Harrison), b. 1796.
8. ABIGAIL (Harrison); d.
9. MARY (Harrison); d.

812. MARTHA CRANE[5] [346], (Elihu,[4] Elihu,[3] Jasper,[2]
Jasper[1]), married May 21, 1785, Rev. John Croes, first P. E.
bishop of New Jersey. He was born at Elizabethtown, N. J.,
June 1, 1762, second son of Jacob and Charlotte Christiana
(Reigart or Reger) Croes, natives of Germany. He died July 30,
1832. She died Feb. 5, 1845. She was called Patty Crane.
Children :

1. CHARLOTTE (Croes), b. April 12, 1786; d. May 7, 1794.
2. JOHN (Croes), b. Sept. 22, 1787.
3. SAMUEL AUSTIN (Croes), b. April 7, 1789; d. Dec. 27, 1827, in
    New Brunswick. N. J.
4. WILLIAM (Croes), b. May 26, 1791; d. March 30, 1714, in New
    Brunswick, N. J.
5. CHARLES (Croes), b. Aug. 17, 1793; d. June 11, 1794.
6. ANNE STRATTON (Croes), b. April 2, 1795; d. Dec. 7, 1872, in
    Brooklyn, and buried in New Brunswick, N. J.
7. PATTY (Croes), b. May 17, 1797; d. Sept. 6, 1846, at Elizabeth,
    N. J.
8. ROBERT BROWN (Croes), b. Aug. 13, 1800, at Swedesborough,
    N. J.

813. Rev. JOHN CROES [2]; m. Sept., 1812, Eleanor Van Mater in
    Monmouth Co., N. J., his father performing the ceremony.
    He d. on Monday, Aug. 20, 1849. Children :
    1. CATHERINE VAN MATER (Croes); b. Aug. 7, 1813.
    2. CHARLOTTE MARTHA (Croes), b. April 4, 1815.
    3. RALPH VAN MATER (Croes), b. May 14, 1817.
    4. ANNA THEODOSIA (Croes), b. July 8, 1819.
    3. ELEANOR RATTOONE (Croes), b. July 15, 1821.
    6. MARY HENRIETTA (Croes), b. May 29, 1824.
    7. JOHN WILLIAM (Croes), b. July 20, 1829.
    8. JOHN (Croes), b. Aug. 27, 1831.

814. Rev. ROBERT BROWN CROES [8]; m. May 10, 1830, Helen
   Robertson, formerly of Philadelphia. She was third daughter of James Robertson, and m. in Monumental Church, Richmond, Va. He d. in Yonkers, N. Y., July 22, 1878. Children:
   1. MARY ROBERTSON (Croes).
   2. JOHN JAMES ROBERTSON (Croes).
   3. HELEN ROBERTSON (Croes).

815. ANNA CRANE[5] [349], (Elihu,[4] Elihu,[3] Jasper,[2] Jasper[1]),
married Joseph Davis, Esq., of Bloomfield, N. J., Jan. 10, 1791.
Children:
   1. ABIGAIL (Davis), b. July 12, 1792.
   2. CALEB S. (Davis), b. Nov. 9, 1794.
   3. CHARLES (Davis), b. Feb. 9, 1797.
   4. MARTHA C. (Davis), b. Nov. 22, 1799.
   5. MARY (Davis), b. June 24, 1802; d. Dec., 1847.
   6. HENRIETTA (Davis), b. Oct. 13, 1806; d. March 9, 1874.
   7. JOSEPH AUSTIN (Davis), b. July 1, 1813.

816. ABIGAIL DAVIS [1]; m. Rev. —— Osborn; both d. Children:
   1. LOUISE (Osborn); m. Rev. —— McDowell.
   2. Dr. EDWARD (Osborn); m.
   3. Dr. JOSEPH (Osborn); m.
   4. HENRY FRANK (Osborn); m. —— Coe; has 8 children.
   5. MIRIAM (Osborn); m.
   6. ELLA (Osborn); m.
   7. CLARA (Osborn); m.
   8. BESSIE (Osborn).
   9. JULIA (Osborn).

817. CALEB S. DAVIS [2]; m. Hannah —— Children:
   1. CHARLES (Davis).
   2. JOSEPH A. (Davis).
   3. EDWARD (Davis).
   4. MARY (Davis).
   5. ANNA (Davis).

818. Dr. CHARLES DAVIS [3]; m. 1st, Mary L. Wilson, June 30, 1825.
   She died Oct. 30. 1832, leaving five children. He m. 2d,
   Matilda Gildersleeve, Jan. 15, 1834. He was an M. D. Children:
   1. ANNA MATILDA (Davis), b. Jan. 7, 1827.
   2. ELEANOR WILSON (Davis), b. July 23, 1828; d. Jan.
      22, 1830.
   3. MARY AUGUSTA (Davis), b. Aug. 9, 1829.
   4. JULIA BUTLER (Davis), b. Oct. 14, 1830; d. May 19,
      1831.
   5. EMILY LOUISA (Davis), b. Oct. 15, 1832; d. March
      16, 1851.
   6. FRANCES GILDERSLEEVE (Davis), b. Nov. 22, 1835.
   7. CHARLES (Davis), b. April 8, 1838.
   8. WILLIAM M. (Davis), b. July 13, 1840.
   9. LUTHER (Davis), b. Nov. 17, 1842; d. in the Army, Aug.
      20, 1863.
   10. CAROLINE GILDERSLEEVE(Davis), b. Jan. 2, 1845; d. May
      20, 1845.
   11. ELLEN GILDERSLEEVE (Davis), b. and d. April 10, 1846.
   12. HELEN VEEDENBURG (Davis), b. and d. July 10, 1847.
   13. ISABELLA (Davis), b. July 21, 1852; d. Aug. 7, 1892.

819. ANNA MATILDA DAVIS [1]; m. Ebenezer Platt, Jr., Jan. 17, 1855.
He was son of Rev. I. W. Platt, and b. April 18, 1823; resided
at Elizabeth, N. J.; was bank teller. He d. Dec. 17, 1878.
Children:
1. CHARLES DAVIS (Platt), b. March 18, 1856.
2. MARY WILSON (Platt), b. Feb. 27, 1858; d. March 2,
1860.
3. ANNA MCCLURE (Platt), b. July 11, 1860; residence at
Morristown, N. J.
4. WILLIAM CLIFFORD (Platt), b. Jan. 22, 1862; residence
at Chicago, Ill. (1897).
5. LUTHER DAVIS (Platt), b. April 21, 1864; residence at
New York city (1897).

CHARLES DAVIS PLATT [1]; m. Aug. 29, 1883, Mary Jane West,
dau. of Stephen Gifford West. Aug., 1883, settled in Morristown, N. J.; a teacher. Children:
1. ELEANOR WILSON (Platt), b. Aug. 24, 1884.
2. DOROTHY (Platt), b. Oct. 9, 1887.
3. RICHARD MORRIS (Platt), b. Dec. 16, 1889.
4. ROGER (Platt), b. Aug. 20, 1891; d. in infancy.
5. JULIA (Platt),   } b. June 30, 1892; { d. 1894.
6. KATHARINE (Platt), }
7. NORMAN H. (Platt), b. Jan. 25, 1894.
8. MARGARET (Platt), b. Aug. 12, 1897.

820. MARY AUGUSTA DAVIS [3]; m. Benjamin Haines, Jr., March 20,
1850. He was son of Richard T. Haines. Resided in Elizabeth, N. J. Children:
1. BENJAMIN (Haines), b. 1851; d. 1871.
2. CHARLES DAVIS (Haines), b. 1853.
3. JOHN J. (Haines); d.
4. RICHARD AUGUSTUS (Haines); d.
5. MARY (Haines); d.
6. HENRY FONDEY (Haines), b. 1868; m. —— Fortune,
N. Y. city.
7. ELEANOR ELIZABETH (Haines), b. 1875.

CHARLES DAVIS HAINES [2]; m. Mary Sabine; residence New
York city; a banker. Children:
1. JULIA (Haines).
2. ALENE (Haines).
3. GUSTAVUS SABINE (Haines).

821. FRANCES GILDERSLEEVE DAVIS [6]; m. Rev. James Edwin
Miller, July, 1858. She d. June, 1872. He d. Nov., 1885.
Children:
1. HUGH WILSON (Miller), b. June 10, 1859.
2. CAROLINE GILDERSLEEVE (Miller), b. April 8, 1862.

822. CHARLES DAVIS [7]; m. Lizzie Day, March 29, 1865. Children:
1. BESSIE CLARK (Day), b. Jan. 3, 1867.
2. CHARLES (Day), b. Aug. 23, 1869; m. Florence Oberly,
April 15, 1896.
3. LUTHER (Day), b. Jan. 8, 1871.
4. WILLIAM NICHOLS (Day), b. Jan. 24, 1873.

823. WILLIAM M. DAVIS [8]; m. Elizabeth Wakeman Weller, April
25, 1866. Children:
1. KATHARINE STIMSON (Davis), b. Sept. 5, 1867.
2. CAROLINE GILDERSLEEVE (Davis), b. Jan. 2, 1869.
3. ELIZABETH TUTTLE (Davis), b. July 31, 1876.
4. MARGARET HOXEY (Davis), b. Oct. 8, 1877.

824. KATHARINE STIMSON DAVIS [1]; m. Wallace McCamant, April 25, 1893. Child:
    1. DAVIS (McCamant),· b. July 24, 1896.

825. MARTHA C. DAVIS [4]; m. Stephen Dickerson. Children;
    1. A daughter (Dickerson), who m. Mr. Winans.
    2. JAMES L. (Dickerson), who m. ——.

826. Dr. JOSEPH AUSTIN DAVIS [7]; m. Caroline Foster; b. d. Children:
    1. JOSEPHINE (Davis).
    2. JULIA (Davis).
    3. CAROLINE (Davis); m. Wm. Sears. Children:
        1. JOSEPH (Sears).
     ·2· A daughter (Sears).

827. ISAAC WATTS CRANE[5] [351], (Elihu,[4] Elihu,[3] Jasper,[2] Jasper[1]) married in 1809 Anna Maria Alberti, of Philadelphia, Pa. She was the daughter of Dr. Geo. Frederick Alberti, who was of a noble German family. His name is recorded as among the earliest school-teachers in Cranetown, now Mont Clair. He was interested in his family history, and considerable information has been secured by means of memoranda he prepared. Children:

828—1. HANNAH PRICE, b. 1810.
829—2. WILLIAM CROES.
830—3. SARAH.
831—4. ANNA MATILDA.
832—5. ISAAC.
    Perhaps other children, who died young.

833. Judge DAVID D. CRANE[5] [362], (David,[4] David,[3] Jasper,[2] Jasper[1]), married Martha Banks, Nov. 30, 1784. She was born Aug. 19, 1766; died Aug. 18, 1844, aged 77 years, 11 months and 30 days.. He served as private and musician in the Revolutionary war; chosen town constable, April 28, 1787, and again in 1788, also pound-master; and constable, 1789. David D. Crane was one of the most prominent and influential men in Newark. He was at various times from 1787 to 1803 chosen overseer of highways. and overseer of the poor. At the annual town meeting held April 14, 1806, he and Israel Crane were elected to serve on the township committee. Mr. Crane was reëlected in 1807, 1808 and 1809. The latter year he was chairman of the Newark committee. He was chosen again on that committee in 1812. In 1820, he was chosen on committee to inquire into the situation of the town docks, and also to secure place for a public burying-ground, and one of the trustees for the town docks, but resigned the latter position in April, 1822. April 13, 1829, he was on committee to see about changing the use of the old burying-ground, and removal of remains there buried to another spot. He died in Newark, N. J., Sept. 11, 1838, aged 74 years, 11 months and 22 days. Children:

834—1. JAMES, b. Jan. 17, 1786.
835—2. JOHN R., b. April 16, 1787.
836—3. SARAH, b. Nov. 8, 1789.
    31

837—4. CATHARINE B., b. Nov. 1, 1792.
838—5. MARTHA, b. March 26, 17—.
839—6. DAVID NOYES, b. Nov. 7, 1804; drowned June 30, 1813.

840.   Capt. JOHN CALEB CRANE[5] [379], (Caleb,[4] Jonathan,[3] Jasper,[2] Jasper,[1]), married Sarah Myer, of Orange, N. J., born April 24, 1760, and lived at Chatham.   In Newark town meeting, April 27, 1789, he was elected highway surveyor.
   Children :

841—1. SAMUEL, b. Feb. 17, 1779; m. Abigail Dodd.
842—2. HENRY, b. Aug. 3, 1781; m. Sarah Day.
843—3. PHEBE, b. Oct. 26, 1784; m. 1st, Elijah Day; 2d, Samuel
          Williams.
844—4. DANIEL, b. April 7, 1787; m. Gertrude Turner.
845—5. LYDIA, b. Sept. 30, 1789; m. David Burnet.
846—6. HANNAH, b. Oct. 6, 1791.
847—7. JOHN CALEB, b. Aug. 10, 1797; m. Matilda Alling.
848—8. SARAH, b. Aug. 10, 1797; m. Isaac B. Lee.
849—9. SIMEON, H., b. March 8, 1800; m. Amanda Burroughs.
850-10. EZRA DARBY, b. Sept. 14, 1803; m. Mercy Woodruff.

851.   HANNAH CRANE[5] [381], (Caleb,[4] Jonathan,[3] Jasper,[2] Jasper[1]), married Simeon Harrison.   He was born in 1741.
   Children :

   1. CALEB (Harrison); m. Katurah Crane, dau. of Isaac Crane.
        See No. 801.
   2. JOHN (Harrison); m. Abby Condit.
   3. HANNAH (Harrison); m. —— Burnside.
   4. SARAH (Harrison); m. —— Mathews.

852.   ELIJAH CRANE[5] [387], (Elijah,[4] Jonathan,[3] Jasper,[2] Jasper[1]), married ——, and lived in Newark, N. J.   Children :

   1. ELIJAH; d. unmarried.
   2. ELIZABETH; d. unmarried.

853.   JONATHAN CRANE[5] [397], (Nehemiah,[4] Jonathan,[3] Jasper,[2] Jasper[1]), married 1st, Rachel Clisbe, who was born Dec. 23, 1752, and died in Newark, N. J., Nov. 3, 1777; married 2d, Sarah ——, who died Jan. 18, 1825.   He was elected overseer of highways at town meeting in Newark, April 14, 1795.   He died at that place Feb. 18, 1805.   Child :

854—1. NEHEMIAH J., born Aug. 13, 1774; m. Mary Ward.

855. BENJAMIN CRANE[6] [425], (Josiah,[5] Edmund,[4] John,[3] John,[2] Jasper[1]), went with his father to Orange Co., N. Y., in the spring of 1784, and settled near the present city of Middletown. He married Phebe Allien, daughter of John Allien, and said to be interested as heir to the Trinity Church property, in the city of New York. Mr. Crane was a farmer and merchant, and remained in Orange County until quite advanced in years, when he removed with his eldest son to Montrose, Pa., where he died, Feb. 12, 1845. His wife also died there. Children :

856—1. JOHN A., b. Jan. 12, 1792.
857—2. JOSIAH, b. Aug. 24, 1795.
858—3. HENRY, b. 1800.
859—4. STEPHEN KITCHELL, b. Jan. 25, 1802.
860—5. WILLIAM MORRISON, b. May 24, 1804.
861—6. VALARIA ANN, b. Nov. 13, 1808; m. Isaac Schultz Corwin.

862. ABRAHAM CRANE[6] [426], (Josiah,[5] Edmund,[4] John,[3] John,[2] Jasper[1]), married Phebe Winans ; lived near Middletown, Orange Co., N. Y. Removed to Ohio, and died in Delaware County, Feb. 17, 1839.

862½-1. JAMES HARVEY; d. in infancy.
863—2. ALFRED WINANS.
864—3. GABRIEL, b. March 30, 1800.
865—4. JOSIAH LEONARD, b. Jan. 19, 1802.
866—5. EDWARD LEWIS, b. Oct. 26, 1803.
867—6. TRYPHENA, b. Dec. 7, 1805.
868—7. JEREMIAH COLEMAN, b. March 30, 1808.
869—8. ARIGAIL K.; m. Jarvis Spafford, in Perrysburg, Ohio; d. there.
870—9. JAMES HARVEY; d. in infancy.
871—10. LAVISA LEONARD; unm.; d. in Perrysburg, Ohio.
872—11. MARIA; m. —— Morrow, of Green County, Ohio; left a daughter who d. unmarried.

873. STEPHEN CRANE[6] [428], (Josiah,[5] Edmund,[4] John,[3] John[2], Jasper[1]), married 1st, Phebe Bailey, June 19, 1802. She was born Dec. 16, 1782, and died May 23, 1808, leaving four children. He married 2d, Dorothy Little, of Middletown, N. Y., Feb. 9, 1809. She was born July 3, 1784, and died June 2, 1854, leaving eight children. For more than twenty years he lived on a portion of the home farm near Middletown, N. Y.; here all his children were born. In religion he was a Presbyterian ; of good education and strictly temperate, not even using tobacco; of medium height, with dark brown hair and

hazel eyes. In the year 1824, he removed with his family to Ohio, making the journey by wagon. The distance to Worthington, Franklin County, from the old home, was about six hundred and forty miles, and twenty-six days were consumed in making the trip. At the time of starting from Middletown, there were other families in the party, but as Mr. Crane declined to travel on the Sabbath day, they became separated; at the end of the journey, however, Mr. Crane arrived two days in advance of the other wing of the party. Ohio was then a sparsely settled country, and, although they found their friends who had previously removed from Orange County, N. Y., to Franklin County, Ohio, it took some little time for the newcomers to adapt themselves to the new surroundings. The next year (1825) they went on to Sunbury, Delaware Co., where they remained through the summer; then a brief stay was made at Monroe, but after another trial at Blendon, Franklin County, the final settlement was made in Licking County. For some years Mr. Crane busied himself in teaching school winters and farming summers. In his latter years he made his home with his son Abram K., until his wife Dorothy died, then he went to live with his eldest son Joseph B., in Illinois. In politics through his early life he had been a Democrat, but in 1860, he cast his first Republican vote for Abraham Lincoln. He died in Chicago, Feb. 26, 1866, and was buried at Tonica, LaSalle County, Ill. Children:

874—1. JOSEPH BAILEY, b. March 4, 1803.
875—2. WARREN, b. Sept. 22, 1804.
876—3. SOLOMON, b. June 22, 1806.
877—4. ABIGAIL KITCHELL, b. Dec. 23, 1807; d. Aug. 11, 1809
878—5. GEORGE LITTLE, b. Dec. 26, 1809.
879—6. JOSIAH, b. March 17, 1812; d. 1842.
880—7. DAVID, } twins; b. Feb. 17, 1814; both d. in infancy.
881—8. JOHN, }
882—9. JAMES, b. May 15, 1815; left home when a lad, and not heard from after.
883—10. ABRAM KITCHELL, b. Feb. 7, 1818.
884-11. PHEBE, b. April 1, 1820.
885-12. ABIGAIL, b. Aug. 26, 1822.

886. ELIZABETH CRANE[6] [429], (Josiah,[5] Edmund,[4] John,[3] John,[2] Jasper[1]), married 1st, John Robbins, in 1806. He died and she married 2d, Mr. Taylor. She died Feb. 8, 1831, in Orange Co., N. Y. Children:

1. CHARLES (Robbins), b. Aug. 10, 1807.
2. MATTHIAS SEELY (Robbins), b. July 24, 1809.
3. AFFIE M. (Robbins), b. Sept. 14, 1811.
4. JOB (Robbins), b. Jan. 26, 1815.
5. ANNA C. (Robbins), b. May 14, 1819.
6. JOSIAH C. (Robbins), b. March 27, 1822.
7. JOHN R. (Taylor), b. 1827; living April, 1899, at Earlville, Ill.

887. SHADRACK CRANE[6] [431], (Ezekiel,[5] Edmund,[4] John,[3] John,[2] Jasper[1]), married Hannah Palmer, Dec. 30, 1794. She

was born July 16. 1773, and died Jan. 22, 1841, in Batavia, N.
Y. He was a civil engineer. He died Oct. 28, 1848, in Napoli,
Cattaraugus Co., N. Y. Children :

888—1. EZEKIEL, b. Jan. 12,1796; had a son who settled in Augusta,
Mich.
889—2. LEWIS ALLEN, b. July 27, 1797.
890—3. ABIGAIL, b. April 17, 1799; d. April 27, 1799.
891—4. NANCY, b. May 24, 1800; m. —— Miller; living (1880),
at Napoli, Cattaraugus Co., N. Y.
892—5. STEVENS, b. March 20, 1802.
893—6. HENRY, b. Oct. 3, 1803; d. July 15, 1805.
894—7. SILAS, b.·April 7, 1805.
895—8. ROSWELL R., b. Sept. 12, 1806.
896—9. JAMES NELSON, b. May 15, 1808.
897-10. SHADRACK, b. Oct. 19, 1809; d. in infancy.
898-11. ANN ELIZA, b. Jan. 28, 1815.
899-12. ALONZO, b. Aug. 31, 1816; d. June 7, 1817.

900. ABIGAIL CRANE[6] [432], (Ezekiel,[5] Edmund,[4] John,[3]
John,[2] Jasper[1]), married William Duvall, formerly of Hackensack, N. J. Child :

1. ISRAEL SMITH (Duvall), b. March 20, 1798.
John S. Clark of Auburn, N. Y., a descendant of this Abigail,
collected considerable data relating to this immediate line,
and was to have furnished the writer with the result of his
researches, but died before carrying out his promise, and
his family failed to respond to subsequent solicitation.

901. SILAS CRANE[6] [433], (Ezekiel,[5] Edmund,[4] John,[3] John,[2]
Jasper[1]), married Ann Stringham Platt, of Canondaga Co., N.
Y., and removed to Michigan. He died Nov. 5, 1848. She
died July 13, 1849. Child :

902—1. FRANCES R.; m. Walter Wright; had one child who m. Mr
Van Brunt.

903. LOYAL CRANE[6] [444], (James,[5] Edmund,[4] John,[3] John,[2]
Jasper[1]), born in Mentz, Cayuga Co., N.·Y., and married there,
Oct. 22, 1834, Sally Ann DeGraff. She was born at Esopus,
Ulster Co., N. Y., Oct. 2, 1813. He removed to Michigan, and
settled at Paw Paw, about 1838 or 1840 ; a farmer. She died
there April 14, 1874. Children :

904—1. JAMES M., b. Oct. 2, 1842.
905—2. SALLY MARIAH; residence, 1408 V St., Washington, D. C.;
she has a son, Harry L. Van Auken.

906. ALONZO CRANE[6] [445], (James,[5] Edmund,[4] John,[3]
John,[2] Jasper[1]), born in Mentz, Cayuga Co., N. Y. He removed to Michigan, about 1838 ; married Eliza Lyle about 1839 ;
was a surveyor by profession ; resided on a farm near Paw Paw,
Mich., where he died in the fall of 1846 (October). Children :

907—1. URSULA L., b. July 10, 1842; m. —— Harrison, and for some
years after her husband died, was superintendent of the
Industrial School for Boys, Norwood Park, Cook Co., Ill.
908—2. EDGAR A., b. July 5, 1844.

909—3. ERASTUS W., b. May 4, 1846; m. Cornelia Wilson, Oct. 15,
      1867. She d. in 1874, and he married again; no children:
      residence, Kalamazoo, Mich.

910. NATHANIEL JONES CRANE[6] [451], (Joseph,[5] Joseph,[4]
Jasper,[3] John,[2] Jasper[1]), married 1st, Amanda Baldwin, daughter of Caleb Baldwin, of Plumfield; d. Feb. 6, 1839; 2d, Elizabeth Jenette Ward, daughter of Dr. Eleazer Ward, Nov. 10,
1840. She was born June 1, 1816, and died at Woodside, N.
J., Sept. 13 or 19, 1870. He was a farmer, and lived in Newark.
Children :

911—1. ANNA FRANCES, b. Feb. 21, 1843.
912—2. ANDREW L.
913—3. JOSEPH J.
914—4. CHARLOTTE E.
915—5. FRANK S.
916—6. JENNIE M.
917—7. SARAH ISABELLE, b. May 26, 1858; d. Dec. 7, 1882.

918. ROBERT CRANE[6] [455], (Moses,[5] Joseph,[4] Jasper,[3]
John,[2] Jasper[1]), married Eliza Cooley. Children :

919—1. ROBERT W.; lived in Brooklyn.
920—2. CHARLES H.; went to Selma, Ala., 1855.

921. HARRY CRANE[6] [456], (Moses,[5] Joseph,[4] Jasper,[3] John,[2]
Jasper[1]), married ——, and was living in 1865 near Paterson, N.
J. Children :

922—1. JAMES; m. Miss Budd, and d. in Albany, N. Y., leaving a
      widow and one daughter.
923—2. CHARLES.
924—3. EDWARD,; lived in Jersey City 1865.
925—4. MOSES; a farmer; lived near his father.
926—5. WILLIAM; lived in Jersey City 1865.
927—6. SARAH; m. —— Spur, of Bloomfield, and lived there.

928. PHEBE CRANE[6] [458], (Moses,[5] Joseph,[4] Jasper,[3] John,[2]
Jasper,[1]), married John H. Timms, a coachmaker, afterwards a
mechanical engineer; a man of great public spirit and inventive
skill, who produced several useful inventions, among them an
axle-box for oiling the journals of railway cars, and which was
adopted quite generally throughout the country. He died at
Newark, N. J., May 9, 1856, leaving one child :

1. THEODORE (Timms); living in Utica, N. Y., in 1865, and in
    the jewelry business. He m. Mary E. Burnet, dau. of Abner
    B. Burnet, of Newark, N. J.

929. JANE CRANE[6] [459], (Moses,[5] Joseph,[4] Jasper,[3] John,[2]
Jasper[1]), married Sanford M. Tower; was living in Harlem in
1865, and had nine children.

930. MARIA CRAIN[6] [474], (William,[5] Jeremiah,[4] Daniel,[3]
John,[2] Jasper[1]), married —— Burt, and died, leaving one child :

1. AMANDA (Burt), b. about 1827; she m. in 1845 Frederick Pring,
    and had one child :
      1. EMILY (Pring), b. about 1850.

931. ACHILLES RAINER CRAIN[6] [476], (William,[5] Jeremiah,[4] Daniel,[3] John,[2] Jasper[1]), married Dec. 9, 1833, Eliza, daughter of William Dunbar. He died in New York city Oct. 8, 1841. Children :

932—1. ORESTES MOTIER, b. Oct. 10, 1834; d. Jan. 2, 1866.
933—2. HORATIO, b. Aug. 2, 1836.

934. JOSEPHUS NICHOLSON CRAIN[6] [477], (William,[5] Jeremiah,[4] Daniel,[3] John,[2] Jasper[1]), married in 1833 Frances E. Guinness. He died of yellow fever at Galveston, Texas, Nov. 12, 1847. Children :

935—1. GEORGE J., b. Aug. 15, 1834.
936—2. THOMAS B., b. April 10, 1836.
937—3. CHARLES S., b. Aug. 29, 1837; d. Sept. 15, 1838.
938—4. FRANCES JOSEPHINE, b. Nov. 13, 1838; m. Mr. Hardy, and had a son.
939—5. WILLIAM GUINNESS, b. July 13, 1842; d. about 1864.
940—6. SARAH E., b. Aug. 28, 1843.
941—7. MARIANNA, b. March 13, 1846.

942. SUSAN CRAIN[6] [478], (William,[5] Jeremiah,[4] Daniel,[3] John,[2] Jasper[1]), married Dennis Gahagan. She died Sept. 22, 1839, at Smithfield, Liberty Co., Texas. Child :

1. IRENE (Gahagan).

943. WILLIAM DAVIS CRAIN[6] [479], (William,[5] Jeremiah,[4] Daniel,[3] John,[2] Jasper[1]), married Aug. 20, 1844, Emily Matilda Blake. Children :

944—1. JOSEPHUS; d. in infancy.
945—2. WILLIAM HENRY, b. Nov. 25, 1848.
946—3. FRANK; d. in infancy.
947—4. CHARLES DAVIS, b. Oct. 12, 1852.

948. ISRAEL CRANE[6] [482], (Matthias,[5] William,[4] Nathaniel,[3] Azariah,[2] Jasper[1]), married in 1796 Fannie Pierson, born March 20, 1773, daughter of Dr. Matthias Pierson, of Orange, N. J., the first resident physician at the " Newark Mountains," and who was great-grandson of Thomas Pierson, one of the first settlers of Newark in 1666, who came from Branford, Conn. Mr. Crane was a graduate of Princeton in 1793. This is probably the Israel Crane called in the Newark town records of Bloomfield, and held various town offices during the years from 1799 to 1814. Was a farmer and merchant, and known as "King" Crane from his extensive and successful mercantile operations. From his store in the stone building, located on the north side of the old road, and standing in 1881 near the residence of his son James, he sent out five and six-horse teams, loaded with merchandise, to be distributed throughout the counties lying west, and even into the borders of the State of Pennsylvania. He died March, 1858. Children :

949—1. MARY STOCKTON, b. 1798; d. 1805.
950—2. ELIZABETH, b. 1800; m. E. Beach.

951—3. MATTHIAS, b. 1802; m. S. Baldwin.
952—4. ABIGAIL, b. 1804; m. Dr. I. Dodd, and d. 1863.
953—5. MARY, b. 1807.
954—6. JAMES, b. 1809; m. Phebe Crane.

955. ABIGAIL CRANE[6] [483], (Matthias,[5] William,[4] Nathaniel,[3] Azariah,[2] Jasper[1]), married William Holmes, of Belleville, N. J. Children:

1. WILLIAM WILSON (Holmes); drowned when young. .
2. ISRAEL (Holmes); m., and has a son a Presbyterian minister in Rockford, Ill., Rev. Mead Holmes.
3. HUGH (Holmes).
4. ELIZABETH (Holmes).
5. SARAH (Holmes).
6. LYDIA (Holmes).

HUGH HOLMES [3]; m. Eliza, dau. of Rev. John Dow. He was a dry goods merchant. Children:
1. ANGALINE (Holmes); m. Cyrus Pierson.
2. SARAH (Holmes); m. John S. Kingsland.
3. ORILLA (Holmes); m. Charles A. Lent.
4. WILLIAM WILSON (Holmes); m. Elizabeth Van Riper; their son Wm. D. has been postmaster at Belleville for several years.
. ANNA ELIZA (Holmes); m. Jas. G. Henkle.
HUGH (Holmes); m. Anna D., dau. of John Williams.
5. JOHN D. (Holmes); d. in infancy.
8. ADOLPHUS M. (Holmes).
9. ABIGAIL (Holmes).

956. Dr. ABIJAH CRANE[6] [485], (Jonathan,[5] William,[4] Nathaniel,[3] Azariah,[2] Jasper[1]), married Mary Jacobus in Newark, N. J., May 10, 1791. She was born in Bergen, May 1, 1770. He was born in Cranetown. Was a physician and farmer. Served in the War of 1812. They resided at Fairfield, N. J. Children:

957—1. SALLY, b. 1798; m. Peter Ryerson 1816 or 1826, and d. 1872; had six children.
958—2. JONATHAN, b. 1800; d. 1837.
959—3. POLLY, b. 1803; m. John Prince in 1826; d. 1829.
960—4. ESTHER, b. 1806; m. Abraham Husk; d. 1866, leaving seven children.
961—5. UZAL A , } twins, b. May 10, 1807; { m. Silas B. Osborne;
962—6. SOPHIAH, }   four children.
963—7. JAMES A., b. 1811; m. Elizabeth Vandyne; three children. He d. 1872.
964—8. HENRY A. R., b. Dec. 11, 1813.

965. UZAL CRANE [6] [486], (Jonathan,[5] William,[4] Nathaniel,[3] Azariah,[2] Jasper[1]), married ——. Child:

1. UZAL.

966. TIMOTHY CRANE[6] [487], (Jonathan,[5] William,[4] Nathaniel,[3] Azariah,[2] Jasper[1]), married ——. Children:

967—1. ZENAS.
968—2. CYRUS.

969. AMOS CRANE[6] [489], (Jonas,[5] William,[4] Nathaniel,[3] Azariah,[2] Jasper[1]), married ——. Child:

970—1. GEORGE.

971. CALVIN SMITH CRANE[6] [491], (Jonas,[5] William,[4] Nathaniel,[3] Azariah,[2] Jasper[1]), married 1st, Nancy, daughter of Samuel Day, of New York, May 10, 1818. She was born Feb. 15, 1793, and died Jan. 9, 1827; 2d, Julia Angelina, daughter of Nathaniel Douglass, April 2, 1829. She was born at Pompton, N. J., in 1800, and died in Caldwell, Jan. 22, 1835; he married 3d, Mary Hier, daughter of John Hier, Oct. 17, 1836. Mr. Crane was a popular teacher, and kept a boarding-school in Caldwell, where he died March 4, 1837. By his first wife he had two children, and also two by his second wife. His last wife died March 4, 1887. Children:

972—1. STEPHEN MUNSON, b. Feb. 13, 1819.
973—2. PHEBE ANN, b. Feb. 5, 1823; m. Stephen Sayre, of Newark, 1851. She d. 1882.
974—3. VAN ZANT, b. Nov. 11, 1826; d. Dec., 1826.
975—4. DELIA, b. June 20, 1830; m. Chas. G. Campbell, of Newark, N. J., May, 1853; d. Sept. 15, 1889.
976—5. WALWORTH DOUGLASS, b. July 8, 1833.
977—6. CATHARINE AUGUSTA, b. Oct. 17, 1837; d. Jan. 20, 1867.

978. BETHUEL CRANE[6] [492], (Jonas,[5] William,[4] Nathaniel,[3] Azariah,[2] Jasper[1]), married Abby Harrison, daughter of Joseph Harrison, Esq., of Livingston. He died in West Orange, N. J., Aug. 26, 1854, nearly 75 years of age. She died Sept. 10, 1854. Children:

979—1. AARON D.
980—2. JONAS SMITH.
981—3. RACHEL; m. Oct. 18, 1827, Stephen C. Moore, merchant at Caldwell, N. J.
982—4. HARRIET, b. about 1828; m.
983—5. ABBY ANN, b. about 1829; d. 1852.

984. HANNAH CRANE[6] [501], (William,[5] William,[4] Nathaniel,[3] Azariah,[2] Jasper[1]), married Cyrus Crane, son of Samuel, of Caldwell, N. J. She died in 1850, aged 68 years. (See No. 1051).

985. SARAH CRANE[6] [502], (William,[5] William,[4] Nathaniel,[3] Azariah,[2] Jasper[1]), married Amos Baldwin, of Orange, N. J. Children:

1. LEWIS (Baldwin).
2. WILLIAM (Baldwin).
3. DANIEL (Baldwin).
4. NATHANIEL (Baldwin).
5. AMOS (Baldwin).
6. SQUIRE (Baldwin).
7. JOANNA (Baldwin).

986. JOSIAH W. CRANE[6] [503], (William,[5] William,[4] Nathaniel,[3] Azariah,[2] Jasper[1]), married June 28, 1808, Fanny Cockefair. He was a farmer, and resided in West Bloomfield,

32

N. J., where he died May 26, 1865. She died there July 21, 1867. He served in the war of 1812. Children:

987—1. ALEXANDER M., b. June 20, 1809; m. Phebe Adeline Baldwin, of Caldwell, N. J, May 20, 1831; d. July 15, 1877.
988—2. JOHN NEWTON, b. Dec. 26, 1810; a minister.
989—3. HENRY L., b. March 5, 1813; m. Elizabeth Marshall, April, 1833; settled in Lacon, Ill.; a minister.
990—4. NAOMI C., b. July 23, 1816; m. Nathaniel L. Baldwin, Nov. 8, 1834; d. Aug. 8, 1882.
991—5. MICHAEL C., b. April 22, 1818; d. Jan. 14, 1829.
992—6. SARAH CAROLINE, b. Feb. 29, 1820; d. June 17, 1882.
993—7. MARGARET C., b. Oct. 23, 1822; m. Samuel Eveland, June 1, 1852; d. July 24, 1892.
994—8. NANCY F., b. Oct. 22, 1825; m. Joseph B. Cockefair, May 7, 1868; d. March 20, 1890.
995—9. MARY P., b. Jan. 17, 1828; m. Samuel Carl, Jr., Aug. 11, 1874; d. Oct. 10, 1887.
996—10. HESTER A., b. April 14, 1831; m. Philip Harrison, of Bloomfield, N. J.
997-11. FRANCES A., b. Sept. 5, 1833; m. Marcus Harrison.

998. WILLIAM CRANE[6] [504], (William,[5] William,[4] Nathaniel,[3] Azariah,[2] Jasper,[1]), married Deborah Woodruff, of Westfield, N. J., and settled in Orange. She died June 2, 1865. He was pound-master, in 1830, 1831 and 1832. Children:

999—1. JOSHUA, b. 1821.
1000—2. EUPHRONIA; m. George Harrison.

1001. JOSHUA CRANE[6] [507], (William;[5] William,[4] Nathaniel,[3] Azariah,[2] Jasper[1]), married Clarissa Fenn, of Dundaff, Pa., and settled in East Bloomfield, N. J. Children:

1002—1. EMMA M. D.; d., aged 16 years.
1003—2. MELVINA P.; d., aged 14 years.
1004—3. WILLIAM JUDSON; d., aged 12 years.
1005—4. SYDNEY H.; d., aged 8 years.
1006—5. ALPHEUS L.; d., aged 5 years.
1007—6. LYDIA B.; d., aged 2 years.

1008. LYDIA CRANE[6] [511], (Oliver,[5] William,[4] Nathaniel,[3] Azariah,[2] Jasper[1]), married Josiah Eliakim Crane, son of Eliakim,[4] John,[3] Azariah,[2] Jasper[1], Sept. 20, 1810. He died June 8, 1845, aged 76. She died Sept. 4, 1848. Children:

1009—1. Dr. LYMAN MARK, b. 1813.
1010—2. CHARLES OLIVER, b. 1815.
1011—3. EDWARD AMES, b. Oct. 19, 1817.
1012—4. JASON, b. Sept. 18, 1821.

1013. STEPHEN FORDHAM CRANE[6] [512], (Oliver,[5] William,[4] Nathaniel,[3] Azariah,[2] Jasper[1]), married, Feb. 22, 1816, Matilda Howell Smith, daughter of Peter and Huldah (Fordham) Smith. She was born March 15, 1791, and died Jan. 18, 1871. He was an elder in the Presbyterian Church, as was his father before him. Children:

1014—1. EMELINE HULDAH, b. Nov. 5, 1817; d. June 23, 1857.
1015—2. SUSAN PHILETTA, b. Aug. 22, 1820.
1016—3. OLIVER, b. July 12, 1822.

1017—4. SARAH URANIA, b. Jan. 17, 1825; d. 1836.
1018—5. HANNAH MARIA, b. Oct. 25, 1827; d. Sept. 7, 1855.
1019—6. STEPHEN SMITH, b. March 12, 1830; d. June 28, 1872.

1020. RACHEL CRANE[6] [513], (Oliver,[5] William,[4] Nathaniel,[3] Azariah,[2] Jasper[1]), married Amos Baldwin, Sept. 9, 1818. He was born March 20, 1792, and died Jan. 27, 1858. She died March 17, 1855. Children :

1. OLIVER CRANE (Baldwin), b. April 23, 1819; d. Jan. 17, 1881.
2. EPHRAIM (Baldwin), b. Sept. 23, 1822.
3. HARVEY (Baldwin), b. April 11, 1825; d. Feb. 16, 1857.
4. SARAH (Baldwin), b. Aug. 2, 1827; m. Mahlon Griffith.
5. SILAS (Baldwin), b. Oct. 2, 1830; d. May 27, 1850.
6. SUSAN M. (Baldwin), b. March 18, 1833; m. Mr. Brooks.
7. PHEBE JANE (Baldwin), b. June 23, 1835; m. Rev. Bently S. Foster.
8. LYDIA (Baldwin), b. Nov. 16, 1836.
9. MARCUS CRANE (Baldwin), b. Aug. 27, 1840; d. Feb. 16, 1857.

1021. OLIVER CRANE BALDWIN [1]; m. Mary C. Osborn, May 21, 1850. Children :
1. MARY VIRGINIA (Baldwin), b. June 7, 1851
. JAMES OSBORN (Baldwin), b. Sept. 1, 1856.
. HOMER T. (Baldwin), b. Dec. 19, 1859.
3. VERNA L. (Baldwin), b. Sept. 21, 1862.
5. AMOS B. (Baldwin), b. July 25, 1874.
6. SAMUEL C. (Baldwin), b. Oct. 25, 1876.

1022. AMOS CRANE[6] [514], (Oliver,[5] William,[4] Nathaniel,[3] Azariah,[2] Jasper[1]), married Rhoda Caroline Ward. He died in Mont Clair, N. J., April 11, 1882, in his 84th year. Children :

1023—1. AMOS S.; d. in infancy.
1024—2. ALFRED JASPER, b. Jan. 18, 1864.

1025. ZOPHAR BALDWIN CRANE[6] [515] (Oliver,[5] William,[4] Nathaniel,[3] Azariah,[2] Jasper[1]), married Julia Freeland, who died Aug., 1874. He died April, 1877. Children :

1026—1. WILLIAM M., b. Jan., 1833.
1026½-2. SUSAN; d. young.
1027—3. MARY LOUISA, b. about 1837.

1028. NATHANIEL MARCUS CRANE[6] [516], (Oliver,[5] William,[4] Nathaniel,[3] Azariah,[2] Jasper[1]), married Julia A. Ostrander, Nov. 7, 1836. They went as missionaries to India, where they spent eight years. He died Sept. 21, 1859. Children :

1029—1. JULIA FRANCES, b. Dec. 21, 1837.
1030—2. CHARLOTTE LOUISA. b. Sept. 17, 1839; d. Sept. 1, 1868.
1031—3. HARRIET JANE, b. Nov. 4, 1840.
1032—4. MARCUS HENRY, b. Dec. 13, 1841; d. March 9, 1860.
1033—5. THEODORE FORDHAM, b. Feb. 24, 1844.
1034—6. CATHERINE EMILY, b. Nov. 21. 1845.

1035. ISAAC WHEELER CRANE[6] [517], (Oliver,[5] William,[4] Nathaniel,[3] Azariah,[2] Jasper[1]), married Elizabeth Burrows. She died April 1, 1855, and he married 2d, Mary L. Turnbull, Aug. 10, 1865. Children :

1036—1. CHARLES; d. Sept., 1864.

1037—2. ANN ELIZABETH; d. about 1880.
1038—3. JOSEPH MARCUS.
1039—4. FANNIE; m. Aug. 2, 1881, Rev. John McCull Anderson; settled in Eldorado, Iowa.

1040. CALEB CRANE[6] [519], (Samuel,[5] Noah,[4] Nathaniel,[3] Azariah,[2] Jasper[1]), married Lydia Personette, who was born Oct. 3, 1767, probably in Orange, N. J. She died May .10, 1863. He was a farmer, and resided in Caldwell, where he was deacon in the Church. He died Jan. 10, 1844, aged 74.

Children :

1041—1. MARIA, b. 1794; d. 1830.
1042—2. SAMUEL GIBSON, b. 1797.
1043—3. ELIZABETH BALDWIN, b. May, 1800.
1044—4. MOSES PERSONETTE. b. Aug. 11, 1801.
1045—5. ZENAS C., b. Oct. 22, 1804.
1046—6. LYDIA P., b. 1809.

1047. ZENAS CRANE[6] [520], (Samuel,[5] Noah,[4] Nathaniel,[3] Azariah,[2] Jasper[1]), married Abbie Grover, of Parsippany; was drowned at the ferry between New York and Brooklyn, Nov. 19, 1801, aged 29 years. Children :

1048—1. CLARINDA; m. —— Hasslet, and had five children.
1049—2. SARAH; m. Samuel Dobbins; d. in Illinois.
1050—3. ZENAS; m., and lived in Jackson, Wayne Co., Ohio.

1051. Col. CYRUS CRANE[6] [523], (Samuel,[5] Noah,[4] Nathaniel,[3] Azariah,[2] Jasper[1]), married Hannah Crane, daughter of William,[5] who married Lydia Baldwin (see No. 984). He lived at Caldwell, N. J., and died in 1827, aged 48. She died in 1850, aged 69. Children :

1052—1. DORCAS, b. Jan., 1807; m. —— Harrison.
1053—2. ASHUR B., b. Nov., 1809.
1054—3. MARCUS E., b. Oct., 1811; d. 1843; unm.
1055—4. MARY B., b. Feb., 1814.
1056—5. JOSEPH B., b. April, 1816; unm.; d. 1832, while studying for the ministry.
1057—6. ELIZABETH M., b. Aug. 13, 1818.
1058—7. SARAH, b. Sept., 1820; d. unmarried.

1059. ELIZABETH CRANE[6] [524], (Samuel,[5] Noah,[4] Nathaniel,[3] Azariah,[2] Jasper[1]), married Matthias Canfield. Children :

1. SAMUEL (Canfield); m. Lydia Bond, and had Geo. M.
2. ESTHER (Canfie d).
3. ELIZA (Canfield).
4. SMITH (Canfield).
5. CYRUS (Canfield).
6. MARY (Canfield).
7. NEWTON (Canfield).

1060. MARY CRANE[6] [525], (Samuel,[5] Noah,[4] Nathaniel,[3] Azariah,[2] Jasper[1]), was called Polly, and married Feb., 1810, Samuel Harrison. He was born 1782. Children :

1. JOANNA (Harrison). b. 1811; m. Ashur Crane, 1850.
2. SAMUEL (Harrison).
3. CYRUS (Harrison).

4. ZENAS (Harrison).
5. MARY (Harrison).
6. MARILLA (Harrison).

1061. Major NATHANIEL S. CRANE[6], [526], (Samuel,[5] Noah,[4] Nathaniel,[3] Azariah,[2] Jasper[1]), married Jane Lee Duryea, Feb., 1809. She died in Caldwell, Jan. 16, 1820. He married 2d, in 1821, Julia F. Hedges; married 3rd, in 1854, Janette E. Cook. He was ruling elder in the Church at Caldwell, and gave $500 to that Church; was a farmer, and died July 8, 1870.

Children:

1062—1. SAMUEL, b. 1810.
1063—2. JOHN T., b. 1813; m. Charlotte Thompson, in 1861.
1064—3. CALEB S., b. 1815; m. Rhoda M. Dodd, in 1838.
1065—4. HENRY W., b. 1817.
1066—5. JANE ELIZA, b. 1819; m. Caleb N. Pierson, in 1839.
1067—6. DELPHENE, b. 1822; d. 1827.
1068—7. JAMES H., b. 1824.
1069—8. PHEBE M., b. 1826.
1070—9. CYRUS E., b. 1829.
1071-10. JULIA H., b. 1835; m. Sept. 12, 1860, Rev. Lemuel Stoughton Potwin, son of Thomas and Sarah (Stoughton) Potwin, of East Windsor, Conn. In 1865, he was associate editor of the American Tract Society, of Boston, Mass.

1072. NATHANIEL CRANE[6] [531], (Joseph,[5] Noah,[4] Nathaniel,[3] Azariah,[2] Jasper[1]), married ——. Children:

1073—1. MORINGTON (or MORMINGTON).
1074—2. PHEBE.
1075—3. IRVING.

1076. NANCY CRANE[6] [541], (Aaron,[5] Job,[4] Azariah,[3] Azariah,[2] Jasper[1]), married Isaac Pierson, M.D., in 1795, and died in 1841. Settled in Orange, N. J. Children:

1. WILLIAM (Pierson), b. 1796.
2. ALBERT (Pierson), b. 1798.
3. PHEBE S. (Pierson), b. 1801.
4. FANNY (Pierson), b. July 22, 1803.
5. GEORGE (Pierson), b. Oct. 16, 1805.
6. EDWARD (Pierson), b. April 27, 1808.
7. AARON (Pierson), b. Feb. 28, 1811.
8. ISAAC (Pierson), b. July 20, 1813.
9. HARRIET (Pierson), b. March 12, 1816.
10. SARAH ANN (Pierson), b. March 21, 1820.

1077. TIMOTHY A. CRANE[6] [546], (Aaron,[5] Job,[4] Azariah,[3] Azariah,[2] Jasper[1]), married Sarah Gould, and resided in Mont Clair, N. J. Children:

1078—1. AARON.
1079—2. MARY C.; m. Samuel D. Mead.
1080—3. ISAAC; m. Emma Crane; had Timothy A.
1081—4. NANCY.
1082—5. JAMES C.; m. Grace Crane.
1083—6. HORACE.

1084. ELIAS B. CRANE[6] [547], (Aaron,[5] Job,[4] Azariah,[3] Azariah,[2] Jasper[1]), married ——. Children:

1085—1. SMITH EMONS, b. 1813; d. 1854.

1086—2. OLIVIA CAROLINE, b. 1815.
1087—3. GEORGE AUGUSTUS, b. 1819; d. 1891.
1088—4. ELIZABETH ANN, b. 1824.
1089—5. WILLIAM HENRY, b. 1830; d. 1887.
1090—6. CHARLES STANTON, b. 1833.

1091. ZENAS SQUIER CRANE[6] [548], (Aaron,[5] Job,[4] Azariah,[3] Azariah,[2] Jasper[1]), married Sept. 4, 1821, Maria Searing, who was born in Philadelphia, Pa., Jan. 22, 1779, and settled in Mont Clair, formerly Cranetown, N. J. He served in the War of 1812 nine months, along the coast below New York city. He held the office of magistrate fifty-three years; judge of the common pleas court twenty-eight years; and master in chancery in the State of New Jersey twenty-two years. He died in 1884, at the age of 91 years, the last survivor of his father's family.
Child:

1092—1. THEODORE.

1093. JACOB G. CRANE[6] [569], (Zebina,[5] Gamaliel,[4] Azariah,[3] Azariah,[2] Jasper[1]), married Nov. 9, 1817, Permelia Dexter, by whom he had two children. She died April 28, 1821. He then married Mary Carr, who bore him six children. She died Feb. 4, 1837, and he married Anna Smith, by whom he had three children. Mr. Crane was an industrious, hard-working man, and succeeded in accumulating a respectable amount of property, which he distributed among his children. He died in 1870 on the farm where he had made his home many years.
Children:

1094—1. ZEBINA, b. July 20, 1818.
1095—2. MYRON, b. Nov. 11, 1819.
1096—3. DAVID, b. June 25, 1822; d. Aug. 22, 1823.
1097—4. CALEB, b. Nov. 28, 1823.
1098—5. SAMUEL, b. Oct. 14, 1826; d. March 31, 1834.
1099—6. DEWITT, b. May 12, 1829; d. March 4, 1833.
1100—7. WILLIAM A., b. May 22, 1831.
1101—8. ALONZO, b. May 4, 1833.
1102—9. J. SMITH, b. Dec. 24, 1837.
1103—10. MARY P., b. June 5, 1839; d. Sept. 19, 1841.
1104—11. JUSTUS B., b. Dec. 26, 1842. In early life went to Chicago, Ill.; studied law, and was a lawyer there.

1105. SUSANNAH CRANE[6] [570], (Zebina,[5] Gamaliel,[4] Azariah,[3] Azariah,[2] Jasper[1]) married 1st, April 18, 1816, Howell Sweezey, by whom she had five children. He died, and she married 2d, William Brown. They settled in one of the western states. Children:

1. ARCHIBALD (Sweezey), b. April 29, 1817; d. Jan. 31, 1822.
2. LAVINA V. (Sweezey), b. Nov. 5, 1819; d. Aug., 1824.
3. ELIZABETH (Sweezey), b. Aug. 3, 1823.
4. SARAH A. (Sweezey), b. Nov. 30, 1825; d. June 3, 1850.
5. SUSANNAH (Sweezey), b. Jan. 29, 1827.
6. WILLIAM H. (Brown), b. March 18, 1832; d. June 12, 1837.
7. MARY (Brown), b. March 13, 1834.
8. HANNAH (Brown), b. May 13, 1836.
9. GEORGE W. (Brown), b. July 21, 1838; m. Abby Ferguson; d. in Louisiana.

10. JULIA (Brown), b. March 19, 1842; m. James.——.
11. FREDERICK (Brown), b. Dec. 23, 1856; d. July 24, 1858.

1106. ELIZABETH SWEEZEY [3]; m. Ezra Morrell, June 22, 1850, and
went west. Children:
    1. STEPHEN WALLACE (Morrell), b. May 9, 1851.
    2. MARY J. (Morrell), b. July 6, 1853.
    3. EZRA WARREN (Morrell), b. Jan. 6, 1855; d. Sept. 25,
       1855.
    4. WILLIAM EZRA (Morrell), b. Oct. 6, 1857; d. Sept. 24,
       1860.
    5. SUSANNAH (Morrell), b. May 3, 1860; d. July 24, 1889.
    6. JOSEPH D. (Morrell), b. Feb. 16, 1863.

1107. STEPHEN WALLACE MORRELL [1]; m. Phœba Ann Spencer,
Jan. 2, 1870. Children:
    1. FRANK L. (Morrell), b. Nov. 16, 1870.
    2. JESSIE W. (Morrell), b. Nov. 9, 1876.

1108. MARY J. MORRELL [2]; m. John C. Dunlap, April 24, 1873.
Children:
    1. CHARLES M. (Dunlap), b. May 12, 1874.
    2. EZRA M. (Dunlap), b. Dec. 28, 1876.
    3. ARTHUR C. (Dunlap), b. March 26, 1878.
    4. ROSCOE P. (Dunlap), b. July 15, 1881. ·

1109. JOSEPH D. MORRELL [6]; m. Estella P. Warner, Aug. 3, 1891.
Children:
    1. MABLE ADELLA (Morrell), b. May 27, 1892.
    2. MARY (Morrell), b. Jan. 23, 1894.

1110. SUSANNAH SWEEZEY [5]; m. Harrison Bishop, Jan. 1, 1844; settled in Illinois; living at last report in Union, McHenry Co.
Children:
    1. EDWIN A. (Bishop), b. Jan. 5, 1845; d. Aug. 19, 1845.
    2. MARY JANETTE (Bishop), b. April 2, 1847; d. May 21,
       1883.
    3. MARIA E. (Bishop), b. Oct. 5, 1848; m. Upton Pierce,
       March 7, 1876.
    4. HENRY H. (Bishop), b. Aug. 9, 1850.
    5. HENRIETTA (Bishop), b. March 30, 1852.
    6. EDGAR C. (Bishop), b. June 20, 1854.
    7. IDA VIOLA (Bishop), b. Oct. 30, 1856; d. April 1, 1865.

1111. MARY JANETTE BISHOP [2]; m. Dwight Bigalow, Oct. 8, 1868; .
d. May 21, 1883. Children:
    1. EARNEST (Bigalow), b. Nov. 18, 1871.
    2. NELLIE (Bigalow), b. Sept. 22, 1874.
    3. WINNIE (Bigalow), b. July 21, 1876.
    4 WALTER (Bigalow), b. Feb. 20, 1878.

1112. HENRY H. BISHOP [4]; m. Elva Brown, Feb. 8, 1880; she d.
without issue; m. 2d, Augusta Hiddel, Jan. 13, 1887.
Children:
    1. HARRISON (Bishop), b. Oct. 8, 1887.
    2. CARRIE (Bishop), b. April 29, 1890.

1113. HENRIETTA BISHOP [5]; m. William Wiley, Nov. 2, 1871.
Child:
    1. SUSIE J. (Wiley), b. May 11, 1874.

1114. EDGAR C. BISHOP [6]; m. Nellie East, Jan. 27, 1878. Children:
    1. DAISY (Bishop), b. Nov. 13, 1879.
    2. JESSIE E. (Bishop), b. July 14, 1880.
    3. ERNIE A. (Bishop), b. Jan. 19, 1882.

    4. ARTHUR E. (Bishop), b. Dec. 1, 1884.
    5. EDGAR C. (Bishop), b. March 30, 1886.
    6. CLARA B. (Bishop), b. Jan. 18, 1889; d. April 10, 1889.
    7. NELLIE MAY (Bishop), b. Dec. 1, 1891.

1115. MARY BROWN [7]; m. Joseph Morrell; she is reported to have
        d. March 20, 1876. Children:
    1. MARY ALICE (Morrell), b. March 3, 1850; m. James J.
        Rarick, Oct. 10, 1872. Children:
        1. JULIA M. (Rarick), b. June 6, 1877; d. March
            31, 1882.
        2. HARRIETT E. (Rarick), b. Aug. 19, 1883.
    2. GEORGE B. (Morrell).
    3. HENRY (Morrell).

1116. ELIZABETH CRANE[6] [571], (Zabina,[5] Gamaliel,[4] Azariah,[3] Azariah,[2] Jasper[1]), married 1st, Abel Brockway, in 1817,
by whom she had one son. After the death of her first husband,
she married 2d, William A. Chatfield, Oct. 16, 1822. She died
at the west, Feb., 1840. Children:

    1. AMOS (Brockway).
    2. SARAH M. (Chatfield), b. Nov. 6, 1824; d. July 18, 1836.
    3. OBED C. (Chatfield), b. April 14, 1827; d. Oct. 8, 1827.
    4. CYNTHIA A. (Chatfield), b. Dec. 11, 1828; d. Oct. 9, 1834.
    5. JAMES (Chatfield), b. Dec. 24, 1831; d. June 24, 1889.
    6. MARTHA (Chatfield), b. April 4, 1834.
    7. DAVID C. (Chatfield), b. Nov. 6, 1836; d. Aug. 26, 1838.

1117. AMOS BROCKWAY [1]; m., and settled in Illinois. Children:
    1. DAVID (Brockway), b. May 8, 1843; m. Jane Moore, 1861;
        d. 1878.
    2. SARAH (Brockway), b. 1845; m. Harmon Willis, March
        10, 1864; d. 1873.
    3. MARY (Brockway), b. June 9, 1847; m. John P. Yates,
        1865; d. 1886.
    4. EDWARD (Brockway), b. Aug. 9, 1849; m. Sarah Calais,
        1872.
    5. GEORGE W. (Brockway), b. Aug. 9, 1853; m. Ada Ward,
        June 1, 1884.
    6. CAROLINE (Brockway), b. Dec. 5, 1855; m. Errol McMil-
        ler. 1880; d Feb. 4, 1890.
    7. AMOS R. (Brockway), b. Aug. 3, 1859; m. Emma Young,
        July 28, 1880. Children:
        1. CLARENCE AUGUSTUS (Brockway), b. May 9, 1881.
        2. WILLIAM GRIFFIN (Brockway), b. June 18, 1883;
            d. Aug. 7, 1883.
        3. MYRTLE IRENE (Brockway), b. July 10, 1884.
        4. AMOS REED (Brockway), b. May 4, 1888.
        5. CHARLES ARTHUR (Brockway), b. Feb. 24, 1891.

1118. JAMES CHATFIELD [5]; m. Sarah C. Briddell, Aug. 24, 1856;
        she d. without issue; m. 2d, Sarah C. Shockley, Jan. 10, 1861.
        Children:
    1. WILLIAM E. (Chatfield), b. Nov. 16, 1861.
    2. EDWIN K. (Chatfield), b. Feb. 21, 1863; m. Hattie Hoag,
        Dec. 23, 1891.
    3. GEORGE S. (Chatfield), b, Feb. 3, 1865.
    4. J. WEBSTER (Chatfield), b. Feb. 24, 1867.
    5. MAUD M. (Chatfield), b. Dec. 6, 1868.
    6. BEULAH (Chatfield), b. Nov. 21, 1871; m. Mark S.
        Nichols.

1119. WILLIAM E. CHATFIELD [1]; m. Mary Bunker, Feb. 18, 1890.
Child:
    1. JAMES (Bunker), b. Sept. 24, 1891.

1120. MARTHA CHATFIELD [6]; m. Edwin R. Kendall, Feb. 22, 1858.
Children:
    1. JENNIE (Kendall), b. Jan. 29, 1859; d. July, 1861.
    2. WM. CHATFIELD (Kendall), b. Oct. 14, 1860.
    3. PRUDIE (Kendall), b. March 23, 1863; d. March, 1869.
    4. JOHN (Kendall), b. March 23, 1865; d. Nov., 1866.
    5. CHARLIE (Kendall), b. Nov. 21, 1866; d. Feb., 1869.
    6. EDWIN ARTHUR (Kendall), b. Aug. 17, 1870.
    7. NELLIE GRANT (Kendall), b. July 3, 1872.
    8. JAMES B. (Kendall), b. April 2, 1874.

1121. HANNAH CRANE[6] [573], (Zabina,[5] Gamaliel,[4] Azariah,[3]
Azariah,[2] Jasper[1]), married Daniel Dean, Dec. 31, 1823. She
died July 13, 1884. Children:
    1. LOUISA (Dean), b. 1824; d. 1830.
    2. JULIA (Dean), b. 1827; d. 1840.
    3. PHILENA (Dean), b. 1829; d. 1845.
    4. DAVID C. (Dean), b. May 21, 1831.
    5. B. H. MILES (Dean), b. April 24, 1834; d. Nov. 30, 1863.
    6. SETH B. (Dean), b. Nov. 2, 1836.
    7. LYDIA (Dean), b. Jan. 2, 1839.
    8. MARY A. (Dean). b. April 2, 1841; m. Chas. D. Curtis, Jan. 3,
       1860; d. Jan. 25, 1893.
    9. JOHN S. (Dean), b. May 14, 1846; d. May 14, 1891.

1122. DAVID C. DEAN [4]; m. April 14, 1858, Lovisa Sweezey. Child:
    1. EDWIN S. (Dean), b. Sept. 29, 1867.

    EDWIN S. DEAN [1]; m. Florence Meaker, April 18, 1889.
    Children:
        1. PAULINE (Dean), b. May 28, 1890.
        2. HAZEL (Dean).

1123. B. H. MILES DEAN [5]; m. Ann Eliza, dau. of James and Anna
(Crane) Brown, March 11, 1853; d. Nov. 30, 1863. She m.
2d, Truman S. Chappell, and had two children. Children:
    1. JULIA ANN (Dean), b. March 4, 1855; m. Wm. H.
       Grandon, Nov. 4, 1880.
    2. HANNAH ANNA (Dean), b. May 14, 1860.
    3. J. C. FREMONT (Dean), b. Oct. 8, 1862.
    4. JAMES W. (Chappell), b. Aug. 12, 1868.
    5. LESTER RAY (Chappell), b. Jan. 28, 1877.

1124. SETH B. DEAN [6]; m. Sept. 21, 1858, Hannah Van Ostrand.
Child:
    1. CHARLES L. (Dean), b. Dec. 13, 1862.

1125. HANNAH ANNA DEAN [2]; m. Henry E. Perry, April 8, 1883.
Child:
    1. MILES W. (Perry), b. June 9, 1884.

1126. J. C. FREMONT DEAN [3]; m. Addie L. Perry, Dec. 24, 1884
Children:
    1. CHARLES W. (Dean), b. May 4, 1887.
    2. MILES H. (Dean), b. Nov. 30, 1888.
    3. SETH W. (Dean),   } twins; b. May 13, 1892.
    4. SIDNEY F. (Dean), }

33

1127.   CHARLES L. DEAN [1]; m. Hattie Maynard, Oct. 26, 1886.
Children:
1.   PAULINE (Dean), b. Nov. 7, 1887.
2.   PAUL (Dean), b. Dec. 27, 1888; d. March 12, 1889.
3.   SETH MAYNARD (Dean), b. July 13, 1890.
4.   DONALDSON J. (Dean), b. Aug. 30, 1891.

1128.   LYDIA DEAN [7]; m. Nov. 2, 1858, Frederick L. Van Ostrand;
settled near Marion, N. Y.   Children:
1.   BYRON D. (Van Ostrand), b. Sept. 15, 1862; m. Eva
Brown, Dec. 12, 1888.
2.   MARY H. (Van Ostrand), b. July 17, 1873; m. Charles
Peer, Dec. 11, 1895.   Child:
1.   LUCILE (Peer), b. Aug. 24, 1897.

1129.   JOHN S. DEAN [9]; m. Dec. 27, 1870, Elizabeth Tremain; was
educated at Marion Collegiate Institute, and Poughkeepsie
Business College; was a merchant and a farmer in Marion,
N. Y.; d. May 14, 1891.   Children:
1.   JENNIE M. (Dean), b. Aug. 19, 1873; m. Clarence
Sweezey, Jan. 18, 1893.
2   NELLIE F. (Dean), b. Dec. 28, 1874; m. Albert Feller,
Oct. 28, 1896.
3.   MILES B. (Dean), b. Jan 24, 1882.
4.   ALBERT L. (Dean), b. April 22, 1884.

1130.   DAVID CRANE[6] [574], (Zebina,[5] Gamaliel,[4] Azariah,[3]
Azariah,[2] Jasper[1]), married Catharine Stolp, Feb. 23, 1832, and
settled in Aurora, Du Page Co., Ill. He died June 2, 1849. She
married 2d, Edgar Gallaway and removed to New York State.
Children:

1131—1.   FREDERICK S., b. June 6, 1833.
1132—2.   FRANCIS, b. Sept. 11, 1836.
1133—3.   EDGAR G., b. Nov. 11, 1837.
1134—4.   JANETTE W., b. Oct. 10, 1840; d. 1860.
1135—5.   ANN AUGUSTA, b. Aug. 13, 1844; d. Nov 20, 1844.
1136—6.   LAURA EMMA, b. June 22, 1847.
1137—7.   DAVID HENRY, b. Sept. 19, 1849.

1138.   OBEDIAH CRANE[6] [575], (Zebina,[5] Gamaliel,[4] Azariah,[3]
Azariah,[2] Jasper[1]), married, May 23, 1830, —— Chichester, and
settled in Michigan. She died about 1844, and he married 2d,
Mary Loey. After living many years on a farm he sold it, and
located near Pontiac, where he died Dec. 21, 1875.   Children:

1139—1.   ANDREW J., b. July 13, 1831.
1140—2.   DIANA M., b. June 11, 1833.
1141—3.   WM. ALONZO, b. May 8, 1835.
1142—4.   MARTHA D., b. May 6, 1838.
1143—5.   DAVID, b. Oct. 22, 1840; d. 1840.
1144—6.   EDWARD, b. 1841; d. 1841.
1145—7.   LYMAN G., b. Sept., 1842.
1146—8.   DAVID, b. Oct. 25, 1845.
1147—9.   OBED, b. Sept. 9, 1847; m. Georgana Willitts.
1148-10.   NORMAN, b. June 9, 1850.
1149-11.   EMMA P., b. March 2, 1854.
1150-12.   ELMER B., b. April 10, 1861.

1151. SARAH ANN CRANE[6] [576], (Zebina,[5] Gamaliel,[4] Azariah,[3] Azariah,[2] Jasper[1]), married Beverly Ketchum, in the year 1830, and settled near Aurora, Ill. She died in March, 1878. Children :

1. ELIJAH B. (Ketchum), b. Nov. 30, 1831; m. 1st, Elizabeth P. Millard; 2d, Jane Whelpley; 3rd, Carrie Wilson.
2. OLIVER C. (Ketchum), b. April 11, 1835; d. June, 1858.
3. DELIA (Ketchum), b. June 5, 1837.
4. MARIA B. (Ketchum), b. July 29, 1840.
5. ELIAS D. (Ketchum), b. Feb. 14, 1844.
6. MARILLA (Ketchum), b. Jan. 31, 1846.
7. EUGENE L. (Ketchum), b. Sept. 23, 1848; m. Mary Nickelson.

1152. MARIA B. KETCHUM [4]; m. Joel W. Clark, Jan. 9, 1858. Children :
1. ORION L. (Clark), b. July 19, 1860; d. Sept. 26, 1861.
2. WALTER C. (Clark), b. Jan. 27, 1867; d. March 27, 1872.
3. LULU MAY (Clark), b. July 24, 1878

1153. ELIAS D. KETCHUM [5]; m. Mary Sayrs, June 21, 1868. Children :
1. IDA LOUISA (Ketchum), b. June 13, 1869; m. Sylvester F. Conoly, July 4, 1885. Mr. Conoly died and she m. 2d, A. E. Phillips, Jan. 27, 1897. Child:
   1. SYLVESTER (Conoly), b. April 20, 1886.
2. STELLA MAY (Ketchum), b. Sept. 28, 1874.
3. JESSIE JOHN (Ketchum), b. Feb. 22, 1876.
4. WILLIAM D. (Ketchum), b. May 27, 1879; d. July 17, 1881.
5. OSCAR (Ketchum), b. and d. April 27, 1880.
6. DAISY BELLE (Ketchum), b. April 12, 1882; d. May 28, 1882.
7. GEORGE ELMO (Ketchum), b. Jan. 21, 1884.
8. HARRY ALBERT (Ketchum), b. Oct. 11, 1885.
9. BENJAMIN F. (Ketchum), b. June 4, 1887.
10. FENELLA FRANCIS (Ketchum), b. Feb., 1893; d. Oct., 1895.

1154. DELIA KETCHUM [3]; m. Samuel Ryder, March 5, 1856. Children :
1. JESSIE JOHN (Ryder), b. Dec. 13, 1858; d. Feb. 18, 1875.
2. WALTER EUGENE (Ryder), b. Dec. 9, 1860; m. Lena Stippet.
3. EDWIN ALBERT (Ryder), b. May 5, 1863; d. March 26, 1882.
4. NETTIE ADELLIA (Ryder), b. Oct. 5, 1865; d. April 11, 1866.
5. MARY ELIZABETH (Ryder), b. Feb. 13, 1867.
6. FREDA AMELIA (Ryder), b. April 11, 1870; d. July 19, 1870.
7. WILLIAM HENRY (Ryder), b. Dec. 5, 1871; d. Oct. 8, 1874.
8. ELLEN LOVINA (Ryder), b. Aug. 18, 1874; d. July 25, 1890.

1155. RACHEL CRANE[6] [578], (Zebina,[5] Gamaliel,[4] Azariah,[3] Azariah,[2] Jasper[1]), married James Kent, in 1830, and settled in Michigan. She died April 12, 1892. Children :

1. HARRIETT (Kent).
2. CATHERINE (Kent).
3. SIMEON (Kent); was a soldier in the Civil War, and lost an arm in the service.

1156. ANNA CRANE[6] [579], (Zebina,[5] Gamaliel,[4] Azariah,[3] Azariah,[2] Jasper[1]), married James Brown, Jan. 10, 1833, and

settled in the State of Illinois, near Naperville. She died about the year 1856. Children:

1. DEWITT C. (Brown), b. May 10, 1834.
2. ANN ELIZA (Brown), b. Feb. 28, 1836; m. B. H. Miles Dean.
3. FRANCIS E. (Brown), b. April, 1838.
4. CHARLES R. (Brown), b. June 14, 1840.
5. MARY ELLEN (Brown), b. May 18, 1842.
6. WILLIAM A. (Brown), b. March 31, 1843; m. Minerva Rash, June 26, 1877.
7. LOUISA AMELIA (Brown), b. June 13, 1844; d. Dec. 13, 1857.
8. SARAH M. (Brown), b. Oct. 25, 1846.
9. JAMES HENRY (Brown), b. Dec. 6, 1848; m. Maria Bruce, Nov. 22, 1871.
10. DAVID G. (Brown), b. Dec. 29, 1849; d. April 6, 1897.
11. MYRON C. (Brown), b. June 26, 1855.

1157. DEWITT C. BROWN [1]; m. Louisa Bean, Oct. 18, 1857; d. Nov. 18, 1890. Children:
    1. ANNA ESTELLA (Brown), b. Oct. 18, 1858; m. Ashley Mott, Feb. 4, 1881.
    2. MARY T. (Brown), b. May 27, 1860.
    3. FRED L. (Brown), b. Dec. 26, 1861.
    4. KATE C. (Brown), b. July 24, 1866.

1158. MARY T. BROWN [2]; m. Albert C. Ames, March 10, 1880. Children:
    1. KATIE (Ames), b. Oct. 9, 1882.
    2. ARTHUR (Ames), b. Oct. 12, 1885.

1159. FRED L. BROWN [3]; m. Mary Bushkamp, Jan. 26, 1886. Children:
    1. FRED L. (Brown), b. April 28, 1888.
    2. ELLA LOUISA (Brown), b. Nov. 21, 1890.
    3. KATIE (Brown), b. Sept. 26, 1896.

1160. KATE C. BROWN [4]; m. Paul Lamb, Jan. 26, 1887. Children:
    1. LEWIS L. (Lamb), b. Feb. 8, 1888.
    2. PAUL E. (Lamb), b. Oct. 17, 1889.

1161. FRANCES E. BROWN [3]; m. Francis M. Church, May 11, 1856. Children:
    1. CORA ESTELLA (Church), b. Aug. 18, 1857; d. Oct. 18, 1860.
    2. MARY ANNA (Church), b. June 1, 1859.
    3. FREDERICK ALONZO (Church), b. June 28, 1862.
    4. FRANCIS ELSWORTH (Church), b. April 1, 1864.
    5. CHARLES EDGAR (Church), b. March 1, 1866.
    6. FLORENCE ADINE (Church), b. March 2, 1869.
    7. SADIE JOSAPHINE (Church), b. July 6, 1871.
    8. EVA MAY (Church), b. Sept. 3, 1873.
    9. ARTHUR EVERITT (Church), b. Oct. 5, 1877; m. Maud Norton, Feb. 10. 1897.
    10. JENNIE BLANCH (Church), b. Dec. 9, 1880; m. Arthur Robertson, Jan. 31, 1898.

1162. MARY ANNA CHURCH [2]; m. Walter D. Mambert, Oct. 1, 1876. Children:
    1. Infant (Mambert), b. May 7, 1880; d. May 11, 1880.
    2. DÉSSIE (Mambert), b. Sept. 25, 1882.
    3. HARRY W. (Mambert), b. June 25, 1890.

1163. FRANCIS ELSWORTH CHURCH [4]; m. Lydia Card, May 5, 1890.
Children :
    1. LYMAN (Church), b. Sept. 12, 1892.
    2. ADA (Church), b. Oct. 2, 1895.

1164. CHARLES EDGAR CHURCH [5]; m. Hannah Card, Feb. 22, 1890.
Child :
    1. RAYMOND (Church), b. May 27, 1891.

1165. FLORENCE A. CHURCH [6]; m. Charles A. Dean, Dec. 22, 1886.
Children :
    1. LOUIE A. (Dean), b. Sept. 25, 1887.
    2. MABEL (Dean), h. Jan. 20, 1890.
    3. PAUL (Dean), b. April 21, 1892.
    4. FRANCES VINETTA (Dean), b. May 13, 1895.

1166. SADIE JOSAPHINE CHURCH [7]; m. William L. Nelson, April 22,
1888. Children :
    1. ETHEL B. (Nelson), b. May 25, 1889.
    2. WADE H. (Nelson), b. Dec. 6, 1891.
    3. REID (Nelson), b. Nov. 12, 1896.

1167. EVA MAY CHURCH [8]; m. Byron Norton, Sept. 9, 1890. Children :
    1. DORA (Newton), b. Dec. 13, 1891.
    2. EARL (Newton), b. Jan. 31, 1893.
    3. MADGE (Newton), b. Aug. 28, 1895.
    4. LOUIS (Newton), b. March 5, 1898.

1168. CHARLES R. BROWN [4]; m. Clarisa Scofield, March 4, 1861.
She d., and he m. Maggie Rash, Feb. 6, 1867. Children :
    1. ADA M. (Brown); d. May 3, 1865.
    2. EDGAR D. (Brown), b. Nov. 28, 1867.
    3. LUELLA S. (Brown), b. March 16, 1869.
    4. JAMES N. (Brown), b. Sept. 10, 1870; m. Olive Brooks,
       March 5, 1895.
    5. JESSIE E. (Brown), b. Nov. 15, 1872.
    6. NELSON J. (Brown).

1169. EDGAR D. BROWN [2]; m. Dora Benbon, Aug. 8, 1894.
Child :
    1. GEORGE (Brown), b. May 26, 1898.

1170. LUELLA S. BROWN [3]; m. C. H. Caswell, Sept., 1893.
Child :
    1. SCOT KENNETH (Brown), b. Sept. 12, 1896.

1171. JESSIE E. BROWN [5]; m. Elmer Crosser, Dec. 12, 1890.
Child :
    1. LEO ELMER (Brown), b. Oct. 7, 1891.

1172. MARY ELLEN BROWN [5]; m. Charles Murrey, Feb. 23, 1859.
She d. April 19, 1865. Children :
    1. JAMES (Murrey), b. Dec. 10, 1859.
    2. WILLIAM C. (Murrey), b. Dec. 25, 1861; m. Vindetta
       R. Whipple, Nov. 7, 1882. Child :
         1. ORION SCOTT (Murrey), b. Aug. 19, 1886.

1173. SARAH M. BROWN [8]; m. Jesse C. Wheaton, Dec. 30, 1866.
Children :
    1. EDITH MAY (Wheaton), b. Jan. 18, 1868; m. Enos W.
       Shaw, Dec. 16, 1896.
    2. HENRY WARD (Wheaton), b. Jan. 22, 1870.
    3. SADIE BROWN (Wheaton), b. July 31, 1886; d. May 18,
       1890.

1174. MYRON CAREY BROWN [11]; m. Viola Musgrove, Nov. 15, 1876. She d., and he m. Jennie S. Gregory, July 3, 1882. He d. April 6, 1897. Children:

1. WALTER ANDREWS (Brown), b. Sept. 9, 1877.
2. MINNIE E. (Brown), b. April 21, 1879.
3. FANNY (Brown), b. May 2, 1883; d. Aug. 23, 1883.
4. BERTIE B. (Brown), b. Sept. 12, 1887.

1175. AARON GRUMMON CRANE[6] [582], (Obediah,[5] Gamaliel,[4] Azariah,[3] Azariah,[2] Jasper[1]), married Nov. 2, 1836, in New York city, Ann Aletta Nuttman. She was born in Newark, N. J., Dec. 22, 1817, and died in New York city Dec. 9, 1879. Had one child that died in infancy. Children:

1176—1. M. A. ADELAIDE, b. Aug. 22, 1837.
1177—2. THOMAS SEXTON, b. Aug. 31, 1839, in Newark, N. J.
1178—3. CHARLOTTE BALDWIN, b. Dec. 6, 1841; d. Dec. 18, 1841.
1179—4. HENRIETTA N., b. Dec. 16, 1842; d. unmarried.
1180—5. VIRGINIA E., b. Oct. 6, 1845.
1181—6. CHARLOTTE W., b. April 24, 1848; m. Judah Lord Taintor, Feb. 17, 1885, in New York, and d. March 29, 1886.

1182. ELIZA GRUMMON CRANE[6] [583], (Obediah,[5] Gamaliel,[4] Azariah,[3] Azariah,[2] Jasper[1]), married Dec. 25, 1835, John B. Akerman. She died in Brooklyn, N. Y., Oct. 25, 1879. Children:

1. EDGAR (Akerman).
2. AARON (Akerman).
3. GEORIANNA (Akerman).
4. HELEN (Akerman).
5. DWIGHT (Akerman).

1183. CHARLOTTE O. CRANE[6] [585], (Obediah,[5] Gamaliel,[4] Azariah,[3] Azariah,[2] Jasper[1]), married in New York city, Dec. 4, 1839, Chauncey L. Norton. She died in that city Nov. 8, 1840. Child:

1. MARGARET (Norton).

1184. TIMOTHY DWIGHT CRANE[6] [587], (Obediah,[5] Gamaliel,[4] Azariah,[3] Azariah,[2] Jasper[1]), married in New York, Jan. 19, 1848, Adeline B. Clinch. He died in Williamsburg, N. Y., Jan. 25, 1860. Children:

1185—1. SARAH.
1186—2. CHARLES.
1187—3. WILLIAM.
1188—4. TIMOTHY.
1189—5. A young babe; died, and was buried with her father.

1190. NEHEMIAH CRANE[6] [592], (John R.,[5] Ezekiel,[4] Azariah,[3] Azariah,[2] Jasper[1]), married Phebe Jones, who was born on Staten Island, Oct. 19, 1780. Settled in Caldwell, N. J. He died Sept. 5, 1821. She died Oct. 27, 1834. Child:

1191—1. NOAH, b. Sept. 21, 1808.

1192. SAMUEL CRANE[6] [604], (Amos,[5] Moses,[4] Azariah,[3] Azariah,[2] Jasper[1]). This Samuel appears to have been the son

of the above Amos, son of Moses, of Parsippany, N. J.; married Mary Crane, daughter of Jacob Crane,[4] from Stephen,[1] of Elizabethtown. She was born Dec. 27, 1771, and died Oct. 25, 1850. Children:

1193—1. EZRA.
1194—2. PHEBE.
1195—3. COOPER WOODRUFF.
1196—4. CALEB.
1197—5. EDWARD.
1198—6. SALLY.

1199. MOSES MASCO CRANE[6] [607], (Stephen,[5] Moses,[4] Azariah,[3] Azariah,[2] Jasper[1]), married Betsey Bignall. He died March 27, 1867, in Michigan (North Lake). He served in the War of 1812. Children:

1200—1. JAMES; soldier in late war; killed in 1863. His home was in Shiawassee Co., Mich.
1201—2. ISRAEL; lived in Clinton Co., Mich.
1202—3. SABRA; m.; d. at Saugatuck, Mich., 1892.

1203. STEPHEN BRANT CRANE[6] [608], (Stephen,[5] Moses,[4] Azariah,[3] Azariah,[2] Jasper[1]), married Eunice McCarthy. Settled at Kalamazoo, Mich., where he died in 1870. He served in the War of 1812. Children:

1204—1. THOMAS; soldier in late war, and killed before Richmond, Va., 1863.

1205—2. STEPHEN.
1206—3. HORACE.
1207—4. DELEVAN.
1208—5. IRA.
1209—6. MARTIN.
1210—7. PHEBE.

1211. POLLY CRANE[6] [609], (Stephen,[5] Moses,[4] Azariah,[3] Azariah,[2] Jasper[1]), married Demming Boardman. Lived in Tyre, N. Y. She died Dec. 17, 1881. Children:

1. WILLIAM (Boardman).
2. AMANDA (Boardman).
3. JANE (Boardman).
4. AMERILLA (Boardman).
5. BURNETT (Boardman).
6. MALCOM (Boardman).
7. CAROLINE (Boardman).
8. CHARLES (Boardman).

1212. ELIZABETH CRANE[6] [611], (Stephen,[5] Moses,[4] Azariah,[3] Azariah,[2] Jasper[1]), married Solomon L. Bignall, Sept. 17, 1823. She died Jan. 29, 1846. He was born in Vergennes, Vt., Jan. 23, 1802 Was a blacksmith and farmer; also justice of the peace. He died April 18, 1877, in Fowlerville, Mich. Children:

1. ANNETTA (Bignall), b. April 20, 1826; m. W. H. Keeler at Seneca Falls N. Y.
2. LEMUEL C. (Bignall), b. Sept. 11, 1829; residence at Holland, Ottawa Co., Mich.

3. MOSES C. (Bignall), b. March 5, 1832; d. Feb. 5, 1892, at St. Louis, Mo.
4. SOLOMON L. (Bignall), b. May 1, 1834.
5. SUSAN E. (Bignall), b. Sept. 1, 1836; m. Mr. Smith at Kansas City, Mo.
6. BURNETT BOARDMAN (Bignall), b. Jan. 16, 1840; residence at St. Charles, Ill.
7. POLLY J. (Bignall), b. Aug. 29, 1843; d. Jan. 11, 1846.

1213. SOLOMON L. BIGNALL [4]; m. at Unadilla, Mich., Jan. 14, 1855, Phebe A. Glenn. She was b. in Washtenaw Co., in that State, Jan. 12, 1837. Mr. Bignall was b. at Lyne, Seneca Co., N. Y. He spent three years and a half recruiting soldiers for the civil war. Was a member of the Michigan legislature in 1864, and again in 1890, where he appeared quite prominent in the introduction of reforms in railway legislation. He is quite an extensive farmer and stock raiser, being the proprietor of "Oak Lawn Farm," located one-quarter of a mile south of the D., L. & N. R. R. depot, in Fowlerville, Mich., where he has his residence. He is also connected with the hardware business in Chicago, Ill., and a manufacturer, being president of the S. L. Bignall Hardware Company. This company manufactures pumps, sinks, soil pipe and fittings, plumbers' and water works specialties, their factory being at St. Charles, Ill. Mrs. Bignall died of paralysis Dec. 13, 1896. Their children, born at Unadilla, Livingston Co., Michigan:

1. EDITH S. (Bignall), b. Dec. 5, 1855; d. Oct. 12, 1860.
2. KATIE E. (Bignall), b. Nov. 25, 1857; d. Jan. 29, 1863.

1214. RACHEL CRANE[6] [612], (Stephen,[5] Moses,[4] Azariah,[3] Azariah,[2] Jasper[1]), married Malcome Burch. She died in 1870. Children:

1. LAWRENCE D. (Burch).
2. STEPHEN B. (Burch).
3. LEONARD (Burch).
4. MARY ELLEN (Burch).
5. WIRT (Burch).
6. MARSDEN (Burch).

1215. JOHN CRANE[6] [613], (Stephen,[5] Moses,[4] Azariah,[3] Azariah,[2] Jasper[1]), married 1st, Jane Compson. Lived at Seneca Falls, N. Y. By a second marriage to Abigail Sears he had four children, but we have not their names. He died Oct., 1893. Children:

1216—1. JOHN HENRY; was a soldier in late war; d. of small-pox at Alexandria, Va., 1863.
1217—2. THERESSA JANE.

1218. CHARLES CRANE[6] [614], (Stephen,[5] Moses,[4] Azariah,[3] Azariah,[2] Jasper[1]), married in 1830 Caroline A. Compson, who died Feb. 2, 1896. He died in 1874. Their home was at Seneca Falls, N. Y. He was an elder in the Presbyterian Church. Children:

1219—1. PHINEAS.
1220—2. AUGUSTA.
1221—3. MARION.

1222—4. VIOLA.
1223—5. EDWARD.
1224—6. ORVILLE.
1225—7. JULIA.
1226—8. ALICE.
1227—9. ELLA.

1228. JONAS CRANE[6] [618], (Ezekiel,[5] Moses,[4] Azariah,[3] Azariah,[2] Jasper[1]), married Sept. 30, 1827, Nancy McBain, who was born Sept. 30, 1807. He was a farmer, and removed to Wayne, Mich., where he died Nov. 18, 1880. She died there May 23, 1841. Children:

1229—1. LUCY AMELIA, b. March 21, 1828; d. Dec. 3, 1847.
1230—2. RUTH ADELIA, b. May 21, 1829.
1231—3. ABIGAIL, } twins, b. Nov. 10, 1832.
1232—4. OBEDIAH, }
1233—5. ALFRED, b. Dec. 9, 1834.
1234—6. GEORGE B., b. March 26, 1837; served in 12th Michigan Infantry; d. in Little Rock, Ark., July 23, 1864.
1235—7. CHARLES M., b. June 18, 1839.
1236—8. GORDON, b. May 3, 1841; d. Nov. 18, 1880.

1237. JULIA CRANE[6] [621], (Benjamin,[5] Stephen,[4] Azariah,[3] Azariah,[2] Jasper[1]), married Hiram Dodd, Feb. 14, 1799. He was son of Moses Dodd, and an elder in the Presbyterian Church of Bloomfield, N. J., and died about 1823. She died in March, 1858, aged 78. Residence at Bloomfield. Children:

1. ABEL JACKSON (Dodd), b. Nov. 3, 1799; d. in California, Sept. 5, 1852.
2. CHRISTIANA (Dodd), b. Aug. 20, 1801; m. Benjamin Fowler.
3. MEHITABEL (Dodd), b. July 23, 1803; d. Jan. 25, 1815.
4. FANNY (Dodd), b. March 10, 1806; m. William Sexton.
5. MOSES (Dodd), b. Feb. 17, 1808.
6. JAIRUS (Dodd), b. Sept. 17, 1811.
7. LOIS CAROLINE (Dodd), b. Oct. 31, 1813; m. Joseph Sandford.
8. STEPHEN H. (Dodd), b. April 25, 1816.
9. BENJAMIN LEWIS (Dodd), b. Oct. 1, 1818.
10. MARGARET (Dodd), b. Nov. 8, 1820; d. Sept., 1831.

1238. Judge BENJAMIN CRANE[6] [622], (Benjamin,[5] Stephen,[4] Azariah,[3] Azariah,[2] Jasper[1]), born in Cranetown, and with his father removed to Morris Co., N. J., in 1805; married 1st, Ellonor Stiles; 2d, Barbara ——. He lived in a brick house, near Pine Brook, Morris Co., N. J. In the spring of 1864 he went on a journey to the western country, and was suffocated April 16 while stopping at a hotel in Fond du Lac, Wis. He was judge of the court of common pleas twenty years, and also a farmer. He held eight commissions under the seal of the governor of New Jersey,—three military, three as justice, commissioner of deeds, and judge. Children:

1239—1. JULIANN.
1240—2. TIMOTHY W.
1241—3. LUCINDA.
1242—4. HETTY M.
1243—5. HARRIET.

34

1244—6. ELIZABETH.
1245—7. ELLEN.
1246—8. BENJAMIN F., b. July 21, 1829.
1247—9. MARIETTA H.
1248-10. BARBARA F.

1249. BARSHEBA CRANE[6] [624], (Benjamin,[5] Stephen,[4] Azariah,[3] Azariah,[2] Jasper[1]), married Phillip Miller. Children:

1. HETTY CAROLINE (Miller).
2. HARRIET (Miller).

1250. JEREMIAH CRANE[6] [625], (Benjamin,[5] Stephen,[4] Azariah,[3] Azariah,[2] Jasper[1]), married ——. Children:

1251—1. BENJAMIN.
1252—2. AMZI.
1253—3. HIRAM; lived in Jersey City; a carpenter.
1254—4. GEORGE.
1255—5. CAROLINE.

1256. AMZI L. CRANE[6] [626], (Benjamin,[5] Stephen,[4] Azariah,[3] Azariah,[2] Jasper[1]), married ——. Lived in Seneca Co., N. Y., 1851. Children:

1257—1. HARRIET; m. John Wolfe.
1258—2. ROSWELL.
1259—3. LOUISE.
1260—4. JAMES.
1261—5. GEORGE.

1262. JOHN CRANE[6] [627], (Benjamin,[5] Stephen,[4] Azariah,[3] Azariah,[2] Jasper[1]), married ——. Children:

1263—1. ALBERT.
1264—2. PHILETTA; m. March 17, 1839, Benjamin L. Dodd.
1265—3. DELIA MAY.
1266—4. CHARLOTTE.
1267—5. HETTY.
1268—6. MARGARET.

1269. IRA CRANE[6] [640], (Azariah,[5] Stephen,[4] Azariah,[3] Azariah,[2] Jasper[1]), married ——. Most of the following children went to New York State:

1270—1. JOHN.
1271—2. DANIEL.
1272—3. AZARIAH.
1273—4. NANCY.
1274—5. KETURAH.
1275—6. PEGGY.
1276—7. THANKFUL.
1277—8. BENJAMIN.

1278. WILLIAM CRANE[6] [644], (Jeremiah,[5] Stephen,[4] Azariah,[3] Azariah,[2] Jasper[1]), married Sarah Jacobus, who was born in Caldwell, N. J., Aug. 17, 1803, and died Feb. 20, 1886, at Little Falls. He was born in Cranetown, now Mont Clair, and settled first at Caldwell, but in 1834 he was living at Newark,

and their four youngest children were born there. He died in
Newark, Oct. 2, 1880. Children:

1279—1. CHARLES, b. July 3, 1823; m. Louisa Munn.
1280—2. AMZI, b. Nov. 27, 1824.
1281—3. JOHN M., b. March 12, 1826; d. March 5, 1829.
1282—4. RICHARD THERON, b. Jan. 12, 1828; m. Mary Cavanaugh.
1283—5. FRANCES EMELINE, b. Feb. 20, 1834; d. Dec. 16, 1850.
1284—6. WILLIAM MUNSON, b. Feb. 23, 1836; m. Emily Vanness.
1285—7. SARAH ELIZABETH, b. Nov. 30, 1838; m. S. T. Budd.
1286—8. MARY ANN AUGUSTA, b. Nov. 8, 1840; m. Charles Campbell, Dec. 14, 1865; he is dead.

1287. IRA CRANE[6] [648], (Jeremiah,[5] Stephen,[4] Azariah,[3]
Azariah,[2] Jasper[1]), married 1st, Margaret Norwood, born July
22, 1813. She died Jan., 1862, and he married 2d, Mary Saunders. He died 1868. Children:

1288—1. JARVIS G., b. Feb. 8, 1831.
1289—2. ANGELINE, b. Jan. 9, 1833.
1290—3. ISRAEL, b. Jan. 16, 1839.

1291. JONAS CRANE[6] [661], (Rufus,[5] Jonas,[4] John,[3] Azariah,[2] Jasper[1]), married ———. Children:

1292—1. WILLIAM R.
1293—2. SAMUEL; was auditor for West Virginia.
1294—3. MARGARET.
1295—4. J. MADISON; d. 1859, out west.
1296—5. JONAS; d. at Richmond, Va., 1856.

1297. ELIZABETH (called BETSEY) CRANE[6] [662], (Rufus,[5]
Jonas,[4] John,[3] Azariah,[2] Jasper[1]), married Josiah Johnson, a
farmer, and lived near Newark, N. J. She died in August,
1840. Children:

1. CATHARINE (Johnson).
2. AARON C. (Johnson).
3. ELIZABETH (Johnson).
4. MATILDA (Johnson).

1298. ABIGAIL CRANE[6] [664], (Rufus,[5] Jonas,[4] John,[3] Azariah,[2] Jasper[1]), married Moses Morehouse. Children:

1. DAVID (Morehouse).
2. REBECCA (Morehouse).
3. WILLIAM (Morehouse).
4. ELIZABETH (Morehouse).
5. ANN (Morehouse).

1299. WILLIAM CRANE[6] [665], (Rufus,[5] Jonas,[4] John,[3] Azariah,[2] Jasper[1]), married 1st, Lydia Dorsett, of Perth Amboy, July
9, 1812. She was born July 19, 1786. He settled in Richmond,
Va., Oct., 1812. She died in Philadelphia, Sept. 26, 1830.
July 20, 1831, he married 2d, Jean Niven Daniel, born at Fal-
mouth, Va., May 10, 1803. He died in Baltimore, Md., suddenly, Sept. 28, 1866, in his 78th year. He removed to the
latter place, in 1834. Was a hide and leather dealer.
Children:

1300—1. WILLIAM CARY.

1301—2. MARY DORSETT.
1302—3. ADONIRAM JUDSON.
1303—4. ELIZABETH.
1304—5. ANDREW FULLER, b. Jan. 17, 1820, at Richmond, Va.
1305—6. HARRIETT N.
1306—7. GEORGE W.
1307—8. LYDIA.
1308—9. FRANCES GREENHOW; d. 1892.
1309-10. ANNE MONCURE; d. in Germany, in 1872.
1310-11. JOHN DANIEL; d. 1871.
1311-12. JAMES CONWAY.
1312-13. WM. WARD, b. March 23, 1844.
1313-14. JOSEPHINE STONE.

1314. REBECCA CRANE[6] [667], (Rufus,[5] Jonas,[4] John,[3] Azariah,[2] Jasper[1]), married John Spear. Child:

1. JOHN (Spear).

1315. RICHARD MONTGOMERY CRANE[6] [668], (Rufus,[5] Jonas,[4] John,[3] Azariah,[2] Jasper[1]), married 1st, Nov. 1, 1820, Elizabeth Gardner, daughter of Elijah and Sarah (Force) Gardner. She died Sept. 7, 1838. He married 2d, Maria H. Coles, by whom he had five children. She was sister of Abraham Coles, manufacturer and dealer in leather, shoes, and trunks. Store on Market street, Newark (1831).

1316—1. SARAH ANN, ⎫ twins, b. Aug., 1821. d. Aug. 8, 1821.
1317—2. ELIZABETH, ⎭
1318—3. DAVID JONES, b. July 19, 1822; d. Dec. 29, 1822.
1319—4. MARY ELIZABETH, b. Jan. 24, 1824.
1320—5. SAMUEL PIERSON, b. Dec. 23, 1825.
1321—6. CAROLINE AMELIA, b. May 9, 1827.
1322—7. GEORGE WASHINGTON, b. Feb. 22, 1829; d. March 13, 1830.
1323—8. CATHARINE MATILDA; d. in infancy.
1324—9. CATHARINE MATILDA, b. Jan. 10, 1834.
1325-10. FRANCES MARIA, b. Feb. 6, 1836.
1326-11. DEINSIS C., b. Aug. 6, 1841.
1327-12. ANN ROGERS, b. May 1, 1843.
1328-13. WILLIAM MONTGOMERY, b. Aug. 16, 1848; d. March 14, 1849.
1329-14. LAURA STOUT, b. Sept. 2, 1850.
1330-15. WILLIAM MONTGOMERY, b. June 15, 1854.

1331. JAMES CAMPBELL CRANE[6] [669], (Rufus,[5] Jonas,[4] John,[3] Azariah,[2] Jasper[1]), married Nov. 18, 1824, Isabella Steel, at Richmond, Va. She was born in Philadelphia, Pa., March 5, 1804, and died at Yanceyville, N. C., Aug. 26, 1863. He was born in Newark, N. J., but went to Richmond, Va., Nov., 1819, then sixteen years of age, and became a very enterprising business man. He was a leather dealer, also president of a fire insurance company, and member of the City Council there, in 1841 to 1844. He died in that city, March 31, 1856. Children:

1332—1. DAVID ROPER.
1333—2. JAMES T.
1334—3. THOMAS.
1335—4. ROBERT.
1336—5. HENRY RAYLAND, b. Jan. 19, 1845.

Through the kindness of Mr. John G. Crane, of Baltimore, Md., the writer was permitted to read a memoir of this good man, James C. Crane. It was written by J. L. Burrows, D.D., pastor of the First Baptist Church, of Richmond, Va., and published at Charleston, S. C., by the Southern Baptist Publication Society, in 1858. Dr. Burrows here pays Mr. Crane the highest compliments for his manly and Christian qualities, and presents him as an ideal for other men to follow. Surely no person could read that little book without entertaining the thought that the Crane family have at least furnished one life to be a worthy example for imitation.

It appears that his brother William located in Richmond, Va., in 1812, and started in the leather trade; that in 1819, James, at the age of sixteen, went there as a clerk in this store. After a few years he was admitted a partner, and soon another store was opened in Baltimore, Md., William attending to that, while James conducted the one at Richmond. In 1842 the partnership was dissolved, William taking the business at Baltimore, and James that at Richmond. As early as March, 1817, Mr. Crane was baptized into the Baptist Church, and ever until his death, walked in the true faith of his Lord and Master, giving freely of his time, talent and means for the furtherance of religion.

1337. SARAH CRANE[6] [674], (Timothy,[5] Samuel,[4] John,[3] Azariah,[2] Jasper[1]), married William Cook, and died Sept. 1, 1822. They lived in Worcester, Otsego Co., N. Y. Children:

1. HORACE (Cook).
2. JOHN (Cook).
3. JILES (Cook).
4. LOUISE (Cook).
5. ESTHER (Cook).
6. SARAH (Cook).

1338. MARY CRANE[6] [675], (Timothy,[5] Samuel,[4] John,[3] Azariah,[2] Jasper[1]), married Sherman Curtis, Jan. 12, 1809. Children:

1. ORVIL (Curtis), b. March 24, 1810.
2. PENMAH (Curtis), b. Aug. 11, 1811.
3. ELIZABETH (Curtis), b. March 12, 1814.
4. MARY (Curtis), b. Oct. 9, 1816.
5. SARAH (Curtis), b. Jan. 8, 1821.
6. ESTHER (Curtis), b. Dec. 2, 1823.
7. ALBERT SHERMAN (Curtis), b. Oct. 5, 1826.

ORVIL CURTIS [1], m. ———, at Litchfield, Mich. Children:
1. ELIZABETH (Curtis).
2. JANE (Curtis).
3. SHERMAN (Curtis).

1339. ALBERT S. CURTIS [7]; m. ———. Children:
1. NETTIE (Curtis).
2. HARRIET (Curtis); m. Dr. Z. L. Baldwin, Niles, Mich.
3. PIERSON CRANE (Curtis); physician at Round Lake, N. Y.
4. ORVIL (Curtis); physician at Buchanan, Mich.

1340. SARAH CURTIS [5]; m. Gad Smith; settled in Ballston, N. Y. Children:
1. SHELDEN D. (Smith).
2. ELIZABETH (Smith).
3. BELINDA (Smith).
4. ———; d. young.

1341. PIERSON CRANE[6] [676], (Timothy,[5] Samuel,[4] John,[3] Azariah,[2] Jasper[1]), married Roxanna Smith, in Charlton, N. Y., Dec. 10, 1818. She was born there, Dec. 17, 1799, and died Feb. 20, 1861. He was a farmer, and died there, March 11, 1874. Children:

1342—1. ZADOCK SMITH, b. Sept. 4, 1819.
1343—2. LAURA, b. March 3, 1821; d. July 16, 1877.
1344—3. TIMOTHY, b. March 7, 1823; d. Feb. 8, 1870.

1345. JONAS CRANE[6] [677], (Timothy,[5] Samuel,[4] John,[3] Azariah,[2] Jasper[1]), married Almira Basley. He died May 15, 1874. Children:

1346—1. ELIZA.
1347—2. ABBA.

1348. EDWIN CRANE[6] [679], (Timothy,[5] Samuel,[4] John,[3] Azariah,[2] Jasper[1]), married Sept. 22, 1831, Mary Parish, of Morean, Saratoga Co., N. Y., born Aug. 22, 1806, at Fort Edward, N. Y., where they settled. He was a gardener, also for twelve years justice of the peace. She died Nov. 4, 1871. He died Nov. 4, 1888. Children:

1349—1. ESTHER, b. Dec. 7, 1832.
1350—2. JULIA, b. Sept. 9, 1834.
1351—3. JOHN, b. Dec. 26, 1836; d. July 10, 1871.
1352—4. GEORGE, b. Dec. 8, 1838.
1353—5. ANDREW, b. March 8, 1841.
1354—6. ELIZA, b. Oct. 2, 1843; m. Charles L. Ketchum, May 11, 1876; resides at Fort Edward.
1355—7. HARRIETT, b. May 25, 1846.

1356. JOHN CRANE[6] [689], (Matthias,[5] John,[4] John,[3] Azariah,[2] Jasper[1]), married Mary Myers, March 3, 1822, in Green Co., Pa., where she was born and where they first settled. Mr. Crane was a farmer and gunsmith. About 1845, they removed to Illinois. He died in Quincy, Ill., Feb. 23, 1869. Children:

1357—1. FREDERICK M., b. Sept., 1822.
1358—2. JOSIAH FERRIS, b. Aug. 10, 1824.
1359—3. JAMES COGGSWELL, b. Dec. 3, 1826; d. May 24, 1844.
1360—4. WILLIAM TANNER, b. Oct. 13, 1828.
1361—5. Infant, b. and d. Aug. 21, 1829.
1362—6. ELIZABETH JANE, b. Dec. 8, 1831.
1363—7. ELLIS FREEMAN, b. Oct. 21, 1833.
1364—8. JOHN A., b. Sept. 10, 1844.

1365. ASA CRANE[6] [709], (Jonas,[5] Benjamin,[4] John,[3] Azariah,[2] Jasper[1]), married Elizabeth Wilson. Settled in Jackson Co., Ind. Children:

1366—1. JONAS; m. Elizabeth Taylor.
1367—2. HANNAH W., b. Aug. 12, 1821; m. Joseph W. Elliott.
1368—3. ELIZA ANN; m. Sylvester Wheadon.
1369—4. HARVEY; m. 1st, Eliza Forey; 2d, Mary Ann Young.

1370. JOSEPH CRANE[6] [711], (Jonas,[5] Benjamin,[4] John,[3] Azariah,[2] Jasper[1]), married Susanna Turnbull. Children:

1371—1. EDWIN M., b. Jan. 22, 1834; d. April 18, 1855.

1372—2. DAVID; d. young.
1373—3. VALINDER T., b. Aug. 9, 1837; living at Roseville, Ill.
1374—4. JOHN; d. young.
1375—5. ELIZABETH R., b. Feb. 11, 1840.
1376—6. HENRIETTA; d. young.
1377—7. JABEZ; d. young.
1378—8. CALISTA; d. in infancy.

1379. PHEBE CRANE[6] [712], (Jonas,[5] Benjamin,[4] John,[3] Azariah,[2] Jasper[1]), married 1st, Edwin Moore; 2d, Capt. Allen Shepard. She died in 1835. The Shepards reside in Brownstown, Ind. Children:

1. EDWIN (Moore), b. Sept. 11, 1826.
2. RHODA ANN (Shepard), b. Oct. 29, 1829; d. Aug. 1, 1897.
3. ABIGAIL LOUISA (Shepard), b. April 1, 1832.

1380. RHODA ANN KITCHELL CRANE[6] [716], Jonas,[5] Benjamin,[4] John,[3] Azariah,[2] Jasper[1]), married John C. Turnbull, a brother of her brother Joseph's wife. She died July 29, 1859. Children:

1. JAMES (Turnbull); d. young.
2. ABIGAIL (Turnbull); d. young.
3. MARY (Turnbull); d. young.
4. ADILINE (Turnbull); d. young.
5. JOHN CARLTON (Turnbull); resides No. 213 East First Ave., Monmouth, Ill.

1381. JABEZ TUNIS CRANE[6] [726], (Obediah M.,[5] Benjamin,[4] John,[3] Azariah,[2] Jasper[1]), born in Ohio. Married, 1847, Mary A. Franklin, a native of Indiana. She was born 1828. Their eldest child was born in Indiana; all the others in Iowa. He was a farmer; residence at Montrose, where some of the family still live. Children:

1382—1. JOHN W., b. 1849; farmer; graduate of Iowa State University; d. in Mills Co., Iowa, 1878.
1383—2. LEROY F., b. 1852; m. 1877 at Montrose, Iowa.
1384—3. GEORGE A., b. 1853; attorney-at-law; d. at Alpine, Col., 1880.
1385—4. JABEZ T., b. 1860 at Montrose, Iowa.
1386—5. ELLSWORTH, b. 1862 at Montrose, Iowa.
1387—6. ELMER E., b. 1866 at Montrose, Iowa.
1388—7. BENJAMIN OTTO, b. 1869 at Montrose, Iowa.
1389—8. ADDIE MAY, b. 1870 at Montrose, Iowa.

1390. JOHN S. CRANE[6] [729], (David,[5] Benjamin,[4] John,[3] Azariah,[2] Jasper[1]), married Margaret ——, of New York city. Child:

1391—1. ELECTA.

1392. OGDEN RIGGS CRANE[6] [732], (David,[5] Benjamin, John,[3] Azariah,[2] Jasper[1]), married Charlotte Amelia ——. Children:

1393—1. CATHERINE ELECTA.
1394—2. GEORGE.
1395—3. CHARLOTTE.

1396. ABRAM RIGGS CRANE[6] [734], (David,[5] Benjamin,[4] John,[3] Azariah,[2] Jasper[1]), married Nancy Mahew. Children:

1397—1. JOHN SMITH.
1398—2. WILLIAM SHULER.
1399—3. GEORGEANNA.

1400. MARIE CRANE[6] [736], (David,[5] Benjamin,[4] John,[3] Azariah,[2] Jasper[1]), married William Danson. Children:

1. JANE A. (Danson).
2. SMITH (Danson); enlisted in 121st Ohio Infantry; served under Grant at Vicksburg; d. there July 16, 1863.
3. MARY (Danson).
4. JOHN A. (Danson); enlisted in 12th New York Battery, Artillery; served through entire war.
5. ISAAC (Danson); enlisted in 32d New York; transferred to 12th; was sergeant; was taken prisoner at Gettysburg; sent to Andersonville; starved there; finally paroled; but d. at Florence, S. C., on his way to Washington, D. C.
6. WILLIAM ROSSELLE (Danson); as soon as he became of age enlisted, but peace was declared before he was assigned.
7. EMMA (Danson).

JANE A. DANSON [1]; m. William Van Eps; residence at Schenectady, N. Y. Children:
1. WILLIAM EDGAR (Van Eps).
2. GRACE I. (Van Eps).
3. ARTHUR D. (Van Eps).
4. ISAAC (Van Eps).
5. CHARLES R. (Van Eps).
6. D. MATTHIAS (Van Eps).

1401. DAVID CRANE[6] [737], (David,[5] Benjamin,[4] John,[3] Azariah,[2] Jasper[1]), married Margaret Adams in Amsterdam, N. Y., May 10, 1838. He died there April 27, 1857. She was living in Amsterdam in December, 1897. Children:

1402—1. ELECTA RIGGS, b. Feb. 17, 1839; m. 1st, Dr. Goldsmith; he d.; m. 2d, Henry Green.
1403—2. SARAH ADAMS, b. Dec. 25, 1840; m. June 27, 1859, Morris Williams. She d. March 10, 1861.
1404—3. NANCY, b. Dec. 25, 1842; m. March 1, 1863, Morris Williams.
1405—4. ALEXANDER A., b. June 17, 1845; m. Mary E. Sullivan, and d. Feb. 21, 1895.
1406—5. HELEN A., b. Sept. 9, 1849; m. John McNernie in 1872.
1407—6. DAVID, b. March 9, 1852.
1408—7. HENRY, b. Sept. 28, 1854.
1409—8. MARTHA, b. Aug. 25, 1857.

1410. OBEDIAH MEEKER CRANE[6] [741], (Caleb Camp,[5] Benjamin,[4] John,[3] Azariah;[2] Jasper[1]), married Julia Carpenter. She was born in November, 1810, in Rensselaer Co., N. Y., where they settled. He was born in Amsterdam, N. Y., and died June 6, 1857. Children:

1411—1. JULIA ANN, b. Aug. 8, 1833; m. —— Buck.
1412—2. CHARLES, b. 1843.

1413. CALEB CAMP CRANE[6] [742], (Caleb Camp,[5] Benjamin,[4] John,[3] Azariah,[2] Jasper[1]), born at Craneville, Montgomery Co.,

N. Y.; married Mary Ann Von Bumble, who was born in 1808. They removed to the city of New York. He died in Brooklyn, N. Y., 1865. She died in 1895. Children:

1414—1. ISAAC B., b. 1830.
1415—2. HENRY M., b. 1836.
1416—3. CALEB CAMP, b. 1840.

1417. EDWARD SAVAGE CRANE[6] [743], (Caleb C.,[5] Benjamin,[4] John,[3] Azariah,[2] Jasper[1]), married Catharine Lawsing. Children:

1417½-1. ADALINE, b. Oct. 31, 1833; m. James Starkweather. Children:
  1. LEONARD (Starkweather).
  2. RALPH (Starkweather).
  3. EARL (Starkweather).
1418—2. LOUISA, b. Jan. 17, 1837; residence at Freeport, Ill.
1419—3. CHARLOTTE, b. Jan. 11, 1840.
1420—4. GEORGE DAVIS, b. Feb. 6, 1842, at Fort Wayne, Ind.

1421. JAMES W. CRANE[6] [746], (Caleb C.,[5] Benjamin,[4] John,[3] Azariah,[2] Jasper[1]), married Almira Lawson. Children:

1422—1. AGNES; m. Ezra Lawson (or Lawsing); d.
1423—2. JAMES W.
1424—3. JONAS H.; d.
1425—4. HARRIET; m. James H. Van Dyke; d.
1426—5. EMMA; d.

1427. ARCHIBALD M. CRANE[6] [751], (Caleb C.,[5] Benjamin,[4] John,[3] Azariah,[2] Jasper[1]), married 1st, Maria B. Breed; she died about 1855; 2d, Jennie Burch, of Racine, Wis.; 3d, Lauzarah Varney at Champaign, Ill., Aug. 27, 1863. He was born in Amsterdam, N. Y., and died at Chatsworth, Ill., March 6, 1879. Children:

1428—1. CORDELIA MARIA, b. 1853; m. Clarence W. Edsall, June, 1871. He d. May 24, 1897.
1429—2. CORA ANNA, b. Sept. 7, 1861; m. John Davis, of Racine, May 12, 1884, and d. 1885.
1430—3. EDWARD SAMUEL, b. July 27, 1865; m.; lives at 141 Marvin Ave., Cleveland, Ohio.
1431—4. SARAH MARIA, b. Sept. 9, 1867; d. Oct., 1867.
1432—5. CHARLES MILVILLE, b. March 5, 1870; m. Ethel M. Sutherland, June 16, 1895.
1433—6. JONAS HALSTEAD, b. April 25, 1874.
1434—7. LAUZARAH VARNEY, b. March 30, 1876.
1435—8. ARCHIE LOUISE, b. Oct. 17, 1879; d. Oct, 30, 1880.

1436. ABNER CRANE[6] [756], (Benjamin,[5] Benjamin,[4] Joseph,[3] Jasper,[2] Jasper[1]), married Miss Fanny Cooper, in 1796, and settled in Bethel, Clermont Co., Ohio, in June, 1814. Before removing to Ohio, he lived just about midway between Newark and Elizabethtown, N. J. He died Sept. 22, 1835. She died Aug. 8, 1833. Children:

1437—1. NANCY, b. April, 1797; m.; had four sons and one daughter.
1438—2. SARAH, b. 1799; m.; had four sons and five daughters.
1439—3. SEARS, b. 1803; d. 1832, in Cincinnati, Ohio, of cholera.

35

1440—4. BENJAMIN, b. April 17, 1805; m.; had seven children.
1441—5. OLIVER, b. 1807; m.; had six children.
1442—6. JOHN, b. 1810; m.; had six children.
1443—7. PHEBE ANN, b. 1813; d. Sept. 11, 1835.

1444. TIMOTHY CRANE[6] [757], (Benjamin,[5] Benjamin,[4] Joseph,[3] Jasper,[2] Jasper[1]), married Elizabeth Conger, and removed to the State of New York, in 1822; in 1823 they lived in Amsterdam, Montgomery Co., which was near East Galway, Saratoga Co., where, it is reported, they have lived. She was aunt to Dr. Stephen Conger, of Newark, N. J., and born May 15, 1774. He was a member of the Baptist Church, and a weaver by trade. Had twenty children, many of whom died in infancy. He died Jan. 31, 1859. She died Jan. 21, 1859.

Children :

1445—1. PHEBE C., b. Oct. 19, 1795; d. July 11, 1829.
1446—2. SILAS, b. Jan. 9, 1797; d. July 29, 1823.
1447—3. LYDIA, b. May 3, 1798; d. Jan., 1815.
1448—4. MARTHA, b. Aug. 8, 1799; d. Jan., 1890.
1449—5. ISAAC W., b. Jan. 10, 1801; d. April, 1856.
1450—6. MATILDA, b. Feb. 11, 1802; d. March 21, 1883; m. ——, and had three daughters.
1451—7. STEPHEN R., b. July 1, 1803; d. March 7, 1884.
1452—8. DAVIE, b. Sept. 1, 1805; d. May 24, 1872.
1453—9. RACHEL, b. Feb. 11, 1807; d. Oct. 7, 1871.
1454—10. ELIZABETH A., b. Nov. 7, 1814; d. Feb. 12, 1832.
1455—11. BENJAMIN FRANKLIN, b. March 28, 1816; d. Jan., 1877.
1456—12. EMILY J., b. March 1, 1820; d. June 6, 1877.
1457—13. LEMUEL C. P., b. Aug. 23, 1822.

1458. DAVIS CRANE[6] [764], (Benjamin,[5] Benjamin,[4] Joseph,[3] Jasper,[2] Jasper[1]), married Sarah Dunham, Oct. 28, 1813. She was born May 7, 1791. They settled in Bethel, Clermont Co., Ohio, when that country was unsettled by white people to any considerable extent. He died July 2, 1872, aged 84 years, 3 months and 22 days. Children :

1459—1. LAFAYETTE, b. Jan. 11, 1815.
1460—2. GEORGE WHITEFIELD, b. June 26, 1820.
1461—3. BARTON STONE, b. May 15, 1823; d. Nov. 30, 1854; unm.
1462—4. PHEBE ANNE, b. March 14, 1829; d. March 20, 1837.

1463. STEPHEN CRANE[6] [768], (Elias,[5] Ezekiel,[4] Joseph,[3] Jasper,[2] Jasper[1]), married Mary Enyart, May 25, 1809. She was born April 15, 1790, and died July 14, 1832. He died Feb. 14, 1860. Children :

1464—1. CYRUS, b. May 2, 1810; d. Aug. 23, 1850.
1465—2. FRANCIS C., b. Jan. 24, 1812; d. Sept. 1, 1874.
1466—3. PHEBE, b. May 20, 1814; d. Aug. 14, 1822.
1467—4. CELIA, b. Aug. 10, 1816; d. Aug. 7, 1822.
1468—5. SQUIRE B., b. Jan. 10, 1818; d. Sept. 23, 1845.
1469—6. JULIA A., b. Nov. 2, 1819; d. March 16, 1855.
1470—7. DAVID, b. June 15, 1823; d. May 30, 1879.
1471—8. HARRIET, b. April 25, 1825.
1472—9. ELIZA, b. Nov. 8, 1827.
1473—10. GEORGE, b. Feb. 6, 1829.

1474. MOSES CRANE[6] [769], (Elias,[5] Ezekiel,[4] Joseph,[3] Jasper,[2] Jasper[1]), married ———. He died July 26, 1822.
Children :

1475—1. URIAH.
1476—2. THOMAS H.
1477—3. DAVID.
1478—4. PHEBE.

1479. WILLIAM CRANE[6] [778], (Elias,[5] Ezekiel,[4] Joseph,[3] Jasper,[2] Jasper[1]), married ———. He died July 2, 1834.
Children :

1480—1. CATHERINE.
1481—2. SYDNEY.
1482—3. AARON; m. ——— Coffin; went west from Ohio; had two or three children.
1483—4. MARTHA A.
1484—5. MARY F.

1485. ABIJAH CRANE[6] [784], (Isaac,[5] Isaac,[4] Joseph,[3] Jasper,[2] Jasper[1]), married Mary Jacobus. He was a printer, as was his father. They resided at Fairfield, where the twins were born. They soon after removed to Newark, N. J. Children :

1486—1. UZAL A., } twins; b. May 10, 1807.   { m. Lucetta B. Gould, dau. of Stephen S. Gould, of New York city; he d. there, Aug. 23, 1884; two sons and a daughter.
1487—2. SOPHIA, }
1488—3. SARAH.
1489—4. JOHN.
1490—5. HENRY ABIJAH ROBERTS, b. Dec. 11, 1813.
1491—6. JAMES; m. a lady of Bergen, and d. of consumption.

1492. ISRAEL C. CRANE[6] [788], (Israel,[5] Israel,[4] Joseph,[3] Jasper,[2] Jasper[1]), married Hannah ———. April, 1822, 1823, and 1824, he was elected overseer of highways for Camptown.
Child :

1493—1. MARY ANN, b. 1815; d. Sept. 2, 1816, aged 1 year and 7 mo.

1494. JOHN JOSIAH CRANE[6] [795], (Josiah,[5] Josiah,[4] Joseph,[3] Jasper,[2] Jasper[1]), married Nov. 7, 1790, Rebeckah Saffer, born at Newark, N. J., Sept. 22, 1769, daughter of Thomas and Mary Saffer. He was a merchant; residence, Newark. He died there in July, 1808. She joined the First Presbyterian Church in Newark, in 1802, and died in New York city, Oct. 26, 1847. Children :

1495—1. SIDNEY, b. Aug. 22, 1791.
1496—2. CHARLES, b. June 30, 1795; d. Aug., 1817, at Charleston, S. C.
1497—3. JULIA, b. Aug. 17, 1797; d. 1873, at New York city.

1498. BENJAMIN CRANE[6] [796], (Josiah,[5] Josiah,[4] Joseph,[3] Jasper,[2] Jasper[1]), married 1st, Elsey Schuyler, March 28, 1804, born March 28, 1787, died July 15, 1806; married 2d, Jane Low, of New York city, April 25, 1807. She was born Aug.

16, 1783, died Dec. 14, 1833. He was born at Lyons Farms,
N. J., and died in New York city, Aug. 26, 1832. Children :

1499—1. ANN MARIA, b. Jan. 18, 1805; d. July 13. 1805.
1500—2. BENJAMIN FRANKLIN, b. Jan. 16, 1808: m. Sept. 15, 1834,
        Amanda F. Chardavoyne; d. Feb. 12, 1839.
1501—3. THEODORE, b. Oct. 8, 1809.
1502—4. ELSEY SCHUYLER, b. Aug. 14, 1811.
1503—5. JOHN JOSIAH, b. June 19, 1813.
1504—6. MADISON, b. Aug. 15, 1815; d. Sept. 26, 1815.
1505—7. AUGUSTUS, b. Jan. 13, 1817; m. Elizabeth Bolles; residence,
        Morristown, N. J.
1506—8. WILLIAM LOW, } b. Jan. 25, 1819; { d. May 19, 1819.
1507—9. EDWARD,   }   { d. Jan. 25, 1819.

1508. PHEBE CRANE[6] [798], (David,[5] Joseph,[4] Joseph,[3]
Jasper,[2] Jasper[1]), married Morris Crane, a carriage maker, of
New York city, and died. Have not been able to fix positively
the line to which Morris Crane belongs. He was born at Elizabethtown, N. J., 1775, and perhaps belongs to the line of
Stephen senior, of that place. After the death of Phebe Crane
he married Abigail Sickles, daughter of Garrett Sickles, who was
a captain under Washington in the Revolutionary war. She was
born in New York city Sept. 1, 1780, and died in Irvington, N.
J., Sept. 6, 1851. Morris Crane died at Springfield, Ill., Aug.
26, 1854, and was buried in Oak Ridge Cemetery. Children :

1. PHEBE; m. James Eaton.
2. CATHERINE; m. Samuel Barry.
3. LUCETTA, b. Oct. 30, 1806; m. Aaron Burr Rumsey.
4. HARRIET; m. Judge Richard Barry.
5. JAMES; d. young.
6. MATTHIAS; m. Elizabeth Morgan.
7. GERARD SICKLES, b. Oct. 25, 1814; m. Elizabeth Frost.
8. RACHEL; m. Charles Smith.

1509. PHEBE CRANE [1]; m. James Eaton, of Irvington, N. J. Chil-
    dren :
    1. JAMES MORRIS CRANE (Eaton), b. Sept. 13, 1828.
    2. THOMAS O. (Eaton).
    3. GEORGE WHEELER (Eaton).
    4. MATTHIAS C. (Eaton).

1510. LUCETTA CRANE [3]; m. Aug. 20, 1833, Aaron Burr Rumsey.
    She d. March 20, 1884, at New Berlin, Ill. He was b. at
    Westport, Conn., May 29, 1803, and d. Feb. 8, 1875, at Good-
    land. Ind. Her daughter Harriet, now Mrs. Francis Taylor,
    in writing about her mother, recites an incident that occurred
    during the civil war that speaks so much for the character of
    the woman that it certainly deserves a place here: " A draft
    of soldiers had been called for in our county. I happened
    to be the one to admit the officer to the house. He told me
    his business, and I called my mother from another room to
    meet him. He told her in an offhand and somewhat offensive
    way that he was taking names of all male members of each
    family in that part of the county preparatory to drafting;
    took out his pen, and opened his great book. I looked at
    my mother, who was an exceedingly handsome woman, with
    faultless physique, wondering what her reply might be. She
    stood a moment; then, with impressive dignity, said: ' Sir,

I have three sons only,—one of them is in a southern prison, another was in the battle of Fort Fisher, and we await the tidings of his death. The last one lies at the point of death in this house from a wound received in a late battle. I have three daughters; if they can be of any service to their country, *take them.*' The great book closed with a slam, and the officer bowed in deepest respect and said, ' Madam, you have done your duty.' " Children:

1. WEBSTER (Rumsey), b. June 13, 1834; d. April 29, 1836.
2. SARAH (Rumsey), b. Feb. 5, 1837; d. April 30, 1867.
3. HARRIET (Rumsey), b. Dec. 5, 1838.
4. GERARD (Rumsey), b. Jan. 6, 1840.
5. CHARLES (Rumsey), b. April 2, 1841.
6. FREDERIC (Rumsey), b. Oct. 4, 1842; d. Nov. 18, 1843.
7. ARTHUR WELLESLEY (Rumsey), b. May 3, 1843.
8. RACHEL SICKLES (Rumsey), b. July 26, 1845.

1511. HARRIET RUMSEY [3]; m. Nov. 21, 1866, Francis Taylor, who was b. in Westport, Conn., Nov. 27, 1821. He d. Dec. 17, 1888, in Manteno, Ill. Her residence (1899) at Springfield, Ill. Children:

1. CHARLES RUMSEY (Taylor), b. Oct. 15, 1867; m. Eva Hensley.
2. WILLIAM FRANCIS (Taylor), b. Aug. 17, 1869; d. Sept. 8, 1893.
3. HARRIET SARAH (Taylor), b. June 27, 1872.
4. FREDERICK DAN (Taylor), b. Feb. 26, 1876.

1512. GERARD RUMSEY [4]; m. Nov. 6, 1867, Adelaide Brayton. She was b. May 13, 1845, in Queensbury, Warren Co., N. Y., and d. Sept. 1, 1885, in Evansville, Kan.; m. 2d, Sarah Josephine Tennyson. He was a soldier in the civil war. Children:

1. WILLIAM BRAYTON (Rumsey), b. Aug. 17, 1868; d. April 2, 1870.
2. HARRY CURTIS (Rumsey), b. Dec. 14, 1870.
3. FLORENCE ADELAIDE (Rumsey), b. Jan., 1876; d. May 16, 1877.
4. FRANKLIN GERARD (Rumsey), b. Jan. 9, 1879.
5. ALTHEA ADELAIDE (Rumsey), b. Jan. 22, 1884.
6. GERARD CLEVELAND (Rumsey), b. Sept. 2, 1888.
7. CHARLES HENRY (Rumsey), b. April 22, 1890; d. July 25, 1890.
8. SOLOMON (Rumsey), b. May 3, 1892; d. Sept. 16, 1893.

1513. CHARLES RUMSEY [5]; m. Jan. 9, 1865, Caroline Hardin. She was b. July 28, 1847, at Corona, N. Y. He was a soldier in the civil war. Children:

1. SARAH MAY (Rumsey), b. Sept. 30, 1866.
2. IDA (Rumsey), b. July 3, 1868; d. Feb. 24, 1869.
3. HELEN MARIA (Rumsey), b. Jan. 18, 1870.
4. EDNA EARLE (Rumsey), b. Jan., 1871.
5. ADA (Rumsey), b. April 12, 1873.
6. JENNIE (Rumsey), b. Oct. 2, 1874; d. April 21, 1896.
7. JESSE S. (Rumsey), b. July 12, 1876.
8. CHARLES (Rumsey), b. Nov. 21, 1877.
9. HERBERT S. (Rumsey), b. March 18, 1880.
10. ERNEST HARDIN (Rumsey), b. July 12, 1882; d. Jan. 15, 1894.
11. FRED EUGENE (Rumsey), b. Nov. 15, 1885; d. April 14, 1887.
12. H—— R—— (Rumsey), b. Jan. 7, 1887; d. July 21, 1889.

1514. ARTHUR WELLESLEY RUMSEY [7]; m. July 10, 1866, at Manteno, Ill., Cordelia Brayton, sister of his brother Gerard's wife. She was b. Oct. 31, 1846, at Queensbury, Warren Co., N. Y. He was a soldier in the civil war. Children:
1. ARTHUR WELLESLEY (Rumsey), b. Aug. 10, 1867.
2. BERTHA BERNICE (Rumsey), b. Nov. 16, 1870.
3. ALBERT BISHOP (Rumsey), b. April 21, 1875.

ARTHUR WELLESLEY RUMSEY [1]; m. Cassie Freer. Child:
1. CHARLES EDGAR (Rumsey), b. Jan., 1892.

RACHEL SICKLES RUMSEY [8]; m. Erastus Bingham Packson, Nov. 21, 1866. They had three sons, only one living:
1. EARNEST.

1515. GERARD SICKLES CRANE [7]; m. Elizabeth Frost, June 27, 1837, in New York city. She was b. in Peekskill, N. Y., July 24, 1813.. Mr. Crane was b. in Jersey City, N. J.; by trade a cabinet maker. He served four years in the United States Army and in the Mexican war with U. S. Grant. He d. in St. Louis, Mo., June 14, 1880. His widow was living Dec. 19, 1897. Their eldest child was b. in New York city; the others in St. Louis, Mo. Children:
1. MARY AUGUSTA; m. Wm. H. Osborne.
2. CATHARINE MARIA.
3. WALTER FROST.
4. LUTHER.
5. ANNA, b. March 2, 1850; d. Nov. 19, 1889.

1516. ELIZA CRANE[6] [799], (David,[5] Joseph,[4] Joseph,[3] Jasper,[2] Jasper[1]), married Aaron Nuttman. He died in the 42d year of his age. She died in the 94th year of her age. Children:

1. ISAAC W. (Nuttman), b. March 16, 1801; m. March 22, 1827; d. Dec. 12, 1872.
2. CAROLINE (Nuttman), b. July 9, 1802; m. Chas. Grant, March 18, 1824; d. Sept. 28, 1854.
3. MARY (Nuttman), b. April 8, 1804; m. May 4, 1825, Mr. Holden; d. Aug. 15, 1832.
4. CLARISSA (Nuttman), b. Feb. 14, 1806; m. Caleb Williams, March 25, 1829; d. Oct. 26, 1888.
5. EMILY (Nuttman), b. Feb. 10, 1808; m. Dr. Thos. Loweree; d. Feb. 3, 1874.
6. HETTY (Nuttman), b. Nov. 6, 1809.
7. AARON (Nuttman), b. April 1, 1812.
8. ELIZA (Nuttman), } twins, b. June 19, 1814.
9. TEMPERANCE (Nuttman), }

1517. HETTY NUTTMAN [6]; m. May 4, 1830; Chas. S. Macknet. Children:
1. THEODORE (Macknet), b. Dec. 13, 1831.
2. CAROLINE A. (Macknet), b. Aug. 17, 1837.

1518. THEODORE MACKNET [1]; m. Eliza A. Dawson. He was a hardware merchant, and lived in Newark, N. J. He had three children; the names of only two appear here:
1. ELIZA DAWSON (Macknet), b. June 3, 1861; m. Robert Clarence Dorsett, of New York city.
2. CARRIE AMANDA (Macknet), b. Nov. 16, 1866; d.

1519. CAROLINE A. MACKNET [2]; m. William H. Woolworth, Nov. 18, 1869. Child:
1. FELIX M. WOOLWORTH, who is m., and has three sons.

1520. KETURAH CRANE[6] [801], (Isaac,[5] Lewis,[4] Elihu,[3] Jasper,[2] Jasper[1]), married in 1791 Caleb Harrison, son of Hannah Crane and Simeon Harrison. He inherited a large estate from his grandfather Caleb Crane, of Orange, N. J., and a portion, if not all, of this estate is now in the possession of the descendants. She died in 1855. He was born in 1770, and died in 1854. Children:

1. SIMEON (Harrison), b. 1792; d. 1799.
2. MARY (Harrison), b. 1793; d. 1815.
3. HANNAH (Harrison), b. 1795.
4. MARGARET (Harrison), b. 1800.
5. PHŒBE (Harrison), b. 1802.
6. SIMEON (Harrison), b. 1804.

1521. HANNAH HARRISON [3]; m. Rev. William Rollinson Whittingham, bishop of Maryland. Children:
    1. EDWARD THOMAS (Whittingham); m. Martha Condit.
    2. MARY (Whittingham); m. Charles Wilmer.
    3. MARGARET (Whittingham).
    4. HARRISON (Whittingham); m. Mrs. Sarah Jones Rogers.

1522. MARGARET HARRISON [4]; m. Joel Wheeler Condit; d. 1896. Children:
    1. MARY HARRISON (Condit); m. Rev. H. S. Bishop.
    2. CHARLOTTE MATILDA (Condit); d. Oct. 4, 1847.
    3. CALEB HARRISON (Condit); m. Eleanor Forrester Barstow. She d. 1886. He d. 1881.
    4. MARGARET (Condit).
    5. SARAH KATHERINE (Condit); m. William Croswell Doane, bishop of Albany.
       ESTELLE (Condit); m. Thomas T. Kinney.
       ALICE CHAPMAN (Condit), b. 1838; d. 1840.
    6. ALICE CHAPMAN (Condit), b. Feb. 9, 1843; m. 1869, Andrew Kirkpatrick. She d. Oct. 28, 1877.

1523. SIMEON HARRISON [6]; m. Abby Maria Condit. Child:
    1. ABBY MARIA (Harrison); who m. Samuel Osborne Rollinson, a cousin of Bishop W. R. Whittingham. Children:
        1. SIMEON HARRISON (Rollinson).
        2. PHŒBE HARRISON (Rollinson).
        3. MARY S. (Rollinson).
        4. WILLIAM (Rollinson).

This family reside in Orange. N. J., at "Mountain Foot," on the estate bequeathed to their grandfather Caleb Harrison by his grandfather Caleb Crane.

1524. HANNAH PRICE CRANE[6] [828], (Isaac W.,[5] Elihu,[4] Elihu,[3] Jasper,[2] Jasper[1]), married Dr. Joseph Gray, in 1834. He died in 1859. She died in 1876. Children:

1. WILLIAM CRANE (Gray); bishop of southern Florida.
2. MARY SADLER (Gray).
3. ANNA ELIZABETH (Gray).
4. EMMA (Gray).
5. EDWIN ALBERTI (Gray).
6. SARAH FRANCES (Gray).
7. CHARLES MCILVAINE (Gray).
8. JOSEPH RIDLEY (Gray); a minister.

1525. WILLIAM CRANE GRAY [1]; m. 1st, in 1863, Margaret Locke
Trent. by whom he had three children; m. 2d, in 1876, Fannie
Campbell Bowers. He is bishop of southern Florida.
Children:

1. MARY FOGG (Gray); d. young.
2. WILLIAM TRENT (Gray); d.
3. JOSEPH ALBERTI (Gray); m. Mary Frances Morgan; resides in
Nashville, Tenn.
4. CAMPBELL (Gray).
5. FANNIE BOWERS (Gray); d. young.

1526. MARY SADLER GRAY [2]; m. Thomas Boardman, of Clarks-
ville, Tenn. She d. in 1860. Child:
1. THOMAS WILLIAM (Gray); d. young.

1527. ANNA ELIZABETH GRAY [3]; m. in 1858, Prof. William Magoffin; residence Newport, Ark. Children:
1. MARY ELIZABETH (Magoffin); d. young.
2. ANNA GRAY (Magoffin).
3. MINNIE EMMA (Magoffin); d. young.
4. MAGGIE TRENT (Magoffin); d. young.
5. FANNIE JOY (Magoffin).
6. WILLIAM GRAY (Magoffin).
7. JAMES (Magoffin); d. young.

1528. ANNA GRAY MAGOFFIN [2]; m. in 1883, Charles T. Bateman;
d. Dec., 1891. Children:
1. ANNA MAGOFFIN (Bateman).
2. MARY EMMA (Bateman).
3. FANNIE GRAY (Bateman).

1528½. FANNIE JOY MAGOFFIN [5]; m. Dec. 7, 1898, John Carolynn
Jones, of Winter Park, Florida. Mr. Jones is a lawyer.

1529. SARAH FRANCES GRAY [6]; m. in 1867, Charles Gore Joy; residence, Abilene, Texas. Children:
1. MARY FRANCES (Joy).
2. EMMA (Joy).
3. CHARLES CHRISTOPHER (Joy).
4. WILLIAM GRAY (Joy); d. young.
5. HANNAH MORE (Joy). ·
6. JOSEPH RIDLEY (Joy).
7. NELLIE (Joy); d. young.
8. J. NINA ALBERTI (Joy).
9. FRANK ROLLINS (Joy).
10. HEBER OTEY (Joy).
11. OPHELIA BILLS (Joy); d. young.
12. MARGUERITE (Joy).

1530. MARY FRANCES JOY [1]; m. in 1888, Theodore Debon Wagner;
residence, Abilene, Texas. Children:
1. EDWIN AUGUSTUS (Wagner); d. young.
2. THEODORE JOY (Wagner).
3. ELIZA CATHERINE (Wagner).
4. CHARLES GORE (Wagner).

1531. EMMA JOY [2]; m. in 1889, Hon. John Howell Cobb; residence, Jenneau, Alaska. He is a lawyer. Child:
1. EDWARD LANG (Cobb).

1532. CHARLES McILVAINE GRAY [7]; m. in 1876, Clara Bills Polk.
He is an Episcopal clergyman, and lives in Ocala, Fla.
Children:
1. HORACE (Gray); d. young.

2. Charles Quintard (Gray).
3. Arthur Rhodefer (Gray).
4. Clara (Gray).
5. Charles McIlvaine (Gray).
6. Ophelia Wilson (Gray).

1533. Joseph Ridley Gray [8]; m. in 1882, Florence Rollius, of Columbia, Mo.; a clergyman of the Episcopal Church, and died in 1886; widow and daughters reside in Columbia, Mo. Children:
1. Mary Rollins (Gray).
2. Florence Price (Gray).

1534. Rev. William Croes Crane, D.D.[6] [829], (Isaac W.,[5] Elihu,[4] Elihu,[3] Jasper,[2] Jasper[1]), married 1st, Caroline Brooks, in 1836; married 2d, Mrs. Charlotte B. Griffith, sister of his first wife. He for many years was rector of the Church in Jackson, Miss., where he died, in 1877; a very eminent divine of the Episcopal Church. Children:

1535—1. Mary Caroline.
1536—2. William Howard.
1537—3. Charles Stone; d. young.
1538—4. Edwin Alberti; d. young.
1539—5. Heber Otey; was an Episcopal clergyman; m. Betty Wharton, of Jackson, Miss; d. in Sherman, Tex., Sept. 3, 1876.
1540—6. Ernestine Alberti; d. without issue.

1541. Sarah Crane[6] [830], (Isaac W.,[5] Elihu,[4] Elihu,[3] Jasper,[2] Jasper[1]), married Arunah Leffingwell, of Woodville, Miss. She was born Sept. 7, 1809, in Middletown, Conn.; settled for a time in New Orleans. Children:

1. Anna (Leffingwell), b. Aug. 8, 1847; d. without issue.
2. Florence (Leffingwell), b. Feb. 27, 1850; d. Oct. 6, 1853.
3. Philura (Leffingwell), b. Aug. 21, 1852; d.
4. Nina (Leffingwell); d. without issue.
5. Arunah (Leffingwell); d.

1542. James Crane[6] [834], (David D.,[5] David,[4] David,[3] Jasper,[2] Jasper[1]), married Phebe Riggs, Dec. 23 or 31, 1808; was cashier of the State Bank, in Elizabeth, N. J. He died April 8, 1851. Children:

1543—1. Martha Banks, b. March 27, 1810; m. Elijah Kellogg, Jan. 30, 1833.
1544—2. John Riggs, b. Sept. 17, 1811; lawyer; member of the Legislature, in 1866; m. Nancy Harrison, Va., Nov. 4, 1847.
1545—3. Mary D., b. Aug. 11, 1813; m. M. M. Woodruff, Oct. 29, 1834.
1546—4. David Noyes, b. Sept. 1, 1815; merchant.
1547—5. James, b. March 6, 1818; M. D.
1548—6. Edward, b. April 3, 1820.
1549—7. Catherine, b. Feb. 15, 1822.
1550—8. Harriett B., b. Feb. 23, 1824.
1551—9. Charles H., b. Dec. 20, 1825.
1552—10. Henry Martyn, b. June 24, 1827; a merchant in New York.

36

1553–11. WILLIAM HALSTED, b. Nov. 24, 1830.
1554–12. CLEMENT BAKER, b. Aug. 2, 1832; unm.; d., aged 47.

1555. Rev. JOHN R. CRANE, D.D.[6] [835], (David D.,[5] David,[4] David,[3] Jasper,[2] Jasper[1]), married Harriett Burnet, May 9, 1816. She was daughter of John and Abigail (Wheeler) Burnet. He was a minister at Middletown, Conn., for many years.
Children :

1556—1. Rev. JAMES BURNET; was colleague pastor, with his father, over the 1st Congregational Church, in Middletown, Conn., 1854-6; hospital chaplain from 1863 to the close of the war; m. 1st, in 1847, and 2d, Kate W. Field, 1861. He d. in Elizabethtown, N. J., Sept. 30, 1868.
1557—2. EDWARD; d. young.
1558—3. JOHN JACOB, b. 1819.
1559—4. GEORGE; d. young.
1560—5. MARIA B.

1561. SAMUEL CRANE[6] [841], (John C.,[5] Caleb,[4] Jonathan,[3] Jasper,[2] Jasper[1]), married Abigail Dodd, who was born Feb. 22, 1781. She died Sept. 17, 1857. Children :

1562—1. ROWENA; d. unmarried.
1563—2. LYDIA; d. unmarried.
1564—3. PHEBE; d. unmarried.
1565—4. JOSEPH D.; d. unmarried.
1566—5. CALEB.

1567. HENRY CRANE[6] [842], (John C.,[5] Caleb,[4] Jonathan,[3] Jasper,[2] Jasper[1]), married Sarah Day. Children :

1568—1. HARRIET.
1569—2. NANCY, b. Jan. 9, 1803.
1570—3. HETTY.
1571—4. WILLIAM.
1572—5. ISAAC.

1573. PHEBE CRANE[6] [843], (John C.,[5] Caleb,[4] Jonathan,[3] Jasper,[2] Jasper[1]), married 1st, Elijah Day, by whom she had a daughter; married 2d, Samuel Williams. Child :

1. ADALINE (Day); d. soon after her marriage.

1574. DANIEL CRANE[6] [844], (John C.,[5] Caleb,[4] Jonathan,[3] Jasper,[2] Jasper[1]), married Gertrude Turner. Children :

1575—1. MARIA; m. Mr. Pine.
1576—2. PHEBE ANN.

1577. LYDIA CRANE[6] [845], (John C.,[5] Caleb,[4] Jonathan,[3] Jasper,[2] Jasper[1]), married David Burnet. She died and he married 2d, Harriet Crane Bunn, widow of Nathan Bunn, and daughter of Henry and Sarah (Day) Crane. See No. 1568.
Children :

1. LEWIS (Burnet).
2. CHARLOTTE (Burnet).
3. NANCY (Burnet),

GABRIEL CRANE.

4. ELIJAH (Burnet).
5. BENJAMIN (Burnet).
6. LYDIA (Burnet).

1578. JOHN CALEB CRANE[6] [847], (John C.,[5] Caleb,[4] Jonathan,[3] Jasper,[2] Jasper[1]), married Matilda Alling. She was born Jan. 13, 1801, and died April 1, 1879, at West Orange, N. J., at the home of her son-in-law, John B. Van Wagenen. He died in Newark, Jan. 13, 1849. He was a prominent business man.
Children :

1579—1. SARAH MARIAH, b. Nov. 28, 1827; d. April 24, 1892.
1580—2. WILLIAM, b. March, 1832; d. May 30, 1832.
1581—3. CAROLINE MATILDA, b. Dec. 10, 1836; m. July 10, 1860, at Newark, N. J., John B. Van Wagenen, who was born Aug. 3, 1835.

1582. SARAH CRANE[6] [848], (John C.,[5] Caleb,[4] Jonathan,[3] Jasper,[2] Jasper[1]), married Isaac B. Lee. Child :

1. EVELINE (Lee); m. John Crane Williams. Children :
   1. BENJAMIN L. (Williams); postmaster at West Orange, N. J.
   2. EZRA CRANE (Williams); resides at West Orange.

1583. Rev. SIMEON HARRISON CRANE[6] [849], (John C.,[5] Caleb,[4] Jonathan,[3] Jasper,[2] Jasper[1]), married 1st, Amanda Taylor, at Lexington, Ky., Oct. 31, 1826. She died July, 1836. He then married 2d, at Madison, Ind., Aug. 28, 1837, Jane Robinson Alling. He died in Lexington, in 1841. He was a Presbyterian minister; graduate of Princeton College in 1822. Jane Robinson Alling was born in Baltimore, Md., Nov. 14, 1808. Children :

1584—1. NATHAN BURROWES, b. Aug. 7, 1827; d. in 1848.
1585—2. JOHN CALEB, b. July 15, 1829; lives at St. Louis, Mo.
1586—3. SARAH MATILDA, b. July 26, 1831; d. March 25, 1893.
1587—4. MARY BURROWES, b. Aug. 18, 1833.
1588—5. SIMEON HARRISON DAVIES, b. Aug. 24, 1836; d. in infancy.
1589—6. ELIZABETH HODGES, b. May 29, 1838; m. Rev. Rufus B. Black; lives in Springfield, Iowa.
1590—7. SIMEON HENRY, b. Feb. 11, 1840.
1591—8. JANE MARY, b. March 10 or May 22, 1842; unm.; lives at Madison, Ind.

1592. EZRA D. CRANE[6] [850], (John C.,[5] Caleb,[4] Jonathan,[3] Jasper,[2] Jasper[1]), married Mary Pierson Woodruff. She was born March 1, 1806, and died Nov. 8, 1897. He died Jan. 1, 1851. Children :

1593—1. ELIZABETH BRITTON, b. Feb. 28, 1829.
1594—2. HENRY MEYER, b. July 28, 1830; d. June 18, 1878.
1595—3. CHARLES FAREL, b. Aug. 29, 1832; d. Sept. 9, 1854.
1596—4. JOSEPH DODD, b. Feb. 3, 1835; d. Aug. 24, 1835.
1597—5. MARY ADALINE, b. June 1, 1837; resides at 17 Prospect Terrace, West Orange, N. J.
1598—6. JOSEPH DODD, b. Dec. 18, 1838; d. Sept. 15, 1839.
1599—7. EZRA HAINES, b. Jan. 25, 1845; lives in Boston, Mass.
1600—8. LOUISA BALDWIN, b. Nov. 29, 1848; d. July 6, 1870.

1601. NEHEMIAH J. CRANE[6] [854], (Jonathan,[5] Nehemiah,[4] Jonathan,[3] Jasper,[2] Jasper[1]), married Mary (called Polly) Ward. She was born in Newark, N. J., March 3, 1777. He was a cooper by trade, at 52 Plane Street, Newark. He died there Nov. 27, 1852, from a fall from a load of apples, Nov. 26. She died Feb. 22, 1853. He served as overseer of highways, 1808; as pound-master in 1815 and 1816. Children:

1602—1. ISAAC WARD, b. April 23, 1799.
1603—2. JOHN CUMMINGS, b. Aug. 11, 1801; d. May 17, 1878.
1604—3. LYDIA ELIZA, b. Jan. 29, 1804; d. Sept. 27, 1805.
1605—4. AMBROSE, b. July 16, 1806.
1606—5. LYDIA, b. Feb. 20, 1809; d. Sept. 28, 1829.
1607—6. ABNER WARD, b. March 5, 1812; d. Aug. 2, 1813.
1608—7. SARAH WARD, b. June 5, 1814; d. Dec. 19, 1818.
1609—8. MARY ELIZABETH, b. Aug. 3, 1816; d. 1888.
1610—9. SARAH WARD, b. Jan. 3, 1819; d. Nov. 16, 1891.
1611-10. PHEBE SMITH, b. July 26, 1821; d. Aug. 12, 1821.

Clara F. Wachler

1612.   JOHN A. CRANE[7] [856], (Benjamin,[6] Josiah,[5] Edmund,[4]
John,[3] John,[2] Jasper[1]), married 1st, Sally Ayres, Dec. 25, 1813,
at Circleville, Orange Co., N. Y., where she was born Dec. 22,
1793.   She died Nov. 7, 1838, and he married 2d, Abigail
Brown, April 6, 1840.   She was born Dec. 25, 1793.   He served
in the War of 1812 from New York State.   Settled in Circleville, and there his children were born.   He died at Montrose,
Pa., Nov. 23, 1867.   Children :

   1613—1. PHEBE JANE, b. Nov. 12, 1814.
   1614—2. JULIA ANN, b. June 24, 1816.
   1615—3. SARAH MARIA. b. Jan. 24, 1820.
   1616—4. OLIVER MORRISON, b. Jan. 5, 1825.

1617.   JOSIAH CRANE[7] '[857], (Benjamin,[6] Josiah,[5] Edmund,[4]
John,[3] John,[2] Jasper[1]), married Oct. 6, 1821, Keziah Saxton
Sturgis, who was born near Circleville, N. Y., Feb. 21, 1805.   She
died Aug. 9, 1884.   He was born Aug. 24, 1795, on the Crane homestead settled by his grandfather Capt. Josiah Crane, in the town of
Wallkill, near Middletown, Orange Co., N. Y.   His early life was
spent with his father working on the farm.   About the age of 16
he met with a serious accident caused by the running away of a
team of horses, depriving him of his left arm near the shoulder,
and almost of his life.   After much suffering he finally recovered ; and, being possessed of a strong intellect and a studious
disposition, he prepared himself for the work of teaching, a vocation he followed for many years.   He was elected justice of the
peace, and also collector of taxes ; both of which offices he held
by reëlection for many years.

In the spring of 1842 he removed to Burlingham, Sullivan
Co., N. Y., where he remained until 1860, and then returned to
his native town, where he spent his remaining years.

Squire Crane, as he was universally known, was a great reader,
a deep thinker, and a ready debater,—a man of decided literary
tastes and culture.   He was greatly respected for his many
Christian virtues and rectitude of character.

Two or three weeks before his death he attended a revival
meeting in a Methodist Church near his home.   Although bent
with the weight of years, and suffering from bodily infirmities, he
walked to the church in the evening, and delivered a powerful
and affecting exhortation to the unconverted.   Those who heard

him said that he spoke like one inspired and conscious of his approaching end.

A few days later he was stricken with apoplexy, and died April 13, 1869. He was buried at the Circleville Presbyterian Church, of which he was one of the founders and an elder for forty years. The whole community loved and respected him during his life and mourned his death. Children :

1618—1. WILLIAM HENRY, b. April 11, 1823.
1619—2. ABIGAIL MARIA, b. Feb. 19, 1825; d. Jan. 16, 1826.
1620—3. ELIZABETH JANE, b. Dec. 5, 1827.
1621—4. PHEBE ANNA, b. Nov. 13, 1830.
1622—5. ANTOINETTE, b. May 19, 1836; d. Sept. 18, 1836.
1623—6. JOSIAH MEEKER, b. March 3, 1838.
1624—7. JAMES MADISON, b. Jan. 13, 1842.
1625—8. MARY EMILY, b. April 21, 1846; d. April 20, 1882.

1626. HENRY CRANE[7] [858], (Benjamin,[6] Josiah,[5] Edmund,[4] John,[3] John,[2] Jasper[1]). The early part of his life was spent on his father's farm; but when a young man he removed to Elk Lake, Susquehanna Co., Pa., where he opened a country store, which he carried on for many years. Jan. 27, 1850, he married Mrs. Judith Simons, who died in 1858. He died in 1870, leaving no children.

1627. STEPHEN KITCHELL CRANE[7] [859], (Benjamin,[6] Josiah,[5] Edmund,[4] John,[3] John,[2] Jasper[1]). He remained at the old homestead until a young man, when he learned the trade of a carpenter, and removed to New Milford, Susquehanna Co., Pa., where he purchased a large tract of wild land, which, with the help of his three sons, he finally succeeded in clearing up and making into good farming land, and dividing the same among them. Jan. 1, 1826, he married Hannah Elsie Hickman, who was born March 22, 1803, and died Dec. 17, 1875. Mr. Crane was a devoted Christian, an active worker in the Presbyterian Church, and for many years superintendent of the Sunday-school, acting until the infirmities of health forced him to relinquish the work. He died at Nicholson, Pa., March 7, 1885, aged 84. Children :

1628—1. ISAAC BENJAMIN, b. Aug. 18, 1826.
1629—2. THOMAS KITCHELL, b. April 26, 1830.
1630—3. HENRY JOSIAH, b. June 27, 1836. .

1631. WILLIAM MORRISON CRANE[7] [860], (Benjamin,[6] Josiah,[5] Edmund,[4] John,[3] John,[2] Jasper[1]), married July 8, 1830, Mary Goble. She was born Sept. 22, 1800. She died Nov. 20, 1845, leaving no children. He married 2d, Sarah Cobb, March 19, 1846. She was born April 18, 1818, and died July 6, 1866, leaving six children. He married 3d, Mrs. Hannah Heb, 1868; no children. Children :

1632—1. WILLIAM HENRY, b. Feb. or Oct. 25, 1847, at Middletown, N. Y.

Josiah L. Crane

1633—2. HOLLOWAY WHITFIELD, b. Feb. 15, 1850, at Middletown, N. Y.; d. at same place March 3, 1870.
1634—3. ALBERT B., b. Sept. 5, 1852, near Milford, Pa.
1635—4. EDWIN THOMAS, b. April 10, 1855, at North Jackson, Pa.
1636—5. SARAH CAROLINE, b. Oct. 16, 1856, at North Jackson, Pa.
1637—6. CHARLES EMMETT, b. Aug. 16, 1860, at North Jackson, Pa.

1638. VALARIA ANN CRANE[7] [861], (Benjamin,[6] Josiah,[5] Edmund,[4] John,[3] John,[2] Jasper[1]), married Isaac Schultz Corwin, Nov. 26, 1829, at Wallkill, Orange Co., N. Y. He was born May 29, 1809. She died at New Milford, Pa., July 23, 1888. Children :

1. SILAS BENJAMIN (Corwin), b. May 20, 1832.
2. ELI EGBERT (Corwin), b. May 16, 1834.
3. HENRY HORTON (Corwin), b. Jan. 17, 1836.
4. ROSETTA ANN (Corwin), b. Sept. 14, 1838; d. July 23, 1888.
5. ARCHIBALD LITTLE (Corwin), b. Nov. 19, 1840; d. Dec. 23, 1851.
6. VALARIA CHARLOTT (Corwin), b. March 16, 1842; d. Dec. 12, 1868.
7. EUNICE OLIVE (Corwin), b. Oct. 11, 1843.
8. MARGARET OPHELIA (Corwin), b. Aug. 16, 1846.
9. WILLIAM SHULTZ (Corwin), b. Feb. 15, 1849.
10. EMMA LOUISA (Corwin), b. Sept. 15, 1850; d. May 21, 1864.
11. SELAH WELLS (Corwin), b. Oct. 17, 1852.

1639. ALFRED WINANS CRANE[7] [863], (Abraham,[6] Josiah,[5] Edmund,[4] John,[3] John,[2] Jasper[1]), married 1st, in Orange Co., N. Y., ———, by whom he had four children ; 2d, Sarah Galpin, a native of New England, and a school teacher. They also had four children, but we have not their names. He died in Delaware Co., Ohio, more than fifty years ago. Children :

1640—1. HENRY PEARSON.
1641—2. WILLIAM.
1642—3. PHŒBE.
1643—4. JANE.

1644. GABRIEL CRANE[7] [864], (Abraham,[6] Josiah,[5] Edmund,[4] John,[3] John,[2] Jasper[1]), married Oct. 13, 1831, Mary Ann Whitmore. She was born June 23, 1807, and died Feb. 9, 1872. He died Aug. 17, 1882. Children :

1645—1. JAMES HARVEY, b. May 24, 1832.
1646—2. HENRY JARVIS, b. June 8, 1835.
1647—3. AMOS WATERS, b. Nov. 7, 1837.
1648—4. CLARA FIDELIA, b. Jan. 1, 1841.
1649—5. JULIA ANN, b. March 4, 1846; d. July 1, 1850.

1650. JOSIAH LEONARD CRANE[7] [865], (Abraham,[6] Josiah,[5] Edmund,[4] John,[3] John,[2] Jasper[1]), married April 15, 1830, Miranda Jones, at Perrysburg, Wood Co., Ohio. She was born at Woodstock, Vt., Jan. 2, 1811. He settled at Perrysburg, and died there May 3, 1851. He was by trade a ship carpenter. She died there Oct. 4, 1878. He was an industrious, kind-hearted man, somewhat reserved in his nature, but an honest, reliable

citizen. She was of a generous, lovable nature, fond of her home and all that made it pleasant and attractive.   Children :

1651—1. CAROLINE MARY, b. July 25, 1831; d. May 9, 1847.
1652—2. HENRY LEWIS, b. May 28, 1836.
1653—3. OLIVIA SPAFFORD, b. Aug. 26, 1844; d. May 11, 1845.
1654—4. WILLIAM HOPKINS, b. June 9, 1846; d. June 3, 1847.
1655—5. WILLIAM ALFRED, b. Aug. 13, 1848.

1656. EDWARD LEWIS CRANE[7] [866], (Abraham,[6] Josiah,[5] Edmund,[4] John,[3] John,[2] Jasper[1]), married Feb. 14, 1830, Sarah Ann, daughter of William Woodward, of Miami Co., Ohio, and born April 17, 1811. He died Jan. 14, 1887. He was born in Orange Co., N. Y., on a farm which is still (1899) retained in the Crane family. He read medicine with Dr. Benjamin Fredenborg at Quemans-on the Hudson, N. Y., and attended medical lectures at Berkshire College, Pittsfield, Mass. Went to Ohio in 1828. First taught school; but soon began the practice of his profession at West Charleston, Miami Co., where he continued to reside until 1857, when he moved to Tippecanoe,—four miles away,—where he spent the remainder of his life. He was a man of striking personality and strong mentality. He was always a student, with the disposition and faculty of going to the bottom of things. He was never a candidate for office, but always kept an active interest in politics, and was in much demand as a public speaker in that line. He certainly was not an orator with eloquence, but was always attentively listened to by the plain people because of his logical, forcible and clear statements. For a country doctor he left a good estate (over $100,000), largely in farming land. He began poor, and was not aided by any inheritance beyond a few hundreds of dollars.   Children :

1657—1. ELIZABETH JANE, b. March 3, 1831; d. Dec. 29, 1831.
1658—2. WILLIAM WOODWARD, b. July 24, 1832.
1659—3.. FREDENBORG, b. Jan. 30, 1834; d. Aug. 13, 1834.
1660—4. ZEBINA, b. June 13, 1836; d. June 10, 1840.
1661—5. VAN ELI, b. Feb. 17, 1839.
1662—6.. ALVINA, b. Jan. 2, 1842.
1663—7. PERRY, b. April 4, 1844; d. Nov. 11, 1848.

1664. TRYPHENA CRANE[7] [867], (Abraham,[6] Josiah,[5] Edmund,[4] John,[3] John,[2] Jasper[1]), married 1st, May 10, 1827, David Bradford of Montgomery Co., Ohio. They had two children; both died in infancy. He died in 1833. She married 2d, Feb. 10, 1836, Ephraim Lindsley, of Dayton, Ohio. Children :

1. MARTHA G. (Lindsley), b. Dec. 18, 1836; m. June 1, 1876, J. H. Bradford of Green Co., Ohio.
2. ABIGAIL S. (Lindsley), b. Jan. 26, 1839.
3. SIMEON (Lindsley), b. Oct. 26, 1840.

1665. SIMEON LINDSLEY [3]; m. Jan. 1, 1866, Mary Hagerman. He was private in Co. I, 11th Ohio Infantry. This was one of

Edward L. Crane

Ohio's best fighting regiments, and Mr. Lindsley did his part to sustain the reputation of his regiment. Children:

1. WALTER G. (Lindsley), b. March 30, 1867; m. Feb. 6, 1896 Leola Moeller.
2. NELLIE (Lindsley), b. Sept. 2, 1869.

1666. NELLIE LINDSLEY [2]; m. Aug. 8, 1893, Samuel Burt Weeks, Dayton, Ohio. Children:

1. BLANCH MARTHA (Weeks), b. March 13, 1896.
2. IRENE, } twins (Weeks), b. Sept. 11, 1897.
3. CLARA, }

1667. JEREMIAH COLEMAN CRANE[7] [868], (Abraham,[6] Josiah,[5] Edmund,[4] John,[3] John,[2] Jasper[1]), married Dec., 1839, Livinia W. Cushman. She was born 1808, and died July 29, 1854, having had five children. He married 2d, Sept., 1869, Roxanna ——, who was born 1817, and died 1888; no children by this union. He died Dec. 24, 1885. Children:

1668—1. EDWARD DUSTIN, b. Dec. 13, 1841; d. May 24, 1842.
1669—2. RUFUS GEORGE, b. Feb. 22, 1813; d. March 11, 1843.
1670—3. HARVEY G., b. Feb. 22, 1843; d Feb. 25, 1844.
1671—4. ABBIE K., b. June 26, 1844; d. Sept. 18, 1850.
1672—5. JULIA ANN, b. Dec. 24, 1847.

1673. JOSEPH BAILEY CRANE[7] [874], (Stephen,[6] Josiah,[5] Edmund,[4] John,[3] John,[2] Jasper[1]), born near Middletown, Orange Co., N. Y.: married Dec. 12, 1832, Hannah Webb, of Middletown. She was born Aug. 4, 1811, and died March 22, 1843. He then married Oct. 6, 1843, Lydia Bennett, who was born Oct. 10, 1804, and d. Sept. 11, 1846. He married 3d, Sarah Jane Martin, who was born June 18, 1820, at Middletown, as was also his second wife. Mr. Crane first settled near the place of his birth; but in the spring of 1845 removed to Franklin Co., Ohio, where he purchased a farm and resided until the fall of 1853, when he removed to La Salle Co., Ill., locating at Tonica, where he remained until the year 1865, when he went to Chicago for the purpose of obtaining better advantages for educating his children. Here he engaged in the lumber business; but a growing deafness caused him to retire from active business. He was a man of sterling worth, absolutely honest and upright in all his dealings. He died Feb. 12, 1874, leaving his family well provided for. He was buried at Tonica. He left three children by his first wife, two by the second, and four by the third wife. The latter died Dec. 31, 1898. Children:

1674—1. PHEBE MARIAH, b. Feb. 10, 1835; d. Jan. 15, 1857; unm.
1675—2. ANNA MELIA, b. April 6, 1838.
1676—3. SOLOMON, b. May 31, 1840.
1677—4. STEPHEN MORTIMER, b. May 26, 1844. He was b. in Orange Co., N. Y. He removed with his parents, first to Ohio in 1845, then to Illinois in 1853. He enlisted at Ottawa, Ill., Aug., 1862, in Houghtelling's Battery, Light Artillery, and was at once ordered to the front. His regiment was engaged at Murfreesboro, which was the first battle in which he participated. He was with Sherman on his march to the sea. On their return, on the morning of March

37

19, 1865, an engagement took place at Bentonville, N. C., where he was instantly killed by a shell from the enemy's gun, striking him upon the head. This was the last battle participated in by Sherman's army, and the last gun fired by the enemy during that engagement. He was postilion in the battery.

1678—5. HANNAH MARGARET. She was b. Oct. 11, 1845, in Franklin Co., Ohio, and was m. April 7, 1864, in Chicago, Ill., to William Stillman Carpenter. He d. in that city Feb. 15, 1866, and she m. George N. Jennings, M. D., April 12, 1888, a practicing physician. Residence Tonica, Ill.

1679—6. MARY ANTONIETT, b. Jan. 24, 1854.

1680—7. EMMA ELIZABETH, b. June 26, 1856.

1681—8. OLIVIA ABIGAIL, b. Nov. 13, 1857.

1682—9. ELSIE MORIA, b. Dec. 27, 1859.

1683. SOLOMON CRANE[7] [876], (Stephen,[6] Josiah,[5] Edmund,[4] John,[3] John,[2] Jasper[1]), married Abigail Moriah Webb at Middletown, N. Y., Dec. 11, 1830. She was born June 10, 1808, and died July 30, 1833. He died May 22, 1834, leaving one child :

1684—1. HIRAM WEBB, b. March 2, 1833.

1685. GEORGE LITTLE CRANE[7] [878], (Stephen,[6] Josiah,[5] Edmund,[4] John,[3] John,[2] Jasper[1]), went with his parents to Ohio in 1824. In 1838 he located in Nelsonville, Athens Co., in that State, and August 5th of that year married Abigail Young, a native of Bar Harbor, Me. He was by trade a stone mason, and was engaged in the construction of both the Ohio and the Hocking Valley canals. He enlisted Oct. 2, 1861, at Nelsonville in Co. G, 18th Ohio V. I., and was mustered in Nov. 5th at Camp Dennison to serve for three years. Was under fire at Bowling Green, Ky. ; Nashville, Tenn. ; Huntsville, Tuscumbia, and Decatur, Ala. He was taken prisoner at Athens, Ala. May 1, 1862, paroled, and sent to Camp Chase, Columbus, Ohio, when, on account of sickness, he was given a discharge furlough, and allowed to go to his home ; was finally discharged May 28, 1863, completely broken in health. He never applied for a pension, although deserving of one. He was a great student of the Bible ; but in religion he might be termed a materialist. The Golden Rule was his creed, and he lived up to the tenets of his profession. He passed about thirty-five years of his life in Nelsonville, where he died Nov. 26, 1874. Children :

1686—1. JOSIAH YOUNG, b. July 1, 1839.

1687—2. LEWIS GEORGE, b. March 9, 1841; d. April 20, 1894.

1688—3. ALMIRA DRAKE, b. Oct. 14, 1842.

1689—4. FRANKLIN HARPER, b. Sept. 14, 1844.

1690—5. LORANIA ABIGAIL, b. July 10, 1846.

1691—6. LYDIA ELLEN, b. May 13, 1848.

1692—7. JASPER NEWTON, b. Dec. 9, 1851; d. Sept. 10, 1878; was wonderfully gifted in designing and drawing; was an invalid for many years.

1693. ABRAM KITCHELL CRANE[7] [883], (Stephen,[6] Josiah,[5] Edmund,[4] John,[3] John,[2] Jasper[1]), married Amy Sophia Smith,

A. K. Crane

Mrs. Dorothy N. Law

Sept. 20, 1862, at Granville, Licking Co., Ohio. She was born in Franklin Co., Vt., March 11, 1832. For fifty years has been a respected and honored resident of Alexandria, Ohio. Children :

1694—1. NETTIE SOPHIA, b. July 9, 1863.
1695—2. GEORGE BERTRAND, b. Oct. 5, 1864.

1696. PHEBE CRANE[7] [884], (Stephen,[6] Josiah,[5] Edmund,[4] John,[3] John,[2] Jasper[1]), married Israel Taylor, Oct. 10, 1838. He died in 1852, and she married 2d, Aug. 30, 1855, Rev. Josiah Sherman. She died Aug. 3, 1899, at the home of her daughter Dorothy N. Law, and she was laid to rest in the churchyard at Alexandria, Ohio, where rest the ashes of her husband and mother. Children :

1. FANNIE ELIZABETH (Taylor), b. June 30, 1839 ; d. Aug. 12, 1840.
2. DOROTHY NORTON (Taylor), b. June 27, 1841.
3. CARRIE EVA (Sherman), b. July 18, 1857 ; d. Sept. 10, 1858.
4. CHARLES KITCHELL (Sherman), b. Jan. 1, 1860, in Alexandria, Ohio.

1697. DOROTHY NORTON TAYLOR [2] ; m. May 10, 1880, Dr. David Hillis Law, who was b. in New York city July 4, 1830, of Scotch-Irish parentage. In 1837 he with his parents removed to Lee Co., Ill., and settled on a farm in the valley of Rock River. In the spring of 1852 he joined a party *en route* overland with teams to California. Returning home in 1856 he entered upon the study of medicine with his brother-in-law, Dr. Oliver Everett, graduating from the College of Physicians and Surgeons at Keokuk, Iowa, class of 1861. He immediately enlisted in Co. A, 13th I. V. I., and became assistant surgeon of that regiment; later detailed as staff surgeon for Gen. Curtis, performing the duties of a battalion surgeon. Later was discharged to accept the commission of lieutenant-colonel in a Missouri regiment; but at that time the war was drawing to a close, and this regiment was not called into action, giving the doctor an opportunity to serve as private surgeon for different generals, who, recognizing his skill and ability, employed him at a salary. After four years of faithful service for his country he resumed his private medical practice, in which he is still (1897) engaged. He owns the farm purchased by his father in 1837, and has upon it a choice herd of cows that furnish milk for the Anglo Swiss Condensing Milk Factory, the largest of the kind in the world. This company has one establishment in Switzerland, one in England, two in Sweden, and a small one at Middletown, N. Y., besides the one at Dixon, Ill. He with his family reside in Dixon, Ill., where he is a member of the G. A. R. Post 299, the Military Order of the Loyal Legion of the United States, a Master Mason, and Knight Templar. Child :
1. JAMES EVERETT (Law), b. Jan. 13, 1882.

1698. CHARLES KITCHELL SHERMAN [4] ; m. in St. Joseph, Mo., Elizabeth Kelso Glaskin, Dec. 12, 1884. Children :
1. CHARLES GLASKIN (Sherman), b. Dec. 9, 1885.
2. WILLIAM CRANE (Sherman), b. Nov. 27, 1889.
3. HELEN LUENNA (Sherman), b. Oct. 25, 1891.

1699. ABIGAIL CRANE[7] [885], (Stephen,[6] Josiah,[5] Edmund,[4] John,[3] John,[2] Jasper[1]), married March 2, 1843, Albert G. Goodspeed. She died Sept. 21, 1854. Children:

1. PHEBE ADELIA (Goodspeed), b. Jan. 19, 1844; d. Dec. 24, 1844.
2. LEWIS G. (Goodspeed), b. Dec. 29, 1844; m. and d. Aug. 8, 1892.
3. DELIA (Goodspeed), b. Jan. 29, 1848; d. March 26, 1866.
4. MATHEW G. (Goodspeed), b. May 15, 1850; d. Sept. 7, 1850.

1700. LEWIS ALLEN CRANE[7] [889], (Shadrack,[6] Ezekiel,[5] Edmund,[4] John,[3] John,[2] Jasper[1]), married Sarah Klady. She was born Jan. 18, 1802, a native of Montezuma, N. Y. He was a mechanic and farmer; was married in Montezuma, N. Y.; resided in Batavia, and afterwards removed to Cooper, Mich., where he died April 9, 1870. She died there March 15, 1889. He served in the war of 1812, at the battle of Fort Erie, in a New York regiment, so stated by his son Billings. He for many years served as supervisor. Children:

1701—1. CHARLOTTE C., b. Feb. 21, 1823.
1702—2. ELIZABETH C., b. Feb. 23, 1826.
1703—3. BILLINGS, b. May 30, 1828.
1704—4. MARY ELIZA, b. Sept. 10, 1840; m. Duncan Furgeson, who d. July 30, 1888.

1705. NANCY CRANE[7] [891], (Shadrack,[6] Ezekiel,[5] Edmund,[4] John,[3] John,[2] Jasper[1]), married Silas Miller. Settled in Napoli, Cattaraugus Co.; N. Y. Children:

1. ANN ELIZA (Miller); m. Judson Sibley.
2. BETSEY MARIA (Miller); m. George Thorp.

1706. STEVENS CRANE[7] [892], (Shadrack,[6] Ezekiel,[5] Edmund,[4] John,[3] John,[2] Jasper[1]), married Clarinda Daw. She was born Sept. 27, 1803, and died in June, 1860, in Genesee Co., N. Y. He was a carpenter, and died at Cascade, Iowa, April 23, 1852. Children:

1707—1. PETER FERRIS, b. Jan. 22, 1827.
1708—2. AUGUSTA AMELIA, b. Feb. 11, 1829.
1709—3. HENRY D., b. March 11, 1831.
1710—4. CHARLES DEWITT, b. Nov. 28, 1833.
1711—5. LEVANT, b Dec. 5, 1835; d. Aug. 8, 1836.
1712—6. DERIAS FISH, b. April 30, 1838.
1713—7. ANN ELIZA, b. Dec. 3, 1842.
1714—8. STEVENS LEVANT, b. Nov. 18, 1844; d. Nov. 28, 1845.

1715. SILAS CRANE[7] [894], (Shadrack,[6] Ezekiel,[5] Edmund,[4] John,[3] John,[2] Jasper[1]), married Celina Gibbs, and had two children before removing west. Reported to have died in Indiana. Children:

1716—1. HENRY.
1717—2. LOUISE.

1718. ROSWELL R. CRANE[7] [895], (Shadrack,[6] Ezekiel,[5] Edmund,[4] John,[3] John,[2] Jasper[1]), born at Metz, Cayuga Co., N. Y. Married Paulina Newman, Sept. 18, 1828, in Covington, Genesee

Wm. A. Crane

Co., N. Y. She was born Dec. 27, 1806, at New Haven, Addison Co., Vt. He died at Anamosa, Iowa, May 25, 1888. She was living in Dec., 1897. Children :

1719—1. MARIA ANTONETTE, b. Oct. 18, 1829; m. —— Fisher.
1720—2. HELEN AMELIA, b. Feb. 19, 1831; m. Col. W. T. Shaw.
1721—3. MARTHA MELVINA, b. June 25, 1833; m. Chilion T. Lampson, grain dealer; d. Jan. 30, 1894.
1722—4. EMILY ADELIA, b. Aug. 25, 1835; m. —— Peet.
1723—5. ORVILLE DEVOLL, b. Jan. 13, 1838; d. May, 1897.
1724—6. LEROY ALBERTI, b. April 19, 1840; a lawyer in Pueblo, Col.
1725—7. ALICE OPHELIA, b. March 27, 1843; m. Judge Holmes at Des Moines.
1726—8. MARCIA THERESA, b. April 17, 1846; m. —— Cox.

1727. JAMES NELSON CRANE[7] [896], (Shadrack,[6] Ezekiel,[5] Edmund,[4] John,[3] John,[2] Jasper[1]), married 1st, Eliza Ann Whitney, Feb. 3, 1829, in Erie Co., N. Y., and settled in New Orleans, La. She died Feb. 18, 1840, and he married 2d, Ann D. Brimley. He died there Sept. 9, 1874. Children :

1728—1. WILLIAM WHITNEY, b. Oct. 30, 1829.
1729—2. ELIZA ANN, b. Dec. 12, 1830.
1730—3. MARY BEAUFORT, b. Aug. 24, 1833.
1731—4. MARTHA CAROLINE, b. June 21, 1835.
1732—5. JAMES BRIMLEY, b. Nov. 28, 1841.
1733—6. WALTER EMMETT, b. June 3, 1843.
1734—7. STEVENS FULLER, b. July 31, 1846.
1735—8. ANN ELIZA, b. July 7, 1848.
1736—9. GEORGE WASHINGTON S., b. Sept. 1, 1851.
1737-10. KATHERINE RACHEL, b. July 28, 1853.
1738-11. FRANKLIN H., b. Jan. 21, 1856.
1739-12. UTICA VOLTAIRE, b. March 25, 1858.

1740. ANN ELIZA CRANE[7] [898], (Shadrack,[6] Ezekiel,[5] Edmund,[4] John,[3] John,[2] Jasper[1]), married Sept. 27, 1841, Hiram Burbank. He was born June 9, 1814. Residence at Napoli, N. Y. Both living in Dec., 1897. Children :

1. FRANCES M. (Burbank), b. Aug. 31, 1847; m. Chas. S. Coburn, Nov. 27, 1891.
2. MIRANDA E. (Burbank), b. Sept. 5, 1850.
3. ALICE N. (Burbank), b. July 6, 1854.

1741. JAMES M. CRANE[7] [904], (Loyal,[6] James,[5] Edmund,[4] John,[3] John,[2] Jasper[1]), married Mary A. Collins at Buchanan, Mich., Sept. 26, 1866. She was born there Oct. 18, 1847, and died April 1, 1894. He served in the Army of the Cumberland in 1862 and 1863. He was a merchant at Paw Paw, Mich., some years; married 2d, Della W. Clark, of Boston, Mass., Nov., 1898. Resides at Washington, D. C. Child :

1741½-1. NATHANIEL D., b. Dec. 5, 1871; d. April 2, 1873.

1742. SALLY MARIAH CRANE[7] [905], (Loyal,[6] James,[5] Edmund,[4] John,[3] John,[2] Jasper[1]), married Aaron Van Auken, of Paw Paw, Mich. They now (1898) reside at 1408 V Street, Washington, D. C. Child :

1. HARRY L. (Van Auken).

1743. EDGAR A. CRANE[7] [908], (Alonzo,[6] James,[5] Edmund,[4] John,[3] John,[2] Jasper[1]), born at Paw Paw, Mich. Graduate of Michigan University, Ann Arbor. Enlisted and served through the war (1862 to 1865) in the Army of the Cumberland and 4th Michigan Cavalry, the company that captured Jefferson Davis at the downfall of the confederacy; married Oct. 15, 1867, at Paw Paw, Nancy P. Abbott, who was born there Sept. 1, 1845; an attorney-at-law. Residence for a time at Chicago, Ill.; subsequently removed to Kalamazoo, Mich. Children:

1744—1. ROBFRT B., b. Nov. 29, 1873, at Chicago, Ill.
1745—2. DANIEL A., b. Dec. 2, 1878, at Chicago, Ill.

1746. ANNA FRANCES CRANE[7] [911], (Nathaniel J.,[6] Joseph,[5] Joseph,[4] Jasper,[3] John,[2] Jasper[1]), married Dec. 7, 1871, Charles Henry Kimball, of Bloomfield, N. J. He was born in New York city Dec. 2, 1843. Children:

1. JEANNETTE WARD (Kimball), b. Sept. 9, 1872; m. Aug. 17, 1895, Abram Ray Tyler, of Brooklyn, N. Y. He was b. Dec. 24, 1868; is organist at New York Ave. M. E. Church, Brooklyn, where they reside. Child:
    1. MARIAN WILLIS (Tyler), b. Nov. 26, 1896.
2. ARTHUR SPENCER (Kimball), b. June 17, 1874; m. Dec. 23, 1896, Anna May Brokaw, of East Orange, N. J., dau. of William G. Brokaw, of that place.

1748. HORATIO CRAIN[7] [933], (Achilles R.,[6] William,[5] Jeremiah,[4] Daniel,[3] John,[2] Jasper[1]), married at Key West, Fla., Dec. 24, 1862, Amelia, daughter of Charles Howe. Their eldest child was born in New York city; next eldest at Key West, Fla.; the third at Vineland, N. J.; and the two youngest at Detroit, Mich. Children:

1749—1. HERBERT HOFFMAN, b. Dec. 17, 1863.
1750—2. EDWARD HOWE, b. Nov. 25, 1865.
1751—3. ANNIE JULIA, b. March 5, 1868.
1752—4. ST. CLAIR, b. April 7, 1872.
1753—5. LUCITA, b. April 7, 1874; d. Jan. 22, 1875.

1754. GEORGE JACKSON CRAIN[7] [935], (Josephus N.,[6] William,[5] Jeremiah,[4] Daniel,[3] John,[2] Jasper[1]), married Emily Bell. Children:

1755—1. FRANCIS E, b. Nov. 25, 1860.
1756—2. GEORGE W., b. Feb. 22, 1867.

1757. THOMAS BENTON CRAIN[7] [936], (Josephus N.,[6] William,[5] Jeremiah,[4] Daniel,[3] John,[2] Jasper[1]), married Jennie Clifford. Children:

1758—1. FRANCES ELIZABETH, b. Dec. 18, 1870.

1759. SARAH ELMIRA CRAIN[7] [940], (Josephus N.,[6] William,[5] Jeremiah,[4] Daniel,[3] John,[2] Jasper[1]), married Henry Mott. Child:

1760—1. HENRIETTA (Mott).

1761. MARIANNA CRAIN[7] [941], (Josephus N.,[6] William,[5] Jeremiah,[4] Daniel,[3] John,[2] Jasper[1]), married July 1, 1865, William A. Doran. Children :

1. WILLIAM JAMES (Doran), b. May 2, 1866.
2. CLARENCE AUGUSTINE (Doran), b. Feb. 6, 1869.
3. ARTHUR PIUS (Doran), b. Jan. 6, 1871; d. May 2, 1871.
4. ELLA (Doran), b. Feb. 17, 1872; d. July 5, 1872.
5. EDWARD (Doran), b. April 4, 1874; d. Aug. 20, 1874.
6. BERTHA AGNES (Doran), b. Oct. 29, 1875.
7. FRANCIS ROWEN (Doran), b. Oct. 14, 1877.
8. CHARLES (Doran), b. Jan. 13, 1879.
9. MARIANNA AGNES (Doran), b. May 19, 1880.
10. LORETTO (Doran), b. Aug. 24, 1881.
11. ARTHUR EDWARD (Doran), b. June 12, 1883.
12. HANNAH ELLA (Doran), b. Nov. 19, 1884.
13. LEONARD EDWARD (Doran), b. Jan. 28, 1889, in New York city.

1762. WILLIAM HENRY CRAIN[7] [945], (William D.,[6] William,[5] Jeremiah,[4] Daniel,[3] John,[2] Jasper[1]), married July 9, 1873, Angeline Genevieve Mitchell. He was born in Galveston, Tex., Nov. 25, 1848; studied law and became a very successful practitioner; a hard worker, without making any effort for show or display; a good speaker with the reputation of an orator already gained, although comparatively a young man. He was a Democrat in politics, and for twelve years represented the Galveston District in Congress, serving on important committees. He was a man of firm convictions, one who could not be moved by other than true and lofty motives to do whatever was set before him to do. While out one evening in Washington he contracted a cold, which, perhaps through lack of proper early treatment, resulted in pneumonia, and caused his death, Feb. 10, 1896, after a week of illness. His family being at the time in Cuero, DeWitt Co., Tex., which place was their home. It had been his intention to retire from politics at the close of the term which he was then serving, and devote his time entirely to his legal profession. He was a kind-hearted, genial, generous person, and quite generally liked as an associate. It was through his efforts that the appropriation was secured for deep-water improvements for Galveston harbor. Children :

1763—1. FRANCIS HENRY, b. Aug. 16, 1874; a lawyer by profession; mayor of Cuero, Tex.; orator there, Decoration Day, 1896; elected mayor, Nov. 24, 1897.
1764—2. ANGELINE G., b. Sept. 15, 1876.
1765—3. JAMES KERR, } twins; b. Aug. 28, 1879.
1766—4. WILLIAM HENRY,
1767—5. NEWTON MITCHELL, b. Dec. 26, 1883.
1768—6. MARY MATILDA, b. Jan. 19, 1887.

1769. Dr. CHARLES DAVIS CRAIN[7] [947], (William D.,[6] William,[5] Jeremiah,[4] Daniel,[3] John,[2] Jasper[1]), married Maggie McCrea Sanford. He is by profession a dentist; residence, Galveston, Tex. Has been deputy collector of customs, at Isabel, Cameron Co. Children :

1770—1. CLAUD DAVIS, b. March 21, 1881

1771—2. ZITA, b. March 28, 1883.
1772—3. ANNIE MATILDA, b. Dec. 16, 1884.
1773—4. CHARLES DAVIS.

1774. MATTHIAS CRANE[7] [951], (Israel,[6] Matthias,[5] William,[4] Nathaniel,[3] Azariah,[2] Jasper[1]), married in 1831, Susan Baldwin, of South Orange, N. J., born in 1813. She was daughter of Jephtha, and granddaughter of Benjamin, which Benjamin was in the fourth generation from John Baldwin, one of the original settlers of Newark, N. J. Children:

1775—1. EDWARD B.
1776—2. ISRAEL, b. Aug. 23, 1835.
1777—3. CATHARINE B.
1778—4. MARY C.
1779—5. ABBY FRANCES.
1780—6. HENRY L.

1781. ABIGAIL CRANE[7] [952], (Israel,[6] Matthias,[5] William,[4] Nathaniel,[3] Azariah,[2] Jasper[1]), married Oct. 29, 1834, Dr. Isaac D. Dodd, of Bloomfield, N. J. Children:

1. MARY FRANCES (Dodd), b. April 4, 1836; d. 1895.
2. SARAH DAVIS (Dodd), b. March 31, 1839; m. Dr. Stubbert.
3. CHARLES HENRY (Dodd), b. Feb. 13, 1843; d. June 17, 1845.
4. ELIZA BEACH (Dodd), b. Sept. 1, 1845; m. ———.

1782. JAMES CRANE[7] [954], (Israel,[6] Matthias,[5] William,[4] Nathaniel,[3] Azariah,[2] Jasper[1]), married Phœbe Crane, daughter of Nathaniel and Rebecca Harrison Crane. Children:

1783—1. JAMES B.
1784—2. REBECCA.
1785—3. FANNY.
1786—4. PHOEBE.
1787—5. CHARLES D.
1788—6. ROSE.

1789. UZAL A. CRANE[7] [961], (Abijah,[6] Jonathan,[5] William,[4] Nathaniel,[3] Azariah,[2] Jasper[1]), married Lucetta B., daughter of Stephen S. Gould, Sept. 2, 1830. She was born in New York city, in 1806. He was a printer. Their eldest child was born in Caldwell, N. J., where Mr. Crane was born. The second child was born in Paterson, but their remaining children were born in New York city. For many years past their residence has been in Brooklyn, N. Y., where he died of paralysis, Aug. 23, 1884. He learned the art of printing in the Law Publishing House of Stephen S. Gould, who was formerly of Gould, Banks, & Co., New York city. Mr. Crane's first venture was editing the *Paterson Courier*, and for some years pursued an active, journalistic life, until he became connected with the New York Post-Office. Subsequent to that he purchased a farm near Indianapolis, Ind., where he resided several years. In the year 1872, he removed to Brooklyn, N. Y. He was a devoted and prominent member of the Christian Church; an Abolitionist and life-long friend of Horace Greeley. Children:

1790—1. CAROLINE HOLMES.

1791—2. ALEXANDER GOULD; was major in the late war; d. Dec. 25, 1876.
1792—3. DAVID BANKS.
1793—4. MARY BANKS.
1794—5. UZAL OGDEN.
1795—6. HENRY PAXTON.

1796. Col. HENRY A. R. CRANE[7] [964], (Abijah,[6] Jonathan,[5] William,[4] Nathaniel,[3] Azariah,[2] Jasper[1]), married Oct. 4, 1837, at St. Augustine, Fla., Angelina M. Allen. She was a native of Fernandina, born March 1, 1818. He was a man of prominence, having held both civil and military offices in Florida. For some years he was a resident of Key West, where he was editor and publisher of a newspaper. His eldest child was born in St. Augustine, the next two at Palatka, the next three at Mellonville, and the youngest at Tampa. Children:

1797—1. HENRY LAFAYETTE, b. Oct. 12, 1838; served in the Confederate Army; proprietor of Orange Grove hotel, at Tampa; judge of probate, Hillsboro Co.
1798—2. CAROLINE B., b. 1841; in 1866 m. Capt. H. Jenks, Key West.
1799—3. EMMA, b. 1843.
1800—4. SOPHIA, b. 1845; m. Peter Crocker, 1862, at Key West.
1801—5. LUCETTA B., b. 1848; m. F. Diaz, 1875.
1802—6. FLORA, b. 1850.
1803—7. FANNIE, b. 1855; d. at Key West, 1869.

1804. STEPHEN MUNSON CRANE[7] [972], (Calvin S,[6] Jonas,[5] William,[4] Nathaniel,[3] Azariah,[2] Jasper[1]), married Jane Piggott at New York. He died June 23, 1894. Child:

1805—1. MARY DAY; m. Rev. D. D. Whedon, D.D., of Newark.

1806. WALWORTH DOUGLASS CRANE[7] [976], (Calvin S.,[6] Jonas,[5] William,[4] Nathaniel,[3] Azariah,[2] Jasper[1]), married Nov. 22, 1857, in Brooklyn, Mary E. Van Leer, of New York city. She was born March 27, 1844. He was a railroad contractor. He died April 17, 1890, at Crosswell, Mich. Child:

1807—1. JOSEPH OWEN, b. Oct. 29, 1858.

1808 JONAS SMITH CRANE[7] [980], (Bethuel,[6] Jonas,[5] William,[4] Nathaniel,[3] Azariah,[2] Jasper[1]), married Hetty E. Baldwin. He died March 18, 1859, aged 43. Children:

1809—1. ANNA H.; d. aged 14.
1810—2. MARY; m. Dr. John Bromly, of Newark, N. J.
1811—3. SARAH F.
1812—4. MARGARET.

1813. Rev. JOHN NEWTON CRANE[7] [988], (Josiah W.,[6] William,[5] William,[4] Nathaniel,[3] Azariah,[2] Jasper[1]), married Hannah Wilde, June 16, 1836, at Mont Clair, N. J. He was a Methodist. She was born in England, Sept. 11, 1810. He died July 9, 1892. Children:

1814—1. FANNY S.
1815—2. ROBERT NEWTON, b. April 1, 1848, at Long Branch, N. J.

38

1816. HESTER ANNE ROGERS CRANE[7] [996], Josiah W.,[6] William,[5] William,[4] Nathaniel,[3] Azariah,[2] Jasper[1]), married Philip Henry Harrison at West Bloomfield, N. J., Oct. 19, 1853. He was born at Livingston, Aug. 24, 1831. He is a contractor. Present residence at Newark. Children all born in Centerville. Children :

1. CAROLINE LANDAU (Harrison), b. July 23, 1854; m. Benj. T. Parkhurst.
2. ELIZA DURYEE (Harrison), b. Sept. 3, 1857; d. Feb. 24, 1862.
3. FANNIE CRANE (Harrison), b. Sept. 16, 1860; m. Oscar H. Condit.
4. KATHARINE SCHUYLER (Harrison), b. Aug. 19, 1864.
5. HARRY LINCOLN (Harrison), b. July 20, 1866; m. May Verges Cresse; a contractor at Newark.
6. LOUIS BALDWIN (Harrison), b. June 18, 1869; a contractor at Newark.
7. EDITH LEE (Harrison), b. Oct. 16, 1870.

1817. FRANCES ALMIRA CRANE[7] [997], (Josiah W.,[6] William,[5] William,[4] Nathaniel,[3] Azariah,[2] Jasper[1]), married Marcus Harrison, Oct., 1854. Residence at Caldwell, N. J. Children :

1. THEODORE FRELINGHUYSEN (Harrison), b. July 26, 1855; m. Nov., 1882, Kate Herdman; and d. Nov. 15, 1895.
2. JOSEPH LESLIE (Harrison), b. Jan., 1862; m. Nora Bond, May 19, 1887; resides at Ventura, Cal.

1818. CHARLES OLIVER CRANE[7] [1010], (Lydia,[6] Oliver,[5] William,[4] Nathaniel,[3] Azariah,[2] Jasper[1]), married ——. Children :

1819—1. ANNIE.
1820—2. SARAH.

1821. EDWARD AMES CRANE[7] [1011], (Lydia,[6] Oliver,[5] William,[4] Nathaniel,[3] Azariah,[2] Jasper[1]), married Amanda Nichols. Children :

1822—1. EDWARD NICHOLS, b. April 5, 1846; lived at Newark
1823—2. CLEMENT; d.
1824—3. FRANK WRIGHT; d.
1825—4. HARRY C.; d.
1826—5. ARTHUR MCAULAY.

1827. JASON CRANE[7] [1012], (Lydia,[6] Oliver,[5] William,[4] Nathaniel,[3] Azariah,[2] Jasper[1]), married Oct. 1, 1845, Amarintha Dodd, daughter of Ira Dodd. She was born Sept. 19, 1821. Children :

1829—1. FREDERICK, b. June 15, 1847.
1830—2. ADELINE C., b. Feb. 19, 1849; d. Sept. 11, 1849.
1831—3. HARRIET, b. Oct. 6, 1850; m. Children :
    1. ARTHUR.
    2. NORMAN.
    3. LAURA.
    4. HAROLD.
    5. HELEN.
1832—4. EDWARD L., b. Dec. 26, 1852; d. Aug. 4, 1853.
1833—5. ANNIE D., b. June 22, 1854; m.; had child Robert

1834—6. HENRY W., b. July 7, 1856; m.; had child Frederick.
1835—7. GEORGE M., b. Aug. 13, 1858; d. Oct. 11, 1858.
1836—8. HELEN W., b. Sept. 27, 1860.
1837—9. LAURA H., b. Aug. 25, 1862; d. Feb. 8, 1879.

1838. SUSAN PHILETTA CRANE[7] [1015], (Stephen F.,[6] Oliver,[5] William,[4] Nathaniel,[3] Azariah,[2] Jasper[1]), married Lemuel F. Corwin in 1846. Children:

1. STEPHEN (Corwin), b. 1849; d. in infancy.
2. OLIVER G. (Corwin), b. 1851; d. 1871.

1839. Rev. OLIVER CRANE[7] [1016], (Stephen F.,[6] Oliver,[5] William,[4] Nathaniel,[3] Azariah,[2] Jasper[1]), married Sept. 5, 1848, Marion Dun Turnbull, daughter of John and Margaret Turnbull, and sailed Jan. 3, 1849, as a missionary to Turkey. He was a graduate of Yale, class of 1845. After spending some years in Turkey he returned home, and in 1864 was installed as pastor of the First Presbyterian Church at Carbondale, Pa. He died in Boston in 1896. Children:

1840—1. LOUINA MATILDA, b. June 21, 1849; d. Jan. 12, 1851.
1841—2. ELIZABETH MARION, b. May 12, 1851.
1842—3. CAROLINE HANNAH, b. Oct. 31, 1852.
1843—4. OLIVER TURNBULL, b. Nov. 14, 1855.
1844—5. LOUINA MARY, b. Aug. 11, 1861; m. H. C. Crane, May 21, 1884. He d. Aug. 23, 1895.

1845. WILLIAM M. CRANE[7] [1026], (Zophar B.,[6] Oliver,[5] William,[4] Nathaniel,[3] Azariah,[2] Jasper[1]), married Anna M. Pierson. Child:

1846—1. WILLIAM W., b. Sept., 1856; m. Nelly Burgess.

1847. MARY LOUISA CRANE[7] [1027], (Zophar B.,[6] Oliver,[5] William,[4] Nathaniel,[3] Azariah,[2] Jasper[1]), married Henry Crane. Child:

1. IDA, b. May 7, 1870.

1848. JULIA FRANCES CRANE[7] [1029], (Nathaniel M.,[6] Oliver,[5] William,[4] Nathaniel,[3] Azariah,[2] Jasper[1]), married Hugh A. Jamieson, and had four children, two of whom died in infancy. She resides at Grinnell, Iowa. Children:

1. MARCUS WILLIAM (Jamieson), b. July 16, 1861.
2. HUGH EUGENE (Jamieson), b. Jan. 9, 1863; d. Sept. 8, 1864.
3. THEODORE FRANCIS (Jamieson), b. March 25, 1864; d. Aug. 1, 1864.
4. CHARLES WETMORE (Jamieson), b. July 9, 1867.

1849. THEODORE FORDHAM CRANE[7] [1033], (Nathaniel M.,[6] Oliver,[5] William,[4] Nathaniel,[3] Azariah,[2] Jasper[1]), married Narcissa B. Taylor. Residence, Grinnell, Iowa. Children:

1850—1. GERTRUDE F.
1851—2. FREDERICK LYLE.
1852—3. MABEL J.

1853. SAMUEL GIBSON CRANE[7] [1042], (Caleb,[6] Samuel,[5] Noah,[4] Nathaniel,[3] Azariah,[2] Jasper[1]), married Lydia S. Crane. She was born in 1800, and died in 1855. Child:

1853½-1. ANN MARIA G.; d. 1839, aged 18 years.

1854. ELIZABETH BALDWIN CRANE[7] [1043], (Caleb,[6] Samuel,[5] Noah,[4] Nathaniel,[3] Azariah,[2] Jasper[1]), married Gershom Freeman. Children:

1. ZENAS G. (Freeman).
2. ELIZA (Freeman).
3. ANNIE MARIA (Freeman).

1855. MOSES PERSONETTE CRANE[7] [1044], (Caleb,[6] Samuel,[5] Noah,[4] Nathaniel,[3] Azariah,[2] Jasper[1]), married at Madison, N. J., June 7, 1831, Sarah B. Hedges. She was a native of that place, and born July 2, 1802. She died in Caldwell, Dec. 29, 1874, where the family resided for many years. He was a farmer. His late residence was at Mandarin, Fla. Children:

1856—1. CALEB G., b. July 26, 1833.
1857—2. WILLIAM WALLACE, b. Oct. 14, 1836; d. April 28, 1837.
1858—3. EDWARD NELSON, b. July 16, 1839; d. Jan. 11, 1840.
1859—4. EDWARD W., b. March 31, 1843.

1860. ZENAS C. CRANE[7] [1045], (Caleb,[6] Samuel,[5] Noah,[4] Nathaniel,[3] Azariah,[2] Jasper[1]), married at Livingston, N. J., Oct. 17, 1833, Mary Harrison, a native of that place, and settled in Caldwell. Their three eldest children died in infancy. Children:

1861—1. MARCUS HARRISON, b. Oct. 10, 1842.
1862—2. ANNA MARIA, b. Oct. 28, 1844.
1863—3. CALEB, b. Oct. 22, 1846.

1864. LYDIA P. CRANE[7] [1046], (Caleb,[6] Samuel,[5] Noah,[4] Nathaniel,[3] Azariah,[2] Jasper[1]), married George C. Steele. Children:

1. GIBSON (Steele).
2. MARIA C. (Steele).
3. GEORGE WHITFIELD (Steele); d. Aug. 27, 1863, of disease contracted at Camp Chase.

1865. ASHUR B. CRANE[7] [1053], (Cyrus,[6] Samuel,[5] Noah,[4] Nathaniel,[3] Azariah,[2] Jasper[1]), married 1st, ———, daughter of Joshua Baldwin; 2d, Joanna Harrison, daughter of Samuel and Mary (Crane) Harrison. She was born in 1811. Children:

1866—1. JOSIAH.
1867—2. SARAH.
1868—3. WILLIAM.
1869—4. MARY.
1870—5. LUCY.
1871—6. PRUDENCE.
1872—7. JOSHUA.
1873—8. HENRY.
1874—9. ELIHU.

1875. ELIZABETH M. CRANE[7] [1057], (Cyrus,[6] Samuel,[5] Noah,[4] Nathaniel,[3] Azariah,[2] Jasper[1]), married Aaron Baldwin, March 7, 1843. Children :

1. SARAH (Baldwin), b. March 13, 1844.
2. IDA HANNAH MARIA (Baldwin), b. June 26, 1845.
3. STEPHEN (Baldwin), b. May 22, 1847.
4. LUCASPE CAROLINE (Baldwin), b. Sept. 17, 1852.
5. GEORGE P. (Baldwin), b. April, 1855.
6. JONAH (Baldwin), } twins, b. Feb. 4, 1858.
7. SILAS K. (Baldwin), }
8. MARCUS Y. (Baldwin), b. Dec. 13, 1862.

1876. SAMUEL CRANE[7] [1062], (Nathaniel S.,[6] Samuel,[5] Noah,[4] Nathaniel,[3] Azariah,[2] Jasper[1]), married Maria Pierson in 1834. She was born in 1813. Children :

1877—1. JANE L., b. 1836; m. —— Steel.
1878—2. NATHANIEL NELSON, b. 1838; m. Euphronia Collier.
1879—3. A. M. GIBSON, b. 1841.
1880—4. ELIZA C., b. 1847; m. —— Pool.

1881. CALEB S. CRANE[7] [1064], (Nathaniel S.,[6] Samuel,[5] Noah,[4] Nathaniel,[3] Azariah,[2] Jasper[1]), married Rhoda M. Dodd in 1838. She died in 1848, aged 32. He was killed by being kicked by a horse, Aug. 30, 1851, while on his way from Ohio to sell his father-in-law Aaron Dodd's farm, the latter having been killed by a blow from a windlass while digging a well. Children :

1882—1. AARON D.
1883—2. HENRY D.
1884—3. MARIA D. } twins.
1885—4. LOUISA W. }

1886. HENRY WILSON CRANE[7] [1065], (Nathaniel S.,[6] Samuel,[5] Noah,[4] Nathaniel,[3] Azariah,[2] Jasper[1]), married at Montville, N. J., March 31, 1842, Sarah Ann Duryea. She was born there Dec. 16, 1821. He was a farmer and contractor, and settled in Boonton, N. J., where all their children except the eldest were born. Gilbert D. was born in Caldwell. Children :

1887—1. GILBERT DURYEA, b. Feb. 5, 1844.
1888—2. CORNELIA JANE, b. Dec. 19, 1846; d. April 9, 1851.
1889—3. EDWARD WILSON, b. Oct. 26, 1849; d. Nov. 30, 1854.
1890—4. LAURA AUGUSTA, b. July 21, 1852.
1891—5. MARY LEE, b. May 3, 1856.
1892—6. CARRIE WILSON, b. Oct. 8, 1859.

1893. JANE ELIZA CRANE[7] [1066], (Nathaniel S.,[6] Samuel,[5] Noah,[4] Nathaniel,[3] Azariah,[2] Jasper[1]), married Caleb N. Pierson in 1839. Children :

1. JOSEPH (Pierson).
2. MARIA (Pierson).
3. JULIA (Pierson).
4. JANETTE (Pierson).
5. WALTER (Pierson).
6. —— (Pierson).
7. CALEB (Pierson).
8. JOHN D. (Pierson).

1894.   James H. Crane[7] [1068], (Nathaniel S.,[6] Samuel,[5] Noah,[4] Nathaniel,[3] Azariah,[2] Jasper[1]), married Abbie Harrison. Children :

1895—1. WILLIE; d. 1850, aged 11 months.
1896—2. ELLA, b. July 8, 1852.

1897.   Mary C. Crane[7] [1079], (Timothy A.,[6] Aaron,[5] Job,[4] Azariah,[3] Azariah,[2] Jasper[1]), married Samuel D. Mead. Children :

  1. HARRIET M. (Mead).
  2. CAROLINE (Mead).
  3. JACOB K. (Mead); m. Children:
    1. CATHERINE (Mead).
    2. MARY C. (Mead).
  4. HORACE C. (Mead).
  5. SARAH G. (Mead).
  6. J. ELLSWORTH (Mead); m. Children:
    1. J. ELLSWORTH, Jr. (Mead).
    2. JACOB K. (Mead).
    3. JENNIE F. (Mead).
  7. ELIZABETH C. (Mead).

1898.   Isaac Crane[7] [1080], (Timothy A.,[6] Aaron,[5] Job,[4] Azariah,[3] Azariah,[2] Jasper[1]), married Emma Crane. Children :

1899—1. EMMA.
1900—2. TIMOTHY A.

1901.   James C. Crane[7] [1082], (Timothy A..[6] Aaron,[5] Job,[4] Azariah,[3] Azariah,[2] Jasper[1]), married Grace Crane. Child :

1902—1. GRACE.

1903.   Smith Emons Crane[7] [1085], (Elias B.,[6] Aaron,[5] Job,[4] Azariah,[3] Azariah,[2] Jasper[1]), married Aug. 20, 1835, Phebe C. Beach. She was born 1811, and died in 1883. He died in 1854. Children :

1904—1. ANNA ALABAMA, b. 1837; m. Nov. 4,. 1856, Benj. Hard; d. 1859.
1905—2. ELIAS BEACH, b. 1838.
1906—3. FREDERICK EMONS, b. 1830.
1907—4. MARY VANCE. b. 1841.
1908—5. HENRY WILBER, b. 1846; d. 1866.
1909—6. AMZI BEACH, b. 1849.

1910.   George Augustus Crane[7] [1087], (Elias B.,[6] Aaron,[5] Job,[4] Azariah,[3] Azariah,[2] Jasper[1]), married ———. He died 1891. Child :

1911—1. LIZZIE CONGER; m. April 24, 1884, David A. Wooley.

1912.   Charles Stanton Crane[7] [1090], (Elias B.,[6] Aaron,[5] Job,[4] Azariah,[3] Azariah,[2] Jasper[1]), married ———. Children :

1913—1. CHARLES HARVEY, b. 1857; d. 1881.
1914—2. ANNA E., b. 1859.
1915—3. BELL D., b. 1864; d. 1871.
1916—4. KATE OSBOURNE, b. 1868; d. 1892.
1917—5. BESSIE DEAN, b. 1872.

1918. ZEBINA CRANE[7] [1094], (Jacob G.,[6] Zebina,[5] Gamaliel,[4] Azariah,[3] Azariah,[2] Jasper[1]), married Jan. 17, 1844, Hannah Peer, daughter of Thomas Peer, of Williamson, Wayne Co., N. Y., and settled in Arcadia, where they resided for a number of years, then removed to Marion. May 15, 1870, his first wife died, and he married 2d, March 23, 1871, Mary Ann Cogswell, daughter of Giles Cogswell. Mr. Crane was a farmer, but late years has lived in the village of Marion. Children:

1919—1. DEWITT C., b. Nov. 8, 1844.
1920—2. EMILY P., b. Feb. 10, 1846.
1921—3. ALONZO B., b. Nov. 11, 1852; m. Lucy L. Niles, Nov. 11, . 1874.
1922—4. MARY A., b. May 17, 1855.

1923. MYRON CRANE[7] [1095], (Jacob G.,[6] Zebina,[5] Gamaliel,[4] Azariah,[3] Azariah,[2] Jasper[1]), married Feb. 26, 1845, Gertrude Hoagland, and removed to one of the western States. He died Nov. 20, 1852. The widow with her three children returned to Wayne Co., N. Y.; she afterwards married William Cogswell, and settled in Williamson. Children:

1924—1. ELIZABETH J., b. Feb. 8, 1846; d. March 24, 1872.
1925—2. WILLIAM ALPHONZO, b. Jan. 4, 1850.
1926—3. C. ELLEN, b. May 13, 1853.

1927. CALEB CRANE[7] [1097], (Jacob G.,[6] Zebina,[5] Gamaliel,[4] Azariah,[3] Azariah,[2] Jasper[1]), married 1st, Harriet Sweezey, March 19, 1846, and settled in the western part of Walworth, N. Y.; a farmer. She died leaving two children. He married 2d, Mary J. Shaw, April 15, 1852; she also died leaving two children, and he married 3rd, Irena Shaw, sister of his second wife, Oct. 10, 1858. He died Sept. 18, 1894. Children:

1928—1. MARIA E., b. Dec. 16, 1846; d. Dec. 22, 1846.
1929—2. MARION F., b. Nov. 3, 1848.
1930—3. JAMES M., b. Sept. 19, 1853.
1931—4. MYRON S., b. Oct. 8, 1854; d. Oct. 6, 1855.
1932—5. MARY A., b. Oct. 5, 1859.
1933—6. WILLIAM C., b. May 11, 1864; m. Lillian B. Smith, March 4, 1891.

1934. ALONZO CRANE[7] [1101], (Jacob G.,[6] Zebina,[5] Gamaliel,[4] Azariah,[3] Azariah,[2] Jasper[1]), married March 21, 1857, Laura Stebbins, and for a time lived in Marion, N. Y., but purchased a farm in Walworth, Wayne Co., about half a mile south of the village, and removed there. For a number of terms has held the office of commissioner of highways to the satisfaction of his constituents. Child:

1935—1. MILLIE L., b. May 2, 1878.

1936. J. SMITH CRANE[7] [1102], (Jacob G.,[6] Zebina,[5] Gamaliel,[4] Azariah,[3] Azariah,[2] Jasper[1]), married 1st, Louisa Dann, March 1, 1863. She died having had one child. He married 2d, Philena Orcutt, Dec. 28, 1870. Children:

1937—1. JACOB ASA, b. Feb. 6, 1864.

1938—2. ANNA LOUISA, b. Nov. 8, 1871.
1939—3. C. BENSON, b. Dec. 6, 1878.

1940. FREDERICK S. CRANE[7] [1131], (David,[6] Zebina,[5] Gamaliel,[4] Azariah,[3] Azariah,[2] Jasper[1]), married Mary Bristol, Dec. 20, 1855. She died July 18, 1887, and he married 2d, Melvina S. Lord, May 20, 1896. Children:

1941—1. HIRAM D., b. Nov. 3, 1856.
1942—2. FRANK H., b. May 13, 1858; d. Sept. 25, 1895.
1943—3. MYRON F., b. March 7, 1860.
1944—4. S. JANETTE, b. April 5, 1863.
1945—5. CARRIE MAY, b. Feb. 5, 1869.

1946. FRANCES CRANE[7] [1132], (David,[6] Zebina,[5] Gamaliel,[4] Azariah,[3] Azariah,[2] Jasper[1]), married Giles Strong, Oct. 1, 1855. Children:

1. EDWARD C. (Strong), b. Oct. 20, 1856.
2. WILBER E. (Strong), b. Dec. 1, 1859; d. Nov. 6, 1869.
3. NETTIE E. (Strong), b. Feb. 8, 1863.
4. MERWIN W. (Strong), b. Feb. 6, 1877.

1947. EDWARD C. STRONG [1];·m. Addie E. Ferry, Dec. 31, 1878
Children:
1. BERTHA (Strong), b. Nov. 25, 1879.
2. MAY (Strong), b. April 28, 1883; d. May 3, 1883.
3. ETHEL MAY (Strong), b. Nov. 8, 1884.
4. ALICE MYRTLE (Strong), b. March 14, 1888.
5. CHARLES EDWARD (Strong), b. Nov. 5, 1889.

1948. NETTIE E. STRONG [3]; m. Edward C. Jenkins, Nov. 30, 1887.
Child:
1. BERTHA (Jenkins), b. April 4, 1889.

1949. EDGAR G. CRANE[7] [1133], (David,[6] Zebina,[5] Gamaliel,[4] Azariah,[3] Azariah,[2] Jasper[1]), married Celinda Griswold, Jan. 13, 1869. Children:

1950—1. DAVID N., b. Nov. 29, 1869; d. April 21, 1872.
1951—2. GEORGE S., b. Dec. 16, 1871; d. May 9, 1883.
1952—3. EDITH M., b. Aug. 30, 1874.
1953—4. CHARLES F., b. Sept. 4, 1877.
1954—5. EDGAR G., b. Nov. 11, 1882.
1955—6. HARRY B., b. Nov. 13, 1886.

1956. LAURA EMMA CRANE[7] [1136], (David,[6] Zebina,[5] Gamaliel,[4] Azariah,[3] Azariah,[2] Jasper[1]), married George M. Sweezey, March 7, 1867. Children:

1. KITTIE MAY (Sweezey), b. Jan. 6, 1868; m. Edgar T. Luce, May 11, 1887.
2. LILLA F. (Sweezey), b. Aug. 29, 1874; m. Frank Sherman Mosher, Oct. 14, 1896.

1957. DAVID HENRY CRANE[7] [1137], (David,[6] Zebina,[5] Gamaliel,[4] Azariah,[3] Azariah,[2] Jasper[1]), married Mary L. Hutchins, Feb. 9, 1871. She died Feb. 7, 1872, and he married 2d, Sarah Maria Hicks, Jan. 27, 1875. Children:

1958—1. FRED, b. Jan. 27, 1872; d. Feb. 27, 1872.
1959—2. MARY ALMIRA, b. Dec. 25, 1877.

1960—3. ARTHUR HICKS, b. Nov. 20, 1880.
1961—4. ORIN DAVID, b. Dec. 17, 1890.

1962. ANDREW J. CRANE[7] [1139], (Obediah,[6] Zebina,[5] Gamaliel,[4] Azariah,[3] Azariah,[2] Jasper[1]), married Lodena Locey. He died Feb. 3, 1874. Children:

1963—1. ALBERT.
1964—2. WILLIAM.
1965—3. FRANKLIN.
1966—4. CHARLES OLIVER.
1967—5. FREDERICK.
1968—6. MAY.

1969. DIANA MARIA CRANE[7] [1140], (Obediah,[6] Zebina,[5] Gamaliel,[4] Azariah,[3] Azariah,[2] Jasper[1]), married Philo J. Crane. Children:

1970—1. RIENZA.
1970½-2. ARISTINE.

1971. WILLIAM ALONZO CRANE[7] [1141], (Obediah,[6] Zebina,[5] Gamaliel,[4] Azariah,[3] Azariah,[2] Jasper[1]), married Elizabeth Purchase, April 2, 1857. He was born in Saginaw, Mich., and was a farmer and teacher. Children:

1972—1. WILLIAM ERASTUS, b. March 14, 1858.
1973—2. RILEY LEONARD, b. Oct. 26, 1860.
1974—3. HIRAM AMBROSE, b. Feb. 13, 1863.
1975—4. MARY ALICE, b. July 30, 1869; m. Myron T. Dodge, Feb. 14, 1891.
1976—5. MILO ALBERT, b. Jan. 21, 1874.
1977—6. BENJAMIN F., b. April 6, 1876.
1978—7. LURA ETHEL, b. May 13, 1885.

1979. MARTHA D. CRANE[7] [1142], (Obediah,[6] Zebina,[5] Gamaliel,[4] Azariah,[3] Azariah,[2] Jasper[1]), married Franklin Crowell. Children:

1. MARY (Crowell), b. Nov. 12, 1861; m. Henry Chayney.
2. WILLIAM H. (Crowell), b. Dec. 20, 1863.
3. IDA (Crowell), b. March 15, 1868.
4. MYRTLE (Crowell), b. Feb. 23, 1873; m. Chas. Rieder.

1980. LYMAN G. CRANE[7] [1145], (Obediah,[6] Zebina,[5] Gamaliel,[4] Azariah,[3] Azariah,[2] Jasper[1]), married Sarah J. Webster, Jan. 3, 1870. Children:

1981—1. LILLA MAY, b. Jan. 8, 1872.
1982—2. VIDA M., b. May 15, 1873.
1983—3. GERTRUDE E., b. July 7, 1874.
1984—4. HATTIE B., b. April 24, 1876.
1985—5. NORA M., b. Dec. 25, 1877.
1986—6. JESSIE D., b. Nov. 3, 1880.
1987—7. DAISY J., b. Nov. 18, 1881.
1988—8. ERNEST L., b. April 20, 1883; d. Sept. 8, 1883.
1989—9. LYMAN G., b. March 20, 1885.

1990. NORMAN CRANE[7] [1148], (Obediah,[6] Zebina,[5] Gamaliel,[4] Azariah,[3] Azariah,[2] Jasper[1]), married Alice Colby, Feb. 12, 1874. He died Dec. 18, 1885. Children:

1991—1. MAUD, b. Feb. 10, 1876.

39

1992—2. NELLIE, b. Aug. 28, 1878.
1993—3. ALVIN N., b. Sept. 24, 1885.

1994. EMMA P. CRANE[7] [1149], (Obediah,[6] Zebina,[5] Gamaliel,[4] Azariah,[3] Azariah,[2] Jasper[1]), married Nathan Knight, Dec. 14, 1875.   Children:

1. LULU J. (Knight), b. Sept. 13, 1879.
2. PEARL (Knight), b. Nov. 20, 1886.

1995. M. A. ADELAIDE CRANE[7] [1176], (Aaron G.,[6] Obediah,[5] Gamaliel,[4] Azariah,[3] Azariah,[2] Jasper[1]), married Jan. 2, 1863, Henry Williams, who died within a month of their marriage.   She married 2d, in Florence, Italy, May 30, 1877, Parla La Villa.   Child:

1. ANNALETTA FRANCESCA CECILIA ITALIA (La Villa).

1996. THOMAS S. CRANE[7] [1177], (Aaron G.,[6] Obediah,[5] Gamaliel,[4] Azariah,[3] Azariah,[2] Jasper[1]), married in Elizabeth, N. J., Oct. 7, 1863, Anna M. Day.   Children:

1997—1. WILLIAM F. D., b. Feb. 22, 186-.
1998—2. ADELAIDE W.
1999—3. MYRA K.
2000—4. LOUISE D.
2001—5. ETHEL WALDRON.

2002. VIRGINIA EWING CRANE[7] [1180], (Aaron G.,[6] Obediah,[5] Gamaliel,[4] Azariah,[3] Azariah,[2] Jasper[1]), married May 16, 1866, Charles Edwin Gilbert.   He was born in Wallingford, Conn., Nov. 8, 1836.   They settled in Hartford, Conn., where they now (1897) reside.   Children:

1. ALBERT WALDRON (Gilbert), b. Nov. 3, 1867.
2. EDWIN RANDOLPH (Gilbert), b. Jan. 18, 1871.
3. CHARLES ALLAN (Gilbert), b. Sept. 9, 1873.

2003. NOAH CRANE[7] [1191], (Nehemiah,[6] John R.,[5] Ezekiel,[4] Azariah,[3] Azariah,[2] Jasper[1]), married Kate A. Matthews.   He was a tanner and currier, doing business in Newark, but residing in Bloomfield, N. J.   Children:

2004—1. E——— J———; residence 229 W. 42d Street, New York city.
2005—2. F——— G———; residence, Chicago, Ill.
2006—3. A daughter, Mrs. C. S. MILLER, wife of Judge Miller, of Ottawa, Ill.

2007. EZRA CRANE[7] [1193], (Samuel,[6] Amos,[5] Moses,[4] Azariah,[3] Azariah,[2] Jasper[1]), married Hetty Brown.   Lived near Rahway, N. J.   Children:

2008—1. AMOS; m. in Cincinnati.
2009—2. MARY; m. Job Tower.
2010—3. JACOB.
2011—4. JAMES.
2012—5. CATHARINE; m. ———, son of Enos Whitehead.

2013. PHEBE CRANE[7] [1194], (Samuel,[6] Amos,[5] Moses,[4]

Azariah,[3] Azariah,[2] Jasper[1]), married Benjamin Garthwait. She died July 3, 1864. Children:

1. MARY ANN (Garthwait).
2. ABBY (Garthwait).
3. SARAH CATHARINE (Garthwait); m. Mr. Spader, Staten Island.

2014. COOPER WOODRUFF CRANE[7] [1195], (Samuel,[6] Amos,[5] Moses,[4] Azariah,[3] Azariah,[2] Jasper[1]), married Ann Meeker. Children:

2015—1. CLARK S., b. March 24, 1829; m. ——— in St. Louis, Mo.
2016—2. JULIA, b. Sept. 26, 1830; m. James W. Palmer; went to California.
2017—3. ABRAHAM S., b. Dec. 24, 1831; went to St. Louis, Mo.
2018—4. HARVEY, b. July 13, 1834; m. Mary ———; had two children.

2019. ALFRED CRANE[7] [1233], (Jonas,[6] Ezekiel,[5] Moses,[4] Azariah,[3] Azariah,[2] Jasper[1]), born at Seneca County, N. Y.; married in Paw Paw, Mich., Oct. 9, 1856, Clarissa Loring. She was born Feb. 14, 1835. He is a farmer. Residence at Oshtemo, Mich. Children:

2020—1. GILES A., b. Aug. 29, 1857; d. Nov. 29, 1883.
2021—2. JONA. B., b. March 2, 1873.

2022. JULIANN CRANE[7] [1239], Benjamin,[6] Benjamin,[5] Stephen,[4] Azariah,[3] Azariah,[2] Jasper[1]), married Martin Vanduyne. Children:

1. ORVIL (Vanduyne).
2. HORACE (Vanduyne).
3. SARAH FRANCES (Vanduyne).
4. ELIZABETH ELLEN (Vanduyne).
5. HARRIET JANE (Vanduyne).
6. HETTY MARIA (Vanduyne).
7. SIMEON (Vanduyne).
8. LUCINDA ANN (Vanduyne).

2023. TIMOTHY W. CRANE[7] [1240], (Benjamin,[6] Benjamin,[5] Stephen,[4] Azariah,[3] Azariah,[2] Jasper[1]), married 1st, Jane Martin; 2d, Catherine Courter. He was a farmer. Children:

2024—1. ANDREW.
2025—2. GEORGE.
2026—3. RHODA.
2027—4. BENJAMIN.
2028—5. NEWTON.
2029—6. MANUS.
2030—7. MARY.
2031—8. SARAH.
2032—9. CATHARINE.

2033. LUCINDA CRANE[7] [1241], (Benjamin,[6] Benjamin,[5] Stephen,[4] Azariah,[3] Azariah,[2] Jasper[1]), married Alexander Freeman, a tinsmith, at Orange, N. J. Children:

1. ADISON (Freeman).
2. JENEVIRA (Freeman).
3. WILBERFORCE (Freeman).

2034. HETTY M. CRANE[7] [1242], (Benjamin,[6] Benjamin,[5] Stephen,[4] Azariah,[3] Azariah,[2] Jasper[1]), married Abram C. Vanduyne, a farmer. Children:

1. MARTHY ANN (Vanduyne).
2. LUCINDA (Vanduyne).
3. JOHN WILSON (Vanduyne).

2035. HARRIET CRANE[7] [1243], (Benjamin,[6] Benjamin,[5] Stephen,[4] Azariah,[3] Azariah,[2] Jasper[1]), married Stephen Vanduyne, a carpenter. Children:

1. NICHOLAS (Vanduyne).
2. MARYETTA (Vanduyne).

2036. ELIZABETH CRANE[7] [1244], (Benjamin,[6] Benjamin,[5] Stephen,[4] Azariah,[3] Azariah,[2] Jasper[1]), married Garrit Miller, a farmer. Child:

1. EPHRAIM (Miller).

2037. ELLEN CRANE[7] [1245], (Benjamin,[6] Benjamin,[5] Stephen,[4] Azariah,[3] Azariah,[2] Jasper[1]), married Enos W. Martin, a blacksmith, at Franklin. Children:

1. SUSAN (Martin).
2. RHODA (Martin).
3. HARRIET FLORINDA (Martin).

2038. BENJAMIN F. CRANE[7] [1246], (Benjamin,[6] Benjamin,[5] Stephen,[4] Azariah,[3] Azariah,[2] Jasper[1]), married in Newark, N. J., Nov. 15, 1853, Sarah M. Eagles. She was born at that place May 7, 1832. He is a real estate agent. Residence at Newark. Children:

2039—1. LAURA E.
2040—2. MARILLA.
2041—3. W. RAE.
2042—4. ANNA M.
2043—5. EUGENE E.
2044—6. BENJAMIN F.
2045—7. LUNORA.
2046—8. EADITH.

2047. AMZI CRANE[7] [1280], (William,[6] Jeremiah,[5] Stephen,[4] Azariah,[3] Azariah,[2] Jasper[1]), married Oct. 17, 1853, Eleanor L., daughter of Hezekiah and Mary Eliza Thompson. She was born Sept. 17, 1833. Children:

2048—1. ELLA FRANCES, b. July 30, 1854.
2049—2. HENRIETTA EAGLES, b. March 28, 1856; m. Capt. J. W. Wescott, Dec. 30, 1878, at Detroit, Mich.
2050—3. WILLIAM THOMPSON, b. Oct. 1, 1858.
2051—4. CHARLES AMZI, b. May 31, 1871.
2052—5. FREDERICK THOMPSON, b. Dec. 1, 1875.

2053. RICHARD THERON CRANE[7] [1282], (William,[6] Jeremiah,[5] Stephen,[4] Azariah,[3] Azariah,[2] Jasper[1]), married Mary H. Cavannah. Children:

2054—1. FREDERICK F.
2055—2. WILLIAM A. C.

2056—3. LIZZIE.
2057—4. EMMA H.

2058. JARVIS G. CRANE[7] [1288], (Ira,[6] Jeremiah,[5] Stephen,[4] Azariah,[3] Azariah,[2] Jasper[1]), married Henrietta Smith.
Children :

2059—1. IRA SEYMOUR; m., and lives in Mont Clair, N. J.
2060—2. FRANK SMITH; m., and lives in Mont Clair, N. J.
2061—3. ALICE BOYD; m., and lives in Mont Clair, N. J.

2062. ANGELINE CRANE[7] [1289], (Ira,[6] Jeremiah,[5] Stephen,[4] Azariah,[3] Azariah,[2] Jasper[1]), married Albert W. Harrison, Oct. 13, 1858. He survives her, and resides near Alexandria, Va., She died Sept. 24, 1896. Children :

1. CLARA B. (Harrison).
2. MARGARET N. (Harrison); m. J. N. Gibbs.
3. MARY C. (Harrison).
4. ALBERT R. (Harrison).

2063. ISRAEL CRANE[7] [1290], (Ira,[6] Jeremiah,[5] Stephen,[4] Azariah,[3] Azariah,[2] Jasper[1]), went from Mont Clair, N. J., to Carbondale, Pa., in the year 1864, and married Dec. 19, 1867, Mary Grant Lathrope. About that time he engaged in the dry goods trade in that place, thus laying the foundation of one of the most prosperous and extensive houses in its line in Carbondale, now known as the Israel Crane Company, dealers in dry goods and carpetings. Mr. Crane died there, Sept. 5, 1891; since which time the business has been continued by the family, under the direction of the eldest son, Dwight L. Children :

2064—1. MARGARET NORWOOD, b. Nov. 12, 1870; d. Aug. 4, 1878.
2065—2. DWIGHT LATHROPE, b. Dec. 12, 1872.
2066—3. MARION FRASER, b. Sept. 7, 1875.
2067—4. ALBERT HARRISON, b. Oct. 3, 1877.

2068. WILLIAM CAREY CRANE, D.D.[7] [1300], (William,[6] Rufus,[5] Jonas,[4] John,[3] Azariah,[2] Jasper[1]), married Catherine Sheppard. He was president of Baylor University, Independence, Tex. Died in 1865. Children :

2069—1. WILLIAM CAREY; m., and has two sons.
2070—2. ANNIE; m., and has three sons and a daughter.
2071—3. CHARLES JUDSON, of the U. S. Army.
2072—4. JAMES THOMAS.
2073—5. GORDON SHEPPARD.
2074—6. BALFOUR DORSETT.
2075—7. ROYSTON CAMPBELL.
2076—8. HARRIET BURNS.

2077. MARY DORSETT CRANE[7] [1301], (William,[6] Rufus,[5] Jonas,[4] John,[3] Azariah,[2] Jasper[1]), married Thomas H. Edmunds. She died in 1864. Children :

1. MARY (Edmunds).
2. THOMAS (Edmunds); supposed to have been drowned during the late war.
3. JAMES (Edmunds).
4. JOSEPHINE (Edmunds).
5. HARRIET (Edmunds); m. Williams S. Reins.

2078. JAMES EDMUNDS [3]; m. Anna Keyser. Children:
1. MARY (Edmunds).
2. CHARLES (Edmunds).
3. ANNA (Edmunds).
4. GRACE (Edmunds).
5. HELEN (Edmunds).
6. JAMES (Edmunds).

2079. ADONIRAM JUDSON CRANE[7] [1302], (William,[6] Rufus,[5] Jonas,[4] John,[3] Azariah,[2] Jasper[1]), married 1st, Susan Maria Clark; 2d, Sarah Ellen Smith. He was a' lawyer at Richmond, Va.; died Jan. 3, 1867; leaving two children by each wife.
Children:
2080—1. CHARLES THOMAS CLARK.
2081—2. MARIA LOVISA; m. Daniel C. Woods; no children.
2082—3. LUCY.
2083—4. ARTHUR.

2084. ANDREW FULLER CRANE[7] [1304], (William,[6] Rufus,[5] Jonas,[4] John,[3] Azariah,[2] Jasper[1]), married March 23, 1840, Mary Clement Lovering, at Baltimore, Md. Was engaged in business with his father. She was born at Georgetown, D. C.,. Nov. 30, 1819. He died in 1885, at which time his firm was one of the most extensive importers of hides in the country.
Children:
2085—1. WILLIAM FULLER, b. June 11, 1842.
2086—2. MARY.
2087—3. ANDREW F.
2088—4. CHARLES CAMPBELL.
2089—5. FLORENCE.
2090—6. ALICE.

2091. HARRIET NEWELL CRANE[7] [1305], (William,[6] Rufus,[5] Jonas,[4] John,[3] Azariah,[2] Jasper[1]), married Francis Burns, of Baltimore, Md. He died Feb., 1866. Children:
1. FRANCIS (Burns).
2. ELIZABETH HIGHLANDS (Burns).

2092. GEORGE WHITFIELD CRANE[7] [1306], (William,[6] Rufus,[5] Jonas,[4] John,[3] Azariah,[2] Jasper[1]), married in California, Encarnacian de Ortega, and died there in 1867. Children:
2093—1. WILLIAM.
2094—2. LYDIA.
2095—3. VIRGINIA.

2096. JAMES CONWAY CRANE[7] [1311], (William,[6] Rufus,[5] Jonas,[4] John,[3] Azariah,[2] Jasper[1]), married Virginia Hall. He died in 1888. Child:
2097—1. JEAN DANIEL.

2098. SARAH ANN CRANE[7] [1316], (Richard M.,[6] Rufus,[5] Jonas,[4] John,[3] Azariah,[2] Jasper[1]), married Samuel Crane Burnett, of Morristown, N. J. Child:
1. LIZZIE (Burnett).

2099. MARY ELIZABETH CRANE[7] [1319], (Richard M.,[6] Rufus,[5] Jonas,[4] John,[3] Azariah,[2] Jasper[1]), married Robert B. Harthorne. Children :

1. MARY (Harthorne).
2. FREDERICK (Harthorne).

2100. SAMUEL PIERSON CRANE[7] [1320], (Richard M.,[6] Rufus,[5] Jonas,[4] John,[3] Azariah,[2] Jasper[1]), married Hellen Lockwood, in California, whither he went in 1849. Children :

2101—1. MARY.
2102—2. EMMA.

2103. CAROLINE AMELIA CRANE[7] [1321], (Richard M.,[6] Rufus,[5] Jonas,[4] John,[3] Azariah,[2] Jasper[1]), married Robert M. Hunter, of Newark, N. J. Children :

1. LIZZIE (Hunter) ; d. young.
2. HELLEN AMELIA (Hunter).
3. SAMUEL CRANE (Hunter).
4. ROBERT (Hunter).
5. HENRY (Hunter).

2104. CATHERINE MATILDA CRANE[7] [1324], (Richard M.,[6] Rufus,[5] Jonas,[4] John,[3] Azariah,[2] Jasper[1]), married John Mulford. Children :

1. MILLIARD M. (Mulford).
2. ROBERT H. (Mulford).
3. MARY (Mulford).
4. SARAH A. (Mulford).

2105. FRANCES M. CRANE[7] [1325], (Richard M.,[6] Rufus,[5] Jonas,[4] John,[3] Azariah,[2] Jasper[1]), married William N. Truax, of New York. Children :

1. RICHARD M. (Truax).
2. FANNIE (Truax).

2106. DAVID ROPER CRANE[7] [1332], (James C.,[6] Rufus,[5] Jonas,[4] John,[3] Azariah,[2] Jasper[1]), married Julia Lumpkin, of Henrico Co., Va., in 1852. Child :

2107—1. JULIA BELLE; m. William C. Fleet, of King and Queen Co., Va.; residence, Huntsville, Tex. Five children.

2108. HENRY RAYLAND CRANE[7] [1336], (James C.,[6] Rufus,[5] Jonas,[4] John,[3] Azariah,[2] Jasper[1]), married Nov. 29, 1871, at Alberton, Baltimore Co., Md., Clara Merryman, who was born at that place Sept. 2, 1844. Mr. Crane served in 2d Corps, C. S. army, northern Virginia, from March 17, 1862, to April 9, 1865, and was wounded at the battle of Chancellorsville. For many years he has resided in Baltimore, Md., where he is engaged in insurance business. Children :

2109—1. LAURA MERRYMAN, b. Oct. 11, 1873.
2110—2. EDITH CAMPBELL, b. Dec. 17, 1876.
2111—3. CLARA ISABEL, b. Sept. 14, 1880.
2112—4. HELEN BOND, b. Sept. 17, 1886.

2113. ZADOCK SMITH CRANE[7] [1342], (Pierson,[6] Timothy,[5] Samuel,[4] John,[3] Azariah,[2] Jasper[1]), married Elizabeth Jennette Donnan. He was a farmer, and lived in Charlton, N. Y., where he was born. She was also born there Jan. 1, 1822. He died Dec. 23, 1872. Children:

2114—1. ALEXANDER, b. June 26, 1847; a magistrate, farmer and surveyor at Charlton, N. Y.
2115—2. WILLIAM PIERSON, b. Aug. 5, 1849; a farmer at Charlton, N. Y.

2116. ELIZA CRANE[7] [1346], (Jonas,[6] Timothy,[5] Samuel,[4] John,[3] Azariah,[2] Jasper[1]), married John Sanders. Children:

1. JONAS (Sanders).
2. FREDERICK (Sanders).
3. ALBERT (Sanders); m. Child:
    1. BELLE CLARA (Sanders).
4. JAMES (Sanders); m. Child:
    1. JOHN (Sanders).
5. MARGARET (Sanders).
6. MYRA (Sanders).

2117. ABBA CRANE[7] [1347], (Jonas,[6] Timothy,[5] Samuel,[4] John,[3] Azariah,[2] Jasper[1]), married Elisha Weld. Children:

1. LOIS (Weld).
2. MARY JANE (Weld).
3. FRANK (Weld).

2118. FREDERICK MYERS CRANE[7] [1357], (John,[6] Matthias,[5] John,[4] John,[3] Azariah,[2] Jasper[1]), married Mary Ann Fisher about the year 1840 in Noble County, Ohio. He was a blacksmith, and about 1858 removed with his family from near Lewisville, Monroe Co., Ohio, to Troy, Iowa, where he very soon after died. Children:

2119—1. MARY JANE, b. about 1844.
2120—2. RICHARD ELLIS, b. about 1848.
2121—3. WILLIAM BOWEN, b. March 14, 1850.

2122. JOSIAH FERRIS CRANE[7] [1358], (John,[6] Matthias,[5] John,[4] John,[3] Azariah,[2] Jasper[1]), married Ellee Ann Kiger in Green County, Pa., Sept. 11, 1845. She was born March 11, 1827, and died in Wetzel County, Va., Sept. 28, 1873. He was a farmer in Green County, Pa., but removed to Wetzel County, Va., about 1857. He was living at Porter's Falls in 1881. Children:

2123—1. MARY JANE, b. Sept. 23, 1847.
2124—2. JAMES K., b. April 25, 1849; m.; farmer.
2125—3. REBECCA ANN, b. April 30, 1851; m. 1873.
2126—4. JOHN T., b. Aug. 5, 1853; m. 1876; farmer.
2127—5. WILLIAM H., b. Jan. 9, 1856; farmer.
2128—6. EZRA S., b. Feb. 28, 1858; d. Oct. 21, 1877.
2129—7. MARTHA ELLEN, b. June 20, 1860; m. in Richie County, Va., 1877.
2130—8. GEORGE J., b. June 20, 1860.
2131—9. SARAH K., b. Oct. 4, 1862; m. 1878 in Richie County, Va.

2132-10. ELLEE ANN, b. Nov. 14, 1865.
2133-11. JOSIAH J., b. May 19, 1867.
2134-12. CHARLES G., b. Aug. 5, 1869.

2135. WILLIAM TANNER CRANE[7] [1360], (John,[6] Matthias,[5] John,[4] John,[3] Azariah,[2] Jasper[1]), married Jan. 1, 1857, at Carlinville, Ill., Eliza Wallace. She was born Aug. 27, 1837, in Sangamon County, Ill. They settled in Virden, Ill., then removed to Austin, Nev. He is a farmer and stock raiser. Residence at Coral Hill, Elkes Co., Nev. Children:

2136—1. GEORGE·WASHT, b. Jan. 5, 1858.
2137—2. SISSIE RAE, b. March 26, 1860; d. Aug. 6, 1861.
2138—3. KNOX A., b. Nov. 16, 1861.
2139—4. A son; d. in infancy.
2140—5. MARY E., b. April 18, 1865, in Austin, Nev.
2141—6. LIZZIE L., b. Jan. 28, 1867, in Austin, Nev.
2142—7. HENRY SHEPHERD, b. Feb. 14, 1869, in South Humboldt, Nev.
2143—8. EMMA FRANCIS, b. Jan. 28, 1871, in South Humboldt, Nev.
2144—9. CHARLES HUMBOLDT, b. Dec. 20, 1872, in South Humboldt, Nev.
2145-10. ANDREW BRADLEY, b. May 15, 1875, in South Humboldt, Nev.
2146-11. JENNEY B., b. Oct. 27, 1877, in South Humboldt, Nev.
2147-12. JAMES MONROE, b. May 11, 1879, in South Humboldt, Nev.

2148. ELLIS FREEMAN CRANE[7] [1363], (John,[6] Matthias,[5] John,[4] John,[3] Azariah,[2] Jasper[1]), married July 2, 1878, at Macomb, Ill., Mary Jane Crow, a native of Vinten County, Ohio. She was born Sept. 15, 1852. He is a farmer. Residence three miles southeast of Macomb, Ill. Child:

2149—1. WILLIAM ELLIS, b. July 25, 1879.

2150. JOHN A. CRANE[7] [1364], (John,[6] Matthias,[5] John,[4] John,[3] Azariah,[2] Jasper[1]), married 1st, Oct. 7, 1866, in Green County, Pa., Charlotty H. Calvert, who was born there Aug. 24, 1844. She died Jan. 26, 1871, in Shelby County, Mo. He married 2d, Mary A. Wilson in Adams County, Neb., Sept. 29, 1879. He is a farmer, and, after residing in Macomb, Ill., for a few years after marriage, removed to Nebraska, and settled in Blaineville. He served in Co. A, 84th Illinois Volunteer Infantry, from 1862 to 1865. Children:

2151—1. ANNIE B., b. Aug. 28, 1867, at Macomb, Ill.
2152—2. HARRY L., b. Sept. 6, 1869, at Macomb, Ill.

2153. JONAS CRANE[7] [1366], (Asa,[6] Jonas,[5] Benjamin,[4] John,[3] Azariah,[2] Jasper[1]), married Elizabeth Taylor. Children reside in Maryville, Mo. Children:

2154—1. HARVEY T.
2155—2. SARAH W.
2156—3. MARIA H.

2157. HANNAH W. CRANE[7] [1367], (Asa,[6] Jonas,[5] Benjamin,[4] John,[3] Azariah,[2] Jasper[1]), married Joseph W. Elliott, Oct. 1, 1842. He died in Jackson County, Ind., March 19, 1860. She died in Lucas County, Iowa, Feb. 19, 1870. Children:

1. HARVEY W. (Elliott).·
40

   2. AMANDA (Elliott), b. Dec. 27, 1844.
   3. PRESLEY O. (Elliott).
   4. OSCAR A. (Elliott).
   5. EMMA E. (Elliott).
   6. CALEB N. (Elliott).
   7. ELIZABETH (Elliott).
   8. MARY JOSEPHINE (Elliott).

  2158. AMANDA ELLIOTT [2]; m. James A. Holmes, April 8, 1868, in Jackson County, Ind. Children:
    1. WALTER EDMOND (Holmes).
    2. ARLEY MAY (Holmes).

  2159. ELIZA ANN CRANE[7] [1368], (Asa,[6] Jonas,[5] Benjamin,[4] John,[3] Azariah,[2] Jasper[1]), married Sylvester Wheadon. Children live at Colorado Springs, Col. Children:

   1. SOPHIA ELIZABETH (Wheadon).
   2. MARY (Wheadon).
   3. JERETTA (Wheadon).
   4. ASA (Wheadon).

  2160. HARVEY CRANE[7] [1369], (Asa,[6] Jonas,[5] Benjamin,[4] John,[3] Azariah,[2] Jasper[1]), married 1st, Eliza Forey, who died, leaving one child; married 2d, Mary Ann Young. Residence at Brownstown, Ind. Children:

2161—1. EVA.
2162—2. LUELLA.
2163—3. NANCY.
2164—4. HARRY.

  2165. VALINDER T. CRANE[7] [1373], (Joseph,[6] Jonas,[5] Benjamin,[4] John,[3] Azariah,[2] Jasper[1]), married Dec., 1855, Aaron F. Byarlay, of Jackson County, Ind., and soon removed from there to Warren County, Ill. He died Sept., 1869, and she married 2d, J. T. Lathrop in 1875. Residence at Roseville, Ill. Children:

   1. ALICE C. (Byarlay); d. in infancy.
   2. EDWIN R. (Byarlay); d. in 1869, aged 11 years.
   3. RHODA A. (Byarlay).
   4. MARY E. (Byarlay).
   5. JOHN M. (Byarlay); d. in infancy.
   6. ESTELLA W. (Byarlay); d. in infancy.
   7. AARON F. (Byarlay).

  2166. RHODA A. BYARLAY [3]; m. Dr. Edward H. Hope, of Red Clay, Georgia, in Dec., 1889. He d. May 29, 1893. She resides at Roseville, Ill. Child:
    1. NIDA (Hope).

  2167. MARY E. BYARLAY [4]; m. Rob H. Fallis, April, 1885. Reside in Chicago, Ill. Child:
    1. HELEN DAVY (Fallis), b. Feb. 7, 1889

  2168. ELIZABETH R. CRANE[7] [1375], (Joseph,[6] Jonas,[5] Benjamin,[4] John,[3] Azariah,[2] Jasper[1]), married William Stansfield in 1859 in Warren County, Ill. Residence at Roseville. Children:

   1. MARTHA (Stansfield).

2. GEORGE (Stansfield); d. in infancy.
3. VICTORIA (Stansfield).
4. BYRON (Stansfield); d. in infancy.
5. FLORA (Stansfield); lives in Hyde, Col.
6. EDWIN (Stansfield); m.; lives in Hyde, Col.
7. WILLIAM (Stansfield); lives in Hyde, Col.
8. CHARLIE (Stansfield); lives in Hyde, Col.
9. NELLIE (Stansfield); d. in infancy.

2169. MARTHA STANSFIELD [1]; m. Orrin McConnell; lives at Colorado Springs, Col. Children:
1. EDWIN (McConnell).
2. WILLIE (McConnell).
3. WALTER (McConnell).
4. VIRA (McConnell).

2170. VICTORIA STANSFIELD [3]; m. Robert Gray, of Roseville, Ill., 1891. Child:
1. EVA (Gray).

2171. ELECTA RIGGS CRANE[7] [1402], (David,[6] David,[5] Benjamin,[4] John,[3] Azariah,[2] Jasper[1]), married 1st, Dr. Goldsmith; 2d, Henry Green. Children:

1. MAGGIE (Goldsmith).
2. HATTIE (Green).
3. ALEXANDER (Green).
4. HENRY (Green).

2172. MAGGIE GOLDSMITH [1]; m. John Showerman. Children:
1. ESTHER (Showerman).
2. ALVIN (Showerman).

2173. NANCY CRANE[7] [1404], (David,[6] David,[5] Benjamin,[4] John,[3] Azariah,[2] Jasper[1]), married Morris Williams, March 1, 1863. Children:

1. JENNIE (Williams).
2. HELEN A. (Williams); m. John L. Hall.

2174. JENNIE WILLIAMS [1]; m. Emery Lum. Children:
1. MORRIS W. (Lum).
2. CHARLES E. (Lum).
3. LOUIS E. (Lum).

2175. HELEN A. CRANE[7] [1406], (David,[6] David,[5] Benjamin,[4] John,[3] Azariah,[2] Jasper[1]), married John McNernie. Children:

1. BLANCH (McNernie).
2. JOHN (McNernie).
3. WILLIAM (McNernie); d., aged 16 years.
4. DAVID (McNernie).
5. WALTER (McNernie).

2176. DAVID CRANE[7] [1407], (David,[6] David,[5] Benjamin,[4] John,[3] Azariah,[2] Jasper[1]), married Margaret Cloehitey. Children:

2177—1. MORRIS W.
2178—2. JOHN.
2179—3. HELEN.
2180—4. HAZEL.
2181—5. ALEXANDER.

2182. JULIA ANN CRANE[7] [1411], (Obediah M.,[6] Caleb C.,[5] Benjamin,[4] John,[3] Azariah,[2] Jasper[1]), married William Buck, March 28, 1852. He is a farmer. Residence at first in Illinois, but removed to Minnesota previous to the birth of their second child. Children:

1. JOHN (Buck), b. Dec. 31, 1852; d. 1860.
2. EDWARD (Buck), b. Dec. 13, 1854.
3. ROSA A. (Buck), b. Sept. 26, 1856.
4. FRANK (BUCK), b. Sept. 6, 1858; d. 1867.
5. HARRIET E. (Buck), b. Oct. 21, 1863.

2183. CHARLES CRANE[7] [1412], (Obediah M.,[6] Caleb C.,[5] Benjamin,[4] John,[3] Azariah,[2] Jasper[1]), married 1st, Eloise M. Edwards, a native of Vermont, born 1851. She died, and he married 2d, Myra Ford, a native of Michigan, born in 1852. He enlisted in 1861 for three years in the 93d Illinois regiment. In the fall of 1864 he enlisted in the 4th Minnesota volunteers. He is a farmer, and resides at Stewartsville, Minn. Children:

2184—1. HERBERT E.
2185—2. G—— D——.

2186. ISAAC B. CRANE[7] [1414], (Caleb C.,[6] Caleb C.,[5] Benjamin,[4] John,[3] Azariah,[2] Jasper[1]), married Virginia A. Smith in 1852. Residence at Brooklyn, N. Y. Children:

2187—1. ISAAC B.
2188—2. VIRGINIA A.

2189. CALEB CAMP CRANE[7] [1416], (Caleb C.,[6] Caleb C.,[5] Benjamin,[4] John,[3] Azariah,[2] Jasper[1]), was born in New York city. Married at Saratoga in 1863 Emily J. Warner. She was born in 1839. In 1864 they removed to Minnesota, and settled in Austin. In 1878 they removed to Anoka, and in 1889 to Minneapolis, where he now resides. For many years he has been in the employ, as secretary and manager, for Hon. W. D. Washburn. Child:

2190—1. ARCHIBALD A., b. 1866, in Austin, Minn. Removed with his parents in 1878 to Anoka, and in 1883 entered the employ of the Anoka National Bank. Nine years later (1887) he went to Minneapolis to accept a situation as cashier of the Flour City National Bank. Here he remained until the year 1895, when he took the position of assistant cashier of the National Bank of Commerce, which has a capital of one million dollars. He married in 1890 Fannie Chase Stevens.

2191. NANCY CRANE[7] [1437], (Abner,[6] Benjamin,[5] Benjamin,[4] Joseph,[3] Jasper,[2] Jasper[1]), married Wesley Swing. Children:

1. GEORGE W. (Swing).
2. ABNER (Swing).
3. JOHN C. (Swing).
4. ELIZABETH (Swing).
5. MARYETTE (Swing).

2192. SARAH CRANE[7] [1438], (Abner,[6] Benjamin,[5] Benja-

min,[4] Joseph,[3] Jasper,[2] Jasper[1]), married Samuel Sims, and had eleven children, two died young; their names not given.
Children :

1. REBECCA (Sims).
2. PHEBE (Sims).
3. NANCY (Sims).
4. OLIVER (Sims).
5. EDWARD (Sims).
6. MELISSA (Sims); m. George McNutt; lives at Williamsburg, O.
7. ELIZA (Sims).
8. AMANDA (Sims).
9. ISOURA (Sims).

2193. BENJAMIN CRANE[7] [1440], (Abner,[6] Benjamin,[5] Benjamin,[4] Joseph,[3] Jasper,[2] Jasper[1]), married Jan. 6, 1806, Patsey Johnson. She was born in Hamilton County, eleven miles from Cincinnati, O., near the spot where Mount Washington now stands. She celebrated her ninety-second birthday Thursday, Jan. 6, 1898, at the home of her daughter, Mrs. T. G. Morehead, Cincinnati, O. Mr. Crane died April 25, 1858. Widow now (1899) has passed her 93d birthday. Children :

2194—1. WESLEY S., b. July 8, 1830.
2195—2. ACHSAH, b. and d. 1832.
2196—3. REBECCA.
2197—4. ABNER, b. 1836; residence in Utah.
2198—5. MARY ELLEN.
2199—6. ELIZABETH.
2200—7. ANNIE.

2201. OLIVER CRANE[7] [1441], (ABNER,[6] Benjamin,[5] Benjamin,[4] Joseph,[3] Jasper,[2] Jasper[1]), married Eliza West.
Children :

2202—1. WILLIAM.
2203—2. PHEBE.
2204—3. MARY E.
2205—4. ISAAC.
2206—5. JAMES M.
2207—6. SARAH E.

2208. JOHN CRANE[7] [1442], (Abner,[6] Benjamin,[5] Benjamin,[4] Joseph,[3] Jasper,[2] Jasper[1]), married Sarah Swing. Children :

2209—1. RUTH.
2210—2. GEORGE.
2211—3. OLIVER.
2212—4. PHILIP.
2213—5. BELLE.
2214—6. HARRIET.
2215—7. BERGEN.
2216—8. PORTER.

2217. SILAS CRANE[7] [1446], (Timothy,[6] Benjamin,[5] Benjamin,[4] Joseph,[3] Jasper,[2] Jasper[1]), married ———. Children :

2218—1. SILAS; m. and d. in California; a physician.
2219—2. JULIA ETTA.
2220—3. HARRIET B.; m. ——— Smith; d. at South Sodus, N. Y.

2221. MARTHA CRANE[7] [1448], (Timothy,[6] Benjamin,[5] Benjamin,[4] Joseph,[3] Jasper,[2] Jasper[1]), married Sedate Padelford, Feb. 8, 1827, and the family removed from New York State to Illinois. Children:

1. MARY E. (Padelford), b. Dec. 14, 1827.
2. JOSEPH C. (Padelford), b. Sept. 26, 1829; d. July 6, 1830.
3. A. JUDSON (Padelford), b. July 26, 1831; minister, Calais, Me.
4. PHEBE AUGUSTA (Padelford), b. Nov. 21, 1833; d. May 18, 1862.
5. MARSHALL MANLY (Padelford), b. Feb. 26, 1836.

2222. ISAAC W. CRANE[7] [1449], (Timothy,[6] Benjamin,[5] Benjamin,[4] Joseph,[3] Jasper,[2] Jasper[1]), married twice. Had a daughter by second wife, Mary Ledyard. Child:

1. ELIZABETH; d., aged 7 years.

2223. STEPHEN V. R. CRANE[7] [1451], (Timothy,[6] Benjamin,[5] Benjamin,[4] Joseph,[3] Jasper,[2] Jasper[1]), married Euna Hendrick, born Feb. 26, 1801. She died in 1859. Child:

2224—1. JOHN HENRY, b. Nov. 30, 1841.

2225. DAVIS CRANE[7] [1452], (Timothy,[6] Benjamin,[5] Benjamin,[4] Joseph,[3] Jasper,[2] Jasper[1]), married March 2, 1833, Elvasinda Mallory. She was a native of Easton, N. Y., born Aug. 25, 1806. He was a railroad agent, and died at Hastings-on-Hudson, May 24, 1872. She died April 24, 1884, at Stanhope, N. J. Their son was born at Schaghticoke Point, N. Y. Child:

2226—1. JOHN JAY, b. Aug. 21, 1841; a minister at Stanhope, N. J.; a graduate of New York University.

2227. BENJAMIN FRANKLIN CRANE[7] [1455], (Timothy,[6] Benjamin,[5] Benjamin,[4] Joseph,[3] Jasper,[2] Jasper[1]), married Emeline Smith, of Yonkers, N. Y. He died Jan. 10, 1888. Children:

2228—1. CORNELIA; m. Theo. M. Banta; lives in Brooklyn, N. Y.
2229—2. BENJ. FRANKLIN; physician; lives in New York.
2230—3. SARAH; d. in infancy.
2231—4. SARAH PRISCILLA; m. J. O. Bertolph; widow; lives in Yonkers, N. Y.
2232—5. LEMUEL MILLER; lives in New York.
2233—6. JAMES FREDERICK; m.; d. leaving two daughters.
2234—7. EMMA; m. James Romer; lives St. Paul, Minn.
2235—8. GERTRUDE; m.; lives Abilene, Tex.

2236. LEMUEL C. P. CRANE[7] [1457], (Timothy,[6] Benjamin,[5] Benjamin,[4] Joseph,[3] Jasper,[2] Jasper[1]), married Sarah Barnetz; residence, San Francisco, Cal. Children:

2237—1. LITTA; m. —— McKinley; one child.
2238—2. CARRA; m. —— Lang; one child.
2239—3. LEMUEL.
2240—4. IRVING.
2241—5. JESSE.
2242—6. DAISY.
2243—7. DOUGLASS.
2243½—8. ——; d. young.

2244. LAFAYETTE CRANE[7] [1459], (Davis,[6] Benjamin,[5] Benjamin,[4] Joseph,[3] Jasper,[2] Jasper[1]), married Dec. 9, 1835, Lydia Harris; she died July 3, 1836. He married 2d, in 1837, Sarah Leeds; she died leaving two children. He married 3rd, Susanna Leeds, sister of his second wife; she also had two children. In April, 1851, they removed to Pike Co., Ill.
Children:

2245—1. EZRA, b. June, 1838.
2246—2. FELIX, b. 1839.
2247—3. ELY L..
2248—4. SARAH ELIZABETH.

2249. GEORGE WHITEFIELD CRANE[7] [1460], (Davis,[6] Benjamin,[5] Benjamin,[4] Joseph,[3] Jasper,[2] Jasper[1]), married Euphema Buck, Feb., 1844. Children:

2250—1. ALBERT, b. Oct. 12, 1844.
2251—2. CYRUS GREELY, b. Feb. 20, 1851.

2252. GEORGE CRANE[7] [1473], (Stephen,[6] Elias,[5] Ezekiel,[4] Joseph,[3] Jasper,[2] Jasper[1]), married Lucy Dyer, at Dubuque, Ia., Sept. 4, 1860. He is a graduate of Miami University, 1851, and resides in Dubuque; a lawyer. Is president of the Northern Iowa Building and Loan Association, with authorized capital of $5,000,000. Children:

2253—1. GEORGE LESLIE.
2254—2. ELTON S.

2255. Col. HENRY ABIJAH ROBERTS CRANE[7] [1490], (Abijah,[6] Isaac,[5] Isaac,[4] Joseph,[3] Jasper,[2] Jasper[1]), was born in Newark, N. J., married in 1837, at St. Augustine, Fla., Sophia A. Allen. She was born on Amelia Island, Fernandina, March 1, 1818. Mr. Crane was a life-long soldier, serving as military instructor. of tactics at Fortress Monroe, before the Seminole war, in which war he took part as captain. He was also actively engaged in the late war; at one time commanding Company A, 2d Florida Calvary, U. S. A. In 1852, published the *Tampa Herald*, the first newspaper of the place. Of late years he has resided at Key West, where he has edited and published several newspapers. He died there June 18, 1888. Children:

2256—1. HENRY L., b. Sept. 25, 1838; m. Dec. 25, 1868, Mrs. Meroba Thurman.
2257—2. CAROLINE BANKS, b. Dec. 6, 1841.
2258—3. EMMA, b. Aug. 31, 1845.
2259—4. SOPHIA M., b. Sept. 6, 1847.
2260—5. LUCETTA E., b. Nov. 8, 1849.
2261—6. FLORA, b. Feb. 25, 1852.
2262—7. FANNIE, b. May 14, 1856; d. Nov. 29, 1868.
2263—8. TIMOTHY WARD, b. Nov. 8, 1859, at Fort Myers; d. at Tampa.

2264. SIDNEY CRANE[7] [1495], (John J.,[6] Josiah,[5] Josiah,[4] Joseph,[3] Jasper,[2] Jasper[1]), married Catherine Heynembourg, in New Haven, Conn., Sept. 10, 1818. She was daughter of

Charles and Mary Heynembourg, of that city. In Dec., 1820, they removed to Columbia, S. C., where he was engaged in mercantile business until his death there, March 13, 1850. She died in Sumter, S. C., Aug. 18, 1872. Children:

2265—1. JOSEPH SIDNEY BREWSTER, b. June 10, 1821; residence (1881) New York city.
2266—2. CHARLES LOUIS, b. July 13, 1823; residence (1881) Sumter, S. C.
2267—3. JAMES BOATWRIGHT, b. Aug. 27, 1826; residence (1881) Batesville, Ark.
2268—4. ELIZABETH SARAH, b. Nov. 12, 1828; m. —— Gregg; residence (1881) Marietta, Ga.

2269. THEODORE CRANE⁷ [1501], (Benjamin,⁶ Josiah,⁵ Josiah,⁴ Joseph,³ Jasper,² Jasper¹), married Sept. 1, 1831, Margaret B. Havens. Died March 12, 1871. Child:

2270—1. JANE E.; m. Wm. Loring Andrews, of New York city.

2271. JOHN JOSIAH CRANE⁷ [1503], (Benjamin,⁶ Josiah,⁵ Josiah,⁴ Joseph,³ Jasper,² Jasper¹), married Sarah W. Briggs. She was born Jan. 14, 1817. Children:

2272—1. JOHN AUGUSTUS.
2273—2. ISAAC BRIGGS; lived and d. in New York city.
2274—3. SARAH.
2275—4. THEODORE B., b. Oct. 6, 1846.
2276—5. CHARLES.
2277—6. EDITH.
2278—7. MARY.
2279—8. ELSIE SCHUYLER.

2280. AUGUSTUS CRANE⁷ [1505], (Benjamin,⁶ Josiah,⁵ Josiah,⁴ Joseph,³ Jasper,² Jasper¹), married March 9, 1848, Mary Elizabeth Bolles, daughter of Nathan and Abby Baldwin Bolles, born June 4, 1823. Residence, Morristown, N. J. Children:

2281—1. MARY, b. Jan. 14, 1849.
2282—2. JULIA, b. June 23, 1850.
2293—3. AUGUSTUS, b. Oct. 27, 1852.
2284—4. BENJAMIN, b. June 19, 1854.

2285. MARY CAROLINE CRANE⁷ [1535], (William C.,⁶ Isaac W.,⁵ Elihu,⁴ Elihu,³ Jasper,² Jasper¹), married in 1866, Gilbert Douglas Sidway, of Jackson, Miss. Children:

1. MARY EMMA (Sidway); m. in 1893, William G. McKay, of Meridian, Miss.
2. CAROLINE CHARLOTTE (Sidway); m. in 1897, E. M. Perkins, of Franklin, Tenn.
3. ERNESTINE ALBERTI (Sidway).
4. CHARLES ALBERTI (Sidway).

2286. WILLIAM H. CRANE⁷ [1536], (William C.,⁶ Isaac W.,⁵ Elihu,⁴ Elihu,³ Jasper,² Jasper¹), married 1st, Mary Field; 2d, Mary Bell Enders. He died in 1888. His family reside in Jackson, Miss. Children:

2287—1. WILLIAM MORTIMER.
2288—2. MARY BELL.

2289—3. DAIZY.
2290—4. ERNEST.
2291—5. LOUISE.

2292. MARTHA BANKS CRANE[7] [1543], (James,[6] (David D.,[5] David,[4] David,[3] Jasper,[2] Jasper[1]), married Elijah Kellogg, Jan. 30, 1833, at Elizabeth, N. J. Children:

1. JAMES (Kellogg).
2. MARY (Kellogg).
3. HARRIETTE (Kellogg).
4. CLEMENTINA (Kellogg).

2293. JOHN RIGGS CRANE[7] [1544], (James,[6] David D.,[5] David,[4] David,[3] Jasper,[2] Jasper[1]), married Nancy Harrison, widow of Robert Harrison, who was nephew of ex-president William Henry Harrison, in Virginia, Nov. 4, 1847. Children:

2294—1. JAMES.
2295—2. HENRY.
2296—3. EDWARD.
2297—4. JOHN JASPER; only one living of this family.
2298—5. LUCY.
2299—6. CATHERINE.

2300. MARY D. CRANE[7] [1545], (James,[6] David D.,[5] David,[4] David,[3] Jasper,[2] Jasper[1]), married Moses M. Woodruff, Oct. 29, 1834. Child:

1. HELEN (Woodruff).

2301. JAMES CRANE, M. D.[7] [1547], (James,[6] David D.,[5] David,[4] David,[3] Jasper,[2] Jasper[1]), married Aletta Hartwell, May 19, 1842, at Somerville, N. J. Children:

2302—1. MARY.
2303—2. CATHERINE.
2304—3. ELIZABETH H.

2305. HENRY MARTYN CRANE[7] [1552], (James,[6] David D.,[5] David,[4] David,[3] Jasper,[2] Jasper[1]), married Louisa Fisk, of Brooklyn, May 19, 1851. He is a merchant in New York city.

2306—1. CLEMENT.
2307—2. HONORA F.
2308—3. ANNIE D.

2309. WILLIAM HALSTED CRANE[7] [1553], (James,[6] David D.,[5] David,[4] David,[3] Jasper,[2] Jasper[1]), married 1st, Catherine Rankin, Nov. 1, 1854; married 2d, Julia D. Gibson, May 6, 1863. He was a merchant. Children:

2310—1. WILLIAM H., b. Aug. 7, 1855; d. Oct. 19, 1857.
2311—2. JOHN RANKIN, b. Nov. 12, 1857; d. May 16, 1874.
2312—3. JAMES, b. Dec. 21, 1859; d. May 14, 1874.
2313—4. ANSON G. P., b. Jan. 24, 1866; d. Sept. 11, 1866.
2314—5. WALTER BEVERLEY, b. Nov. 13, 1867.

2315. CATHERINE CRANE[7] [1549], (James,[6] David D.,[5] David,[4] David,[3] Jasper,[2] Jasper[1]), married 1st, Capt. William

41

Chandler, U. S. N., Sept. 29, 1847; married 2d, Abraham Barker, of Philadelphia, Pa.; no issue. Children :

1. WALTER (Chandler).
2. MARGARET (Chandler).

2316. HARRIETTE B. CRANE[7] [1550], (James,[6] David D.,[5] David,[4] David,[3] Jasper,[2] Jasper[1]), married 1st, Lieut. W. B. Beverly, U. S. N., June 10, 1846, by whom she had no children; married 2d, William B. Cooper, July 1, 1860, by whom she had a daughter; married 3rd, William B. Hamilton; no issue. Child :

1. ALLICE B. (Cooper).

2317. JOHN JACOB CRANE, M.D.[7] [1558], (John R., D.D.,[6] David D.,[5] David,[4] David,[3] Jasper,[2] Jasper[1]), was born in Middletown, Conn. Graduate of Princeton College; studied medicine, and for many years practiced his profession in the city of New York. He possessed marked ability, and soon became one of the ablest physicians in that great metropolis, acquiring an extensive practice, which brought him abundant riches. May 12, 1847, he married Jane B. Young, who became the mother of his three children. She died; and he, in the year 1873, married Mrs. Caroline Suydam, widow of Frederick Suydam, and daughter of Stephen Whitney. The united fortunes of Dr. Crane and the widow Suydam it is said amounted to about six million dollars, the care of. which demanded so much time and attention that Mr. Crane felt obliged to discontinue his practice, although he gave considerable time to travelling, making frequent trips across the Atlantic. and visiting nearly every prominent city in the world. After his second marriage he made his home in New Haven, Conn., and "Ivy Nook," as his place was called, with its beautiful trees and rare flowers, was the pride and admiration of not only New Haven people, but all who gave it a visit. Here he died March 4, 1889, in the 70th year of his age, and was buried at Middletown. Children :

2318—1. HENRY WARD; d. young.
2319—2. ROBERT REMSON; d. 1886.
2320—3. MARY GEORGINA; m. John B. Mills, Esq.

2321. CALEB CRANE[7] [1566], (Samuel,[6] John C.,[5] Caleb,[4] Jonathan,[3] Jasper,[2] Jasper[1]), married Nov. 25, 1840, Sarah P. Gardiner, daughter of Robert and Nancy Crane Gardiner. He died Sept. 13, 1845, leaving two daughters. Feb. 10, 1865, she married Alsop Purdy. He was killed on railroad July 20, 1894. Children :

2322—1. JULIA H.; d. Oct. 11, 1861.
2323—2. JOANNA M.; d. March 16, 1863.
2324—3. LOUISA G. (Purdy); m. Dr. G. M. Swain.

2325. HARRIET CRANE[7] [1568], (Henry,[6] John C.,[5] Caleb,[4] Jonathan,[3] Jasper,[2] Jasper[1]), married Nathan Bunn, who died leaving three children. She then married David Burnet, a wid-

ower whose first wife was Lydia Crane (see No. 1577). By him she had seven children, but only four lived to grow up.
Children :

1. LEWIS D. (Bunn).
2. SARAH E. (Bunn).
3. JAMES (Bunn).
4. WILLIAM (Burnet).
5. HARRIET (Burnet).
6. EMMA (Burnet).
7. MARY (Burnet).

2326. HARRIET BURNET [5]; m. Alfred Pruden. Children :
1. FRANK (Pruden).
2. FRED (Pruden).
3. ORLIE (Pruden).
4. LEWIS B. (Pruden).
5. GERTRUDE (Pruden).
6. HERBERT (Pruden).

2327. NANCY CRANE[7] [1569], (Henry,[6] John C.,[5] Caleb,[4] Jonathan,[3] Jasper,[2] Jasper[1]), married Robert Gardiner, April 11, 1821, by whom she had one child. Child :
1. SARAH P. (Gardiner), b. Feb. 7, 1822; m. Caleb Crane.

2328. HETTY CRANE[7] [1570], (Henry,[6] John C.,[5] Caleb,[4] Jonathan,[3] Jasper,[2] Jasper[1]), married James Bower. Children :
1. HANNAH M. (Bower).
2. DAVID (Bower).
3. ISAAC C. (Bower).
4. WILLIAM H. (Bower).
5. LEWIS D. (Bower).
6. JOSEPH C. (Bower).

2329. MARIA CRANE[7] [1575], (Daniel,[6] John C.,[5] Caleb,[4] Jonathan,[3] Jasper,[2] Jasper[1]), married ——— Pine. Children :
1. THEODORE (Pine); an artist; resides in Chicago, Ill.
2. ELIZA (Pine).

2330. JOHN CALEB CRANE[7] [1585], (Simeon H.,[6] John C.,[5] Caleb,[4] Jonathan,[3] Jasper,[2] Jasper[1]), married Elizabeth Crowe in 1855. The eldest child was born in Madison, Ind.; the other children were born in Memphis, Tenn.; but his late residence is at St. Louis, Mo. He is a steamboat master, and for many years has been engaged in running steamboats between St. Louis, Mo., and New Orleans, La. Children :

2331—1. CHARLES LOUIS, b. April 27, 1856; d. May 21, 1881.
2332—2. HARRY NYE, b. April 30, 1857; lives at St. Louis, Mo.
2333—3. MARY HATTIE, b. Jan. 30, 1861; lives at St. Louis, Mo.

2334. SARAH MATILDA CRANE[7] [1586], (Simeon H.,[6] John C.,[5] Caleb,[4] Jonathan,[3] Jasper,[2] Jasper[1]), married April 23, 1856, Otis B. Sappington, of Baltimore, Md. He was born Jan. 1, 1832. She resides at Seymour, Ind. He met his death at the burning of the steamers *United States* and *America* on the Ohio River, Dec. 4, 1868. Children :
1. CHARLES C. (Sappington), b. Dec. 22, 1860; m. Julia Smith; lives at Chicago, Ill.

   2. MARY W. (Sappington), b. Nov. 25, 1864; lives in Madison,
         Ind.
   3. OTIS B. (Sappington), b. Aug. 16, 1869; lives in Louisville, Ky.;
         m. Bertha Hennesey, March 9, 1890.

2335. MARY BURROWES CRANE[7] [1587], (Simeon H.,[6] John
C.,[5] Caleb,[4] Jonathan,[3] Jasper,[2] Jasper[1]), married David White
at Lexington, Ky., March 27, 1849.   Children born in Madison,
Ind.   Children :

   1. SIMEON HARRISON (White), b. 1850; lives in St. Louis, Mo.
   2. ANNIE BURROWES (White), b. 1854; m. J. E. Cartwright; lives
         in St. Louis, Mo.
   3. DAVID M. (White), b. 1855; m. Josie B. Rice at St. Louis, Mo.,
         Nov. 14, 1876; d. at Denver, Col., 1880.
   4. FREDERICK CUMBAUGH (White), b. 1858.

2336. SIMEON HENRY CRANE[7] [1590], Simeon H.,[6] John C.,[5]
Caleb,[4] Jonathan,[3] Jasper,[2] Jasper[1]), married Mary Ellen Potter,
June 29, 1865.   Residence at Chicago, Ill., where he is a member of the firm of John Alling & Co., wholesale hardware merchants.   He served in the late war; was captain in Co. C,
67th Indiana regiment.   Child :

2336½.-1. MARIAH POTTER, b. Feb. 9, 1867.

2337. ISAAC WARD CRANE[7] [1602], (Nehemiah J.,[6] Jonathan,[5]
Nehemiah,[4] Jonathan,[3] Jasper,[2] Jasper[1]), married Dec. 5, 1828,
in Newark, N. J., Hannah Smith Condit, born above Orange
Mountains, N. J., Aug. 18, 1808.   They resided in Newark and
New York city.   He was by occupation a cabinet-maker.   He
died July 9, 1879.   Children :

2338—1. MARY WARD.
2339—2. ALEXANDER TAYLOR.
2340—3. NEHEMIAH; d.
2341—4. JEPHTHA; d.
2342—5. ISAAC SMITH.
2343—6. JONATHAN N.
2344—7. WILLIAM B.; d.
2345—8. EDWARD PAYSON.
2346—9. SARAH CORDELIA, b. May 13, 1843, in New York city; by
           occupation a teacher.
2347-10. THEODORE F., b. Dec. 1, 1844, in New York city.
2348-11. ALBERT F.; d.

2349. JOHN CUMMINGS CRANE[7] [1603], (Nehemiah J.,[6]
Jonathan,[5] Nehemiah,[4] Jonathan,[3] Jasper,[2] Jasper[1]), married in
Newark, N. J., Oct. 5, 1825, Mary C. Pike.   She was a native
of Newark also, and born Sept. 13, 1804.   By trade he was a
saddler.   For forty-five years he was a ruling elder in the Third
Presbyterian Church in Newark.   He died May 17, 1878.   Children :

2350—1. WILLIAM TENNETT, b. Nov. 18, 1826; harness-maker; d.
           Jan. 12, 1868, at Lisbon, Ill.
2351—2. SARAH ELIZABETH H., b. May 7, 1830.
2352—3. ABBY ANN WARD, b. June 28, 1832; d. June 27, 1871.

2353—4. JOHN NEHEMIAH, b. April 28, 1835; d. April 4, 1850.
2354—5. ABNER WARD, b. Oct. 2, 1840; d. April 25, 1861.

2355. AMBROSE CRANE[7] [1605], (Nehemiah J.,[6] Jonathan,[5] Nehemiah,[4] Jonathan,[3] Jasper,[2] Jasper[1]), married Lydia Pike. Children:

2356—1. EMMA; m. Mr. Skinner.
2357—2. MARTHA; m. Mr. Cleveland.
2358—3. HENRY.
2359—4. LOUISE; d.
2360—5. STEPHEN.
2361—6. CAROLINE; d.

2362. MARY ELIZABETH CRANE[7] [1609], (Nehemiah J.,[6] Jonathan,[5] Nehemiah,[4] Jonathan,[3] Jasper,[2] Jasper[1]), married James Vanderpoel. Children:

1. JAMES (Vanderpoel).
2. MARY ELIZABETH (Vanderpoel).
3. JULIA LEWIS (Vanderpoel).
4. JANE CROCKETT (Vanderpoel).
5. ALBION ALEXANDER (Vanderpoel).
6. MARTHA WARD (Vanderpoel).
7. FRANK (Vanderpoel).
8. CYRUS EDWARD (Vanderpoel), b. 1858; d. 1879.

EIGHTH GENERATION.

2363. PHEBE JANE CRANE[8] [1613], (John A.,[7] Benjamin,[6] Josiah,[5] Edmund,[4] John,[3] John,[2] Jasper[1]), married March 3, 1836, Hiram Dollaway. He was born July 3, 1813; was a farmer. After his death she married 2d, John Washburn, Sept. 19, 1867. He died Sept. 24, 1887. She (1898) still living.
Children, born at Montrose, Pa. :

1. MATHEW (Dollaway), b. April 19, 1839.
2. SILAS KIRBY (Dollaway), b. May 15, 1841.
3. JOHN W. (Dollaway). b. March 24, 1843.
4. OLIVER MORRISON (Dollaway), b. Feb. 23, 1845.
5. HIRAM (Dollaway), b. Dec. 25, 1846.
6. GEORGE S. (Dollaway), b. Sept. 4, 1848.
7. ALBERT C. (Dollaway), b. April 25, 1850.
8. SARAH E. (Dollaway), b. Aug. 1, 1852.

2364. JULIA ANN CRANE[8] [1614], (John A.,[7] Benjamin,[6] Josiah,[5] Edmund,[4] John,[3] John,[2] Jasper[1]), married Silas Hulse Kirby, Nov. 13, 1841. He was born in Circleville, Orange Co., N. Y.; was a builder; died Dec. 2, 1894. She died Jan. 13, 1895. Children, born in Middletown, N. Y. :

1. SARAH JANE (Kirby), b. June 13, 1844.
2. GEORGE HENRY (Kirby), b. May 25, 1847.
3. ANNA MARIA (Kirby), b. Oct. 6, 1849.
4. ABIGAIL (Kirby), b. Aug. 4, 1852.
5. EMMET HOYT (Kirby), b. Nov. 14, 1857.
6. HARVEY EVERETT (Kirby), b. July 26, 1858.

2365. SARAH MARIA CRANE[8] [1615], (John A.,[7] Benjamin,[6] Josiah,[5] Edmund,[4] John,[3] John,[2] Jasper[1]), married Zipron Cobb, Jr., May 9, 1837, of Circleville, Orange Co., N. Y.; a merchant. Removed to Montrose, Susquehanna Co., Pa., where children were born. Children :

1. JOHN WELSEY (Cobb), b. Sept. 7, 1838.
2. SARAH ANN (Cobb), b. April 9, 1840.
3. MARY ELIZABETH (Cobb), b. Aug. 6, 1841.
4. PHEBE ADELINE (Cobb), b. Jan. 17, 1843.
5. AUGUSTA (Cobb), b. Feb. 12, 1845.
6. GEORGE NELSON (Cobb), b. May 5, 1847.
7. HANNAH JANE (Cobb), b. Dec. 28, 1849.
8. HENRY LEWIS (Cobb), b. Feb. 22, 1852.
9. HARRIET ELIZA (Cobb), b. Aug. 23, 1855.
10. ALICE FLORA (Cobb), b. May 21, 1858.

2366. OLIVER MORRISON CRANE[8] [1616], (John A.,[7] Benjamin,[6] Josiah,[5] Edmund,[4] John,[3] John,[2] Jasper[1]), married Ann M. Smith, Oct. 17, 1846, at Montrose, Pa. He was a merchant

Rev. J. E. CRANE, M.A., Ph.D.

and farmer, also sheriff for Susquehanna Co. He died at Montrose, Dec. 24, 1891. Children:

2367—1. CHARLES LYMAN, b. July 31, 1853.
2368—2. JOHN PHINEAS, b. May 22, 1855, at Bridgewater.
2369—3. MARY EUGENIE, b. Sept. 15, 1857, at Bridgewater. •

2370. WILLIAM HENRY CRANE[8] [1618], (Josiah,[7] Benjamin,[6] Josiah,[5] Edmund,[4] John,[3] John,[2] Jasper[1]), was a great-grandson of Capt. Josiah Crane, who served as a captain through the Revolutionary war. He was by occupation a farmer, and died on the place where he was born, March 11, 1897. He married Mary Jane Gillen, July 29, 1842. She was born May 30, 1819, and was the eldest daughter of John Gillen, Esq., of Fair Oaks, N. Y., and granddaughter of Thomas Gillen, who was born in London, England, and who came to this country just before the Revolutionary war, and enlisted in the Continental army, serving seven years and a half under Washington's immediate command, as one of his life guards. (See *Rollin's History of United States*). Children:

2371—1. JOHN JUDSON, b. March 27, 1843.
2372—2. HARRISON HORTON, b. Oct. 1, 1844.
2373—3. HANNAH ANN, b. Feb. 22, 1847.
2374—4. CHARLES G., b. Feb. 15, 1849; d. Jan. 10, 1884.
2375—5. SARAH ELIZABETH, b. Jan. 23, 1851; a teacher in New York city.
2376—6. Rev. JOSIAH ELMER, A.M., Ph.D., b. April 27, 1853, at Fair Oaks, Orange Co., N. Y. His early life was spent on the farm. Feeling he was called for the ministry, he prepared himself and entered Rutgers College, at New Brunswick, N. J., graduating in 1881, and from Rutgers Seminary in 1884, receiving the degree of A.M., and in 1896, the degree of Ph.D., from Martyn College, Washington, D. C. He was ordained as a minister of the (Dutch) Reformed Church, in 1884. His first charge was Rocky Hill, N. J., where he remained a number of years, when he was called to the Church at Schodack, on the Hudson, N. Y., where he is at present (1899). He married, Sept. 3, 1885, Ida Augusta Moon, of Salisbury, Conn., who was born, Oct. 16, 1862. No children.
2377—7. JAMES EMMET DURYEA, b. Dec. 23, 1856.
2378—8. MARY EMMERETTE, b. Feb. 23, 1859.
2379—9. ELDORA ADALAIDE, b. June 24, 1862.

2380. ELIZABETH JANE CRANE[8] [1620], (Josiah,[7] Benjamin,[6] Josiah,[5] Edmund,[4] John,[3] John,[2] Jasper[1]), born at the old Crane homestead, Orange Co., N. Y., married John Leebody, Dec. 10, 1846. He was born Jan. 2, 1820. Children:

1. JAMES (Leebody), b. April 28, 1848.
2. ANNIE J. (Leebody), b. July 17, 1849.
3. ROBERT (Leebody), b. July 2, 1851.
4. HATTIE J. (Leebody), b. July 13, 1856.
5. ADELIA E. (Leebody), b. June 10, 1860.

2381. PHEBE ANNA CRANE[8] [1621], (Josiah,[7] Benjamin,[6] Josiah,[5] Edmund,[4] John,[3] John,[2] Jasper[1]), born at the old Crane

homestead, Orange Co., N. Y.; married Dec. 19, 1852, Hugh
Nesbith Wolfe, a native of Mendham, Morris Co., N. J., born
Jan. 28, 1830. Children:

1. EMMA FRANCES (Wolfe), b. Dec. 15, 1853.
2. CARRIE (Wolfe), b. June 24, 1856.
3. GEORGE WASHINGTON (Wolfe), b. Jan. 25, 1866.
4. DAISY (Wolfe), b. Aug. 11, 1869.

2382. JOSIAH MEEKER CRANE[8] [1623], (Josiah,[7] Benjamin,[6]
Josiah,[5] Edmund,[4] John,[3] John,[2] Jasper[1]), was born on a farm
near Middletown, Orange Co., N. Y.; married at Newark, N.
J., June, 1865, Jane Clara Wolfe, and settled in Jersey City,
where he has been a very successful contractor and builder.
Children :

2383—1. ALTHEA GARRISON, b. Sept. 13, 1866; d. Dec. 31, 1890.
2384—2. JENNIE MAY, b. May 20, 1873; m. Chas. V. A. Walsh, April
            22, 1896.
2385—3. HOWARD M., b. Dec. 2, 1875; d. July 16, 1876.
2386—4. ADA TAYLOR, b. May 30, 1881.

2387. JAMES MADISON CRANE[8] [1624], (Josiah,[7] Benjamin,[6]
Josiah,[5] Edmund,[4] John,[3] John,[2] Jasper[1]), was born near Circleville, Orange Co., N. Y. He received the advantages of the
district school, as well as of a private school, and after
teaching for two years, entered the State Normal School, at
Albany, and was graduated therefrom July 3, 1863. Since
which time he has taught school continuously. For three months
at Roslyn, N. Y., three years at Walden, but since Sept., 1866,
he has been engaged at Newburg; Dec., 1897, was principal
of the Newburg Free Academy, a position he had then held for
nearly twelve years. July 7, 1890, he received the degree of A.
M. from Union College, Schenectady. After completing a
course of study he received the degree of Master of. Pedagogy
from the New York University, June 6, 1893. Since residing in
Newburg, Mr. Crane has for several years been a member of
the board of water commissioners, and for three years was its
president. Nov. 2, 1864, he married Mary A., daughter of John
B. Tears, of Walden. She died within a few years, leaving a
daughter. July 17, 1872, he married 2d, Elizabeth P., daughter
of John Murray and Margaret Patterson. She was born Sept.
2, 1853, at Irvington, N. Y. Children :

2388—1. JENNIE H., b. Dec. 30, 1867; d. Oct. 1, 1882.
2389—2. EDITH ELIZABETH, b. Oct. 12, 1873; m. Herbert Calhoun
            Reed, of Stamford, Conn., Oct. 6, 1897.
2390—3. JAMES TILDEN, b. Dec. 31, 1875, at Yale.

2391. MARY EMILY CRANE[8] [1625], (Josiah,[7] Benjamin,[6]
Josiah,[5] Edmund,[4] John,[3] John,[2] Jasper[1]), born April 21, 1846,
at Burlingham, Sullivan Co., N. Y.; married Cornelius W.
Todd, Dec. 2, 1868. He was born Oct. 7, 1833. She died
April 20, 1882. Child :

1. GEORGE (Todd), b. Dec. 13, 1869.

JAMES M. CRANE.

2392. Isaac Benjamin Crane[8] [1628], (Stephen K.,[7] Benjamin,[6] Josiah,[5] Edmund,[4] John,[3] John,[2] Jasper[1]), married Dec. 30, 1852, Mary Ann Gunn. She was born Aug. 28, 1833. Resided in Susquehanna County, Pa. Children:

2393—1. Mary Hannah, } twins, b. April 20, 1854; { d. Oct. 23, 1871.
2394—2. Isaac Kitchell,
2395—3. Phebe Jane, b. March 2, 1858.
2396—4. George Delmer, b. May 7, 1859; d. March 28, 1875.
2397—5. Cynthia Mariah, b. March 19, 1861.
2398—6. Lottie Alvira, b. April 14, 1863.

2399. Rev. Thomas Kitchell Crane[8] [1629], (Stephen K.,[7] Benjamin,[6] Josiah,[5] Edmund,[4] John,[3] John,[2] Jasper[1]), reared on a farm near Montrose, Pa., and for a time worked at the trade of a blacksmith; but being endowed with deep religious convictions, and feeling a desire to serve the Master in the great work of the ministry, he attended a course of study at Auburn Seminary, graduating May 8, 1873; received his degree, and was ordained a minister of the Presbyterian Church. After preaching three years he died Feb. 20, 1876, at the Presbyterian Hospital from the effect of an operation; thus abruptly ending what had promised to be a useful and exceedingly profitable career. He married 1st, Aug. 24, 1854, Phebe Louise Crane, who died Nov. 6, 1867; 2d, Sept. 2, 1873, Rosetta M. Rounds, who died Nov. 23, 1873. Children:

2400—1. Hannah Amelia, b. April 15, 1858; d. March 8, 1878.
2401—2. Sarah Estella, b. Sept. 30, 1859; d. June 4, 1875.
2402—3. Henry Payson, b. Nov. 5, 1864; d. Feb. 8, 1868.
2403—4. William Kitchell, b. Jan. 4, 1867; d. April 9, 1868.

2404. Rev. Henry Josiah Crane[8] [1630], (Stephen K.,[7] Benjamin,[6] Josiah,[5] Edmund,[4] John,[3] John,[2] Jasper[1]), after spending his boyhood days with his father on the farm he prepared to enter the New York University, New York city, graduating from there June 20, 1860, and from Union Theological Seminary three years later. Receiving his degree he was ordained minister of the gospel for the Presbyterian Church. He also received in 1865 the degree of medicine, and in 1873 the degree of D.D. From 1863 to 1871 he was settled at Wysox, Pa.; 1871 to 1875 at Hunter, N. Y.; then two years at Gibson, Pa.; and from 1877 to 1889 at Nicholson. During the latter year he located at Uniondale, where he was given charge of the Presbyterian Church of that place. Dr. Crane's labors have been crowned with no small degree of success, over fifteen hundred people having been added to the church under his administrations. He married in New York city, June 27, 1860, Charlotte Ann Morgan. Children:

2405—1. Tululah Eugenie, b. April 6, 1866.
2406—2. Howard Crosby, b. July 24, 1878.

2407. William Henry Crane[8] [1632], (William M.,[7] Benjamin,[6] Josiah,[5] Edmund,[4] John,[3] John,[2] Jasper[1]), born at Mid-

42

dletown, N. Y.   Married Catherine Wiseman, Oct. 23, 1866, at
New Milford, Pa., where they settled.   She died Feb. 21, 1896,
and he married Nettie Nowlan, March 18, 1897.   Children:

2408—1.   WILLIAM EMMETT, b. April 10, 1869.
2409—2.   CALLIE EDITH, b. Jan. 11, 1872; m. Clarence G. Brewer,
          Aug. 29, 1894.

2410.   ALBERT B. CRANE[8] [1634], (William M.,[7] Benjamin,[6]
Josiah,[5] Edmund,[4] John,[3] John,[2] Jasper[1]), married May L.
Martin, May 25, 1879, at North Jackson, Pa., where they set-
tled.   Children:

2411—1.   NELLIE E., b. Dec. 8, 1880.
2412—2.   BERTON C., b. May 16, 1884.
2413—3.   EDNA L., b. May 2, 1886.
2414—4.   SARAH H., b. July 9, 1891.

2415.   EDWIN THOMAS CRANE[8] [1635], (William M.,[7] Benjamin,[6] Josiah,[5] Edmund,[4] John,[3] John,[2] Jasper[1]), married Mary
Emma Cavanagh, May 21, 1883.   She was born at Jefferson,
Kan., July 24, 1866.   In his boyhood days he worked on a farm
in Pennsylvania, and, to obtain something of an education, did
chores for his board, and went to school; in this way fitting himself to teach a common district school, following that occupation
about four years.   About the year 1879 he went to Kansas, continuing his teaching there two years, when he secured a situation
as travelling salesman.   Was postmaster at Goffs, Nemaha Co.,
Kan., during President Harrison's administration.   He owns a
good farm, and still continues the travelling business.   His home
is at Centralia, Kan.; is an active member of the M. E. Church
there, as is also his wife.   Children:

2416—1.   MAURICE EDWIN, b. April 25, 1886, at Grasshopper, Atchi-
          son Co., Kan.
2417—2.   ERNEST THOMAS, b. Aug. 2, 1887, at Grasshopper, Atchison
          Co., Kan.
2418—3.   ETHEL MAY, b. Nov. 10, 1888, at Harrison, Nemaha Co.,
          Kan.
2419—4.   NELLIE MYRTLE, b. Aug. 14, 1893, at Harrison, Nemaha Co.,
          Kan.
2420—5.   ALMA IRENE,   } twins, b. Sept. 10, 1896, at Harrison, Ne-
2421—6.   ALTA JOSEPHINE, } maha Co., Kan.

2422.   SARAH CAROLINE CRANE[8] [1636], (William M.,[7] Benjamin,[6] Josiah,[5] Edmund,[4] John,[3] John,[2] Jasper[1]), married
James E. Washburn, Aug. 29, 1874.   Children:

1.   LEON E. (Washburn), b. Aug. 7, 1876.
2.   GUY LIVINGSTON (Washburn), b. May 22, 1879.
3.   EDITH MAY (Washburn), b. Sept. 2, 1883; d. Dec. 18, 1887.
4.   GALE CONRAD (Washburn), b. Jan. 29, 1891.

2423.   CHARLES EMMETT CRANE[8] [1637], (William M.,[7] Benjamin,[6] Josiah,[5] Edmund,[4] John,[3] John,[2] Jasper[1]), married Belle
Stanley, Dec. 24, 1888.   She died Dec 28, 1894.   He then married Feb. 4, 1896, Minnie V. Gillespie.   Child:

2424—1.   GERTRUDE ALICE, b. Dec. 27, 1896.

Henry J. Crane

2425. JAMES HARVEY CRANE[8] [1645], (Gabriel,[7] Abraham,[6] Josiah,[5] Edmund,[4] John,[3] John,[2] Jasper[1]), married May 25, 1862, Mary Ann Rideout, who was born Sept. 15, 1834. Mr. Crane was senior member of the firm of J. H. Crane & Sons, dairymen. He was killed by being run over by cars on his own farm June 13, 1898. He enlisted as home guard in the organization known as the "Squirrel Hunters," for the defence of Cincinnati, Ohio, in the spring of 1864, when Kirby Smith appeared in the vicinity of that city, threatening a raid upon that portion of the State of Ohio. He was mustered in United States service for one hundred days. Children:

2426—1. CHARLES, b. March 30, 1863; d. March 4, 1864.
2427—2. ISAAC GABRIEL, b. Nov. 29, 1864; m. Feb. 20, 1896, Jessie M. Jelleff.
2428—3. HARVEY A, b. May 10, 1868.
2429—4. JIMMIE, b. Aug. 27, 1870; d. March 27, 1871.
2430—5. IRVING JAMES, b. March 27, 1875.
2431—6. MARY ANN, b. April 17, 1877.

2432. HENRY JARVIS CRANE[8] [1646], (Gabriel,[7] Abraham,[6] Josiah,[5] Edmund,[4] John,[3] John,[2] Jasper[1]), married July 7, 1865, Mary A. Ford, who was born Jan. 7, 1839, and died April 26, 1880. Mr. Crane is one of the firm of Crane Brothers, market gardeners. He enlisted as private Oct. 10, 1861; Nov. 15, promoted to orderly; Jan. 18, 1862, second lieutenant; and captain March 23, 1862, for meritorious conduct at the battle of Winchester; was wounded at Fort Wagner, S. C., July 18, 1863; was before Richmond; and mustered out Jan. 18, 1865. Children:

2433—1. LOTTIE FORD, b. April 20, 1866; d. April 15, 1870.
2434—2. HARRY HYATT, b. June 4, 1869; attended Franklin College, 1884—1887; m. Josephine Jelleff.
2435—3. AUGUSTA, b. May 28, 1871; d. Aug. 7, 1872.
2436—4. GRACE ENID, b. May 4, 1873; graduated from Lake Erie Seminary, Painesville, Ohio, June, 1894.
2437—5. FRANK GOODWIN, b. April 13, 1875; graduated at Brown University, June, 1898.
2438—6. CLARA LOUISE. b. Aug. 30, 1876; attending Lake Erie Seminary, 1898.
2439—7. DANIEL BRADLEY, b. Jan. 18, 1879.

2440. AMOS WATERS CRANE[8] [1647], (Gabriel,[7] Abraham,[6] Josiah,[5] Edmund,[4] John,[3] John,[2] Jasper[1]), married March 22, 1865, Emma Cook, who was born June 17, 1845. Mr. Crane graduated from Dartmouth College, Hanover, N. H., June, 1862. He also enlisted in the "Squirrel Hunters," in company with his brother; and it was genuine patriotic service this organization rendered in placing themselves between the possible attacks of the daring confederate raiders and the homes of wives, mothers and daughters of the soldiers already engaged in the service of the Union at the front. He was mustered out in the fall of 1864. Children:

2441—1. ALICE, b. Dec. 12, 1865; m. Aug., 1895, Charles Kuhns.
2442—2. EMILY FIDELIA, b. Dec. 19, 1867; m. June, 1894, August Reihing.

2443—3. EDWARD LOUIS, b. March 26, 1870.
2444—4. MARY ANN, b. April 25, 1872; d. June 17, 1872.
2445—5. CORA EMMA, b. Oct. 4, 1876; d. Dec. 10, 1876.
2446—6. FANNIE LOUISA, b. Nov. 23, 1877.
2447—7. EUNICE LAURA, b. Nov. 23, 1885.
2448—8. CARL AMOS, b. July 13, 1891.

2449. HENRY LEWIS CRANE[8] [1652], (Josiah L.,[7] Abraham,[6] Josiah,[5] Edmund,[4] John,[3] John,[2] Jasper[1]), served in the civil war in Co. C, 21st Regt., O. V. I., in the call for three months men; on duty in West Virginia. At the close of that term he enlisted in the United States Navy, and served on the United States steamer *Montgomery* (cruiser), in D. G. Farragut's fleet, in the vicinity of the West Indies and the Bermuda Islands. He was a teacher by occupation. Residence at Perrysburg, Wood Co., Ohio. He married Dec. 31, 1863, at Perrysburg, Mary Ann Purvis. She was a native of that place, born Sept. 15, 1838. She died March 7, 1869. Children:

2450—1. MARY CAROLINE, b. Aug. 8, 1865; d. June 6, 1867.
2451—2. EDWARD LEWIS, b. July 14, 1868; d. March 7, 1869.

2452. WILLIAM WOODWARD CRANE[8] [1658], (Edward L.,[7] Abraham,[6] Josiah,[5] Edmund,[4] John,[3] John,[2] Jasper[1]), married June 8, 1858, Anna Martha Weakley, daughter of Edward T. Weakley, of New Carlisle, Clark Co., O. He was born on the Woodward farm, in sight of Tippecanoe; attended district school in West Charleston; one year at Dayton Academy, then in charge of Milo G. Williams; two years at the Methodist High School, Springfield, O.; read medicine with his father, Dr. Edward L. Crane; and graduated from the medical department, of Western Reserve College, Cleveland, O. At the breaking out of the war in 1861, he was appointed by the governor to take charge (as one of a committee of three) of the recruiting in Miami County and caring for soldier's families. He assisted in organizing the 44th Ohio Infantry, and the 71st Ohio Volunteer Infantry, of the latter he was made assistant surgeon. He went into camp in November, 1861, and was mustered out at Huntsville, Ala., Jan., 1865. Has since served five years as surgeon of the 3rd regiment, Ohio National Guards. After the war he engaged in manufacturing and farming. In the line of stockbreeding his work will be most enduring. First on record with the idea of building up a breed of hornless cattle of the shorthorn type; first and only president of the American Polled Durham Breeders' Association. He has continued this line of work for nearly twenty-five years, with the gratification of seeing that which in the beginning was held in disfavor, and thought to be but an idle hobby, to be accepted as a decided improvement in domestic cattle; his work having been classed by competent judges as "beneficient and important to the cattle industry of the country." Children:

2453—1. WILLIAM, b. April 23, 1862.

Henry L. Crane

2454—2. EDWARD L., b. May 13, 1865; assistant cashier, Tippecanoe
National Bank; received his education at Tippecanoe, O.,
East Hampton, Mass., and in Germany; m. Aug. 31,
1893, Enora, daughter of Furnes Kerr, of Miami Co., O.

2455—3. WOODWARD, b. Jan. 16, 1873; d. June 2, 1874.

2456—4. WILSON, } twins; b. Feb. 11, 1875; { d. Aug. 1, 1875.
2457—5. WEAKLEY, }

2458. VAN ELI CRANE[8] [1661], (Edward L.,[7] Abraham,[6]
Josiah,[5] Edmund,[4] John,[3] John,[2] Jasper[1]), married Jan. 17,
1877, Jean Mallory, of St. Clair Co., Mich. She died April 19,
1884; he then married 2d, Anna Doretta Lindeman Schafer, of
Port Huron, Mich. He attended the schools of West Charleston,
O., and took a practical course at Farmer's College, near Cincin-
nati; served in the war of the Rebellion in the Ohio Volunteer
Infantry, from May to Sept., 1864. Children :

2459—1. VAN JEAN, b. April 10, 1878.
2460—2. GRACE LOUIS, b. July 21, 1879; d. Nov. 23, 1890.
2461—3. VIRGINIA MARGARETTA, b. Jan. 23, 1888.
2462—4. OLIVIA CAROLINE, b. Aug. 22, 1889.
2463—5. GRACE COLUMBIA, b. July 30, 1892.

2464. ALVINA CRANE[8] [1662], (Edward L.,[7] Abraham,[6]
Josiah,[5] Edmund,[4] John,[3] John,[2] Jasper[1]), married Thomas J.
Sheets, of Clear Spring, Md., Oct. 16, 1861; served in the war
of the Rebellion, U. S. N., Mississippi Squadron. August, 1862,
was yeoman, master-mate, and signal officer. Honorably discharged, Nov., 1863, on account of continued disability; died at
Tippecanoe, O. Business was suspended in the town during his
funeral. He was a manly and honorable gentleman. Children :

1. MINNIE (Sheets), b. Jan. 23, 1863; d. in infancy.
2. EDWARD (Sheets), b. June 8, 1864; d. in infancy.
3. LEWIS T. (Sheets), b. Sept. 30, 1865; lawyer, and now (1898)
mayor of Tippecanoe, O.
4. ANNA E. (Sheets), b. Feb. 27, 1876; educated at schools in
Tippecanoe, and Female Seminary, Oxford, O.

2465. JULIA ANN CRANE[8] [1672], (Jeremiah C.,[7] Abraham,[6]
Josiah,[5] Edmund,[4] John,[3] John,[2] Jasper[1]), married at Perrysville,
O., Nov. 12, 1868, John F. Schroder. Children :

1. ELLA B. (Schroder), b. Oct. 5, 1869.
2. EMILY LAVINA (Schroder), b. Aug. 14, 1871; m. at Kansas City,
Mo., Nov. 7, 1893, Jay O. Caldwell.
3. ARTHUR COLEMAN (Schroder), b. Nov. 25, 1873.
4. CLARA HARTER (Schroder), b. March 7, 1876.
5. FRANK FERN (Schroder), b. Sept. 5, 1877; d. Sept. 23, 1877.
6. ETHEL MAY (Schroder), b. March 6, 1882.

2466. ANNA MELIA CRANE[8] [1675], (Joseph B.,[7] Stephen,[6]
Josiah,[5] Edmund,[4] John,[3] John,[2] Jasper[1]), married Adrien
Grafton Robinson, May 15, 1861, at Tonica, Ill. He was born
April 12, 1839, at Peru, Oxford Co., Me., removing from there
with his parents in the year 1854, to La Salle Co., Ill., and
engaged in farming. After the breaking out of the late war, he
enlisted at Tonica, Aug., 1862, in the 104th regiment, Illinois

Volunteer Infantry, and served until the close of the war, being discharged at Louisville, Ky., June, 1865. He was in the following engagements : Kentsville, Tenn., Hoover's Gap, Elk River, Bailey's Cross Roads, Chickamauga, Waldron's Ridge; after which on account of ill health was ordered to Louisville for light duty, where he remained until mustered out, as above stated. Returning home he again resumed farming, in which he has been successful, adding to his original eighty acres until he now (1897) has a six-hundred-acre farm, making a specialty of breeding fine cattle, short-horns being his favorite. This year he decided to retire from active labor, and enjoy the fruit of his toil. He receives a pension from the government of eight dollars per month. Children :

1. VESTA ALMA (Robinson), b. Nov. 26, 1866; d. Aug. 28, 1868.
2. GERTRUDE LILIAN (Robinson), b. Oct. 11, 1869.
3. MARGARET CRANE (Robinson), b. March 3, 1873.
4. ERNEST BAILEY (Robinson), b. Dec. 25, 1876.

2467. SOLOMON CRANE[8] [1676], (Joseph B.,[7] Stephen,[6] Josiah,[5] Edmund,[4] John,[3] John,[2] Jasper[1]), enlisted at Joliet, Ill., June 14, 1861, in Co. H, 20th Reg., I. V. I. After serving for a time in Missouri, was taken ill at Bird's Point, and transferred to the hospital, at Mound City; from there his father took him, as soon as he was able, to his home, receiving his discharge for inability, Nov., 1861. He is a member of the U. S. Grant Post, No. 28, G. A. R., of Chicago, Ill. He married at Bloomington, Sept. 6, 1865, Mary Porter, and settled in Chicago, in 1867, and for nearly a quarter of a century has been engaged in the coal business there, and is the owner of valuable real estate, in the northern division of the city. Children :

2468—1. HARRIET PORTER, b. Sept. 19, 1866; d. June 21, 1885.
2469—2. ALFRED BAILEY, b. March 16, 1873; m. Grace Elizabeth Ismon, at Chicago, Ill., June 30, 1898.

2470. EMMA ELIZABETH CRANE[8] [1680], (Joseph B.,[7] Stephen,[6] Josiah,[5] Edmund,[4] John,[3] John,[2] Jasper[1]), married in Chicago, Ill., Jan. 28, 1886, W. Heristel Eaton. Children :

1. RUTH (Eaton), b. Nov. 3, 1886.
2. EDITH MAY (Eaton), b. Nov. 23, 1889.
3. EUGENE BAILEY (Eaton), b. March 3, 1892.

2471. HIRAM WEBB CRANE[8] [1684], (Solomon,[7] Stephen,[6] Josiah,[5] Edmund,[4] John,[3] John,[2] Jasper[1]), married April 10, 1855, Julia Ann Messinger, of Pennsylvania. He died Feb. 14, 1859, at Lowell, Ill. She died April 10, 1886, at Ashley, Penn. Children :

2472—1. SAMUEL EDGAR, b. Sept. 26, 1856.
2473—2. JESSIE AMANDA, b. Dec. 25, 1857.
2474—3. HATTIE WEBB, b. Feb. 25, 1859; m. Samuel A. Miller, April 26, 1882; d. April 27, 1884.

2475. JOSIAH YOUNG CRANE[8] [1686], (George L.,[7] Stephen,[6]

Solomon Crane

Josiah,[5] Edmund,[4] John,[3] John,[2] Jasper[1]), married Sarah E. Hatfield, Oct. 4, 1863. Children:

2476—1. CHARLES COSSINS, b. June 28, 1864; m. Bertie Davis, 1890.
2477—2. LEROY ELMER, b. Sept. 25, 1867; m. Maggie Hardy, Sept. 5, 1892.
2478—3. MELVANIA LANIA, ⎱ b. Jan. 19, 1870; ⎰ m. John Chunk, 1893.
2479—4. MELVANIA ALENIA, ⎰ ⎱ m. Thomas Hardy, 1893.
2480—5. FLORENCE BERTHA, b. Aug. 4, 1872; m. George Lewis, Oct. 10, 1890.

2481. LEWIS GEORGE CRANE[8] [1687], (George L.,[7] Stephen,[6] Josiah,[5] Edmund,[4] John,[3] John,[2] Jasper[1]), lived in Nelsonville, O., where he was born, until the war, when he enlisted, July 14, 1861; mustered in Aug. 13, at Camp Dennison, Cincinnati, 39th O. V. I., and for a time stationed at Camp Colerain, Cincinnati. He re-enlisted Jan. 1, 1864, at Chattanooga, Tenn., and appointed corporal sergeant, Feb. 26, 1864. During the winter of 1861 and 1862, was engaged with his regiment in battles and skirmishes at New Madrid, Liberty, Syracuse, Lexington, Springfield, and New Mexico, Mo. He also was at Island No. 10, Fort Pillow, and Memphis, Tenn., Corinth, Vicksburg, Iuka, and Holly Springs, Miss., Resaca, Dallas, Kennesaw, and Atlanta, Ga., where he was wounded, July 22, 1864; sent to the hospital, and two days later his left leg was amputated. He reached home Nov. 1, 1864. On July 9, 1865, by order of the war department was discharged a veteran. During his four years' service, he received two furloughs, Feb. 26, 1862, from Jefferson City, Mo., on account of illness, and Jan. 1, 1864, from Chattanooga. He was of a sympathetic, charitable disposition, and constantly caring for the needy and unfortunate. He received a pension of thirty dollars per month. Married Feb. 11, 1868, Diana Fay; died April 20, 1894. Children:

2482—1. LEWIS MILTON, b. June 29, 1869.
2483—2. ASHFORD BYRON, b. Oct. 24, 1872.
2484—3. VENORA MAY, b. Feb. 20, 1879.
2485—4. NETTIE SYLVIA, b. Aug. 22, 1882.
2486—5. PERLIA HARVEY, b. July 16, 1890.

2487. ALMIRA DRAKE CRANE[8] [1688], (George L.,[7] Stephen,[6] Josiah,[5] Edmund,[4] John,[3] John,[2] Jasper[1]), married Henry M. Harold, at Zanesville, O., Dec. 10, 1866. Children:

1. HYLA MISSOURI (Harold), b. Sept. 20, 1868, in Kansas City, Mo.
2. FRANKLIN HOOK (Harold), b. Nov. 28, 1870, in Kansas City, Mo.
3. MAUD KANSAS (Harold), b. Aug. 1, 1872; m. James Verity, Aug. 18, 1892.
4. DEE ETTIE LITTLE (Harold), b. Aug. 31, 1875; m. William Allen Goodspeed, June 5, 1892.

2488. FRANKLIN HARPER CRAIN[8] [1689], (George L.,[7] Stephen,[6] Josiah,[5] Edmund,[4] John,[3] John,[2] Jasper[1]), July 28, 1861, when less than seventeen years of age, he enlisted in Co. C, 39th

Reg., O. V. I., in the same regiment with his brother Lewis G., and took part in all the engagements with that regiment for three years, not losing a single day from active duty, and escaping all bodily harm throughout his army life. In May, 1865, was severely injured in a stone quarry, and has never fully recovered from that accident. He is now (1897) secretary and treasurer of the Republican Club, at Glen Ebon, O., where he resides. He married April 3, 1872, Hannah Matheny.

Children:

2489—1. WASHINGTON IRVING, b. April 14, 1873.
2490—2. RUBY RENORA, b. June 20, 1876; m. George Hook, May, 1893.
2491—3. RULY MAY, b. April 3, 1879.

2492. LORANIA ABIGAIL CRANE[8] [1690], (George L.,[7] Stephen,[6] Josiah,[5] Edmund,[4] John,[3] John,[2] Jasper[1]), married Dec. 24, 1875, John Killett, of Bradford, Yorkshire, England. She died Jan. 20, 1885. Child:

1. JOHN (Killett), b. Oct. 18, 1877; m. Sylvia Maud Bateman, Sept. 25, 1896.

2493. LYDIA ELLEN CRANE[8] [1691], (George L.,[7] Stephen,[6] Josiah,[5] Edmund,[4] John,[3] John,[2] Jasper[1]), married Dec. 13, 1873, Herbert Graves, of Cumberland, England. Children:

1. ROBERT RODERIC (Graves), } twins, b. June 2, 1875.
2. SOLOMON CHARLES (Graves), }
3. ABBIE JANE, b. Nov. 12, 1877.
4. LYDIA ELLEN, b. Jan. 9, 1884.
5. GEORGE HERBERT, b. Jan. 31, 1889.
6. THOMAS JASPER, b. Oct. 23, 1891.

2494. NETTIE SOPHIA CRANE[8] [1694], (Abram K.,[7] Stephen,[6] Josiah,[5] Edmund,[4] John,[3] John,[2] Jasper[1]), married Harry Thomas Smith, Sept. 4, 1883. He also was a native of Alexandria, Ohio, and born Feb. 17, 1861. Child:

1. FREDERIC GUY (Smith), b. July 7, 1884.

2495. GEORGE BERTRAND CRANE[8] [1695], (Abram K.,[7] Stephen,[6] Josiah,[5] Edmund,[4] John,[3] John,[2] Jasper[1]), married June 10, 1891, at Findlay, Ohio, Pett Kerr, a native of that place, born Oct. 8, 1861. Children:

2496—1. LEONARD KERR, b. Feb. 11, 1894; d. Aug. 28, 1894.
2497—2. GEORGE BERTRAND, b. May 31, 1895.

2498. CHARLOTTE C. CRANE[8] [1701], (Lewis A.,[7] Shadrack,[6] Ezekiel,[5] Edmund,[4] John,[3] John,[2] Jasper[1]), married George F. Nichols, Aug., 1839. She died in 1868. Children:

1. WILLIAM R. (Nichols).
2. MARIAN J. (Nichols).
3. FRANCES A. (Nichols); m. John Harrison Pierce; d. April, 1888.
4. LAURA (Nichols); m. William Abbot.
5. AGNES E. (Nichols); d. Sept., 1897.
6. LEWIS C. (Nichols).
7. GEORGE O. (Nichols).

2499. ELIZABETH CORDELIA CRANE[8] [1702], (Lewis A.,[7] Shadrack,[6] Ezekiel,[5] Edmund,[4] John,[3] John,[2] Jasper[1]), married George Higby, Feb. 8, 1853. He died Oct., 1868, leaving two children. She married 2d, Col. William T. Shaw, and resided in Anamosa, Iowa. Children:

   1. GEORGE HENRY (Higby), b. Nov. 16, 1853.
   2. ENOCH IVES (Higby), b. Feb. 10, 1855; d. Sept. 16.
   3. SARAH FRANCES (Higby), b. Sept. 17, 1858.
   4. ALBERT BILLINGS (Higby), b. July 4, 1862; d. Jan. 5, 1863.

  2500. SARAH FRANCES HIGBY [3]; m. Henry S. Dutton, Jan. 1, 1882.
     Children b. in Anamosa, Iowa. Children:
     1. MARY LOUISE (Dutton), b. Aug. 1, 1887.
     2. WILLIAM LAWRENCE (Dutton), b. April 15, 1894.

2501. BILLINGS CRANE[8] [1703], (Lewis A.,[7] Shadrack,[6] Ezekiel,[5] Edmund,[4] John,[3] John,[2] Jasper[1]), married in February, 1863, Jane E. Deming, who was born in Cooper, Mich., in 1836, and resided there; a farmer. He served as supervisor from 1878 to 1887. He died April 15, 1894. Children:

2502—1. JAY D., b. July, 1868.
2503—2. SARAH ELECTA, b. March, 1878.

  2504. PETER FERRIS CRANE[8] [1707], (Stevens,[7] Shadrack,[6] Ezekiel,[5] Edmund,[4] John,[3] John,[2] Jasper[1]), married Ann Eliot. He died in Ottawa, Kan. Children:

2505—1. FRANK E.; lives at Ottawa, Kan.
2506—2. GEORGE; lives at Spokane, Wash.
2507—3. CHARLES; travelling man.
2508—4. HENRY DAWS; lives at Rossland, B. C.

  2509. AUGUSTA AMELIA CRANE[8] [1708], (Stevens,[7] Shadrack,[6] Ezekiel,[5] Edmund,[4] John,[3] John,[2] Jasper[1]), married Henry McCray. She died in Anamosa, Iowa. Child:

   1. ALBERT (McCray); lives at Agricola, Kan.

2510. HENRY D. CRANE[8] [1709,] (Stevens,[7] Shadrack,[6] Ezekiel,[5] Edmund,[4] John,[3] John,[2] Jasper[1]), married Dec. 25, 1858, in Cascade, Dubuque Co., Iowa, Rossella A. Wightman, who was born in Granville, Ohio, Jan. 31, 1835. Mr. Crane is a miller. Residence at Ottawa, Kan. Child:

2511—1. LULU, b. July 7, 1868, in Cascade, Iowa.

2512. CHARLES DEWITT CRANE[8] [1710], (Stevens,[7] Shadrack,[6] Ezekiel,[5] Edmund,[4] John,[3] John,[2] Jasper[1]), married Dec. 13, 1866, at Cascade, Iowa, Angelica B. Anderson. She was born in Dubuque, Aug. 5, 1842. For many years he has been a dry goods merchant in Ottawa, Kan. Children:

2513—1. ALBERT WALLACE, b. Dec. 30, 1867; d. Feb. 15, 1869, at Cascade.
2514—2. ADA BELLE, b. Aug. 21, 1869.
   43

2515. DERIAS FISH CRANE[8] [1712], (Stevens,[7] Shadrack,[6] Ezekiel,[5] Edmund,[4] John,[3] John,[2] Jasper[1]), married Eliza D. Carmine. Child:

2516—1. MARGARET MAY.

2517. ANN ELIZA CRANE[8] [1713], (Stevens,[7] Shadrack,[6] Ezekiel,[5] Edmund,[4] John,[3] John,[2] Jasper[1]), married Duncan Ferguson in 1860 at Cascade, Iowa. She died in Anamosa, Iowa. Children:

1. HATTIE (Ferguson); m. Mr. Feehan; lives in Murray, Idaho.
2. CLARA (Ferguson); m. Mr. Moffett; lives in Anamosa, Iowa.

2518. MARIA ANTONETTE CRANE[8] [1719], (Roswell R.,[7] Shadrack,[6] Ezekiel,[5] Edmund,[4] John,[3] John,[2] Jasper[1]), married Dec. 15, 1850, Israel Fisher, of Anamosa, Iowa. He was engaged in milling and merchandise business. He died Aug., 1897. Children:

1. FLORENCE (Fisher), } twins; { d
2. FLORA (Fisher),
3. ROLLA (Fisher); d.
4. WALTER (Fisher), } twins; { d..
5. CLARA (Fisher),
6. NELLIE (Fisher).
7. MARTHA (Fisher).

2519. HELEN AMELIA CRANE[8][1720], (Roswell R.,[7] Shadrack,[6] Ezekiel,[5] Edmund,[4] John,[3] John,[2] Jasper[1]), born in Dexter, Mich. Married May 11, 1854, Col. William T. Shaw, grocer, banker and real estate dealer in Anamosa, Iowa. Children:

1. HELEN LOUISE (Shaw), b. June 8, 1855.
2. ANTONETTE M. (Shaw), b. Nov. 7, 1859; d. May 11, 1862

2520. EMILY ADELIA CRANE[8] [1722], (Roswell R.,[7] Shadrack,[6] Ezekiel,[5] Edmund,[4] John,[3] John,[2] Jasper[1]), born at Kalamazoo, Mich.; married May 12, 1856, Daniel Ario Peet, a merchant in Anamosa, Iowa, but recently removed to California, near Los Angeles, he and his wife being in poor health. Children:

1. GEORGE SHAW (Peet); m. Bessie Williams.
2. EMILY ELNORA (Peet); m. Charles Wilde.

2521. ORVILLE D. CRANE[8] [1723], (Roswell R.,[7] Shadrack,[6] Ezekiel,[5] Edmund,[4] John,[3] John,[2] Jasper[1]), married 1st, Mary Barton; 2d, Susie Sutzin. He died in Red River, New Mexico, May 6, 1897. His widow resides at The Dalles, Oregon. He was editor and publisher of a newspaper. Children:

2522—1. MARC.
2523—2. PERLINA.
2524—3. BESSIE.
2525—4. MARCIA.
2526—5. HENRY.
2527—6. ANNA.
2528—7. JENNIE.
2529—8. WINNIE.

2530. LEROY ALBERTI CRANE[8] [1724], (Roswell R.,[7] Shadrack,[6] Ezekiel,[5] Edmund,[4] John,[3] John,[2] Jasper[1]), born at Otsego, Mich. Married in 1864 Carrie M. Hall. He is a lawyer. Residence, Pueblo, Col. Was a captain in 14th Iowa Infantry from 1861 to 1864. Children :

2531—1. CORA; d.
2532—2. WILLIAM.
2533—3. HELEN.
2534—4. EDWIN; d.
2535—5. DANIEL.
2536—6. JOSEPHINE.
2537—7. ROY.

2538. ALICE OPHELIA CRANE[8] [1725], (Roswell R.,[7] Shadrack,[6] Ezekiel,[5] Edmund,[4] John,[3] John,[2] Jasper[1]), born at Otsego, Mich. Married Judge Calvin P. Holmes, July 9, 1863. Residence, Des Moines, Iowa. Child :

1. MABEL (Holmes).

2539. MARCIA THERESA CRANE[8] [1726], (Roswell R.,[7] Shadrack,[6] Ezekiel,[5] Edmund,[4] John,[3] John,[2] Jasper[1]), born at Otsego, Mich. Married Archibald B. Cox, Nov. 16, 1865. He was a hotel-keeper in Marshalltown, Iowa, for over twenty years. He died April 3, 1897. Child :

1. ARCHIBALD M. (Cox).

2540. WILLIAM WHITNEY CRANE[8] [1728], (James N.,[7] Shadrack,[6] Ezekiel,[5] Edmund,[4] John,[3] John,[2] Jasper[1]), married at New Orleans, La., July 17, 1858, by Rev. Mr. Hedges, to Ruth Ann McFadden. She was born in 1840, and died July 9, 1868, in that city, where they resided. He died Oct. 31, 1880. Children :

2541—1. WILLIAM WHITNEY, b. Sept. 29, 1859.
2541½-2. HORACE BEAN, b. Sept. 30, 1863; d. July 21, 1867.

2542. ISRAEL CRANE[8] [1776], (Matthias,[7] Israel,[6] Matthias,[5] William,[4] Nathaniel,[3] Azariah,[2] Jasper[1]), married in 1866 Anna Barnes. He is a graduate of Princeton, 1854; now (1897) a merchant in New York. Child :

2542½-1. PERCY S.

2543. JOSEPH OWEN CRANE[8] [1807], (Walworth D.,[7] Calvin S.,[6] Jonas,[5] William,[4] Nathaniel,[3] Azariah,[2] Jasper[1]), was born in New York city, and married there Nov. 23, 1881, Meta M. Smith, who was born Feb. 6, 1859, at Petrolia, Pa. She was a graduate of Vassar College. He graduated at Columbia College in 1881. He is engaged in stock brokerage business, and his late residence is at Warwick Avenue, South Orange, N. J. Child :

2544—1. LEWIS DOUGLASS, b. Nov. 22, 1882, in New York city.

2545. ROBERT NEWTON CRANE[8] [1815], (John N.,[7] Josiah W.,[6] William,[5] William,[4] Nathaniel,[3] Azariah,[2] Jasper[1]), mar-

ried Mary Frances Allen at St. Louis, Mo., Nov. 12, 1873. She was born there Dec. 23, 1853. He is a graduate of Wesleyan University, Middletown, Conn, 1867; was United States consul at Manchester, Eng., from March, 1874, to Nov., 1877. He is an attorney and counsellor-at-law. Residence, St. Louis, Mo. Children:

2546—1. GERARD B. ALLEN, b. June 12, 1875, at Manchester, Eng.
2547—2. ROBERT EUGENE, b. Jan. 8, 1879, at St. Louis, Mo.

2548. EDWARD NICHOLS CRANE[8] [1822], (Edward A.,[7] Lydia,[6] Oliver,[5] William,[4] Nathaniel,[3] Azariah,[2] Jasper[1]), married June 9, 1875, Cordelia Catharine Matthews. She was born in Craneville, now Cranford, N. J., Feb. 9, 1853. He is a member of the firm of Crane & Co., manufacturers of saddlery hardware. Residence, Newark, N. J. Children:

2549—1. HELEN MATTHEWS, b. Feb. 27, 1876.
2550—2. EDNA NICHOLS, b. Nov. 20, 1878.
3. JASPER.
4. AMANDA.
5. CORDELIA.
6. EDWARD.

2551. ELIZABETH MARION CRANE[8] [1841], (Oliver,[7] Stephen F.,[6] Oliver,[5] William,[4] Nathaniel,[3] Azariah,[2] Jasper[1]), married Rev. John S. Gardner, June 28, 1876. Children:

1. JOHN CRANE (Gardner), b. May 17, 1877.
2. OLIVER CRANE (Gardner), b. Sept. 27, 1878.
3. MARION CRANE (Gardner), b. Sept. 28, 1881.
4. WILLIAM (Gardner),   } twins, b. July 8, 1884; both d. in infancy
5. AUGUSTA (Gardner),

2551½. CAROLINE HANNAH CRANE[8] [1842], (Oliver,[7] Stephen F.,[6] Oliver,[5] William,[4] Nathaniel,[3] Azariah,[2] Jasper[1]), married Jan. 13, 1880, Edward C. Lyon. Children:

1. EDWARD CRANE (Lyon), b. Oct. 26, 1880.
2. MARION CRANE (Lyon), b. Nov. 12, 1881.
3. OLIVER CRANE (Lyon), b. March 1, 1885.
4. WAYNMAN CRANE (Lyon), b. Dec. 4, 1890.

2552. OLIVER TURNBULL CRANE[8] [1843], (Oliver,[7] Stephen F.,[6] Oliver,[5] William,[4] Nathaniel,[3] Azariah,[2] Jasper[1]), married Gertrude Boyd, Jan. 6, 1892. Children:

2553—1. GERTRUDE, b. Oct. 31, 1892.
2554—2. DAVID BOYD, b. Nov., 1894.

2555. CALEB G. CRANE[8] [1856], (Moses P.,[7] Caleb,[6] Samuel,[5] Noah,[4] Nathaniel,[3] Azariah,[2] Jasper[1]), born in Caldwell, N. J.; married there Jan. 9, 1853, Mary J. Maynard, also of that place. She died at Mandarin, Fla., May 20, 1873. He married 2d, at Newark, N. J., April 20, 1875, Eva D. Leverich, of that place. He was alderman for the first ward of the city of Newark in 1869, 1870, 1871 and 1872; also lieutenant-colonel of N. J. S. M. He has been engaged in growing oranges

at Mandarin, Fla. Their three eldest children were born in Caldwell, N. J.; the fourth in Newark. Children:

2556—1. ELLA AMELIA, b. April 3, 1854.
2557—2. WALDO MAYNARD, b. Dec. 25, 1856.
2558—3. SARAH AUGUSTA, b. April 14, 1861.
2559—4. MARY ERNESTINE, b. May 17, 1865.

2560. EDWARD W. CRANE[8] [1859], (Moses P.,[7] Caleb,[6] Samuel,[5] Noah,[4] Nathaniel,[3] Azariah,[2] Jasper[1]), married Elmira M. Crane, and lived in Newark, N. J. Child:

2561—1. EDWARD LINCOLN, b. Aug. 3, 1868; went to Sanborn, Dak.

2562. MARCUS HARRISON CRANE[8] [1861], (Zenas C.,[7] Caleb,[6] Samuel,[5] Noah,[4] Nathaniel,[3] Azariah,[2] Jasper[1]), married Effie Muzzy in May, 1869, and settled in Urbana, Ohio, where he is engaged in the manufacture of stoves. Children:

2563—1. EDGAR MELVIN.
2564—2. MARIA STEEL; d. 1888.
2565—3. FRANCES.

2566. ANNA MARIA CRANE[8] [1862], (Zenas C.,[7] Caleb,[6] Samuel,[5] Noah,[4] Nathaniel,[3] Azariah,[2] Jasper[1]), married Oct. 5, 1871. Children:

1. ROBERT.
2. LYNN LOCKWARD.

2567. CALEB CRANE[8] [1863], (Zenas C.,[7] Caleb,[6] Samuel,[5] Noah,[4] Nathaniel,[3] Azariah,[2] Jasper[1]), married May, 1877, in Paterson, N. J. He is a farmer. Child:

2568—1. LEWIS MARTIN.

2569. ELIAS BEACH CRANE[8] [1905], (Smith E.,[7] Elias B.,[6] Aaron,[5] Job,[4] Azariah,[3] Azariah,[2] Jasper[1]), married Feb. 10, 1861, Alice A. King. He died in 1875. Children:

2570—1. ISABEL W., b. Jan. 30, 1862.
2571—2. BESSIE K., b. Jan. 29, 1866.
2572—3. HENRY WILBUR; d. in infancy.

2573. FREDERICK EMONS CRANE[8] [1906], (Smith E.,[7] Elias B.,[6] Aaron,[5] Job,[4] Azariah,[3] Azariah,[2] Jasper[1]), married May 31, 1872, Emma Nichols. Children:

2574—1. WATSON WILBUR, b. Feb. 29, 1873.
2575—2. ALMONA M., b. April 7, 1875.

2576. MARY VANCE CRANE[8] [1907], (Smith E.,[7] Elias B.,[6] Aaron,[5] Job,[4] Azariah,[3] Azariah,[2] Jasper[1]), married Dec. 18, 1872, Jacob W. Hadden. Children:

1. AMZI (Hadden), b. Nov. 5, 1873.
2. CLARENCE W. (Hadden), b. Nov. 11, 1875.

2577. AMZI BEACH CRANE[8] [1909], (Smith E.,[7] Elias B.,[6] Aaron,[5] Job,[4] Azariah,[3] Azariah,[2] Jasper[1]), married Jan. 7, 1874, Charlotte Turner. Children:

2578—1. MARY MACKAY, b. Feb. 16, 1875.

2579—2. WILLIAM HERBERT, b. June 16, 1877.
2580—3. ALICE GERTRUDE, b. Feb. 19, 1882.
2581—4. AMZI BEACH, b. Jan. 16, 1884.
2582—5. JOHN GARRETT, b. Oct. 28, 1885.
2583—6. CHARLOTTE, b. Dec. 5, 1886.

2584. ANNA E. CRANE[8] [1914], (Charles S.,[7] Elias B.,[6] Aaron,[5] Job,[4] Azariah,[3] Azariah,[2] Jasper[1]), married Charles R. Pickard, in 1880. Child:

1. ROBERT A. (Pickard), b. 1881.

2585. KATE OSBOURNE CRANE[8] [1916], (Charles S.,[7] Elias B.,[6] Aaron,[5] Job,[4] Azariah,[3] Azariah,[2] Jasper[1]), married Thomas McCallie, in 1890. Child:

1. THOMAS CRANE (McCallie), b. 1892.

2586. DEWITT C. CRANE[8] [1919], (Zebina,[7] Jacob G.,[6] Zebina,[5] Gamaliel,[4] Azariah,[3] Azariah,[2] Jasper[1]), married 1st, Sept. 8, 1869, Cora Harrison. She died and he married 2nd, March 30, 1871, Elizabeth Smith. She died leaving a son. He married 3d, Katherine Van Valkenburg, April 7, 1881. Mr. Crane was educated at the Marion Collegiate Institute, at Marion, N. Y., and at the Business College, Poughkeepsie, N. Y.; settled on a farm on the western portion of Marion, but subsequently removed to the village of Newark, Wayne Co. Children:

2587—1. FRED W., b. Dec. 7, 1875.
2588—2. EDITH J., b. Jan. 1, 1887.

2589. EMILY P. CRANE[8] [1920], (Zebina,[7] Jacob G.,[6] Zebina,[5] Gamaliel,[4] Azariah,[3] Azariah,[2] Jasper[1]), married Henry D. Stebbins, Dec. 29, 1869, and settled on a farm in the western part of Walworth, N. Y. Some years later they removed to Palmyra, but his late residence is upon a portion of the farm where she was reared. Children:

1. CORA H. (Stebbins), b. Feb. 13, 1871.
2 LUCY B. (Stebbins), b. March 4, 1874; m. Arthur Pratt, April 26, 1895.
. MYRON E. (Stebbins), b. March 9, 1876.
. ELLA MAY (Stebbins), b. Aug. 1, 1878.
. ARTHUR G. (Stebbins), b. Oct. 5, 1880.
6. ROBERT Z. (Stebbins), b. Jan. 5, 1887.

2590. MARY A. CRANE[8] [1922], (Zebina,[7] Jacob G.,[6] Zebina,[5] Gamaliel,[4] Azariah,[3] Azariah,[2] Jasper[1]), married Richard B. McOmber, Nov. 26, 1874. Children:

1. ORRA (McOmber), b. Feb. 5, 1876; m. Thos. B. Witherden, May 5, 1896. Child:
    1. BENJAMIN THOMAS (Witherden), b. Feb. 13, 1897.
2. ISRAEL Z. (McOmber), b. Oct. 7, 1881.

2591. ELIZABETH J. CRANE[8] [1924], (Myron,[7] Jacob G.,[6] Zebina,[5] Gamaliel,[4] Azariah,[3] Azariah,[2] Jasper[1]), married Newton H. Garlock, Jan. 8, 1866. She died March 24, 1872.

Children :

1. ALFRED A. (Garlock), b, May 13, 1867.
2. JENNIE B. (Garlock), b. Jan. 2, 1869.
3. ELLEN V. (Garlock), b. Oct. 18, 1870.

2592. ALFRED A. GARLOCK [1]; m. Nellie Smith, April 4, 1894.
Children :
1. SIBYL E. (Garlock).
2. WINIFRED M. (Garlock).
3. GEORGE D. (Garlock).

2593. WILLIAM ALPHONZO CRANE[8] [1925], (Myron,[7] Jacob
G.,[6] Zebina,[5] Gamaliel,[4] Azariah,[3] Azariah,[2] Jasper[1]), married
Lydia E. Robinson, Nov. 13, 1883. Children :

2594—1. ELLA MAY, b. Sept. 24, 1884.
2495—2. MAY GERTRUDE, b. Nov. 26, 1886.
2596—3. MYRON W., b. Feb. 6, 1889.

2597. C. ELLEN CRANE[8] [1926], (Myron,[7] Jacob G.,[6]
Zebina,[5] Gamaliel,[4] Azariah,[3] Azariah,[2] Jasper[1]), married Albert
Seeley, Jan. 1, 1872. He died and she married 2d, George
Cheatem, Jan. 24, 1894. The family reside in Williamson, N.
Y., where Mr. Cheatem is a hardware merchant. One child by
second husband.

2598. MARION F. CRANE[8] [1929], (Caleb,[7] Jacob G.,[6]
Zebina,[5] Gamaliel,[4] Azariah,[3] Azariah,[2] Jasper[1]), married Lydia
L. Lawrence, Nov. 28, 1880. Children :

1. CHESTER A., b. Nov. 18, 1882; d. June 19, 1884.
2. ADA ALMEDA, b. Sept. 12, 1884.
3. HARRIET MAY, b. March 22, 1886.
4. WALTER CALEB, b. April 1, 1888.
5. CLARENCE ALONZO, b. April 6, 1890.

2599. JACOB ASA CRANE[8] [1937], (J. Smith,[7] Jacob G.,[6]
Zebina,[5] Gamaliel,[4] Azariah.[3] Azariah,[2] Jasper[1]), married March
4, 1885, Bertha Hodge. She died and he married 2d, Dec. 14, -
1893, Carrie Eldridge. Children :

2600—1. MARY L., b. May 17, 1886; d. Aug. 8, 1886.
2601—2. ANNA GRACE, b. Feb. 25, 1888.
2602—3. GEORGE D., b. Feb. 28, 1891; d. Aug. 31, 1891.
2603—4. ALBERT L., b. May 22, 1895.
2604—5. ELMER J., b. May 22, 1895.
2605—6. FLOYD WILLIAM, b. Jan. 30, 1897.

2606. HIRAM D. CRANE[8] [1941], (Frederick S.,[7] David,[6]
Zebina,[5] Gamaliel,[4] Azariah,[3] Azariah,[2] Jasper[1]), married Nellie
M. Flanders, Sept. 8, 1887. Children :

2607—1. INA, b. June, 1891.
2608—2. OLIVE, b. July 21, 1895.

2609. MYRON F. CRANE[8] [1943], (Frederick S.,[7] David,[6]
Zebina,[5] Gamaliel,[4] Azariah,[3] Azariah,[2] Jasper[1]), married Mary
L. Snow, Aug. 3, 1882. Children :

2610—1. MARY C., b. May 10, 1885; d. Sept. 29, 1886.

2611—2. LOTTIE M., b. Oct. 22, 1887.
2612—3. GLADYS N., b. Oct. 25, 1888.

2613. CARRIE MAY CRANE[8] [1945], (Frederick S.,[7] David,[6] Zebina,[5] Gamaliel,[4] Azariah,[3] Azariah,[2] Jasper[1]), married Frank Patten, Aug. 20, 1891. Children :

1. BYRON C. (Patten), b. June 14, 1892.
2. BARBARY (Patten), b. Sept. 1, 1893.
3. EVERITT FRANK (Patten), b. July 7, 1895.

2614. WILLIAM ERASTUS CRANE[8] [1972], (William A.,[7] Obediah,[6] Zebina,[5] Gamaliel,[4] Azariah,[3] Azariah,[2] Jasper[1]), was born in Lyons, Mich., married in Ann Arbor, Ada Tremper, June 17, 1884; graduate of the law department, Michigan University, 1882. He is an attorney-at-law. Children :

2615—1. LLOYD, b. April 5, 1886.
2616—2. GLADYS, b. April 23, 1890.

2617. RILEY LEONARD CRANE[8] [1973], (William A.,[7] Obediah,[6] Zebina,[5] Gamaliel,[4] Azariah,[3] Azariah,[2] Jasper[1]), married Clara Duprau, Dec., 1882. Children :

2618—1. MABEL, b. March, 1885.
2619—2. LAURA, b. May, 1888.
2620—3. CORA, b. Dec., 1889.

2621. HIRAM AMBROSE CRANE[8] [1974], (William A.,[7] Obediah,[6] Zebina,[5] Gamaliel,[4] Azariah,[3] Azariah,[2] Jasper[1]), married Lucy Steckhart, April, 1885. Children :

2622—1. GEORGE EARLE, b. July, 1886.
2623—2. WINIFRED MAY, b. May, 1891.

2624. WILLIAM F. CRANE[8] [2085], (Andrew F.,[7] William,[6] Rufus,[5] Jonas,[4] John,[3] Azariah,[2] Jasper[1]), served in the confederate army, Oct. 15, 1861, to Jan. 3, 1865; enlisting as private, Co. C, 1st Md. C. S. Cavalry, subsequently made ordnance officer, Maryland Line, under Gen. R. E. Lee's command. He married Florence Bangs, in Washington, D. C., Sept. 28, 1872. She was a native of that city, born March 21, 1853. Mr. Crane has been employed in the United States Treasury Department, Washington; occupation, bookkeeper; residence, Georgetown, D. C. Child :

2625—1. DORSET, b. Aug. 18, 1878.

2626. CHARLES THOMAS CLARK CRANE[8] [2080], (Adoniram J.,[7] William,[6] Rufus,[5] Jonas,[4] John,[3] Azariah,[2] Jasper[1]), married Annie Lovering. Children :

2627—1. CHARLES LOVERING.
2628—2. ROBERT TREAT.
2629—3. JOHN ALDEN.

2630. MARY CRANE[8] [2086], (Andrew F.,[7] William,[6] Rufus,[5] Jonas,[4] John,[3] Azariah,[2] Jasper[1]), married William R. Devries. Children :

1. W. L. (Devries); minister in Washington, D. C.

2. MARY (Devries); married Frank Frick.
3. LYDIA (Devries).

2631. CHARLES CAMPBELL CRANE[8] [2088], (Andrew F.,[7] William,[6] Rufus,[5] Jonas,[4] John,[3] Azariah,[2] Jasper[1]), married Maria Virginia Zell. She died leaving six children. He married 2d, Miss Hawes. Children:

2632—1. ELIZABETH.
2633—2. CAMPBELL.
2634—3. OLIVER.
2635—4. FLORENCE.
2636—5. GEORGE.
2637—6. ANDREW.

2638. FLORENCE CRANE[8] [2089], (Andrew F.,[7] William,[6] Rufus,[5] Jonas,[4] John,[3] Azariah,[2] Jasper[1]), married George N. Appold. Child:

1. SARAH (Appold).

2639. ALICE CRANE[8] [2090], (Andrew F.,[7] William,[6] Rufus,[5] Jonas,[4] John,[3] Azariah,[2] Jasper[1]), married George H. Bayne. Child:

1. GEORGE (Bayne).

2640. MARY JANE CRANE[8] [2119], (Frederick M.,[7] John,[6] Matthias,[5] John,[4] John,[3] Azariah,[2] Jasper[1]), married 1st, Bennett Curtis; 2d, C. T. Green. A grocer. Residence (1880), Elkhart, Ind. Children:

1. WILLIAM LIBERTY (Curtis).
2. LOUVETTA (Curtis); d. aged 3½ years.

2641. RICHARD ELLIS CRANE[8] [2120], Frederick M.,[7] John,[6] Matthias,[5] John,[4] John,[3] Azariah,[2] Jasper[1]), married 1st, Libby Miller; 2d, Lenorah Winebrenner. Residence (1880), Elkhart, Ind. Children:

2642—1. FRANK.
2643—2. LUELLA.

2644. WILLIAM BOWEN CRANE[8] [2121], (Frederick M.,[7] John,[6] Matthias,[5] John,[4] John,[3] Azariah,[2] Jasper[1]), married Sept. 2, 1874, at Cleveland, O., Frances C. Whitney. Residence (1880), Cleveland, O. Children:

2645—1. MARY FRANCES, b. June 2, 1875.
2646—2. WILLIAM FREDERICK, b. Jan. 17, 1878.

2647. WESLEY S. CRANE[8] [2194], (Benjamin,[7] Abner,[6] Benjamin,[5] Benjamin,[4] Joseph,[3] Jasper,[2] Jasper[1]), married Caroline E. Reilly, Jan. 5, 1860. He served in the 153d Regt., O. N. G., Co. C, during the civil war as musician, 100 days' service, or three-months man. Residence at Bethel, Ohio. Children:

2648—1. FRANCIS E., b. Nov. 12, 1860; a teacher; is principal of the Columbia School in Avondale, Cincinnati, Ohio.
2649—2. A son, b. 1864; d. June, 1864; two weeks old.

44

2650—3. HARRY L., b. March 7, 1866; teacher; principal of the
Oakley Schools, Cincinnati, Ohio.

2651—4. ANNIE, b. May 16, 1870; m. S. J. Casey; residence, Love-
land, Ohio.

2652. REBECCA CRANE[8] [2196], (Benjamin,[7] Abner,[6] Benja--
min,[5] Benjamin,[4] Joseph,[3] Jasper,[2] Jasper[1]), married Walter W.
Burke. She died. Child:

1. JAMES (Burke); resides near Bethel, Ohio.

2653. ABNER CRANE[8] [2197], (Benjamin,[7] Abner,[6] Benja-
min,[5] Benjamin,[4] Joseph,[3] Jasper,[2] Jasper[1]), married Melvina
Clemenson. ·Lives in Mount Pleasant, San Pete Co., Utah.
Children :

2654—1. ANNIE.
2655—2. WILLIAM WALTER.

2656. MARY ELLEN CRANE[8] [2198], (Benjamin,[7] Abner,[6]
Benjamin,[5] Benjamin,[4] Joseph,[3] Jasper,[2] Jasper[1]), married
William Swing. She died. Children:

1. LIZZIE (Swing).
2. IDA (Swing); lives in Mattoon, Ill.

2657. ELIZABETH CRANE[8] [2199], (Benjamin,[7] Abner,[6]
Benjamin,[5] Benjamin,[4] Joseph,[3] Jasper,[2] Jasper[1]), married
Charles Goodwin. She died. Children live in Cincinnati, Ohio.
Children :

1. JAMES (Goodwin).
2. THOMAS (Goodwin).

2658. ANNIE CRANE[8] [2200], (Benjamin,[7] Abner,[6] Benjamin,[5] Benjamin,[4] Joseph,[3] Jasper,[2] Jasper[1]), married T. G.·
Moorehead, and live at Walnut Hills, Cincinnati, Ohio. Her
mother makes her home with this daughter, and it was at their
home that the mother celebrated her ninety-third birthday Jan.
6, 1899. Child:

1. WALTER (Moorehead).

2659. JOHN HENRY CRANE[8] [2224], (Stephen V. R.,[7] Timothy,[6] Benjamin,[5] Benjamin,[4] Joseph,[3] Jasper,[2] Jasper[1]), married
Sarah Jackson, Sept. 30, 1863. She was born in 1839, and died
May 15, 1887. Residence at Galway, N. Y.; is travelling
agent for Miller's Falls Co., of New York city. Child:

2660—1. WILLIAM JACKSON, b. April 26, 1865; m. Harriette Stewart,
June 10, 1896. She was b. Sept. 12, 1869. They reside on
the Crane farm in Galway, Mr. Crane being in the fourth
generation of the family that have lived on this farm.

2661. CAROLINE BANKS CRANE[8] [2257], (Henry A. R.,[7]
Abijah,[6] Isaac,[5] Isaac,[4] Joseph,[3] Jasper,[2] Jasper[1]), born at
Palatka, Fla. Married May 9, 1864, John Harry Jenks, a
native of Bath, Me. He was born March 10, 1834. Settled at
Key West, Fla. Children:

1. JOHN HENRY ALLEN (Jenks), b. May 8, 1865.

2. BENJAMIN DEAN (Jenks), b. Jan. 17, 1867.
3. ALEXANDER CYRUS (Jenks), b. Jan. 22, 1869..

2662. SOPHIA M. CRANE[8] [2259], (Henry A. R.,[7] Abijah,[6] Isaac,[5] Isaac,[4] Joseph,[3] Jasper,[2] Jasper[1]), born at Mellonsville, Fla. Married April 3, 1867, at Key West, Peter J. Crocker, and settled at Tampa. Children:

  1. FANNY.M. C. (Crocker), b. July 7, 1873. .
  2. FLORA M. A. (Crocker), b. April 12, 1877; d. Jan. 17, 1883.
  3. HENRY C. (Crocker), b. Dec. 30, 1881; d. July 31, 1882.
  4. CARRIE M. E. (Crocker), b. July 25, 1883; d. June 11, 1884, at Sarasota, Fla.

2663. LUCETTA E. CRANE[8] [2260], (Henry A. R.,[7] Abijah,[6] Isaac,[5] Isaac,[4] Joseph,[3] Jasper,[2] Jasper[1]), born at Mellonsville, Fla. Married at Key West, Jan. 7, 1873, Juan Francisco y Diaz y Fernandez. Children:

  1. ANGELIQUE (Fernandez), b. Oct. 31, 1873; m. Albert F. Shultz, who for many years held the office of clerk of the criminal court at Key West, Fla., having been reëlected for highly creditable service.
  2. MARIA DIAZ (Fernandez), b. Oct. 4, 1877.

2664. JOSEPH SIDNEY BREWSTER CRANE[8] [2265], (Sidney,[7] John J.,[6] Josiah,[5] Josiah,[4] Joseph,[3] Jasper,[2] Jasper[1]), married Harriet Draper in Hartford, June 9, 1853. She was born in Greenfield, Mass., Jan. 10, 1829. He graduated at South Carolina College in 1840, and University of Pennsylvania in 1844. Their eldest child was born in Columbia, S. C.; all the other children in New York city, where he located as a practicing physician. Children:

2665—1. CATHARINE, b. June 26, 1856.
3666—2. AMELIA B., b. Nov., 1863.
2667—3. CHARLES SIDNEY, b. Oct., 1866.
2668—4. CHARLTON W., b. Jan., 1872.

2669. JAMES BOATWRIGHT CRANE, M.D.[8] [2267], (Sidney,[7] John J.,[6] Josiah,[5] Josiah,[4] Joseph,[3] Jasper,[2] Jasper[1]), married in Sumter, S. C., March 12, 1857, Frances A. Wilson. She was a native of that place, and born Nov. 6, 1830. She is a graduate of Darlington Female College, Darlington, S. C. He is a graduate of the Medical College, State of South Carolina, of 1851, and a practicing physician at Batesville, Ark. Children:

2670—1. SIDNEY WILSON, b. Dec. 1, 1858.
2671—2. KATHERINE F., b. July 7, 1860; was teacher in Arkansas College, Batesville.
2672—3. ARTHUR J., b. May 20, 1866.
2673—4. CHARLTON J., b. Feb. 12, 1870.
2674—5. MARY W., b. March 25, 1873.

2675. JOHN AUGUSTUS CRANE[8] [2272], (John J.,[7] Benjamin,[6] Josiah,[5] Josiah,[4] Joseph,[3] Jasper,[2] Jasper[1]), married in 1865 Harriet Faile, daughter of Edward G. and Ann Valentine Faile. She died Dec. 14, 1897. Children:

2676—1. JOHN JOSIAH, b. Oct. 17, 1866.

2677—2. WILLIAM AUGUSTUS, b. Nov. 4, 1873.
2678—3. ANNIE.

2679. THEODORE B. CRANE[8] [2275], (John J.,[7] Benjamin,[6] Josiah,[5] Josiah,[4] Joseph,[3] Jasper,[2] Jasper[1]), married in Brooklyn, N. Y., April 30, 1873, Margaret B. Wilmot, of Toronto, born Feb. 17, 1852. Children :

2680—1. SARAH H., b. Feb. 21, 1875, in Savannah, Ga.
2681—2. THEODORE.

2682. Rev. EDWARD PAYSON CRANE[8] [2345], (Isaac W.,[7] Nehemiah J.,[6] Jonathan,[5] Nehemiah,[4] Jonathan,[3] Jasper,[2] Jasper1), born in New York city; became a Congregational minister. April, 1879, he located in Minnesota. He served in the late war as chaplain of the 39th New Jersey Volunteers, from Oct., 1864, to the close of the war; was with Grant before Petersburg. Married Oct. 25, 1865, at Madison, N. J., Mary Ward Griswold, who was born May 31, 1841, in Columbia, N. J. His residence, July, 1879, was High Forest, Olmsted Co., Minn.
Children :

2683—1. CHAUNCEY CAROL, b. Nov. 19, 1867, in Greenville, Orange Co., N. Y.
2684—2. ARTHUR GRISWOLD, b. Sept. 1, 1877, in Davenport Centre, Delaware Co., N. Y.

2685. THEODORE F. CRANE[8] [2347], (Isaac W.,[7] Nehemiah J.,[6] Jonathan,[5] Nehemiah,[4] Jonathan,[3] Jasper,[2] Jasper1), was born in New York city, and married in Pennsylvania, June 1, 1867, Mary C. Allen, who was born at Harmony, N. J., Sept. 25, 1842; settled in Newark. He is a photo artist. Children :

2686—1. MINNIE C.
2687—2. HARRY A.
2688—3. EDWARD F.
2689—4. DAISY H.
2690—5. MARY E.
2691—6. THEODORE F.

2692. SARAH ELIZABETH CRANE[8] [2351], (John C.,[7] Nehemiah J.,[6] Jonathan,[5] Nehemiah,[4] Jonathan,[3] Jasper,[2] Jasper1), married Dr. Seigfried Neumann, of Koenigsberg, Prussia.
Children :

1. MARY AMELIA (Neumann), b. Sept. 24, 1851; d. Feb. 29, 1876.
2. ALEXANDER CUMMINGS (Neumann), b. Oct. 17, 1853.
3. ROSA ELIZABETH (Neumann), b. Nov. 8, 1855; d. April 6, 1864.
4. LOUIS WARD (Neumann), b. Sept. 20, 1859; d. Jan. 20, 1896.
5. LILLIE HERMENIA (Neumann).
6. STELLA ADELAIDE (Neumann).

2693. CHARLES LYMAN CRANE[9] [2367], (Oliver M.,[8] John A.,[7] Benjamin,[6] Josiah,[5] Edmund,[4] John,[3] John,[2] Jasper[1]), married Armind Tompkins, at Montrose, Pa., Dec. 20, 1874. About 1879, he removed to Nebraska; was engaged in banking business. Children:

2694—1. LEWIS.
2695—2. CELIA.
2696—3. FRED.
2697—4. GRACE.
2698—5. ALICE.

2699. JOHN PHINEAS CRANE[9] [2368], (Oliver M.,[8] John A.,[7] Benjamin,[6] Josiah,[5] Edmund,[4] John,[3] John,[2] Jasper[1]), married Lucy Evelyn Jackson, March 15, 1877, at Cohoes, N. Y., where she was born, Jan. 25, 1858. He is a minister of the Methodist Church, Troy conference. Children:

2700—1. GEORGE PARKER, b. July 17, 1878, at Bridgewater, Sus-
              quehanna Co., Pa.
2701—2. JOHN DIXON, b. Jan. 26, 1881, at Wells, Hamilton Co., N. Y.
2702—3. ALICE LOUISE, b. April 9, 1882, at Cohoes, Albany Co., N. Y.

2703. MARY EUGENIE CRANE[9] [2369], (Oliver M.,[8] John A.,[7] Benjamin,[6] Josiah,[5] Edmund,[4] John,[3] John,[2] Jasper[1]), married at Montrose, Pa., Charles Henry Van Loan, Jan. 15, 1876. He was born Dec. 25, 1850. Children:

1. EUGENE M. (Van Loan), b. May 2, 1877.
2. NELLY MARIE (Van Loan), b. Nov. 5, 1878.
3. BESSIE BELLE (Van Loan), b. Jan. 5, 1880.
4. CHARLES PAUL (Van Loan), b. July 23, 1893.

2704. JOHN JUDSON CRANE[9] [2371], (William H.,[8] Josiah,[7] Benjamin,[6] Josiah,[5] Edmund,[4] John,[3] John,[2] Jasper[1]), was born at Fair Oaks, Orange Co., N. Y., March 27, 1843; married Rose A. Terry, Nov. 21, 1866. She was also a native of Fair Oaks, and was born Jan. 6, 1844. Mr. Crane lived on the farm with his father until a young man, and while yet in his teens went to New York city. He was there at the time of the first draft for the civil war, and among those drafted, but failed to pass the physical examination, was advised by the examining surgeon to leave the city at once, and go back on the farm. Realizing his condition he acted on the suggestion, resigning a good position. Some years later he returned to the city, but on account of his

health was again compelled to return to the farm. Mr. Crane has been elected tax collector for the town in which he lives. Child:

2705—1. LULU MAY, b. March 18, 1869 : d. Aug. 12, 1870.

2706. HARRISON HORTON CRANE[9] [2372], (William H.,[8] Josiah,[7] Benjamin,[6] Josiah,[5] Edmund,[4] John,[3] John,[2] Jasper[1]), was born at Burlingham, Sullivan Co., N. Y. His boyhood days were spent on a farm. In the spring of 1861, he went to Middletown, N. Y., and entered the employ of Scott, Sayer and Scott to learn the tinsmith and hardware trade, but about four years later he went to New York city, and secured a position with Lord and Taylor. In Feb., 1865, he left the latter firm to accept a position in the National Park Bank, where he remained about fifteen years, when he resigned that charge to engage in the dairy restaurant business with his brother Charles G. Crane, and which for a number of years they conducted on the temperance plan. For the past ten years, he has been in partnership with the house of Cantrell, shoe dealers, West Twenty-third Street, New York city. He resides at Middletown, N. Y., and when the town became a city, was elected first president of the Common Council. He married May 10, 1870, at St. Paul's M. E. Church, Newark, N. J., Mary Elizabeth Morehouse, of Newark, N. J. She was born July 6, 1845; daughter of the late Samuel Baldwin Morehouse and Sarah Hall.
Children, born in New York city:

2707—1. GRACE, b. Nov. 18, 1872.
2708—2. HARRISON DINSMORE, b. Dec. 24, 1874.
2709—3. CLAUDE GRANVILLE, b. July 29, 1876 ; was graduated from Middletown High School, in 1896, and the same year entered the college of physicians and surgeons, Columbia University, of New York city, receiving the degree of M. D., 1898.

2710. CHARLES GEORGE CRANE[9] [2374], (William H.,[8] Josiah,[7] Benjamin,[6] Josiah,[5] Edmund,[4] John,[3] John,[2] Jasper[1]), was born Feb. 15, 1849, at Fair Oaks, Orange Co., N. Y. He married Marie Eugenia Dickinson, of Newark, N. J., May 18, 1875, where he made his residence, doing business in New York city. He died Jan. 10, 1884. Children :

2711—1. HERBERT ROYAL, b. March 22, 1876.
2712—2. ALICE MAWBRY, b. Dec. 30, 1878.
2713—3. HOWARD DICKINSON, b. July 29, 1881.
2714—4. CHARLES GEORGE, b. July 21, 1883.

2715. JAMES EMMETT DURYEA CRANE[9] [2377], (William H.,[8] Josiah,[7] Benjamin,[6] Josiah,[5] Edmund,[4] John,[3] John,[2] Jasper[1]), was born Dec. 23, 1856, at Fair Oaks, Orange Co., N. Y. His early life was spent on the farm, later went to New York city. He married June 19, 1889, Edith May Wilkinson, daughter of Walter Weed and Cynthia Corwin Wilkinson, of Middletown, N. Y., born May 23, 1862. In 1889 he went to Milton, Penn.,

where he remained a few years, and then returned to his native town, locating on a farm, where he now resides. Children:

2716—1. PAUL WILKINSON, b. June 19, 1890, at Milton, Penn.
2717—2. FAITH, b. Sept. 8, 1891, at Milton, Penn.
2718—3. ELSIE, b. Aug. 24, 1893, at Milton, Penn.; d. Dec. 26, 1897.
2719—4. OLIVE, b. Aug. 18, 1895, at Fair Oaks, Orange Co., N. Y.
2720—5. ISABELLA, b. March 1, 1898, at Fair Oaks, Orange Co., N. Y.; d. July 30, 1898.

2721. MARY EMMERETTE CRANE[9] [2378], (William H.,[8] Josiah,[7] Benjamin,[6] Josiah,[5] Edmund,[4] John,[3] John,[2] Jasper[1]), born at Fair Oaks, Orange Co., N. Y., Feb. 23, 1859. Married Dec. 28, 1882, Stanley S. Arthur at Fair Oaks. He was born Aug. 18, 1857. Children:

1. HAZEL CRANE (Arthur), b. Sept. 22, 1885, at Corsicana, Texas.
2. GRACE CRANE (Arthur), b. Feb. 25, 1895, at Chelsea, Indian Ter.

2722. ELDORA ADELAIDE CRANE[9] [2379], (William H.,[8] Josiah,[7] Benjamin,[6] Josiah,[5] Edmund,[4] John,[3] John,[2] Jasper[1]), born June 24, 1862, at Fair Oaks, Orange Co., N. Y. Married Dec. 25, 1880, at that place, John Nelson Mance, who was born at Circleville, N. Y., Dec. 31, 1857. Child:

1. MABEL CRANE (Mance), b. Oct. 31, 1884, at the Crane homestead in Middletown, Orange Co., N. Y.

2723. MARY HANNAH CRANE[9] [2393], (Isaac B.,[8] Stephen K.,[7] Benjamin,[6] Josiah,[5] Edmund,[4] John,[3] John,[2] Jasper[1]), married Jan. 15, 1873, Frederic Leonard Allen. He died July 15, 1884. She then married Minor L. Stephens, May 5, 1894· Lived in Susquehanna County, Pa. Children:

1. PERCY BENTLY (Allen), b. June 27, 1874.
2. HARRY CLARENCE (Allen), b. Sept. 23, 1879; d. April 29, 1891.

2724. PHEBE JANE CRANE[9] [2395], (Isaac B.,[8] Stephen K.,[7] Benjamin,[6] Josiah,[5] Edmund,[4] John,[3] John,[2] Jasper[1]), married Dec. 6, 1875, Oliver Royce. Children:

1. LILLIE MAY (Royce), b. May 10, 1879; d. Jan. 27, 1889.
2. EDWIN DOUGLAS (Royce), b. Aug. 9, 1882.
3. GEORGE WALTER (Royce), b. July 26, 1890.

2725. CYNTHIA MARIAH CRANE[9] [2397], (Isaac B.,[8] Stephen K.,[7] Benjamin,[6] Josiah,[5] Edmund,[4] John,[3] John,[2] Jasper[1]), married Feb. 27, 1884, Jeremiah Eli Goff. Lived in Susquehanna County, Pa. Children:

1. ELLEN MYRTLE (Goff), b. Jan. 26, 1885.
2. HARRY WALTER (Goff), b. Sept. 3, 1886; d. Oct. 4, 1897.
3. CARRIE BELLE (Goff), b. July 30, 1896.

2726. TULULAH EUGENIE CRANE[9] [2405], (Henry J.,[8] Stephen K.,[7] Benjamin,[6] Josiah,[5] Edmund,[4] John,[3] John,[2] Jasper[1]), received a careful education, taking the degree of A.B. Married Alonzo Clark Stevens, Dec. 19, 1888. Children:

1. MILDRED EUGENIE (Stevens), b. Nov. 1, 1889.
2. MORGAN COLVIN (Stevens), b. Jan. 25, 1891.

3. CLARK CRANE (Stevens), b. Jan. 19, 1894.

2727. WILLIAM EMMETT CRANE[9] [2408], (William H.,[8] William M.,[7] Benjamin,[6] Josiah,[5] Edmund,[4] John,[3] John,[2] Jasper[1]), born near New Milford, Pa. Married July 24, 1894, Grace DeVoe. Child:

2728—1. HENRY DEVOE, b. Jan. 14, 1896, at Binghamton, N. Y.

2729. HARRY HYATT CRANE[9] [2434], (Henry J.,[8] Gabriel,[7] Abraham,[6] Josiah,[5] Edmund,[4] John,[3] John,[2] Jasper[1]), married Oct. 30, 1889, Josephine S. Jelleff, who was born June 17, 1868. Children:

2730—1. ALFRED HYATT, b. Nov. 25, 1891.
2731—2. MARY JOSEPHINE, b. March 6, 1897.

2732. SAMUEL EDGAR CRANE[9] [2472], (Hiram W.,[8] Solomon,[7] Stephen,[6] Josiah,[5] Edmund,[4] John,[3] John,[2] Jasper[1]), married Maud A. Walrath, Sept. 17, 1890. She was born at Fort Plain, Montgomery Co., N. Y., April 27, 1860. He is a conductor on West Shore Railway, New York State. Child:

2733—1. JESSIE WALRATH, b. June 11, 1894.

2734. JESSIE AMANDA CRANE[9] [2473], (Hiram W.,[8] Solomon,[7] Stephen,[6] Josiah,[5] Edmund,[4] John,[3] John,[2] Jasper[1]), married July 8, 1873, Adam D. Smith. He was born March 2, 1847. Children:

1. EDNA MAUD (Smith), b. July 28, 1874; d. Sept. 1, 1874.
2. EDWARD FRANK (Smith), b. June 10, 1875; dentist at Wilkes-barre, Pa.
3. LENA WEBB (Smith), b. Dec. 12, 1878.
4. GAINS EUGENE (Smith), b. Jan. 16, 1881; d. Feb. 1, 1883.

2735. JAY D. CRANE[9] [2502], (Billings,[8] Lewis A.,[7] Shadrack,[6] Ezekiel,[5] Edmund,[4] John,[3] John,[2] Jasper[1]), married Fanny Ellen Munn, March 18, 1891. Residence, Cooper, Mich. Children:

2736—1. JULIAN ERNEST.
2737—2. ALICE ISABELLE.

2738. WILLIAM WHITNEY CRANE[9] [2541], (William W.,[8] James N.,[7] Shadrack,[6] Ezekiel,[5] Edmund,[4] John,[3] John,[2] Jasper[1]), born in New Orleans, La.; was educated there, graduating from the high school. He early in life became connected with the militia, serving in New Orleans from Sept. 14, 1874, to Jan. 9, 1877; was first lieutenant and adjutant in 2d Infantry, 1st Div., Louisiana S. Nat. Guard; colonel and aide-de-camp to His Excellency the Governor of Louisiana; staff officer with rank of brigadier-general to Major-General J. H. Leathers, commanding the southern division Essenic army; member of the Southern Yacht Club and its house committee; member of the Century Road Club of America, and State Centurian of Louisiana; member of Southern Wheelman, Washington Artillery, Chess, Checkers and Whist Club, as well as other social

and athletic bodies. He is past master of Corinthian Lodge, No. 190, F. and A. M.; Concorde Chapter, No. 2, Royal Arch Masons; Jacques DeMolay Commandery, No. 2; Knights Templar, 32° A. and A. S. R.; Jerusalem Temple, Nobles of the Mystic Shrine; secretary of Orleans Senate, No. 302, K. A. E. O.; and at present (1897) travelling freight agent for the Illinois Central Railroad. Residence, Jackson, Tenn. Married July 28, 1881, Ellen Janet Murphy. Children:

2739—1. LAURA RUTH, b. Oct. 23, 1882.
2740—2. ROBERT WHITNEY, b. Feb. 17, 1886.

2741. ISABEL W. CRANE[9] [2624], (Elias B.,[8] Smith E.,[7] Elias B.,[6] Aaron,[5] Job,[4] Azariah,[3] Azariah,[2] Jasper[1]), married Oct. 18, 1881, Henry B. Graves. Children:

1. ALICE K. (Graves), b. Aug. 27, 1882.
2. CLIFFORD C. (Graves), b. Nov. 4, 1883.
3. HENRY B. (Graves), b. Oct. 10, 1885; d. Dec. 7, 1886.
4. ISABEL (Graves), b. March 28, 1888.
5. CHARLES P. (Graves), b. June 19, 1890.

2742. BESSIE K. CRANE[9] [2625], (Elias B.,[8] Smith E.,[7] Elias B.,[6] Aaron,[5] Job,[4] Azariah,[3] Azariah,[2] Jasper[1]), married May 25, 1886, Wilson H. Brown. Child:

1. HAIDEE (Brown), b. Jan. 30, 1888.

2743. JOHN JOSIAH CRANE[9] [2676], (John A.,[8] John J.,[7] Benjamin,[6] Josiah,[5] Josiah,[4] Joseph,[3] Jasper,[2] Jasper[1]), married June 20, 1888, Annie Morrison Kitching. Child:

2744—1. DOROTHY, b. 1889.

45

TENTH GENERATION.

2745.   HARRISON DINSMORE CRANE[10] [2708], (Harrison H.,[9] William H.,[8] Josiah,[7] Benjamin,[6] Josiah,[5] Edmund,[4] John,[3] John,[2] Jasper[1]), married Nov. 28, 1895, at Milton, Penn., Nellie Gaskell Hastings, daughter of William Penn Hastings, Esq. She was born at Punxsutawney, Jefferson Co., Penn., May 10, 1873.   Mr. Crane is a commercial traveller; residence (1899), Middletown, N. Y.   Children:

2746—1. DOROTHY HASTINGS, b. Oct. 11, 1896; d. Feb 2, 1898.
2747—2. EDITH HASTINGS, b. May 13, 1899.

STEPHEN CRANE, OF ELIZABETHTOWN, NEW JERSEY, AND HIS DESCENDANTS.

FIRST GENERATION.

1. STEPHEN CRANE,[1] born about 1630 or 1635. Some have claimed he was born as early as 1619, but that date seems too early from a careful consideration of the whole subject. Tradition says he came from England or Wales between the years 1640 and 1660. He was one of the original settlers of Elizabethtown, and one of the company of colonists who planted the first English settlement in what is now the State of New Jersey. He was called one of the "Elizabethtown Associates," and was there as early as 1665, for he took the oath of allegiance to Lord King Charles II. and his successors February 19th of that year. The deed by which the first settlers claimed their land was dated Oct. 28, 1664, so that the fall of 1664 or spring of 1665 would be quite as early as it is safe to fix the date of the settlement. In 1675 he obtained from the proprietors of East Jersey a patent to confirm his title to lands in Elizabethtown; dates given below. In 1710 he executed a deed to his son Nathaniel, giving him his house lot, with other pieces of land in Elizabethtown; and, in describing the bounds of these lands, they were said to be bounded on lands of John Crane, Daniel Crane, Jeremiah and Azariah Crane. The fact that he settled within such close proximity to the family of Jasper Crane might indicate that there was a family connection existing between them; but up to the present time no proof of any blood relationship has come to light. Samuel H. Congar, Esq., late librarian of the New Jersey Historical Society, who gave careful consideration to the subject, wrote that "this Stephen was probably nearly related to Jasper Crane, of Newark," and that he came to New Jersey from Connecticut. Rev. Jonathan T. Crane was also of the opinion that he was a relative of Jasper. Isaac Watts Crane, Esq., in December, 1848, stated that it was his opinion that this Stephen was either a son or a brother of Jasper Crane, of Newark,—that the Elizabethtown Cranes claim descent from Jasper. We first meet with him at Elizabethtown where he lived; prior to the year 1664 we have no knowledge of his origin beyond tradition. He was active in resisting the claims of the proprietors in the great land

dispute, which was never settled. His name appears as defendant in the Elizabethtown bill in chancery, schedule No. 8, page 104. The answer to this bill was printed in 1752. This land was surveyed to him in the year 1676,—one Warren for 120 acres in Elizabethtown, dated March 28th; another of 156 acres, October 2d; still another of 156 acres, November 30th. One of these 156-acre lots was bounded by Crane's Brook, east by the Mill Creek, and east by the highway. His six-acre house lot was a part of this tract. By his will, dated 1709, he bequeathed to his son John a certain piece of land within the bounds of Elizabethtown, and died a few years later.

Rev. Elias N. Crane contributes the following, found among the papers of his father, Rev. Elias W. Crane, son of Noah, and the account purports to come from Mr. Isaac Crane, of Elizabethtown, son of Caleb, Jr., great-great-grandson of Stephen senior: "About 1625 A. D., thirty years before Elizabeth Town, N. J., was setttled, during the persecutions of the Puritans in England under Queen Elizabeth, the ancestor of the Crane family came to America. His name was Stephen. The ship in which he came is supposed to have sailed from the west of England, favored at embarkation by a fog, which allowed escape in case of pursuit. When the fog passed away the ship was out of sight of land. It is said to have sunk at Amboy, N. J., but all on board were saved. Stephen Crane and his fellow voyagers settled Elizabeth Town, named for Queen Elizabeth, who confirmed the purchase of lands from the Indians." This Isaac Crane was born July 20, 1766, about one hundred years after the settlement of Elizabeth Town, and it would seem that at that time there might have been some connecting link to bind the history of the early settlement to the period in which this Isaac Crane lived. We often find one life to span that interim; certainly two would have done it from father to son; it could have been handed down to Isaac or some other member of the family. But let us analyze this bit of history. If this Stephen Crane came to America, as indicated, in 1625, for the purpose of assisting in establishing a settlement, he must have been twenty or twenty-five years of age, and we know he lived until 1710; therefore he would be one hundred and five years old at his death, a very improbable event; again, in the natural course of things, his children would have been born twenty or thirty years earlier than they were born. People exposed to the hardships of those days seldom reached the age of seventy-five and children were born to them usually before the parents were seventy or even sixty-five years old. Again, if Stephen had been in this country thirty years before the settlement of Elizabeth Town, we should find some record of it somewhere. From all that can be proven, this Stephen Crane was born about 1630 or 1635 in England, and probably was son of Jasper, perhaps by a former marriage. It is said that his wife was a Danish woman, with red hair, and

that nearly all the Cranes in and about Elizabethtown and West-field, N. J., are descendants from this pair.   Children :

2—1. JOHN; d. Feb., 1723.
3—2. JEREMIAH; d. 1742.
4—3. DANIEL, b. 1672-3; d. Feb. 24, 1724.
5—4. NATHANIEL, b. 1680; d. 1755.

SECOND GENERATION.

6. JOHN CRANE[2] [2], (Stephen[1]), married Esther Williams, daughter of Samuel and Esther (Wheeler) Williams, and lived in Elizabethtown, N. J.   In 1713 he was chosen one of the overseers of highways; Aug. 2, 1720, was appointed one of seven committeemen to perform some duty for the town.   He died in February, 1723, leaving a will dated Feb. 7, 1722, and proved Feb. 16, 1723 (see Trenton, Liber A, page 238), in which he mentioned his brother Jeremiah and ten children.   Three of his sons were minors at the time of his death.   His saw and grist mill located on the Rahway River he gave to his sons John and Joseph, which property was retained in the family many years. Esther Williams Crane made a will March 17, 1742, proved Sept. 17. 1748, in which she named Jacob DeHart one of the executors.   December, 1714, John Crane purchased one hundred acres of land on the east side of Rahway River.   He also owned land on the southwest side of the river, where the village of Cranford is now located.   Children :

7—1. JOHN, b. about 1700; went to Westfield; d. 1763.
8—2. MATTHIAS.
9—3. BENJAMIN, b. about 1710; m. Esther Woodruff.
10-4. SAMUEL, b. about 1712.
11-5. ABIGAIL, b. Jan. 25, 1703; m. Jacob DeHart, and d. before 1777; he d. 1777 at Elizabethtown.
12-6. JOSEPH.
13-7. ESTHER; probably m. John Davis.
14-8. SARAH.
15-9. REBECCA.
16-10. DEBORAH.

17. JEREMIAH CRANE[2] [3], (Stephen[1]), married Susannah ———— . He was admitted among the second generation of associates in 1699, and the same year signed a petition to the king. He died in 1742, his wife being administratrix of his estate. Child :

18—1. JAMES, b. 1712; d. Sept. 2, 1777.

19. DANIEL CRANE[2] [4], (Stephen[1]), married Hannah (or Susannah) Miller, daughter of William Miller and sister to Alderman William Miller.   In 1699 he signed a petition to the king with his brother Jeremiah.   He died Feb. 24, 1723–4.   His will mentioned five sons.   Children :

20—1. DANIEL, b. 1703; d. Feb. 25, 1723–4. aged 20.
21—2. JONATHAN, b. April 19, 1705; d. in Westfield, Jan., 1766.

22—3. WILLIAM.
23—4. STEPHEN, b. 1709; d. June 23, 1780.
24—5. DAVID, b. about 1712; may have gone to Maryland.

25. NATHANIEL CRANE[2] [5], (Stephen[1]), married Demaris ———. He died Jan. 13, 1755. She was born in 1684, and died Oct. 9, 1745. Children :

26—1. NATHANIEL; m. Mary, dau. of John Price.
27—2. CALEB, b. 1715; d. Dec. 19, 1773.
28—3. JONATHAN, b. 1719; d. 1780.
29—4. CHRISTOPHER; moved to Westfield; had one son, Nathaniel.
30—5. MOSES; m. Johanna Miller; had one son, Noah.
31—6. PHEBE; m. John Chandler's father.
32—7. MARY; m. 1st, ——— Chandler; 2d, ——— Dayton; mother of Gen. Elias Dayton.

33. JOHN CRANE[3] [7], (John,[2] Stephen[1]), married and removed to Westfield, N. J. He succeeded to the Crane homestead, also the saw-mill and the grist-mill. He died Sept. 11, 1763. Children :

34—1. JOHN, b. April 20, 1723.
35—2. STEPHEN.
36—3. JACOB; went to Canada soon after the Revolutionary war
37—4. ISAAC.
38—5. JOSEPH, b. 1741; d. June 7, 1778.

39. MATTHIAS CRANE[3] [8], (John,[2] Stephen[1]), married. He was Mayor of the Borough of Elizabeth, N. J., under the British government, so says Jacob Woodruff Crane, of Newark, N. J. Children :

40—1. MATTHIAS; m. ——— Meeker, daughter of Joseph Meeker.
41—2. JACOB, b. 1745; m. Phebe Crane, daughter of Stephen Crane, Esq., mayor.
42—3. ANDREW; m. Anne Burroughs, daughter of John Burroughs.
43—4. ELIHU; removed to Ohio.
44—5. JOHN, b. March 4, 1761; m. Mary, daughter of Benjamin Cleveland.
44½-6. ———; m. George Mitchell.

45. BENJAMIN CRANE[3] [9], (John,[2] Stephen[1]), married Esther Woodruff, born 1711. She died Feb. 22, 1809, aged 98. Children :

46—1. BENJAMIN, b. about 1732; m. Phebe Halsey.
47—2. ELEAZER; m. Susan Day.

48. ABIGAIL CRANE[3] [11], (John,[2] Stephen[1]), married Jacob De Hart, March 3, 1723–4, by Mr. Edward Vaughn, who was rector of St. John's Episcopal Church, in Elizabeth. Mr. De Hart was born Dec. 28, 1699, and died Sept. 21, 1777, in the 67th year of his age. She died June 10, 1770, in the 67th year of her age. In the St. John's churchyard at Elizabeth, N. J., may be found an old tomb-stone with the following: "In memory of Jacob De Hart, who died 1777, and his wife Abigail Crane, who died previously." Jacob De Hart was associated with Stephen Crane in the dispute against the claims of certain titles to lands in Elizabethtown, N. J. Children :

49—1. MATTHIAS, b. Dec. 27, 1723–4.
50—2. JOANNA, b. 1725; d. Oct. 2, 1735.
51—3. JOHN, b. July 25, 1727; d. June 1, 1795.

52. JAMES CRANE[3] [18], (Jeremiah,[2] Stephen[1]), married ———— Miller. He died Sept. 2, 1777, aged 65. Child:

53—1. JAMES, b. 1739; d. Oct. 17, 1819, aged 80.

54. JONATHAN CRANE[3] [21], (Daniel,[2] Stephen[1]), married Mary ————. She died in 1766, aged 62. He died in West-field, Jan., 1766, aged 61. Children:

55—1. HANNAH, b. July 24, 1728.
56—2. MARY, b. Nov. 1, 1730.
57—3. SARAH, b. May 24, 1733; d. March 1, 1738.
58—4. REBECCA, b. July 12, 1740; m. Deacon Joseph Achur, and was grandmother to John D. Norris of Elizabethtown, N. J.

59. STEPHEN CRANE[3] [23], (Daniel,[2] Stephen[1]), was one of the leading patriots of New Jersey during the Revolution, under the Colonial Government; a man of considerable note in his day, although he was sheriff of Essex County under George III., and judge of the Court of Common Pleas during the agitation con-cerning the Stamp Act, he became an ardent patriot, and was elected a member of the first Continental Congress, which met in 1774, and did much efficient work on committees on supplies, etc., serving two terms. The engraving "The first Prayer in Congress," contains his portrait. He was also a member of the New Jersey legislature and senate. His homestead was about one and one-half miles from Elizabeth, near the point where the road to Galloping Hill leaves the road to Mulfords. The spot is in sight, and on the north side, of the Central Railroad. The old well was on the opposite side of the road from the house where he lived, and which was a few years ago still standing in firm preservation, and under a large oak tree. He was one of the first trustees of the First Presbyterian Church in Elizabeth, and mayor of the Borough. He married Phebe ————, born 1714, and died Aug. 28, 1776, aged 62. He died June 23, 1780. Children:

60—1. DANIEL, b. Jan. 3, 1735.
61—2. STEPHEN, b. Oct. 14, 1737; killed by British soldiers.
62—3. ELIZABETH, b. March 10, 1740.
63—4. DAVID, b. Nov. 27, 1742.
64—5. WILLIAM, b. 1747.
65—6. PHEBE, b. June 2, 1750; m. Capt. Jacob Crane, son of Matthias. (See No. 133.)
66—7. JOSEPH, b. May 20, 1752; m. 1st, Susannah Ross; 2d, Miss Van Vechten.
67—8. JONATHAN, b. May 15, 1754; killed by the Hessian soldiers, June 1780.
68—9. CATHARINE, b. Oct. 8, 1756.

69. DAVID CRANE[3] [24], (Daniel,[2] Stephen[1]), sometime in the early part of the eighteenth century, left his brothers, Stephen and William, at Elizabethtown, N. J., and removed to the State of Maryland, settling in Chestertown, Kent County, where he established himself in the business of tanning and currying

46

leather. He married Elizabeth Rickets, of that place, and died quite young. Children :

70—1. DAVID, b. Sept. 19, 1743.
71—2. SARAH; d. without issue.

72. NATHANIEL CRANE[3] [26], (Nathaniel,[2] Stephen[1]), married Mary, daughter of John Price, who was son of Benjamin Price, who settled on Long Island about 1639, and from there went to Elizabethtown, N. J. Children :

73—1. MARY; m. Stephen Parsell.
74—2. DAVID; m. 1st, —— Lyon; 2d, Jane Lee.

75. CALEB CRANE[3] [27], (Nathaniel,[2] Stephen[1]), married 1st, Mary, daughter of Edward Searls; 2d, Elizabeth, daughter of Charles Townley, Aug. 27, 1760. His first wife was born in 1722, and died April 2, 1758. He died Dec. 19, 1773, leaving a will which was recorded, 1774, by which he left a grist-mill and saw-mill on the Elizabeth River, to his sons, Caleb, Nehemiah and Jacob. Children :

76—1. ELIZABETH.
77—2. CALEB, b. 1739.
78—3. NEHEMIAH, b. 1743.
79—4. JACOB, b. 1748.
80—5. MARY, b. March 14, 1753.
81—6. JOANNA; was 2d wife of Waters Burrows.
82—7. ABIGAIL, b. 1761; m. 1st, Amos Clark; 2d, Robert Clark; she d. April 30, 1827. .
83—8. NATHANIEL, b. Nov. 24, 1762.

84. JONATHAN CRANE[3] [28], (Nathaniel,[2] Stephen[1]), married Sarah, daughter of Alderman William Ross, and removed to Morris County with six sons and four daughters. He died of consumption, April 14, 1780. They are buried in the old cemetery at Morristown. She was received into the First Church at Morristown, Nov. 1772, and died Feb. 3 or 5, 1787, aged 63. Children :

85—1. JONATHAN; served in the war of 1776, and d. unmarried.
86—2. ICHABOD; m. and removed west after erecting a headstone in the burying-ground at Morristown. N. J.; no inscription.
87—3. MOSES; m., and had two or three children.
88—4. DEMARIS; m. Timothy Stiles.
89—5. SARAH, b. July 24, 1755; m. Samuel Freeman, Aug. 28, 1774.
90—6. PHEBE; m. —— Kirkpatrick.
91—7. ELIZABETH; m. —— Wells; lived in Morristown, and had two daughters.
92—8. JOHN, b. 1748; m., Sept. 19, 1774, Mary O'Harah.
93—9. WILLIAM, b. 1753; m. Lydia Edminster. She was b. 1754; d. May 13, 1777. He died prior to July 28, 1776.
94-10. AARON; m. Mary Hathaway, Jan. 27, 1774. He d. 1775 or 1776, leaving a widow, who had Damaris, b. Aug. 9, 1776.

95.   CHRISTÒPHER CRANE[3] [29], (Nathaniel,[2] Stephen[1]), married and removed to Westfield; died 1760; will names children. Children :

96—1.   NATHANIEL; m. Jane Hubbard, daughter of Rev. Mr. Hubbard.
97—2.   NEHEMIAH.
98—3.   JACOB.
99—4.   CALEB.

100.   MOSES CRANE[3] [30], (Nathaniel,[2] Stephen[1]), married Johanna Miller; removed to Westfield, N. J.   Child :

101—1.   NOAH; went west.

102. JOHN CRANE[4] [34], (John,[3] John,[2] Stephen[1]), married 1st, Huldah Grant; 2d, Miss Bedell, sister of Jacob Bedell, of Westfield; 3rd, a widow Force, by whom he had no children. He died Sept. 12, 1807. He succeeded to the Crane homestead, mills, etc. Children:

103—1 ELIJAH; m. a daughter of David Ross, of Westfield.
104—2. JOHN, b. June 17, 1755; m. Phebe Ross, sister of Elijah's wife.
105—3. SARAH; m. Isaac Kendricks of Westfield.
106—4. MARY; m. Aaron Sayres, of Westfield.
107—5. BEDELL, by 2d wife.

108. ISAAC CRANE[4] [37], (John,[3] John,[2] Stephen[1]), married Mary, daughter of John Miller, and removed from Westfield to Passaic Valley, and purchased a tract of land containing 178 acres, being lot No. 1, and part of No. 2, Corsen's survey of Elizabethtown lots, where he made his home. It was located above the first mountain, and south of the Joseph Corry Farm. Children:

109—1. JONATHAN; d. Dec. 14, 1770.
110—2. ISAAC MILLER; d. April 28, 1784.
111—3. MARY, b. 1761; m. Samuel Parsons; d. Nov. 11, 1850.
112—4. MARTHA, b. 1763; m. Nathaniel Bonnel, Jan. 15, 1783; d. June 30, 1846.
113—5. HULDAH, b. 1764; m. Abner Stiles, Feb. 18, 1786; d. June 24, 1835.
114—6. SALLY, b. 1769; m. Nathan Elmer, Nov. 4, 1792; d. July 19, 1838.

115. JOSEPH CRANE[4] [38], John,[3] John,[2] Stephen[1]), married Ruth Miller, sister to Isaac's wife, and removed from Westfield to the Passaic Valley, and settled on a farm of 154 acres, which he purchased of Nathaniel Smith in May, 1764; located on the north, and adjoining his brother Isaac's. His farm extended to the River. He died June 7, 1778. The widow went with her sons to Ohio, and died there, over 90 years of age. Children:

116—1. SAMUEL; m. Abby Roberts, Nov. 7, 1792.
117—2. JOHN, b. about 1770; m. Sept. 23, 1792, Betsy, daughter of Jonathan Mulford, Jr.
118—3. STEPHEN; m. Esther Thompson; went to Ohio.
119—4. JONATHAN; m. Keziah Tappin; went to Ohio.
120—5. ABNER; m. Huldah Robinson; went to Ohio.
121—6. JOSEPH, b. 1771; m. Sally Bebout, daughter of William, and lived on the Bebout farm.
122—7. MOSES; m. Susannah Dilts, of Warren Co., O.

123—8.   JOANNA, b. about 1777; m. April 1, 1797, William Valentine; went to Redstone.
124—9.   ANNAR, b. about 1762; m. Benjamin Corrington, Nov. 13, 1782; went to Ohio.
125—10. RUTH, b. about 1765; m. William Hale, July 5, 1785.
126—11. ELIZABETH, b. about 1774; m. Daniel Doty, May 1, 1794; went to Middletown, O.

127.   ANDREW CRANE[4] [42], (Matthias,[3] John,[2] Stephen[1]), married Glory Anne Burroughs, daughter of John Burroughs. Children :

128—1.   THOMAS B., b. 1769; m. Margaret Shotwell.
129—2.   JOHN, b. 1772; m. Mary Wade.
130—3.   ROBERT, b. 1775; m. Fanny Pool.
131—4.   EZEKIEL; m. 1st, Ann Shotwell; 2d, Betsy Meeker.
132—5.   SALLY; m. Ezekiel Williams.

133.   Capt. JACOB CRANE[4] [41], (Matthias,[3] John,[2] Stephen[1]), married Phebe Crane, daughter of Stephen Crane, Esq., mayor, in 1770. He died July 25, 1811. He served in the French and Indian wars, and was a non-commissioned officer under the British government in the war with Canada. Children :

134—1.   STEPHEN, b. 1760; m. Elizabeth Trotter.
135—2.   JACOB, b. 1774; m. Sarah Sayre.
136—3.   PHEBE; m. John Stiles.
137—4.   MATTHIAS, b. Nov. 24, 1780; m. 1st, Prudence Lum, Nov. 22, 1802; 2d, Sally Lum, a sister; he d. July 25, 1825.

138.   JOHN CRANE[4] [44], (Matthias,[3] John,[2] Stephen[1]), married Mary, daughter of Benjamin Cleveland. She was born July 11, 1763, and died March 5, 1837. He died April 7, 1840. Children :

139—1.   AARON.
140—2.   MATTHIAS, b. June 30, 1785; m. Eliza Glendening.
141—3.   CHARLES.
142—4.   ELIHU; m. Susan, dau. of Robert Crane, son of Andrew.
143—5.   PHEBE.
144—6.   BETSY.

145.   J——— CRANE[4] [44½], (Matthias,[3] John,[2] Stephen[1]), married George Mitchell. Children :

146—1.   ELIHU (Mitchell); m. ——— Crane.
147—2.   JACOB (Mitchell); m. Sarah Williams.
148—3.   HANNAH (Mitchell); not m.
149—4.   NATHANIEL (Mitchell); m.
150—5.   SUSAN (Mitchell); not m.

151.   BENJAMIN CRANE[4] [46], (Benjamin,[3] John,[2] Stephen[1]), married Phebe Halsey, daughter of Joseph Halsey, who lived between Elizabethtown and Rahway. Benjamin lived in Westfield. Children :

152—1.   BENJAMIN, b. Nov. 29, 1761; m. Sarah Thompson.
153—2.   ABIGAIL, b. Nov. 22, 1762; d. young.
154—3.   NORRIS, b. Feb. 9, 1764; m. Jane Dunham, and d. Feb 21, 1846.
155—4.   JOHN, b. April 18, 1765.

156—5.   PHEBE, b. Dec. 19, 1766; m. John Johnson; no children.
157—6.   SARAH, b. April 12, 1771; m. John Ogden, Jan. 31, 1801, at
         Green Village, Morris Co.; she was buried at Madison,
         N. J. He d. Aug. 8, 1826; she d. March 8, 1854.
158—7.   ABIGAIL, b. Sept. 14, 1774; d. young.

159.   ELEAZER CRANE[4] [47], (Benjamin,[3] John,[2] Stephen[1]).
He was called of Elizabethtown, N. J.   Married Susan Day,
and had three sons.   His grandson William Watrous Crane says
this Eleazer Crane was a soldier in the Revolutionary war, and
served with the New Jersey troops; was taken prisoner at the
battle of Long Island, Aug. 27, 1776, and imprisoned in the old
French Episcopal Church on Pine Street, New York city, where
he soon died.   She was the daughter of David Day, Esq., son of
George Day.   After the death of Mr. Crane she married Matthias
Allen, and had two daughters, Elizabeth and Susan; the latter
married John Morrison.   Children:

160—1.   ABNER.
161—2.   JOSHUA.
162—3.   DAVID DAY, b. Oct. 26, 1769.

163.   JAMES CRANE[4] [53], (James,[3] Jeremiah,[2] Stephen[1]),
married Sarah ———— (one record says married Mary ————),
who was born in 1744, and died March 21, 1805.   He died Oct.
17, 1819, aged 80.   During the latter part of his life he was
familiarly called "Uncle Jammey," and lived near Miller Crane's
residence on Cherry Street, Elizabeth, N. J.   Children:

164—1.   STEPHEN; m. Phebe Gurthwait.
165—2.   JEREMIAH.
166—3.   BETSY; m. James Woodruff.
167—4.   RACHEL; not m.
168—5.   ANNA; not m.
169—6.   NANCY; not m.

170.   STEPHEN CRANE[4] [61], (Stephen,[3] Daniel,[2] Stephen[1]),
married 1st, Phebe Morse, born in 1738, and died March 10,
1786; 2d, Jane Haines (or Harris).   He died Feb. 11, 1796.
[Have two dates given for his death, one report says he was
killed by British soldiers].   Children:

171—1.   ELIZABETH, b. Nov. 14, 1757; m. Stephen Hout.
172—2.   SUSAN, b. Aug. 14, 1759.
173—3.   DANIEL, b. Sept. 5, 1761; m. Prosia Dorman; lived near
         Morristown; d. 1810; had child living in New York city.
174—4.   PHEBE, b. Feb. 7, 1764; m. ———— Woodruff; had son in
         Springfield.
175—5.   NANCY, b. May 17, 1766; m. Obed Meeker.
176—6.   MARGARET, b. Oct. 7, 1768; m. Jacob Bonnel, July 9, 1789;
         d. Jan. 16, 1832.
177—7.   HANNAH, b. May 30, 1770; m. Jonathan Squire, of Westfield.
178—8.   MARY, b. Oct. 8, 1772; m.; d. young.
179—9.   JENET SINCLAIR, b. Oct. 9, 1776.
180—10. ESTHER, b. June 5, 1778; m. Recompence Squire, of
         Westfield.
181-11. JONATHAN, b. Oct. 25, 1780; m. Hetty Winans, sister of Noah
         Crane's wife.

By second wife:

182–12. MARY, b. Aug. 8, 1787; unm.
183–13. SARAH, b. Dec. 3, 1790; m. Nehemiah Crane, son of Jacob
         and Phebe Woodruff.
184–14. SOLOMON, b. Feb. 25, 1792; m. —— Mulford, and d.
         in June, 1832.

185. ELIZABETH CRANE[4] [62], Stephen,[3] Daniel,[2] Stephen[1]),
perhaps married Samuel Bonnel. Children:

186–1. JANE (Bonnel).
187–2. LEWIS (Bonnel).

188. DAVID CRANE[4] [63], (Stephen,[3] Daniel,[2] Stephen[1]),
married Anne Sayre, Nov. 21, 1762. She was born May 23,
1742, and died Nov. 24, 1805. In 1806 he married 2d, Agnes
Neaty Cooper, daughter of John Cooper, but had no children by
her. She died Sept. 4, 1833, aged 61 years. He was an alderman;
died Aug. 20, 1822, aged 79 years. Children:

189–1. DAVID, b. Feb. 7, 1772; d. Sept. 27, 1791.
190–2. SARAH, b. May 13, 1778; d. Sept. 16, 1778.
        All were buried in Union Cemetery, Connecticut Farms, N. J.

191. Gen. WILLIAM CRANE[4] [64], (Stephen,[3] Daniel,[2] Stephen[1]), was lieutenant of artillery in the army that accompanied
Gen. Montgomery to Quebec; he was severely wounded in the
ancle in the attack on that city, which wound gave him much
trouble in after years, necessitating amputation of the leg, even
this operation did not wholly relieve him. Ulceration again
appeared, and he died July 30, 1814, thirty-nine years after
receiving the wound. After the close of the war he became
major-general of the militia. During the last war with England,
he held a major-general's command in the New Jersey militia,
and was for a time posted at Sandy Hook, to defend New York
city. He was twice married; his second wife being Abigail
Miller, daughter of Benjamin, born 1763, and died July 22,
1825. Children:

192–1. WILLIAM MONTGOMERY, b. Feb. 1, 1776, in Elizabethtown, N. J.
        He entered the United States Navy; was midshipman, May
        23, 1799; became lieutenant, July 20, 1803; commander,
        March 4, 1813; captain, Nov. 22, 1814. He served with
        distinction through the war of 1812. July, 1827, he was
        appointed commander of the squadron in the Mediterranean
        Sea. He was distinguished before Tripoli. In 1842, he
        became chief of the Bureau of Ordnance. He died by his
        own hand, in Washington, D. C., March 18, 1846, aged 61
        years; no cause given for his rash act.
193–2. ICHABOD B.; colonel in U. S. A., in 1851; was commander
        of Governor Island.
194–3. JOSEPH H.; m. Julia Elliot; lived in Dayton, O.; judge of the
        Supreme Court, Ohio; d. Nov. 12, 1851.
195–4. MARIAH; lived with brother Joseph; unmarried.
196–5. JOANNA, b. 1800; m. John Magie; d. Jan. 30, 1820, leaving
        dau. Julia.
197–6. PHEBE, b. 1795; d. Feb. 28, 1820; unmarried.

198. JOSEPH CRANE[4] [66], (Stephen,[3] Daniel,[2] Stephen[1]), married 1st, Susannah Ross. She died Oct. 22, 1781, aged 32. He married 2d, Margaret Van Vechten, of Somerville. He was sheriff of the County, also judge, and resided in Elizabethtown, N. J. He was living there at the time of the Revolutionary war.
  Children :

199—1. ANN, b. Jan. 20, 1773.
200—2. SUSANNA, b. Dec. 12 or 23, 1774; m. Henry Weaver; went to Trenton, Butler Co., O.
201—3. WILLIAM, b. Oct. 23, 1778; m. Sarah Townley.
202—4. NANCY; m. Abraham Van Sickle; went to Trenton, O.
203—5. RICHARD Van Vechten, b. Dec. 29, 1785.
204—6. DAVID, b. April 18, 1788; lived on river St. Josephs, O.
205—7. CATHARINE, b. Nov. 7, 1791; d. Sept. 6, 1806.
206—8. SALLY; d. unmarried.
207—9. JOHN, b. April 17, 1796; m. Sarah Conover; was major of militia; d. Covington, Ky., March 15, 1864; was buried at Hamilton, O.
208-10. MICHAEL Van Vechten, b. June 17, 1800; d. unmarried about 1848.

209. DAVID CRANE[4] [70], (David,[3] Daniel,[2] Stephen[1]), was born in Chester Town, Kent Co., Md. ; he succeeded to his father's business—that of a tanner and currier; married Mary Reed, sister to Col. Philip Reed who commanded at the battle of Caulk's Field, where Sir Peter Parker fell, in 1814. Mr. Crane while serving as captain, dispersed a squad of Tories at Clows' Fort, in the edge of Delaware, near the close of the Revolutionary war. Mary Reed was born May 19, 1746, and died Dec. 28, 1804. Mr. Crane died March 2, 1816. Children :

210—1. ELIZABETH, b. Jan. 1, 1766; d. Nov., 1822.
211—2. MARGARET, b. Nov. 1, 1767; d. March 24, 1791.
212—3. DAVID, b. Sept. 7, 1769; m. and lived in Harford, Md.; d. July 12, 1806, leaving no issue.
213—4. WILLIAM, b. March 19, 1771.
214—5. ROGER, b. Oct. 5, 1772.
215—6. THOMAS, b. March 20, 1774.
216—7. MARY, b. Oct. 19, 1776.
217—8. STEPHEN, b. June 28, 1778; d. Feb. 24, 1814; no issue.
218—9. JOHN, b. Jan. 24, 1780.
219-10. SARAH, b. Aug. 25, 1781; d. Aug. 31, 1781.
220-11. SARAH, b. March 2, 1783; d. Feb. 27, 1795.
221-12. PHILIP, b. Jan. 7, 1785.
222-13. JONATHAN, b. Sept. 28, 1788.

223. MARY CRANE[4] [73], (Nathaniel,[3] Nathaniel,[2] Stephen[1]), married Stephen Parsel. Children :

224—1. SALLY (Parsel); m. 1st, —— Mulford; 2d, Wm. Pierson; 3d, Wm. Christie.
225—2. ABBY (Parsel); m. William Stiles.
226—3. MARY (Parsel); m. Chas. Tooker.
227—4. NANCY (Parsel); m. 1st. —— Scott; 2d, Abner Pierce; 3d, Stephen Parsel.

228. DAVID CRANE[4] [74], (Nathaniel,[3] Nathaniel,[2] Stephen[1]),

married 1st ——— Lyon; 2d, Jane Lee, mother of Drake. Rev.
E. N. Crane says 2d wife was a Drake. Children:

229—1. ELIAS, b. 1766; m. Elizabeth Sarles, and removed to Ohio,
in 1790; had a son a doctor.
230—2. HANNAH; d. young.
231—3. ANDREW DRAKE, b. May 7, 1781; of New York city.

232. ELIZABETH CRANE[4] [76], (Caleb,[3] Nathaniel,[2] Stephen[1]), married Jeremiah Garthwaite. He died 1815. She died
March, 1817. Children:

1. CALEB (Garthwaite); m. ——— Williams; had four children,
all girls.
2. ISAAC (Garthwaite); m. Mary Wilcox; had ten children; d.
about 1812.
3. JACOB (Garthwaite); m. ——— Scudder, of Westfield; had two
children; d. May 9, 1828.
4. JEREMIAH (Garthwaite); m. Sally Ludlow; had seven children.
5. DANIEL (Garthwaite), b. Feb. 3, 1784; m. Abigail B. Frazee, of
Westfield, Jan. 17, 1807; had eleven children; d. Sept. 29,
1826.
6. NEHEMIAH (Garthwaite); m. Elizabeth Young, of New York;
had three children; d. 1852.
7. MARY (Garthwaite); d. when a young woman.
8. JOANNA (Garthwaite); was 2d wife of Andrew Miller, of New
Brunswick; had eight children.
9. PHEBE (Garthwaite); m. James Mooney; had nine children.

233. DANIEL GARTHWAITE [5], m. Abigail Basset Frazee of Westfield, Jan. 17, 1807. She was b. April 15, 1785. He d. Sept.
29, 1826. Children:
1. MATTHIAS (Garthwaite), b. April, 1808; m. Maria Hatfield.
2. SUSAN (Garthwaite), b. Oct. 13, 1809; m. Henry Hatfield.
3. CHARLOTTA (Garthwaite), b. July 27, 1811; m. Zopha
Hatfield.
4. LETITIA K. (Garthwaite), b. June 7, 1813; m. John
Umston.
5. JOANNA (Garthwaite), b. March 26, 1815; m. S. D.
Barnet.
6. HANNAH OSBORNE (Garthwaite), b. Jan. 13, 1817; m.
William Morgan.
7. JEREMIAH (Garthwaite), b. Aug. 20, 1819; m.
8. ELIZABETH CRANE (Garthwaite), b. Oct. 22, 1821; m.
A. D. Gibbons.
9. PHEBE (Garthwaite), b. Nov. 21, 1823; d. Dec. 13,
1824.
10. PHEBE MARIA (Garthwaite), b. May 8, 1826; m. William
Ross.

234. JEREMIAH GARTHWAITE [6]; m. Mary Freeman, Oct. 13, 1845.
Children:
1. SOLOMON (Garthwaite), b. July 19, 1846.
2. LIZZIE ANN (Garthwaite), b. March 6, 1848.
3. MATTHIAS F. (Garthwaite), b. March 5, 1850; d. March
19, 1852.
4. LOUISA B. (Garthwaite), b. March 8, 1852; d. Sept. 3,
1853.

47

5. DANIEL BASSETT (Garthwaite), b. Sept. 12, 1854; d. Jan. 12, 1860.
6. OSCAR BARNETT (Garthwaite), b. April 28, 1859.

235. CALEB CRANE[4] [77], (Caleb,[3] Nathaniel,[2] Stephen[1]), married Mary Arnett in 1764. She was the daughter of James and Jemima (Pierson) Arnett. She was born in 1744, and died Dec. 3, 1822. He died April 9, 1777. His widow married Capt. Jeremiah Ballard in November, 1778, who was a magistrate of the town and mayor of the borough. He died Sept. 4, 1828.
Children :

236—1. ISAAC, b. July 20, 1766; m. Abigail Price, Nov. 15, 1791.
237—2. CALEB, b. 1771; d. 1776.

238. NEHEMIAH CRANE[4] [78], (Caleb,[3] Nathaniel,[2] Stephen1), married Esther, daughter of Cooper Woodruff and granddaugter of Benjamin Price, from England or Wales to Long Island, and thence to Elizabethtown, about 1666. He died April 4, 1777. The widow married John Potter, Nov. 11, 1789; had no children.
Children :

239—1. JOB.
240—2. CHARITY ; m. Stephen Meeker.
241—3. ESTHER; m. Noah Sayre; had no children.

242. JACOB CRANE[4] [79], (Caleb,[3] Nathaniel,[2] Stephen[1]), married Phebe, daughter of Cooper Woodruff, born 1748, a sister of his brother Nehemiah's wife. She died July 26, 1806. In 1777 and 1778 he was running the mill left him and his brothers by his father. He died Jan. 11, 1817. Children :

243—1. MARY, b. Dec. 27, 1771; m. Samuel, son of Amos Crane, and d. Oct. 25, 1850.
244—2. NOAH, b. June 10, 1773; m. Martha Winans in 1795; d. Feb. 24, 1831.
245—3. ELIZABETH, b. Feb. 9, 1776; m. 1st, Moses Parsnet; 2d, Andrus Parsell.
246—4. CALEB, b. March 4, 1778; m. Elizabeth Dalton, of Long Island.
247—5. NEHEMIAH, b. March 6, 1780; d. young.
248—6. JACOB, b. Aug. 28, 1781; m. 1st, Jenet; 2d, Susan; daughters of Obed Meeker.
249—7. PHEBE, b. Oct. 25, 1783; d. young.
250—8. NEHEMIAH, b. Oct. 10, 1785; m. Sarah, dau. of Stephen Crane.
251—9. ABIGAIL, b. Aug. 20, 1787; m. Elias Winans, and d. Nov. 5, 1853.

252. MARY CRANE[4] [80], (Caleb,[3] Nathaniel,[2] Stephen[1]), married John Robertson, April 30, 1776. He was born Oct. 29, 1749, and died March 2, 1823. She died Dec. 26, 1830.
Child :

1. CALEB (Robertson), b. 1782; m. Mary Hines Halsey, April 23, 1803, and d. March 22, 1857.

253. CALEB ROBERTSON [1]; m. Mary Hines Halsey, April 23, 1803. He d. March 22, 1857. Children :
1. JOHN (Robertson), b. May 1, 1806; m. Harriet Brookfield.

2 ICHABOD HALSEY (Robertson), b. Oct. 10, 1808; m. Mary Jane Stansbury.

3. JOHN DENNIS MORRIS (Robertson), b. Nov. 2, 1813; m. Lydia Kenedy.

4. DANIEL HALSEY (Robertson), b. Aug. 27, 1816; m. Susan S. Limbarger.

5. AMOS T. (Robertson), b. Jan. 22, 1820; m. Ann D. Emens.

254. AMOS T. ROBERTSON [5]; m. Ann D. Emens, Dec. 11, 1845. She was b. Aug. 9, 1826. Children:

1. WILLIAM C. (Robertson), b. Jan. 28, 1847.
2. ADELAIDE CELESTA (Robertson), b. May 15, 1854; d. Jan. 11, 1855.

255. NATHANIEL CRANE[4] [83], (Caleb,[3] Nathaniel,[2] Stephen[1]), married Mary Woodruff, born in 1764, a sister of his brother Jacob's wife. She died Sept. 12, 1792, when he married Sarah, daughter of Elder Moses Miller. She was born in 1768, and died May 15, 1832. He died Aug. 31, 1825. Children:

256—1. JOB, b. Aug. 8, 1787; m. Mary B. Woodruff, Jan. 11, 1814; d. Dec. 17, 1848.
257—2. ELIHU, b. 1789; d. Sept. 12, 1793.
258—3. ELIHU JEWELL, b. Dec. 9, 1797; m. Eliza, dau. of Kennedy Miller, Jan. 28, 1819.
259—4. MOSES MILLER, b. Dec. 16, 1799; m. Phebe S. Williams.
260—5. HENRY BAKER, b. Jan. 12, 1803; d. Sept. 19, 1813.
261—6. ELIZABETH TOWNLEY, b. Sept. 1, 1804; m. David P. Kenyon.
262—7. MARY WOODRUFF, b. Nov. 25, 1806.
263—8. ABIGAIL CLARK, b. Oct. 2, 1812; m. Charles A. Kiggins.

264. DEMARIS CRANE[4] [88], (Jonathan,[3] Nathaniel,[2] Stephen[1]), Jan. 6, 1779, married Timothy Stiles, son of Jonathan Stiles, of New Vernon, Morris Co., N. J. They removed to Ontario, near Geneva. Children:

1. PHEBE (Stiles).
2. SALLY (Stiles).
3. BETSY (Stiles).

265. SARAH CRANE[4] [89], (Jonathan,[3] Nathaniel,[2] Stephen[1]), married Samuel Freeman, who was born Jan. 21, 1753. Children:

1. MARY (Freeman), b. Sept. 10, 1774; m. Timothy Axtel; had ten children.
2. PHEBE (Freeman), b. Nov. 27, 1775.
3. ELIZABETH (Freeman), b. April 8, 1777; m. Daniel Pruden; had eleven children.
4. STEPHEN (Freeman), b. May 2, 1780; m. Esther Burnet; had ten children.
5. LEWIS (Freeman), b. Dec. 9, 1784; m. Electa Voorhees; had five children.
6. JOHN ROSS (Freeman), b. April 6, 1786.
7. SARAH (Freeman), b. Jan. 9, 1788; m. Jerry Kitchel; had six children.
8. HULDAH (Freeman), b. Aug. 28, 1791; m. Samuel Kirk; had five children.

266. PHEBE FREEMAN [2]; m. John Burnet, July 21, 1799. He was
b. March 7, 1774, and d. June 11, 1857. She d. Oct. 11, 1861.
Children:
  1. JAMES B. (Burnet), b. March 28, 1800.
  2. SAMUEL C. (Burnet), b. July 6, 1802.
  3. SARAH (Burnet), b. Aug. 31, 1803.
  4. JOHN F. (Burnet), b. Oct. 9, 1815.

267. JOHN ROSS FREEMAN [6]; m. Rachel Pierson, Feb. 7, 1808. She
was b. July 27, 1782. He d. Nov. 25, 1859. Children:
  1. TIMOTHY G. (Freeman), b. July 4, 1810; m. Elizabeth
    Fellows, Sept. 13, 1837.
  2. MARY E. (Freeman), b. Dec. 4, 1811.
  3. SAMUEL (Freeman), b. April 22, 1815; d. Aug. 5, 1863.
  4. SARAH (Freeman), b. April 22, 1815; m. Silas D. Cory,
    March 16, 1853.
  5. ABRAHAM PIERSON (Freeman), b. June 22, 1817; m.
    Elizabeth Lex.
  6. FRANCIS SMITH (Freeman), b. March 29, 1821; m.
    Sarah C. Smith, Aug. 29, 1852.
  7. CATHERINE CAROLINE (Freeman), b. March 29, 1821; m.
    Elias D. Roy, Jan. 26, 1848.
  8. ELIJAH P. (Freeman), b. July 29, 1823; m. Sarah J.
    Close, Jan. 14, 1858.
  9. JOANNA C. (Freeman), b. Jan. 29, 1826; d. Feb. 16, 1843.

268. PHEBE CRANE[4] [90], (Jonathan,[3] Nathaniel,[2] Stephen[1]),
married ———— Kirkpatrick. Child:

  1. HANNAH (Kirkpatrick).

269. JOHN CRANE[4] [92], (Jonathan,[3] Nathaniel,[2] Stephen[1]),
married Mary O'Harah, Sept. 19, 1774, at Morristown, N. J.,
where they settled. He died of fever May 22, 1783, aged 35.
She married John Cummins, Dec. 24, 1786. Child:

270—1. JAMES, b. 1776; d. July 3, 1777.

271. AARON CRANE[4] [94], (Jonathan,[3] Nathaniel,[2] Stephen[1]),
went with his father to Morris County, N. J., and settled in or
near Morristown. He married Mary Hathaway, Jan. 27, 1774,
and died in 1775 or 1776. Child:

272—1. DAMARIS, b. Aug. 9, 1776.

273. NOAH CRANE[4] [101], (Moses,[3] Nathaniel,[2] Stephen[1]),
married Phebe Crane. Went west with his children, and lived
with them in Ohio. Children:

274—1. MOSES.
275—2. EPHRIAM.
276—3. WILLIAM.
277—4. NOAH.

FIFTH GENERATION.

278. ELIJAH CRANE[5] [103], (John,[4] John,[3] John,[2] Stephen[1]), married —— Ross, daughter of David Ross. Children:

279—1. STEPHEN; m. Miss Williams.
280—2. DAVID; m. Miss Denman, dau. of Andrew Denman, of Westfield.
281—3. HULDA; m. William Miller.

282. JOHN CRANE[5] [104], (John,[4] John,[3] John,[2] Stephen[1]), married Phebe Ross, a sister of his brother Elijah's wife. He and his father before him lived about five miles west of Elizabeth, N. J. He died May 14, 1837, and was buried at Westfield. He also came in possession of the Crane homestead and the mill property. Children:

283—1. REBECCA; m. Major Jotham Potter.
284—2. JOHN GRANT, b. March 16, 1782; m. Sally Pearson.
285—3. ELIZABETH; m. Thomas Moore.
286—4. PHEBE; m. Benjamin Potter.
287—5. MARY ANN; m. Nathan Winans, son of Aaron Winans, of Elizabethtown.
288—6. ELIAS, b. April 24, 1789; m. Esther Maxwell.
289—7. JOSIAH, b. June 4, 1791; m. Electa Ross; he d. Aug. 7, 1873.
290—8. HULDAH; m. John Potter.
291—9. SARAH.

292. SARAH CRANE[5] [105], (John,[4] John,[3] John,[2] Stephen[1]), married Isaac Hendricks, of Westfield, N. J. Child:

1. HULDA (Hendricks); m. Aaron Pease.

293. MARY CRANE[5] [111], (Isaac,[4] John,[3] John,[2] Stephen[1]), married Samuel Parsons (son of William Parsons, Jr.), born 1758. He died Dec. 25, 1822. She died Nov. 11, 1850, aged 89 years, 10 months. Children:

1. CLOE (Parsons); d. April 7, 1788.
2. POLLY (Parsons).
3. LEWIS (Parsons), b. 1784; d. April 6, 1789.
4. ISAAC CRANE (Parsons), b. 1786; d. March 24, 1849.
5. SALLY (Parsons); m. 1st, John Codington; 2d, William Petty.
6. CLOE (Parsons); m. Aaron McKinstry, son of John McKinstry, of Lamberton.
7. BETSY (Parsons); m. Jonathan Ketchum; lived in Newark.
8. SQUIRE (Parsons); m. —— Jennings.

294. MARTHA CRANE[5] [112], (Isaac,[4] John,[3] John,[2] Stephen[1]),

married Nathaniel Bonnel, Jan. 15, 1783. He died April 15, 1814, aged 58. She died June 30, 1846, aged 83. Children:

1. PHILEMON (Bonnel), b. March 29, 1785; m. Rachel Noe, June 26, 1806.
2. HULDA (Bonnel), b. Sept. 1, 1787; m. 1st, Timothy D. Pettit.
3. JONATHAN CRANE (Bonnel), b. Sept. 27, 1790; m. Phebe Ward, Nov. 2, 1814.
4. MARY (Bonnel), b. Feb. 29, 1792; m. Charles Day, Jan. 9, 1813.
5. JANE (Bonnel), b. July 3, 1795; m. J. M. Stiles.
6. ELIZABETH (Bonnel), b. Feb. 11, 1797; m. Mathias Osborn.
7. SARAH (Bonnel), b. Feb. 17, 1799; m. James T. Lennington.
8. MALINE MILLER (Bonnel), b. July 22, 1802; m. Eliza D. Walker.

295. HULDAH CRANE[5] [113], (Isaac,[4] John,[3] John,[2] Stephen[1]), married Abner Stiles, Feb. 18, 1786, and resided in New Providence; was an elder in the Presbyterian Church. He died Aug. 29, 1831. She died June 24, 1835, aged 71. Children:

1. ELIJAH (Stiles); m. Jane Wade.
2. WILLIAM (Stiles); m. Hannah B. Smith.
3. HULDA GRANT (Stiles); m. John Thompson.
4. JOHN M. (Stiles); m. Jane Bonnel.
5. CLOE (Stiles); m. Ezra Fairchild.
6. ABNER (Stiles); m. Charlotte Bonnel.
7. APOLLOS (Stiles); m. Mary Bryant.

296. SAMUEL CRANE[5] [116], (Joseph,[4] John,[3] John,[2] Stephen[1]), married 1st, Abby Roberts, Nov. 7, 1792; 2d, Jane Bonnel. She was born in April, 1763. He removed to Preston County, West Virginia, in 1790. He served in the war of 1812 under Col. Jonathan Crane, and was a brave soldier. His widow Jane died March 26, 1848, in Fountain County, Ind. He carried on farming and milling. He died in December, 1821. Children:

297—1. JONATHAN; had a son, Isaac R. Crane, at Warsaw, Mo.
298—2. SMITH; removed to Belleville, Ill., and from there to Blackhawk.
299—3. SAMUEL; d. 1833 with cholera at Osage, Mo.
300—4. JOSEPH; died in a fit.
301—5. JOHN, b. Aug. 26, 1799; m. Nancy Dunam.
302—6. JACOB; d. on the home farm on Muddy Creek, W. Va.
303—7. CALVIN, b. Aug. 4, 1805.
304—8. ELIZABETH; m. Isaac Romine; settled in Warren County, Ohio.

305. JOHN CRANE[5] [117], (Joseph,[4] John,[3] John,[2] Stephen[1]), married Betsy Mulford, daughter of Jonathan Mulford, Sept. 23, 1792. She died March 9, 1828. He died July 18, 1843. Children:

306—1. JONATHAN MULFORD; died when a young man.
307—2. ELIAS; went to Ohio, and died there.
308—3. HULDA; m. Levi Wilcox; went to Illinois.
309—4. ORPHA; m. Erastus P. Crosfield; went to Ohio; had one son, John Edgar Crosfield.
310—5. DEBORAH; m. Ezra Ludlo.
311—6. SYLVESTER; m. Hulda Bonnel.
312—7. MARY; m. Aaron H. Laning.
313—8. DANIEL; m. Catherine Rogers; went to Indiana.

314—9. HARRIET; m. Samuel G. Benedict; went to Illinois.
315-10. ELIZABETH; m. Samuel F. Day; went to Ohio.

316. ABNER CRANE[5] [120], (Joseph,[4] John,[3] John,[2] Stephen[1]), married Huldah Robinson, and lived near·Red Lion, in Warren Co., Ohio. He died in April, 1848. Children:

317—1. LYDIA ROBINSON; m. George Lease.
318—2. ISAAC R.
319—3. ABBY R.; m. Andrew Coffin.
320—4. ABRAHAM R.; m. Ruth Romaine.
321—5. HANNAH R.; m. William Lease, a brother to George.
322—6. SAMUEL R,; m. Ellen Jane Dearth.
323—7. HULDAH R. ANNE; m. John Decker.
324—8. ABNER EDWIN R.; m. Sarah Jones.
325—9. RUTH JANE R.

326. JOSEPH CRANE[5] [121], (Joseph,[4] John,[3] John,[2] Stephen[1]), married Sally Bebout, and lived on the Bebout farm. He died June 3, 1829, aged 58. She died Aug. 31, 1825, aged 47, in New Providence, N. J. Children:

327—1. WILLIAM BEBOUT; m. Deborah Conklin, April 24, 1820.
328—2. ELIZA; m. Levi Clark.
329—3. IRA.
330—4. NANCY.
331—5. RUTH; m. Linus H. Stevens.
332—6. JACOB.
333—7. ARETUS; m. Serepta Doty.
334—8. HANNAH; d. about 19 years of age.
335—9. CATHERINE; m. Daniel Doty, son of Daniel, of Middletown, Ohio.
336-10. JOSEPH.
337-11. SARAH WHEELER.

338. MOSES CRANE[5] [122], (Joseph,[4] John,[3] John,[2] Stephen[1]), married Susan (or Susannah) Dilts in Ohio, and removed to Indiana. Children:

339—1. SILAS; m. Jane Romaine, daughter of Isaac.
340—2. WHITLEY; m. Betsey Robinson.
341—3. NELSON; m. Sarah Maloy.
342—4. POLLY; m. Cornelius Bogart.
343—5. ALFRED; m. Mary Ann Bogart, sister of Cornelius.
344—6. DAVISON; Indiana.
345—7. ELIAS; Indiana.
346—8. JOSEPH; m. Hannah Snorff.
347—9. RUTH ANNA; Indiana.
348-10. RACHEL; Indiana.
349-11. MOSES MILLER.

350. ELIZABETH CRANE[5] (called BETSY) [126], (Joseph,[4] John,[3] John,[2] Stephen[1]), married Daniel Doty, May 1, 1794, and moved from New Jersey to Middletown, O., about 1796. He was born March 23, 1765, and died May 8, 1848.
Children:

1. JOEL (Doty), b. Feb. 9, 1795; drowned at 11 years of age.
2. NOAH (Doty), b. May 6, 1796; d. in his 7th year.
3. JOHN (Doty), b. Dec. 15, 1797; m. Peggy Jewel.

4. DANIEL (Doty), b. Aug. 9, 1799; m. 1st, Molly Burgess: 2d, Catherine Crane, daughter of Joseph.
5. BETSEY (Doty), b. Jan. 16, 1801; m. Ambrose Doty.
6. HULDAH (Doty), b. Jan. 8, 1803; m. John Williamson.
7. ORPHA (Doty), b. June 8, 1804; m. Thos. Van Tile.
8. SEREPTA (Doty), b. Feb. 16, 1806; m. 1st, James Jewel; 2d, Aretus Crane, son of Joseph.
9. JOSEPH (Doty), b. Jan. 7, 1808; m. Mary Vail.
10. JAMES M. (Doty), b. Oct. 8, 1809; m. Susan Andre.
11. JERUSHA (Doty), b. Jan. 9, 1814; m. Simeon Taylor.
12. ELIAS (Doty), b. June 23, 1815; m. Pamela Bogart.

351. THOMAS B. CRANE[5] [128], (Andrew,[4] Matthias,[3] John,[2] Stephen[1]), married Margaret Shotwell. Lived in Elizabethtown, N. J. Children:

352—1. MARIAH; m. William M. Crane, son of Stephen, son of James[4]; had three children.
353—2. ANN; m. James Crane, son of Stephen, son of James[4]; had three children.
354—3. ANDREW; m. Hannah Meeker; had eight children.
355—4. JOHANNAH.
356—5. HENRIETTA; m. James Tatout; had two children.
357—6. SUSAN; m. John Bennet; had two children.
358—7. JONATHAN; m. Ann Maggie Crane, daughter of Stephen, son of James[4].

359. JOHN CRANE[5] [129], Andrew,[4] Matthias,[3] John,[2] Stephen[1]), married Mary Wade. Children:

360—1. HORRACE; m. Mary ———; had three children.
361—2. DAVID; went south.
362—3. JONATHAN; m. Keziah, daughter of widow Betsey Crane; had four children.
363—4. ELIZABETH; m. Jacob Clark; had seven children.
364—5. HANNAH; m. Jacob Ludlow; had seven children.
365—6. ANDREW, b. June 22, 1818; in Boston.
366—7. BENJAMIN; m. Elizabeth ———, in Delhi; had two children.
367—8. ABBY; m. Henry Roll; had two children.

368. ROBERT CRANE[5] [130], (Andrew,[4] Matthias,[3] John,[2] Stephen[1]), married Fanny Pool. Children:

369—1. SUSAN; m. George Crane, son of John and Mary (Cleveland) Crane.
370—2. WILLIAM; m. Mary Clark.
371—3. DUTILLA; m. William Luster (or Lester).

372. EZEKIEL CRANE[5] [131], (Andrew,[4] Matthias,[3] John,[2] Stephen[1]), married 1st, Ann Shotwell; 2d, Betsey Meeker. Children:

373—1. ANN; m. John Sharp; had four children.
374—2. ELIZABETH; m. Elijah Gary (or Garey); had three children.
375—3. EZEKIEL; m. in Morristown; had three children.

376. SALLY CRANE[5] [132], (Andrew,[4] Matthias,[3] John,[2] Stephen[1]), married Ezekiel Williams. Children:

1. WILLIAM (Williams); m. Abby Mulford.
2. CRANE (Williams); went south; m. Susan ———.
3. BETSY (Williams); m. Elias Woodford.
4. DAVID (Williams); m. Charlotte Haines.

5. GLOWANNE (Williams); m. Otis Woodruff.
6. SALLY (Williams); m. Henry Terrill.

377. STEPHEN CRANE[5] [134], (Jacob,[4] Matthias,[3] John,[2] Stephen[1]), married Elizabeth Trotter. He removed to the city of New York in 1806, and was engaged as a custom-house officer until his death. He was born in Essex Co., N. J., in 1760, and died Dec. 6, 1829. Children :

378—1. JOHN, b. Oct. 26, 1786; m. Dec. 11, 1811; d. Sept. 27, 1828.
379—2. WILLIAM, b. Sept. 12, 1788; m. 1st, Margaret Conklin; 2d, Margaret Force.
380—3. PHILIP, b. May 19, 1792; d. Dec. 12, 1822, leaving one son, who after his father's death went to Pennsylvania.
381—4. STEPHEN, b. May 29, 1794; m. Sarah Joy.
382—5. SARAH HASTING, b. Aug. 19, 1796; m. Charles Gregory.
383—6. ELIZABETH, b. Aug. 6, 1799; m. Charles Winfield.
384—7. SUSAN, b. Dec. 5, 1801; d. 1870.
385—8. GEORGE W., } twins, b. Nov. 17, 1803; { d. March, 1805.
386—9. RASHO,
387-10. HENRIETTA, b. Oct. 14, 1805; m. Richard M. Moore.

388. JACOB CRANE[5] [135], (Jacob,[4] Matthias,[3] John,[2] Stephen[1]), married Sarah Sayre in 1799. She was born in Union Township, N. J., and died in Newark, Dec. 9, 1863, aged 85. He died in Newark, July 4, 1848. Resided at Lyons Farms, Newark, N. J. Children :

389—1. ELIZABETH, b. 1800; d. 1837, unmarried.
390—2. JOANNAH, b. 1802; m. Lewis Little, 1833.
391—3. PHEBE. b. 1804; m. Obediah Lyon, 1834; she was his 2d wife. (See No. 780).
392—4. DAVID WARNER, b. April 3, 1808; m. 1st, Phebe Woodruff; 2d, Sarah Brown, 1830.
393—5. JACOB, b. Aug. 11, 1810; m. 1st, Letty Pearson; 2d, Ellen M. Horg, 1835.
394—6. SARAH, b. 1813; m. Edward Earle, 1835; d. Sept., 1865.
395—7. WILLIAM ALEXANDER, b. 1815; m. 1st, Frances Garthwaite; 2d, Mary Earle, 1840.

396. PHEBE CRANE[5] [136], (Jacob,[4] Matthias,[3] John,[2] Stephen[1]), married John Stiles. Children :

1. DAVID (Stiles); m. Betsy Winans.
2. PHEBE (Stiles); m. Jonathan Garthwaite.
3. JOHN (Stiles).
4. WILLIAM (Stiles); m. Mary Meeker; he d. Jan. 27, 1896.
5. MARY (Stiles); m. Linus Little.
6. HARRIOT (Stiles); m. Luke Higgins.
7. BETSY (Stiles); m. W. William Connet.
8. SALLY (Stiles); m. Jonas Winans.
9. CHARLOTTE (Stiles); m. A. Parkhurst.

397. MATTHIAS CRANE[5] [137], (Jacob,[4] Matthias,[3] John,[2] Stephen[1]), married 1st, Nov. 27, 1802, Prudence Lum, born 1799, by whom he had one child, Prudence; 2d, in 1808, Sally (or Sarah) Lum, born Oct. 21, 1781; sister of his first wife. He was a farmer, carpenter and wheelwright; served in the war of 1812 [so says his son William Henry]. First wife Prudence died
48

Dec. 23, 1804; second wife Sally died Sept. 25, 1868. He died July 3. One account says that he married 1st, Nov. 22, 1802, and died July 25, 1825. Children:

398—1. PRUDENCE, b. Sept. 24, 1804; m. Obadiah Lyon; for 2d wife, he m. Phebe, daughter of Jacob and Sarah Sayre Crane.
399—2. MATTHIAS BRANT, b. Dec. 27, 1808; m. Margaret Winans; had four children.
400—3. DAVID LUM, b. Sept. 28, 1811; m. Rachel ———; had three children:
401—4. JOHN CLARK, b. April 10, 1814; m. 1st, Catherine Williams; 2d, ———; had one child.
402—5. SAMUEL, b. Sept. 30, 1816; m. Sarah Ann Nelson; had five children.
403—6. WILLIAM HENRY, b. Dec. 1, 1818; m. Julia Ann Atwater, of Florida; had two children.
404—7. JANE ELIZABETH, b. Jan. 15, 1821; d. unmarried.
405—8. STEPHEN JOY, b. Nov. 20, 1824; m. Eve Finiley; had two children.

406. MATTHIAS CRANE[5] [140], (John,[4] Matthias,[3] John,[2] Stephen[1]), married Eliza Glendening, in New York city. He was by trade a carpenter, and resided in the city of New York; served in the war of 1812. He died in Newark, N. J., Feb. 20, 1853. Children:

407—1. JOHN, b. Nov. 27, 1809; m. Rebecca T. Glendening.
408—2. SQUIRE M.; m. 1st, Jane Ann Forrister; 2d, Miss Pollard; no children.
409—3. ALFRED H.
410—4. MATTHIAS; went to Kansas, where he married.
411—5. JOB S.; m. 1st, Miss Tompkins; 2d, Miss Mayo; no children; he is president of The J. S. Crane Carriage Hardware Co., of Newark, N. J.

412. BENJAMIN CRANE[5] [152], (Benjamin,[4] Benjamin,[3] John,[2] Stephen[1]), married Sarah Thompson. Children:

413—1. JOHN; m. Mary Clark, of Westfield.
414—2. ABIGAIL; m. David Keyt.
415—3. ESTHER; d. at the age of 18 or 20 years.
416—4. HEZEKIAH THOMPSON; m. Amanda Osborn.
417—5. PHEBE; m. 1st, Francis Randolph; 2d, Geo. R. King.
418—6. CHARLOTTE KING; m. H. Baker.
419—7. NORRIS; went to Cincinnati, O., and m. there.
420—8. JACOB THOMPSON; went to Cincinnati, O., and d. there unmarried.
421—9. BENJAMIN; m. Electa Baker; was her 2d husband.
422—10. DAVID JOHNSON; m. Ann Eliza Roll.
423—11. MOSES THOMPSON; m. Eliza Scudder.

424. NORRIS CRANE[5] [154], (Benjamin,[4] Benjamin,[3] John,[2] Stephen[1]), married Jane Dunham, and died Feb. 21, 1846. She was born near Long Hill, Morris Co., N. J., May 13, 1765, and died June 23, 1848. His grandson Sineus Benjamin says his grandmother's name was Jane Tappan. They lived at what was known as Long Hill. Children:

425—1. NANCY, b. Sept. 29, 1790; m. William Pearson Conklin.
426—2. ISAAC, b. Oct. 25, 1792; m. 1st, Polly ———; 2d, Anne Parrot.

427—3. SALLY, b. March 27, 1797; m. Peter Parrot.
428—4. JOHN, b. Sept. 29, 1799; m. Abby Flatt.
429—5. BENJAMIN, b. April 16, 1802; m. Julia Bebout, Dec. 2, 1824.
430—6. ALBERT, b. March 17, 1804; m. a daughter of Anderson French.
431—7. MARY, b. March 16, 1807; m. Israel Bebout, Jan. 4, 1843.

432. DAVID DAY CRANE[5] [162], (Eleazer,[4] Benjamin,[3] John,[2] Stephen[1]), was born in Elizabethtown, N. J.; married May 16, 1789, Hannah Cleveland, who was also a native of Elizabethtown, and born Oct. 21, 1774. She died in New York city, Feb. 13, 1847. Mr. Crane was a merchant and died in Brooklyn, June 21, 1851. Children:

433—1. ALETTA, b. March 23, 1790.
434—2. SUSAN, b. April 10, 1792; m. John Gable, Oct. 20, 1820; d Sept. 12, 1822.
435—3. ABNER, b. March 27, 1794; d. Sept. 28, 1805.
436—4. SARAH POTTER,
437—5. PHEBE THOMPSON, } b. Oct. 14, 1796. } m. Dec. 3, 1827, John Tiebout; d. Aug. 5, 1828.
438—6. MATTHIAS ALLEN, b. Dec. 23, 1798; d. April 14, 1805.
439—7. DAVID, b. May 17, 1801; m. 1st, Margaret Marsh, March 29, 1827. She d. Jan. 14, 1850; m. 2d, Jane L. Isham, May 6, 1851; no children; he d. March 27, 1881.
440—8. BETSEY ALLEN, b. June 25, 1803; d. March 1, 1807.
441—9. MARIA, b. Oct. 1, 1805; d. Aug. 14, 1806.
442—10. WILLIAM WATROUS, b. Dec. 2, 1807, in New York city.
443—11. ROBERT THOMPSON, b. Feb. 16, 1810; left home and never heard from.
444—12. ANN MARIA, b. Feb. 8, 1812; d. April 22, 1885.
445—13. ALEXANDER PATTERSON, b. Dec. 29, 1814.
446—14. ELIZABETH, b. April 9, 1819; m. Albert Gallatin Howe, Sept. 7, 1839; she d. May 8, 1840; no children.

447. STEPHEN CRANE[5] [164], (James,[4] James,[3] Jeremiah,[2] Stephen[1]), married Phebe Garthwaite, who was born Aug. 16, 1784, and died April 29, 1829. He died Feb. 14, 1846. Children:

448—1. JAMES, b. Feb. 10, 1803; d. Oct. 9, 1803.
449—2. JAMES, b. Oct. 21, 1804.
450—3. WILLIAM M., b. Dec. 24, 1806.
451—4. STEPHEN, b. 1807.
452—5. JOSEPH, b. March 16, 1809; d. March 22, 1810.
453—6. PRUDENCE, b. Aug. 20, 1811; d. April 27, 1812.
454—7. ELIAS G., b. April 18, 1813; unmarried.
455—8. MARY E., b. Oct. 21, 1816; m. James Ervin; no children.
456—9. PRUDENCE, b. June 5, 1819; d. May 28, 1820.
457—10. ANN M., b. Jan. 23, 1825; m. 1st, Jonathan Crane, son of Thomas B. and Margaret (Shotwell) Crane; 2d, David Williams; living, March, 1899, Roselle, N. J.

458. JEREMIAH CRANE[5] [165], (James,[4] James,[3] Jeremiah,[2] Stephen[1]), married Margaret Hatfield. Children:

459—1. SARAH.
460—2. ELIZABETH (or BETSY).
461—3 HANNAH.

462—4. JEREMIAH.
463—5. ROBERT.
464—6. ANN.
465—7. JOHN.
466—8. JOSEPH.

467. BETSY CRANE[5] [166], (James,[4] James,[3] Jeremiah,[2] Stephen[1]), married Joseph Woodruff [so says Ann M. (Crane) Williams, of Roselle, N. J.] Child:

1. JAMES (Woodruff); m. ———. Children:
   1. JOSEPH (Woodruff).
   2. JOHN (Woodruff).
   3. JAMES (Woodruff).
   4. ELIZABETH (Woodruff).
   5. SARAH (Woodruff).
   6. JANE (Woodruff).

468. ELIZABETH CRANE[5] [171], (Stephen,[4] Stephen,[3] Daniel,[2] Stephen[1]), married Stephen Hout. Children:

1. STEPHEN (Hout), b. Feb. 13, 1777.
2. SAMUEL (Hout), b. Jan. 13, 1782.

469. DANIEL CRANE[5] [173], (Stephen,[4] Stephen,[3] Daniel,[2] Stephen[1]), married Prosia Dorman, and lived near Morristown. He died in 1810, after which she married again. She died Nov. 3, 1821. Children:

470—1. CHARLES, b. Aug. 8, 1788.
471—2. PHEBE, b. Dec. 3, 1790; m. George Marsh; he d. Aug. 16, 1833; she d. April 25, 1842.
472—3. CATHERINE, b. Feb. 25, 1793.
473—4. ELIZABETH, b. Jan. 23, 1802.
474—5. PROSIA, b. Sept. 27, 1803.
475—6. SUSAN, b. March 10, 1809.

476. PHEBE CRANE[5] [174], (Stephen,[4] Stephen,[3] Daniel,[2] Stephen[1]), married ——— Woodruff. Children:

1. DAVID (Woodruff).
2. HANNAH (Woodruff).

477. NANCY CRANE[5] [175], (Stephen,[4] Stephen,[3] Daniel,[2] Stephen[1]), married Obed Meeker. Children:

1. JENETT (Meeker); m. Jacob Crane at the mill.
2. AGNES (Meeker); m. Benjamin Kirby; had two children.
3. SUSAN (Meeker); m. Jacob Crane [at the mill], 2d wife.
4. ANN (Meeker); m. Cooper Woodruff Crane. Children:
   1. CLARK S. (Crane); went to St. Louis.
   2. JULIA (Crane); m. James W. Palmer; went to Colorado.
   3. ABRAHAM S. (Crane); went to St. Louis.
   4. HARRY [or HENRY] (Crane); m. Mary———.
5. MARIA (Meeker); m. Morris Howard, and had seven children.

478. MARGARET CRANE[5] [176], (Stephen,[4] Stephen,[3] Daniel,[2] Stephen[1]), married Jacob Bonnel. She died Jan. 16, 1832. He died Feb. 23, 1841. Children:

1. CHARLES (Bonnel), b. Dec. 19, 1789; m. Abigail Woodruff.
2. UNICE (Bonnel), b. Jan. 21, 1792; d. July 20, 1793.
3. ANNA (Bonnel), b. Dec. 10, 1793.

4   VASTITE (Bonnel), b. Dec. 10, 1795.
5. MARIAH (Bonnel), b. Feb. 14, 1799; d. Oct. 1, 1799.
6. AMOS (Bonnel), b. Feb. 9, 1801; d. Sept. 30, 1802.
7. EZRA (Bonnel), b. Aug. 24, 1802; m. Amy Underhill.
8. JOB (Bonnel), b. Dec. 7, 1806; d. Dec. 18, 1806.
9. MARGARET (Bonnel), b. Jan. 23, 1809; m. Caleb Underhill.
10. AGNES (Bonnel), b. Oct. 1, 1811; m. George Chesline.

479. HANNAH CRANE[5] [177], (Stephen,[4] Stephen,[3] Daniel,[2] Stephen[1]), married Jonathan Squire, of Westfield, N. J. He was born May 16, 1766. She died May 10, 1832. Children:

1. JOHN (Squire), b. Aug. 31, 1794; d. young.
2. JOBE (Squire), b. Oct. 20, 1796; m. Mary Coles; d. July 27, 1854.
3. ELIZA (Squire), b. Sept. 21, 1799.
4. DAVID (Squire), b. Feb. 5, 1802; d. 1805.
5. DAVID (Squire), b. April 14. 1805; d. Sept. 26, 1829.
6. NANCY (Squire), b. Nov. 18, 1806; d. Aug. 24, 1822.
7. JANE (Squire), b. Jan. 14, 1809; m. Jacob G. Crane, son of Noah Crane.
8. WILLIAM CRANE (Squire), b. Jan. 8, 1812; m. Catherine Craig.

480. JONATHAN CRANE[5] [181], (Stephen,[4] Stephen,[3] Daniel,[2] Stephen[1]), married Hetty Winans. He died May 27, 1850. Children:

481—1. JANE, b. Nov. 27, 1803; d. Oct. 12, 1854.
482—2. JASON, b. Aug. 15, 1805; m. Jan. 21, 1845; d. Aug. 15, 1848.
483—3. ABIGAIL, b. Jan. 1, 1808: d. March 11, 1847.
484—4. JULIA A., b. Nov. 25, 1810; m. Feb. 3, 1839.
485—5. MARTHA, b. Feb. 15, 1812.
486—6. STEPHEN, b. June 29, 1815; d. Nov. 5, 1853.
487—7. BYERSON, b. Feb. 13, 1817; m. Jan. 5, 1840.
488—8. ELIAS H., b. April 25, 1819; m. Sept. 25, 1845.

489. ICHABOD B. CRANE[5] [193], (William,[4] Stephen,[3] Daniel,[2] Stephen[1]), was born at Elizabethtown, N. J. He entered the United States Army; was appointed second lieutenant of Marines in January, 1809; and captain of the Third Artillery, April 25, 1812; brevet major for meritorious services Nov. 13, 1813; major of Fourth Artillery, Sept. 15, 1825; lieutenant-colonel of Second Artillery, Nov. 3, 1832; colonel of First Regiment United States Artillery, June 27, 1843; and governor of the Military Asylum at Washington, May, 1851, to November, 1853. He died at Port Richmond, Staten Island, N. Y., Oct. 5, 1857. He married Charlotte A. Rainger, of Barre, Mass., Aug. 27, 1825, and March 26, 1828, they sold land in Barre she received from Dr. Ephraim Brooks, of that place, at which time Major Crane lived in Newport, R. I. They also disposed of more of this land in the year 1829. Child:

490—1. CHARLES HENRY, b. July 19, 1825, at Newport, R. I., where his father, an United States Army officer, was then stationed. At the time of entering Yale College his father was stationed at Norfolk, Va. He graduated from there in the class of 1844. Four years later (Feb. 14, 1848,) he was appointed to the United States Army from Massachusetts; after receiving several promotions was on March 13, 1865, made brevet brigadier-general for meritorious

services during the war of the rebellion; and on July
28, 1866, he was promoted to be colonel and assistant surgeon-general. In 1882 he received the appointment of
surgeon-general, as successor to Surgeon-General Barnes.
Several candidates were presented for this position, some
of them bearing exceedingly strong petitions; but the long
and faithful service rendered by Dr. Crane, together with
his thorough qualification for the position, won for him
the appointment over the other competitors. He was one
of the surgeons who attended President Lincoln after
being shot by Wilkes Booth. He died at his home in
Washington, D. C., Oct. 10, 1883. For several weeks he
had been troubled with a throat disease, accompanied by
hemorrhages, but attended to his official duties up to
within about a week of his death. Dr. Crane was tall
and of large frame. The funeral was held at Washington; burial at Shelter Island. The War Department and
its bureaus were closed during the day out of respect to
his memory. He left a widow.

491. Hon. JOSEPH H. CRANE⁵ [194], (William,⁴ Stephen,³
Daniel,² Stephen¹), married Julia Ann Elliot. He lived in
Dayton, Ohio; was elected member of the United States Congress, and was judge of the supreme court of the State of Ohio
at the time of his death. He died Nov. 12, 1851. Children:

492—1. MARIA; m. Joshua Clements; had one child, Joseph Clements
493—2. WILLIAM.
494—3. WILBRA.
495—4. JAMES.
496—5. HENRIETTA.
497—6. JOSEPH; m. Sarah Schenck.
498—7. CLEMENTS.

499. JOANNA CRANE⁵ [196], (William,⁴ Stephen,³ Daniel,²
Stephen¹), married John Magie. She died Jan. 30, 1820. Child:

1. JULIA.

500. SUSANNA CRANE⁵ [200], (Joseph,⁴ Stephen,³ Daniel,²
Stephen¹), married Henry Weaver, and went to Ohio. He was
born April 15, 1761; is said to have served on a privateering
vessel during the Revolutionary war; was confined in old Mill
prison, England, and released in January, 1784. Married
Hannah Meeker about 1787. She soon left him, returning to her
family. He afterwards eloped, it is said, with Susan Crane, she
not yet sixteen years of age. They were married May 1, 1790,
and removed to Columbia County, in what was then Northwest
Territory, and about six miles from Cincinnati, then called Fort
Washington. Here he carried on farming and surveying. In
1792 he helped to establish Tucker's Station, midway between
Cincinnati and Fort Hamilton. In 1794 he received from Gov.
St. Clair an appointment as justice of the peace for Hamilton
County. After the conclusion of the treaty with the Indians by
Gov. Wayne, in 1795, Mr. Weaver removed to a tract of land
near Middletown, Butler County; and about 1801 purchased land
in Madison township, on Elk Creek, where he resided at his

death, which occurred Aug. 17, 1829. He was buried at Trenton, Butler Co., Ohio. About 1805 he was appointed associate judge of the court of common pleas for Butler County, resigning July 20, 1829. Mrs. Weaver died Jan. 22, 1851. Children:

1. NATHANIEL L. (Weaver), b. March 22, 1791.
2. ANN (Weaver), b. July 7, 1793; m. Jacob Randall Clauson.
3. WILLIAM (Weaver), b. Dec. 20, 1795.
4. JANE (Weaver), b. Feb. 11, 1798; m. Robert E. Duffield.
5. SUSAN (Weaver), b. April 20, 1800; d. Nov. 18, 1800.
6. JOHN GREENWOOD (Weaver), b. Oct. 8, 1801; m. Lucy Bowman.
7. ABRAHAM (Weaver), b. Jan. 9, 1804.
8. SAMUEL (Weaver), b. Nov. 6, 1806; m. Ruth McNeal.
9. MARY (Weaver), b. March 2, 1809; m. James Baird.
10. JOSEPH (Weaver), b. July 27, 1811; d. Aug. 28, 1811.
11. ELIZA GREENWOOD (Weaver), b. Nov. 18, 1812.
12. SUSAN (Weaver), b. April 5, 1815; d. April. 1817.
13. HENRY (Weaver), b. Oct. 4, 1818; d. Oct. 6, 1818.
14. ISAAC CLARK (Weaver), b. Nov. 26, 1820.

501. WILLAM CRANE[5] [201], (Joseph,[4] Stephen,[3] Daniel,[2] Stephen[1]), married in the year 1802 Sarah Townley, of Elizabeth, N. J., who was born Oct. 26, 1776. He was born Oct. 23, 1778. He died June 4, 1830, at Elizabeth. She died Aug. 18, 1832. He was a farmer, surveyor and justice of the peace; resided in Connecticut Farms, now known as Union, Essex Co., N. J. Children:

502—1. ANNE, b. Nov. 20, 1803; d. Aug. 6, 1805.
503—2. DAVID ROSS, b. Jan. 8, 1806; m. Phebe Ann Harllam.
504—3. AGNES COOPER, b. Aug. 6, 1809; m. Rev. Curtis Tulley; had dau. Hellen.
505—4. RICHARD TOWNLEY, b. Sept. 14, 1812; m. Jane T. Dolbier, Children:
    1. THEODORE T. D. CRANE.
    2. FREDERICK T. D. CRANE.
506—5. JOSEPH WILLIAM, b. Dec. 14, 1815; m. Harriet J. Wilcox.
507—6. JONATHAN T., b. June 18, 1819; m. Mary Hellen Peck.

508. NANCY CRANE[5] [202], (Joseph,[4] Stephen,[3] Daniel,[2] Stephen[1]), married Abraham Van Sickle. Went to Trenton, Ohio. Children:

1. SUSAN (Van Sickle); m. 1st, Mr. Long; 2d, Mr. Bailey; 3d, Mr. Brown.
2. HENRY (Van Sickle).
3. MARIA (Van Sickle).
4. CATHERINE (Van Sickle).
5. JOSEPH (Van Sickle).

509. RICHARD CRANE[5] [203], (Joseph,[4] Stephen,[3] Daniel,[2] Stephen[1]), married ———. Resides in Ohio. Child:

1. A daughter; m. John Trotter; residence at Macoupin County, Illinois. Children: CLARK; OSCAR; GEORGE.

510. DAVID CRANE[5] [204], (Joseph,[4] Stephen,[3] Daniel,[2] Stephen[1]), born April 18, 1788. Married Elizabeth Huff, and settled in Butler County, Ohio; a farmer. He died in Cass

County, Mich., about 1850. She died in Piasa, Macoupin Co., Ill., Oct. 9, 1880. Children:

511—1. LEONARD W., b. Feb. 1, 1813; killed by Indians in 1866.
512—2. NANCY, b. June 20, 1817; d. about 1854; unmarried.
513—3. ELIZABETH; m. Mr. B. Gard; d.
514—4. JOANNA; m. Allen Rodgers, Champaign, Ill.
515—5. ISAAC; lives at Piasa, Macoupin Co., Ill.
516—6. DAVID; m.; had one son, WILLIE; lives at Rich Coffe, Texas.
517—7. JOHN; d. about 1862; unmarried.
513—8. CATHARINE; m. Josephus Rich, Prairie Round, Cass Co., Mich.

519. JOHN CRANE[5] [207], (Joseph,[4] Stephen,[3] Daniel,[2] Stephen[1]), married Sarah Conover. Children:

520—1. WILLIAM; m. Rachel Cranford. Children: JOHN; WILLIAM.
521—2. JOEL; m. Sarah Warner.
522—3. MARGARET; m. H. M. Moore.
523—4. TRYPHENA; m. Thomas Davis. Children: CHARLES; MARGARET; THOMAS.
524—5. GEORGE W.
525—6. MARIAH.
526—7. MARY.
527—8. JOHN C.
528—9. JANE C.
529-10. JOSEPH.

530. WILLIAM CRANE[5] [212], (David,[4] David,[3] Daniel,[2] Stephen[1]), a planter; lived the greater portion of his life in Kent County, Md. Married three times: 1st, Ann Pearce, April 6, 1797; she died Oct. 6, 1800, leaving a daughter. 2d, Esther Blackiston, Jan. 15, 1803; she died Dec. 8, 1824. No children by second wife. He married 3d, Feb. 13, 1827, the widow of William Banks Wakeman, whose maiden name was Araminta Bowers Hynson. She died May 29, 1835, aged 40. Mr. Crane was paymaster in the Kent County regiment in the war of 1812. He died March 4, 1838. Children:

531—1. MARY ANN b. March 18, 1800.
532—2. WILLIAM BOWERS, b. Dec. 18, 1827; was a physician; went to Kansas, and d.
533—3. THOMAS RICHARD, b. March 29, 1830; living (1898) in Baltimore, Md.

534. ROGER CRANE[5] [214], (David,[4] David,[3] Daniel,[2] Stephen[1]), went to sea from Philadelphia, Pa., and became captain of a merchantman. Married Eleanor, daughter of William Fullerton and his wife Eleanor Donaldson, of that city. She is said to have been a relative of Gen. Jackson. He died March 20, 1819, and she married his brother Philip. Children:

535—1. MARY; m. Dr. Griffin; no children.
536—2. DAVID; d.; unm.
537—3. ELEANOR D.; m. Samuel Hilt, of Philadelphia.
538—4. ADELINE.
539—5. PHILIP SAMUEL, } twins.
540—6. SARAH ELIZABETH, }

541. THOMAS CRANE[5] [215], (David,[4] David,[3] ˉDaniel,[2] Stephen[1]), married Oct. 3, 1803, Mary Ingraham, of Kent County, Md. She was born May 26, 1782, and settled at Church Hill, Queen Anne's Co. He died June 26, 1823. She died Feb. 20, 1852. She left five daughters; reside at Baltimore. Children :

542—1. THOMAS, b. Aug. 19, 1804; d. July 18, 1808.
543—2. RACHEL, b. Dec. 9, 1806; d. July 28, 1896.
544—3. MARY, b. March 2, 1809; m. Israel Day; d. Oct., 1890.
545—4. EDWARD, b. May 15, 1811; d. Oct. 2, 1811.
546—5. ELIZABETH, b. Jan. 19, 1813; living Dec., 1898.
547—6. DAVID, b. Oct. 5, 1815; d. July 30, 1841.
548—7. JANE, b. Oct. 14, 1817; d. June 15, 1893.
549—8. MARGARET ANN, b. July 22, 1820: d. Jan. 1, 1870.
550—9. SARAH MATILDA, b. Oct., 1822; d. 1823.

551. MARY CRANE[5] [216], (David,[4] David,[3] Daniel,[2] Stephen[1]), married James Blackiston, and settled on the estate he purchased of his father, a large tract of land situated in the upper portion of Kent County, Md., called " Brighthelmstone," and where he was born. It was a part of his grandfather James Blackiston's estate. She died Jan. 17, 1859. Mr. Blackiston lost his property late in life through endorsing obligations for others. Children :

1. JONATHAN (Blackiston); d. in infancy.
2. MARY M. (Blackiston); m. her cousin Thomas Medford Blackiston; their only child, MARY ELIZABETH, m. Dr. James A. Perkins, of Chestertown, Md. They have eight sons and a daughter. Mary M. d. April 10, 1845, aged 36 years, 4 months, 9 days.
3. KATHARINE AMANDA (Blackiston).
4. DAVID CRANE (Blackiston), b. Feb. 19, 1809; m. Rachel Mott Hooton, April 4, 1837. She was dau. of Andrew and Mary (McKenzie) Hooton; b. Sept. 30, 1809. She d. Feb. 9, 1884. He d. Dec. 24, 1888. Children :
    1. MARY HOOTON (Blackiston), b. April 2, 1838; d. Aug. 16, 1839.
    2. CATHARINE AMANDA (Blackiston), b. Nov. 28, 1839; m. Alfred Stille, M.D., June 14, 1899. Residence, Philadelphia, Pa.
    3. MARY JANE (Blackiston), b. April 12, 1841.
    4. MOTT HOOTON (Blackiston), b. Aug. 31, 1842; d. Sept. 2, 1842.
    5. ANDREW HOOTON (Blackiston), b. May 21, 1844; d. Aug. 30, 1878.
    6. DAVID JAMES (Blackiston), b. Feb. 23, 1846; m. Elizabeth Bruce, Jan. 26, 1870. He is a lawyer by profession, and several times chosen mayor of Cumberland, Md.

ANDREW HOOTON (Blackiston) [5]; m. Elizabeth Pearre, of Cumberland, Md., May 21, 1874. Children :
    1. ANDREW HOOTON (Blackiston), b. April 21, 1877.
    2. GEORGE PEARRE (Blackiston), b. May 18, 1879.

552. JOHN CRANE[5] [218], (David,[4] David,[3] Daniel,[2] Stephen[1]), at an early age left his home in Kent Co., Md., and
49

went to sea, about the year 1800. While sailing as mate of an East Indian merchant vessel, the captain died, leaving the mate, then but eighteen years of age, in command of the ship. The trip proved successful, and the owners were so well pleased with the conduct of the young commander that he was continued some years in that position, and until he married, and at the solicitation of friends, gave up the seafaring life, and removed to Harford, where his brother David had been living, but then deceased. Later he resided for a time in Queen Anne's County, but shortly prior to his death, he took up his residence in Chester Town, where he died Jan. 15, 1827. He married Anne ———.

Children :

552½-1. ———; followed a seafaring life many years, then was a stevedore, at Mobile, New Orleans, and later at Galveston, Tex., where he died about 1873.
553—2. ANN; m. John A. Hall. and settled in Queen Anne's Co., Md.
554—3. MARY; m. William Hendrix.
555—4. DAVID HENRY, b. Oct. 11, 1816.
556—5. PHILIP.

557. PHILIP CRANE[5] [221], (David,[4] David,[3] Daniel,[2] Stephen[1]), served in the war of 1812; was wounded at the battle of Caulk's Field, in 1814. He settled first in Kent Co., Md., later went to New Orleans, La. He married Eleanor Fullerton Crane, widow of his brother Roger.

Mrs. Alfred Stille furnishes the following, which was related to her by her father David Crane Blackiston: " The battle of Caulk's Field was fought near Tolchester, about ten miles below Chester Town, Kent Co., Md., Aug. 30, 1812. There was great consternation among the people of Chester Town, because Sir Peter Parker, commander of the British forces, made oath on landing that he ' would burn Chester Town, or eat breakfast in hell.'

"The American forces were under command of Col. Philip Reed, and several of David Crane's sons were in the engagement, having volunteered as soon as danger appeared. Philip, who was named for his kinsman, Col. Philip Reed, was among the number. The British lost fifteen men and Sir Peter Parker was mortally wounded by a stray buckshot, and died before reaching his boat. Thus Chester Town and other places along the shore were spared the proposed destruction. Philip Crane received a wound in the hip early in the engagement, but dropping on his knees continued to load and fire until the battle was over, and, as the shot which struck Sir Peter Parker came from the direction of Philip Crane, it was supposed he fired the fatal shot. After the close of the battle, Peter Crane was carried' from the field, and his wound cared for, although he was lame throughout his life."

Child :

558—WILLIAM FULLERTON, b. April 22, 1820, Kent Co., Md.

559. JONATHAN CRANE[5] [222], (David,[4] David,[3] Daniel,[2] Stephen[1]), married Nov. 12, 1815, Catherine Miers, daughter of Stephen Miers and Juliana Thomas his wife. He studied medicine, and located in Church Hill, Md.; was also a local Methodist preacher. Mrs. Crane died March 6, 1828. He married 2d, ———, and had Charles, died in infancy; married 3d, Julia Baker, born in 1817; had five children by third wife. He died July 21, 1855. Children:

560—1. MARY, b. Sept. 3, 1816; d. April 11, 1835.
561—2. STEPHEN MIERS, b. March 23, 1818; d. Nov., 1854.
562—3. JAMES OSBORN, b. Sept. 14, 1820; d. Oct. 11, 1821.
563—4. WILLIAM HENRY, b. Feb. 4, 1822; d. July 28, 1822.
564—5. JULIANN, b. July 14, 1823; d. Sept. 28, 1823.
565—6. THOMAS HENRY, b. Feb. 7, 1825; d. Feb. 8, 1887.
566—7. CATHERINE ELIZA, b. Sept. 14, 1827; d. July 17, 1828.
567—8. JULIA ANN, b. Aug. 27, 1839.
568—9. JONATHAN, b. 1840; d. 1853.
569-10. DAVID, b. 1841; d. in infancy.
570-11. SARAH CATHARINE, b. 1843; d. 1871.
571-12. EMILY, b. 1845; d. in infancy.

572. ELIAS CRANE[5] [229], (David,[4] Nathaniel,[3] Nathaniel,[2] Stephen[1]), married Elizabeth Searles, and removed to Ohio, in 1790. Was a Methodist minister; died in Leesville, Carroll Co., O.: had a son a doctor. Child:

573—1. ELIHU*; m. and had a son James Lyon Crane. This Elihu lived in Berea, Cuyahoga Co., O.

574. ANDREW DRAKE CRANE[5] [231], (David,[4] Nathaniel,[3] Nathaniel,[2] Stephen[1]), was a carpenter by trade; was born and resided in Elizabeth, N. J., also in New York. He was a soldier in the war of 1812. He married Elizabeth Woodruff, April 30, 1808. She was born Aug. 11, 1773. Two other of their children died young. Children:

575—1. DAVID, b. March 19, 1809, in Elizabeth, N. J.
576—2. JANE LEE; d. Mt. Stirling, Ill.
577—3. ELIAS F., b. Oct. 1, 1819, in New York.

578. ISAAC CRANE[5] [236], (Caleb,[4] Caleb,[3] Nathaniel,[2] Stephen[1]), married Abigail Price, daughter of Thomas Price and Abigail Ogden his wife, Nov. 15, 1791. She was born Sept. 8, 1766, and died May, 1832. He was much interested in matters of family history, and to him the descendants are indebted for the preservation of some of the early records relating to their ancestors. He was an elder in the Presbyterian Church for forty

---

*Did he marry Anxious Chaney, mother of Regin Baker Crane, who died in De Kalb Co., Ind., March 7, 1860 ? Regin Baker Crane married Mary Jane Chaney, and had John Wesley Crane, born Jan. 8, 1845; clergyman, M. E. Church; was settled at Kansas, Ill.; married Sept. 1, 1870, Amanda Hallett, Valparaiso, Ind. .Children: MINNIE GERTRUDE; ALBERT CLARK; JESSE V.

years, and has been styled the " School Teacher." His home was in Elizabethtown, N. J. Children :

579—1. JEREMIAH BALLARD, b. Sept. 20, 1792; m. Mary P. Clark; d. Aug. 8, 1829.
580—2. JONATHAN EDWARDS, b. July 22, 1794; m. Mary P. Thompson.
581—3. CALEB, b. Sept. 15, 1796; d. Dec. 31, 1796.
582—4. CALEB I., b. Dec. 9, 1797; d. March, 1832.
583—5. MARY BALLARD, b. April 26, 1800; d. Oct. 24, 1824.
584—6. THOMAS OGDEN, b. July 4, 1803; d. Aug. 18, 1803.
585—7. THOMAS OGDEN, b. Sept. 23, 1804; m. 1st, Elizabeth Price; 2d, Berthia Miller.

586. CHARITY CRANE[5] [240], (Nehemiah,[4] Caleb,[3] Nathaniel,[2] Stephen[1]), married Stephen Meeker. Children :

1. NEHEMIAH (Meeker).
2. PHEBE (Meeker); m. Aaron Bonnell, Jan. 1819.
3. MARY (Meeker); m. William Stiles, son of John and Phebe (Crane) Stiles, daughter of Capt. Jacob Crane.
4. ESTHER (Meeker); m. Nehemiah Sayre.
5. CHARITY.

587. MARY CRANE[5] [243], (Jacob,[4] Caleb,[3] Nathaniel,[2] Stephen[1]), married Samuel Crane, a son of Amos, perhaps son of Moses, fourth generation from Jasper. She died Oct. 25, 1850. Children :

1. EZRA; m. Hetty Brown; near Rahway, N. J.
2. PHEBE; m. Benjamin Garthwait.
3. COOPER WOODRUFF; m. Ann Meeker.
4. CALEB; a dwarf.
5. EDWARD; a dwarf.
6 SALLY.

588. NOAH CRANE[5] [244], (Jacob,[4] Caleb,[3] Nathaniel,[2] Stephen[1]), married Martha Winans, 1795. He died Feb. 25, 1831. She died March 31, 1862. She was sister to Jonathan Crane's wife, and born May 7, 1777. He owned and worked a large farm, also a grist and saw mill, at Elizabethtown, N. J. Children : .

589—1. ELIAS WINANS, b. March 18, 1796.
590—2. PHEBE, b. Feb. 19, 1798.
591—3. JONATHAN, b. Sept. 14, 1800.
592—4. ABIGAIL WINANS, b. Oct. 24, 1803.
593—5. JACOB GOZEN, b. Aug. 13, 1806.
594—6. HENRIETTA PARLEE, b. July 16, 1810.
595—7. ISAAC C., b. Aug. 4, 1817; d. of yellow fever at Mobile, 1843.
596—8. ABRAHAM WINANS, b. Nov. 3, 1820; d. of typhoid fever, at Elizabethtown, 1848.

597. CALEB CRANE[5] [246], (Jacob,[4] Caleb,[3] Nathaniel,[2] Stephen[1]), married Elizabeth Dalton, of Long Island. Children :

598—1. JULIA ANN, b. Jan., 1807; m. 1st, John Scudder, in Aug., 1826; 2d, Thomas Strang.
599—2. ELIZA, b. March, 1809.

600. ELIZABETH CRANE[5] [245], (Jacob,[4] Caleb,[3] Nathaniel,[2] Stephen[1]), married 1st, Moses Parsnet, by whom she had one daughter; 2d, Andrew Parsel. Children:

1. PHEBE (Parsnet).
2. MOSES (Parsel)
3. ANDRUS (Parsel).
4. ELIZA (Parsel).
5. SARAH (Parsel).

601. JACOB CRANE[5] [248], (Jacob,[4] Caleb,[3] Nathaniel,[2] Stephen[1]), married 1st, Janet, daughter of Obed Meeker. She was born 1784, and died Aug. 21, 1824. He afterwards married Susan Meeker, sister of his first wife, who after the death of Mr. Jacob Crane, married, in 1828, Nehemiah Crane, by whom she had one child, who died in 1831. Children:

602—1. MOSES, b. Nov. 21, 1803; d. Dec. 28, 1826.
603—2. OBEDIAH, b. Feb. 28, 1805; d. Sept. 28, 1805.
604—3. OBEDIAH, b. Dec. 10, 1806; d. July 10, 1811.
605—4. NOAH, b. Dec. 10, 1808; m. widow Scribner, of South Carolina.
606—5. OBEDIAH, b. July 10, 1812; d. Aug. 10, 1812.
607—6. OBED MEEKER, b. Oct. 6, 1813.
608—7. ANN, b. 1815; m. Thos. Sanders, of North Carolina, 1832.
609—8. JOB SQUIER, b. 1822; m. in North Carolina.
610—9. JANNETTE S., b. 1826; d. July 10, 1875.

611. NEHEMIAH CRANE[5] [250], (Jacob,[4] Caleb,[3] Nathaniel,[2] Stephen[1]), married Sarah, daughter of Stephen Crane, born Dec. 3, 1790. She died Sept. 22, 1828. He was a miller and lived in Elizabeth, N. J. Children:

612—1. HINES; m. Cornelia ———; d. leaving a son.
613—2. JACOB B.; m. Hannah ———.
614—3. JOSEPH WARREN; m. ——— Winans; had five children.
615—4. ELIAS WINANS; m. 1st, ——— Crane, daughter of Solomon, son of Stephen, Esq.; 2d, ——— Mulford.

616. ABIGAIL CRANE[6] [251], (Jacob,[4] Caleb,[3] Nathaniel,[2] Stephen[1]), married Elias Winans, and died Nov. 5, 1853. Children:

1. JACOB CRANE (Winans); m. Sarah M. Hedden. Children:
    1. SARAH ALICE (Winans), b. Sept. 22, 1835.
    2. CAROLINE B. (Winans), b. April 28, 1844.
    3. MARY ELIZABETH (Winans), b. Nov. 12, 1850.
    4. HARRIET BALIS (Winans), b. 1852.
2. PHEBE WOODRUFF (Winans), b. Feb. 20, 1814; m. Samuel B. Hedden, May 12, 1833. Children:
    1. ELIAS WINANS (Hedden), b. April 6, 1834; m. Jane Crane, Dec. 10, 1863.
    2. ELIZA DAY (Hedden), b. April 20, 1836.
    3. SARAH MARSH (Hedden), b. Aug. 23, 1839; m. A. C. Brown, Oct. 11, 1850.
    4. JACOB WINANS (Hedden), b. May 16, 1844; m. Mary V. Crane, Dec. 18, 1873.
    5. HENRIETTA DORNING (Hedden), b. June 19, 1846.
    6. JAMES MARSH (Hedden), b. Feb. 5, 1849.

617. JOB CRANE[5] [256], (Nathaniel,[4] Caleb,[3] Nathaniel,[2] Stephen[1]), married Mary B. Woodruff, Jan. 11, 1814. She was born March 10, 1788, and died Aug. 15, 1873. He died Dec. 17, 1848. Children:

618—1. JANE WOODRUFF, b. Nov. 6, 1814.
619—2. MARY MITCHEL, b. May 28, 1816; m. Rev. Benjamin Cory, Nov. 18, 1835.
620—3. WILLIAM WOODRUFF, b. Sept. 10, 1819; m. Charity B. Clark, Oct. 7, 1846.
621—4. SARAH WOODRUFF, b. Feb. 27, 1822; d. Jan. 8, 1836.
622—5. JOB SYMMES, b. April 23, 1825; m. Helen B. Watkins.
623—6. ELIZA, b. April 18, 1828; d. Dec. 16, 1832.
624—7. JULIA ANN, b. May 26, 1833; m. Feb. 7, 1838.

625. ELIHU JEWELL CRANE[5] [258], (Nathaniel,[4] Caleb,[3] Nathaniel,[2] Stephen[1]), married Eliza, daughter of Samuel Kennedy Miller. She was born April 27, 1802, and died Aug. 18, 1878. He died Jan. 8, 1853. Children:

626—1. SARAH ELIZABETH, b. Feb. 23, 1830; d. June 4, 1850.
627—2. NATHANIEL MARTIN, b. Aug. 19, 1835; m. Julia A. Harris, Oct. 6, 1858.
628—3. WILLIAM EDWIN, b. Feb. 28, 1839; d. March 18, 1839.

629. MOSES MILLER CRANE[5] [259], (Nathaniel,[4] Caleb,[3] Nathaniel,[2] Stephen[1]), married Phebe S. Williams, Feb. 24, 1825. She died Feb. 5, 1869. He died Nov. 27, 1874. Children:

630—1. ELIAS SPENCER, b. Jan. 28, 1826; d. Feb. 16, 1840.
631—2. ANNA WILLIAMS, b. April 15, 1828; m. Abram C. Miller, Sept. 15, 1847.
632—3. JANE ELIZA, b. Feb. 12, 1833; m. John N. Earl, Dec. 25, 1855.
633—4. JOHN WILLIAMS, b. Dec. 23, 1834; m. Anna E. Wilson, Dec. 21, 1859.
634—5. CHARLES HENRY, b. Dec. 31, 1837; d. Feb. 13, 1840.

635. ELIZABETH TOWNLEY CRANE[5] [261], (Nathaniel,[4] Caleb,[3] Nathaniel,[2] Stephen[1]), married David P. Kenyon, June 21, 1828, and died March 12, 1877. Children:

1. JAMES HENRY (Kenyon), b. May 19, 1829.
2. SARAH CRANE (Kenyon), b. March 13, 1832.
3. JOB CRANE (Kenyon), b. Nov. 19, 1834.
4. DAVID RANDOLPH (Kenyon), b. Oct. 30, 1836.
5. CHARLES SPENCER (Kenyon), b. June 15, 1843.
636. JAMES HENRY KENYON [1]; m. Margaret Ann Dietz, Dec. 3, 1855. She was b. June 2, 1833, and d. Sept. 12, 1867. Children:
   1. DAVID PALMER (Kenyon), b. Oct. 18, 1856.
   2. SARAH ELIZABETH (Kenyon), b. Nov. 1, 1858.
   3. WILLIAM HENRY (Kenyon), b. Aug. 14, 1862.
   4. MARY CRANE (Kenyon), b. May 21, 1867; d. July 2, 1867.
637. SARAH CRANE KENYON [2]; m. William Augustus Pembrook, Dec. 1, 1858. Children:
   1. WILLIAM AUGUSTUS (Pembrook), b. April 14, 1860; d. June 18, 1866.
   2. THEODORE KENYON (Pembrook), b. March 5, 1862.

638. JOB CRANE KENYON [3]; m. Mary Amanda Bowne, Oct. 18, 1870. Children :
    1. EDWARD (Bowne), b. Feb. 15, 1872.

639. DAVID RANDOLPH KENYON [4]; m. Elizabeth Carhart, Dec. 2, 1863. Children :
    1. MINNIE MATILDA (Kenyon), b. March 24, 1865.
    2. ANGELINE DALES (Kenyon), b. Nov. 16, 1867.
    3. CHARLES CARHART (Kenyon), b. Aug. 9, 1871.

640. CHARLES SPENCER KENYON [5]; m. Margaret M. Runyon, Sept. 15, 1869. Children :
    1. MARA CRANE (Kenyon), b. Aug. 27, 1870.
    2. PALMER (Kenyon), b. July 31, 1872; d. Sept. 17, 1872.
    3. LIZZIE EDDOWES (Kenyon), b. June 16, 1873.

641. ABIGAIL CLARK CRANE[5] [263], (Nathaniel,[4] Caleb,[3] Nathaniel,[2] Stephen[1]), married Charles A. Kiggins, March 30, 1837, son of Charles and Hannah (Paul) Kiggins. Children :
    1. ISAAC CRANE (Kiggins), b. Oct. 4, 1838.
    2. CHARLES SYMMES (Kiggins), b. Aug. 19, 1843.
    3. THEODORE AUGUSTUS (Kiggins), b. Aug. 14, 1848; d. Sept. 16, 1850.

642. ISAAC CRANE KIGGINS [1], m. June 21, 1864, Julia M., daughter of Rev. Benjamin Cory. She was born Dec. 26, 1840. Children :
    1. JENNIE CORY (Kiggins), b. Sept. 3, 1865.
    2. GRACE (Kiggins), b. March 17, 1869.
    3. WILLARD AUGUSTUS (Kiggins), b. Nov. 5, 1870.
    4. NICHOLAS MURRY (Kiggins), b. 1879.

643. MOSES CRANE[5] [274], (Noah,[4] Moses,[3] Nathaniel,[2] Stephen[1]), married ———, and settled in Butler Co., O. Children :

644—1. NOAH.
645—2. STEPHEN.

646. NOAH CRANE[5] [277], (Noah,[4] Moses,[3] Nathaniel,[2] Stephen[1]), married Elizabeth Pierce, at or near Lebanon, O. He learned the art of printing at Morristown, N. J., and on removing to Ohio, settled first at " Lower Springfield," a suburb of Cincinnati, and set up the first " form " of the *Liberty Hall and Cincinnati Gazette*. He subsequently removed to Trenton, Butler Co., which place, first called Bloomfield, was laid out by the Cranes, both names having been taken, no doubt, from their New Jersey homes. He died in the year 1810, of typhoid fever. Child :

647—1. WILLIAM MILLER, b. Feb. 20, 1808, at Lebanon, O.

648. STEPHEN CRANE[6] [279], (Elijah,[5] John,[4] John,[3] John,[2] Stephen[1]), married ——— Williams. Children:

649—1. JOHN MARSH.
650—2. WILLIAMS.
651—3. MARIAH; m. Elias Potter, son of Jothan (or Jonathan) Potter, of Union, and all the family removed to Peoria, Ill.

652. REBECCA CRANE[6] [283], (John,[5] John,[4] John,[3] John,[2] Stephen[1]), married Major Jothan Potter, son of John. Children:

1. SUSAN (Potter); m. Joseph Potter.
2. ELIZABETH (or BETSEY) (Potter); m. David Crane, and had OLIVER.
3. ELIAS (Potter); m. Mariah Crane, dau. of Stephen[6].

653. JOHN GRANT CRANE[6] [284], (John,[5] John,[4] John,[3] John,[2] Stephen[1]), married Sarah, daughter of William Pearson, and resided about five miles west of Elizabeth, N. J. He died March 9, 1814, in Westfield. She died Aug. 27, 1873, in Elizabeth. Children:

654—1. JOHN DAVIS, b. Aug. 3, 1807; m. Catherine, dau. of William B. Potter.
655—2. WILLIAM; m. ———, dau. of John Miller, of Westfield.

656. ELIZABETH CRANE[6] [285], (John,[5] John,[4] John,[3] John,[2] Stephen[1]), married Thomas, son of Robert Moore, of Woodbridge. Children:

1. DAVID (Moore).
2. ROBERT (Moore).
3. JOHN (Moore).
4. ISRAEL (Moore).
5. PHEBE (Moore).

657. PHEBE CRANE[6] [286], (John,[5] John,[4] John,[3] John,[2] Stephen[1]), married Benjamin, brother of Major Jothan Potter. Children:

1. SUSAN (Potter); m. Joseph Potter.
2. ELIZABETH (Potter).
3. REBECCA (Potter); m. Israel Rowland.
4. JOHN (Potter); m. Phebe Ball.
5. HANNAH (Potter); m. Mr. Fornote.
6. PHEBE (Potter); m. David Bird.

658. ELIAS CRANE[6] [288], (John,[5] John,[4] John,[3] John,[2] Stephen[1]), married Esther, daughter of John Maxwell. He was

elder in a church at Union, N. J. He died July 19, 1869. Children:

659—1. JOHN; m. Sarah Cutter; residence at Roselle, N. J.
660—2. PHEBE; m. Silas, son of Abraham Miller.
661—3. SUSAN; m. Isaac Williams.
662—4. ELIAS M.
663—5. AMZI A., b. Nov. 6, 1829, in Essex County, N. J.

664. JOSIAH CRANE[6] [289], (John,[5] John,[4] John,[3] John,[2] Stephen[1]). married Electa, daughter of John Ross, of Union, N. J., and lived where Col. Jacob Crane formerly did. He died Aug. 7, 1873. Children:

665—1. MARY ROSS, b. Feb. 11, 1813; m. Hampton Cutter.
666—2. JOHN GRANT, b. June 17, 1817; m. Abby Miller.
667—3. ANN ELIZABETH, b. Aug. 9, 1819; m. Jacob Williams.
668—4. JOSIAH, b. Dec. 6, 1822; m. Sarah Jane Miller.

669. HULDAH CRANE[6] [290], (John,[5] John,[4] John,[3] John,[2] Stephen[1]), married John, brother of Major Jothan Potter. Child:

1. MARY H. (Potter).

670. JONATHAN CRANE[6] [297], (Samuel,[5] Joseph,[4] John,[3] John,[2] Stephen[1]), married. He died Feb. 25, 1859. Child:

671—1. ISAAC K.; residence at Warsaw, Mo.

672. JOHN CRANE[6] [301], (Samuel,[5] Joseph,[4] John,[3] John,[2] Stephen[1]), married March 16, 1820, Nancy Dunham. She was born in Fayette County, Pa., Aug. 19, 1798. He was justice of the peace and farmer, and resided in Preston County, W. Va. He died Nov. 15, 1858. in Harford County, Md., where he went with a drove of horses and cattle; took cold, and died of typhoid pneumonia. We give an extract from a newspaper notice of his death:

" DIED—November 15, 1858, at the residence of Dr. Abraham Street, Harford County, Md., JOHN CRANE, Esq., of Preston County, Va., aged 59 years, 2 months and 19 days. Mr. Crane was a prominent citizen of Preston, his native county, and will be much lamented and greatly missed by an extensive circle of friends. He was eminently a business man. Twenty-three years since he emigrated to the beautiful portion of the county known as 'The Pine Swamp.' Under the hand of industrial enterprise the wilderness was rapidly changed to fruitful fields. At the time of his death Mr. Crane had in his plantation one thousand acres of improved land in the midst of a prosperous and growing settlement. A thriving little town had arisen upon his premises, which, in honor of its founder, is called Craneville. For many years he has been the medium of exchange between the eastern markets and the principal stock dealers of the county. But he lived not for this world alone. Twenty-seven years since, with his companion, he embraced the gospel,

and was baptized into the Baptist Church." She died July 28, 1878. Children :

673—1. SMITH, b. Feb. 28, 1821.
674—2. SAMUEL, b. Sept. 10. 1822.
675—3. ELIZABETH, b. July 14, 1824.
676—4. ELISHA, b. May 17, 1826.
677—5. ALLEN DUNHAM, b. Jan. 8, 1828; m. Hannah Bruin; he d. in St. Louis, Mo., May 12, 1882, his late residence.
678—6. JANE, b. Jan. 5, 1830.
679—7. AMANDA, b. May 10, 1831.
680—8. SARAH, b. May 8, 1833; d. May 21, 1837.
681—9. LOVILA, b. May 7, 1835.
682-10. JACOB WILBER, b. May 21, 1838.
683-11. JOHN BONNELL, b. Jan. 5, 1840.

684. JACOB CRANE[6] [302], (Samuel,[5] Joseph,[4] John,[3] John,[2] Stephen[1]), married Mary Elliott. He died Oct. 1, 1859, on the old home farm on Muddy Creek, where his father settled. Children :

685—1. WILLIAM BONNELL, b. May 5, 1824; d. March 14, 1873.
686—2. SAMUEL ELLIOTT, b. Oct. 6, 1828; d. March 8, 1894.

687. CALVIN CRANE[6] [303], (Samuel,[5] Joseph,[4] John,[3] John,[2] Stephen[1]), married Jane Elliott, who was born June 14, 1806, and lived near Willey, Preston Co., W. Va. She died Feb. 25, 1886, aged 79 years, 8 months and 11 days. He died June 28, 1886, aged 80 years, 6 months and 28 days. Children :

688—1. LOUISA J., b. Nov. 21, 1828.
689—2. JOSEPHAS ELLIOTT, b. April 20, 1830.
690—3. SAMUEL BONNELL, b. March 22, 1832.
691—4. ISAAC M., b. June 30, 1834; d. Dec. 9, 1836.
692—5. MARY ANN, b. April 3, 1836.
693—6. ELIZABETH, b. Feb. 15, 1838.
694—7 MARTIN LUTHER, b. April 5, 1840.
695—8. JOHN CALVIN, b. Dec. 17, 1841.
696—9. JARVIS K., b. Jan. 10, 1844; d. Feb. 10, 1864.
697-10. RUTH R., b. Feb. 12, 1846.
698-11. RACHEL R., b. Jan. 12, 1851; d. Feb. 15, 1851.

699. ELIZABETH CRANE[6] [304], (Samuel,[5] Joseph,[4] John,[3] John,[2] Stephen[1]), married Feb. 25, 1809, Isaac Romine. Settled in Warren County, Ohio, and removed from there to Stone Bluff, Fountain Co., Ind., where she died Sept. 21, 1878, aged 87 years and 4 months. Children :

1. SMITH (Romine), b. Dec. 1, 1809; m. Gainor Forman; d. April 17, 1841.
2. RUTH (Romine), b. Feb. 14, 1811; d. April, 1855.
3. JANE (Romine), b. May 3, 1812; d. Nov. 23, 1898.
4. JESSE (Romine), b. Sept. 22, 1813; d. Nov., 1889.
5. SAMUEL (Romine), b. Dec. 26, 1817; d. Aug. 24. 1820.
6. PRUDENCE (Romine), b. Aug. 22, 1819; d. Nov. 13, 1823.
7. JOHN (Romine). b. June 6, 1822; d. Aug., 1855.
8. ISAAC M. (Romine), b. Sept. 22, 1823; d. Dec. 31, 1859.
9. ELIJAH (Romine), b. March 10, 1825; d. Sept., 1851.
10. SARAH A. (Romine), b. March 13, 1827.
11. JACOB BONNELL (Romine), b. Aug. 8, 1828.
12. DAVID S. (Romine), b. Feb. 4, 1830; d. April, 1852.

700. SARAH A. ROMINE [10]; m. John M. Galloway; residence near
Stone Bluff (post-office), Ind. Children :
   1. GEORGE A. (Galloway).
   2. JOHN A. (Galloway).
   3. D. S. (Galloway).
   4. MILLER R. (Galloway).
   5. OWEN S. (Galloway).
   6. ANNA ELIZABETH (Galloway).
   7. RUTH BELL (Galloway).

701. GEORGE A. GALLOWAY [1]; m. Laura A. Ward. daughter of
Archibald and Joanna (Crane) Ward, Sept. 22, 1874, by Mary
Thomas Clark; residence, Fountain, Ind. Children :
   1. MYRTLE M. (Galloway), b. Nov. 3, 1877.
   2. CHAUNCEY W. (Galloway), b. Jan. 30, 1880.
   3. LELIA B. (Galloway), b. Feb. 5, 1882.
   4. NELSON J. (Galloway), b. Sept. 2, 1884.
   5. SARAH J. (Galloway), b. Nov. 27, 1886.
   6. COURTLAND P. (Galloway), b. Jan. 18, 1889.
   7. GLENN G. (Galloway), b. Jan. 4, 1891.
   8. IRENE L. (Galloway), b. Dec. 6, 1894.

702. ANNA ELIZABETH GALLOWAY [6]; m. ——— Huber, June, 1889.
Child :
   1. DALE GALLOWAY (Huber).

703. RUTH BELL GALLOWAY [7]; m. Joseph J. Crane, son of Henry
and Eliza (Sharp) Crane, Sept. 9, 1875. Residence, Summer-
town, Lawrence Co., Tenn. Children :
   1. WILBERT L., born March 19, 1876.
   2. LEOLINE.

704. HULDA CRANE[6] [308], (John,[5] Joseph,[4] John,[3] John,[2]
Stephen[1]), married Levi Wilcox, and removed to Illinois.
Children :

   1. DAVID B. (Wilcox); d. at about 20 years of age.
   2. AMAR (Wilcox); m. 2d, William Atkinson.
   3. OPHA (Wilcox).
   4. ELIAS CRANE (Wilcox); d. about 14 years of age.
   5. ALBERT (Wilcox).
   6. FRANCIS (Wilcox).
   7. MULFORD (Wilcox).
   8. JOHN (Wilcox).
   9. MARY (Wilcox).

705. ORPHA CRANE[6] [309], (John,[5] Joseph,[4] John,[3] John,[2]
Stephen[1]), married Dr. Erastus Darwin Crossfield, and removed
to Warren Co., O. Had two children, one died in infancy.
Child :

   1. JOHN EDGAR (Crossfield); lives in Indiana.

706. DEBORAH CRANE[6] [310], (John,[5] Joseph,[4] John,[3] John,[2]
Stephen[1]), married Ezra Ludlow, son of Joseph, and lived in
Elizabeth, N. J. Children :

   1. LEVI MULFORD (Ludlow); went to California.
   2. FRANCIS (Ludlow); d. in infancy.
   3. JOHN JOSEPH (Ludlow).
   4. ERASTUS (Ludlow); d. in infancy.
   5. ERASTUS (Ludlow).

6. JOHN EDGAR (Ludlow).
7. GEORGE (Ludlow).
8. JAMES F. MEEKER (Ludlow).

707. SYLVESTER CRANE[6] [311], (John,[5] Joseph,[4] John,[3] John,[2] Stephen[1]), married Hulda Bonnel, daughter of Philomon; settled in Iowa, and died there, near Valisco. Children:

708—1. RACHAEL; d., aged 8½ years.
709—2. JOHN.
710—3. ELIAS.

711. MARY CRANE[6] [312], (John,[5] Joseph,[4] John,[3] John,[2] Stephen[1]), married Aaron H. Laning. She died in Grinnell, Ia., about 1886. Children:

1. LAURA BURNET (Laning); m. and lives in Grinnell, Ia.
2. ORPHA JANE (Laning); m. and d. in Illinois.
3. JOHN JOSEPH (Laning); d. in childhood.

712. DANIEL CRANE[6] [313], (John,[5] Joseph,[4] John,[3] John,[2] Stephen[1]), married Catherine Rogers and settled in Indiana, where they lived for a time, then removed to Iowa, and with his brother Sylvester, took up government land, near Valisca, in the southwestern part of the State. In the early seventies he went to California, and from there to Seattle, Wash., whither his daughter had gone. Children:

713—1. SARAH E.
714—2. LAURA.
715—3. BELLE.
716—4. MULFORD; d. in the army near the close of the late war.

717. HARRIET CRANE[6] [314], (John,[5] Joseph,[4] John,[3] John,[2] Stephen[1]), married Samuel G. Benedict; went to Indiana, 1835, and lived near Crawfordsville. Children:

1. GOODRICH (Benedict).
2. WILLIAM (Benedict); lives in Indiana.
3. ORPHA (Benedict).
4. ALMIRA (Benedict).
5. ELIZABETH (Benedict); m. ——— Prebble, and lives in Indiana.

718. ELIZABETH CRANE[6] [315], (John,[5] Joseph,[4] John,[3] John,[2] Stephen[1]), married Samuel Thomas Day, and removed to Ohio. He died Feb. 8, 1892. Children:

1. WILBUR FISK (Day).
2. WATERS BARROWS (Day).
3. JOHN CRANE (Day).
4. BENJAMIN (Day).
5. PENNINGTON MULFORD (Day).
6. STEPHEN SYLVESTER (Day).
7. FRANKLIN (Day).
8. MARY (Day).

719. WILLIAM BEBOUT CRANE[6] [327], (Joseph,[5] Joseph,[4] John,[3] John,[2] Stephen[1]), married 1st, April 24, 1820, Deborah

Conklin, daughter of Benjamin, by whom he had three children ; married 2d, Mundulency Potter. Children :

- 720—1. ELIAS.
- 721—2. MULFORD.
- 722—3. JERUSHA.
- 723—4. ELIZABETH.
- 724—5. HANNAH.
- 725—6. SARAH.
- 726—7. JOHN.
- 727—8. JACOB.

728. ELIZA CRANE[6] [328], (Joseph,[5] Joseph,[4] John,[3] John,[2] Stephen[1]), married Levi Clark, son of Daniel. Children :

1. JEREMIAH (Clark).
2. JOSEPH (Clark).
3. JOHN WESLEY (Clark).
4. SARAH ELIZABETH (Clark).
5. CHARLES (Clark).
6. PITMAN (Clark).
7. IRA (Clark).
8. DANIEL SEELY (Clark).
9. ABIGAIL (Clark).
10. MORRIS (Clark).

729. IRA CRANE[6] [329], (Joseph,[5] Joseph,[4] John,[3] John,[2] Stephen[1]), was born Oct. 10, 1808, married in Crawfordsville, Ind., Fannie Wilhite. She died in 1861. His late residence was Lake City, Minn., where he was a merchant tailor. He removed there with his children in 1865; here he died May 20, 1889. Children :

- 730—1. CLARENCE; d. young.
- 731—2. ANN E.
- 732—3. LENA: m. Allen Devoe; no children.
- 733—4. MARY; m. James Crawford; no children.
- 734—5. CATHARINE; m. H. R. Merrill, in California.
- 735—6. JULIA.
- 736—7. THEODORE I.
- 737—8. CHARLES E.; m. Cora Wickham..
- 738—9. EDWARD C., b. March 14, 1855, in Indiana; m. Maud Dodge: lives Granite Falls, Minn.

739. RUTH CRANE[6] [331], (Joseph,[5] Joseph,[4] John,[3] John,[2] Stephen[1]), married Linus H. Stevens, son of Christopher. Removed to Bloomfield, N. J., and from there to Indiana, and from there to Illinois. Children :

1. HANNAH JANE (Stevens).
2. PHEBE ANNA (Stevens).
3. JOSEPH CRANE (Stevens).

740. ARETUS CRANE[6] [333], (Joseph,[5] Joseph,[4] John,[3] John,[2] Stephen[1]), married his cousin Serepta, daughter of Daniel Doty. Children :

- 741—1. ALBERT.
- 742—2. JOSEPH.
- 743—3. SARAH.
- 744—4. WILLIAM.
- 745—5. ELIAS.

746. ANDREW CRANE⁶ [365], (John,⁵ Andrew,⁴ Matthias,³ John,² Stephen¹), was born at Elizabeth, N. J. He married Elizabeth Bradbury, Aug. 29, 1846. He is said to have lived near Boston, and died Jan. 4, 1873, aged 54 years, 6 months and 7 days. Widow lived in Somerville, Mass. Children :

747—1. IDELADE BRADBURY, b. Sept. 13, 1853.
748—2. ALICE ELIZABETH, b. July 15, 1857.
749—3. ARTHUR WADE, b. May 21, 1859.
750—4. MABEL HASTINGS, b. April 2, 1865.

751. WILLIAM CRANE⁶ [379], (Stephen,⁵ Jacob,⁴ Matthias,³ John,² Stephen¹), married 1st, Margaret Conklin, Dec. 17, 1817; she died Aug. 18, 1836; 2d, May 24, 1837, Margaret J. Force; she was born May 4, 1804, in Morristown, N. J. He was a carpenter and builder, and carried on business in New York city. He died in Rahway, N. J., Jan. 27, 1863. His widow Margaret died Jan. 12, 1892. Children :

752—1. CHARLES C., b. July 29, 1819; m. Hannah W. Wade; had six children.
753—2. ALFRED E., b. Nov. 6, 1821; d. Aug., 1824.
754—3. MARY E., b. June 31, 1824; m. H. Moore; d. March 31, 1890.
755—4. MARGARET, b. June 29, 1826.
756—5. WILLIAM E., b. Aug. 18, 1828.
757—6. GEORGE T., b. Feb. 12, 1831; m. M. Moore; had one child.
758—7. ALFRED, b. May 17, 1833; d. Oct., 1833.
759—8. STEPHEN SQUIER, b. Aug. 11, 1838; m. Sarah Briggs; had three children.
760—9. AUGUSTUS B., b. Aug. 10, 1840; m. —— Hues.
761-10. EMMA L., b. Feb. 2, 1842; m. Samuel S. Martin.
762-11. ALFRED T., b. April 1, 1844; m. Gertrude V. Martin.

763. STEPHEN CRANE⁶ [381], (Stephen,⁵ Jacob,⁴ Matthias,³ John,² Stephen¹), married 1st, in 1822, Sarah Joy, who was born in 1800, by whom he had one child. By his second wife Eliza M. Lum he had no issue. He died Oct. 11, 1828. His first wife died Dec. 19, 1823. Child:

764—1. AUGUSTUS BAINBRIDGE, b. Aug. 10, 1823.

765. SARAH HASTING CRANE⁶ [382], (Stephen,⁵ Jacob,⁴ Matthias,³ John,² Stephen¹), married Dec. 20, 1815, Charles Gregory. Children :

1. ADALINE H. (Gregory).
2. GEORGE W. (Gregory), b. 1819.
3. JAMES L. (Gregory), b. March 6, 1822.

766. ADALINE H. GREGORY [1]; m. John Croft, April 26, 1846. She d. May 29, 1861. Children :
    1. WILLIAM R. (Croft), b. April 12, 1851; resides at Toledo, Ohio.
    2. ADALINE HARRIOT (Croft), b. Oct., 1852; d. Oct. 29, 1857.

767. GEORGE W. GREGORY [2]: m. Harriot Phelps, March 30, 1848; residence at Raymond, S. Dak. Children :
    1. CHARLES P. (Gregory), b. June 24, 1849.
    2. HARRIOT J. (Gregory), b. Jan. 10, 1853; d. Sept. 10, 1853.

3. ELLA H. (Gregory), b. April 1, 1856; d. Oct. 19, 1857.
4. LAWRENCE E. (Gregory), b. April 19, 1859.

768. JAMES LAWRENCE GREGORY [3]; m. Ann Maria Buck, Oct. 24, 1838. Children:
1. AUGUSTUS CARRIN (Gregory), b. Oct. 14, 1839.
2. MARY (Gregory); m. Joseph Jennings, Hopewell, N. Y.

769. AUGUSTUS CARRIN GREGORY [1]; m. Lucy J. Woodriff, Oct. 28, 1866. He served as a soldier in the civil war. Residence at Decatur, Ind. Children:
1. ROBERT BUCK (Gregory), b. Oct. 18, 1868.
2. CORDELIA IANTHA (Gregory), b. March 11, 1872.

770. GEORGE WASHINGTON CRANE[6] [385], (Stephen,[5] Jacob,[4] Matthias,[3] John,[2] Stephen[1]), was a merchant in New York city, and married there June 22, 1837, Mary Ann Haviland. She was a native of Patterson, Putnam Co., N. Y.; born Dec. 4, 1813. He was a farmer, and died in Rutland, Wis., May 23, 1855, whither he went in 1838 or 1839. She died Jan. 28, 1890.

Children:

771—1. STEPHEN, b. April 30, 1838.
772—2. DAVID H., b. Dec. 20, 1839; d. April 12, 1857.
773—3. ESTHER ANN, b. Jan. 9, 1842.
774—4. RICHARD MOORE, b. Oct. 7, 1843.
775—5. GEORGE WILLIS, b. Nov. 27, 1845; d. June 22, 1855.
776—6. RASHO, b. Nov. 13, 1847; d. July 23, 1864, in Andersonville prison.
777—7. CLARA AUGUSTA, b. Dec. 16, 1849.
778—8. HENRIETTA LAVINA, b. Jan. 11, 1852.

779. JOANNAH CRANE[6] [390], (Jacob,[5] Jacob,[4] Matthias,[3] John,[2] Stephen[1]), married Lewis Little, 1833. Children:

1. HENRY (Little).
2. ELIZABETH (Little).

780. PHEBE CRANE[6] [391], (Jacob,[5] Jacob,[4] Matthias,[3] John,[2] Stephen[1]), married Obediah Lyon in 1834. She was his second wife, he having married for his first wife Prudence, daughter of Matthias and Prudence (Lum) Crane. This Prudence Crane left a daughter, Henrietta C. Lyon, born at North Castle, N. Y., April 13, 1825, who married Elnathan Todd, and had John C. and Harriot A. They lived at Long Ridge, Conn.

Child:

1. EMMA (LYON).

781. DAVID WARNER CRANE[6] [392], (Jacob,[5] Jacob,[4] Matthias,[3] John,[2] Stephen[1]), married 1st, Phebe Woodruff, March 22, 1831; she was born Jan. 27, 1810, and died Feb. 7, 1842; 2d, Sarah E. Bragaw, Jan. 18, 1843; she was born July 3, 1820, and died March 20, 1891. He was by trade a mason, and resided in Newark, N. J. He died Oct. 17, 1886. Children:

782—1. MOSES WOODRUFF, b. March 2, 1832.
783—2. JONATHAN, b. and d. July 10, 1833.
784—3. JACOB WARNER, b. July 15, 1834.
785—4. ISAAC BRAGAW, b. Dec. 11, 1843.

786—5. PHEBE WOODRUFF, b. June 4, 1845.
787—6. DAVID WARNER, b. Feb. 6, 1847; d. young.
788—7. SARAH MATILDA, b. April 4, 1849; d. young.
789—8. CHARLOTTE ELIZABETH, b. Feb. 7, 1851.
790—9. EMMA, b. Sept. 29, 1852; d. young.
791-10. JOSEPH FEWSMITH. b. Jan. 18, 1854; d. young.
792-11. CATHERINE DORMUS, b. Sept. 6, 1855.
793-12. WILLIAM WARNER. b. May 16, 1857; d. young.
794-13. JANE BARRON, b. March 6, 1859.
795-14. SARAH ELIZABETH, b. Nov. 28, 1860.
796-15. ELLEN WILTSEY, b. June 16, 1862; d. young.

797. JACOB CRANE[6] [393], (Jacob,[5] Jacob,[4] Matthias,[3]
John,[2] Stephen[1]), married Letty H. Pierson, March 11, 1835,
at Morristown, N. J., and settled there. He was a coal merchant. She was born Oct. 2, 1813. His first wife died June
19, 1856, at Morristown, N. J. He married 2d, Ellen M.
Hory (or Horg). He died Feb. 23, 1895. Children:

798—1. EDWARD P., b. July 15, 1836.
799—2. SARAH P., b. Nov. 25, 1838; residence at Morristown, N. J.
800—3. DAVID WARNER, b. Sept. 17, 1840; residence at 118 West 23d
        Street, New York city.
801—4. MARCUS F., b. July 13, 1842; d. Aug. 23, 1863.
802—5. JULIA R., b. April 8, 1845; residence at Elizabeth, N. J.
803—6. ANNA R., b. July 24, 1850; d. Oct. 6, 1851.
804—7. CLARA R., b. Oct. 12, 1852; residence at Morristown, N. J.

805. SARAH CRANE[6] [394], (Jacob,[5] Jacob,[4] Matthias,[3]
John,[2] Stephen[1]), married Edward Earle, in 1835, and settled
on a portion of the Capt. Jacob Crane place, near the Magie
neighborhood. She died in 1865. Children:

1. EDWARD BENTON (Earle).
2. WILLIAM ALEXANDER (Earle); m. Dec. 19, 1866, Phebe Ogden
    Magie. Children:
    1. ELIZABETH H. (Earle), b. Nov. 15, 1867; d. Feb. 17, 1875.
    2. EDWARD (Earle), b. July 22, 1870.
    3. J. MAGIE (Earle), b. Nov. 20, 1871; d. March 3, 1892.
    4. LILLIAN O. (Earle), b. Aug. 1, 1873.
    5. CLARENCE ALEXANDER (Earle), b. Nov. 23, 1874.
    6. RICHARD S. (Earle), b. June 14, 1876.

806. WILLIAM ALEXANDER CRANE[6] [395], (Jacob,[5] Jacob,[4]
Matthias,[3] John,[2] Stephen[1]), married 1st, Frances Garthwaite;
2d, Mary Earle, of Lyons Farms, N. J. Children by 2d wife:

807—1. JOANNA, b. Aug., 1854.
808—2. WILLIAM.
809—3. PHEBE.

810. MATTHIAS BRANT CRANE[6] [399], (Matthias,[5] Jacob,[4]
Matthias,[3] John,[2] Stephen[1]), married Dec. 27, 1832, Margaret
Winans; 2d, Abby Moore. He died Feb. 7, 1894. All chil-
dren by his first wife:

811—1. SARAH FRANCES, b. Oct. 27, 1835.
812—2. MARIETTA A., b. Dec. 28, 1836.
813—3. ANN. b. Feb. 11, 1842.
814—4. JOHN W., b. Oct. 5, 1847; d.

815. DAVID LUM CRANE[6] [400], (Matthias,[5] Jacob,[4] Matthias,[3] John,[2] Stephen[1]), married 1st, Feb. 13, 1833, Rachel Eckert; 2d, Ann White. Children by first wife:

816—1. ELMIRA ROY, b. Jan. 30, 1834; m. Amos A. Jayne.
817—2. THEODORE F., b. Dec. 27, 1836; m. Kate Hallock.
818—3. DAVID LUM, b. Nov. 17, 1839; d. Feb. 13, 1862.

819. JOHN CLARK CRANE[6] [401], (Matthias,[5] Jacob,[4] Matthias,[3] John,[2] Stephen[1]), married 1st, Catherine Williams; 2d, ———. He died in 1840. Child:

820—1. EDWIN BOOTH.

821. SAMUEL CRANE[6] [402], (Matthias,[5] Jacob,[4] Matthias,[3] John,[2] Stephen[1]), married Sarah Ann Nelson, Nov. 11, 1846. Children:

822—1. CAMILLA; m. A. B. Miller.
823—2. GEORGE S.
824—3. ELLA E.
825—4. NELSON I.

826. Rev. WILLIAM HENRY CRANE[6] [403], (Matthias,[5] Jacob,[4] Matthias,[3] John,[2] Stephen[1]), married April 3, 1849, Annie Julia Atwater, who was born in St. Mary's, Ga., May 24, 1824. They were married in Quincy, Gadsden Co., Fla., where they reside. He is a teacher and Presbyterian minister, and a graduate at Princeton, 1844. Children:

827—1. HENRY ALEXANDER, b. Jan. 3, 1850.
828—2. MARY ATWATER.
829—3. SARAH ELIZABETH, b. Aug. 2, 1852.
830—4. EDWIN DUFF, b. April 1, 1854.
831—5. MATTIE POTTER.
832—6. WILLIAM POTTER HENTZ, b. May 11, 1861.
833—7. ROBERT SCOTT, b. Dec. 19, 1863.
834—8. JAMES ELIHU, b. Jan. 2, 1866.

835. STEPHEN JOY CRANE[6] [405], (Matthias,[5] Jacob,[4] Matthias,[3] John,[2] Stephen[1]), married Eva Finley. Children:

836—1. SARAH W., b. Aug. 29, 1853.
837—2. EVA JOY, b. Dec. 27, 1855; m. James M. Cullen, Feb. 10, 1880.
838—3. THEODORE K., b. Jan. 18, 1873.

839. JOHN CRANE[6] [407], (Matthias,[5] John,[4] Matthias,[3] John,[2] Stephen[1]), married Rebecca T. Clendening, March 29, 1835, in Newark, N. J., where they resided. He was a chair finisher by trade. Children:

840—1. JOHN F. WARD, b. March 5, 1837.
841—2. LETTICA, b. Feb. 28, 1839.
842—3. ALFRED W. B., b. March 17, 1841.
843—4. FRANCES E. S., b. Oct. 20, 1843.
844—5. WILLIAM SCOTT, b. March 31, 1845.

845. SQUIER M. CRANE[6] [408], (Matthias,[5] John,[4] Matthias,[3] John,[2] Stephen[1]), married Jane A. Femester (or Forrister). Had four children, the two youngest were:

846—1. ANNA E.

51

847—2. HORACE F.

848. ALFRED H. CRANE[6] [409], (Matthias,[5] John,[4] Matthias,[3] John,[2] Stephen[1]), married Mary A. B. Tompkins, Oct., 1836, at Newark, N. J. She was born there Dec. 9, 1820. He was a carriage-smith by trade, and died in Camden, June 28, 1849. Children:

849—1. JANE B.
850—2. JOHN M., b. April 26, 1864; lives at Wilkes Barre, Pa.
851—3. WALTER T.

852. JOHN CRANE[6] [413], (Benjamin,[5] Benjamin,[4] Benjamin,[3] John,[2] Stephen[1]), married Mary Clark, of Westfield, N. Y. Children:

853—1. BENJAMIN F.
854—2. ABIGAIL.
855—3. BETSEY ANN.

856. ABIGAIL CRANE[6] [414], (Benjamin,[5] Benjamin,[4] Benjamin,[3] John,[2] Stephen[1]), married David Heyt. Children:

1. JAMES (Heyt).
2. ANNE ELIZA (Heyt).

857. HEZEKIAH THOMPSON CRANE[6] [416], (Benjamin,[5] Benjamin,[4] Benjamin,[3] John,[2] Stephen[1]), married Amanda Osborn. Child:

858—1. JOHN.

859. PHEBE CRANE[6] [417], (Benjamin,[5] Benjamin,[4] Benjamin,[3] John,[2] Stephen[1]), married Francis Randolph. He died leaving two children. She then married again and had other children. Children:

1. BENJAMIN (Randolph).
2. SARAH ANN (Randolph).

860. BENJAMIN CRANE[6] [421], (Benjamin,[5] Benjamin,[4] Benjamin,[3] John,[2] Stephen[1]), married Electa Baker, and resided at Paterson, N. J. Children:

861—1. CATHERINE SHELTS; d. aged 5 years.
862—2. ALFRED B.
863—3. MARGARET BAKER.
864—4. BENJAMIN HENRY.
865—5. SARAH THOMPSON.
866—6. JOAN.
867—7. JANE.
868—8. ELECTA; d. young.

869. DAVID JOHNSON CRANE[6] [422], (Benjamin,[5] Benjamin,[4] Benjamin,[3] John,[2] Stephen[1]), married Ann Eliza Roll.

870—1. JAMES.
871—2. JACOB THOMPSON; d. at the age of 2½ years.
872—3. DAVID NEWTON.
873—4. GEORGE KING.
874—5. ISAAC ROLL.
875—6. JOHN.

876—7. HEZEKIAH.
877—8. BENJAMIN F.

878. MOSES THOMPSON CRANE[6] [423], (Benjamin,[5] Benjamin,[4] Benjamin,[3] John,[2] Stephen[1]), married Eliza Scudder.⁻
Children :

879—1. THEODORE AUGUSTUS.
880—2. SARAH ANN.

881. ISAAC CRANE[6] [426], (Norris,[5] Benjamin,[4] Benjamin,[3] John,[2] Stephen[1]), married 1st, Polly Parrot; 2d, Anne Parrot. By first wife had three children.   Children :

882—1. ABRAHAM; m. Margaret Ayres.
883—2. WILLIAM, b. Jan. 30, 1820; m. Mary Cole.
884—3. ANNE.
885—4. MARY.
886—5. JOHN HALSEY.
887—6. ALBERT.
888—7. ISAAC.

889. SALLY CRANE[6] [427], (Norris,[5] Benjamin,[4] Benjamin,[3] John,[2] Stephen[1]), married Peter Parrot.   Children :

1. JANE (Parrot); m. William Force.
2. HETTY (Parrot); m. Sylvester Force.
3. PHEBE (Parrot); m. William High.
4. HANNAH (Parrot).
5. JOHN (Parrot).

890. JOHN CRANE[6] [428], (Norris,[5] Benjamin,[4] Benjamin,[3] John,[2] Stephen[1]), married Abby Flatt, was, 1879, residing in New York city.   Children :

891—1. PHEBE.
892—2. NORRIS.
893—3. CAROLINE.
894—4. CHARLOTTE.
895—5. HANNAH.
896—6. BENJAMIN.

897. BENJAMIN CRANE[6] [429], (Norris,[5] Benjamin,[4] Benjamin,[3] John,[2] Stephen[1]), married Julia Ann Bebout, Dec. 2, 1824. She was daughter of Stephen Bebout.   Lived in Green Village, Morris Co., N. J.   Children :

898—1. JOHN OGDON, b. May 22, 1827.
899—2. FANNY.
900—3. SINEUS B., b. June 3, 1831.
901—4. SARAH JANE, b. Sept., 1834.

902. ALBERT CRANE[6] [430], (Norris,[5] Benjamin,[4] Benjamin,[3] John,[2] Stephen[1]), married ———, daughter of Anderson French.
Children :

903—1. JANE.
904—2. LUCY.
905—3. MARY.
906—4. GEORGE.
907—5. JAMES.

908. MARY CRANE[6] [431], (Norris,[5] Benjamin,[4] Benjamin,[3] John,[2] Stephen[1]), married Israel Bebout, Jan. 4, 1843. He was born Oct. 30, 1799. Children :

1. HELEN TODD (Bebout).

909. ALETTA CRANE[6] [433], (David D.,[5] Eleazer,[4] Benjamin,[3] John,[2] Stephen[1]), married Oct. 28, 1809, William Patterson. He was born May 1, 1786. She died Dec. 22, 1856. Children :

1. AMANDA (Patterson), b. Sept. 5, 1810; m. Nov. 27, 1831, Zenas Hurd.
2. ARAMINTA ALETTA (Patterson), b. July 27, 1812; m. Oct. 28, 1836, Henry Exall, and d. Sept., 1883.
3. WILLIAM TURNER (Patterson), b. Dec. 28, 1815; m. Mrs. Sarah Lowrey, and d. Sept. 14, 1894.
4. EDGAR CRANE (Patterson), b. May 1, 1817; m. July 9, 1845, Jane Wilson.
5. HENRY AUGUSTUS (Patterson), b. Sept. 26, 1819; m. July 18, 1844, Eleanor S. Wright, and d. Feb. 9, 1897.

910. SARAH POTTER CRANE[6] [436], (David D.,[5] Eleazer,[4] Benjamin,[3] John,[2] Stephen[1]), married April 6, 1824, William Tiebout. He was born March 2, 1801, and died April 26, 1873. She died Feb. 13, 1878. Children :

1. DAVID CRANE (Tiebout), b. Aug. 22, 1825; m. Mary Ann Morrison.
2. JOHN (Tiebout), b. Oct. 23, 1827; m. 1st, Caroline Holmes Crane; 2d, Lucetta Banks Gould.
3. PHEBE JANE (Tiebout).
4. HANNAH MARIA (Tiebout); d. Oct. 3, 1883.
5. MARGARET BRUCE (Tiebout).
6. WILLIAM TODD (Tiebout), b. March 19, 1839; m. Mary Agnes Wildes.
7. SARAH ELIZABETH (Tiebout), b. Jan. 27, 1843.

911. WILLIAM WATROUS CRANE[6] [442], (David D,[5] Eleazer,[4] Benjamin,[3] John,[2] Stephen[1]), born in New York city; married there Jan. 25, 1830, Nancy McAlpin, a native of Belfast, Ireland. She was born Jan. 20, 1809. She died in Brooklyn, Sept. 12, 1873. He died Aug. 11, 1883. Children :

912—1. WILLIAM WATROUS, b. Sept. 14, 1831.
913—2. HANNAH JANE, b. March 21, 1833; d. April 21, 1836.
914—3. DAVID DAY, b. Feb. 2, 1835; d. Aug. 19, 1836.
915—4. ALFRED CAMPBELL, b. April 26, 1837.
916—5. CATHARINE, b. March 28, 1839; d. Dec. 2, 1843.
917—6. ANN MARIA, b. June 5, 1841; d. June 12, 1841.
918—7. HAROLD, b. Nov. 2, 1842; d. June 9, 1844.
919—8. ANN MARIA, b. Aug. 6, 1844.
920—9. HAROLD LESLIE, b. Feb. 4, 1846.
921—10. DAVID DAY, b. Sept. 20, 1849; d. July 8, 1861.

922. ALEXANDER PATTERSON CRANE[6] [445], (David D.,[5] Eleazer,[4] Benjamin,[3] John,[2] Stephen[1]), married Dec. 9, 1838, Angelina Hurrell. He died Aug. 26, 1881. She died Sept. 18, 1894. Left one child :

923—1. EDITH HAWTHORNE; m. April, 1889, Robert S. Simmons; they have (1899) one child.

925. JAMES CRANE[6] [449], (Stephen,[5] James,[4] James,[3] Jeremiah,[2] Stephen[1]), married Ann, daughter of Thomas B. and Margaret (Shotwell) Crane. Children :

926—1. JACOB S. ; was colonel of 39th Wisconsin regiment, and served in the civil war.
927—2. PHEBE ANN.
928—3. HENRIETTA F.
929—4. MARTIN LUTHER; served in the 1st Wisconsin Volunteer Infantry in the civil war, and received a wound that caused his death.

930. WILLIAM M. CRANE[6] [450], (Stephen,[5] James,[4] James,[3] Jeremiah,[2] Stephen[1]), married Maria Crane, sister of his brother James' wife. She was the daughter of Thomas B. and Margaret (Shotwell) Crane. Children :

931—1. STEPHEN, b. Dec. 5, 1830, at Elizabethtown, N. J.
932—2. THOMAS ; residence at Ansonia, Conn.
933—3. WILLIAM HENRY.

934. JASON CRANE[6] [482], (Jonathan,[5] Stephen,[4] Stephen,[3] Daniel,[2] Stephen[1]), married Jan. 21, 1845. He died Aug. 15, 1848. Children :

935—1. ABIGAIL, b. Sept. 21, 1846.
936—2. ESTHER A., b. Oct. 22, 1848.

937. BYERSON CRANE[6] [487], (Jonathan,[5] Stephen,[4] Stephen,[3] Daniel,[2] Stephen[1]), married Jan. 5, 1840. Children :

938—1. GEORGE H., b. July 4, 1842.
939—2. ESTHER A., b. March 31, 1844; d. March 30, 1847.

940. ELIAS H. CRANE[6] [488], (Jonathan,[5] Stephen,[4] Stephen,[3] Daniel,[2] Stephen[1]), married Sept. 25, 1845. Children :

941—1. MARY E., b. July 7, 1846.
942—2. ELIAS H., b. Feb. 15, 1848.
943—3. JACOB B., b. Sept. 28, 1854.

944. MARIA CRANE[6] [492], (Joseph H.,[5] William,[4] Stephen,[3] Daniel,[2] Stephen[1]), married Dr. John Clements. Child :

1. JOSEPH (Clements).

945. JOSEPH CRANE[6] [497], (Joseph H.,[5] William,[4] Stephen,[3] Daniel,[2] Stephen[1]), married Sarah, daughter of Lieut. Finley Schenck, of the United States Navy. Child :

946—1. JOSHUA CLEMENTS, b. 1834.

947. DAVID ROSS CRANE[6] [503], (William,[5] Joseph,[4] Stephen,[3] Daniel,[2] Stephen[1]), was born Jan. 8, 1806; married March, 1828, Phebe Ann Hallam, daughter of Lewis Hallam, of New York, born May 17, 1811. He died Jan. 12, 1848, at Elizabeth, N. J. Children :

948—1. WILLIAM LEWIS, b. April 20, 1829 ; d. June 28, 1887.
949—2. SARAH ANNA, b. May 16, 1830; d. Jan. 10, 1832.
950—3. SARAH TOWNLEY, b. Nov. 29, 1832.
951—4. ROBERT BURRELL, b. Nov. 27, 1835 ; lost at sea, 1853.

952—5. DAVID ROSS, b. July 7, 1838; d. Jan. 11, 1842.
953—6. ELIZA LANGDON, b. Sept. 20, 1840.
954—7. DAVID ROSS, b. March 1, 1843.
955—8. JONATHAN M. M., b. May 6, 1845; d.
956—9. SUSANNA ROSS, b. Nov. 8, 1847; d.

957. AGNES COOPER CRANE[6] [504], (William,[5] Joseph,[4] Stephen,[3] Daniel,[2] Stephen[1]), married Nov. 17, 1836, Rev. Curtis Tulley, a Methodist minister. She died Jan. 15, 1867, at Morristown, N. J. Child:

  1. HELEN WILLIAMS (Tulley).

958. RICHARD TOWNLEY CRANE[6] [505], (William,[5] Joseph,[4] Stephen,[3] Daniel,[2] Stephen[1]), married Jane Thompson Dolbear, Sept. 24, 1835, in Newark, N. J. She was born at Connecticut Farms, now Union, N. J., Feb. 26, 1818. His·occupation has been that of a sash, door and blind manufacturer, and a farmer; late residence, Millstone, N. J., but died in Camden, Dec. 18, 1886. He learned the sash and blind making trade of Baker & Ward, of Newark. He afterwards removed to Brooklyn, where he remained nine years. Returning to Newark, in 1847, he carried on his business at No. 589 West Broad Street (now Clinton Avenue) for nearly twenty years.

Sept. 24, 1885, Mr. and Mrs. Crane celebrated their golden wedding at the residence of the youngest son, at Lyons Farms, where a large gathering of relatives and friends greeted the venerable couple. Mr. Crane was a musical amateur, and was connected with several musical societies. He was chorister of the First Congregational Church, of Clinton Street, Newark, for eleven years. Mr. Crane was a man of exceptionally regular and temperate habits, irreproachable in all his business relations, and of a retiring, sensitive nature. He was best appreciated and loved by his most intimate friends; and possessing a keen sense of humor, he was a most genial companion.

Children :

959—1. THEODORE TULLEY, b. Oct. 12, 1837, in Newark.
960—2. FREDERIC WILLARD CURTIS, b. Nov. 1, 1842, in Brooklyn, N. Y.

961. JOSEPH W. CRANE[6] [506], (William,[5] Joseph,[4] Stephen,[3] Daniel,[2] Stephen[1]), married Oct. 18, 1837, Harriet J. Wilcox, daughter of Ezekiel. She died leaving one child, and he married 2d, Emma S. Brookfield, daughter of Lewis P. Brookfield, of Spring Valley, Sept. 25, 1839. He died Jan. 1, 1865, in Wilmington, O. Children :

962—1. HARRIET JEMIMA, b. July 15, 1838.
963—2. LEWIS WILLIAM, b. Sept. 25, 1840.
964—3. CHARLES AUGUSTUS, b. July 26, 1842.

965. Rev. JONATHAN TOWNLEY CRANE, D.D.,[6] [507], (William,[5] Joseph,[4] Stephen,[3] Daniel,[2] Stephen[1]), was born at Connecticut Farms, now Union, N. J., June 18, 1819; graduated at Princeton, 1843, and became a minister of the Methodist Episco-

pal denomination. In 1856 the degree of Doctor of Divinity
was conferred on him by Dickinson College, of Carlisle, Pa.
He married in New York city, Jan. 18, 1848, Mary Helen Peck,
a native of Wilkes Barre, Pa., born April 10, 1827, and daughter
of Rev. George Peck. Dr. Crane was an able and most successful preacher. In 1844 he was assigned to the Parsippany
Circuit; in 1849, was elected president of the Conference Seminary, Pennington, and successfully filled the position until 1858,
when he resigned and became pastor of Trinity Church, Jersey
City; 1868, was made presiding elder of the Newark District;
1872, was chosen presiding elder of the Elizabeth District, here
he remained four years, and was then assigned to the Cross
Street Church, Paterson, remaining there until 1878, when he
went to Port Jervis, where he died Feb. 16, 1880. He was a
very earnest worker, a genial, dignified, companionable person.
In his home life he perhaps shone the brightest. He was author
of the following books: " Essay on Dancing," published in
1848; '' The Right Way, or Practical Lectures on the Deca-
logue,"1853; "Popular Amusements," 1869; '' Arts of Intoxica-
tion," 1870; "Holiness the Birthright of all God's Children,"
1874; '' Methodism and its Methods," 1875. Children:

966—1. MARY HELEN.
967—2. GEORGE PECK.
968—3. JONATHAN TOWNLEY.
969—4. WILLIAM HOWE.
970—5. AGNES ELIZABETH.
971—6. EDMUND BRYAN.
972—7. WILBER FISKE.
973—8. ELIZABETH TOWNLEY.
974—9. LUTHER PECK.
975—10. MYRA BLANCHE.
976—11. BLANCHE.
977—12. JESSE T.
978—13. JESSE T.
979—14. STEPHEN.

980. LEONARD W. CRANE[6] [511], (David,[5] Joseph,[4] Stephen,[3]
Daniel,[2] Stephen[1]), married Catharine Hall, in Cass Co., Mich.
He was a farmer, and lived in Volinia, where he was postmaster.
He was killed in Arizona, about June, 1866, by Apache
Indians, at a place called Morol Springs. Children:

981—1. ANN, b. Nov. 16, 1837; m. Jasper Gleason.
982—2. ELI, b. Nov. 26, 1839.
983—3. ELIZA, b. June 4, 1842; d. July 3, 1845.
984—4. JAMES LEWIS HERBERT, b. Jan. 8, 1852.

985. DAVID CRANE[6] [516], (David,[5] Joseph,[4] Stephen,[3]
Daniel,[2] Stephen[1]), married ———. Child:

986—1. WILLIE; lives at Rich Coffe, Tex.

987. WILLIAM CRANE[6] [520], (John,[5] Joseph,[4] Stephen,[3]
Daniel,[2] Stephen[1]), married Rachael Cranford. Children:

988—1. JOHN.

989—2. WILLIAM.

990. MARY ANN CRANE[6] [531], (William,[5] David,[4] David,[3] Daniel,[2] Stephen[1]), married Nathaniel Maginnis, of Kent Co., Md. Children:

1. SARAH CORNELIA (Maginnis); m. Dr. Robinson.
2. WILHELMENIA (Maginnis).
3. WILLIAM (Maginnis).

991. WILLIAM BOWERS CRANE, M.D.,[6] [532], (William,[5] David,[4] David,[3] Daniel,[2] Stephen[1]), married June 20, 1850, Sarah Henrietta Osborne, of Kent Co., Md. He was a practicing physician, in Baltimore for a time, then removed to St. Joseph, Mo., and practiced there until his death, in the year 1865. Children:

992—1. FLORENCE HYNSON, b. April 1, 1851.
993—2. ALICE LORRAINE, b. Aug. 15, 1853.
994—3. HENRIETTA OSBORNE, b. Feb. 16, 1856.
995—4. WILLIAM BOWERS, b. Feb. 18, 1858.

996. ELEANOR DONALDSON CRANE[6] [537], (Roger,[5] David,[4] David,[3] Daniel,[2] Stephen[1]), married Samuel R. Hilt, of Philadelphia, Pa. Children:

1. DAVID (Hilt).
2. GEORGE (Hilt).
3. CHARLES (Hilt).

997. PHILIP SAMUEL CRANE[6] [539], (Roger,[5] David,[4] David,[3] Daniel,[2] Stephen[1]), married 1st, Louise MacKellar. She died, and he married 2d, Emma Dewees. Child:

998—1. ROGER; d.

999. SARAH ELIZABETH CRANE[6] [540], (Roger,[5] David,[4] David,[3] Daniel,[2] Stephen[1]), married Hamlet Pearson, of Philadelphia, who was born in Chester, Pa., 1814. He died 1859. She died Oct. 22, 1895. Children:

1. SAMUEL SHAW (Pearson), b. Sept. 4, 1842; served in the 13th Pennsylvania Cavalry; d. in the Civil war, Dec. 15, 1863.
2. MARY LOUISE (Pearson), b. Aug. 5, 1845.
3. ELEANOR CRANE (Pearson), b. Dec. 2, 1847.
4. JANE SHAW (Pearson), b. Sept. 4, 1851.

1000. MARY LOUISE PEARSON [2]; m. Dec. 27, 1871, William Francis Mattingly, of Washington, D. C., attorney-at-law, office in Washington, and his son is associated with him under the firm name of W. F. Mattingly & Son. Children:
　　1. MARIE LOUISE (Mattingly); m. Robert Treat Paine, Jr., of Boston.
　　2. WILLIAM FRANCIS (Mattingly).
　　3. GENEVIEVE PEARSON (Mattingly).

1001. ELEANOR CRANE PEARSON [3]; m. John P. Nicholson, recorder-in-chief for the Loyal Legion. Child:
　　1. ELEANOR LOUISE (Nicholson).

1002. JANE SHAW PEARSON [4]; m. Charles R. Roberts. Child:
　　1. CHARLES HAMLET (Roberts).

1003. MARY CRANE[6] [554], (John,[5] David,[4] David,[3] Daniel,[2] Stephen[1]), married William Hendrix ; died leaving but one son, a resident of Church Hill, Queen Anne's Co , Md., and an officer of that County (1878). Child :

1. DAVID H. (Hendrix).

1004. Major DAVID HENRY CRANE[6] [555], (John,[5] David,[4] David,[3] Daniel,[2] Stephen[1]), married in 1842, Eugenia Cruikshank. She and her children died. He married 2d, Maria Louisa Crnikshank, half-sister of his first wife, Dec., 1858. When a lad he learned the trade of a printer, in Philadelphia, with Mr. Tillinghast Collins. Returned to Kent Co., Md., and conducted a paper called *The Kent News*, some years. He then removed to Church Hill, and in company with his brother-in-law John A. Hall, conducted a store there. He sold out, and for twenty-five years was a farmer, and became well-to-do in worldly goods. But with the breaking out of the war reverses began, and by endorsing for others, lost heavily. Major Crane was a man honored and appreciated for his good character and attainments. In 1863, was sent by the Union party to the State Senate, and for several years held a commission as major in the State militia, of Maryland. After losing his property, Major Crane taught school at Church Hill. He was a man of unusual intelligence, strict integrity and enjoyed the full confidence of his neighbors.
Children :

1005—1. EUGENIA A., b. June 27, 1861 ; m. Levi C. Clough.
1006—2. PHILIP GEORGE, b. Sept. 8, 1864 ; m. Rosa Wicks.
1007—3. MARY ANN, b. March 8, 1867 ; m. Frederick Newton.

1008. PHILIP CRANE[6] [556], (John,[5] David,[4] David,[3] Daniel,[2] Stephen[1]), married Margaret Ann Crane, daughter of Thomas, and settled in Baltimore, Md. Had three daughters, two are living (Dec., 1898). Children :

1009—1. SARAH ELIZABETH ; m. —— Fairbanks ; resides in Baltimore, Md.
1010—2. ANNIE ; m. Mr. Simms, a methodist minister. He and his wife are missionaries to the Indians ; residence Oklahoma.

1011. WILLIAM FULLERTON CRANE[6] [558], (Philip,[5] David,[4] David,[3] Daniel,[2] Stephen[1]), married Feb. 29, 1844, Mary Clay Weer, of Kent County, Md. The ceremony was performed by Rev. Thomas Smith. Oct. 4, 1862, he enlisted as first lieutenant in Co. G, 157th P. V. ; Dec. 1, 1864, was commissioned captain, and mustered in Jan. 16, 1865, as captain of Co. B, 157th P. V., and held that position until March, 1865 ; honorably discharged as captain of Co. D, 191st P. V., May 10, 1865 ; was clerk in post-office department, Washington, D. C. Mr. Crane died Aug. 21, 1889, at Laurel, Md. Children :

1012—1. WILLIAM FULLERTON, b. May 2, 1845, in Kent County, Md.
1013—2. LIZZIE WEER, b. Nov. 1, 1846, in Philadelphia, Pa.

1014—3. MARY ELLEN, b. July 1, 1849, in Louisville, Ky.
1015—4. PHILIP DONALDSON, b. Aug. 23, 1851, in Louisville, Ky.
1016—5. FRANK EDWARDS, b. Feb. 14, 1856, in Louisville, Ky.; m.
         Mrs. Marcia Reubendale, Albuquerque, N. M.
1017—6. BERTHA DONALDSON, b. April 4, 1859, in Kent County, Md.;
         m. Nov. 25, 1885, James A. Wheeler at Laurel, Md.

1018. STEPHEN MIERS CRANE[6] [561], (Jonathan,[5] David,[4]
David,[3] Daniel,[2] Stephen[1]), married 1st, Mary E., daughter of
Giles Hicks, and sister to Ex-Gov. Thomas H. Hicks, of Mary-
land, afterwards elected to United States Senate, which office he
held up to the time of his death. She died, leaving four chil-
dren. His second wife was Josephine, daughter of Dr.
George O. Trenchard, of Church Hill, Queen Anne's Co., Md.
Went from New Jersey to Maryland many years ago. They lived
near Church Hill. He died Nov., 1854. His first wife died
Oct., 1846. Children :

1019—1. WILLIAM H.; m. Maggie R. Lucas; lived in Church Hill,
         Md., and d. there, 1864.
1020—2. STEPHEN M.; residence Baltimore, Md.
1021—3. THOMAS HENRY; m. Annie E. Hickman.
1022—4. JOHN GILES, b. Dec. 9, 1844; residence Baltimore, Md.
1023—5. JONATHAN, b. 1846; d. in infancy.
1024—6. GEORGE O. T.; d. in infancy.
1025—7. GEORGE T., b. 1850; m. Clara Washington; d. in Philadel-
         phia.
1026—8. CURTIS EDWARD, b. 1853; m. Belle Fountain; lives in
         Chestertown, Md.
1027—9. ANNIE, b. 1855; m. William Lawrence, of Baltimore.

1028. THOMAS HENRY CRANE, M.D.[6] [565], (Jonathan,[5]
David,[4] David,[3] Daniel,[2] Stephen[1]), graduate of University of
Maryland, 1845. Married 1st, April 16, 1849, Ellen Sophia,
daughter of Ebenezer Thomas Massey and his wife Emily Ann.
She died July 23, 1853. He married 2d, Jan. 16, 1855, Anne
E., daughter of William F. and Anne E. (Rochester) Smith.
He settled in Millington, Kent Co., Md., where he was highly
esteemed as a physician and a citizen, his practice extending over
the counties of Kent and Queen Anne's. He died Feb. 8, 1887.
The portrait here given was made from a photograph taken when
he was 57 years of age. Children :

1029—1. HENRY MASSEY, b. Dec. 1, 1850; residence at Philadelphia,
         Pa.
1030—2. EDWARD THOMAS, b. Jan. 17, 1853; m. H. L. Paysaunt;
         cigar manufacturer; lives at Philadelphia, Pa.
1031—3. WILLIAM FRISBY, b. Sept. 23, 1855; d. Sept. 24, 1855.
1032—4. WILLIAM SMITH, b. Dec. 2, 1856; d. April 10, 1861.
1033—5. ELLA, b. Feb. 8, 1858; d. Feb. 22, 1858.
1034—6. GERTRUDE, b. March 7, 1859; d. Aug. 12, 1860.
1035—7. ROBERT EVERETT, b. Sept. 18, 1860; d. March 3, 1889.
1036—8. JOHN ALBERT, b. Aug. 28, 1862; m. Oct. 31, 1888, Emilie
         Ann, daughter of B. H. C. Massey.
1037—9. ANNA MATILDA, b. Aug. 11, 1867.
1038-10. HARRIET AUGUSTA, b. July 22, 1870; d. May 27, 1893.
1039-11. JONATHAN HEBER, b. Sept. 17, 1872.

THOMAS HENRY CRANE, M.D.

1040. JULIA ANN CRANE[6] [567], (Jonathan,[5] David,[4] David,[3] Daniel,[2] Stephen[1]), married Albert Halsey Brown, of Newark, N. J. Children :

1. WILBER VINCENT (Brown), b. March 27, 1860.
2. IRVING C. (Brown), b. May 12, 1865.

> WILBER VINCENT BROWN [1]; m. in 1884, Addie E. Fish, of Boston, Mass. Child :
> 1. IRVING FREDERICK (Brown), b. 1893.

> IRVING CHESTER BROWN [2]; m. Jessie Craig Ellis in 1896. Child :
> 1. MARGARET ELLIS (Brown), b. 1897.

1041. DAVID CRANE[6] [575], (Andrew Drake,[5] David,[4] Nathaniel,[3] Nathaniel,[2] Stephen[1]), was born at Elizabeth, N. J., and resided in New York city. At the age of 24 years he married, April 5, 1832, Charlotte Stewart, and about two years afterwards removed to New Albany, Ind., where they both died,—he Dec. 20, 1876. She was born in or near New York city June 30, 1810. Children :

1042—1. THEODORE DRAKE, b. Jan. 22, 1833, in New York city.
1043—2. JANE WOOD, b. Jan. 11, 1835, in New Albany; d. July 10, 1835.
1044—3. ELIZABETH JANE LEE, b. Sept. 3, 1836.
1045—4. ELIAS FLAVEL, b. June 25, 1840.
1046—5. LEWIS STEWART, b. Aug. 14, 1842.
1047—6. ALEXANDER HENRY, } twins, b. Jan. 7, 1846; { d. July 27.
1048—7. WILLIAM EDGAR, } { 1846.
1049—8. DAVID HENRY, b. Sept. 17, 1852.

1050. ELIAS F. CRANE[6] [577], (Andrew Drake,[5] David,[4] Nathaniel,[3] Nathaniel,[2] Stephen[1]), was born in New York city; married April 12, 1842, in Philadelphia, Pa., Catharine B. Priest. She was born in New York, April 11, 1821, and for a time they resided in New York city, but removed to Mount Sterling, Ill., where he was a merchant and president of the First National Bank. He was deeply interested in the genealogy of his family, and furnished considerable data that he had collected relating to the early families, principally in the line of Jasper. Child :

1051—1. FREDERIC D., b. in New York city March 26, 1843.

1052. JEREMIAH BALLARD CRANE[6] [579], (Isaac,[5] Caleb,[4] Caleb,[3] Nathaniel,[2] Stephen[1]), married Mary P. Clark, Nov. 20, 1816. She was born in June, 1799, and was the daughter of Noah Clark, of Springfield, N. J. He died Aug. 8, 1829. Children :

1053—1. ELIZABETH CLARK, b. June 3, 1818.
1054—2. ABIGAIL OGDEN, b. Nov. 28, 1819.
1055—3. BENJAMIN C., b. April 25, 1822; in 1866 was in Central America.

1056. JONATHAN EDWARDS CRANE[6] [580], (Isaac,[5] Caleb,[4] Caleb,[3] Nathaniel,[2] Stephen[1]), married Dec. 15, 1817, Mary

P., daughter of Elias and Fanny (Britton) Thompson. She was born Oct. 29, 1796, and died Oct. 5, 1834. He died Oct. 4, 1828. Children :

1057—1. ELIAS THOMPSON, b. Aug. 15, 1818; d. Aug. 1, 1819.
1058—2. ISAAC ARNETT, b. Nov. 19, 1819.
1059—3. ELIAS OGDEN, b. Oct. 11, 1821.
1060—4. JOSEPH TOOKER, b. April 9, 1824.
1061—5. ABEL, b. March 1, 1826; d. March 8, 1826.
1062—6. JONATHAN THOMPSON, b. Feb. 8, 1827.

1063. THOMAS OGDEN CRANE[6] [585], (Isaac,[5] Caleb,[4] Caleb,[3] Nathaniel,[2] Stephen[1]), married July 6, 1826, Elizabeth, daughter of Eliphalet and Elizabeth Price. She was born Aug. 26, 1807, and died Dec., 1837. He married 2d, Oct. 5, 1842, Bethia P. Miller, of Morris County. She was born April 22, 1817. He died Sept., 1878. Children :

   1. Infant, b. 1829; d.
1064—2. MARY ELIZABETH, b. Sept. 8, 1830; d. April, 1832.
1065—3. ALONZO DE LAVERGNE, b. Sept. 9, 1832; d. Oct. 22, 1854.
1066—4. ISAAC ARNETT, b. April 1, 1844; d.
1067—5. THOMAS OGDEN, b. 1846; d. Oct., 1848.
1068—6. MARY ELIZABETH, b. Feb. 12, 1851; d. June, 1875.

1069. Rev. ELIAS WINANS CRANE[6] [589], (Noah,[5] Jacob,[4] Caleb,[3] Nathaniel,[2] Stephen[1]), married July 7, 1819, Hannah Margaretta, daughter of Judge John Johnson, of Newton, N. J. She was born June 9, 1786. He graduated at Princeton in 1814, and Princeton Theological Seminary in 1818. He was pastor of the Presbyterian Church at Springfield, N. J., from 1820 to 1826, and at Jamaica, L. I., from 1826, until his death, which occurred suddenly Nov. 10, 1840. His 1st wife died Oct. 18, 1827, and he married 2d, Sarah, daughter of Capt. Samuel Wickham Rogers, June 30, 1829, at Jamaica, L. I. She died Nov. 23, 1853. Children :

1070—1. HANNAH ROY, b. May 15, 1820.
1071—2. MARTHA WINANS. b. Feb. 28, 1822.
1072—3. DELINDA HOPKINS, b. Oct. 29, 1823.
1073—4. ELIZABETH WOODRUFF, b. Sept. 4, 1825; d. Dec. 25, 1825.
1074—5. ELIAS NETTLETON, b. Jan. 4, 1827.
1075—6. SAMUEL WICKHAM, b. July 31. 1830; d. Jan. 3, 1831.
1076—7. JAMES LOVETT, b. Oct. 23, 1832.
1077—8. JOHN McDOWELL, b. Dec. 8, 1833.
1078—9. ROBERT CORNELL, b. Oct. 1, 1835; d. May 27, 1836.

1079. PHEBE CRANE[6] [590], (Noah,[5] Jacob,[4] Caleb,[3] Nathaniel,[2] Stephen[1]), married Nov. 30, 1820, John Vanderveer, of Rocky Hill, N. J. She died at Elizabeth, N. J., Jan. 29, 1874. He died previous to that date. Children :

   1. ELIAS WINANS CRANE (Vanderveer), b. Oct., 1821; d. Sept., 1822.
   2. ANDREW H. (Vanderveer), b. 1823; not m.
   3. ELIAS WINANS CRANE (Vanderveer), b. 1825; m. Emily Carter, of Madison, N. J.
   4. MARTHA ANN (Vanderveer), b. 1827; m. Joseph Ralston, of Elizabeth, N. J.

5. NOAH (Vanderveer). b. 1828; drowned 1840.
6. MARGARETTA HANNAH (Vanderveer), b. 1840; m. Oct., 1857, John A. Miller.
7. JANE S. (Vanderveer), b. 1843; m. Nov., 1857, Isaac S. Connett.

1080. JONATHAN CRANE[6] [591], (Noah,[5] Jacob,[4] Caleb,[3] Nathaniel,[2] Stephen[1]), married Henrietta Middlebrook, of New York city. He died of yellow fever at Mobile, Ala., Oct. 12, 1837. Children:

1081—1. GEORGE L., b. Nov., 1830; d. 1836.
1082—2. CAROLINE, b. Nov., 1832; d. May 14, 1863.
1083—3. JONATHAN H., b. 1834; m. May 2, 1872, Eliza Crannell.
1084—4. HENRIETTA, b. Jan., 1838; d. June, 1840.

1085. ABIGAIL WINANS CRANE[6] [592], (Noah,[5] Jacob,[4] Caleb,[3] Nathaniel,[2] Stephen[1]), married Joseph Dayton Price, of Elizabethtown, N. J. She died Aug. 16, 1830. Children:

1. W. FURMAN (Price), b. Nov. 13, 1828; m. in 1854.
2. ABBY WINANS (Price). b. June, 1830; m. E. Edwards in 1851.

1086. JACOB GOZEN CRANE[6] [593], (Noah,[5] Jacob,[4] Caleb,[3] Nathaniel,[2] Stephen[1]), married Jane Squier, of Rahway, N. J., daughter of Jonathan Squier and Hannah Crane. She was born Jan. 14, 1809, and died May 10, 1869. He died Dec. 3, 1864. Children:

1087—1. ANN SQUIER, b. April 18, 1831; m. John A. Gunn, of New York, April 10, 1852.
1088—2. NOAH, b. Jan. 13, 1833; d. Dec. 12, 1834.
1089—3. WILLIAM SQUIER, b. June 22, 1834; d. Oct. 5, 1835.
1090—4. NOAH, b. Nov. 15, 1836; d. April 18, 1861.
1091—5. HANNAH ELIZABETH, b. Nov. 25, 1838.
1092—6. MARTHA WINANS, b. June 3, 1841.
1093—7. JANE SQUIER, b. May 24, 1844; m. Thos. Price, Newark, Nov., 1876.
1094—8. FRANCES OAKLEY, b. Aug. 9, 1846.
1095—9. JONATHAN SQUIER, b. Oct. 21, 1851; d. Oct. 4, 1859.

1096. HENRIETTA PARLEE CRANE[6] [594], (Noah,[5] Jacob,[4] Caleb,[3] Nathaniel,[2] Stephen[1]), married Melyne W. Halsey, of Elizabethtown, N. J., 1834. He died March 6, 1873. Children:

1. NOAH CRANE (Halsey), b. May 21, 1835; d. April 21, 1856.
2. MARY CHAPMAN (Halsey), b. Oct. 17, 1837; d. April 9, 1859.
3. CATHERINE PRICE (Halsey), b. Feb. 19, 1839; d. March 26, 1841.
4. SARA WINANS (Halsey), b. Sept. 19, 1841; m. James C. Ogden, Jan. 6, 1877; d. Aug. 15, 1878.
5. ISAAC CRANE (Halsey), b. Dec. 8, 1843; d. July 3, 1844.
6. MELYNE WINANS (Halsey), } b. Feb. 23, 1851; { d. Feb. 17, 1854.
7. HENRIETTA CRANE (Halsey), }
8. ABRAHAM WOODRUFF (Halsey), b. March 22, 1853.

1097. ELIZA CRANE[6] [599], (Caleb,[5] Jacob,[4] Caleb,[3] Nathaniel,[2] Stephen[1]), married William Ross, son of James. Children:

1. DELIA M. (Ross), b. June 9, 1827; m. John M. Prudden.
2. WILLIAM (Ross), b. May 10, 1828; m. Amelia Everhart.

3. ELIZA CRANE (ROSS), b. Nov. 8, 1830; d. Dec. 24, 1833.
4. THOMAS STRANG (ROSS), b. March 13, 1833; m. Hester Griffith.
5. LIDA (ROSS), b. April 18, 1834; m. Edward Everett.
6. JULIA CRANE (ROSS), b. Oct. 29, 1836; m. F. W. Hotchkiss.
7. FRANK ROBINSON (ROSS), b. April 25, 1839.
8. ALICE (ROSS), b. May 3, 1841; d. Oct. 18, 1852.
9. GEORGE GRIER (ROSS), b. July 23, 1845; m. Mattie Dickinson.
10. ELLA (ROSS), b. Sept. 2, 1847.
11. MARY DARLING (ROSS), b. March 20, 1850.

1098. NOAH CRANE[6] [605], (Jacob,[5] Jacob,[4] Caleb,[3] Nathaniel,[2] Stephen[1]), married the widow Scribner, of South Carolina, by whom he had one child. She died and he married 2d, Henrietta Pearson, daughter of Col. Abraham Winans, of Newark, N. J. She died in Sumter, S. C., Oct. 20, 1863. He died Nov. 28, 1868. Child:

1098½-1. SARAH; d. young.

1099. ANN CRANE[6] [608], (Jacob,[5] Jacob,[4] Caleb,[3] Nathaniel,[2] Stephen[1]), married Thomas Sanders, of North Carolina, in 1832. Children:

1. NOAH (Sanders).
2. WARREN (Sanders).
3. MEEKER (Sanders).
4. JENET (Sanders.)

1100. JOSEPH WARREN CRANE[6] [614], (Nehemiah,[5] Jacob,[4] Caleb,[3] Nathaniel,[2] Stephen[1]), married Nov. 12. 1834, in New York city, Charity Winans, who was born in that city. June 24, 1816. He was a contractor and builder; died in Rochester, N. Y., June 13, 1873. Children:

1101—1. ALONZO J.
1102—2. WILLIAM E.
1103—3. ELIAS W., b. Feb. 13, 1845.
1104—4. FRANK ALYMER, b. Feb. 24, 1850.
1105—5. AMANDA.
1106—6, EMMA.
1107—7. BERTHA.

1108. MARY MITCHEL CRANE[6] [619], (Job,[5] Nathaniel,[4] Caleb,[3] Nathaniel,[2] Stephen[1]), married Nov. 18, 1835, Rev. Benjamin Cory, son of Mulford Cory, and grandson of elder Benjamin Cory. Children:

1. JULIA MARIA (Cory), b. Dec. 26, 1840; m. Isaac C. Kiggins.
2. JANE WOODRUFF (Cory), b. Feb. 24, 1843; d. Dec. 5, 1860.
3. MARY ELIZABETH (Cory), b. March 14, 1845; m. Dr. F. W. Seward.
4. BENJAMIN MULFORD (Cory), b. June 29. 1847; d. May 14, 1848.
5. SARAH CRANE (Cory), b. June 3, 1849; d. Nov. 15, 1860.

1109. WILLIAM WOODRUFF CRANE[6] [620], (Job,[5] Nathaniel,[4] Caleb,[3] Nathaniel,[2] Stephen[1]), married Oct. 7, 1846, Charity B. Clark, daughter of Job, born July 4, 1820; also great-great-

great-granddaughter of Stephen Crane[1]. Mr. William Crane was born Sept. 10, 1819, and died July 12, 1885. Children:

1110—1. JOB CLARK, b. Feb. 21, 1848; m. Florence W. Langdon, May 3, 1876.
1111—?. MARY JANE, b. Nov. 21, 1850; m. Campbell T. Hedge, Nov. 6, 1878.
1112—3. WILLIAM SEARING, b. Nov. 4, 1852; d. May 15, 1854.
1113—4. SARAH ANNA, b. Jan. 26, 1855.
1114—5. AUGUSTUS STOUT, b. June 27, 1858.
1115—6. NELLIE MORTON, b. July 7, 1861.

1116. Dr. JOB SYMMES CRANE[6] [622], (Job,[5] Nathaniel,[4] Caleb,[3] Nathaniel,[2] Stephen[1]), married Helen B. Watkins, March 8, 1854, and settled in Elizabeth, N. J., where he was born, and became a very skilful physician; continuing the practice of his profession until 1894, when he was stricken with paralysis, but recovered somewhat, and two years later, 1896, he died in St. Augustine, Fla., whither he had gone for his health.
Children:

1117—1. AGNES OGILVIE, b. Feb. 13, 1855.
1118—2. FANNY WATKINS, b. June 23, 1859.
1119—3. DE WITT, b. March 20. 1863.
1120—4. HELEN BERTHA, b. June 1, 1870.

1121. NATHANIEL MARTIN CRANE[6] [627], (Elihu J.,[5] Nathaniel,[4] Caleb,[3] Nathaniel,[2] Stephen[1]), married Julia A. Harris, Oct. 6, 1858. He died June 26, 1870. Children:

1122—1. SARAH ELIZABETH, b. Sept. 5, 1859.
1123—2. FRANCIS ELIHU, b. April 4, 1861; m. Emma Wright Myers, Oct. 20, 1892; lives in Amsterdan, N. Y.

1124. ANNA WILLIAMS CRANE[6] [631], (Moses M.,[5] Nathaniel,[4] Caleb,[3] Nathaniel,[2] Stephen[1]), married Abram C. Miller, Sept. 15, 1847, and died Oct. 12, 1854. Child:

1. ANNA IRENE (Miller), b. July 18, 1851; d. May 8, 1853.

1125. JANE ELIZA CRANE[6] [632], (Moses M.,[5] Nathaniel,[4] Caleb,[3] Nathaniel,[2] Stephen[1]), married Dec. 25, 1855, John N. Earl, son of Robert C. Children:

1. ANNA MILLER (Earl), b. Oct. 4, 1858.
2. ROBERT NELSON (Earl), b. May 17, 1862.
3. MILLER CRANE (Earl), b. March 21, 1864.
4. JOHN THOMPSON (Earl), b. June 5, 1873.

1126. JOHN WILLIAMS CRANE[6] [633], (Moses M.,[5] Nathaniel,[4] Caleb,[3] Nathaniel,[2] Stephen[1]), married Dec. 21, 1859, Anna Elizabeth Wilson, daughter of John Wilson, from North Shields, England, and Nancy Lyon, daughter of Amos, of Lyons Farms, N. J. Their home is on the land originally granted by Governor Carteret to Stephen Crane senior, and been in the possession of the family since that time. Children:

1127—1. MOSES MILLER, b. Jan. 15, 1864.
1128—2. HENRY WILSON, b. May 7, 1874.

1129. WILLIAM MILLER CRANE[6][647], (Noah,[5] Noah,[4] Moses.[3] Nathaniel,[2] Stephen[1]), was an attorney-at-law; a man of uncommon ability, and acquired considerable distinction in his profession, which occupation he followed for fifty years. Some of his cases were carried before the Supreme Court of the United States, having the name of Salmon P. Chase, as associate lawyer, attached to some of his briefs before that court. His legal attainments were of high order, and his opinions on questions of law were generally accepted as final. At the age of seventy-two years he fell on the ice, and fractured his hip, which made him a cripple for about twelve years. He died at Fort Wayne, Ind., Dec. 14, 1891, aged 83 years, 9 months and 24 days. Children all born at St. Mary's, Ohio :

1130—1. CALVIN DENNISON, b. Oct. 4, 1837.
1131—2. ELVIRA MARIA, b. Oct. 4, 1840; d. at Fort Wayne, Ind.
1132—3. SUSAN ELIZABETH, b. Dec. 10, 1842; m. ——— Hoagland; residence Fort Wayne, Ind.
1133—4. WILLIAM RUFUS, b. Dec. 26, 1845; d. in infancy.
1134—5. WILLIAM METCALF, b. Jan. 27, 1847; residence Albia, Ia.
1135—6. ELI, b. Jan. 29, 1852; d. in infancy.
1136—7. NATHAN BRADFORD, b. Dec. 2, 1853; d. about 1866.

1137. Mariah Crane[7] [651], (Stephen,[6] Elijah,[5] John,[4] John,[3] John,[2] Stephen[1]), married Elias Potter, and removed to Peoria, Ill. Children :

   1. Susan Elizabeth (Potter).
   2. Emeline (Potter).
   3. Catherine (Potter).
   4. Louisa (Potter).

1138. John Davis Crane[7] [654], (John G.,[6] John,[5] John,[4] John,[3] John,[2] Stephen[1]), married Catharine Haines, daughter of William B. Potter, of Connecticut Farms, and settled at Westfield, N. J. Children :

1139—1. William Grant, b. Nov. 27, 1838; d. at Augusta, Ga., Feb. 27, 1843.
1140—2. Annie N., b. Oct. 4, 1841; d. July, 1876.
1141—3. Sarah Catharine, b. Oct. 29, 1843.
1142—4. Albert Grant, b. April 13, 1847.
1143—5. John Joseph, b. Nov. 11, 1849.

1144. John Crane[7] [659], (Elias,[6] John,[5] John,[4] John,[3] John,[2] Stephen[1]), married Sarah Cutter (or Carter), Jan. 14, 1837, and settled in Roselle, N. J. She died Sept. 4, 1854. [Have been unable to get a reply to inquiries about this family, but believe they had the following children, and from our best information he married 2d, Hannah Cutter, sister of his first wife, Aug. 4, 1857]. Children :

1145—1. Mary H., b. Feb. 4, 1838.
1146—2. Anna A., b. May 17, 1839.
1147—3. Sarah C., b. March 4, 1842.
1148—4. Esther, b. Aug. 29, 1843.
1149—5. John M., b. Nov. 14, 1845.
1150—6. Frederic, b. July 18, 1847.
1151—7. David C., b. June 4, 1849.
1152—8. William C., b. June 19, 1858.

1153. Phebe Crane[7] [660], (Elias,[6] John,[5] John,[4] John,[3] John,[2] Stephen[1]), married Silas Miller. Children :

   1. Charlotte (Miller).
   2. Abram (Miller).
   3. Jonas (Miller).
   4. Mary (Miller).

1154. Susan Crane[7] [661], (Elias,[6] John,[5] John,[4] John,[3] John,[2] Stephen[1]), married Isaac Williams. Children :

   1. John (Williams).
   2. Louisa (Williams).

1155. ELIAS M. CRANE[7] [662], (Elias,[6] John,[5] John,[4] John,[3] John,[2] Stephen[1]), married Louisa Miller; went west, and was residing in 1899 at Chambridge, Ill. Children :

  1156—1. BRITTON.
  1157—2. SARAH.
  1158—3. JOSIE.
  1159—4. WINFERD.
  1160—5. JOHN.
  1161—6. ELIZABETH.

1162. AMZI A. CRANE[7] [663], (Elias,[6] John,[5] John,[4] John,[3] John,[2] Stephen[1]), married Emmeline C. Potter in Peoria County, Ill., Sept. 13, 1854. She was born July 24, 1835. He is a farmer; residence at Osco, Ill. Children :

  1163—1. FRANKLIN P., b. July 9, 1855.
  1164—2. HARRIET M., b. March 1, 1859.
  1165—3. ANNIE E., b. Aug. 1, 1861.

1166. MARY ROSS CRANE[7] [665], (Josiah,[6] John,[5] John,[4] John,[3] John,[2] Stephen[1]), married Hampton, son of William Cutter, of Woodbridge, N. J. Children :

  1. JOSIAH (Cutter), b. Nov. 11, 1836; d.
  2. WILLIAM HENRY (Cutter), b. June 22, 1840; living (1898) at Woodbridge, N. J.
  3. SARAH ANNA (Cutter), b. May 6, 1845; living (1898) at Woodbridge, N. J.
  4. EMILY (Cutter), b. May 31, 1852; living (1898) at Woodbridge, N. J.

1167. JOHN GRANT CRANE[7] [666], (Josiah,[6] John,[5] John,[4] John,[3] John,[2] Stephen[1]), married Abby, daughter of John Miller. He died June 15, 1893, aged 76. She died Feb. 17, 1875, aged 54 years, 10 months and 7 days. Children :

  1168—1. SARAH LOUISA, b. 1840; m. James C. Runyon; reside at Middletown, N. J.
  1169—2. MARY ELIZABETH. b. 1842; m. Jesse P. Woodruff, Jamaica, L. I.
  1170—3. PHILIP ALFRED, b. 1844; m. Hattie Shackley; he d. 1885.
  1171—4. WILLARD GRANT, b. 1846; m. Charlotte Melissa Stapleton.
  1172—5. JOHN CHANCELOR. b. 1848.
  1173—6. JAMES WALACE. b. 1850; m. Emma Miller.
  1174—7. ADDIE A., b. 1852.
  1175—8. MILLER L., b. 1860.
  1176—9. EMMA L., b. 1862.

1177. ANN ELIZABETH CRANE[7] [667], (Josiah,[6] John,[5] John,[4] John,[3] John,[2] Stephen[1]), married Jacob, son of Moses Williams, of Union, N. J. Mr. Williams died, and his widow lived in New Orleans, La. Children :

  1. HAMPTON (Williams); d.
  2. SARAH M. (Williams); d.
  3. NATHANIEL (Williams); living (1898) at Elizabeth, N. J.
  4. ELECTA R. (Williams); living (1898) at New Orleans, La.

1178.   JOSIAH CRANE[7] [668], Josiah,[6] John,[5] John,[4] John,[3] John,[2] Stephen[1]), married Sarah Jane, daughter of Jacob Miller.   Residence at Pictou, Ont.   Children :

1179—1.   DAVID; living (1898) at Canadensis, Pa.
1180—2.   GEORGE H.; living (1898) at Connescon, Ont.

1181.   SMITH CRANE[7] [673], (John,[6] Samuel,[5] Joseph,[4] John,[3] John,[2] Stephen[1]), married Mary Catharine Morris, Nov. 16, 1847.   She was born in Preston Co., W. Va., Aug. 10, 1827 ; a descendant of Robert Morris, of Philadelphia, Pa., and settled in Kingwood, Preston Co., W. Va., where for many years Mr. Crane was clerk of the circuit court.   Previous to July 2, 1863, at which date he was called to this clerkship, he was, from July 1, 1852, clerk of the Preston County court.   Child :

1182—1.   JOHN MORRIS, b. Sept. 22, 1853.

1183.   SAMUEL CRANE[7] [674], (John,[6] Samuel,[5] Joseph,[4] John,[3] John,[2] Stephen[1]), married Abigail Kelley, Nov. 9, 1848. Children :

1184—1.   CORDELIA, b. June 25, 1849.
1185—2.   JOHN, b. July 31, 1850.
1186—3.   WILLIAM ALLEN, b. Dec. 20, 1852 ; m. Laura Bell Feather, Feb. 4, 1884.
1187—4.   VIRGINIA, b. June 7, 1855.
1188—5.   SERENA, b. Dec. 12, 1857.
1189—6.   NANCY, b. Jan. 13, 1860.
1190—7.   MARSHALL, b. Jan. 15, 1861.
1191—8.   WINFIELD SCOTT, b. April 1, 1864.

1192.   ELIZABETH CRANE[7] [675], (John,[6] Samuel,[5] Joseph,[4] John,[3] John,[2] Stephen[1]), married Sept. 26, 1841, Henry Albright, of Cranesville, W. Va.   Children :

1.   MARCELLUS (Albright), b. Feb. 22, 1843.
2.   JACOB (Albright), b. Aug. 21, 1844.
3.   NANCY JANE (Albright), b. Oct. 23, 1845.
4.   JOHN C. (Albright), b. Sept. 29, 1847.
5.   DAVID A. (Albright), b. June 2, 1849.
6.   HENRY N. (Albright), b. April 29, 1851.
7.   AMANDA (Albright), b. April 15, 1853.
8.   ARBANUS SYLVESTER (Albright), b. Nov. 8, 1855.
9.   SUSANAH E. (Albright), b. May 6, 1858 ; m. Charles Lee ; residence, Michigan.

1193.   MARCELLUS ALBRIGHT [1] ; m. Dora Gaston. Children : ALICE ; ADA ; SUSAN ; FRANK.

1194.   NANCY JANE ALBRIGHT [3] ; m. Edmund Albright.   Children : MARGARET ; GEORGIA ; VICTOR.

1195.   DAVID A. ALBRIGHT [5] ; m. I. Alice Frankhouser.   Children : VERNON ; STELLA ; RUBY ; WILBER.

1196.   ARBANUS SYLVESTER ALBRIGHT [8] ; m. Z. Olive Falkenstein. Children : OKEY RUSSELL, b. March 25, 1888 ; NELLIE, b. Dec. 10, 1892.

1197.   ELISHA CRANE[7] [676], John,[6] Samuel,[5] Joseph,[4] John,[3]

John,[2] Stephen[1]), married Sept. 10, 1847, Mary Ann Fike. She was born May 19, 1827. Residence, Lincoln, Ill.
Children :

1198—1. MARSHALL ALLEN, b. Sept. 18, 1848.
1199—2. JOHN FRANKLIN, b. Aug. 9, 1851; d. Oct. 30, 1857.
1200—3. MARTHA ALICE, b. May 20, 1853.

1201. JANE CRANE[7] [678], John,[6] Samuel,[5] Joseph,[4] John,[3] John,[2] Stephen[1]), married Edmund Otto, of Cranesville, W. Va., Nov. 17, 1847. Children :

1. NANCY (Otto), b. Nov. 24, 1848.
2. EMILY (Otto), b. Sept. 20, 1850; m. Charles F. M. Jeffers, Sept. 20, 1874.
3. ELISHA ALLEN (Otto), b. June 5, 1852.
4. NAOMI (Otto), b. Feb. 15, 1857.
5. JOHN FRANKLIN (Otto), b. March 8, 1862; d. Sept. 11, 1865.
6. MARY FLORENCE (Otto), b. March 11, 1866; m. James M. Wolfe, March 5, 1885; d. Sept. 7, 1885.
7. LESLIE WILBER (Otto), b. Sept. 4, 1873.

1202. NANCY OTTO [1]; m. Obediah Metheney, Jan. 11, 1872. Children : LETITIA; ARTIE M.

1203. NAOMI OTTO [4]; m. Andrew S. Teats, April 2, 1870; residence, Oakland, Md. Children : NELLIE; LAURA; LESTER; MINNIE F.; CHARLES R.; GRACE; FOSTER.

1204. LESLIE WILBER OTTO [7]; m. Anna Wells, July 4, 1894. Child : PEARL ADONIA (Otto), b. June 6, 1895.

1205. AMANDA CRANE [679], married April 3, 1853, Jacob S. Hyde, of Brandville, W. Va. He was born Sept. 27, 1829. Served as captain in 6th W. Va. Cavalry, Co. L, from 1861 to 1865, and died March 12, 1865, at Annapolis, Md.
Children :

1. HENRY CLAY HANNIBAL (Hyde), b. Jan. 23, 1855; d. Oct. 22, 1899.
2. DORA MELISSA (Hyde), b. March 16, 1857.
3. JOSEPHINE (Hyde), b. Jan. 28, 1859; d. Nov. 9, 1880.
4. NANCY ELIZABETH (Hyde), b. Aug. 12, 1860; d. Jan. 23, 1869.
5. FREMONT GREELY (Hyde), b. Jan. 22. 1863; m. Elizabeth Cornelius; is a jeweller at Oakland, Md.

1206. HENRY CLAY HANNIBAL HYDE [1]; m. Ida May Martin, of Kingwood, W. Va., Oct. 30, 1889. Children :
    1. HAROLD EDWARD (Hyde), b. March 2, 1891.
    2. RUTH (Hyde), b. March 31, 1893.

1207. DORA MELISSA HYDE [2]; m. T. W. Scott; residence at New Haven, Pa. Children :
    1. HELEN WARD (Scott).
    2. MABEL CLARE (Scott).
    3. THOMAS W. (Scott).
    4. JOSEPHINE L. (Scott).
    5. DORA PAULINE (Scott).

1208. LAVILA CRANE[7] [681], (John,[6] Samuel,[5] Joseph,[4] John,[3] John,[2] Stephen[1]), married Charles Stone, of Uniontown,

Pa., and removed to Texas, where he died. The family then removed to Chicago, Ill., where she died in 1898. Children:

1. ANNA D. (Stone).
2. VIOLA CRANE (Stone); m. —— Chapman.
3. MATTIE (Stone).

1209. JACOB WILBER CRANE[7] [682], (John,[6] Samuel,[5] Joseph,[4] John,[3] John,[2] Stephen[1]), married in Findlay, Ohio, June 20, 1865, Mary E. Wykes. He served in the United States Volunteers from West Virginia in 1864 and 1865. For some years he was a commercial traveller. Residence (1899) at Springfield, Ohio. Mrs. Crane was born Oct. 13, 1845, in Lorain County, Ohio. Children:

1210—1. LESLIE WILBER, b. March 15, 1868, in Fremont, Ohio.
1211—2. CLARA EUGENIA, b. March 12, 1871, in Fremont, Ohio.

1212. JOHN BONNELL CRANE[7] [683], (John,[6] Samuel,[5] Joseph,[4] John,[3] John,[2] Stephen[1]), married Mary E. Fleming in Fairmont, Marion Co., W. Va., Nov. 28, 1867. She was born in that County Sept. 13, 1845. Mr. Crane served in the rebellion; was regimental quartermaster-sergeant. Was for six years recorder for the County of Marion, and clerk of the court for Marion County more than nine years, and was still in office at the time this record was sent in. He was also clerk of the board of supervisors of that County for the years 1867, 1868, 1869 and 1871. Residence at Fairmont. He died Aug. 5, 1898. Children:

1213—1. GEORGIA T., b. Jan. 21, 1869; m. John H. Hough.
1214—2. JOHN R., b. June 8, 1875; d. Sept. 1, 1875.
1215—3. NELLIE D., b. Feb. 9, 1877.
1216—4. HARRY B., b. Dec. 11, 1879.
1217—5. JOHN B.

1218. WILLIAM BONNELL CRANE[7] [685], (Jacob,[6] Samuel,[5] Joseph,[4] John,[3] John,[2] Stephen[1]), married Rachel Elliott, Oct. 19, 1852. She was born June 10, 1829, and died Sept. 26, 1889. Children:

1219—1. SILAS FULLER, b. Nov. 8, 1853.
1220—2. CHARLES CLARENDON, b. March 31, 1856; d. June 24, 1857.
1221—3. MARSHALL WELLINGTON, b. Feb. 18, 1858; d. Sept. 22, 1887.
1222—4. EUDORA CORNELIA, b. Dec. 13, 1859; d. Sept. 7, 1893.
1223—5. JENNIE OLIVE, b. Oct. 16. 1861; d. April 10, 1894.
1224—6. WILLIAM ELLIOTT, b. March 19, 1864; d. Oct. 18, 1864.
1225—7. CHESTER CLAY, b. May 22, 1866; d. July 24, 1894.

1226. SAMUEL ELLIOTT CRANE[7] [686], (Jacob,[6] Samuel,[5] Joseph,[4] John,[3] John,[2] Stephen[1]), married Malinda, daughter of Samuel Fiske. She was born May 21, 1833, in Preston County, W. Va. Removed to Lee's Summit, Mo., where they died,—he March 8, 1894; she Aug. 13, 1897. Children:

1227—1. CHARLES CRITTENDEN, b. Nov. 11, 1858, at Preston, W. Va
1228—2. VICTORIA.
1229—3. WILBERT F.

1230—4. HOWARD.
1231—5. TROY LINCOLN.
1232—6. WILLIAM BONNELL.
1233—7. LILLIE.

1234. LOUISA J. CRANE[7] [688], (Calvin,[6] Samuel,[5] Joseph,[4] John,[3] John,[2] Stephen[1]), married 1st, Nov. 22, 1849, William Rigg. He was born Nov. 20, 1826, and died Dec. 20, 1854, aged 28 years, leaving a daughter. She married 2d, March 25, 1858, Salathiel J. Posten. He was born Oct. 27, 1831, and died Aug. 9, 1897, aged 65 years, 9 months and 12 days. Children:

1. OPHELIA ANN (Rigg), b. March 28, 1853.
2. RHENA BELL (Posten), b. Jan. 1, 1859.
3. WILLIAM OSCAR (Posten), b. Dec. 15, 1861.

1235. OPHELIA ANN RIGG [1]; m. Dec. 5, 1871, Caleb Joshua Trippett. He was b. May 14, 1846. Children:
    1. HALLIE B. (Trippett), b. April 28, 1876.
    2. CLYDE H. (Trippett), b. June 7, 1877.

1236. RHENA BELL POSTEN [2]; m. Dec. 28, 1881, Scott T. Jones. He was b. May 10, 1858. Children:
    1. HARLAND LIVINGSTON (Jones), b. Oct. 25, 1882.
    2. GRACE MAY (Jones), b. March 9, 1886.

1237. WILLIAM OSCAR POSTEN [3]; m. April 10, 1890, Sallie McCauley Shipley. She was b. July 17, 1864. Child:
    1. WILLIAM FLOYD (Posten), b. Nov. 30, 1895.

1238. JOSEPHAS ELLIOTT CRANE[7] [689], (Calvin,[6] Samuel,[5] Joseph,[4] John,[3] John,[2] Stephen[1]), married Feb. 20, 1870, Lizzie Engle. She was born Nov. 24, 1850. Children:

1239—1. WILLIAM REED, b. Aug. 20, 1870; m. Mattie Casteel, Feb. 19, 1896.
1240—2. ORLANDO CHESTER, b. July 4, 1874; m. Mollie Celia Joyce, Sept. 9, 1895.
1241—3. ADA ELLEN, b. Jan. 12, 1878.
1242—4. CLYDE FOREST, b. Oct. 31, 1879.

1243. SAMUEL BONNELL CRANE[7] [690], (Calvin,[6] Samuel,[5] Joseph,[4] John,[3] John,[2] Stephen[1]), married Dec. 28, 1854, Ruth A. Forman. She was born Nov. 19, 1832. Children:

1244—1. BENJAMIN F., b. Nov. 6, 1855.
1245—2. THOMAS W., b. Dec. 9, 1857.
1246—3. JENNIE R., b. Nov. 3, 1859.
1247—4. CHARLES C., b. March 13, 1862.
1248—5. JARVIS D., b. March 29, 1864.
1249—6. JOHN C., b. Sept. 17, 1867.
1250—7. IDA MAY, b. July 12, 1870; d. March, 1889.
1251—8. WILLIAM E., b. July 3, 1874.

1252. MARY ANN CRANE[7] [692], (Calvin,[6] Samuel,[5] Joseph,[4] John,[3] John,[2] Stephen[1]), married July 1, 1855, John F. Wotring. He was born March 18, 1834. Children:

1. ALICE BELL (Wotring), b. June 26, 1856.
2. ARTHUR CLARENCE (Wotring), b. June 6, 1858.
3. ARTENIS OSCAR (Wotring), b. Oct. 2, 1861.

4. IDA MAY (Wotring), b. July 1, 1864; d. same day.
5. DORAH JANE (Wotring), b. March 20, 1866; d. June 26, 1870.
6. RUTH OPHELIA (Wotring), b. Feb. 26, 1868.
7. BRUCE BONNELL (Wotring), b. Aug. 24, 1870.

1253. ALICE BELL WOTRING [1]; m. Feb. 25, 1877, William J. McComb. Children:
1. ARTHUR A. (McComb), b. Sept. 23, 1878.
2. FRANKLIN (McComb), } twins, b. Jan. 1, 1880.
3. MARY (McComb), }
4. RHUBEN (McComb), b. Feb. 14, 1882.
5. LAWRENCE (McComb), b. June 12, 1886.
6. CLYDE ((McComb), b. Dec. 3, 1889.
7. THOMAS McComb), b. Sept. 28, 1893.

1254. ARTHUR CLARENCE WOTRING [2]; m. Feb. 26, 1879, Josephine Fairbanks. Children:
1. RHENA M. (Wotring), b. Oct. 1, 1879.
2. CORA E. (Wotring), } twins, b. Oct. 24, 1883.
3. DORA J. (Wotring), }
4. HARLON H. (Wotring), b. July 23, 1888.
5. LILLIAN R. (Wotring), b. Nov. 15, 1892.
6. MILDRED M. (Wotring), b. April 7, 1894.
7. CECIL J. (Wotring), b. May 5, 1887.

1255. ARTENIS OSCAR WOTRING [3]; m. Sept. 18, 1886, Blanche Robbins. Child:
1. ARMENIA (Wotring), b. Feb. 13, 1889.

1256. ELIZABETH CRANE[7] [693], (Calvin,[6] Samuel,[5] Joseph,[4] John,[3] John,[2] Stephen[1]), married Dec. 25, 1856, Peter L. Cramer. He was born Sept. 17, 1833, and died March 25, 1890. Children:

1. CHARLES WILBERT (Cramer), b. Dec. 3, 1858; m. Lida Spindler, Aug. 7, 1886.
2. MARTIN LUTHER (Cramer), b. July 15, 1863.
3. JOHN CALVIN (Cramer), b. June 12, 1868.
4. R. BRUCE WHEELER (Cramer), b. Oct. 24, 1876.
5. WORLEY H. (Cramer), b. Nov. 5, 1877; d. Jan. 12, 1879.

1257. MARTIN LUTHER CRAMER [2]; m. Feb. 22, 1889, Jennie F. Cox. Children:
1. BLONDIA BRICE (Cramer), b. Aug. 30, 1894.
2. ORLANDO CHESTER (Cramer), b. Dec. 9, 1897.

1258. JOHN CALVIN CRAMER [3]; m. Nov. 4, 1891, Nettie M. Welch. Children:
1. LAURA MAUD (Cramer), b. Oct. 5, 1892.
2. CLAUD J. (Cramer), b. April 10, 1894.
3. ROBERT McKENLEY (Cramer), b. April 9, 1896.
4. MILDRED BLANCH (Cramer), b. Feb. 12, 1898.

1259. MARTIN LUTHER CRANE[7] [694], (Calvin,[6] Samuel,[5] Joseph,[4] John,[3] John,[2] Stephen[1]), married Jan. 17, 1867, Mary Jane Smith. She was born May 15, 1842, and died Dec. 10, 1897. Children:

1260—1. CLAY, b. June 1, 1868; m.
1261—2. SMITH, b. Feb. 20, 1870; d. Sept. 1, 1892.
1262—3. GREELY, b. March 30, 1873; m.
1263—4. LULU RUTH, b. June 6, 1883.

1264. JOHN CALVIN CRANE[7] [695], (Calvin,[6] Samuel,[5] Joseph,[4] John,[3] John,[2] Stephen[1]), married Feb. 15, 1866, Margery Ruhamah Bishoff. She was born Dec. 9, 1848. Children:

1265—1. DEE, b. Jan. 19, 1867; m.
1266—2. CLOYD MOUNTAIN, b. June 21, 1868; m.
1267—3. SPENCER, b. Dec. 26, 1872; m. Myrtle Welch, Jan. 16, 1895.
1268—4. FRANK WILLEY JORDAN, b. March 31, 1881.

1269. RUTH R. CRANE[7] [697], (Calvin,[6] Samuel,[5] Joseph,[4] John,[3] John,[2] Stephen[1]), married Oct. 8, 1872, A. S. Baumgardner. He was born Feb. 12, 1852. She was an adopted daughter. Child:

1. ANNIE H. V. (Baumgardner), b. Oct. 24, 1881.

1270. ANN E. CRANE[7] [731], (Ira,[6] Joseph,[5] Joseph,[4] John,[3] John,[2] Stephen[1]), married Abram P. Watson. Settled in Crawfordsville, Ind. Child:

1. MARY E. (Watson).

1271. JULIA CRANE[7] [735], (Ira,[6] Joseph,[5] Joseph,[4] John,[3] John,[2] Stephen[1]), married Frank Kelloge. Removed to Alameda, Cal. Children:

1. MAUD (Kelloge).
2. PAUL (Kelloge).
3. FRANK (Kelloge).

1272. THEODORE I. CRANE[7] [736], (Ira,[6] Joseph,[5] Joseph,[4] John,[3] John,[2] Stephen[1]), married Jennie Workman. Residence at Lake City, Minn. He is a dealer in watches, diamonds, jewelry, etc.; of the firm of Crane Brothers. Child:

1273:—1. FRANCES.

1274. CHARLES C. CRANE[7] [752], (William,[6] Stephen,[5] Jacob,[4] Matthias,[3] John,[2] Stephen[1]), married Nov. 7, 1843, Hannah A. Wade He resides at Hooker, Trempealeau Co., Wis. She died April 1, 1891. He died Oct. 3, 1895. Children:

1275—1. JULIA A., b. Sept. 10, 1847; m. Feb. 22, 1869.
1276—2. ANN M., b. July 8, 1849; m. March 19, 1868.
1277—3. SARAH R., b. Oct. 14, 1852; m. Oct. 25, 1882.
1278—4. WILLIAM A. E., b. Dec. 21, 1853.
1279—5. LILLIAN J., b. Oct. 16, 1858.
1280—6. CHARLES E., b. Jan. 5, 1865.

1281. WILLIAM E. CRANE[7] [756], (William,[6] Stephen,[5] Jacob,[4] Matthias,[3] John,[2] Stephen[1]), married Nov. 25, 1868, Elizabeth Devalor. Residence at Stamford, Conn. She died Oct. 12, 1892. Children:

1282—1. EVA MAY, b. May 23, 1870; d. Sept. 12, 1870.
1283—2. ROBERT FLETCHER, b. Nov. 20, 1871; d. May 1, 1895.

1284. GEORGE T. CRANE[7] [757], (William,[6] Stephen,[5] Jacob,[4] Matthias,[3] John,[2] Stephen[1]), married April 30, 1852, Matilda Moore. Reside at Williamsburgh, L. I., N. Y. Children :

1285—1. WILLIAM GIBBY, b. Nov. 1, 1854; drowned Sept. 15, 1864, at Columbia, S. C.
1286—2. VIOLA, b. June 3, 1868; d. of diphtheria Oct. 15, 1875.
1287—3. MARY LOUISA, b. Oct. 27, 1871.

1288. STEPHEN SQUIER CRANE[7] [759], William,[6] Stephen,[5] Jacob,[4] Matthias,[3] John,[2] Stephen[1]), born in Essex County, N. J. Married Feb. 25, 1857, at Williamsburgh, L. I., N. Y., Sarah Elizabeth Briggs. She was born in New York city July 4, 1836. He enlisted in 1861, and served in the late war. He resides at Yonkers, N. Y.; is a merchant; has been there since 1869; after marriage and to that date his home was at Williamsburgh. Children :

1289—1. WILLIAM GILBERT BRIGGS, b. Feb. 5, 1858.
1290—2. GERTRUDE AMELIA, b. March 27, 1860.
1291—3. EMMA LOUISA, b. Aug. 1, 1864.
1292—4. SUSAN ELIZABETH, b. March 8, 1866.
1293—5. CHRISTIANA, b. Aug. 27, 1867; m. March 13, 1899, Clark L. Waters.
1294—6. JOSEPH T., b. Dec. 1, 1869.
1295—7. STEPHEN S., b. Feb. 18, 1872.
1296—8. HENRY W., b. Sept. 19, 1875.

1297. AUGUSTUS B. CRANE[7] [760], (William,[6] Stephen,[5] Jacob,[4] Matthias,[3] John,[2] Stephen[1]), married Sept. 28, 1864, Eunice Hughs, and settled in Rahway, N. J. Children :

1298—1. MARGARET EMMA, b. and d. July 6, 1865.
1299—2. WILLIAM AUGUSTUS, b. Aug. 7, 1866.
1300—3. JOSEPH WILLIAM, b. Oct. 2, 1868.
1301—4. DAVID FRANKLIN, b. Nov. 13, 1870.
1302—5. STEPHEN SQUIER, b. April 19, 1873; d. March 9. 1874.
1303—6. EUNICE RHODES, b. March 8, 1875; d. March 25, 1875.
1304—7. MARY AUGUSTA, b. Oct. 1, 1876.
1305—8. EUNICE, b. June 10, 1880.

1306. EMMA L. CRANE[7] [761], (William,[6] Stephen,[5] Jacob,[4] Matthias,[3] John,[2] Stephen[1]), married July 30, 1857, Samuel S. Martin. Residence at Williamsburgh, L. I., N. Y. He died April 3, 1891. Children :

1. FRANCIS JOSEPH (Martin), b. April 10, 1859; d. March 10, 1861.
2. EDWIN AUGUSTUS (Martin), b. Aug. 30, 1862.
3. ELLA (Martin), b. April 9, 1864; d. Nov. 23, 1864.
4. GEORGE ELDRIDGE (Martin), b. Dec. 11, 1865; d. Jan. 11, 1874.
5. ALBERT EARL (Martin), b. April 9, 1868.
6. SAMUEL MASON (Martin), b. June 16, 1869; d. Aug. 1, 1869.

1307. ALFRED T. CRANE[7] [762], (William,[6] Stephen,[5] Jacob,[4] Matthias,[3] John,[2] Stephen[1]), married Nov. 23, 1864, Gertrude V. Martin, and settled at Rahway, N. J., where she died June 7, 1898. Children :

1308—1. MARY M., b. Nov. 6, 1865; d. Sept. 13, 1875.

54

1309—2. GEORGE W., b. Nov. 24, 1866; m. Winifred Cox, July
         23, 1891.
1310—3. CLARA, b. Oct. 31, 1868.
1311—4. ALFRED T., b. Jan. 28, 1873.

1312. AUGUSTUS B. CRANE[7] [764], (Stephen,[6] Stephen,[5]
Jacob,[4] Matthias,[3] John,[2] Stephen[1]), married Jan. 31, 1844,
Lovinia Baldwin. She was born Aug. 24, 1824. Residence at
Mount Pleasant, Racine Co., Wis. Children:

1313—1. WILLIAM AUGUSTUS, b. Sept. 11, 1844; m. Nov. 11, 1867.
1314—2. JAMES HENRY, b. July 7, 1848; m. Jan. 6, 1873.
1315—3. SARAH LOVINIA, b. March 17, 1852.
1316—4. GEORGE STEPHEN, b. Aug. 19, 1855; drowned May 15, 1863.

1317. STEPHEN CRANE[7] [771], (George W.,[6] Stephen,[5]
Jacob,[4] Matthias,[3] John,[2] Stephen[1]), served in the war of the
rebellion, Army of the Potomac, from 1863 to the close of the
war. Married Melissa Hyden. Children:

1318—1. GEORGE WILLIS, b. Feb. 23, 1862; d. 1864.
1319—2. LESLIE, b. 1865; d. April 12, 1872.
1320—3. LULU LONORA, b. Oct. 18, 1868.
1321—4. STANLEY, b. 1870; d. April 12, 1872.

1322. ESTHER ANN CRANE[7] [773], (George W.,[6] Stephen,[5]
Jacob,[4] Matthias,[3] John,[2] Stephen[1]), married William H. Dudley. Children:

1. LILLIA M. (Dudley), b. April 19, 1863.
2. LIZZA M. (Dudley), b. April 13, 1866; d. Sept. 27, 1867.
3. FRANK L. (Dudley), b. March 4, 1868; d. Aug. 9, 1878.
4. CHESTER H. C. (Dudley), b. Aug. 25, 1879.
5. AVERY A. (Dudley), b. Jan. 31, 1882.

1323. RICHARD MOORE CRANE[7] [774], (George W.,[6] Stephen,[5]
Jacob,[4] Matthias,[3] John,[2] Stephen[1]), born in Racine, Wis.
Married at Patch Grove, Grant Co., Wis., Aug. 5, 1873, Mary
Ella Shultz. She was born March 12, 1852. Mr. Crane enlisted
and served in the late war in the 7th Regt., Wisconsin Infantry,
from March 29, 1862, to May 20, 1865; was wounded May 25,
1864, at North Anna River. He graduated at Wisconsin State
University, Law Department, in 1872. He is an attorney and
banker at Marion Centre, Marion Co., Kan. Children:

1324—1. WILBER SHULTZ, b. Nov. 20, 1877; d. Aug. 6, 1878.
1325—2. RICHARD MOORE, b. Oct. 28, 1879.
1326—3. HELEN BERTHA, b. April 21, 1883.
1327—4. CLARA, b. Jan. 23, 1889.

1328. CLARA AUGUSTA CRANE[7] [777], (George W.,[6] Stephen,[5]
Jacob,[4] Matthias,[3] John,[2] Stephen[1]), married Rodolph Blanchard.
Children:

1. HENRY WARD (Blanchard), b. Nov. 3, 1870; d. March 1, 1887.
2. FRANK ADOLPH (Blanchard), b. Nov. 30, 1874.
3. RAY MOORE (Blanchard), b. July 26, 1880.
4. WILLIAM CLYDE (Blanchard), b. Sept. 26, 1890.

1329. HENRIETTA LAVINA CRANE[7] [778], (George W.,[6]
Stephen,[5] Jacob,[4] Matthias,[3] John,[2] Stephen[1]), married Rev.

William A. Lyman, and in 1880 were living in Windsor, Dane Co., Wis. She is a graduate of State University, Madison, Wis. Children :

1. ROLO LU VERNE (Lyman), b. March 4, 1878.
2. MARION VINNETTE (Lyman), b. March 22, 1880.
3. EDNA IRENE (Lyman), b. Sept. 15, 1882.
4. WILLIAM AZRO (Lyman), b. June 30, 1885.
5. CARAL GENEVIEVE (Lyman), b. Sept. 25, 1889.

1330. MOSES WOODRUFF CRANE[7] [782], (David W.,[6] Jacob,[5] Jacob,[4] Matthias,[3] John,[2] Stephen[1]), married Oct. 17, 1855, Sarah Frances, daughter of Matthias Brant and Margaret (Winans) Crane. Children :

1331—1. MARGARET WINANS, b. July 20, 1856; m. J. Brookfield, April 11, 1883.
1332—2. MARY MAXWELL, b. Aug. 12, 1858; m. E. W. Hedden, March 16, 1882.
1333—3. MATTHIAS BRANT, b. Dec. 27, 1860; d. Dec. 13, 1862.
1334—4. WILLIE, b. Jan. 19, 1865; d. Feb. 14, 1865.
1335—5. FANNY WOODRUFF, b. May 28, 1866; d. Jan. 18, 1873.
1336—6. NELLIE, b. Sept. 9, 1867; d. Oct. 7, 1867.
1337—7. JACOB WARNER, b. March 15, 1878.

1338. JACOB WARNER CRANE[7] [784], (David W.,[6] Jacob,[5] Jacob,[4] Matthias,[3] John,[2] Stephen[1]), married Jan. 1, 1859, at Newark, N. J., Susan Bragaw. She was born there May 27, 1838. He is a mason by occupation. Residence at Newark. Children :

1339—1. CHARLES ADAMS, b. Dec. 21, 1859.
1340—2. DAVID WARNER, b. March 19, 1861; drowned at Budd's Lake, July 6, 1878.
1341—3. MOSES WOODRUFF, b. Oct. 9, 1863; m. Minnie W. Weinrick.
1342—4. EMMA SOUTHWORTH, b. Oct. 8, 1865; m. Willis G. Hillman.
1343—5. FRANKLIN SPENCER, b. Nov. 21, 1867.
1344—6. HERBERT QUINCEY, b. April 2, 1870; m. Daisey F. Bolus.
1345—7. SALLY DOREMUS, b. April 10, 1872; m. Ottomar A. Black.
1346—8. CHARLOTTE ELIZABETH, b. Oct. 23, 1874.
1347—9. DANIEL DODD, b. July 7, 1877.
1348-10. ROBERT CLARK, b. Aug. 8, 1879.

1349. ISAAC BRAGAW CRANE[7] [785], (David W.,[6] Jacob,[5] Jacob,[4] Matthias,[3] John,[2] Stephen[1]), married Ella G. Roe, June 17, 1874. Children :

1350—1. MABEL, b. April 3, 1876.
1351—2. FLORENCE, b. May, 1877.

1352. PHŒBE WOODRUFF CRANE[7] [786], (David W.,[6] Jacob,[5] Jacob,[4] Matthias,[3] John,[2] Stephen[1]), married George W. Bates, Dec. 28, 1864. Children :

1. DAVID WARNER (Bates), b. Jan. 31, 1870
2. ISAAC CRANE (Bates), b. Oct. 31, 1878.
3. GRACE ELIZABETH (Bates), b. Nov. 4, 1884.

1353. CATHERINE DOREMUS CRANE[7] [792], (David W.,[6]

Jacob,[5] Jacob,[4] Matthias,[3] John,[2] Stephen[1]), married William Brant Burnett, Dec. 4, 1878. Children:

1. D. FREDERICK (Burnett), b. Sept. 20, 1879.
2. WILLIAM B. (Burnett), b. Nov. 20, 1880.

1354. EDWARD P. CRANE[7] [798], (Jacob,[6] Jacob,[5] Jacob,[4] Matthias,[3] John,[2] Stephen[1]), born in Elizabethtown, N. J. Married July 4, 1862, in Paterson, Sarah F. Mandeville, who was born at Pompton Plains, Jan. 16, 1840. He was a builder. Residence at Brooklyn, N. Y. He died April 26, 1893. Children:

1355—1. CHARLES EDWARD, b. Nov. 30, 1864; d. June 15, 1898.
1356—2. JACOB IRVING, b. May 14, 1867.
1357—3. LETTY MANDEVILLE, b. Nov. 1, 1869.
1358—4. MABEL ELOISE, b. July 28, 1872.
1359—5. ADA MIRIAM, b. April 3, 1875.
1360—6. ROBERT ELLIS, b. Aug. 6, 1883.

1361. SARAH FRANCES CRANE[7] [811], (Matthias B.,[6] Matthias,[5] Jacob,[4] Matthias,[3] John,[2] Stephen[1]), married Moses, grandson of Jacob Crane, of Lyons Farms, N. J., and son of David Warner Crane. He died Nov., 1882. Children:

1. MARIETTA, b. July 20, 1856.
2. MARY M., b. Aug. 12, 1858.
3. MATTHIAS B., b. Dec. 27, 1860.
4. WILBER, b. Jan. 19, 1865.
5. FANNY, b. May 26, 1866.
6. NELLY, b. Sept. 9, 1867.
7. JACOB W., b. March 15, 1878.

1362. MARIETTA A. CRANE[7] [812], (Matthias B.,[6] Matthias,[5] Jacob,[4] Matthias,[3] John,[2] Stephen[1]), married Edward Benton Earle, of Lyons Farms, N. J. Children:

1. ELIZABETH L. (Earle)b b. June 13, 1860.
2. EDWARD F. (Earle). . Aug. 9, 1862; m. Annie Leypold, Sept. 13, 1885.
3. ANN MAY (Earle), b. May 12, 1865.
4. WILLIAM A. (Earle), b. Aug. 19, 1867; m. Feb. 15, 1892, Maude Conway.
5. MARIETTA B. (Earle), b. April 10, 1870.
6. FANNY CRANE (Earle), b. June 4, 1873; d. May 25, 1883.
7. ALICE M. Earle), b. Jan. 14, 1876.
8. SARAH MARGARET (Earle), b. Jan. 12, 1877; d. June 1, 1879.
9. GRACE (Earle), b. Jan. 17, 1879.
10. FLORANCE A. (Earle), b. Jan. 1, 1880.
11. GEORGE M. (Earle), b. Jan. 15, 1882.

1363. JOHN F. WARD CRANE[7] [840], (John,[6] Matthias,[5] John,[4] Matthias,[3] John,[2] Stephen[1]), served in the late war, from April, 1861, to Nov., 1865, on the Union side. Married in Newark, N. J., Nov. 14, 1860, Mary E. Inslee, who was born Jan. 29, 1837, in Paterson, N. J. For many years was an accountant with residence in Newark. Child:

1364—1. WILLIAM HALL, b. Nov. 14, 1861.

1365. ALFRED W. B. CRANE[7] [842], (John,[6] Matthias,[5] John,[4] Matthias,[3] John,[2] Stephen[1]), served in the late war, in 2d N.

J. Vols., 1861 to 1862, principally in Virginia. Married in
Newark, N. J., Nov. 23, 1864, Sarah Matilda Matlock. She
was born Dec. 5, 1842, and died Nov. 26, 1866. He then
married 2d, Nov. 4, 1868, Margaret Elizabeth M. Stoy, a
native of Philadelphia, Pa. He is a dentist. Residence,
Newark. Children :

1366—1. JOHN H., b. Aug. 23, 1865.
1367—2. EDITH FOWLE, b. Jan. 1, 1870.
1368—3. FRANK MURRAY, b. Jan. 7, 1872.

1369. FRANCIS E. S. CRANE[7] [843], (John,[6] Matthias,[5] John,[4]
Matthias,[3] John,[2] Stephen[1]), was born in Newark, N. J., and
married there Dec. 22, 1870. Abby E. Dennis, who was born
there, Jan. 2, 1847. He is a machinist. Children :

1370—1. WILLIAM BARNET, b. Feb. 4, 1874.
1371—2. FRANCIS ELLSWORTH, b. Jan. 16, 1876.

1372. ABRAHAM CRANE[7] [882], (Isaac,[6] Norris,[5] Benjamin,[4]
Benjamin,[3] John,[2] Stephen[1]), married Margaret Ayres, daughter
of Richard, of Long Hill, N. J. Children :

1373—1. GEORGE.
1374—2. ABRAHAM, } twins.
1375—3. MARGARET, }
1376—4. JOANNA.
1377—5. RICHARD.
1378—6. WILLIAM.
        Son, } twins.
        Daughter, }

1379. WILLIAM CRANE[7] [883], (Isaac,[6] Norris,[5] Benjamin,[4]
Benjamin,[3] John,[2] Stephen[1]), married May 28, 1849, Mary Cole,
daughter of Elias, of Scotch Plains, N. J. Child :

1380—1. CORNELIUS.

1381. JOHN OGDEN CRANE[7] [898], (Benjamin,[6] Norris,[5] Ben-
jamin,[4] Benjamin,[3] John,[2] Stephen[1]), married Mary Fletcher
Searing. He was a farmer, and lived near Green Village, N. J.
His wife died about 1873, leaving two children. Children :

1382—1. ELLA.
1383—2. HARRY.

1384. SINEUS B. CRANE[7] [900], [Benjamin,[6] Norris,[5] Benjamin,[4] Benjamin,[3] John,[2] Stephen[1]), married in New Vernon,
Morris Co., N. J., Dec. 9, 1856, Caroline M. Mills. She was
born in that place, Oct. 6, 1835. Their eldest child was born in
Green Village; the second one in New Vernon. They then
removed to Berwick, Warren Co., Ill., but in 1865, they settled
in Roseville, where they have since remained. Children :

1385—1. AUGUSTA MATILDA, b. Jan. 1, 1858.
1386—2. JOSEPH HALSTEAD, b. Aug. 25, 1859.
1387—3. ALFRED MILLS, b. Jan. 27, 1862.
1388—4. FRANK LEWIS, b. May 4, 1863.
1389—5. ELIPHALET COOPER, b. Nov. 17, 1865.
1390—6. LUELLA CAROLINE, b. July 3, 1869.

1391—7. JULIA, b. Oct. 17, 1871.
1392—8. HENRY MILLS, b. Dec. 27, 1873.
1393—9. SARAH, b. March 28, 1876.
1394-10. SINEUS BEBOUT, b. Sept. 25, 1879.

1395. SARAH JANE CRANE[7] [901], (Benjamin,[6] Norris,[5] Benjamin,[4] Benjamin,[3] John,[2] Stephen[1]), married Oscar Lindsley, a farmer; resides near Green Village, N. J. Children:

1. DEWITT CLINTON (Lindsley).
2. JULIA (Lindsley).
3. HERBERT (Lindsley); d. in childhood.
4. HARRIET (Lindsley).
5. MARY AUGUSTA (Lindsley).

1396. WILLIAM WATROUS CRANE[7] [912], (William W.,[6] David D.,[5] Eleazer,[4] Benjamin,[3] John,[2] Stephen[1]), married in San Francisco, Cal., Nov. 29, 1856, Hannah S. Austin. He is an attorney-at-law, and resides in that city (Nov., 1881). Child:

1397—1. MARY NANCY; m. June 10, 1884, Horace Potter Hussey. Children:
    1. EVELYNE (Hussey), b. March 21, 1885.
    2. JOSEPH G. (Hussey), b. April 9, 1886; d. Aug. 11, 1886.
    3. Son (Hussey), b. March 1, 1893; d. March 2, 1893.
    4. AUSTIN CRANE (Hussey), b. Aug. 1, 1896.

1398. ALFRED CAMPBELL CRANE[7] [915], (William W.,[6] David D.,[5] Eleazer,[4] Benjamin,[3] John,[2] Stephen[1]), married Feb. 7, 1866, Sophy Cass Hall. He died May 19, 1893. She died Oct. 14, 1898. Children:

1399—1. LEONARD ALFRED, b. Jan. 14, 1868.
1400—2. CATHARINE MCALPINE, b. June 7, 1870.
1401—3. FRANK HALL, b. Feb. 8, 1875.

1402. ANN MARIA CRANE[7] [917], (William W.,[6] David D.,[5] Eleazer,[4] Benjamin,[3] John,[2] Stephen[1]), married Oct. 8, 1862, Walsingham A. Miller. He was born April 10, 1840. She died May 21, 1882. Child:

1. LILLIE COX (Miller), b. Dec. 24, 1863; d. Aug. 28, 1864.

1403. HAROLD LESLIE CRANE[7] [920], (William W.,[6] David D.,[5] Eleazer,[4] Benjamin,[3] John,[2] Stephen[1]), married Dec. 3, 1867, Elsie Elizabeth Dillon. She was born Feb. 8, 1841, and was a daughter of Robert and Charlotte Matilda (Lyon) Dillon, of New York. Mr. Crane is an importer. Children:

1404—1. ROBERT DILLON, b. Jan. 9, 1869; m. April 11, 1893, Annie Edna Walton, b. Sept. 1, 1870.
1405—2. WILLIAM WATROUS, b. Oct. 1, 1873.

1406. STEPHEN CRANE[7] [931], (William M.,[6] Stephen,[5] James,[4] James,[3] Jeremiah,[2] Stephen[1]), married Calista Johnson, at Ansonia, Conn., Oct. 4, 1853. He was by trade a clock maker; was a soldier in the civil war; served in the 3d,

Conn. regiment, returning Sept., 1864; was policeman in Ansonia, 1870 to 1881. She was born in Seymour, Conn., Dec. 2, 1836. Children:

1407—1. F. S.
1408—2. A. F.
1409—3. CALISTA JANE.
1410—4. LESLIE D.
1411—5. WILLIE A.
1412—6. LOUIE L.
1413—7. FRANK E.

1414. THEODORE T. CRANE[7] [959], (Richard T.,[6] William,[5] Joseph,[4] Stephen,[3] Daniel,[2] Stephen[1]), married in Flemington, N. J., Aug. 31, 1861, Ruth E. Thatcher, of Everittstown, where she was born, Nov. 22, 1840. She died Aug. 24, 1891, at Clarksboro. Mr. Crane is a local preacher of the Methodist Episcopal Church, and a teacher of music; residence, Camden, N. J. He married 2d, June 24, 1896, Henrietta Dod Miller. Children:

1415—1. HELEN ELIZABETH, b. June 27, 1863.
1416—2. CHARLES THATCHER, b. Feb. 23, 1866; m. Marie Cheeseman, Sept. 2, 1896.

1417. FREDERIC WILLARD CURTIS CRANE[7] [960], (Richard T.,[6] William,[5] Joseph,[4] Stephen,[3] Daniel,[2] Stephen[1]), served in the late war, in Pennsylvania, 1864. Married 1st, June 28, 1866, Hattie Ricker, at Newark, N. J. She died Nov. 10, 1868, and he married 2d, at Lyons Farms, N. J., Oct. 18, 1870, Phebe Townley Dod, who was born in Newark, Oct. 10, 1841. They reside at Lyons Farms, where he is an accountant; also elder in the Presbyterian Church. Children:

1418—1. LAURA DOD, b. Dec. 4, 1871; d. Dec. 24, 1873.
1419—2. JESSIE FLORENCE, b. May 3, 1873; d. Aug. 23, 1876.
1420—3. RAYMOND TOWNLEY. b. May 31, 1875.
1421—4. ARTHUR DOD, b. Sept. 7, 1877.
1422—5. CLARENCE BROWN, } twins, b. April {
1423—6. WILLARD WARD, }   9, 1879; { d. Aug. 11, 1879.

1424. ELI CRANE[7] [982], (Leonard W.,[6] David,[5] Joseph,[4] Stephen,[3] Daniel,[2] Stephen[1]), was born in Cass Co., Mich.; married in Malvern, Ia., Sept. 12, 1882, Phidelia A. Darling. She was born in Malvern, June 17, 1858. He is a carpenter; residence, Hawarden, Sioux Co., Ia. Child:

1425—1. HATTIE W., b. Sept. 1, 1883.

1426. WILLIAM FULLERTON CRANE[7] [1012], (William F.,[6] Philip,[5] David,[4] David,[3] Daniel,[2] Stephen[1]), was born in Kent Co., Md.: enlisted Sept. 20, 1861, in Co. K, 8th Reg., Pa. V. Cav., 2d Brigade, 2d Div. Cav. Corps, at the age of sixteen. He was in the battles of Chancellorsville, May 1–4, 1863; Smithville, July 5; Boonsborough, July 8; Jones Cross Roads, July 10; Sulphur Springs, Oct. 11, 1863; Bethesda Church, June 2, 1864; Gains Mills, June 3, 1864; orderly to Gen. Wright, June,

1864, 6th A. C.; Aug., 1864, corps standard bearer; captured
Sept. 28, 1864, at battle of Hatchers Run, Va., and held a
prisoner of war at Salisbury, N. C., five months; promoted
to sergeant, June, 1865; discharged Aug. 11, 1865, at Richmond, Va. He was married Nov. 4, 1872, to Alice M. Green, at
Washington, D. C., by Rev. John C. Smith. He died in Kansas
City, Mo., May 13, 1890. Children:

1427—1. GERTRUDE ELEANORE, b. Oct. 3, 1877, at Albuquerque,
   N. M.
1428—2. ALICE LOUISE, b. Feb. 4, 1879, at Albuquerque, N. M.
1429—3. WILLIAM LUCIOUS, b. May 31, 1886, at Albuquerque, N. M.

1430. LIZZIE WEER CRANE[7] [1013], (William F.,[6] Philip,[5]
David,[4] David,[3] Daniel,[2] Stephen[1]), was married to Isaac B. Ruff,
in Washington, D. C., by Rev. John C. Smith, Jan. 3, 1871.
Children:

 1. RENA GENEVIEVE (Ruff), b. March 10, 1873, at Washington,
   D. C.
 2. GRACE EDNA (Ruff), b. June 16, 1876, at Laurel, Md.
 3. FLORENCE GENEVA (Ruff), b. Aug. 23, 1882, at Laurel, Md.

1431. RENA GENEVIEVE RUFF [1]; m. Oct. 3, 1893, Frank H. Knowlton, at Laurel, Md., by Rev. Jas. Nicols. Child:
   1. LESTER (Knowlton), b. Aug. 13, 1894, at Washington,
    D. C.

1432. STEPHEN M. CRANE[7] [1020], (Stephen M.,[6] Jonathan,[5]
David,[4] David,[3] Daniel,[2] Stephen[1]), married Mary J. Dobler,
Oct. 29, 1890; lives in Baltimore, Md.; served in the Union
army during the civil war. Children:

1433—1. MARY D.
1434—2. STEPHEN.
1435—3. JOHN MORRIS.
1436—4. AMY HICKS.

1437. THOMAS HENRY CRANE[7] [1021], (Stephen M.,[6] Jonathan,[5] David,[4] David,[3] Daniel,[2] Stephen[1]), married 1863, Annie
E. Hickman, of Virginia. He served in the Union Army during
the civil war. Children:

1438—1. MOLLIE; d. young.
1439—2. STEPHEN R.; d. young.
1440—3. WILLIAM FULLER; living in Baltimore, Md.

1441. JOHN GILES CRANE[7] [1022], (Stephen M.,[6] Jonathan,[5]
David,[4] David,[3] Daniel,[2] Stephen[1]), was born near Church Hill,
Queen Anne Co., Md. At the age of seven years, he went to
live with a cousin, Nathaniel Meginnis, in Kent Co., Md. He
married in 1873, Miss M. L. Moffett, a native of Kent County.
He served in the Union army during the civil war. He came out
of the army broken in health, and has been an invalid many
years; resides in Baltimore, Md. Children:

1442—1. WILLIAM M.
1443—2. WALTER M.
1444—3. CHARLES P.

1445—4. BERTHA, b. 1880.
1446--5. ALICE MAY, b. 1891.
———; d. in infancy.

1447. HARRIET AUGUSTA CRANE[7] [1038], (Thomas H.,[6] Jonathan,[5] David,[4] David,[3] Daniel,[2] Stephen[1]), married June 8, 1892, William S. Collins. She died May 27, 1893. Child:

1. HARRIET CRANE (Collins), b. May 14, 1893.

1448. THEODORE DRAKE CRANE[7] [1042], (David,[6] Andrew D.,[5] David,[4] Nathaniel,[3] Nathaniel,[2] Stephen[1]), married in New Albany, Ind., June 4, 1863, Carrie Edwards; resides at present (Jan., 1897), in Louisville, Ky. Child:

1449—1. CHESTER A.

1450. ELIZABETH JANE LEE CRANE[7] [1044], (David,[6] Andrew D.,[5] David,[4] Nathaniel,[3] Nathaniel,[2] Stephen[1]), was born in New Albany, Ind., and married at that place, April 25, 1857, John Eugene Crane, son of Curtis, and a lineal descendant in the seventh generation from Benjamin Crane, of Wethersfield, Conn. (See page 191). Children:

1. LOTTIE STEWART, b. Sept. 11, 1858.
2. NANNIE MONTGOMERY, b. June 28, 1861.
3. JESSIE BROWN, b. Sept. 21, 1863; d. Aug. 4, 1864.
4. LOUISE BARNEY, b. Jan. 2, 1866.
5. JENNIE LEE, b. Dec. 16, 1868.
6. STELLA BROWN, b. March 29, 1872.

1451. ELIAS FLAVEL CRANE[7] [1045], (David,[6] Andrew D.,[5] David,[4] Nathaniel,[3] Nathaniel,[2] Stephen[1]), was born in New Albany, Ind.; married Sophia Angel, Feb. 23, 1870, in Delavan, Ill., where the widow now (1897) resides. He died in Mason City, Ill., May 6, 1872. Child:

1452—1. LOTTIE ANGEL, b. in Mason, Ill.

1453. LEWIS STEWART CRANE[7] [1046], (David,[6] Andrew D.,[5] David,[4] Nathaniel,[3] Nathaniel,[2] Stephen[1]), married May 14, 1872, Anna Catharine Ragner, and settled in New Albany, Ind. Children:

1454—1. HARRIE.
1455—2. STEWART.

1456. WILLIAM EDGAR CRANE[7] [1048], (David,[6] Andrew D.,[5] David,[4] Nathaniel,[3] Nathaniel,[2] Stephen[1]), married Oct. 23, 1869, Carrie E. Walch, at Mt. Sterling, Ill., where the family reside. Mrs. Crane died July 7, 1895. Children:

1457—1. JESSE HOLMES, b. Oct. 23, 1870.
1458—2. LEWIS YATES, b. Feb. 15, 1877; d. Feb. 23, 1880.
1459—3. EDGAR LEON, b. Oct. 3, 1879.

1460. DAVID HENRY CRANE[7] [1049], (David,[6] Andrew D.,[5] David,[4] Nathaniel,[3] Nathaniel,[2] Stephen[1]), married in Chicago, Ill., Jan. 16, 1873, Anna M. Nelson. Child:

1461—1. KATHARINE.
55

1462. FREDERICK DRAKE CRANE[7] [1051], (Elias F.,[6] Andrew D.,[5] David,[4] Nathaniel,[3] Nathaniel,[2] Stephen[1]), married in Rushville, Ill., Feb. 28, 1867, Adelaide Wells. She was a native of that place. She was born in 1844. He resides at Mt. Sterling, where he is a merchant. Children:

1463—1. FRANK WELLS.
1464—2. LEWIS BURTON.
1465—3. FREDERIC PRIEST; d. Aug., 1873.
1466—4. KATE PRIEST.
1467—5. JAMES L.
1468—6. ADELAIDE EDITH.

1469. ELIZABETH CLARK CRANE[7] [1053], (Jeremiah B.,[6] Isaac,[5] Caleb,[4] Caleb,[3] Nathaniel,[2] Stephen[1]), married George C. Haswell, July 17, 1855, and removed to California. Child:

1. GRACE HEDGES (Haswell).

1470. ISAAC ARNETT CRANE[7] [1058], (Jonathan E.,[6] Isaac,[5] Caleb,[4] Caleb,[3] Nathaniel,[2] Stephen[1]), married Oct. 21, 1847, Sarah, daughter of John Duncan, of Evansville. She was born May 16, 1831. Children:

1471—1. MARY THOMPSON, b. March 22, 1849; m. William Bogart at New York, Dec. 9, 1870.
1472—2. ANNIE DUNCAN, b. July 19, 1856; d. Nov. 22, 1861.

1473. ELIAS OGDEN CRANE[7] [1059], (Jonathan E.,[6] Isaac,[5] Caleb,[4] Caleb,[3] Nathaniel,[2] Stephen[1]), married Sept. 6, 1843, Eliza Ann, daughter of Peter Hueston, of Newark, N. J. She was born June 12, 1827. Removed in 1866 to Kansas. Children:

1474—1. PETER HUESTON, b. Oct. 20, 1844.
1475—2. LAURENT, b. Oct. 5, 1858.

1476. JOSEPH TOOKER CRANE[7] [1060], (Jonathan E.,[6] Isaac,[5] Caleb,[4] Caleb,[3] Nathaniel,[2] Stephen[1]), married July 3, 1847, Rachel, daughter of Stewart Crowell, of Rahway. She was born Aug. 7, 1825. Children:

1477—1. MARY T., b. Oct. 25, 1848; d. Sept. 27, 1857.
1478—2. LAURA FRANCES b. April 20, 1852; d. Jan. 25, 1857.
1479—3. WILLIAM, b. Nov. 7, 1854.
1480—4. LOUIS FRANK, b. April 2, 1857.
1481—5. ALONZO, b. May 24, 1860.
1482—6. CHARLES, b. Dec. 10, 1862.
1483—7. STEWART, b. Nov. 18, 1865.

1484. JONATHAN THOMPSON CRANE[7] [1062], (Jonathan E.,[6] Isaac,[5] Caleb,[4] Caleb,[3] Nathaniel,[2] Stephen[1]), married Aug. 30, 1846, Hannah, daughter of William Runyon. She was born March 8, 1828. Child:

1485—1. ABENETHY, b. Jan. 17, 1852.

1486. HANNAH ROY CRANE[7] [1070], (Elias W.,[6] Noah,[5] Jacob,[4] Caleb,[3] Nathaniel,[2] Stephen[1]), born at Springfield, N. J. Married Jan. 22, 1841, John Aster Gunn at Jamaica, L.

I., N. Y. She died Aug. 3, 1850. He died May 22, 1877.
Children :

1. MARGARETTA LOUISA (Gunn), b. Sept. 10, 1842; d. Aug. 13, 1877.
2. MARTHA WINANS (Gunn), b. May 6, 1844; d. Aug. 19, 1844.
3. AMELIA (Gunn), b. July 19, 1846; d. Sept. 5, 1847.
4. MARY ANTONETTE (Gunn), b. Nov. 1, 1848; d. July 17, 1849.
5. EDWARD EARL (Gunn), b. April 15, 1850; d. Aug. 3, 1850.

1487. MARTHA WINANS CRANE[7] [1071], (Elias W.,[6] Noah,[5]
Jacob,[4] Caleb,[3] Nathaniel,[2] Stephen[1]), born in Springfield, N. J.
Married Oct. 6, 1847, in New York city, Henry N. Beach, Esq.
She died at Orange, N. J., June 29, 1874.   Children :

1. CAROLINE BRINSMADE (Beach), b. July 27, 1849, in Jamaica, L.
   I., N. Y.
2. GERTRUDE RICHARDS (Beach), b. March 1, 1851, in New York
   city; d. Feb. 26, 1856.
   . HENRY CRANE (Beach), b. Nov. 28, 1852, in New York city.
4. LOUISA JOHNSON (Beach), b. July 15, 1854, in New York city;
   d. June 3, 1855.
5. FRANCES JANNIE (Beach), b. Oct. 14, 1855, in New York city.
6. ANNA JOSEPHINE (Beach), b. June 17, 1862.
7. MARGARET ELIZABETH (Beach), b. Feb. 15, 1864, at Orange, N.
   J.; d. Dec. 3, 1865.

1488. DELINDA HOPKINS CRANE[7] [1072], (Elias W.,[6] Noah,[5]
Jacob,[4] Caleb,[3] Nathaniel,[2] Stephen[1]), born in Springfield, N.
J.   Married May 9, 1849, Jeremiah Ross at Elizabethtown, N.
J.   She died there May 10, 1855.   Child :

1. HENRY CRANE (Ross), b. Sept. 26, 1854. He is a lawyer; residence at Elizabethtown, N. J.

1489. Rev. ELIAS NETTLETON CRANE[7] [1074], (Elias W.,[6]
Noah,[5] Jacob,[4] Caleb,[3] Nathaniel,[2] Stephen[1]), born at Jamaica,
L. I., N. Y.   Graduated at College of New Jersey, Princeton,
in 1852, and from the Theological Seminary there in 1855, and,
following in the footsteps of his father, became a Presbyterian
minister, and was pastor of the church at New Vernon, N. J.,
from 1856 to 1862.   During the latter year he was chaplain in the
175th Regt., New York Vols.; United States Christian commission agent for eastern Virginia from Sept., 1863, to July, 1865;
for many years seaman's chaplain at Norfolk, Va., commissioned by the American Seaman's Friend Society, Aug. 1, 1865.
He married April 21, 1864, at Plainfield, N. J., Mary Elizabeth
Pruden ; born Aug. 27, 1829. She was a native of New Vernon.
He died May 27, 1895.   Children, all born in Norfolk :

1490—1. WILLIAM LINCOLN, b. Oct. 17, 1866; d. Dec. 13, 1866.
1491—2. CHARLES IRA, b. Jan. 30, 1868; d. July 31, 1868.
1492—3. VIRGINIA MAY, b. May 3, 1869; d. May 4, 1869.

1493. JAMES LOVETT CRANE[7] [1076], (Elias W.,[6] Noah,[5]
Jacob,[4] Caleb,[3] Nathaniel,[2] Stephen[1]), born at Jamaica, L. I.,
N. Y.   Married 1st, Jane Amanda, daughter of James H.
Reeves, of Jamaica, L. I., N. Y., in 1857. She died. He

married 2d, Feb. 6, 1862, Mary Reed Alexander, of Williamsburgh, L. I. He died Feb. 12, 1896. Children:

1494—1. JAMES RITCHIE, b. Dec. 21, 1862.
1495—2. JOHN McDOWELL, b. Feb. 14, 1867.
1496—3. CHARLES HARRINGTON, b. April 15, 1869; m. Caroline Smith; d. Nov. 15, 1894.
1497—4. CAROLINE BROWN, b. Sept. 2, 1873.
1498—5. HARRIET SEABURY, b. Jan. 3, 1877.
1499—6. ALEXANDER STEPHEN, b. Jan. 2, 1879.

1500. JOHN McDOWELL CRANE[7] [1077], (Elias W.,[6] Noah.[5] Jacob,[4] Caleb,[3] Nathaniel,[2] Stephen[1]), born at Jamaica, L. I., N. Y. Married May 7, 1861, Harriet, daughter of John Seabury, of Jamaica, and settled there. For many years he was cashier of the National Shoe and Leather Bank, located at 271 Broadway, corner of Chambers Street, New York city, and for several years was president of the village of Jamaica. Feb. 1, 1883, he was elected president of the Bank where he had served so long and faithfully, and has been honored by a reëlection from that time forward, and still (1897) holds that position of great responsibility. Children:

1501—1. ALDEN SEABURY, b. March 23, 1862.
1502—2. WARREN SEABURY, b. June 10, 1866.

1503. ELIAS W. CRANE[7] [1103], (Joseph W.,[6] Nehemiah,[5] Jacob,[4] Caleb,[3] Nathaniel,[2] Stephen[1]), born in Rochester, N. Y. Married at West Sand Lake, Sept. 8, 1878, Charlotte Schlenk, and settled in Rochester; a contractor and builder. She was born in New York city Nov. 30, 1854. Child:

1504—1. GEORGE W., b. July 26, 1879.

1505. JOB CLARK CRANE[7] [1110], (William W.,[6] Job,[5] Nathaniel,[4] Caleb,[3] Nathaniel,[2] Stephen[1]), married Florence W. Langdon, May 3, 1876. Children:

1506—1. ELSIE LANGDON, b. April 23, 1877.
1507—2. NELLIE CLARK, b. May 23, 1879.
1508—3. MARJORIE IVES, b. Feb. 8, 1886.
1509—4. CHARLES WILLIAM, b. Oct. 25, 1887.

1510. MARY JANE CRANE[7] [1111], (William W.,[6] Job,[5] Nathaniel,[4] Caleb,[3] Nathaniel,[2] Stephen[1]), married Nov. 6, 1878, Campbell Hedge. Children:

1. MABEL LEA (Hedge), b. Aug. 20, 1885.
2. EDITH (Hedge), b. Dec. 23, 1887.

1511. AUGUSTUS STOUT CRANE[7] [1114], (William W.,[6] Job,[5] Nathaniel,[4] Caleb,[3] Nathaniel,[2] Stephen[1]), married Oct. 4, 1882, Minerva Carlisle Lea, daughter of Gabriel M. and Phœbe S. Lea. She was born July 11, 1860. Mr. Crane published in the year 1874 a pamphlet containing a very brief genealogical record of some of the descendants of Stephen Crane, of Elizabethtown. The writer has enjoyed the benefit of that little volume, which brought so much pleasure to many of those descendants,

and is greatly indebted, not only to the publisher, but to all those who assisted him in that work. Children :

1512—1. ROY AUGUSTUS, b. Aug. 14, 1883; d. Aug. 21, 1884.
1513—2. ETHEL MINERVA, b. April 23, 1886; d. Dec. 28, 1892.
1514—3. FREDERICK LEA, b. Feb. 12, 1888.
1515—4. HELEN CLARK. b. March 20, 1889.
1516—5. RALPH WILLIAM AUGUSTUS, b. Feb. 6, 1897.

1517. CALVIN DENNISON CRANE[7] [1130], (William M.,[6] Noah,[5] Noah,[4] Moses,[3] Nathaniel,[2] Stephen[1]), married Oct. 22, 1863, Carrie Rosa Kroff. She died May 4, 1897. Mr. Crane has made his home in Dayton, Ohio, although of late years he has passed some time in Missouri and Oklahoma Territory. He is a surveyor, teacher, inventor and author. Children :

1518—1. CORLESTA CARRIE, b. June 23. 1865, at Shelby County, Ind.;
m. ——— Hodges. Children: DAISY and MARION.
1519—2. CALVIN DENNISON, b. Aug. 9, 1867; residence at Aguas Calientes, Mex.
1520—3. HALIE MAE, b. Jan. 25, 1872; residence at Cascade, Col.

1521. WILLIAM METCALF CRANE[7] [1134], (William M.,[6] Noah,[5] Noah,[4] Moses,[3] Nathaniel,[2] Stephen[1]), married at Fort Wayne, Ind., June 14, 1881, Inez May Reid. She was born at that place Dec. 21, 1855, and settled at Albia, Iowa, where their children were born. Children :

1522—1. REID ISAAC, b. April 2, 1883.
1523—2. WILLIAM METCALF, b. May 8, 1885.
1524—3. INEZ MAY, b. March 27, 1887.
1525—4. LOUISA MATILDA, b. Sept. 2, 1888.
1526—5. CARLE HODGES, b. Oct. 11, 1890.
1527—6. CALVIN DENNISON, b. Nov. 4, 1892; d. Dec. 17, 1892.

1528. SARAH LOUISA CRANE[8] [1168], (John G.,[7] Josiah,[6] John,[5] John,[4] John,[3] John,[2] Stephen[1]), married James C. Runyon, and settled in Middletown, N. Y. Children :

1 IDA C. (Runyon).
2. JOHN G. (Runyon) ; m. and has one child, FRANCIS.

1529. MARY ELIZABETH CRANE[8] [1169], (John G.,[7] Josiah,[6] John,[5] John,[4] John,[3] John,[2] Stephen[1]), married Jessie P. Woodruff. He died ; widow lives in Jamaica, L. I., N. Y. Children :

1. FRED P. (Woodruff) ; m. ———. Children :
    1. KENNETH (Woodruff).
    2. FRED (Woodruff).
2 MARY (Woodruff).

1530. WILLARD GRANT CRANE[8] [1171], (John G.,[7] Josiah,[6] John,[5] John,[4] John,[3] John,[2] Stephen[1]), married in 1868, Charlotte Melissa Stapleton, of Hillier, Canada. He is a chemist and perfumer, manufacturer of soap, soap powder, etc. ; residence, Auburn. N. Y. Children :

1531—1. BERT WILLFRED, b. Nov. 2, 1869, at Geneseo, Ill.
1532—2. BESSIE WINIFRED, b. June 22, 1877, at Cranford, N. J.

1533. JOHN CHANCELOR CRANE[8] [1172], (John G.,[7] Josiah,[6] John,[5] John,[4] John,[3] John,[2] Stephen[1]), married Sarah Crane, of Cranford, N. J , daughter of William. Children :

1534—1. FANNY E.
1535—2. GRACE L.

1536. JAMES WALACE CRANE[8] [1173], (John G.,[7] Josiah,[6] John,[5] John,[4] John,[3] John,[2] Stephen[1]), married Emma Miller ; residence, Elizabeth, N. J. Child :

1537—1. WALACE M.

1538. JOHN MORRIS CRANE[8] [1182], (Smith,[7] John,[6] Samuel,[5] Joseph,[4] John,[3] John,[2] Stephen[1]), married Margaret Barker Wardwell, of Swampscott, Mass., Oct. 3, 1883, at Mexico, Mo. ; residence, Kingwood, W. Va. Mr. Crane has given special attention to collecting data for his immediate family, and has rendered great assistance to the writer. Child :

1539 —1. STANHOPE ORDWAY, b. April 2, 1886.

1540. VIRGINIA CRANE[8] [1187], (Samuel,[7] John,[6] Samuel,[5] Joseph,[4] John,[3] John,[2] Stephen[1]), married David S. Livengood, Oct. 9, 1873. Children :

1. ALDINE KEEFER (Livengood), b. Oct. 27, 1874.
2. SAMUEL WILBERT (Livengood), b. Aug. 13, 1876.
3. EFFA ESTELLA (Livengood), b. June 7, 1879.
4. THEODOSIA (Livengood), b. Feb. 7, 1882.
5. IDA MEDELLA (Livengood), b. May 2, 1883.
6. GIRTIE MAY (Livengood), b. April 5, 1887.
7. GEORGIA ANNA (Livengood), b. Feb. 26, 1891.
8. CHESTER (Livengood), b. Jan. 15, 1893.
9. ICY BLANCH (Livengood), b. April 1, 1895.
10. MARY ESTHER (Livengood), b. June 9, 1898.

1541. WINFIELD SCOTT CRANE[8] [1191], (Samuel,[7] John,[6] Samuel,[5] Joseph,[4] John,[3] John,[2] Stephen[1]), married Allitia May Feather, June 13, 1891. Children :

1542—1. DON, b. Jan. 23, 1892.
1543—2. GUY, b. Jan. 2, 1894.
1544—3. STANLEY, b. April 29, 1896.
1545—4. ZENITH FAY, b. April 15, 1898.

1546. MARSHALL ALLEN CRANE[8] [1198], (Elisha,[7] John,[6] Samuel,[5] Joseph,[4] John,[3] John,[2] Stephen[1]), married Clara Susan, daughter of Jno. M. and Martha S. Poorman, of Williamsville, Ill., April 6, 1876. Children :

1547—1. FLORA GRAYBILL, b. Aug. 21, 1877.
1548—2. JESSIE PALMER, b. Jan. 26, 1879.
1549—3. JOHN POORMAN, b. Nov. 12, 1880.
1550—4. SMITH, b. July 3, 1883.

1551. MARTHA ALICE CRANE[8] [1200], (Elisha,[7] John,[6] Samuel,[5] Joseph,[4] John,[3] John,[2] Stephen[1]), married Dec. 25, 1873, Harlan W. Sanford, b. June 25, 1847. Children :

1. MARSHALL CRANE (Sanford), b. Oct. 26, 1874; d. Nov. 20, 1893.
2. ELMER HARLAN (Sanford), b. Nov. 7, 1878.

1552. SILAS FULLER CRANE[8] [1219], (William B.,[7] Jacob,[6] Samuel,[5] Joseph,[4] John,[3] John,[2] Stephen[1]), married Isabelle May Brosius, Feb. 16, 1881. Residence, Parkersburg, W. Va. Children :

1553—1. WILLIAM BONNELL, b. Nov. 17, 1884.
1554—2. CHESTER HOWELL, b. Dec. 7, 1887; d. July 20, 1888.
1555—3. SILAS FULLER, b. Jan. 15, 1889.
1556—4. JOHN PAUL JONES, b. June 15, 1892.

1557. MARSHALL WELLINGTON CRANE[8] [1221], (William B.,[7] Jacob,[6] Samuel,[5] Joseph,[4] John,[3] John,[2] Stephen[1]), married Kate Townsend, of Oakland, Md., Dec. 1, 1886. He died Sept. 22, 1887. Child :

1558—1. MARSHALL WELLINGTON, b. Sept. 18, 1887.

1559. EUDORA CORNELIA CRANE[8] [1222], (William B.,[7] Jacob,[6] Samuel,[5] Joseph,[4] John,[3] John,[2] Stephen[1]), married

Frank Scott Riley, Oct. 16, 1878. She died Sept. 7, 1893. He died Feb. 8, 1898. Children:

1. WILLIAM HARRY (Riley), b. March 13, 1880; d. Oct. 28, 1880.
2. ADAH MAY (Riley), b. Aug. 3, 1881.
3. ALBERT LEE (Riley), b. Aug. 21, 1886.
4. JAMES CASSELL (Riley), b. Dec. 5, 1888; d. June 13, 1892.
5. FRANCES VIRGINIA (Riley), b. July 19, 1891; d. Oct. 23, 1891.

1560. CHARLES CRITTENDEN CRANE[8] [1227], (Samuel E.,[7] Jacob,[6] Samuel,[5] Joseph,[4] John,[3] John,[2] Stephen[1]), married June 21, 1882, at Chicago, Ill., Alice M. Buzzard, who was born at Elkhart City, Logan Co., Ill., Aug. 8, 1861. Residence, Aurora Springs, Mo. Children:

1561—1. ETHEL MAY, b. March 21, 1885.
1562—2. CHARLES MERREL, b. July 31, 1890.
1563—3. MABEL LEOTA, b. Sept. 16, 1893.
1564—4. SAMUEL ELLIOTT, b. Feb. 9, 1897.
1565—5. GRACE, b. and d. Jan. 26, 1888.

1566. BENJAMIN F. CRANE[8] [1244], (Samuel B.,[7] Calvin,[6] Samuel,[5] Joseph,[4] John,[3] John,[2] Stephen[1]), married Civilla C. White. Children:

1567—1. LLOYD W.
1568—2. ALMA A.
1569—3. LAWRENCE B.
1570—4. ROBERT L.; d. in infancy.
1571—5. DELLA M.
1572—6. LEO F.
1573—7. MAMIE F.; d. in infancy.
1574—8. WILMER L.

1575. THOMAS W. CRANE[8] [1245], (Samuel B.,[7] Calvin,[6] Samuel,[5] Joseph,[4] John.[3] John.[2] Stephen[1]), married Agnes Pospeshil. Children:

1576—1. FRANK.
1577—2. ALBERT.
1578—3. RUSSELL.

1579. JENNIE R. CRANE[8] [1246], (Samuel B.,[7] Calvin,[6] Samuel,[5] Joseph,[4] John,[3] John,[2] Stephen[1]), married James A. DeBerry. Children:

1. EFFIE; d., aged five years.
2. BESSIE; d., aged three years.
3. STANLEY E.
4. HAZEL R.

1580. CHARLES C. CRANE[8] [1247], (Samuel B.,[7] Calvin,[6] Samuel,[5] Joseph,[4] John,[3] John,[2] Stephen[1]), married Jennie Allen. Children:

1581—1. SAMUEL.
1582—2. DOROTHY.

1583. JARVIS D. CRANE[8] [1248], (Samuel B.,[7] Calvin,[6] Samuel,[5] Joseph,[4] John,[3] John,[2] Stephen[1]), married Elizabeth Berrier. Children:

1584—1. HARRY.

1585—2. RUTH.
1586—3. JAY.
1587—4. MAY.

1588. JOHN C. CRANE[8] [1249], (Samuel B.,[7] Calvin,[6] Samuel,[5] Joseph,[4] John,[3] John,[2] Stephen[1]), married Elizabeth C. Wright. Children:

1589—1. CLARENCE G.
1590—2. LAURA P.

1591. CLAY CRANE[8] [1260], (Martin L.,[7] Calvin,[6] Samuel,[5] Joseph,[4] John,[3] John,[2] Stephen[1]), married June 5, 1889, Arette May Conner. She was born July 5, 1871. Children:

1592—1. GAY ELKINS, b. March 13, 1892.
1593—2. DOLPHA ALBERT, b. June 3, 1896.

1594. GREELY CRANE[8] [1262], (Martin L.,[7] Calvin,[6] Samuel,[5] Joseph,[4] John,[3] John,[2] Stephen[1]), married March 27, 1895, Mollie A. Feather. She was born Jan. 7, 1874. Child:

1595—1. DANIA, b. Oct. 15, 1896.

1596. DEE CRANE[8] [1265], (John C.,[7] Calvin,[6] Samuel,[5] Joseph,[4] John,[3] John,[2] Stephen[1]), married June 7, 1889, Annie Forman. She was born July 17, 1865. Children:

1597—1. HARLEY L., b. March 31, 1891.
1598—2. NINA H., b. Dec. 5, 1892.
1599—3. MARGERY N., b. June 10, 1896.

1600. CLOYD MOUNTAIN CRANE[8] [1266], (John C.,[7] Calvin,[6] Samuel,[5] Joseph,[4] John,[3] John,[2] Stephen[1]), married Oct. 16, 1891, Lona M. Feather. She was born March 13, 1868. Children:

1601—1. JESSIE, b. Nov. 1, 1893.
1602—2. MARY WILLARD, b. Aug. 22, 1897.

1603. GERTRUDE AMELIA CRANE[8] [1290], (Stephen S.,[7] William,[6] Stephen,[5] Jacob,[4] Matthias,[3] John,[2] Stephen[1]), married Thomas L. Jewell. Children:

1. FREDERICK E. (Jewell), b. May 11, 1881.
2. SARAH ELIZABETH (Jewell), b. March 16, 1882.
3. THOMAS L. (Jewell), b. June 21, 1883.
4. EDGAR CRANE (Jewell), b. May 31, 1884; d. Sept. 30, 1884.
5. AMY LOUISA (Jewell). b. May 21, 1886.
6. RAYMOND ASHLAND (Jewell), b. May 26, 1887.
7. STEPHEN SQUIER (Jewell), b. Aug. 17, 1889.
8. BERTHA MAY (Jewell), b. Dec. 3, 1890.
9. HAROLD MALCOM (Jewell), b. June 18, 1892; d. July 30, 1892.
10. GERTY GLADES (Jewell), b. Sept. 28, 1893.
11. GEORGE ARTHUR (Jewell), b. Sept. 29, 1894.
12. ADA GRACE (Jewell), b. Oct. 30, 1895.
13. CHRISTIANA (Jewell), b. Oct. 16, 1897.
14. JESSEY BRIGG (Jewell), } twins, b. Nov. 22, 1898.
15. JOSEPH CRANE (Jewell), }

1604. EMMA LOUISA CRANE[8] [1291], (Stephen S.,[7] William,[6] Stephen,[5] Jacob,[4] Matthias,[3] John,[2] Stephen[1]), married Theodore Keeler, Jr.   Children :

1. GERTIE RUTH (Keeler), b. Dec. 7, 1888.
2. EDGAR HERBERT (Keeler), b. April 10. 1890.
3. EDNA ELIZABETH (Keeler), b. March 25, 1891.
4. MIRA ALACE (Keeler), b. July 20, 1893.
5. KENNETH JAMES (Keeler), b. April 16, 1897.
6. HENRY MALCOM (Keeler), b. Dec. 22, 1898.

1605. JOSEPH T. CRANE[8] [1294], (Stephen S.,[7] William,[6] Stephen,[5] Jacob,[4] Matthias,[3] John,[2] Stephen[1]), married Ida McFarland, June 29, 1897.   Child :

1606—1. JOSEPHINE McFARLAND, b. Nov. 30, 1898.

1607. WILLIAM AUGUSTUS CRANE[8] [1313], (Augustus B.,[7] Stephen,[6] Stephen,[5] Jacob,[4] Matthias,[3] John,[2] Stephen[1]), married Nov. 11, 1867, Laura T. Lathrop.   Children :

1608—1. LOUISA LOVINIA, b. July 16, 1868; m. Aug. 19, 1896, Marcus C. Wadmond.
1609—2. GEORGE AUSTIN, b. Feb. 7, 1870; m. March 30, 1897, Mable Barker.
1610—3. GENEVIVE. b. Dec. 7, 1871.
1611—4. CHARLES AUGUSTUS, b. Nov. 17, 1874.
1612—5. HERBERT WILBER, b. April 5, 1878.
1613—6. LUCY LUCINDA, b. Nov. 25, 1883; d. May 3, 1893.

1614. JAMES HENRY CRANE[8] [1314], (Augustus B.,[7] Stephen,[6] Stephen,[5] Jacob,[4] Matthias,[3] John,[2] Stephen[1]), married Jan. 15, 1873, Clara A. Cogswell.   She was born March 25, 1851.   Children :

1615—1. ORTON ALBERT, b. Oct. 31, 1873.
1616—2. ARCHER B., b. June 2, 1875.
1617—3. WALTER S., b. May 23, 1879.
1618—4. MERTON E., b. July 13, 1887.

1619. CATHARINE McALPINE CRANE[8] [1400], (Alfred C.,[7] William W.,[6] David D.,[5] Eleazer,[4] Benjamin,[3] John,[2] Stephen[1]), married Wallace R. Farrington, Oct. 26, 1896.   Child :

1. JOSEPH RIDER (Farrington), b. Oct. 15, 1897.

1620. ALDEN SEABURY CRANE[8] [1501], (John M.,[7] Elias W.,[6] Noah,[5] Jacob,[4] Caleb,[3] Nathaniel,[2] Stephen[1]), married Cornelia Deans Tucker, Sept. 5, 1893.   Children :

1621—1. HARRIET SEABURY, b. June 11, 1894.
1622—2. CORNELIA TUCKER, b. Jan. 11, 1896.

NINTH GENERATION.

1623. BERT WILLFRED CRANE[9] [1531], (Willard G.,[8] John G.,[7] Josiah,[6] John,[5] John,[4] John,[3] John,[2] Stephen[1]), married Henrietta Vicors, of Auburn, N. Y., where they reside.
Child :

1624—1. EARL HEWITT, b. Jan. 14, 1897.

1625. HERBERT WILBER CRANE[9] [1612], (William A.,[8] Augustus B.,[7] Stephen,[6] Stephen,[5] Jacob,[4] Matthias,[3] John,[2] Stephen[1]), married May 18, 1896, Mildred Ellerson or Edlerson.
Children :

1626—1. WILLIAM VERNON, } twins, b. Feb. 11, 1897.
1627—2. JAMES VICTOR,

ADDENDA.

In compiling records for this volume several families have been discovered that it was impossible to place with absolute certainty in either of the four main lines given in the body of the work; but that all records collected may be preserved and made available for future reference, they have been placed in this *addenda*, thus giving an opportunity for others to solve the problem.

There is reason for believing that this Thomas Crane went from Connecticut to New Hampshire, and that he was a descendant of Benjamin, of Wethersfield. We know that certain members of that family settled in that State, and in the County of Cheshire.

1. THOMAS CRANE, of Richmond, N. H., married in Winchester, N. H., Aug. 4, 1768, Sarah Barrus, daughter of Abraham Barrus, of Cumberland, where she was born Aug. 11, 1747. Probably Cumberland, R. I. They settled on lot No. 13. He died in Nova Scotia. She died in Richmond, N. H. Children:

  2—1. ABRAHAM.
  3—2. JAMES, b. Feb. 28, 1773.
  4—3. MARY (or POLLY), b. May 27.
  5—4. WILLIAM, b. Jan. 5.
  6—5. JOHN, b. Nov. 6, 1776.
  7—6. THOMAS, b. June 3.

8. ABRAHAM CRANE [2]; married Nancy Ingalls, and lived for some years in New Hampshire. He died in Madison County, N. Y., Sept., 1841. She died there March, 1831. Children:

  1. BROUGHTON. 2. IRA. 3. JAMES.
  9—4. WHEELER J., b. Feb. 13, 1806.
  5. MATILDA. 6. NANCY.

10. JAMES CRANE [3]; married in Richmond, N. H., March 3, 1800, Anna Archer. Lived in St. Johnsbury and Danville, Vt. Children:

  1. JAMES.
  11—2. CHARLES, b. July 6, 1819, in St. Johnsbury, Vt.
  3. GEORGE. 4. ABIGAIL; m. George Soper.

12. MARY CRANE [4]; married Solomon Gatwell (or Sartwell), and removed to Pennsylvania. Child:

  1. CORDELIA (Gatwell).

13. WILLIAM CRANE [5]; married in Richmond, N. H., April
20, 1800, Rhoda Aldrich. He lived in Dalton, N. H., where
four, at least, of his children were born. He was a cooper by
trade. He afterwards removed to Bethlehem, where he died
about 1824. She died 1861, aged 82. Children :

     1. MOSES, b. March 2, 1803.   2. PATTY, b. Aug. 2, 1805.
14—3. OTIS, b. April 17, 1807.
     4. VIANA, b. Aug. 2, 1809.
15—5. SARAH.
16—6. HUSEA.
17—7. MARTHA.
18—8. LAVINA.
19—9. ELIZA.
20—10. ALVIN.
21—11. OBED, b. Jan. 18, 1817.
    12. CORDELIA; d. in Lowell, 1845.

22. JOHN CRANE [6]; married in Richmond, N. H., Feb. 27,
1800, Linda (or Lyndia) Harris, born March 15, 1783, at
Richmond, N. H. Went from Richmond, and lived in Dalton,
N. H., in 1798, and was a school teacher for many years; also a
farmer. Elected member of the New Hampshire legislature
two years. He died in Dalton, Aug., 1848. She also died the
same month and year. Children :

23—1. NAHUM, b. Nov. 12, 1801.
    2. LYDIA, b. May 6, 1804; m. ——— Phillips; settled in Lunenburgh, Vt.
24—3. ONO, b. Nov. 26, 1806, in Whitefield, N. Y.
25—4. WILLIAM B., b. April 1, 1811, in West Concord, Vt.
26—5. LUKE H., b. April 2, 1817, in Plaistow, N. H.

27. THOMAS CRANE [7]; settled in Brookline, Vt., and had
one son, a minister, who was settled at Northampton, Mass. He
may have had other children; not been able to obtain any information from the family. Child :

28—1. Rev. D——— M———. He d. in Northampton, Mass.; m. Bathsheba
    Phillips, of Newfane, Vt. She was b. March 1, 1811.

29. Rev. WHEELER J. CRANE[3] [9]; studied at Hamilton Seminary, although, on account of poor health, he did not pursue a full
course. Married at Hamilton, N. Y., June 7, 1829, Miss A.
Biddell. She was born in Greenfield, Saratoga Co., N. Y.,
March 30, 1806. Mr. Crane served a long and useful life as a
Baptist minister; preached in Cayuga County, N. Y., and Genesee County. April, 1879, he was living in Bergen, and had then
been a Baptist minister fifty years. Children :

30—1. CHARLES, b. July 10, 1831; m. in Indiana, May 12, 1856; d. Feb. 9,
    1868.
31—2. Rev. CEPHAS BENNETT, b. March 28, 1833. Graduate of Rochester
    University in 1858; from Theological Seminary in 1860. Was
    pastor of the South Baptist Church, Hartford, Conn., nearly
    eighteen years, and for many years pastor of the First Baptist
    Church, Boston, Mass. A strong, vigorous preacher, and
    greatly beloved by his people. He married in Hartford, Conn.,
    Nov., 1865.
32—3. FRANK W., b. Dec. 25, 1835; m. in Genesee County, N. Y., Dec. 23,
    1861. He is a physician; graduate of Buffalo Medical College in
    1865.

33. CHARLES CRANE [11]; married Mary Fiske. She was born July 13, 1820, in Guildhall, Vt. Settled in Danville, Vt., where all his children were born. Children:

1. JOHN, b. Sept. 27, 1843. 2. CALISTA J., b. Dec. 3, 1845. 3. DENZIL M., b. Feb. 19, 1848. 4. EDWIN E., b. Sept. 20, 1850. 5. EMMA, b. May 28, 1856; d. Sept. 22, 1878. 6. FRANK A., b. Aug. 19, 1859. 7. NELSON H., b. Aug. 27, 1863.

34. OTIS CRANE [14], married in Bethlehem, N. H., 1831, Jane, daughter of Aaron Kinney, of Bethlehem, N. H. He died March, 1881, aged 74. She was born in 1811. He was a farmer. Children:

1. DANIEL B., b. 1831 in Bethlehem. 2. MARCELLUS, 3. ——— ; both d. in infancy.

35. SARAH CRANE [15], married Hosea Streeter, son of David. Children:

1. SARAH (Streeter); m. Mr. Butterfield. 2. MARTHA (Streeter); m. Silas Newt at St. Johnsbury, Vt. 3. WILLIAM (Sreeeter). 4. HOSEA (Streeter). 5. ARNOLD (Streeter).

36. HOSEA CRANE [16], married Olive Fisher. He died 1863. Children:

1. MELVINA, b. Sept. 1831; m. 1870, Jesse Hughs, of Bethlehem, N. H. 2. BETSY ANN. 3. LOUISA, b. Feb., 1835; m. 1859, James Cobb, of Nashua, N. H. 4. WILLIAM, b. Aug. 29, 1838; m. Martha W. Brown. 5. JOSEPH F., b. Sept. 24, 1878. 6. LUTHER WILLIAM, b. April, 1839; killed in battle of the Wilderness, 1864. 7. AMY; d.

37. MARTHA CRANE [17], married L. Phillips. Children:

1. NATHANIEL (Phillips). 2. JESSE (Phillips); m. Dora Little, of Bethlehem, N. H. 3. ROBERT (Phillips); m. Eliza Streeter. 4. DAVID (Phillips); m. Lucy Ann Little, sister of Dora.

38. LAVINA CRANE [18], married Robert Streeter. She died 1863. Children:

1. MARIA (Streeter); m. Thomas Nuss, of Littleton, N. H. 2. ELIZA (Streeter); m. Robert Phillips, of Bethlehem, N. H. 3. OTIS (Streeter); m. ——— Watson; have INA. 3. AMASA (Streeter). 4. JANE (Streeter). 5. ELLEN (Streeter).

39. ELIZA CRANE [19], married Allen Bennett, of Swanzey, N. H., and lived in Milford, N. Y. Child:

1. A son, ——— (Bennett).

40. ALVIN CRANE [20]; m. Betsy Streeter. Children:

1. A daughter; d. in infancy. 2. VIANTA. 3. MARTHA. 4. FRANK.

41. OBED CRANE [21], married Eliza, daughter of Simeon Bolles, of Bethlehem, N. H. Children:

42—1. EDWIN, b. Aug. 3, 1845; m. Ella Blandin, of Bethlehem, N. H.
43—2. ALLEN, b. July 28, 1847; m. Ann Brown, of Bethlehem, N. H.
3. MARIA, b. Dec. 27, 1849; d. Sept., 1863. 4. JENNETTE, b. Dec., 1851; d. Sept., 1863. 5. OSMAN, b. March 27, 1858. 6. ELDEN, b. March 17, 1860.

44. NAHAM CRANE [23], born in Dalton, N. H. Married at Littleton, March 12, 1830, Margaret Nix. She was born in

Stansted, Lower Canada, Nov. 16, 1799. In 1879 he was living in Merrimac, Mass.; a farmer. Children :

    1. LAURA H., b. Dec. 12, 1831, in Dalton, N. H.; d. May 28, 1833.
45—2. WILLIAM, b. July 8, 1833; m. in Medfield, Mass.
46—3. MOSES B., b. Feb. 13, 1835; m. in Brownsville. Ore.
    4. PERSIS R. ,b. Dec. 31, 1837. 5. ELIZA R., b. March 17, 1842. 6.
       MARY A, b. June 29, 1849.

47. ONO CRANE [24], born in Dalton, N. H. Married Oct. 8, 1835, Rosira Phillips in Bethlehem, where she was born Feb. 26, 1816. They settled in Whitfield, where he was a farmer. She died there Feb. 2, 1879. Children :

    1. LOANZA. 2. LYDIA. 3. DENZIL. 4. LOVELL. 5. MARY. 6. AL-
       MIRA. 7. REUBIN. 8. ISAAC. 9. LAURA.

47½. WILLIAM B. CRANE [25], born in Dalton, N. H. Married in Lunenburgh, Vt., Nov. 23, 1837, Abigail Snow, who was born in Keene, N. H., May 10, 1811, and settled in Dalton, N. H. He enlisted, and served in the Army of the Potomac in Virginia in 1864. Has been honored with public office in his native town; also in Concord, Vt., to which place he removed. Children :

    1. HORTENSIA B., b. Oct. 15, 1838; d. Nov. 4, 1872. 2. JOSEPHINE, b.
       April 15, 1841; d. Nov. 5, 1841. 3. JOSEPHINE, b. Oct. 12, 1843.
       4. AZARIAH S., b. Nov. 25, 1845; served in Virginia in 1864 in the
       civil war.

48. LUKE H. CRANE [26], married in Plaistow, N. H., Aug. 21, 1845, Mary N. Currier. She was a native of that town, and born 1815. Children :

    1. MARY ELVINA. 2. ALLISON B. 3. LURENA A.

49. EDWIN CRANE[4] [42], married Ella Blanding, of Bethlehem, N. H. Children :

    1. CHARLES. 2. MYRON. 3. WILBUR. 4. ELIZABETH. 5. CAROLINE.

50. ALLEN CRANE [43], married Ann Brown, of Bethlehem, N. H. Child :

    1. NINNIE, b. 1874.

51. WILLIAM CRANE [45], married Ella M. Richards in Medfield, Mass., Feb. 18, 1865. She was born in Medway, Feb. 17, 1847. For several years he was station agent of B., C. & F. R. R.; also reporter for Boston newspapers, while his home was in Medfield, Mass. Children :

    1. EDITH SARGENT, b. Feb. 20, 1866. 2. AGNES FRANCIS, b. March 4,
       1869. 3. FLORA MAY, b. April 30, 1871. 4. ALVAN RICHARDS,
       b. Dec. 4. 1875; d. Sept. 14, 1879. 5. AUSTIN WILLIAM, b. May 19,
       1877; d. Sept. 16, 1879. 6. ETHEL PERSIS, b. Jan. 17, 1885.

52. MOSES B. CRANE [46], married Mary S. Perry, Oct. 9, 1870, at Brownsville, Ore. She was born in South Wales, April 6, 1844. Children :

    1. MAGGIE M., b. in Albany, Ore. 2. LIZZIE P., b. in Albany, Ore.
       3. EDGAR N., b. in Brownsville, Ore. 4. GEORGE W., b. in
       Brownsville. Ore. 5. STELLA E., b. in Brownsville, Ore.

No doubt the following are descendants from New Jersey Cranes, and perhaps from Jasper:

The wife of Chilion Crane (59) writes that Jesse Crane, born at Hanover, N. J., was father of Asa and Jesse Crane, brothers, who settled in Bridport, Vt. But Mahlon Crane (58) wrote that he thought his grandfather's name was Abijah, that he died, leaving four young boys, names as given below. David probably served in the Revolutionary war, from Morris Co., N. Y., and Daniel from Essex.

    1. DANIEL; served in the Revolutionary war, and was killed. 2 DAVID; left New Jersey at the close of the Revolutionary war, and not heard from.
53—3. ASA, b. July 16, 1758; his granddaughter says Asa's father was Jesse Crane.
54—4. JESSE, b. Aug. 29, 1760.

55. ASA CRANE [53], born in New Jersey on the banks of the Passaic River; lived there until after his marriage. His son Mahlon writes that his father was with Washington's army four years; was at Valley Forge with the army; was near by when Major Andre was taken and hanged; was at the battle of Monmouth, N. J.; also at the battle of Princeton, where he was wounded in the leg. Was a Revolutionary pensioner. Married Abigail Young, Dec. 28, 1784. She was born Sept. 26, 1765, and died Jan. 5, 1839. He died Sept. 23, 1848, at Bridport, Vt. She died there also. As near as it can be ascertained he was born at or near Hanover Neck, N. J., and married, and lived there until his three eldest children were born. The family then removed to Goshen, Orange Co., N. Y., where they remained a few years, when they removed to Lumberland, Ulster Co. Here they lived about ten years, when in the year 1808 they removed to Bridport, Vt., where his brother was then living. In the official register of officers and men of New Jersey in the Revolutionary war we find the name of Asa Crane, Morris County, also Somerset 1st battalion, also State troops, and also Continental army, which quite likely refers to this Asa Crane; and as serving in Capt. Piatt's company, 1st battalion, second establishment; also in militia. The following information was obtained by Mrs. Johnson, a granddaughter of Asa Crane: "He enlisted in May, 1778, in the Revolutionary war, and served as private for nine months in Capt. Daniel Piatt's company, Col. Ogden's regiment, Gen. Maxwell's brigade, New Jersey line. He was stationed at this time at Valley Forge and Mt. Holly. He was engaged in the battle of Monmouth, and was honorably discharged at Elizabethtown, N. J. He also served several times in other tours of military service, but records did not say where. He applied for a pension from Addison County, Vt., April 1, 1818. The pension was allowed, and he received it regularly until his death, which

57

occurred in 1849 or 1850. These facts were obtained from the pension office." Children :

- 1. CALVIN, b. Aug. 24, 1787; m. Jemima Quick, and removed to Pike County, Pa.; a farmer.
- 56—2. ABIJAH, b. Nov. 14, 1789; d. at Clinton, N. Y.
- 57—3. PHEBE, b. April 15, 1792.
- 58—4. MAHLON, b. Jan. 3, 1795, in Goshen, Orange Co., N. Y.
- 59—5. CHILION, b. Dec. 20, 1797.
- 60—6. SALLY, b. March 27, 1801.
- 61—7. JESSE, b. June 1, 1803, in New Jersey, on Delaware River.
- 8. MARY, b. Oct. 10, 1805; d. March 30, 1830. 9. ELIZABETH, b. June 5, 1808; d. unmarried.

62. JESSE CRANE [54], married Jan. 1, 1784, Mary Mulford, who was born Dec. 12, 1765. He was born in New Jersey, and settled in Bridport, Vt., in the year 1800, and was the first of the two brothers to go to Vermont; a farmer. They were members of the Presbyterian Church, and he was a deacon. He died March, 1824. She died Dec. 27, 1838. There was a Jesse Crane who served in Capt. Stephen Munson's company, Easton's battalion, Morris County, N. J.; also in Continental army, and in fourth battalion, second establishment; also in militia. Children :

- 1. KETURAH, b. Dec. 30, 1784; m. Edmon Grandy; d. July 22, 1863. 2. SARAH, b. June 28, 1786; m. Mitchell Kugman; d. Aug. 7, 1862. 3. MARY, b. Aug. 20, 1788; d. Oct. 13, 1796.
- 63—4. ELIJAH, b. April 23, 1790; d. Sept. 25, 1865.
- 64—5. DAVID A., b. Sept. 25, 1792.
- 65—6. MULFORD, b. Oct. 14, 1795; d. July 9, 1870.
- 66—7. PHINEAS, b. March 15, 1798; d. March 3, 1865.
- 67—8. JESSE, b. Nov. 26, 1800.
- 68—9. WHITFIELD, b. Jan. 21, 1802.
- 10. MARIA, b. March 7, 1805; d. Jan. 12, 1813.
- 69-11. LYMAN, b. Dec. 8, 1806.

70. ABIJAH CRANE [56], born in New Jersey. Married Sept. 27, 1823, Hannah Emerson Hall. She was born in Middle Granville, N. Y., Nov. 8, 1798; died in Clinton, June 12, 1846. He was a soldier in the war of 1812, and engaged in the battle of Plattsburgh, N. Y. Graduate of Middlebury College, Vermont; ordained minister in the Presbyterian Church; settled as pastor in 1824 over the Church in Hampton, N. Y.; and from 1833 till his death secretary and general agent of the American Home Missionary Society for central New York. He organized the first temperance society west of Albany in or about the year 1825. He died May 14, 1847, at Clinton, N. Y. Children :

- 71—1. EDWIN HALL, b. May 31, 1825.
- 72—2. LOUIS H. DeLOSS, b. July 7, 1826.
- 3. HELEN EVEREST, b. Oct. 18, 1828; d. in Dodgeville, Wis., Jan., 1856.
- 73—4. JAMES E., b. Aug. 17, 1830.
- 74—5. EMILIA ROYCE, b. Jan. 18, 1834.
- 6. GEORGE WHITFIELD, b. March 31, 1836, in Utica, N. Y.; d. March 1863.

75. PHEBE CRANE [57], married Moses Southard, Aug., 1820, and settled in Michigan. Had one child :

- 1. HARRIET (Southard); m. Luman Moon; residence at Flint, Mich.

76. MAHLON CRANE [58], was born in Goshen, Orange Co., N. Y. Married in Bridport, Addison Co., Vt., Abigail Reed, Aug. 3, 1821. He was by trade a hatter, and also a farmer. She was born in Vermont in 1801, and died in Chicago, Ill., Nov. 9, 1872. He died in Gardner, Ill., June 27, 1887. Children:

77—1. MARY ANGELINE. b. Sept. 9, 1821.
    2. WILLIAM PARSONS, b. Jan. 29, 1824; d. 1868 in Holly, Mich.
78—3. PHEBE ELIZA, b. Nov. 19, 1825.
    4. HARRIET ADALINE, b. Sept. 30, 1827; m. Benj. H. Hebard. He served in the civil war; lived in Chicago, Ill. She d. April 12, 1899, at the home of her daughter, Mrs. N. E. Dillie, Chicago.
79—5. THADDEUS PEMBROOK. b. Sept. 9, 1829.
80—6. SARAH LUCINDA, b. 1833.
81—7. CHARLES HENRY. b. Oct. 10, 1835.
82—8. EDWIN ASA, b. Dec. 31, 1838.
83—9. HELEN CORNELIA, b. Dec. 23, 1841.

84. CHILION CRANE [59], born at Back Mills (or Lumberland), Ulster Co., N. Y. Married at Addison, Vt., Nov. 13, 1822, Cynthia Holeman, a native of Salisbury, Vt.; born March 4, 1804. He settled at Bridport, Vt.; a farmer. He died there Oct. 25, 1872. Children:

    1. MELISSA A.; never m.
85—2. CALVIN E.
    3. WALTER DENNISON CRANE; m. 1st, Mary Jane Smith at Franklin, Vt. She d., having had two children that d. in infancy; m. 2d, Alice E. Grow, Oct., 1892, at Derby, Vt. They had one child that d. in infancy. He d. at Newport, Vt., March 11, 1898. 4. SARAH A. 5. HENRY MELVIN CRANE; m. 1st, Jane Smith, of Ashtabula, Ohio; m. 2d, —— in Ohio; m. 3d, —— in Michigan. Had three children by second wife, but all d. in infancy. 6. EDWARD CRANE; m. J. Nelson at Galesburg, Ill.; had one child, d. in infancy. He d. at Janesville, Minn., March 4, 1887. 7. LORIN P., b. 1835; m. Ida Fletcher, 1862; importer in New York city. He served in United States army in the civil war.
86—8. CYRUS R.
    9. CHAUNCY M. CRANE; m. Emma Samson at Wybridge, Vt. He was killed at Spottsylvania Court House, Va., in battle. No children.
87—10. ROLLIN C.
88—11. WILLIAM HARRISON.
    12. GEORGE CARLOS; m. Elizabeth Rennyson, of New York city; no children. 13. CASSIUS P., b. Sept. 6, 1846; farmer at Bridport, Vt.

89. SALLY CRANE [60], married Clement Miner, Jan., 1825. He died May 17, 1837, and she married 2d, Mr. Hodge. She died July 5, 1841. Children:

    1. MARTHA A. (Miner); m. John Kingman; had: LUCY; ELLA; FLORA; IDA. 2. MARY C. (Miner); m. Julius J. Crane. 3. NANCY M. (Miner); m. Cornelius Abernethy; had: CORA; CLEMENT; ALSON; ABBIE; MATTIE; MILO. 4. CHAMPLIN C. (Miner); m. Ann Sturdevant; had: BENJAMIN C. and HELEN A. 5. SARAH A. (Hodge).

90. JESSE CRANE [61], married Sept. 22, 1835, Amanda H. Hamilton, a native of Bridport, Vt. She was born May 7, 1814. Settled in Bridport; a farmer and clothier. The farm on which he lived and died he purchased when at the age of 21. He died 1889. Children:

    1. ALBERT A., b. Dec. 13, 1836; was teacher three years in Middlebury College, Vermont; served in the civil war; enlisted Oct., 1861;

reënlisted March, 1864; was 1st lieutenant, and killed in the battle of the Wilderness. May 5. 1864. 2. BYRON W., b. June 5, 1838; served in the civil war; was 2d lieutenant; m. Lucy Jewett Howe; farmer.

91—4. EMMA L., b. Nov. 18, 1841; teacher at Howard University, Washington; D. C.
  5. HARRIET E., b. June 30, 1843; teacher, Middlebury, Vt.; d. Dec. 8, 1863.
92—6. JENNIE A., b. Oct. 19, 1844.
  7. SARAH L., b. Oct. 30, 1846; educated at Middlebury, Vt.; teacher there and in Washington. D. C.; since 1893 employed in treasury department. 8. FLORA M., b. Dec. 13, 1852; graduate of Holyoke College in 1874; taught 4 years at Moody's School, Northfield, Mass., and 12 years teacher at Washington. D. C., High School; in 1899 was teaching in Tennessee.
93—3. JAMES E., b. May 16, 1840.

94. ELIJAH CRANE [63], born in Hanover, Morris Co., N. J. Married Eliza C. Young at Vergennes, Vt., Jan. 8, 1841. She was born in Hanover, N. J., Aug. 19, 1805. He served in the war of 1812. Settled in Bridport, Vt.; a farmer. He died Sept. 25, 1865, leaving an only child :

95—1. CHARLES E., b. Oct. 31, 1841.

96. DAVID A. CRANE [64], born in New Jersey. Married Lydia Bascom. He died Jan. 31, 1872. One David Crane was allowed payment on a bill by the governor and council of Vermont, Nov. 6, 1819, and an order passed Nov. 8, 1820, to pay the same. Was it this one or David E., Jr.? Children :

  1. CHARLES E. 2. GEORGE B. 3. ADELIA.
97—4. JULIUS J., b. Jan. 14, 1824.
  5. MARY S. 6. SAMUEL B. 7. RODNEY B.

98. MULFORD CRANE [65], married. Died July 9, 1870. Child :

  1. EDWIN; residence at Ypsilanti, Mich.

99. PHINEAS CRANE [66], married. Died March 3, 1865. Had five children. Children :

  1. ACHSA. 2. HENRY; residence at Pope Creek, Mercer Co., Ill.

100. JESSE CRANE [67], born in Bridport, Vt.; a farmer; also a tanner and currier of leather. Married Sept. 29, 1825, Ann Eliza Rogers, a native of Addison, and born Oct. 18, 1806. She died in Bridport, Feb. 11, 1865. He died there Jan. 13, 1879. Perhaps had other children. Children :

101—1. FRANKLIN C., b. July 17. 1826. in Addison, Vt.
102—2. JOSEPH R., b. Aug. 13, 1834.

103. WHITFIELD CRANE [68], born at Bridport, Vt. Married Salome G. Stagg, Nov. 1, 1827. She was a native of Panton, Addison Co., Vt. She was born May 3, 1809. He died at Potsdam, N. Y., Dec. 23, 1844. Their three eldest children were born in Panton; the others in Potsdam, N. Y. Children :

  1. JOSIAH, b. June 26, 1828; d. Aug. 23, 1829. 2. HENRY FAYETTE, b. Jan. 31. 1833; residence at San Francisco, Cal.
104—3. GEORGE WHITFIELD, b. March 25, 1835.
  4. DELIA MARIA, b. Aug. 15, 1837; m. S. H. Pitcher: d. May 11, 1874.
  5. VIOLA ELLEN, b. June 5, 1841; m. Robert Stafford. 6. BYRON GRANDY, b. Feb. 24, 1843. 7. RHODA ELVIRA, b. April 4, 1845.

105. LYMAN CRANE [69], married Sarah Skinner, April 28, 1835. She was born in Jericho, Vt., in 1802. He settled in Stockholm, St. Lawrence Co., N. Y. He was a clothier. He died June 27, 1875. Children:

    1. MARY ELIZA, b. Nov. 29, 1838; m. E. S. Burnett; residence at Brookings. S. D.; has a son, E. A. BURNETT, professor of agriculture in the college there.

    106—2. EDGAR L., b. June 25, 1841.

107. EDWIN HALL CRANE [71], born in Hampton, Oneida Co., N. Y. Graduated at Hamilton College with the highest honors in 1844, and at Andover Theological Seminary in 1849, and was ordained a Presbyterian minister, and went as a missionary to the Nestorians under the A. B. C. F. M. He married Ann Eliza Cowles, Aug., 1852, and died Aug. 27, 1854, at the mission station of Gawar, in the mountains of Koordistan, Persia. Children:

    1. MORRIS GRANT, b. 1853, in Ooroomiah, Persia; d. Sept. 6, 1854. 2. EDWIN HALL, b. Nov. 6, 1854, in Ooroomiah, Persia; was in Danville, N. Y.

108. LOUIS H. DE LOSS CRANE [72], graduate of Hamilton College in 1845; studied law with Hon. Willis Hall of New York; admitted to the bar in 1849. He removed to Beloit, Wis., in 1853, where he taught school for a time. There he married Lucy, daughter of Major Burrell, formerly of Stockbridge, Mass. Subsequently and for several years he was chief clerk of the Wisconsin legislature. Offering his services to the government at the outbreak of the civil war, he soon rose rapidly from a second lieutenant in the 3d Wisconsin regiment of volunteers to lieutenant-colonel, participating in all the actions of that regiment till he met his death at the battle of Cedar Mountain, Va., while heroically rallying his men at the last stand made on that disastrous day. Several of their children died in infancy. Child:

    1. MARY L., b. Nov., 1858; m. James L. Perkins at Beloit, Wis.

109. JAMES EELLS CRANE [73], born in Hampton, N. Y. Served as second lieutenant in 3d Wisconsin regiment, and aide-de-camp to Maj.-Gen. Ruger in the civil war, receiving honorable mention for services in the battles of Chancellorsville and Gettysburg. Was for many years a merchant in Paris, France; also in New York city; an importer of rich tapestries and choice fabrics, a business that caused him to make frequent trips across the Atlantic, having made the passage about forty times. Married March 1, 1866, Ann Elizabeth Coleman at Warren, Conn. Children:

    1. SPENCER COLEMAN, b. Dec. 19, 1868, in New York city. 2. ANNIE WINSLOW, b. Jan. 9, 1871, at Newton, Mass.

110. EMILIA ROYCE CRANE [74], born in Utica, N. Y. Married Charles Anthony at Gouverneur, N. Y., June, 1867, where they settled.

Children :

> 1. HERBERT (Anthony), b. Dec. 20, 1868. 2. HELEN EMERSON (Anthony), b. Feb. 26. 1875.

111. MARY ANGELINE CRANE [77], born in Addison, Vt. Married Joseph Van Vleck, Jan. 21, 1845, in Penfield, N. Y.; a farmer. Children :

> 1. EDGAR D. (Van Vleck), b. in Penfield. 2. MAHLON CRANE (Van Vleck). 3. THADDEUS J. (Van Vleck). 4. ELIZABEH H. (Van Vleck). 5. FRANK H. (Van Vleck). 6. CARRIE L. (Van Vleck). 7. ELLA M. (Van Vleck). 8. CHARLES E. (Van Vleck).

112. PHEBE ELIZA CRANE [78], born in Bridport, Vt. Married George F. Spencer, of Wayne County, N. Y., July 2, 1851, in Penfield, N. Y.; a farmer. She died July 10, 1898, at her home in Gardner, Ill. Children :

> 1. ALICE (Spencer). 2. LIBBIE (Spencer). 3. IDA (Spencer).

113. THADDEUS PEMBROOK CRANE [79], (Mahlon, Asa), born in Waybridge, Vt. Married at Elmira, N. Y., June 12, 1856, Phebe E. Thompson, of Preston, N. Y. She was the daughter of Robert Thompson, of Addison, N. Y., who was a soldier in the war of 1812. Mr. Crane was a farmer; residence at Gardner, Ill. Children :

> 1. CHARLES T.; d. Sept. 14, 1862. 2. FRANK E.; d. Sept. 13, 1862.
> 114—3. FRED E., b. April 21, 1865.
> 4. NELLIE E. 5. HARRIE V.

115. SARAH LUCINDA CRANE [80], born in Perington, N. Y. Married William J. Hipp, May 31, 1854, in Rochester, N. Y. He was born in Brydon, 1826; by trade a carpenter. Settled at Penfield, N. Y. Children :

> 1. CARRIE C. (Hipp), b. Dec. 27, 1855; d. Feb. 8, 1862. 2. HATTIE L. (Hipp), b. Sept. 21, 1857. 3. MINNIE E. (Hipp), b. Dec. 21, 1860; m. Feb. 8, 1891, at E. Pembroke, N. Y. 4. ELLA M. (Hipp), b. April 2, 1864. 5. BERTON R. (Hipp), b. June 14, 1866; m. Dec. 25, 1890. 6. EVA B. (Hipp), b. June 25, 1868. 7. CLARA R. (Hipp), b. Aug. 1, 1870. 8. EDWIN C. (Hipp), b. April 8, 1872. 9. WILLIAM M. (Hipp), b. Nov. 8, 1874. 10. ETTA A. (Hipp), b. June 15, 1876. 11. ARTHUR H. (Hipp), b. July 13, 1880.

116. CHARLES HENRY CRANE [81], married Eliza Phelps, of Chicago, Ill., in 1862. Residence at 235 S. Oakley Avenue, Chicago. He is foreman at P., Ft. W. & C. R. R. freight house, No. 2 W. Madison Street. Children :

> 1. CHARLES PHELPS, b. 1865. 2. CLARA, b. 1868.

117. Edwin ASA CRANE [82], born in Penfield, N. Y. Married Jan. 14, 1874, in Chicago, Ill., Gertrude A. Wheeler, of Milford, N. Y.; born 1849. Mr. Crane has been president of the Board of Education at Braidwood, Ill., where he resides, and where he is a merchant. Children :

> 1. GEORGE H., b. Jan. 15, 1876. 2. EDWIN A., b. 1880.

118. HELEN CORNELIA CRANE [83]. She went to Gardner, Ill., about 1863. Married Albert Collins, of Elburn, Ill., 1866,

and lived on a farm near Elburn, Kane Co., until her death, May, 1893. Children :

    1. HARRY (Collins). 2. MINNIE (Collins). 3. FRANK (Collins).

119   CALVIN ERASTUS CRANE [85], married P. Coraine Samson at —— , Vermont, July 15, 1856. Children :

    1. JULIA E. 2. WALTER E. 3. MERRILL C. 4. IDA L. 5. CHAUN-
      CY. 6. CHARLES W. 7. WINDOM C. 8. ALICE M. 9. E——— ;
      d. at Minneapolis, Minn., Feb., 1896.

120. CYRUS R. CRANE [86], married 1st, Orella Pond at Franklin, Mass. She had one child, who died in infancy. He married 2d, in New York city, Marie L. Dufour. He died at Housatonic, Mass., July 21, 1888. Children :

    1. LOUISE M. 2. NINA.

121. ROLLIN CHILION CRANE [87], (Chilion, Asa), married 1st, Lucy Griffith, of Minnesota, who had one child ; married 2d, Alice Magson at Mooers, N. Y. ; had three children. Children :

    1. JAMES OSCAR. 2. EDWARD. 3. ROLLIN. 4. JESSIE.

122. WILLIAM HARRISON CRANE [88], married Grace Cornell at Clifton, N. J. Had six children ; two died in infancy. Children :

    1. LEONORE. 2. CARLTON. 3. MAY. 4. ARNOLD.

123. EMMA L. CRANE [91], educated in the common schools of her native town ; also at the Young Ladies' Seminary, Middlebury, Vt. Taught in the district schools of Addison County, Vt. ; also in the Ladies' Seminary ; and later in the public schools at Washington, D. C. In 1873 she married James Bowen Johnson, then of Washington, D. C., but a native of Royal Oak, Mich. He was born in 1830, and settled in Washington, where he died Jan. 10, 1899. Children :

    1. FLORA LOUISE PRISCILLA (Johnson), b. July 14, 1875. She was
      educated in schools in Washington, D. C., and Ladies' Seminary,
      Andover, Mass. 2. PAUL BOWEN ALDEN (Johnson), b. March
      23, 1878. He was educated at the schools in Washington, enter-
      ing Yale College in 1897 ; still (1899) pursuing his studies there.

124. JENNIE A. CRANE [92], educated at Burlington, Vt., and West Lebanon, N. H. Married Charles W. Prentiss, of Washington, D. C., in May, 1868, where she was a teacher, and where they have since made their home. Children :

    1. ALBERT N. (Prentiss), b. Feb. 14, 1870 ; entered Middlebury Col-
      lege in 1888 ; remained one year, and returned to Washington to
      enter the employ of the government ; m. Edith Meeus, Sept. 1898.
      2. HATTIE E. (Prentiss), b. July 16, 1873 ; d. same day. 3.
      LUCIA (Prentiss), b. July 16, 1873 ; d. same day. 4. CHARLES W.
      (Prentiss), b. Aug. 14. 1874 ; educated at Washington, D. C., and
      Middlebury College ; graduated 1896 with honors ; now (1899) as
      past graduate in Harvard. 5. JEAN M. (Prentiss), b. Sept. 23,
      1877 ; d. June 3, 1882. 6. CARLOS B. (Prentiss), b. April 21,
      1879 ; d. May 19, 1882.

125. FRANKLIN C. CRANE[3] [101], married Oct. 20, 1852,

Eliza Ann Kitchell. She was born at Bridport, Vt., April 28, 1822, where they settled. He was a farmer.

Children :

    1. CLARENCE F., b. Aug. 6, 1855. 2. SADIA JANE S., b. Aug. 17, 1857.

126. JOSEPH R. CRANE[3] [102], farmer, Bridport, Vt. Married Mary J. Smith, Feb. 23, 1858, at Addison, Vt., where she was born Sept. 4, 1834. Children :

    1. CLAYTON E., b. June 4, 1861. 2. ALBERT S., b. Dec. 24, 1863. 3. WILLIE J., b. Jan. 28, 1866; d. June 23, 1875.

127. GEORGE WITFIELD CRANE[3] [104], married March 8, 1865, at Philipsburg, Province of Quebec, Maria Louise Hoyle, where she was born Sept. 7, 1840. He served in the civil war; was under Butler at New Orleans in 1862. By trade a carpenter. Residence in Worthington, Minn.

Children :

    1. MARY LOUISE, b. Feb. 20, 1866, in Potsdam, N. Y. 2. FRANK MALCOM, b. July 6, 1869, in Potsdam, N. Y. 3. NELLIE EUNICE.

128. JAMES E. CRANE [93], after laying the foundations for a liberal education, failing health compelled him to relinquish that object, and he took up bee culture, and is at present writing considered the most extensive bee keeper in the State of Vermont. He also spends a portion of his time writing for publication and lecturing. In 1870 he married Emily Joslin, of Waitsfield, Vt. She died, and he married her sister Dora, by whom he had :

    1. PHILIP. 2. THEODORA.

129. CHARLES E. CRANE [95], married in New Haven, Vt., Sept. 8, 1868, Helen E. Sturdivant. She was a native of that place; born May 18, 1844. He is a farmer; resides at Bridport, Vt. Child :

    1. MYRTIE ELIZA, b. Aug. 29, 1869; m. ARTHUR E. Brown. Children : EFFIE MAY; ALICE EVA.

130. JULIUS J. CRANE [97], married at Bridport, Vt., Jan. 3, 1849, Mary C. Miner, who was a native of that place; born June 2. 1830. He represented his town in the legislature of Vermont in 1876. He is a farmer. Children :

131—1. THERON M. b. Sept. 10, 1850.
    2. HELEN. 3. FREDERICK C., b. Oct. 13, 1856.

131½. THERON M. CRANE [131], a mechanic; residence at Bridport, Vt. Married Lizzie A. Burneau, Dec. 9, 1874. She was born in Bridport, Sept. 25, 1859. Child :

    1. ALLAN R., b. July 1, 1877.

132. EDGAR L. CRANE[3] [106], served in the civil war from Oct. 5, 1861, to Aug. 1, 1865, in 60th New York Infantry; twice wounded at Gettysburg; was with Sherman on his march to the sea, and at the surrender of Lee. Mar-

ried April 26, 1868, Ruby E. Partridge; a farmer at N. Stockholm, N. Y. Children :

1. ANNA D., b. April 23, 1869. 2. LYMAN P., b. May 7, 1870; m. Minnie E. Curtis, Dec. 28, 1897. Child: EVA ANNA, b. Dec. 6. 1898. 3. SOLON E., b. Oct. 8, 1871. 4. MARY E., b. Dec. 14, 1873. 5. SARAH A., b. Nov. 7, 1875. 6. EDNA L., b. Sept. 6, 1879. 7. ANSEL F., b. Feb. 19, 1883. 8. FRED W., b. Nov. 9, 1884.

133. FRED E. CRANE[4] [114], (Thaddeus P.,[3] Mahlon,[2] Asa1), married March 13, 1888, Isabella McGorman at Gardner, Ill., where she was born Feb. 15, 1865; a farmer, Gardner, Ill. Children :

1. CHARLES HENRY, b. Dec. 27, 1888. 2. ETHEL E., b. Oct. 20, 1890. 3. BERT E., b. Sept. 25, 1892. 4. ALICE H., b. May 8, 1895.

Probably descendants of Jasper; certainly originally from New Jersey, according to reports received.

134. MOSES CRANE, born about 1750 in New Jersey. Married about 1773 or 1774, and settled in the town of Edinburgh, Saratoga Co., N. Y., about the year 1793. His wife died, and he went to New Jersey, where, it is related by his grandson John Grinnell, he had a call to preach, and did not return to care for his children. Stephen and Jane, being considerably older than their sisters, put them out in good families, and looked after them until grown up. Children :

135—1. STEPHEN, b. 1776.
136—2. JANE, b. 1777.
3. LOTTIE; m. Stephen Carr. 4. SALLY; m. Isaac Cady in Augusta, Oneida Co., N. Y.

STEPHEN CRANE[2] [135], (Moses[1]). He was born in Poughkeepsie, N. Y., and married Elsie Grinnell, and for thirty-five years carried on farming with his brother-in-law, Isaiah Grinnell. Their two eldest children were born in Edinburgh, Saratoga Co. They afterwards lived in Augusta, Oneida Co.; Pompey, Onondaga Co.; Fabius; and then in 1819 went to Spafford, where he died May 16, 1851, aged 75 years. Mrs. Crane died March 12, 1844. Children :

1. SALLY, b. about 1796; m. Samuel Ellis. She had 12 children; five of them were living Feb., 1897. Children: KATHARINE, the eldest, lives in Fabius; b. Sept., 1815. IRA, lives in Gilman. Iowa. SYLVIA, lives in De Ruyter, N. Y. JACKSON. ROBERT, lives in Pompey, N. Y.
137—2. JERA.
3. LYDIA; m. Isaac Griffin; d. at Otisco, N. Y. 4. LUCINDA. 5. POLLY; m. T omas Whiting in 1821; had two sons and four daughters. 6. GEORGE; m. Octavia Billings, and had four daughters and one son.
138—7. SAMUEL, b. April 4, 1815, in Fabius, N.Y.; d. June 10, 1887.
8. HARRIET.

139. JANE CRANE[2] [136], (Moses), married Isaiah Grinnell, brother of her brother Stephen's wife. Mr. Grinnell carried on farming with his wife's brother Moses Crane for thirty-five years.

58

He was born 1773; died Jan. 19, 1862, aged 89. She died May 24, 1866, also aged 89. Children:

1. EZRA (Grinnell), b. 1794; d. June 9, 1862. 2. JOHN (Grinnell), b. Dec. 4, 1796; living Jan., 1882. 3. BETSEY (Grinnell), b. March 18, 1799; m. Alanson Tinkham; d. 4. CHLOE (Grinnell), b. 1801; m. R. M. Tinkham, and d. 1877. 5. MAJOR (Grinnell), b. 1803; d. 1869. 6. AMOS (Grinnell), b. 1805; living in 1882. 7. ANNA (Grinnell), b. 1807; m. Weston Wetherbee, and d. 1858. 8. ELIZA (Grinnell), b. 1809; m. William Tyler; d. 1879. 9. SEYMOUR (Grinnell), b. 1813; living 1882. 10. SALLY (Grinnell), b. March 18, 1816; m. Elijah Griffin. 11. ANSEL (Grinnell), b. Aug. 30, 1818; living 1882.

JOHN GRINNELL [2], married three times. His first wife was Miss Tinkham, sister to Alanson and R. M. Tinkham, his brothers-in-law. She died, leaving six children. Two years later he married again. By this marriage he had two children. She died, and in 1847 he married his third wife, who was living in January, 1882, having had one child, a daughter, born about 1850. In the fall of 1820, Mr. Grinnell left his home in ———, and took up wild land in Barre, Genesee Co. (since 1824 Orleans County), for the purpose of making a home, and will give the story as he penned it: "I told you the trade with the Tinkham boys; they married my sisters, and I married theirs. I located my land in the fall of 1820, and built a place to come to in the winter. There was not much snow that winter, and one of the Tinkham boys and I had a pair of three-year-old steers between us. We bought a pair of old wagon wheels, made a cart, yoked the steers, took our axes, cooking utensils, bed clothes, two cows, and started for our new home. From second day of April until fore part of June we kept our own house, boarding ourselves; our cows both gave milk, and we got some baking done about a mile away at our nearest neighbor. We took turns cooking. Sunday morning we had shortcake and butter. One would do the chores, milking, &c., while the other would attend to the cooking, make the butter, &c. About the middle of June our wives' fathers came out with wagons, bringing their goods. Our nearest neighbors were west one mile, north two and a half miles, east three miles, south ten miles, the Indian Reservation lying between us, and settlers south. I now (1882) have a home farm of 197 acres, with three houses and four barns, and a 62½ acre timber lot. We are half way between Rochester and Buffalo. We raised last season one thousand bushels of wheat and forty acres of barley now on the ground. I have seven boys;—two that work my farm; one living three miles south of here; one in St. Clair County, Mich.; another in Coldwater, that State; one in Chicago at the stock yards; and one in Iowa.

"I cannot tell you the name of the town in New Jersey Uncle Stephen found his father Moses Crane; but he afterwards came to New York State to see his children in Spafford, Onondaga Co., and my father and mother and Uncle Stephen came with him to my house to see us; that was the only time I saw Grandfather Moses

Crane. Uncle Stephen and my father farmed it together in partnership thirty-five years. They removed from Saratoga County to Oneida Co., town of Augusta, and from there to Pompey, Onondaga County, and from there just over the line into Fabius, then to Spafford, where they died. I left Barre in 1854, having purchased a farm in Shelby, an adjoining town, and three miles distant, where I now reside."

140. JERA (or JERRA) CRANE[3] [137], married in Spafford, Onondaga County, N. Y., Orissa Fisher, Dec. 25, 1821. Settled in Barre, Orleans Co., N. Y.; a farmer. He was born in Saratoga County. She was born in Cherry Valley, Otsego Co. He died Nov. 23, 1878. Children:

141—1. STEPHEN, b. March 24, 1828.
2. JUDSON. 3. HARRISON. 4. ALONZO. 5. GEORGE. 6. LEWIS.

142. SAMUEL CRANE[3] [138], married Almira Shaw, Oct. 7, 1837. He was a farmer, and lived in Spafford, N. Y., and died June 10, 1887. Children:

1. Dr. ELLIS. 2. EARL. 3. HARLEY. 4. GEORGE.

143. STEPHEN CRANE[4] [141], (Jera,[3] Stephen,[2] Moses[1]), married Aug. 22, 1849, Mary Elizabeth, daughter of Deacon Floyd Starr and his wife Parthenia (Abbot) Gates, and settled in Norwich, Conn., where Mr. Crane carries on the nursery business, making a specialty of choice shrubs and ornamental shade trees. She died Nov. 25, 1879, in Norwich. Children:

1. FLOYD HENRY, b. Nov. 16, 1851; studied law; lived in New York city (1879). 2. CARRIE P., b. Nov. 24, 1857; m. Oct. 11, 1877. 3. HARRIET ORISSA, b. June 27, 1860; d. March, 1862. 4. SARAH MARGARET, b. Dec. 22, 1862.

---

144. MOSES CRANE, married 1st, Sarah Peters; 2d, Nancy Stone. He with his eldest son was at one time engaged in the foundry business, and carried on other iron works in New York city, but removed to western New York with his family at quite an early day. He is said to have had a brother Samuel, who was father of Elijah Crane, the Quaker, in Michigan; also two sisters, one of whom married Mr. Beaman; the other, Mr. Suthard. By his first marriage Moses Crane had four children, and by the second five. He died in Detroit, Mich., July 8, 1829. Children:

145—1. MOSES, b. Aug. 15, 1801, in New Jersey, it is said.
2. HENRY; settled at Lansing, Mich. 3. HARRIET; m. Mr. Henry. 4. ———; m. David Eaton, brother of Eliza. 5. SAMUEL; settled in Ohio. 6. ALFRED; d. in Adrian, Mich., 1885; son: H——— E.
146—7. JACOB CROOK.
8. ———ALBERT; settled at La Salle, Ill.; d.; sons: FRANK; JAMES; very extensive farmers. 9. PETER; was a railroad man. 10. PHILANDER; a railroad man; d. in hospital, Washington, D. C., winter of 1898.

MOSES CRANE [145], married Eliza Eaton; born 1811; sister of David Eaton, husband of his sister. He died in York, Washtenaw Co., Mich., May 31, 1868. She died Oct. 2, 1890.

Children :

147—1. Lauren H., b. Nov. 10, 1830, in Clarkson, Monroe Co., N. Y.
148—2. Ann Eliza, b. 1833; m. Roger Crippen.
    3. Rufus H., b. May 24, 1836.
    4. Mary; m. —— Van Winkle.

Lauren H. Crane [147], married Harriet Mason, Dec. 27, 1853, in Bedford, Monroe Co., Mich.; a farmer; residence at Augusta, Washtenaw Co., Mich. Children:

1. Mary Eliza, b. Dec. 28, 1857. 2. Dewey Mason, b. July 12, 1862. 3. George Chester, b. June 16, 1865.

Ann Eliza Crane [148], married Roger Crippen, a farmer; residence at York, Mich. Children:

1. Rufus, b. Jan. 26, 1855. 2. Clarence, b. Dec. 2, 1856. 3. Mennie, b. Nov. 10, 1857. 4. Luella, b. Jan. 1, 1859. 5. Lewis, b. Feb. 26, 1864. 6. Perry, b. Aug. 10, 1866. 7. Lillian, b. Dec. 4, 1867. 8. Carrie, b. Jan. 13, 1870. 9. Frank, b. Feb. 26, 1871. 10. Ernest, b. Dec. 19, 1873.

Jacob Crook Crane [146], married Geraldine Letitia Gadd, Oct. 3, 1835, in Paris, Ont. He died in Victoria, B. C., in 1879. Children:

149—1. Thomas Crook, b. 1838; d. in Burr Oak, Mich., June 17, 1890. 2. Albert; d., aged 20 years, in British Columbia. 3. George; d., aged 3 years. 4. Henry A., b. 1849; d. in Buffalo, N. Y., Oct. 20, 1894.

Thomas Crook Crane [149], married March 20, 1861, Elizabeth Ann Cochran in Richwood, Ont.; removed from Canada to Michigan in 1876; carried on farming and creamery business until his death, June 17, 1890. Child:

1. Jairus William, b. June 1, 1862. In 1883 he with his uncle Henry A. Crane went to Oswego, N. Y., and were engaged in the lumber business with Crane, Belden & Co., of Oswego and Syracuse, N. Y. He married Oct. 9, 1889, Alice E. Griswold in Tecumseh, Mich., and settled in Elmhurst, Ill., a suburb of Chicago, but June, 1897, removed to Minnesota, where he now (1899) resides, being western agent for Hunter, Walton & Co., extensive dealers in butter and cheese. Children: 1. Bertha Maud, b. Sept. 20, 1890. 2. George Griswold, b. May 28, 1893. 3. Mildred Ruth, b. Jan. 14, 1899.

---

150. Thomas G. Crane, born June 22, 1789, at Cape May, N. J. Married Ann Bates. She was born at Newton, N. J., Nov. 1, 1796; died Nov. 15, 1852. He was a carpenter and joiner. In the spring of 1828 he removed to what is now Hamilton, Ont.; died Oct. 27, 1837. Children:

1. James Bates, b. Oct. 12, 1818, at Newton, N. J. 2. John Smith, b. 1820, at Newton, N. J. 3. Frances Elizabeth, b. at New Jersey. 4. Sarah, b. at New Jersey. 5. Joseph, b. 1830, in Ontario; m. Jane Robinson; residence at Schell City, Mo. 6. Benjamin Stocton, b. at Saginaw, Mich. 7. Jane, b. in Ontario.

151. James Bates Crane [1], married Eliza Lymburner.

He was a carpenter and builder at Barford, Ont. Late residence at Springfield, Ont. Children:

> 1. WILLIAM S., b. April 12, 1842. 2. CHARLES H.. b. Aug. 1, 1843. 3. NANCY JANE, b. March 29, 1846. 4. SARAH ELIZABETH, b. Jan. 14, 1849. 5. MARY MALINDA, b. April 17, 1852.

152. JOHN SMITH CRANE [2], married April 15, 1849, Grace Elizabeth Wheeler. He was a cooper by trade; settled at Paris, Ont. Children:

> 1. SARAH ANN, b. Aug. 13, 1850. 2. MARIA JANE, b. May 7, 1852. 3. JAMES EDWARD, b. April 25, 1855. 4. ROBERT HENRY, b. Sept. 16, 1858. 5. MARY ELIZABETH, b. Sept., 1862; d. Sept. 14, 1863. 6. JACOB WESLEY, b. and d. March 6, 1864; 7. ELLEN MATILDA, b. March 6, 1865. 8. ROSE EMMA, b. April 18, 1867. 9. LOUISA D., b. May 2, 1870; d. Sept. 11, 1871.

------

153. Dr. JOEL CRANE, born Jan. 20, 1779, it is said at Newark, N. J. Married June 20, 1804, Olive Mitchell; born April 11, 1774, at South Britain, Conn. He was a farmer and physician. Settled in Southbury, Conn. Was representative in the Connecticut legislature in 1813–14–15. Removed to Vermillion, Erie Co., Ohio, where he died Aug. 3, 1844. She died there Sept. 21, 1857. Children:

> 1. SIMEON M. 2. MARY ANN. 3. WILLIAM H. 4. CHARLES E.; d. young.

154. SIMEON M. [1], born March 24, 1805. Married Sept. 3, 1838, at Vermillion, Ohio, Olive Rockwell; born Sept. 29, 1820, at Painesville. Settled in Florence, Erie Co. He died at Oberlin, March 4, 1876. She died there March 24, 1876. The first three children were by his former wife. Children:

> 1. Dr. CHARLES E.; settled at Green Bay, Wis. 2. SAMUEL J.; settled in New York. 3. GEORGE M.; killed in the civil war. 4. ANNA; residence at Orange County, Fla. 5. JOEL R. 6. OLIVE A. 7. LAURA A. 8. MARY E. 9. BURT D.; residence at Orange County, Fla.

155. JOEL R. CRANE [5], born Dec. 1, 1845, in Birmingham, Erie Co., Ohio. Married Oct. 30, 1872, Frankie A. Broadwell; born at Columbia, Sept. 5, 1852. He is a furniture manufacturer at Oberlin, Ohio. He served in the civil war in the 4th army corps from Sept. 2, 1862, to July 25, 1865. Child:

> 1. LESLIE M., b. March 29, 1874, at Bellevue, Ohio.

------

156. ELIJAH CRANE, born in New York city. His wife Mary was born in Darien, near Norwalk, Conn. He was a maker of ladies' shoes. His last residence was at Adrian, Mich., where he

died. It is said his father was born in Cranetown, N. J. Their son :

1. MATTHEW F. CRANE, b. in New York city March 3, 1815; was a carpenter and joiner; m. in that city March 13, 1836, Maria Van Orden; she was b. there Oct. 10, 1816. He enlisted Sept. 3, 1861, in Co. K, 51st Regt., New York Infantry. Children : 1. MARY T., b. Dec. 2, 1838, at Ann Arbor, Mich.; m. in 1862 in Chicago, Ill. 2. SARAH R., b. Feb. 28, 1841, at Raisin, Mich. 3. WILLIAM, b. March 28, 1843, at New York city; residence at Colorado. 4. ABBIE T., b. July 13, 1845, at Raisin, Mich. 5. JOSEPHINE S., b. Dec. 7, 1848, at Bedford, Mich.; residence at Green Point. 6. GEORGE THEODORE, b. Jan. 22, 1851, at Bedford, Mich.; residence at Brooklyn, N. Y.

---

157. JOHN P. CRANE, married Mary, daughter of William DeCamp, who died in 1777, prisoner of war, in New York. Their son Charles Crane married Elizabeth Williams, and had :

1. OSCAR B. CRANE, b. March 15, 1828, in Newark, N. J.; m. there Oct. 5, 1855, Mary Harrison; b. Jan. 24, 1818. Children, b. in Newark : 1. MARY F., b. Nov. 4, 1856. 2. IDA C., b. Jan. 6, 1859. 3. OSCAR H. L., b. Nov. 2, 1861.

---

158. MOSES CRANE, married Lydia Jones. Their son :

1. ARCHIBALD D. CRANE, born in New York State, July 2, 1830. Married Dec. 25, 1849, in that State, Jane Haynes. He served in the civil war; was corporal in Co. H, 36th Regt. Wisconsin Vols., and a pensioner. Residence at Garden City, Minn. Children : 1. LUCAS. 2. MARY ANTONETTE. 3. ALICE. 4. FRANCES. 5. DAVID. 6. MELVIN. 7. FREDDIE.

The following five brothers lived in or near Mifflin, Mifflin Co., Pa. They were from New Jersey it is supposed. Mr. O. W. Crane, of Newark, Ohio, writes, "the name of their father was Joseph;" others say "John." Children :

1. JOSEPH CRANE, b. 1765; m.; 2. EVAN, b. 1772, in Cumberland County. 3. GEORGE. 4. ROBERT, b. Aug. 24, 1776. 5. BENJAMIN.

159. JOSEPH CRANE [1], married Mary Smiley. He died in Juniata County, Pa., in 1836. His son James S. says his father was called a Jerseyman. Children :

1. MATHEW, b. 1795. 2. GEORGE. 3. JAMES S., b. Oct. 27, 1815, in Mifflin County, Pa.

160. EVAN CRANE [2], about the year 1808 removed to Salt Creek Township, Muskingum Co., seven miles east of Zanesville, Ohio. Married 1st, Sidona Wells. She died April 30, 1807. Married 2d, Mrs. Amelia Eddington, a widow, whose maiden name was Wales. She died in May, 1332. He died

March 13, 1850. Was drafted in the war of 1812, but soon discharged. He was a farmer. Children :

1. ABRAHAM. 2. GEORGE. 3. JOSEPH, b. Jan. 12, 1802. 4. JAMES. 5. BENJAMIN. 6. SIDONA. By 2d wife: 7. MARY. 8. DOROTHY. 9. SUSAN. 10. SARAH. 11. ROBERT. 12. MATTHEW EVAN, b. Feb. 24, 1819.

161. ROBERT CRANE [4], married in 1805 Jane Taylor, of Huntington County, Pa. She was born Aug. 22, 1778. He was a cooper and farmer. Served in the war of 1812. He died Nov. 21, 1843, at Chandlersville, Ohio. She died there Aug. 24, 1853. Child :

1. ROBERT TAYLOR, b. 1807.

162. MATTHEW CRANE [1], born in 1795. Married Martha Rodgers, a native of Lancaster. Pa.; born 1802. He removed to Muskingum County, near Zanesville, Ohio, in 1820. He was a carpenter. He died in Washington, Ill., Oct. 1, 1855, or Sept. 27, 1856. The two dates are given for his death. She died Jan. 13, 1896. Children :

1. VIOLET; d. in infancy. 2. JOSEPH, b. April 6. 1822, at Zanesville, Ohio. 3. JAMES R., b. Sept. 14, 1824, at Zanesville, Ohio. 4. JANE M.; m. B. E. Miles. 5. GEORGE W. 6. MILTON B. 7. CHARLES A.; postmaster. 8. THOMAS ASHTON, b. Jan. 5, 1830. 9. WILLIAM H.; an M.D.; d. 1877.

163. JAMES S. CRANE [3], married Dec. 24, 1841, Martha Helmick, in Muskingum County, Ohio, He was a carpenter. Residence at Dresden, Ohio. Served in the civil war about Nashville, Tenn., in 1863 and 1864. He was justice of the peace in 1864, and 1880 still holding the office. Children :

1. CAROLINA A. 2. MARY ELIZA. 3. RUSSELL BURGESS. 4. ANNA BELL. 5. JENNETTE D. 6. MARIA JANE.

164. JOSEPH CRANE [3], married March 9, 1826, Eliza Clark, in Muskingum County. Ohio. He was a farmer. She was born in New York State, Dec. 28, 1806. She died Jan. 1, 1830. Child :

1. EVAN JOSEPH, b. April 26, 1827, in Muskingum County, Ohio; m. Cassandria Geyer.

165. MATTHEW EVAN CRANE [12], married Mary M. Huff, Feb. 14, 1845. Children :

1. F. A., b. Feb. 16, 1846; merchant at Newark, Ohio. 2. O. W., b. July 6, 1851; merchant at Newark, Ohio.

166. ROBERT TAYLOR CRANE [1], born in Pennsylvania in 1807. Married Rhoda Hector in Taylorsville, Ohio. Settled in Muskingum County, Ohio; a carpenter. He died in Dresden, Ohio, Aug. 30, 1841. She died June 7, 1877, in Chandlersville, Ohio. Child :

1. BENJAMIN BAILY, b. Aug. 10, 1834; m. Sarah E. Doty.

167. JOSEPH CRANE[4] [2], (Mathew.[3] Joseph,[2] Joseph[1]), married Mary E. Bates, May 20, 1852, at St. Louis, Mo. She was

born Nov. 27, 1831, in Newtown, Ky. He was a miller. Residence at California, Mo., where he died. Child:

1. EDWARD BATES, b. April 30, 1853.

168. JAMES R. CRANE [3], married Leva A. Burton, Sept. 13, 1855, at Washington, Ill., where he settled. He was a notary public and real estate dealer. He died Jan. 2, 1897. She died Feb. 9, 1899. Children:

1. MARY B., b. Dec., 1856; m. Joseph V. Graff, Oct. 5, 1882. She is a graduate of the Normal School, Peoria, Ill., 1877. He is a member of Congress, and on the committee on claims of the 55th Congress.
2. MARTHA RODGERS, b. April 24, 1860; m. Frank Snyder Heiple, Oct. 21, 1880. Children: 1. GERTRUDE. 2. MARY. 3. MAUDE. 4. ROBERT. 5. FRANK. 6. ELI E. 7. DONAL. 8. HAROLD.
3. ROBERT. b. Jan. 6, 1863; d. Aug. 24, 1875.
4. LEVA A., b. June 14, 1869.
5. JOHN RAE, b. Nov. 15, 1876.

169. JANE M. CRANE [4], married Nov. 27, 1845, Benjamin Eustice, son of Joseph B. and Elizabeth (Buckingham) Miles. He was born Oct. 11, 1818. Residence at Washington, Ill. Children:

1. PHILO BUCKINGHAM (Miles), b. Dec. 12, 1849. 2. CHARLES CRANE (Miles), b. Aug. 1, 1852. 3. ELIZABETH MARTHA (Miles), b. May 29, 1855. 4. MATHEW CRANE (Miles), b. April 7, 1859; d. Aug. 1, 1860. 5. LUCY ALDERSON (Miles), b. July 30, 1861. 6. JOSEPH CRANE (Miles), b. Nov. 27, 1865. 7. CATHERINE BELINDA (Miles), b. March 2, 1868.

170. GEORGE W. CRANE [5], married Mollie Gorin. Children:

1. FRANK. 2. CLARENCE. 3. FRED.

171. MILTON B. CRANE [6], married Belle Jaynes in St. Louis in 1860. Children:

1. VIOLET; m. Bert Brown. 2. BURT. 3. OZARK J. 4. GRACE. 5. CHAUNCEY.

172. CHARLES A. CRANE [7], married Laura Parker. Children:

1. JAMES C., and 2. WILLIAM T.; both residing (1895) in St. Louis, Mo.

173. THOMAS ASHTON CRANE [8], married March 23, 1854, Emily Ann Kingsbury. He was a farmer in Tazewell County, Ill. He died March 22, 1872. She was born in Rochester, N. Y., Dec. 28, 1834; died March 31, 1872. Children:

1. LEWIS F., b. March 31, 1856. 2. ADDIE MARION. 3. EDWIN ASHTON. 4. MATHEW AMHERST. 5. EMILY JOSEPHINE. 6. CHARLES MILTON. 7. JAMES ROGERS; d. Dec. 30, 1867. 8. HELEN KINGSBURY. 9. MARTHA JANE. 10. BESSIE FRANCES.

173½. MATHEW AMHERST, married June 20, 1883, Anna Ruhrrup, a native of Muscatine, Iowa. She was born Oct. 7, 1862. He was a merchant at De Witt, Neb., in 1884. Child:

1. HENRY ASHTON, b. Jan. 17, 1884.

174. EVAN JOSEPH CRANE [1], married Cassandria Geyer, Nov. 4, 1851, in Muskingum County, Ohio, where she was born May 2, 1828. He was postmaster, notary public and a merchant in Iberia, Ohio. Children:

    1. MARION CLARK, b. Sept. 10, 1852. 2. ROSETTA CAROLINE, b. Feb. 1. 1855. 3. GEORGE WINFIELD, b. July 7, 1857. 4. FLORENCE MAY, b. Jan. 1, 1862. 5. DELLA VIOLINDER, b. July 14, 1865.

175. BENJAMIN BAILEY CRANE [1], married Sarah E. Doty at Cardington, Ohio, Dec. 31, 1864. She was born in Morrow County, Ohio, Jan. 3, 1842. He served in the civil war in 3d O. V. I., in 1861, 1862 and 1863. He graduated at Bartlett's Commercial School, Cincinnati, in 1855, and followed the insurance business. Children:

    1. FRED L., b. Nov. 11, 1865. 2. ANNA and MARY, twins, b. Sept. 8, 1867; 3. MARY; d. Feb. 13, 1874. 4. CORA BELL C., b. Oct. 15, 1869. 5. NELLIE, b. Dec. 6, 1874; d. April 12, 1876.

---

176. Captain AMBROSE CRAIN served in the Revolutionary war. His son, JOSEPH CRAIN, m. Mary, daughter of Andrew Moore, Esq., and had several children, among them Col. RICHARD M. CRAIN, b. Nov., 1777, in West Hanover Township, Lancaster (now Dauphin County), Pa. He was their fifth son, and he married Elizabeth, daughter of Hon. Robert Whitehill, of East Pennsborough Township, Cumberland Co., Pa. He was a well known citizen of that State, of high social standing and extensive means. He served with distinction in the War of 1812. He died Oct. 16, 1852. Children:

    1. JOSEPH; m. Rebecca Wills. 2. ELEANOR REED; m. Dr. William W. Ruthford, of Harrisburg, Pa. 3. MARY ADELINE; m. 1st, Dr. James Jarkin; 2d, Dr. A. T. Dean; 3d, Isaac Van Horn, Esq. 4. ELIZABETH; m. Leopold Wykoff, of Philadelphia. 5. AGNES; d. unm.

---

177. JAMES H. CRAIN, M. D., of Beechwood, Pulaski Co., Ill., reports the following, which leads to the belief that some connection existed with the family above: "My grandfather's name was Joseph, who, with his brothers, took part in the Revolution. They spelled their name Crain, and settled on the Susquehanna River, southeast of Harrisburg, at an early day. Family names were Richard, Joseph, Andrew and John. My father John Crain, with several brothers, left Pennsylvania, coming down the Ohio River in a flatboat to Maysville, Ky., in the last century. After spending some time there they removed to Franklin, Ohio, and later to Springfield, Clark Co., Ohio. Dr. Joseph Crain, of Chambersburgh, was son of Richard, a brother of my father."

178. JOHN CRAIN, born six miles southeast of Harrisburg, Pa. Married ——— Reeder; but another report says he mar-

59

ried Nancy Milholin. He was a farmer at Springfield, Ohio, and perhaps was twice married. Children:

> 1. JOSEPH MILTON, b. Sept. 2, 1807.   2. JAMES H., b. Aug. 30, 1827.

179.   JOSEPH MILTON [1], married in Springfield, Ohio, April 22, 1830, Dulsena A. Donavon, who was born in Maysville, Ky., Oct. 14, 1812. She died Sept. 30, 1853, in New Carlisle, Ohio. He was a cabinet maker. He died at Villa Ridge, Ill., Oct. 11, 1876. Children:

> 1. JOHN REEDER. 2. WILLIAM R. 3. JOHN REEDER CRAIN, b. in Springfield, Ohio; m. S. R. Townsley, Dec. 6, 1853. He was a saddle and harness maker at Jamestown, Ohio; a captain in the United States service in the civil war from 1861 to 1865. Children: 1. CALVIN L., b. Dec. 30, 1855. 2. FRANK W., b. Feb., 1859. 3. ALBERT C., b. Oct., 1873.

180.   WILLIAM R. CRAIN [2], born in Springfield, Ohio. Married March 2, 1862, in Caledonia, Ill., Mary A. Spence, who was born there Feb. 2, 1844. He was a farmer; residence at Villa Ridge, Ill. He served in the civil war in 81st Illinois Infantry from Aug. 5, 1862, to Aug. 5, 1865. Children:

> 1. JAMES L., b. June 13, 1866. 2. WARREN E., b. Jan. 5, 1869. 3. EMMA, b. March 6, 1870. 4. ALMA, b. Sept. 15, 1872. 5. LEWIS F., b. Dec. 25, 1873. 6. MARY, b. May 30, 1875. 7. WILLIAM R., b. Dec. 19, 1877.

181.   JAMES H. CRAIN, M. D. [2], was a practicing physician at Buchwood, Pulaski County, Ill.; graduate of College of Physicians and Surgeons, New York city, in 1850. Married Nancy J. Wilson. Children:

> 1. RYDAL. 2. CORAL. 3. FESTAL. 4. CLAUDE.

---

182.   BENJAMIN CRAIN, of Ogelthorpe County, Ga., was a farmer, and about the year 1800 removed to the State of Kentucky. John, his only son, was born in Kentucky in 1801; also a farmer. Married in Covington, Washington Co., Ill. Anna Higgins. She died there in 1831. This John Crain was a member of both the house and senate of the Illinois legislature. He died in 1872, leaving an only son:

183.   JOSEPH ADDISON, born Jan. 8, 1831; a lawyer; graduate of Harvard Law School in 1856. Settled at Freeport, Ill., where he married Feb. 7, 1860, Vennete Sweet, a native of that place. She was born 1840. He held the office of United States register in bankruptcy in 1867—1878. Children:

> 1. KATHARINE, b. Sept. 14, 1860; d. Feb. 21, 1864. 2. JOHN SWEET, b. Dec. 14, 1864; d. Nov. 18, 1866. 3. VENNETE SWEET, b. Sept. 27, 1867; graduate of Wellesley College in 1888. 4. CHARLES FREDERICK, b. July 21, 1872; graduate of West Point, June 12, 1894, and commissioned second lieutenant of 19th Infantry, U. S. A.; went to Porto Rico with his regiment, and there promoted to first lieutenant, and assigned to 15th Infantry, and sent with that regiment to Cuba. 5. ETHEL GORDON, b. Oct. 13, 1876.

Lieut. Crain furnished the following, taken from records at Lexington, Ga., Dec. 14, 1895, and there is nothing further about the family there :

June 28, 1799.—Marriage license issued to George Crain and Amelia Thompkins.
January 12, 1801.—Marriage license to William Crain and Nellie Humphries.
June 16, 1803.—Marriage license to Spencer Crain and Polly Thompkins.

---

184. BENJAMIN CRANE, born at Harrisburg, Pa., in 1755 Married Elizabeth ——— ; born in Lycoming County, Pa., in 1775. She died in Miami County, Ohio, in 1862. He was a farmer. He died in Troy, Ohio, April, 1819. His son :

185—1. SAMUEL CRANE. b. March 12, 1808, in Lycoming County, Pa.; m. Ann Mills, Oct. 8, 1829, in Green County, Ohio. where she was b. Oct. 29, 1807. He was a merchant. He d. Jan. 16, 1876, at Columbus, Ga. Their son :

186—1. WILLIAM H. CRANE. b. June 22, 1838, at Fletcher, Ohio; m. Dec. 25, 1860, at Columbus, Ga , Emily Gidion, a native of Stewart County, Ga. He served in the confederate army in Virginia. He was a merchant at Columbus, Ga. Children: 1. CHARLEY A., b. May 24, 1863; d. June 20, 1864. 2. SAMUEL C., b. Sept. 16, 1864. 3. ANNA C., b. Jan. 29, 1866. 4. ROSA, b. April 6, 1868.

The following is reported by·William Strain Crain, La Fayette, Ind. :

187. ANDREW CRAIN, born 1759 in Scotland. Married Jane Strain at the north of Ireland. Was a tanner. Came to this country about 1784 with his brothers John, William and Joseph, and settled in Pennsylvania, and then removed together to Ohio. Was private in the Revolutionary war. He died in 1825. Children :

188—1. WILLIAM STRAIN, b. Sept. 5, 1812, in Green County, Ohio; went to Indiana in 1829.; m. July 14, 1842, Marietta A. Taylor. who was b. April 2, 1819, in Colesville, N. J. He served in the Black Hawk war. He was a grocer at La Fayette, Ind. Had six children; three of them d. young; names not given: 1. CHARLES HICKS. M. D., b. Dec. 7, 1854; physician at La Fayette, Ind.; m. Jennie W. Vernon. Oct. 1, 1879. ' 2. RICHARD ELDRIDGE, b. Dec. 11, 1856. 3. WILLIAM SAWYER, b. Feb. 9, 1858.

2. JAMES, b. June 16, 1816, in Clark County, Ohio; settled in White County, Ind.

---

189. LEWIS CRANE, formerly of Newark, N. J., by trade a builder. His grandson Andrew W. Crane says this Lewis had a brother George Crane who lived in Newark, N. J. Lewis married Phebe DeCamp, who died in Newark, N. J. He died in Hopkinsville, Warren Co., Ohio, Oct. 4, 1856, whither he went with his son Edward from New York State about 1840.

Children :

1. SARAH ; m. —— Kearn, or Kearny; settled in Lebanon, Ohio.2.
   CAROLINE ; m. —— Roof. 3. EDWARD, b. May 18, 1803.4.
   GEORGE ; d.; no issue. 5. ANTOINETTE.

190. EDWARD CRANE [3], married Oct. 15, 1828, Evaline S.
Durkee. She was born July 4, 1808, at Auburn, Cayuga Co.,
N. Y. He was a harness-maker and carriage trimmer and
farmer. Resided in Jordan, N. Y., many years. He died in
Hopkinsville, Warren Co., Ohio, March 27, 1860. Children :

1. HORACE D., b. Oct. 5, 1829, at Jordan, N. Y. 2. CAROLINE L.; m.
   —— Hopkins, at Hopkinsville, Ohio. 3. ANDREW W., b. May
   10, 1833. 4. CELESTIA ; d.; no issue. 5. DWIGHT K., b. June 21,
   1839, at Seneca Falls, N. Y. 6. DAY OTIS, b. Oct. 6, 1841, at Lebanon, Ohio. 7. SENECA. 8. GEORGE. 9. EDWARD G.

191. HORACE D. CRANE [1], married Ella Whitton, Aug. 21,
1856, in Warren County, Ohio. She was born Aug. 8, 1835, in
Cincinnati. First residence at Mainville, Warren Co., Ohio.
By occupation he was a steamboat man. Children :

1. DAVID W., b. Aug. 8, 1857 at Mainville. 2. EDWARD, b. Oct. 27,
   1858, at Mainville. 3. LOUIE, b. Feb. 18, 1860, at Mainville. 4.
   EVA, b. Feb. 18, 1860, at Mainville. 5. EDITH, b. June 28, 1863,
   at Mainville; m. John Weaver. 6. ELLA, b. Dec. 25, 1866, in
   Clermont County, Ohio. 7. LAURA, b. July 22, 1868, in Cler-
   mont County, Ohio. 8. MARK, b. June 20, 1870, in Warren
   County, Ohio. 9. HARRY, b. Feb. 17, 1875, in Mississippi. 10.
   FRANK, b. Oct. 10, 1876, in Mississippi.

192. ANDREW W. CRANE [3], married April 6, 1861, Mary
E. Wager, a native of Deerfield, Ohio. She was born June 16,
1840. He was a carpenter and builder. Late residence at
Nashville, Tenn. Children :

1. HARRY, b. 1862; d. 1863. 2. LILIE MAY, b. 1864. 3. LULEO LAKE,
   b. 1866. 4. ANDREW WALTER, 5. ELLA WALDREN, twins, b.
   1868. 6. DAY OTIS, b. 1871. 7. MARY EVALINE, b. 1873. 8.
   BESSEY L., b. 1876.

193. DWIGHT K. CRANE [5], married Dec. 31, 1861, Orena
E. Gilman, in Mainville, Warren Co., Ohio. She was born in
Cincinnati, Nov. 1, 1836. Children :

1. DELOSS ORIN, b. Dec. 13, 1862, near Hopkinsville, Ohio; d. March
   10, 1868, in Westboro, Clinton Co., Ohio. 2. CORA ELIZA, b. Jan.
   2, 1865, near Hopkinsville, Ohio; d. Oct. 12, 1870, in Buckley, Ill.
   3. CLYDE C., b. April 1, 1872, in Flora, Clay Co., Ill. 4. GUY
   GILMAN, b. May 19, 1874, in Flora, Clay Co., Ill.

194. DAY OTIS CRANE [6], married at Springfield, Mo., Oct.
25, 1877, Georgianna B. Morhisen. He served in the civil war
from April 6, 1861, to September, 1865 ; was captain of volunteers. He is an attorney-at-law. Residence at Washington, D.
C. Child :

1. DONN P., b. Sept. 1, 1878, at Springfield, Mo.

---

195. GEORGE CRANE, born March 22, 1766. Married Catharine Quiggle. She was born in 1766. He purchased in 1799 a

tract of 300 acres on the west branch of the Susquehanna River, near Jersey Shore, Lycoming Co., Pa. The property is well known as the "Crane Farm," and now (February, 1879,) still in the possession of his descendants, and under the highest state of cultivation. He died Dec. 25, 1819 She died March 4, 1813. Children:

> 1. GEORGE, b. June 2, 1792; m. Lucretia Covenhoven. 2. MICHAEL, m. Maria Covenhoven, Oct. 10, 1831; moved to Illinois after marriage; she d. Dec., 1878, in Kansas. 3. CATHARINE; m. ——— Nichols; she d. in Wisconsin, July 1, 1861. 4. ———; m. Charles Stewart. 5. FANNY; m. Abijah Smith; she d. June 26, 1832.

196. Col. GEORGE CRANE [1], married Lucretia Covenhoven, Feb. 22, 1816. She was born Oct. 29, 1795; died Aug. 5, 1849, aged 53 years and 9 months. Lucretia Covenhoven was daughter of Robert Covenhoven, who was of Dutch parentage, but a native of Monmouth County, N. J. He was married in New Jersey, Feb. 22, 1778, barely escaping the grasp of a troop of Hessians, who appeared on the spot during the marriage ceremony. He served under Gen. Washington; participated in the battles at Trenton and Princeton. He served under Gen. Sullivan as a spy and guide in his celebrated expedition in Pennsylvania up the north branch of the Susquehanna in 1779 to the Indian country. He was in the unfortunate company commanded by Lieut. Boyd, and among the few that escaped the dreadful massacre. He also acted as a spy, and frequently alone, and was a prominent actor in the skirmishes and battles with the Indians on the west branch and its tributaries, experiencing many narrow escapes from death. When peace was restored he settled permanently on the west branch of the Susquehanna, near Jersey Shore, Lycoming Co., Pa., and after the death of his wife for a time made it his home with his son-in-law Col. George Crane. Children:

> 1. CATHARINE, b. Nov. 5, 1816; m. W. C. Sanderson. 2. ROBERT, b. Nov. 21, 1818; m. Elizabeth M. Strickler. 3. GEORGE WASHT, b. Jan. 30, 1821; m. Emma A. Gouter, Jan. 15, 1845; no children. 4. MICHAEL QUIGGLE, b. Feb. 7, 1823; m. Hannah C. Bailey. 5. MERCIE KELSIE, b. May 4, 1825; m. J. J. Sanderson. 6. RICHARD M., b. Sept. 3, 1827; d. June 15, 1830. 7. LUCRETIA ANN, b. March 2, 1829; m. 1st, J. M. Strickler; m. 2d, S. H. Fredericks. 8. JAMES VAN BUREN, b. April 28, 1834; m. Frances O. Bailey, Jan. 5, 1860; he d. Dec. 11, 1878; no children.

197. CATHARINE CRANE [1], married W. C. Sanderson, Jan. 10, 1837. (This may be Sanduson or Sanderson). Children:

> 1. WILLIAM H. (Sanderson); m. Sallie W. Malone. 2. ELLEN (Sanderson), d. May 4, 1840. 3. MARY FRANCES (Sanderson); m. A. O. Furst; she d. Sept. 27, 1877. 4. GEORGE CRANE (Sanderson); m. Laura Grafius. 5. LAURA (Sanderson); m. Daniel Detwiler. 6. ELIZABETH JANE (Sanderson); m. George L. Potter. 7. CREACIE CRANE (Sanderson). 8. EMMA C. (Sanderson).

198. MERCIE KELSIE CRANE [5], married John J. Sanderson, Jan. 10, 1843. Children:

> 1. GEORGE L. (Sanderson); m. Mary L. White. 2. CREACIE ELIZABETH (Sanderson); m. John A. Gamble. 3. MARGARET A.

(Sanderson). 4. VIRGINIA (Sanderson); m. H. C. Trump. 5.
ELLEN KATE (Sanderson). 6. MERCIE (Sanderson).

199. ROBERT CRANE [2], married Elizabeth M. Strickler,
May 6' 1846. Children :

    1. JANE S., b. Aug. 14, 1847; m. Dr. J. K. Lineaweaver, June 2, 1868.
      2. GEORGE, b. Aug. 29, 1849; m. Emily M. Gossler, Nov. 21.
      1778. 3. CREACIE, b. June 31, 1851; m. H. O. Chapman, June 18,
      1874. 4. ROBERT, b. May 30, 1853; m. Alice M. Hershey, Dec. 5,
      1878. 5. ELIZABETH M., b. Oct. 16, 1859.

200. LUCRETIA ANN CRANE [7], married J. M. Strickler, Nov.
7, 1848. Children :

    1. PAUL STRICKLER.
    2. CREACIE, } twins; { m. B. T. Malone.
    3. JENNIE, }   { m. George Shipman.

201. MICHAEL Q. CRANE [4], married Hannah C. Bailey,
Feb. 21, 1850. Children :

    1. HARVEY; m. Belle Hancock. 2. GEORGE. 3. EDWARD. 4.
      HARRY. 5. ELLA; m. William Wagner.

202. JANE S. CRANE [1], married Dr. J. K. Lineaweaver,
June 2, 1868. Children :

    1. ROBERT C. (Lineaweaver), b. May 25, 1869; d. Nov. 24, 1869. 2.
      JANET C. (Lineaweaver), b. July 19, 1873. 3 JOHN (Linea-
      weaver), b. June 5, 1876; d. Nov. 18, 1878.

203. CREACIE CRANE [3], married O. H. Chapman, June 18,
1874. Child :

    1. BESSIE (Chapman), b. April 25, 1876.

Cranes of St. Mary's County, Md. :

204. THOMAS CRANE, married Elizabeth, daughter of Dr.
James Armstrong, of St. Mary's County, Md., and had 12 children; but names of only four have been obtained :

    1. JAMES ARMSTONG, b. June 17, 1758. 2. SARAH; m. Major Henry
      Watts. 3. HELEN; m. ——— Bean. 4. ROBERT; last heard of
      in Cincinnati.

205. JAMES ARMSTRONG CRANE [1], married Jan. 10, 1790,
Mary Abell. He died Sept. 1, 1836. He lived in St. Mary's and inherited from his father the Herring Creek farm, a fine estate,
which has been in the family more than two hundred years. The
old Crane burying ground is on this estate, which has but recently
passed out of the hands of the Cranes. He had 12 children;
several died in childhood and unmarried. The following left
descendants :

    1. ELIZABETH; m. Mathew Abell; had: 1. JAMES CRANE (Abell);
      d. in Texas. 2. ALEXANDER (Abell); d. west.
    2. CATHARINE; m. Henry Watts; had: 1. WILLIAM (Watts). 2.
      MARY ELIZABETH (Watts). 3. HENRY (Watts).
    3. SUSANNA; m. John Milburn; had: 1. GEORGE ROBERT (Milburn).
      2. SUSAN CRANE (Milburn).

4. MARY; m. Thomas Young; she d. May, 1897, in Washington, D. C.,
   aged 92; had: 1. SARAH CRANE (Young). 2. Dr. JAMES
   THOMAS (Young); residence at Washington, D. C.
5. GEORGE; m. three times, 1st, Susanna Bennett. 6. ROBERT. 7.
   JAMES EDWARD.

206. GEORGE CRANE [5], married three times; Susanna
Bennett was the mother of his children. Children :

1. ANN MARIA; m. 1st, Lewis Smith; 2d, Edward S. Abell, by whom
   she had: 1. JOHN H. 2. SUSAN.
2. JOHN ABELL; m. twice, and had children; among them: 1. GEORGE;
   was in Chicago.
3. MARY ABELL; m. Rev. Andrew Sutton, of Baltimore.
4. RAVAUD KEARNEY; a prominent physician in St. Mary's County,
   Md., but d. early in life, leaving a daughter, who married.

207. ROBERT CRANE [6], married Sarah Brent Watts. Both
died. Their residence at Baltimore. Children :

1. Prof. ROBERT BRENT; single. 2. SUSAN WATTS; single. 3.
   HENRY WATTS; m. ——Gresham; has three children. 4. RA-
   VAUD KEARNEY; m. —— Hodgkins; no children. 5. SARAH
   VIRGINIA; single. 6. KATIE; single.

208. JAMES EDWARD CRANE [7], married Sarah Amanda
Spencer. He died in 1861, aged 50. She died in 1876, aged
65. They had six children; four died in early childhood.
Children :

1. JAMES PARRAN. 2. WILLIAM SOMERSET; single; residence in St.
   Mary's County.

209. Judge JAMES PARRAN CRANE [1], married 1st, Laura A.
Hammett. She died 1885, leaving three children. He married 2d,
Mollie Dent. Mr. Crane is a lawyer, and since 1882 has been on
the bench of the seventh judicial circuit of Maryland, having
been reëlected in 1897 for a second term of fifteen years. Children :

1. KATHARINE SPENCER. 2. GEORGIE E. 3. THOMAS SPENCER. 4.
   LAURA AMANDA. 5. JAMES DOUGLASS. 6. CHARLES FRANKLIN.

Judge Crane writes that the ancestors of the Maryland Cranes
were Church of England people, and, with few exceptions, continue in that faith; and that Judge Peter Crane, of Maryland,
said he believed they were all related, although some spelled their
name differently.

---

210. PETER WOOD married Anne GANTT, of Maryland.
Settled in Woodville, Prince George's Co., Md. For seventy
years the Wood family have lived here. Children :

1. THOMAS (Wood); m. —— Crain, granddaughter of Capt. John
   Crain. 2. ELIZABETH (Wood); m. Col. Robert Alex Crain. 3.
   A daughter (Wood); m. —— Crain. 4. JOHN (Wood): m.
   —— CRAIN.

211. —— CRAIN, married Miss Wood. Children :

1. Judge PETER W. CRAIN, of Annapolis and Baltimore, Md. 2.
   Dr. ROBERT CRAIN. 3. CATHARINE CRAIN; m. Bailey Crain.
   4. ELIZA CRAIN; m. Mr. Morgan.

212. Captain JOHN CRAIN, married Mary Bailey. Was captain of a company in war of 1812; a Presbyterian by faith. He changed the spelling of his name to Crain, and lived in Springfield in the old family mansion, near Middleburgh, Fauquier Co., Va., where his children were born. He was a well-to-do planter of high standing in the community, and as his children married he gave them liberal portions; all had fine farms and good homes. A sister of Capt. Crain married Col. Bronaugh, aid to Gen. Washington when Braddock was killed, and assisted in burying him. Children:

> 1. JOHN. 2. JAMES. 3. BAILEY. 4. MARY. 5. ROBERT ALEXANDER, b. Nov. 4, 1789; m. Elizabeth, dau. of Peter Wood. 6. A daughter; m. —— Sanford.

213. JOHN CRAIN [1], married —— Lane, daughter of Col. Lane. Children:

> 1. JOHN, b. about 1805; went to Louisiana about 1828; first of the family to go; d. in Louisiana, aged about 23. 2. JOSEPH LANE; d. in Louisiana; was a civil engineer; second to go. 3. WARNER; removed to Texas. 4. HUMPREY; was a lawyer; also a doctor; d. of yellow fever in 1838 or 1839 in Alexandria, La. 5. EPAMINONDES; d. in New Orleans while on his way to Texas from Virginia.

214. BAILEY CRAIN [3], married Catherine Crain, whose mother was Miss Wood, of Maryland. Child:

> 1. A daughter, who m. Judge Michael Ryan, and removed to Alexandria, La.

215. MARY CRAIN [4], married —— Sullivan. Child:

> 1. WARNER (Sullivan), who removed with his uncle Col. Robert Alexander Crain to Louisiana.

216. Col. ROBERT ALEXANDER CRAIN [5], married Feb. 9, 1814, Elizabeth, daughter of Peter Wood, of Woodville, Prince George's Co., Md. Her mother was Anne Gantt, also of that county in Maryland. The year prior to his marriage he made a trip to Louisiana on a visit, and was so much pleased with the country that in 1821 he, with his family, removed to that State, locating at Rapides Parish, where he established a cotton plantation; Texas then was a part of Mexico. The route travelled in making the journey to Louisiana was via Pittsburgh, Pa., down the river to Louisville, Ky., thence down the Mississippi River to Natchez, where they visited Col. Wood, a relative of Mrs. Crain, who went there from Maryland, and was then a wealthy planter, and from Natchez on to Rapides Parish. Mrs. Crain was cousin to Mrs. Margaret (née Smith), wife of Gen. Zachary Taylor, one of whose daughters was first wife of Jefferson Davis. She died Sept. 27, 1850. He died Aug. 27, 1852, at Roselawn, Rapides Parish, La., at the home of his son-in-law, C. H. Blanchard. Children:

> 1. JANE ADALINE, b. April 2, 1816, in Woodville, Prince George's Co., Md. 2. LAWRENCE P., b. 1818, in Springfield, Va. 3. FRANCES AMELIA, b. July 21, 1821, near Alexandria, La. 4. ROBERT

ALEXANDER, b. 1823. 5. WALTER O. 6. ALFRED BLANCHARD,
b. 1830; a physician, d. in California, June 12, 1852. 7. PEN, b.
July 4, 1837.

———— CRAIN [6], married ———— Sanford. Child:

1. JOHN (Sanford); m. Amy, a daughter of Capt. Nathaniel Green
Wilkinson, of the United States army. Residence at Tyrone.
Her mother was Georgianna Blanchard.

217. JANE ADALINE CRANE [1], married December 12,
1834, at the home of her father, Oak Hill, La., Dr. Levon
Luckett, of Fauquier County, Va. She was born at the Wood
family mansion in Prince George's County, Md., and in
1822 removed with her parents to Rapides Parish, La. After her
marriage they settled in Alexandria. To this good woman we
are deeply indebted for nearly every particle of information
respecting this line of Maryland and Virginia families, and from
her letters written to Mr. Herbert Henry Crain, of Key West,
Fla., these records have been chiefly taken. She writes: "The
Virginia Crains and my father's family are undoubtedly the
direct descendants of one of the brothers who came from Wales
and settled in that State (Virginia), and scattered out as his pos-
terity increased, into the adjoining State of Maryland and the
far off State of Louisiana. The number of my grandchildren
is 42 or 43, and of my great-grandchildren enough to settle
a small colony." She writes further: "Tradition says the
three brothers who came over from Wales were wealthy and of
high standing. One settled in Virginia (my grandfather's ancestor); one in Maryland; a descendant of the latter married my
grandfather Wood's sister, and Judge Peter Crain, of Annapolis,
Md., was a son." (See page 583.)

There were others of the name. One was Dr. Robert Crain.
They were contemporaries with my grandfather's family, and
distantly related. Their names I do not remember. They settled in Prince George's and Charles Counties, Md., and my uncle
Bailey Crain married one of the daughters. One of the brothers
went to New Jersey. Children:

1. ROBERT LEVON (Luckett), b. Dec. 12, 1837. 2. LETITIA ELIZA-
BETH (Luckett), b. Dec. 19, 1839. 3. FRANCES BERKELEY (Luck-
ett), b. Nov. 7, 1841. 4. ELLEN (Luckett), b. Nov. 9, 1843. 5.
DELIA APHIA (Luckett), b. Nov., 1845. 6. HENRY PAYTON
(Luckett), b. Aug. 9, 1847. 7. ADALINE (Luckett), b. March 31,
1849. 8. CORA (Luckett), b. Dec. 12, 1850.

Dr. Robert L. Luckett, aged 57 years, died at the family
residence in Cotile Ward, Rapides Parish, La., Wednesday,
April 24, 1895, at 1 o'clock P. M. He had been seriously ill for
several weeks. He was born in Rapides Parish, son of the late
Dr. Levon Luckett and Adeline Crain. Dr. Robert married
Miss Angelica Marye, sister of Mr. L. V. Marye, of Alexandria, in 1861. Fourteen children were born; ten now survive.
Dr. Robert L. Luckett was a gallant confederate soldier. He
left for the front as lieutenant in Capt. Davidson's company;

60

afterwards appointed surgeon, and served in the army in Tennessee in that capacity. He leaves four sisters and one brother,—Mrs. Samuel Flower, of New Orleans; Mrs. Lizzie Vance, of Louisville, Ky.; Mrs. H. A. Thompson, of Boyce, La.; Mrs. J. P. Hickman, of Alexandria; and Mr. Henry P. Luckett, of Cotile Ward, this parish. He was a democrat, and very popular man. He served in the legislature in 1874; constitutional convention in 1879; State senator, representing Rapides and Vernon Parishes in 1880, serving four years; appointed United States marshal for the western district of Louisiana by President Cleveland in 1893, holding the office at the time of his death. He was an ardent anti-lottery advocate, and did much to check the evil. It was Bob Luckett that was made chairman of the committee that visited the McEnery-Wickliffe convention at Baton Rouge. His conduct then showed him to be a man of courage and strong convictions. He willingly served the poor without remuneration as their physician. His death was a severe blow to his native Parish and to the State.

218.	Capt. LAWRENCE P. CRAIN [2], married 1st, Martha, daughter of Dr. Flournoy, of Greenwood, Texas. She lived about a year, and died, leaving an infant son, which died, aged about six months. Capt. Crain was born in Springfield, Va.; was captain of a company of volunteers that went to the Mexican war from Shreveport, Caddo Parish, La. By profession he was a lawyer, and ranked high. He died in New Orleans, Jan. 27, 1858, on his way to Cuba for his health, having returned from the Mexican war in ill health. His remains were buried in Shreveport. He was educated at the University of Virginia, and graduated with distinctive honors, and carried on the practice of law for some years in Shreveport. He married 2d, Adalaide, daughter of Gov. Stokes, of North Carolina. Children :

     1. LAWRENCE; d. in infancy. 2. ROBERT CAMPBELL; was member of Louisiana legislature; d. of heart disease. 3. JOHN. 4. LAWRENCE SIDNEY; residence (1890), at Shreveport, La. 5. MONTFORT STOKES; a lawyer; (b. 1853), resided at Shreveport in 1853, where he d. March 3, 1890, leaving a wife and daughter.

219.	FRANCES AMELIA CRAIN [3], married Col. Cary Hansford Blanchard. She died at Roselawn, La., July 3, 1855. He died there Oct. 26, 1861. Was born in 1805. He was son of Cary Edward Blanchard, of Virginia, and Amy Newton, of Norfolk, Va., his wife. Children :

     1. CARY EDWARD (Blanchard), b. Dec. 14, 1846. 2. NEWTON CRAIN (Blanchard), b. Jan. 29, 1849. 3 FRANCIS ALEXANDER (Blanchard). 4. CHARLES HENRY (Blanchard), b. Jan. 26, 1853.

220.	CARY EDWARD BLANCHARD [1], married Mary Lucretia Davidson of Highland Plantation, Rapides Parish, La., and settled at Boyce. Children :

     1. FRANCES CRAIN (Blanchard), b. March 9, 1876. 2 CARY EDWARD (Blanchard), b. July 1, 1877. 3. MARTHA DAVIDSON (Blanchard), b. July 11, 1880. 4. NEWTON CRAIN (Blanchard), b. Nov. 25, 1883.

221. NEWTON CRAIN BLANCHARD [2], married December, 1873, Mary Emma, daughter of Capt. W. W. Barret, of Shreveport, La. His home is in Alexandria, La. He was elected member of congress from his district in 1880. In politics he is a democrat; an able and successful lawyer. Children:

    1. A son (Blanchard). 2. A daughter (Blanchard).

222. FRANCIS ALEXANDER BLANCHARD [3], married Sarah, daughter of Capt. W. W. Barret, of Shreveport, La. Children:

    1. A daughter .(Blanchard). 2. A daughter (Blanchard). 3. A son (Blanchard). 4 THOMAS (Blanchard)

223. CHARLES HENRY BLANCHARD [4], married Jan. 19, 1876, M. E. Jones. Children:

    1. EVELYN (Blanchard), b. March 13, 1878; d. Sept. 8, 1887. 2. FRANK ALEXANDER (Blanchard), b. Sept. 18, 1879. 3. ROBERT MATTHEW (Blanchard), b. Oct. 18, 1881. 4. CHARLES HENRY (Blanchard), b. Nov. 10, 1883. 5. LAWRENCE CRAIN (Blanchard), b. March 23, 1885.

224. Lieut. ROBERT ALEXANDER CRAIN [4] born in Virginia. Educated at West Point; served through the Mexican war; was first lieutenant on Gen. De Russey's staff. At the close of the war he returned to his home in Louisiana, and became a planter in Caddo Parish. When the civil war began he enlisted in the southern cause, and served through that war in Gen. Breckenridge's division. After peace was declared he again returned to Louisiana, and made his home with his sister Mrs. Luckett, at Ashbourne, on the Red River, where he died March 6, 1872.

225. Capt. WALTER O. CRAIN [5]. He, at the age of sixteen, and while Mason was secretary of the navy, entered the Naval Academy at Annapolis as a cadet, and afterwards served for a period of ten years in the United States navy prior to the civil war. When the war began he withdrew from the navy and served as captain in the confederate navy. After the close of the war he resided in Shreveport, La.

226. Dr. PEN CRAIN [7], was born at Oakhill, in Louisiana; a physician. Resides at Compti, on the Red River, La. Children:

    1. ROBERT ALEXANDER, b. July 2, 1879. 2. PEN, b. 1881.

227. Dr. ROBERT LEVEN LUCKETT [1], born in Alexandria, La. Entered Yale College at the age of about fourteen, and finished his education at the University of Virginia. Studied medicine at the age of twenty-one; graduating with distinction at twenty-three from the Louisiana Medical College at New Orleans. He married Nov. 27, 1861, Mary Angelica Marye, of Virginia, granddaughter of Mr. De Geñeres, the Spanish gov-

ernor of San Domingo at the time of the insurrection there, after which he came to the United States. Children :

1. ROBERT EDWARD (Luckett), b. Oct. 1, 1862; d. May 18, 1863. 2. ROBERT LEVEN (Luckett), b. Nov. 11, 1864. 3. CONSTANCE ADALINE (Luckett), b. July 17, 1866. 4. HENRY MARYE (Luckett), b. March 17, 1868; d. Sept. 28, 1883. 5. CORA MARY (Luckett), D. March 17, 1870. 6. ELLEN FLOWER (Luckett), b. March 17, 1870. 7. EDWARD FLOWER (Luckett), b. May 18, 1873. 8. MARY ELIZABETH (Luckett), b. May 20, 1873; d. June 17, 1884. 9. SAMUEL FLOWER (Luckett), b. March 10, 1877. 10. FRANCIS BARKELY (Luckett), b. Dec. 19, 1879. 11. MARSOLINA EUGENIA (Luckett), b. May 17, 1881. 12. MARY ELIZABETH (Luckett), b. Aug. 28, 1883. 13. HENRY FLOWER (Luckett), b. July 11, 1885. 14. GEORGE VICTOR (Luckett), b. July 12, 1887.

228. LETITIA ELIZABETH LUCKETT [2], married Hamilton M. Vance. Residence at New Orleans, La. Children :

1. LIZZIE LUCKETT (Vance), b. Sept. 3, 1863, at Ashbourne; m. Charles Hausford Shield, of Virginia; residence at Louisville, Ky. 1. MARGARET JOHNSTONE (Shield), b. Nov. 7, 1889. 2. LUCKETT (Vance), b. July, 1866. 3. JOSEPH BYRNE (Vance), b. Jan., 1868; m. Adaline Thompson, Feb. 2, 1889.

229. FRANCES BERKELEY LUCKETT [3], married Dec. 16, 1868, Robert K., son of Judge Walke, of Dayton, Ohio, and nephew to Commodore Walke, United States navy. She died in Longview, Texas, Jan. 1, 1882. Children :

1. ADALINE (Walke), b. Aug., 1875. 2. JOHN (Walke), b. March, 1880.

230. ELLEN LUCKETT [4], married April 4, 1866, Capt. Samuel Flower, C. A. Residence at New Orleans, La. Children :

1. SAMUEL (Flower), b. Feb., 1867. 2. HENRY HAYES (Flower), b. April, 1869. 3. ROBERT HENRY (Flower), b. 1871. 4. NELLIE (Flower), b. Aug. 13, 1874; d. in infancy. 5. NELLIE (Flower), b. Aug., 1875. 6. BALDWIN STUART (Flower), b. Dec. 25, 1876.

231. DELIA APHIA LUCKETT [5], married Capt. James G. P. Hooe. He died in 1868, leaving a son. She then married James P. Hickman. Child:

1. LEVEN LUCKETT (Hooe), b. March 23, 1866; a graduate in law; residence at Alexandria, La.

232. HENRY PAYTON LUCKETT [6], married July 23, 1875, Cornelia Petrovic. Residence at Ashbourne, La. Children :

1. LEVEN (Luckett), b. June 11, 1876. 2. DELIA (Luckett), b. Jan. 18, 1878. 3. PHILIP NOLAND (Luckett), b. Nov. 29, 1880. 4. CHARLES FLOWER (Luckett), b. Oct. 18, 1882. 5. HENRY PAYTON (Luckett), b. March 28, 1884; d. 1885. 6. ROBERT MADDOK (Luckett), b. Oct. 9, 1886; d. Oct. 20, 1886. 7. BESSIE THORNTON (Luckett), b. Jan. 11, 1888. 8. AMY STAFFORD (Luckett), b. 1889.

233. ADALINE CRAIN LUCKETT [7], married Henry A. Thompson, who was born Sept. 9, 1850. Children :

1. ADALINE (Thompson); m. Joseph B. Vance, Feb. 2, 1889. 2. HENRY (Thompson). 3. ROBERT (Thompson).

234. CORA LUCKETT [8], married Feb. 24, 1871, James P. Hickman. She died May 28, 1884, leaving eight children. He

then married Delia Aphia (Luckett) Hooe, a sister of his first wife. Residence at New Hope, La. Children:

> 1. ROBERT LUCKETT (Hickman), b. Sept. 11, 1872; d. Aug. 11, 1888. 2. CORA (Hickman), b. March 1, 1874. 3. MARY EMMA (Hickman), b. May 12, 1875; d. Sept. 6. 1887. 4. LILIAN (Hickman), b. Nov. 6, 1876. 5. MARY VANCE (Hickman), b. Oct. 17, 1878. 6. NEWTON BLANCHARD (Hickman), b. April 15, 1880. 7. JAMES PASCAL (Hickman), b. Aug. 1, 1881. 8 WILLIAM PRESTON (Hickman), b. May 28, 1884.

235. —— CRAIN, his given name may have been James, or, possibly, Lewis (is said to have had a half-brother John Smith Crain), was a native of Maryland or Virginia. He married Agness Hardgrove, a native of Maryland; born near Baltimore. He joined the soldiers as they marched by his farm in Virginia, and went to serve in the war of 1812. He died of yellow fever at Norfolk. She died in Utica, Mo., May 20, 1879, leaving a son Lewis Crain, born May 12, 1807, in Hampshire County, West Va. This Lewis Crain married Hannah Warfield in that County in Dec., 1831. She was born June 4, 1804. He was a farmer in Utica, Mo., where he d. Dec. 16, 1880. She d. there May 19, 1878. Children:

> 1. GEORGE W., b. and d. 1832; 2. JESSE, b. July 11, 1833, at Madison, Ind.; served in Co. H, 73d Regt., Indiana Vol. Infy., from 1862 to 1864; m. Eliza Lemon. Feb. 20, 1879; merchant at Utica, Mo., and is deeply interested in his family history. 3. ELIZABETH A., b. at Logansport. Ind., Aug. 25, 1836. 4. SUSANNAH, b. 1837; d. 1846. 5. JOHN, b. 1838; d. 1862; in service in Tennessee; private. in Co. H, 73d Ind. Vol. Infy. 6. SARAH C., b. 1841; d. Jan. 15, 1877. 7. ISAAC H., b. Jan. 19, 1842. 8. MARY J., b. Sept. 23, 1845; m. Frank S. Mitchell, Oct. 14, 1867, Utica, Mo.

235½. ISAAC H. CRAIN [7], married at Utica, Mo., Aug. 7, 1870, Luella Ford, a native of La Salle, Ill.; was born Aug. 7, 1851. He served in the civil war in 29th Regt., Indiana Vol. Infy., from 1862 to 1864. His first wife died Nov. 7, 1875, and he married 2d, Mattie Syford, at Chillicothe, March 4, 1880. Children:

> 1. CARY E., b. Nov. 7, 1871. 2. VYULA M., b. May 9, 1874. 3. LEWIS J., b. Jan. 10, 1881.

236. JAMES CRAIN, born about 1734, is reported to have married a woman of German extraction from Pennsylvania, and settled at Stanton, Va.; a farmer, and a deeply religious man. His son:

> 1. SAMUEL CRAIN, b. 1761; served in the Revolutionary war from 1780 to its close, and was with Washington at the surrender of Cornwallis; a farmer. and resided in Virginia until 1798, when he removed, with his family of eight children, to Fleming County, Ky. Was twice married; 1st, about 1783; 2d, Oct., 1819, in Bath County, Ky., Jane B. Moffett, who was b. there March 2, 1791. By 2d m. he had six children. He d. June 25, 1825, in Fleming County, Ky. She d. in Illinois, Dec. 24, 1862. A son, JOHN ALLEN CRAIN, was

b. Nov. 5, 1822; m. 1st, May 23. 1848. E. J. Manson, who was b.
April 23, 1828; she d. Aug. 1, 1854; 2d, in Morgan Co., Ill., May 27.
1856, E. M. Kennedy; she was b. April 11, 1836; graduate of Jack-
sonville Female College. He was a merchant; residence at Waverly,
Ill. Children: 1. MARY JANE. b. April 28, 1849. 2. LUCY ALLEN,
b. Aug. 31, 1851. 3. EMMA M., b. Dec. 23, 1852. 4. CLARA E., b.
July 4, 1854. 5. KATE KENNEDY, b. April 7, 1857. 6. ELLA S.,
b. May 11, 1859. 7. JOHN O., b. July 23. 1862. 8. CHARLES E.,
b. Sept. 21, 1864. 9. DEMSY CHASE, b. Nov. 11, 1866. 10. AMY
P., b. Oct. 31, 1871. 11. MANA S., b. Dec. 31, 1868. 12. THOMAS
H., b. Aug. 21, 1873.

237.   WILLIAM CRAIN, born in 1784 (son of the above Samuel
and wife Sarah ———), was a farmer in Fleming County, Ky.,
and died there in 1868.   By his wife Sarah ———, born in Virginia in 1794, and died in Fleming County, Ky., in 1875, he had :

1. JAMES SIMEON. b. June 17, 1828, who served in the Mexican war
    in 1847 and 1848. May 3, 1864, m. in Sutter County, Cal., Julia
    Lord; b. in New York in 1844; residence (1879) in Gridley, Cal.
    He was county supervisor. Children, b. in Bath County: 1. FI-
    DELLA, b. 1865· 2. CHARLES, b. 1867. 3. JAMES, b. 1871.

---

238.   WILLIAM CRANE, married Rachel L. ———.   Was a
civil engineer, and for several terms city engineer at Memphis,
Tenn.   Was first lieutenant in the confederate service from 1860
to 1864.   His wife died in 1858.   He died at Gainesville, Ala.,
1868.   A son :

1. JOSEPH CRANE. b. Jan. 20. 1847; was a confederate soldier 1860 to
    1864; m. at Meridian, Miss., Sept. 2. 1874, Annie E. Warren; b.
    1853, at Barton, Miss. He was a merchant at Port Gibson, Miss.,
    and had an uncle living (about 1880) at Augusta, Ga. Children:
    1. JOSEPH WILLIAM, b. May 5, 1876. 2. ANNIE LEE, b. Feb. 21,
    1878.

---

239.   THOMAS CRANE, married ——— Lee.   He had a son,
Tarleton Lee Crane, born in Virginia in 1784.   He married in
Kentucky, Polly Beagles. a native of North Carolina.   She died
in Missouri in 1843.   He was a farmer; died in Missouri in
1849, leaving a son :

1. JOEL CRANE. b. in Kentucky. June 16, 1839; m. in California, July
    7, 1853, Jane E. Davidson, a native of Kentucky; residence
    at Santa Rosa, Cal. Children: 1. ELLIS T., b. May 17, 1854. 2.
    WILLIAM C., b. Nov. 16, 1855. 3. ISABELLE K., b. March 4, 1857.
    4. MARTHA JANE, b. Sept. 14, 1858. 5. OLIVE OATMAN, b. Feb.
    1, 1860. 6. JOEL LEE, b. June 11, 1862; accidentally drowned
    May 30, 1879. 7. WALTER JACKSON, b. Dec. 29, 1865. 8. ALEX-
    ANDER THOMAS, b. Aug. 29, 1867.

---

240.   JAMES CRANE, born March 20, 1790, in North Carolina;
a farmer.   He married Britanea Brown ; born Nov. 10, 1812, in
North Carolina.   She died in Currituck County, March 13, 1868,

leaving a son, Thomas J. Crane, born May 11, 1830, in Pasquotank County. He married Aug. 23, 1855, in Currituck County, Lizzie Dawdy, who was born there Feb. 13, 1834. He was a farmer, and served in the confederate army. Children :

> 1. HAYWOOD B., b. Sept. 30, 1857. 2. ALEXIS. 3. THOMAS. 4. PATRICK. 5. CHARLES H. 6. WILSON. 7. NANCY J. 8. MARTHA A. 9. LIZZIE.

---

241. RICHARD CRANE, married———, and had :

> 1. WILLIAM; lived in Illinois. 2. GEORGE RICHARD, settled in Indiana. 3. JANE. 4. CHARLES CRANE, b. in Virginia, June 11, 1816; a farmer; m. 1847, in Illinois, Sarah Miller, a native of Ohio; b. Aug. 9, 1827, and settled in Sangamon County, Ill. Children: 1. GEORGE W., b. June 17, 1849. 2. CHARLES M.; residence near Dawson, Ill. 3. FRANCIS A.; residence at Decatur, Ill. 4. JOHN M.; residence at Dawson, Ill. 5. NATHAN E.; b. at Dawson, Ill. 6. CLARA J.

242. GEORGE W. CRANE [1], married Mary I. White, Jan., 1870, a native of Montgomery County, Ill. She was born March 19, 1855. He was postmaster; notary public at Kenneth, Kan.; assessor three years in Montgomery County, Ill.; and treasurer in Sheridan County, Kan., two terms. Children :

> 1. CHARLES F., b. Nov. 7, 1875, in Montgomery County, Ill. 2. ARRILLA ARIZONA, b. April 2, 1878, in Montgomery County, Ill.

---

243. Since printing page 68 the following has been received, which turns attention to No. 356—6, on page 65, as being the Abel Crain who was father of Abel, John and Orange Crain :

" The above Abel Crain, Sr., married twice, and had four children by first wife. He, about the year 1806, married 2d, Mrs. Anna Blanchard. He was living near Whitby, Ontario, at the time of the war of 1812, and was drafted into the English army, but refused to serve only as drummer. He, with twelve others, deserted, and crossed the river into the United States. After the war he returned to his family in Canada, and was arrested for deserting and stealing a boat by which he had made his escape, and harboring American prisoners; was tried and acquitted, but his property was confiscated. He then removed with his family to the United States, and settled in Ohio. He died in the spring of 1837. She died in the fall of the same year."
Children :

> 1. EZEKIEL. 2. ANNA. 3. MARIA. 4. LUCIA. 5. ORANGE; b. Aug. 28, 1808, at Stanstead, Quebec. 6. PHEBE, b. March 10, 1810; d. near Whitby, Ont. 7. ABEL, b. Dec. 4, 1811, near Whitby, and d. in Castroville, Cal., April 2, 1884. 8. JOHN, b. Nov. 21, 1813, near Whitby, Ont.; d. June 11, 1884.

244. ORANGE CRAIN [5], married Abigail Williams, of Whitby, and died in Spring Valley, Minn., Jan. 30, 1886. Set-

tled first in Michigan, but removed to Minnesota in 1855. Children :

> 1. HARRIET C.; late residence at Valley Springs, S. D. 2. ORANGE E.
> 3. OZIAS. 4. DORAH. 5. DELIA.

245. JOHN CRAIN [8], married Ursula M. Albro, May 4, 1836, in Michigan. Removed to Indiana; then to Franklinville, McHenry Co., Ill.; and in 1854 to Minnesota, and named the locality where he settled Free Soil Prairie (now Wykoff), which is now the railroad station. Children :

> 1. CHARLES.W.; residence at Aberdeen, S. D. 2. E—— S——; residence at Walton, Kan. 3. PHEBE; residence at Spring Valley, Minn. 4. JOHN H.; d. April 19, 1843. 5. E —— H.; residence at Spring Valley, Minn. 6. H ——A ——; d. Aug. 3, 1870. 7. M—— L——; d. May 4, 1853. 8. GEORGE J.; residence at Spring Valley, Minn. 9. LESTER A.; residence at Webster, S. D.

INDEX I.

61

Date.		No.	Date.		No.	Date.		No.
1830	Azor B.,	2229		Cassandra B.,	1445	1829	Charlotte J.,	1680
1884	Azor B.,	2703		Cassie L.,	2692		Charlotte L.,	827
				Catharine,	997		Charlotte L.,	2279
	B			Catharine A.,	2353		Charlotte R.,	1862
				Catharine C.,	1220	1845	Charles W.,	1691
	Barnabas,	305		Catharine J.,	2634	1810	Chauncy,	1063
	Barney A.,	984		Cecilia A.,	1132	1782	Chauncy,	1140
1770	Belden,	1335		Celestia C.,	2540		Channcy G.,	1143
	Belle,	2089		Celestia E.,	891		Chester C.,	2454
1630	Benjamin,	1		Charlie F.,	2740	1745	Chloe,	145
1656	Benjamin,	2		Charles,	273		Chloe P.,	2075
1694	Benjamin,	112	1791	Charles,	284		Christobelle,	2555
1640	Benjamin,	350	1812	Charles,	1065		ChristopherC.,	2731
	Benjamin,	51	1788	Charles,	1434		Clair,	1962
	Benjamin,	750	1797	Charles,	1645		Clara,	1943
1793	Benjamin,	850		Charles,	1952		Clara,	2428
1798	Benjamin,	853		Charles,	1916	1854	Clara A.,	2550
1832	Benjamin D.,	2238	1793	Charles,	1337		Clara A.,	1575
	Benjamin E.,	908		Charles,	1412		Clara E.,	2493
	Benjamin F.,	1966		Charles,	969		Clara E.,	1833
	Benjamin F.,	1829	1873	Charles,	1963	1818	Clara F.,	897
	Benjamin R.,	781		Charles,	2461		Clara L.,	2513
	Benjamin T.,	2292	1892	Charles,	2546		Clarance O.,	2542
1704	Benonie,	55	1836	Charles E.,	2538	1807	Clareuda,	1544
	Berdella J.,	2181	1818	Charles A.,	1718		Clarinda,	2300
	Bertha,	1392		Charles A.,	1432		Clarinda P.,	1446
	Bernice,	2578	1853	Charles A.,	2366		Clarissa,	1584
	Bessie E.,	1570	1861	Charles A.,	2467	1792	Clarissa,	1096
	Bessie S.,	2662	1891	Charles A.,	2577	1812	Clarissa,	1380
1873	Bessie,	2688		Charles A.,	2761		Clifford,	2425
	Bessie A.,	2710	1867	Charles B.,	2576		Clinton L.,	1794
1793	Betsy,	1171		Charles B.,	2697		Clorinda,	2262
	Betsy,	1458	1871	Charles C.,	1927	1787	Clorinda,	1323
	Betsy,	1368	1850	Charles D.,	2568		C. Lyle,	2547
1798	Betsy,	2236		Charles D.,	1720	1706	Comfort,	44
	Betsey,	1080		Charles E.,	2404		Cora,	2500
	Betsey P.,	1084		Charles E.,	1769		Cora,	2081
	Betsey A.,	2130	1858	Charles E.,	2147		Cora,	2743
	Blanche A.,	1618	1853	Charles E.,	2660		Cora E.,	2152
	Bonnie M.,	2665	1845	Charles E.,	2508		Cora M.,	2594
	Burdette,	1185		Charles E.,	2779		Cornelia,	2234
	Byron W.,	2484		Charles F.,	1066		Cornelia M.,	1641
			1842	Charles F.,	1169		C. Spencer,	924
	C			Charles F.,	2734	1747	Curtis,	278
			1845	Charles G.,	2195	1777	Curtis,	728
	Calista R.,	1732		Charles H.,	1267	1781	Curtis,	1149
	Calvin C.,	1679		Charles J.,	1884	1842	Curtis,	2620
	Carl H.,	1945		Charles J.,	2778		Curtis L.,	2593
	Carlos,	1207		Charles L.,	1722		Cylena D.,	1733
	Carlos O.,	1777	1832	Charles L.,	2050	1800	Cynthia,	1484
	Caroline,	935	1898	Charles L.,	2666		Cynthia A.,	2772
	Caroline,	1125		Charles R.,	1106		Cynthia G.,	1907
1840	Caroline E.,	2054	1852	Charles S.,	2384		Cyrenus C.,	932
	Caroline,	2645		Charles S.,	2621		Cyrus M.,	1779
	Caroline E.,	2003		Charles S. B.,	1593		Cyrus S.,	2502
	Caroline T.,	1915		Charles T.,	1804			
1806	Caroline E.,	2278		Charity L.,	917		**D**	
1820	Caroline M.,	1619		Charity M.,	889			
	Caroline M.,	1681	1816	Charity M.,	896		Daniel,	140
1800	Carso,	1406		Charity T.,	382	1763	Daniel,	616
	Carso,	2746	1802	Charlotte,	1413	1798	Daniel,	1474
	Carrie,	1965		Charlotte,	2094		Daniel C.,	911
1866	Carrie,	2447		Charlotte,	1163	1857	Daniel C.,	1817
	Carrie A.,	1798	1826	Charlotte,	2314		David L.,	2589
1876	Carrie A.,	2525		Charlotte,	1393		Daniel G.,	2076
	Carrie E.,	2732		Charlotte,	1420	1769	Daniel O.,	1083
1858	Carrie E.,	2751		Charlotte,	1443	1813	Daniel W.,	1381
1860	Carrie M.,	2313		Charlotte,	1471		Daniel W.,	2363
	Carrilena,	2713		Charlotte E.,	2145	1816	Darius,	1985

Date	Name	No.
	Florence,	2166
	Florence A.,	2681
	Florence I.,	2146
	Frances,	1005
1856	Frances A.,	1501
	Frances A.,	2153
	Frances A.,	2745
	Frances D.,	1871
	Frances E.,	2487
	Frances J.,	1644
	Frances M.,	1837
	Francis,	185
	Francis,	967
	Francis,	1640
	Francis,	2204
	Francis B.,	2129
	Frank,	968
1851	Frank,	1182
	Frank,	1905
1873	Frank,	2499
	Frank B.,	2755
	Frank E.,	2062
1879	Frank E.,	2161
	Frank G.,	1440
	Frank L.,	1946
	Frank P.,	2197
	Frank S.,	1748
1871	Frank S.,	2656
1869	Frank S.,	2739
	Frankie,	1627
	Franklin,	1058
	Franklin H.,	2149
	Franklin L.,	2070
1840	Franklin L.,	2072
	Franklin L.,	2654
	Franklin O.,	2069
	Fred,	965
	Fred,	1906
	Fred,	1953
	Fred B.,	1978
	Fred E.,	1062
	Fred G.,	2747
	Frederick,	1187
	Frederick B.,	2383
1847	Frederick H.,	1692
	Frederick H.,	1728
	Frederick R.,	2686

G

Date	Name	No.
	Garritt B.,	1395
	George,	190
1788	George,	803
1834	George,	1235
1851	George,	1268
1863	George,	1715
1808	George,	1752
	George.	1925
1861	George,	2200
	George,	2203
	George,	2700
	George,	2714
	George A.,	1556
1850	Georgia A.,	1662
	George A.,	1900
1870	George A.,	1920
	George A.,	2093
1878	George A.,	2512
1868	George A.,	2610

Date	Name	No.
	George B.,	2301
	George C.,	818
	George C.,	1144
	George D.,	2057
	George E.,	1612
	George E.,	1686
	George F.,	2782
	George D.,	2079
	George H.,	1617
	George H.,	1928
1846	George H.,	2033
	George H.,	2135
1869	George H.,	2444
	George L.,	2244
1836	George L.,	2249
1842	George O.,	2013
	George P.,	2442
	George P.,	2722
	George R.,	1124
1808	George R.,	1494
	George R.,	2002
1831	George S.,	2490
	George V.,	1775
1857	George W.,	2368
1854	George W.,	2523
	George W.,	2655
	George W.,	2762
	Georgia,	2694
	Georgiana A.,	2764
	Geraldine,	1411
1791	Gerard,	682
1815	Gerard,	1557
	Gerard,	2408
	Gertrude,	1180
	Gertrude A.,	2360
	Gilbert,	1468
	Gilbert,	2193
	Gilman,	2037
	Gilman C.,	2631
	Gladys V.,	2769
	Glen,	1970
	Grace,	335
	Grace E.,	2376
	Gratia,	987

H

Date	Name	No.
1689	Hannah,	28
1692	Hannah,	96
1706	Hannah,	56
1702	Hannah,	136
1744	Hannah,	277
	Hannah,	1079
	Hannah,	2209
	Hannah,	2324
	Hannah,	2464
1818	Hannah A.,	915
	Hannah A.,	2554
	Hannah M.,	939
	Harold,	2709
	Harrie D.,	2658
1803	Harriet,	869
1829	Harriet,	1594
1802	Harriet,	1678
1803	Harriet,	1699
	Harriet,	2047
1843	Harriet,	2194
1808	Harriet,	2272
1827	Harriet,	2623

Date	Name	No.
	Harriet,	2698
	Harriet A.,	2622
1848	Harriet E.,	2723
	Harriet M.,	2186
	Harriet N..,	1841
	Harriette,	1153
	Harriette,	1172
	Harris W.,	2759
	Harrison,	2310
	Harry,	1629
	Harry,	2468
	Harry J.,	2649
	Harry S.,	2663
	Harry W.,	1717
1817	Harvey,	1254
	Harvey,	2257
	Harvey H.,	1265
	Hattie,	1165
	Hattie A.,	2510
1858	Hattie E.,	2127
	Hattie E.,	2080
	Hattie E.,	2606
	Hattie M.,	1613
	Hazel,	2544
	Hazel,	2775
	Helen,	1816
1849	Helen,	2190
	Helen,	2783
	Helen A.,	2537
	Helen B.,	2682
	Helen E.,	2162
	Helen E.,	2381
	Helen F.,	2633
	Helen M.,	937
1845	Helen M.,	1803
	Helen M.,	1880
1851	Helen M.,	2065
	Helen M.,	2647
	Hendrick,	2027
	Henrietta,	1723
	Henrietta,	2137
1785	Henry,	730
1784	Henry,	1422
	Henry,	1897
	Henry,	2086
	Henry,	2138
	Henry B.,	2781
	Henry D.,	2382
	Henry F.,	960
	Henry H.,	1209
	Henry J.,	2479
	Henry M.,	2389
1863	Henry R.,	2443
	Henry S.,	1608
	Henry V. B.,	2614
	Herbert,	2687
	Herold A.,	2777
1721	Hezekiah,	174
1748	Hezekiah,	312
1747	Hezekiah,	454
1781	Hezekiah,	795
1773	Hezekiah,	1111
1797	Hezekiah,	1226
	Hezekiah A.,	2176
	Hezekiah B.,	2022
	Hezekiah C.P.,	1090
1805	Hiram,	1486
	Hiram A.,	2391
1817	Hiram H.,	927

Date.		No.	Date.		No.	Date.		No.
	Samuel H.,	2504		Sophronia,	2005		**V**	
	Samuel G.,	1134		Stanley P.,	2569			
1830	Samuel L.,	828		Stella B.,	2677		Van Buren,	2609
	Samuel L.,	782		Stella E.,	1792		Vernon E.,	1951
	Samuel,	784	1879	Stella B.,	1983		Viancy,	1365
	Samuel L. G.,	2126	1734	Stephen,	249		Viancy,	1003
	Samuel O.,	952	1769	Stephen,	695		Violetta,	1344
1814	Samuel O.,	1853	1770	Stephen,	1285		Virgia A.,	2474
	Samuel P.,	1133		Stephen,	2245		Virginia E.,	1403
1804	Samuel R.,	1742	1819	Stephen G.,	928			
1680	Sarah,	73		Stephen H.,	2446			
1687	Sarah,	27		Stephen T.,	2445		**W**	
	Sarah,	48	1704	Susan,	35			
1707	Sarah,	138	1802	Susan,	1485		Wade O.,	1784
1735	Sarah,	150		Susan,	1600		Wallace S., ᵤ	1661
	Sarah,	195		Susan A.,	2277		Walter,	999
	Sarah,	548		Susan V.,	1257		Walter,	1436
1750	Sarah,	549		Susan E.,	1640		Walter,	1957
1757	Sarah,	638		Susan H.,	844	1865	Walter,	2370
1772	Sarah,	783		Susanna,	369		Walter B.,	1378
1762	Sarah,	351		Susanna,	959		Walter C.,	2465
	Sarah,	348		Sumner L.,	1793	1858	Walter L.,	2180
1781	Sarah,	399		Sylvester E.,	940		Walter G.,	1148
	Sarah,	363		Sylvester F.,	916		Walter L.,	1872
	Sarah,	353		Sylvester,	2169		Walter O.,	1789
1780	Sarah,	1319	1842	Sylvester,	2170		Walter V.,	1954
	Sarah,	1433		Sylvester R.,	936		Ward,	1290
	Sarah,	964		Sylvia,	852	1770	Wareham,	1095
	Sarah,	977		Syrene H.,	1426		Wareham B.,	1099
	Sarah,	1410					Warren S.,	1170
1847	Sarah,	2189		**T**		1802	Warren S.,	1183
1859	Sarah A.,	1664					Washington,	1367
1834	Sarah A.,	1637		Tamer,	1287	1788	Weltham,	244
	Sarah A.,	1515		Tamer A.,	1309		Welthan,	1351
	Sarah A.,	1135	1728	Thaddeus,	228		Whiting,	739
	Sarah A.,	1977	1753	Thaddeus,	230	1749	William,	287
	Sarah E.,	1984	1780	Thaddeus,	672	1744	William,	527
1840	Sarah E.,	1483	1795	Thaddeus,	1535	1775	William,	279
1851	Sarah E.,	2402	1824	Thaddeus,	1585		William,	736
	Sarah J.,	2470	1845	Thaddeus,	2416	1785	William,	832
	Sarah E.,	2730		Thaddeus B.,	2432		William,	1076
1842	Sarah E.,	1850	1777	Thalia,	714		William,	1721
1852	Sarah E.,	1931	1786	Theda,	681	1860	William,	1958
	Sarah J.,	1088	1720	Theoda,	81	1847	William,	1986
1836	Sarah J.,	2052		Theodore W.,	1487		William A.,	1726
	Sarah L.,	2770		Theodorey,	147		William B.,	1863
1856	Sarah J.,	2725		Theodosha,	420		William C.,	1857
	Sarah H.,	857		Theodosha,	496	1826	William C.,	2100
	Sarah H.,	2252		Theodotia L.,	918		William D.,	1866
	Sarah M.,	1352		Thirza,	899		William E.,	2693
	Sarah M.,	1448	1812	Thirza N.,	912		William H.,	838
	Sarah M. A.,	1996		Thirza M.,	1326		William H.,	1639
	Sarah W.,	1625	1797	Thomas,	247	1842	William H.,	1659
	Seth,	142	1801	Thomas,	1569	1845	William H.,	2063
	Seth,	264		Thomas A.,	829		William F.,	2667
	Sewall L.,	2048		Thomas C. T.,	2552	1816	William H.,	867
	Sewall H.,	2642		Thomas S.,	1480		William H.,	883
	Sewall,	2646		Thomas,	2150	1840	William H.,	1266
	Sheldon C.,	2683	1783	Timothy,	1215	1817	William H.,	2372
	Sherburne H.,	1424	1780	Tirzah,	994		William H.,	1606
	Sibyl,	1998		Trumau L.,	1729	1847	William H.,	2561
1723	Silas,	143		T. Chandler,	842		William M.,	1888
1743	Silas,	334					William N.,	2398
1780	Silas,	769					William G.,	1757
	Silas H.,	839		**U**		1852	William F.,	2142
	Silvea D.,	2572					William J.,	819
	Sobrina,	378	1832	Ustacia,	2608		William S.,	1910
1750	Solomon,	589	1870	Ustacia,	2615		William W.,	1126
	Sophia,	1933					William W.,	2586

INDEX I.

NAMES OTHER THAN CRANE.

DESCENDANTS OF BENJAMIN.

62

Taylor, Helen M., 1385
Howard W.
Mary B.
William F.
Sarah M., 1494
Harriet M., 2138
Tenney, Andrew P. F.. 1990
Asa P.
Daniel C.
James G.
Jonathan.
Judith A.
Lydia A.
Thomas. Harriet N., 2193
Thompkins, Dilazon. 1347
Thompson, Elizabeth, 186
Eunice, 186
H. Hale, 1022
Job, 186
Leslie J., 1826
Julinette, 1022
Lucina, 1022
Nancy M., 1022
Rhoda, 186
Russell, 1826
Susan C., 2176
William, 421
William, 1826
Violet, 1826
Titus, Charlotte, 672
Todd, Abigail, 248
Elizabeth.
John.
Jonathan.
Mary.
Matilda.
Sarah.
Timothy.
Tousey, Amanda, 547
Arabella, 545
Benjamin, 546
Charles, 546
Edward, 547
Frank, 547
George, 547
Henry, 545
John E., 546
Mary A., 545
Sinclair, 546
William, 546
Zerah. 545
Townsend, Martha A., 1307
Zilpha, 2459
Trask, Clarrisa J., 1461
Delos R.
Edwin W.
Gilbert C.
Luella J.
Ozell.
Riverus H.
Simon.
Travis, Emeline, 2235
Gilbert.
Treat, James, 118
Prudence W., 742
Trescott, Charles, 512
Trowbridge, Ada, 1321

Adah Z., 1319
Allerton M.
Alvah.
Arabella.
Aralinda.
Amanda, 1320
Cora B., 1321
Cornelia, 1319
Cornelia, 1320
Edwin M., 1320
George P., 1320
Eliza, 1321
John C., 1320
Phineas B., 1319
Sarah B., 1319
William C., 1319
William R., 1320
Tunnicliff, Persis N., 1857
Tupper, Leland E., 2580
Lella E., 2580
Tuttle, Hattie, 2099
Lottie.
Millie.
Perry.
Zervey.
Twining, Betsey, 778
Tyler, Mary, 160

U

Underwood, Julia R., 1604
Susan J., 2126
Upham, Lucy, 1915
Mary, 1915
Zenas, 1915

V

Van Alstine, Melinda, 955
Vance, Charles, 649
David.
Frank L.
Hattie.
Jane.
Louis.
William.
Wilson.
Vanderveer, Adaline, 2520
Van Vlirt. Ellen, 1952
Varney, Noble, 1732
Vaugh, Cordelia S., 1690
Vaughn. Rowena, 692
Wakefield. Betsey, 2320
Wakely, Elizabeth, 114
Wakeman. George M., 2314
Levi.
Martha C.
Thaddeus.
William.
Walcott. Emily L., 2005
Eunice, 194
Hiram, 2005
Hiram H., 2005
James M., 2005

Jane M., 2005
Julia M., 2005
Julius, 2005
Francis N., 2005
Louisa, 2131
Sophronia M., 2005
Waldo, Ruth, 97
Waldron. Maria, 903
Walter, Erastus, 2541
Guy L., 2541
Minnie, 2541
Walworth. Clara A., 2745
John D., 2745
Warner, Abigail, 68
Hannah, 70
John, 69
Jonathan. 72
Mary, 72
Solomon B., 706
William, 65
William, 71
Daniel, 550
Belden N., 550
Harriet, 550
Sally, 550
Washburn, Emma A., 2292
George A., 2718
Waterman, Anna, 2362
Lucy, 143
Waters, A. Frank, 2381
Franklin, 2381
Watrous, Eleazer, 1322
William, 1322
Harriet, 2589
Watson, Esther C., 2712
Ellen F., 1507
Mark S., 1507
Richard P., 1507
Winslow B., 1507
Winslow C., 1507
Watts, Fannie, 419
Webb, Ann, 191
Alice.
Darius.
Ebenezer.
Elizabeth.
Elizabeth, 2255
Hannah, 191
Jerusha.
Jonathan.
Welch, Abigail, 573
Betsey, 575
John, 573
Laura, 573
Paul, 573
Peter, 576
Marvin, 574
Rachel, 573
Sally, 573
Samuel, 573
Martha, 557
Wells, David, 1999
Henry.
Horace.
Huldah.
John.
Joshua.
Julia A.

INDEX II.

CHRISTIAN NAMES OF CRANES.

DESCENDANTS OF JOHN.

INDEX II.

NAMES OTHER THAN CRANE.

DESCENDANTS OF JOHN.

INDEX III.

CHRISTIAN NAMES OF CRANES.

DESCENDANTS OF JASPER.

D

Date	Name	No.
	Daisy,	2242
	Daisy H.,	2689
	Daisy J.,	1987
	Daizy,	2289
1684	Daniel,	48
1721	Daniel,	52
	Daniel,	460
	Daniel,	181
	Daniel,	385
	Daniel,	409
	Daniel,	529
	Daniel,	605
1800	Daniel P.,	610
1787	Daniel,	1574
	Daniel,	1271
	Daniel,	2535
	Daniel A.,	1745
	Daniel B.,	2430
1751	Daniel P.,	615
1693	David,	113
	David,	43
1721	David,	357
1756	David,	141
	David,	273
	David,	728
	David,	306
1756	David,	797
	David,	554
	David,	1130
	David,	710
	David,	1401
	David,	1146
	David,	2176
	David,	1470
	David,	1477
1785	David B.,	773
	David B.,	1792
	David B.,	2554
1763	David D.,	833
	David H.,	1957
	David N.,	1546
	David R.,	2106
1788	Davis,	1458
1805	Davis,	2225
	Deborah,	602
	Deborah F.,	685
	Deinsis C.,	1326
	Delevan,	1207
	Delia,	975
1642	Delivered,	4
	Delia M.,	1265
	Derias F.,	2515
	Diana M.,	1969
	Dorcas,	120
1764	Dorcas,	236
1777	Dorcas,	522
1807	Dorcas,	1052
	Dorothy,	2744
	Dorothy H.,	2746
	Dorset,	2625
	Douglass,	2243
	De Witt C.,	2586
	Dwight L.,	2065

E

Date	Name	No.
	Eadith,	2046

Date	Name	No.
	Edgar A.,	1743
	Edgar G.,	1940
1787	Edgar G.,	1954
1740	Edgar M.,	2563
1760	Edie,	466
	Edith,	2277
	Edith C.,	2110
	Edith E.,	2389
	Edith H.,	2747
	Edith J.,	2588
	Edith M.,	1952
1692	Edmand,	131
	Edna L.,	2413
	Edna N.,	2550
	Edward,	924
	Edward,	1197
	Edward,	1223
1820	Edward,	1548
	Edward,	2296
	Edward,	2548
	Edward.	
	Edward A.,	705
	Edward A.,	1821
	Edward B.,	1775
	Edward F.,	2688
	Edward H.,	1750
1803	Edward L.,	1656
	Edward L.,	2443
	Edward L.,	2454
	Edward L.,	2561
	Edward N.,	2548
	Edward P.,	2682
1803	Edward S.,	1417
	Edward S.,	1430
	Edward W.,	2560
1804	Edwin,	1348
1855	Edwin T.,	2415
	Eldora A.,	2722
	Eleazer,	528
	Electa,	735
	Electa,	1391
	Electa R.,	2171
	Electy Z.,	749
	Eliakim,	266
1793	Eliakim,	269
	Elias,	272
1753	Elias,	766
	Elias,	321
	Elias B.,	1084
	Elias B.,	2569
1689	Elihu,	105
1726	Elihu,	344
1771	Elihu,	350
	Elihu,	1874
1716	Elijah,	386
1751	Elijah,	207
	Elijah,	387
	Elijah,	852
	Elisha,	635
	Eliza,	652
	Eliza,	1516
	Eliza G.,	1182
	Eliza,	2116
	Eliza,	1354
	Eliza A.,	2159
	Eliza,	1472
	Eliza A.,	1729
	Eliza C.,	1880
	Elizabeth,	64

Date	Name	No.
	Elizabeth,	537
	Elizabeth,	197
1787	Elizabeth,	219
1740	Elizabeth,	296
1760	Elizabeth,	332
	Elizabeth,	375
	Elizabeth,	886
	Elizabeth,	440
	Elizabeth,	1059
	Elizabeth,	559
	Elizabeth,	1116
	Elizabeth,	1212
	Elizabeth,	1297
	Elizabeth,	727
	Elizabeth.	950
	Elizabeth S.,	2268
	Elizabeth,	2036
	Elizabeth,	1303
	Elizabeth,	2657
	Elizabeth,	2632
	Eliz beth H.,	2304
	Elizabeth A.,	1088
	Elizabeth B.,	1854
	Elizabeth B.,	1593
	Elizabeth C.,	2498
	Elizabeth J.,	1362
1827	Elizabeth J.,	2380
	Elizabeth J.,	2591
	Elizabeth M.,	1875
	Elizabeth M.,	2551
	Elizabeth R,	2168
	Ella,	1227
	Ella,	1896
	Ella A.,	2556
	Ella F.,	2048
	Ella M.,	2594
	Ellen,	416
	Ellen,	420
	Ellen,	2037
	Ellen A.,	2132
	Ellis F.,	2148
	Ellsworth,	1386
	Elmer B.,	1150
	Elmer E.,	1387
	Elmer J.,	2604
	Emeline H.,	1014
	Emma E.,	2470
	Emma P.,	1994
	Emma,	1426
	Emma,	1799
	Emma,	1899
	Emma H.,	2057
	Emma,	2102
	Emma F.,	2143
	Emma,	2234
	Emma,	2356
	Elmira,	581
	Elmira M.,	2560
	Elsey S.,	1502
	Elsie S.,	2279
	Elsie M.,	1682
	Elton S.,	2254
	Ely L.,	2247
	Erastus W.,	909
	Ernest,	2290
	Ernest T.,	2417
	Ernestine A.,	1540
	Esther,	167
	Esther,	681

Date.		No.
	Henry,	537
1781	Henry,	1567
1800	Henry,	1626
1854	Henry,	1408
	Henry,	1716
	Henry,	1847
	Henry,	1873
	Henry,	2295
	Henry,	2358
	Henry,	2526
	Henry A. R.,	1796
	Henry A. R.,	2255
	Henry D.,	2510
	Henry D.,	1883
	Henry D.,	2508
1896	Henry D.,	2728
1836	Henry J.,	2404
1835	Henry J.,	2432
	Henry L.,	989
1836	Henry L.,	2449
	Henry L.,	1797
	Henry M.,	1415
1827	Henry M.,	2305
1830	Henry M.,	1594
	Henry P.,	1640
	Henry P.,	1795
	Henry R.,	2108
	Henry S.,	2142
	Henry W.,	1886
	Henry W.,	1834
	Herbert H.,	1749
	Herbert E.,	2184
	Herbert R.,	2711
	Hester A. R.,	1816
	Hetty,	537
	Hetty,	1267
	Hetty,	2328
	Hetty M.,	2034
	Hiram,	1253
	Hiram A.,	2621
	Hiram D.,	2606
	Hiram W.,	2471
	Honora F.,	2307
	Horace,	418
	Horace,	1083
	Horace,	1206
	Horatio,	1748
	Howard C.,	2406
	Howard D.,	2713

I

Date.		No.
	Ida,	1847
	Ina,	2607
	Ira,	1269
1808	Ira,	1287
	Ira,	1208
	Ira S.,	2059
	Irving,	1075
	Irving,	2240
	Irving J.,	2430
	Isaac,	233
1709	Isaac,	304
1770	Isaac,	239
	Isaac,	781
1766	Isaac,	336
1746	Isaac,	800
	Isaac,	555
	Isaac,	636

Date.		No.
	Isaac,	733
	Isaac,	782
	Isaac,	832
	Isaac,	1898
	Isaac,	1572
1808	Isaac B.,	281
1830	Isaac B.,	720
1826	Isaac B.,	2186
	Isaac B.,	2392
	Isaac B.,	2187
	Isaac,	2205
	Isaac B.,	2273
	Isaac G.,	2427
	Isaac S.,	2342
	Isaac W.,	827
1808	Isaac W.,	1035
1801	Isaac W.,	2222
1799	Isaac W.,	2337
	Isabel W.,	2741
1713	Israel,	312
1755	Israel,	787
	Israel,	948
	Israel,	647
	Israel,	1201
	Israel,	2063
1835	Israel,	2542
	Israel C.,	1492

J

Date.		No.
	Jabez,	708
1797	Jabez,	740
1819	Jabez T.,	1381
	Jabez T.,	1385
	Jacob,	564
	Jacob,	2010
	Jacob A.,	2599
1795	Jacob G.,	1093
	James,	51
1723	James,	441
1754	James,	367
	James,	713
	James,	722
1812	James,	731
1802	James,	785
	James,	1542
1786	James,	882
	James,	922
1809	James,	1782
	James,	1200
	James,	1260
	James,	1491
1818	James,	2301
	James,	2011
	James,	2294
	James A.,	963
1826	James B.,	2669
	James B.,	1556
	James B.,	1732
	James B.,	1783
1803	James C.,	1331
1794	James C.,	686
	James C.,	1901
	James C.,	2096
1856	James E. D.,	2715
	James F.,	2233
	James H.,	1894
1832	James H.,	2425
	James K.,	1765

Date.		No.
	James K.,	2124
1842	James M.,	2387
	James M.,	1930
	James M.,	2147
	James M.,	2206
	James M.,	1741
	James M.,	446
	James N.,	1727
	James T.,	1333
	James T.,	2390
	James T.,	2072
	James W.,	1421
	James W.,	1423
1686	Jane,	84
	Jane,	65
	Jane,	550
	Jane,	929
	Jane,	467
	Jane,	534
	Jane,	558
	Jane;	1643
1822	Jane D.,	753
	Jane E.,	2270
	Jane E.,	1893
	Jane L.,	1877
	Jane M.,	1591
	Jarvis G.,	2058
	Jason,	705
	Jason,	1827
16—	Jasper,	1
1651	Jasper,	28
1679	Jasper,	42
	Jasper,	2548
	Jasper N.,	1692
	Jay D.,	2735
	Jean D.,	2097
1716	Jedediah,	356
1802	Jedediah,	359
	Jennie,	2528
	Jennie M.,	916
	Jennie M.,	2384
	Jenny B.,	2146
	Jeremiah,	149
	Jeremiah,	643
	Jeremiah,	1250
1808	Jeremiah C.,	1667
	Jerusha,	326
	Jesse,	2241
	Jesse D.,	1986
	Jessie A.,	2734
	Jessie W.,	2733
	Joanna,	58
1718	Joanna,	337
1760	Joanna,	234
	Joanna,	779
	Joanna,	325
	Joanna,	341
	Joanna,	701
	Joanna M.,	2323
	Job,	185
1635	John,	9
1671	John,	35
1695	John,	85
	John,	36
	John,	258
	John,	699
	John,	329
	John,	368
1766	John,	408

Date.		No.	Date.		No.	Date.		No.
	Lucy,	2298		Martha C.,	1731		Mary E.,	2703
	Luella,	2162		Martha D.,	1979	1859	Mary E.,	2721
	Luella,	2643		Martha E.,	2129		Mary E.,	2559
	Lulu,	2511		Martha M.,	1721		Mary E.,	2690
	Lunora,	2045		Martin,	1209		Mary F.,	2645
	Luther,	762		Martin L.,	440		Mary F.,	1484
	Lydia,	153	1693	Mary,	24		Mary G.,	2320
	Lydia,	248		Mary,	39		Mary H.,	2333
	Lydia,	493	1735	Mary,	246	1854	Mary H.,	2723
	Lydia,	1008		Mary,	119		Mary J.,	2731
	Lydia,	553		Mary,	128		Mary J.,	2640
1789	Lydia,	1577		Mary,	174		Mary J.,	2123
	Lydia,	1307	1755	Mary,	209		Mary L.,	1891
	Lydia,	2094	1762	Mary,	235		Mary L.,	1847
	Lydia E.,	2493		Mary,	276		Mary M.,	1768
	Lydia P.,	1864		Mary,	786		Mary M.,	2578
	Lyman G.,	1980		Mary,	315		Mary P.,	995
	Lyman G.,	1989		Mary,	324		Mary V.,	2576
	Lyman M.,	704		Mary,	340		Mary W.,	2338
	Lyman M.,	1009		Mary,	345		Mary W.,	2674
				Mary,	372		Matilda,	1450
	M			Mary,	465		Matthias,	92
				Mary,	505		Matthias,	481
	M. A. Adelaide,		1784	Mary,	1060	1765	Matthias,	684
		1995		Mary,	535	1802	Matthias,	1774
	Mabel,	2618		Mary,	590		Maud,	1991
	Mabel J.,	1852		Mary,	616		Maurice E.,	2416
	Manus,	2029		Mary,	537		May,	1968
	Marc,	2522		Mary,	653		Mehitabel,	177
	Marcia T.,	2539		Mary,	1338		Mehitabel,	539
	Marcia,	2525	1807	Mary,	953		Mehitabel,	594
	Marcus H.,	2562		Mary,	1810		Melissa J.,	414
	Mark,	561		Mary,	1869		Melvania A.,	2479
	Margaret,	271		Mary,	2009	1645	Mercy,	17
	Margaret,	376		Mary,	2030	1647	Micah,	6
	Margaret,	1268		Mary,	2630		Mentor,	616
	Margaret,	1294		Mary,	2101		Millie L.,	1935
	Margaret,	1812		Mary,	2278		Milo A.,	1976
	Margaret C.,	993		Mary,	2281		Minnie C.,	2686
	Margaret M.,	2516		Mary,	2302		Myra K.,	1999
	Margaret R.,	725	1816	Mary A.,	725		Myron,	1923
	Maria,	930		Mary A. A.,	1286		Myron F.,	2609
	Maria,	560		Mary A.,	1597		Myron W.,	2596
	Maria,	872	1854	Mary A.,	1679		Morington,	1073
	Maria,	1041		Mary A.,	2590		Morris W.,	2177
	Maria,	2329		Mary A.,	1932	1731	Moses,	210
	Maria A.,	2518		Mary A.,	1959		Moses,	454
	Maria B.,	1560		Mary A.,	1975		Moses,	193
	Maria D.,	1884		Mary A.,	2431		Moses,	616
	Maria L.,	2081		Mary B.,	1793		Moses,	1474
	Maria H.,	2156		Mary B.,	1055		Moses,	925
	Maria P.,	2336½	1833	Mary B.,	2335		Moses M.,	1199
	Marianna,	1761		Mary B.,	1730		Moses P.,	1855
	Marie,	1400		Mary C.,	747			
	Marilla,	2040		Mary C.,	1897			
	Marion,	1221		Mary C.,	2285		**N**	
	Marion F.,	2598		Mary D.,	1805			
1875	Marion F.,	2066		Mary D.,	2077		Nancy,	1076
1759	Martha,	690	1813	Mary D.,	2300		Nancy,	1705
	Martha,	311		Mary E.,	410		Nancy,	1081
1762	Martha,	812		Mary E.,	415		Nancy,	1273
	Martha,	654		Mary E.,	2099		Nancy,	2173
	Martha,	838	1816	Mary E.,	2362	1797	Nancy,	2191
	Martha,	1409	1846	Mary E.,	2391		Nancy,	2327
	Martha,	2221	1840	Mary E.,	1704		Nan y,	2163
	Martha,	2357		Mary E.,	2140		Nancy F.,	994
	Martha A.,	1483		Mary E.,	2656		Naomi C.,	990
1810	Martha B.,	2292		Mary E.,	2204	1680	Nathaniel,	60

Date.		No.
	Sarah,	13
1683	Sarah,	33
	Sarah,	46
1734	Sarah,	121
	Sarah.	160
	Sarah,	183
	Sarah,	230
	Sarah,	274
1735	Sarah,	293
	Sarah,	303
1762	Sarah,	334
	Sarah,	347
	Sarah,	369
	Sarah,	374
	Sarah.	380
	Sarah,	406
	Sarah,	463
	Sarah,	985
	Sarah,	510
	Sarah,	533
	Sarah,	566
	Sarah,	537
	Sarah.	1337
1783	Sarah,	763
	Sarah,	805
	Sarah,	1541
	Sarah,	836
1797	Sarah,	1582
	Sarah,	927
	Sarah,	1049
	Sarah,	2192
	Sarah,	1488
	Sarah,	1820
	Sarah,	1867
	Sarah,	2031
	Sarah,	2274
	Sarah A.,	1151
	Sarah A.,	2098
	Sarah A.,	1403
	Sarah A.,	2558
	Sarah C.,	992
1856	Sarah C.,	2422
1843	Sarah C.,	2346
	Sarah E.,	2503
	Sarah E.,	1759
	Sarah F.,	421
	Sarah E.,	1285
	Sarah E.,	2207
	Sarah F.,	1811
	Sarah E.,	2248
	Sarah E. H.,	2692
	Sarah E.,	2375
	Sarah H.,	2414
1875	Sarah H.,	2680
	Sarah L.,	917
	Sarah K.,	2131
	Sarah M.,	1431
	Sarah M.,	1579
1831	Sarah M.,	2334
1820	Sarah M.,	2365
	Sarah P.,	2231
1819	Sarah W.,	1610
	Sarah W.,	2155
	Sayres,	241
	Sayres,	682
	Sears,	761
	Sears,	1439
1773	Shadrack.	857
1791	Sidney,	2264

Date.		No.
	Sidney W.,	2670
	Silas,	180
	Silas,	383
1780	Silas,	901
1805	Silas,	1715
1797	Silas,	2217
	Silas,	2218
	Simeon,	551
1800	Simeon H.,	1583
1840	Simeon H.,	2336
	Smith E.,	1903
1725	Solomon,	45
1806	Solomon,	1683
1840	Solomon,	2467
	Sophia,	565
	Sophia,	982
	Sophia,	1487
	Sophia,	1800
	Sophia M.,	2662
	St. Clair,	1752
	Stephen,	220
1735	Stephen,	400
	Stephen,	401
	Stephen N.,	410
	Stephen,	176
	Stephen,	606
	Stephen,	628
1733	Stephen,	292
	Stephen,	358
1780	Stephen,	873
	Stephen,	438
1778	Stephen,	1463
	Stephen,	1205
	Stephen,	2360
	Stephen B.,	1203
	Stephen F.,	1013
1802	Stephen K.,	1627
1844	Stephen M.,	1677
	Stephen M.,	1804
	Stephen R.,	2223
	Stephen S.,	1019
	Stevens,	1706
	Stevens F.,	1734
	Susan,	942
	Susan F.,	1838
	Susannah,	1105
	Sydney,	1481
	S. Janette,	1944

T

Date.		No.
	Thankful,	1276
	Theodore,	1092
1809	Theodore,	2269
	Theodore,	2641
	Theodore B.,	2679
	Theodore F.,	1849
1844	Theodore F.,	2685
	Theodore F.,	2691
	Theressa J.,	1217
1778	Thomas,	542
	Thomas,	1334
	Thomas B.,	1757
	Thomas H.,	1476
1830	Thomas K.,	2399
	Thomas S.,	1996
1726	Timothy,	232
1770	Timothy,	238
1760	Timothy,	672

Date.		No.
	Timothy,	966
1771	Timothy,	1444
	Timothy,	788
	Timothy,	1344
	Timothy A.,	1077
	Timothy A.,	1900
	Timothy D.,	1184
	Timothy W.,	2023
	Timothy W.,	2263
1805	Tryphena,	1664
	Tululah E.,	2726

U

		No.
	Uriah,	1475
	Ursula L.,	907
	Utica V.,	1739
	Uzal,	307
	Uzal,	965
	Uzal A.,	1789
	Uzal A.,	1486
	Uzal O.,	1794

V

Date.		No.
1808	Valaria A.,	1638
	Valinder T.,	2165
	Van Eli,	2458
	Van Jean,	2459
	Van Zant,	974
	Venora M.,	2484
	Vida M.,	1982
	Viola,	1222
	Virginia E.,	2002
	Virginia,	2095
	Virginia A.,	2188
	Virginia M.,	2461

W

Date.		No.
	Waldo M.,	2557
	Walter,	462
	Walter B.,	2314
	Walter C.,	2598
	Walter E.,	1733
	Walworth D.,	1806
	Warren,	875
	Washington I.,	2489
	Watson W.,	2574
	Weakly,	2457
	Wesley S.,	2647
	William,	154
1775	William,	473
1759	William,	497
	William,	402
	William,	490
	William,	998
	William,	597
	William,	616
1797	William,	1278
1790	William,	1299
1799	William,	1479
	William,	926
	William,	1571
	William,	1641
	William,	1868
	William,	1964
	William,	2093

INDEX III.

NAMES OTHER THAN CRANE.

DESCENDANTS OF JASPER.

INDEX IV.

CHRISTIAN NAMES OF CRANES.

DESCENDANTS OF STEPHEN.

Date		No.	Date		No.	Date		No.
	Mary,	526		Nathaniel,	96		Rachel,	348
	Mary,	535	1835	Nathaniel M.,	1121		Rachel,	543
	Mary,	1003	1743	Nehemiah,	238		Ralph W. A.,	1516
1809	Mary,	544		Nehemiah,	97	1847	Rasho,	776
	Mary,	733	1785	Nehemiah,	611		Raymoud T.,	1420
	Mary,	885		Nehemiah,	183		Rebecca,	15
	Mary,	905		Nehemiah,	601	1740	Rebecca,	58
	Mary A.,	287		Nellie C.,	1507		Rebecca,	652
1800	Mary A.,	990		Nellie D.,	1215		Regin B.,*	573
1836	Mary A.,	1252		Nellie M.,	1115		Reid I.,	1522
	Mary A..	828		Nelson,	341		Richard,	1377
1867	Mary A.,	1007		Nelson I..	825	1843	Richard M.,	1323
1876	Mary A.,	1304		Nina H.,	1598	1879	Richard M.,	1325
	Mary D.,	1433		Noah,	273	1812	Richard T.,	958
1816	Mary E.,	455	1773	Noah,	588		Richard V.,	509
	Mary E.,	754		Noah,	646	1775	Robert,	368
	Mary E.,	941	1808	Noah,	1098		Robert,	463
1849	Mary E.,	1014		Noah,	644		Robert C.,	1348
1816	Mary M.,	1108	1836	Noah,	1090		Robert D.,	1404
1851	Mary E.,	1068	1764	Norris,	424		Robert E.,	1035
	Mary E.,	1529		Norris,	419	1883	Robert E.,	1360
	Mary H.,	966		Norris,	892		Robert F.,	1283
	Mary H..	1145					Robert S.,	833
	Mary J.,	1510		**O**		1810	Robert T.,	443
	Mary L.,	1287				1772	Roger,	534
1813	Mary R.,	1166	1813	Obed M.,	607		Russell,	1578
	Mary T.,	1471		Orlando C.,	1240		Ruth,	125
1858	Mary M.,	1332		Orpha,	705		Ruth,	739
	Mary N.,	1397		Orton A.,	1615		Ruth,	1585
1806	Mary W.,	262					Ruth A.,	347
	Mary W.,	1602		**P**			Ruth J. R.,	325
	Mattie P.,	831				1846	Ruth R.,	1269
	Matthias,	39		Peter H.,	1474			
1780	Matthias,	397		Phebe,	31		**S**	
	Matthias,	406		Phebe,	136			
	Matthias,	410		Phebe,	268	1769	Sally,	114
1808	Matthias B.,	810		Phebe,	273		Sally,	376
	May,	1587		Phebe,	396	1797	Sally,	889
	Merton E.,	1618		Phebe,	143		Sally,	587
	Michael V. V.,	208	1766	Phebe,	156		Sally D.,	1345
	Miller L.,	1175	1764	Phebe,	476	1712	Samuel,	10
	Moses,	100	1795	Phebe,	197		Samuel,	296
	Moses,	87		Phebe,	657		Samuel,	299
	Moses,	338	1804	Phebe,	780	1816	Samuel,	821
	Moses,	643		Phebe,	859	1822	Samuel,	1183
1803	Moses,	602	1790	Phebe,	471		Samuel,	587
	Moses,	1361	1798	Phebe,	1079		Samuel,	1581
1799	Moses M.,	629		Phebe,	1153	1832	Samuel B.,	1243
	Moses M.,	349	1828	Phebe,	809	1828	Samuel E.,	1226
1864	Moses M.,	1127		Phebe,	891	1897	Samuel E.,	1564
	Moses T.,	878		Phebe,	587		Samuel R.,	322
1832	Moses W.,	1330		Phebe A.,	927		Sarah,	14
1863	Moses W.,	1341	1796	Phebe T.,	437	1755	Sarah,	265
	Mulford,	716	1845	Phebe W.,	1352		Sarah,	292
	Mulford,	721	1785	Philip,	557	1771	Sarah,	157
	Myra B.,	975	1792	Philip,	380	1790	Sarah,	183
				Philip S.,	997		Sarah,	291
	N			Philip,	1008		Sarah,	805
				Philip A.,	1170		Sarah,	459
	Nancy,	169		Philip D.,	1015		Sarah,	725
1766	Nancy,	477		Philip G.,	1006		Sarah,	743
	Nancy,	508		Polly,	342		Sarah,	611
	Nancy,	330	1803	Prosia,	474		Sarah,	1157
	Nancy,	425	1804	Prudence,	398	1876	Sarah,	1393
	Nancy,	512		Prudence,	780		Sarah,	1533
1860	Nancy,	1189					Sarah A.,	880
1680	Nathaniel,	25		**R**		1855	Sarah A.,	1113
	Nathaniel,	72				1843	Sarah C.,	1141
1762	Nathaniel,	255		Rachel,	167	1842	Sarah C.,	1147

INDEX IV.

NAMES OTHER THAN CRANE.

DESCENDANTS OF STEPHEN.

INDEX TO ADDENDA.

67

The general Court of Connecticut colony ordered that no young, unmarried man, unless he were a public officer or had a servant, could keep house alone, except by license of the town under a penalty of 20 shillings per week, and that no head of a family should entertain such young man under a like penalty, without liberty of the town. Hard lines! The joys of single blessedness were much alloyed, it would seem. Today it is different. The bachelor is happy—let us hope that he is happy. He certainly is independent. It is easy for him to explain why it is manifestly impossible for him to undertake matrimony—"a crazy experiment."

Related Families.

The Parkes of New England and the Cranes are related. Richard Parke, colonist, married Margery Crane in England. They had two daughters. One, Isabel Parke, became the wife of Francis Whitmore.

The important family connection is with the Treats, with Richard Treat and wife, Alice Gaylard, the colonists. They settled at Wethersfield, Ct., in 1637, where Richard became a man of social standing, prominent in civic affairs. His son, Robert Treat, was governor of Connecticut, and died at Milford, Ct., in 1710, aged 83 years. He was commander in chief of the Connecticut quota of men engaged in King Philip's war and had the rank of major.

Robert was re-elected governor for many years, but at the age of 86 he declined re-election. He was one of those who saved Connecticut's charter when it was demanded by Andros, October 31, 1687.

Governor Treat had sisters. They married into the families of Deming, Hollister and Campfield. The governor married first, Jane, daughter of Edmund Tapp, and second, Elizabeth, daughter of Elder Michael Powell. This

was Elizabeth's third matrimony. Her other husbands Richard Hollingsworth, a Richard Bryan. The gover Elizabeth.

In records of Newark, N the Cranes and Treats abo were among the early set town, moving there from N

Records of the Cranes an found in the following bc necticut quarterly magazin ford County," by Trumbull; ain," by Andrews; "Early tlers," by Hinman; "Norw leck; "Milford Tombstone 1 "Hartford Probate Records field," by Stiles, and genea families of Coleman, Hollis Wolcott, Hall, Goodwin a the last named by Noah W records are available in " Colonial Wars" and of the Colonial Dames," for New

As to the Webster family Robert, son of Governor Jo married, in 1672, Susanna was probably a sister of Treat.

The Coat of Arm

The armorial of the Cran shown was a fesse between crosslets.

This is similar to the coat by Jasper Crane, colonial ar the exception, that besides thereare, also three rings,

Several armorials are asc Cranes—grants for special valor. One coat of arms crane for crest, a "crane or, en crane.

A list of genealogies pu be forwarded to any one stamp. Special research wi taken, if desired, and drawi of arms in their proper color All inquiries will be answere ly if a postage stamp is en ters may be addressed to M M. Smith, Chappaqua, county, New York.

CPSIA information can be obtained
at www.ICGtesting.com
Printed in the USA
BVOW06s1539300617
488220BV00020B/612/P